MW00718607

MANAGEMENT

CONCEPTS • APPLICATIONS • SKILL DEVELOPMENT

ROBERT N. LUSSIER, Ph.D

SPRINGFIELD COLLEGE
SPRINGFIELD, MASSACHUSETTS

SOUTH-WESTERN College Publishing

An International Thomson Publishing Company

Acquisitions Editor: Randy Haubner
Project Manager: Christine Sofranko
Production Editor: Marci Dechter
Internal Design: Delgado Design
Infographic Art: Boston Graphics
Photo Research: Jennifer Mayhall
Photo Editing: Charlotte Goldman
Production House: WordCrafters Editorial Services, Inc.
Cover Design: Michael H. Stratton

Library of Congress Cataloging-in-Publication Data
Lussier, Robert N.
Management : concepts, applications and skill development. 1e / by Robert N. Lussier
p. cm.
Includes bibliographical references and index.
ISBN 0-538-85126-0 (alk. paper)
1. Management—Problems, exercises, etc. 2. Supervision of employees—Problems, exercises, etc. I. Title
HD31.L84 1996
658'.0076—dc20 96–15162
CIP

1 2 3 4 5 6 7 8 9 VH 4 3 2 1 0 9 8 7 6

Printed in the United States of America

International Thomson Publishing

To my wife Marie and our six children:

Jesse, Justin, Danielle, Nicole, Brian, and Renee

CONTENTS IN BRIEF

CONTENTS

PART ONE INTRODUCTION

PART TWO PLANNING SKILLS

PART FOUR LEADING SKILLS

PART FIVE CONTROLLING SKILLS

PREFACE

The world of management has changed and so has how it is taught. Increasing numbers of students want more than just an understanding of the concepts of management. They also want skills they can use in their everyday life at work. It's not enough to learn about management; they want to learn how to *BE* managers. This is why I wrote this book.

INTEGRATION

Based on my experience teaching the management course for over twenty years, I developed course materials that develop students into managers. As the title of this book implies, it involves a balanced, three-pronged approach to the curriculum:

- a clear understanding of management concepts;
- the application of management concepts for critical thinking in the real world; and
- the development of management skills.

I wrote this text and its supporting ancillary package to support these three distinct but integrated parts. This text follows a management functions approach covering all the traditional concepts and current topics. The applications develop students' critical-thinking skills as they require them to apply specific concepts to their own work experience (part time, summer, or full time), to short situations, and to cases. In addition, this text meets the challenge of the AACSB and SCANS call for skills development. Since I wrote almost every exercise and application in the package, the material is completely integrated to create a seamless experience in the classroom.

FLEXIBILITY

Because these three key elements of concepts, applications, and skills are integrated throughout the chapters, you won't find them in broad general sections. However, they are identified clearly and are delineated in some detail for your reference in this preface. Recognizing the diverse needs of students and faculty, they can be used flexibly to fit any classroom. Instructors can create their course by using only features that fit with their objectives.

Concepts

This text covers all key management topics and concepts. It is comprehensive in scope as shown by the detailed learning objectives at the front of each chapter. Each objective is reinforced and identified throughout the chapter. Key terms are placed in the margin to emphasize the vocabulary of management for students.

FEWER CHAPTERS/SYSTEMS INTEGRATION

Businesses today no longer operate in traditional departments isolated by function. To understand management, students must understand the interrelationships of the various business functions. My text is written from this perspective. The business is shown as a system; managers work within a system of relationships. I focus on viewing the organization as a whole and the interrelationship of its parts. The text emphasizes systems in four ways: the interrelationship of management functions, the interrelationship of the functional areas/departments, systems thinking versus reductionist thinking, and use of traditional systems theory.

As a result, rather than having 20-24 chapters, my text has 17 chapters because of fusing topics to better correlate with business today. Figures scattered throughout the text reinforce the integrated learnings through visual appeal. The result is a leaner, more realistic book.

493
Chapter 15 • Control Systems: Financial Control and Productivity

to customers, which requires damage control and warranty cost. This is particularly problematic with services, such as manicures and haircuts and auto repairs, which are delivered as they are produced. The best solution is to prevent poor quality from ever happening in the first place. Doing so creates a win-win situation by minimizing warranty cost and maximizing customer satisfaction.

Functional Area/Department Control Systems

Although in most organizations the only functional area that actually transforms the inputs into the outputs of goods and services (which are called *products*) that are sold to customers is the operations department, all functional departments use the systems process. Figure 15–2 illustrates how this is done; it

Figure 15–2
Systems Processes for Functional Areas/Departments

Systems Process

Inputs Preliminary Control → Transformation Process Concurrent Control → Outputs Rework Control → Customer for Output Damage Control

Feedback

Operations Department Systems Process

Raw Materials → Make the Product → Finished Product → Marketing Department

Marketing Department Systems Process

Finished Product → Sales Presentation → Completed Sale → Customer

Human Resources Department Systems Process

Recruited and Present Employees → Attracting, Developing, and Retaining Systems → New and More Productive Employees → Employees are a Major Input to All Departments

Finance Department Systems Process

Revenues, Borrowed Funds, and Owners' Funds → Recording Transactions and Overseeing the Budgeting Process → Budgeted Funds, Financial Statements, and Other Reports → Inputs to All Departments and Payments to Stakeholders

Information (MIS) Department Systems Process

Data Collection from All Departments and External Sources → Transforming Data Into Information → Information → Inputs to All Appropriate Employees in All Departments

New Product Development Systems Process

Data Collection from Potential Customers, Actual Customers, and All Departments → Transforming Ideas into New Products (Major Changes to a Product Can Be Considered New) → Plan for a New Product → Inputs to the Operations Department that Creates the Product, and to All Appropriate Employees in All Departments Involved with the New Product

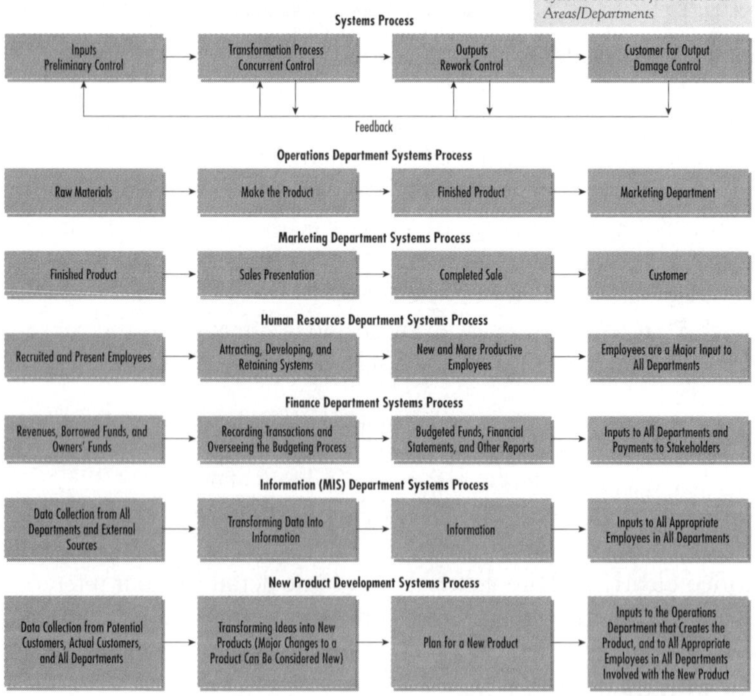

Concepts

CURRENT MANAGEMENT ISSUES

Because this text takes an integrated approach to the subject of management, it is not cluttered with extraneous boxes. Instead, current topics as described by the AACSB such as globalization, diversity, ethics and social responsibility, quality and TQM, productivity, participative management and teams, and small business are covered throughout the chapters. In particular, each chapter ends with a Current Management Issues section that discusses many of these topics, including future trends. Students are shown the relationship between traditional management topics and current management issues today.

tions and it could have ended in an argument. The cans were straight. The employee was not praised for the slow work pace. However, if the praise had not worked, the manager should have used another reinforcement method.[27]

In the opening case, Donna should give Susan praise for increasing performance to encourage her to continue this behavior. Praise is an effective positive reinforcement when used with a variable interval schedule.

SKILLBUILDER

PUTTING THE MOTIVATION THEORIES TOGETHER WITHIN THE MOTIVATION PROCESS

Motivation is important because it helps to explain why employees behave the way they do. At this point, you may be wandering: How do these theories fit together? Is one the best? Should I try to pick the correct theory for a given situation? The groups of theories are complementary; each group of theories refers to a different stage in the motivation process. Each group of theories answers a different question. Content motivation theories answer the question; What needs do employees have that should be met on the job? Process motivation theories answer the question; How do employees choose behavior to fulfill their needs? Reinforcement theory answers the question; What can managers do to get employees to behave in ways that meet the organizational objectives?

In the first section of this chapter you found that the motivation process went from need to motive to behavior to consequence to satisfaction or dissatisfaction. Now let's make the motivation process a little more complex by incorporating the motivation theories, or answers to the preceding questions, into the process. See Figure 11–6 for an illustration. Note that Step 4 loops back to Step 3 because, according to reinforcement theory, behavior is learned through consequences. Step 4 does not loop back to Steps 1 or 2 because reinforcement theory is not concerned with needs, motives, or satisfaction; it focuses on getting employees to behave in predetermined ways, through conseuqences provided by managers. Also note that Step 5 loops back to Step 1 because meeting needs is ongoing; meeting our needs is a never-ending process. Finally, be aware that, according to two-factor theory, Step 5, satisfaction or dissatisfaction, is not on one continuum but on two separate continuums (satisfied to not satisfied or dissatisfied to not dissatisfied), based on the level of need being met (motivator or maintenance).

1. Need
(Unmet need or want to be satisfied at work)
Content Motivation Theories
Hierarchy of Needs Theory
ERG Theory
Two-Factor Theory
Acquired Needs Theory

2. Motive
(Selecting behavior to satisfy need)
Process Motivation Theories
Equity Theory
Goal-Setting Theory
Expectancy Theory

3. Behavior
(Employee action to satisfy need)

4. Consequence
(Manager behavior and/or natural outcome of employee action)
Reinforcement Theory

5. Satisfaction or Dissatisfaction
(The degree to which the need is met and for how long before dissatisfaction reoccurs, creating an unmet need)

Figure 11–6
The Motivation Process with the Motivation Theories

CURRENT MANAGEMENT ISSUES

Organizational *reward systems* (pay, benefits, and so on, Chapter 9) must be designed to motivate employees. A reward system is effective if it attracts new peo-

Women tend to place more importance on convenient work hours, good interpersonal relations, and the opportunity to learn.

8. Explain the major difference between the Japanese and U.S. approach to motivating employees.

have (organizations, including General Foods and Texas Instruments, offer the opportunity to increase skills to attain raises); a variety of bonuses (cash, gifts, trips, etc.) for suggestions for improvements; profit-sharing programs (at Lincoln Electric, employees in recent years have received approximately their annual wages and double in profit-sharing payouts alone).

Diversity. Within the United States, we have a *diversified work force;* what motivates one person may not motivate another. For example, men tend to place more importance on having a lot of autonomy in their jobs, whereas women place more importance on convenient work hours, good interpersonal relations, and the opportunity to learn.[28] However, there are always exceptions; don't over generalize. The needs of a student working part time, a single parent working full time, a person who is not married working full time, and a retired person working part time will tend to be different.

Globalization. When you expand the business to other countries, the diversity continues to increase in complexity. The motivation theories you have studied were developed largely in America. As organizations become *global,* managers must be aware of the cultural limitation to theory generalizations. In 1980 it was recognized that motivational concerns vary globally.[29] A survey revealed distinct differences among U.S. salespeople and Japanese and Korean salespeople, but not between salespeople in the two Asian countries.[30] An example from NAFTA countries includes a U.S. firm in Mexico that gave workers a raise to motivate them to work more hours. The raise actually motivated the employees to work less hours because they could now make enough money to live and enjoy life (one of their primary values) in less time, so why should they work more hours? In Sweden there is a very high tax rate on overtime pay that makes it very difficult to motivate employees to work more hours based on money.

Intrinsic motivation of higher-level needs tends to be more relevant to developed countries than to Third World countries in which most people are on a lower level of hierarchy of need than those in developed countries. The term *self-actualization* is not translatable in the Chinese language. Even in developed countries, the level of needs focus varies. In the United States, people tend to be motivated by higher-level needs of self-actualization (do your own thing) and esteem; in Greece and Japan security is more important, while in Sweden, Norway, and Denmark, people are more concerned with social needs. McClelland's acquired need for achievement is more predominant in the United States. *Achievement* is difficult to translate into most other languages. Therefore, acquired achievement need has limited use outside of the United States and Canada unless managers are willing to train employees to acquire the need for achievement.

One major cultural difference is in the focus on individualistic versus group approaches to business. Individualistic societies (the United States, Canada, Great Britain, Australia) tend to value self-accomplishment. Collective societies (Japan, Mexico, Singapore, Venezuela, Pakistan) tend to value group accomplishment and loyalty.[31] Cultural differences suggest that self-actualization, achievement, and esteem needs tend to be met from group membership in Japan and from individualism in the United States.

Expectancy theory holds up fairly well, cross-culturally, because it is flexible. It allows for the possibility that there may be differences in expectations

Concepts

Quality and TQM. To be successful in business requires continually increasing *quality* and *customer value*. Continuous improvement does not come from a few major decisions every few years. It comes from continually coming up with creative ideas that become innovations. TQM encourages the use of the decision-making model and math techniques such as statistical process controls. Decisions made with TQM should take a systems effect approach. In other words, a decision should not be made in isolation. Consider how the decision being made will affect other areas and plan changes in all necessary areas.

Productivity. As employees develop creative ways to transform inputs into outputs, *productivity* increases. Generally, when poor decisions are made, problems are not eliminated and opportunities are not taken advantage of. Therefore, poor decisions lead to lower levels of productivity.

Ethics and Social Responsibility. Ethics (Chapter 2) should be at the heart of decisions and human relations (Chapter 3). The golden rule, four-way test, and/or the stakeholders' approach to ethics may be used when making decisions. When evaluating alternatives, individuals or groups should consider how they affect stakeholders. In the area of *social responsibility*, important decisions must be made about the level of commitment and which specific actions the company will take. Coca-Cola believes that it should give back to the communities that have been so good to the company wherever it does business. To this end, it made the decision to establish the Coca-Cola Foundation with the mission of fostering and promoting a favorable environment for business growth by supporting education

Small Business. It are more important t panies, like Coca- New Coke, it co profitable durin cision, they c Wentworth o sion to open itors forced

CHAPTER SU

The chapter summary is organized to answer th learning objectives for Chapter 4.

1. Explain the relationship among objec problem-solving, and decision-making.
The three terms are interrelated as follows. Manag responsible for setting and achieving organization jectives. When managers do not meet objectives, a lem results. When a problem exists, decisions m made about what, if any, action must be taken.

2. Explain the relationship among the ma ment functions, decision-making, and pro solving.

and nonprogrammed decisions and among the conditions of certainty, uncertainty, and risk.
The difference between programmed and nonprogrammed decisions is in the recurrence, routine, and significance of the decision to be made. Nonprogrammed decisions include nonrecurring, nonroutine, significant decisions. Recurring, routine, and nonsignificant decisions are programmed decisions.

The difference in decision-making conditions is based on the degree of certainty of the outcome of the decision. With certainty you know the outcome of alternatives, with risk you can assign probabilities to the outcomes, and with uncertainty you do not know the outcomes of alternatives.

5. Describe when to use the decision-making model versus the bounded rationality model and group versus individual decision-making.
Use the decision-making model with group decision-making when a nonprogrammed decision with high risk or uncertainty exists. Use the bounded rationality model with an individual decision when a programmed decision with low risk or certainty exists. However, this is a general guide; there may be exceptions to the rule.

6. State the difference between an objective and "must" and "want" criteria.
An objective is the end result you want from making the decision. The "must" criteria are the requirements that an alternative must meet to be selected as the decision. The "want" criteria are desirable but are not necessary for the alternative to be selected as the decision.

7. State the difference between creativity and innovation.
Creativity is a way of thinking that generates new ideas. Innovation is the implementation of new ideas for products and processes.

8. List and explain the three stages in the creative process.
The three stages are: (1) preparation; familiarity with the problem; (2) incubation and illumination; incubation is taking a break from the problem and illumination is the point at which one gets the idea for the solution; (3) evaluation; making sure the idea will work before it becomes an innovation.

9. Describe the difference among quantitative, the Kepner-Tregoe, and cost-benefit analysis techniques for analyzing and selecting an alternative.
Quantitative and Kepner-Tregoe are management science approaches; cost-benefit is not. Quantitative methods use math subjectively to select the alternative with the highest value. Kepner-Tregoe uses objective math, with some subjectivity in selecting and weighting criteria, to select the alternative with the highest value. Cost-benefit analysis is primarily based on subjective analysis, with some math, but alternatives do not have a final number value to compare.

10. Define the following key terms (in order of appearance in the chapter):
Select one or more methods: (1) fill in the missing key terms from memory, (2) match the key terms from the end of the review with their definitions below, or (3) copy the key terms in order from the list at the beginning of the chapter.

A _____ exists whenever objectives are not being met.

_________ is the process of taking corrective action in order to meet objectives.

_________ is the process of selecting an alternative course of action that will solve a problem.

The _________ steps include classifying and (1) defining the problem or opportunity, (2) setting objectives and criteria, (3) generating alternatives, (4) analyzing alternatives and selecting the most feasible, (5) planning and implementing the decision, and (6) controlling.

With _________, recurring or routine situations, the decision-maker should use decision rules or organizational policies and procedures to make the decision.

With _________, significant and nonrecurring and nonroutine situations, the decision-maker should use the decision-making model.

The three _________ include certainty, risk, and uncertainty.

_____ are the standards that an alternative must meet to be selected as the decision that will accomplish the objective.

_____ is the implementation of a new idea.

_____ is a way of thinking that generates new ideas.

The three stages in the _________ are (1) preparation, (2) incubation and illumination, and (3) evaluation.

With the _____ cus on defending the solv up with criticisms of w _____ is the n ternatives withou ating alternative agreement on a

KEY TERMS

brainstorming	decision-making	nominal grouping
consensus mapping	decision-making conditions	nonprogrammed decision
creative process	decision-making model	problem
creativity	devil's advocate	problem-solving
criteria	innovation	programmed decision

REVIEW AND DISCUSSION QUESTIONS

1. Are problem-solving and decision-making really important? Explain.
2. Why is it necessary to determine the decision structure and decision-making conditions?
3. What is the current trend in using groups to solve problems and make decisions?
4. Which potential disadvantage of group problem-solving and decision-making do you think is most common?
5. Is a decrease in sales or profits a symptom or a cause of a problem?
6. Would a maximum price of $1,000 to spend on a stereo be an objective or a criterion?
7. Are creativity and innovation really important to all types of businesses? Is it important to evaluate creativity before it becomes an innovation?
8. Have you ever made a decision with information that was not timely, of quality, complete, and/or relevant? If yes, explain.
9. What is the major difference between nominal grouping and consensus mapping?
10. Why are generating and analyzing alternatives separate steps in the decision-making model?
11. Have you ever used any of the techniques for analyzing and selecting an alternative? If yes, which one?
12. Do you know anyone who has been the victim of escalation of commitment? If yes, explain.

CASE

Carolyn Blakeslee's Art Calendar®

(This case also serves as the basis for Exercises 4–1 and 4–2.)

In 1986, Carolyn Blakeslee founded *Art Calendar*, a monthly publication for visual artists. Art Calendar provides information (approximately 15 pages) about grants, shows, and other forums to which artists can submit their work, as well as some topical freelance columns. *Art Calendar* is folksy in appearance and is mailed second class.

Carolyn started *Art Calendar* as a part-time business in a room in her home. She believed that half the people who received her first brochure would want to subscribe to her publication. She was heartbroken when only 3 percent subscribed. Later, she was happy to learn that 3 percent isn't bad in publishing. Regardless of her disappointment, eight out of the first ten years, circulation revenues doubled. Art *Calendar* grew to become artists' definitive source of information.

END OF CHAPTER MATERIAL REINFORCEMENT OF CONCEPTS

Each chapter ends with a Chapter Summary and Glossary. The summary reinforces every Learning Objective. The unique glossary aspect of the summary enables the readers to choose the key terms themselves, making it an active glossary. In addition, at least ten Review and Discussion Questions that support and reinforce the key conceptual learnings appear in the chapter.

TEST BANK ASSESSMENT OF CONCEPTS

Over half of the questions in the test bank (print and electronic) assess student knowledge of the managerial concepts taught in the text.

Applications

Powerful learning takes place when theory is put within the context of the real world. Using this text, students are challenged to apply the concepts they learn to actual business situations, especially as they have experienced them personally. Students must *think critically* as they apply specific concepts to their own work experience, short situations, and cases.

OPENING CASE AND INTERNET

At the beginning of each chapter information about an actual manager and organization is presented. Throughout the chapter, how the manager/organization applies the management concepts is discussed. The student gets a real-world example illustrated extensively throughout the chapter beginning with the opening pages. These cases reflect a mix of large, medium, and small businesses, both for profit and nonprofit organizations. As appropriate, an Internet address referring students to that company's WWW site is provided, allowing students to do further research on the organization. Use of the Internet is optional.

Skill Development

1. You should develop your skill to analyze a company's environment and management practices (Skill-Building Exercise 2–1).

This analysis requires conceptual skills. Having the skill to analyze your company's environment and management practices, and those of its competitors, will make you a more valuable employee. This skill is especially important if you want to progress to higher levels of management. The primary management function skill developed is planning. The primary management roles developed are informational and decisional. The SCANS skill competencies of resources, information, and especially systems, as well as basic and thinking foundation skills are developed.

Frederick W. Smith thought of the idea of an overnight delivery system by air freight to accommodate time-sensitive shipments such as medicines, computer parts, and electronics. Smith presented the idea in a term paper to a professor in college and received a grade of "C." On March 12, 1973, Smith tested his service by delivering six packages. FedEx began operations officially on April 17 with a total of 186 packages shipped. FedEx lost a million dollars a month for the first 27 months.

FedEx developed the hub-and-spokes system now widely imitated in the airline industry. Using this system, all shipments are flown to a centralized hub, sorted, loaded onto planes, and dispatched. By November 1988, Federal Express was able to deliver as many as a million packages in one night. FedEx was the first in its industry to offer innovative ideas and services including overnight package delivery, the Overnight Letter (1981), 10:30 A.M. next-day delivery (Fall 1982), package tracking in vans, real-time package tracking over the phone (1981), time-definite service for freight, Saturday delivery, and pickup service.

Applications

WORK APPLICATIONS

Throughout the chapter there are scattered open-ended questions (approximately ten per chapter) that require the students to explain how the text concepts apply to their own work experience. Student experience can be present, past, summer, full-time, or part-time employment. The questions cause the students to bridge the gap between theory and their real world.

107

Chapter 4 • Creative Problem-Solving and Decision-Making Skills

certainty, the manager knows the outcome of each alternative in advance. When making a decision under conditions of *risk*, the manager does not know the outcome of each alternative in advance, but can assign probabilities to each outcome. Under conditions of *uncertainty*, lack of information or knowledge makes the outcome of each alternative unpredictable so the manager cannot determine probabilities.

Nonprogrammed Decision (Significant and nonrecurring and nonroutine) (Longer period of time to make decisions)

Programmed Decision (Nonsignificant, recurring, and routine) (Shorter period of time to make decisions)

Figure 4–1
Decision Structure Continuum

As an example, suppose you were considering making an investment. If you were considering bonds, money market accounts, and certificates of deposit, you would know the payoff of each of the alternatives and would make a decision with *certainty* as to the interest paid. If you consider well-established stocks like Coca-Cola, Mobil Oil, and GM, through research you could assign probabilities of each stock going up (such as 40%, 35%, and 25%) and you would know the dividend paid. However, if you considered investing in two new companies with new innovative products, you could not be sure of the return, nor could you assign probabilities to them. When Coca-Cola introduced New Coke, it incurred a *risk*. If the company had been certain of the outcome of the decision, it would not have made it. It was a condition of risk because the company had conducted research with over 190,000 consumers through taste tests. The overwhelming majority preferred the taste of New Coke over Coca-Cola.

Work Application

3. Give an example of a programmed and a nonprogrammed decision and their decision conditions from an organization you work or have worked for.

Management makes most decisions under conditions of risk. However, upper-level managers tend to make more uncertain decisions than lower-level managers. When making decisions under uncertainty, it is difficult to determine the needed resources to solve the problem or create an opportunity.[7] Although risk and uncertainty cannot be eliminated, they can be reduced. Figure 4–2 illustrates the decision-making conditions continuum.

5. Describe when to use the decision-making model versus the bounded rationality model and group versus individual decision-making.

Decision-Making Model. There are two primary decision models: the rational model and the bounded rationality model. With the *rational model*, the decision-maker attempts to use *optimizing*, selecting the best possible alternative. With the *bounded rationality model*, the decision-maker uses *satisficing*, selecting the first alternative that meets the minimal criteria. The decision-making model presented as Model 4–1 is the rational model. With satisficing, only parts, or none, of the model would be used.

Uncertainty — Risk — Certainty

(outcome of alternatives unpredictable) — (outcome of alternatives predictable)

Figure 4–2
Decision-Making Conditions Continuum

You need to remember which model to use and when. The more unstructured the decision and the higher the degree of risk and uncertainty, the greater the need to spend the time conducting research with the aid of the decision-making model. Optimize (select the best possible alternative) when you are making nonprogrammed high-risk or uncertain decisions. Satisfice (select the first alternative that meets the minimum criteria) when you are making programmed low-risk or certain decisions. Figure 4–4 on page 110 il-

APPLYING THE CONCEPT

Every chapter contains a series of three to five Applying the Concepts boxes that require the student to determine the management concept being illustrated in a specific short example. There are 20 objective questions per chapter for development of student critical-thinking skills.

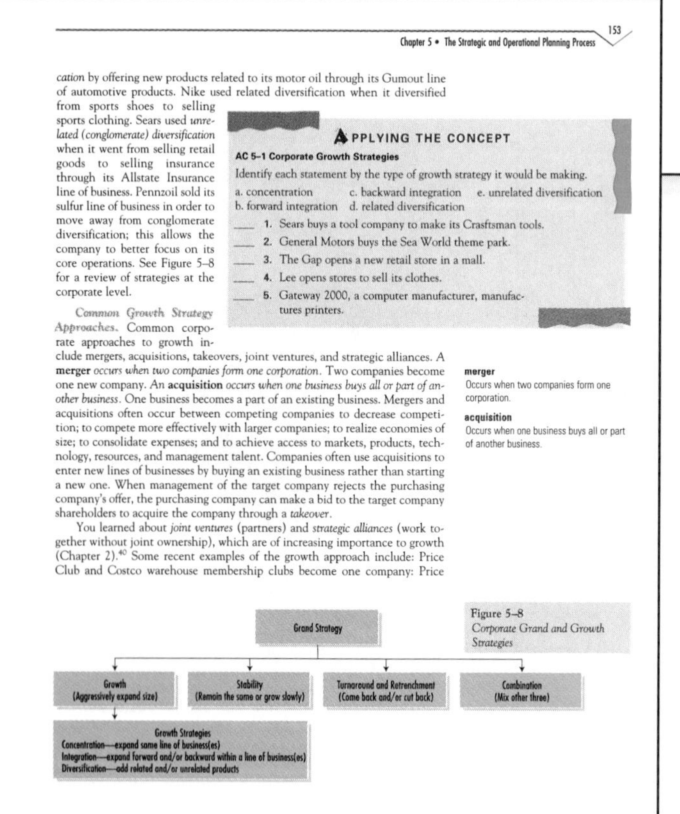

153

Chapter 5 • The Strategic and Operational Planning Process

cation by offering new products related to its motor oil through its Gumout line of automotive products. Nike used related diversification when it diversified from sports shoes to selling sports clothing. Sears used *unrelated (conglomerate) diversification* when it went from selling retail goods to selling insurance through its Allstate Insurance line of business. Pennzoil sold its sulfur line of business in order to move away from conglomerate diversification; this allows the company to better focus on its core operations. See Figure 5–8 for a review of strategies at the corporate level.

APPLYING THE CONCEPT

AC 5–1 Corporate Growth Strategies

Identify each statement by the type of growth strategy it would be making.

a. concentration c. backward integration e. unrelated diversification
b. forward integration d. related diversification

___ 1. Sears buys a tool company to make its Crafstman tools.
___ 2. General Motors buys the Sea World theme park.
___ 3. The Gap opens a new retail store in a mall.
___ 4. Lee opens stores to sell its clothes.
___ 5. Gateway 2000, a computer manufacturer, manufactures printers.

Common Growth Strategy Approaches. Common corporate approaches to growth include mergers, acquisitions, takeovers, joint ventures, and strategic alliances. A **merger** *occurs when two companies form one corporation.* Two companies become one new company. An **acquisition** *occurs when one business buys all or part of another business.* One business becomes a part of an existing business. Mergers and acquisitions often occur between competing companies to decrease competition; to compete more effectively with larger companies; to realize economies of size; to consolidate expenses; and to achieve access to markets, products, technology, resources, and management talent. Companies often use acquisitions to enter new lines of businesses by buying an existing business rather than starting a new one. When management of the target company rejects the purchasing company's offer, the purchasing company can make a bid to the target company shareholders to acquire the company through a *takeover*.

merger
Occurs when two companies form one corporation.

acquisition
Occurs when one business buys all or part of another business.

You learned about *joint ventures* (partners) and *strategic alliances* (work together without joint ownership), which are of increasing importance to growth (Chapter 2).[40] Some recent examples of the growth approach include: Price Club and Costco warehouse membership clubs become one company: Price

Grand Strategy

Growth (Aggressively expand size) | Stability (Remain the same or grow slowly) | Turnaround and Retrenchment (Come back and/or cut back) | Combination (Mix other three)

Growth Strategies
Concentration—expand same line of business(es)
Integration—expand forward and/or backward within a line of business(es)
Diversification—add related and/or unrelated products

Figure 5–8
Corporate Grand and Growth Strategies

Applications

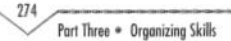

END-OF-CHAPTER CASE AND INTERNET

Following the review questions, students are presented with another actual manager and organization. The student learns how the manager/organization applies the management concepts from that chapter. Again, the businesses in the cases are large, medium, and small from both the for profit and nonprofit sectors. Each case is followed by ten multiple-choice questions and several open-ended questions. The questions require the student to apply management practices and concepts to the actual organization. As appropriate, an Internet address referring students to that company's WWW site is provided, allowing students to do further research on the organization. Use of the Internet is optional.

__________ is an OD technique that uses a questionnaire to gather data that are used as the basis for change.

__________ is an OD technique designed to help work groups increase structural and team dynamics performance.

__________ is an OD technique that is designed to improve team dynamics.

__________ is the planned change to realign the organization with its environment.

KEY TERMS

core values of TQM
forcefield analysis
learning organization
levels of culture
management information systems (MIS)
OD interventions
organizational culture
organizational development (OD)
organizational revitalization
process consultation
stages of the change process
survey feedback
team-building
types of change

REVIEW AND DISCUSSION QUESTIONS

1. How do the management functions relate to change?
2. How does the systems affect relate to the four types of change?
3. List the four stages in the change process.
4. Which of the five reasons for resisting change do you believe is most common?
5. Which of the six ways to overcome resistance to change do you believe is the most important?
6. What is the difference between a strong and weak
7. What are the two types of innovations?
8. List the six characteristics of an innovative culture.
9. Do you agree with the core values of TQM or would you recommend changing them? If yes, state your core values for TQM.
10. Which change model do you prefer? Why?
11. Have you ever worked for a firm that went through any type of organizational revitalization? If yes, explain it.

CASE

of business, best known to the public, was its photographic products. The Japanese came out with the 35-millimeter camera, while Kodak ignored the market for too long and gave the first mover advantage to the Japanese companies. Kodak also unsuccessfully spent years and millions of dollars on developing an instant camera to compete with

Polaroid, and got sued in the process for patent infringement. In the film area it lost market share to Fuji and other companies. On top of the heavy competition, the price of silver rose dramatically. Kodak was in a crisis because silver was a critical raw material in its photographic products.

Planning for Change

Top managers identified three major factors contributing to problems at Kodak. First, costs were too high. Second, information at the bottom of the operation was not being shared throughout the company, and managers were not being held accountable for performance. Third, staff specialists developed strategic planning but it was not implemented by the line managers. In other words, the planning process was not working. Based on these factors, departmentalization was considered to be the cause of many of Kodak's problems.

Kodak's functional departments focused on manufacturing, marketing, R&D, and finance. However, the top managers believed that the company had to respond to the global environment based on businesses rather than functions. With functional departments, no one was responsible for performance. The decision was made to change from functional to divisional departmentalization. The next decision was how to plan and implement the departmental change. A common approach was to have a group of four or five managers make the new organization chart behind closed doors and then dictate the change.

Managers were concerned about making the reorganization a success, so they decided to use participative management to implement the change following these steps: The top three managers developed a new organization. Then they met with the nine line managers, who would be affected by the change, and explained the new organization and the rationale as to why it was required. Part of the rationale was to become more competitive by developing new products at a faster rate. Top managers simply told the nine line managers to go off and think about the reorganization and then come back and discuss it. Line managers were to challenge, question, understand, improve, and most importantly to feel as though it is "our" reorganization. After four months, the team of 12 had a reorganization plan.

The team of 12 was expanded to the top 50 managers who went through roughly the same process. At the end of five months, 62 managers had a reorganization plan. The 62 widened to the top 150 managers. However, their job was not to rework the departmentalization; they were to develop a specific plan for the divisional implementation.

The next step was to appoint people to the top jobs in the new organization. Appointments were made based on assessment of talent, with seniority second in importance. Most of the top 150 managers involved in the process had new jobs. But more importantly, the large majority of managers supported the reorganization regardless of their new jobs. The preparation for change took 14 months.

Implementing Change

Kodak's reorganization began with a 12 percent reduction of employees over a two-year period. Most left voluntarily for other jobs, retirement, and so on. Over time, the number of managers was reduced by about 25 percent, and Kodak stopped its habit of promoting managers from within. Over a five-year period, nearly 70 percent of the key managers were new to their jobs.

Next, nearly 30 independent business units were created and given the responsibility for developing and implementing their own strategy and worldwide profit performance. The export strategy changed, depending on the business unit, all the way to the direct investment level. The business units were grouped into traditional imaging businesses, image-intensive information technology, and plastic polymers. Kodak acquire[…] into pharmaceutic[…] group.

In order t[…] markets, and […] were split u[…] The relati[…] different […] its busin[…] terms, ea[…] oping th[…] geograph[…] of that t[…]

Each […] uation o[…]

to generate a return that exceeded an internally established cost of equity, reflecting its own level of risk and market conditions. Businesses unable to attain the required rate of return were put on probation, and if they did not reach the goal, they were dismantled or divested.

Kodak's reorganization was successful by most measures. It improved its financial, productivity, and market share performance. Kodak's performance improved at a rate four times the U.S. average for several years in a row.

Select the best alternative for the following questions. Be sure you are able to explain your answers.

___ 1. The forces for change at Kodak came from the ___ environment.

a. external b. internal c. both

___ 2. The type of change Kodak made was primarily a ___ change.

a. strategy c. technology
b. structure d. people

___ 3. Top management at Kodak took so long, 14 months, coming up with a plan for change because it was concerned about the ___ stage in the change process.

a. denial c. exploration
b. resistance d. commitment

___ 4. Managers at Kodak may have resisted the change for ___ reasons.

a. uncertainty d. loss
b. inconvenience e. control
c. self-interest f. all of these

___ 5. The primary way to overcome resistance to change used at Kodak was

a. develop a trust climate
b. plan
c. state why change is needed and how it will affect employees
d. create a win-win situation
e. involve employees
f. provide support

___ 6. Part of the reason for Kodak's change in departmentalization was to develop a more innovative culture.

a. true b. false

___ 7. Kodak changed to a TQM culture.

a. true b. false

___ 8. Kodak used OD in its change process.

a. true b. false

___ 9. Kodak followed the steps in the comprehensive change model.

a. true b. false

___ 10. Kodak's change can be considered an organizational revitalization.

a. true b. false

11. Discuss the systems affect of Kodak's reorganization.

12. It took 14 months to plan the change, and the organizational design was not changed dramatically from the original top three managers' plan. Would it have been faster just to have dictated the change? Using hindsight, would you have dictated the change or used participation as Kodak did?

For current information on Kodak, use Internet address http://www.kodak.com. For ideas on using the Internet, see the Appendix.

Applications

APPENDIX:

HOW TO RESEARCH CASE MATERIAL USING THE INTERNET

Students familiar and not so familiar with the Internet will find this appendix a practical tool for using the Internet to gain more information about various companies. Whether researching the companies and addresses listed with the text cases or completing other class projects, this short guide shows students how to find the most current information on businesses in our information age.

ENVIRONMENT
MANAGING CHANGE
LEADERSHIP
CONTROL SYSTEMS
HUMAN RESOURCES
QUALITY
PLANNING
TEAMWORK
DECISION MAKING

BUSINESSLINK VIDEOCASES

Student learning is enhanced by seeing actual managers tackling real management problems within their workplace. The Lussier package contains nine videocases provided free to adopters. Each videocase centers around the decisions made by managers from the topic of a given chapter. All videos pose critical-thinking questions to be answered by students. BusinessLink Video Cases are integrated at the end of each chapter. All BusinessLink Video Cases have extensive supporting print material for both instructors and students.

69

Chapter 2 • The Environment: Quality, Globalization, Ethics, and Social Responsibility

VIDEOCASE

The Changing U.S. Health Care Environment:
Central Michigan Community Hospital

The U.S. health care environment is undergoing major changes. The average age of the American population is increasing. This is due to aging of the post-war baby boom generation and life-extending medical technologies which have increased the average life span for both men and women. The population has also become more health conscious, enabling senior citizens in their seventies and eighties to lead active lives. At the same time, there are major concerns about the cost of health care. Employers, consumers, and government—the major payers of health care bills—are seeking ways to contain health costs while maintaining quality and access to medical services. New technologies are constantly being developed, and they are often very expensive.

In response to these social, economic, and technological trends, hospitals and doctors have come under pressure to better manage delivery of health care services and costs. Hospitals and doctors are joining together, sometimes in cooperation with insurance companies, to control costs and provide services. These cooperative arrangements are sometimes called *managed care* or *health maintenance organizations*. These newly formed cooperative hospital/doctor groups are now competing with one another to provide coverage to growing elderly (Medicare) and poor (Medicaid) populations, while keeping costs under control.

Central Michigan Community Hospital (CMCH) is a nonprofit regional referral system which includes a full-service 151-bed hospital; a medical staff of over 120 doctors; READYCARE, a walk-in urgent care center; wellness services; occupational medicine; home health care; plus numerous other services. In 1994, CMCH was honored as one of the "Top 100 Hospitals in the U.S." But changes in the U.S. health care environment are affecting CMCH. CMCH has been evaluating these environmental changes and how they could influence the future of their regional health system.

TEST BANK (ASSESSING APPLICATION ABILITY) AND INSTRUCTOR MANUAL REINFORCEMENT OF APPLICATIONS

The test bank includes application questions that include work application questions, questions similar to "applying the concepts" questions, and some short cases with accompanying critical-thinking questions. The Instructor's Manual contains detailed answers for all of the application features.

Skills

The difference between learning about management and learning to be a manager is the acquisition of skills. My text focuses on skill development so students can use what they learn on the job. While the skill material is integrated throughout the text, instructors can choose how to incorporate the material into their classroom experience – individually or as groups, inside the class or as outside group projects. Instructors can also determine the extent to which they want to use behavior modeling as the basis for skill development in their classroom, if at all.

I use the term "skill building" in this text only if students can actually develop a skill that can be used on the job. The features listed below include true skill building, such as step-by-step models, skill-building exercises, and behavior model videos. Other features support skill building, such as self-assessments and group exercises. Students will know they are working on a skill when they see this icon in the margin.

SKILL DEVELOPMENT GOALS

Following a chapter's Learning Objectives, the chapter's Skill Development Goals are listed. Specific skills that can be learned through the use of the chapter and its exercises are detailed. The goals identify the management function, skill, role, and SCANS competencies taught in that chapter.

Skill Development

SKILLBUILDER 1. You should develop your skill at setting priorities (Skill-Building Exercise 7–1).

Setting priorities is an organizing skill that utilizes conceptual and decision-making skills. The exercise develops your decisional role skill of resource allocator. The SCANS skill competencies of using resources, information, and systems, as well as basic, thinking, and personal qualities foundation skills are also developed.

SKILLBUILDER 2. You should develop your delegating skills (Skill-Building Exercise 7–2).

Delegating is an organizing skill that utilizes human and communication skills. This exercise develops your interpersonal leader skills, informational skill of monitor, and decisional skill of resource allocator. The SCANS skills competencies of using resources, information, and systems, as well as basic, thinking, and personal qualities foundation skills are developed.

lfred Chandler determined the need to match the organization's strategy and structure (Chapter 1). In other words, for the strategy to be implemented successfully, the organization must have a compatible structure. When the strategy changes, the structure follows (form follows function). As firms change, the organization structure must also change. The need for change will be illustrated throughout the chapter with the CMP Publications integrated case.

The husband and wife team of Gerry and Lilo Leeds founded CMP Publications in 1971. They have grown, at their goal of 20 percent a year, from 1 to 14 business newspapers and magazines, which are leaders in their respective markets. Sales exceed $380 million a year. They compete in the high growth high-tech markets.

The Leeds's original structure called for centralized authority with Gerry and Lilo making all important decisions. As CMP grew, it became increasingly difficult for employees to personally meet with the Leeds. Employees began to line up outside the office at 8:00 in the morning and there was a constant waiting line. Important decisions that required a quick response, due to rapidly changing environments, were often delayed. The

Skills

STEP-BY-STEP MODELS

The book contains 24 detailed sets of how-to steps for handling day-to-day management functions. They are integrated into the context of the chapter or skill-building exercise being taught. For example, models teach how to set objectives and priorities, how to handle a complaint, how to discipline an employee, etc. This feature directly teaches students how to be managers.

policy that allows employees to feel free to come to you with a complaint. It is much better to get complaints out in the open and try to resolve them than to have employees complaining to everyone else about you. In this section you will learn how to handle complaints, and Skill-Building Exercise 2–1 will help you develop this skill.

The Complaint-Handling Model

7. List and explain the steps in the complaint-handling model.

When employees come to you with a complaint, try not to take it personally as a reflection on you or your management ability. Even the best managers have to deal with complaints. Do not become defensive and try to talk the employee out of the complaint. You can use the complaint-handling model to help you resolve complaints when employees come to you. *The* **complaint-handling model** *involves (1) listening to the complaint and paraphrasing it; (2) having the complainer recommend a solution; (3) scheduling time to get all the facts and/or make a decision; (4), developing a plan, and (5) implementing the plan and following up.* A discussion of each step follows.

complaint-handling model
(1) Listen to the complaint and paraphrase it. (2) Have the complainer recommend a solution. (3) Schedule time to get all the facts and/or make a decision. (4) Develop a plan. (5) Implement the plan and follow up.

step 1. **Listen to the Complaint and Paraphrase It.** This is a very important step. Listen to the full story without interruptions and paraphrase it (repeat it back to the complainer in your own words) to ensure accuracy. Listening and paraphrasing are necessary because if you cannot accurately state the complaint, you cannot resolve it. Paraphrasing is very important because employees often do not know how to state their complaint accurately. They often talk about one issue when something else is causing the problem. Your paraphrasing helps them see the difference and adjust accordingly. As the manager, it's your job to determine the true cause of the complaint.

When listening to the complaint, distinguish facts from opinions. There will be times when employees think they know the facts, when in reality they do not. For example, a more experienced employee may have heard that a less experienced worker earns the same wages. The experienced employee may complain. When the manager states the facts—that the experienced worker is paid more (it may be best not to state the specific amount)—the complaint may be dropped immediately.

It is also helpful to identify the person's feelings about the complaint and to determine the employee's motives for the complaint.

Have the Complainer Recommend a Solution. After you have paraphrased the complaint and the employee has agreed with the paraphrasing, you should ask the complainer to recommend a solution. The complainer may know a good solution you may not think of. Requesting a solution does not mean that you have to implement it. In some cases, the recommended solution may not solve the problem. Moreover, the solution may not be fair to others. Some recommendations may not be possible. In such cases, you should let the employee know that the solution is not possible and explain why. step 2.

step 3. **Schedule Time to Get All the Facts and/or Make a Decision.** Since employee complaints often involve other people, you may find it necessary to check records or to talk to others. It is often helpful to talk to your boss or your peers, who may have had a similar complaint; they may be

Model 3–1
The Complaint Model

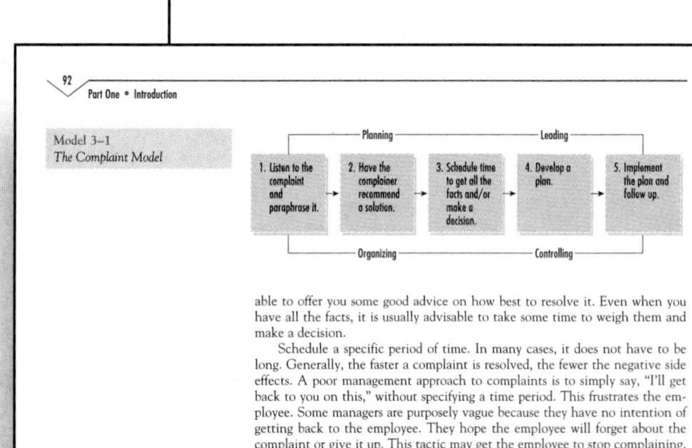

able to offer you some good advice on how best to resolve it. Even when you have all the facts, it is usually advisable to take some time to weigh them and make a decision.

Schedule a specific period of time. In many cases, it does not have to be long. Generally, the faster a complaint is resolved, the fewer the negative side effects. A poor management approach to complaints is to simply say, "I'll get back to you on this," without specifying a time period. This frustrates the employee. Some managers are purposely vague because they have no intention of getting back to the employee. They hope the employee will forget about the complaint or give it up. This tactic may get the employee to stop complaining, but it may also cause productivity and turnover problems.

Work Application

8. Identify a complaint you brought to a manager. State the complaint and identify which steps in the complaint-handling model the manager did or did not follow. If you have never complained, interview someone who has.

Develop a Plan. After getting all the necessary facts and advice from others, you should develop a plan. The plan may be developed by simply using the complainer's recommended solution. However, when you do not agree with the complainer's solution, explain why, and either work with the employee to find an alternative or present your own plan. The level of the employee's participation in planning should be based on his or her capability level. step 4.

In cases where you decide not to take any action to resolve the complaint, you should clearly explain why you chose not to do so. State that if employees are not satisfied, they can appeal the decision to another level. The complainer should be told how to appeal the decision. In a nonunion organization, the usual step is to go to the manager's boss. In a union organization, the first step usually is to go to the union steward, who often accompanies the employee during the meeting with the supervisor.

step 5. **Implement the Plan and Follow Up.** It is important to make sure that the plan is implemented through follow-up methods. It may be appropriate to set a follow-up meeting. It is also advisable to make a written documentation of all meetings and actions taken by you and others.

See Model 3–1 for a review of the five steps just discussed.

SKILLBUILDER

CURRENT MANAGEMENT ISSUES

In this chapter we discussed *diversity* and *globalization* and diversity. *Ethics* is an important concept as it relates to diversity. If you use ethical behavior, it will improve your human relations. If you use unethical behavior, for example, if you

Skills

SKILL-BUILDING EXERCISES

Each chapter contains at least one Skill-Building Exercise, all class tested to be the best found in any text in the market. Full support of over 27 activities can be found in the Instructor's Manual including detailed information, timing, answers, etc. All exercises and their use are optional in the classroom. There are two primary types of exercises:

A. Individual Focus: Approximately 60 percent are those in which participants are required to make individual decisions prior to or during class. These can be shared in class for discussion or, in large class settings, the instructor may elect to go over recommended answers;

B. Role Play Focus: Less than 40 percent are those in which participants are presented with a model and given the opportunity to use the model, usually in groups of three.

276 
Part Three • Organizing Skills

SKILL-BUILDING EXERCISE 8–1

Identifying Resistance to Change

Preparing for Skill-Building Exercise 8–1

Below are ten statements made by employees asked to make a change on the job. Identify the source and focus of their resistance using Model 8–1. Because it is difficult to identify intensity of resistance on paper, skip the intensity factor. However, when you deal with people on the job, you need to identify their intensity. Place the number of the box (1–9) that represents and best describes the major resistance.

___ 1. "But we never did the job that way before. Can't we just do it the same way as always?"

___ 2. The tennis coach asked Jill, the star player, to have Louise as her doubles partner. Jill said, "Come on, Louise is a lousy player. Betty is better; don't break us up." The coach disagreed and forced Jill to accept Louise.

___ 3. The manager, Winny, told Mike to stop letting everyone in the department take advantage of him by sticking him with extra work. Mike said, "But I like my coworkers and I want them to like me, too. If I don't help people they may not like me."

___ 4. "I can't learn how to use the new computer. I'm not smart enough to use it."

___ 5. The police sergeant asked Chris, the patrol officer, to take a rookie cop as her partner. Chris said, "Do I have to? I broke in the last rookie, Wayne. He and I are getting along well."

___ 6. The employee went to Chuck, the manager, and asked him if she could change the work-order form. Chuck said, "That would be a waste of time; the current form is fine."

___ 7. Diane, an employee, is busy at work. The manager tells her to stop what she is doing and begin a new project. Diane says, "The job I'm working on now is more important."

___ 8. "I don't want to work with that work team. It has the lowest performance record in the department."

buy our smoke detector system. I don't think its unethical. Our competitors do it."

Doing Skill-Building Exercise 8–1 in Class

Objective
To develop your ability to identify resistance to change so that you can improve your skill at overcoming resistance and implement changes effectively.

Preparation
You should have determined the resistance to change for the ten preparation statements.

Experience
You will get feedback on how well you identified resistance to change.

Procedure (10–30 minutes)
Option 1. Break into groups of four to six and share your priorities. Try to reach a group consensus on each of the ten priorities. When the groups are finished, one member records priorities for the entire class to see. After all groups are finished, the instructor goes over the recommended answers.

Option 2. The instructor calls on students to get their priorities to each task. The instructor goes over the recommended answer for each item after a student(s) gives a priority.

Option 3. The instructor goes over the recommended answers without student involvement.

Conclusion
The instructor leads a class discussion and/or makes concluding remarks.

Application (2–4 minutes)
What did I learn from this experience? How will I use this knowledge in the future?

the sharing questions.

Chapter 9 • Human Resources Management: Staffing 315

SKILL-BUILDING EXERCISE 9–1

Selecting a Tennis Coach[68]

Preparing for Skill-Building Exercise 9–1

You are in your first year as athletic director at a local high school. While planning your human resources needs, you realize the tennis coach position will be open. You must staff the position. The compensation for the job is set in the budget. It is to be paid in one lump sum at the end of the season. It is competitive with the pay of other tennis coaches in the area.

Recruiting

Because you have no recruiting budget, you do some internal recruiting and contact some athletic directors in your area to spread the word about the opening. You recruit three candidates for the coaching position. Following is a brief listing of their qualifications.

Candidate A has been a history teacher at your school for ten years. This person was the tennis coach for two years. It's been five years since the teacher coached the team. You don't know why the candidate stopped coaching or how good a job was done. Candidate A never played competitive tennis. However, someone told you the candidate plays regularly and is pretty good. You guess the teacher is about 35 years old.

Candidate B works as a supervisor on the 11 P.M. to 7 A.M. shift for a local business. This candidate has never coached before. However, the person was a star player in high school and college. Candidate B still plays in local tournaments and you see the name in the paper now and then. You guess this candidate is about 25 years old.

Candidate C has been a basketball coach and physical education teacher at a nearby high school for the past five years. The person has a master's degree in physical education. You figure it will take the person 20 minutes to get to your school. Candidate C has never coached tennis, but did play on the high school team. The candidate plays tennis about once a week. You guess the person is about 45 years old.

Preparing for the Interviews

Follow the six interview preparation steps in Model 9–1. For step 1, there are no job descriptions and specifications. Because there are only three candidates, you have decided to interview them all, even if they do not meet your job specifications.

Conducting the Interviews

During the in-class part of this exercise you will conduct a job interview. Be sure to bring your preparation—written questions on a form—material for class use.

Doing Skill-Building Exercise 9–1 in Class

Objectives
To perform a job analysis and to develop skills in employment selection interviewing.

Preparation
You should have your form with a list of questions for candidates.

Experience
You will discuss your preparation. You will also conduct a job interview, be an interviewee, and observe an interview.

Procedure 1 (5–10 minutes)
Break into groups of five or six, pass your preparation materials around to the other members, and discuss them. You may make changes to improve your preparation. For example, you may want to add some good questions you did not think of.

Procedure 2 (3–5 minutes)
Break into groups of three; do not divide into the same groups used in procedure 1. Make one or two groups of two, if necessary. Each person selects one of the three candidates (A, B, or C) he or she will role-play during the interview. Use your own name, but assume you have the person's qualifications; ad lib realistically.

Procedure 3 (25–75 minutes)
1-1. *Interview 1 takes place.* The person who chose A is the interviewer, B is the interviewee, and C is the observer. A conducts the interview using his or her interview materials, while B answers the questions. C observes quietly, and gives feedback on how well the interview went. (If there are only two in your group, B is also the observer.) You may not be able to ask all your questions in the allotted time (5 to 20 minutes). Keep the opening short and be sure to close when you are ready to or the time is up.

1-2. *Integration* (3–5 minutes). C gives his or her observation of the interview. All three group members discuss the interview and how it could be improved. Do not go on to the next interview until you are told to do so.

2-1. *Interview 2 takes place.* B is the interviewer, C is the interviewee, and A is the observer. Follow the guidelines for 1-1.

2-2. *Integration.* Follow the guidelines for 1-2.

3-1. *Interview 3 takes place.* C is the interviewer; A is the interviewee; and B is the observer. Groups of two join other triads as observers. Follow the guidelines for 1-1.

Skills

SITUATIONAL MANAGEMENT
HANDLING COMPLAINTS
DECISION MAKING
DELEGATION
EMPLOYMENT INTERVIEWING
TRAINING
SITUATIONAL COMMUNICATIONS
GIVING PRAISE
INITIATING CONFLICT RESOLUTION
MEDIATING CONFLICT RESOLUTION
COACHING
DISCIPLINE

BEHAVIOR MODEL VIDEOS

To reinforce the development of skills for students, the Lussier package includes twelve Behavior Model Videos, unique to the Management curriculum. The videos demonstrate managers successfully handling common management functions such as handling complaints, delegating tasks, conducting job interviews, etc. Students learn from watching the videos and/or using them in conjunction with Skill-Building Exercises. Material in the text integrates the videos into the chapters. Ideas for using all videos are detailed in the Instructor's Manual.

SELF-ASSESSMENT EXERCISES

Scattered throughout the text are 16 Self-Assessment Exercises. Students complete these assessments in order to gain personal knowledge of self. All information for completing and scoring the assessments is contained within the text. Self-knowledge leads students to an understanding of how they can and will operate as managers in the real world. Many of the assessments are tied to exercises within the book, thus enhancing the impact of the activities.

28 Part One • Introduction

__ 8. As CEO, Bill Gates has greater need for which skills?

a. technical over conceptual
b. conceptual over technical
c. a balance

__ 9. As CEO, how does Bill Gates spend more time.

a. planning and organizing
b. leading and controlling
c. a balance

__ 10. Which approach does Bill Gates most likely take to management?

a. classical c. management science
b. behavioral d. integrative

11. Give examples of some of the tasks Bill Gates performs in each of the four management functions.

12. Give examples of some of the tasks Bill Gates performs in each of the three management roles.

13. Do you think you would like to work for Bill Gates? Explain your answer.

For current information on Microsoft, use Internet address http://www.microsoft.com. For ideas on using the Internet, see the Appendix.

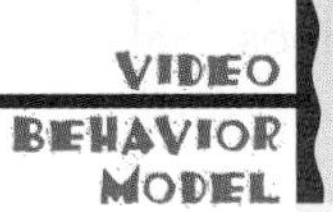

Behavior Model Video 1–1, Situational Management, shows Laura, a bank branch manager, who manages tellers who are not collecting fees. Laura's boss, Celeste, discusses the situation with her. The video illustrates the four management styles, explained in Skill-Building Exercise 1–1.

Objective
To better understand the four situational management styles.

Procedure 1 (10–20 minutes)
The instructor shows Behavior Model Video 1–1. As you view each of the four scenes, identify the four situational management styles and select the one being used by the manager.

Scene 1. __ a. autocratic (S1A)
Scene 2. __ b. consultative (S2C)
Scene 3. __ c. participative (S3P)
Scene 4. __ d. empowerment (S4E)

After viewing each of the four scenes, identify/match the style used by the manager by placing the letter of the style on the scene line.

Option A: View all four scenes and identify the style used by the manager. After viewing all four scenes, discuss them. The correct answers are given in the video.

Option B: After each scene, the class discusses the style used by the man-
...h of the four
...re other styles
...ppropriate) for

Chapter 10 • Communicating 335

Notice that the second statement takes the pressure off the employee. The sender is asking for a check on his or her ability, not that of the employee. These types of requests for paraphrasing should result in a positive attitude toward the message and the sender. They show concern for the employee and for communicating effectively.

Delta Airlines' communication objective was to inform travel agents of its decision to cap their commissions. Delta selected the written fax to send the message. Delta did not check understanding because it knew the feedback would be negative. What type of feedback would you give to a person who told you that you will do the same work, but you will be paid less, possibly half as much, for doing it? The written fax was chosen because it does not often encourage a response. Many travel agents that target business travelers had their revenues cut dramatically. They needed to book passengers on airlines that did not have a cap. However, this is not always possible. Therefore, to help cut the lost revenue, they needed to pass on some of the cost to the client. Many travel agents appropriately met face-to-face with clients to go over the cap situation and discuss added fees.

Work Application

6. Recall a past or present boss. How effective was this person at getting feedback? Was the boss open to feedback and aware of nonverbal communication? Did the boss ask questions and ask you to paraphrase?

SKILL BUILDER

RECEIVING MESSAGES

The third step in the communication process requires the receiver to decode the message and decide if feedback is needed. With oral communication, the key to successfully understanding the message is listening.

Listening Skills

Complete Self-Assessment Exercise 10–1 to determine how good a listener you are, then read the tips for improving listening skills in the message-receiving process.

SELF-ASSESSMENT EXERCISE 10–1

Listening Skills

Select the response that best describes the frequency of your actual behavior. Place the letter A, U, F, O, or S on the line before each of the 15 statements.
A—almost always U—usually F—frequently
O—occasionally S—seldom

__ 1. I like to listen to people talk. I encourage others to talk by showing interest, smiling, nodding, and so forth.
__ 2. I pay closer attention to people who are more similar to me than people who are different from me.
__ 3. I evaluate people's words and nonverbal communication ability as they talk.
__ 4. I avoid distractions; if it's noisy, I suggest moving to a quiet spot.
__ 5. When people come to me and interrupt me when I'm doing something,

Skills

STUDENT ASSESSMENT SOFTWARE

All of the Self-Assessment Exercises can be completed and scored electronically using the Student Assessment Software. The outcome of the assessments will be a personal profile of the student as manager. The software also contains content concept reinforcement through vocabulary and review questions. The software is available separately.

EXERCISES

Many chapters contain exercises that enhance classroom learning but are not directly tied to developing skills. These tend to center around group projects and classroom discussions for the creation of an active learning environment.

TEST BANK (ASSESSING SKILL DEVELOPMENT) AND INSTRUCTOR MANUAL REINFORCEMENT OF SKILLS

Every Skill-Building Exercise in the text has reinforcement and assessment questions for it in the corresponding test bank chapter, a unique feature of the Lussier text package.
The Instructor's Manual contains detailed answers for all of the skills features in the text including timing, information, answers, logistics for instructor use, and follow-up questions for student debriefing.
The manual also explains how to test on skill-building.

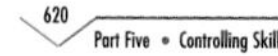
620 Part Five • Controlling Skills

SKILL-BUILDING EXERCISE 17–1

Economic Order Quantity

Preparing for Skill-Building Exercise 17–1

Calculate the EOQ for each of the four following situations:

__ 1. R = 2,000, S = $15.00, H = $5.00
__ 2. H = $10.00, R = 7,500, S = $40.00
__ 3. R = 500, H = $15.00, S = $35.00
__ 4. S = $50.00, H = $25.00, R = 19,000

Doing Skill-Building Exercise 17–1 in Class

Objective
To develop your skill at calculating EOQ.

Preparation
You should have calculated EOQ for the four situations in the preparation section.

Procedure 1 (10–20 minutes)
Option A. The instructor goes over the correct EOQ answers in class.
Option B. The instructor has students come to the front of the class and go over the EOQ answers.

Conclusion
The instructor leads a class discussion and/or makes concluding remarks.

Application (2–4 minutes)
What did I learn for this experience? How will I use this knowledge in the future?

____

____

Sharing
Volunteers give their answers to the application section.

EXERCISE 17–1

Implementing the Management Functions

Preparation for Exercise 17–1

You should have studied planning, organizing and staffing, leading, and controlling.

Doing Exercise 17–1 in Class

Objective
To develop skill at implementing the management functions.

Preparation
The preparation is to have studied the prior chapters covering the management functions.

Experience
During the in-class exercise, you will be either a member of Production Company that produces a product to make a profit or a customer and supplier who buys the product and

Procedure 1 (3–4 minutes)
Break into as many groups of five as possible while still having at least half as many students as the number of teams. The students in the groups are members of Production Company and will produce the product described below. This is not an ongoing product that is sold; it is a one-time order from one customer. All other students will be customers and suppliers. At least one student must be assigned to each group as its customer and/or supplier; if necessary, customer/suppliers may have more than one group. Teams should spread out as much as possible. Suppliers are given stacks of paper to sell to the groups. Customers/suppliers should sit close to their Production Company team and listen and observe. However, they may not communicate in any way with the team.

Procedure 2 (10 minutes)
Suppliers give each Production Company team ten free papers for planning purposes. Using the contract with cus-
ement) sheet ac-
team must plan
during the ten-
w much raw ma-
team must plan
as organize and

Chapter 17 • Operations, Quality, and Information Control Systems 621

Production Company Contracts with Customer and Supplier and Profit or Loss Statement
(To be filled out by customer/supplier with Production Company)

Customer Contract
Bid: number of products Production Company contracts to build during the period. ________*
The customer will not buy any products above the bid amount.
Agreed price per product that meets inspection: $25,000.
Number of products accepted ______ × $25,000 = $ ________
Agreed penalty charge of $30,000 for each product not delivered on time.
Number not produced ______ × $30,000 = – $ ________
Check paid by customer to Production Company. $ ________
Fine for unethically making products before or after time period,
If caught deduct $100,000 from amount of check to be paid to customer.

Supplier Contract
Number of raw material paper purchased ________ × $10,000 = $ ________*
Raw material of unused paper cannot be used for other jobs. However, the supplier agrees to buy it back at a penalty.
Number of returned unfolded papers ________ × $8,000 = – $ ________
All work-in-process cannot be sold after the contract period, nor returned to the supplier at a penalty fee. However, the supplier will buy it as scrap.
Number of folded papers ________ × $5,000 = – $ ________
Cost of Goods Sold (CGS) Check given to supplier from Production Company. $ ________

Profit or Loss Job Statement
Revenue (amount of check received from customer) $ ________
Cost of Goods Sold (variable cost, check given to supplier) – ________
Gross Profit $ ________
Expenses (fixed cost for the period including labor, overhead, etc.) – $ 250,000
Profit or Loss Before Taxes $ ________
Taxes (If you have a profit, multiply 25% tax rate times profit) – $ ________
Net Income or Loss $ ________

*Filled out prior to production. All others lines filled-out after production period.

Steps for Making the Product

1. Fold the paper in half; unfold. Then fold it in half in the other direction; unfold.

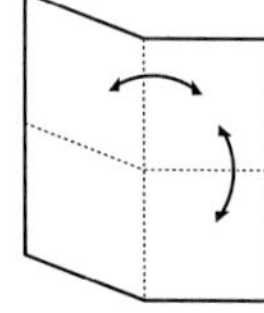

2. Turn the paper over. Fold the paper in half diagonally; unfold. Then fold it in half diagonally in the other direction.

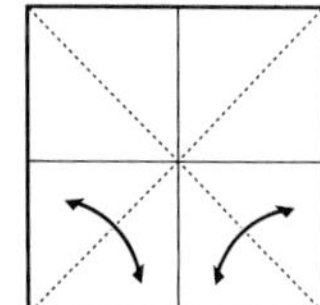

Ancillary Support

Just as businesses must be integrated across functions and departments for success, text and ancillary material must also integrate to create the optimum student learning experience. Many of our key supplements have been described to you as part of the support for our three-pronged approach to the management curriculum. The list below describes all elements of the text package to create a successful classroom environment. All instructor supplements are free to adopters. I personally wrote the Instructor's Manual, wrote and reviewed much of the test bank, created all the acetate transparencies, and edited every Behavior Model Video script to assure the development of the best integrated learning features for management.

STUDENT SUPPLEMENTS

Study Guide. The study guide consists of the following per chapter: Chapter Pretest, Chapter Summary, Key Term Review, Review Questions (including t/f and multiple choice), and answers to all questions.

Student Assessment Software. This unique tool allows students to combine the elements of the study guide with the creation of a personal management profile based on an assessment of the student's personality attributes. All of the Self-Assessment Exercises can be completed and scored electronically using the Student Assessment Software. The outcome of the assessments will be a personal profile of the student as manager. The software also contains content concept reinforcement through vocabulary and review questions.

BusinessLink Videocase Student Guide. Another unique learning tool, the BusinessLink Videocase Student Guide, provides students with extensive materials describing the companies in the videocases including annual reports, critical-thinking questions, and Internet sites for students. The guide makes the profiled companies come alive.

INSTRUCTOR SUPPLEMENTS

Instructor's Manual. I wrote the manual to assure every faculty member would receive complete integrated support for teaching. The manual contains the following for each chapter of the book: a detailed outline for lecture enhancement, Work Application Student Sample Answers, Review and Discussion Questions Answers, Applying the Concept Answers, Answers to Case Questions, Instructions on Use of Videos, and Skill-Building Exercise and other Exercise Ideas (including set-up and timing). The IM also includes ideas on how to use the special features of the text in the classroom with an emphasis placed on creating an interactive learning environment.

Electronic Instructor's Manual. The entire manual is available to instructors on disk for custom manipulation of outlines and other material for class preparation.

Ancillary Support

Test Bank. A unique feature of the text package is the test bank structured around the three-pronged approach of the book: concepts, applications, and skills. Questions assessing each aspect of student learning in these three areas are delineated and included for each chapter. No other book on the market attempts to assess student skill development.

Electronic Test Bank. All test questions are available in electronic Windows-based format for automatic test generation.

Teaching Transparencies. Over one hundred acetate transparencies will support the package. All are referenced within the Instructor's Manual for use in lectures.

PowerPoint. All teaching transparencies are available in electronic format for a more flexible and professional presentation in the classroom.

Behavior Model Videos. To reinforce the development of skills for students, the Lussier package includes twelve Behavior Model Videos, unique to the Management curriculum. The videos demonstrate managers successfully handling common management functions such as handling complaints, delegating tasks, conducting job interviews, etc. Students learn from watching the videos and/or using them in conjuction with Skill-Building Exercises. Material in the text integrates the videos into the chapters. Ideas for using all videos are detailed in the Instructor's Manual.

BusinessLink Videocases. Accompanying and integrated within the text are nine BusinessLink Videocases. Each case centers around topics key to management understanding within a profile of a real business organization solving real-world problems. They create added variety in the classroom presentation and stimulate students to learn about organizations, teams, and management.

BusinessLink Videocase Manual. A special supplement accompanies the BusinessLink videocases that includes the entire script for each video with cues for instructor enhancement, critical-thinking questions and answers, detailed company backgrounds, and additional embellishments for use of the videos in the classroom.

Summary of Key Innovations

My goal is to make both students and instructors successful in the classroom by providing learning features that not only teach about management but help students become managers. Here's the special ways in which we do it:

- The three-pronged approach to the curriculum: concepts, applications, skills.
- Flexibility – use any or all of the features that work for you!
- Assessment of this approach through a three-section test bank: concepts, applications, skills.
- Unique skill-building exercises that develop skills for use on the job.
- Fewer chapters with a systems approach to the subject of management.
- Internet linkages including a helpful appendix.
- An unsurpassed video package: 12 Behavior Models; 9 BusinessLink Videocases.

Acknowledgments

The authorship of a publishing project of this magnitude is only one aspect of a complex process. Many hardworking individuals gave great effort to create this text and package. I wish to express my gratitude to many of these key contributors, especially the fine people at South-Western College Publishing/ITP. Having worked with a number of major publishers over the years, South-Western is the best. First of all, Gary Bauer and Tom Bormann got this project off the ground with their fine tuning of my vision and suggestions. Christine Sofranko took over direction of the project to spearhead its development and marketing. Editor-in-Chief, Valerie Ashton, has been unwavering in her strong support of the project and its goals. I also wish to thank my Art Director, Debbie Kokoruda, my Production Editors, Marci Dechter and Laura Cleveland, and my Video Editor, Sherie Skladany. My secretary, Mechele Holbrook, also provided great support.

I wish to thank my mentor and coauthor of many publications, Joel Corman, for his advice and encouragement during and after my graduate education at Suffolk University. I also wish to thank Dr. Abbas Nadim, Dr. David Morris, and Dr. Judith Neal, doctoral faculty at the University of New Haven. Thanks, Dr. Nadim (Ph.D., Wharton School; protégé of Russell Ackoff) for educating me in the ways of systems theory which is used throughout this book. Thanks too to Dr. Morris for influencing the development of more figures that integrate the material through the use of visuals.

In addition, the reviewers of the project provided me with great ideas and inspiration for writing. The reviewers overwhelmingly confirmed the basic philosophical premise behind the book – teaching students how to *BE* managers – and I am very grateful for their valuable input:

Ann Devine
Alverno College

Julie Derrick
Brevard Community College

Cheryl Macon
Butler Community College

Jim Thornton
Champlain College

Joseph Byers
Community College of Allegheny County

Sam Dunbar
Delgado Community College

Phil Bauccio
Dowling College

Diane Coggiano
Fitchburg State College

Edward Hamburg
Gloucester County College

Irving Mason
Herkimer County Community College

Charles Duffy
Iona College

James Armstrong
John Tyler Community College

John Dixon
Lee College

Allan Levy
Macomb County Community College

Richard Paulson
Mankato State University

Nancy Ray-Mitchell
McLennan Community College

Nancy Higgins
Montgomery College

Duane Schecter
Muskegon Community College

Ken Esterline
Northwest State Community College

Randy Wade
Rogue Community College

John Mack
Salem State College

Larry Bailey
San Antonio College

Olene Fuller
San Jacinto College-North

Gary Clark
Sinclair Community College

Brian Peach
University of West Florida

I hope everyone who uses this text enjoy teaching from these materials as I do.

Robert N. Lussier
Springfield College

Photo Credits

pp. 3, 4: © 1996 Mark Richards/Contact Press Images. **p. 4:** Courtesy of Bonnie Castonguary. **p. 7:** © Walter Hodges/Tony Stone Images. **p. 16:** © Doug Menuez 1990. **p. 27:** © REUTERS/Dick Baldwin/ARCHIVE PHOTOS. **pp. 39, 40:** Courtesy FedEx. **p. 53:** © Charlesworth/SABA. **p. 60:** © Robbie McClaran. **p. 64:** © Martin Rogers/Tony Stone Images. **pp. 71, 72:** © Andy Sacks/Tony Stone Images. **p. 75:** © E. Lee White. **p. 90:** © REUTERS/Dennis Owen/ARCHIVE PHOTOS. **P. 95:** Courtesy KFC Corporation. **pp. 101, 102:** © Paul Chesley/Tony Stone Images. **p. 104:** © Philip Amdal. **p. 114:** Courtesy of Sprint. **p. 124:** Courtesy Carolyn Blakeslee. **pp. 137, 138:** Courtesy Peter Clark/Jiffy Lube. **p. 151:** Courtesy Mary Kay Inc. **p. 163:** Courtesy Ford Motor Company. **p. 166:** Mattel Photos © 1994 Mattel, Inc. All Rights Reserved. Used with permission. **pp. 175, 176:** © Dan Bosler/Tony Stone Images. **p. 181:** © Terry Vine/Tony Stone Images. **p. 198:** Photography by Erik Von Fischer/Photonics. **p. 201:** Courtesy Southwest Airlines. **pp. 207, 208:** Courtesy of Lilo and Gerry Leeds/CMP Publications. **p. 212:** Courtesy Tyson Foods. **p. 224:** © SuperStock. **p. 245:** © REUTERS/Mark Cardwell/ARCHIVE PHOTOS. **p. 246:** Courtesy of IBM Corporation. **p. 249:** © David Joel/Tony Stone Images. **p. 258:** Courtesy of Hewlett-Packard Company. **pp. 281, 282:** Courtesy Scitor Corporation. **p. 308:** © Andrew Sacks/Tony Stone Images. **p. 312:** © Edward Caldwell. **pp. 319, 320:** © 95 Mugshots/The Stock Market. **p. 328:** © PhotoDisc. **p. 343:** © Dilip Mehta/Contact Press Images. **p. 345:** Courtesy Wal-Mart Stores. **pp. 359, 360:** Courtesy of Donna Brogle. **p. 369:** © Will & Deni McIntyre/Tony Stone Images. **p. 380:** Courtesy The Lincoln Electric Company. **p. 384:** Courtesy Arthur Friedman. **pp. 389, 390:** © Hans Neleman. **p. 397:** AP/Wide World Photos. **p. 407:** © 1996 Nation's Business/T. Michael Keza. **p. 410:** © John Sheridan. **pp. 417, 418:** © Roger Tully/Tony Stone Images. **p. 425:** © Steven Peters/Tony Stone Images. **p. 441:** © Charles Gupton/Tony Stone Images. **p. 444:** © Andy Sacks/Tony Stone Images. **pp. 453, 454:** © Danny Turner. **p. 456:** © Reuters/Bettmann. **p. 476:** © Dan Ham/Tony Stone Images. **p. 482:** © Steven Peters/Tony Stone Images. **pp. 489, 490:** Courtesy MOCON. **p. 499:** c Ted Horowitz/The Stock Market. **p. 519:** © PhotoDisc. **p. 523:** © William Taufic/The Stock Market. **pp. 535, 536:** Courtesy W.K. Kellogg Foundation. **p. 550:** Phil Huber/Black Star. **p. 568:** © Sal DiMarco Jr./Black Star. **p. 571:** © William Taufic/The Stock Market. **pp. 579, 580:** © Chris Usher. **p. 582:** © John Madere/The Stock Market. **p. 590:** Courtesy the Boeing Co. **p. 618:** © Sharon Guynup.

Management: Past and Present

Learning Objectives

After studying this chapter, you should be able to:

1. Describe a manager's responsibility.
2. List and explain the three management skills.
3. List and explain the four management functions.
4. Explain the three management roles: interpersonal, informational, and decisional.
5. List the hierarchy of management levels.
6. Describe the three different types of managers: general, functional, and project.
7. Describe the differences among management levels in terms of skills needed and functions performed.
8. State the major similarity and difference between the classical and behavioral theorists.
9. Describe how the systems theorist and the contingency theorist differ from the classical and behavioral theorists.
10. Define the following **key terms** (in order of appearance in the chapter):

    manager
    manager's resources
    performance
    management skills
    technical skills
    human and communication skills
    conceptual and decision-making skills
    management functions
    planning
    organizing
    leading
    controlling
    management role categories
    levels of management
    types of managers
    classical theorists
    behavioral theorists
    management science theorists
    systems theorists
    sociotechnical theorists
    contingency theorists

Skill Development

1. You should develop your situational management skills (Skill-Building Exercise 1–1).

   To be more specific, you should develop your conceptual and decision-making management skills by analyzing situations and selecting the appropriate management style that best meets the needs of the situation. Using the most appropriate management style for a given situation will help you understand the appropriate human and communication skills to use for the situation. The primary management function skill developed is leadership. The primary management roles developed through this exercise are the interpersonal role and decisional role. The SCANS skill competencies of information and systems, as well as basic and thinking foundation skills are developed.

he Gap, Inc., started with a single Gap store on Ocean Avenue in San Francisco in 1969. Within 25 years it grew to become a leader in retailing with over 1,500 stores, annual sales exceeding $3.7 billion, and earnings of $320 million. The Gap is a specialty retailer that operates stores selling casual apparel for men, women, and children under five brand names: Gap, Gap Kids, babyGap (over 825 U.S. stores), Old Navy (over 125 U.S. stores), and Banana Republic (over 200 U.S. stores). Some of the Gap stores combine these product lines and others are single-line stores. Personal care products and shoes have been introduced recently at The Gap to provide customers with still more reasons to shop the stores.

Stores in the United States are located in 48 states, including all of the 50 largest metropolitan statistical areas. Gap international stores are in Puerto Rico, Canada, the United Kingdom, France, Japan, Wales, and Scotland. Virtually all stores are leased, and no stores are franchised or operated by others.

The Gap is customer-driven. In other words, all

The Gap offers internships to college students, which can lead to challenging management careers after graduation.

Gap employees focus on the customer as the most important part of the job. Evidence of this dedication to customers is The Gap's policy of greeting each customer at the door to make him or her feel welcomed and to determine how the employees can help the customer. All store managers work with customers and are evaluated and promoted based on how well they deal with customers.

The Gap offers college graduates challenging management careers. The company offers internship positions to college students; interns who perform well are offered full-time management jobs after graduation. In addition, The Gap has a promotion policy that enables the talented, harder working managers to continually advance. Those who are willing to relocate increase the speed at which they climb the corporate ladder. Important management practices at The Gap include goal-setting and training.

Although the title of this chapter is "Management: Past and Present," you will first study what management is, what it takes to be a successful manager, what managers do, and differences among managers. These topics apply to both the past and present. Then, you will study the evolution of management from past to present, and finally timely hot topics in management that will continue to be important issues in future years.

Bonnie Castonguary, a store manager at The Gap.

WHAT IS MANAGEMENT?

An Interview with a Manager

This interview with Bonnie Castonguary, a store manager at The Gap, provides an overview of the manager's job and responsibility.

Author: When did you start with The Gap and what was your progression to your present job as store manager?

Bonnie: I started in November of 1990 as a store manager in training. In September of 1991 I replaced a woman on maternity leave as acting store manager. In January of 1992 I had my first store. In August of 1993 and October of 1994 I was promoted to larger stores with more sales volume. My next career advancement is to general manager whereby I would still be in one store, but I would assist the district manager by overseeing other stores in my district.

Author: Briefly describe your job.

Bonnie: The following general summary is taken from "The Gap, Inc. Position Overview Store Management" form, which is two pages long. It begins with the general summary and is followed by details of each part of the summary for each level of management.

> The Store Management team manages the sales, operations and personnel functions of the store to ensure maximum profitability and compliance with company procedures. The team includes Assistant Managers, Associate Managers, the Store Manager and/or General Manager.

In Figure 1–1, Bonnie describes a typical Monday.

Figure 1–1
A Day in the Life of a Manager

8:00 A.M.
- Enter the store and walk the sales floor to ensure a proper close took place the night before.
- Project the payroll cost for the week as a percentage of my forecasted sales, and call it in.
- Perform opening procedures on the controller (computer that records sales transactions and inventory count for all cash registers in the store).

8:30 A.M.
- Walk the sales floor with visual staff and assign projects for them to create new displays for merchandise during the day (create a "to do" list for employees and myself).

9:00 A.M.
- Before the store opens, call voice mail for messages left by other store managers or my boss, the district manager.
- Make business telephone calls for the day.

9:30 A.M.
- Assign sales associates to store zones.
- Put money in computer cash register drawers.

10:00 A.M.
- Open the store.
- Make sure sales associates are zoned out on the floor for proper floor coverage.
- Make sure everyone who enters the store is greeted and has their needs determined.
- Floor coverage. (Help out as needed—greet customers, assist customers with sales, stock shelves, changing room, etc.)

12:00 P.M.
- Do business analysis for previous month from operating statement and gross margin reports.

12:30 P.M.
- Floor coverage as needed for staggered employee breaks.

1:30–2:30 P.M. My break then:
- Prepare customer request transfers (merchandise our store has but other stores do not have) to be delivered. Enter transfers into computer and get merchandise.

3:00 P.M.
- Leave for district meeting.

3:15 P.M.
- Drop off transfers and pick up another store manager; continue on to district meeting.

4:00 P.M.
Meeting is conducted by district manager with the seven general and store managers. Meeting begins with discussion of the following topics and ends with a walk-through of the store at which the meeting is held.
- Previous week's sales, previous week's payroll, payroll projections for next month (cost as a percentage of sales), cleanliness and standards of the stores.
- New information items, mail, general discussion, questions, etc.
- Store walk-through. During a walk-through, the host store manager discusses new display ideas that the other store managers may want to use. In addition, the other store managers give the host manager ideas for improving the store visualization as well. In other words, this is a time to share ideas that will help all team members in the Gap district.

6:00 P.M.
- Call my store to see how sales are going for the day, then leave for home.

Author: What do you like best about being a manager?

Bonnie: You don't have time to get bored on the job because you are always doing something different.

Author: What do you like least about being a manager?

Bonnie: Dealing with difficult performance problems of employees and customers, and always being on call. When I'm not at work, I'm still on call when there are problems at the store. This could mean going to the store at 2:00 A.M. to shut off the alarm.

Author: What advice would you give to college graduates without any full-time work experience who are interested in a management career after graduation?

Bonnie: You need to be dedicated and hard working. You must take great pride in your work. You have to be willing to take on a lot of responsibility. Remember, your employees are always looking to you to set the example; when you make a mistake (which you will do), it affects your staff. You have to be a self-starter. As a store manager you have to motivate employees, but your boss is not around much to motivate you.

1. Describe a manager's responsibility.

The Manager's Responsibility

manager
The individual responsible for achieving organizational objectives through efficient and effective utilization of resources.

manager's resources
Human, financial, physical, and informational resources.

A **manager** *is responsible for achieving organizational objectives through efficient and effective utilization of resources.* A few terms in this definition should be explained. *Efficient* refers to doing things right, to maximizing the utilization of resources. *Effective* refers to doing the right thing in order to attain the objective, or the degree to which a manager achieves objectives. *The* **manager's resources** *include human, financial, physical, and informational.*

Human Resources. Human resources are people. Managers are responsible for getting the job done through employees. People are the manager's most valuable resource. Note that in the day in a life of a manager, Bonnie did not attempt to create all the visual displays herself. She accomplished this objective through her staff. As a manager you should hire the best people available. These employees must then be trained to use the organization's other resources to maximize productivity. Throughout this book we will focus on working with employees to accomplish organizational objectives.

Financial Resources. Most managers have a budget stating how much it should cost to operate their department/store for a set period of time. In other words, a budget defines the financial resources available. The manager is responsible for seeing that the department does not waste any of the available resources. Bonnie placed cash in the drawers before opening the store. She also projected payroll cost as a percentage of sales to reach profit objectives. Bonnie is responsible for maximizing profitability at The Gap.

Physical Resources. Getting the job done requires effective and efficient use of physical resources. In a retail store like Bonnie's, this includes the store building, merchandise to be sold, the fixtures that display the merchandise, and the computer used to record sales and inventory. It also involves the inventory in the back room and supplies such as price tags, hangers, charge slips, and so on. Managers are responsible for keeping the equipment in working condition and for making sure that necessary materials and supplies are available. Deadlines might be missed and present sales and future business lost if physical resources are not available and used and maintained properly.

Informational Resources. Managers need information from a variety of sources.[1] The controller (computer) is used to store and retrieve information within and among Gap stores. When Bonnie was checking her voice mail, making calls, giving employees directions on setting up displays, and attending the district meeting with store walk-through, she was using informational resources. Sharing information with teammates will influence your success as a manager.[2] Information continues to increase in importance as a means of increasing the speed of doing business in a competitive global environment.

Work Application

1. Describe the specific resources used by your present/past boss. Give the manager's job title and department.

The level of organizational **performance** *is based on how effectively and efficiently managers utilize resources to achieve objectives.* Managers are responsible for and evaluated on how well they meet organizational objectives through effective and efficient utilization of resources. The current trend is to require managers to achieve objectives with fewer resources.[3] Today's managers are expected to work as team leaders[4] with a diversity of team members.[5]

performance
Means of evaluating how effectively and efficiently managers use resources to achieve objectives.

Today's managers are expected to work as team leaders with a diversity of team members.

WHAT DOES IT TAKE TO BE A SUCCESSFUL MANAGER?

Now that you have an idea of what management is, you will learn some of the qualities and skills necessary to be a successful manager.

Management Qualities

Over the years, numerous researchers have attempted to answer the question, "What does it take to be a successful manager?" In a *Wall Street Journal* Gallup survey, 782 top executives in 282 large corporations were asked, "What are the most important traits for success as a supervisor?"[6] Before you read what these executives stated, complete Self-Assessment Exercise 1–1 to find out if you have what it takes to become a successful manager.

SELF-ASSESSMENT EXERCISE 1–1

Management Traits Questionnaire

The following 15 questions relate to some of the qualities needed to be a successful manager. Rate yourself on each item by placing the number 1–4 that best describes your behavior for each item.

4—The statement is not very descriptive of me.

3—The statement is somewhat descriptive of me.

2—The statement is descriptive of me.

1—The statement is very descriptive of me.

___ 1. I enjoy working with people. I prefer to work with others rather than working alone.

___ 2. I can motivate others. I can get people to do things they may not want to do.

___ 3. I am well liked. People enjoy working with me.

___ 4. I am cooperative. I strive to help the team do well, rather than to be the star.

___ 5. I am a leader. I enjoy teaching, coaching, and instructing people.

___ 6. I want to be successful. I do things to the best of my ability to be successful.

___ 7. I am a self-starter. I get things done without having to be told to do them.

___ 8. I am a problem-solver. If things aren't going the way I want them to, I take corrective action to meet my objectives.

___ 9. I am self-reliant. I don't need the help of others.

___ 10. I am hard working. I enjoy working and getting the job done.

___ 11. I am trustworthy. If I say I will do something by a set time, I do it.

___ 12. I am loyal. I do not do or say things to intentionally hurt my friends, relatives, or coworkers.

___ 13. I can take criticism. If people tell me negative things about myself, I give them serious thought and change when appropriate.

___ 14. I am honest. I do not lie, steal, or cheat.

___ 15. I am fair. I treat people equally. I don't take advantage of others.

___ Total score (add numbers on lines 1–15; the range of your score is 15–60)

In general, the lower your score, the better your chances of being a successful manager. If you are interested in being a manager someday, you can work on improving your integrity (items 11–15), industriousness (items 6–10), and ability to get along with people (items 1–5) both in this course and in your personal life. As a start, review the traits listed here. Which ones are you strongest and weakest in? Think about how you can improve in the weaker areas, or preferably, write out a plan.

Work Application

2. Identify a specific manager, preferably one who was or is your boss, and explain what makes him or her successful or unsuccessful. Give examples.

The executives in the Gallup survey identified integrity, industriousness, and the ability to get along with people as the three most important traits for successful managers. Other traits included business knowledge, intelligence, leadership ability, education, sound judgment, ability to communicate, flexibility, and ability to plan and set objectives. The executives also identified seven traits that lead to failure in a manager: having a limited viewpoint, not being able to understand others, not being able to work with others, being indecisive, lacking initiative, not assuming responsibility, and lacking integrity. Other failure traits included lack of ability to change, reluctance to think independently, inability to solve problems, and desire for popularity.

Management Skills

2. List and explain the three management skills.

Today, there is a need for good management skills.[7,8] Experience, training, and education in courses similar to this one will help you develop good management skills. Because management skills are so important, the focus of this book is on skill-building. The key to success is perseverance through hard work. If you work at it, you can develop your management skills through this course. The concepts in this book also can and should be used in your daily life.

Robert Katz conducted a study over 20 years ago that is still widely quoted today. Katz identified three skills needed to be an effective administrator: technical, human, and conceptual.[9] Over the years other researchers have added administrative, communication, political, and problem-solving and decision-making skills. For our purposes, **management skills** *include (1) technical, (2) human and communication, and (3) conceptual and decision-making.*

management skills
(1) technical, (2) human and communication, and (3) conceptual and decision-making.

technical skills
The ability to use methods and techniques to perform a task.

human and communication skills
The ability to work with people in teams.

conceptual and decision-making skills
The ability to understand abstract ideas and select alternatives to solve problems.

Technical Skills. **Technical skills** *are the ability to use methods and techniques to perform a task.* When managers are working on budgets they may need computer skills in spreadsheet software such as Lotus 1-2-3 or Excel. Bonnie needs computer skills to open the store, record transfers, and record sales. Most employees are promoted to their first management position primarily because of their technical skills. Technical skills vary widely from job to job; therefore, this course does not focus on developing technical skills. However, in Chapters 6 and 15 you will learn to use planning and decision-making tools and financial and budgetary tools.

Human and Communication Skills. **Human and communication skills** *are the ability to work with people in teams.* Without communication skills, you cannot be an effective team member or manager.[10] Today, employees want to participate in management.[11] Therefore, there is an increase in the use of teams with an emphasis on good human relations.[12] Another area of human skills includes political skills. How well you get along with employees will affect your management success. You do not have to like people—although it does help—to have a good working relationship. Most of Bonnie's day was spent working with employees and customers. The Gap position overview for store managers states that excellent communication skills are needed to be a manager. Throughout this book, you will learn how to work with a diversity of people, develop human resource skills, improve communication skills, motivate and lead others, manage teams, develop power and political skills, manage conflict, and improve employee performance.

Conceptual and Decision-Making Skills. **Conceptual and decision-making skills** *are the ability to understand abstract ideas and select alternatives to solve problems.* Another term for conceptual skills is *systems thinking,* or the ability to understand an organization/department as a whole and the interrelationship among its parts. As businesses compete in a continually diversifying global environment, creative analysis and judgment,[13] currently referred to as *critical thinking,* are needed to resolve conflict and solve problems.[14] An important part of Bonnie's job is to make decisions about what merchandise to carry, how to display the merchandise, and which people to hire. Throughout this book, you will learn how to develop your conceptual and planning skills. For a review of the management skills, see Figure 1–2.

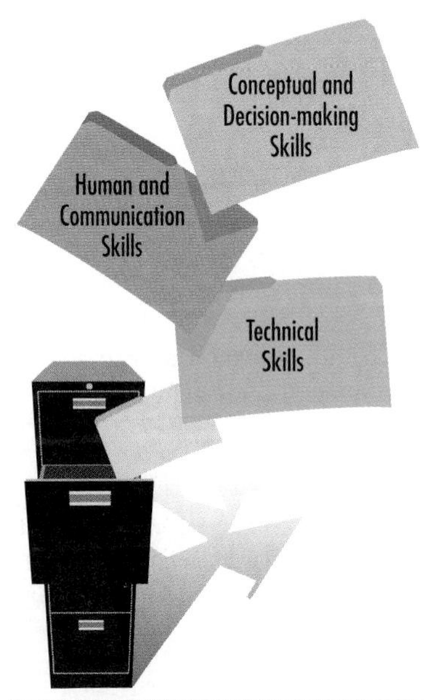

Figure 1–2
Management Skills

Work Application

3. Select a manager, preferably one who is or was your boss, and state the specific technical, human, communication, conceptual, and decision-making skills he or she uses on the job.

Skills and Tasks for Jobs: SCANS

The U.S. Secretary of Commerce's Commission on Achieving Necessary Skills (SCANS) conducted a study to determine the necessary skills and tasks for jobs. The commission members identified five competencies (resources, interpersonal skills, information, systems, and technology) and a three-part foundation (basic skills, thinking skills, and personal qualities) of skills for personal qualities needed for solid job performance. A more detailed explanation of the skills identified by SCANS will be presented later in this chapter.

The Ghiselli Study

Professor Edwin Ghiselli conducted a study to determine the traits necessary for success as a manager.[15] Ghiselli identified six traits as important, although not all are necessary for success. These six traits, in reverse order of importance, include: (6) initiative, (5) self-assurance, (4) decisiveness, (3) intelligence, (2) need for occupational achievement, and (1) supervisory ability. The number-one trait, supervisory ability, includes skills in planning, organizing, leading, and controlling. Ghiselli's four areas of supervisory ability are more commonly referred to as the *management functions*, which you will learn about in the next section.

APPLYING THE CONCEPT

AC 1–1 Management Skills

Identify each skill in the following five situations as being one of the following:

a. technical b. human and communication c. conceptual and decision-making

____ 1. The ability to see things as a whole and as the interrelationship of their parts.

____ 2. The ability to motivate employees to do a good job.

____ 3. The ability to perform departmental jobs such as data entry in a computer.

____ 4. The ability to determine what's going wrong and correct it.

____ 5. The ability to write memos and letters.

WHAT DO MANAGERS DO?

Having discussed what management is, and what it takes to be a successful manger, our next question is, "What do managers do?" In this section, you will learn about the four functions performed by managers and the three roles that all managers play.

3. List and explain the four management functions.

Management Functions

As stated earlier, managers get the job done through others. A manager plans, organizes, leads, and controls resources to achieve organizational objectives. If managers run a machine, wait on customers, or put up a store display, they are performing nonmanagement or employee functions. *The four* **management functions** *include:*

management functions Planning, organizing, leading, and controlling

- *planning*
- *organizing*
- *leading*
- *controlling*

This book is organized around the four management functions. Each of the four management functions serves as a title for a part of the book, and three to five chapters are devoted to developing skills in each functional area. Here, and in later chapters, each function is explained separately. However, you should realize that the four functions are a systems process; they are interrelated and are often performed simultaneously.

Planning. Planning is typically the starting point in the management process. To be successful, organizations need a great deal of planning.[16] People in organizations need goals and plans to achieve them.[17] **Planning** *is the process of setting objectives and determining in advance exactly how the objectives will be met.* Managers commonly have to schedule employees and the work to be performed and develop budgets. Bonnie has to schedule employees to work and select merchandise to be sold. At 8:30 A.M. Bonnie planned what displays the visual staff would create. Your ability to perform the planning function is based on your conceptual and decision-making management skills.

planning
The process of setting objectives and determining in advance exactly how the objectives will be met.

Organizing. To be successful requires organization.[18] A manager must also design and develop an organizational system to implement the plans. **Organizing** *is the process of delegating and coordinating tasks and resources to achieve objectives.* Managers allocate and arrange resources. An important part of coordinating human resources is to assign people to various jobs and tasks. At 8:30 A.M. Bonnie delegated the responsibility to develop the merchandise displays to the visual staff. At 9:30 A.M. Bonnie assigned sales associates to zones to fill the sales floor. An important part of organizing, sometimes listed as a separate function, is staffing. *Staffing* is the process of selecting, training, and evaluating employees; Bonnie has full responsibility for staffing her store. Your ability to organize is based on a blend of conceptual and decision-making skills and human and communication skills.

organizing
The process of delegating and coordinating tasks and resources to achieve objectives.

Leading. In addition to planning and organizing, a manager must work with employees as they perform their tasks on a daily basis. **Leading** *is the process of influencing employees to work toward achieving objectives.* Managers must communicate the objectives to employees and motivate them to achieve the objectives.[19] An important part of Bonnie's job involves communicating with, motivating, and leading individuals and teams. Bonnie coaches her employees as they perform their jobs. Your ability to lead is based on human and communication skills.

leading
The process of influencing employees to work toward achieving objectives.

Controlling. Only three out of ten people do the things they say they will do.[20] Therefore, objectives will not be met without follow-through. **Controlling** *is the process of establishing and implementing mechanisms to ensure that objectives are achieved.* An important part of controlling is measuring progress toward the achievement of the objective and taking corrective action when necessary.[21] Throughout the day Bonnie was controlling. She started her day by checking the previous night's closing and turning on the computer. From 10:00 to 12:00 and 12:30 to 1:30 Bonnie was making sure there was full floor coverage at all locations, and filling in where needed to maintain coverage. Your ability to control is based on conceptual and decision-making and human and communication skills.

controlling
The process of establishing and implementing mechanisms to ensure that objectives are achieved.

Work Application

4. Identify a specific manager, preferably one who was or is your boss, and give examples of how that person performs each of the four management functions.

Nonmanagement Functions

All managers perform the four functions of management. A manager's job is to get the work done through employees. However, many managers also perform nonmanagement, or employee, functions as well. For example, Bonnie spent from 10:00 to 12:00 and 12:30 to 1:30 primarily waiting on customers, which is an employee or nonmanagement function. If Bonnie personally made a photocopy of the business analysis she was working on, this would be a nonmanagement function as well. Many managers, like Bonnie, are called working managers because they perform both management and employee functions. When Bonnie is promoted to general manager, she will spend less time performing nonmanagement functions and virtually no time when she becomes a district manager.

APPLYING THE CONCEPT

AC 1–2 Management Functions

Identify whether each of the five situations describes one of the four management functions listed or is a nonmanagement function.

a. planning b. organizing c. leading d. controlling e. nonmanagement

____ **6.** The manager is showing an employee how to set up a machine for production.

____ **7.** The manager is determining how many units were produced during the first half of the shift.

____ **8.** An employee has been absent several times. The manager is discussing the situation and trying to get the employee to improve attendance.

____ **9.** The manager is conducting a job interview to fill the position of a retiring employee.

____ **10.** The manager is fixing a broken machine.

The Systems Relationship among the Management Functions

The management functions are not a linear process. Managers do not usually plan, then organize, then lead, and then control. The functions are distinct yet interrelated. Managers often perform these functions simultaneously. In addition, each function depends on the others. For example, if you start with a poor plan, the objective will not be met even though things are well organized, led, and controlled. Also, if you start with a great plan, but are poorly organized, or poorly lead, the objective may not be met. Plans without controls are rarely implemented effectively. Figure 1–3 illustrates this process. Remember that the management functions are based on setting (planning) and achieving (organizing, leading, and controlling) objectives.

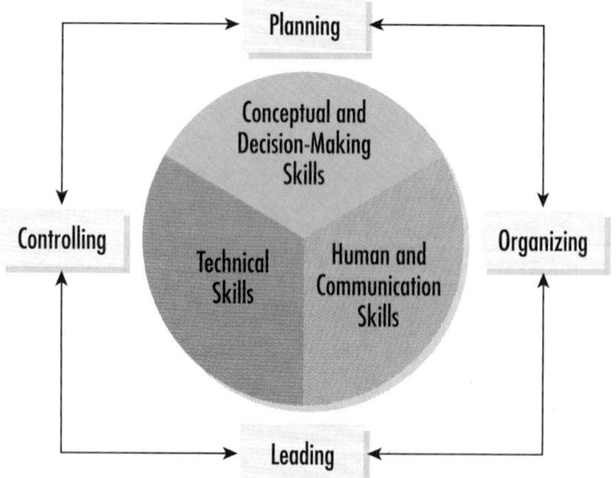

Figure 1–3
Management Skills and Functions

SCANS and the Management Functions

To better understand the relationship among SCANS and the management skills and functions, see Figure 1–4. Following each SCANS skill (in parentheses), is a listing of the management skills and functions which help to develop the SCANS skill.

Management Roles

Henry Mintzberg identified ten roles that managers undertake to accomplish the management functions of planning, organizing, leading, and controlling. A *role* is a set of expectations of how one

Workplace Know-How

The know-how identified by SCANS is made up of five competencies and a three-part foundation of skills and personal qualities needed for solid job performance. These include:

COMPETENCIES. Effective workers can productively use:

1. **Resources.** Allocating time, money, materials, space, staff. (Resources relates to technical and conceptual and decision-making skills, and to the planning, organizing, and controlling management functions.)
2. **Interpersonal Skills.** Working on teams, teaching others, serving customers, leading, negotiating, and working well with people from culturally diverse backgrounds. (Interpersonal skills relates to the human and communication skills, and to the organizing and leading management functions.)
3. **Information.** Acquiring and evaluating data, organizing and maintaining files, interpreting and communicating, and using computers to process information. (Information relates to the technical, human, and communication management skills, and to the organizing, leading, and controlling management functions.)
4. **Systems.** Understanding social, organizational, and technological systems; monitoring and correcting performance; and designing or improving systems. (Systems relates to the conceptual and decision-making management skill, and to the planning, organizing, and controlling management functions.)
5. **Technology.** Selecting equipment and tools, applying technology to specific tasks, and maintaining and troubleshooting technologies. (Technology relates to the technical management skill, and to the planning, organizing, and controlling management functions. Chapters 6, 7, 15, and 17 help to develop technology skills.)

THE FOUNDATION. Competence requires:

1. **Basic Skills.** Reading, writing, arithmetic and mathematics; speaking and listening. (All the management skills and functions need the basic skills. Reading skills can be developed through reading this book. Chapters 6 and 15 require some math. Speaking skills can be developed through class activities. Chapter 10 provides suggestions for improving writing, speaking, and listening skills.)
2. **Thinking Skills.** Thinking creatively, making decisions, solving problems, seeing things in the mind's eye, knowing how to learn, and reasoning. (All the management skills and functions need the thinking skills, especially conceptual and decision-making management skills. Chapter 4 focuses exclusively on thinking skills.)
3. **Personal Qualities.** Individual responsibility, self-esteem, sociability, self-management, and integrity. (Personal qualities affect our management skills and how we perform the management functions. Personal qualities can be developed throughout this book; each chapter has one or more self-learning exercises which focus on personal qualities.)

Source: U.S. Secretary's Commission on Achieving Necessary Skills. *Skills and Tasks for Jobs: A SCANS Report for America 2000*. Washington, DC: U.S. Department of Commerce, National Technical Information Services, 1992, p. 6.

Information in parentheses added by the author.

Figure 1–4
The Relationship Between SCANS and the Management Skills and Functions

will behave in a given situation. Recent studies have supported Mintzberg's management role theory.[22,23,24] Mintzberg grouped these roles into three categories.[25] *The* **management role categories** *include:*

- *interpersonal*
- *informational*
- *decisional*

4. Explain the three management roles: interpersonal, informational, and decisional.

management role categories
Interpersonal, informational, and decisional.

Interpersonal Roles. Interpersonal roles include figurehead, leader, and liaison. When managers play interpersonal roles, they use their human and communication management skills as they perform the necessary management function. Managers play the *figurehead role* when they represent the organization or department in ceremonial and symbolic activities. Bonnie played the figurehead

Work Application

5. Identify a specific manager, preferably one who was or is your boss, and give examples of how that person performs each of the three manager role categories. Be sure to identify at least one of the three or four roles listed under interpersonal, informational, and decisional roles.

role when she greeted visitors and gave them a tour of the store. Managers play the *leader role* when they motivate, train, communicate with, and influence others. Throughout the day, Bonnie performed the leader role as she directed employees to maintain floor coverage. Managers play the *liaison role* when they interact with people outside of their unit to gain information and favors. Bonnie was a liaison at the district meeting, which included the store walk-through.

Informational Roles. Informational roles include monitor, disseminator, and spokesperson. When managers play informational roles, they use their human and communication management skills. Managers play the *monitor role* when they read and talk to others to receive information. Bonnie was continually monitoring the situation to ensure full floor coverage. Managers play the *disseminator role* when they send information to others. Bonnie played the disseminator role when she was at the district meeting. Managers play the *spokesperson role* when they provide information to people outside the organization. Bonnie played the spokesperson role when she made business calls in the morning and gave the interview to the author of this book.

Decisional Roles. Decisional roles include entrepreneur, disturbance-handler, resource-allocator, and negotiator. When managers play decisional roles they use their conceptual and decision-making management skills. Managers play the *entrepreneur role* when they innovate and initiate improvements. Bonnie had the visual staff set up new displays to help improve store sales. Managers play the *disturbance-handler* role when they take corrective action during disputes or crisis situations. Bonnie had to deal with a customer who was not satisfied that an employee would not give a cash refund for merchandise returned. Managers play the *resource-allocator* role when they schedule, request authorization, and perform budgeting and programming activities. Bonnie allocated sales associates to cover the floor. Managers perform the *negotiator role* when they represent their department or organization during nonroutine transactions. Bonnie played the negotiator role when she made business calls to outside contractors.

APPLYING THE CONCEPT

AC 1–3 Management Roles

Identify each of the five roles below as:

a. interpersonal b. informational c. decisional

____ **11.** The manager discusses the new union contract with union representatives.

____ **12.** The manager shows an employee how to fill-out the form.

____ **13.** The manager reads *The Wall Street Journal* with a cup of coffee first thing in the morning.

____ **14.** The manager develops new total quality management (TQM) techniques.

____ **15.** The sales manager discusses a complaint with a customer.

As businesses continue to compete in a diversified global economy, environment and technology affect interpersonal, informational, and decisional roles.[26] See Figure 1–5 for a review of these three categories of ten roles.

5. List the hierarchy of management levels.

DIFFERENCES AMONG MANAGERS

Differences occur in levels of management, types of managers, management skills needed, management functions performed, large versus small business managers, and profit versus not-for-profit managers.

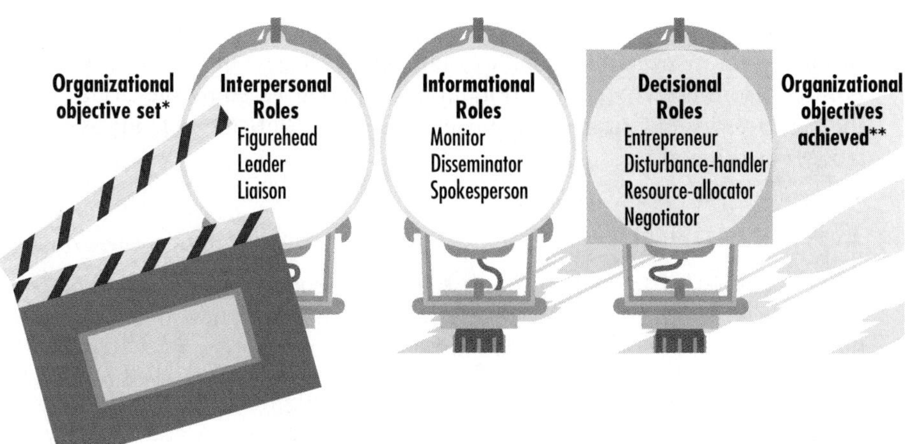

*Note that the starting place is with organizational objectives. Therefore, read the boxes from left to right.

**Managers play the necessary roles, while performing management functions, to achieve organizational objectives.

Figure 1–5
Ten Roles Managers Play

The Three Levels of Management (and Operative Employees)

The three **levels of management** *include top, middle, and first-line.* They are also called strategic, tactical, and operational. The three levels relate to each other as described here.

levels of management
Top, middle, and first-line.

Top Managers. These executive positions have titles such as chairman of the board, chief executive officer (CEO), president, or vice president. Most organizations have relatively few top management positions. Top managers are responsible for managing the entire organization or major parts of it. They develop and define the organization's purpose, objectives, strategies, and long-term plans. They report to other executives or boards of directors and supervise the activities of middle managers.

Middle Managers. People holding these positions have titles such as sales manager, branch manager, or department head. Middle managers are responsible for implementing top management's strategy by developing short-term operating plans. They generally report to executives and supervise the work of first-line managers.

First-Line Managers. Examples of the titles at this level include crew leader, supervisor, head nurse, and office manager. These managers are responsible for implementing middle managers' operational plans. They generally report to middle managers. Unlike those at the other two levels of management, first-line managers do not supervise other managers; they supervise operative employees.

Operative Employees. Operative employees are the workers in an organization who do not hold management positions. They report to first-line managers. They make the products, wait on customers, perform repairs, and so on.

Based on The Gap organization structure, Bonnie is a first-line manager because she has operative employees reporting directly to her. Recall that Bonnie told the visual staff what to do for the day. However, within her store, she is in a sense the top manager. Bonnie is also a middle manager in the sense that she

Work Application

6. Identify the three levels of management in a specific organization by level and title. Be sure to list the organization's name.

reports to a higher level district manager and has three first-line managers—two associate managers and one assistant manager—reporting directly to her. Bonnie's store usually has a minimum of 30 operative employees. But, during the busy seasons of Christmas and back-to-school, there are as many as 50 employees working at her store.

6. Describe the three different types of managers: general, functional, and project.

Types of Managers

types of managers General, functional, and project.

The three **types of managers** *include general, functional, and project.* Top-level and some middle managers are *general managers* because they supervise the activities of several departments that perform several different activities. Middle and first-line managers are often *functional managers* that supervise the activities of related tasks. Bonnie is a functional manager because she is responsible for overseeing the functions performed at her store.

Project managers at General Mills coordinate employees and other resources to develop and produce a new breakfast cereal.

The four most common functional areas include operations/production, marketing, finance/accounting, and human resources/personnel management. A production manager is responsible for making a product such as a Ford Mustang, whereas an operations manager is responsible for providing a service such as a loan by Bank America. However, both product and service organizations now use the broader term *operations*. A marketing manager is responsible for selling and advertising products and services. The accounting manager is responsible for keeping records of sales and expenses (accounts receivable and payable) and determining profitability, whereas the financial manager is responsible for obtaining the necessary funds and investments. The term *finance* is commonly used to mean both accounting and financial activities. The human resources (replaces the old term *personnel*) manager is responsible for forecasting future employee needs and recruiting, selecting, evaluating, and compensating employees. This manager also ensures that employees follow legal guidelines and regulations.

A *project manager* coordinates employees and other resources across several functional departments to accomplish a specific task, such as to develop and produce a new breakfast cereal for Kellogg's or General Mills, or a new model aircraft at Boeing.

The current business trend is to cut management levels,[27] particularly middle managers, and to bridge the gap between levels. Organizations are also developing less rigid management structures, such as self-managed teams, which increases the need for human relations and communication skills. See Figure 1–6 for an example of an organization chart showing the levels and functions of management.

Work Application

7. Identify which type of boss you have now or have had. If that person is or was a functional manager, be sure to specify the functional tasks of the department.

7. Describe the differences among management levels in terms of skills needed and functions performed.

Management Skills

All managers need technical, human and communication, and conceptual and decision-making skills. However, the need for these skills varies with the level of management. Although various studies have been conducted to determine the exact need for each skill by each level of management, discrepancies in the results exist. It is generally agreed that at all three levels of management, the need for human and communication skills remains fairly constant. However, top-level managers have a greater need for conceptual and decision-making skills, whereas first-line managers have a greater need for technical skills. This is logical because as you move up the management levels, you have to be able

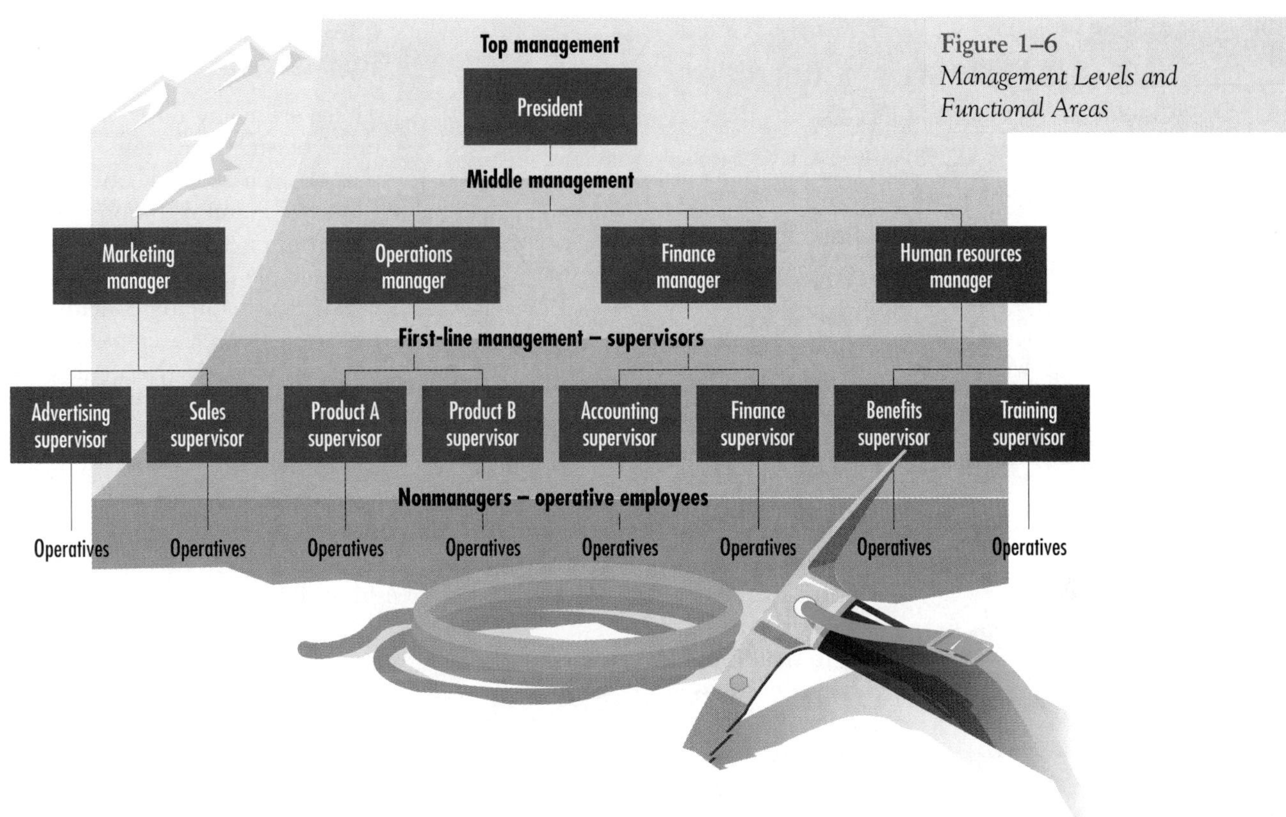

Figure 1–6
Management Levels and Functional Areas

to conceptualize how more departments interrelate. At the first-line level you need to be concerned primarily with day-to-day production of the product. Middle managers tend to need a balance of all three skills, but needs vary from organization to organization.

Management Functions

All managers perform the four management functions: planning, organizing, leading, and controlling. However, the time spent on each function varies with the level of management. Studies of the amount of time managers spend on each function are inconclusive. However, it is generally agreed that supervisors spend more time leading and controlling, middle-level managers spend equal time on all four functions, and top managers spend more time planning and organizing. Figure 1–7 summarizes this difference in management level as well as the varying skills needed.

Management Level	Primary Management Skills Needed	Primary Management Functions Performed
Top	Conceptual and human skills	Planning and organizing
Middle	Balance of all three	Balance of all four
First-Line	Technical and human skills	Leading and controlling

Figure 1–7
Differences among Management Levels in Skills Needed and Functions Performed

APPLYING THE CONCEPT

AC 1–4 Differences among Management Levels

Five descriptions follow (16–20). Identify the level of management as:

a. top b. middle c. first-line

____ **16.** Supervises the operative employees.

____ **17.** Has greater need for conceptual than technical skills.

____ **18.** Spends more time leading and controlling.

____ **19.** Reports to an executive.

____ **20.** Has a more balanced need for the management skills and functions.

Large versus Small Business Managers

There are many different definitions of small business. For our purposes, based on one Small Business Administration (SBA) definition, a small business is independently owned and operated, is not dominant in its field, and has fewer than 500 employees. In large businesses there may be more than three levels of management, whereas in a small business the owner may be the only manager. Large firms tend to be more formal and complex in structure. In small businesses, managers tend to be less specialized than in large firms. Bonnie works for a large organization—The Gap. Her independent store resembles a small business, but it has the support of a large organization.

In small businesses the managers are often more technically oriented than in larger businesses, whose managers are further removed from the products and services and customers. Planning in large businesses is often more formalized with written plans; small business owners tend to have plans but are less formal in developing them. Large businesses tend to make greater use of sophisticated computerized control systems; small businesses rely more on direct observation.[28] For example, large- and medium- and some small-sized companies have computerized inventory records that keep track of how much of each item has been sold and is in inventory. The computer is used to determine when to reorder inventory. However, many small business owners keep inventory records on paper, or in their heads, and know when to reorder by looking at the shelves.

The importance of roles varies from large to small firms. In small businesses, the most important roles are entrepreneur and spokesperson. It takes entrepreneurial skills to start a new business and a spokesperson to promote the business. In large businesses the more important role is resource-allocator, and the least important role is entrepreneur. Small business managers tend to rate lower on the leader and informational roles than managers in large firms.[29,30] Although prior studies have identified entrepreneurial skills as less important for large business, today, large businesses are seeking people with entrepreneurial skills. *Entrepreneurs* start new businesses. In large organizations, *intrapreneurs* start new lines of business within a larger business with the support of its resources. Companies such as 3M, General Electric, and Bristol Myers encourage intrapreneurship.

Profit versus Not-for-Profit Managers

Is the manager's job the same in the profit and not-for-profit organization? Although some noteworthy differences exist, the answer is yes.[31] All managers need management skills, perform the same management functions, and play the same roles regardless of the organization type. Bonnie works for a profit business.

Two primary areas of difference between the profit and not-for-profit organization include measuring performance and staffing. The primary measure of performance for profit organizations is the bottom-line profit. Not-for-profit organizations have no universal measure of performance. The United Way, Boy and Girl Scouts, library, and registry of motor vehicles have different performance measurements. In addition, profit organizations pay workers. However, in many not-for-profit organizations some of the workers are unpaid volunteers.

Throughout this text you will develop management skills universally valuable to all organizations. But, more importantly, you will develop skills that will help you become the person that you want to be in your private and professional life.

A BRIEF HISTORY OF MANAGEMENT

8. State the major similarity and difference between the classical and behavioral theorists.

There are two primary reasons why you should be concerned about the history of management: to better understand current developments and to avoid repeating mistakes. Early literature on management came from management practitioners who wrote about their experiences and attempted to extrapolate basic principles. More recent literature comes from researchers. There are different classifications of management approaches or what are often called schools of management thought. In this section you will learn about five approaches to management: classical, behavioral, quantitative, systems, and contingency.

Classical Theory

The **classical theorists** *focus on the job and management functions to determine the best way to manage in all organizations*. In the early 1900s, managers began an organized approach to increasing performance by focusing on the efficiency of managing jobs. This focus later changed to a concern for managing departments and organizations. Scientific management stressed job efficiency through the development of technical skills, while administrative theory stressed rules and the structure of the organization.

classical theorists
Researchers who focus on the job and management functions to determine the best way to manage in all organizations.

Scientific Management. Frederick Winslow Taylor (1856–1915), an engineer known as the Father of Scientific Management, focused on analyzing and redesigning jobs more efficiently. He searched for the best way to maximize performance. As a result of his work, he developed several "scientific management" principles. Some of his major principles include:

1. Develop a procedure for each element of a worker's job.
2. Promote job specialization.
3. Scientifically select, train, and develop workers.
4. Plan and schedule work.
5. Establish standard methods and times for each task.
6. Use wage incentives such as piece rates and bonuses.[32]

Frank Gilbreth (1868–1924) and his wife Lillian Gilbreth (1878–1972) developed time and motion studies to develop more efficient work procedures. Their work was popularized in a book, movie, and television sitcom entitled

Cheaper by the Dozen, a reference to their application of scientific management practices to their family of 12 children. When Frank died, their children ranged in age from 2 to 19 years old. Lillian continued her work as a consultant. However, she changed the focus of her work to pioneer industrial psychology. Lillian became a professor of management at Purdue University, and is commonly referred to as the First Lady of Management.

Another person who made important contributions to scientific management was Henry Gantt (1861–1919). He developed a method for scheduling work over a period of time that is still widely used today. You will learn how to develop a Gantt Chart in Chapter 6.

Administrative Theory. Henri Fayol (1841–1925) was a French engineer known as the Pioneer of the Principles and Functions of Management. He made a clear distinction between operating and managerial activities. Fayol identified five major functions of management: planning, coordinating, organizing, controlling, and commanding. In addition to his five management functions, Fayol also developed 14 principles that are still used today.[33] Most principles of management textbooks are organized and presented based on the functions of management.

Two other contributors to administrative management are Max Weber (1864–1920) and Chester Barnard (1886–1961). Max Weber was a German sociologist who developed the *bureaucracy concept*. His concept of bureaucracy did not include a lot of red tape and inefficiency: its aim was to develop a set of rules and procedures to ensure that all employees were treated fairly. Chester Barnard studied authority and power distributions in organizations. He raised awareness of the informal organization—cliques and naturally occurring social groupings within formal organizations.

Mary Parker Follett (1868–1933) stressed the importance of people rather than engineering techniques. Follett contributed to administrative theory by emphasizing the need for worker participation, conflict resolution, and shared goals. The trend today is toward increasingly higher levels of employee participation. Barnard and Follett's contributions led to the development of behavioral theory.

Companies still successfully use classical management techniques today. McDonald's system of fast food service is one good example of a company using these techniques. Managers at Monsanto also use classical techniques, such as time and motion studies, and organization principles that you will learn about in Chapter 7. Large organizations that are downsizing to cut cost by laying off employees and becoming more efficient are using a classical management approach.

Behavioral Theory

behavioral theorists
Researchers who focus on people to determine the best way to manage in all organizations.

The **behavioral theorists** *focus on people to determine the best way to manage in all organizations*. In the 1920s, management writers began to question the classical approach to management and changed their focus from the job itself to the people who perform the job. Like the classicists, behaviorists were looking for the best way to manage in all organizations. However, the behavioral approach to management stressed the need for human skills rather than technical skills.

Elton Mayo (1880–1949) pioneered the *human relations* movement. Mayo headed a group of Harvard researchers in conducting the Hawthorne Studies, a landmark study of human behavior in Western Electric's Hawthorne plant (Cicero, Illinois) from 1927 to 1932. Like Taylor, Mayo wanted to increase performance; however, he wanted to determine the best work environment as his means to the end result. These researchers suggested that a manager's treatment of people had an important impact on their performance. In other words, treating people as special and meeting their needs frequently results in increased performance. The *Hawthorne effect* refers to the phenomenon that just studying people affects performance.[34]

Abraham Maslow (1908–1970) developed the *hierarchy of needs theory*.[35] Maslow is one of the earliest researchers to study motivation, and motivation is still a major area of research. You will learn more about Maslow's hierarchy of needs and other motivation theories in Chapter 11.

Douglas McGregor (1906–1964) developed *Theory X and Theory Y*. McGregor contrasted the two theories, based on the assumptions that managers make about workers. Theory X managers assume that people dislike work and need managers to plan, organize, and closely direct and control their work in order for them to perform at high levels. Theory Y managers assume that people like to work and do not need close supervision. McGregor did not give specific details on how to manage; he suggested a reorientation in managerial thinking.[36] You will learn how Theory X and Theory Y affect motivation and performance in Chapter 11.

Behaviorists felt that a happy employee would be productive. However, later research suggested that a happy worker is not necessarily a productive worker. As you can see, the classical and behavioral theories are very different, yet both claimed to have the best method of managing in all organizations.

The behavioral approach to management is still evolving and is being used in organizations. The current term for studying people at work is the *behavioral science approach*, which draws from economics, psychology, sociology, and other disciplines. Most of the material in the organizing and leading chapters is based on behavioral science research. Bonnie and managers all over the globe use behavioral sciences in dealing with people.

Management Science

The **management science theorists** *focus on the use of mathematics to aid in problem-solving and decision-making*. During World War II (1940s) a research program began to investigate the applicability of quantitative methods to military and logistics problems. After the war, business managers began to use management science (math). Some of the mathematical models are used in the areas of finance, management information systems (MIS), and operations management. The use of computers has led to an increase in the use of quantitative methods by managers all over the globe. Because management science stresses decision-making skills and technical skills, it is more closely aligned with classical management theory than behavioral theory. You will learn more about management science in the planning and controlling chapters. Management science is not commonly used in the organizing and leading management functions.

management science theorists
Researchers who focus of the use of mathematics to aid in problem-solving and decision-making.

9. Describe how the systems theorist and the contingency theorist differ from the classical and behavioral theorists.

Integrative Perspective

The integrative perspective has three components: systems theory, sociotechnical theory, and contingency theory.

systems theorists
Researchers who focus on viewing the organization as a whole and as the interrelationship of its parts.

Systems Theory. The **systems theorists** *focus on viewing the organization as a whole and as the interrelationship of its parts.* In the 1950s, there was an attempt to integrate the classical, behavioral, and management science theories into a holistic view of the management process. An organizational system transforms inputs (resources) into outputs (products and/or services).

According to Russell Ackoff, the commonly used classical approach to problem-solving is a reductionism process. Managers tend to break an organization into its basic parts (departments), understand the behavior and properties of the parts, and add the understanding of the parts together to understand the whole. They focus on making independent departments operate as efficiently as possible. The reductionism approach cannot yield an understanding of the organization, only knowledge of how it works. Because the parts of a system are interdependent, even if each part is independently made to perform as efficiently as possible, the organization as a whole will not perform as effectively as possible. For example, all-star athletic teams are not known to be the best teams and may not be able to beat an average team in the league.[37]

Systems theory stresses the need for conceptual skills in order to understand how the subsystems (departments) interrelate and contribute to the organization as a whole. For example, the marketing, operations, and financial departments' (subsystems) actions affect each other; if the quality of the product goes down, sales may decrease, causing a decrease in finances. Before managers in one department make a decision, they should consider the interrelated effects it will have on the other departments. The organization is a system (departments), just as the management process is a system (planning, organizing, leading, and controlling), with subsystems (parts of departments) that affect each other. So, in other words, when you have a problem to solve, do not break it into pieces; focus on the whole.

According to Harold Koontz,[38] Daniel Katz and Robert Kahn,[39] and others, the systems approach recognizes that the organization is an open system because it interacts with, and is affected by, the external environment. For example, government laws affect what the organization can and cannot do, the economy affects the organization's sales, and so on. You will learn more about open systems and the organizational environment in the next chapter.

Over the years, systems theory lost some of its popularity. However, today one of the major trends is toward total quality management (TQM), which takes a systems approach to management. You will learn more about TQM in Chapters 2, 8, and 17.

sociotechnical theorists
Researchers who focus on integrating people and technology.

Sociotechnical Theory. The **sociotechnical theorists** *focus on integrating people and technology.* Also during the 1950s and 1960s, Trist, Bamforth, Emery,[40] and others developed sociotechnical systems. They realized, as today's managers do, that you must integrate both people and technology. To focus on one at the exclusion of the other leads to lower levels of performance. Much of current behavioral science work is in agreement with sociotechnical theory.

contingency theorists
Researchers who focus on determining the best management approach for a given situation.

Contingency Theory. The **contingency theorists** *focus on determining the best management approach for a given situation.* In the 1960s and 1970s, management researchers wanted to determine how the environment and technology affected the organization.

Tom Burns and George Stalker conducted a study to determine how the *environment* affects a firm's organization and management systems. They identified two different types of environments: stable (where there is little change) and innovative (great changes); and two types of management systems: mechanistic (similar to bureaucratic classical theory) and organic (nonbureaucratic, more similar to behavioral theory). They concluded that in a stable environment the mechanistic approach works well, whereas in an innovative environment the organic approach works well.[41]

Joan Woodward conducted a study to determine how *technology* (the means of producing products) affects organizational structure. She found that organizational structure did change with the type of technology. Woodward concluded that the mechanistic or classical approach worked well with mass-production technology (autos on an assembly line), whereas the organic or behavioral approach worked well with small-batch (custom-made products) and long-run process (oil refinery) technology.

Comparing Theories

Recall that the classical and behavioral theorists claimed to have the best management approach for all organizations. In contrast, combined contingency researchers stated that there is no best way to manage all organizations. Contingency theorists do not tell managers how to manage; they tell managers to examine their situations and use the best of the other theories. Unlike systems theorists, contingency theorists do not truly try to integrate the classical, behavioral, and management science theories. They recommend using the best theory for a given situation. However, contingency theorists would recommend that managers use the systems approach when determining which approach to take in meeting objectives. Throughout this text, you will learn to take an integrative perspective using systems and contingency theories to ensure that you maximize development of your management skills. In fact, in the Skill-Building Exercise you are going to learn how to be a situational manager.

CURRENT MANAGEMENT ISSUES

At the end of each chapter you will find a discussion of the current management topics as they apply to the chapter. The current hot topics include: globalization, diversity, ethics and social responsibility, quality, productivity, participative management, teams, and small business. These issues will be addressed in more detail in subsequent chapters.

Globalization. The trend toward doing business in other countries continues. Exxon, considered to be a U.S. company, earns about 70 percent of its revenues from sales outside America. U.S. companies use parts from other countries. For example, the Ford Crown Victoria includes parts made in Mexico, Japan, Spain, Germany, and England. Even small business owners must compete with foreign companies for customers. If you are employed by a U.S. company, you may be asked to work in a foreign country for a period of time. You need human skills to work with people from other cultures.

Diversity. Managing diversity is important for many reasons. The U.S. work force is becoming increasingly diverse as the twenty-first century approaches. Statisticians show that most organizations are experiencing gender, culture, and age diversity within their labor forces.[42] Over the next decade, 85 percent of the labor force increase will be minorities and women.[43] It has been estimated that by the year 2030 less than 50 percent of the people in the United States will be white. Therefore, managing diversity will constitute a large portion of management's agenda throughout the 1990s and into the next century.[44] Organizations need to manage diversity to survive.[45] The bottom-line result of failing to embrace diversity is lost profits.[46] A diverse work force will outperform a homogeneous one,[47] and successful organizations are stressing diversity as a competitive advantage.[48]

Ethics and Social Responsibility. In recent years there has been increased emphasis on business ethics.[49,50] *Ethics*, the moral standard of right and wrong behavior, varies throughout the global environment. Often, what is unethical is also illegal, but this is not always true. The Gap is socially responsible and includes statements about the Gap Foundation, Community Action Programs, and Corporate Sourcing in its annual report. You will learn more about ethics and social responsibility in Chapter 2.

Quality and Total Quality Management (TQM). As the global economy continues to expand, the need to offer quality products and services becomes more important to survival.[51] The expression many organizations are using to reflect the importance of quality is total quality management (TQM). Two important parts of TQM are strong customer focus (like The Gap) and continual improvement in all dimensions of operations.[52] The Ford slogan, "Quality is Job 1," emphasizes the importance the company places on quality.

Productivity. Productivity is a performance measure relating outputs to inputs. To compete on a global basis, organizations must continue to increase employee productivity. To increase performance managers are expected to do more with less. To compete with the Japanese, Xerox halved both the number of employees and the amount of time needed to design a product. Harley-Davidson reduced total plant employment by 25 percent while cutting the time it takes to make a motorcycle by more than half. Two current issues related to productivity are downsizing and re-engineering.

Participative Management. Employees are an organization's greatest resource. The trend today is toward increasing the level of employee participation. To compete in a global environment, managers must move information, knowledge, rewards, and power down to the lowest levels in organizations.[53] They must also get information from lower levels. You will learn more about participative management throughout the book.

Teams. As part of the growth of participative management, more emphasis is being placed on teamwork as the major means of increasing productivity.[54] It has long been recognized that team participation in decision-making results in better decisions and more commitment to their implementation.[55,56]

Small Business. As introduced in this chapter, differences exist between how small and large businesses are managed. In each chapter, you will learn about these differences as they relate to the topics presented in the chapter.

CHAPTER SUMMARY AND GLOSSARY

The chapter summary is organized to answer the ten learning objectives for Chapter 1.

1. Describe a manager's responsibility.
A manager is responsible for achieving organizational objectives through efficient and effective use of resources. *Efficient* refers to doing things right, and *effective* refers to doing the right thing. The manager's resources include human, financial, physical, and informational.

2. List and explain the three management skills.
The three management skills are technical, human and communications, and conceptual and decision-making. Technical skills are the ability to use methods and techniques to perform a task. Human and communication skills are the ability to work with people in teams. Conceptual and decision-making skills are the ability to understand abstract ideas and select alternatives to solve problems.

3. List and explain the four management functions.
The four management functions are planning, organizing, leading, and controlling. Planning is the process of setting objectives and determining in advance exactly how the objectives will be met. Organizing is the process of delegating and coordinating tasks and resources to achieve objectives. Leading is the process of influencing employees to work toward achieving objectives. Controlling is the process of establishing and implementing mechanisms to ensure that the organization achieves its objectives.

4. Explain the three management roles: interpersonal, informational, and decisional.
Managers play the interpersonal role when they act as figurehead, leader, and liaison. Managers play the informational role when they act as monitor, disseminator, and spokesperson. Managers play the decisional role when they act as entrepreneur, disturbance-handler, resource-allocator, and negotiator.

5. List the hierarchy of management levels.
The three hierarchy levels are top (operations executive), middle (marketing manager), and first-line (accounting supervisor).

6. Describe the three different types of managers: general, functional, and project.
A general manager supervises the activities of several departments/units that perform different activities. Functional managers supervise related activities such as operations, finance, marketing, and human resources management. A project manager coordinates employees and other resources across several functional departments to accomplish a specific task.

7. Describe the differences among management levels in terms of skills needed and functions performed.
Top managers have a greater need for conceptual and decision-making skills than first-line managers. Middle managers have a need for a balance of all three skills. First-line managers have a greater need for technical skills than top managers.

8. State the major similarity and difference between the classical and behavioral theorists.
Both the classical and behavioral theorists wanted to find the best way to manage in all organizations. However, the classicist focused on the job and management functions, whereas the behaviorist focused on people.

9. Describe how the systems theorist and the contingency theorist differ from the classical and behavioral theorists.
The classical and behavioral and the systems theorists differ in the way they conceptualize the organization and its problems. The classical and behavioral theorists use a reductionist approach by breaking the organization into its component parts to conceptually understand the whole (sum of parts = whole). Systems theorists look at the organization as a whole and the interrelationship of its parts to conceptually understand the whole (whole = interrelationship of parts).

The classical and behavioral theorists seek the best management approach in all organizations. The contingency theorists propose that there is no best approach for all organizations; they seek to determine which management approach will work best in a given situation.

10. Define the following key terms (in order of appearance in the chapter):
Select one or more methods: (1) fill in the missing key terms from memory, (2) match the key terms from the end of the review with their definitions below, or (3) copy the key terms in order from the list at the beginning of the chapter.

A ______ is responsible for achieving organizational objectives through efficient and effective utilization of resources.

The __________ include human, financial, physical, and informational.

The level of organizational ______ is based on how effectively and efficiently managers use resources to achieve objectives.

__________ include technical, human and communication, and conceptual and decision-making.

__________ are the ability to use methods and techniques to perform a task.

______________ are the ability to work with people in teams.

______________ are the ability to understand abstract ideas and select alternatives to solve problems.

The four __________ include planning, organizing, leading, and controlling.

______ is the process of setting objectives and determining in advance exactly how the objectives will be met.

______ is the process of delegating and coordinating tasks and resources to achieve objectives.

______ is the process of influencing employees to work toward achieving objectives.

______ is the process of establishing and implementing mechanisms to ensure that objectives are achieved.

The ______________ include interpersonal, informational, and decisional.

There are three __________: top, middle, and first-line.

There are three __________: general, functional, and project.

The __________ focus on the job and management functions to determine the best way to manage in all organizations.

The __________ focus on people to determine the best way to manage in all organizations.

The __________ focus on the use of mathematics to aid in problem-solving and decision-making.

The __________ focus on viewing the organization as a whole and as the interrelationship of its parts.

The __________ focus on integrating people and technology.

The __________ focus on determining the best management approach to a given situation.

KEY TERMS

behavioral theorists
classical theorists
conceptual and decision-making skills
contingency theorists
controlling
human and communication skills
leading
levels of management
management functions
management role categories
management science theorists
management skills
manager
manager's resources
organizing
performance
planning
sociotechnical theorists
systems theorists
technical skills
types of managers

REVIEW AND DISCUSSION QUESTIONS

1. What is management, and why is it important to learn about management?
2. What are the three management skills? Do all managers need these skills?
3. What are the four functions of management? Do all managers perform all four functions?
4. What are the three management roles? Do all managers perform all three roles?
5. What are the three types of managers? Is there really a difference among them?
6. What is the major theme of contingency theory?

CASE

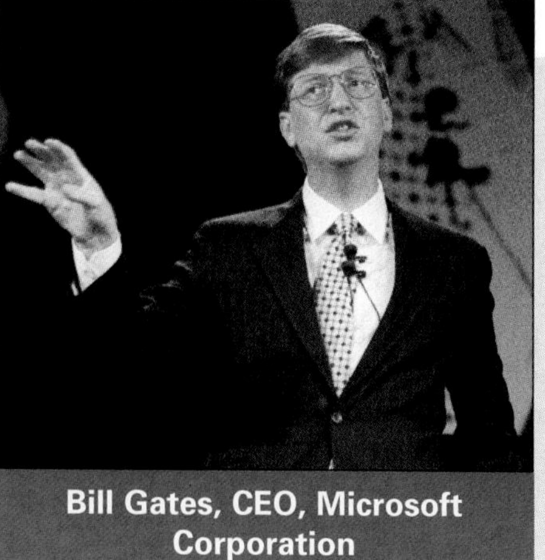
Bill Gates, CEO, Microsoft Corporation

In 1978, Bill Gates and Paul Allen launched Microsoft, which grew from a small business into a giant. Microsoft surpassed the value of IBM ($26.76 versus $26.48 billion). Bill Gates's 30 percent stock ownership has been valued at over $7 billion. The phenomenal growth of Microsoft is directly related to Gates's dedication to innovation and hard work. Over 120 million PCs run on the Microsoft MS-DOS operating system worldwide. Microsoft has over 30 percent of the market share and outsells its three largest competitors—Lotus, Novell, and WordPerfect—combined.

Bill Gates, known as a demanding boss, encourages creativity and recognizes employee achievements. He demands that his colleagues be well informed, logical, vocal, and thick-skinned. Employees often spend long hours interacting in teams. Teams that develop and market programming languages must present their ideas at the so-called "Bill" meeting. During Bill meetings, Gates often interrupts presentations to question facts and assertions. He is known to shout criticism and challenges at team members who are expected to stand up to him with good answers.

Bill Gates actively participates in and coordinates small units devoted to functional areas such as programming and marketing, but he delegates authority to managers to run their departments. Each part of the company is independent, yet Gates is the glue that holds it all together. Gates's overall business goals and plan for Microsoft, known as the Microsoft Vision, are clearly stated and effectively communicated throughout the company. His long-range vision, "Information at Your Fingertips," will take at least a decade to realize. He believes that any piece of information that the public wants should be available. Gates talks about how the company's current success sprang from the bets it made years ago and stuck with. The bets for the 1990s include multimedia, interactive TV, object-oriented programming, and far-out projects such as a wallet PC.

Select the best alternative for the following questions. Be sure you are able to explain your answers.

___ 1. Which resource played the most important role in the success of Microsoft?

a. human c. financial
b. physical d. informational

___ 2. Which of the management skills is stressed most in the case study?

a. technical
b. human and communication
c. conceptual and decision-making

___ 3. Which one of the management functions is stressed most in the case study?

a. planning c. leading
b. organizing d. controlling

___ 4. Bill Gates' participation in and coordination of small units, but delegating authority to managers to run them is an example of the ___ management function.

a. planning c. leading
b. organizing d. controlling

___ 5. Which primary management role did Bill Gates use to achieve success?

a. interpersonal–leader
b. informational–monitor
c. decisional–negotiator

___ 6. Bill Gates is at which level of management?

a. top
b. middle
c. first-line

___ 7. Which type of manager is Bill Gates?

a. general b. functional c. project

___ 8. As CEO, Bill Gates has greater need for which skills?

a. technical over conceptual
b. conceptual over technical
c. a balance

___ 9. As CEO, how does Bill Gates spend more time.

a. planning and organizing
b. leading and controlling
c. a balance

___ 10. Which approach does Bill Gates most likely take to management?

a. classical c. management science
b. behavioral d. integrative

11. Give examples of some of the tasks Bill Gates performs in each of the four management functions.

12. Give examples of some of the tasks Bill Gates performs in each of the three management roles.

13. Do you think you would like to work for Bill Gates? Explain your answer.

For current information on Microsoft, use Internet address http://www.microsoft.com. For ideas on using the Internet, see the Appendix.

Behavior Model Video 1–1, Situational Management, shows Laura, a bank branch manager, who manages tellers who are not collecting fees. Laura's boss, Celeste, discusses the situation with her. The video illustrates the four management styles, explained in Skill-Building Exercise 1–1.

Objective
To better understand the four situational management styles.

Procedure 1 (10–20 minutes)
The instructor shows Behavior Model Video 1–1. As you view each of the four scenes, identify the four situational management styles and select the one being used by the manager.

Scene 1. ___ a. autocratic (S1A)
Scene 2. ___ b. consultative (S2C)
Scene 3. ___ c. participative (S3P)
Scene 4. ___ d. empowerment (S4E)

After viewing each of the four scenes, identify/match the style used by the manager by placing the letter of the style on the scene line.

Option A: View all four scenes and identify the style used by the manager. After viewing all four scenes, discuss them. The correct answers are given in the video.

Option B: After each scene, the class discusses the style used by the manager. The instructor states the correct answer after each of the four scenes.

Procedure 2 (2–5 minutes)
Select the one style that you would use in this situation. Are other styles also appropriate? Which style would you not use (not appropriate) for

this situation. Next to each style listed above, write the letter A for appropriate or N for not appropriate.

Discussion
Option A: In groups of four to six, answer the following questions.

Option B: As a class answer the follwing questions.

1. Which style(s) are not appropriate to use in this situation?
2. Which styles(s) are appropriate to use in this situation?
3. Is there one style most appropriate in this situation? If yes, which one?

Conclusion
The instructor may make concluding remarks.

Application (2–4 minutes)
What did I learn from this exercise? How will I use this knowledge in the future?

____

____

Sharing
Volunteers give their answers to the application section.

SKILL-BUILDING EXERCISE 1–1

Situational Management[57]

Preparing for Skill-Building Exercise 1–1

In this exercise you will learn your preferred management style and how to analyze a situation in order to select the appropriate management style.

Determining Your Preferred Management Style

Before reading about situational management, complete Self-Assessment Exercise 1–2 which follows to determine your preferred management style.

SELF-ASSESSMENT EXERCISE 1–2

Determining Your Preferred Management Style

Following are 12 situations. Select the one alternative that most closely describes what you would do in each situation. Don't be concerned with trying to pick the right answer; select the alternative you would really use. Circle a, b, c, or d. Ignore the C ___ and S ___, which will be explained later in this chapter and used in class in Skill-Building Exercise 1–1.

C ___ 1. Your rookie crew seems to be developing well. Their need for direction and close supervision is diminishing. What do you do?

a. Stop directing and overseeing performance unless there is a problem. S ___

b. Spend time getting to know them personally, but make sure they maintain performance levels. S ___

c. Make sure things keep going well; continue to direct and oversee closely. S ___

d. Begin to discuss new tasks of interest to them. S ___

C ___ 2. You assigned Jill a task, specifying exactly how you wanted it done. Jill deliberately ignored your directions and did it her way. The job will not meet the customer's standards. This is not the first problem you've had with Jill. What do you decide to do?

a. Listen to Jill's side, but be sure the job gets done right. S ___

b. Tell Jill to do it again the right way and closely supervise the job. S ___

c. Tell her the customer will not accept the job and let Jill handle it her way. S ___

d. Discuss the problem and solutions to it. S ___

C ___ 3. Your employees work well together; the department is a real team. It's the top performer in the organization. Because of traffic problems, the president okayed staggered hours for departments. As a result, you can change your department's hours. Several of your workers have suggested changing. What action do you take?

a. Allow the group to decide the hours. S ___

b. Decide on new hours, explain why you chose them, and invite questions. S ___

c. Conduct a meeting to get the group members' ideas. Select new hours together, with your approval. S ___

d. Send around a memo stating the hours you want. S ___

C ___ 4. You hired Bill, a new employee. He is not performing at the level expected after one month's training. Bill is trying, but he seems to be a slow learner. What do you decide to do?

a. Clearly explain what needs to be done and oversee his work. Discuss why the procedures are important; support and encourage him. S ___

b. Tell Bill that his training is over and it's time to pull his own weight. S ___

c. Review task procedures and supervise his work closely. S ___

d. Inform Bill that his training is over and that he should feel free to come to you if he has any problems. S ___

C ___ 5. Helen has had an excellent performance record for the last five years. Recently you have noticed a drop in the quality and quantity of her work. She has a family problem. What do you do?

a. Tell her to get back on track and closely supervise her. S ___

b. Discuss the problem with Helen. Help her realize that her personal problem is affecting her work. Discuss ways to improve the situation. Be supportive and encourage her. S ___

c. Tell Helen you're aware of her productivity slip and that you're sure she'll work it out soon. S ___

d. Discuss the problem and solution with Helen and supervise her closely. S ___

C ___ 6. Your organization does not allow smoking in certain areas. You just walked by a restricted area and saw Joan smoking. She has been with the organization for ten years and is a very productive worker. Joan has never been caught smoking before. What action do you take?

a. Ask her to put the cigarette out and then leave. S ___

b. Discuss why she is smoking and what she intends to do about it. S ___

c. Give her a lecture about not smoking and check up on her in the future. S ___

d. Tell her to put the cigarette out, watch her do it, tell her you will check on her in the future. S ___

C ___ 7. Your employees usually work well together with little direction. Recently a conflict between Sue and Tom has caused problems. What action do you take?

a. Call Sue and Tom together and make them realize how this conflict is affecting the department. Discuss how to resolve it and how you will check to make sure the problem is solved. S ___

b. Let the group resolve the conflict. S ___

c. Have Sue and Tom sit down and discuss their conflict and how to resolve it. Support their efforts to implement a solution. S ___

d. Tell Sue and Tom how to resolve their conflict and closely supervise them. S ___

C ___ 8. Jim usually does his share of the work with some encouragement and direction. However, he has migraine headaches occasionally and doesn't pull his weight when this happens. The others resent doing Jim's work. What do you decide to do?

a. Discuss his problem and help him come up with ideas for maintaining his work; be supportive. S ___

b. Tell Jim to do his share of the work and closely watch his output. S ___

c. Inform Jim that he is creating a hardship for the others and should resolve the problem by himself. S ___

d. Be supportive but set minimum performance levels and ensure compliance. S ___

C ___ 9. Barbara, your most experienced and productive worker, came to you with a detailed idea that could increase your department's productivity at a very low cost. She can do her present job and this new assignment. You think it's an excellent idea. What do you do?

a. Set some goals together. Encourage and support her efforts. S ___

b. Set up goals for Barbara. Be sure she agrees with them and sees you as being supportive of her efforts. S ___

c. Tell Barbara to keep you informed and to come to you if she needs any help. S ___

d. Have Barbara check in with you frequently so that you can direct and supervise her activities. S ___

C ___ 10. Your boss asked you for a special report. Frank, a very capable worker who usually needs no direction or support, has all the necessary skills to do the job. However, Frank is reluctant because he has never done a report. What do you do?

a. Tell Frank he has to do it. Give him direction and supervise him closely. S ___

b. Describe the project to Frank and let him do it his own way. S ___

c. Describe the benefits to Frank. Get his ideas on how to do it and check his progress. S ___

d. Discuss possible ways of doing the job. Be supportive; encourage Frank. S ___

C ___ 11. Jean is the top producer in your department. However, her monthly reports are constantly late and contain errors. You are puzzled because she does everything else with no direction or support. What do you decide to do?

a. Go over past reports, explaining exactly what is expected of her. Schedule a meeting so that you can review the next report with her. S ___

b. Discuss the problem with Jean and ask her what can be done about it; be supportive. S ___

c. Explain the importance of the report. Ask her what the problem is. Tell her that you expect the next report to be on time and error-free. S ___

d. Remind Jean to get the next report in on time without errors. S ___

C ___ 12. Your workers are very effective and like to participate in decision-making. A consultant was hired to develop a new method for your department using the latest technology in the field. What do you do?

a. Explain the consultant's method and let the group decide how to implement it. S ___

b. Teach them the new method and supervise them closely. S ___

c. Explain the new method and the reasons that it is important. Teach them the method and make sure the procedure is followed. Answer questions. S ___

d. Explain the new method and get the group's input on ways to improve and implement it. S ___

To determine your preferred management style, follow these steps:

1. Circle the letter you selected for each situation. The column headings (S-A through S-E) represent the management style you selected. S1A = Autocratic, S2C = Consultative, S3P = Participative, S4E = Empowerment

	S1A	S2C	S3P	S4E
1.	c	b	d	a
2.	b	a	d	c
3.	d	b	c	a
4.	c	a	d	b
5.	a	d	b	c
6.	d	c	b	a
7.	d	a	c	b
8.	b	d	a	c
9.	d	b	a	c
10.	a	c	d	b
11.	a	c	b	d
12.	b	c	d	a
Totals	___	___	___	___

2. Add up the number of circled items per column. The highest is your preferred management style. Is this the style you tend to use most often?

Your management style flexibility is reflected in the distribution of your answers. The more evenly distributed the numbers are between S-A, S-C, S-P, and S-E, the more flexible your style is. A score of 1 or 0 in any column may indicate a reluctance to use the style.

Note: There is no "right" management style. This part of the exercise is designed to enable you to better understand the style you tend to use or prefer to use.

Analyzing the Situation

Now that you have determined your preferred management style, you will learn about the four management styles and when to use each. According to contingency theorists, there is no best management style for all situations. Instead, effective managers adapt their style to individual capabilities or a group situation.[58] Studies have shown that manager–employee interactions can be classified into two distinct categories: directive and supportive.

- *Directive behavior*. The manager focuses on directing and controlling behavior to ensure that the task gets done. The manager tells employees what to do and when, where, and how to do the task and closely oversees performance.
- *Supportive behavior*. The manager focuses on encouraging and motivating behavior without telling the employee what to do. The manager explains things and listens to employee views, helping employees make their own decisions through building up confidence and self-esteem.

In other words, when you, as a manager, interact with your employees, you can focus on directing (getting the task done), supporting (developing relationships), or both.

These definitions lead us to the question, "What style should I use and why?" The answer depends on the situation, which is determined in part by the capability of the employees. In turn, there are two distinct aspects of capability:

- *Ability*. Do the employees have the knowledge, experience, education, skills, and so forth to do a particular task without direction from you as the manager?
- *Motivation*. Do the employees have the confidence to do the task? Do they want to do the task? Are they committed to performing the task? Will they perform the task without your encouragement and support?

Determining Employee Capability. Employee capability may be measured on a continuum from low to outstanding, which you, as a manager, determine. You select the capability level that best describes the employees' ability and motivation for the specific task.

- *Low (C1)*. The employees can't do the task without detailed directions and close supervision. Employees in this category are either unable or unwilling to do the task.
- *Moderate (C2)*. The employees have moderate ability and need specific direction and support to get the task done properly. The employees may be highly motivated but still need direction due to lack of ability.
- *High (C3)*. The employees have high ability but may lack the confidence to do the job. What they need most is support and encouragement to motivate them to get the task done.
- *Outstanding (C4)*. The employees are capable of doing the task without direction or support.

Most people perform a variety of tasks on the job. It is important to realize that employee capability may vary depending on the specific task. For example, a bank teller may be a C4 for routine transactions but a C1 for opening new or special accounts. Employees tend to start working with a C1 capability, needing close direction. As their ability to do the job increases, you can begin to be supportive and probably stop supervising closely. As a manager, you must gradually develop your employees from C1 to C2 to C3 or C4 levels over time.

The Four Management Styles

As mentioned, the correct management style depends on the situation, which in turn, is a function of employee capability. Each of the four management styles also involves various degrees of supportive and directive behavior. The four situational management styles are autocratic, consultative, participative, and empowerment.

- *Autocratic style (S1A)* involves high-directive/low-supportive behavior (HD/LS) and is appropriate when interacting with low-capability employees (C1). When interacting with employees, give very detailed instructions describing exactly what the task is and when, where, and how to perform it. Closely oversee performance and give some support. The majority of time with the employees is spent giving directions. Make decisions without input from the employees.
- *Consultative style (S2C)* involves high-directive/high-supportive behavior (HD/HS) and is appropriate when interacting with moderately capable employees (C2). Give specific instructions as well as overseeing performance at all major stages through completion. At the

same time, support the employees by explaining why the task should be performed as requested and answering their questions. Work on relationships as you sell the benefits of completing the task your way. Give fairly equal amount of time to directing and supporting employees. When making decisions, you may consult employees, but still have the final say. Once you make the decision, which can incorporate employees' ideas, direct and oversee their performance.

- *Participative style (S3P)* is characterized by low-directive/high-supportive behavior (LD/HS) and is appropriate when interacting with employees with high capability (C3). When interacting with employees, spend a small amount of time giving general directions and a great deal of time giving encouragement. Spend limited time overseeing performance, letting employees do the task their way while focusing on the end result. Support the employees by encouraging them and building up their self-confidence. If a task needs to be done, don't tell them how to do it; ask them how they will accomplish it. Make decisions together or allow employees to make the decision subject to your limitations and approval.
- *Empowerment style (S4E)* entails low-directive/low-supportive behavior (LD/LS) and is appropriate when interacting with outstanding employees (C4). When interacting with these employees, merely let them know what needs to be done. Answer their questions, but provide little, if any, direction. It is not necessary to oversee performance. These employees are highly motivated and need little, if any, support. Allow these employees to make their own decisions subject to your limitations although approval will not be necessary. Other terms for empowerment would be *laissez-faire* or *hands off*; let them alone to do their own thing.

Model 1–1 summarizes the four management styles.

Applying the Situational Management Model

You're already familiar with the following situation from Self-Assessment Exercise 1–2, which was part of the exercise for determining your management style. Now you're going to apply the information in Model 1–1 to this situation. (Later, in Skill-Building Exercise 1–1, you may deal with the remaining 11 situations in class.)

To begin, identify the employee capability level in each situation, listed in the top of Model 1–1. Indicate the capability level by placing the number 1 through 4 on the line marked "C" to the left of the situation. Next, determine the management style that each response (a, b, c, or d) represents and indicate that style by placeing the letter A, C, P, or E) on the line marked "S" at the end of each response. Finally, identify the response you think is most appropriate by placing a checkmark next to it. Now use Model 1–1 to select the management style that will result in the optimum performance of the task.

C ___ **1.** Your rookie crew seems to be developing well. Their need for close supervision is diminishing. What do you do?

a. Stop directing and overseeing performance, unless there is a problem. S ___

b. Spend time getting to know them personally, but make sure they maintain performance levels. S ___

c. Make sure things keep going well; continue to direct and oversee closely. S ___

d. Begin to discuss new tasks of interest to them. S ___

Let's see how well you did.

1. As a rookie crew, their capability started at C-1, but they have now developed to the C-2 level. If you put the number 2 on the C line, you were correct.
2. Alternative a is the E—empowerment style. There is low direction and support. Alternative b is the C—consultative style. There is both high direction and support. Alternative c is the A—autocratic style. There is high direction but low support. Alternative d is the P—participative style. There is low direction and high support (in discussing employee interests).
3. If you selected b as the match, you were correct. However, in the business world there is seldom only one way to handle a situation successfully. Therefore, in this exercise, you are given points based on how successful your behavior would be in each situation. In situation 1, b is the most successful alternative because it involves developing the employees gradually; it's a three-point answer. Alternative c is the next best alternative, followed by d. It is better to keep things the way they are now rather than trying to rush employee development, which would probably cause problems. So c is a two-point answer, and d gets one point. Alternative a is the least effective because you are going from one extreme of supervision to the other. This is a zero-point answer because the odds are great that this style will cause problems that will negatively affect your management success.

The better you match your management style to employees' capabilities, the greater your chances of being a

Model 1–1
Situational Management Model

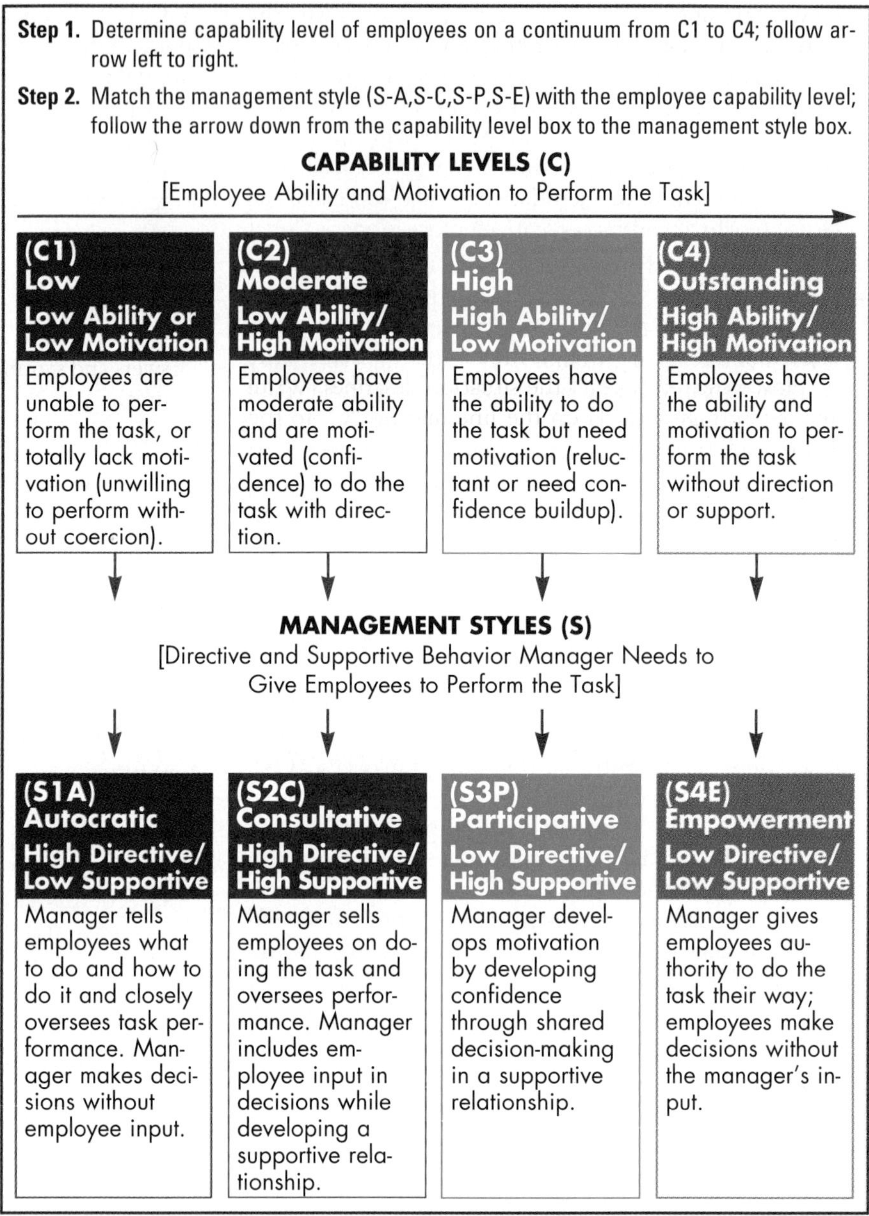

successful manager. During the in-class part of Skill-Building Exercise 1–1, you will apply the model to the remaining situations and be given feedback on your success at applying the model as you develop your situational management skills.

Step 1. Determine capability level of employees on a continuum from C1 to C4; follow arrow left to right.
Step 2. Match the management style (S-A,S-C,S-P,S-E) with the employee capability level; follow the arrow down from the capability level box to the management style box.
CAPABILITY LEVELS (C)
[Employee Ability and Motivation to Perform the Task]
(C1) Low
Low Ability or Low Motivation
Employees are unable to perform the task, or totally lack motivation (unwilling to perform without coercion).
(C2) Moderate
Low Ability/ High Motivation
Employees have moderate ability and are motivated (confidence) to do the task with direction.
(C3) High
High Ability/ Low Motivation
Employees have the ability to do the task but need motivation (reluctant or need confidence buildup).
(C4) Outstanding
High Ability/ High Motivation
Employees have the ability and motivation to perform the task without direction or support.
MANAGEMENT STYLES (S)
[Directive and Supportive Behavior Manager Needs to Give Employees to Perform the Task]
(S1A) Autocratic
High Directive/ Low Supportive
Manager tells employees what to do and how to do it and closely oversees task performance. Manager makes decisions without employee input.
(S2C) Consultative
High Directive/ High Supportive
Manager sells employees on doing the task and oversees performance. Manager includes employee input in decisions while developing a supportive relationship.
(S3P) Participative
Low Directive/ High Supportive
Manager develops motivation by developing confidence through shared decision-making in a supportive relationship.
(S4E) Empowerment
Low Directive/ Low Supportive
Manager gives employees authority to do the task their way; employees make decisions without the manager's input.

Doing Skill-Building Exercise 1–1 In Class

Objectives

1. To learn to use the situational management model.
2. To develop your ability to supervise employees using the appropriate situational management style for their capability level.

Procedure

You will apply the Situational Management Model 1–1 to the situations in Self-Assessment Exercise 1–2. Your instructor will give you the recommended answers which will enable you to determine your success at selecting the appropriate style.

Video (XX minutes)
Behavior Model Video 1–1 may be shown to illustrate how to use the situational management model and the four management styles. Use the form on page 28 to record answers.

Step 1 (3–8 minutes)

The instructor reviews the situational management model and explains how to use the model for situation 2 in Self-Assessment Exercise 1–2.

1. Determine the capability level of employees. For each situation, use the top row in Model 1–1 to identify the employee capability level the situation describes. Write the level (1 through 4) on the line marked "C" to the left of each situation.
2. Match the management style with the employee capability level. The management match is below the capability level in the model. Identify the management style that each response (a through d) represents. Indicate the style (S1A, S2C, S3P, or S4E) on the line marked "S" at the end of each response. Finally, choose the management style best for each situation by making a checkmark next to the appropriate response (a, b, c, or d).

Step 2 (25–45 minutes)

1. Turn to situation 3 in Self-Assessment Exercise 1–2 and to Model 1–1. Apply the model to the situation and select the best course of action (3 to 4 minutes). The instructor will go over the answers and scoring (3 to 4 minutes).
2. Divide into teams of two or three. Apply the model as a team to situations 4 through 6. Team members may select different answers if they don't agree (6 to 10 minutes). Do not do situations 7 through 12 until you are told to do so. Your instructor will go over the answers and scoring for situations 4 through 6 (5 to 8 minutes).
3. As a team, select your answers to situations 7 through 12 (11 to 15 minutes). Your instructor will go over the answers and scoring for situations 7 through 12 (2 to 4 minutes).

Conclusion
The instructor may lead a class discussion and make concluding remarks.

Application (2–4 minutes)
What did I learn from this experience? How will I use this knowledge in the future?

____

____

Sharing
Volunteers give their answers to preceding applications.

EXERCISE 1–1

Getting to Know You[59]

Objectives

1. To get acquainted with some of your classmates.
2. To gain a better understanding of what the course covers.
3. To get to know more about your instructor.

Procedure 1 (5–8 minutes)
Break into groups of five or six, preferably with people you do not know. Each member tells his or her name and two or three significant things about himself or herself. After all the members are finished, they may ask each other questions to get to know each other better.

Procedure 2 (4–8 minutes)
Can anyone in the group call the others by name? If so, he or she should do so. If not, have each member repeat his or her name. Follow with each member calling all members by name. Be sure each person knows everyone's first name.

Discussion Question
What can you do to improve your ability to remember people's names?

____

____

____

Procedure 3 (5–10 minutes)
Elect a spokesperson or recorder for your group. Look over the following categories and decide what specific statements or questions you would like your spokesperson to ask the instructor based on these categories. The spokesperson will not identify who asked the questions. You do not have to have questions for each area.

1. *Course expectations*. What do you hope to learn from this course? Your instructor will comment on your expecta-

tions and tell the class whether the topics are a planned part of the course.

2. *Doubts or concerns*. Is there anything about the course that you don't understand? Express any doubts or concerns that you may have or ask questions for clarification.
3. *Questions about the instructor*. List questions to ask the instructor in order to get to know him or her better.

Procedure 4 (10–20 minutes)
Each spokesperson asks the instructor one question at a time until all questions from Procedure 3 have been answered. Spokespeople should skip questions already asked by other groups.

Conclusion
The instructor may make concluding remarks.

Application (2–4 minutes)
What did I learn from this experience? How will I use this knowledge in the future?

____

____

Sharing
Volunteers may give their answers to the preceding questions.

The Environment: Quality, Globalization, Ethics, and Social Responsibility

Learning Objectives

After studying this chapter, you should be able to:

1. Explain the five internal environmental factors: management, mission, resources, systems process, and structure.
2. List and explain the need for the two primary principles of total quality management (TQM).
3. Describe how the nine external environmental factors—customers, competitors, suppliers, labor force, shareholders, society, technology, governments, and economies—can affect the internal business environment.
4. State the difference among a domestic, international, and multinational business.
5. Of the six ways to take a business global, list the lowest and the highest cost and risk.
6. Explain the stakeholders' approach to ethics.
7. Discuss the differences in the four levels of social responsibility: obstruction, obligation, reaction, and involvement.
8. Explain the difference between downsizing and re-engineering.
9. Define the following **key terms** (in order of appearance in the chapter):

   internal environment
   mission
   stakeholders
   systems process
   quality
   customer value
   total quality management (TQM)
   external environment
   international business
   multinational corporation (MNC)
   global sourcing
   joint venture
   direct investment
   ethics
   stakeholders' approach to ethics
   social responsibility
   downsizing
   re-engineering

Skill Development

1. You should develop your skill to analyze a company's environment and management practices (Skill-Building Exercise 2–1).

   This analysis requires conceptual skills. Having the skill to analyze your company's environment and management practices, and those of its competitors, will make you a more valuable employee. This skill is especially important if you want to progress to higher levels of management. The primary management function skill developed is planning. The primary management roles developed are informational and decisional. The SCANS skill competencies of resources, information, and especially systems, as well as basic and thinking foundation skills are developed.

rederick W. Smith thought of the idea of an overnight delivery system by air freight to accommodate time-sensitive shipments such as medicines, computer parts, and electronics. Smith presented the idea in a term paper to a professor in college and received a grade of "C." On March 12, 1973, Smith tested his service by delivering six packages. FedEx began operations officially on April 17 with a total of 186 packages shipped. FedEx lost a million dollars a month for the first 27 months.

FedEx developed the hub-and-spokes system now widely imitated in the airline industry. Using this system, all shipments are flown to a centralized hub, sorted, loaded onto planes, and dispatched. By November 1988, Federal Express was able to deliver as many as a million packages in one night. FedEx was the first in its industry to offer innovative ideas and services including overnight package delivery, the Overnight Letter (1981), 10:30 A.M. next-day delivery (Fall 1982), package tracking in vans, real-time package tracking over the phone (1981), time-definite service for freight, Saturday delivery, and pickup service.

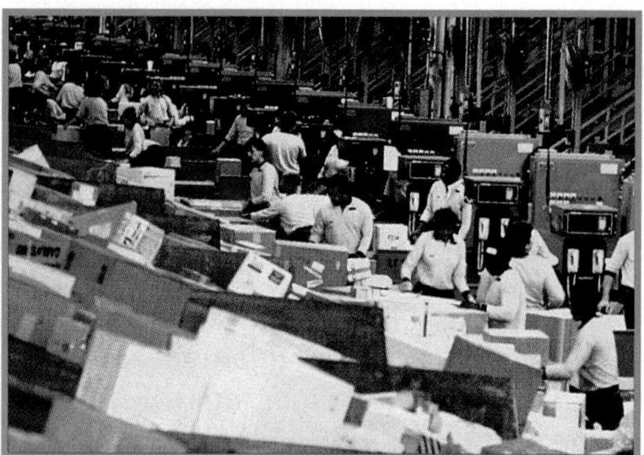

Federal Express is able to deliver as many as 2 million packages per night to 186 countries.

FedEx now delivers an average of two million pieces per night to 186 countries. As you will learn in this chapter, FedEx's success is based on its internal environment and its ability to adapt to its external environment.[1]

For current information on Federal Express, use Internet address http://www.fedex.com. For ideas on using the Internet, see the Appendix.

1. Explain the five internal environmental factors: management, mission, resources, systems process, and structure.

internal environment
Factors that affect an organization's performance from within its boundaries.

THE INTERNAL ENVIRONMENT

Profit and nonprofit organizations are created to produce products and/or services for customers. *The organization's* **internal environment** *includes the factors that affect its performance from within its boundaries.* They are called internal factors because they are within the organization's control, as opposed to external factors, which are outside of the organization's control. The five internal environmental factors that you will learn about in this section are management, mission, resources, the systems process, and structure.

Work Application

For each application in this chapter use a different, or at least several different, organizations for your examples.

1. State the mission of an organization, preferably an organization you work or have worked for.

Management

Managers are responsible for the organization's performance. They perform the functions of planning, organizing, leading, and controlling. The leadership style used and the decisions made by managers from the top down affect the performance of the organization. Top managers often receive credit for the success or failure of the organization because they have control over their behavior, even though it is affected by the external environment. Clearly, FedEx would not be the success it is today without its founder and CEO, Frederick W. Smith. Bonnie Castonguary (Chapter 1) directly affects the performance of her Gap store. You will learn how to be an effective manager and develop management skills throughout this book. However, effective managers realize the need for employee participation in management of the organization.[2] Employees want input into how organizations are run.[3]

mission
An organization's purpose or reason for being.

stakeholders
People whose interests are affected by organizational behavior.

Mission

The organization's **mission** *is its purpose or reason for being.* Developing the mission is top management's responsibility. The mission should identify present

Federal Express is committed to our PEOPLE–SERVICE–PROFIT philosophy. We will produce outstanding financial returns by providing totally reliable, competitively superior global air-ground transportation of high priority goods and documents that require rapid, time-certain delivery. Equally important, positive control of each package will be maintained utilizing real-time electronic tracking and tracing systems. A complete record of each shipment and delivery will be presented with our request for payment. We will be helpful, courteous, and professional to each other and the public. We will strive to have a completely satisfied customer at the end of each transaction.

Figure 2–1
Federal Express Mission Statement

and future products. The term *product* is commonly used to include both goods and services. According to Deming, the major reason businesses fail is that management doesn't look ahead. Under management's directives, the organization produces the wrong product—one with no market, or too small a market.[4] Managers with vision change the organization's mission by offering products in demand by customers. According to a survey, worker loyalty is being eroded by management's failure to develop and convey missions with clear objectives.[5] Figure 2–1 shows that Federal Express has a clear mission statement. Notice the objective to satisfy each customer.

Professor and consultant Russell Ackoff stated that the mission should include objectives that allow for measurement and evaluation of performance. The mission should state how the organization differs from its competitors. What unique advantage does the organization have to offer customers?[6] The mission should be relevant to all stakeholders. **Stakeholders** *are people whose interests are affected by organizational behavior*. Some of the stakeholders include employees, shareholders, customers, suppliers, the government, and so on. More about these stakeholders appears throughout this chapter.

The mission is also known as the ends the organization strives to attain. The other internal environmental factors are considered the means to achieve the ends. See Figure 2–2 for an illustration. Note that managers develop the mission and set objectives, but the managers are a means to the end. Managers are not an end in and of themselves. As a manager, you may not write the mission statement, but you will be responsible for helping to achieve it.

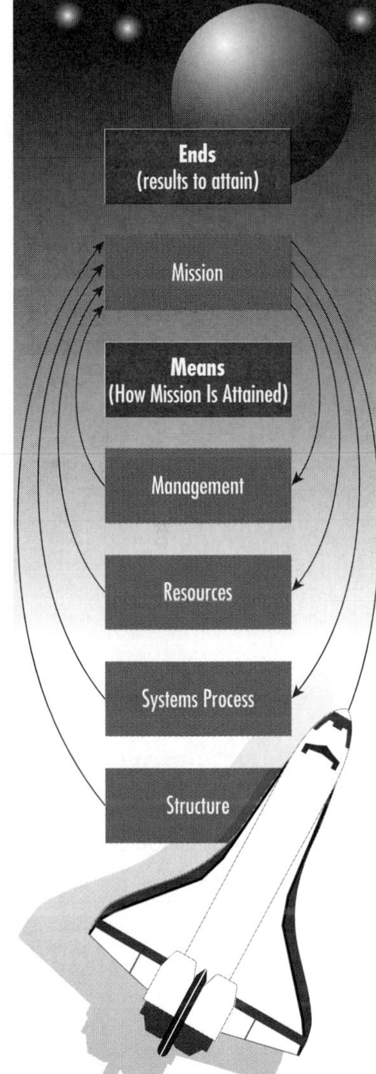

Figure 2–2
Internal Environment Means and Ends

Resources

Organizations have resources to accomplish their mission. As stated in Chapter 1, organizational resources include human, financial, physical, and informational. *Human resources* are responsible for achieving the organization's mission and objectives. They come up with the creative ideas that result in changes that increase an organization's performance. FedEx's People–Service–Profit philosophy states that when the company puts its people first, they will provide outstanding service, which in turn will lead to profits. FedEx has over 98,000 employees delivering over two million packages daily to 186 countries. *Physical resources* at FedEx include approximately 457 aircraft and 29,000 ground vehicles. COSMOS, the FedEx computer system, is critical to timed delivery with tracking. *Financial resources* are necessary to purchase and maintain the physical resources and to pay employees. In 1994, FedEx had revenues of over $8 billion and a net profit of $204,370,000. *Informational resources* come primarily through COSMOS, but FedEx also has its own internal TV network called FXTV that reaches more than 1,200 facilities worldwide via a closed-circuit satellite hookup. As a manager, you will be responsible for using these four resources to achieve the organization's mission.

The Systems Process

systems process
The method used to transform inputs into outputs.

The **systems process** *is the method used to transform inputs into outputs*. The systems process has four components:

1. *Inputs*. Inputs are the startup forces that provide the organization with operating necessities. The inputs are the organization's resources (human, financial, physical, and informational). At FedEx, the primary input is the two million packages to be delivered to 186 countries daily.
2. *Transformation*. Transformation is the conversion of the inputs into outputs. At FedEx, the packages (input) go to the hub (transformation) where they are sorted for delivery.
3. *Outputs*. Outputs are the products offered to customers. At FedEx, the packages are delivered to customers.
4. *Feedback*. Feedback provides a means of control to insure that the inputs and transformation process are producing the desired results. COSMOS is used as a means of feedback to help ensure that all packages are delivered on time.

Work Application

2. Illustrate the systems process for an organization, preferably one you work or have worked for.

A manufacturing firm like Ford Motor Company uses raw materials and components such as steel, plastic and metal parts, rubber tires, and so on (inputs) as it makes cars (outputs) on the assembly line (transformation process). The Gap purchases clothes (inputs) from manufacturers to display and sell for cash or on credit (transformation process) to customers (outputs). The customer can be internal or external, and the output of one system can be an input to another system. For example, Ford could buy its tires from Goodyear. The tires would be an output of Goodyear and an input for Ford, making Ford Goodyear's external customer. Within Ford, one department could mold fenders (outputs) and send them to the assembly line (inputs). Departments within the same organization are internal customers. In the previous example, Ford and Goodyear would be stakeholders to each other.

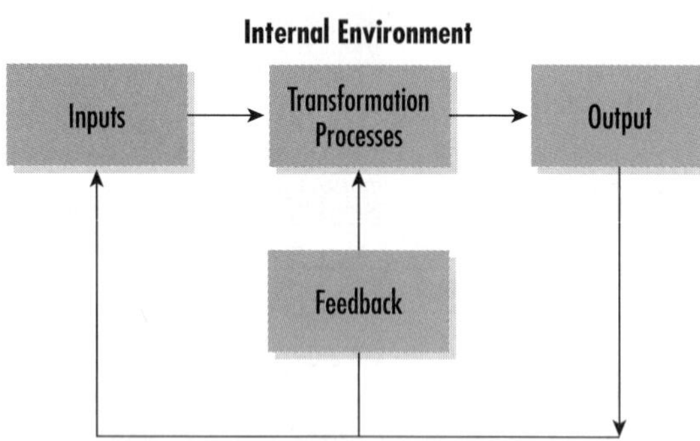

Figure 2–3
The Systems Process

Managers with a systems perspective view the organization as a process rather than as separate departments for finance, marketing, operations, and human resources. The focus is on the interrelationship of all of these functions as the inputs are converted into outputs. As a manager, you will use your conceptual skills to understand the systems process in order to help the organization achieve its mission. See Figure 2–3 for an illustration of the systems process.

quality
Comparing actual use to requirements to determine value.

customer value
The purchasing benefits used by customers to determine whether or not to buy a product.

Quality. Quality is an internal factor because it is within the control of the organization. *Customers determine* **quality** *by comparing actual use to requirements to determine value*. **Customer value** *is the purchasing benefits used by customers to determine whether or not to buy a product*. Customers don't simply buy a product itself. They buy the benefit they expect to derive from that product. Value is what motivates us to buy products. When the author bought a computer and software, it was not for the equipment itself; it was for the benefits of being able to word process this book's manuscript. It was quicker, easier, and cheaper to word process the manuscript than to hand-write it and have someone else type it. The computer had value to it so the author bought it.

Quality and value are important components of all organizations because they attract and retain customers. If a customer uses FedEx to send a package that gets delivered on time, and the customer perceives the cost to be worth it, the customer perceives FedEx to be of value and will continue to send packages through FedEx; if not, the customer will go to another source. Quality and value are continually being redefined in a competitive market. If United Parcel Service (UPS) offers faster service for less money, it will be perceived as a value and FedEx will lose customers to UPS.

Total Quality Management (TQM). TQM is the commonly used term for stressing quality within an organization. TQM uses a systems perspective because it is not a program for one department, but a responsibility of everyone (total) in the organization. **Total quality management (TQM)** *is the process that involves everyone in the organization focusing on the customer to continually improve product value.* Four primary principles of TQM follow:[7]

2. List and explain the need for the two primary principles of total quality management (TQM).

total quality management (TQM) The process that involves everyone in the organization focusing on the customer to continually improve product value.

1. *Focus on delivering customer value.* As stated previously, if an organization is to be successful, it must offer value to attract and retain customers.

2. *Continually improve the system and its processes.* Principle 2 is closely related to Principle 1. Quality and value continue to change, and if the organization is satisfied with old standards and wants to stay the same, the organization will lose customers to competitors. IBM is an example of a company that did not change from mainframe computers to PCs fast enough and has had problems with its systems process. As a result, IBM has lost sales to Compaq, Apple, Packard-Bell, and others, making it fourth in PC sales in 1993. Toyota's Lexus division's motto, "The Relentless Pursuit of Perfection," indicates the need to focus on Principles 1 and 2. Principles 1 and 2 are the basis for the definition of TQM.

3. *Focus on managing processes rather than people.* Employees transform inputs into outputs through systems process. If managers want to improve employee performance, they need to focus on the process rather than the people. This is because employees only execute processes based on their own skills and the other resources the organization provides to help them. Juran and Deming found that only 15 to 20 percent of all work problems were worker-controlled.[8] Therefore, 80 to 85 percent of the problems are caused by systems process problems, not people; this is often called the 85–15 rule. A poor input may not be able to be transformed into an effective output. If a package were placed in a FedEx box without a proper mailing address, it is not the fault of the employee who picked up the package. It is the system that allows people to drop off packages that are picked up later without having the mailing address checked by an employee.

4. *Work in teams to execute processes efficiently and effectively.* A single employee rarely obtains inputs, converts them to outputs, delivers them to customers, and services the output. In an organization in which employees are responsible for various steps in the systems process, a need for teamwork exists. In Chapter 13 you will learn more about teams.

Work Application

3. Identify the quality and value of a product you purchased recently.

FedEx is dedicated to quality and value, and its dedication is evident in its "quality improvement process," which stems from its People–Service–Profit philosophy. FedEx has more than 75 quality professionals, hired from within the organization, who train people in quality courses, assist quality team activity, promote success stories, and serve as consultants for special corporatewide initiatives. Their mission is to customize quality training, communication, measurement, and rewards according to their division's special needs. In 1990 FedEx was the first company to win the Malcolm Baldrige National Quality Award in the service category. As a manager, you must understand the importance of quality and customer value, and continually strive to achieve them through processes as a team member.

APPLYING THE CONCEPT

AC 2–1 The Internal Environment

Identify each statement by its internal environmental factor.

a. management c. resources e. structure
b. mission d. systems process

____ **1.** "We take these chemicals and make them into a liquid, which then goes into these molds. When it's hard, we have outdoor chairs."

____ **2.** "We deliver pizza and buffalo wings."

____ **3.** "It's the people here that make this company what it is."

____ **4.** "As we grew we added a new department for human resources services."

____ **5.** "Management does not trust us. All the major decisions around here are made by top-level managers."

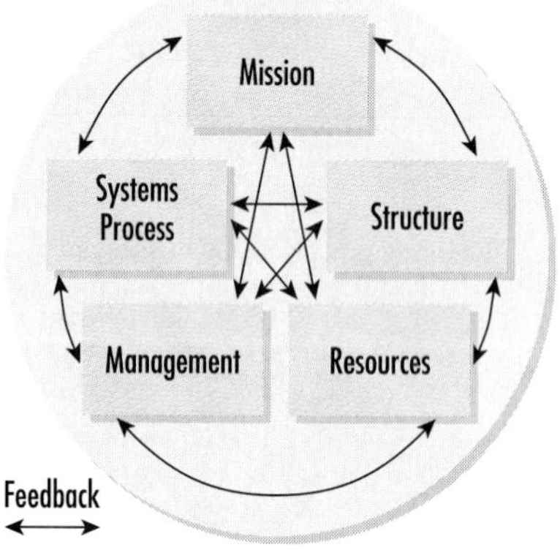

Figure 2–4
Internal Environment Components

Structure

Structure refers to the way in which the organization groups its resources to accomplish its mission. As discussed in Chapter 1, an organization is a system. An organization, being a system, is structured into departments such as finance, marketing, production, personnel, and so on. Each of these departments affects the organization as a whole, and each department is affected by the other departments. Organizations structure resources to transform inputs into outputs. All of the organization's resources must be structured effectively to achieve its objectives. As a manager you will be responsible for part of the organization's structure—a department. You will learn more about organizational structure in Chapters 7 through 9. See Figure 2–4 for a review of the internal environment components.

3. Describe how the nine external environmental factors—customers, competitors, suppliers, labor force, shareholders, society, technology, governments, and economies—can affect the internal business environment.

THE EXTERNAL ENVIRONMENT

external environment
The factors that affect an organization's performance from outside its boundaries.

The organization's **external environment** *includes the factors that affect its performance from outside its boundaries.* Although managers can control the internal environment, they have very limited influence over what happens outside the organization. The nine major external factors are customers, competition, suppliers, labor force/unions, shareholders, society, technology, governments, and the economy.

Customers

Customers have a major effect on the organization's performance through purchasing products. Without customers there is no need for an organization. Effective managers today realize the need to offer customers products of value to them. Continually improving customer value is often the difference between success and failure in business. Effective managers develop a mission that offers value to customers. Using its structure and resources through its systems process, the organization offers the products to the targeted customers. According to FedEx's mission statement, its primary value is delivering "high priority goods and documents that require rapid, time-certain delivery . . . with real time tracking . . . as employees strive for a completely satisfied customer at the end of each transaction." Managers must change the organization's mission and products as value to customers changes. If they do not, they will lose customers to competitors as has happened with PC sales at IBM.

Is Customer Service Important? A study by the Strategic Planning Institute revealed that the organizations with high service strategies increased their market share by 6 percent per year and their return on sales was 12 percent. The organizations with low service strategies had a decrease in market share of 2 percent and a return on sales of only 1 percent. So there is no question that service has an economic impact.[9] Service is an important part of value. This, among other reasons, is why TQM focuses on creating customer value. The better you create customer value, the more successful your management career will be.

Competition

Organizations must compete for customers. Competitors' strategic moves affect the performance of the organization. FedEx was the first to offer overnight delivery by 10:30 A.M., but its primary competitor, United Parcel Service (UPS), was first to introduce overnight delivery by 8:30 A.M. followed by same-day delivery. FedEx is matching UPS's services to keep its customers.[10] When a company is the first to increase customer value, the competitors may permanently lose customers even though they match the value. Other major competitors of FedEx include Roadway Package System (RPS), Airborne, and Express Mail–U.S. Postal Service, plus many other regional companies.

Another important area of customer value is pricing. When a competitor changes prices, firms tend to match prices to keep customers; for example, the increasing speed and dropping prices of PCs. Another example is that when RJR Nabisco raised its cigarette prices, its competitors Philip Morris and Brown & Williamson quickly matched them.[11] If its competitors did not match the price increase, RJR most likely would have dropped its prices to match theirs. Competition is increasing as the global economy expands.

Effective managers develop missions with strategies that offer a unique advantage over the competition. The organization uses its resources and structure through the transformation process to develop unique products. Pizza Hut was unique with its restaurants. Domino's Pizza developed free delivery guaranteed within 30 minutes (which was later changed), and took business away from Pizza Hut and others. Now, because of the competition, Pizza Hut and others also offer free delivery. Little Caesar's is unique in offering two pizzas and crazy bread, but it did not offer free delivery until 1995. The better you are at competing for customers, the more successful the organization will be.

Time-based competition, which focuses on increasing the speed of going from product idea to delivery to customers, is a current trend. You will learn about time-based competition in Chapters 5 and 17.

Work Application

4. Give an example of how one firm's competitors have affected that business.

Suppliers

Many organizations' resources come from outside the firm. Organizations often buy land, buildings, machines, equipment, natural resources, and component parts from suppliers. Therefore, an organization's performance is affected by suppliers. General Motors (GM) built the Saturn plant to make four models of Saturn cars. GM developed a separate Saturn dealership network to sell its cars. However, in its first year, due to production problems, Saturn dealers received only half of their allocation of cars. GM supplies Saturn dealerships. If GM doesn't deliver the cars and/or they are of poor quality, the dealer's performance is adversely affected. FedEx's delivery depends on its planes and trucks which it purchases through suppliers. To be an effective manager you need to realize the importance of suppliers and develop close working relationships with them; this is an important part of TQM.

Labor Force

The employees of the organization have a direct effect on its performance. Management recruits human resources from the available labor force outside its boundaries. The firm's mission, its structure, and its systems process are major determining factors of the capability levels employees need to meet objectives. The skills needed by FedEx employees differ from those needed by Gap employees.

Unions also provide employees for the organization. Unions are considered an external factor because they become a third party when dealing with the organization. Most UPS employees are members of the Teamsters Union while FedEx employees do not have a major union. In a unionized organization, the union, rather than the individual employee, negotiates an agreement with management. In nonunionized firms, there is a threat of employees' organizing to form a union. The union has the power to strike. When a union strikes, revenues and wages are lost. The 1994 baseball strike is one example.

Shareholders

The owners of a corporation, known as shareholders, have a significant influence on management. Most shareholders of large corporations are generally not involved in the day-to-day operation of the firm, but they do vote for the directors of the corporation. The board of directors is also generally not involved in the day-to-day operation of the firm. However, it hires and fires top management. The top manager reports to the board of directors. If the organization does not perform well, managers can be fired. John Akers is now the former chairman and CEO of IBM. Shareholders hold over 56 million shares of FedEx stock. As a manager you may be given the opportunity to own stock in the company you work for.

Society

Members of society may also exert pressure on the management of an organization to change. Individuals and groups have formed to pressure business for changes. People who live in the area of a business do not want it to pollute the air or water or otherwise abuse the natural resources. Societal pressures have brought about tougher pollution requirements. Tuna companies used to kill dolphins when catching tuna. However, due to societal pressure, many companies now put claims on tunafish cans stating that they are "dolphin safe." Society is pressuring business to be socially responsible and ethical. You will learn more about ethics and social responsibility later in this chapter.

Technology

The rate of technological change will continue to increase. Few organizations operate today as they did even a decade ago. Products not envisioned a few years ago are now being mass-produced. The computer has changed the way organizations conduct and transact business. Computers are often a major part of a firm's systems process. Telecommunications has been growing for a century and may be poised to explode into a wave of new products.[12]

New technologies often change product use. Atari was the first company to successfully offer home video games. However, Nintendo, with its superior technology, took over the market. In 1995, it was estimated that Sega would outsell Nintendo in U.S. retail sales of video games (including hardware and software sales) based on introducing its new generation, called Saturn, before Nintendo (time-based competition).[13] Sony set an unexpectedly low price for its new PlayStation video-game player, using compact disk technology, increasing pressure on industry rivals.[14] Microsoft announced technology to give its next operating system a performance boost for playing fast-moving computer games. The PC industry hopes to overtake sales of Sega, Nintendo, Sony, and other game-only machines.[15]

New technology creates opportunities for some companies and a threat to others. FedEx prides itself in using technology. FedEx was the first to develop the hub system that enabled overnight delivery and its real-time tracking system for all packages using COSMOS. On the other hand, the fax machine created a threat to FedEx, offering instant delivery. Fortunately, the bulk of FedEx revenues comes from packages. Many years ago thousands of baby diaper services existed; but due to the technological advance of the disposable diaper (which later created an environmental problem), most went out of business. If you want your management career to continue, you must keep up with the latest technology in your field. Be the first to volunteer to learn new things.

Work Application

5. Give an example of how technology has affected one or more organizations, preferably one you work or have worked for.

Governments

Foreign, federal, state, and local governments all set laws and regulations that businesses must obey. These laws remain pretty much intact through generations of political turnover, even though their interpretations, guidelines, and enforcement do depend heavily on the government officials of the time. The government environment is sometimes referred to as the political and legal environment.

The auto industry has been required to decrease the amount of pollution its cars emit into the air. Airlines have been told to decrease the noise level of their planes. Businesses can no longer dump their waste in our waterways. The Occupational Safety and Health Administration (OSHA) sets safety standards that must be met. Organizations cannot sell drugs without FDA approval. The Americans with Disabilities Act (ADA) compelled businesses to change many employment practices.[16] In other words, to a large extent, business may not do whatever it wants to do; the government tells business what it can and cannot do. Sears-owned Allstate Insurance left the state of Massachusetts due to the unfavorable government environment.

Governments create both opportunities and threats for businesses. A number of years ago, the state of Maine changed the legal drinking age from 21 to 18. Dick Peltier opened a bar targeted for the 18- to 20-year-old group which became very successful. However, a few years later, the state increased the legal drinking age. Dick virtually lost his business overnight.

Organizations and governments are working together to develop free trade between countries. The General Agreement on Tariffs and Trade (GATT) is an international organization to which over 100 countries belong. GATT works to develop general agreements between all members and it acts as a mediator between member countries who cannot resolve differences or when one country feels another is using unfair practices. A GATT panel can order unfair practices stopped or allow the country claiming unfair practices to retaliate. There are European trade alliances, the largest being the European Union (EU), formerly called the European Community, which consists of 12 full-member countries: Belgium, Denmark, France, Greece, Ireland, Italy, Luxembourg, The Netherlands, Portugal, Spain, the United Kingdom, and Germany. Since late 1992, the EU is a single market without national barriers to travel, employment, investment, and trade. The European Free Trade Association (EFTA) includes Austria, Finland, Iceland, Norway, Sweden, and Switzerland in one market. But these countries plan to join the EU, and Czechoslovakia, Hungary, and Poland have agreed to open their markets to EU products by the end of the decade.

The U.S.–Canada agreement was expanded to include Mexico in the North American Free Trade Agreement (NAFTA), which was created in 1993 and implemented in 1994. In the next 10 to 15 years, as many as 20,000 separate tariffs are expected to be eliminated to allow free trade among member countries. There is talk of expanding NAFTA to include alliances with Central and South America. The Pacific Rim countries—Japan, China, Korea, Taiwan, Indonesia, Malaysia, the Philippines, Thailand, Hong Kong, and Singapore—have formed a trading block called Pacific Asia. For an illustration of these trading blocs see Figure 2–5. These agreements between governments also affect the way firms conduct business in a global environment. Global business will be presented later in this chapter.

Economy

The organization has no control over economic growth, inflation, interest rates, foreign exchange rates, and so on, yet these things have a direct impact on its performance. In general, as measured by gross national product (GNP) and gross domestic product (GDP), businesses do better when the economy is growing than during times of decreased GNP/GDP, or recession. The last U.S. recession occurred during the last quarter of 1990 and the first two quarters of 1991. Since then the economy has been growing at an unsteady rate. If business activity is slow, there are less packages to ship, so FedEx is affected as well.

During periods of inflation, businesses experience increased costs, which cannot always be passed along to consumers. This results in decreased profits. When interest rates are high, it costs more to borrow money, which may affect

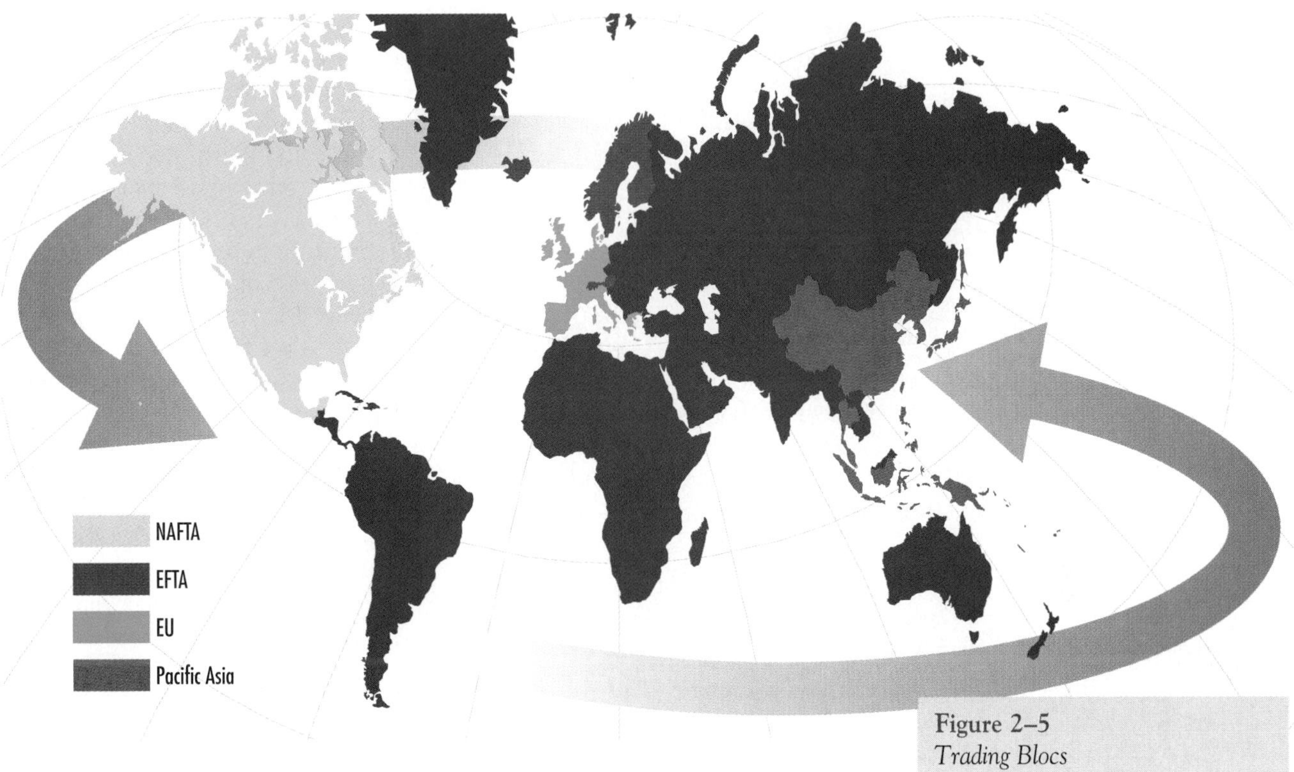

Figure 2–5
Trading Blocs

profits. Foreign exchange rates affect businesses both at home and abroad. When the dollar is weak, foreign goods are more expensive in the United States, and vice versa. A weak dollar helps to create opportunities for the United States. When the dollar is weak against the yen, Japanese auto makers have to increase prices or reduce profits. As Japanese auto prices increase, Americans tend to buy more U.S. cars, and other products as well. With the depressed dollar, U.S. businesses do well in Europe too.[17] An understanding of economics, and more importantly global economics, can help you to advance to top-level management.

Interactive Management

According to Russell Ackoff, unlike reactive managers (who make changes only when forced to by external factors) and responsive managers (who try to adapt to the environment by predicting and preparing for change before they are required to do so), interactive managers design a desirable future and invent ways of bringing it about. They believe we are capable of creating a significant part of the future and controlling its effects on us. They try to prevent, not merely prepare for, threats and to create, not merely exploit, opportunities. Rather than react or respond, interactive managers make things happen for their benefit and for that of their stakeholders. They plan to do better in the future than presently deemed possible. Interactive managers pursue ideals that they know can never be attained but that can be continuously approached. With the accelerating rates of change, interactive managers try to design the systems they control in order to increase their ability to actively learn and adapt. Experience is no longer the best teacher; it is too slow, ambiguous, and imprecise. Experimentation replaces experience. Interactive managers are willing to make any change necessary to bring the organization closer to its ideal design.[18] In the early 1970s, people believed that overnight delivery was not possible, but this did not stop Smith from making overnight delivery become a reality through Federal Express. Do you have any great ideas for a new business or a way to help an existing business create customer value?

As a business grows, the complexity of its internal and external environments increases. The major factor increasing the complexity of the environment is the globalization of markets; managers believe it will have the greatest effect on their businesses.[19] For a review of the organizational environment, see Figure 2–6. Think about the complexity of FedEx's environment. FedEx does business in 186 countries. Therefore, it has to follow the rules and regulations of 186 different governments in countries with different economies, labor forces, societies, and so on. In the next two sections you will learn about conducting business in a global environment.

APPLYING THE CONCEPT

AC 2–2 The External Environment

Identify each statement by its external environmental factor.

a. customers	d. labor force	g. technology
b. competition	e. stockholders	h. governments
c. suppliers	f. society	i. economy

____ **6.** "Procter & Gamble has developed a new biodegradable material to replace the plastic liner on its diapers so that they don't take up landfill space for so long."

____ **7.** "At one time, AT&T was the only long-distance company, but then MCI, Sprint, and others came along and have taken away some of its customers."

____ **8.** "I applied for a loan to start my own business, but I might not get it because money is tight these days, even though interest rates are high."

____ **9.** "The owners of the company have threatened the CEO. They say they will fire the CEO if the business does not improve this year."

____ **10.** "Management was going to sell our company to PepsiCo, but the government said we would be in violation of Antitrust laws. What will happen to our company now?"

4. State the difference among a domestic, international, and multinational business.

CONDUCTING BUSINESS IN A GLOBAL ENVIRONMENT

In this section you will learn about global business, how to take a business global, and practices of large global companies and small international businesses.

Competing in the global environment is necessary to any company's survival.[20] Even most small local businesses do, or will, compete with global companies at home. Managers, particularly in large companies, are embracing global management systems.[21] Of the largest 500 global companies, grouped according to country, the United States has more than any other country.[22] The global environment is characterized by rapidly transforming economies, instant communication, interconnected business alliances, closed relationships with suppliers, and rapidly changing technology.[23] The question is no longer, "Should the business go global?" It's "How do we go global and how fast?"[24]

The primary reason for conducting business globally is to increase sales and profits. If you start a *domestic business* (business conducted in only one country) in the United States, you have around 250 million people as potential customers. If you expand to transact business (buy and sell some inputs and out-

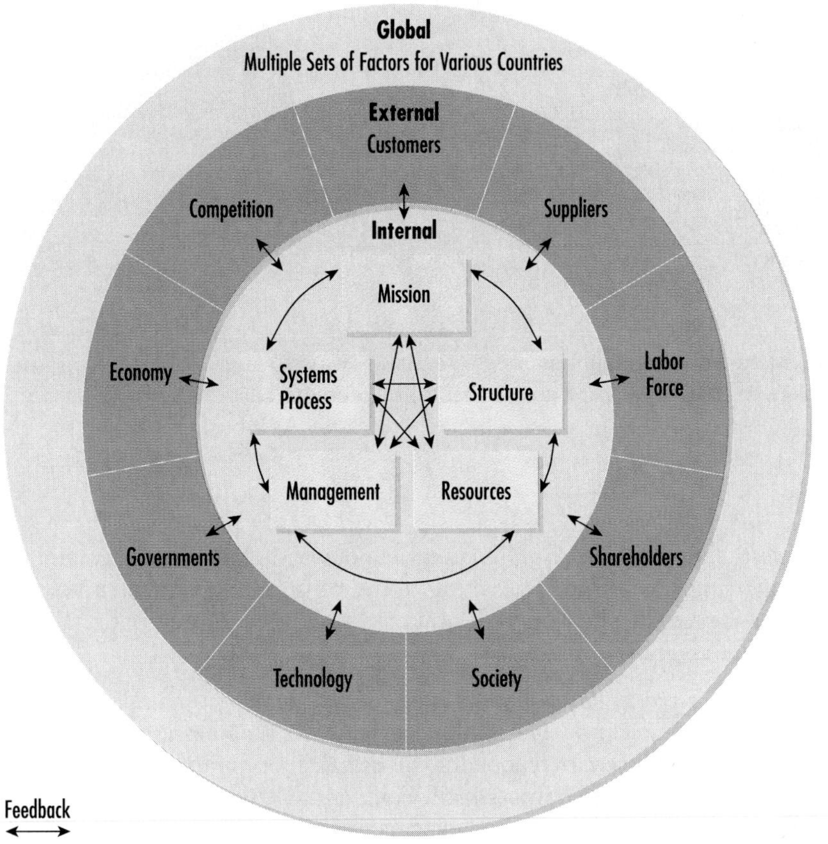

Figure 2–6
The Organizational Environment

puts) in Canada and Mexico (NAFTA countries), you increase your population market to around 360 million. At this point, you would have an international business. An **international business** *is primarily based in one country but transacts business in other countries*. If you expand to the EU by setting up business operations in one of the 12 countries and transact business throughout the EU, you have 330 million more potential customers, for a total of around 700 million. At the point when you have significant operations (an established place of conducting business at home and in a least one other country and have sales outside your home country of 25 percent or more), you would have a multinational or global business. A **multinational corporation (MNC)** *has significant operations in more than one country*. Larger MNCs with established places of conducting business in many countries and with sales outside the home country exceeding 50 percent include: Gillette, Colgate, Coca-Cola, IBM, Digital Equipment, NCR, Dow Chemical, Xerox, Alfac, Rhône-Poulene Rorer, Exxon, Mobil, Texaco, Motorola, Citicorp, Bank of Boston, Avon, and Hewlett-Packard. Nestlé is based in Vevy, Switzerland, and gets over 98 percent of its revenues and has over 95 percent of its assets outside of Switzerland. McDonald's has over 14,250 restaurants in 73 countries with around 5,000 of them outside the United States.[25] You may never start your own global business, but you may become an international manager. An *international manager* manages across a number of countries and cultures simultaneously.[26]

international business
A business primarily based in one country that transacts business in other countries.

multinational corporation (MNC)
A business with significant operations in more than one country.

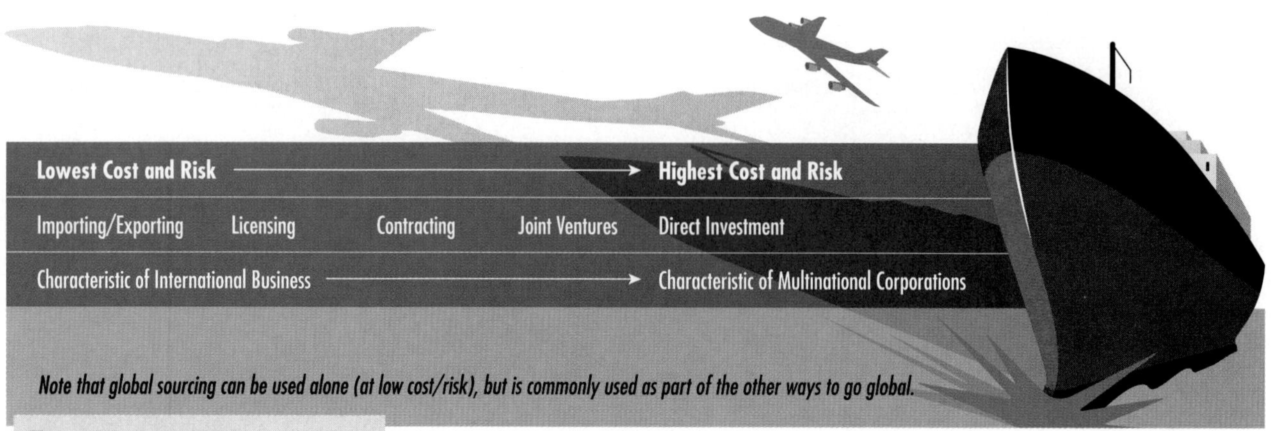

Figure 2–7
Taking a Business Global

Taking a Business Global

5. Of the six ways to take a business global, list the lowest and the highest cost and risk.

A domestic business can go global in six major ways: global sourcing, importing and exporting, licensing, contracting, joint ventures, and direct investment. Figure 2–7 presents them in order by cost and risk and international versus MNC use.

global sourcing
The utilization of worldwide resources.

Global Sourcing. **Global sourcing** *is the utilization of worldwide resources*. It is also called *outsourcing*. The difference between a domestic manager and a global manager is where they look for the best deal on inputs and a location for transforming inputs into outputs. GM, Ford, and Chrysler use foreign material, supplies, and parts in their U.S.-made cars. For several years now, Chrysler has been making cars in Canada that are sold in the United States. MNCs cannot help but chase the lowest-cost workers around the globe.[27] One of the major barriers to passing NAFTA was the threat of losing jobs to Mexico through maquiladoras. *Maquiladoras* are light-assembly plants built in Mexico, near the U.S. border, to take advantage of the low-cost labor. Both international corporations and MNCs use global sourcing. As an international manager you will need to scan the globe, not just the United States, for the best deals.

Importing and Exporting. With *importing*, the domestic firm buys the products from the foreign firms and sells them at home. Pier 1 Imports and U.S. auto dealerships selling Japanese and German cars are examples. With *exporting*, the domestic firm sells its products to a foreign buyer. Ford exports cars to Japanese dealerships.

Licensing. Under a *licensing* agreement, one company allows another to use its assets, such as brand name, trademark, technology, patent, and copyright. For a fee, Walt Disney allows companies around the world to make all kinds of products using Mickey Mouse and the Lion King. A common form of licensing is the *franchise* in which the franchiser provides a combination of trademark, equipment, materials, training, managerial guidelines, consulting advice, and cooperative advertising to the franchisee for a fee and a percentage of the revenues. McDonald's, Pizza Hut, Subway, and Holiday Inn, for example, have franchise operations all over the world.

Contracting. With *contract manufacturing*, you have a foreign firm manufacture the goods while retaining the marketing process. Sears uses this approach in Latin America and Spain. Contract manufacturers make products with Sears' name on them, and Sears sells them in its stores. With *management contracting*, the seller provides management services for the foreign firm. Hilton operates hotels all over the world for local owners. All kinds of contract services can be provided.

Joint Venture. A **joint venture** *is created when firms share ownership (partnership) of a new enterprise.* Chrysler and Austrian Motors established a joint venture called Eurostar to manufacture and sell minivans in Europe. Toyota and GM have a joint venture in California. The two firms share the costs and risk, but both lose some control over how business is conducted and they must share the rewards. A *strategic alliance* is an agreement but does not necessarily involve shared ownership. Kodak, Fuji, Canon, and Minolta have agreed to work together to develop new types of film. Kodak and Fuji will manufacture the film and Canon and Minolta will produce cameras to use it. However, about half of all strategic alliances fail.[28]

joint venture
Created when firms share ownership (partnership) of a new enterprise.

Direct Investment. **Direct investment** *occurs when a company builds or purchases operating facilities (subsidiaries) in a foreign country.* Ford, Chrysler, and GM have production facilities in Europe. Becoming an MNC takes at least a joint venture, but the auto industry uses a combination of joint ventures and direct investments. The auto company trend is to make the cars closer to where they are sold.[29] The three U.S. automakers are all MNCs with direct investments, but they also use the lowest levels of global expansion, importing, and exporting, as well.

direct investment
Occurs when a company builds or purchases operating facilities (subsidiaries) in a foreign country.

In its pursuit of global expansion to 186 countries, FedEx made direct investments by purchasing 20 different companies. A few include Gelco Express (a worldwide courier servicing 84 countries, 1984), Lex Wilkinson and Lex Systemline (United Kingdom, 1986), Cansica (Canada, 1987), Island Couriers (Latin America, 1987), Daisei Companies (Japan, 1988), Flying Tigers (worldwide, 1989), and Aeroenvios S.A. de C.V. (Mexico, 1990). Clearly, FedEx is an MNC.

Practices of Large Global Companies

MNCs have a global management team, strategy, operations and products, technology and R & D, financing, and marketing.[30]

Global Management Team. Leading global companies have top-level managers who are foreign nationals and subsidiaries managed by foreign nationals. Cross-culturally trained managers frequently travel to understand the cultures in which they do business. The fast management track now leads overseas; global companies want top managers who have been around the world.[31] In Chapter 3 you will learn about diversity in global cultures.

The sales force at Nestlé was created to build a relationship with Thailand's rapidly developing supermarket industry.

Global Strategy. The entire global company has one strategy and structure, not one per subsidiary. Global dimensions are balanced for worldwide coordination to attain economies of scale and the local dimension that enables the country manager to respond to local consumer needs and counter local competition. There is no home-country preference. All subsidiaries are involved in global sourcing. Global strategy utilizes direct investment, joint ventures, and strategic alliances.

Global Operations and Products. Global companies have standardized operations worldwide to attain economies of scale, and they make products to be sold worldwide, not just in local markets. In the mid-1990s Ford sold different cars in Europe and the United States with different operating equipment. However, Ford's stated goal is to have the same type of facilities producing the same cars that will be sold in NAFTA, EU, and other countries by the year 2000.[32] Unit headquarters are placed in the country with the best resources to do the job, rather than in the home country. AT&T's corded telephone operation is headquartered in France, Du Pont's electronics in Japan, and IBM's networking systems in the United Kingdom.[33]

Global Technology and R&D. Technology and research and development (R&D) are centralized in one country, rather than duplicated at each subsidiary, to develop world products. Global sourcing of technology and R&D is used. For example, Ford had Mazda develop its Probe, which Ford produces.

Global Financing. MNCs search world markets to get the best rates and terms when borrowing money for the long term; short-term financing is largely in individual countries using local financial institutions. Product prices are quoted in foreign currencies, rather than the home currency. MNCs sell stock in their subsidiary to the people in that country. They manage currency exchange—as well as global purchasing, currency hedging, currency risk exposure, and other important corporate functions—on an international basis.

Global Marketing. Global products and marketing are adapted for local markets. When McDonald's went to India, it had a problem. Can you guess what it was? If you said the cow is sacred in India and most people there will not eat an all-beef patty, you are correct. So McDonald's sells its Big Mac in India, but it's not beef. Advertisements are often developed by local agencies. Products used to be developed in the home market and then brought to other countries later, but the trend is toward global introduction of products (time-based competition). Gillette introduced its Sensor razor in the United States (during the 1990 Super Bowl) and 19 other countries at virtually the same time with the same advertisement. What do you think is the best single frozen global food? If you said pizza, you are correct. "It lasts well in the freezer and everybody loves it."[34]

FedEx follows these practices with strong emphasis on global delivery of packages using standardized operations. For a review of the list of practices of large global companies see Figure 2–8.

Figure 2–8
Practices of Large Global Companies

Practices of Small International Companies

You do not have to be a big fish to swim in international waters.[35] Peter Drucker said that CEOs, even of small companies, need to think globally or they will be unemployed. It is actually easier for small companies to operate without much regard for national boundaries, and they can usually make changes much faster than large MNCs. The most successful global companies are small specialized niche players with one product or product line.[36] However, large MNCs have more resources than small businesses. Therefore, small firms tend to be international businesses rather than global companies, and they cannot follow all six practices of leading MNCs.[37] Let's examine the differences between large MNCs and small international businesses using the six practices.

Global Management Team. Small business owners often do not have, and cannot afford to hire, foreign managers. However, consultants and agents can be hired to do the job.

Global Strategy. While MNCs can afford to use direct investment and joint ventures as their strategy for going global, most small business don't have the money. They tend to use importing and exporting and global sourcing strategies to go global.

Global Operations and Products. While MNCs can afford to have their own operating facilities in many countries, most small businesses cannot. Therefore, they tend to provide fewer operating facilities, use contracting, or they export to others who have the operating facilities. Small businesses can make standard products that can be sold globally.

Global Technology and R&D. Other than high-tech companies, most small businesses have a small or no budget for technology and R&D. However, many scan the globe and copy the latest developments quickly rather than developing them.

Global Financing. Generally, unlike MNCs, small businesses cannot borrow money from one country and invest it in another. To go global, many small business owners turn to the Export-Import Bank. Eximbank is a government agency responsible for aiding the export of U.S. goods and services through a variety of loan guarantees and insurance programs. Besides Eximbank, a small business may be able to get a loan in the country in which it plans to do business. This should be a consideration when selecting a country in which to do business.

Work Application

6. Select a business and identify its level of globalization and as many of its global practices as you can.

Global Marketing. Small businesses can use export management companies, agents, and distributor services to conduct their marketing. In addition, small business managers can attend trade shows, network through trade centers, and advertise in industry publications.

BUSINESS ETHICS

Business graduates have been called ethically naïve.[38] In recent years there has been an increased emphasis on business ethics.[39,40] You cannot go too many days without hearing or reading, in the mass media, some scandal related to unethical and/or unlawful behavior.[41] **Ethics** *are the standards of right and wrong that influence behavior*. Right behavior is considered ethical and wrong behavior is considered unethical. Government laws and regulations are designed to govern business behavior. However, ethics goes beyond legal requirements. The differ-

ethics
Standards of right and wrong that influence behavior.

ence between ethical and unethical behavior is not always clear. What some countries consider unethical, other countries consider ethical. For example, in the United States it is ethical to give a gift but unethical to give a bribe (a gift as a condition of attaining business). However, the difference between a gift and a bribe is not always clearcut. In some countries giving bribes is the standard business practice. In this section you will learn that ethical behavior does pay, some simple guides to ethical behavior, and about managing ethics.

Does Ethical Behavior Pay?

Generally, the answer is yes. Recall from Chapter 1 that one of the qualities necessary to being a successful manager is integrity. Using ethical behavior is part of integrity. Using good human relations skills is also exercising good ethics.[42] At first, you may be richly rewarded for acting unethically, but retaliation follows, trust is lost, and productivity declines.[43] If you get caught in a lie, people will not trust you and it becomes difficult to get ahead in the organization. Organizations are interviewing job applicants carefully in order to avoid hiring unethical employees.[44] Good business and good ethics are synonymous. Ethics is at the heart and center of business, and profits and ethics are intrinsically related.[45]

Simple Guides to Ethical Behavior

Every day in your personal and professional life, you face decisions in which you can make ethical or unethical choices. You make your choices based on your past learning from parents, teachers, friends, managers, coworkers, and so forth. Your combined past makes up what many refer to as your conscience, which helps you to choose right from wrong in a given situation. Following are some guides that can help you make the right decisions.

Golden Rule. Following the Golden Rule will help you to use ethical behavior. The golden rule is:

"Do unto others as you want them to do unto you."

or

"Don't do anything to anyone that you would not want them to do to you."

Four-Way Test. Rotary International developed the four-way test of the things we think and do to guide business transactions. The four questions are: (1) Is it the truth? (2) Is it fair to all concerned? (3) Will it build goodwill and better friendship? (4) Will it be beneficial to all concerned? When making your decision, if you can answer yes to these four questions it is probably ethical.

6. Explain the stakeholders' approach to ethics.

stakeholders' approach to ethics
Creating a win-win situation for all stakeholders so that everyone benefits from the decision.

Stakeholders' Approach to Ethics. *Under the* **stakeholders' approach to ethics,** *when making decisions, you try to create a win-win situation for all relevant stakeholders so that everyone benefits from the decision.* The higher up in management you go, the more stakeholders you have to deal with. You can ask yourself one simple question to help you to determine if your decision is ethical from a stakeholders' approach:

"Am I proud to tell relevant stakeholders my decision?"

If you are proud to tell relevant stakeholders your decision, it is probably ethical. If you are not proud to tell others your decision, or you keep rationalizing it, the decision may not be ethical. If you are not sure if a decision is ethical, talk to your boss, higher-level managers, ethics committee members, and other people with high ethical standards. If you are reluctant to ask others for advice on an ethical decision because you may not like their answers, the decision may not be ethical.

In 1982, Johnson & Johnson's Tylenol was poisoned by someone not working for the company, which resulted in the death of eight people. Chairman James Burke made the decision to protect the public and at great cost recalled all Tylenol capsules and halted production. From the stakeholders' perspective, everyone benefited. Customers benefited because any poisoned capsules were destroyed. J&J lost money in the short run but benefited in the long run because people had confidence in the company and continued to buy the product. If J&J focused on not losing money in the short run, it would have lost customers forever, and not only of its Tylenol product. Employees also benefited because they did not lose jobs, which most likely would have happened if J&J had kept the capsules on the shelf and denied any fault.

Unfortunately, there are times when decisions must be made that do not benefit all stakeholders. For example, if business is slow, a layoff may be necessary. Usually, the employees who get laid off do not benefit from the decision. Many large companies that permanently lay off employees offer severance pay and outplacement services to help them get jobs with other organizations.

Managing Ethics

An organization's ethics are based on the collective behavior of its employees. If each individual is ethical, the organization will be ethical too. The starting place for ethics is you.[46] Are you an ethical person? Exercise 2–1 at the end of this chapter will help you to answer this question. From the management perspective, managers should set guidelines for ethical behavior, set a good example, and enforce ethical behavior.

Codes of Ethics. Codes of ethics, also called codes of conduct, state the importance of conducting business in an ethical manner and provide guidelines for ethical behavior. Most large businesses have written codes of ethics. See Figure 2–9 for the code of ethics at Exxon Company, U.S.A.

Top Management Support. It is the responsibility of management from the top down to develop codes of ethics, to ensure that employees are trained and instructed on what is and what is not considered ethical behavior, and to enforce ethical behavior. However, the primary responsibility is to lead by example. Employees tend to look to managers, especially top managers, for examples of behavior. If managers are not ethical, employees will not be ethical. Jack S. Llewellyn, President and CEO of Ocean Spray, believes that the CEO has to be the model for ethical standards, that written policy statements are not worth anything, and that managers will treat customers and workers fairly if the CEO does.

Enforcing Ethical Behavior. If employees are rewarded rather than punished for their unethical behavior, they will conduct unethical business practices. Many organizations have developed ethics committees that act as judge

Figure 2–9
Summary Code of Ethics of Exxon Company, U.S.A.

Business Ethics

- Our Company policy is one of strict observance of all laws applicable to its business.
- A reputation for scrupulous dealing is itself a priceless Company asset.
- We do care how we get results.
- We expect candor at all levels and compliance with accounting rules and controls.

Conflict of Interest

- Competing or conducting business with the Company is not permitted, except with the knowledge and consent of management.
- Accepting and providing gifts, entertainment, and services must comply with specific requirements.
- An employee may not use Company personnel, information, or other assets for personal benefit.
- Participating in certain outside activities requires the prior approval of management.

Work Application

7. Select a business and identify how it manages ethics.

and jury to determine if unethical behavior has been conducted and what the punishment should be for violating company policy. More companies are establishing ethics offices, with a director or vice president who reports directly to the CEO, to establish ethics policies, listen to employees' complaints, conduct training, and investigate abuses such as sexual harassment.[47]

As a means of enforcing ethical behavior, employees should be encouraged to engage in internal whistle-blowing. *Whistle-blowing* occurs when employees expose what they believe to be unethical behavior by their fellow employees. Whistle-blowers can go internally to management and report unethical behavior or they can go to external sources like the government or newspapers. According to the law and ethics, whistle-blowers should not suffer any negative consequences. Would you report unethical behavior by fellow employees to your boss or upper-level managers? If upper-level managers engage in, or support, unethical behavior, would you go outside the organization to report it? It is not easy to say whether or not you would be a whistle-blower without being in a specific situation, but some day you may be faced with that decision.

By living its People–Service–Profits philosophy, FedEx is considered to be an ethical company. FedEx has a code of ethics that stresses the achievement of the highest possible standards of business and personal ethics.

SOCIAL RESPONSIBILITY

social responsibility
The conscious effort to operate in a manner that creates a win-win situation for all stakeholders.

Ethics and social responsibility are closely related. **Social responsibility** *is the conscious effort to operate in a manner that creates a win-win situation for all stakeholders*. Ethical behavior is often socially responsible and vice versa. In this section you will learn about social responsibility to stakeholders, that it pays to be socially responsible, and the four levels of social responsibility.

Social Responsibility to Stakeholders

Companies have a social responsibility to try to create a win-win situation with all nine external categories of stakeholders, as well as the internal stakeholders—the employees you learned about earlier in this chapter. For *customers*, the company must provide safe products and services with customer value. For *society*, the company should improve the quality of life, or at least not destroy the environment. The company must compete fairly with *competitors*. Through *technology*, the company should develop new ways of increasing customer value and the quality of life. The company must work with *suppliers* in a cooperative manner. It must abide by the laws and regulations of *government*. The company must strive to provide equal-employment opportunities for the *labor force*. It must act financially responsible in relation to the *economy*. The company must provide *shareholders* with a reasonable profit. It must provide *employees* with safe working conditions with adequate pay and benefits.

APPLYING THE CONCEPT

AC 2–3 Stakeholders

Identify each statement by its stakeholder:

a. employees c. society e. suppliers
b. customers d. competitors f. government

____ **11.** "We are going to fight that utility company to stop it from putting a nuclear power plant in our town."

____ **12.** "I bought this cigarette. It exploded in my face when I lit it, causing me an injury."

____ **13.** "The town board is very political, so you have to play games if you want to get a liquor license."

____ **14.** "I'm sorry to hear your retail sales are down; we will have to cut back our production."

____ **15.** "I bid on the job, but PIP's got the contract to print the material."

Does It Pay to Be Socially Responsible?

Various researchers have tried to determine the relationship between social responsibility and financial performance. However, results based on financial performance alone have been inconsistent. An alternative performance measure based on stakeholders' response was tested and a relationship was established between social responsibility and performance.[48] Overall stock prices do not fall based on the announcement of some corporate illegalities, but they do fall when bribery, tax evasion, or violations of government contracts are announced.[49] In a survey, 88 percent of respondents stated that they were more inclined to buy from companies that are socially responsible than from companies that are not.[50] Although there is no clear link between social responsibility and bottom-line profits, we can at least say that it does not hurt performance. Therefore, social responsibility does pay because company stakeholders benefit.

Levels of Social Responsibility

7. Discuss the differences in the four levels of social responsibility: obstruction, obligation, reaction, and involvement.

Historically, capitalism was based on Adam Smith's ideas and practices. Smith stated that in the long run, public interests are served by individuals and businesses pursuing their own self-interest, and that government should play a limited role. Milton Friedman, economist and Nobel laureate, agrees with Smith; when a business makes a profit it is being socially responsible. A corporation has

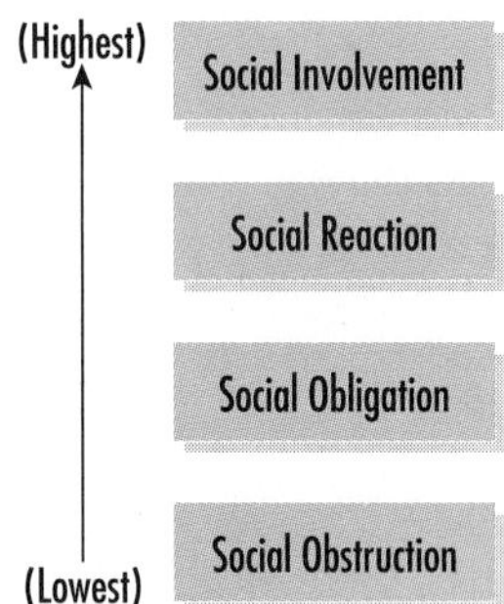

Figure 2–10
Levels of Social Responsibility

no responsibility to society beyond that of obeying the law and maximizing profits for shareholders.[51] On the other extreme, Sethi stated that CEOs have been accused of not placing a high value on social responsibility and has suggested that socially responsible policies be a part of company mission statements.[52] Most managers' and employees' views fall between these two extremes. Sethi identified four levels of social responsibility: social obstruction, social obligation, social reaction, and social involvement. For an illustration of the four levels of social responsibility, see Figure 2–10.

Social Obstruction. Under *social obstruction,* managers deliberately perform, or request employees to perform, unethical or illegal business practices. For example, Ashland Oil was found guilty of setting prices with other contractors in order to charge higher prices for highway work in Tennessee and North Carolina. Ashland managers also wrongfully fired two employees because they refused to cover up illegal company payments. In such cases, whistle-blowing and strong government penalties can help to prevent social obstruction.

Work Application

8. Select a business and identify its level of social responsibility for a specific issue.

Social Obligation. Under *social obligation,* managers meet only the minimum legal requirements. For example, Philip Morris was pressured by social groups to stop using its cartoon character Joe Camel to advertise cigarettes because he appeals to young people. Legally, Philip Morris can use Joe Camel and decided to ignore the request and continue to use him.

Social Reaction. Under *social reaction,* managers respond to appropriate societal requests. If Philip Morris elects to drop the use of Joe Camel, due to continued social pressure, this will be social reaction. Some tuna companies stopped killing dolphins due to societal pressure. They now place "dolphin safe" on their labels as a sign of social responsibility. However, the most common type of social reaction takes place when civic groups go to a company and ask for donations for the arts, college scholarships, antidrug programs, and so on; sponsorship of sports teams; or the use of company facilities for meetings or sports team use. Companies, including IBM and Exxon, also match employee contributions to worthwhile charitable causes.

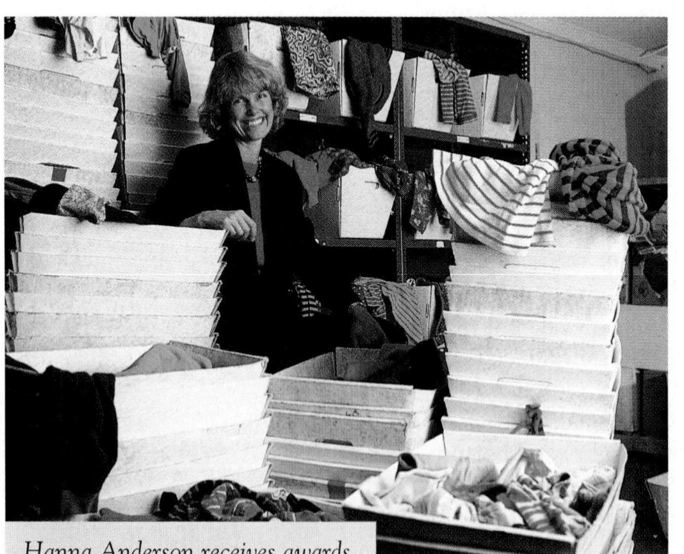

Hanna Anderson receives awards for community involvement, which includes a program called Hannadowns that donates clothing to local charities and disaster relief.

Social Involvement. Under *social involvement,* managers voluntarily initiate socially responsible acts. McDonald's was socially involved when it established Ronald McDonald houses to help the families of sick children. FedEx is at the social involvement level of social responsibility. FedEx was the first to invest in a noise-reduction program to enable 727-100 aircraft to fly at Stage 3 noise levels (the quietest noise levels certified by the FAA). FedEx worked with Pratt & Whitney to develop noise reduction kits for its 727-series aircraft. New aircraft purchases will meet Stage 3 noise levels. FedEx has actively worked with Congress to create a clean fuel fleet program for vehicles. It currently uses some alternate-fuel vehicles. FedEx collects used motor oil and contracts with outside firms to collect and recycle the oil. FedEx uses recycled paper when possible, and all paks, tubes, and boxes are 100 percent recyclable. FedEx encourages employees to devote personal time to community service.

Overall, many organizations can be classified as being at one of the four levels of social responsibility. However, an organization can be on different levels for different issues. For example, Philip Morris is on the social obligation level when it comes to Joe Camel, but it does give generously to social requests and it has initiated social involvement programs.

APPLYING THE CONCEPT

AC 2–4 Levels of Social Responsibility

Identify each statement by its level of social responsibility.

a. social obstruction c. social reaction
b. social obligation d. social involvement

____ **16.** "I agree that a Boys and Girls Club downtown would be beneficial to our city. We will give you $1,000 for the project."

____ **17.** "I'm disappointed with the reading levels of employees coming from our local high school. Betty, I want you to contact the principal and see if you can work together to develop a program to improve reading skills."

____ **18.** "Bill, the auditor will be here next week, so we'd better make sure that the missing inventory we took does not show up as missing."

____ **19.** "We stopped killing seals with clubs because of the bad press we were receiving. Now we use guns, which is more expensive."

____ **20.** "As of June 1 the new regulations go into effect. We will have to cut the amount of waste we dump into the river by half. Get the lowest bidder to pick up the other half and dispose of it.

Social Audit. A *social audit* is a measure of a firm's social behavior. Many large businesses set social objectives and thus try to measure if they have met the objectives.[53] Many large corporations include a social audit in their annual report.

CURRENT MANAGEMENT ISSUES

8. Explain the difference between downsizing and re-engineering.

The focus of this chapter was on many of the current management issues (globalization, ethics, quality, teams, and a comparison of small versus large businesses). In the next chapter we look at diversity and some of the other issues differently. Under the issue of *diversity*, it should be clear to you that as the globalization of business continues, the work force becomes more diversified, and the issues become more important.

downsizing
The process of cutting organizational resources to get more done with less as a means of increasing productivity.

To increase *productivity* many firms are downsizing. **Downsizing** *is the process of cutting organizational resources to get more done with less as a means of increasing productivity*. The primary area of cutting is human resources. Many large organizations have reported plans to cut jobs by the thousands as part of cost-cutting programs. In the short run, executives have reported productivity gains due to work-force reductions, contracting out for goods and services, and shedding some units.[54] Current research on performance of companies that have downsized indicates that past cuts are hurting current and future profits, especially in firms that have cut research and marketing.[55] Researchers indicate that nearly half of the 1971–1982 mergers failed, resulting in subsequent divestment. The price was paid by U.S. workers, who were needlessly laid off in record numbers through downsizing, for the sake of higher stock values.[56] Yes, to be competitive in a global market, companies must do more with less, but simply cutting jobs and requiring the remaining employees to do the same jobs of two or three people does not work in the long run. An alternative to downsizing is re-engineering, which does involve downsizing in a systematic manner.

re-engineering
The radical redesign of work to combine fragmented tasks into streamlined processes that save time and money.

Re-engineering *involves the radical redesign of work to combine fragmented tasks into streamlined processes that save time and money* (time-based competition). With re-engineering you start with a fresh approach which assumes there are no current jobs. You design the process so that *teams* are involved in *participative management* responsibility for acquiring inputs all the way through to transforming them into outputs. Re-engineered work usually requires fewer workers and far fewer managers. In the aftermath of re-engineering, employees are no longer cogs in the wheel; they are the wheel.[57] With traditional operations (and simple downsizing), everyone does a little thing, so it's hard to get much satisfaction out of piecemeal work. However, with re-engineering, teams work on a whole process and have a real sense of closure because they have the power to make decisions and can point to an outcome and say, "I made that happen." In addition, re-engineering squeezes out nonvalue-added work, so there is a lot more money to go around.[58] Re-engineered jobs tend to be much more rewarding than traditional jobs.[59] The details of how to implement re-engineering are beyond the scope of this text. Entire books have been written on the subject. For our purposes, you should have a basic understanding of what it is rather than how to do it.

CHAPTER SUMMARY AND GLOSSARY

The chapter summary is organized to answer the nine learning objectives for Chapter 2.

1. Explain the five internal environment factors: management, mission, resources, systems process, and structure.

Management refers to the people responsible for an organization's performance. Mission is the organization's purpose or reason for being. The organization has human, physical, financial, and informational resources to accomplish its mission. The systems process is the method of transforming inputs into outputs as the organization accomplishes its mission. Structure refers to the way in which the organization groups its resources to accomplish its mission.

2. List and explain the need for the two primary principles of total quality management (TQM).

The two primary principles of TQM are: (1) focus on delivering customer value and (2) continually improve the system and its processes. To be successful, businesses must continually offer value to attract and retain customers. Without customers you don't have a business.

3. Describe how the nine external environmental factors—customers, competitors, suppliers, labor force, shareholders, society, technology, governments, and economies—can affect the internal business environment.

Customers should decide what products the business offers, for without customer value there are no customers or business. *Competitors'* business practices, such as features and prices, often have to be duplicated in order to maintain customer value. Poor-quality inputs from *suppliers* result in poor-quality outputs without customer value. Without a qualified *labor force*/employees, products and services will have little or no customer value. *Shareholders*, through an elected board of directors, hire top managers and provide directives for the organization. *Society* pressures business to perform or not perform certain activities, such as pollution. The business must develop new *technologies*, or at least keep up with them, to provide customer value. *Governments* set the rules and regulations that business must adhere to. *Economic* activity affects the organization's ability to provide customer value. For example, inflated prices lead to lower customer value.

4. State the difference among a domestic, international, and multinational business.

A domestic firm does business in only one country. An international firm is primarily based in one country but transacts business with other countries. MNCs have significant operations in more than one country.

5. Of the six ways to take a business global, list the lowest and the highest in cost and risk.

Importing/exporting is the lowest and direct investment is the highest cost and risk; global sourcing can be part of either method.

6. Explain the stakeholders' approach to ethics.

Under the stakeholders' approach to ethics, you create a win-win situation for the relevant parties affected by the decision. If you are proud to tell relevant stakeholders about your decision, it is probably ethical. If you are not proud to tell stakeholders, or you keep rationalizing the decision, it may not be ethical.

7. Discuss the differences in the four levels of social responsibility: obstruction, obligation, reaction, and involvement.

Participation in social responsibility goes from a low to high level. Under social obstruction, managers conduct unethical, illegal behavior. Under social obligation, managers meet only the minimum legal requirements. Under social reaction, managers respond to societal requests. Under societal involvement, managers voluntarily initiate socially responsible acts.

8. Explain the difference between downsizing and re-engineering.

Downsizing is the process of cutting organizational resources to get more done with less as a means of increasing productivity. Re-engineering involves the radical redesigning of work to combine fragmented tasks into streamlined processes that save time and money. Downsizing simply focuses on cutting resources, whereas re-engineering focuses on developing new jobs.

9. Define the following key terms (in order of appearance in the chapter):

Select one or more methods: (1) fill in the missing key terms from memory, (2) match the key terms from the end of the review with their definitions below, or (3) copy the key terms in order from the list at the beginning of the chapter.

The organization's __________ includes the factors that affect the organization's performance from within its boundaries.

The organization's ______ is its purpose or reason for being.

______ are people whose interests are affected by organizational behavior.

The __________ is the method for transforming inputs into outputs.

Customers determine ______ by comparing actual use to requirements to determine value.

__________ is the purchasing benefits expected by customers to determine whether or not to buy a product.

______________ is a process that involves everyone in the organization focusing on the customer to continually improve product value.

The organization's __________ includes the factors that affect its performance from outside its boundaries.

An __________ is primarily based in one country but transacts business in other countries.

A ______________ has significant operations in more than one country.

__________ is the utilization of worldwide resources.

A __________ is created when firms share ownership (partnership) of a new enterprise.

__________ occurs when a company builds or purchases operating facilities (subsidiaries) in a foreign country.

______ are the standards of right and wrong that influence behavior.

Under the ______________, when making decisions you try to create a win-win situation for all relevant stakeholders so that everyone benefits from the decision.

__________ is the conscious effort to operate in a manner that creates a win-win situation for all stakeholders.

______ is the process of cutting organizational resources to get more done with less as a means of increasing productivity.

______ involves the radical redesign of work to combine fragmented tasks into streamlined processes that save time and money,

KEY TERMS

customer value
direct investment
downsizing
ethics
external environment
global sourcing
internal environment
international business
joint venture
mission
multinational corporation (MNC)
quality
re-engineering
social responsibility
stakeholders
stakeholders' approach to ethics
systems process
total quality management (TQM)

REVIEW AND DISCUSSION QUESTIONS

1. Do you believe that most organizations really focus on creating customer value? Explain.
2. Do you think that all organizations should use TQM? Explain your answer.
3. What is the relationship among management and mission, resources, the systems process, and structure? Which of these internal factors are ends and which are means?
4. What major technology change has had the greatest impact on the quality of your life?
5. Is NAFTA of more benefit or harm to the United States?
6. Should government regulation of business be increased, decreased, or remain the same as it is now?
7. Can you list any international and global companies in the area of your college?
8. For some of the companies you listed in question 7, can you identify their method(s) of going global?
9. Do you believe that if you use ethical behavior it will pay off in the long run?
10. Do you have your own guide to ethical behavior that you follow now? Will you use one of the guides from the text? If yes, which one and why?
11. Can ethics be taught and learned?
12. Do you believe that companies benefit from being socially responsible? If yes, how?
13. As a CEO, what level of social responsibility would you use?
14. With global sourcing, downsizing, and re-engineering, U.S. workers lose jobs. Are these practices ethical and socially responsible?

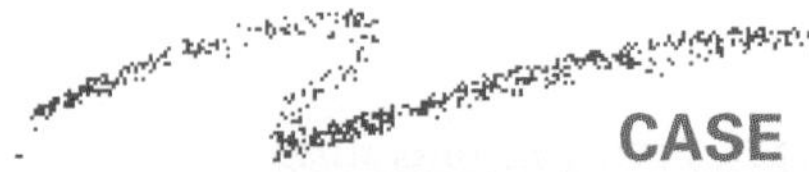

CASE

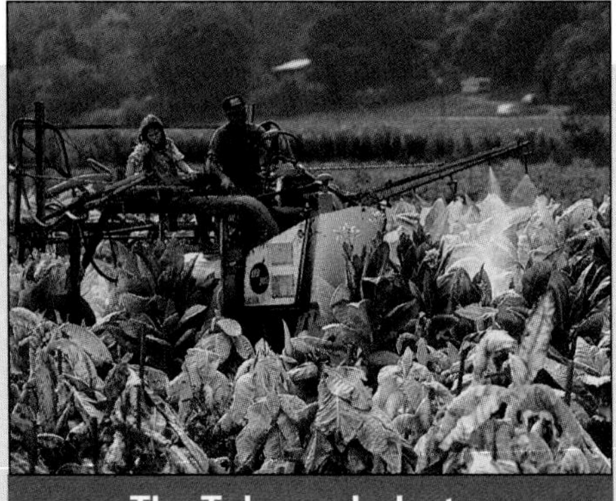

The Tobacco Industry

Over the years there has been pressure on the tobacco companies [major competitors include R. J. Reynolds (part of RJR Nabisco), Philip Morris, and Brown & Williamson] to limit or even stop the sale of tobacco products in the United States. With researchers reporting that cigarette smoking is hazardous to peoples' heath, the Surgeon General mandated that warning labels be placed on all packs of cigarettes. In government buildings and many private buildings, smoking is not allowed. In many other buildings smoking is only permitted in designated areas. Restaurants tend to have smoking and nonsmoking areas, and some do not allow smoking. There have been a variety of advertisements geared toward young people stating the health dangers of smoking, and others indicating that smoking is not the "in thing." Teens have been portrayed as having bad breath and losing dates with attractive people because they smoke. Philip Morris has been asked to stop using Joe Camel to promote its cigarettes because he appeals to young people. People with cancer and other health problems have tried to bring lawsuits against the tobacco companies for damages. Tobacco companies have been accused of putting substances into their cigarettes to make them addictive. A relative of one of the founders of a major tobacco company did an antismoking advertisement apologizing for his family. There are investment funds with special holdings of stock in companies considered "socially conscious" that will not buy tobacco company stocks.

In spite of the pressure, tobacco companies are profitable and claim that they provide customers with a product they want. With cigarette profits, the sale of stock, and debt, tobacco companies have diversified to provide other means of income. Philip Morris bought Miller Beer, General Foods, and Kraft. R. J. Reynolds and Nabisco are now one company. Despite pressure and diversification, the tobacco companies are not about to stop selling cigarettes. Tobacco companies do not force people to buy their cigarettes. As long as people continue to smoke, some business will provide the cigarettes, so why shouldn't it be RJR and Philip Morris? If either of these two companies stopped selling cigarettes, it would just mean more business for the other one. If they both stopped selling cigarettes, some new company would provide them, so long as it is profitable. Besides, the government collects a lot of taxes on the sale of cigarettes, and the tobacco companies pay taxes on their cigarette profits, which in turn help to pay for programs that help the poor. The tobacco industry provides many thousands of people with jobs, and thousands of businesses sell cigarettes at a profit.

Even before all the antismoking pressure in the United States, tobacco companies realized the potential for increased sales overseas. The Asian market alone sells more than $90 billion worth of cigarettes annually. In fact, over ten years ago, the U.S. government helped RJR and Philip Morris send cigarettes into the Asian market by threatening to boycott goods from Japan, Taiwan, and Korea. China has over one billion people and over 90 percent of the males smoke. The Chinese manufacture and smoke well over one trillion cigarettes a year. Smoking-related illnesses are the top Asian health risk. Yet, Asian governments do little in terms of requiring warning labels, prohibiting sales to minors, or banning smoking. Taiwan has a cigarette brand called "Long Life," and the Japanese warning label simply reads, "Please don't smoke too much."

Fewer than 10 percent of Asian women and adolescents smoke, and U.S. tobacco companies promised not to go after them. However, Philip Morris advertises a cigarette geared to women (Virginia Slims), and RJR sponsored three concerts featuring a popular Hong Kong rock star with the admissions price being five empty packs of Winston cigarettes. American and Taiwanese officials have complained that U.S. companies have hired people to hand out cigarettes to 12-year-olds at amusement parks.[60]

Select the best alternative for the following questions. Be sure you are able to explain your answers.

___ 1. Tobacco companies provide a quality product with customer value.

a. true b. false

___ 2. RJR and Philip Morris have shareholders.

a. true b. false

___ 3. Technology has had a major effect on the tobacco industry.

a. true b. false

___ 4. The primary pressure on the tobacco industry is coming from the ___ external factors.

a. customers and competition
b. society and governments
c. suppliers and labor
d. economy and competition
e. shareholders and technology

___ 5. GATT, NAFTA, EU, and Pacific Asia have the power to affect tobacco companies' performance.

a. true b. false

___ 6. RJR and Philip Morris are ___ companies.

a. domestic c. MNC
b. international

___ 7. Based on information in the case, the primary way RJR and Philip Morris took the business global to Asia was ___.

a. exporting d. joint venture
b. licensing e. direct investment
c. contracting

___ 8. Tobacco companies have been accused of unethical practices.

a. true b. false

___ 9. Managers at RJR and Philip Morris appear to be strongly enforcing ethical behavior in Asia.

a. true b. false

___ 10. Overall, in the United States, tobacco companies are on the ___ level of social responsibility.

a. social obstruction
b. social obligation
c. social reaction
d. social involvement

11. Are the tobacco companies ethical? Explain your answer.

12. Are the tobacco companies socially responsible? In other words, do they make a conscious effort to operate in a manner that creates a win-win situation for all stakeholders?

13. If the U.S. government passed a law making the sale of cigarettes illegal, how would each of the nine external factors benefit and/or be hurt?

14. Should the U.S. government pass a law making the sale of cigarettes illegal?

For information on RJR and Philip Morris, use Internet address http://www.streethrt.com. For ideas on using the Internet, see the Appendix.

SKILL-BUILDING EXERCISE 2–1

The Organizational Environment and Management Practices Analysis

Preparing for Skill-Building Exercise 2–1

For this exercise you will select a specific organization. It is recommended that you select an organization you work or have worked for. Answer the questions as they relate to the business you selected. You may contact people in the organization to get your answers. Write your answers to all questions.

The Internal Environment

1. Identify the top managers and briefly discuss their leadership style.
2. State the organization's mission.
3. Identify some of the organization's major resources.
4. Explain the organization's systems process. Be sure to discuss how the organization ensures quality and customer value.
5. Identify the organization's structure by listing its major departments.

The External Environment

(Within your answer to this section's questions, be sure to state how each of these external factors affects the organization.)

6. Identify the organization's target customers.
7. Identify the organization's major competitors.
8. Identify the organization's major suppliers.
9. What is the major labor force the organization recruits from?
10. Does the organization have shareholders? Is the stock listed on one of the three major stock exchanges? If yes, which one?
11. How does the organization affect society and vice versa?
12. Describe some of the past, present, and future technology of the organization's industry. Is the organization a technology leader?
13. Identify the governments that affect the organization. Be sure to list some of the major laws and regulations affecting the business.
14. Explain how the economy affects the organization.

Globalization

15. Is the organization a domestic, international, or global company?
16. If the organization is international or global, list and briefly describe its global activities (exporting, etc.).
17. If the organization is international or global, list and briefly describe its practices (management team, strategy, etc.).

Ethics

18. Does the organization have any guides to ethical behavior? If yes, explain.
19. How does the organization manage ethics? Does it have a code of ethics (what's in it)? Does top management lead by good ethical example? Are ethical behaviors enforced (how)?

Social Responsibility

20. Overall, on which level of social responsibility does the organization operate? Identify some of the things the organization does to be socially responsible and the level of social responsibility.

Doing Skill-Building Exercise 2–1 in Class

Objective
To develop the conceptual skill to analyze an organization's environmental and management practices.

Preparation
You should have completed the organizational environment preparation before class.

Experience
The primary skill-building comes from the preparation for this exercise. Class members will share their preparation to reinforce learning.

Options (10–30 minutes)

1. The class breaks into groups of three to five members. Each member tells the others his or her answers to the preparation. One student's example may be selected and presented to the entire class.
2. The instructor calls one member of the class to give his or her answers to the preparation. Several students may be called on to give their answers.
3. The instructor calls on different students to give answers to different parts of the preparation.

Conclusion
The instructor may make concluding remarks.

Application (2–4 minutes)
What did I learn from this experience? How will I use this knowledge in the future?

____

____

Sharing
Volunteers give their answers to the application section.

EXERCISE 2–1

Ethics and Whistle-Blowing

Preparing for Exercise 2–1

SELF-ASSESSMENT EXERCISE 2–1

Is Your Behavior Ethical?

For this exercise you will be using the same set of statements twice. The first time you respond to them, focus on your own behavior and the frequency with which you use it. On the line preceding the question, place the number 1–5 that represents how often you did, do, or would do the behavior if you had the chance. These numbers will allow you to determine your level of ethics. You can be honest without fear of having to tell others your score in class. Sharing ethics scores is not part of the exercise.

The second time you use the statements, focus on other people in an organization that you work or have worked for. Place an "O" on the line after the number if you observed someone doing this behavior. Also place a "W" on the line if you reported (whistle-blowing) this behavior within the organization or externally.

Column 1	Frequently			Never
	1	2	3	4	5
Column 2	O—observed	W—reported		

College

___ 1. ___ Cheating on homework assignments.

___ 2. ___ Passing in papers that were completed by someone else, as your own work.

___ 3. ___ Cheating on exams.

Job

___ 4. ___ Coming to work late and getting paid for it.

___ 5. ___ Leaving work early and getting paid for it.

___ 6. ___ Taking long breaks/lunches and getting paid for it.

___ 7. ___ Calling in sick to get a day off, when not sick.

___ 8. ___ Socializing or goofing off rather than doing the work that should be done.

___ 9. ___ Using the company phone to make personal calls.

___ 10. ___ Doing personal work while on company time.

___ 11. ___ Using the company copier for personal use.

___ 12. ___ Mailing personal things through the company mail.

___ 13. ___ Taking home company supplies or merchandise and keeping it.

___ 14. ___ Taking home company tools/equipment without permission for personal use and returning it.

___ 15. ___ Giving company supplies or merchandise to friends or allowing them to take them without saying anything.

___ 16. ___ Putting in for reimbursement for meals and travel or other expenses that weren't actually eaten or taken.

___ 17. ___ Using the company car for personal business.

___ 18. ___ Taking spouse/friends out to eat and charging it to the company expense account.

___ 19. ___ Taking a spouse/friend on business trips and charging the expense to the company.

___ 20. ___ Accepting gifts from customers/suppliers in exchange for giving them business.

To determine your ethics score, add up the numbers 1–5. Your total will be between 20 and 100. Place the number here ___ and on the continuum below that represents your score.

Unethical   Ethical

20—30—40—50—60—70—80—90—100

Discussion Questions

1. For the college items 1–3, who is harmed and who benefits from these unethical behaviors?
2. For job items 4–20, select the three (circle their numbers) you consider the most severe unethical behavior. Who is harmed and who benefits by these unethical behaviors?
3. If you observed unethical behavior but didn't report it, why didn't you report the behavior? If you did blow the whistle, why did you report the unethical behavior? What was the result?
4. As a manager it is your responsibility to uphold ethical behavior. If you know employees are doing any of these unethical behaviors, will you take action to enforce compliance with ethical standards?

Doing Exercise 2–1 in Class

Objective
To better understand ethics and whistle-blowing and what you will do about unethical behavior.

Preparation
You should have completed the preparation for this exercise.

Experience
You will share your answers to the preparation questions, but are not requested to share your ethics score.

Procedure 1 (5–10 minutes)
The instructor writes the numbers 1–20 on the board. For each statement students raise their hands if they observed this behavior, and again if they reported the behavior. The instructor writes the numbers on the board. (Note: Procedures 1 and 2A may be combined.)

Procedure 2 (10–20 minutes)
Option A: As the instructor takes a count of the students who have observed and reported unethical behavior, he or she leads a discussion on the statements.

Option B: Break into groups of four to six and share your answers to the four discussion questions at the end of the preparation part of this exercise. The groups may be asked to report their general consensus to the entire class. If so, select a spokesperson before the discussion begins.

Option C: The instructor leads a class discussion on the four discussion questions at the end of the preparation part of this exercise.

Conclusion
The instructor may make concluding remarks.

Application (2–4 minutes)
What did I learn from this exercise? How will I use this knowledge in the future?

____

____

Sharing
Volunteers give their answers to the application section.

VIDEOCASE

The Changing U.S. Health Care Environment: Central Michigan Community Hospital

The U.S. health care environment is undergoing major changes. The average age of the American population is increasing. This is due to aging of the post-war baby boom generation and life-extending medical technologies which have increased the average life span for both men and women. The population has also become more health conscious, enabling senior citizens in their seventies and eighties to lead active lives. At the same time, there are major concerns about the cost of health care. Employers, consumers, and government—the major payers of health care bills—are seeking ways to contain health costs while maintaining quality and access to medical services. New technologies are constantly being developed, and they are often very expensive.

In response to these social, economic, and technological trends, hospitals and doctors have come under pressure to better manage delivery of health care services and costs. Hospitals and doctors are joining together, sometimes in cooperation with insurance companies, to control costs and provide services. These cooperative arrangements are sometimes called *managed care* or *health maintenance organizations*. These newly formed cooperative hospital/doctor groups are now competing with one another to provide coverage to growing elderly (Medicare) and poor (Medicaid) populations, while keeping costs under control.

Central Michigan Community Hospital (CMCH) is a nonprofit regional referral system which includes a full-service 151-bed hospital; a medical staff of over 120 doctors; READYCARE, a walk-in urgent care center; wellness services; occupational medicine; home health care; plus numerous other services. In 1994, CMCH was honored as one of the "Top 100 Hospitals in the U.S." But changes in the U.S. health care environment are affecting CMCH. CMCH has been evaluating these environmental changes and how they could influence the future of their regional health system.

Managing Diversity: Human Skills

Learning Objectives

After studying this chapter, you should be able to:

1. Explain the difference among prejudice, stereotypes, and discrimination.
2. Describe how increased markets and lower employee costs are advantages of diversity.
3. Discuss the difference between valuing diversity and managing diversity.
4. List two important parts of diversity training.
5. Explain the relationship between the stakeholders' approach to ethics and to human skills.
6. Describe how global diversity affects the implementation of the management functions.
7. List and explain the steps in the complaint-handling model.
8. Define the following **key terms** (in order of appearance in the chapter):

   diversity
   ethnocentrism
   prejudices
   stereotypes
   discrimination
   glass ceiling
   sexual harassment
   disability
   valuing diversity
   managing diversity
   mentors
   golden rule of human relations
   stakeholders' approach to human relations
   customs
   complaint
   complaint-handling model

Skill Development

1. You should develop your skill to better handle complaints (Skill-Building Exercise 3–1).

   Handling complaints takes human and communication skills and is an important part of the decisional roles: the disturbance-handler and negotiator roles and possibly the resource-allocator role, depending on the complaint. The SCANS skill competencies of using resources, interpersonal, information, and systems, as well as the basic, thinking, and personal qualities foundation skills are also developed.

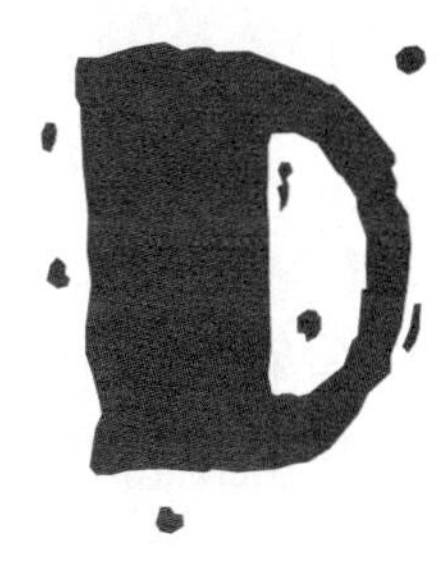

igital Equipment Corporation, a computer manufacturer, operates in 72 countries, with headquarters in Maynard, Massachusetts. Digital pioneered the trend toward valuing and managing a diverse work force. The company built two plants in 1972 and 1980 to give women and minorities opportunities to grow and develop before being assigned to other Digital facilities.

Unlike many companies today that are just beginning to recognize the importance of diversity, back in the early 1980s Digital was encouraging every employee to reach his or her full potential. Barbara Walker was hired to expand Digital's equal employment opportunity and affirmative action program to diversity. Individual differences were valued and celebrated, rather than tolerated, which is the traditional view.

Walker was given the title "Manager of Valuing Differences." Digital's Valuing Differences Program and philosophy are based on the conviction that the broader the spectrum of differences in the workplace, the higher the synergy among employees and the more creative are workers' ideas, which leads to higher levels of organizational performance.

Digital's goals were to gain the competitive advantage of a more effective work force, higher morale, and a reputation for being a better place to work through its diversity efforts. Digital wants to continue to be able to attract and retain the best talent in the labor market.

Employees at Digital learn to value diversity, as evidenced by this blind technician on the computer assembly line.

Training in valuing differences helps employees understand prejudice and stereotypes and how to avoid discrimination based on them. Employees learn to value differences. The Valuing Differences Program includes various cultural boards of directors and valuing differences boards of directors, which include a number of senior managers. These boards promote openness to individual differences, encourage managers to be committed to diversity goals, and sponsor celebrations of racial, gender, and ethnic differences. For example, Digital celebrates Hispanic Heritage Week and Black History Month.

Digital has achieved a diverse work force. The Boston factory has employees from 44 countries who speak 19 languages. To accommodate differences, company announcements are printed in English, Chinese, French, Spanish, Portuguese, Vietnamese, and Haitian Creole.[1]

For current information on Digital Equipment Corporation, use Internet address http://www.digital.com. For ideas on using the Internet, see the Appendix.

DIVERSITY: AN OVERVIEW

The old stereotype of the United States as a "melting pot" where ethnic and racial differences were blended into an American puree has changed. In reality, many ethnic and most racial groups retained their identities but did not express them at work. Today, minorities do not want to drop their identities, and the law states that they don't have to. The Civil Rights Act made ethnic and gender discrimination illegal. But, more importantly, contemporary managers don't want people to drop their identities. They realize that diversity affects the bottom line,[2] that a diverse work force will outperform a homogeneous one,[3] and that managers are using diversity as a competitive advantage.[4] In this section you will learn where diversity came from, some important terms, and about diverse groups and what they want.

From Equal Employment and Affirmative Action to Diversity

Equal employment opportunity (EEO) was primarily a battle against racism and prejudice. As the name implies, the EEO stresses treating all employees equally.

The goal of affirmative action (AA) was to correct the past exclusion of women and minorities from organizations. AA is a recruitment tool used to hire and promote minorities and women. The government and business had numerical quotas which required a certain percentage of women and minorities in certain positions. It became expected practice to hire and promote less qualified women and minorities to meet quotas. However, majority-group members complained of reverse discrimination. As a result, the government and business have moved away from percentages and quotas. While progress has been made, most women and minorities under EEO and AA are still at the bottom of most organizations. In other words, EEO and AA have not worked.[5]

Diversity programs are replacing EEO and AA programs as the titles EEO and AA are disappearing from the titles of executives' responsibilities.[6] Employers are embracing the idea of *diversity*, the un-affirmative action without quotas, timetables, or written moral obligations. Diversity places a premium on having some "qualified" women and minorities in management because they are expected to be different from white males in ways that can help the bottom line.[7] However, when you get rid of AA numerical goals, you can have diversity without promoting minorities and women. The net result of eliminating AA is a reduced number of "qualified" minorities. In turn, the goal of diversity is difficult to realize.[8] "Diversity is more palatable than AA, but it obscures the truth. AA is still necessary because most firms still do not hire and promote women and minorities as readily as they do white males—no matter how much they embrace, support, manage, nurture, foster, or promote diversity."[9] Only time will tell if AA will be a part of diversity, or if AA will be eliminated.

Important Terms

1. Explain the difference among prejudice, stereotypes, and discrimination.

When we talk about diversity, we are referring to characteristics of individuals that shape their identities and their experiences in the workplace. **Diversity** *refers to the degree of differences among members of a group or organization.* If you are wondering if diversity is really all that important, the answer is yes. There is a total lack of homogeneity in this world.[10] Over the next decade, 85 percent of the labor force increase will be minorities and women.[11] It has been estimated that by the year 2030 less than 50 percent of the U.S. population will be white. Diversity in the workplace is a major concern of managers.[12] Therefore, managing diversity will constitute a large portion of management's agenda throughout the 1990s and into the next century.[13]

diversity
The degree of differences among members of a group or organization.

Some of the problems we have in dealing with a diversity of people include ethnocentrism, prejudice, stereotypes, and discrimination. Ethnocentrism refers to our natural tendency to judge other groups—cultures, countries, customs, and so on—less favorably than our own. **Ethnocentrism** *is the belief that one's own group is superior to others.* Prejudices and stereotypes are related to ethnocentrism. **Prejudices** *are preconceived judgments of a person or situation.* If someone were to ask you, "Are you prejudiced?" you would probably say "no." However, we all tend to prejudge people and situations. First impressions are powerful prejudices. If you have ever not listened closely because you already knew what a person was going to say, you've experienced prejudice. **Stereotypes** *are positive or negative assessments or perceived attributes toward people or situations.* The phrases "all ____ (fill in the blanks) are cheap, ____ are lazy, ____ are criminals, ____ don't really want to work, ____ are too emotional, and ____

ethnocentrism
The belief that one's own group is superior to others.

prejudices
Preconceived judgments of a person or situation.

stereotypes
Positive or negative assessments or perceived attributes toward people or situations.

Work Application

1. Give an example of when you, or someone you know, were discriminated against for any reason on a job.

discrimination
Unjust behavior for or against a person or situation.

cannot jump," are negative stereotypes. The problem is that people can prejudge others based on the stereotypes without getting to know the individual. Based on ethnocentrism, we tend to stereotype one of our own group as better than someone in another group without even knowing the person.

To prejudge or stereotype a person in and of itself is not harmful; we all tend to do this. However, we must be aware of our prejudices and stereotypes and make sure we get to know the person as an individual. If you discriminate based on ethnocentrism or your prejudices and stereotypes, you cause harm to yourself and others. **Discrimination** *is unjust behavior for or against a person or situation.* We have all been discriminated against at one time or another because we were in some way different than the other people in the group.

The use of discrimination in business prevents equal-employment opportunity. Discrimination is both unethical and illegal. Historically, the five areas where discrimination in employment is most common include recruitment, selection, compensation (white males still make more money than other groups), upward mobility, and evaluation.

To illustrate the difference among prejudice, stereotypes, and discrimination, assume that Carl is a manager and is in the process of hiring a new employee. There are two qualified candidates: Pete, a member of Carl's group; and Ted, a member of another group. Carl is subject to ethnocentrism and stereotypes people of Ted's group as not being as productive on the job as members of his group. Carl is also aware of his ethnocentrism and stereotypes and believes that people of Ted's group deserve a break and knows that the company is interested in a diversified work force. Carl has a few options.

APPLYING THE CONCEPT

AC 3–1 Prejudice/Stereotype versus Discrimination

Identify each statement made by a white male as being

a. prejudice/stereotype b. discrimination

____ **1.** "Here comes Jamal (a tall African-American); I bet he will talk about basketball."

____ **2.** "I select Pete as my partner. Karen, you team up with Betty for this assignment"

____ **3.** "I cannot continue to work with you today, Sue. Is it your time of the month?"

____ **4.** "I do not want to work the night shift. Can you force me to change?"

____ **5.** "The boss hired a new good-looking blond secretary. I bet she's not very bright."

Carl can select a candidate and discriminate based on prejudice for Pete (as being a member of his group) or Ted (as being a member of a group that deserves a break, and management wants diversity). Selecting an employee based solely on group membership is clearly illegal discrimination. Carl can be aware of his prejudices yet try not to let them influence his decision. Carl can interview both candidates and select the person who is best qualified for the job. If no significant difference exists between the candidates' qualifications, Carl could hire Ted; then there would be no discrimination. This option is legal and ethical and is the generally recommended approach.

Diverse Groups and What They Want

People are diverse in many ways. Within the work force, as Figure 3–1 illustrates, the major groups include race/ethnicity, religion, gender, age, ability, and other.

You are aware that an organization cannot discriminate against a minority. Who is legally considered a minority? A minority is just about anyone who is not a white male, of European heritage, or adequately educated. The Equal Employment Opportunity Commission (EEOC) guidelines minority list includes Hispanics, Asians, African-Americans, Native Americans, and Alaskan natives. Women are also protected by law from discrimination in employment, but the EEOC does not consider them to be a legal minority. The law also protects disadvantaged young people, disabled workers, and persons over 40. The EEOC has 47 field offices across the nation. It offers seminars for employees who feel they aren't getting a fair shake, and it operates a WATTS line (1-800-USA-EEOC) around the clock to provide information on employee rights.

For our business management purposes, we will define majority and minority groups in a different manner than the law requires. The majority group holds the decision-making power and resources and may not be the largest number. The minority group lacks power, and may be the largest number. For example, most health-care organizations hire more women employees than men. However, the people with the power are typically the white male doctors and administrators. Also, some companies hire more people of color than whites, yet the whites tend to hold the management positions. There are also businesses owned by people of color that employ whites who are the minority group. On the other hand, Ben and Jerry hired an African-American as CEO of their company.

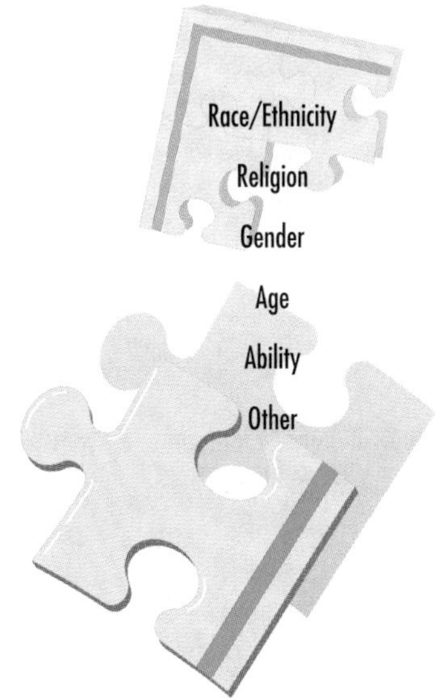

Figure 3–1
Diverse Work-Force Groups

As a manager you will most likely have employees with different races/ethnicities, religions, genders, ages, abilities, and other diversities.

Race/Ethnicity. According to the Hudson Institute, in its *Workforce 2000* report, African-Americans and Hispanics need to be fully integrated into the economy. This is particularly urgent between now and the year 2000.[14]

- *People of color want* to be valued as unique individuals, as members of ethnically diverse groups, as people of different races, and as equal contributors. They want to establish more open, honest, working relationships with people of other races and ethnic groups. And they want the active support of white people in fighting racism.
- *White people want* to have their ethnicity acknowledged. They want to reduce discomfort, confusion, and dishonesty in dealing with people of color. They want to build relationships with people of color based on common goals and concerns and mutual respect for differences.[15]

Ben and Jerry's CEO, Robert Holland, is new to the ice cream business, but he has the operational expertise to take the company to higher levels.

Religion. A manager must make reasonable accommodations for employees' religious beliefs. For example, employees should be allowed to take religious holidays off. In some countries, employees stop working at set times and pray. Therefore, a manager needs to adjust.

Gender. Before you learn about gender, complete Self-Assessment Exercise 3–1 to determine your attitude toward women at work.

SELF-ASSESSMENT EXERCISE 3–1

Women at Work

For each of the following ten statements, select the response that best describes your honest belief about women at work. Place the number 1, 2, 3, 4, or 5 on the line before each statement.

5—Strongly agree 4—Agree 3—Not sure 2—Disagree 1—Strongly disagree

___ 1. Women lack the education necessary to get ahead.
___ 2. Women working has caused rising unemployment among men.
___ 3. Women are not strong enough or emotionally stable enough to succeed in high-pressure jobs.
___ 4. Women are too emotional to be effective managers.
___ 5. Women managers have difficulty in situations calling for quick and precise decisions.
___ 6. Women work to earn extra money rather than to support a family.
___ 7. Women are out of work more often than men.
___ 8. Women quit work or take long maternity leaves when they have children.
___ 9. Women have a lower commitment to work than men.
___ 10. Women lack motivation to get ahead.
___ Total

To determine your attitude score, add up the total of your ten answers and place it on the total line and on the following continuum.

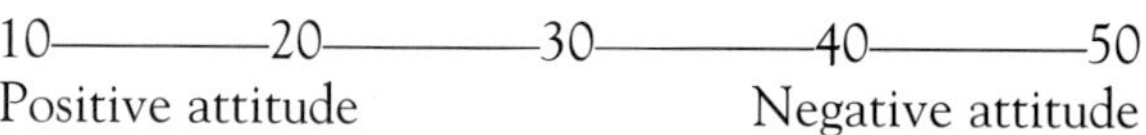

Each statement is a commonly held attitude about women at work. However, through research, all of these statements have been shown to be false, or are considered myths about women at work. Such statements stereotype women unfairly and prevent women from gaining salary increases and promotions.

The traditional family in which the husband worked and the wife was not employed is no longer the majority; two-income marriages are now the norm.[16] However, on average, men put in less than half as much time as women on housework and child care.[17] According to the U.S. Bureau of Labor Statistics, by the year 2000 nearly 80 percent of women of working age are expected to be employed, and women will comprise almost half of the total work force.

Do women get equal treatment at work today? According to the Census Bureau, in spite of the Equal Pay Act, which requires equal pay for the same job, women's average hourly earnings are 70 percent of men's.[18] Although there has been progress in the promotion of minority group members and women, the glass ceiling still exists. *The* **glass ceiling** *refers to the invisible barrier that prevents minorities and women from advancing beyond a certain level in organizations.* Women hold about 37 percent of all domestic U.S. management positions.[19] However, women hold less than 5 percent of top management positions at large companies[20] and only 3 percent of all international management positions over-

glass ceiling
The invisible barrier that prevents minorities and women from advancing beyond a certain level in organizations.

seas. The most difficult part of an international management assignment for women is getting the job, not succeeding once they get overseas.[21] Women are also more commonly sexually harassed than men at work. **Sexual harassment** *is any unwelcome behavior of a sexual nature.*

APPLYING THE CONCEPT

AC 3–2 Sexual Harassment

Identify whether the following behavior is

a. sexual harassment b. not sexual harassment

____ **6.** Ted tells Claire she is sexy and he'd like to take her out on a date.

____ **7.** Sue tells Josh he will have to go to a motel with her if he wants to be recommended for a promotion.

____ **8.** On the walls near Joel and Kathy's desks, they each hung pictures of nude men and women in view of other employees who walk by.

____ **9.** For the third time, after being politely told not to, Pat tells Chris an explicitly sexual joke.

____ **10.** Ray puts his hand on his secretary Lisa's shoulder as he talks to her.

- *Women want* recognition as equal partners and the active support of male colleagues. They want organizations to proactively address work and family issues.
- *Men want* the same freedom to express their emotions as women have. They want to be perceived as allies, not as the enemy. And they want to bridge the gap between dealing with women at home and work.[22]

sexual harassment
Any unwelcome behavior of a sexual nature.

As a manager you should realize that both males and females want a balance between work and family.

Age. You will be working with older customers and workers. Middle-aged people are the fastest-growing population group, while the number of young adults is on the decline.[23] According to the Census Bureau, by the year 2000, 36 percent of the population will be over 45 years of age. There are 77 million baby boomers approaching their 50s. Companies, such as AlliedSignal, which denies the charges, have faced age-discrimination charges by ex-employees.[24] Such legal cases can be very expensive.

- *Young and old people want* more respect for their life experiences and to be taken seriously. They want to be challenged, not patronized, by their peers and organizations.[25]

Ability. Skill levels vary greatly in most organizations from the technical and professional to the lower-level jobs. Education levels also vary greatly. More people are graduating from college than there are job openings for them, while the number of illiterates continues to increase. As a manager you may have employees with a diversity of skills and education levels.

The Americans with Disabilities Act (ADA) compelled businesses to change many employment practices. The law requires employers with at least 25 workers to make "reasonable accommodations" for qualified workers and job applicants with disabilities as well as to avoid discriminating against them.[26] According to the Equal Employment Opportunity Commission (EEOC), *people with significant physical or mental impairment that substantially limits a major life activity are considered to have a* **disability.** The EEOC later defined an impairment as a physiological disorder affecting at least one body system or a mental or psychological disorder.[27] The term *disabled* replaces the old term *handicapped* because the word tends to have a negative connotation.

disability
Significant physical or mental impairment that substantially limits a major life activity.

About two out of three people with disabilities do not work, even though about 80 percent of them want to work. Many of those who do work say coworkers will not socialize with them.[28] In many cases, a person with a disability can do just as good, or better, a job as a nondisabled employee. In fact, a survey revealed that 88 percent of corporate department heads and 91 percent of equal-employment officers at 921 companies rated employees with disabilities as "good" or "excellent" workers.[29] Marriott Corporation has a 105 percent annual employee turnover rate, but the turnover rate of employees with disabilities is only 8 percent. McDonald's created the McJobs program in 1981 to recruit, train, and retain employees with disabilities. Over 9,000 people with disabilities have been trained.

You have to look at a person's abilities rather than his or her disabilities. As a manager, you may be held personally liable for violating the ADA.[30]

- *People with disabilities want* greater acknowledgment of, and focus on, abilities rather than on disabilities alone. They want to be challenged by colleagues and organizations to do their best. They want to be included, not isolated.
- *Physically able people want* to develop more ease in dealing with people with disabilities. They want to appreciate abilities in addition to understanding disabilities. And they want to give honest feedback and appropriate support without being patronizing or overprotective.[31]

Work Application

2. Identify the diversity of people in a department/organization you work or have worked for.

Other. People are different in a limitless number of other ways. A few of the commonly listed differences include military status, sexual preference, expectations and values, lifestyles, socioeconomic class, work styles, and function and/or position within the organization. As an employee and manager, you should deal with all people in an ethical and legal manner.

In this section, although you have learned what different groups want, remember that these are generalities; not all members of these groups want these things. Be careful not to use lists to stereotype people; get to know them as individuals.

ADVANTAGES AND CHALLENGES OF DIVERSITY

In this section you will learn about the advantages and challenges of diversity, which Figure 3–2[32] lists.

Advantages	Challenges
Ethical and social responsibility	Discrimination
Increased markets	Mistrust and tension
Lower employment cost	Lower cohesiveness
Improved decision-making	Communication problems
Better quality management team	
Flexibility	

Figure 3–2
Advantages and Challenges of Diversity

Advantages of Diversity

Ethical and Social Responsibility. As you learned in Chapter 2, ethical and social responsibility pays.

Increased Markets. When a company has a diversified work force, employees can provide valuable information about minority markets because they are part of the market. Minorities can also give ideas for new products that create customer value in these new markets. For example, a cosmetics company that offers products only to whites is not servicing minority markets well. The company with minority employees will generally create better customer value than one with an all-white work force.

2. Describe how increased markets and lower employee costs are advantages of diversity.

Lower Employment Cost. Attracting, retaining, and motivating employees is costly. Recruiting, hiring, and training one employee may cost thousands of dollars, depending on the employment level. When they do not believe that people in their group are treated fairly, or are discriminated against, good employees will quit and go to work where they have opportunities, and costs will be higher. Employees who feel that they are being treated unfairly will not be motivated to perform at high levels.

Improved Decision-Making. A group of all-white males who work together tends to think alike. Diverse group members tend to have different perspectives and offer more approaches to problem-solving. Diverse groups tend to offer more creative and innovative ideas because they are freer to deviate from the traditional white male approaches and practices. This is especially true when the decisions to be made affect minorities. The government has been criticized because in the past it has repeatedly used all-white male groups to solve minority problems.

Better Quality Management Team. As you learned in Chapter 2, leading multinational companies have diverse management teams because they are of higher quality.

Flexibility. People who work with a diversity of people tend to be more capable of making changes to accommodate others. As you learned in Chapter 2, flexibility is needed to be successful because you need continuous improvement to offer increasing customer value. A flexible work force that can change quickly is an advantage over work forces that cannot.

Challenges of Diversity

Discrimination. A major challenge for all of us is to be aware of our prejudices and stereotypes, but not to discriminate for or against people who are of the same or are of a different race/ethnicity, religion, gender, age, ability, and so on.

Mistrust and Tension. It is natural for people to want to associate with people like themselves. People who do not get to know people different from themselves tend to mistrust other groups. In an environment in which members do not trust each other, stress and tension are common and reaching an agreement on problems can be difficult. The traditional management versus union mentality is an example. A major challenge for all of us is to get to know members of other groups personally so that our fear, mistrust, and tension will not create problems in a diverse group.

Lower Cohesiveness. Cohesiveness refers to how well group members "stick together" or get along and conform to group expectations. Generally, homogeneous groups are more cohesive than diverse groups. A major challenge for all of us is to get to know members of our work groups personally so that we can all stick together. You will learn more about cohesiveness in Chapter 13.

Communication Problems. Time is lost when all members of a group do not speak the same language, or when additional time is needed for interpreta-

Work Application

3. Describe a work situation in which you encountered any one of the advantages or challenges of diversity. Be sure to identify the advantage or challenge by its text name.

tion. Difficulties include misunderstandings, inaccuracies, and inefficiencies when using information resources. A major challenge for all of us is to be patient and to take the necessary time to communicate correctly the first time rather than to solve problems caused by miscommunication later.

Company policies requiring employees to speak only English create tensions and lawsuits. The EEOC stated that English-only rules may violate civil rights laws, unless an employer can show they are necessary for conducting business.[33] In some areas of the United States, and especially on a global basis, if a company had an English-only rule it would not have a work force. In the United States and on a global scale, you need to communicate with people using their language, not yours, if you want to create customer value.

Keep in mind that although there are challenges to diversity, the advantages outweigh the negative side as demonstrated by companies like Digital Equipment.

VALUING AND MANAGING DIVERSITY

In this section you will learn the difference between valuing diversity and managing diversity. You will also learn about managing diversity policies and practices, diversity training, and the management functions and diversity.

3. Discuss the difference between valuing diversity and managing diversity.

Valuing Diversity versus Managing Diversity

Valuing diversity focuses on understanding, respecting, and valuing differences among employees (mental activity), whereas managing diversity builds on valuing differences. Both require top management support (behavioral activity).[34] Valuing diversity focuses on interpersonal qualities, such as race, gender, and age, whereas managing diversity looks at the diverse *needs* of employees, not the cultural diversity of employees. Managing diversity also requires putting policies and procedures in place to meet the diverse needs of employees.[35] For our purposes, **valuing diversity** *emphasizes training employees of different race and ethnicity, religions, genders, ages, abilities, and with other differences to function effectively together.* **Managing diversity** *emphasizes fully utilizing human resources through organizational actions that meet all employees' needs.* Valuing diversity is an important part of managing diversity. However, managing diversity goes beyond valuing diversity to focus on the diverse quality of employees' work–life needs, such as child care, family leave, and flexible work and holiday schedules.[36] Next, you will learn more about managing diversity and some of the ways in which organizations meet diverse employee needs.

valuing diversity
Emphasizes training employees of different race and ethnicity, religions, genders, ages, abilities, and with other differences to function effectively together.

managing diversity
Emphasizes fully utilizing human resources through organizational actions that meet all employees' needs.

Managing Diversity

There are four major areas of managing diversity, which Figure 3–3 presents.

Top Management Support and Commitment. Managing diversity must have top management support and commitment to be effective. Companies committed to managing diversity can follow the lead of nonprofit organizations which have more diverse management teams.[37] One way to communicate support for diversity to employees and the external environment (Chapter 2) is to incorporate it into the mission statement and to set objectives. True commit-

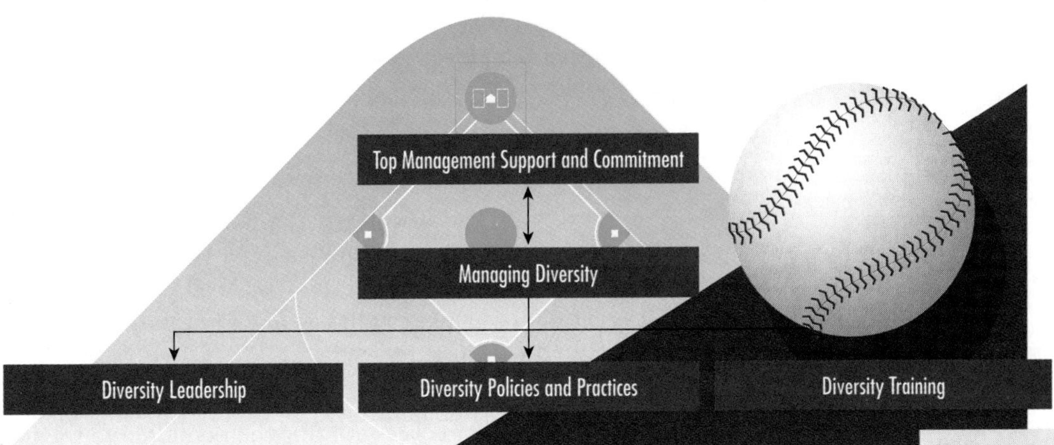

Figure 3–3
Managing Diversity

ment to diversity should include directly linking management compensation to accomplishing diversity objectives. Baxter Health Care, Coca-Cola, The Federal National Mortgage Association, and Merck all tie managers' compensation to their performance in diversity efforts. Adequate funding must be allocated to diversity and leadership must be established.

Diversity Leadership. Organizations committed to diversity have established offices or committees to coordinate the companywide diversity effort and to provide feedback to top management. For example, Digital Equipment Corporation has a manager of valuing differences, Honeywell has a director of work force diversity, and Avon has a director of multicultural planning and design.

In addition to diversity directors, committees are commonly used to enable specific diverse groups to identify problem areas in polices, practices, and attitudes and make recommendations where change is needed. Digital uses Core Groups, Equitable Life Assurance Society has Business Resource Groups that meet regularly with the CEO, and U.S. West has a 33-member Pluralism Council. At Honeywell employees with disabilities formed a council. To move a diversity of employees to higher levels in the organization, Mobil Oil has a special committee of executives who select women and minorities with high potential for high-paying and critical line positions. Honeywell has a team to evaluate the career progress of women, minorities, and employees with disabilities and to devise ways to move them up through the ranks.

Diversity Policies and Practices. To manage diversity, organizations must develop policies that directly affect how employees are treated. For the organization to truly offer equal employment opportunities, it must actively recruit, train, and promote a diverse work force without discrimination. Policies and procedures must also be developed to handle problems that arise from diversity. For example, if an African-American woman complains of not being promoted due to race discrimination, how the complaint is handled will send a message throughout the organization. If excessive burden of proof is placed on the African-American woman, she is discouraged from complaining. And if the punishment for discrimination is minor for the guilty party, employees will get the message that discrimination against African-Americans is an accepted practice. Later in this chapter you will learn how to handle complaints.

Organizations offer a wide variety of ongoing practices and procedures to meet the diverse needs of their employees. Some of the practices include

- *Diversity training programs*—to help employees value differences; you will learn more about training in this section.
- *Training and development*—to prepare diverse people for present and future jobs.
- *Flexible, often called cafeteria, benefits programs*—to allow employees to select their benefits.
- *Flexible work schedules*—to enable employees to set their own hours to start and end work, within limits.
- *Telecommuting*—to let employees work at home.
- *Child care centers*—to allow employees to bring their children to the job site.
- *Family leave*—to allow time off to care for a child or other relative.
- *Counseling*—to help deal with job and family pressure and substance abuse.
- *Role models and mentoring programs*—to help prepare lower-level employees for progression. **Mentors** *are higher-level managers who prepare high-potential employees for advancement.*
- *Wellness programs*—to keep employees in good health through exercise and diet, and to help them stop smoking.

mentors
Higher-level managers who prepare high-potential employees for advancement.

Unfortunately, many organizations involved in downsizing and re-engineering (Chapter 2) are ignoring some of the practices that help employees balance work and family issues. For re-engineering to be successful, organizations cannot simply ask employees to redesign their work without there being something in it for them. Managers of successful re-engineering programs at Merck and First Tennessee National realize that work and family initiatives are not a frill, but a "driving force" behind quality-improvement efforts. Merck and First Tennessee answered the "what's in it for me" question by asking employees to redesign work so that it allows them to have a life while doing their jobs well. Employees discuss how work is done and how it could be done better. Then, employees' desire to lead balanced work and family lives draws them into streamlining efforts.[38] This is the stakeholder approach which creates a win-win situation for the employees and company (Chapter 2).

Work Application

4. Give examples of any actions taken by an organization to promote diversity.

4. List two important parts of diversity training.

Diversity Training

The number of organizations that are offering diversity training is on the increase.[39] Organizations of all types are training their employees to value group differences. Some of the many organizations that offer diversity programs include Levi Strauss & Company, McDonald's Corporation, Nestlé Beverage Company, Avon, Prudential, Hewlett-Packard, and LIMRA. One important part of diversity training is making people aware of the meaning and importance of valuing diversity and to make them aware of their prejudices and stereotypes so that they do not use them to discriminate. A second part of diversity training is making it clear to all employees what it takes to get ahead in the organization. In most companies, the "rules" for success are ambiguous, unwritten, and can even be inconsistent with written policy. Valuing diversity includes teaching the unwritten rules and changing the rules to benefit a diverse work force.

Following are some examples of diversity training programs. LIMRA developed a customized diversity seminar with these objectives for employees: (1) to understand the current and changing demographics of the work force, (2) to view the company's business as part of a global work force and economy, (3) to recognize how prejudice and discrimination can inhibit business success, and (4) to recruit from and market to targeted multicultural markets in their territory.[40] Avon Products began its managing diversity program as an effort to move away from assimilation (trying to get diverse people to be like white males) as a corporate value and to raise awareness of negative stereotypes and how they affect the workplace. Avon's success is evident in the number of women who have advanced to management positions.[41] Hewlett-Packard introduced its managing diversity program as part of the management-development curriculum required of all managers. The program stresses diversity as a competitive advantage.[42]

Diversity training works. Survey feedback was used to evaluate the diversity programs at National Transportation Systems, General Computer, and United Communications. The data suggest that exposure to diversity issues affects workplace attitudes. Discussions of cultural differences and attempts to eliminate negative stereotypes are often beneficial to employees and may enhance their communication and morale.[43] A diversity training exercise, Exercise 3–1, is included at the end of this chapter.

Work Application

5. Have you, or anyone you know, gone through diversity training? If yes, describe the program.

The Management Functions and Diversity

To successfully manage a diverse work force requires technical, human and communication, and conceptual and decision-making skills anchored within the four basic functions of management.

Planning. Planning is the process of setting objectives and determining in advance exactly how the objectives will be met (Chapter 1). Valuing and managing diversity don't just happen; they take planning. Planning begins with setting objectives. Diversity objectives could be to recruit and/or promote a specific number of minorities to specific jobs and to have all employees complete diversity training. With the diversity training goal, a training program must be developed through careful planning to determine the objectives of the training, material to be used, when and where the training will take place, who will conduct the training, and so on. Once objectives are set and plans are made to achieve them, organizing, leading, and controlling become involved at the implementation phase.

Organizing. Organizing is the process of delegating and coordinating tasks and resources to achieve objectives (Chapter 1). The diversity training needs to be coordinated so that employees can attend without interrupting customer service. The staffing component of organizing is critical to achieving diversity because managers must make special efforts to select and train a diversity of employees.

Leading. Leading is the process of influencing employees to work toward achieving objectives (Chapter 1). Employees look to management, especially top management, to lead by example (Chapter 2). For the diversity training to be successful, managers must attend and see to it that their employees attend too. Managers should influence employees to value diversity on the job.

APPLYING THE CONCEPT

AC 3–3 Management Functions and Diversity

Identify each statement by its management function

a. planning b. organizing c. leading d. controlling

____ **11.** "I am pleased with your progress on the assignment and with how well you are getting along."—Manager to a diverse group.

____ **12.** "Our goal is to have about the same percentage of Hispanic managers as we have Hispanic workers."

____ **13.** "To date, our Hispanic management percentage has gone from 3 to 8 percent, with a constant Hispanic employment of 28 percent."

____ **14.** "Ted, Wonita, José, Jamal, Betty, and Carl—I want you to work together to come up with a solution to this customer complaint."

____ **15.** "OK, then, we agree that we will show video B and conduct exercises X, Y, and Z during the training sessions."

Controlling. Controlling is the process of establishing and implementing mechanisms to ensure that objectives are achieved (Chapter 1). Management should evaluate the diversity training program. Department managers must also follow up to make sure that what was learned in training is used on the job. Managers must continually monitor how well their department is meeting diversity objectives and take corrective action, when needed, to meet the objectives.

To have effective human relations with all types of people, you need to be tolerant of their differences and try to understand why they are different, have empathy for them and their situation, and communicate openly with them. Be aware of your human tendency to prejudge and stereotype others and be sure to avoid discrimination.

HUMAN RELATIONS SKILLS

Recall the best and worst manager you ever had. Why did you select these managers? The odds are great that one of the reasons that you chose the best manager is because he or she took a personal interest in you, and the one that you selected as the worst manager treated you just as a means of getting the job done. According to James Champy, co-author of *Re-Engineering the Corporation*, "The biggest lie told by most corporations, and they tell it proudly, is that 'people are our most important assets.' Total fabrication. They treat people like raw material."[44] We all want to be accepted for who we are, not just for what we can do for someone else. Hopefully, you will treat human resources as people.

As you learned in Chapter 1, human skills are important in business. In this section, and throughout the text, you will learn about human skills. To be more specific, topics include the golden rule of human relations and the stakeholders' approach to human relations, human relations guidelines—do's and don'ts, and handling human relations problems.

The Golden Rule of Human Relations and the Stakeholders' Approach to Human Relations

Human relations are interactions among people. To be successful in business, you must be able to get along well with a diversity of people. Using ethical behavior (Chapter 2) will help you to develop good human relations. Let's slightly change the golden rule and stakeholders' approach to ethics to better relate to human relations.

The Golden Rule of Human Relations. The **golden rule of human relations** *is:*

Treat others as you want them to treat you and/or as they want to be treated.

golden rule of human relations
Treat others as you want them to treat you and/or as they want to be treated.

In other words, keep the golden rule "don't do anything to anyone that you would not want them to do to you" and add "do things for them that you would want them to do for you and/or that they would want you to do for them." When you are interacting with people who are different from you, remember that they may not want to be treated the way you do, so go out of your way to treat them the way they want to be treated. For example, you and your friends may use certain words (or do things) that people different from you don't like to hear (see). So don't say/do these things around them.

The Stakeholders' Approach to Human Relations. Under the **stakeholders' approach to human relations,** *you try to create a win-win situation so that all parties benefit from your interactions with them.* As you engage in human relations, ask yourself: "Am I just looking out for me, just the other person(s), or am I looking out for both me and the other person(s)?" In other words, it's better not to be selfish or selfless; it's better for both of you to benefit whenever possible.

5. Explain the relationship between the stakeholders' approach to ethics and to human skills.

stakeholders' approach to human relations
Creating a win-win situation so that all parties benefit from your interactions with them.

To develop any skill takes conscious effort and work. If you want to be good at tennis, you don't just play once a month; you practice regularly. The same principle holds true for human relations skills; it takes continuous work. The beauty of human relations is that you get so many opportunities to practice your skills. If you work hard to follow the golden rule of human relations and the stakeholders' approach to human relations with "everyone," you will improve your human relations skills. Digital offers skills training programs that focus on developing human skills as part of diversity training. Next you will learn some specifics that can help you develop human skills with a diversity of people.

Human Relations Guidelines—Do's and Don'ts

The lists of do's and don'ts in Figure 3–4 are not meant to be all-inclusive. As you read the do's and don'ts, be aware that you will view these concepts from your own cultural perspectives. Warning: All lists of do's and don'ts encourage stereotyping that assumes people from the same group are mostly alike. This is not true.

APPLYING THE CONCEPT

AC 3–4 Human Relations Do's and Don'ts

Identify each statement as something you should do or should not do.

a. do b. don't

____ **16.** Ignore differences when assigning a task.

____ **17.** Speak up when others do things that offend you.

____ **18.** Assume communication takes place when no one asks a question.

____ **19.** Minimize differences by focusing on similarities.

____ **20.** Assume that certain people are better at and prefer to do certain tasks.

Handling Human Relations Problems

Even though you follow the human relations guidelines, in any organization there are bound to be times when you disagree with others. You may be assigned to work with a person you do not like. When you encounter these human relations problems, you have to decide whether to avoid resolving the problem or to confront the person to solve it. In

Do's

Some of the things you *should* do to develop effective human relations include:

- Be aware of your prejudices and stereotypes, and do not discriminate based on them.
- Use the golden rule of human relations and the stakeholders' approach to human relations.
- Expect discomfort when interacting with people who are different from you. As you get to know people, discomfort will lessen. Hopefully, it will be eliminated.
- Take a personal interest in others; get to know people as individuals, not just about them. Use peoples' names when you talk to them. Realize that they play more roles than worker: parent, sports player/fan, coach, scout leader, and so on.
- Encourage pride in your own and others' heritage and other differences, but don't gloat about yours over others.
- Gently and honestly discuss differences you may have that you don't understand.
- Ask if there are things that you say or do that are confusing or upsetting and what might be done to reduce such difficulties.
- Speak up when someone does something that is offensive to you. If you ignore the situation you send the message that you are in agreement with such behavior. For example, "I don't appreciate racial jokes; please don't tell me any more." "I'm uncomfortable when you touch me. Don't do it again or I will report you for sexual harassment." In Chapter 14 you will develop your conflict resolution skills.
- Be appreciative when others tell you of any offense you may have caused.
- Think before you speak and act. If there is any question about it being offensive, don't say or do it.
- Allow people to do things their own way. There is always more than one way to do a task.
- Trust others.

Don'ts

Some of the things you *should not* do, that will hurt human relations, include:

- Think or expect people to think, act, react, or behave the way that you do.
- Judge others' values, attitudes, or behavior to be wrong just because they are different from yours.
- Assume you have communicated just because there are no questions. You will learn effective communication skills in Chapter 10.
- Ignore differences when assigning work and making teams; benefit from diversity.
- Assume anyone is more suited for anything; give everyone the opportunity to do it.
- Think for, or speak for, others; let them represent themselves.
- Assume that a person's statement/behavior is the same as that of the others in that group.
- Call differences personality conflicts; resolve conflicts. In Chapter 14 you will develop your conflict-resolution skills.
- Minimize differences by focusing on similarities.
- Assume everyone has the same options in situations as you do.
- Take everything personally.
- Expect to be trusted without earning trust.

Figure 3–4
Human Relations Guidelines: Do's and Don'ts

most cases it is advisable to solve human relations problems rather than to ignore them. Problems usually get worse instead of solving themselves. When you decide to resolve a human relations problem, you have at least three alternatives:

1. Change the Other Person. Whenever a human relations problem occurs, it is easy to blame others and expect them to make the necessary changes in their behavior to meet our expectations. In reality, few human relations problems can be blamed entirely on one party. Both parties usually contribute to the problem. Blaming the other party without taking some responsibility usually results in resentment and defensive behavior. The more we force people to change to meet our expectations, the more difficult it is to maintain effective human relations.

Work Application

6. Select at least two do's and two don'ts you should focus on to improve your human relations. Explain why you selected these four as you list them.

2. Change the Situation. If you have a problem getting along with the person or people you work with, you can try to change the situation by working with another person or other people. You may tell your boss you cannot work with so and so because of a personality conflict and ask for a change in jobs. There are cases where this may be the only solution. However, when you complain to the boss, the boss often figures that you are the problem not the other party. Blaming the other party and trying to change the situation enables us to ignore our behavior, which may be the actual cause of the problem.

3. Change Yourself. Throughout this book, you will be examining your own behavior. In many situations, your own behavior is the only thing you can control. In most human relations problems, the best alternative is to examine the other party's behavior and to try to understand why he or she is doing and saying such things. Then examine your own behavior to determine why you are behaving the way you are. In most cases, the logical choice is to change your own behavior. This does not mean doing whatever other people request. In fact, you should be assertive. You are not being forced to change; rather, you are changing your behavior because you elect to do so. When you change your behavior the other party may also change. Human relations skills require being flexible.

GLOBAL DIVERSITY

U.S. managers using traditional American management styles often fail in an overseas business culture because managing diversity goes well beyond business etiquette. Companies need to train employees in language, local culture, and local business practices so they can be successful globally.[45] When conducting business with foreign firms, and more importantly in foreign countries, be aware of cultural differences. To have successful human relations, you must be flexible and adapt to other peoples' ways of behaving; you are the foreigner and cannot expect others to change for you.

In this section you will learn about diversity in customs, time, work ethics, pay, laws and politics, ethics, and participative management. Figure 3–5 lists global diversities. As you read, realize that you are presented with stereotypical generalities in which exceptions occur. The examples are not meant to judge "right" and "wrong" behavior. They are intended to illustrate cross-cultural differences that affect human relations.

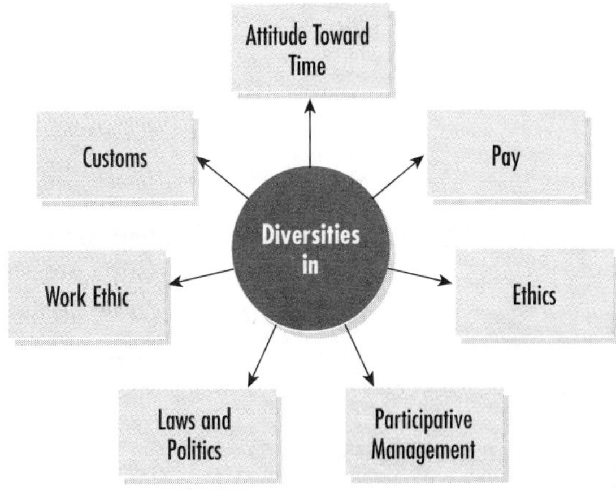

Figure 3–5
Global Diversities

Diversity in Customs. **Customs** *are the accepted way of conducting business.* The Japanese place a high priority on human relations, participative management, and teamwork.[46] If you try to be an individual star, you will not be successful in Japan. If you are very outspoken, you will be considered impolite in

customs
Accepted ways of conducting business.

Japan. If you refuse to be involved in receiving and giving gifts, you will offend Japanese people. Many Japanese companies start the day with exercises and company cheers. If you do not actively participate, you will be an outsider.

In Europe, management has more cultural than technical aspects. It deals with value systems and religious backgrounds and is organized more as a language than as a set of techniques.[47] Power and politics (Chapter 14) are important in the United States, but they are even more important in France. It is important for a French manager to be seen as holding great power. Teamwork is less important in France. An essential part of the French morning routine for many men is to kiss most of the women of equivalent class to themselves.[48] Unexpected kissing could create an embarrassing situation for you.

Americans prefer to speak face-to-face from a greater distance than people of most other countries. If you back away or turn to the side from others, they may follow you and create a dance, and you may be considered cold and standoffish. During face-to-face communications, Latinos tend to touch each other more than Americans. Jumping when unexpectedly touched could create an embarrassing situation.

Gestures vary from country to country. For example, Americans prefer eye contact. However, if you talk to young Puerto Ricans they will look down as a mark of respect when speaking to adults because eye contact is rude. In Australia making the "V" sign with the hand is considered an obscenity rather than a sign of victory. Former President Bush found this out after flashing the "V" sign to the Australian crowds in 1992.

Diversity in Attitudes Toward Time. Americans typically view time as a valuable resource that is not to be wasted, and socializing is often considered a waste of time. However, it would be considered impolite to start a business meeting with Hispanics without engaging in a certain amount of relaxed small talk. If you try to rush business deals without slowly developing personal relationships with Japanese managers, you will not be successful in obtaining Japanese business accounts.

American and Swiss businesspeople usually expect you to be precisely on time for an appointment. However, if you arrive on time for an appointment with a manager in other countries, you may be kept waiting for an hour. If you call a meeting in some countries, most members will be late and some may not show up at all. When they do show up they may express that punctuality was not one of their priorities. They may expect you to wait up to an hour for them. If you get angry and yell, you could harm human relations.

Diversity in Work Ethics. The work ethic—viewing work as a central interest and a desirable goal in life—varies all over the world. Generally, the Japanese have a higher work ethic than Americans and Europeans. With a high work ethic, and the acceptance of automation, many Japanese plants are the most productive in the world. Although there is not much difference in work ethic between Americans and Europeans, Americans are more productive even though Europeans are usually better trained than Americans.

Americans are relatively good at extracting value from poorly prepared workers, which is important when working with illiterate people all over the world. However, in some cultures, managers and employees have little interest in being productive. These relaxed attitudes do not do much for the bottom line of global businesses that are trying to change work ethics.

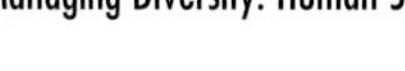

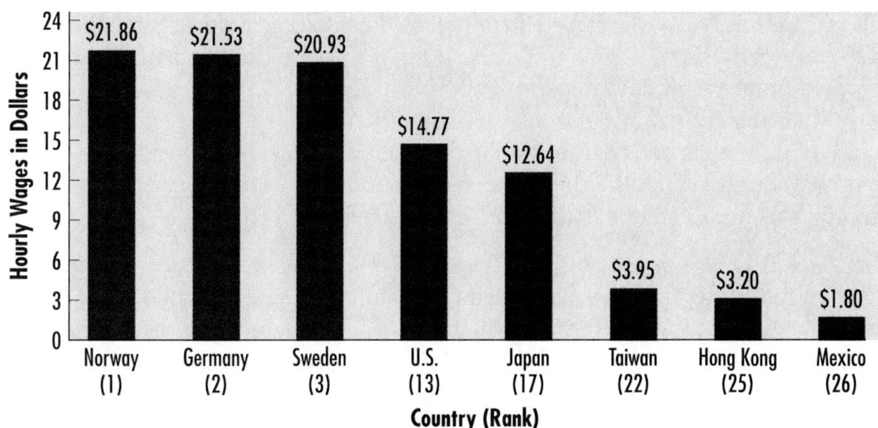

Figure 3–6

Diversity in Pay. Americans, in general, are no longer the world's highest paid employees. The Japanese and Europeans have caught up and earn as much as Americans. Focusing on only factory workers, according to the U.S. Department of Labor, 12 countries pay a higher hourly rate than Americans. Employees of Third-World countries are paid much less than employees in developed countries. Figure 3–6 shows hourly wages for a number of countries.

Pay systems also must vary in some countries to meet employee values. One of the trends in American pay has been pay for performance. However, some cultures value being paid for loyalty and following orders.[49] Paying a salary works well in some countries, but not in others.

Diversity in Laws and Politics. The legal and political environment becomes increasingly complex as the multinational company does business all over the world. Employee health and safety laws are generally more protective of employees in developed countries than in Third-World countries. Labor laws also vary widely from country to country. Western European nations offer good benefits, including a required four- to six-week vacation, paid holidays, and sick and family leave. When compared by countries, German auto employees work about 1,600 hours a year, Americans work 2,000 hours, and Japanese work 2,300 hours. Such differences change the actual labor cost per hour. It is also easier to terminate employees in some countries than in others.

In some countries, government structure and politics are much more stable than in others. A change in government can mean changes in business practices overnight. Some countries have literally taken away American business plants and equipment and sent the Americans home without any compensation.

Diversity in Ethics. When conducting global business you must rethink business ethics.[50] In the United States and other countries, it is illegal to take and give bribes for doing business. However, in many countries bribing is the standard practice of doing business. An American businessperson complained to a local telephone company manager that the service person showed up and asked for a bribe, which was refused, so the telephone worker left without installing the phone. The telephone company manager told the businessperson that the matter would be investigated, for a fee (bribe).

Diversity in Participative Management. In Third-World nations, employees need basic skills training and are not capable of participating in man-

Work Application

7. Give an example of when you, or someone you know, experienced one or more of the seven global diversity areas.

agement decisions without being trained to do so. Some cultures value participation in management whereas others are not interested. In some cultures employees simply want, and need, to be told what to do.

Management–labor relations vary globally. In France, management and labor are more polarized than in America, whereas in Japan they are more cooperative. You should realize that management and human relations become more complex as management styles change from country to country.

6. Describe how global diversity affects the implementation of the management functions.

Global Diversity and the Functions of Management. What works well in the United States does not necessarily work in other countries. To successfully manage globally, the international manager must plan, organize, lead, and control differently based on the characteristics of the culture of the country. It is fine to come up with a general set of principles, but global companies cannot try to detail everything. With restaurants in 73 countries, McDonald's employment practices and philosophies, in essence, are similar around the world. However, this does not mean that McDonald's implements these practices the same way from one country to the next. That is where cultural differences come into play. McDonald's managers must have good leadership styles. However, the characteristics of leadership may vary greatly from place to place. McDonald's does not say exactly how someone has to do something. To do so would be unfair and culturally inappropriate.[51] Digital is skilled at managing a diverse work force with operations in 72 countries and employees from 44 countries in one factory in Boston.

McDonald's opened its largest restaurant in Beijing, China, in 1992. It is a symbol of China's new affluence and openness to the outside world.

HANDLING COMPLAINTS

As a manager, you should strive to use the stakeholders' approach to ethics by creating a win-win situation for all stakeholders so that everyone benefits (Chapter 2) by your decisions. The traditional approach to management treated all employees the same, to ensure equality. Under the contemporary approach to diversity, employees are treated as individuals. For example, under traditional management all workers started and finished at the same time; there were no exceptions. Under diversity management, exceptions are made for good reasons such as starting a little earlier/later to accommodate child care needs or to attend a college class.

complaint
Occurs when an employee is not satisfied with a situation and seeks change.

Under the traditional, and probably more so under diversity, management, no matter how hard you try to do a good job and satisfy all employees' needs, complaints will arise. A **complaint** *occurs when an employee is not satisfied with a situation and seeks change*. Many employees complain at work but do not take the complaint to a manager who can resolve it. It is advisable to use an open-door policy that allows employees to feel free to come to you with a complaint. It is much better to get complaints out in the open and try to resolve them than to have employees complaining to everyone else about you. In this section you will learn how to handle complaints, and Skill-Building Exercise 2–1 will help you develop this skill.

The Complaint-Handling Model

7. List and explain the steps in the complaint-handling model.

When employees come to you with a complaint, try not to take it personally as a reflection on you or your management ability. Even the best managers have to deal with complaints. Do not become defensive and try to talk the employee out of the complaint. You can use the complaint-handling model to help you resolve complaints when employees come to you. *The* **complaint-handling model** *involves (1) listening to the complaint and paraphrasing it; (2) having the complainer recommend a solution; (3) scheduling time to get all the facts and/or make a decision; (4), developing a plan, and (5) implementing the plan and following up.* A discussion of each step follows.

complaint-handling model
(1) Listen to the complaint and paraphrase it. (2) Have the complainer recommend a solution. (3) Schedule time to get all the facts and/or make a decision. (4) Develop a plan. (5) Implement the plan and follow up.

step 1. **Listen to the Complaint and Paraphrase It.** This is a very important step. Listen to the full story without interruptions and paraphrase it (repeat it back to the complainer in your own words) to ensure accuracy. Listening and paraphrasing are necessary because if you cannot accurately state the complaint, you cannot resolve it. Paraphrasing is very important because employees often do not know how to state their complaint accurately. They often talk about one issue when something else is causing the problem. Your paraphrasing helps them see the difference and adjust accordingly. As the manager, it's your job to determine the true cause of the complaint.

When listening to the complaint, distinguish facts from opinions. There will be times when employees think they know the facts, when in reality they do not. For example, a more experienced employee may have heard that a less experienced worker earns the same wages. The experienced employee may complain. When the manager states the facts—that the experienced worker is paid more (it may be best not to state the specific amount)—the complaint may be dropped immediately.

It is also helpful to identify the person's feelings about the complaint and to determine the employee's motives for the complaint.

step 2. **Have the Complainer Recommend a Solution.** After you have paraphrased the complaint and the employee has agreed with the paraphrasing, you should ask the complainer to recommend a solution. The complainer may know a good solution you may not think of. Requesting a solution does not mean that you have to implement it. In some cases, the recommended solution may not solve the problem. Moreover, the solution may not be fair to others. Some recommendations may not be possible. In such cases, you should let the employee know that the solution is not possible and explain why.

step 3. **Schedule Time to Get All the Facts and/or Make a Decision.** Since employee complaints often involve other people, you may find it necessary to check records or to talk to others. It is often helpful to talk to your boss or your peers, who may have had a similar complaint; they may be

Model 3–1
The Complaint Model

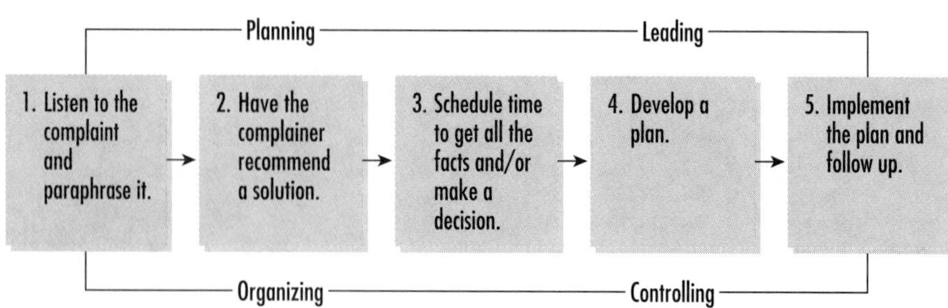

able to offer you some good advice on how best to resolve it. Even when you have all the facts, it is usually advisable to take some time to weigh them and make a decision.

Schedule a specific period of time. In many cases, it does not have to be long. Generally, the faster a complaint is resolved, the fewer the negative side effects. A poor management approach to complaints is to simply say, "I'll get back to you on this," without specifying a time period. This frustrates the employee. Some managers are purposely vague because they have no intention of getting back to the employee. They hope the employee will forget about the complaint or give it up. This tactic may get the employee to stop complaining, but it may also cause productivity and turnover problems.

Work Application

8. Identify a complaint you brought to a manager. State the complaint and identify which steps in the complaint-handling model the manager did or did not follow. If you have never complained, interview someone who has.

step 4.

Develop a Plan. After getting all the necessary facts and advice from others, you should develop a plan. The plan may be developed by simply using the complainer's recommended solution. However, when you do not agree with the complainer's solution, explain why, and either work with the employee to find an alternative or present your own plan. The level of the employee's participation in planning should be based on his or her capability level.

In cases where you decide not to take any action to resolve the complaint, you should clearly explain why you chose not to do so. State that if employees are not satisfied, they can appeal the decision to another level. The complainer should be told how to appeal the decision. In a nonunion organization, the usual step is to go to the manager's boss. In a union organization, the first step usually is to go to the union steward, who often accompanies the employee during the meeting with the supervisor.

step 5.

Implement the Plan and Follow Up. It is important to make sure that the plan is implemented through follow-up methods. It may be appropriate to set a follow-up meeting. It is also advisable to make a written documentation of all meetings and actions taken by you and others.

See Model 3–1 for a review of the five steps just discussed.

SKILLBUILDER

CURRENT MANAGEMENT ISSUES

In this chapter we discussed *diversity* and *globalization* and diversity. *Ethics* is an important concept as it relates to diversity. If you use ethical behavior, it will improve your human relations. If you use unethical behavior, for example, if you lie to people, you will not be trusted and you will not have good human relations.

When conducting business in diverse markets, having employees who represent people in these markets can help to improve the *quality* and customer value of these products. In addition, a diverse work force is more flexible and can change the quality of the products in all markets at a faster rate than a homogeneous work force. A diverse work force is also more *productive* than a homogeneous work force. With a diverse work force, employee costs are lower, which leads to higher productivity.

Teams with diverse members tend to make better decisions through *participative management*. With diversity you tend to get a better quality management team. And diversity is as important to *small business* as it is to large business.

CHAPTER SUMMARY AND GLOSSARY

This chapter summary is organized to answer the eight learning objectives for Chapter 3.

1. Explain the difference among prejudice, stereotypes, and discrimination.

Prejudices are the preconceived judgments of a person or situation. Stereotypes are positive or negative assessments or perceived attributes toward people or situations. Discrimination is unjust behavior for or against a person or situation. A major difference is that people tend to use prejudices and stereotypes, but they do not have to act on them with discriminatory behavior.

2. Describe how increased markets and lower employee costs are advantages of diversity.

Having diverse employees can provide information on potential customers and provide new product ideas to offer customer value that provides new business. A company that truly provides equal opportunity for a diverse work force will have lower costs for recruiting, retaining, and motivating employees than a company that does not.

3. Discuss the difference between valuing diversity and managing diversity.

Valuing diversity emphasizes training employees of different race and ethnicity, religions, genders, ages, and abilities as well as other differences to function effectively together, whereas managing diversity emphasizes fully utilizing human resources through organizational actions that meet all employees' needs. Managing diversity includes valuing diversity but goes beyond it by taking action to ensure that the work force is diverse.

4. List two important parts of diversity training.

The first part of diversity training makes people aware of the meaning and importance of valuing diversity. The second part makes it clear to all employees what it takes to get ahead in the organization.

5. Explain the relationship between the stakeholders' approach to ethics and to human skills.

With the stakeholders' approach you try to create a win-win situation so that all stakeholders benefit. With ethics the focus is on making ethical decisions, whereas with human relations the focus is on interacting with people.

6. Describe how global diversity affects the implementation of the management functions.

With global diversity, management practices that work well in one country may not work at all in another. Therefore, when performing the management functions of planning, organizing, leading, and controlling, the manager must do so based on the characteristics of the customs and culture of the country.

7. List and explain the steps in the complaint-handling model.

(1) Listen to the complaint and paraphrase it; listen then repeat the complaint back to the complainer in your own words. (2) Have the complainer recommend a solution; ask the complainer how he or she would resolve the complaint without guaranteeing you will use the suggestion. (3) Schedule time to get all the facts and/or make a decision; it is often necessary to talk to others for information and suggestions. (4) Develop a plan; specify the action that will resolve the complaint or state why no action will be taken to resolve it. (5) Implement the plan and follow up; be sure the action steps of the plan are followed and resolve the complaint.

8. Define the following key terms (in order of appearance in the chapter):

Select one or more methods: (1) fill in the missing key terms from memory, (2) match the key terms from the end of the review with their definitions below, or (3) copy the key terms in order from the list at the beginning of the chapter.

______ refers to the degree of differences among members of a group or organization.

______ is the belief that one's own group is superior to others.

______ are the preconceived judgments of a person or situation.

______ are positive or negative assessments toward or perceived attributes of people or situations.

______ is unjust behavior for or against a person or situation.

The ______ refers to the invisible barrier that prevents minorities and women from advancing beyond a certain level in organizations.

__________ is any unwelcome behavior of a sexual nature.

People with significant physical or mental impairment that substantially limits a major life activity are said to have a ______ .

__________ emphasizes training employees of different race and ethnicity, religions, genders, ages, and abilities as well as other differences to function effectively together.

__________ emphasizes fully utilizing human resources through organizational actions that meet all employees' needs.

______ are higher-level managers who prepare high-potential employees for advancement.

The ______________ is: "Treat others as you want them to treat you."

Under the ______________ , you try to create a win-win situation so that all parties benefit from your interactions with them.

______ are the accepted way of conducting business.

A ______ occurs when an employee is not satisfied with a situation and seeks change.

The __________ involves: (1) listening to the complaint and paraphrasing it; (2) having the complainer recommend a solution; (3) scheduling time to get all the facts and/or make a decision; (4) developing a plan, and (5) implementing the plan and following up.

KEY TERMS

complaint
complaint-handling model
customs
disability
discrimination
diversity
ethnocentrism
glass ceiling
golden rule of human relations
managing diversity
mentors
prejudices
sexual harassment
stakeholders' approach to human relations
stereotypes
valuing diversity

REVIEW AND DISCUSSION QUESTIONS

1. Do you believe that affirmative action quotas should be used in business today?
2. Do you agree that minorities, women, disadvantaged youth, the disabled, and people over 40 should be given legal protection against discrimination?
3. Turn to the section on diverse groups and what they want and find the statements about what people want that relate to you and your group. Do you want these things? Would you add or cut any of the statements?
4. Have you or anyone you know been sexually harassed? If so, describe the situations in language acceptable to everyone.
5. Have you ever worked with a person with a disability? If yes, what was the disability and how did you get along with this person? If you have a disability explain your work experience to the class.
6. Do you agree with the list of advantages and challenges of diversity? Would you add or cut any?
7. Do you know anyone who is or was a mentor or mentoree? If yes, explain the situation.
8. List the four management functions. Is any one of the functions more important in managing diversity?
9. What is your opinion of the golden rule of human relations and the stakeholders' approach to human relations?
10. Can you give other examples of global diversities?

CASE

A Diversity of Success

James G. Kaiser graduated from UCLA in 1968 and took a job as sales representative with Corning Inc. He worked his way up the ranks to senior vice president and general manager of Corning's technical products division and Latin America, Asia-Pacific Exports divisions. Kaiser runs a $200 million business unit that develops, produces, and sells 40,000 products and technologies. Kaiser believes his success results from his people-oriented approach to management in which he gives his subordinates the power to make their own decisions. Kaiser is committed to helping fellow African-Americans by making sure that they come along, that they are taught, and that the system works for them. He has done so by working directly with other African-Americans as understudies, by playing an instrumental role in Corning's cultural diversity initiative, and as president of the Executive Leadership Council, a national organization based in Washington, D.C. made up of 60 senior-level African-American managers that has helped hundreds of black executives develop their careers.

In 1976 **Julie Stasch** joined Stein & Company, a major real estate developer in Chicago. In 1991 she became president. Stasch was dissatisfied with the low number of women in high-paid, skilled construction jobs. Both contractors and unions claimed that they would love to have more women. But contractors don't hire women because the unions don't have any, and unions don't have any women because contractors don't want to hire them. So Stasch created the Female Employment Initiative (FEI) with ten influential women from contracting and non-profit groups in Chicago. As paid consultants by Stein & Company, committee members encourage women to seek skilled construction jobs, help train them, and work with employers to make job sites more women-friendly. As a result, 85 of the 500 tradespeople who built the 30-story Ralph H. Metcalfe Federal Building, 75 of the workers who built U.S. Gypsum's headquarters, and 200 of the workers who built the convention center and sports arena in Chicago were women.

Colonel **Harland Sanders** (1890–1980) started Kentucky Fried Chicken in 1952. But it wasn't until after he was forced to sell his restaurant because the interstate bypassed the place he'd been operating for 25 years that he really got started on franchising the business, at the age of 66. He traveled about a quarter of a million miles a year making sure the stores were run right, because his name was on them. He loved teaching the young folks and raising a little hell once in a while when things were not going exactly right at the stores. He called himself a one-man consumer protection agency.

Sanders worked hard to help get the Age Discrimination in Employment Act amended. The Colonel gave testimony before the U.S. Congressional Committee on Aging on May 25, 1977. He stated that he was dead against forced retirement at age 65. "Folks should be allowed to work as long as they want to and as long as they can do the job. We older folks have a lot to contribute." Sanders used examples of contributions by people after the age of 65. Benjamin Franklin was 70 years old when he was appointed to the committee that wrote the Declaration of Independence. When Franklin was 81 years old, he played a major role in getting it ratified. If Ben had been forced to retire, we might not have had a constitution or a country. Thomas Jefferson brought about the founding of the University of Virginia when he was 67. Thomas Edison kept inventing things long after his 65th birthday. George Marshall was 67 when he designed the European Recovery program, for which he received the Nobel Prize. The Colonel stated that these are dramatic examples, but that there are lots of folks like him who contribute in more common ways. Working was his hobby. He liked staying active and facing real business challenges.

PepsiCo, Inc., acquired KFC in 1986. Today, KFC has more than 9,500 restaurants around the world. KFC serves more than six billion customers each day, employs nearly 200,000 people, and has annual sales of more than $7 billion.

Select the best alternative to the following questions. Be sure you are able to explain your answers.

___ 1. Kaiser, Stasch, and Sanders have less focus on

a. equal employment opportunity
b. affirmative action
c. diversity

___ 2. Of the three groups, which one would you say had the most difficult stereotype to overcome?

a. African-Americans b. women c. elders

___ 3. Discrimination has been common for

a. African-Americans c. elders
b. women d. all three groups

___ 4. Julie Stasch developed FEI to break the glass ceiling.

a. true b. false

___ 5. Which major advantage of diversity is not relevant to Stasch and FEI?

a. ethical and social responsibility
b. increased market
c. lower employee cost
d. improved decision-making
e. better quality of management
f. flexibility

___ 6. For the three diverse groups in the case study, which one of the challenges would be the least relevant?

a. discrimination
b. mistrust and tension
c. lower cohesiveness
d. communication problems

___ 7. Kaiser, Stasch, and Sanders have more concern for

a. valuing diversity b. managing diversity

___ 8. Which person more clearly stated that he or she was a mentor?

a. Kaiser b. Stasch c. Sanders

___ 9. Which individual needs to be most personally concerned with global diversity?

a. Kaiser b. Stasch c. Sanders

___ 10. Which individual was most concerned with diversity in pay?

a. Kaiser b. Stasch c. Sanders

11. What can you learn from Kaiser, Stasch, and Sanders?

12. Which of the three people would you say has made the more important contribution?

For current information on KFC, use Internet address http://www.pepsi.com. For ideas on using the Internet, see the Appendix.

Behavior Model Video 3–1, Handling Complaints, has been made for Chapter 3. The video illustrates a manager, Cassandra, handling a complaint from Andrew about being passed over for promotion. Cassandra follows the steps described in the model on pages 91 and 92.

SKILL-BUILDING EXERCISE 3–1

Handling Complaints[52]

Preparing for Skill-Building Exercise 3–1

During class you will be given the opportunity to role-play handling a complaint. Select a complaint. It may be one you brought to a manager, one that was brought to you, one you heard about, or one you made up. Fill in the information below for the person who will role-play bringing you a complaint to resolve. Explain the situation and complaint. List pertinent information about the other party that will help him or her play the role of the complainer (relationship with manager, knowledge, years of service, background, age, values, etc.). Review Model 3–1 and think about what you will say and do when you handle this complaint.

____

____

____

____

____

____

____

COMPLAINT OBSERVER FORM

During the role-play, observe the handling of the complaint. Determine whether the manager followed the steps below during the exercise, and how well. Try to have a positive and an improvement comment for each step in the complaint model. Be specific and descriptive. For all improvement comments, have an alternative positive behavior (APB). What could have been done or said that was not?

Step 1. How well did the manager listen? Was the manager open to the complaint? Did the manager try to talk the employee out of the complaint? Was the manager defensive? Did the supervisor get the full story without interruptions? Did the manager paraphrase the complaint?

Positive: ____

____

Improvement: ____

____

Step 2. Did the manager have the complainer recommend a solution? How well did the supervisor react to the solution? If the solution could not be used, did the supervisor explain why?

Positive: ____

____

Improvement: ____

____

Step 3. Did the manager schedule time to get all the facts and/or make a decision? Was it a specific date? Was it a reasonable length of time?

Positive: ____

____

Improvement: ____

____

Step 4. Did the manager and employee develop a plan?

Positive: ____

____

Improvement: ____

____

Step 5. Implement the plan and follow up (This step will not be appropriate for the in-class exercise.)

Positive: ____

____

Improvement: ____

____

Doing Skill-Building Exercise 3–1 in Class

Objective
To experience and develop skills in resolving complaints.

Preparation
You should be prepared to handle a complaint.

Experience
You will initiate, respond to, and observe a complaint role-play. Then you will evaluate the effectiveness of its resolution.

Procedure 1 (2–3 minutes)
Break into as many groups of three as possible. If there are any people not in a triad, make one or two groups of two. Each member selects a number 1, 2, or 3. Number 1 will be the first to initiate a complaint role-play, then 2, followed by 3.

Procedure 2 (5–12 minutes)

A. Number 1 (the manager) tells Number 2 (the complainer) his or her complaint information from the preparation for this exercise. Once Number 2 understands, role-play (Procedure B). Number 3 is the observer.
B. Role-play the complaint. Put yourself in this person's situation, ad-lib. Number 3, the observer, writes his or her observations on the complaint observer form, found on the previous page.
C. Integration. When the role-play is over, the observer leads a discussion on the effectiveness of the conflict resolution. All three should discuss the effectiveness; Number 3 is not a lecturer. Do not go on until told to do so.

Procedure 3 (5–12 minutes)
Same as Procedure 2, only Number 2 is now the manager, Number 3 is now the complainer, and Number 1 is the observer.

Procedure 4 (5–12 minutes)
Same as Procedure 2, only Number 3 is the manager; Number 1 is the complainer; and Number 2 is the observer. Groups of two may join other groups as observers.

Conclusion
The instructor leads a class discussion and/or makes concluding remarks.

Application (2–4 minutes)
What did I learn from this experience? How will I use this knowledge in the future?

____

____

Sharing
Volunteers give their answers to the application section.

EXERCISE 3–1

Diversity Training

Preparing for Exercise 3–1

In preparation for this exercise, write out the answers to the following questions.

Race and Ethnicity

1. I am of ______ race and ethnicity(s).
2. My name is ______. It is significant because it means ______ and/or I was named after ______.
3. One positive thing about being a ______ is ______.
4. One difficult or embarrassing thing about being a ______ is ______.

Religion

1. I am of ______ religion.
2. One positive thing about being a ______ is ______.
3. One difficult or embarrassing thing about being a ______ is ______.

Gender

1. I am of ______ gender.
2. One positive thing about being a ______ is ______.
3. One difficult or embarrassing thing about being a ______ is ______.
4. Men and women are primarily different in ______ because ______.

Age

1. I am ______ years old.
2. One positive thing about this age is ______.
3. One difficult or embarrassing thing about being this age is ______.

Ability

1. I am of ______ (high, medium, low) ability in college and on the job. I do/don't have a disability.
2. One positive thing about being of ______ ability is ______.
3. One difficult or embarrassing thing about being of ______ ability is ______.

Other

1. The major other way(s) in which I'm different from other people is ______.
2. One positive thing about being different in this way is ______.
3. One difficult or embarrassing thing about being different in this way is ______.

Prejudice, Stereotypes, Discrimination

1. Identify how you have been prejudged, stereotyped, and discriminated against.

____

____

____

____

____

Doing Exercise 3–1 in Class

Objectives
To increase your understanding of the value of diversity and being different. The more you value diversity, the more effort you will place on developing good human relations with a diversity of people.

Preparation
You should have answered the preparation questions for this exercise.

Experience
You will share your answers to the preparation questions for this exercise.

Procedure 1 (2–3 minutes)
Break into groups of four to six with as much diversity as possible. The instructor will check the diversity levels and reassign people to groups to improve diversity, if necessary. Select a spokesperson to give the group's best one or two example answers to the prejudice, stereotype, discrimination question; it is not necessary to report on any other areas.

Procedure 2 (10–30 minutes)
The instructor sets a time limit and selects the topics in the preparation to be discussed. Start with areas of differences first, but be sure to allow time, about 5 minutes, to complete the prejudice, stereotype, discrimination question. If you finish the question to be reported before the time is up, go over other areas of differences that were not assigned by the instructor.

Procedure 3 (5–20 minutes)
The spokesperson from each group gives the one or two best examples of prejudice, stereotype, discrimination.

Conclusion
The instructor may lead a class discussion and/or make concluding remarks.

Application (2–4 minutes)
What did I learn from this experience? How will I use this knowledge in the future?

____

____

Sharing
Volunteers give their answers to the application section.

Creative Problem-Solving and Decision-Making Skills

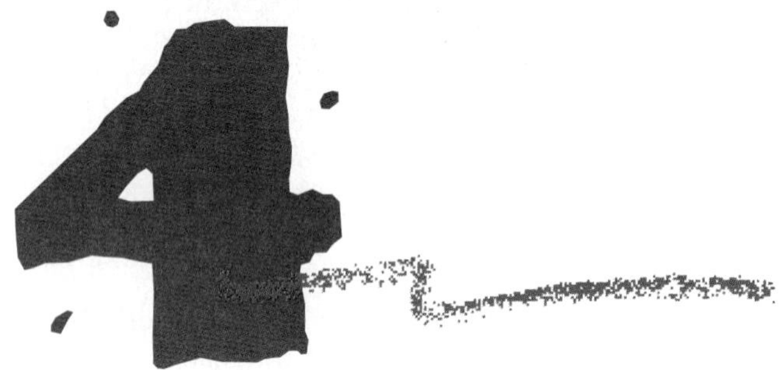

Learning Objectives

After studying this chapter, you should be able to:

1. Explain the relationship among objectives, problem-solving, and decision-making.
2. Explain the relationship among the management functions, decision-making, and problem-solving.
3. List the six steps in the decision-making model.
4. Describe the difference between programmed and nonprogrammed decisions and among the conditions of certainty, uncertainty, and risk.
5. Describe when to use the decision-making model versus the bounded rationality model and group versus individual decision-making.
6. State the difference between an objective and "must" and "want" criteria.
7. State the difference between creativity and innovation.
8. List and explain the three stages in the creative process.
9. Describe the difference among quantitative, Kepner-Tregoe, and cost-benefit analysis techniques for analyzing and selecting an alternative.
10. Define the following **key terms** (in order of appearance in the chapter)

    problem
    problem-solving
    decision-making
    decision-making model
    programmed decision
    nonprogrammed decision
    decision-making conditions
    criteria
    innovation
    creativity
    creative process
    devil's advocate
    brainstorming
    nominal grouping
    consensus mapping

Skill Development

1. You can develop your problem-solving and decision-making skills by learning to use the decision-making model (Skill-Building Exercise 4–1).

   This skill is part of conceptual and decision-making management skill. Decision-making is used when performing all four management functions and the five SCANS competencies. This skill is part of the decisional management role and SCANS thinking skills.

2. You can develop your skill at knowing which level of participation to use in a given decision-making situation (Skill-Building Exercise 4–2).

oca-Cola began as a five-cents-a-glass local pharmacy soda fountain drink on May 8, 1886, and has become the world's favorite soft drink. The Coca-Cola script has become the best known and most admired trademark in the history of commerce, recognized by nearly all of the world's population. The Coca-Cola Company is clearly in touch with the simple desire of people everywhere to pause, refresh, and enjoy. Satisfying this need is the core of Coca-Cola's global success—yesterday, today, and tomorrow.

The Coca-Cola Company is the world's largest producer and distributor of soft drink syrups and concentrates. Coca Cola sells products through bottlers, fountain wholesalers, and distributors in more than 195 countries around the globe. In 1994, company products represented approximately 46 percent of total flavored, carbonated soft drink unit case volume consumed worldwide. Also, Coca-Cola has become the world's largest marketer and distributor of juice and juice drink products (Minute Maid, Hi-C, Bright & Early, and Bacardi tropical fruit mixers). However, the company's soft drink products generate 89 percent of revenues and 97 percent of income.

The Coca-Cola Company is clearly in touch with the simple desire of people everywhere to pause, refresh, and enjoy.

Management's primary objective is to increase shareowner value over time, which it has done. If you bought one share of Coca-Cola stock (KO) in 1919 for $40, in 1994 it was worth around $135. If you had bought 800 shares, through stock splits you'd have 2,304 shares. Over the past five years, earnings per share from continuing operations grew at an average annual compound rate of 18 percent, and return on common equity increased from 39.4 to 52 percent. The major factor for growth has been worldwide expansion of sales. In fact, the U.S. and Canadian soft drink sales account for 32 percent of sales, while 68 percent are international. Led by Cuban born Roberto Goizueta, chairman of the board and CEO, the company's goal for the 1990s is to expand its global business system to reach increasing numbers of consumers.

The decision to go global started in Canada back at the turn of the 20th century; in 1906 bottling plants had been established in Cuba and Panama. However, in 1923, making Coca-Cola available around the world became an organized part of the business. This creative decision made Coca-Cola the world leader it is today. Along the way many problems needed to be solved and their solutions led to its present success. However, even Coca-Cola has made poor decisions, such as introducing New Coke. Coke has momentum because it continues to remain disciplined and focused no matter what the external environment might be.[1]

For current information on Coca-Cola, use Internet address http://www.cocacola.com. For ideas on using the Internet, see the Appendix.

PROBLEM-SOLVING AND DECISION-MAKING: AN OVERVIEW

The ability to solve problems in innovative ways is one of the top four qualities employers want.[2] One of the major reasons managers are hired is to solve problems and make decisions.[3] Making bad decisions can destroy careers and companies.[4] Some decisions affect the health, safety, and wellbeing of consumers, employees, and the community. Some writers state that a manager makes about 80 decisions daily, or one every 5 or 6 minutes, and others claim the total is in the hundreds.[5] No one can say for sure how many decisions you will make as a manager, but you should realize that your problem-solving and decision-making skills will affect your career success. As with all the management skills, problem-solving and decision-making can be developed.

This section will cover what a problem is and the relationship among objectives, problem-solving, and decision-making; the relationship among the management functions, decision-making, and problem-solving; the problem-solving and decision-making model; and your preferred decision-making style.

The Relationship among Objectives, Problem-Solving, and Decision-Making

1. Explain the relationship among objectives, problem-solving, and decision-making.

As a manager, you and your boss may set objectives together or your boss may simply assign objectives for you to achieve. When you do not meet your objectives, you have a problem. When you have a problem, you must make decisions. The better you can develop plans that prevent problems before they occur, the fewer problems you will have and the more time you will have to take advantage of opportunities. Seeking opportunities to continuously increase customer value requires the same consideration as solving existing problems.

A **problem** *exists whenever objectives are not being met.* In other words, you have a problem whenever a difference exists between what is actually happening and what you and your boss want to happen. If the objective is to produce 1,500 units per day, but the department produces only 1,490, a problem exists. Recall from Chapter 2 that the system causes 85 percent of the problems in organizations, not its people. **Problem-solving** *is the process of taking corrective action in order to meet objectives.* **Decision-making** *is the process of selecting an alternative course of action that will solve a problem.* Decisions must be made when you are faced with a problem. The first decision concerns whether or not to take corrective action.

problem
Occurs when objectives are not being met.

problem-solving
The process of taking corrective action in order to meet objectives.

decision-making
The process of selecting an alternative course of action that will solve a problem.

No constant link exists between problems and decision-making. Some problems cannot be solved, and others do not deserve the time and effort it would take to solve them. However, your job requires you to achieve organizational objectives. Therefore, you will have to attempt to solve most problems. Following the suggestions in this chapter can help you develop your problem-solving and decision-making skills.

Work Application

1. Give an example of when a job objective was not met. Identify the problem created and the decision made in regard to the objective not being met.

The Relationship among the Management Functions, Decision-Making, and Problem-Solving

2. Explain the relationship among the management functions, decision-making, and problem-solving.

All managers perform the same four functions: planning, organizing, leading, and controlling. While performing these functions, managers must make decisions. Recall (Chapter 2) that conceptual and decision-making skills are one of the three skills needed for success in management. In fact, making decisions precedes taking action. For example, when planning, managers must make decisions about objectives and when, where, and how they will be met. When organizing, managers must make decisions about what to delegate and how to coordinate the department's resources. When staffing, managers must decide who to hire and how to train and evaluate employees. To lead, managers must decide how to influence employees. To control, managers must select methods to ensure that they meet objectives. When managers perform management functions with skilled decision-making, they have fewer problems to solve.

Pepsi Cola wanted to create an opportunity by increasing customer value. Pepsi had an objective to increase its market share by getting Coca-Cola

Coca-Cola's loyal customers felt that the introduction of New Coke decreased customer value. The company agreed and reintroduced Coca-Cola Classic.

drinkers to switch to Pepsi. To do so, Pepsi successfully created the "Pepsi challenge." Pepsi advertised that people preferred Pepsi to Coke. Pepsi did not change its product to increase customer value. Instead, the company used advertising to give people the perception of a superior product, and the perception itself created customer value. Coca-Cola had a problem because it was losing sales to Pepsi Cola. To solve the problem, Coca-Cola made the decision to introduce New Coke. The New Coke decision caused additional problems with Coke's loyal customers who felt the decision decreased, rather than increased, customer value. Three months later, Coca-Cola admitted the poor decision and made the decision to reintroduce Coca-Cola Classic. We'll discuss the New Coke decision in more detail as we cover the steps in the decision-making model.

You should realize that if you don't achieve organizational objectives, you will have problems that require decision-making. If you make poor decisions or if you do not perform the management functions proficiently, you will create problems for yourself. Throughout this book you will develop management function skills, and in this chapter you will develop problem-solving and decision-making skills.

Work Application

2. Give a job example of when a manager was performing a management function and made a poor decision. Explain the management function and the problem created by the poor decision.

The Decision-Making Model

3. List the six steps in the decision-making model.

decision-making model
The steps are (1) classifying and defining the problem or opportunity, (2) setting objectives and criteria, (3) generating creative and innovative alternatives, (4) analyzing alternatives and selecting the most feasible, (5) planning and implementing the decision, and (6) controlling.

The **decision-making model** *steps are (1) classifying and defining the problem or opportunity, (2) setting objectives and criteria, (3) generating creative and innovative alternatives, (4) analyzing alternatives and selecting the most feasible, (5) planning and implementing the decision, and (6) controlling.* Model 4–1 lists these steps. Notice that the steps do not simply go from start to finish. At any step you may have to return to a prior step to make changes. For example, if you are in the sixth step, controlling, and the implementation is not going as planned (step 5), you may have to backtrack to prior steps to take corrective action by generating and selecting a new alternative or changing the objective. If you have not defined the problem accurately, you may have to go back to the beginning.

Following the steps in the model will not guarantee that you make good decisions. However, using the model will increase your chances of success in problem-solving and decision-making. Consciously use the model in your daily life, and you will improve your ability to make decisions. The remainder of this chapter provides the details of the model so that you can develop your creative problem-solving and decision-making skills. But before you do so, learn your preferred decision-making style in Self-Assessment Exercise 4–1.

SELF-ASSESSMENT EXERCISE 4–1

Decision-Making Styles

Individuals differ in the way they approach decisions. To determine if your decision-making style is reflexive, reflective, or consistent, answer the eight questions by selecting the choice that best describes how you make decisions. Place a number 1–5 on the line before each question.

This behavior is common for me. This behavior is not common for me.
1————2————3————4————5

___ 1. Overall, I make decisions quickly.
___ 2. When making decisions, I go with my first thought or hunch.
___ 3. When making decisions, I don't bother to recheck my work.
___ 4. When making decisions, I gather little or no information.
___ 5. When making decisions, I consider very few alternative options.
___ 6. When making a decision, I usually make it well before the deadline.
___ 7. When making a decision, I don't ask others for advice.
___ 8. After making a decision, I don't look for other alternatives or wish I had waited longer.
___ Total score

To determine your style, add up the numbers 1 through 5 that represent your answers. The total will be between 8 and 40. Place an X on the continuum line below that represents your score.

Reflexive Consistent Reflective
8————20————30————40

Following is an explanation of each style. A group also has a preferred decision-making style, based on how its members make decisions. You could answer the eight questions by changing the "I" to "we" and referring to a group rather than to yourself.

Reflexive Style. A reflexive decision-maker likes to make quick decisions (shooting from the hip) without taking the time to get all the information that may be needed and without considering all alternatives. On the positive side, reflexive decision-makers are decisive; they do not procrastinate. On the negative side, making quick decisions can lead to waste and duplication when the best possible alternative is overlooked. Employees view a reflexive decision-maker as a poor manager if the manager consistently makes bad decisions. If you use a reflexive style for important decisions, you may want to slow down and spend more time gathering information and analyzing alternatives.

Reflective Style. A reflective decision-maker likes to take plenty of time to make decisions, gathering considerable information and analyzing several alternatives. On the positive side, the reflective type does not make hasty decisions. On the negative side, the reflective type may procrastinate and waste valuable time and other resources. The reflective decision-maker may be viewed as wishy-washy and indecisive. If you use a reflective style, you may want to speed up your decision-making. As Andrew Jackson once said, "Take time to deliberate; but when the time for action arrives, stop thinking and go on."

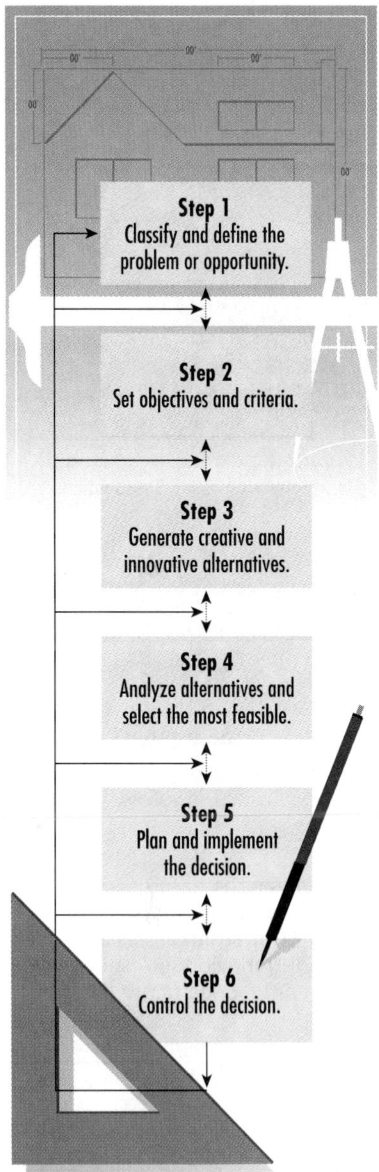
Step 1
Classify and define the problem or opportunity.
Step 2
Set objectives and criteria.
Step 3
Generate creative and innovative alternatives.
Step 4
Analyze alternatives and select the most feasible.
Step 5
Plan and implement the decision.
Step 6
Control the decision.

Model 4–1
The Decision-Making Model

Consistent Style. Consistent decision-makers tend to make decisions without rushing or wasting time. They know when they have enough information and alternatives to make a sound decision. Consistent decision-makers tend to have the best record for making good decisions. They tend to follow the decision-making steps in Model 4–1 when appropriate. The next section will teach you when to make quick decisions without the model and when to take your time and use the model.

APPLYING THE CONCEPT

AC 4–1 Steps in Decision-Making

Identify the step in the decision-making model that each statement represents.

a. Step 1 b. Step 2 c. Step 3 d. Step 4 e. Step 5 f. Step 6

____ **1.** "We will use the brainstorming technique to solve the problem."

____ **2.** "Betty, is the machine still jumping out of sequence, or has it stopped?"

____ **3.** "I don't understand what we are trying to accomplish."

____ **4.** "What symptoms have you observed to indicate that a problem even exists?"

____ **5.** "Linear programming should be used to help us in this situation."

CLASSIFY AND DEFINE THE PROBLEM OR OPPORTUNITY

The first step in the decision-making model requires defining the problem or opportunity. In this section you will learn how to classify the problem, select the appropriate level of participation, and determine the cause of problems.

4. Describe the difference between programmed and nonprogrammed decisions and among the conditions of certainty, uncertainty, and risk.

Classify the Problem

Problems may be classified in terms of the decision structure involved, the conditions under which a decision will be made, and the decision-making model used.

programmed decisions
With recurring or routine situations, the decision-maker should use decision rules or organizational policies and procedures to make the decision.

nonprogrammed decisions
With significant and nonrecurring and nonroutine situations, the decision-maker should use the decision-making model.

Decision Structure. *With* **programmed decisions,** *recurring or routine situations, the decision-maker should use decision rules or organizational policies and procedures to make the decision.* For example, a specified amount of inventory will be reordered every time stock reaches a specified level. *With* **nonprogrammed decisions,** *significant and nonrecurring and nonroutine situations, the decision-maker should use the decision-making model.* To be significant, a decision must be expensive (purchasing major assets) and/or have major consequences (new product or reduction of employees) for the department or organization. Nonprogrammed decisions take longer to make than programmed decisions.

You must be able to differentiate between the two types of decision structures[6] because they provide a guideline as to how much time and effort you should spend to make effective decisions. Coca-Cola made a nonprogrammed decision when it developed New Coke. Upper-level managers tend to make more of the nonprogrammed decisions than lower-level managers, who make more programmed decisions.

decision-making conditions
Certainty, risk, and uncertainty.

Decision-Making Conditions. The three **decision-making conditions** *are certainty, risk, and uncertainty.* When making a decision under the conditions of *certainty*, the manager knows the outcome of each alternative in advance. When making a decision under conditions of *risk*, the manager does not know the outcome of each alternative in advance, but can assign probabilities to each outcome. Under conditions of *uncertainty*, lack of information or knowledge makes the outcome of each alternative unpredictable so the manager cannot determine probabilities.

Nonprogrammed Decision
(Significant and nonrecurring and nonroutine)
(Longer period of time to make decisions)

Programmed Decision
(Nonsignificant, recurring, and routine)
(Shorter period of time to make decisions)

Figure 4–1
Decision Structure Continuum

As an example, suppose you were considering making an investment. If you were considering bonds, money market accounts, and certificates of deposit, you would know the payoff of each of the alternatives and would make a decision with *certainty* as to the interest paid. If you consider well-established stocks like Coca-Cola, Mobil Oil, and GM, through research you could assign probabilities of each stock going up (such as 40%, 35%, and 25%) and you would know the dividend paid. However, if you considered investing in two new companies with new innovative products, you could not be sure of the return, nor could you assign probabilities to them. When Coca-Cola introduced New Coke, it incurred a *risk*. If the company had been certain of the outcome of the decision, it would not have made it. It was a condition of risk because the company had conducted research with over 190,000 consumers through taste tests. The overwhelming majority preferred the taste of New Coke over Coca-Cola.

Work Application

3. Give an example of a programmed and a nonprogrammed decision and their decision conditions from an organization you work or have worked for.

Management makes most decisions under conditions of risk. However, upper-level managers tend to make more uncertain decisions than lower-level managers. When making decisions under uncertainty, it is difficult to determine the needed resources to solve the problem or create an opportunity.[7] Although risk and uncertainty cannot be eliminated, they can be reduced. Figure 4–2 illustrates the decision-making conditions continuum.

5. Describe when to use the decision-making model versus the bounded rationality model and group versus individual decision-making.

Decision-Making Model. There are two primary decision models: the rational model and the bounded rationality model. With the *rational model*, the decision-maker attempts to use *optimizing*, selecting the best possible alternative. With the *bounded rationality model*, the decision-maker uses *satisficing*, selecting the first alternative that meets the minimal criteria. The decision-making model presented as Model 4–1 is the rational model. With satisficing, only parts, or none, of the model would be used.

Figure 4–2
Decision-Making Conditions Continuum

You need to remember which model to use and when. The more unstructured the decision and the higher the degree of risk and uncertainty, the greater the need to spend the time conducting research with the aid of the decision-making model. Optimize (select the best possible alternative) when you are making nonprogrammed high-risk or uncertain decisions. Satisfice (select the first alternative that meets the minimum criteria) when you are making programmed low-risk or certain decisions. Figure 4–4 on page 110 illustrates which model to use when, with other factors.

Select the Appropriate Level of Participation

When a problem exists, the manager must decide who should participate in solving it.[8] As a rule of thumb, only the key people involved with the problem should participate. However, the current trend in management favors increased employee participation. Thus, the major question is not whether managers should allow employees to participate in problem-solving and decision-making, but when and how this should be done. When solving problems and making decisions, you should use the management style appropriate to the situation (autocratic, consultative, participative, or empowerment). You learned about situational management in Chapter 1 (Skill-Building Exercise 1–1). In Skill-Building Exercise 4–2 the situational management model is expanded to cover decision-making. For now, you will learn about two levels of participation: individual and group decision-making. However, realize that even though the trend is toward group decision-making, some people want to be involved in group decision-making while others do not.

Figure 4–3 lists the potential advantages and disadvantages of using groups to make decisions. The key to success when using groups is to maximize the advantages while minimizing the potential disadvantages.

APPLYING THE CONCEPTS

AC 4–2 Classify the Problem

Classify the five problems according to the structure and condition under which the decision is being made.

a. programmed, certainty
b. programmed, uncertainty
c. programmed, risk
d. nonprogrammed, certainty
e. nonprogrammed, uncertainty
f. nonprogrammed, risk

____ **6.** "When I graduate from college I will buy an existing business rather than working for someone else."

____ **7.** Sondra, a small business owner, has had a turnaround in business; it's now profitable. She wants to keep the excess cash liquid so that she can get it quickly if she needs it. How should she invest it?

____ **8.** A purchasing agent must select new cars for the business. This is the sixth time in six years he has made this decision.

____ **9.** In the early 1970s, investors had to decide whether to start the World Football League.

____ **10.** A manager in a department with high turnover must hire a new employee.

Potential Advantages of Group Problem-Solving and Decision-Making. When group members have something to contribute, five potential advantages accrue:

1. *Better-quality decisions*. The old saying, "two heads are better than one," is generally true. Groups usually do a better job of solving complex problems than the best individual in the group. Using groups to solve problems and make decisions is appropriate for significant nonprogrammed decisions made under conditions of risk or uncertainty.

Figure 4–3
Potential Advantages and Disadvantages of Using Group Decision-Making

Potential Advantages	Potential Disadvantages
1. Better-quality decisions	1. Wasted time and slower decision-making
2. More information, alternatives, creativity, and innovation	2. Satisficing
3. Better understanding of the decision	3. Domination and goal displacement
4. Greater commitment to the decision	4. Conformity and groupthink
5. Improved morale and motivation	
6. Good training	

2. *More information, alternatives, creativity, and innovation.* A group of people usually has more information than an individual. A diverse group offers different points of view and a variety of alternative solutions. Creative or innovative ideas (or products) often do not come from the work of one person, but from the combined input of members building on each others' ideas.

3. *Better understanding of the decision.* When people participate in decision-making, they usually understand the alternatives presented and why the one selected was the best alternative. This allows easier implementation of the decision.

4. *Greater commitment to the decision.* Researchers have shown that people involved in making a decision increase their commitment to make implementation of the decision a success.

5. *Improved morale and motivation.* Participation in problem-solving and decision-making is rewarding and personally satisfying to the people involved. People who can say "I was a part of making and implementing that decision" have higher levels of morale and motivation than people who cannot.

6. *Good training.* Group participation allows employees to better understand problems faced by the organization. With the trend toward using groups, allowing participation in decision-making trains people to work in groups by developing group process skills.

Potential Disadvantages of Group Problem-Solving and Decision-Making. Groups need to be careful to avoid the following disadvantages:

1. *Wasted time and slower decision-making.* It takes longer for a group to make a decision. Employees involved in problem-solving and decision-making are not on the job producing. Thus, group involvement costs the organization time and money. When the group's decision is of higher quality than the best individual's decision, time is usually not wasted by using the group. In addition, meetings must be conducted effectively to ensure they don't waste time. You will find out how to conduct meetings in Chapter 13. For programmed decisions of certainty or low risk, individual decision-making would generally be more cost effective than group decision-making.

2. *Satisficing.* Groups more likely will satisfice than an individual, especially when group meetings are not run effectively. Members may take the attitude, "Let's get it over with and get out of here." Part of the reason groups satisfice more than individuals is responsibility. When one person is responsible, that person stands out if a good or poor decision is made. But, with a group usually no one person gets the blame or credit for the decision, so attendance and commitment are often lower.

3. *Domination and goal displacement.* One group member, or subgroup, may dominate and nullify the group decision. Subgroups of individuals may develop and destructive conflict may result. *Goal displacement* occurs when an individual or subgroup tries to get its own decision accepted, dominates for personal reasons, rather than meeting the original goal of finding the best solution.

4. *Conformity and groupthink.* Group members may feel pressured to go along with the group's decision without questioning it out of fear of not being accepted or not wanting to cause conflict. Groupthink occurs when members withhold different views in order to appear in agreement. This nullifies the ad-

Work Application

4. Give an example of a group and individual decision made in an organization you work or have worked for. For the group decision, identify the potential advantages and disadvantages encountered by the group.

vantage of diversity. Conformity is especially problematic in highly cohesive groups because members want to get along. Conformity is less problematic in groups that value diversity because group members seek differences.

In general, when you have a significant nonprogrammed decision with high risk or uncertainty, use group decision-making. When you have a programmed decision with low risk or certainty, use individual decision-making. Exercise 4–1, Individual versus Group Decision-Making, gives you the opportunity to compare the same decision under both approaches.

One individual did not simply make the New Coke decision. However, Coca-Cola may not have utilized the advantages and may have suffered from some of the disadvantages of group decision-making.

To be successful at decision-making, you need to identify the type of problem to be solved, and the level of participation to use. In Skill-Building Exercise 4–2, Situational Management: Decision-Making, you will develop this skill. Figure 4–4 puts together the concepts from this section to help you better understand how to classify problems. However, this is a general guide; there may be exceptions to the rule.

Relationship among:
Decision-Making Structure

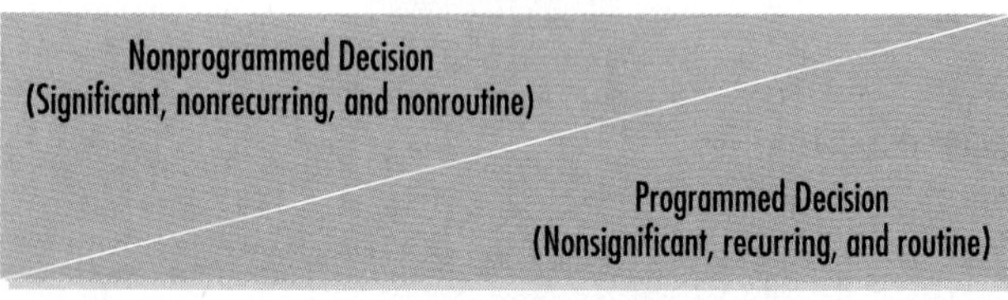

Decision-Making Conditions

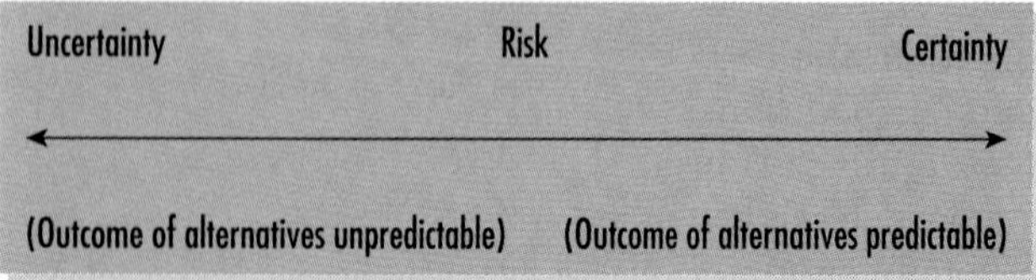

Which Decision Model to Use

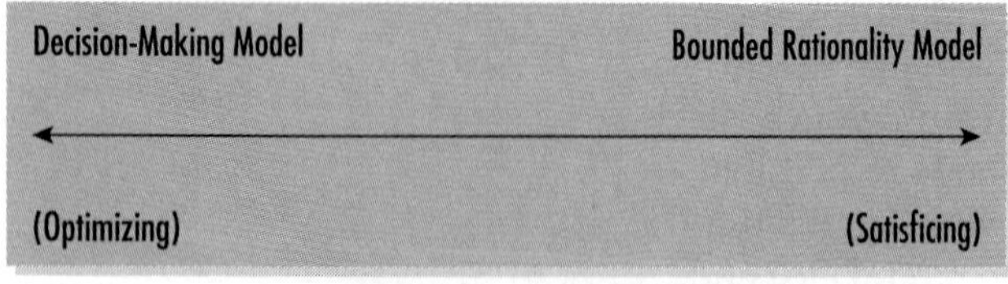

When to Use Group or Individual Decision-Making

Figure 4–4
Classifying the Problem or Opportunity Continuums

Define the Problem or Opportunity

After you have classified the problem or opportunity, you or the group must clearly define it accurately. Defining the problem accurately requires conceptual skills.

Due to job time pressures, especially in downsized organizations, managers must often hurry to solve problems and make decisions. In a hurry, they may neglect the first step in problem-solving. Rushing to solve a problem that is not correctly defined often leads to a decision that does not solve the problem—haste makes waste. An important part of defining the problem is to distinguish symptoms from the cause of the problem.

Distinguish Symptoms from the Cause of the Problem. To do this, list the observable and describable occurrences (symptoms) that indicate a problem exists. Once you do this, you must determine the cause of the problem. If you eliminate the cause, the symptoms should disappear. For example, Sam, an employee with six years on the job, has been an excellent producer. However, in the last month, Sam has been out sick or late more times than he was in the past two years. What is the problem? If you say "absenteeism" or "lateness," you are confusing symptoms and causes. They are symptoms of the problem, but don't tell you why the problem has occurred. If you don't eliminate the original and subsequent causes, problem symptoms will reappear.

At Coca-Cola the symptom of the problem was lost market share to Pepsi. Coca-Cola defined the cause of the problem to be the taste of the product. Pepsi is sweeter than Coke. On the opportunity side, Pepsi defined an opportunity in marketing its Crystal Pepsi product. However, under this nonprogrammed decision of risk, Crystal was not a success.

Microsoft made the decision to seek opportunity by gaining control over software and operating systems (the core of the PC—MS-DOS and Windows). One of the greatest mysteries remains how IBM, the world's largest computer maker that practically created the PC market, miscalculated the opportunity for software and operating systems and allowed Microsoft to take control. In missing the early opportunity, IBM created later problems of growth. Microsoft is now a larger company than IBM. In an attempt to create opportunities, IBM has had more failure than success with software and its operating system OS/2, which cost $2 billion. Unable to be successful on its own, in June 1995, IBM offered to buy Lotus Development Corporation for $3.3 billion.[9] Lotus agreed to be acquired by IBM for $3.52 billion.[10] Only time will tell if IBM will ever create opportunities in these areas.

Remember that, as a decision-maker, you must define the problem correctly in order to solve it. When making significant nonprogrammed decisions of high risk or uncertainty, you need to take your time and clearly distinguish symptoms from causes of the problem.

Work Application

5. Define a problem from an organization you work or have worked for. Be sure to clearly distinguish the symptoms from the causes of the problem.

SET OBJECTIVES AND CRITERIA

6. State the difference between an objective and "must" and "want" criteria.

Generally, with programmed decisions, the objective and criteria have been set. Therefore, you need not follow steps 2–4 of the decision-making model. However, with nonprogrammed decisions you should follow all the steps in the decision-making model. Therefore, the second step for the individual or group to follow in the model requires setting objectives and developing criteria.

Setting objectives helps managers to make better decisions.[11] Groups take longer than individuals to set objectives and criteria, but groups that set their own objectives perform better than those that do not.[12] Having multiple criteria helps to optimize the decision.[13]

Set Objectives. The objective must state what the decision should accomplish. It can be to solve a problem or to take advantage of an opportunity.

Set Criteria. You should also specify the criteria for achieving the objective. **Criteria** *are the standards that an alternative must meet to be selected as the decision that will accomplish the objective*. You should distinguish "must" and "want" criteria. "Must" criteria have to be met in order for the alternative to be acceptable, whereas "want" criteria are desirable but not necessary for the alternative to be acceptable. With satisficing, you stop with the first acceptable alternative; with optimizing, you seek to select the best possible option.

criteria
The standards that an alternative must meet to be selected as the decision that will accomplish the objective.

An example of an objective and criteria for hiring a manager might be as follows. The problem is that a store manager has quit, and a new manager must be hired. The objective is to hire a store manager by June 30, 19XX. The required "must" criteria include a college degree and a minimum of five years' experience as a store manager. The preferred "want" criterion is that the person should be a minority-group member. The hiring manager wants to hire a minority employee but will not hire one who does not meet the "must" criteria. In addition, if a significantly more qualified white person applies for the job, he or she will be offered the job. In this situation you would optimize the decision rather than satisfice. We will discuss criteria again later in this chapter.

Work Application

6. Identify some of the qualification criteria (college degree, years of experience, etc.) for jobs at an organization you work or have worked for. Distinguish any "must" and "want" criteria.

At Coca-Cola, the objective was to gain back customers who had switched to Pepsi. The exact criteria needed to accomplish this objective are not available.

It will take time and effort to develop objectives and criteria for decisions, but doing so will result in better decisions.

GENERATE CREATIVE ALTERNATIVES

After the problem is defined and objectives and criteria are set, the decision-maker may generate possible alternatives (step 3 of the decision-making model) for solving the problem or creating the opportunity. Usually many possible ways exist to solve a problem; in fact, if you don't have two or more alternatives, you don't have to make a decision. Toyota has a set-based concurrent engineering method by which the company thinks about sets of design alternatives for prototype car models, rather than pursuing one design.[14]

With programmed decision-making, the alternative is usually predetermined. However, with nonprogrammed decision-making, more time and effort are needed to come up with new creative and innovative ideas. In this section you will find out about innovation and creativity, using information and technology to generate alternatives, and group methods for generating creative alternatives.

7. State the difference between creativity and innovation.

Innovation and Creativity

innovation
The implementation of a new idea.

Innovation. An **innovation** *is the implementation of a new idea.* Two important types of innovations are product innovation (new things) and process innovation (new ways of doing things). *Product innovations* are changes in outputs (goods or service) to increase consumer value, or new outputs. *Process innovations* are changes in the transformation of inputs into outputs. Coca-Cola introduced New Coke, Diet Coke, and other products, and has been working on its processes to cut cost. The success of innovative products comes from knowing the customer and making every sale result in a satisfied customer.[15] Managers can raise the level of innovation in their organizations by encouraging employees to develop skills in generating multiple alternatives to solve problems and create opportunities.[16]

creativity
A way of thinking that generates new ideas.

Creativity. **Creativity** *is a way of thinking that generates new ideas.* Adelphi University provides an example of a creative solution that became an innovation. The university wanted to expand its graduate business program. However, many potential students felt that they did not have the time to further their education. The alternative that Adelphi developed was the "classroom on wheels," which offers classes four days a week on commuter trains into and out of New York City. Some creative ideas are never converted successfully into products or processes. RJR Tobacco had a creative idea to sell smokeless cigarettes under the name Premier. RJR test marketed Premier in limited areas, but pulled the product from the market with an estimated loss of more than $300 million.[17]

8. List and explain the three stages in the creative process.

creative process
The three stages are (1) preparation, (2) incubation and illumination, and (3) evaluation.

The Creative Process. No definite relationship exists between intelligence and creativity; everyone has creative capability. *The three stages in the* **creative process** *are (1) preparation, (2) incubation and illumination, and (3) evalua-*

tion. Following these guidelines, summarized in Figure 4–5, can help you improve your creativity. As with the decision-making model, you may have to return to prior stages.

1. *Preparation*. The manager must become familiar with the problem by getting others' opinions, feelings, and ideas, as well as the facts. When solving a problem or seeking opportunities, look for new angles, use imagination and invention, and don't limit yourself to the boundaries of past thinking. Generate as many possible solutions as you can think of without making a judgment.

2. *Incubation and illumination*. After generating alternatives, take a break; sleep on the problem. Take some time before working on the problem again. During the incubation stage, you may gain an insight into the solution as your subconscious works on the problem—illumination. Have you ever worked hard on something and become discouraged but found that when you gave up or took a break, the illumination solution came to you? Illumination can also happen while working on the problem or during incubation. Illumination is sometimes referred to as the "Ah ha, now I got it" phenomenon.

3. *Evaluation*. Before implementing a solution, you should evaluate the alternative to make sure the idea is practical. A good approach to use when evaluating a decision, not before, is the devil's advocate. *With the* **devil's advocate** *approach, group members focus on defending the solution while others try to come up with reasons the solution will not work*. Devil's advocate evaluation usually leads to more creativity as the idea is improved upon.

Organizations encourage creativity; therefore, companies like Pitney Bowes are training employees to develop their problem-solving and decision-making skills.[18] Fuji, Omron, Shimizu, and Shiseldo, for example, have developed training programs that emphasize creativity.

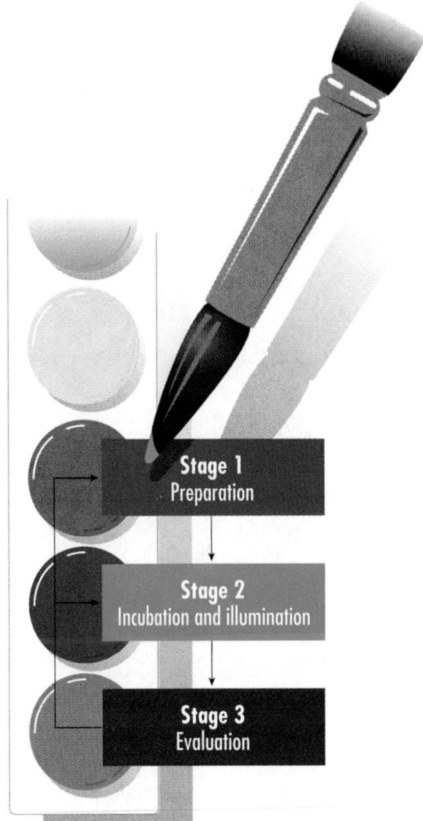

Figure 4–5
Stages in the Creative Process

devil's advocate
Group members focus on defending the solution while others try to come up with reasons the solution will not work.

Using Information and Technology to Generate Alternatives

Coca-Cola CEO Gonizueta has described the ideal managers of the 21st century as internationalists with multilingual, multicultural capabilities who use facts, information, and knowledge to make decisions. Decisions should be based on solid information rather than intuition.[19] However, when generating alternatives the question comes up, "How much information, and alternatives, do I need and where should I get it?" There is no simple answer. The more important the decision, generally, the more information and alternatives you need. To optimize, you select the best possible alternative. However, if you get too much information, the decision becomes too complex, and the optimal alternative may not be selected.[20]

Useful information has four characteristics: (1) timeliness, (2) quality, (3) completeness, and (4) relevance, which Figure 4–6 illustrates. *Timeliness* refers to whether or not you can get the information in time to make a decision. *Quality* refers to the accuracy of the information. People can be easily misled by false information, especially when it comes from group members.[21] When members are closed-minded to selecting more than one alternative, they may give false information to get the decision they want, or they may withhold informa-

Work Application

7. Give an example of how you, or someone else, solved a problem using the stages in the creative process. Be sure to list the steps and whether illumination came during incubation or while working on the problem.

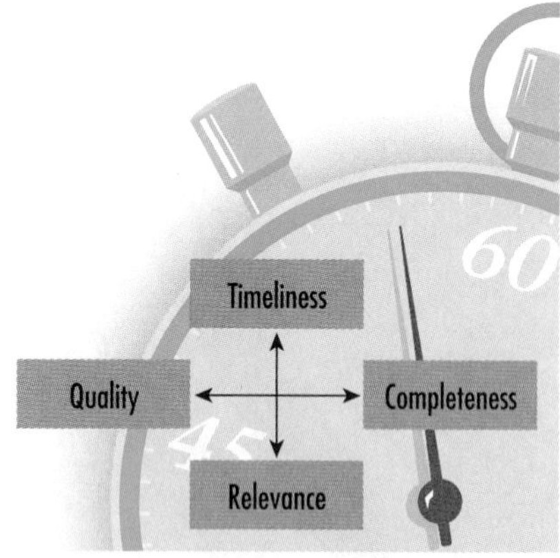

Figure 4–6
Characteristics of Useful Information

tion,[22] which is part of completeness. *Completeness* refers to amount of data collected. *Relevance* refers to how closely and how importantly the information pertains or relates to the decision objectives. Good criteria will help you to select and eliminate information and alternatives.

Technology, especially telecommunications and computers, has shown considerable potential for problem-solving and decision-making.[23] One study revealed that using computer idea-generating software does help individuals develop alternative solutions more creatively.[24] Teleconferencing enables people from all over the world to have a group meeting without getting together. You will learn more about information in Chapter 17.

Using Groups to Generate Creative Alternatives

A group usually generates and analyzes alternatives when it has the greatest potential difficulties of satisficing, dominance, and groupthink, especially with established work groups. To avoid these difficulties, you need to be careful that the group does not just list a limited number of alternatives and quickly move to accept one.[25]

When the problem has been classified as one a group should solve, a variety of methods are available using group participation to generate creative alternative solutions. A discussion of five of the more popular techniques, which Figure 4–7 illustrates, follows.

brainstorming
The process of suggesting possible alternatives without evaluation.

Brainstorming. **Brainstorming** *is the process of suggesting many possible alternatives without evaluation.* The group is presented with a problem and asked to develop as many solutions as possible. Members should be encouraged to make wild, extreme suggestions. They should also build on suggestions made by others. However, members should not react in any way, favorably or unfavorably, to any of the members' contributions, including their own. When selecting

Teleconferencing enables people from all over the world to have a group meeting without getting together.

members for a brainstorming group, try to include a diversity of people; 5 to 12 people make up a good-sized group.[26] Status differences should be ignored. Everyone should have an equal voice.[27] None of the alternatives should be evaluated until all possible alternatives have been presented. Brainstorming is commonly used and companies are training employees to use it[28] for problems requiring creative ideas such as solving problems and naming a new product or service.

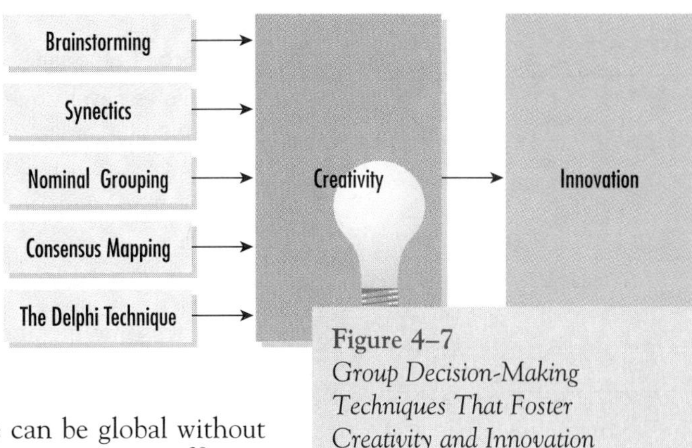

Figure 4–7
Group Decision-Making Techniques That Foster Creativity and Innovation

Electronic brainstorming (EBS) uses computers to generate alternatives. Participants synchronously send ideas without getting together. With EBS, people can be global without getting together, and numbers of participants do not have to be limited.[29]

Synectics. *Synectics* is the process of generating novel alternatives through role-playing and fantasizing. Synectics focuses on generating novel ideas rather than a quantity of ideas. At first, the leader does not even state the exact nature of the problem so that group members avoid preconceptions. For example, when Nolan Bushnell wanted to develop a new concept in family dining, he began by discussing leisure activities generally. Bushnell then moved to leisure activities having to do with eating out. The idea that came out of this synectic process was a restaurant–electronic game complex where families could entertain themselves while eating pizza and hamburgers. The complex is called Chuck E. Cheese Showbiz/Pizza Time Inc.

Nominal Grouping. **Nominal grouping** *is the process of generating and evaluating alternatives using a structured voting method.* This process usually involves six steps:

nominal grouping
The process of generating and evaluating alternatives using a structured voting method.

1. *Listing.* Each participant generates ideas in writing.
2. *Recording.* Each member presents one idea at a time and the leader records them where everyone can see them. This continues in a round-robin manner until all ideas are posted.
3. *Clarification.* Alternatives are clarified through a guided discussion, and any additional ideas are listed.
4. *Ranking.* Each employee rank-orders the top three ideas; low ranked alternatives are eliminated.
5. *Discussion.* Rankings are discussed for clarification, not persuasion. During this time, participants should explain their choices and their reasons for making them.
6. *Vote.* A secret vote is taken to select the alternative.

Nominal grouping is appropriate to use in situations in which groups may be affected by domination, goal displacement, conformity, and groupthink, because it minimizes these affects.

Consensus Mapping. **Consensus mapping** *is the process of developing group agreement on a solution to a problem.* If a consensus cannot be reached, the group does not make a decision for change. It differs from nominal grouping because there can be no competitive battle in which a vote is taken and a solution is

consensus mapping
The process of developing group agreement on a solution to a problem.

Figure 4–8
Responses That Kill Creativity

- It can't be done.
- We've never done it.
- Has anyone else tried it?
- It will not work in our department/company/industry.
- It cost too much.
- It isn't in the budget.
- Let's form a committee.

Work Application

8. Give example decisions in which it would be appropriate for managers where you work or have worked to use brainstorming, nominal grouping, or consensus mapping.

forced on some members of the group. The Japanese call this approach *Ringi*.[30] Consensus mapping can be used after brainstorming. The principal difference is that in consensus mapping the group categorizes or clusters ideas rather than choosing a single solution. A major benefit of consensus mapping is that because the solution is the group's, members generally are more committed to implementing it.

The Delphi Technique. The *Delphi technique* involves using a series of confidential questionnaires to refine a solution. Responses on the first questionnaire are analyzed and resubmitted to participants on a second questionnaire. This process may continue for five or more rounds before a consensus emerges. Managers commonly use the Delphi technique for technological forecasting such as projecting the next computer breakthrough and its effect on a specific industry.[31] By knowing what is to come, managers can make creative decisions to plan for the future.

Upper-level managers commonly use synectics and the Delphi technique for a specific decision. Brainstorming, nominal grouping, and consensus mapping techniques are frequently used at the department level with work groups. Be on guard against responses that kill creativity. Figure 4–8 lists some of these statements. If your employees make such statements, make everyone realize that this demonstrates a negative attitude and is unproductive.

APPLYING THE CONCEPT

AC 4–3 Using Groups to Generate Alternatives

In the five situations, identify the most appropriate group technique to use in generating alternatives.

a. brainstorming b. synectics c. nominal grouping
d. consensus mapping e. Delphi

____ 11. Upper-level management wants to develop some new toys. They called in a consultant who is leading groups of employees and children together to come up with ideas.

____ 12. The department is suffering from morale problems and the manager doesn't know what to do about it.

____ 13. The manager must choose new matching desks for the ten employees in the office.

____ 14. The manager wants to reduce waste in the production department to cut cost and increase productivity.

____ 15. Top managers want to project future trends in the banking industry, as part of their long-range planning.

Decision Trees

After you come up with your alternatives, and subalternatives under them, you may want to make a decision tree. A *decision tree* is a diagram of alternatives. The diagram gives a visual picture of the alternatives which makes it easier for some people to analyze them. A decision tree appears in the case at the end of this chapter.

At Coca-Cola, to stop customers from switching to Pepsi, a few of the alternatives included: to do nothing, to come up with an advertising campaign to offset "the Pepsi challenge," to introduce New Coke while keeping Coca-Cola, and to replace Coca-Cola with New Coke.

ANALYZE ALTERNATIVES AND SELECT THE MOST FEASIBLE

9. Describe the difference among quantitative, Kepner-Tregoe, and cost-benefit analysis techniques for analyzing and selecting an alternative.

Notice that step 3 of the decision-making model, generate alternatives, and step 4, analyze alternatives and select the most feasible, are two different steps. This is because generating and evaluating alternatives at the same time tends to lead to satisficing and wasting time discussing poor alternatives rather than optimizing.

In evaluating alternatives, you should think forward and try to predict the possible outcome of each. Be sure to compare alternatives to the objectives[32] and criteria, set in step 2 of the decision-making model. In addition, compare each alternative to the others.[33] This section presents three popular alternative analysis techniques: quantitative, Kepner-Tregoe, and cost-benefit.

Quantitative Techniques

One of the five approaches to management is management science (Chapter 1) which uses math to aid in problem-solving and decision-making. Quantitative techniques objectively use math to aid in analyzing alternative solutions. Five quantitative techniques follow; Chapter 17 will present other quantitative techniques. This will make you aware of the techniques; it will not make you a mathematician. If you are interested in the actual calculations, you should take a course in quantitative analysis.

Managers may not be expected to compute the math for all types of quantitative techniques. However, if you know when to use these techniques, you can seek help from specialists within or outside the organization. Going to your boss and suggesting using any of these techniques appropriately will show initiative on your part.

Break-Even Analysis. Break-even analysis allows calculation of the volume of sales or revenue that will result in a profit. It involves forecasting the volume of sales and the cost of production. The break-even point occurs at the level where no profit or loss results. For example, Coca-Cola could have computed how many bottles of New Coke would have to be sold to break even. In Exercise 15–1, you will learn how to compute break-even analysis.

Capital Budgeting. These techniques are used to analyze alternative investments. The payback approach allows calculation of the number of years it will take to recover the initial cash invested. The alternative having the quickest payback is preferred. Another technique computes the average rate of return. It is appropriate when the yearly returns differ. A more sophisticated technique, the *discounted cash flow* method, takes into account the time value of money. It assumes that a dollar today is worth more than a dollar in the future. Organizations including AMF, Kellogg, Procter & Gamble, and 3M use discounted cash flow. Coca-Cola used capital budgeting techniques when it made the decisions to buy Minute Maid and Hi-C brand juice and juice drinks. You will learn more about capital budgeting in Chapter 15.

Work Application

9. Give example decisions in which it would be appropriate for managers in an organization you work or have worked for to use the quantitative techniques of break-even analysis, capital budgeting, linear programming, queuing theory, and probability theory. Select any two.

Linear Programming. Optimum allocation of resources is determined using linear programming (LP). The resources managers typically allocate include time, money, space, material, equipment, and employees. Companies primarily use LP for programmed decisions under conditions of certainty or low risk. LP is widely applied to product-mix decisions. Lear Siegler, Inc., uses LP when determining work flow, to optimize the use of its equipment and production. Bendix Corporation uses LP to minimize transportation (shipping) costs for its truck fleet.

Queuing Theory. This technique attacks waiting time. An organization can have any number of employees providing service to customers. If the organization has too many employees working at one time, they will not be waiting on customers and money paid to them is lost. If the organization has too few employees working at one time, it can lose customers who don't want to wait for service, and this results in lost revenue. Queuing theory helps the organization balance these two costs. Retail stores use queuing theory to determine the optimum number of checkout clerks; airports to determine the optimum number of takeoffs and landings on runways; and production departments to schedule preventive maintenance on equipment.

Probability Theory. Probability theory enables the user to make decisions under the condition of risk. The user assigns a probability of success or failure to each alternative. The user then calculates the expected value, which is the payoff or profit from each combination of alternatives and outcomes. The calculations are usually done on a payoff matrix or decision tree by multiplying the probability of the outcome by the benefit or cost. Probability theory is used to determine whether to expand facilities and to what size; to select the most profitable investment portfolio; and to determine the amount of inventory to stock. You could use it to choose a job.

APPLYING THE CONCEPT

AC 4–4 Selecting Quantitative Methods

Select the appropriate quantitative method to use in the following five situations:

a. break-even b. capital budgeting c. linear programming
d. queuing theory e. probability theory

____ **16.** The manager of a small clothing store wants to determine the quantity of items for sale to place on the shelves.

____ **17.** Claude must decide whether to repair his favorite old machine or to replace it with a new one.

____ **18.** Bentley wants to invest money to make a profit.

____ **19.** The manager of a fast-food restaurant wants to even the work load in the store. At times employees hang around with nothing to do and at other times they work for hours without stopping.

____ **20.** The video store owner wants to know how many times a video must be rented out to make it worth adding to the rental list.

The Kepner-Tregoe Method

The Kepner-Tregoe method combines the objective quantitative approach with some subjectivity. The subjectivity comes from determining "must" and "want" criteria and assigning value weights to them. It is a technique for comparing alternatives using the criteria selected in step 2 of the problem-solving and decision-making model. It is helpful when comparing purchase options such as machines, computers, and trucks, and when selecting people to be hired and promoted. Figure 4–9 shows an example of its use. You should refer to the exhibit to clarify the discussion.

Must Criteria		**Car 1**	**Car 2**	**Car 3**	**Car 4**
Cost under $9,000		Yes	Yes	Yes	Yes
Available within one week		Yes	Yes	Yes	No
Want Criteria		**Meets Criteria**			
	Importance*	1 WS**	2 WS**	3 WS**	4 WS**
Gas mileage	7 ×	5 = 35	6 = 42	8 = 56	
Sporty	8 ×	5 = 40	7 = 56	4 = 32	
Blue	3 ×	10 = 30	0 = 0	0 = 0	
AM/FM stereo	5 ×	7 = 35	8 = 40	3 = 15	
Cruise control	2 ×	1 = 2	0 = 0	0 = 0	
Good condition	10 ×	5 = 50	6 = 60	8 = 80	
Low mileage	6 ×	6 = 36	4 = 24	5 = 30	
Few years old	7 ×	3 = 21	5 = 35	5 = 35	
Total weighted score		249	257	248	

*Indicates quantity of importance [on a scale of 10 (high) to 1 (low)] assigned to each as a weight.

**Weighted score.

Figure 4–9
The Kepner-Tregoe Method for Analyzing Alternatives

step 1. **Compare each alternative to the must criteria.** Eliminate any alternative that does not meet the "must" criteria. To illustrate, let's state that our objective is to buy a car within two weeks. This is a nonprogrammed decision, which you will decide by yourself. Figure 4–9 lists the "must" and "want" criteria for each alternative. (These correspond to steps 2 and 3 in decision-making model 4–1.) As you can see, alternative car 4 does not meet all the "must" criteria and is eliminated.

step 2. **Rate each "want" criterion on a scale of 1 to 10 (10 being most important).** Figure 4–9 lists these in the "importance" column. They range from 2 to 10. Note that you do not rank from 1 to 8. The same number may be used more than once, 7 for example.

step 3. **Assign a value of 1 to 10 (10 being the highest) to how well each alternative meets the "want" criteria.** These values can be compared for each car; they are shown in the vertical columns labeled car 1 through 4. Again, many factors can have equal weight, 5 for example.

step 4. **Compute the weighted score (WS) for each alternative** by multiplying (horizontally) the importance value by the "meets criteria" value for each car. Next, add the total weight for each car, each "want" criterion (vertically).

step 5. **Select the alternative with the highest total weighted score** as the solution to the problem. Car 2 should be selected because it has the highest weighted score of 257 versus 248 and 249 for the other cars. Selecting car 2 assumes you rely entirely on your decision model and not partially on your own instinct, intuition, or judgment.

Cost-Benefit (Pros and Cons) Analysis

The management science approaches, quantitative methods, and the Kepner-Tregoe method are objective mathematical approaches to comparing alternatives. However, times occur when the benefit received for the cost is uncertain, making management science approaches unusable. Cost-benefit analysis is a technique for comparing the cost and benefit of each alternative course of action using subjective intuition and judgment along with math. With the pros and cons analysis, you identify the advantages, which can be considered the benefits, and disadvantages, which can be considered the cost, of each alternative. Figure 4–10 compares the three approaches to analyzing and selecting alternatives.

Cost-benefit analysis is more subjective than management science techniques. Therefore, when using cost-benefit with groups, the group should do a critical evaluation of all alternatives.[34] Using a method such as the devil's advocate approach can help the group to avoid the potential problems of satisficing, dominance, and groupthink. The group should also be careful of the way alternatives are presented for evaluation,[35] and the order of presentation can affect the decision. Alternatives presented in a negative way tend not to be selected, and people tend to remember best what they hear first and last.

Research has been conducted to compare the quality of individual decisions when the person consults with others prior to making the final decisions. Results suggest that consulting others increases confidence, but not the accuracy of the decision. This may to be due to the fact that when people consult others they tend to seek information or approval for their decision, rather than having the other person act as a devil's advocate and making them justify the solution.[36]

Social responsibility is a condition under uncertainty in which cost-benefit is appropriate. If you have three nonprofit organizations ask for money for a project they want you to sponsor, you can compare the cost of each, but which one will give the most benefit to the company and other stakeholders? Unlike management science quantitative techniques and Kepner-Tregoe, cost-benefit has no single bottom line number to compare in which you select the objective alternative.

Ben Franklin is said to have used the pros and cons, an offshoot of using cost-benefit. Ben would take a piece of paper and draw a line down the middle. On one side, he would list the pros and on the other the cons for using each alternative. Ben would then select the best alternative. Many people think about the cost and benefits or pros and cons without writing them down. You should write them down in order to improve comparisons of alternatives for important decisions.

Regardless of the method used to analyze alternatives, the one selected should be the optimal alternative that meets the criteria established in step 2 of the decision-making model. If none of the alternatives meet the criteria, you

Figure 4–10
Alternative Analysis Techniques Continuum

Quantitative Techniques	Kepner-Tregoe Method	Cost-Benefit
←		→
(Objective)		(Subjective)
(Maximal use of math to make the decision)		(Minimal use of math to make the decision)

have two basic options: (1) return to step 2 and change the criteria to select the best alternative and (2) return to step 3 and generate more alternatives.

Coca-Cola selected the alternative to replace Coca-Cola with New Coke rather than to offer it as an additional soft drink alternative for those who prefer a sweeter cola taste. After all, research taste tests indicated that people preferred New Coke to Coca-Cola.

Work Application

10. Give an example decision in which it would be appropriate for managers where you work or have worked to use the Kepner-Tregoe method and the cost-benefit analysis

PLAN, IMPLEMENT THE DECISION, AND CONTROL

The final two steps in the decision-making model involve planning and implementing the decision, step 5, and controlling, step 6.

Plan. After making a decision, you develop a plan of action with a schedule for implementation. You will learn the details of planning in the next two chapters.

Implement the Plan. After a decision has been made and plans developed, the plans must be implemented. Communicating the plan to all employees is critical to successful implementation. You will learn about communication in Chapter 10. It may be necessary to delegate assignments to others. You will learn about delegating in Chapter 7. Coca-Cola developed plans to make New Coke, to advertise it, and to deliver it.

Control. Control methods should be developed while planning. Checkpoints should be established to determine whether the alternative chosen is solving the problem. If not, corrective action may be needed. Managers should not be locked into a decision and wind up throwing good money after bad. When managers will not admit that they made a bad decision and change, they are in the process known as *escalation of commitment*. When you make a poor decision, you should admit the mistake and try to rectify it by going back over the steps in the decision-making model. At Coca-Cola, three weeks after introducing New Coke, management admitted its mistake and brought back Coca-Cola, with the new name Coca-Cola "Classic" to distinguish it from New Coke. In 1992 Coca-Cola changed the name of New Coke to Coke II, which is no longer available in all areas.

CURRENT MANAGEMENT ISSUES

Globalization. Managers face an important decision about *globalization*. Managers who ignore making decisions about going global, global expansion, or at least how to compete against global competition will have competitive problems.

Participative Management, Teams, and Diversity. The current trend involves increasing levels of *participation in management* through *teams*. Employees want to be involved in decision-making. When the type of problem is appropriate for group decision-making, it is important to have a *diversity* of participants to increase the quality of decision-making. Management should train employees to value diversity and to work together in teams to take advantage of the benefits of diversity and group decision-making, while minimizing the potential disadvantages.

Quality and TQM. To be successful in business requires continually increasing *quality* and *customer value*. Continuous improvement does not come from a few major decisions every few years. It comes from continually coming up with creative ideas that become innovations. TQM encourages the use of the decision-making model and math techniques such as statistical process controls. Decisions made with TQM should take a systems effect approach. In other words, a decision should not be made in isolation. Consider how the decision being made will affect other areas and plan changes in all necessary areas.

Productivity. As employees develop creative ways to transform inputs into outputs, *productivity* increases. Generally, when poor decisions are made, problems are not eliminated and opportunities are not taken advantage of. Therefore, poor decisions lead to lower levels of productivity.

Ethics and Social Responsibility. Ethics (Chapter 2) should be at the heart of decisions and human relations (Chapter 3). The golden rule, four-way test, and/or the stakeholders' approach to ethics may be used when making decisions. When evaluating alternatives, individuals or groups should consider how they affect stakeholders. In the area of *social responsibility*, important decisions must be made about the level of commitment and which specific actions the company will take. Coca-Cola believes that it should give back to the communities that have been so good to the company wherever it does business. To this end, it made the decision to establish the Coca-Cola Foundation with the mission of fostering and promoting a favorable environment for business growth by supporting educational and related community needs.

Small Business. It's hard to say if problem-solving and decision-making are more important to the large or small business. However, if most large companies, like Coca-Cola, make a poor decision, like replacing Coca-Cola with New Coke, it costs them money but they can afford it. Coca-Cola was still very profitable during the New Coke years. If small businesses make a major poor decision, they cannot afford it, and it can mean the end to the business. Tom Wentworth opened a sandwich shop and was doing well, so he made the decision to open a second shop. The second shop failed to the point where the creditors forced Tom to sell the assets of both shops to pay their bills.

CHAPTER SUMMARY AND GLOSSARY

The chapter summary is organized to answer the ten learning objectives for Chapter 4.

1. Explain the relationship among objectives, problem-solving, and decision-making.
The three terms are interrelated as follows. Managers are responsible for setting and achieving organizational objectives. When managers do not meet objectives, a problem results. When a problem exists, decisions must be made about what, if any, action must be taken.

2. Explain the relationship among the management functions, decision-making, and problem-solving.
The three terms are interrelated as follows. When managers perform the functions of planning, organizing, leading, and controlling, they make decisions. If managers lack proficiency at performing the management functions, they will have many problems.

3. List the six steps in the decision-making model.
The steps in the decision-making model are (1) defining the problem, (2) setting objectives and criteria, (3) generating alternatives, (4) analyzing alternatives and selecting the most feasible, (5) planning and implementing the decision, and (6) controlling.

4. Describe the difference between programmed

and nonprogrammed decisions and among the conditions of certainty, uncertainty, and risk.

The difference between programmed and nonprogrammed decisions is in the recurrence, routine, and significance of the decision to be made. Nonprogrammed decisions include nonrecurring, nonroutine, significant decisions. Recurring, routine, and nonsignificant decisions are programmed decisions.

The difference in decision-making conditions is based on the degree of certainty of the outcome of the decision. With certainty you know the outcome of alternatives, with risk you can assign probabilities to the outcomes, and with uncertainty you do not know the outcomes of alternatives.

5. Describe when to use the decision-making model versus the bounded rationality model and group versus individual decision-making.

Use the decision-making model with group decision-making when a nonprogrammed decision with high risk or uncertainty exists. Use the bounded rationality model with an individual decision when a programmed decision with low risk or certainty exists. However, this is a general guide; there may be exceptions to the rule.

6. State the difference between an objective and "must" and "want" criteria.

An objective is the end result you want from making the decision. The "must" criteria are the requirements that an alternative must meet to be selected as the decision. The "want" criteria are desirable but are not necessary for the alternative to be selected as the decision.

7. State the difference between creativity and innovation.

Creativity is a way of thinking that generates new ideas. Innovation is the implementation of new ideas for products and processes.

8. List and explain the three stages in the creative process.

The three stages are: (1) preparation; familiarity with the problem; (2) incubation and illumination; incubation is taking a break from the problem and illumination is the point at which one gets the idea for the solution; (3) evaluation; making sure the idea will work before it becomes an innovation.

9. Describe the difference among quantitative, the Kepner-Tregoe, and cost-benefit analysis techniques for analyzing and selecting an alternative.

Quantitative and Kepner-Tregoe are management science approaches; cost-benefit is not. Quantitative methods use math subjectively to select the alternative with the highest value. Kepner-Tregoe uses objective math, with some subjectivity in selecting and weighting criteria, to select the alternative with the highest value. Cost-benefit analysis is primarily based on subjective analysis, with some math, but alternatives do not have a final number value to compare.

10. Define the following key terms (in order of appearance in the chapter):

Select one or more methods: (1) fill in the missing key terms from memory, (2) match the key terms from the end of the review with their definitions below, or (3) copy the key terms in order from the list at the beginning of the chapter.

A ______ exists whenever objectives are not being met.

__________ is the process of taking corrective action in order to meet objectives.

__________ is the process of selecting an alternative course of action that will solve a problem.

The ____________ steps include classifying and (1) defining the problem or opportunity, (2) setting objectives and criteria, (3) generating alternatives, (4) analyzing alternatives and selecting the most feasible, (5) planning and implementing the decision, and (6) controlling.

With __________, recurring or routine situations, the decision-maker should use decision rules or organizational policies and procedures to make the decision.

With __________, significant and nonrecurring and nonroutine situations, the decision-maker should use the decision-making model.

The three ______________ include certainty, risk, and uncertainty.

______ are the standards that an alternative must meet to be selected as the decision that will accomplish the objective.

______ is the implementation of a new idea.

______ is a way of thinking that generates new ideas.

The three stages in the __________ are (1) preparation, (2) incubation and illumination, and (3) evaluation.

With the __________ approach, group members focus on defending the solution while others try to come up with criticisms of why the solution will not work.

______ is the process of suggesting many possible alternatives without evaluation.

__________ is the process of generating and evaluating alternatives using a structured voting method.

__________ is the process of developing group agreement on a solution to a problem.

KEY TERMS

brainstorming
consensus mapping
creative process
creativity
criteria
decision-making
decision-making conditions
decision-making model
devil's advocate
innovation
nominal grouping
nonprogrammed decision
problem
problem-solving
programmed decision

REVIEW AND DISCUSSION QUESTIONS

1. Are problem-solving and decision-making really important? Explain.
2. Why is it necessary to determine the decision structure and decision-making conditions?
3. What is the current trend in using groups to solve problems and make decisions?
4. Which potential disadvantage of group problem-solving and decision-making do you think is most common?
5. Is a decrease in sales or profits a symptom or a cause of a problem?
6. Would a maximum price of $1,000 to spend on a stereo be an objective or a criterion?
7. Are creativity and innovation really important to all types of businesses? Is it important to evaluate creativity before it becomes an innovation?
8. Have you ever made a decision with information that was not timely, of quality, complete, and/or relevant? If yes, explain.
9. What is the major difference between nominal grouping and consensus mapping?
10. Why are generating and analyzing alternatives separate steps in the decision-making model?
11. Have you ever used any of the techniques for analyzing and selecting an alternative? If yes, which one?
12. Do you know anyone who has been the victim of escalation of commitment? If yes, explain.

CASE

Carolyn Blakeslee's Art Calendar®

(This case also serves as the basis for Exercises 4–1 and 4–2.)

In 1986, Carolyn Blakeslee founded *Art Calendar*, a monthly publication for visual artists. Art Calendar provides information (approximately 15 pages) about grants, shows, and other forums to which artists can submit their work, as well as some topical freelance columns. *Art Calendar* is folksy in appearance and is mailed second class.

Carolyn started *Art Calendar* as a part-time business in a room in her home. She believed that half the people who received her first brochure would want to subscribe to her publication. She was heartbroken when only 3 percent subscribed. Later, she was happy to learn that 3 percent isn't bad in publishing. Regardless of her disappointment, eight out of the first ten years, circulation revenues doubled. *Art Calendar* grew to become artists' definitive source of information.

Carolyn did not expect the business to become so successful. Over the years the business became more complex and time-consuming. Without employees, it was no longer possible to read all the mail during her daily five miles on a stationary bike. The part-time hours became more than full-time. Carolyn, like many women, wants to have it all. She wants to meet financial goals and devote time to her family (she really enjoys motherhood, spending time with her husband), her own artwork, and leisure pursuits. Carolyn reached that point in the life of successful small businesses where she had to make a decision based on three major alternatives: (1) maintain, (2) expand, or (3) sell the business.

1. *Maintain the folksy nature of the publication*. In this area, she does have at least two subalternatives: (a) continue to work full time doing all the work herself, or (b) hire some help so that she can cut back her hours to part time.

2. *Expand the business by making it more professional*. This alternative does have at least three subalternatives: (a) continue to work full time and personally do most of the work herself to professionalize the publication with clerical-level employees; (b) continue to work full time and make the major decisions about going professional, but hire an experienced person(s) to work with; or (c) cut back her hours to part time by making the major decisions about going professional, but hiring experienced people to do the work. If this alternative is selected, decisions about expansion must be made.

3. *Sell the business*. If Carolyn does sell the business, she has to make a decision about future employment with at least four major alternatives: (a) continue to work in the business as an employee of the new owner(s)—full or part time; (b) start a new business; (c) get a job working for someone else—full or part time; or (4) stop working and devote more time to her family and leisure activities.

The three alternatives, with subalternatives, are presented in the accompanying decision tree. With the decision tree you first write down all the alternatives that lead to one possible decision. Can you think of other alternatives not listed that should be? After listing the alternatives, you analyze them and select the alternative and the subalternative as the decision.

Decision Tree

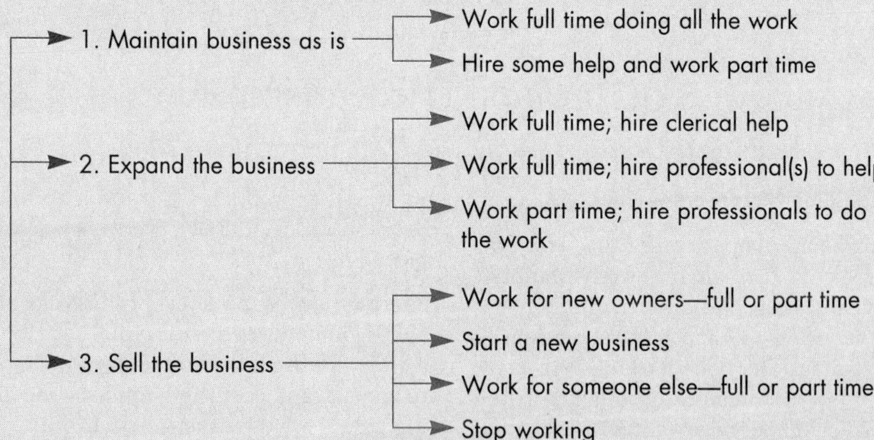

Select the best alternative to the following questions. Be sure you are able to explain your answers.

___ 1. Carolyn Blakeslee does not perform the management function(s) of

a. planning c. leading
b. organizing d. controlling

___ 2. The decision structure facing Carolyn is

a. programmed b. nonprogrammed

___ 3. The decision-making condition facing Carolyn is

a. certainty b. risk c. uncertainty

___ 4. In making this decision, the ___ model would be appropriate.

a. rational b. bounded rationality

___ 5. Should Carolyn set objectives and criteria for the decision?

a. yes b. no

___ 6. In deciding to maintain, expand, or sell, creativity and innovation are not critical.

a. true b. false

___ 7. The information in the case lacks the ___ that Carolyn needs to make her decision.

a. timeliness c. completeness
b. quality d. relevance

___ 8. Which technique would be most appropriate for Carolyn's decision?

a. brainstorming
b. synectics
c. nominal grouping
d. consensus mapping
e. Delphi
f. none of these are appropriate

___ 9. Which method for analyzing and selecting an alternative is most appropriate for Carolyn's decision?

a. quantitative technique
b. Kepner-Tregoe
c. cost-benefit

___ 10. Which alternative will be the most complex to plan, implement, and control?

a. maintain
b. expand
c. sell

11. List the pros and cons for each alternative from Carolyn's perspective, which may be different from yours. Be sure to state the risk of not expanding and expanding.

12. If you were in Carolyn's situation, would you maintain, expand, or sell? Assume you could get a check in the amount equal to ten years' full-time salary upon the sale.

SKILL-BUILDING EXERCISE 4–1

Making a Decision Using the Decision-Making Model

Preparing for Skill-Building Exercise 4–1

Select a significant problem or opportunity that you now face. Remember, a problem exists when objectives are not being met. In other words, there is a difference in what is happening and what you want to happen. The problem or opportunity may be from any facet of your life—work, college, sports, a relationship, a purchase to be made in the near future, where to go on a major date, and so on. Use the decision-making model outline below to write down and solve your problem or take advantage of the opportunity.

Step 1. Classify and Define the Problem or Opportunity

Decision structure. Do you need to make a programmed or nonprogrammed decision?

Decision condition. Is it uncertainty, risk, or certainty?

Decision-making model. Is the rational or bounded rationality model appropriate? (Continue to follow all steps in the decision-making model even if bounded rationality is appropriate.)

Select the appropriate level of participation. Should an individual or group be used? (If a group decision is appropriate, use a group for the following steps in the model. But remember to take advantage of, and minimize the disadvantages of, using groups as you make the decision.)

Define the problem or opportunity. List the symptoms and causes, then write a clear statement of the problem or opportunity you will make a decision about.

___

___

___

___

Step 2. Set Objectives and Criteria

Write out what is to be accomplished by making the decision and the standards that the alternative must meet to be selected as the decision that will accomplish the objective. (Specify "must" and "want" criteria if appropriate for the decision.)

Objective: ______________________________

____

Criteria: (must) ______________________________

(want) ______________________________

Step 3. Generate Creative Alternatives

What information do you need? (Remember that information must be timely, of quality, complete, and relevant to be useful.) Will you use any technology?

If you are using a group, will brainstorming, nominal grouping, or consensus mapping be used?

List your alternatives (at least three) below; number them. If a decision tree will be helpful, make one.

____

____

____

____

____

____

Step 4. Analyze Alternatives and Select the Most Feasible

Are quantitative, Kepner-Tregoe, or cost-benefit (pro and con) analysis appropriate? Use one below.

____

____

____

____

____

Step 5. Plan and Implement the Decision

Write out your plan for implementing the decision. Be sure to state the controls you will use to make sure you know if the decision is working. How can you avoid escalation of commitment?

____

____

____

____

____

____

____

Step 6. Controlling

After implementing the decision, come back and make notes about progress on solving the problem or opportunity. Indicate any need for corrective action, and if you need to, return to prior steps in the decision-making model.

____

____

____

____

____

Doing Skill-Building Exercise 4–1 in Class

Objective
To develop your problem-solving and decision-making skills by learning to use the decision-making model.

Preparation
You should have made a personal decision using the model preparation pages for this exercise.

Experience
You will share your decision with a small group of students who will give you feedback.

Procedure (10–20 minutes)

1. Break into groups of three to five people. One at a time, go through the steps in making your decision. At each step, group members give feedback such as pointing out any errors, offering suggestions on how to improve the written statements, providing additional alternatives, listing more pros and cons not thought of, stating which alternatives others would select, and so on.
2. Same as 1, but the group selects the best decision to be presented to the entire class.

Conclusion
The instructor may lead a class discussion and/or make concluding remarks.

Application (2–4 minutes)
What did I learn from this experience? How will I use this knowledge in the future?

____

____

____

Sharing
Volunteers give their answers to the application section.

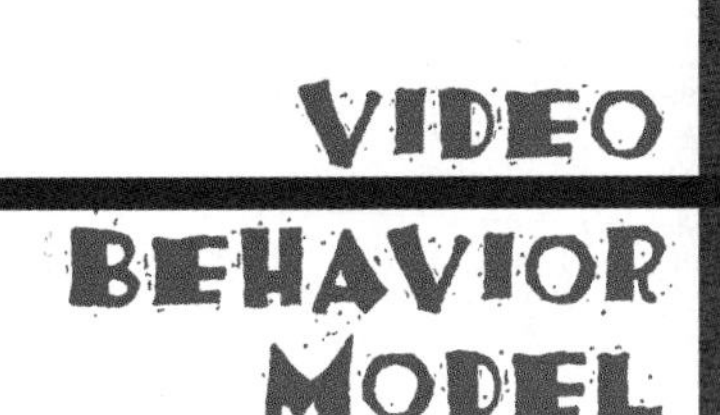

Behavior Model Video 4–1, Situational Management: Decision-Making, shows the human resources director, Richard, meeting with a supervisor, Denise, to discuss training changes. The video illustrates the four situational management styles, explained in Skill-Building Exercise 4–2.

Objectives
To better understand the four situational management decision-making styles.

Procedure 1 (10–20 minutes)
The instructor shows Video Module 4–1, Situational Management: Decision-Making Styles. As you view each of the four scenes, identify the management decision-making style being used by the manager. Write the letters and number of the style on the scene line after each scene.

Scene 1. ______ Autocratic (S1A)
Scene 2. ______ Consultative (S2C)
Scene 3. ______ Participative (S3P)
Scene 4. ______ Empowerment (S4E)

Option A. View all four scenes and identify the style used by the manager. Select the one style that you would use in this situation. Are other styles also appropriate? Which style would you not use (not appropriate) for this situation? Next to each style listed, write the letter A for appropriate or *N* for not appropriate. After everyone is done, the instructor leads a class discussion and/or gives the correct answers.

Option B. After each scene the class discusses the style used by the manager. The instructor states the correct answer after each of the four scenes.

Conclusion
The instructor may lead a class discussion and/or make concluding remarks.

Application (2–4 minutes)
What did I learn from this exercise? How will I use this knowledge in the future?

____

____

____

Sharing
Volunteers give their answers to the application section.

SKILL-BUILDING EXERCISE 4–2

Situational Management: Decision-Making[37]

Preparing for Skill Building Exercise 4–2

Note: This exercise is an extension of the Situational Management Model from Skill-Building Exercise 1–1 (Chapter 1). If you have not read the preparation part of the exercise, read it before continuing.

Managers today recognize the trend toward participation in decision-making and are open to using participation. It is frustrating for managers to decide when to use participation and when not to, and what level of participation to use. You are about to learn how to use a model that will develop your skill at selecting the appropriate management style to meet the needs of the situation. First, let's examine ways in which groups can be used to generate solutions.

Selecting the Appropriate Situational Management Decision Style

In addition to capability level, Situational Management Model, you must also consider time, information, and acceptance. As a manager you follow two steps in selecting the appropriate situational management decision style for problem-solving and decision-making: diagnosing the situation and selecting the appropriate style.

Step 1. Diagnose the Situation. The first step involves diagnosing the situational variables, including time, information, acceptance, and employee capability.

Time. You must determine whether you have enough time to include employees in decision-making. View time as yes (you have time to use participation) or no (you do not have time to use participation). If you do not have time, you should use the autocratic style (S1A), regardless of preference. When you do not have time to include employees in problem-solving and decision-making, you ignore the other three variables; they are irrelevant if you do not have time. If you say yes you have time, any styles may be appropriate. You use the other three variables to select the style. In other words, when there isn't enough time to include participation, time is the most important factor. However, when there is time, it becomes the least important factor.

Time is a relative term. In one situation, a few minutes may be considered a short time period, but in another a month may be a short period of time. Time is not wasted when the potential advantages of using participation are realized.

Information. You must decide if you have enough information to make a quality decision alone. The more information you have, the less need for participation; the less information you have, the greater the need for participation. If you have all the necessary information, you have no need for employee participation, and the autocratic style (S1A) is appropriate. When you have some information, but need more that can be obtained by asking questions, the consultative style (S2C) may be appropriate. If you have little information, the appropriate style may be participative (S3P—group discussion) or empowerment (S4E—group makes the decision).

Acceptance. You must decide whether employee acceptance of the decision is critical to implementing the decision. The more employees will like a decision, the less need for participation; the more employees will dislike a decision, the greater the need for participation. If you make the decision alone, will the employees or group willingly implement it? If the employees or group will be accepting, the appropriate style is probably autocratic (S1A). If the employee or group will be reluctant, the appropriate style may be consultative (S2C) or participative (S3P). If they will probably reject the decision, the participative (S3P) or empowerment style (S4E) may be appropriate. Recall that when groups make decisions, they are more understanding, accepting, and committed to implementing the decision

Capability. You must decide whether the employees or group have the ability and motivation to be involved in problem-solving and decision-making. Do the employees or group have the experience and information needed to be involved? Will employees put the organization's or department's goals ahead of personal goals? Do the employees want to be involved in problem-solving and decision-making? Employees are more willing to participate when the decisions personally affect them. If the employees' or group's capability level is low (C1), an autocratic style (S1A) may be appropriate. When capability is moderate (C2), a consultative style (S2C) may be appropriate. If capability level is high (C3), a participative style (S3P) might be adopted. If capability is outstanding (C4), choose the empowerment style (S4E). Note that you should only use the empowerment style with employees who have outstanding capability levels, regardless of the informational and acceptance factors. Remember that the employees' or group's capability level can change from situation to situation.

Step 2. Select the Appropriate Management Style. After considering the four variables, you select the appropriate style. In some situations, all variables will indicate that the same style is appropriate. In other cases, the appropriate style is not so clear. For example, you could be in a situation in which you have time to use any style, may have all the information necessary (autocratic), employees may be reluctant (consultative or participative), and their capability may be moderate (consultative). In situations where different styles are indicated for different variables, you must determine which variable should be given more weight. In the preceding example, assume that acceptance was critical for successful implementation of the decision. Acceptance takes precedence over information. Because the employees involved have moderate capability, the consultative style would be appropriate. Model 4–2 summarizes use of the four situational management styles in decision-making.

Using the Situational Management: Decision-Making Model

We will apply the model to the following situation; more situations are presented later in this exercise.

______ Manager Ben can give only one of his employees a merit pay raise. He has a week to make the decision. Ben knows how well each employee performed over the past year. The employees really have no option but to accept getting or not getting the pay raise, but they can complain to upper management about the selection. The employees' capability levels vary, but as a group they have a high capability level under normal circumstances.

______ time ______ information
______ acceptance ______ capability

Step 1. Diagnose the Situation. Ben has plenty of time to use any level of participation (place a Y for yes on the time line below the situation). He has all the information needed to make the decision (place S1A on the information line). Employees have no choice but to accept the decision (place S1A on the acceptance line). And the group's capability level is normally high (place S3P on the capability line).

Step 2. Select the Appropriate Style for the Situation. There are conflicting styles to choose from (autocratic and participative): yes time S1A information S1A acceptance S3P capability. The variable that should be given precedence is information. The employees are normally capable, but in a situation like this they may not put the department's goals ahead of their own. In other words, even if employees know who deserves the raise, they may fight for it anyway. Such a conflict could cause future problems. Some possible ways to make the decision include the following:

Autocratic (S1A). The manager would select the person to be given the raise without discussing it with any employees. Ben would simply announce the decision after submitting it to the payroll department.

Consultative (S2C). The manager would get information from the employees concerning who should get the raise. Ben would then decide who would get the raise. He would announce the decision and explain the rationale for it. He might invite questions and discussion.

Participative (S3P). The manager could tentatively select the employee who gets the raise, but be open to change if a group member convinces him that someone else should. Or Ben could explain the situation to the group and lead a discussion concerning who should get the raise. After considering the group's input, Ben would make the decision and explain the rationale for it. Notice that the consultative style does not allow for discussion as the participative style does.

Empowerment (S4E). The manager would explain the situation and allow the group to decide who gets the raise. Ben may be a group member. Notice that this is the only style that allows the group to make the decision.

The autocratic style is appropriate for this situation. The consultative style is also a good approach. However, the participative and empowerment styles use too much participation for the situation. Your skill at selecting the appropriate decision-making management style should improve through using the model for the ten situations below.

Deciding Which Situational Management Decision-Making Style to Use

Following are ten situations calling for a decision. Select the appropriate problem-solving and decision-making style. Be sure to use Model 4–2 when determining the style to use. First determine the answers to the variables on the lines below the situation. Then place the style on the line before the number.

S1A—autocratic S2C—consultative S3P—participative S4E—empowerment

___ 1. You have developed a new work procedure that will increase productivity. Your boss likes the idea and wants you to try it in a few weeks. You view your employees as fairly capable and believe that they will be receptive to the change.

______ time ______ information
______ acceptance ______ capability

___ 2. There is new competition in your industry. Your organization's revenues have been dropping. You

Model 4–2
Situational Management: Decision-Making

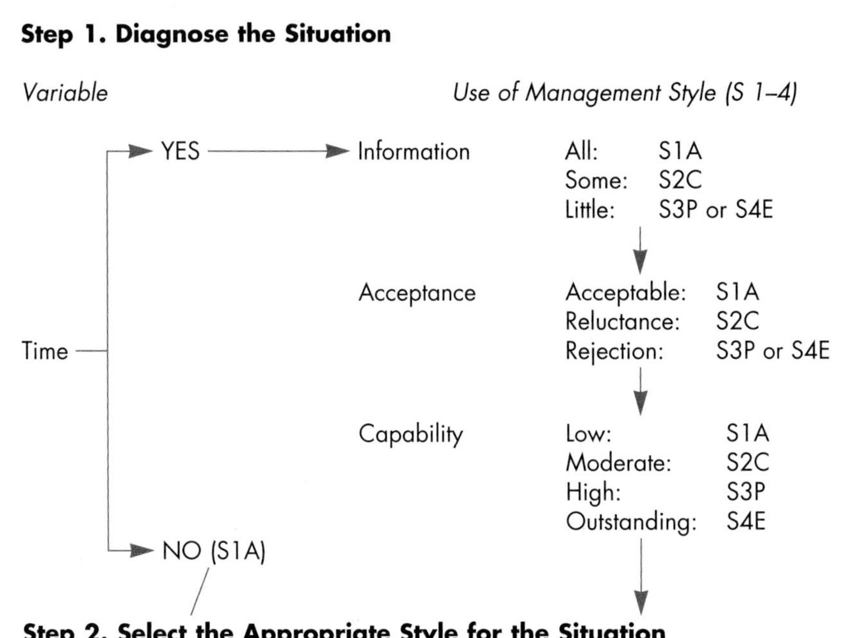

Step 2. Select the Appropriate Style for the Situation

Autocratic (S1A) No participation	Consultative (S2C) Limited participation	Participative (S3P) High participation	Empowerment (S4E) Complete participation
The *manager makes the decision alone* and announces it after the fact. An explanation of the rationale for the decision may be given.	The *manager consults individuals or the group for information and then makes the decision.* Before implementing the decision, the manager explains the rationale for the decision and sells the benefits to the employees. The manager may invite questions and have a discussion.	The *manager may present a tentative decision to the group* and ask for its input, and change the decision if the input warrants a change. *Or the manager presents the problem to the group for suggestions.* Based on employee participation, the manager makes the decision and explains its rationale.	The manager presents the situation to the group and describes any limitations to the decision. *The group makes the decision.* The manager may be a group member with equal input. Note that empowerment should only be used with employees with outstanding capability.

Level of Participation →

Note that with the autocratic, consultative, and participative styles the manager retains the power to make the decision; with empowerment the group makes the decision.

have been told to lay off 3 of your 15 employees in two weeks. You have been supervisor for over three years. Normally, your employees are very capable.

______ time ______ information
______ acceptance ______ capability

__ 3. Your department has been facing a problem for several months. Many solutions have been tried and failed. You've finally thought of a solution, but you're not sure of the possible consequences of the change required or of acceptance by your highly capable employees.

______ time ______ information
______ acceptance ______ capability

__ 4. Flex-time has become popular in your organization. Some departments let each employee start and end work when he or she chooses. However, because of the cooperation required of your employees, they must all work the same eight hours. You're not sure of the level of interest in changing the hours. Your employees are a very capable group and like to make decisions.

______ time ______ information
______ acceptance ______ capability

__ 5. The technology in your industry is changing too fast for the members of your organization to keep up. Top management hired a consultant who has made recommendations. You have two weeks to decide what to do about the recommendations. Your employees are usually capable; they enjoy participating in the decision-making process.

______ time ______ information
______ acceptance ______ capability

__ 6. A change has been handed down by top management. How you implement it is your decision. The change takes effect in one month and it will affect everyone in your department. Their acceptance is critical to the success of the change. Your employees are usually not interested in making routine decisions.

______ time ______ information
______ acceptance ______ capability

__ 7. Your boss called to tell you that someone requested an order for your department's product; the delivery date is very short. She asked you to call her back with a decision about taking the order in 15 minutes. Looking over the work schedule, you realize that it will be very difficult to deliver the order on time. Your employees will have to push hard to make it. They are cooperative, capable, and enjoy being involved in decision-making.

______ time ______ information
______ acceptance ______ capability

__ 8. Top management has decided to make a change that will affect all of your employees. You know that they will be upset because it will cause them hardship. One or two may even quit. The change goes into effect in 30 days. Your employees are very capable.

______ time ______ information
______ acceptance ______ capability

__ 9. You believe that productivity in your department could be increased. You have thought of some ways to do it, but you're not sure of them. Your employees are very experienced; almost all of them have been in the department longer than you have.

______ time ______ information
______ acceptance ______ capability

__ 10. A customer offered you a contract for your product with a quick delivery date. The offer is open for two days. To meet the contract deadline, employees would have to work nights and weekends for six weeks. You cannot require them to work overtime. Filling this profitable contract could help get you the raise you want and feel you deserve. However, if you take the contract and don't deliver on time, it will hurt your chances of getting a big raise. Your employees are very capable.

______ time ______ information
______ acceptance ______ capability

Doing Skill-Building Exercise 4–2 in Class

Objective
To develop your skill at knowing which level of participation to use in a given decision-making situation. You will learn to use the Situational Management: Decision-Making Model.

Experience
You will try to select the appropriate problem-solving and decision-making style for each of the ten situations in the preparation for this exercise.

Preparation
You should have completed the preparation for this exercise unless told not to do so by your instructor.

Procedure 1 (10–15 minutes)
Behavior Model Video 4–1, is shown to illustrate the four decision-making styles. Use the form on page 128 to record answers.

Procedure 2 (10–20 minutes)
Behavior Model Video 4–1, Situational Management Decision-Making, may be shown. The instructor reviews Model 4–2 and explains how to use it to select the appropriate management style for the first situation.

Procedure 3 (4–8 minutes)
Students working alone complete situation 2 using the model, followed by the instructor going over the recommended answers.

Procedure 4 (10–20 minutes)
Break into teams of two or three. Apply the model to situations 3 through 5 as a team. You may decide to change your original answers. The instructor goes over the recommended answers and scoring for situations 3 through 5. Do not continue with situation 6 until the instructor goes over the answers to situations 3 through 5.

Procedure 5 (10–20 minutes)
In the same teams, select decision-making styles for situations 6 through 10. The instructor will go over the recommended answers and scoring.

Conclusion
The instructor may lead a class discussion and/or make concluding remarks.

Application (2–4 minutes)
What did I learn from this experience? How will I use this knowledge in the future?

____

____

____

Sharing
Volunteers give their answers to the application section.

EXERCISE 4–1

Individual versus Group Decision-Making

Preparing for Exercise 4–1

To complete this exercise you must read the Case and answer questions 1–10, on pages 124–126.

Doing Exercise 4–1 in Class

Objective
To compare individual and group decision-making to better understand when to use a group to make decisions.

Preparation
As preparation you should have answered questions 1–10 of the Case.

Experience
You will work in a group that will answer the same ten case questions and then analyze the results to determine if the group or one of its members had the higher score.

Procedure 1 (1–2 minutes)
Place your answers to ten case questions in the "individual answer" column in the table on page 134.

Procedure 2 (15–20 minutes)
Break into teams of five, with smaller or larger groups as necessary. As a group, come to an agreement on the answers to the Case questions. Place the group answers in the "group answer" column. Try to use the consensus mapping rather than the nominal grouping technique in arriving at the answers.

Procedure 3 (4–6 minutes)
Scoring. The instructor will give the recommended answers. Determine how many you got right as an individual and as a group. Total your individual and the group's scores.

Compute the average individual score by adding all the individual scores and dividing by the number of group members. Write it here: ______ Average.

Now compute the difference between the average individual score and the group score. If the group's score is higher than the average individual score, you have a gain (+) of points; if the group score is lower, you have a loss (−) of points. Write it here: ______ and circle one (+ or −).

Determine the highest individual score. Write it here: ______.

Determine the number of individuals who scored higher than the group's score ______.

Procedure 4 (5–10 minutes)—*Integration*
As a group, discuss the advantages or disadvantages of being in a group while making the decisions in this exercise.

Question number	*Individual answer*	*Group answer*	*Recommended answer*	*Individual score*	*Group score*
1. ______	______	______	______	______	______
2. ______	______	______	______	______	______
3. ______	______	______	______	______	______
4. ______	______	______	______	______	______
5. ______	______	______	______	______	______
6. ______	______	______	______	______	______
7. ______	______	______	______	______	______
8. ______	______	______	______	______	______
9. ______	______	______	______	______	______
10. ______	______	______	______	______	______
Total scores	______	______	______	______	______

Potential Advantages

1. *Better quality decisions*. Did your group make better decisions? Was the group's score higher than the highest individual score? If not, why not? Were knowledgeable members nonassertive? Were they listened to?
2. *More information, alternatives, creativity, and innovation*. Did the group get members to think about alternatives they did not consider as individuals? Did your group use the devil's advocate approach?
3. *People understand the decision*. Did members understand the reason for group answers?
4. *People are committed to the decision*. Did group members accept the group's answers?
5. *Improved morale and motivation*. Were members more satisfied making the decisions in a group or as individuals?

Potential Disadvantages

1. *Wasted time*. Did the group waste time? Was the time spent worth the benefits (i.e., a higher group score)?
2. *Satisficing*. Did the group satisfice or optimize answers? Because no one person was held responsible for the group's answers, did members have an "I don't care" attitude?
3. *Domination and goal displacement*. Did any one person or subgroup dominate? Did everyone participate? Did any member(s) seem more interested in getting their answer accepted, rather than getting the best answer?
4. *Conformity and groupthink*. Were members nonassertive when presenting their answers in order to be accepted? Did group pressure force them to agree with the majority?

Improvements

Overall, were the advantages of using a group greater than the disadvantages? If your group were to continue to work together, how could it improve its decision-making ability? Write your answer below.

____

____

____

____

Conclusion
The instructor may lead a class discussion and/or make concluding remarks.

Application (2–4 minutes)
What did I learn from this experience? How will I use this knowledge in the future?

____

____

____

Sharing
Volunteers give their answers to the application section.

EXERCISE 4–2

Brainstorming

Preparing for Exercise 4–2

To complete this exercise you must have read the Case, pages 124–125.

Doing Exercise 4–2 in Class

Objective and Experience
To participate in a brainstorming session.

Procedure 1 (8–12 minutes)
Assume that Carolyn has made the decision to expand *Art Calendar*. She has asked you to help her by giving her some creative ideas for expansion.

As class members give ideas, the instructor and/or class member(s) records them for all to see. Follow the rules of brainstorming:

1. Do offer any ideas that come to you without evaluating them. Crazy is good.
2. Do not evaluate any ideas presented (criticism or praise).
3. Do not question or discuss any ideas. This follows brainstorming.
4. Do improve and combine ideas presented—without evaluation.

Procedure 2 (10–20 minutes)
For each idea presented during brainstorming, question and discuss the ideas to get agreement (vote if large class) on it being rated worth using or not worth using. Cross off ideas not worth using. Try to come up with agreement (vote) for the top three ideas that would be implemented by Carolyn first. Other ideas could be used later.

Conclusion
The instructor may lead a class discussion and/or make concluding remarks.

Application (2–4 minutes)
What did I learn from this experience? How will I use this knowledge in the future?

____

____

____

Sharing
Volunteers give their answers to the application section.

The Strategic and Operational Planning Process

Learning Objectives

After studying this chapter, you should be able to:

1. Describe the difference between strategic and operational plans.
2. State the difference among the three levels of strategies: corporate, business, and functional.
3. Explain the reason for conducting an industry and competitive situation analysis.
4. Explain the reason for conducting a company situation analysis.
5. State how competitive advantage and benchmarking are related.
6. Discuss how goals and objectives are similar yet different.
7. List the steps in the writing objectives model.
8. Describe the four grand strategies: growth, stability, turnaround and retrenchment, and combination.
9. Describe the three growth strategies: concentration, integration, and diversification.
10. Discuss the three business-level adaptive strategies: prospecting, defending, and analyzing.
11. List the four major functional operational strategy areas.
12. Define the following **key terms** (in order of appearance in the chapter):

    strategic planning
    operational planning
    strategic process
    strategy
    three levels of strategies
    corporate-level strategy
    business-level strategy
    functional-level strategy
    situation analysis
    SWOT analysis
    competitive advantage
    benchmarking
    goals
    objectives
    writing objectives model
    management by objectives (MBO)
    grand strategy
    corporate growth strategies
    merger
    acquisition
    business portfolio analysis
    adaptive strategies
    functional strategies

Skill Development

1. You can learn to write effective objectives (Skill-Building Exercise 5–1).

2. You can learn to develop a strategic plan for a business (Skill-Building Exercise 5–2).

These skills are part of conceptual and decision-making management skills. These exercises develop your planning and decisional roles skills. The exercises also develop the SCANS skill competencies of using resources, information, and systems, as well as basic and thinking foundation skills.

Jiffy Lube of Utah began operations in Utah and Colorado. James Hindman bought the company and changed the name to Jiffy Lube International in 1979.

Hindman was the new football coach at Western Maryland College. After graduating with a physical education degree, Peter Clark worked as a graduate assistant coaching football and worked for Hindman for two years as he completed his master's degree and for another two years as a coach and teacher. Hindman asked Pete to work for him at Jiffy Lube. Hindman sent Pete to Utah for three months to learn how to operate Jiffy Lubes. Pete came back to Baltimore as director of training and began to teach people who bought Jiffy Lube franchises how to run them. Pete developed a procedures manual and later became operations manager. After setting up a hundred Jiffy Lubes, Pete decided to quit working for Jiffy Lube and become a franchisee.

Pete became a 50 percent partner with Steve Spinelli in two Jiffy Lube service centers in western Massachusetts. Pete and Steve developed several more service centers. They then became 25 percent partners with Rich Heritage (50 percent) and developed service centers in the Hartford,

Connecticut area. Pete, Steve, and Rich joined with John Sasser to buy nine existing service centers in New York that were not being run well and to develop more service centers. This combined Jiffy Lube business was called American Oil Change, totaled 47 service centers in New England and New York, and employed around 700 people. Pennzoil bought Jiffy Lube International and began to aggressively buy back successful franchises. In 1991, Pete and his partners sold their 47 service centers to Pennzoil's Jiffy Lube.

Pete Clark and his partners own six Jiffy Lubes and employ about 70 people.

At the same time, Pete became a 33⅓ percent partner with his two brothers, James and Paul Clark, who started two centers in Pittsfield, Massachusetts, and a 50 percent partner with his wife Korby's sister Gail Bowman in Worcester, Massachusetts. In 1994, Pete and his brothers sold the Pittsfield Jiffy Lubes to Pennzoil's Jiffy Lube. Today, Pete and Korby are 50 percent owner of six Jiffy Lubes in the Worcester area, with Gail as a 25 percent partner. Gail sold half of her share of the business and moved to Illinois. A new 25 percent partner, Dave Macchia, serves as the operations manager.

Since 1991, at age 37, Pete no longer works full time managing his Jiffy Lube operations. He presently helps Dave run the business, and spends more time in community service, coaching, and with his family. Pete spends many hours working for the Jimmy Fund. Pete has been a football coach at Trinity College, a baseball coach at Agawam High School, and coaches his children's Agawam basketball, baseball, and softball teams.

Throughout this chapter you will learn more about the large businesses of Pennzoil and the small business franchise of Bowman-Clark, Inc. (Pete and his partners currently own six Jiffy Lubes which employ around 70 people).[1]

For current information on Jiffy Lube, use Internet address http://www.jiffylube.com. For ideas on using the Internet, see the Appendix.

STRATEGIC AND OPERATIONAL PLANNING

Chapter 1 defined planning as the process of setting objectives and determining in advance exactly how the objectives will be met. In Chapters 5 and 6 we expand on planning to include a variety of types of plans. In this section you will learn about the planning process and the levels of strategic planning. But first you should understand the importance of planning.

In Chapter 4 you learned the importance of creativity that leads to innovation of new products. Simply having a great idea does not automatically guarantee success. In fact, about eight of every ten (80 percent) product introductions fail. The primary reason for failure is poor planning.[2] A few examples include Weyerhaeuser's UltraSofts baby diapers, R.J. Reynolds' smokeless cigarette Premier, General Mills' Benefit cereal, and Anheuser-Busch's LA Beer.[3] Even highly successful products fail due to poor planning. Harvey Harris started a business, Grandmother Calendar Company, selling elaborate cut-rate personalized calendars. Orders came in much faster than he could fill them, so Harvey diverted money needed for day-to-day expenses to expand capacity. He got output up to 300 calendars a day, but orders came in at a rate of 1,000 a day. As Christmas got closer, tens of thousands of orders went unfilled. Because most orders were to be paid by credit card, Harvey would not get paid until he shipped the calendars. Checks, including paychecks for around 100 employees, began to bounce, ceased altogether, and Harvey stopped business operations. Harvey admits that making mistakes, poor decisions, and poor planning caused the business to fail.[4]

The Strategic Process

1. Describe the difference between strategic and operational plans.

strategic planning
The process of developing a mission and long-range objectives and determining in advance how they will be accomplished.

operational planning
The process of setting short-range objectives and determining in advance how they will be accomplished.

Strategic planning *is the process of developing a mission and long-range objectives and determining in advance how they will be accomplished.* **Operational planning** *is the process of setting short-range objectives and determining in advance how they will be accomplished.* The difference between planning, strategic planning, and operational planning is primarily the timeframe and management level involved. Planning does not specify a timeframe. Strategic planning includes developing a mission statement and long-term objectives. *Long-term* generally means that it will take longer than one year to achieve the objective. Strategic plans are commonly developed for five years, and reviewed and revised every year so that there is always a five-year plan. Top-level managers develop strategic plans. Operational plans have *short-term* objectives that will be met in one year or less. Middle and first-line managers develop operational plans. Some organizations also distinguish *tactical plans* from strategic and operational plans. Tactical plans have an intermediate range between strategic and operational plans. Many organizations combine tactical and operational plans and call them both tactical or operational. We will combine them and call them *operational planning*.

Work Application

1. Give an example strategic and operational objective from an organization you work or have worked for.

Through the strategic process, upper-level managers develop the long-range plans and the middle and lower-level managers develop the operational plans to accomplish the long-range objectives. Following the means-end chain (Chapter 2), top managers determine the ends and the middle- and lower-level managers determine the means to accomplish the ends. The key to a successful strategic process is the coordination of the strategic and operational plans—bridging the gap between levels.[5]

strategic process
The steps are (1) developing the mission, (2) analyzing the environment, (3) setting objectives, (4) developing strategies, and (5) implementing and controlling strategies.

The steps in the **strategic process** *are (1) developing the mission, (2) analyzing the environment, (3) setting objectives, (4) developing strategies, and (5) implementing and controlling strategies.* Developing strategies takes place at three levels. This section presents developing strategies followed by developing the mission. Other section of this chapter cover the other steps. See Figure 5–1 for an illustration of the strategic process. Notice that the process does not simply go linear from steps 1–5 and end. As the arrows indicate, you need to return to prior steps and make changes as an ongoing process. You should also realize that the strategic process includes the four functions of management. After the plans have been developed, organizing (delegating responsibility for achieving objec-

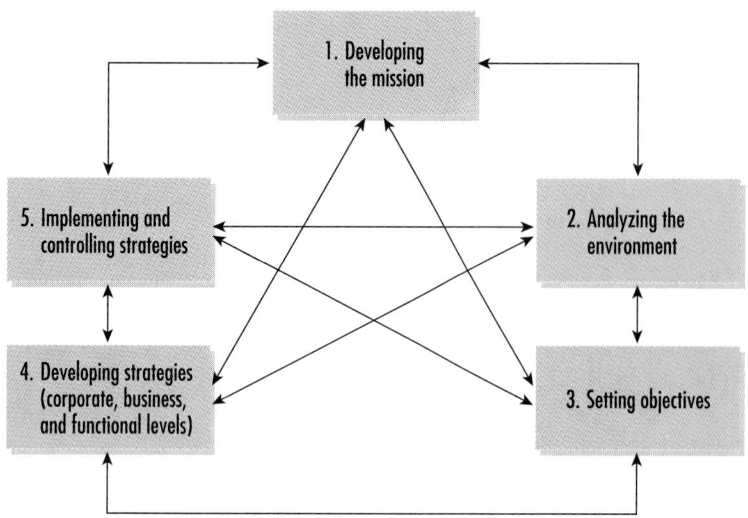

Figure 5–1
The Strategic Process

tives), leading (influencing employees to achieve objectives through communication and motivation), and controlling (taking action to monitor progress and taking corrective action when needed) are needed to continue the process. As a final note, there is no universally accepted strategic list of process steps.

Levels of Strategies

2. State the difference among the three levels of strategies: corporate, business, and functional.

strategy
A plan for pursuing the mission and achieving objectives.

three levels of strategies
Corporate, business, and functional.

corporate-level strategy
The plan for managing multiple lines of businesses.

business-level strategy
The plan for managing one line of business.

functional-level strategy
The plan for managing one area of the business.

A **strategy** *is a plan for pursuing the mission and achieving objectives. The* **three levels of strategies** *are corporate, business, and functional.* The primary difference is the planning focus, which narrows as strategy moves down the organization, and the management level involved in developing the strategy. You will learn more about these three levels of strategies in separate sections later in this chapter. For now, we will simply define each so that you will understand the difference among the three levels.

The **corporate-level strategy** *is the plan for managing multiple lines of businesses.* Many, especially large, companies actually consist of several businesses. Philip Morris has a Philip Morris tobacco line of business, Miller Beer, and Kraft General Foods. General Motors has GM Automobiles, Electronic Data Systems, and Hughes Electronics. Jiffy Lube is one of Pennzoil's lines of business. However, most, especially small, businesses are only in one line of business, Pete Clark's business being one example. Therefore, they do not require corporate strategy.

The **business-level strategy** *is the plan for managing one line of business.* Each of Philip Morris's and General Motors' lines of business has its own strategy for competing in its industry environment. In 1906, after accidentally discovering a way to make ready-to-eat cereal, Keith Kellogg started Kellogg Company. To this day, Kellogg has continued to focus on this single line of business. Pete Clark, with partners, has focused on one line of business.

The **functional-level strategy** *is the plan for managing one area of the business.* The functional areas, discussed in prior chapters, are marketing, finance and accounting, operations/production, human resources, and others based on the line of business. Each of Pete's six Jiffy Lube managers is involved with these functional areas. See Figure 5–2 for an illustration of strategic and operational levels.

Work Application

2. Does a business you work or have worked for have multiple lines of business? If yes, list them.

Developing the Mission

Developing the mission is the first step in the strategic process. However, after analyzing the environment you should reexamine the mission to see if it needs to be changed. The mission is important because it is the foundation of the other four steps in the strategic process. In the ongoing business that has already developed a mission, the task is to critically review the mission and to change it if necessary.[6] The organization's mission is its purpose or reason for being (Chapter 2). The mission states what business(s) the company is in now and will be in the future. A mission creates a vision of where the company is headed

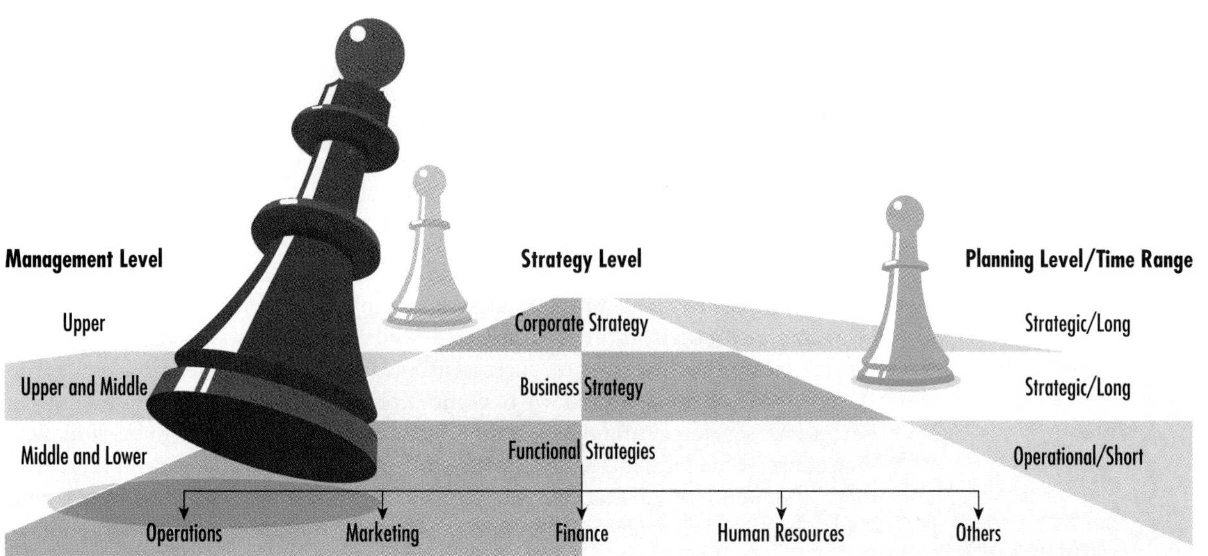

Figure 5–2
Strategic and Operational Levels

and why. It contains the expectations the organization strives to achieve.[7] You may want to review the Federal Express mission statement in Chapter 2, Figure 2–1. Pete stated his Jiffy Lube mission as: "Our business is the automobile oil-changing service business. We provide a timely, high-quality service to provide customer satisfaction."

Pete and others[8] realize the importance of focusing and developing a strategic process from the customer's perspective. CEOs strive to increase customer satisfaction by improving products and reducing delivery times (time-based competition).[9] Pete has no clear definition of quality because the customer determines quality (Chapter 2). It is the customers' perception of how they were treated when they come in for service. If customers perceive they have been treated well, they come back the next time they need their oil changed. Customer satisfaction is so important that many companies focus on it as a corporate strategy, and companies with a customer satisfaction strategy generally outperform those that are not customer satisfaction oriented.[10]

The number of organizations that develop strategic plans has been increasing. Much of the growth comes from the nonprofit sector, following the lead of successful major corporations. There are a variety of software packages that aid in the development of strategic planning.[11]

ANALYZING THE ENVIRONMENT

The process of strategic planning should be externally focused.[12] A business strategy must be congruent with the capabilities of the firm and its external environment.[13] The internal and external environmental factors (Chapter 2) are analyzed as step 2 in the strategic process,[14] which determines congruence. Another term for analyzing the environment is situation analysis. A **situation analysis** *draws out those features in a company's environment that most directly frame its strategic window of options and opportunities*. The situation analysis has three parts: industry and competitive analysis, company situational analysis

situation analysis
Draws out those features in a company's environment that most directly frame its strategic window of options and opportunities.

(SWOT), and competitive advantage. Keep in mind that companies with multiple lines of business must conduct an environmental analysis for each line of business.

3. Explain the reason for conducting an industry and competitive situation analysis.

Industry and Competitive Situation Analysis

Industries vary widely in their business makeup, competitive situation, and growth potential. To determine the attractiveness of an industry requires answering questions such as: How large is the market? What is the growth rate? How many competitors are there? Pete described his industry as the automotive service industry. The market size is around 250,000 people, and since the Worcester area is saturated with competitors, little growth potential exists. Pete's (six service centers) major direct competitors are Ready Lube (four service centers, one under construction), Oil Doctor (two service centers), and the many independent gas stations, service centers (Firestone, Goodyear, etc.), and dealerships that also change oil. Michael Porter developed the five competitive forces as a tool for analyzing the competitive environment.[15]

Five Competitive Forces. Competition in an industry is a composite of five competitive forces:

1. *The rivalry among competing sellers in the industry.* Porter calls this the scrambling and jockeying for position. How do businesses compete for customers (price, quality, speed, and so on)? How competitive is the industry? Coca-Cola and Pepsi and AT&T, MCI, and Sprint are competitive rivals. The company needs to anticipate competitive moves.
2. *Threat of substitute products and services.* Companies in other industries may try to take customers away. Very Fine Juice, Snapple, Gatorade, and others have gone after soda drinkers to substitute juice drinks.
3. *Potential new entrants.* How difficult and costly is it for new businesses to enter the industry as competitors? Does the company need to plan for new competition? Coke and Pepsi don't have to be too concerned about new competition, but the local small business video store may have to compete with a new Blockbuster.
4. *Power of suppliers.* How much does the business depend on the supplier? If the business has only one major supplier, without alternatives available, the supplier has great bargaining power over the business. Coca-Cola has great power over independently owned Coca-Cola bottlers because it is the sole supplier. However, the small video store can buy its videos from any number of suppliers, who have little power over it.
5. *Power of buyers.* How much does the business depend on the buyer? If the business has only one major buyer, or a few, without alternatives available, the buyer has great bargaining power over the business. GM told its suppliers that they would have to cut their prices or lose business. Many of the businesses that sell to GM had no bargaining power and lowered their prices.

Companies use industry and competitive situation analysis primarily at the corporate strategy level to make decisions regarding which lines of business to enter and exit and how to allocate resources among lines of business. This will be explained in more detail later in this chapter. Pennzoil bought Jiffy

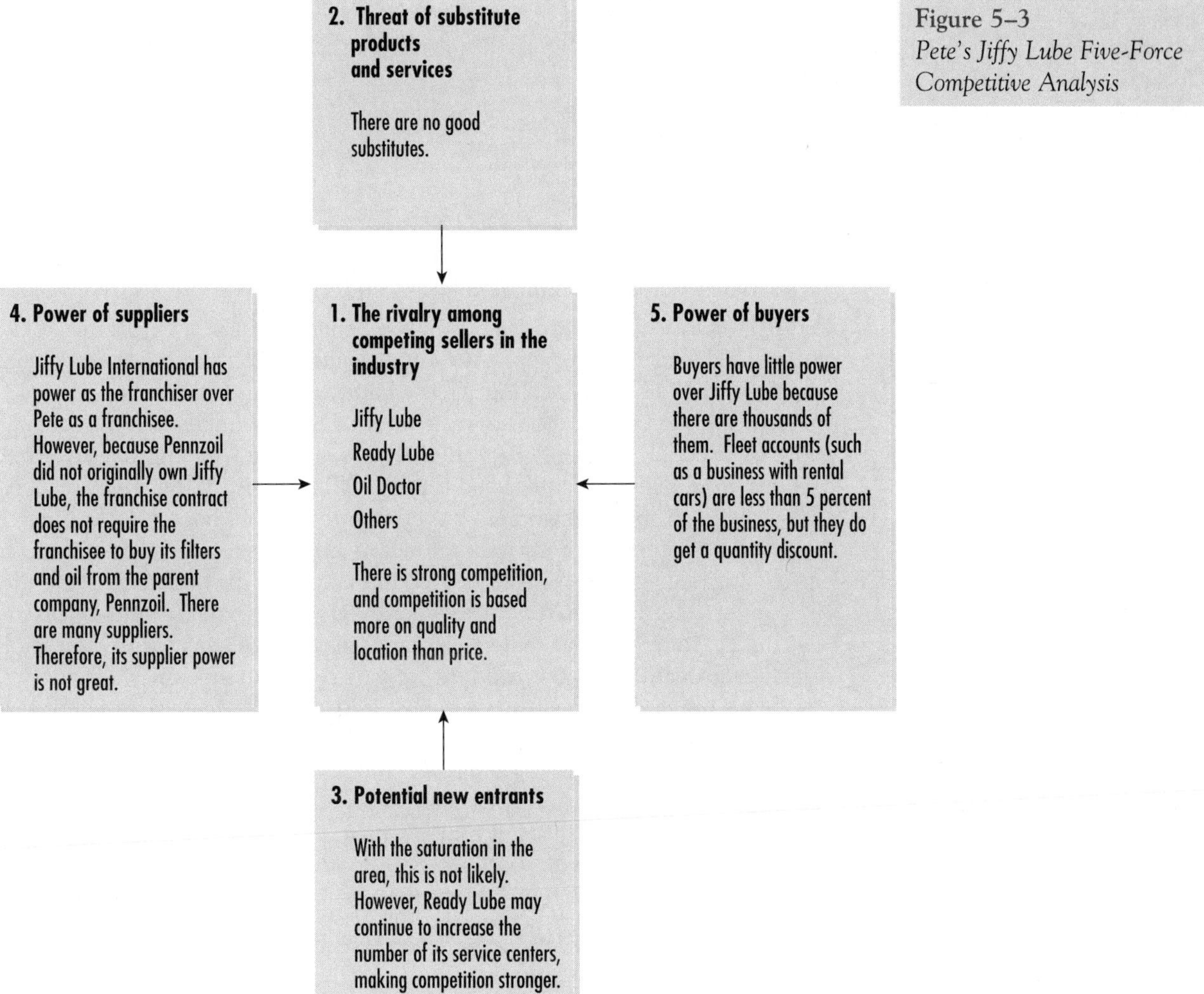

2. Threat of substitute products and services
There are no good substitutes.
4. Power of suppliers
Jiffy Lube International has power as the franchiser over Pete as a franchisee. However, because Pennzoil did not originally own Jiffy Lube, the franchise contract does not require the franchisee to buy its filters and oil from the parent company, Pennzoil. There are many suppliers. Therefore, its supplier power is not great.
1. The rivalry among competing sellers in the industry
Jiffy Lube
Ready Lube
Oil Doctor
Others
There is strong competition, and competition is based more on quality and location than price.
5. Power of buyers
Buyers have little power over Jiffy Lube because there are thousands of them. Fleet accounts (such as a business with rental cars) are less than 5 percent of the business, but they do get a quantity discount.
3. Potential new entrants
With the saturation in the area, this is not likely. However, Ready Lube may continue to increase the number of its service centers, making competition stronger.

Figure 5–3
Pete's Jiffy Lube Five-Force Competitive Analysis

Lube because it was an attractive industry to enter. Pete also used industry and competitive analysis to make the decision to keep his Jiffy Lubes in the Worcester area rather than selling them to Pennzoil, which is still an option. But he does not continually conduct an industry and competitive analysis like Pennzoil does. See Figure 5–3 for a competitive analysis of Pete's Jiffy Lube in the Worcester area. Overall, Pete does not think the industry is attractive to new entrants, but it is attractive for him to stay in this line of business in this area.

Work Application

3. Do a simple five-force competitive analysis for a company you work or have worked for. Use Figure 5–3 as an example.

Company Situation Analysis (SWOT)

4. Explain the reason for conducting a company situation analysis.

The company situation analysis is used at the business strategy level to determine the strategic issues and problems that need to be addressed through the next three steps of the strategic process. A complete company situation analysis has five key parts, listed in Figure 5–4:

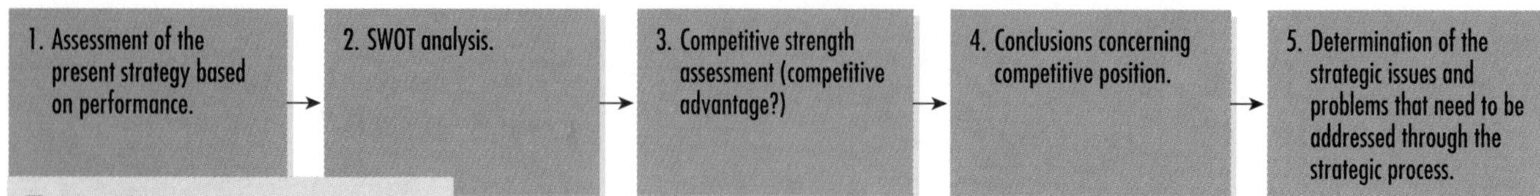
1. Assessment of the present strategy based on performance.
2. SWOT analysis.
3. Competitive strength assessment (competitive advantage?)
4. Conclusions concerning competitive position.
5. Determination of the strategic issues and problems that need to be addressed through the strategic process.

Figure 5–4
Company Situation Analysis Steps

1. *Assessment of present strategy based on performance*. This can be a simple statement or a more complex comparison of performance indicators (market share, sales, net profit, return on assets, and so on) over the last five years.
2. *SWOT analysis. An organization's internal environmental strengths and weaknesses and external environmental opportunities and threats are determined through a* **SWOT analysis.** SWOT is a highly recommended strategic tool.[16] Wal-Mart asked its pet food suppliers to do a SWOT analysis; it sent them a 33-page Vendor Planning Packet. Due to Wal-Mart's buying power of $49 billion, most suppliers completed the SWOT analysis.[17] The SWOT analysis is based on the environment covered in detail in Chapter 2. As a quick review, the internal environmental factors analyzed for *strengths* and *weaknesses* are management, mission, resources, systems process, and structure. The external environmental factors analyzed for *opportunities* and *threats* are customers, competitors, suppliers, labor force, shareholders, society, technology, governments, and the economy. Figure 5–4 contains a SWOT analysis for Pete's Jiffy Lube. The primary opportunity that Hindman realized for Jiffy Lube came out of a threat to the small local gas station. During the 1973 oil embargo, there was little gas available, and many small gas stations who also performed service went out of business. Hindman knew that oil should be changed every 3,000 miles, but that few people changed it that often because of the long wait at service stations. So Hindman took advantage of the opportunity to provide customer value through buying Jiffy Lube of Utah.

SWOT analysis
An organization's internal environmental strengths and weaknesses and external environmental opportunities and threats are determined.

3. *Competitive strength assessment (competitive advantage?)*. For a strategy to be effective, it must be based on a clear understanding of competitors.[18] The critical success factors for the line of business are compared to each major competitor. *Critical success factors* are the few major things that the business must do well to be successful. Through the competitive strength assessment, the organization may elect to develop a competitive advantage. Because all organizations do not elect to develop competitive advantages, it is covered separately as the final part of this section. Organizations may apply two common approaches. Assign each factor a rating of 1 (weak) to 10 (strong) and add up the ratings to determine the ranking of competitors. The second approach uses the same rating system, but weights the critical success factors by importance. The total of the weights equals 1.00. The weight is multiplied by the rating to get a score for each firm on each factor. Scores are totaled to determine the ranking of competitors. Figure 5–5 gives an example of the weighted method for Pete's Jiffy Lube.
4. *Conclusions concerning competitive position*. How is the business doing compared to its competition? Are things improving, slipping, etc?
5. *Determination of the strategic issues and problems that need to be addressed through the strategic process*. Based on parts 1 through 4, what needs to be done in the future to improve competitive position?

Work Application

4. List a couple of the major strengths and weaknesses of an organization you work or have worked for.

1. Assessment of the Present Strategy Based on Performance
Our present strategy is working well. Our performance has been profitable, even during economic downturn in the late 1980s into 1990–1991, but has been strong since 1992.

2. SWOT Analysis
Strengths. Our major strength is the reputation we have developed by being the first company to focus on quick oil change. Being first, we also have selected the prime locations for our service centers. We have a strong management team with a clear mission. A major strength is tight budgetary control over our resources. Our information resource computer enables us to have a complete history of all work done on each car. We continually focus on cost cutting. Our systems process and structure are strong and allow us to lube a car in 10 to 15 minutes.

Weakness. Our one weakness concerns employees who provide the service and interact with customers. Changing oil is not a high-skill, high-paying job. Therefore, we have to be careful to hire employees capable of being responsible and using the good human relations skills we teach them. An irresponsible employee who makes a mistake, such as not putting the oil plug back in so the oil leaks as the person drives the car, can cost money and lost customers.

Opportunity. In the Worcester area, we could put in one more service center, and we could expand into other areas. I see our primary opportunity in offering new services, which we have done over the years. In addition to an oil change, we offer air conditioning, radiator, PVC, and lights services. Jiffy Lube International continues to test new services and lets franchises know which ones work. During better economic times we have the opportunity to service more cars.

Threats. Our major immediate threat comes from the government. Environmental protection requires us to meet standards. For example, new air conditioning systems that do not use freon require us to purchase new machines to service newer cars. This is expensive and it takes up space to have two machines. The Occupational Safety and Health Administration (OSHA) also requires us to meet standards. Through government influence, a major long-term threat is the technology of the electric car. Electric cars do not need an oil change.

3. Competitive Strength Assessment
(rating: 1 (low) to 10 (high) for each firm) (rating × weight –)

Critical success factors	*Weight*	*Jiffy Lube*	*Ready Lube*	*Oil Doctor*
Training	.60	10—6.0	8—4.8	2—1.2
Quality perception	.20	9—1.8	7—1.4	2—0.4
Timely service	.20	8—1.6	8—1.6	3—0.6
Total	1.00	9.4	7.8	2.2

Note: There is a system affect among the critical success factors. Training is the most important factor, because through the training employees learn to deliver quality perception by professional interaction with customers, and they learn to do the job right in a timely manner. Slow service will influence the quality perception.

3. Competitive Advantage
Our competitive advantage is our name recognition and quality image with key locations. Being an industry leader, Jiffy Lube does most of its benchmarking among its own service centers. Franchises are provided with all kinds of statistics that allow us to compare our business to others.

4. Conclusions Concerning Competitive Position
We are the leading, or strongest, competitor and will continue to be through continual improvement of quality service.

5. Determination of the Strategic Issues and Problems That Need to Be Addressed Through the Strategic Process
The three primary areas my Jiffy Lube needs to focus on are: (1) keeping up with Jiffy Lube International research and using new ideas for improving my business; (2) keeping up with the environmental issues; and (3) continuing to monitor Ready Lube which is aggressively trying to take our customers. For example, they are moving across the street from us at their new location.

Figure 5–5
Pete's Jiffy Lube Company Situation Analysis

5. State how competitive advantage and benchmarking are related.

Competitive Advantage

Recall that developing a competitive advantage is an optional part of step 3 of the company situation analysis. Through strategic planning, a competitive advantage should be created.[19] Many organizations are focusing on developing competitive advantages based on high quality and time-based competition.[20] A **competitive advantage** *specifies how the organization offers unique customer value.* It answers the questions: What makes us different from our competition? Why should a person buy our product or service rather than the competitions'? A sustainable competitive advantage (1) distinguishes the organization from its competitors, (2) provides positive economic benefits, and (3) cannot be readily duplicated. The key to producing sustainable competitive advantage is effective management of people.[21]

competitive advantage
Specifies how the organization offers unique customer value.

Pizza Hut had a competitive advantage for restaurant dining before Domino's arrived. Domino's did not compete head on with restaurants; it made free delivery its competitive advantage. Little Caesar started by offering two-pizza deals and crazy bread as a competitive advantage. Some competitive advantages are not sustainable because they are easily copied. Pizza Hut and many local pizza places started to deliver years ago, and Little Caesar began delivery in 1995. However, the creator, such as Domino's and Jiffy Lube, often gets the name recognition and reputation that the followers don't have. If you ask people for the name of a company that delivers pizza and a place to get a quick oil change, most will say Domino's and Jiffy Lube. Jiffy Lube International advertising in 1994 emphasized the quality of both Jiffy Lube and Pennzoil motor oil with the theme, "If it doesn't say Jiffy Lube, it just isn't Jiffy Lube"; this was used to maintain its name competitive advantage.

When a successful business has a competitive advantage, competitors often copy it rather than developing a competitive advantage. Ready Lube and Oil Doctor don't really have a competitive advantage, other than different locations that are more convenient for some customers. It is also difficult to differentiate one product from others that are highly similar. What is Pennzoil's competitive advantage over the many other brands of oil, or Texaco's over other brands of gasoline?

Businesses also use low cost or price as a competitive advantage. If you walk into a supermarket to buy a cola, you will most likely find local brands priced lower than Coke and Pepsi in order to offer customer value. Many stations that compete with Mobil, Exxon, and other national gas stations sell gas at a lower price. The fast oil-change service centers in Pete's area charge about the same price.

Competitive advantage, also called comparative advantage, has developed into a theory called the *comparative advantage theory of competition.*[22] A consulting firm with the name The Competitive Business Advantage Business works with companies to develop a competitive advantage.[23] If you ever consider starting a business, be sure to answer the questions What will make my business different from the competition's? Why should a person buy my product or service rather than the competition's? If you don't have an answer, you will not have a competitive advantage, and you may not be able to get enough customers to have a successful business. Skill-Building Exercise 5–2 requires you to develop a strategic plan for a business that you may be interested in starting some day.

Work Application

5. Does a company you work or have worked for have a competitive advantage? If yes, state it. If no, state how it is the same as competitors.

Two related concepts of competitive advantage are core competency and benchmarking. A *core competency* is what a firm does well. Core competencies are a strength.[24] By identifying core competencies, new products and services can be created that take advantage of the company strengths. For example, Honda has a core competency in engines. It went from cars and motorcycles, which are based on engines, to garden tillers, lawn mowers, snowblowers, snowmobiles, power generators, and outboard motors. **Benchmarking** *is the process of comparing an organization's products and processes with those of other companies.* The idea of benchmarking is to legally and ethically find out about other products and processes and to copy them or improve upon them. Most benchmarking takes place within an industry to eliminate competitive advantages. For example, Ready Lube and Oil Doctor basically resemble Jiffy Lube. Pizza Hut and Little Caesar copied Domino's delivery. However, looking at noncompetitors can provide good ideas that create a competitive advantage. McDonald's in mid-Manhattan copied free delivery.[25] Copying and improving on others' ideas can help the business to develop a competitive advantage, to eliminate one, or both. For example, Burger King copied McDonald's fast-food process, and often its locations, but it differentiates itself by inviting customers to "have it your way" and stating, "Our burgers are flame broiled, not fried like McDonald's."

benchmarking
The process of comparing an organization's products and processes with those of other companies.

After completing the situation analysis, go back and review the mission to see if it needs to be changed. Remember that the situation analysis is an ongoing process, referred to as *scanning the environment*. It tells you what is going on in the external environment that may require change in order to continually improve customer value. See Figure 5–5 for a company situation analysis.

SETTING OBJECTIVES

Successful strategic management requires a commitment to a defined set of objectives by management.[26] After developing a mission and completing a situation analysis, you are ready for the third step in the strategic process: setting objectives that flow from the mission to address strategic issues and problems identified through the situation analysis. Managers should have multiple objectives that are prioritized to allow focus on the more important one.[27] In Chapter 7 you will learn how to prioritize.

Objectives are end results; they do not state how the objective will be accomplished. Achieving the objective is the next step, in the strategic process. In this section you will learn the difference between goals and objectives, how to write objectives, the criteria for effective objectives, and about management by objectives (MBO).

6. Discuss how goals and objectives are similar yet different.

Goals and Objectives

Some people use the terms *goal* and *objectives* synonymously. You should be able to distinguish between them. **Goals** *state general targets to be accomplished.* **Objectives** *state what is to be accomplished in singular, specific, and measurable terms with a target date.* Goals are commonly used and are very useful, but objectives are needed to develop plans and to know if the end result is achieved. For example, Jiffy Lube's goal is perfect service for every customer. This goal is

goals
General targets to be accomplished.

objectives
What is to be accomplished in singular, specific, and measurable terms with a target date.

Figure 5–6
Pennzoil Goals and Objectives for its Oil and Gas Division

Goal
- To raise our performance to the top quartile of our peers.
  To reach the top quartile, we have set four specific objectives.

Objectives
- Annual reserve replacement of 180 percent.
- Replacement cost of $4.30 per barrel of oil equivalent (boe).
- Operating cost, including general and administrative, of $4.25/boe.
- Return on assets of 10 percent after taxes.

Work Application

6. State one or more goals from an organization you work or have worked for.

very useful for providing guidance for employee actions, but how can this be measured? How do you know if you have perfect service? Goals are often translated into objectives. For an example, see Figure 5–6.

7. List the steps in the writing objectives model.

writing objectives model
(1) infinitive + (2) action verb + (3) singular, specific, and measurable result to be achieved + (4) target date.

Writing Objectives

To help ensure that they will be met, objectives should be written and kept in a visual place, such as on your desk or wall rather than in a policy handbook.[28] To help you to write effective objectives that meet the criteria you will learn next, use the writing objectives model. *The parts of the* **writing objectives model** *are (1) infinitive + (2) action verb + (3) singular, specific, and measurable result to be achieved + (4) target date*. Model 5–1 shows the model, which is adapted from Max E. Douglas's model. Other example objectives will be provided with each criteria.

Criteria for Objectives

An effective objective includes four "must" criteria listed in steps 3 and 4 of the writing objectives model. For each criteria, an example of an ineffective objective will be presented, followed by a correction of the objective to make it effective.

Model 5–1
Writing Objectives Model

Organizing → Controlling → Leading → Planning

Four parts of the model:
(1) infinitive +
(2) action verb +
(3) singular, specific, and measurable result to be achieved +
(4) target date

Example from Wal-Mart:[29]
To increase sales per square foot from $325 to $400 by December 1996.
(1) + (2) + (3) + (4)

Singular Result. To avoid confusion, each objective should contain only one end result. With multiple objectives listed together, one may be met and the other(s) may not be. The example comes from Wal-Mart stores.[30]

Ineffective Objective	To increase pet food sales by 25% and to achieve a 5.4% market share.
Effective Objectives	To increase pet food sales by 25% by December 1996. To achieve a 5.4% market share of pet foods during 1996.

Specific. The objective should state the exact level of performance expected. The first example is generic; the second is based on the American Paper Institute.[31]

Ineffective Objective	To maximize profits in 1998. (How much is "maximize"?) To recycle 40% by year end 1995. ($40% of what—glass, paper? type of paper?)
Effective Objectives	To earn a net profit of $1 million in 1998. To recycle 40% of all paper by year end 1995.

Measurable. If people are to achieve objectives, they must be able to observe and measure their progress regularly to determine if the objective has been met. The following example is a Jiffy Lube goal.

Ineffective Objective	Perfect service for every customer. (How do you measure service?)
Effective Objective	To attain a 90% customer "excellent" satisfaction rating for 1999.

Target Date. A specific date should be set for accomplishing the objective. When people have a deadline, they usually try harder to get the task done on time than when they are simply told to do it when they can. We don't tend to get around to it until we have to. The example is based on Logical Water (a software company that developed Quesheet, a program that helps businesses find better ways to achieve their objectives).[32]

Ineffective Objective	To become a multimillionaire. (By when?)
Effective Objective	To become a multimillionaire by December 1997.

It is also more effective to set a specific date than to give a time span because you can forget when the period began and should end. The following example is based on GTE:[33]

Somewhat Effective	To double international business to $5 billion annually within five years.
Effective Objective	To double international business to $5 billion annually by year end 2000.

Some objectives are ongoing and do not require a stated date. The target date is indefinite until it is changed. The following well-known examples come from 3M and General Electric:

Effective Objectives	To have 25% of sales coming from products that did not exist five years ago. To be number one or two in world sales in all lines of business.

Work Application

7. Using the writing objectives model, write one or more objectives for an organization you work or have worked for that meet the criteria objectives should meet.

GE will get out of any line of business in which it is not, or does not, have the potential to become number one or two in the world.

In addition to the four "must" criteria, there are three "want" criteria.

Difficult but Achievable (Realistic). A number of studies show that individuals perform better when assigned difficult but achievable objectives rather than objectives that are too difficult or too easy or when simply told "do your best."[34] You will learn the details in Chapter 11. *Realistic* is a subjective concept; therefore, it is a "want" rather than a "must" criterion.

Participatively Set. Groups that participate in setting their objectives generally outperform groups with assigned objectives (Chapter 4). Managers should use the appropriate level of participation for the employees' capabilities. Because it is not always appropriate to have the group set objectives, it is a "want" rather than a "must" criterion.

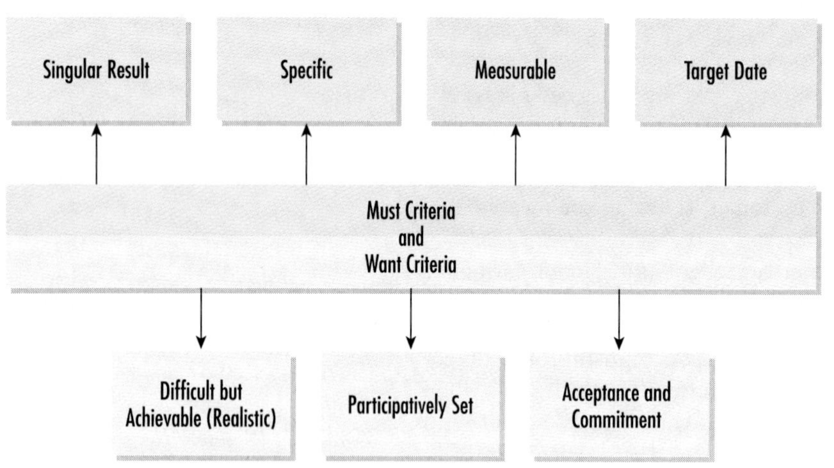

Figure 5–7
Criteria Objectives Should Meet

Acceptance and Commitment. For objectives to be met, employees must accept them. If employees do not commit to strive for the objective, even if you meet the preceding criteria, they may not meet the objective. Participation helps get employees to accept objectives (Chapter 4). Because acceptance and commitment vary from individual to individual and times occur when managers must set objectives that employees will not like, acceptance and commitment are "want" criteria. For a review of the criteria objectives should meet, see Figure 5–7.

SKILLBUILDER

Management by Objectives (MBO)

management by objectives (MBO) The process in which managers and their employees jointly set objectives for the employees, periodically evaluate the performance, and reward according to the results.

Managers need to learn to point workers to a common goal. MBO attempts to do this. **Management by objectives (MBO)** *is the process in which managers and their employees jointly set objectives for the employees, periodically evaluate the performance, and reward according to the results.* Other names for MBO include work planning and review, goals management, goals and controls, and management by results.

For a program to truly be MBO, it should be organizationwide. MBO starts at the top of the management hierarchy and works its way down to the workers. Each level of management's objectives must contribute to the next level's objectives. The process is known as the *hierarchy of objectives*. To be successful, MBO takes a lot of commitment, time, and participation.

MBO has met with both success and failure.[35] A major reason has been the lack of commitment and follow-through on management's part. MBO often fails because employees believe that management is insincere in its efforts to include employees in the decision-making process. Employees feel that management has already set the objectives and made the plans for implementation before talking to them. Management uses MBO as a public relations exercise instead of actually valuing the employees' input. You can use the MBO process successfully with your subordinates if you commit and truly involve employees rather than trying to make them believe that your objectives are theirs.

The three steps of MBO include:

step 1. **Set Individual Objectives and Plans.** With each subordinate, the manager jointly sets objectives. The objectives are the heart of the MBO program and should meet the criteria discussed earlier.

step 2. **Give Feedback and Evaluate Performance.** Xerox Learning Systems stated that giving feedback is the most important management skill. Employees must know how they are progressing toward their objectives.[36] Communication is the key factor in determining MBO's success or failure. Thus, the manager and employee must meet frequently to review progress. The frequency of evaluations depends on the individual and the job performed. However, most managers probably do not conduct enough review sessions.

step 3. **Reward According to Performance.** Employees' performance should be measured against their objectives. Employees who meet their objectives should be rewarded through recognition, praise, pay raises, promotions, and so on.

Mary Kay Cosmetics rewards its employees with awards ceremonies, free trips, and even a pink Cadillac.

CORPORATE-LEVEL STRATEGY

After the mission has been developed, the situational analysis has been completed, and objectives have been set, the strategy, step 4 of the strategic process, should be developed at the corporate, business, and functional levels. In this section you will learn about corporate level strategy: grand strategy, corporate growth strategies, portfolio analysis, and the product life cycle.

Grand Strategy

8. Describe the four grand strategies: growth, stability, turnaround and retrenchment, and combination.

grand strategy
The overall corporate-level strategy of growth, stability, turnaround and retrenchment, or a combination thereof.

Grand strategy *is the overall corporate-level strategy of growth, stability, turnaround and retrenchment, or a combination thereof.* Each grand strategy reflects a different objective. Let's discuss each separately.

Growth. With a *growth strategy*, the company makes aggressive attempts to increase its size through increased sales. You will learn more about growth strategies under "Corporate Strategies."

Stability. With a *stability strategy*, the company attempts to hold and maintain its present size or to grow slowly. Many companies are satisfied with the status quo, for example, the WD-40 Company (petroleum-based lubricant) whose product is found in 75 percent of U.S. homes. Pete's Jiffy Lube has a stability strategy.

Turnaround and Retrenchment. *Turnaround strategy* is an attempt to reverse a declining business as quickly as possible. *Retrenchment strategy* is the divestiture or liquidation of assets. They are listed together because most turnarounds include retrenchment. Turnaround strategies generally attempt to improve cash flow by increasing revenues, decreasing cost, reducing assets, or combining these strategies. Texaco made one of the most successful U.S. turnarounds by selling $7 billion in assets and cutting its labor force by close to 11,000. General Motors, which used to have a 40 percent market share of U.S. autos, has increased the quality of its cars and developed a new Saturn line of cars to regain lost market share.

Pennzoil sold substantially all of the domestic assets of its sulphur division. Pete and his partners sold 50 Jiffy Lubes to Pennzoil. A *spinoff* is a form of retrenchment in which the company sells one of its business units to employees who form a separate company. ITT divided itself into three publicly traded companies in one of the largest-ever U.S. corporate breakups.[37] James River had a spinoff of most of its nonconsumer paper and packaging operations.[38]

Work Application

8. State the grand strategy for an organization you work or have worked for.

Combination. A corporation may pursue growth, stability, and turnaround and retrenchment across different lines of business. Pennzoil, like many other companies, has had the grand strategy to buy and sell business lines. You will learn more about this combination under "Portfolio Analysis."

9. Describe the three growth strategies: concentration, integration, and diversification.

Corporate Growth Strategies

corporate growth strategies
Concentration, backward and forward integration, and related and unrelated diversification.

The company that wants to grow has three major options. **Corporate growth strategies** *include concentration, backward and forward integration, and related and unrelated diversification*.

Concentration. With a *concentration strategy*, the organization grows aggressively in its existing line(s) of business. Wal-Mart continues to open new stores. Pennzoil plans to aggressively increase the number of customers served (around 18 million in 1994) by opening more Jiffy Lube service centers (over 1,150 in 1994). Jiffy Lube plans to open 456 service centers in Sears Auto-Service Centers around the United States.[39]

Integration. With an *integration strategy*, the organization enters a forward or backward line(s) of business. *Forward integration* occurs when the organization enters a line of business closer to the final customer. *Backward integration* occurs when the organization enters a line of business far away from the final customer. Pennzoil began refining oil in 1886 and it backward-integrated into extracting oil in 1989. When Pennzoil acquired Jiffy Lube, its forward integration objectives included gaining control over service centers that would be used to sell more of its motor oil. This gave Pennzoil three lines of business: (1) the extraction of oil (raw material), (2) the refinery to produce motor oil, to (3) the final consumer's auto engine at Jiffy Lube. Some manufactures, like Bass shoes, have opened factory outlet stores to forward-integrate, thus bypassing traditional retail stores and selling their products directly to the customer.

Diversification. With a *diversification strategy*, the organization goes into a related or unrelated line of products. Pennzoil uses *related (concentric) diversifi-*

cation by offering new products related to its motor oil through its Gumout line of automotive products. Nike used related diversification when it diversified from sports shoes to selling sports clothing. Sears used *unrelated (conglomerate) diversification* when it went from selling retail goods to selling insurance through its Allstate Insurance line of business. Pennzoil sold its sulfur line of business in order to move away from conglomerate diversification; this allows the company to better focus on its core operations. See Figure 5–8 for a review of strategies at the corporate level.

APPLYING THE CONCEPT

AC 5–1 Corporate Growth Strategies

Identify each statement by the type of growth strategy it would be making.

a. concentration
b. forward integration
c. backward integration
d. related diversification
e. unrelated diversification

____ **1.** Sears buys a tool company to make its Crasftsman tools.

____ **2.** General Motors buys the Sea World theme park.

____ **3.** The Gap opens a new retail store in a mall.

____ **4.** Lee opens stores to sell its clothes.

____ **5.** Gateway 2000, a computer manufacturer, manufactures printers.

Common Growth Strategy Approaches. Common corporate approaches to growth include mergers, acquisitions, takeovers, joint ventures, and strategic alliances. A **merger** *occurs when two companies form one corporation*. Two companies become one new company. *An* **acquisition** *occurs when one business buys all or part of another business*. One business becomes a part of an existing business. Mergers and acquisitions often occur between competing companies to decrease competition; to compete more effectively with larger companies; to realize economies of size; to consolidate expenses; and to achieve access to markets, products, technology, resources, and management talent. Companies often use acquisitions to enter new lines of businesses by buying an existing business rather than starting a new one. When management of the target company rejects the purchasing company's offer, the purchasing company can make a bid to the target company shareholders to acquire the company through a *takeover*.

merger
Occurs when two companies form one corporation.

acquisition
Occurs when one business buys all or part of another business.

You learned about *joint ventures* (partners) and *strategic alliances* (work together without joint ownership), which are of increasing importance to growth (Chapter 2).[40] Some recent examples of the growth approach include: Price Club and Costco warehouse membership clubs become one company: Price

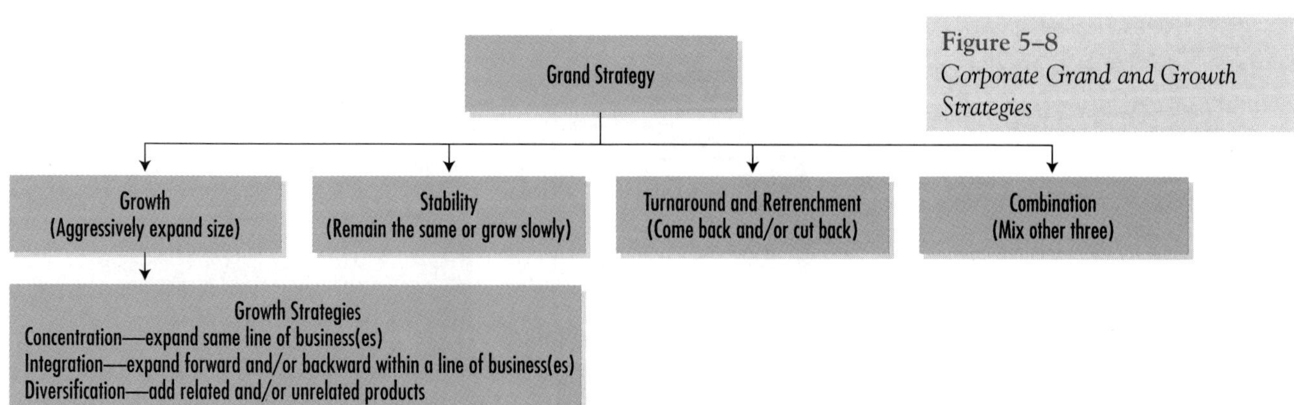

Figure 5–8
Corporate Grand and Growth Strategies

Work Application

9. Identify any growth strategies used by an organization you work or have worked for. Be sure to identify the type of growth strategy and if any mergers, acquisitions, takeovers, joint ventures, or strategic alliances were used.

Costco. Nellcor and Puritan-Bennett[41] and First Data and First Financial Management[42] merged. Vencor acquired Hillhaven, and Crown Cork & Seal acquired CarnaudMetalbox for $4 billion to become the leader in global packaging.[43] Pennzoil acquired Jiffy Lube and Coenerco, a Canadian oil and gas company. Pennzoil also has joint ventures with Brooklyn Union Gas Company (to distribute natural gas), Conoco (Excel Paralubes—to produce base oils), and Petrolite Corporation (Bareco Products—to market wax products).

Portfolio Analysis

business portfolio analysis
The corporate process of determining which lines of business it will be in and how it will allocate resources among them.

Business portfolio analysis *is the corporate process of determining which lines of business it will be in and how it will allocate resources among them.* A *business line*, also called a *strategic business unit (SBU)*, is a distinct business having its own customers that is managed reasonably independently of other businesses within the corporation. What constitutes a SBU varies from company to company, but they can be divisions, subsidiaries, or single product lines. Pennzoil has the following primary businesses: oil and gas (natural), motor oil and refined products, and franchise operations (Jiffy Lube). PepsiCo has soft drinks, Kentucky Fried Chicken, Frito-Lay, Pizza Hut, Taco Bell, and 7Up International. The industry and competitive situation analysis (five competitive forces) for each line of business, step 2 of the strategic process, is used to analyze a portfolio. Another method, the BCG Matrix, puts each line of business into one matrix.

BCG Growth-Share Matrix. A popular approach to analyzing a portfolio is the Boston Consulting Group (BCG) Growth-Share Matrix. The author developed a BCG matrix for Pennzoil, shown in Figure 5–9. The four cells of the matrix are as follows:

- **Cash cows** generate more resources than they need, often with low growth, but with high market share. Examples of cash cows include

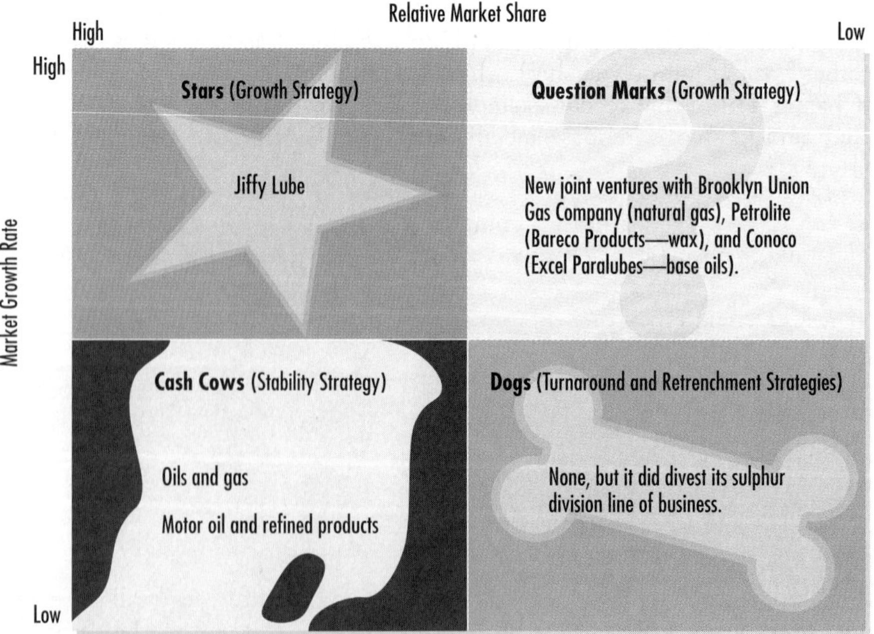

Figure 5–9
Pennzoil's BCG Matrix (Combination Strategy)

Cola-Cola Classic and Crest toothpaste. Cash cows tend to have stability strategies.

- **Stars** are emerging businesses with high growth and market share. Stars require continuing investment of profits into the product, rather than using the funds with a "question mark," to continue growth until they become cash cows. The mini-van became a star for Chrysler and Diet Coke became one for Coca-Cola. Stars tend to have growth strategies.
- **Question marks** are entries into any new businesses with negative returns in a high-growth market, beginning with low market share. Question marks need investments from other lines of business to develop into stars. But, they can become dogs. Maytag acquired Hoover's European unit in hopes of making it a star. However, about five years later it sold Hoover for a $170 million losts.[44] Question marks tend to have growth strategies.
- **Dogs** have low returns in a low-growth market and have low relative market share. Dogs are often divested or liquidated when they no longer provide acceptable profits. Black and white televisions and record turntables have become dogs, and audio tape-players will become dogs because of compact disc players. Dogs tend to have turnaround and retrenchment strategies.

The portfolio analysis (using combination strategy) provides managers with ideas about how to allocate cash and other resources among business lines (as well as which corporate strategies to use). Generally, managers take resources from the cash cows (stability strategy) and allocate them to the question marks, and possibly the stars (growth strategies). Any cash from dogs is also given to question marks and stars, as well as any resources from their sale (retrenchment strategy).

The number of stars and question marks should be balanced with cash cows to finance them, and dogs should be avoided and sold or used as tax write-offs. As SBUs become cash cows, new question marks can be developed. Selection of new business lines to enter is based on the industry and competitive analysis you learned about in step 2 of the strategic process. The new lines of business are growth strategies of integration or diversification.

A company in a single line of business cannot conduct a business portfolio analysis. However, it should perform a *product portfolio analysis*. The BCG business portfolio matrix can also be used to analyze a product line. For example, McDonald's started with a simple hamburger and fries. Over the years McDonald's introduced new products such as the Big Mac. The Big Mac started as a question mark, became a star, and then joined the cash cow hamburger and fries. McDonald introduced pizza as a question mark, but rather than become a star it became a dog and was dropped from most restaurants. A company like Levi Strauss, with a variety of products, can classify each product to balance bringing in new products with the profits from cash cows, like 501 jeans, while phasing out dogs.

BUSINESS-LEVEL STRATEGY

Recall that step 4 of the strategic process is to develop strategies at all three levels. After the organization has followed the first three steps for the corporate level, it must do the same for each line of business. Each line of business must develop its own mission, analyze its own environment (Figure 5–5 shows a company situation analysis for a single line of business), set its own objectives, and develop its own strategy. For the organization with a single line of products, such as Pete's Jiffy Lube, its corporate and business level strategies are the same. For the organization with multiple lines of business, linking corporate strategy with operations at the business unit level determines its success.[45] In this section you will learn about adaptive strategies, competitive strategies, and how to change strategies along the product life cycle.

10. Discuss the three business-level adaptive strategies: prospecting, defending, and analyzing.

Adaptive Strategies

Each line of business needs its own strategy. However, it can be confusing to have the same strategy names at the corporate and business levels. The business level commonly uses the *adaptive strategies*, and they correspond with the grand strategies. However, they emphasize adapting to changes in the external environment and entering new markets as a means of increasing sales. Figure 5–10 illustrates selecting the adaptive strategy based on the changing environment and growth rate, with corresponding grand strategies. Each adaptive strategy reflects a different objective. *The business-level* **adaptive strategies** *include prospecting, defending, and analyzing.*

adaptive strategies
Prospecting, defending, and analyzing

Prospecting Strategy. The *prospecting strategy* calls for aggressively offering new products and/or entering new markets. Wal-Mart continues to open new stores to enter new markets. Pete's Jiffy Lube grew to operate over 50 service centers with the addition of partners. However, recall that growth has to be concentrated or related diversification. If it's integration or unrelated diversification, you need new lines of business and you no longer have a single line of business. The prospector strategy resembles the growth grand strategy and works appropriately in fast-changing environments with high growth potential.

Work Application

10. Identify the adaptive strategy used by an organization you work or have worked for. Be sure to describe how it used the strategy.

Defending Strategy. The *defending strategy* calls for staying with the present product line and markets, and maintaining or increasing customers. Pete uses the defending strategy with his six Jiffy Lubes. Defending resembles the stability grand strategy, and works appropriately in a slow-changing environment with low growth potential.

Analyzing Strategy. The *analyzing strategy* calls for a midrange approach between the prospector and defender. Analyzers move into new market areas at a cautious, deliberate pace and/or offer a core product group and seek new opportunities. Procter & Gamble has several established consumer products, including Pampers and Crest toothpaste, and occasionally offers innovations such

Figure 5–10
Selecting Adaptive Strategies

Rate of Environmental Change	Potential Growth Rate	Adaptive Strategy	Similar to Grand Strategy
Fast	High	**Prospector**	Growth
Moderate	Moderate	**Analyzer**	Combination
Slow	Low	**Defender**	Stability

as Aleve to compete with other pain relievers such as Bayer, Tylenol, and Advil. McDonald's, using the Big Mac and pizza example from product portfolio analysis, is using an analyzing strategy. Analyzing resembles the combination grand strategy, and works appropriately in moderately changing environments with moderate growth potential.

Although the adaptive strategies have no strategy similar to turnaround and retrenchment, strategic business units may need to use this strategy to cut back or stop selling dog products. If the firm does not replace dogs with new products, it may eventually go out of business.

APPLYING THE CONCEPT

AC 5–2 Adaptive Strategies

Identify each statement by the type of adaptive strategy it represents.

a. prospecting b. defending c. analyzing

____ 6. Industry leader Coca-Cola's primary strategy in the saturated U.S. cola market.

____ 7. Nabisco comes out with new "umum" cookie to compete with Keebler's "umum" cookies.

____ 8. Friendly Ice Cream opens restaurants in the State of Washington.

____ 9. IBM pioneers a computer that can be folded up and put in your pocket.

____ 10. Domino's strategy when Pizza Hut started to copy delivering pizza.

Competitive Strategies

Michael Porter identified three effective business-level *competitive strategies:* differentiation, cost leadership, and focus.[46]

Differentiation Strategy. With a differentiation strategy, the company stresses its competitive advantage over its competitors. Nike, Ralph Lauren Polo clothing, Calvin Klein, and others place their names on the outside of their products to create a prestigious differentiation from the competition. Differentiation strategy somewhat resembles the prospector strategy.

Cost Leadership. With a low-cost leadership strategy, the company stresses lower prices to attract customers. To keep its prices down, it must have tight cost control and efficient systems process. Wal-Mart has had success with this strategy. Cost leadership somewhat resembles the defender strategy.

Focus. With a focus strategy, the company focuses on a specific regional market, product line, or buyer group. With a particular target segment, or market niche, the firm may use a differentiation or cost leadership strategy. *Ebony* and *Jet* magazines target African-Americans, MTV focuses on young people, and Rolex watches have a niche of upper-income people. Right Guard deodorant aims at men and Secret aims at women. The focus strategy somewhat resembles the analyzer strategy.

Product Life Cycle

The product life cycle refers to a series of stages that a product goes through over time. The four stages of the *product life cycle* are introduction, growth, maturity, and decline. The speed at which products go through the life cycle varies. Many products, like Tide detergent, stay around for many years, while fad products, like pet rocks, the hula hoop, and pogs may only last months. Figure 5–11 illus-

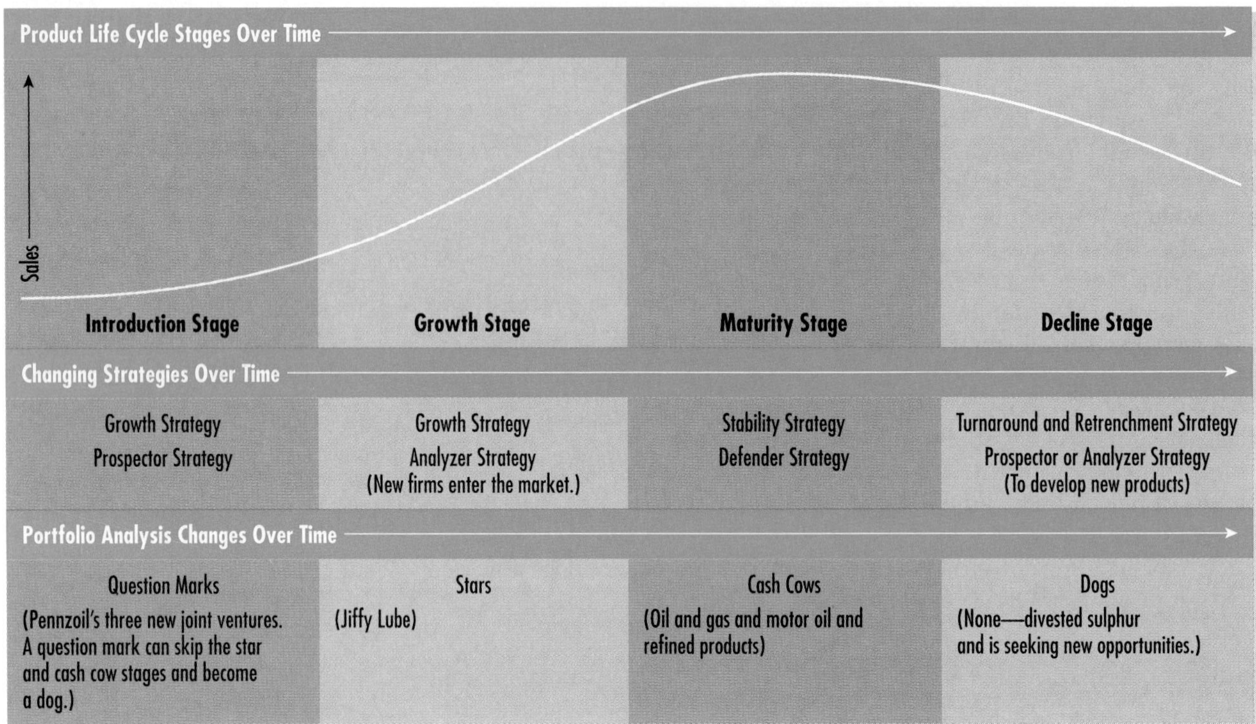

Figure 5–11
Pennzoil Strategies Through the Product Life Cycle Stages

trates the appropriate portfolio analysis, corporate grand strategy, and business-level adaptive strategy for each stage of the product life cycle for Pennzoil.

Introduction Stage. As a growth strategy, the prospector introduces a new product that has a differentiation strategy because it is new; it can also use a focus strategy. It emphasizes getting the product accepted. Resources are used to promote (advertise) the product and to get production going. It is common to charge a high price to try to get back the investment. Jiffy Lube introduced the quick oil change. Introduction products are usually question marks in the business portfolio; Pennzoil's three joint ventures are in their introduction stages.

Work Application

11. Identify the stage in the product life cycle for an organization you work or have worked for. Is the strategy you identified in Work Application 10 the appropriate strategy for this stage of the product life cycle? Explain your answers.

Growth Stage. As a continuing growth strategy, rapid sales growth takes place. When analyzers see that the prospector is doing well, they copy the product through benchmarking. Analyzers may use a differentiation, focus, or low-cost strategy to gain sales through the growth stage. Resource focus emphasizes quality and systems process improvements to gain economies of scale. Prices are often lowered, which reduces profits per unit, to gain market share. U.S. HealthCare cut prices to build market share. Apple Computer has been slow to lower its prices to match IBM compatibles, electing to keep its high-profit strategy. Apple has not had the growth rate of IBM compatibles. Because of lower sales of Apple systems, software makers have been discouraged from developing Apple software, which in turn hurts its growth.[47] Analyzers (Ready Lube, Oil Doctor, and other) have copied Jiffy Lube and tend to use a focus strategy in regional markets. The portfolio stars, like Jiffy Lube, are usually in the growth stage.

Maturity Stage. At the maturity stage, sales growth continues slowly, levels off, and begins to decline. In a saturated market, the growth strategy changes to one of stability (defender). The low cost becomes more important, and cost-cutting efforts are emphasized. Quick oil change (Jiffy Lube) is still in the growth stage but growth is limited due to its nearing maturity. Mature products (Pennzoil oil and gas and motor oil and refined products) are usually cash cows in the portfolio.

APPLYING THE CONCEPT

AC 5-3 Product Life Cycle

Select the stage of the product life cycle of each of the following products.

a. introduction b. growth c. maturity d. decline

____ **11.** Mobil gasoline.

____ **12.** Computers with 5/ floppy drives.

____ **13.** Home carpeting (rugs).

____ **14.** Cellular telephones.

____ **15.** The fold-up computer that fits in your pocket.

Decline Stage. In the decline stage, sales drop. The strategy changes from stability–defend to turnaround and retrenchment and prospector or analyzer. Procter & Gamble uses a turnaround strategy with its personal care products, such as Tide, calling them new and improved to revitalize sales in order to prevent decline to the point of retrenchment. A product can be in the decline stage and remain profitable, such as black and white TVs, for many years. In the portfolio, products in the decline stage are dogs and may be divested. The prospector or analyzer strategy comes into play to develop new products.

Remember that the various grand and adaptive strategies complement one another. You need to select the appropriate strategy based on the mission, situation analysis (including industry and competitive, portfolio, and product life cycle analysis), and objectives.

FUNCTIONAL-LEVEL OPERATIONAL STRATEGIES

11. List the four major functional operational strategy areas.

In prior sections you learned about long-range strategic planning. You will now learn about operational-level planning. The functional departments must develop strategies for achieving the business-level mission and objectives. **Functional strategies** *include marketing, operations, finance, human resources, and others*. The situation analysis also takes place at the functional levels to determine strengths and weaknesses. The functional departments also develop objectives and strategies for achieving them. The business-level strategy, the competition, and stage of the product life cycle will have a major impact on the functional areas' strategies. In the fast-changing environment, large businesses are often criticized for being too slow to convert business-level strategy into operational strategies.[48] We will briefly discuss each function. You may have taken, or will take, one or more entire courses on each function.

functional strategies
Marketing, operations, finance, human resources, and others.

Marketing Strategy

The marketing department has the primary responsibility for knowing what the customer wants, or how to add customer value, and it defines the target market. Marketing has responsibility for the four Ps: product, promotion, place, and price.

In other words, the marketing department makes decisions about which products to provide, how they will be packaged, how they will be advertised, where they will be sold and how they get there, and how much they will be sold for.

If the growth prospector business-level strategy is used, marketing will be involved in planning and implementing new products and/or markets to enter. If the stability defender strategy is selected, marketing will not be concerned about new products or markets or new product advertising. If the analyzer strategy is used, marketing will take a midrange approach between prospecting and defending. If the turnaround and retrenchment strategy is used, marketing will be involved in selecting products to drop and/or markets to exit.

Operations Strategy

The operations (or production) department has responsibility for systems processes that convert inputs into outputs. Operations focuses on quality and efficiency in producing the products which marketing determines will provide customer value. You will learn more about operations in Chapter 17.

If the growth prospector business-level strategy is used, operations will be involved in planning for and producing the new products. Aggressive growth may require new operations facilities. If the stability defender strategy is selected, operations will devote its full energy to improving quality and efficiency and cutting costs. If the analyzer strategy is used, operations will take a midrange approach between prospecting and defending. If the turnaround and retrenchment strategy is used, operations will be involved in cutting back systems processes.

Human Resources Strategy

The human resources department has responsibility for working with all functional departments in the areas of recruiting, selecting, training, evaluating, and compensating employees. You will learn more about human resources in Chapter 9.

If the growth prospector business-level strategy is used, human resources will be involved in planning for and expanding the number of employees. If the stability defender strategy is selected, human resources will devote its full energy to improving quality and efficiency. If the analyzer strategy is used, it will take a midrange approach. If the turnaround and retrenchment strategy is used, human resources will be involved in laying off employees.

Finance Strategy

The finance strategy has at least two parts: (1) financing the business activities by raising money through the sale of stock (equity) or bonds/loans (debt), deciding on the debt to equity ratio, and paying off the debt and dividends (if any) to shareholders and (2) keeping records of transactions, developing budgets, and reporting financial results (income statement and balance sheets). A third area of finance in many organizations includes optimum use of cash reserves, or the area of investing as a means of making money. Some organizations, including Texas Instruments and 3M, are developing separate strategic and operational budgets. You will learn more about finance in Chapter 15.

If the growth prospector business-level strategy is used, finance will be involved in planning for and raising money to pay for the functional area budgets, and dividends will be low, if any are given. If the stability defender strategy is used, finance will focus on paying off debt and will generally pay a dividend. If the analyzer strategy is used, it will take a midrange approach. If the turnaround strategy is used, finance may both raise money and sell assets to pay for the comeback. With a retrenchment strategy, finance will be involved in the sale of assets, and dividends are generally not paid, or are low.

Work Application

12. Identify the functional area of an organization you work or have worked for. What was its operational strategy?

Other Functional Strategies

Based on the type of business, any number of other departments will also need to develop a strategy. One area that varies in importance is research and development (R&D). Businesses that sell a good usually allocate greater resources (budgets) for R&D than service businesses. Businesses in high-tech industries require more R&D than low-tech businesses. And a prospector strategy requires more resources for R&D than an analyzer strategy because the prospector offers the new product (IBM) while the analyzer copies the prospector (clones).

APPLYING THE CONCEPT

AC 5–4 Functional Strategies

Identify each statement's type of functional strategy.

a. marketing c. finance e. other
b. operations d. human resources

____ **16.** The department responsible for cleaning up and fixing things.
____ **17.** The department that sends out the bills.
____ **18.** The primary department that transforms inputs into outputs.
____ **19.** The department that decides where the product will be sold.
____ **20.** The department responsible for labor relations.

Pete has a small business; therefore, he does not have separate functional departments like Jiffy Lube International. Pete uses a stability defender strategy and gets advertising assistance from Jiffy Lube, but he also has an ongoing ad campaign run by a local ad agency. Pete's Jiffy Lubes have tight control of quality and train employees to follow the systems process. Service center managers perform most of the human resource functions. Having paid off most of the debt for the assets of the six Jiffy Lubes, Pete is borrowing money to buy the real estate on which the service centers do business. Pete also has tight budgetary control for revenue and expenses.

IMPLEMENTING AND CONTROLLING STRATEGIES

The first four steps in the strategic process involve planning. The fifth and final step involves implementing and controlling strategies to ensure that the mission and objectives, at all three levels, are achieved. Top and middle managers are more involved with the planning while the lower-level functional managers and employees *implement* the strategies on a day-to-day basis. Successful implementation of strategies requires effective and efficient support systems throughout the organization. As the strategy must fit the environment, it must also fit the multiple factors responsible for its implementation. Throughout Chapters 6 through 14, you will learn these factors and how to use them to implement strategy.

As the strategies are being implemented, they must also be controlled. *Controlling* is the process of establishing and implementing mechanisms to ensure that objectives are achieved. An important part of controlling is measuring progress toward the achievement of the objective and taking corrective action when needed. An important part of controlling is staying within the budget when appropriate and being flexible and changing it when necessary to meet changes in the environment. You will develop your controlling skills in Chapters 15 through 17.

Pete has specific financial objectives for each Jiffy Lube for the next five years. They are revised every year and are broken down to a weekly figure for each year. The revenue budget is based on how many cars should be serviced each week. Then, based on the number of cars to be serviced, the expenditure budget is set. The difference between revenue and expenses is computed each week to determine profits, and a formal monthly financial statement is prepared. Pete and Dave monitor the weekly profits. If they deviate significantly from the budget, Dave will visit the service center to see why the objective was not met and to take corrective action. Every month all employees of each service center meet, before or after business hours, to go over the next month's objectives. They also use weekly meetings to review progress and to discuss ways of improving service for greater customer value.

Pete's Jiffy Lube uses another very important quality-control technique, the mystery shopper. Dave or Pete select the mystery shopper, a person unknown to the people at a Jiffy Lube, to go to a Jiffy Lube for service. After the service, the mystery shopper meets with Dave or Pete and fills out a form that evaluates the quality of service. Following the evaluation, Dave or Pete goes over the evaluation with the service center manager to let him or her know the strengths and weaknesses (areas to improve). Service center managers then go over the evaluation with their employees. Managers know that the sporadic mystery shopper evaluations affect pay raises. Pete feels that the mystery shopper gives the customer's view of the quality of the service offered at Jiffy Lube.

Work Application

13. Give examples of controls used for an organization you work or have worked for.

CURRENT MANAGEMENT ISSUES

Global. The trend toward *global* business is creating growth opportunities for all types of organizations. Pennzoil's major strategic goal is to become a global oil and gas company; a low-cost, efficient refiner; and a worldwide marketer of Pennzoil motor oil and other quality products. To go global requires a strategic plan with a carefully developed growth strategy. Important decisions include which countries to do business in (environmental analysis is critical) and which method to use to go global (global sourcing, importing and exporting, licensing, contracting, joint ventures and strategic alliances, or direct investment). See Chapter 2 for a review of how to go global and for the strategic practices of leading global companies.

Diversity. Doing business in multiple countries with a *diversity* of cultures requires that global strategies include plans to value and manage diversity (Chapter 3). Diversity exists in U.S. and Japanese multinational companies' perceptions of industry globalization potential, desired global strategy response, organizationally derived ability to introduce global strategy, and resulting performance. The Japanese have more globalized strategies than do Americans.[49] The organizing principle driving Japanese strategic planning is the desire to establish a strong market position, whereas the organizing principle behind the strategic planning of American managers is the desire to create a competitive advantage of differentiation.[50]

Ethics and Social Responsibility. *Ethics* is not separate from strategic management because managers should be using ethical decision-making throughout the strategic process.[51] Managers must consider the stakeholders as they develop ethical strategies. Creating a win-win situation for stakeholders develops trust and a commitment to the implementation of strategies.[52] Pete is very ethical and *socially responsible*. He frequently puts in more hours for the Jimmy Fund than he does for Jiffy Lube, especially during the strategic planning and implementing of the golf tournament, which raises around $175,000 a year for the Jimmy Fund. Empirical research has suggested that companies using a prospector strategy have a significantly greater proportion of firms with higher social responsibility performance than companies using the defender strategy.[53]

Quality and TQM. In essence, every strategy concerns the way organizations utilize resources to create products and services with customer value. This point is the foundation of TQM. Applying TQM tools and techniques provides continuous improvement of systems and processes that lead to greater customer value. Companies around the world use TQM to develop a competitive advantage.[54] Ford successfully developed and implemented an elaborate strategy to improve the quality of its automobiles, driven by the slogan, "Quality Is Job 1."

Ford successfully developed and implemented an elaborate strategy to improve the quality of its automobiles.

Productivity. Many organizations are downsizing and using re-engineering strategies to increase *productivity* and to gain a competitive advantage.[55] Downsizing is a retrenchment grand strategy. However, according to strategy expert C. K. Prahalad, downsizing is used too often and imaginative growth strategies too little.[56]

Participative Management and Teams. With the trend toward *participation* and *teamwork*, more organizations have empowered employees to make the decisions on how to implement the strategies, as long as they meet the objectives.[57] It is becoming common for teams to set their own objectives and to develop the plans to achieve them. TQM does not use MBO because it promotes individualism rather than teamwork.

Small Business. The value of strategic planning for *small business* has been questioned. Researchers have provided support stating that small businesses with specific strategic plans outperform those without plans.[58] However, strategic plans for small business don't have to be long and complex.[59] Pete's strategy, presented in this chapter, illustrates this point. Well-developed strategies for growth are especially important.[60] Companies have failed by growing too quickly; Grandmother Calendar, discussed in the opening section of this chapter, is an example. There is a major distinction between the strategic plans for an existing business, which were presented in this chapter, and a new entrepreneurial start-up business. A *business plan* is an entrepreneurs' strategy for opening a new business. The business plan is important not only for running the business but also for lenders and/or investors to use to make the decision to be associated with the business. Therefore, a key part of the business plan presents detailed information on the funds needed to start and run the business. A five-year cash flow of projected (pro forma) revenues and expenses is an essential part of the business plan.[61] You will learn to develop a basic entrepreneurial strategy that could be used as part of a business plan in Skill-Building Exercise 5–2, Entrepreneurial Strategic Planning.

CHAPTER SUMMARY AND GLOSSARY

The chapter summary is organized to answer the 12 learning objectives for Chapter 5.

1. Describe the difference between strategic and operational plans.

The primary difference is timeframe and management level involved. Strategic planning involves developing a mission and long-range objectives and plans. Operational plans involve short-range objectives and plans. Upper-level managers develop strategic plans and lower-level managers develop operational plans.

2. State the difference among the three levels of strategies: corporate, business, functional.

The primary difference is the focus, which narrows as strategy moves down the organization, and the management level involved in developing the strategy. Corporate-level strategy focuses on managing multiple lines of business. Business-level strategy focuses on managing one line of business. Functional-level strategy focuses on managing an area of a business line. Upper-level managers develop corporate- and business-level strategy, and lower-level managers develop functional strategy.

3. Explain the reason for conducting an industry and competitive situation analysis.

The industry and competitive situation analysis is used to determine the attractiveness of an industry. It is primarily used at the corporate strategy level to make decisions regarding which lines of business to enter and exit, and how to allocate resources among lines of business.

4. Explain the reason for conducting a company situation analysis.

The company situation analysis is used at the business strategy level to determine the strategic issues and problems that need to be addressed through the strategic process.

5. State how competitive advantage and benchmarking are related.

Competitive advantage and benchmarking are related because if a company decides to have a competitive advantage, it will use benchmarking against noncompetitors to use their ideas to be different from the competition. If the company decides not to have a competitive advantage, it will benchmark against the leading competitor and copy it. In addition, many firms will copy competitors' good ideas while trying to differentiate themselves in some other way.

6. Discuss how goals and objectives are similar yet different.

Goals and objectives are similar because they both state what is to be accomplished. Goals are often translated into objectives. They also differ in detail. Goals state general targets, whereas objectives state what is to be accomplished in singular, specific, and measurable terms with a target date.

7. List the steps in the writing objectives model.

The parts of the writing objectives model are: (1) infinitive + (2) action verb + (3) singular, specific, and measurable result to be achieved + (4) target date.

8. Describe the four grand strategies: growth, stability, turnaround and retrenchment, and combination.

With a growth strategy, the firm aggressively pursues increasing its size. With a stability strategy, the firm maintains the same size or grows slowly. With a turnaround strategy, the firm attempts a comeback; with retrenchment, it decreases in size. With a combination strategy, the other three strategies are used across different lines of business.

9. Describe the three growth strategies: concentration, integration, and diversification.

With a concentration strategy, the firm grows aggressively in its existing line(s) of business. With integration, the firm grows by entering a forward or backward line(s) of business. With diversification, the firm grows by adding related or unrelated products.

10. Discuss the three business-level adaptive strategies: prospecting, defending, and analyzing.

With the prospecting strategy, the firm aggressively offers new products/services and/or enters new markets. Prospecting is a growth strategy used in fast-changing environments with high growth potential. With the defending strategy, the firm stays with its product/line and markets. Defending is a stability strategy used in slow-changing environments with low growth potential. With the analyzing strategy, the firm moves into new markets cautiously and/or offers a core product group and seeks new opportunities. Analyzing is a combination strategy used in moderately changing environments with moderate growth potential.

11. List the four major functional operational strategy areas.

The four major functional operational strategy areas are marketing, operations, human resources, and finance. There are other functional department strategies based on the organization's needs.

12. Define the following key terms (in order of appearance in the chapter):

Select one or more methods: (1) fill in the missing key terms from memory, (2) match the key terms from the end of the review with their definitions below, or (3) copy the key terms from the list at the beginning of the chapter.

__________ is the process of developing a mission and long-range objectives and determining in advance how they will be accomplished.

__________ is the process of setting short-range objectives and determining in advance how they will be accomplished.

The steps in the __________ are (1) developing the mission, (2) analyzing the environment, (3) setting objectives, (4) developing strategies, and (5) implementing and controlling strategies.

A ______ is a plan for pursuing the mission and achieving objectives.

The __________ include corporate, business, and functional.

The __________ is the plan for managing multiple lines of business.

The __________ is the plan for managing one line of business.

The __________ is the plan for managing one area of the business.

A __________ draws out those features in a company's environment that most directly frame its strategic window of options and opportunities.

Through a __________, the organization's internal environmental strengths and weaknesses and external environmental opportunities and threats are determined.

__________ specifies how the organization offers unique customer value.

__________ is the process of comparing the organization's products/services and processes with those of other companies.

______ state general targets to be accomplished.

______ state what is to be accomplished in singular, specific, and measurable terms with a target date.

The parts of the ______________ are: (1) infinitive + (2) action verb + (3) singular, specific, and measurable result to be achieved + (4) target date.

______________ is the process in which managers and their employees jointly set objectives for the employee, periodically evaluate the progress, and reward according to the results.

__________ is the overall corporate-level strategy of growth, stability, turnaround and retrenchment, or a combination.

______________ include concentration, backward and forward integration, and related and unrelated diversification.

A ______ occurs when two companies form one corporation.

An ______ occurs when one business buys all or part of another business.

The ______________ is the corporate process of determining which lines of businesses it will be in and how it will allocate resources among them.

The business-level ______ include prospecting, defending, and analyzing.

______ include marketing, operations, finance, human resources, and others.

KEY TERMS

acquisition
adaptive strategies
benchmarking
business-level strategy
business portfolio analysis
competitive advantage
corporate growth strategies
corporate-level strategy
functional-level strategy
functional strategies
goals
grand strategy
management by objectives (MBO)
merger
objectives
operational planning
situation analysis
strategic planning
strategic process
strategy
SWOT analysis
three levels of strategies
writing objectives model

REVIEW AND DISCUSSION QUESTIONS

1. In your own words, why are strategic and operational planning important?
2. Is there a difference between a plan and a strategy?
3. Should all businesses have corporate-, business-, and functional-level strategies?
4. Should a mission statement be customer-focused?
5. Why is a situational analysis part of the strategic process?
6. Should all businesses have a competitive advantage?
7. Is it ethical to copy other companies' ideas through benchmarking?
8. Are both goals and objectives necessary for a business?
9. Is it important to write objectives?
10. As a manager, would you use MBO?
11. Which growth strategy would you say is the most successful?
12. What is the difference between a merger and an acquisition?
13. Is there a difference between grand strategies and adaptive strategies?
14. Why would a business use a focus strategy rather than appeal to all customers?
15. Give examples of "other" functional departments.

CASE

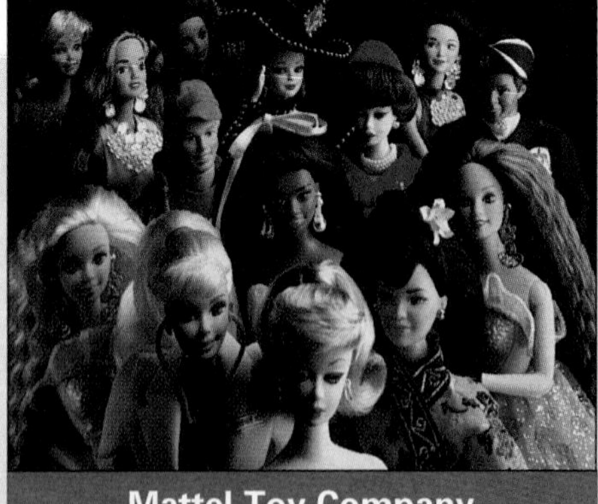
Mattel Toy Company

Mattel, Inc., is the largest toy company in the world. Its competitors include Hasbro, Tyco Toys, and others. To offer a broader range of products, which helps it to compete on a global basis, the toy industry went through a great deal of consolidation. For example, Mattel bought Fisher-Price, but it keeps the Fisher-Price name on its product line of preschool and infant toys. In addition, increased consolidation of retail distribution channels has affected the toy industry. The large specialty toy stores and discount retailers, including Toys 'R' Us, Wal-Mart, Kmart, and Target, have increased their share of the market. As a result, these retailers have increased their business with large toy companies that have financial stability and their ability to advertise and distribute toys on a global scale.

Large retailers are making it difficult to standardize toys because they each seem to want the product they sell to be a little bit different. They require changes in palletization, product packaging, and labeling. Retailers demand the product when they want it and in the quantity they want; this is called just-in-time delivery. It is difficult to coordinate manufacturing and retail needs.

Mattel is changing the way it does business to meet the changing ways of retailers. Mattel has reengineered key business processes. It established a team of company and outside people to work on a project called Reengineering the Order Management Process (ROMP). ROMP determined the specific amount of each product available to every customer. Exchange of information between large retailers and Mattel is needed to allow them to keep up with "what's hot and what's not." Mattel now closely monitors consumer acceptance of particular products through electronic data interchange with large retailers. This allows Mattel to quickly respond to the needs of the faster sales times in the retail store.

Mattel's approach to conducting business is to focus on a few core product lines that account for most of its revenues. The core product lines for Mattel include Barbie fashion dolls, clothing, and accessories; Hot Wheels vehicles and accessories; Disney products; and Fisher-Price products. With a strong core product line bringing most of the revenues, Mattel reduces its reliance on new products (question marks) which can be expensive and risky.

Mattel's core products spend a long time in the growth and maturity stages, while most of its new products tend to go through the product life cycle quickly. Mattel uses licensing agreements from companies with established images to help ensure success with new products. Mattel negotiates licensing agreements to create lines of dolls and other toys based on Disney's animated films such as *Pocahantas*, *Aladdin*, and *Snow White and the Seven Dwarfs*. In 1996, Mattel won an exclusive pact with Disney's TV and film properties, expanding an important but sometimes difficult partnership that provides about 12 percent of its revenue. Mattel also has licensing agreements companies such as Twentieth Century Fox, Turner Entertainment Co., and Viacom.

Mattel realized that buying Fisher-Price and aggressively expanding global distribution was the best way to compete. Globalization provides increased sales volume of core products and extends the product life cycles of new products. Mattel continues to use outsourcing of some of its basic business functions. Mattel purchases some designs from independent toy inventors, and it contracts with independent manufacturers to produce some of its products. Mattel and Fisher-Price had domestic and international operations that were redundant.

Mattel benefits from NAFTA, for which it lobbied strongly, because it lowers its costs in both Mexico and Canada. NAFTA lowered the 20 percent duties on U.S.-made toys sold in Mexico. These tariffs are scheduled to be phased out over a ten-year period. Production costs of manufacturing in Mexico decreased because the raw materials and component parts from U.S. companies are no longer taxed when they enter Mexico.

Mattel has decreased the cost of importing by making its major seaport transactions electronically (paperless). The electronic system increases the speed, while decreasing errors and penalties, of processing imports through customs. The system reduces the time it takes to get the imports from the ship to the shelves (time-based competition). The time and cost saving are important because the majority of Mattel's products are imported. Mattel is committed to continuing to create customer value through continuous improvement in its products and processes.

Select the best alternative for the following questions. Be sure you are able to explain your answers.

___ 1. The information in this case refers primarily to

a. strategic planning b. operational planning

___ 2. Which of the five competitive forces is of major focus for Mattel?

a. competitive rivalry
b. threat of substitute products
c. potential new entrants
d. power of suppliers
e. power of buyers

___ 3. Mattel does not have a competitive advantage over its competitors.

a. true b. false

___ 4. Mattel's global grand strategy is

a. growth c. turnaround and retrenchment
b. stability d. combination

___ 5. Mattel's corporate growth strategy is

a. concentration
b. forward integration
c. backward integration
d. related diversification
e. unrelated diversification

___ 6. The Mattel and Fisher-Price strategic approach was a(n)

a. merger c. joint venture
b. acquisition d. strategic alliance

___ 7. The appropriate portfolio analysis for Mattel is

a. business b. product

___ 8. Mattel's business-level adaptive strategy for products only, not markets, is

a. prospecting b. defending c. analyzing

___ 9. Mattel's primary competitive strategy is

a. differentiation b. cost leadership c. focus

___ 10. In the United States, toys are in which stage of the product life cycle?

a. introduction c. mature
b. growth d. decline

11. Should Mattel have the same adaptive strategy for markets as it does for products? Explain.

12. Should Mattel have the same adaptive strategy for global and domestic operations? Explain.

13. Conduct an industry and competitive situation analysis using the five-force competitive analysis. Use Figure 5–3 as an example.

14. Conduct a SWOT analysis for Mattel.

15. Write some possible goals and objectives for Mattel.

SKILLBUILDER

SKILL-BUILDING EXERCISE 5–1

Writing Objectives

Preparing for Skill-Building Exercise 5–1

For this exercise, you will first work at improving objectives that do not meet the criteria for objectives, then you will write nine objectives for yourself.

Part 1

For each of the following objectives, write the missing criteria and rewrite the objective so that it meets all "must" criteria. When writing objectives use the model:

infinitive + action verb + singular, specific, and measurable result + target date

1. To improve our company image by year end 2000.

   Criteria missing: ______________

   Improved objective: ______________________________

   ____

2. To increase the number of customers by 10 percent.

   Criteria missing: ______________

   Improved objective: ______________________________

   ____

3. To increase profits during 1999.

   Criteria missing: ______________

   Improved objective: ______________________________

   ____

4. To sell 5 percent more hot dogs and soda at the baseball game on Sunday, June 13, 1998.

   Criteria missing: ______________

   Improved objective: ______________________________

   ____

Part 2

Write three educational, personal, and career objectives you want to accomplish. Your objectives can be as short-term as something you want to accomplish today or as long-term as 20 years from now. Be sure your objectives meet the criteria for effective objectives.

Educational Objectives

1. ______________________________

2. ______________________________

3. ______________________________

Personal Objectives

1. ______________________________

2. ______________________________

3. ______________________________

Career Objectives

1. ______________________________

2. ______________________________

3. ______________________________

Doing Skill-Building Exercise 5–1 in Class

Objective
To develop your skill at writing objectives.

Preparation
You should have corrected and written objectives in the preparation before class.

Experience
You will get feedback on how well you corrected the four objectives and share your written objectives with others.

Options (8–20 minutes)

1. The instructor goes over suggested corrections for the four objectives in part 1 of the preparation, then calls on class members to share their written objectives (part 2) with the class.
2. The instructor goes over suggested corrections for the four objectives in part 1 of the preparation, then the class breaks into groups of four to six to share their written objectives.
3. Break into groups of four to six and go over the corrections for the four objectives in part 1. Tell the instructor when your group is done, but go on to part 2. Share your written objectives until all groups are finished with the four corrections. The instructor goes over the corrections and may allow more time for sharing objectives. Give each other feedback for improving your written objectives during part 2.

Conclusion
The instructor may lead a class discussion and/or make concluding remarks.

Application (2–4 minutes)
What did I learn from this experience? How will I use this knowledge in the future?

____

Sharing
Volunteers give their answers to the application section.

SKILL-BUILDING EXERCISE 5–2

Entrepreneurial Strategic Planning

Preparing for Skill-Building Exercise 5–2

Would you like to be your own boss? Have you ever given any thought to owning your own business? For this exercise you are asked to select a business you would like to start some day. To assess your entrepreneurial qualities on ten dimensions, complete Self-Assessment Exercise 5–1 before continuing with this exercise. Answer the questions honestly without fear of sharing your answers during class.

SELF-ASSESSMENT EXERCISE 5–1

Entrepreneurial Qualities

Place a checkmark on the scale that best describes you.

1. I have a strong desire to be independent. — I have a weak desire to be independent.

   ____ ____ ____ ____ ____ ____
   6 5 4 3 2 1

2. I enjoy taking reasonable risks. — I avoid taking risks.

   ____ ____ ____ ____ ____ ____
   6 5 4 3 2 1

3. I avoid making the same mistakes. — I repeat the same mistakes.

   ____ ____ ____ ____ ____ ____
   6 5 4 3 2 1

4. I can work without any supervision. — I need supervision to motivate me to work.

   ____ ____ ____ ____ ____ ____
   6 5 4 3 2 1

5. I seek out competition. — I avoid competition.

   ____ ____ ____ ____ ____ ____
   6 5 4 3 2 1

6. I enjoy working long, hard hours. — I enjoy taking it easy and having plenty of personal time.

   ____ ____ ____ ____ ____ ____
   6 5 4 3 2 1

7. I am confident of my abilities. — I lack self-confidence.

   ____ ____ ____ ____ ____ ____
   6 5 4 3 2 1

8. I need to be the best/successful. — I'm satisfied being average.

   ____ ____ ____ ____ ____ ____
   6 5 4 3 2 1

9. I have a high energy level. — I have a low energy level.

   ____ ____ ____ ____ ____ ____
   6 5 4 3 2 1

10. I stand up for my rights. — I let others take advantage of me.

    ____ ____ ____ ____ ____ ____
    6 5 4 3 2 1

Scoring. Add up the 10 numbers below your checkmarks. The total number will be between 10 and 60. Place your score on the continuum below.

Entrepreneurial Qualities
Strong 60——50——40——30——20——10 Weak

Generally, the higher/stronger your entrepreneurial score, the better your chance of being a successful entrepreneur. However, simple paper-and-pencil surveys are not always good predictors. If you had a low score and really want to start a business, you may be successful. But, realize that you don't have all the typical entrepreneurial qualities.

An important part of any business plan is determining how much it will cost to start the business and to project the financial cash flow for the first five years. The financials are beyond the scope of this course, so just prepare a strategic plan without financials. Assume that money is not an issue because you hit the lottery for $50 million. Select a type of single-line business you want to start and give it a name and a general location with which you are familiar. To develop your strategy, use the following working strategic process papers. If you have absolutely no interest in owning your own business, you may select an existing business.

Before you begin the strategic process, list the name of the business and its major goods and/or services.

Company name: ______________________________

Products: ______________________________

____

Step 1. Developing a Mission

Write a mission for your business. You may want to have a general mission in mind, but wait to write it after completing step 2.

____

____

____

Step 2. Analyzing the Environment

Develop a five-force competitive analysis using Figure 5–3 as an example; then do a company situation analysis.

Five-Force Competitive Analysis

2. Threat of substitute products and services

4. Power of suppliers

1. The rivalry among competing sellers in the industry

5. Power of buyers

3. Potential of new entrants

Company Situation Analysis

1. SWOT analysis.

Strengths	*Opportunities*
______________	______________
______________	______________
______________	______________

Weaknesses	*Threats*
______________	______________
______________	______________
______________	______________

2. Competitive advantage (if any). You may do a competitive strength assessment, but it is not required.

____

____

____

3. Conclusions concerning competitive position.

____

____

____

4. Determine the strategic issues and problems that need to be addressed through the strategic process.

____

____

____

Step 3. Setting Objectives

List three goals or objectives.

____

____

____

Step 4. Developing Strategies

Being in a single line of business, you do not need a grand strategy or to conduct a portfolio analysis. However, you should have an adaptive and competitive strategy based on the product life cycle.

Stage of the product life cycle: ______________________

Adaptive and competitive strategy (explain each briefly):
____
____
____

Step 5. Implementing and Controlling Strategies

List a few major controls you will use to implement the strategy. ______________________________
____
____

Doing Skill-Building Exercise 5–2 in Class

Objective
To develop your strategic planning skills.

Preparation
You should have completed the entrepreneurial strategic plan preparation.

Experience
You will share your entrepreneurial strategic plan in class.

Options (8–20 minutes)

1. Students present their strategic plan to the entire class.
2. Break into groups of three to five and share your strategic plans. Sharing answers to Self-Assessment Exercise 5–1 is not part of this exercise.
3. Same as option 1 but the group selects its best strategic plan to be presented to the entire class.

Conclusion
The instructor may lead a class discussion and/or make concluding remarks.

Application (2–4 minutes)
What did I learn from this experience? How will I use this knowledge in the future?
____
____
____

Sharing
Volunteers give their answers to the application section.

VIDEOCASE

A Study in Planning: Kropf Fruit Company

A family-owned fruit processor, Kropf Fruit Company, faced the problem of massive consolidation among its potential customers. To survive, it needed a strategic plan. The two possibilities were to remain a medium-sized regional packer, or to grow to a major packing and processing company. Kropf chose to use SWOT as a planning tool. Top management analyzed its strengths, weaknesses, opportunities, and threats. A major weakness was limited temperature-controlled storage space. A major opportunity was building greater storage space, and a major threat was the new types of fruit imported from overseas.

Using SWOT, the company developed a strategic plan to increase in size through such means as doubling its acreage and expanding its storage and packing facility. Kropf's ten-year plan was supported by many short-range plans.

Plans and Planning Tools

Learning Objectives

After studying this chapter, you should be able to:

1. State the difference between standing and single-use plans.
2. Explain why contingency plans are often needed.
3. Discuss the relationship between the strategic process and sales forecasting.
4. Describe the difference between qualitative and quantitative sales forecasting techniques.
5. Discuss the difference between the jury of executive opinion and the three composite sales forecasting techniques.
6. Explain the difference between the past sales and time series sales forecasting techniques.
7. Describe the similarities and differences between the planning sheet, Gantt chart, and PERT network.
8. Explain the use of a time log.
9. List and briefly describe the three step in the time-management system.
10. Define the following **key terms** (in order of appearance in the chapter):

    standing plans
    policies
    procedures
    rules
    single-use plans
    contingency plans
    sales forecast
    market share
    qualitative sales forecasting techniques
    quantitative sales forecasting techniques
    time series
    scheduling
    planning sheets
    Gantt charts
    PERT
    critical path
    time management
    time management system

Skill Development

1. You can develop your skill in using the Gantt chart and PERT network (Skill-Building Exercise 6–1).

2. You can develop your time management skills which will enable you to get more done in less time with better results (Skill-Building Exercise 6–2).

   These skills are part of conceptual and decision-making skills. These exercises develop your planning and resource-allocator decisional role skills. The SCANS skill competencies of using resources, information, and systems, basic and thinking foundation skills; and the personal quality of self-management are also developed.

atoya Washington graduated with a doctorate in business and began to teach at a midwestern university. Latoya was a bit disappointed with her education because she felt it was too theoretical and without enough application and practical value—or skill building. She began to develop her own material and used it in her class, which students really liked. In her second year as a college professor, Latoya began a consulting firm, Washington Training and Development Services (WT&DS). Latoya developed a modular approach to offer skill development for business managers. Some of the modules she offers include setting objectives and developing plans, problem-solving and decision-making, participation in decision-making, time management, scheduling, interview skills, performance appraisal skills, situational leadership, communication skills, conflict skills, and women in management.

Latoya developed a brochure as a means of promoting her services. The WT&DS mission statement, taken from the inside cover of her brochure is: "We are dedicated to training people and developing their skills in order to maximize performance and productivity on the job, while enhancing individual careers." The first page contains a table of contents with three parts: (1) Why WT&DS?—which gives reasons for an organization to use her services. The text of the brochure states her qualifications and competitive advantage. (2) About WT&DS training and development. The text explains her approach to conducting training sessions, and how company employees can use the skills developed on the job to increase performance and productivity. (3) Training and development modules—a listing of all the modules offered. The text explains the content of each module and the time needed. Although the module approach makes it seem like Latoya is offering a set of rigid programs, she does tailor the materials of each module to meet the customer needs, at additional cost.

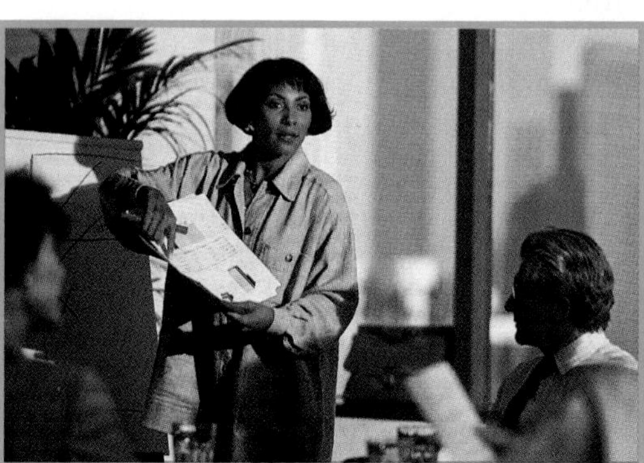

Latoya Washington developed a modular approach to offer skill development for business managers. She promotes her services with a brochure.

Latoya began to market her business by cold-calling possible clients. Over the telephone she would briefly describe her business and try to get an appointment to go and meet with the person in charge of training and development to discuss her services in more detail, and to leave a brochure. After each meeting she would follow up the discussion with a thank-you-for-your-time letter, restating how the organization could benefit from her services. The letter was based on specific things the person told her during the meeting. The letter was an attempt to get the person to commit to a training program. The letter also stated that Latoya would follow up the letter with a phone call to answer questions, to close a sale.

After gaining some clients, Latoya started to market her business with a monthly letter to all prospective organizations (300) in the area. The letters gave updated information on training from publications, and always stated that a brochure was available upon request and that she would be pleased to make a personal visit if the person wanted more information. Latoya got to the point of not having to make any more cold calls because she developed a client base that kept her busy. In fact, Latoya is so busy that she is seriously considering giving up her college job and consulting full time.[1]

A researcher has indicated that managers use various management tools in an effort to improve performance. But, no relationship exists between financial performance and the number of tools used, choice of tools, or satisfaction with the tools used. However, and more importantly, a strong positive relationship does exist between satisfaction with financial results and the firm's ability to build distinctive customer service capabilities. In other words, its not how many tools you use; it is using them correctly to develop customer value that is important.[2]

Although the title of Chapter 5 is "Strategic and Operational Planning," it placed more emphasis on strategic planning. This chapter places more emphasis on operational planning. In this chapter you will learn more about planning, sales forecasting tools, scheduling tools, and time management tools that you can use to improve your operational planning skills.

PLANS

In this section you will learn about the planning dimensions, standing plans versus single-use plans, contingency plans, why managers don't plan, and indicators of poor planning.

Planning Dimensions

Plans can be characterized by at least five dimensions: (1) The management *level* that develops the plan. (2) The *type of plan*—strategic or operational. (3) The *scope* of the plan covered. The plan can be broad in scope, such as for the entire organization, or for a business unit, or it can be narrow, such as for a functional department or for just a part of a department or even for one employee. (4) *Time*—long- or short-range. (5) *Repetitiveness*—single use or standing plan. In the last chapter you covered the first four dimensions. Next, you will cover the repetitiveness of plans. But, first see Figure 6–1 for an illustration of the planning dimensions. Note that upper managers do more single-use planning and that lower levels deal more with standing plans. However, this does not mean that lower-level managers don't make single-use plans.

Standing versus Single-Use Plans

1. State the difference between standing and single-use plans.

According to the repetitive dimension of plans, plans may be either *standing plans*, which are made to be used over and over again (repeated), or *single-use*, which are made to be used only once (nonrepetitive). Figure 6–2 illustrates the different types of standing and single-use plans.

Standing Plans. Operational strategies determine how objectives will be accomplished. This may be done by developing standing plans, which save future planning and decision-making time. **Standing plans** *include policies, procedures, and rules developed for handling repetitive situations.* Their purpose is to guide employees' actions in decision-making. Union contract agreements become standing plans.

standing plans
Policies, procedures, and rules developed for handling repetitive situations.

Policies *provide general guidelines to be followed when making decisions.* Policies exist at all levels within organizations. The board of directors develops

policies
General guidelines to be followed when making decisions.

Management Level	Type of Plan	Scope	Time	Repetitiveness
Upper and Middle	Strategic	Broad	Long-Range	Single-Use
Middle and Lower	Operational	Narrow	Short-Range	Standing Plan

Figure 6–1
Planning Dimensions

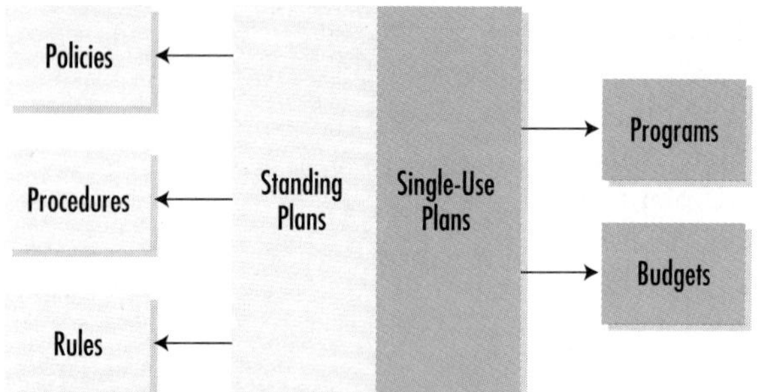

Figure 6–2
Standing versus Single-Use Plans

policies, with the input of top management, for the entire organization. The manager implements these company policies. In doing so, managers often establish policies for their own employees. External groups such as the government, labor unions, accrediting associations, and so forth dictate some policies. For example, the government requires organizations to offer equal opportunity to all, and labor unions require collective bargaining.

Examples of policy statements include: "The customer is always right." "We produce high-quality goods and services." "We promote qualified employees from within." "Employees will receive due process in grievances." Notice that policy statements are intentionally general guides that leave it to employees' discretion on how to implement them. As a manager, your daily decisions will be guided by policies. It will be your job to interpret, apply, and explain company policies to your employees. In situations where no policy exists, ask your boss to establish one or issue one yourself to be used when the situation recurs. Latoya's policy is: "To develop skills that will be used on the job to increase performance and productivity." How this is done varies from training program to training program. The policy helps Latoya to focus on this important issue.

procedures
A sequence of actions to be followed in order to achieve an objective.

Procedures *are a sequence of actions to be followed in order to achieve an objective*. They are also called *standard operating procedures* (SOPs) and *methods*. Procedures are more specific than policies; they entail a series of decisions rather than a single decision and may involve more than one functional area. For example, sales, accounting, production, and shipping personnel may all have to follow a set procedure in order to meet a client's needs. Procedures ensure that all recurring, routine situations are handled in a consistent, predetermined manner. Many organizations have procedures for purchasing, taking inventory, settling grievances, and so forth. Small firms often do not. Latoya teaches employees procedures, such as the steps in decision-making (Chapter 4), as part of her training programs.

rules
State exactly what should or should not be done.

Rules *state exactly what should or should not be done*. Employees have no discretion on how to implement rules and regulations. Most rules and regulations leave little or no room for interpretation. Examples include: "No smoking or eating in the work area." "Everyone must wear a hard hat on the construction site." "Stop at a red light." Violating rules usually involves penalties that vary in severity according to the seriousness of the violation and the number of offenses. As a manager, you will be responsible for establishing and enforcing rules in a uniform manner. Latoya does have a no smoking rule during training.

Work Application

1. Give an example of a policy, a procedure, and a rule from an organization you work or have worked for.

Policies, procedures, and rules are all standing plans. However, they differ in terms of their definition and purpose. Policies provide general guides, procedures set a sequence of activities, and rules govern specific actions. The amount of detail varies for each type of standing plan, yet standing plans guide behavior in recurring situations. It is not always easy to distinguish between a policy, a procedure, and a rule. However, you should do so in order to know when you have the flexibility to do it your way and when you do not. The proper use of standing plans can help an organization meet objectives.

single-use plans
Programs and budgets developed for handling nonrepetitive situations.

Single-Use Plans. **Single-use plans** *include programs and budgets developed for handling nonrepetitive situations*. Single-use plans, unlike standing plans, are developed for a specific purpose and probably will not be used again in the same form. However, a single-use plan may be used as a model for future programs or budgets. A strategy is a single-use plan.

A *program* describes a set of activities and is designed to accomplish an objective over a specified time period. Programs are not meant to exist over the life of the organization. A program may have its own policies, procedures, budget, and so forth. It might take several years or less than a day to complete a given program. Examples include the development of a new product, expansion of facilities, or research and development to find a cure for a disease. Latoya develops programs for her clients.

When developing a program, you may find these procedure guidelines helpful: (1) Set project objectives. (2) Break the project down into a sequence of steps. (3) Assign responsibility for each step. (4) Establish starting and ending times for each step. (5) Determine the resources needed for each step. If you use the operational planning, shown later in Figure 6–4, page 186, you will be following these guidelines.

A *budget* is the funds allocated to operate a department for a fixed period of time. Many people fear budgets because they have low math or accounting skills. In reality, most budgets require planning skills rather than mathematical skills. When developed, a budget is a planning tool, and when implemented, it is a control tool. You will learn budgeting details in Chapter 15. Latoya uses a budget.

Work Application

2. Give an example of a program you were involved in at work.

APPLYING THE CONCEPT

AC 6–1 Identifying Plans

Identify each type of plan by categories:

Objective	*Standing Plan*	*Single-Use Plan*
a. objective	b. policy	e. program
	c. procedure	f. budget
	d. rule	

____ 1. "Quality is job one." (Ford Motor Company)

____ 2. President John F. Kennedy's plan to land someone on the moon.

____ 3. To increase our market share by 10 percent next year.

____ 4. Employees having babies will be given a two-month maternity leave.

____ 5. How much will it cost to operate your department next month?

____ 6. Wear safety glasses while touring the factory.

____ 7. Forms for leaves of absence must be approved by the manager and submitted to the personnel office one month in advance of their effective dates.

____ 8. Maintain the reject rate on staplers under 5 percent.

____ 9. "Never take unfair advantage of anyone the firm deals with." (J.C. Penney)

____ 10. You may spend $1,000 to conduct that seminar.

Contingency Plans

2. Explain why contingency plans are often needed.

No matter how effectively you plan, there will be times when things go wrong that prevent you from achieving your objectives. Often things that go wrong are beyond your control (85-15 rule, Chapter 2). For example, a machine may break down or an employee may call in sick. When the uncontrollable occurs, you should be prepared with a backup, or contingency plan. **Contingency plans** *are alternative plans to be implemented if uncontrollable events occur*. If a key employee calls in sick, another employee fills in to do the job. Construction work is usually contingent upon the weather. If it's nice, they work outside; if it is not, they work indoors. Shippers have contingency plans to use in case of a strike by the Teamsters truck driver union.[3] Microsoft developed a way to uncouple soft-

contingency plans
Alternative plans to be implemented if uncontrollable events occur.

ware for its Windows 95 as a contingency plan to use if the Justice Department takes antitrust action against the company.[4]

To develop a contingency plan for your department, you should answer three questions:

- What might go wrong in my department?
- How can I prevent it from happening?
- If it does occur, what can I do to minimize its effect?

Work Application

3. Describe a situation in which a contingency plan is appropriate. Explain the plan.

The answer to question 3 is your contingency plan. When developing single-use plans, ask everyone involved what can go wrong and what should be done if it does go wrong. Also ask others within and outside the organization who have implemented similar plans. They may have encountered problems you haven't thought of, and they may have good contingency plans to offer you.

Why Managers Don't Plan

In the course of conducting training programs for managers, Latoya has found that by far the most common reason for not planning is lack of time. "I'm too busy putting out fires to plan" is a typical statement. This is one reason why you will learn about time management in this chapter. Latoya responds by asking the manager to think of the last few "fires," or crises, in the department. Were they caused by something the manager did or did not do? Many crises could have been avoided if the manager had planned. Why can managers always find time to do a job over, but can't find the time to plan the job right the first time? Successful planners have fewer crises; they are in control of their departments. Nonplanners run out of control from one crisis to the next. Planning is a continuous activity. Plans do not have to be complicated or take a lot of time. Later in this chapter, you will learn about planning tools.

A second reason managers don't plan is their tendency toward action. When a crisis occurs, many managers don't feel comfortable stopping to think and plan how to deal with it. They are more comfortable taking immediate action, but this often leads to further crises. For example, Jed, a manager, got a rush order from his boss. Jed immediately stopped all production and began work on the rush order. An hour later, Jed's employees told him that although the order was half done, they ran out of the red material needed to finish. Since the customer wanted all red, they had to begin production again in green, of which there was an ample supply. As a result of the rush job, two other orders near completion were sent out late. Both orders were for good customers. If Jed had taken the time to plan, all three customers could have been better served, and labor hours and material saved. There is an old saying, "When you fail to plan, you plan to fail."

Work Application

4. How would you rate the planning ability of your present or past boss? Give examples of any indicators of poor planning.

Indications of Poor Planning

Signs of poor planning include:

- *Objectives not met*. Missed deadlines, delivery dates, and schedules, or work not done on time.
- *Crises*. Pushing through rush jobs and using overtime to complete jobs.

- *Idle resources*. Physical, financial, or human resources kept waiting for the manager to assign tasks.
- *Lack of resources*. Necessary resources not available when needed.
- *Duplication*. The same task being done more than once.

SALES FORECASTING TOOLS

3. Discuss the relationship between the strategic process and sales forecasting.

Forecasting is the process of predicting what will happen in the future. Organizations conduct a variety of forecasts during the environmental analysis, including economic forecasts, technological forecasts, and government regulation forecasts, (Chapter 2). However, the sales forecast is generally considered the most important organizational forecast. The sales forecast or sales budget should take past experience, present condition, and future trends and patterns into account.[5] In other words, it should be based on the environmental analysis. Sales forecasting is one of the most important parts of the strategic planning process.[6] By improving its sales forecasting, Broadway Department Stores increased sales by 35 percent and turnover of merchandise by 18 percent in one year.[7]

A **sales forecast** *predicts the units and/or dollar volume of products to be sold during a specified period of time*. The sales forecast is important because of the systems affect. The short-term sales forecast is commonly conducted by the marketing department for one year and is set by the sales manager, with approval and possible adjustment by upper management.[8] However, the sales forecast affects the marketing department because it serves as the basis for the sales quotas for the sales representatives. The operations department uses the sales forecast to schedule how much of the product or service to produce. Marketing must monitor operations inventory levels and customer inventory levels to adjust sales forecasts as needed.[9] The sales forecast affects the finance department because it has to determine how much money it will take in before it can determine how much money it can budget to spend; the sales forecast is the basis of the cash flow projection used to determine specific borrowing needs. The human resources department is affected by the need to increase or decrease the number of employees to meet the sales forecast.

sales forecast
Predicts the units and/or dollar volume of products to be sold during a specified period of time.

U.S. Boeing and European Airbus predict that total airplane sales will reach $1 trillion by 2014.

When forecasting sales, the stage of the product life cycle must be determined to take into consideration the future growth potential.[10] Sales forecasts are commonly based on industry sales forecasts which consider the product life cycle. For example, jet manufacturers U.S. Boeing and European Airbus conducted separate 20-year sales forecasts and predicted that total airplane sales will reach $1 trillion by 2014. Boeing puts global demand at about 15,400 airplanes and Airbus estimates about 15,000. Both companies based the forecast on three environmental reasons for the growth: growth in passenger traffic, aging fleets that need replacement, and a return to profitability by the whole airline industry.[11]

Based on the total number of products to be sold in an industry, many large companies predict what amount or percentage of industry sales they will make—their *market share*. A **market share** *is the percentage of industry sales made by one organization*. For example, Microsoft has more than a 30 percent market share in the software industry—more than its three largest rivals combined.[12] Professional and trade publications are available that predict industry sales that

market share
The percentage of industry sales made by one organization.

4. Describe the difference between qualitative and quantitative sales forecasting techniques.

qualitative sales forecasting techniques
Use primarily subjective judgment, intuition, experience, and opinion to predict sales.

quantitative sales forecasting techniques
Use objective, mathematical, past sales data to predict sales.

you can use to help you when analyzing the environment and sales forecasting. You take local conditions, especially competition, into account when predicting your company sales.

You should also realize that the sales forecast should be a part of the business-level strategy. When the prospector growth strategy is used, sales projections will go up at aggressive rates in future years. But with the analyzer, defender, or retrenchment strategies, sales will go up slightly, stay about the same, or go down.

Sales forecasting techniques can be classified as qualitative or quantitative. **Qualitative sales forecasting techniques** *use primarily subjective judgment, intuition, experience, and opinion to predict sales.* Some math may be used. **Quantitative sales forecasting techniques** *use objective, mathematical, past sales data to predict sales.* However, organizations commonly use a combination of quantitative and qualitative techniques to increase accuracy. In this section you will learn about each sales forecasting technique, which Figure 6–3 illustrates.

Qualitative (subjective)	Quantitative (objective)
Individual Opinion	Past Sales
Jury of Executive Opinion	Time Series
Sales Force Composite	Regression
Customer Composite	
Operating Unit Composite	
Survey	

Figure 6–3
Sales Forecasting Techniques

5. Discuss the difference between the jury of executive opinion and the three composite sales forecasting techniques.

Qualitative Sales Forecasting Techniques

Qualitative techniques include individual opinion, jury of executive opinion, sales force composite, customer composite, operating unit composite, and survey. You should realize that only qualitative techniques can be used with a new product or by a new company because they have no past sales to quantitatively base the forecast on.

Individual Opinion. You probably predict what will happen in the future based on your personal experience and past events. People often use their intuition to make judgments about the future and to form an *individual opinion.* A person starting a new business all alone has no other option but to make an educated (based on environmental analysis) individual opinion. Latoya used this sales forecasting technique when she started her business.

Jury of Executive Opinion. With the *jury of executive opinion,* a group of managers and/or experts use their pooled opinions to forecast sales. The common format is a group meeting to share ideas and to attempt to reach a consensus agreement of sales. However, the Delphi technique (Chapter 4) is also used. You have to decide if the group or individual decision-making style is appropriate (Chapter 4). Jury of executive opinion is commonly used with partners. Pete and Dave agree on the sales forecasts for their six Jiffy Lube service centers. Interactive retail had sales of around $240 million in 1994 and predicted sales of $6.9 billion by 2000.[13]

Sales Force Composite. The *sales force composite* combines the forecasts of each salesperson. Each salesperson predicts his or her sales for the future period; these are totalled to give a composite sales forecast for the company. Sales reps tend to know their customers and can be a good source. However, many company managers believe that their salespeople are too optimistic, and they balance the composite with other sales forecast techniques.[14] A sales force composite works well when professional sales reps sell relatively expensive products (or total orders) with a clear base of customers or territory such as IBM computers.

Customer Composite. The *customer composite* is the total forecast of each major customer. You ask each major customer to predict how much they will buy during the future period. The total for each customer is added to give a composite sales forecast for the company. Customers tend to know their buying needs. Customer composite works well when an organization has relatively few customers with large volume sales, such as Mattel Toys with the large retailers Toys 'R' Us, Wal-Mart, Kmart, and Target.

Operating Unit Composite. An *operating unit composite* is the total sales forecast for multiple units. Businesses with multiple operating units, such as chain stores The Gap and Edwards Supermarkets, commonly predict the sales for each operating unit then add them together to get the total company sales forecast. Pete and Dave do this with their six Jiffy Lubes.

A variation of the operating unit composite is the *department composite*. A business with multiple revenue departments (such as a supermarket with meat, dairy, produce, etc.) can treat each department as an operating unit. Each department forecasts its sales and the composite is used to predict total sales for the operating unit. Edwards Supermarkets could use the department composite for each store, and the operating unit composite for all stores.

An offshoot of the operating unit composite is the *product composite* in which a business with multiple products determines the sales for each product/service and combines them as a total operating unit sales forecast.

Work Application

5. Explain how any of the qualitative sales forecasting techniques can be, or preferably actually are, used by a company you work or have worked for.

Survey. A survey utilizes mail questionnaires or telephone or personal interviews to predict future purchases. A sample of people is surveyed and a forecast for the entire population is made based on the responses. Businesses commonly use a survey to forecast the sales of a new product or service. For example, new Downy laundry softener samples were mass-mailed to all people in a given area. A week later, a sample of people were called to see if they used the product, if they liked the product, and if they would buy it the next time they need a softener. Surveys are also commonly used in the development of a new product to improve it before the final product is sold.

Quantitative Sales Forecasting Techniques

6. Explain the difference between the past sales and time series sales forecasting techniques.

Quantitative techniques include past sales, time series, and regression. Any of the preceding qualitative techniques can be combined with quantitative techniques as long as the products and companies have existed long enough to have a history of sales. There is no definite time period for a history of sales. But time series and regression techniques need at least a year, and more years will give better results. Coca-Cola charts annual sales in each of the ten successive previous years.

Past Sales. The *past sales* technique assumes that past sales will be repeated, or may be subjectively adjusted for environmental factors. For example, a local pizza shop owner can say that on a typical Friday night it will sell 100 pizzas. Therefore, today it will prepare to sell 100 pizzas. However, if the weather were very poor, the forecast could be subjectively cut to 75 pizzas. If it were a holiday when people tend not to cook, the sales forecast could increase to 125.

time series
Used to predict future sales by extending the trend line of past sales volume over time.

Time Series. **Time series** *is used to predict future sales by extending the trend line of past sales volume over time*. With time series you plot the sales for a week,

Work Application

6. Explain how any of the quantitative sales forecasting techniques can be, or preferably actually are, used by a company you work or have worked for.

month, quarter, year, etc., to find a trend which is then projected into the future to predict sales. The trend line can be extended by hand and the sales estimated (if the trend line is going up, you increase the sales forecast; if it is level, you keep it the same; and if it is going down, you decrease the sales forecast), but using a computer time series program is much more accurate. For example, the local pizza shop could plot sales by year to determine the trend and to predict sales by extending the trend line and possibly changing the 100-pizza standard.

Time series can also be used to plot days and months to determine day and month seasonal trends. With time series, adjustments for environmental factors are still used, but are more objective. Therefore, a typical Monday could be 60 pizzas and Friday could be 100; Friday night in June could be 110 pizzas, while in April it could be 90. Using time series can make the prediction more accurate so that not too much or little is prepared to maximize profits. Chatham Apothecary on Cape Cod used time series to predict monthly sales. Bernie and Carolyn Young keep inventory levels that meet demand, but adjust them for environmental weather factors to maximize sales. Latoya used time series to predict her second-year sales in business. She learned that July and August were slow months, but September and January were busy.

Regression. *Regression* is a mathematical modeling technique used to predict sales based on other variables. Regression, beyond the scope of this book, is taught in statistics classes.

APPLYING THE CONCEPT

AC 6–2 Sales Forecasting Techniques

Identify the most appropriate sales forecast for the following organizations. Items 11 through 13 use qualitative techniques and items 14 and 15 use quantitative techniques.

Qualitative	*Quantitative*
a. Individual opinion	g. Past sales
b. Jury of executive opinion	h. Time series
c. Sales force composite	i. Regression
d. Customer composite	
e. Operating unit composite	
f. Survey	

____ **11.** Pick n' Pay supermarket chain.

____ **12.** Hall Greeting Cards with a sales force that calls on specific stores in the sales area.

____ **13.** Tyson is starting his own sole proprietorship selling his own new, very different perfume.

____ **14.** Jim and Betty run a mom-and-pop variety store.

____ **15.** General Motors automobiles.

7. Describe the similarities and differences between the planning sheet, Gantt chart, and PERT network.

SCHEDULING TOOLS

After the marketing department has completed its sales forecast and received customer orders for the product, the operations department transforms inputs into outputs to create customer value. You will learn more about operations management in Chapter 17. To ensure customer value, many organizations include customer input in scheduling.[15] This is particularly important with just-in-time operations. Schedules are the part of the operational plan that specify the details for transforming inputs into outputs. Effective scheduling often requires the coordination of the flow of inputs into outputs through various stages, possibly departments, until the output is a finalized product or service.[16] Recall that all employees are involved with transforming inputs into outputs, not just the operations department.

Scheduling *is the process of listing activities that must be performed to accomplish an objective; activities are listed in sequence with the time needed to complete each activity*. The details of the schedule answer the what, when, where, how, and who questions. When scheduling, you should define the job and assure the availability of resources when needed.[17] All managers are involved in scheduling resources, including scheduling their time, which you will learn about in the next section on time management.

scheduling
The process of listing activities that must be performed to accomplish an objective; activities are listed in sequence with the time needed to complete each activity.

More organizations are using computers to schedule resources.[18] A variety of computer scheduling software programs are available.[19] However, teaching you to schedule using a computer is beyond the scope of this course. But, you will learn to use a simple planning sheet, a Gantt chart, and PERT network by paper and pencil in this section. If you must do complex scheduling like that done at Westhoff Tool and Die, you will need to learn to use a computer. Westhoff uses a computer to track 80 projects. The computer schedules each machine in the plant on a chart, with copies given to six managers who supervise 60 operators.

Before learning about these three scheduling techniques, let's discuss two simple techniques you may have already used: the calendar and the to-do list. The *calendar* is used to write down important things that must be done on specific days, or times during the day. You can buy special planning calendars. The *to-do list* is commonly just a piece of paper (or you can buy special pads) used to write down the important things that must be done today, or soon. Scheduling calendars and to-do lists are also available in many inexpensive computer software packages. You will learn to use a more complex to-do list that includes setting priorities in the next chapter.

The Planning Sheet

Planning sheets *state an objective and list the sequence of activities, when each activity will begin and end, and who will complete each activity to meet the objective*. The planning sheet in Figure 6–4 shows a transformation process for a monthly marketing letter, developed by Latoya for WT&DS, which she mails to 300 potential customers. Stop reading to review Figure 6–4 and identify the plan used based on the five planning dimensions (Figure 6–1). The answer is at the bottom of the figure. The planning sheet works for plans with independent sequential steps of activities needed to accomplish the objective.

planning sheets
State an objective and list the sequence of activities, when each activity will begin and end, and who will complete each activity to meet the objective.

Set Objectives. Before you can determine how you will do something, you should decide what it is you want to accomplish. So the first step in planning is to clearly state the end result you desire, using the writing objectives model in Chapter 5. After setting the objective, fill in who is responsible for achieving the objective, starting and ending date, priority (high, medium, low), and control checkpoints to use to monitor progress.

Plan and Schedule. List the sequence of steps stating what, where, how, resources needed, and so on in the first column. In the "when" column you place the start and end time for each step. The third column contains the party responsible for each step.

Steps 2 through 4 and 7 could be eliminated if Latoya had all letters printed in their entirety on the word processor, rather than using a printer to duplicate them, and if she sent the letters first class instead of bulk rate. The reasons she

Figure 6–4
WT&DS Operational Plan

OBJECTIVE: To mail a personalized form letter to all target clients by the 15th of each month.
Responsible: Joel **Starting date:** 1st of each month
Due date: 15th of each month **Priority:** High
Control checkpoints: 7th and 12th of each month

Activities (steps of what, where, how, resources needed, and so on)	**When** Start		**End**	**Who**
1. Type the letter on the word processor.	1st		2nd	Latoya
2. Deliver letter to printer.	3rd	or	4th	Joel
3. Letters are printed on WT&DS stationery.	5th		6th	printer
4. Pick up letters at printer.	6th	or	7th	Joel
5. Use mail merge to type names and addresses on letters and envelopes.	7th		9th	Joel
6. Each letter is signed by Latoya, folded, and put in an envelope.	10th		11th	Joel
7. Bundle to meet bulk mailing specifications.	12th		13th	Joel
8. Deliver to U.S. Postal Bulk Mail Center.	13th			Joel
9. Mail letters.	14th	or	15th	U.S. Mail

Based on the five planning dimensions: (1) This plan is developed by Latoya, who is the only manager; no real level. (2) The type of plan is operational. (3) The scope is narrow. (4) The time is short-range. (5) Its repetitiveness is standing plan procedure.

included these steps were cost (first-class mail costs more than twice as much as bulk mail) and personalization. Latoya wanted potential clients to feel as though they received a personal letter rather than a form letter. Placing the client's name on the letter and having her signature on the letter personalizes the letters to overcome the bulk-rate feeling. Latoya's original plan was to word process each letter and mail them all bulk rate. But the U.S. Postal Service informed Latoya that personalized word-processed letters could not be mailed bulk rate. Latoya wanted both personalization and bulk-rate savings. Latoya and the bulk mail manager agreed that Latoya could place the name and address and signature on the printed letter, but that the letters could not be word processed to qualify for bulk rate.

It took time to develop this plan, but the time spent paid off in two major ways. First, she mailed the letters on time. Latoya started with the "we'll do it when we have time" approach, and letters were sent out late, and not at all one month. Second, Joel, listed in the "who" column of Figure 6–4, is a student employed by WT&DS. The turnover time for her student employees is usually one year. This plan saves training time when a new student comes on board. Latoya gives the new student a copy of the plan, which shows the entire process and the student's role and contribution.

You can easily make copies of the operational plan sheet for your own use by writing/typing in the bold information as a template.

Work Application

7. Give an example of a plan that would be appropriate to schedule using the planning sheet in an organization you work or have worked for.

Gantt Chart

Gantt charts *use bars to graphically illustrate a schedule and progress toward the objective over a period of time.* The different activities to be performed are usually shown vertically, with time shown horizontally. The resources to be allocated, such as people or machines, are commonly shown on the vertical axis. Or a variety of projects to be accomplished within a department can be shown on the same chart. Gantt charts, like the planning sheet, are appropriate for plans with independent sequential steps needed to accomplish the objective. The Gantt chart has the advantage over the planning sheet in that it places progress toward the objective on the chart as a control technique. In other words, a Gantt chart is both a planning and control tool.

Gantt charts
Use bars to graphically illustrate a schedule and progress toward the objective over a period of time.

Graphic illustrations of production were used when the Great Pyramids of Egypt were built. Henry Gantt popularized their use at the turn of this century (Chapter 1). Today, these bar diagrams are used extensively for allocating resources. WT&DS's planning sheet could be turned into a Gantt chart by changing the "when" column to show the days 1 through 15 instead of "start" and "end"; the rows would contain the bars to represent the number of days needed for each step. Though not shown in Figure 6–5, a Grant chart can have a column for stating who, or what department or machine, and so on has responsibility for completing the activity or project, similar to the "who" column in the planning sheet. The "who" column especially helps when multiple people, departments, machines, and so on will be used to complete the project.

Figure 6–5 illustrates a Gantt chart for multiple orders in an operations department. Each order bar represents the starting to ending time, and the darker color part completion to date. Using the chart, you can see at a glance how orders are progressing. If you become aware that a project is behind schedule, you can take corrective action to get it back on schedule. Assume that today is day 1 of week 3 in May (end of dark color of bar should be directly under 3 to be on schedule). What is the status of each of the four projects on the chart in Figure 6–5? The answer is at the bottom of the figure.

Work Application

8. Give an example of a plan that would be appropriate to schedule using a Gantt chart in an organization you work or have worked for.

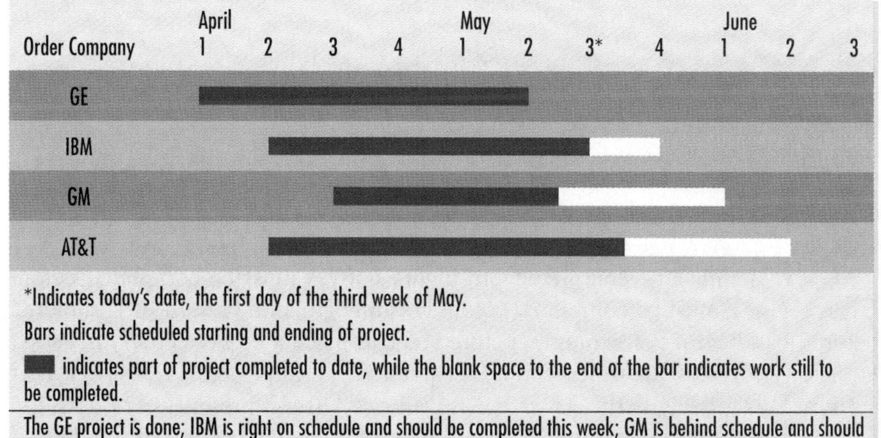
Order Company
April
1
2
3
4
May
1
2
3*
4
June
1
2
3
GE
IBM
GM
AT&T
*Indicates today's date, the first day of the third week of May.
Bars indicate scheduled starting and ending of project.
indicates part of project completed to date, while the blank space to the end of the bar indicates work still to be completed.
The GE project is done; IBM is right on schedule and should be completed this week; GM is behind schedule and should be complete during the fourth week in May; AT&T is ahead of schedule and should be completed during the first week of June.

Figure 6–5
Multiple-Project Gantt Chart (Order by Week)

Performance Evaluation and Review Technique (PERT)

PERT
A network schedule that illustrates the dependence of activities.

critical path
The most time-consuming series of activities in a PERT network.

Multiple activities are independent when they can be performed simultaneously; they are dependent when one activity must be completed before the next activity can begin. The planning sheet and Gantt chart are useful tools when the activities follow each other in a dependent series. However when activities follow both dependent and independent series of each other, PERT (critical path) is more appropriate. **PERT** *is a network schedule that illustrates the dependence of activities*. Figure 6–6 shows a PERT network.

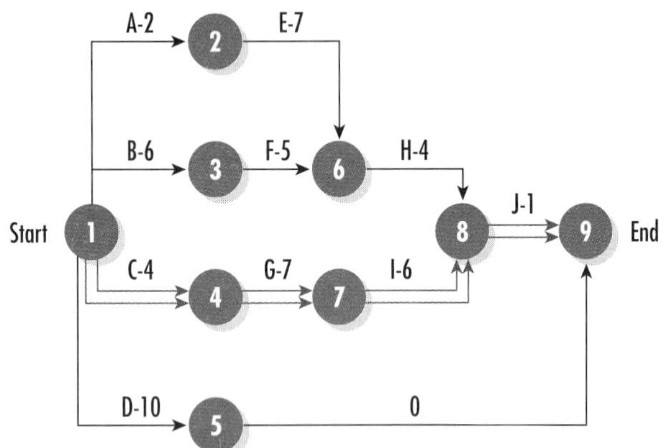

Circles = Events
Arrows and Letter = Activities
Numbers = Time in days
Double Arrows = The critical path, or how long it should take to complete the project

Figure 6–6
PERT Network

The key components to PERT are activities, events, times, the critical path, and possibly cost. With complex programs, it is common to have multiple activities represent one event. For example, in producing a car, building the engine would be an event because it would require multiple activities to complete. Time can be measured in any one of a variety of ways (seconds, minutes, hours, days, weeks, months, years, etc.) to determine the critical path. The critical path is important to know because it determines the length of time it will take to complete a project by determining how long each activity will take.[20] *The* **critical path** *is the most time-consuming series of activities in a PERT network*. It is shown by the double lines in Figure 6–5. Any delay of steps in the critical path will delay the entire project. Many organizations are focusing on shortening the time it takes to complete each activity to save time (time-based competition).[21] Cost for each activity can also be placed with the time.

Developing a PERT Network. The following steps explain how the PERT network in Figure 6–6 was completed:

step 1. **List all the activities/events that must be completed to reach the specific objective.** Assign each a letter. In the example, we have ten activities labeled A through J.

step 2. **Determine the time it will take to complete each activity/event.** In Figure 6–6, time is measured in number of days as follows: A-2, B-6, C-4, D-10, E-7, F-5, G-7, H-4, I-6, and J-1.

step 3. **Arrange the tasks on the diagram in the sequence in which they must be completed.** In Figure 6–6, A must be completed before E can begin; E must be completed before H can begin; and H must be completed before J can begin. For example, before you can place a box of cereal on a shelf for sale (J), it must be ordered (A), received (E), and priced (H). Notice that activity D is independent. An arrow as well as a letter represents each activity. The numbered circles signify the completion of an event leading to the desired outcome. All activities originate and terminate at a circle. In Figure 6–6, 1 represents the start of the project and 9 its end or completion.

Work Application

9. Give an example of a plan that would be appropriate to schedule using a PERT network in an organization you work or have worked for.

step 4.

Determine the critical path. To do this, you must total the time it takes for each path from start (1) to end (9). Path 1–2–6–8–9 takes 2 + 7 + 4 + 1 days for a total of 14 days. Path 1–3–6–8–9 takes 6 + 5 + 4 + 1 days for a total of 16. Path 1–4–7–8–9 takes 4 + 7 + 6 + 1 days for a total of 18 days. Path 1–5–9 takes 10 + 0 days for a total of 10 days. The critical path, indicated by the double arrow, is 1–4–7–8–9. The program or project should take 18 days to complete. If the job is supposed to be done in two weeks, you know before you even start that it cannot be done on time. You would have to change the completion date, or maybe even abandon the project.

To summarize this section, the operational planning sheet and Gantt chart are commonly used to develop procedures for routine standing plans, whereas PERT is commonly used for single-use program plans for a complex project with dependent activities. However, all three types of schedules can be used as either standing or single-use plans. You will develop your scheduling skills through Skill-Building Exercise 6–1.

APPLYING THE CONCEPT

AC 6–3 Scheduling Tools

Select the most appropriate scheduling tool for each situation.

a. Planning Sheet b. Gantt c. PERT

____ **16.** A production department has six different types of machines and eight products.

____ **17.** Ted will develop a plan for building a new house.

____ **18.** Karen will develop procedures for a new method of providing a service.

____ **19.** A plan will be created for building a new submarine.

____ **20.** The training department wants to schedule the use of its rooms and courses.

TIME MANAGEMENT TOOLS

Time has become an important aspect of a company's competitive advantage.[22] Fast delivery of products and services creates customer value. Companies, such as Motorola, Cadillac, and Texas Instruments now focus on time,[23] whereas, Federal Express and Jiffy Lube based their business on time-based competition from the start. Motorola, and other companies have discovered that poor productivity and inadequate customer service are related to poor time management.[24] Time management skills will have a direct affect on your productivity and career success.[25]

time management
Techniques that enable people to get more done in less time with better results.

Time management *refers to techniques that enable people to get more done in less time with better results.* Time is one of a manager's most valuable resources and time wasted can never be replaced. However, many managers do not use their time effectively because they have never been taught the importance of prioritizing activities and using a time management system.[26] Of the companies that do offer training, time management is the most widely taught skill.[27] Franklin Quest Company earns over $35 million a year from time management seminars and materials.[28] Latoya teaches time management skills to clients. Bowles, deputy to chief of staff, worked with President Clinton to develop his time management skills.[29] Unfortunately, many managers don't actually put the time management skills they learn into practice on the job on a regular basis.[30]

In this section, you will learn ways to analyze your present use of time, how to use the time management system, and time management techniques.

Developing time management skills is also an effective way to reduce stress (Chapter 14), increase personal productivity, and experience inner peace. One can possibly gain control of one's life by controlling one's time.[31]

8. Explain the use of a time log.

Analyzing Time Use

The first step to successful time management requires determining how time is spent and wasted.[32] Working long hours is often a sign of poor time management; it's not how long or hard you work that counts; it's results that count.[33] People often do not realize how they waste their time until they analyze time use. For example, managers waste an average of 15 minutes a day on hold on the telephone, which adds up to two weeks per year per person.[34] Managers who are aware of this time waster can plan to do something, such as read mail, while they wait, rather than doing nothing. An analysis of how you use your time will indicate areas for improvement. You need to break habits that waste time.[35]

The Time Log. The *time log* is a daily diary that tracks your activities and enables you to determine how you spend your time. You use one time log for each day. Figure 6–7 gives an example. You should keep track of your time every day over a period of one or two typical weeks. Try to keep the time log with you throughout the day. Fill in each 15 minute time slot, if possible, describing what you did. In Chapter 1, Figure 1–1, you saw the time log used by Bonnie, The Gap manager. Use Figure 6–7 as a template to develop your own time logs.

Analyzing Time Logs. After keeping time logs for five to ten working days, you can analyze the information recorded as follows. Write notes in the evaluation column, using the abbreviations listed on the next page:

Figure 6–7
Daily Time Log

Daily Time Log for: Day ____________________ Date ________________

Starting Time	Evaluation of Time Use
8:00	
8:15	
8:30	
8:45	
9:00	
9:15	
9:30	
9:45	
10:00	
etc., to Ending Time	

- Review the time logs to determine how much time you are spending on your primary responsibilities with high priorities (HP) and low priorities (LP). How do you spend most of your time?
- Identify areas where you spend too much time (TT).
- Identify areas where you do not spend enough time (NT).
- Identify major interruptions (I) that keep you from doing what you want to get done. How can you eliminate them?
- Identify tasks you are performing that you could delegate to someone else (D). Look for nonmanagement tasks. To whom can you delegate these tasks? (You will develop delegation skills in Chapter 7.)
- How much time does your boss control (B)? How much time do your employees control (E)? How much time do others (O) outside your department control? How much time do you actually control (M)? How can you gain more control of your own time?
- Look for crisis situations (C). Were they caused by something you did or did not do? Do you have recurring crises? How can you plan to help eliminate recurring crises? Do you have effective contingency plans?
- Look for habits, patterns, and tendencies. Do they help or prevent you from getting the job done? How can you change them to your advantage?
- List three to five of your biggest time wasters (W). What can you do to help eliminate them?
- Ask yourself, "How can I manage my time more efficiently?"

After analyzing how President Clinton used his time, Bowles eliminated extraneous activities from his calendar.[36] Throughout the remainder of this section, you will learn ideas to help you answer these ten questions.

Work Application

10. Identify your three biggest time wasters, preferably with the use of the time log. How can you cut down or eliminate these time wasters?

A Time Management System

9. List and briefly describe the three steps in the time-management system.

Time management remains one of the most daunting challenges confronting people in unconventional work contexts.[37] The time management system you will learn has a proven record of success with thousands of managers. Managers should try it for three weeks. After that time, they can adjust it to meet their own needs.

The problem managers face is not a shortage of time, but effective use of their time. Could you use an extra two hours every day? Experts say that most people waste at least this much time every day. The average manager could improve time use by 20 percent.

The four key components of the time management system are:

- *Priorities*. Seldom, if ever, do we have enough time to do everything we want to do. However, there is always time to do what is really important. Priorities determine what is more important and should be determined in terms of your major responsibilities. Spending time on high-priority tasks saves time on trivial concerns.[38]
- *Objectives*. Managers should develop goals.[39] You should set weekly objectives[40] following the guidelines stated in Chapter 5.
- *Plans*. You should develop operational plans to meet your objectives.

- *Schedules*. You can use the planning sheet, Gantt chart, and PERT for scheduling. You should schedule each week and work day.

Time management systems all boil down to developing a plan and sticking to it as much as possible.[41] *The* **time management system** *involves planing each week, scheduling each week, and scheduling each day.*

time management system
Planning each week, scheduling each week, and scheduling each day.

step 1. **Plan Each Week.** On the last day of each week, plan the coming week. You can also begin the week with planning it. Do this each and every week. Using your previous week's plan and departmental objectives, fill in a plan for the week on the weekly planner sheet, using Figure 6–8 as a template. Start by listing the objectives you want to accomplish during the week.[42] These should be nonroutine things, not routine tasks you perform weekly or daily. For example, if an employee's annual review is coming up, set an objective to do it.

After setting a few major objectives, list major activities necessary to accomplish each objective in column 1. If the objective calls for multiple activities, use one of the three scheduling tools. Priorities should be high, medium, or low. All high priorities must be done that week; others can be pushed into the next week if necessary. To continue our example, you will need to plan for completing the appraisal form, making an appointment with the employee, and planning for completing the performance review. The performance appraisal is a high (H) priority. You will develop performance appraisal skills in Chapter 15.

The last two columns to fill in are the "Time Needed" and "Day to Schedule." To continue our example, assume it will take you 20 minutes to prepare for the performance appraisal and about a half-hour to complete it. The day to schedule could be your relatively quiet day. Total the time it will take to achieve your objectives for the week. Is the total time realistic considering you still need time for routine tasks and unexpected events? With experience, you will learn if you are too optimistic about how much you can plan for and accomplish in one week. Planning too much is frustrating and causes stress when

Figure 6–8
Weekly Planner

Plan for the week of: ______________________
Objectives:

Activities	Priority	Time Needed	Day to Schedule
Total time for the week			

you cannot get it all done.[43] On the other hand, if you do not plan enough activities, you will end up wasting time.

step 2.

Schedule Each Week. Scheduling your work gets you organized to achieve your objectives for the week.[44] You may make a schedule for the week while you plan it or afterwards, whichever you prefer. Planning and scheduling the week should take about 30 minutes. Figure 6–9 gives you a template for a weekly schedule. Start scheduling by filling in uncontrollable time slots, set weekly meetings, for example. Then, schedule controllable events like performance appraisals. Most managers should leave about 50 percent of the week unscheduled to accommodate unexpected events. Your job may require more or less unscheduled time. With practice, you will perfect weekly planning and scheduling.

The key to time management is not to prioritize your schedule, but to schedule your priorities weekly and daily.[45]

step 3.

Schedule Each Day. At the end of each day you should schedule the following day. Or you can schedule your day first thing in the morning.[46] This should take 15 minutes or less. Base the day's schedule on your plan and schedule for the week, using the template in Figure 6–10. Going from the weekly to a daily schedule allows time to adjust for unplanned events. Begin by scheduling the activities over which you have no control, such as meetings you must attend. Leave your daily schedule flexible. As stated, most managers

Figure 6–9
Weekly Schedule

Schedule for week of: ______________________

	Mon.	Tues.	Wed.	Th.	Fri.
Starting Time 8:00 8:15 8:30 8:45					
9:00 9:15 9:30 9:45					
10:00 etc., to Ending Time					

Figure 6–10
Daily Schedule

Schedule for day of: ____________________

Starting Time
8:00
8:15
8:30
8:45

9:00
9:15
9:30
9:45

10:00
etc., to Ending Time

need about 50 percent of their time unscheduled to handle unexpected events. Some scheduling tips follow:

- Don't be too optimistic; schedule enough time to do each task. Many managers, including the author, find that estimating the time something will take, and then doubling it, works well. With practice, you should improve.
- Once you have prioritized and scheduled tasks, focus on only one at a time.[47] According to Peter Drucker, a few people seem to do an incredible number of things. However, their impressive versatility is based mainly on doing one thing at a time.[48]
- Schedule high-priority items during your "prime time," when you perform at your best. For most people it is early in the morning. However, some people are slow starters and perform better later in the day. Determine your prime time and schedule the tasks that need your full attention. Do routine things, such as checking your mail, at other times.
- Try to schedule a time for unexpected events. Tell employees to see you with routine matters during a set time, such as 3 P.M. Have people call you, and call them, during this set time.
- Do not do an unscheduled task before determining its priority. If you are working on a high-priority item and you receive a medium-priority matter, let it wait. Often even the so-called urgent matters can wait.

The time management system works well for managers who have to plan for a variety of nonrecurring tasks. For managers and employees who deal primarily with routine tasks, the time management system may not be necessary. For people in routine situations, the use of a good to-do list that prioritizes items may be all they need. In the next chapter you will learn about the to-do list. Skill-Building Exercise 6–2 gives you the opportunity to develop your time management skills by using the time management system. Forms similar to Figures 6–8 through 6–10 can be purchased in pad, book, and even computer versions.[49] However, you can make your own full-page copies using the templates from the figures.

SKILLBUILDER

Work Application

11. From the 50 time management techniques listed in Self-Assessment Exercise 6–1, choose the three most important techniques you "should" be using. Explain how you will implement each technique.

Time Management Techniques

Self-Assessment Exercise 6–1 contains 50 time management techniques arranged by management function. Planning and controlling are placed together because they are so closely related. Organizing and leading are separated.

After you have completed the Self-Assessment Exercise, implement the items you check as "should do." Once you are using all the "should do" items, work on your "could do" items to continually improve your time management skills. After implementing all the "should do" and "could do" items, reread the "does not apply" column to see if any of the items apply at that time.

SELF-ASSESSMENT EXERCISE 6–1

Time Management Techniques

A list of 50 ideas that can be used to improve your time management skills follows. Place a checkmark in the appropriate box for each item.

Planning and Controlling Management Functions	Should Do	Could Do	Do Now	Does Not Apply to Me
1. Use the time management system.	☐	☐	☐	☐
2. Use a to-do list and prioritize the items on it. Do the important things rather than the urgent things.	☐	☐	☐	☐
3. Get an early productive start on your top-priority items.	☐	☐	☐	☐
4. During your best working hours (prime time) do only high-priority items; schedule unpleasant or difficult tasks during prime time.	☐	☐	☐	☐
5. Don't spend time performing unproductive activities to avoid or escape job-related anxiety. It doesn't really work. Get the job done.	☐	☐	☐	☐
6. Throughout the day ask yourself, "Should I be doing this—now?"	☐	☐	☐	☐
7. Plan before you act.	☐	☐	☐	☐
8. Plan for recurring crises to eliminate crises (contingency planning).	☐	☐	☐	☐
9. Make decisions. It is better to make a wrong decision than none at all.	☐	☐	☐	☐

10. Schedule enough time to do the job right the first time. Don't be too optimistic about the amount of time it takes to do a job. ☐ ☐ ☐ ☐
11. Schedule a quiet hour to be interrupted only by true emergencies. Have someone take messages or ask people to call you back. ☐ ☐ ☐ ☐
12. Establish a quiet time for the entire organization or department. The first hour of the day is usually the best time. ☐ ☐ ☐ ☐
13. Schedule large blocks of uninterrupted (emergencies-only) time for projects and so forth. If this doesn't work, hide somewhere. ☐ ☐ ☐ ☐
14. Break large (long) projects into parts (time periods). ☐ ☐ ☐ ☐
15. Before abandoning a scheduled item to do something unscheduled, ask the priority question: "Is the unscheduled event more important than the scheduled event?" If not, stay on schedule. ☐ ☐ ☐ ☐
16. Schedule a time for doing similar activities (for example, make and return calls, write letters and memos). ☐ ☐ ☐ ☐

Organizing Management Function

17. Schedule unexpected event time and let people know the time. Ask people to see or call you during your scheduled unexpected time (professors have office hours), unless it's an emergency. Answer mail and do routine things while waiting for people to contact you. If people ask to see you—"Got a minute?"—ask whether it can wait until your scheduled unexpected event time. ☐ ☐ ☐ ☐
18. Set a scheduled time, agenda, and time limit for all visitors, and keep on topic. ☐ ☐ ☐ ☐
19. Keep a clean, well organized work area/desk. ☐ ☐ ☐ ☐
20. All non-work-related or distracting objects should be removed from your work area/desk. ☐ ☐ ☐ ☐
21. Do one task at a time. ☐ ☐ ☐ ☐
22. With paperwork, make a decision at once. Don't read it again later and decide. ☐ ☐ ☐ ☐
23. Keep files well arranged and labeled with an active and inactive file section. When you file an item, put a throw-away date on it. ☐ ☐ ☐ ☐
24. Call rather than write and visit, when appropriate. ☐ ☐ ☐ ☐
25. Delegate someone else to write letters, memos, and so forth. ☐ ☐ ☐ ☐
26. Use form letters and form paragraphs in a word processor. ☐ ☐ ☐ ☐
27. Answer letters (memos) on the letter itself. ☐ ☐ ☐ ☐
28. Have someone read and summarize things for you. ☐ ☐ ☐ ☐
29. Divide reading requirements with others and share summaries. ☐ ☐ ☐ ☐

30. Have calls screened to be sure the right person handles it. ☐ ☐ ☐ ☐
31. Plan before calling. Have an agenda and all necessary information ready; take notes on the agenda. ☐ ☐ ☐ ☐
32. Ask people to call you back during your scheduled unexpected time. Ask about the best time to call them. ☐ ☐ ☐ ☐
33. Have a specific objective or purpose for every meeting you conduct. If you cannot think of an objective, don't have the meeting. ☐ ☐ ☐ ☐
34. For meetings, invite only the necessary participants and keep them only as long as needed. ☐ ☐ ☐ ☐
35. Always have an agenda for a meeting and stick to it. Start and end as scheduled. ☐ ☐ ☐ ☐
36. Set objectives for travel. List everyone you will meet with. Send (call) them agendas and have a file folder for each with all necessary data for your meeting. ☐ ☐ ☐ ☐
37. Combine and modify activities to save time. ☐ ☐ ☐ ☐

Leading Management Function

38. Set clear objectives for subordinates with accountability; give them feedback and evaluate results often. ☐ ☐ ☐ ☐
39. Don't waste others' time. Don't make subordinates wait idly for decisions, instructions, or materials, in meetings, and so on. Wait for a convenient time, rather than interrupting your subordinates/others and wasting their time. ☐ ☐ ☐ ☐
40. Train your subordinates. Don't do their work for them. ☐ ☐ ☐ ☐
41. Delegate activities in which you do not need to be personally involved, especially nonmanagement functions. ☐ ☐ ☐ ☐
42. Set deadlines earlier than the actual deadline. ☐ ☐ ☐ ☐
43. Use the input of your staff. Don't reinvent the wheel. ☐ ☐ ☐ ☐
44. Teach time management skills to your subordinates. ☐ ☐ ☐ ☐
45. Don't procrastinate; do it. ☐ ☐ ☐ ☐
46. Don't be a perfectionist—define "acceptable" and stop there. ☐ ☐ ☐ ☐
47. Learn to stay calm. Getting emotional only causes more problems. ☐ ☐ ☐ ☐
48. Reduce socializing without causing antisocialism. ☐ ☐ ☐ ☐
49. Communicate well. Don't confuse employees. ☐ ☐ ☐ ☐
50. If you have other ideas not listed above, add them here ☐ ☐ ☐ ☐

CURRENT MANAGEMENT ISSUES

Globalization. To compete in a *global* marketplace, businesses must implement their strategic plans through the functional operational level. As competition increases globally, the need for accurate environmental and sales forecasts[50] and schedules become increasingly important. Therefore, planning tools become a necessity.

Diversity, Ethics, and Social Responsibility. In order for organizations to value and manage *diversity*, they must forecast employee needs and develop plans and schedules to implement diversity programs. Good time management skills can also allow employees more time to focus on developing good human relations with a diversity of workers. It is ethical and socially responsible to use planning tools to create a win-win situation for all stakeholders.

Quality and TQM. Customers continue to demand that products and services be delivered to them in the quickest way possible. Organizations are realizing that they can gain a competitive advantage over competitors by meeting customers' time demands.[51] Therefore, time is a competitive weapon which has become a part of many TQM systems.[52] Companies that emphasize TQM focus on delivering customer value and continuously improving systems processes, and they use planning tools to do these things. Just-in-time is an important part of TQM, and schedules are critical to being on time.[53] Time management has a focus on completing priority tasks, and using time management with TQM helps employees focus on customer value.[54]

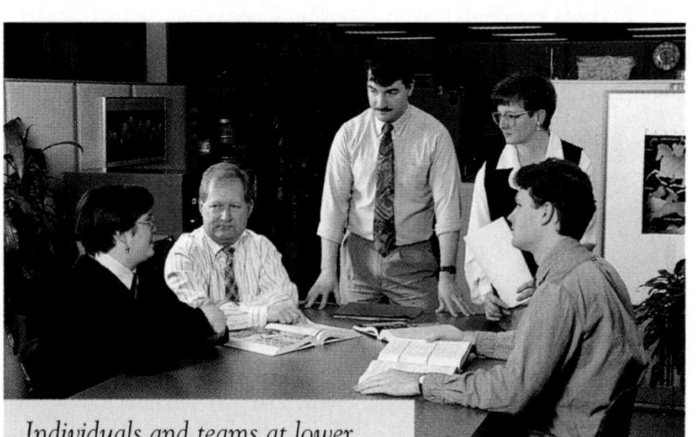

Individuals and teams at lower levels in the organization are being trained to use planning tools as they are empowered to take on more responsibility.

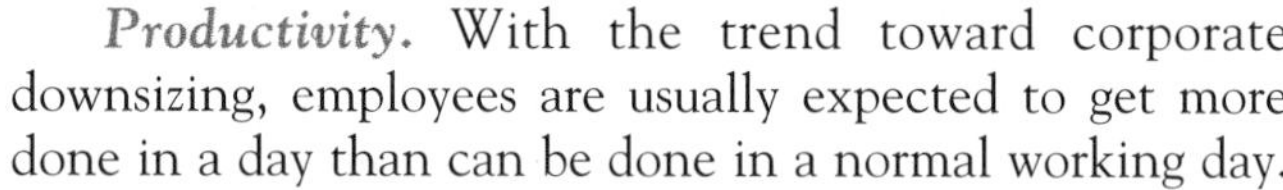

Productivity. With the trend toward corporate downsizing, employees are usually expected to get more done in a day than can be done in a normal working day. Time management skills can help increase productivity. An important part of re-engineering is to develop new processes that save time and other resources, and planning tools are used for this purpose.

Participative Management and Teams. As part of the trend toward *participative management*, individuals and *teams* at lower levels in the organization are being trained to use planning tools as they are empowered to take on more responsibility for developing and implementing functional operational strategies. Employees, not management, increasingly schedule their own work and manage their own time.

Small Business. Both large and small businesses can benefit greatly from planning tools. The major difference in their use concerns the level of sophistication. Large companies tend to have training budgets with expert training personnel to teach employees planning tools, and/or they hire expert consultants like Latoya Washington. Small businesses do not tend to have training budgets or expert trainers. Employees are taught less sophisticated planning tools on the job, or develop them on their own.

CHAPTER SUMMARY AND GLOSSARY

This chapter summary is organized to answer the ten learning objectives for Chapter 6.

1. State the difference between standing and single-use plans.

The major difference is repetitiveness. Standing plans include policies, procedures, and rules developed for handling repetitive situations. Single-use plans include programs and budgets developed for handling nonrepetitive situations.

2. Explain why contingency plans are often needed.
Contingency plans are alternative plans to be implemented if uncontrollable events occur. There are many events that the manager cannot control, that could prevent objectives from being achieved. By predicting what could go wrong and planning how to handle it if it does, managers increase the chances of successfully achieving objectives.

3. Discuss the relationship between the strategic process and sales forecasting.
Sales forecasting is a part of the strategic process. A short-term (one-year) sales forecast is prepared at the functional operational level, usually by the marketing department. It is based on the environmental analysis and the business-level strategy.

4. Describe the difference between qualitative and quantitative sales forecasting techniques.
The difference between qualitative and quantitative sales forecasting is based on the objective use of math. Qualitative sales forecast techniques are based on subjective judgment, intuition, experience, and opinion, with some math. Quantitative techniques are based on objective mathematical past sales data to predict sales. However, a combination of the two methods can be used with existing products and organizations to improve forecasting.

5. Discuss the difference between the jury of executive opinion and the three composite sales forecasting techniques.
The jury of executive opinion seeks a consensus of agreement from managers and/or experts. The composite methods combine the forecasts of salespeople, customers, or operating units to get a total company sales forecast without an agreed upon consensus. The composite techniques are more objective, are based more on math, than the jury of executive opinion.

6. Explain the difference between the past sales and time series sales forecasting techniques.
With past sales, future sales are predicted to be the same or are subjectively adjusted for environmental factors. With time series, future sales are predicted based on extending the trend line based on sales volume over time. Adjustments for environmental factors are more objective.

7. Describe the similarities and differences between the planning sheet, Gantt chart, and PERT network.
Similarities include the fact that all three are scheduling techniques and list activities that must be performed to accomplish an objective. Activities are listed in sequence with the time needed to complete each. The primary difference concerns their format and use.

Planning sheets state an objective and list the sequence of activities, when each activity will begin and end, and who will complete each activity to meet the objective. *Gantt charts* use bars to graphically illustrate a schedule and progress toward the objective over a period of time. Gantt charts, like planning sheets, are appropriate for plans with independent sequential steps of activities needed to accomplish the objective. The Gantt chart has the advantage over the planning sheet in that it places progress toward the objective on the chart as a control technique. *PERT* is a network schedule that illustrates the dependence of activities. When activities are both dependent and independent of each other, PERT is more appropriate.

8. Explain the use of a time log.
A time log is a daily diary used to analyze how time is spent and wasted. Through a time log analysis, one knows areas to work on to improve time use.

9. List and briefly describe the three steps in the time management system.
The steps in the time management system are (1) Plan each week. The week is planned by determining the objectives and activities necessary to achieve the objective. (2) Schedule each week. The week is scheduled by selecting days and times to perform the activities necessary to achieve the week's objectives. (3) Schedule each day. The day is scheduled by selecting the times to perform the activities necessary to achieve the week's objectives. Going from a weekly to a daily schedule allows time to adjust for unplanned events.

10. Define the following key terms (in order of appearance in the chapter):
Select one or more methods: (1) fill in the missing key terms from memory, (2) match the key terms from the end of the summary with their definitions below, or (3) copy the key terms in order from the list at the beginning of the chapter.

__________ include policies, procedures, and rules developed for handling repetitive situations.

______ provide general guidelines to be followed when making decisions.

______ are a sequence of actions to be followed in order to achieve an objective.

______ state exactly what should or should not be done.

__________ include programs and budgets developed for handling nonrepetitive situations.

__________ are alternative plans to be implemented if uncontrollable events occur.

__________ is the prediction of the units and/or dollar volume of products to be sold during a specified period of time.

__________ is the percentage of industry sales made by one organization.

______________ use primarily subjective judgment, intuition, experience, and opinion to predict sales. Some math may be used.

______________ use objective mathematical past sales data to predict sales.

__________ is used to predict future sales by extending the trend line of past sales volume over time.

______ is the process of listing activities that must be performed to accomplish an objective; activities are listed in sequence with the time needed to complete each.

__________ state an objective and list the sequence of activities, when each activity will begin and end, and who will complete each activity to meet the objective.

__________ use bars to graphically illustrate a schedule and progress toward the objective over a period of time.

______ is a network schedule that illustrates the dependence of activities.

______ is the most time-consuming series of activities in a PERT network.

__________ refers to techniques that enable people to get more done in less time with better results.

The ______________ involves planing each week, scheduling each week, and scheduling each day.

KEY TERMS

contingency plans
critical path
Gantt charts
market share
PERT
planning sheets
policies
procedures
qualitative sales forecasting techniques
quantitative sales forecasting techniques
rules
sales forecast
scheduling
single-use plans
standing plans
time management
time management system
time series

REVIEW AND DISCUSSION QUESTIONS

1. What are the five planning dimensions?
2. What is the difference between a policy, a procedure, and a rule?
3. Why do some managers fail to plan?
4. Why is sales forecasting important?
5. When can't you use quantitative sales forecasting techniques?
6. Why is scheduling important?
7. What does a Gantt chart show that the planning sheet and PERT don't show?
8. When would you use a PERT network rather than Gantt chart?
9. Why are time management skills important?
10. What does a time log show?
11. What are the four key components of the time management system?
12. If you schedule each week, why do you have to schedule each day too?
13. Can you think of any other important current management issues not listed?

CASE

Southwest Airlines

Southwest Airlines started as a small business with four planes in 1971. But its chairman, president, and CEO, Herb Kelleher, has turned Southwest into the fifth largest U.S. carrier with around 226 planes and revenues of over $2.7 billion. It has been profitable in all but its first two years, and profits have exceeded $75 million. What makes this success story even more remarkable is the fact that companies including TWA, Delta, American, and United were reporting huge losses and retrenching while Southwest had a growth prospector strategy.

Southwest used a focus and low-cost strategy to get where it is today. Rather than compete head on with major airlines, Southwest selected a niche focus in short-haul point-to-point flights. Its average flight is only 55 minutes. Therefore, it essentially has no hubs, does not make connections with, or transfer baggage to, other carriers. Southwest flies to fewer cities, but it offers more frequent flights to those cities than its competitors. For example, it has 39 roundtrip daily flights between Dallas and Houston, 23 roundtrip Phoenix and Los Angeles, and 20 roundtrip between Las Vegas and Phoenix.

Southwest's cost per available seat mile is 6.5 cents versus 9 cents at American and 15 cents at USAir. Southwest's average yearly salary and benefits for each unionized worker is $43,707 versus $58,816 at Delta; the industry average is $45,692. Southwest has one of the lowest debt to equity ratios (49 percent) and the highest Standard & Poor's credit rating among U.S. airlines. Southwest planes spend an average of 20 minutes at the gate between flights, while the industry average is around 60 minutes. Therefore, Southwest planes spend about 11 hours per day in the air while the industry average is 8 hours, despite the fact that it has more frequent shorter flights than the competition.

The mission at Southwest concerns inexpensive, simple, and focused airline service. Based on its low cost, it offers low fares. Southwest's average fare is under $60. In some areas the competition was charging $300. Needless to say, competitors had to drop their prices to compete with Southwest, and some decided to get out of Southwest's markets because they cannot compete. Southwest costs less than comparable inter-city bus prices in most of its markets. CEO Kelleher has said, "Southwest has created a solid niche making the automobile our main competition."

To achieve its mission of inexpensive, simple service, Southwest has only one type of plane: the fuel-efficient Boeing 737. This standardization allows lower inventory cost for spare parts, and allows specialization and minimizes training of flight and maintenance crews. Southwest has the lowest employee turnover in the industry at 7 percent.

To keep cost and fares down, Southwest uses a "no frills" approach to operations. It has no first-class or business section. It has no computerized reservation system because it does not offer reserved seats. Agents issue reusable numbered plastic cards on a first-come first-aboard to pick seats basis. Southwest does not offer meals or movies. However, low-cost and no frills do not mean low quality. In fact, Southwest is the only airline to win the U.S. Department of Transportation's "triple crown" monthly citation for the best on-time performance, fewest lost bags, and fewest overall complaints—not once, but four years in a row.

Select the best alternative for the following questions. Be sure you are able to explain your answers.

____ 1. Southwest gains efficiency primarily from its

a. standing plans b. single-use plans

___ 2. To be the low-cost operator in the airline business is a(n)

a. objective c. procedure e. program
b. policy d. rule f. budget

___ 3. Being a "no-frills" airline is a company

a. objective c. procedure e. program
b. policy d. rule f. budget

___ 4. To get its planes back in the air in about 15 minutes for an average of 11 trips a day, Southwest relies heavily on

a. objective c. procedure e. program
b. policy d. rule f. budget

___ 5. Southwest most likely uses the ___ qualitative sales forecasting technique.

a. sales force composite
b. customer composite
c. operating unit composite
d. survey

___ 6. Southwest most likely uses the ___ quantitative sales forecasting technique.

a. past sales b. time series

___ 7. For scheduling flights, the ___ scheduling tool would be most appropriate for use at Southwest.

a. planning sheet b. Gantt chart c. PERT

___ 8. Following Southwest's growth strategy, the ___ scheduling tool would be most appropriate for entering new markets.

a. planning sheet b. Gantt chart c. PERT

___ 9. Time is a competitive advantage at Southwest.

a. true b. false

___ 10. Time management skills are an important part of Southwest's success.

a. true b. false

11. Is Southwest customer-focused?

12. Could Southwest be as fast at getting its planes back into the air (15 minutes) if it offered long-distance flights?

13. Should Southwest grow by offering long-distance flights?

For current information on Southwest Airlines, use Internet address http://www.iflyswa.com. For ideas on using the Internet, see the Appendix.

SKILL-BUILDING EXERCISE 6–1

Developing a Plan to Open a Record Shop[55]

Preparing for Skill-Building Exercise 6–1

You have decided to open and manage (your name) Record Shop on April 1. It is now late December. You plan to move in one month before the store is scheduled to open in order to set up. During March, your assistant will help you set up and you will train him or her. You will start to implement the plan on January 2.

Assume that you have decided to use a (1) Gantt chart and (2) PERT network. Develop both, in order of your preference, following the text guides for their development, assuming that you have identified the activities and completion times listed below. (The activities may not be given in sequence.)

a. Lease the store fixtures to display your CDs, records, and tapes; it will take two weeks to receive and arrange them.
b. Order and receive records/tapes/CDs. This takes one week.
c. Recruit and select an assistant (three weeks or less).
d. Install the fixtures, paint, decorate, and so on (two weeks).
e. Form a corporation (four weeks).
f. Make arrangements to buy records/tapes/CDs on credit (two weeks).
g. Find a store location (six weeks or less).
h. Unpack and display records and tapes (one week).
i. Train the assistant (one week).
j. Select the records/tapes/CDs you plan to stock (one week).
k. Determine start-up cost and cash outflow per month through April 30. Your rich uncle will lend you this amount (one week).

1. Gantt Chart. When developing the Gantt chart, use the format on the next page, based on weeks. You may want to change the letter sequence to match starting dates.

Gantt Chart

Activity	January				February				March				April
(letter)	1	2	3	4	1	2	3	4	1	2	3	4	1
___													
___													
___													
___													
___													
___													
___													
___													
___													
___													
___													

2. PERT. When developing the PERT chart below, from start draw arrows to your circle for the independent activities. Inside the circle place the letter of the activity. On the arrow to the activity, place the number of weeks it will take to complete it. Then draw an arrow to the end. Also from start, draw the first dependent activity followed by the next dependent activity and so on until the last one; then draw an arrow to end. Be sure to put the number of weeks and activity/event letters on your network. After all activities are listed, determine the critical path and draw the second arrow to indicate it. *Hint:* You should have five arrows to activities coming from start; you can start the process with selecting music independently or finding a store location.

PERT
(with critical path)

Start **End**

Doing Skill-Building Exercise 6–1 in Class

Objective
To develop your planning skill using a Gantt chart and PERT network.

Preparation
You should have completed the Gantt and PERT to open your record shop.

Experience
You will be given feedback on your plans.

Procedure (10–20 minutes)
The instructor goes over the recommended Gantt and PERT.

Discussion and Conclusion
Is Gantt or PERT more appropriate for this type of plan?

Application (2–4 minutes)
What did I learn from this experience? How can I use this knowledge in the future?

____

____

Sharing
Volunteers give their answers to the application section.

SKILL-BUILDING EXERCISE 6–2

Time Management System[56]

Preparing for Skill-Building Exercise 6–2

For this exercise you will need to make full-page copies of Figures 6–8 through 6–10 to serve as templates. Before using the time management system, it is helpful, but not necessary, to keep a time log for one or two typical weeks.

Step 1. Plan Your Week. Using Figure 6–8, develop a plan for the rest of this week. Begin with today.

Step 2. Schedule Your Week. Using Figure 6–9, schedule the rest of this week. Be sure to schedule a 30-minute period to plan and schedule next week, preferably on the last day of this week.

Step 3. Schedule Your Day. Using Figure 6–10, schedule each day. Do this for every day at least until the class period for which this exercise is assigned.

Be sure to bring your plans and schedules to class.

Doing Skill-Building Exercise 6–2 in Class

Objective
To develop your time management skills to enable you to get more done in less time with better results.

Preparation
You need your completed time management plans and schedules.

Experience
You will share and discuss your plans and schedules for the week and your daily schedules.

Procedure 1 (5–10 minutes)
Break into groups of four to six and share and discuss your plans and schedules. Pass them around so that you can make comparisons. The comparisons serve as a guide to improving future plans and schedules.

Conclusion
The instructor leads a class discussion and makes concluding remarks.

Application (2–4 minutes)
What did I learn from this experience? How will I use this knowledge in the future?

____

____

Sharing
Volunteers give their answers to the application section.

VIDEOCASE

A Study in Decision-Making: Next Door Food Store

Next Door Food Store is a chain of thirty convenience stores and gas stations. Management must make two fundamental decisions: (1) what distribution channels to use and (2) what items to stock in the stores. The company explored two alternative distribution strategies: build a warehouse or use wholesalers. Their stocking decision had to consider an offer of $50,000 from Coca-Cola to stock Coke products exclusively. Accepting the offer would mean not stocking any Pepsi products. Is the Coke offer worth it? Next Door Food Store was also seeing changes in merchandising strategies among its competitors. The company needed to determine how to identify and respond to new merchandising trends.

Organizing Concepts and Delegating Work

Learning Objectives

After studying this chapter, you should be able to:

1. Explain the difference between a flat and tall organization.
2. Describe the similarity and difference among liaisons, integrators, and boundary roles.
3. Discuss the difference between formal and informal and centralized and decentralized authority.
4. List and briefly explain the four levels of authority.
5. Describe the relationship between line and staff authority.
6. Explain what an organization chart is and list the four things it shows.
7. Discuss the difference between internal and external departmentalization.
8. State the similarities and differences between matrix and divisional departmentalization.
9. Explain the difference between job simplification and job expansion.
10. Describe the job characteristics model and what it is used for.
11. Explain how to set priorities by listing the three priority questions and how you assign and delegate high, medium, and low priority.
12. List the four steps in the delegation model.
13. Define the following **key terms** (in order of appearance in the chapter):

    span of management
    responsibility
    authority
    delegation
    levels of authority
    line authority
    staff authority
    centralized authority
    decentralized authority
    organization chart
    departmentalization
    divisional structure
    job design
    job enrichment
    job characteristics model
    priority determination questions
    delegation model

Skill Development

SKILLBUILDER **1.** You should develop your skill at setting priorities (Skill-Building Exercise 7–1).

Setting priorities is an organizing skill that utilizes conceptual and decision-making skills. The exercise develops your decisional role skill of resource allocator. The SCANS skill competencies of using resources, information, and systems, as well as basic, thinking, and personal qualities foundation skills are also developed.

2. You should develop your delegating skills (Skill-Building Exercise 7–2).

Delegating is an organizing skill that utilizes human and communication skills. This exercise develops your interpersonal leader skills, informational skill of monitor, and decisional skill of resource allocator. The SCANS skills competencies of using resources, information, and systems, as well as basic, thinking, and personal qualities foundation skills are developed.

lfred Chandler determined the need to match the organization's strategy and structure (Chapter 1). In other words, for the strategy to be implemented successfully, the organization must have a compatible structure. When the strategy changes, the structure follows (form follows function). As firms change, the organization structure must also change. The need for change will be illustrated throughout the chapter with the CMP Publications integrated case.

The husband and wife team of Gerry and Lilo Leeds founded CMP Publications in 1971. They have grown, at their goal of 20 percent a year, from 1 to 14 business newspapers and magazines, which are leaders in their respective markets. Sales exceed $380 million a year. They compete in the high growth high-tech markets.

The Leeds's original structure called for centralized authority with Gerry and Lilo making all important decisions. As CMP grew, it became increasingly difficult for employees to personally meet with the Leeds. Employees began to line up outside the office at 8:00 in the morning and there was a constant waiting line. Important decisions that required a quick response, due to rapidly changing environments, were often delayed. The

Gerry and Lilo Leeds founded CMP Publications in 1971.

Leeds decided to reorganize CMP.

The Leeds broke the company into divisions which essentially created semiautonomous companies within CMP. Each division had a manager who was given the authority to run the division and to make it grow. Division managers report to the publications committee which oversees the divisions to ensure that they operate within CMP's mission and growth strategy. The publications committee consists of the Leeds and the division managers who meet regularly to discuss current business issues.

In this chapter you will learn some principles of organization and about authority, then you will learn to organize an entire firm, jobs, and yourself.

For current information on CMP Publications, use Internet address http://www.techweb.com/techweb. For ideas on using the Internet, see the Appendix.

PRINCIPLES OF ORGANIZATION

Organizing is the second function of management and was defined as the process of delegating and coordinating tasks and resources to achieve objectives. The four resources you organize are human, physical, financial, and information (Chapter 1). On an organizationwide basis, organizing refers to grouping activities and resources. As a manager, you must organize your departmental resources to achieve the functional operating objectives.[1]

Henri Fayol did pioneering work in administrative theory (Chapter 1). Many of the principles of organization that Fayol developed are still in use today. In this section, you will learn eight of the ten principles: unity of command and direction, chain of command, span of management, division of labor, coordination, balanced responsibility and authority, delegation, and flexibility. Figure 7–1 illustrates the organization principles. Later in this chapter you will learn about departmentalization and integration.

Figure 7–1
Principles of Organization

- Unity of command and direction
- Chain of command
- Span of management (flat and tall organizations)
- Division of labor (specialization)
- Coordination
- Balanced responsibility and authority
- Delegation
- Flexibility
- Departmentalization
- Integration

Unity of Command and Direction

Unity of command means that each employee should report to only one boss. *Unity of direction* means that all activities should be directed toward the same objective. The general objective should be to create customer value. Unity of direction starts with the organization's mission and is carried out through the strategic process. Gerry and Lilo Leeds reorganized CMP into divisions with managers to provide unity of command. However, the divisions report to the publications committee which provides unity of direction for the divisions.

Chain of Command

Chain of command, also known as the Scalar Principle, is the clear line of authority from the top to the bottom of the organization. All members of the firm should know to whom they report and who, if anyone, reports to them. The chain of command forms a hierarchy and is illustrated in the organization chart, which you will learn about in this chapter. This is a vertical separation based solely on differences in authority and responsibility.

The chain of command also identifies the formal path for communications. It is generally wise to handle your affairs through this chain of command. However, times occur when you will have to go to a higher authority, for example, when your boss is unavailable. In most organizations, it is also common for people from different departments to communicate outside the chain of command. It is best to conform to the practices of the organization, but don't betray confidences. If you talk about people behind their back, they usually find out. Reliance Steel and Aluminum Company changed its chain of command.[2] CMP divisions set up a clear chain of command within each division. The Leeds now work closely with the division managers.

Work Application

1. Follow the chain of command from your present/past position to the top of the organization. Start by identifying anyone who reported to you, then list your boss's title, your boss's boss's title, to the top manager's title.

Span of Management

1. Explain the difference between a flat and tall organization.

span of management
The number of employees reporting to a manager.

The **span of management** *refers to the number of employees reporting to a manager.* The fewer employees supervised, the smaller or narrower the span of management, also called *span of control.* The more employees supervised, the greater or wider the span. There is no best number of employees to manage. However, it is generally believed that lower-level managers can have a wider span of control than higher-level managers. The Leeds narrowed their span of control by organizing into divisions. Now they work with division managers rather than with all levels of employees as they did with the past structure.

The number of employees reporting to a manager should be limited to a number that can be effectively supervised. The proper span of management depends on the nature of work, management methods, subordinate ability, personalities, congruency of goals, organization size, self-control, and the manager's ability to supervise employees effectively. Positive factors of a wide span of management include delegation of authority, clear policies, and positive behavioral effects on employees who have more freedom. Positive factors of a narrow span include close supervision, control, and fast communication.[3]

V. A. Graicunas developed a formula for determining the span of management when you know the number of possible relationships between the manager and subordinates. For example, with manager Juan and two subordinates,

Colleen and Rick, six possible relationships can occur. Juan can talk to Colleen and Rick separately (2). Juan can meet with Colleen and Rick and interact with both of them (2). Juan may not be present when Colleen talks to Rick, or Rick to Colleen (2). The number of possible relationships increases geometrically as shown below.

Number of Subordinates	*Number of Possible Relationships*
3	18
6	222
9	2,376
12	24,708
18	2,359,602

Work Application

2. Identify your boss's span of management, or your own if you are or were a manager. How many levels of management are there in this organization? Is it a flat or tall organization?

With the span of management comes the height of the organizational levels. A *flat organization* exists when there are few levels with wide spans of management. A *tall organization* exists when there are many levels with narrow spans of management. Figure 7–2 illustrates flat versus tall organizations. Notice that the flat structure has only two levels of management and the tall structure has four.

Figure 7–2
Flat versus Tall Organizations

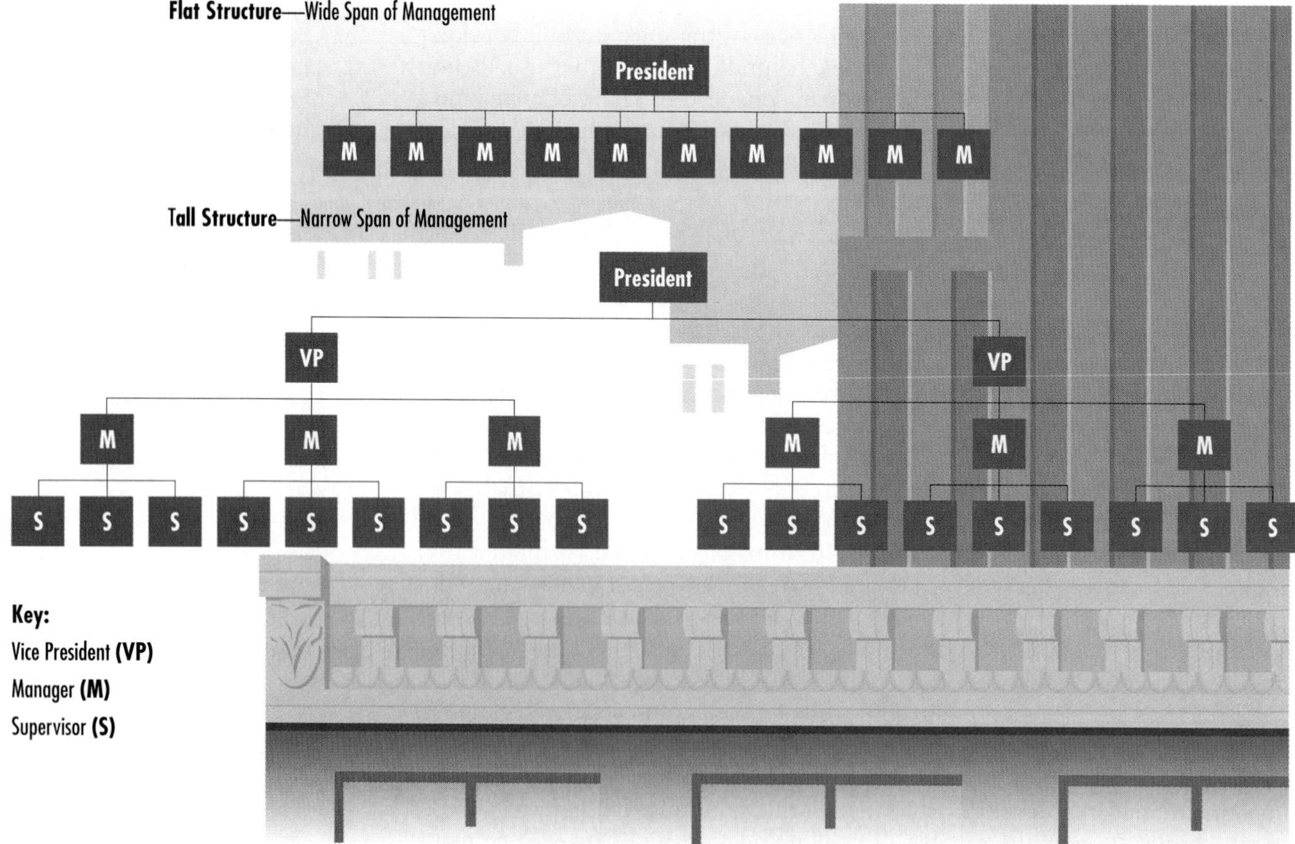

Division of Labor

With the *division of labor*, employees have specialized jobs. Related functions are grouped together under a single boss. Employees generally have specialized jobs in a functional area such as accounting, production, or sales. Managers usually perform less specialized functions as they move up the management ladder. However, a debate in management literature exists over whether managers should be generalists or specialists. The Leeds developed a clear division of labor when they organized into divisions.

Lawrence and Lorsch coined the terms *differentiation* and *integration*.[4] Differentiation refers to the need to break the organization into departments, while integration refers to the need to coordinate the departmental activities. The eight principles of organization are used to this end.

Coordination

2. Describe the similarity and difference among liaisons, integrators, and boundary roles.

Coordination means that all departments and individuals within the organization should work together to accomplish the strategic and operational objectives and plans. Coordination is the process of integrating organizational/departmental tasks and resources to meet objectives. Coordination requires conceptual skills. It is important that you coordinate all your department's resources.

The unity of command and direction, chain of command, span of management, balanced responsibility and authority, and standing plans are used to coordinate activities. Other means of coordination include:

- *Direct contact* between people within and between departments.
- *Liaisons* who work in one department and coordinate information and activities with one or more other departments.
- *Committees* made up of people from the different departments being coordinated, such as the publications committee at CMP.
- *Integrators*, such as product or project managers, who do not work for any department but coordinate departmental activities to reach an objective.
- *Boundary roles* in which employees coordinate efforts with people in the external environment. Employees in sales, customer service, purchasing, public relations, and others play boundary roles. People outside the organization form their impression of the organization based on the employees in boundary roles; most never even see or talk to a manager. Employees in boundary roles also acquire information about the environment which is used for ongoing environmental analysis.

Balanced Responsibility and Authority

Balanced responsibility and authority mean that the responsibilities of each individual in the organization are clearly defined. Each individual is also given the authority needed to meet these responsibilities and is held accountable for meeting them. Based on the acceptance theory of authority, when you delegate responsibility and authority, you do not give them away; you share them.

responsibility
The obligation to achieve objectives by performing required activities.

authority
The right to make decisions, issue orders, and utilize resources.

Responsibility *is the obligation to achieve objectives by performing required activities.* When strategic and operational objectives are set, the people responsible for achieving them should be clearly identified. Managers are responsible for the results of their organizations/divisions/departments even though they do not actually make the goods or provide the services.

Authority *is the right to make decisions, issue orders, and utilize resources.* As a manager you will be given responsibility for achieving departmental objectives. You must also have the authority to get the job done. Authority is delegated. The chief executive officer (CEO) is responsible for the results of the entire organization and delegates authority down the chain of command to the lower-level managers who are responsible for meeting operational objectives. To have true authority, you must gain the trust of your subordinates, peers, and boss.[5]

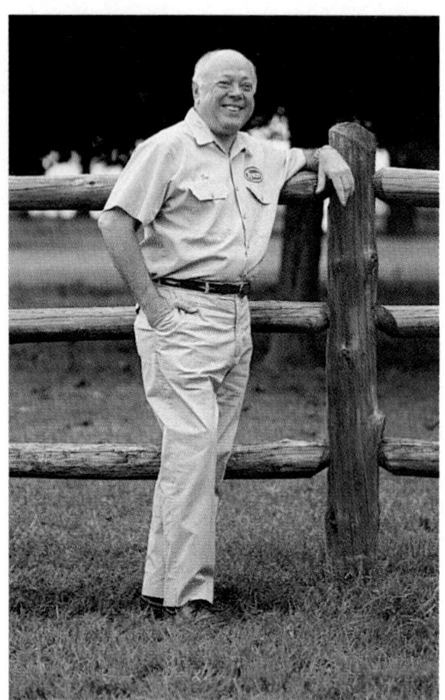
As CEO of Tyson Foods, Don Tyson is responsible for the results of the entire organization.

Accountability is the evaluation of how well individuals meet their responsibility. All members of the organization should be evaluated periodically and held accountable for achieving their objectives. To this end, some companies keep track of the numbers and even names of employees who make the products. If the product is defective, they know who is responsible. There is debate over who medical doctors are responsible and accountable to. Are medical doctors responsible to their patients, the organizations they work for, insurance companies, or the government?[6]

Managers are accountable for everything that happens in their departments. As a manager, you should delegate responsibility and authority to perform tasks, but you should realize that you can never delegate your accountability. For example, Jamal, a middle manager, delegated responsibility and authority for filling a special customer's order to supervisor Dave. As a supervisor should, Dave delegated the responsibility to employee Chris, who is accountable to Dave. The order was not sent out on time. The organization lost the customer. Following the chain of command, Jamal went to Dave who is accountable to him. Dave took the blame because he is accountable for his employee's performance. Dave, in turn, went to Chris, who is accountable to him.

Delegation

delegation
The process of assigning responsibility and authority for accomplishing objectives.

Delegation *is the process of assigning responsibility and authority for accomplishing objectives.* Responsibility and authority are delegated down the chain of command. In the preceding example, Jamal and Dave delegated. Delegation is an important skill for managers;[7] therefore, it will be covered in detail later in this chapter.

Flexibility

Work Application

3. Does an organization you work or have worked for encourage following the standing plans or flexibility? Explain your answer.

Flexibility means that there will always be exceptions to the rule. Based on management training, many employees focus on company rules rather than creating customer satisfaction. For example, the rule is no sales slip with returned merchandise, no cash refund. This rule helps to protect the store from people who steal merchandise and then return it for cash. A well-known, excellent customer comes into the store and demands a cash refund without a sales slip. In analyzing the situation, the employee realizes that the store has a good chance of losing a good customer. Should the employee follow the rules and lose a good customer, or be flexible and keep the good customer?

AUTHORITY

In this section, you will learn about formal and informal authority, types of authority, line and staff authority, and centralized and decentralized organizational authority.

> **APPLYING THE CONCEPT**
>
> **AC 7–1 Principles of Organization**
>
> Identify each statement in terms of the following organizational principles:
>
> a. unity of command and direction
> b. chain of command
> c. span of management
> d. division of labor
> e. coordination
> f. balanced responsibility and authority
> g. delegation
> h. flexibility
>
> ____ **1.** "Karl told me to pick up the mail. When I got to the post office, I did not have a key, so the postal worker wouldn't give me the mail."
>
> ____ **2.** The players on the football team are on the offensive or defensive squad.
>
> ____ **3.** "My job is frustrating at times because I work in a matrix structure and sometimes my department manager tells to do one thing while my project manger tells me to do something else at the same time."
>
> ____ **4.** Middle manager: "I want an employee to deliver this package but I can't order one to do it directly. I have to have one of my supervisors give the order."
>
> ____ **5.** "There has been an accident, and the ambulance is on the way. Juan, call Doctor Rodriguez and have her get to emergency room C in 10 minutes. Pat, get the paperwork ready. Karen, prepare emergency room C."

Formal and Informal Authority

Formal Authority. *Formal authority* (or structure) includes the specified relationships among employees. It is the sanctioned way of getting the job done. Formal authority starts at the top of the organization and is delegated down the chain of command. The organization chart illustrates formal authority and shows the lines of authority and the lines of communication. A job description states the employees' formal authority. However, formal authority does not fully describe how an organization actually gets things done.

3. Discuss the difference between formal and informal and centralized and decentralized authority.

Informal Authority. *Informal authority* (or structure) includes the patterns of relationships and communication that evolve as employees interact and communicate to get their jobs done. It is the unsanctioned way of getting the job done. Informal authority can be used to overcome the burdens and limitations that formal authority imposes on employees. Informally, employees can often get things done quicker, and even do things that seem impossible. Electronic mail (computer messages) and voice mail (telephone answering machines) have enhanced informal communication with anyone in the organization without going through the chain of command. Informal authority will always exist; the issue is to make sure it supports the organization's attainment of its mission and objectives.

Scope of Authority. The scope of authority narrows as it flows down the organization. The president has more authority than a vice president, who has more authority than a manager, who has more authority than a supervisor. Responsibility and authority are delegated and flow down the organization, whereas accountability flows up the organization, as Figure 7–3 illustrates.

As a manager, you will be given formal authority, but you will have to earn informal authority. The real test of authority is whether employees will accept and carry out your orders. To gain informal authority, people must trust you.[8] As do all organizations, CMP has both formal and informal authority. The Leeds have the greatest scope of authority as owners and top managers of CMP.

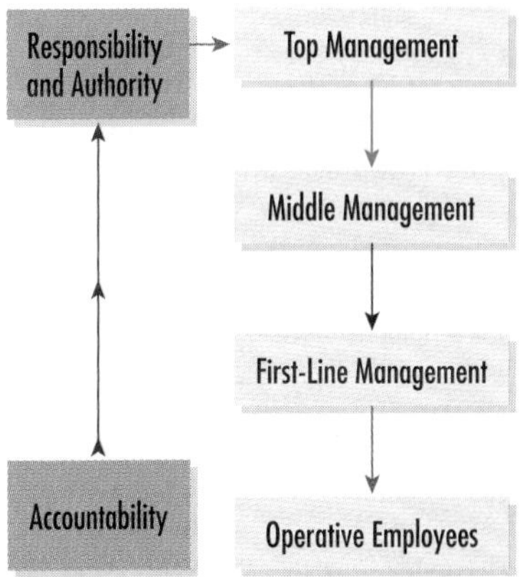

Figure 7–3
Scope of Authority

4. List and briefly explain the four levels of authority.

Levels of Authority

You should know your formal authority.[9] For example, what level of authority does a nurse have to alter a medical record that is believed to be in error? Levels of authority can vary from task to task.

levels of authority
Inform, recommend, report, and full.

The **levels of authority** *are inform, recommend, report, and full.*

1. *Inform authority.* The person informs the boss of possible alternative actions. The boss has the authority to make the decision. People in secretarial and clerical positions often have only inform authority because the job calls for gathering data for others.
2. *Recommend authority.* The person lists alternative actions, analyzes them, and recommends one action. However, the person may not implement the recommendation without the boss's okay. The boss may require a different alternative if he or she does not agree with the recommendation. Committees are often given recommend authority.
3. *Report authority.* The person may freely select a course of action and carry it out. However, afterward the person must report the action taken to the boss. Nurses have the authority to alter medical records, when the situation calls for it. The doctor who wrote the original entry should be informed of the alteration.[10]
4. *Full authority.* The person may freely make decisions and act without the boss's knowledge. For the most part, the Leeds gave the division managers full authority to run their semiautonomous divisions. However, even with full authority, many people consult their boss for advice.

To illustrate, Tania, a manager, needs a new machine. If Tania had no authority, it would be up to her boss to get one. With inform authority, Tania would give her boss a list of possible machines to try and a description of their features, prices, and so forth. With recommend authority, Tania would analyze the machines' features and suggest which one to purchase. With report authority, Tania would actually purchase a machine, but would have to tell her boss about it, possibly by sending him or her a copy of the purchase order. With full authority, Tania would purchase the machine without having to tell her boss about it.

Work Application

4. List and explain your level of authority for a specific task in an organization.

5. Describe the relationship between line and staff authority.

Line and Staff Authority

line authority
The responsibility to make decisions and issue orders down the chain of command.

staff authority
The responsibility to advise and assist other personnel.

Line authority *is the responsibility to make decisions and issue orders down the chain of command.* Line managers are primarily responsible for achieving the organization's objectives, and staff people provide them with a service to help them.[11] **Staff authority** *is the responsibility to advise and assist other personnel.* Operations and marketing are usually line departments. But, some organizations include financial activities too. Human resources management, public relations, and data processing are almost always staff departments.

Line departments would not be as successful without the support of staff departments since every line objective has its human, financial, and data components.[12] The line departments are internal customers of the staff department. Therefore, line and staff department members should strive to form a collaborative partnership.[13]

The following example will make the line staff relationship clearer. Maurice, a production (line) manager, needs a new employee. The human resources (staff) department will assist by recruiting possible candidates. Human resources may conduct interviews and tests and advise Maurice of the results. It may recommend the top candidates for an interview. The line manager decides who to hire, with the advice and assistance of staff. The operations department also needs the services of the purchasing and maintenance department. In some organizations, such as IBM and Bechtel, employees rotate between line and staff positions.

Functional Authority. The staff's primary role is to advise and assist, but situations occur in which they can give orders to line personnel. *Functional authority* is the right of staff personnel to issue orders to line personnel in established areas of responsibility. For example, the maintenance department assists production by keeping the machines operating. If maintenance determines that a machine is unsafe, the department may issue an order to a line manager not to use the machine. Or a payroll manager may order a line manager to have employees fill in time cards to specifications.

Dual Line and Staff Authority. Staff managers may have both staff and line authority. For example, Ted, a public relations (staff) manager, advises and assists all departments in the organization. However, Ted also has line authority within his own department and issues orders (a line function) to his employees.

General and Specialist Staff. *General staff* work for only one manager. Often called "assistant to," they help the manager in any way needed. *Specialist staff* help anyone in the organization who needs it. Human resources, finance, accounting, public relations, and maintenance offer specialized advice and assistance.

The Leeds and division managers are all line managers. Division managers may use the services of the printing, finance, and human resources departments.

Work Application

5. Identify one or more line and staff positions in an organization you work or have worked for. Also identify staff as general or specialist.

Centralized and Decentralized Authority

The major difference between centralized and decentralized authority is who makes the important decisions. *With* **centralized authority,** *important decisions are made by top managers. With* **decentralized authority,** *important decisions are made by middle- and first-level managers.*

centralized authority
Important decisions are made by top managers.

decentralized authority
Important decisions are made by middle- and first-level authority.

The major advantages of centralization include control (uniform procedures are easier to control, and fewer risks are taken) and reduced duplication of work (few employees perform the same tasks, and specialized staff may be fully utilized). The major advantages of decentralization include efficiency and flexibility (decisions are made quickly by people familiar with the situation) and development (managers are challenged and motivated to make decisions and solve their own problems). Which type of authority works best? There is no simple answer. Sears, General Electric, and General Motors have successfully used decentralized authority, and General Dynamics, McDonald's, and Kmart have successfully used centralized authority.

Authority is a continuum, with decentralized and centralized at each end.

Centralized authority ———————————— Decentralized authority

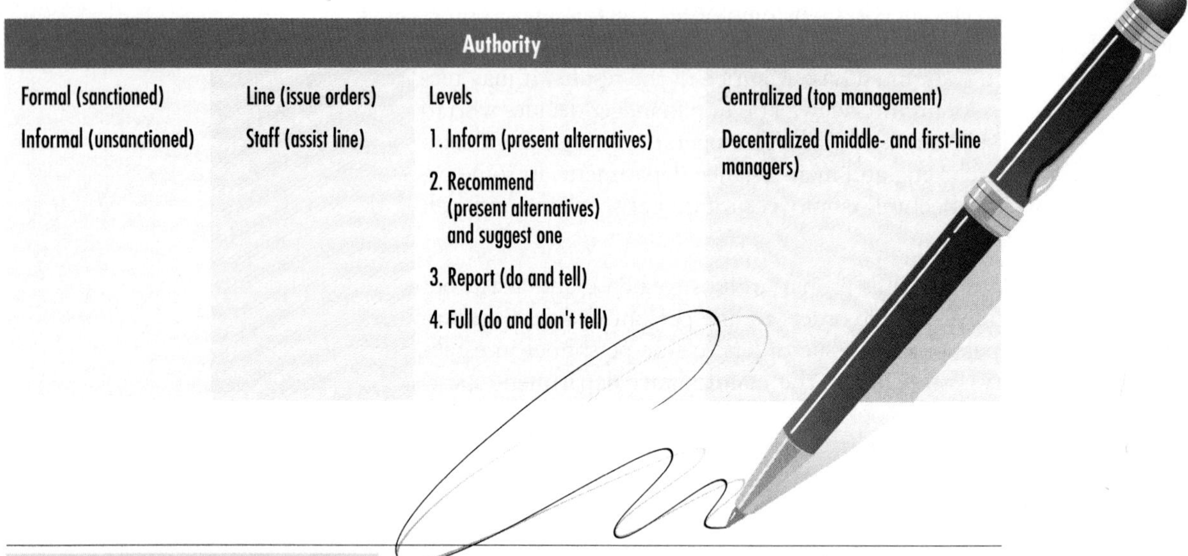

Authority
Formal (sanctioned)
Informal (unsanctioned)
Line (issue orders)
Staff (assist line)
Levels
1. Inform (present alternatives)
2. Recommend (present alternatives) and suggest one
3. Report (do and tell)
4. Full (do and don't tell)
Centralized (top management)
Decentralized (middle- and first-line managers)

Figure 7–4
Authority

Work Application

6. Describe the type of authority (centralized or decentralized) used in an organization you work or have worked for.

With the exception of very small companies, which tend to be centralized, most organizations lie somewhere between the two extremes, but can be classified overall. The key to success seems to be having the right balance between the two extremes. For example, General Motors is primarily decentralized, but it maintains centralized control over such areas as strategic planning and resource allocation. Production and sales are often decentralized, whereas finance and labor relations are centralized to provide uniformity and control throughout an organization. Top managers are decentralizing authority to the business-unit-level managers,[14] and the business-level managers are empowering teams.[15]

The Leeds started CMP with centralized authority. But, as the company grew, it became time-consuming to make all the decisions. Therefore, the Leeds decentralized authority to the division managers. See Figure 7–4 for a review of authority.

ORGANIZATIONAL DESIGN

Now that you know the basics of organization, you will learn about organizing an entire firm. *Organizational design* refers to the arrangements of positions into work units/departments and the interrelationship among them within the organization. The organizational design is illustrated through the organization chart and type of departmentalization.

6. Explain what an organization chart is and list the four things it shows.

Organization Chart

organization chart
A graphic illustration of the organization's management hierarchy and departments and their working relationships.

The formal organizational authority/structure defines the working relationships between the organization's members and their jobs and is illustrated through an organization chart. An **organization chart** *is a graphic illustration of the organization's management hierarchy and departments and their working relationships*. Each box represents a position within the organization, and each line indicates the reporting relationships and lines of communication.

Figure 7–5, an adaptation of General Motors' organization, illustrates four major aspects of a firm.

- *The level of management hierarchy*. The CEO and presidents are top-level management, the vice presidents and managers are middle-level management, and the supervisors are first-level management.
- *Chain of command*. As you follow the vertical lines you can see that the division presidents report to the CEO. The managers report to vice presidents, and supervisors report to the managers.

APPLYING THE CONCEPT

AC 7–2 Authority

Identify each statement by the type of authority.

a. formal
b. informal
c. level
d. line
e. staff
f. centralized
g. decentralized

____ 6. "My job is interesting, but it is frustrating when I recommend employees to the production and marketing managers and they do not hire them."

____ 7. "It is great working for an organization that encourages everyone to share information with everybody else."

____ 8. "Managers here have the autonomy to run their departments the way they want to."

____ 9. "I'm not sure if I'm suppose to get a list of company cars for Wendy, or recommend one of them to her."

____ 10. "That is a great idea. I'll talk to our boss Pete, and if he likes it, he'll let us present the idea to his boss Jean."

- *The division and type of work*. GM divides work by type of automobile: Buick, Cadillac, Chevrolet, Oldsmobile, and Pontiac. Each vice president within a division is responsible for a function, or type of work, such as marketing, production, or finance. The production middle managers

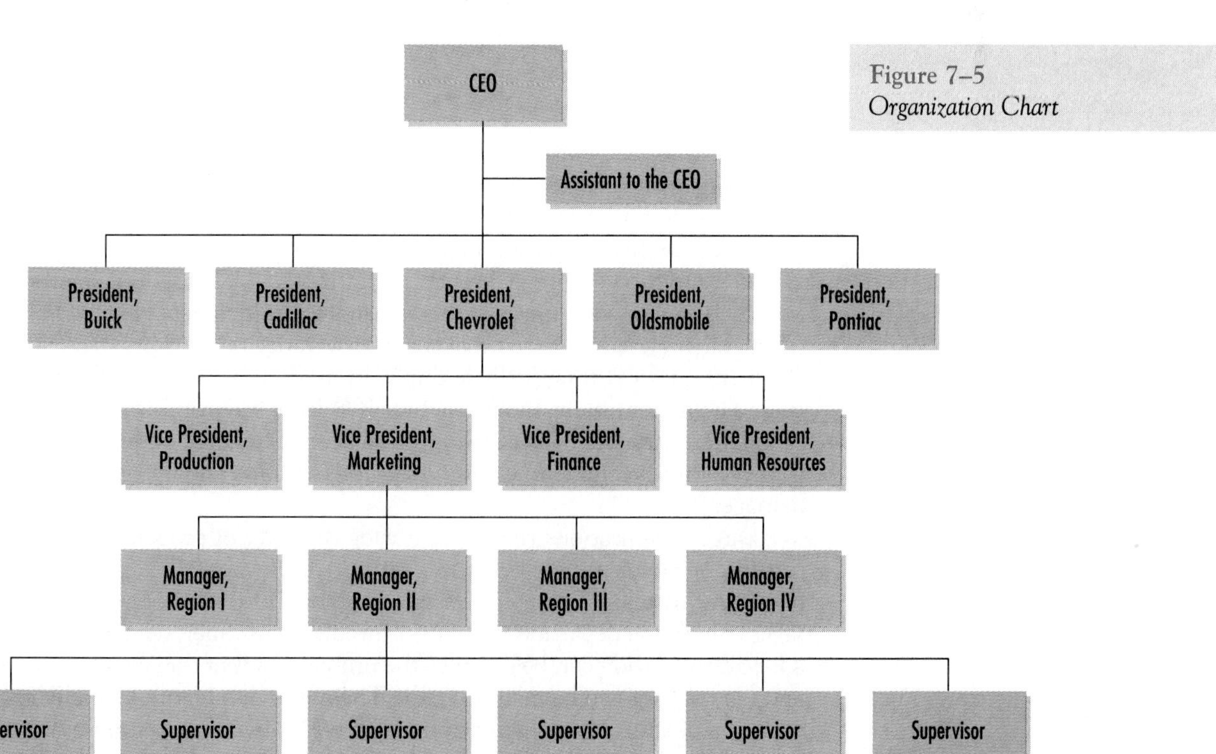

Figure 7–5
Organization Chart

are responsible for specific automobile models such as Corvette or Camaro. The supervisors are responsible for specific phases of production: engine, frame, body, paint, and so forth.

- *Departmentalization.* An organizational chart shows how the firm is divided into permanent work units. GM is organized primarily by product. Throughout this section organization charts will be used to illustrate the various types of departmentalization.

Note that each vice president of the Chevrolet Division has middle managers reporting to him or her, and each middle manager has supervisors reporting to him or her. The other four divisions—Buick, Cadillac, Oldsmobile, and Pontiac—all have their own vice presidents, middle managers, and supervisors, as Chevrolet does. The assistant to the CEO is a *general* staff, and the finance and human resources departments are *specialist* staff.

An organization chart does not show the day-to-day activities performed or the structure of the informal organization.

At large organizations it is difficult to use organization charts because of the large number of positions and reporting relationships. It is also difficult to keep an updated organization chart as companies grow and change reporting relationships.

7. Discuss the difference between internal and external departmentalization.

Departmentalization

departmentalization
The grouping of related activities into units.

Departmentalization *is the grouping of related activities into units.* Departments may be created with an internal or external focus. Departmentalization around the internal operations or functions that the employees perform and the resources needed to accomplish the unit's work is called *functional departmentalization*. External or output departmentalization is based on activities that focus on factors outside the organization; this is called *product, customer, and territory departmentalization*.

Functional Departmentalization. Functional departmentalization involves organizing departments around essential input activities, such as production, sales, and finance, that are managerial or technological functions. The top of Figure 7–6 illustrates functional departmentalization.

The functional approach is the form most widely used by small organizations. The major advantages of this internal focus include: (1) it is cost efficient; (2) managing is easier because of the narrow range of skills involved in each department; and (3) there is little duplication of effort because of the specialization. The major disadvantages include: (1) little attention is paid to any single product or customer because all must be accommodated; and (2) this approach is not readily adaptable to change; decisions are often slow to get through to top managers.

Large organizations that have a wide diversity of products or types of customers, or cover a wide territory, cannot departmentalize effectively around functions. Instead, they focus on factors external to the company. The advantages of external departmentalization (product, customer, territory) include: (1) adequate attention can be given to the unique needs of the individual customer; and (2) changes can be made quickly. The major disadvantages include: (1) duplication of effort; the organization may have, for example, production and sales departments for each product; and (2) managing is more difficult because a wide range of skills (general versus specialty) are needed.

Product (Service) Departmentalization. Product (service) departmentalization involves organizing departments around products or services. Companies with multiple products commonly use product departmentalization. Each department may become a self-contained company, making and selling its own product or service. Retail stores like Sears have product departments. Sears is increasing its apparel department by transferring furniture and appliances to separate Homelife and Brand Central stores.[16] Deloitte & Touche reorganized by separating consulting from its auditing and tax practices, thus creating a new product department.[17] The second organizational chart in Figure 7–6 shows an example of product departmentalization

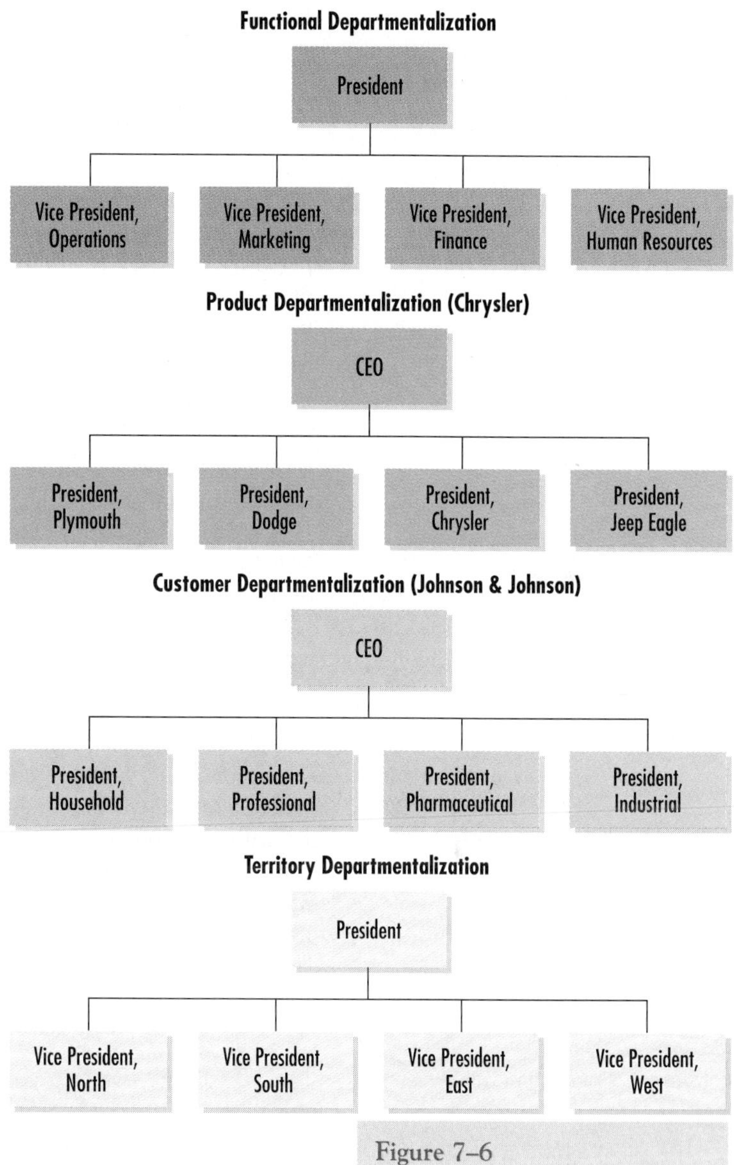

Figure 7–6
Departmentalization

Customer Departmentalization. Customer departmentalization involves organizing departments around the needs of different types of customers. The product may be changed and a different sales team may serve each group of customers. For example, IBM reorganized by customer because needs varied by industry and size of firm.[18] Like many companies using customer departmentalization, IBM sells many of the same products/computers, or only slightly different ones, to different customers. However, the marketing is usually different. Organizations that offer a wide diversity of products often use customer departments, as do some nonprofit organizations. For example, a counseling center may offer drug counseling, family counseling, and so on. However, these usually are not self-contained units. The third organization chart in Figure 7–6 illustrates customer departmentalization.

Territory (Geographic) Departmentalization. Territory (geographic) departmentalization involves organizing departments in each area in which the enterprise does business. The federal government does this. For example, the Federal Reserve System is divided into 12 geographic areas centered in cities such as Boston, New York, and San Francisco. Many large retailers (Wal-Mart and Kmart, for example) are departmentalized by territory. Coca-Cola has U.S. and International departments. McDonnell Douglas reorganized its military business along geographic lines.[19] Often the customers in each territory have different needs, for example, for winter clothes in the North and South. The last organization chart in Figure 7–6 illustrates territory departmentalization.

8. State the similarities and differences between matrix and divisional departmentalization.

Multiple Departmentalization

Many organizations, particularly large, complex organizations, use several of the departmental structures described to create a *hybrid* organization. Any mixture of structures can be used. Some organizations have functional departments with one manufacturing facility, and sales are departmentalized by territory with separate sales managers and salespeople in different areas.

General Motors (Figure 7–6) uses multiple departmentalization. It is departmentalized by car brand (product). However, each division is functionally departmentalized because each has its own production, marketing, finance, and human resources departments. GM is also departmentalized by territory—managers of regions I through IV.

Matrix Departmentalization. Matrix departmentalization combines the functional and product departmental structures. With matrix departmentalization, the employee works for a functional department and is also assigned to one or more products or projects. The major advantage of matrix departmentalization is flexibility. It allows the enterprise to temporarily organize for a project. With this structure, functional departments do not have to be duplicated for each project or product. The major disadvantage is that each employee has two bosses—a functional boss and a project boss—which violates the unity of command principle. Role conflict can result when two people give orders. Coordination can also be difficult. Rank Xerox and Boeing use a formal matrix structure. Figure 7–7 illustrates a matrix structure.

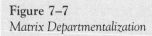

divisional structure
Departmentalization based on semiautonomous strategic business units.

Divisional Departmentalization. **Divisional structure** *departmentalizes based on semiautonomous strategic business units* (Chapter 5). In essence, you have coordinated companies within a company. Within the divisional (or M-Form) structure, any mixture of the other forms of departmentalization may also be used by the company and within divisions. Divisional structure is common for large, complex global businesses with a diversity of products and services to aid

Figure 7–7
Matrix Departmentalization

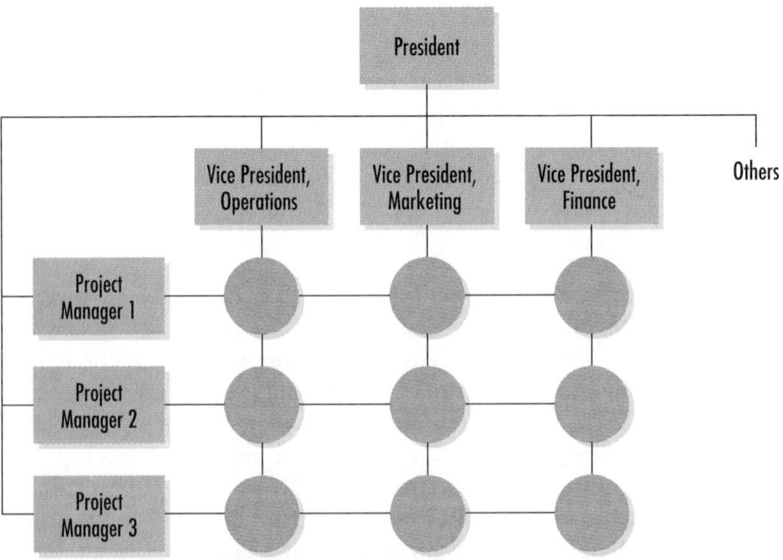

in portfolio management (Chapter 5). Westinghouse uses divisional departmentalization to organize its dozens of divisions.

The number of divisions is an important consideration. The more divisions, the more managers and the higher the cost. However, the divisions are also more specialized to deal with a changing environment.[20] Philip Morris reorganized its food business by merging Kraft and General Foods into a single company division.[21] It now has three major divisions (cigarettes, Miller Beer, and Kraft General Foods) rather than four. The Leeds reorganized CMP into divisions.

The *conglomerate* (holding company or H-Form) structure departmentalizes based on autonomous profit centers. Companies with unrelated diversified businesses units use the conglomerate structure. Top management focuses on portfolio management to buy and sell businesses without great concern for coordinating divisions. ITT and Newell use the conglomerate structure. Johnson & Johnson has 166 separate companies that are encouraged to act independently. Some presidents see their bosses only four times a year at company headquarters.

APPLYING THE CONCEPT

AC 7–3 Departmentalization

Identify the five organizational charts below as being departmentalized by one of the following methods:

a. function
b. product/service
c. customer
d. territory
e. matrix
f. divisional

____ **11.** Washington Consulting Company

President
Manager, Strategic Planning | Manager, Training & Development | Manager, Marketing Research

____ **12.** Jones Publishing Company

President
Manager, EL-Hi Books | Manager, College Books | Manager, Retail Books

____ **13.** Worldwide Marriage Encounter—USA

Executive Team
Coordinators, Zone 1 | Coordinators, Zone 2 | Coordinators, Zone 3 | Coordinators, Zone 4

____ **14.** Best Company International

CEO
President, West Service Stations | President, Long Sports Equipment | President, Jones Consultants | President, Timer Rentals

____ **15.** Production department of metal toys company

Manager
Supervisor, Plating and Molding | Supervisor, Assembly | Supervisor, Painting

Other Designs. Other designs include contingency theory, networks, new venture, and high involvement.

Contingency theory includes mechanistic versus organic (Burns and Stalker), technology (Woodward), and strategy and structure (Chandler). Refer back to Chapter 1 for a review.

Network structures describe the interrelationship among different organizations. Networks are often flexible temporary arrangements among suppliers, customers, and/or competitors. Companies using strategic alliances and outsourcing form networks held together by contract and performance agreements. For example, Apple Computer lacked the capacity to produce its entire line of PowerBook computers, so it contracted with Sony to manufacture the least expensive version. Apple ended the network after Sony produced 100,000 units in the first year.

New venture units, or skunkworks, consist of a group of employees who volunteer to work to develop new products or ventures for companies. They use a form of matrix structure. New products become a part of traditional departmentalization, are developed into new departments, or grow into divisions. Boeing, Genentech, Hewlett-Packard, IBM, Monsanto, NCR, Westinghouse, and 3M have used skunkworks.

Work Application

7. Draw a simple organization chart for an organization you work or have worked for. Identify the type of departmentalization and staff positions, if any, used.

High involvement, or greenfields, use a team approach to organize a new facility. Rather than change a traditional facility, many organizations are creating new smaller facilities, between 100 and 200 employees, based on the input of employees. High involvement organizations are flat; employee work teams make the decisions. You will learn about these in the next section. Cummins Engine, General Foods, Mead, Procter & Gamble, Sherwin-Williams, and TRW have all developed greenfields.

JOB DESIGN

job design
The process of combining tasks that each employee is responsible for completing.

Tasks to be performed by organizations are grouped into functional departments, and the tasks are further grouped into jobs for each employee. **Job design** *is the process of combining tasks that each employee is responsible for completing.* Job design is crucial because it affects job satisfaction and productivity.[22] Therefore, jobs should be carefully designed to enhance productivity, work quality, motivation, and job satisfaction.[23] To do so, jobs must combine social and technical features[24] (Chapter 1).

Jobs can be designed by one of three major groups: (1) time and motion experts who analyze the job to determine the best method and the amount of time it should take to do the task, (2) managers who supervise the jobs, and (3) employees who perform the jobs. Employees are the most knowledgeable about their jobs and can make effective changes. Empowering employees to be involved in designing their own jobs motivates them to increase productivity.[25] Many organizations, including GE and Pizza Hut, are asking employees to suggest ways to redesign their work.[26]

As you will learn in this section, jobs can contain few tasks, called simplified, or they can contain many tasks, called expanded. You can use a job characteristics model to design jobs. Jobs are also being designed for work teams, and there are job-scheduling options.

9. Explain the difference between job simplification and job expansion.

Job Simplification

Job simplification is used to make jobs more specialized. It is based on the organizing principle of division of labor and Taylor's scientific management (Chapter 1). The idea behind job simplification is to work smarter, not harder. *Job simplification* is the process of eliminating, combining, and/or changing the work sequence to increase performance. Have employees break the job down into steps (flowchart) and see if they can:

- *Eliminate*. Does the task have to be done at all? If not, don't waste time doing it.
- *Combine*. Doing more than one thing at a time often saves time. Make one trip to the mail room at the end of the day instead of several throughout the day.
- *Change sequence*. Often a change in the order of doing things results in a lower total time.

Jobs that are too simple and boring can lead to lower levels of productivity. However, when used appropriately, work simplification can be effective at motivating employees. Often people don't hate the job, just some aspect of it. Rather than ignoring or simply putting up with these hated aspects, they can change them. Intel decided that it was not necessary to fill out a voucher for expenses amounting to less than $100. Work volume went down by 14 percent in 30 days. GE developed its Work Out Program to improve and eliminate work, and Pizza Hut credits up to a 40 percent increase in store sales due to job simplification.[27] The Leeds simplified jobs at CMP when they created specialized divisions.

Work Application

8. Describe how a job at an organization you work or have worked for could be simplified. Be sure to specify if you are eliminating, combining, or changing the sequence of the job.

Job Expansion

Job expansion is the process of making jobs less specialized. Jobs can be expanded through job rotation, job enlargement, and job enrichment.

Job Rotation. Job rotation involves performing different jobs for a set period of time. For example, employees making a car on an assembly line could rotate so that they get to work on different parts. Some of the employees work on building the chassis one week; the next week they put the body on the chassis; the third week they put engines in the cars; and the fourth week they work on the interior. On week five, they rotate back to chassis. Many organizations develop conceptual skills in management trainees by rotating them through various departments. A few of the companies that have used job rotation include Bethlehem Steel, Dayton Hudson, Ford, Motorola, National Steel, and Prudential Insurance. Unfortunately, once employees master the various jobs, those jobs can be considered specialized and boring.

job enrichment
The process of building motivators into the job by making it more interesting and challenging.

Job Enlargement. Job enlargement involves adding tasks to broaden job variety. For example, rather than rotate jobs, the car workers could combine tasks into one job. There could be two jobs instead of four. AT&T, Chrysler, GM, IBM, and Maytag are a few of the companies that have used job enlargement. Unfortunately, adding more simple tasks to a simple job is often not a great motivator.

Job Enrichment. **Job enrichment** *is the process of building motivators into the job itself by making it more interesting and challenging.* Job enrichment increases productivity.[28] Job enrichment works with jobs of low motivation potential with employees who want their jobs enriched. Some employees are happy with the jobs the way they are. Organizations including AT&T, General Motors, IBM, Maytag, Monsanto, Motorola, Polaroid, and Traveler's Insurance Company have used job enrichment successfully. The Leeds created enriched jobs for the division managers by giving them the power to run their divisions as semi-autonomous companies.

Work Application

9. Describe how a job at an organization you work or have worked for could be expanded. Be sure to specify if you are using job rotation, job enlargement, or job enrichment and how the job is changed.

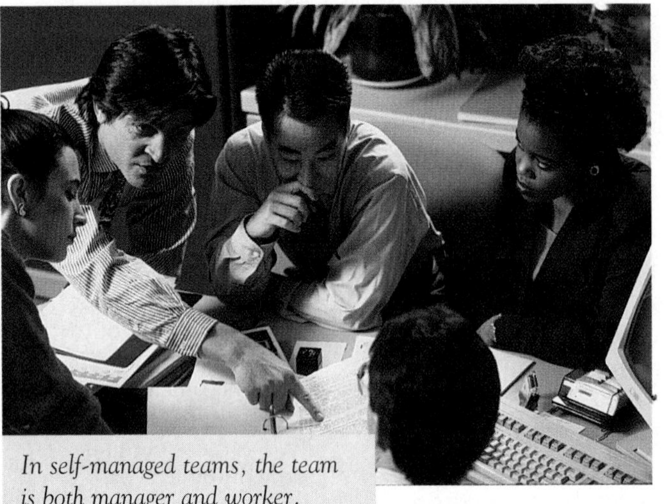
In self-managed teams, the team is both manager and worker.

A simple way to enrich jobs is for the manager to delegate more variety and responsibility to employees. You will learn what to delegate, and how, later in this chapter. A more complex method of enriching jobs is presented in the job characteristics model, presented later in this section.

Work Teams

The traditional approach to job design has been to focus on individual jobs. Today, the trend is shifting to designing jobs for work teams, or rather, teams are redesigning members' jobs.[29] The development of work teams is a form of job enrichment. Two common types of work teams are integrated and self-managed.

Integrated Work Teams. Integrated work teams are assigned a number of tasks by the manager, and the team gives specific assignments to members and is responsible for rotating jobs. For example, the foreman of a cleaning company could drop off groups of employees at job sites and go over tasks to be completed. The teams would decide who does what and how. The foreman would go to the various job sites to see how the work was progressing, and to transport employees to new job sites when they have finished.

Self-Managed Work Teams. Self-managed work teams are assigned a goal, and the team plans, organizes, leads, and controls to achieve the goal. Usually, self-managed teams operate without a designated manager; the team is both manager and worker. Teams commonly select their own members and evaluate each other's performance. The cleaning company integrated work team could become a self-managed team by assigning the goal (number of sites to be cleaned for the day/week) and allowing the team, not the foreman, to determine the sequence of job sites. The team, not foreman, would check its own progress. High-involvement, greenfields are characterized by self-managed teams.[30] Chrysler used teams to develop the Viper sports car. AT&T uses teams at its submarine systems plant in New Jersey. The teams reduced cost by more than 30 percent, over two years, and saved the plant from being closed.

Work Application

10. Describe how an organization you work or have worked for uses, or could use, teams. Be sure to specify if the teams are integrated or self-directed.

Work teams have been successful.[31] Team-based work systems are emerging as key source of sustained competitive advantage.[32] However, members need to be trained to work together as a team. In Chapter 13 you will learn about, and be trained in, teamwork. See Figure 7–8 for a review of the types of job designs and the job characteristics model, to be discussed next.

10. Describe the job characteristics model and what it is used for.

The Job Characteristics Model

job characteristics model Comprised of core job dimensions, critical psychological states, and employee growth-need strength; designed to improve quality of life for employees and productivity for the organization.

The job characteristics model provides a conceptual framework for designing enriched jobs. Individuals or a team can use the model to enrich jobs. *The* **job characteristics model** *comprises core job dimensions, critical psychological states, and employee growth-need strength to improve quality of working life for employees and productivity for the organization.* Hackman and Oldham[33] developed the job characteristics model.

Job Simplification	Job Expansion	Work Teams	Job Characteristics Model
Eliminate	Job rotation, switch jobs	Integrated	Core dimensions
Combine	Job enlargement, more tasks	Self-managed	Critical psychological states
Change sequence	Job enrichment, delegate		Performance and work outcomes
			Employee growth-need strength

Figure 7–8
Job Designs

Core Job Dimensions. Core job dimensions include five dimensions that determine a job's personal (quality of working life for employees) and work (productivity for the organization) outcomes.

1. *Skill variety* is the number of diverse tasks that make up a job and the number of skills used to perform the job. By increasing skill variety, you can increase personal and work outcomes.
2. *Task identity* is the degree to which an employee performs a whole identifiable task. Having an employee put together an entire television, rather than just placing the screen in the set, can increase job identity and personal and work outcomes.
3. *Task significance* is the perception of the importance of the task to others—the organization, the department, coworkers, and/or customers. Creating the perception of significance can increase personal and work outcomes.
4. *Autonomy* is the degree to which the employee has discretion to make decisions in planning, organizing, and controlling the task performed. Higher levels of autonomy can lead to higher levels of personal and work outcomes.
5. *Feedback* is the extent to which employees find out how well they perform their tasks. Receiving quick, accurate feedback from the job itself, or from others, can increase personal and work outcomes.

Critical Psychological States. The three critical psychological states, developed through core job dimensions, determine a job's personal and work outcomes.

A. *Experienced meaningfulness of the work* is based on (1) skill variety, (2) task identity, and (3) task significance. The greater these core dimensions are, the greater the experienced meaningfulness of work, and the greater the personal and work outcomes.
B. *Experienced responsibility for outcomes of the work* is based on dimension 4, autonomy. The greater the autonomy, the greater the experienced responsibility for outcomes of the work, and the greater the personal and work outcomes.
C. *Knowledge of the actual results of the work activities* is based on dimension 5, feedback. The greater the feedback, the greater the knowledge of results of the work, and the greater the personal and work outcomes.

Performance and Work Outcomes. Performance and work outcomes are the four benefits of the critical psychological states which are created by the five core job dimensions:

Figure 7–9
The Job Characteristics Model

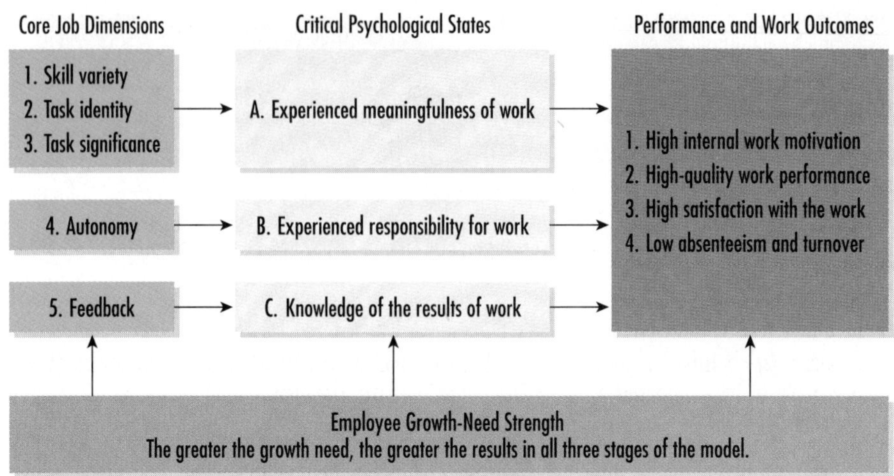

1. High internal work motivation.
2. High-quality work performance.
3. High satisfaction with the work.
4. Low absenteeism and turnover.

Employee Growth-Need Strength. Employee growth-need strength determines the employees' interest in having the five core dimensions improved, which determines the critical psychological states and personal and work outcomes. Generally, the stronger the employees' growth-need, the more interested they are in improving the five core dimensions and the critical psychological states, and the greater the personal and work outcomes. You will learn more about needs and motivation in Chapter 11. Figure 7–9 illustrates this process. Note that employee growth-need strength is at the bottom of the model because in essence it holds up the other parts of the model. In other words, if employees are not interested in enriching their jobs, the job characteristics model will fail.

APPLYING THE CONCEPT

AC 7–4 Job Designs

Identify the way each of the jobs is being designed as:

a. job simplification c. job enlargement e. work teams
b. job rotation d. job enrichment f. job characteristic model

____ **16.** "Jill, I'm delegating a new task to you to provide you with more challenge."

____ **17.** "Sales reps who have business lunches with clients that are under $20 no longer need to provide a sales receipt."

____ **18.** "We'd like to change your job so that you can develop new skills, complete entire jobs by yourself so that the job is more meaningful, let you do the job the way you want to, and let you know how you are doing."

____ **19.** "To make your job less repetitive, we are going to add three new tasks to your job responsibility."

____ **20.** "I'd like you to learn how to run the switchboard so that you can fill in for Ted while he is at lunch."

ORGANIZING YOURSELF AND DELEGATING

Successful managers are effective at setting priorities[34] and delegating work.[35] Dr. Rudenstine, president of Harvard University, stayed home for two weeks because he was too exhausted to work. People close to him said that to survive as president, Dr. Rudenstine must change his management style. He will have to learn to prioritize and delegate responsibility.[36]

Now that you understand how organizations and jobs are designed, its time to learn how to organize yourself by setting priorities and delegating work.

Setting Priorities[37]

11. Explain how to set priorities by listing the three priority questions and how you assign and delegate high, medium, and low priority.

One important aspect of organizing a department, a job, and yourself is setting priorities. At any given time, several tasks must be performed. How you, as a manager, select the *priority* order in which these tasks will be completed will affect your career success.[38] To prioritize successfully, list tasks that you must perform on a to-do list[39] and then assign each task a priority[40] to rank the order of performance.[41] After prioritizing tasks, focus on accomplishing only one task at a time.[42]

Priority Determination Questions. In order to determine the importance of tasks, you ask yourself three questions about the task that needs to be completed. **Priority determination questions** *ask: Do I need to be personally involved? Is the task my responsibility or will it affect the performance or finances of my department? When is the deadline? Is quick action needed?* Figure 7–10 also lists the priority determination questions.

priority determination questions
Do I need to be personally involved? Is the task my responsibility or will it affect the performance or finances of my department? When is the deadline? Is quick action needed?

1. *Do I need to be personally involved because of my unique knowledge or skills?* (yes or no) There are times when you are the only one who can do the task, and you must be involved.
2. *Is the task within my major area of responsibility or will it affect the performance or finances of my department?* (yes or no) You must oversee the performance of your department and keep the finances in line with the budget.
3. *When is the deadline? Is quick action needed?* (yes or no) Should you work on this activity right now, or can it wait? Time is a relative term. The key is to start the task soon enough so that you will meet the deadline. People often miss deadlines because they don't start the task soon enough.

Assigning Priorities. After the three questions are answered, a high, medium, or low priority can be assigned to each activity:

- *Delegate (D):* The task is delegated if the answer to question 1 (Do I need to be personally involved?) is no. If the answer to question 1 is no, it is not necessary to answer questions 2 and 3 because a priority is not assigned to the task. However, planning the delegation and delegating the task are prioritized.
- *High (H) Priority:* A high priority is assigned if you answer yes to all three questions. You need to be involved; it is your major responsibility, and quick action is needed.
- *Medium (M) Priority:* A medium priority is assigned if you answer yes to question 1 (you need to be involved) but no to question 2 (it is not your major responsibility) or no to question 3 (quick action is not needed; it can wait).
- *Low (L) Priority:* A low priority is assigned if you answer yes to question 1 (you need to be involved) but no to both questions 2 and 3. It is not your major responsibility, and quick action is not needed.

Figure 7–10
Priority Determination Questions

1. Do I need to be personally involved because of my unique knowledge or skills? (yes or no)
2. Is the task within my major area of responsibility or will it affect the performance or finances of my department? (yes or no)
3. When is the deadline? Is quick action needed? (yes or no)

Assigning a Priority	Priority Determination Questions				Priority
D Delegate priority (N) No to question 1 H High priority (YYY) Yes to all three questions M Medium priority (YNY or YYN) Yes to questions 1 and 2 or 3 L Low priority (YNN) Yes to question 1 and No to questions 2 and 3	#1	#2	#3		
Task	1. Do I need to be involved?	2. Is it my responsibility or does it affect performance or finance of my company?	3. Is quick action needed?	Deadline	

Model 7–1
Prioritized To-Do List

The Prioritized To-Do List. Refer to Model 7–1 for a copy of the prioritized to-do list. The steps to using the prioritized to-do list are:

1. *Write the task* that you must perform on the task line.
2. *Answer the three priority questions* by placing a Y (yes) or N (no) in the column. Also place the deadline and time needed to complete the task in their

columns. The deadline and time needed are used with lower-level priorities that change into high priorities as the deadline approaches. You many want to write in the deadline to start the task rather than the completion deadline.

3. *Assign a priority* to the task by placing the letter D (delegate), H (high), M (medium), or L (low) in the priority column. Use the box at the top left of the prioritized to-do list to determine priority based on the Y or N answers to the priority determination questions. If you write D, set a priority on when to delegate the task.
4. *Determine which task to complete now*. You may have more than one high priority, so select the most important one. When all high priorities are completed, go to medium followed by low.

Work Application

11. Using Model 7–1, list three to five tasks you must complete in the near future and prioritize them.

Update the tasks on the prioritized to-do list and *add new ones*. As time passes, the items prioritized medium and low become high. There is no set rule for how often to update, but do it at least daily. As new tasks come up, be sure to add them to your to-do list and prioritize them. In doing so, you will avoid stopping performing a high-priority task to work on a lower-level task.

As stated in Chapter 6, if you have a management job with a large variety of changing tasks with the need for more long-range planning, you may want to use the time management system. You can use the prioritized to-do list with the time management system for daily scheduling. If you have a job with a small variety of changing tasks and short-range time planning, you may simply use the prioritized to-do list to keep yourself organized and focused on high-priority tasks.

Complete Skill-Building Exercise 7–1 to develop your skill at setting priorities using the prioritized to-do list. The prioritized to-do list includes ten tasks for you to prioritize. But, more importantly, make copies of the prioritized to-do list and use it on the job.

Delegation

Delegation is the process of assigning responsibility and authority for accomplishing objectives. Telling employees to perform tasks that are part of their job design is issuing orders, not delegating. Delegating refers to giving employees new tasks. The new task may become a part of a redesigned job, or it may simply be a one-time task.

Benefits of Delegation. When managers delegate, they have more time to perform high-priority tasks.[43] Delegation gets tasks accomplished and increases productivity.[44] Delegation trains employees and improves their self-esteem; it also eases the stress and burden on managers.[45] Delegating is a means of enriching jobs and can result in improved performance and work outcomes.

Obstacles to Delegation. Managers become used to doing things themselves.[46] Managers fear that the employee will fail to accomplish the task,[47] or will show them up. Recall that you can delegate responsibility and authority, but not your accountability. Managers believe they can perform the task more efficiently than others.[48] Some managers don't realize that delegation is an important part of their job, others don't know what to delegate, and some don't know how to delegate. If you let these, or other reasons, keep you from delegating, you could end up like Dr. Rudenstine, president of Harvard University. The

Work Application

12. Describe an obstacle to delegation or sign of delegating too little that you have observed.

Leeds set up a division structure and delegated the responsibility for running the divisions to the division managers.

Signs of Delegating Too Little. The signs of delegating too little include: (1) taking work home, (2) performing employee tasks, (3) being behind in work, (4) continual feeling of pressure and stress, (5) rushing to meet deadlines, (6) deadlines not met, and (7) employees' seeking approval before acting.

Delegation Decisions

An important part of delegation is knowing which tasks to delegate.[49] Successful delegation is often based on selecting what task to delegate and to whom to delegate it.[50]

What to Delegate. As a general guide, use your prioritized to-do list and delegate anything that you do not have to be personally involved with because of your unique knowledge or skill. Some possibilities include the following:

- *Paperwork*. Have employees write reports, memos, letters, and so on.
- *Routine tasks*. Have employees check inventory, schedule, order, and so on.
- *Technical matters*. Have top employees deal with technical questions and problems.
- *Tasks with developmental potential*. Give employees the opportunity to learn new things. Prepare them for advancement by enriching their jobs.
- *Solving employees' problems*. Train them to solve their own problems; don't solve problems for them unless they lack capability.

What Not to Delegate. As a general guide, do not delegate anything that you need to be personally involved with because of your unique knowledge or skill. Typical examples include:

- *Personnel matters*. Performance appraisals, counseling, disciplining, firing, resolving conflicts, and so on.
- *Confidential activities*. Unless you have permission to do so.
- *Crises*. There is no time to delegate.
- *Activities delegated to you personally*. For example, if you are assigned to a committee, do not assign someone else without permission.

Determining to Whom to Delegate. Once you have decided what to delegate, you must select an employee to do the task. When selecting an employee to delegate to, be sure that he or she has the capability to get the job done right by the deadline. Consider your employees' talents, interests, and motivation when making a selection. You may consult with several employees to determine their interest before making the final choice.

12. List the four steps in the delegation model.

delegation model
(1) explain the need for delegating and the reason for selecting the employee; (2) set objectives that define the responsibility, the level of authority, and the deadline; (3) develop a plan; (4) establish control checkpoints and hold employees accountable.

Delegating with the Use of a Model

After determining what to delegate and to whom, you must plan for and delegate the tasks. *The* **delegation model** *steps are: (1) explaining the need for delegat-*

ing and the reasons for selecting the employee; (2) setting objectives that define responsibility, the level of authority, and the deadline; (3) developing a plan; (4) establishing control checkpoints and holding employees accountable. Following these four steps can increase your chances of successfully delegating. As you read, you will see how the delegation model is used with the job characteristics model, core job dimensions, and critical psychological states to influence performance and work outcomes.

step 1. **Explain the Need for Delegating and the Reasons for Selecting the Employee.** It is helpful for the employee to understand why the assignment must be completed. In other words, how will the department or organization benefit? Informing employees helps them realize the importance of the task (experienced meaningfulness of work). Telling the employee why he or she was selected should make him or her feel valued. Don't use the "it's a lousy job but someone has to do it" approach. Be positive; make employees aware of how they will benefit from the assignment.[51] If step 1 is completed successfully, the employee should be motivated, or at least willing, to do the assignment.

step 2. **Set Objectives That Define Responsibility, the Level of Authority, and the Deadline.** The objectives should clearly state the end result the employee is responsible for achieving by a specific deadline. You should also define the level of authority the employee has, as the following choices illustrate:

1. Make a list of all supplies on hand and present it to me each Friday at 2:00 (inform authority).
2. Fill out a supply purchase order and present it to me each Friday at 2:00 (recommend authority).
3. Fill out and sign a purchase order for supplies; send it to the purchasing department with a copy put in my in-basket each Friday by 2:00 (report authority).
4. Fill out and sign a purchase order for supplies and send it to the purchasing department each Friday by 2:00, keeping a copy (full authority).

step 3. **Develop a Plan** Once the objectives are set, a plan is needed to achieve them. It is helpful to write the objectives, with the level of authority, and develop the plan on an operational plan sheet (Chapter 6 Figure 6–4). The plan may be written on the operational planning sheet.

When developing a plan, be sure to identify the resources needed to achieve the objectives, and give the employee the authority necessary to obtain the resources. Inform all parties the employee must work with of his or her authority. For example, if an employee is doing a personnel report, you should contact the personnel department and tell them the employee must have access to the necessary information.

The level of autonomy for developing the plan to accomplish the task should be based on the employee's capability level. Refer to Skill-Building Exercise 1–1 for details on selecting the management style appropriate for the employee's capability level. Part of the plan may be to train the employee and

Model 7–2
Steps in the Delegation Model

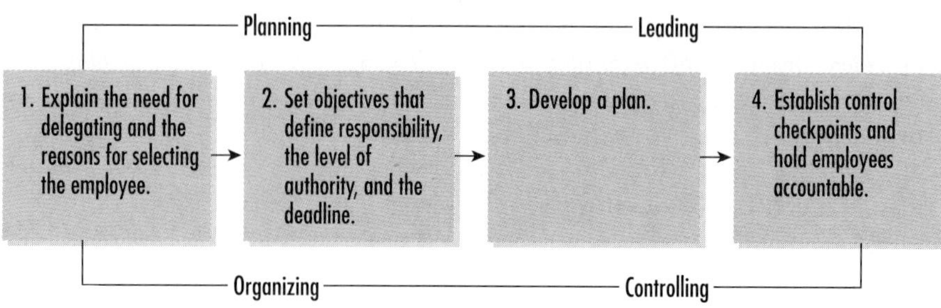

develop the employee's autonomy and experienced responsibility for work. For example, the employee may start with inform authority and progress to full authority over time for a job enlargement task.

Establish Control Checkpoints and Hold Employees Accountable. For simple, short tasks, a deadline without control checkpoints is appropriate. However, it is often advisable to check progress at predetermined times (control checkpoints) for tasks that have multiple steps and/or will take some time to complete. This builds information flow into the delegation system right from the start. You and the employee should agree on the form (phone call, visit, memo, or detailed report) and timeframe (daily, weekly, or after specific steps are completed but before going on to the next step) for information regarding the assignment. When establishing control, consider the employee's capability level. The lower the capability, the more frequent the checks; the higher the capability, the less frequent the checks.

Work Application

13. Select a manager you work or have worked for and analyze how well he or she implements the four steps of delegation. Which steps does the manager typically follow and not follow?

It is helpful to list the control checkpoints in writing on an operational planning sheet, making copies of the finished plan so that the parties involved and you as the delegating manager have a record to refer to. In addition, all parties involved should record the control checkpoints on their calendars. If the employee to whom the task was delegated does not report as scheduled, follow up to find out why the person did not report, and get the information. You should evaluate performance at each control checkpoint to date and upon completion to provide feedback that develops knowledge of the results of work. Providing praise for progress and completion of the task motivates employees to do a good job.[52] You will learn how to give praise in Chapter 11.

Model 7–2 summarizes the four steps of the delegation process. In Skill-Building Exercise 7–2, you will be given the opportunity to use the model to delegate a task to develop your delegation skills.

CURRENT MANAGEMENT ISSUES

Globalization. With the trend toward *globalization*, multinational companies (MNCs) need to develop rigid designs and rely on technology to coordinate strategic business units.[53] MNCs need to be more flexible for the following reasons:

1. Unity of direction is important for the MNC.
2. Following the chain of command is often neglected in order to compete in a dynamic environment.

3. The span of management is increasing through the use of flat organizational structures with fewer staff members.
4. Division of labor is becoming less specialized.
5. Coordination is becoming increasingly important and difficult across national boundaries.
6. Delegation of responsibility and authority is decentralized as it is going down to lower levels in the organization.

MNCs use multiple departmentalization and commonly use the divisional structure.

Diversity and Teams. Jobs need to be designed differently based on the *diversity* of global employees. For example, job enrichment and work teams are working well in the United States. However, in diverse developing countries employees are concerned with meeting their basic needs. A simplified job would be a motivator and work well.

Ethics and Social Responsibility. Companies using strategic business units (Chapter 5) should take extra precautions in implementing a decentralized divisional structure because it can unwittingly transform the organization into a socially unresponsive or, worse, socially irresponsible entity.[54] When going outside the chain of command and working with the informal structure, employees must be *ethically and socially responsible*. Managers must design jobs and delegate tasks in an ethically and socially responsible manner so that employees can be ethical and socially responsible.

Quality, TQM, and Participation. TQM emphasizes flexibility and the importance of aligning systems parts to deliver customer value as the coordinating mechanism. TQM organizations coordinate through information technology and open communications (informal authority), rather than through the chain of command. The TQM approach attempts to eliminate non-value-adding (job simplification) tasks and layers of management (flat structure), simplify communication flow, speed up decision-making, and encourage *participation* and employee involvement.

TQM also emphasizes the importance of continuously improving systems and processes that cut across organizational boundaries through cross-functional *teams*. Work teams are used to increase employee *participation* in decision-making, improving activities, planning, and communicating with other teams. Teams are given the authority to design enriched jobs (job expansion).

With the TQM focus on the customer, some companies are reorganizing. For example, in response to customer complaints about inefficient service, Eastman Kodak reorganized its Professional & Printing Imaging division.[55] Some organizations, including Dana Corporation, Federal Express, Nordstrom, and Wal-Mart, have developed an upside-down organization chart with the customer at the top of the chart and management at the bottom. The upside-down chart reminds everyone in the organization that their job is to provide customer value, and to make managers realize that their role is to support employees in providing customer value. Figure 7–11 shows an upside-down organization chart.

Productivity. In the quest for increased *productivity*, many organizations have downsized and re-engineered. Both approaches design changes in the organization structure known as reorganization. Downsizing and re-engineering

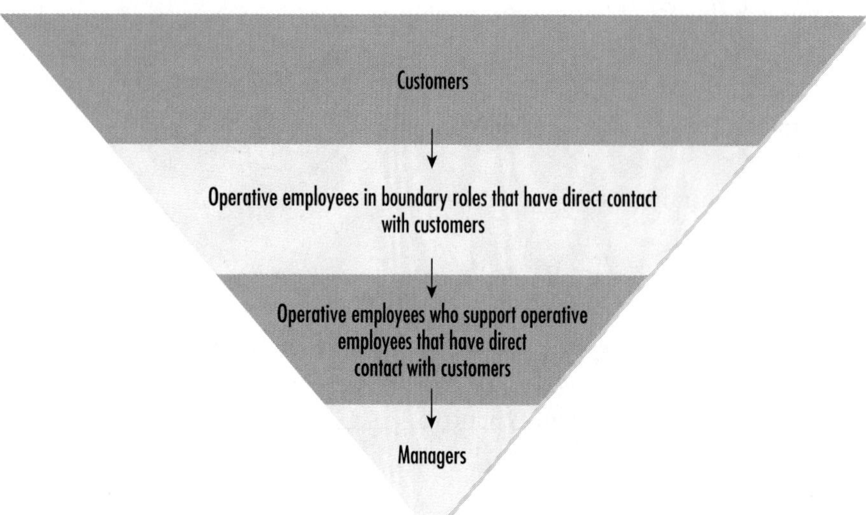

Figure 7–11
Upside-Down Organization Chart

widen the span of management, flatten the structure, and eliminate staff positions. Re-engineering projects often include job enrichment and the use of work teams, which are the means to increase productivity.[56] The high-involvement greenfields are an approach to re-engineering. Empirical research has shown that the conglomerate form of unrelated, diversified, autonomous departmentalization has not been productive for the majority of companies using it. Companies that have used retrenchment strategies and divested unrelated business units to focus on a core-competency-related lines of semiautonomous divisions have had higher levels of performance.[57]

Small Business. Small businesses commonly do not have unity of command, have expanded jobs, and use informal authority rather than following the chain of command. They also have few, if any, staff members. For example, purchasing would be just a part of someone's job in a small company, whereas it would be the entire job in a large company. Small companies commonly use centralized authority and functional departmentalization. Flexibility and the ability to change quickly are strengths of the small company. Many large companies are trying to be more like small entrepreneurial companies and are using the divisional structure to create semiautonomous small businesses. High-involvement greenfields create small businesses divisions.

CHAPTER SUMMARY AND GLOSSARY

The chapter summary is organized to answer the 13 learning objectives for Chapter 7.

1. Explain the difference between a flat and tall organization.

A flat organization has a few levels of management with wide spans of management. A tall organization has many levels of management with narrow spans of management.

2. Describe the similarity and difference among liaisons, integrators, and boundary roles.

They are similar because they are all coordination techniques. Liaisons and integrators are similar because they coordinate internally, whereas boundary roles coordinate efforts with customers, suppliers, and other people in the external environment. Liaisons and integrators are different because liaisons work in one department and coordinate with other departments, whereas integrators coordinate department activities without working for any department.

3. Discuss the difference between formal and informal and centralized and decentralized authority.
Formal authority is the sanctioned relationships and ways of getting the job done, whereas informal authority is the unsanctioned relationships and ways of getting the job done. With centralized authority top managers make important decisions; with decentralized authority middle- and first-line managers make important decisions.

4. List and briefly explain the four levels of authority.
(1) *Inform*—the person simply presents an alternative. (2) *Recommend*—the person presents alternatives and suggests one. (3) *Report*—the person takes action and then tells the boss. (4) *Full*—the person takes action and does not have to tell the boss about it.

5. Describe the relationship between line and staff authority.
The staff personnel advise and assist line personnel, who are responsible for making decisions, and issue orders down the chain of command.

6. Explain what an organization chart is and list the four things it shows.
An organization chart is a graphic illustration of the organization's management hierarchy and departments and their working relationships. It shows the level of management hierarchy, chain of command, division and type of work, and departmentalization.

7. Discuss the difference between internal and external departmentalization.
Internal, or input, departmentalization focuses on functions performed within the organization. External, or output, departmentalization focuses on the product, customer, or territory in which the organization does business.

8. State the similarities and differences between matrix and divisional departmentalization.
They are similar because they are both multiple departmentalization methods. Matrix combines the functional and product departmental structures to focus on projects. Divisional structure departmentalizes based on semiautonomous strategic business units to focus on portfolio management.

9. Explain the difference between job simplification and job expansion.
Job simplification is used to make jobs more specialized by eliminating, combining, and/or changing the sequence of work. Job expansion is used to make jobs less specialized by rotating employees, enlarging the job, and/or enriching the job to make it more interesting and challenging.

10. Describe the job characteristics model and what it is used for.
The job characteristics model is a conceptual framework for designing enriched jobs. It comprises core job dimensions, critical psychological states, and employee growth-need strength. It is used to improve the quality of working life for employees and productivity for the organization.

11. Explain how to set priorities by listing the three priority questions and how you assign and delegate high, medium, and low priority.
(1) Do I need to be personally involved because of my unique knowledge or skills? (2) Is the task within my major area of responsibility or will it affect the performance or finances of my department? (3) When is the deadline? Is quick action needed? A delegate priority is assigned when the answer to question 1 is no (N). A high priority is assigned when the answers to questions 1–3 are yes (YYY). A medium priority is assigned when the answer to question 1 is yes and the answers to question 2 or 3 is no (YNY or YYN). A low priority is assigned when the answer to question 1 is yes and the answers to questions 2 and 3 are no (YNN).

12. List the four steps in the delegation model.
The delegation model steps are: (1) explaining the need for delegating and the reasons the employee was selected; (2) setting objectives that define responsibility, the level of authority, and the deadline; (3) developing a plan; (4) establishing control checkpoints and holding employees accountable.

13. Define the following key terms (in order of appearance in the chapter):
Select one or more methods: (1) fill in the missing key terms from memory, (2) match the key terms from the end of the summary with their definition below, or (3) copy the key terms in order from the list at the beginning of the chapter.

The __________ refers to the number of employees reporting to a manager.

______ is the obligation to achieve objectives by performing required activities.

______ is the right to make decisions, issue orders, and utilize resources.

______ is the process of assigning responsibility and authority to achieve objectives.

The __________ are inform, recommend, report, and full.

__________ is the responsibility to make decisions and issue orders down the chain of command.

__________ is the responsibility to advise and assist other personnel.

With __________, important decisions are made by top managers.

With __________, important decisions are made by middle- and first-line managers.

An __________ is a graphic illustration of the organization's management hierarchy and departments and their working relationships.

__________ is the grouping of related activities into units.

__________ departmentalizes based on semiautonomous strategic business units.

__________ is the process of combining tasks that each employee is responsible for completing.

__________ is the process of building motivators into the job by making it more interesting and challenging.

The __________ comprises core job dimensions, critical psychological states, and employee growth-need strength to improve quality of working life for employees and productivity for the organization.

__________ ask: Do I need to be personally involved? Is the task my responsibility or will it affect the performance or finances of my department? When is the deadline, is quick action needed?

The __________ steps are: (1) explaining the need for delegating and the reasons for selecting the employee; (2) setting objectives that define responsibility, the level of authority, and the deadline; (3) developing a plan; (4) establishing control checkpoints and holding employees accountable.

KEY TERMS

authority
centralized authority
decentralized authority
delegation
delegation model
departmentalization
divisional structure
job characteristics model
job design
job enrichment
levels of authority
line authority
organization chart
priority determination questions
responsibility
span of management
staff authority

REVIEW AND DISCUSSION QUESTIONS

1. What is the difference between unity of command and direction?
2. What is the relationship between the chain of command and the span of management?
3. What do the terms *diversification* and *integration* mean?
4. What is the difference between responsibility and authority?
5. Can accountability be delegated?
6. How does the scope of authority change throughout the organization and what is the flow of responsibility, authority, and accountability?
7. What is the difference between a general and specialist staff?
8. What does an organization chart show? What doesn't it show?
9. What is the difference between product and customer departmentalization?
10. What is the difference between a network structure, skunkwork, and greenfield?
11. What is job design and why is it necessary?
12. What is the difference between an integrated and self-managed work team?
13. What is the importance of employee growth-need strength to the job characteristics model?
14. Why is it important to update priorities on a to-do list?
15. As a simple guide, what one question do you ask to determine what and what not to delegate?
16. Why is each of the four steps in the delegation model necessary?

CASE

General Motors and Saturn

Alfred Sloan received an engineering degree from MIT and went to work for Hyatt Roller Bearing Company in Newark, New Jersey, for $50 a month. Seeing no future at Hyatt, Sloan quit. A few years later, Sloan heard that Hyatt was in financial trouble and might be liquidated. Sloan's father and an associate put $500 into the business with the agreement that Alfred would run the company with a turnaround strategy. At age 40, Sloan sold Hyatt to William Durant, the founder of General Motors (GM), for $13.5 million. Sloan worked his way up the GM corporate ladder and became president in 1923.

At the end of 1920, GM was in a crisis and its future was in doubt. The company's success had grown out of control. Sloan was part of the team that developed a turnaround strategy based on reorganization of GM. Sloan's reorganization was designed to solve the company's problems of operating multiple units with different products made by different divisions.

Sloan based the reorganization on his basic concept of decentralized operations with coordinated control. Decentralization was the emphasis because it produced initiative, responsibility, management development, decision-making close to the action, and flexibility. All were needed to adapt to a changing environment.

Sloan developed a tall organization structure. Self-contained divisions were created to perform groups of functions with an executive in charge. The divisions were grouped and an executive was put in charge of each group. Corporate headquarters had an advisory staff and a financial staff, with no line authority. In other words, Sloan is the father of decentralized divisional departmentalization. After decades of success, Sloan retired in 1956. Lee Iacocca, who turned Chrysler from near bankruptcy to profitability, called Sloan "the greatest genius ever in the auto business." The MIT business school and journal bear his name—The Sloan School of Management and the *Sloan Management Review*.

In the 1980s, and even earlier, GM was once again having problems. GM was slow to respond to changing consumer taste. More Americans were buying Japanese cars because they liked the designs and high quality. By the early 1990s, GM was losing tens-of-billions of dollars a year, which forced its board to install new management. GM returned to profitability under its new president, John Smith, Jr.

GM has lost market share over the past decade while its major domestic competitor Ford has increased market share. GM's market share fell from over 40 percent in 1985 to a low of around 32 percent by mid-1995. During the same period, Ford's market share increased 7 points from around 20 to 27 percent. Each point of market share represents $2.5 billion in sales. Alex Trotman, chairman since January 1994, is working toward his goal to make Ford number one in world auto sales. Trotman has put Ford through a double-time reorganization, cutting out three layers of management and combining its North American and European arms into a single $92 billion-a-year business. GM said it has abandoned its costly prior market share strategy for a profitability strategy, and is not worried about Ford taking over as number one. Market analysts criticized Ford's market share strategy because it has hurt its profit margin. Chrysler, though the smallest American auto maker, has been setting the profitability standard for the industry.[58]

Back in the early 1980s, GM set the goal to make cars that were every bit as good as those made by the Japanese with a low price. However, GM did not want its image and present business systems and processes at that time to influence the achievement of its goal. So, it made the decision to set up an entirely new division called Saturn. GM invested over $3.5 billion in the Saturn project before it sold a single car in the fall of 1990.

The new Saturn plant was built in Spring Hill, Tennessee. A team of 99 people from the United Auto Workers and GM literally designed the company from scratch. Team members used benchmarking to come up with a superior-built car. They scoured the globe examining successful manufacturing operations to learn what they could do to improve quality and cut costs. The plant was designed with flexible equipment so that one assembly line could make different car models in response to changing market demands. Unlike the traditional assembly line in which workers stay put and the line moves, Saturn teams of assembly workers ride along with the car bodies on a slowly moving platform so they remain engaged with the evolving car shell. The platform can be raised and lowered.

Saturn's 4,500 workers participate in decision-making at all levels because union members sit on major committees. Saturn has fewer managers than the typical GM plant, and their role is different. At Saturn, they are advisors to the teams of 15 or so workers who have full responsibility and authority to do the job the way they want to. Team members can work with anyone in the organization to get the job done. Team members are trained technically and learn how to perform as an effective team. For example, they learn cooperative work methods, conflict management, and group dynamic skills. Original workers received 700 hours of training; new workers receive around 175 hours of training.

Saturn has been a design and sales success. Customers like the reliability, low price, and courteous dealer service. Buyers have ranked Saturn sixth in customer satisfaction. This is an exceptional rating because competitors with higher ranks include Lincoln and Mercedes which cost three to five times as much as the average $11,000 sticker price of a Saturn. However, Saturn has not been a profit success.

Saturn has had problems producing the quantity of high-quality cars it needs to be profitable. The company has had trouble meeting production objectives. In its first year, the objective was to build 150,000 cars; it actually built 50,000. To meet consumer demand and become profitable, management added a second and third shift to boost production to 310,000 cars. However, as production has gone up, quality has suffered. Employees have stated that management is willing to trade off quality for quantity, that if quality goes down, the company will be at risk of losing customers, and that they may get laid off like employees at other GM plants. Employees have stated that the cooperative spirit between management and labor is threatened.

Select the best alternative for the following questions. Be sure you are able to explain your answers.

___ 1. The Saturn plant is a move toward greater unity of direction than other GM plants.

a. True b. False

___ 2. Saturn developed ___ as the primary means of coordination.

a. direct contact d. integrators
b. liaisons e. boundary roles
c. a committee

___ 3. The Saturn plant was designed to be a ___ structure than other GM plants.

a. flatter b. taller

___ 4. Within the Saturn plant, authority is

a. centralized b. decentralized

___ 5. Today, GM uses ___ departmentalization.

a. functional d. territory
b. product e. matrix
c. customer f. divisional

___ 6. Saturn is based primarily on ___ design.

a. network b. skunkworks c. greenfield

___ 7. The Saturn plant primarily uses job

a. simplification c. enlargement
b. rotation d. enrichment

___ 8. Saturn uses ___ work teams.

a. integrated b. self-managed

___ 9. Based on the job characteristics model, jobs at Saturn have ___ levels of core job dimensions and critical psychological states.

a. high b. low

____10. Managers at Saturn are reluctant to delegate.

a. True b. False

11. Which TQM concepts does Saturn use?

12. Are production volume and high quality incompatible objectives?

13. Do you think Saturn will become a major profitable success story for GM? Better yet, go to the library and/or on the Internet and find out how it is doing by using Saturn in a computer search.

For current information on Saturn, use Internet address http://www.Saturncars.com. For ideas on using the Internet, see the Appendix.

SKILL-BUILDING EXERCISE 7–1

Setting Priorities[58]

Preparing for Skill-Building Exercise 7–1

For this exercise assume that you are the first-line manager of a production department in a large company. A prioritized to-do list with ten tasks is on the next page. Assign priorities to each task by following the prioritized to-do list steps:

1. Write the task that you must perform on the task line. The ten tasks have been written in for you. When you use the to-do list for your own tasks, it is not recommended that you number them. They are numbered for class use so it is easier to know which task is being discussed.
2. Answer the three priority determination questions by placing a Y for yes or N for no in the columns labeled 1, 2, and 3. Because you are not the actual manager of this department, do not fill in the deadline/time needed column.
3. Assign a priority to the task by placing the letter D (delegate), H (high), M (medium), or L (low) in the priority column. Use the box at the top left of the prioritized to-do list to determine the priority based on the Y or N answers to the priority questions.
4. Determine which task to complete now. You may have more than one high priority, so select the most important one to do now—or first.

Doing Skill-Building Exercise 7–1 in Class

Objective
To develop your skill at setting priorities.

Preparation
You should have assigned a priority to the ten tasks on the to-do list preparation.

Experience
You will get feedback on how well you prioritized.

Procedure (10–30 minutes)
Option 1. Break into groups of four to six and share your priorities. Try to reach a group consensus on each of the ten priorities. After a group has finished, one member records priorities for the entire class to see. After all groups have finished, the instructor goes over the recommended answers.
Option 2. The instructor calls on students to get their priorities to each task. The instructor goes over the recommended answer for each item after a student(s) gives a priority.
Option 3. The instructor goes over the recommended answers without student involvement.

Conclusion
The instructor leads a class discussion and/or makes concluding remarks.

Application (2–4 minutes)
What did I learn from this experience? How will I use this knowledge in the future?

____

____

Sharing
Volunteers share their priorities lists with the class.

Prioritized To-Do List	Priority Determination Questions				
	#1	#2	#3		
D Delegate priority (N) No to question 1 H High priority (YYY) Yes to all three questions M Medium priority (YNY or YYN) Yes to questions 1 and 2 or 3 L Low priority (YNN) Yes to question 1 and No to questions 2 and 3					
Task	1. Do I need to be involved?	2. Is it my responsibility or does it affect performance or finance of my company?	3. Is quick action needed?	Deadline	Priority
1. Tom, the sales manager, told you that three customers stopped doing business with the company because your products have decreased in quality.					
2. Your secretary, Michele, told you that there is a salesperson waiting to see you. He does not have an appointment. You don't do any purchasing.					
3. Molly, a vice president, wants to see you to discuss a new product to be introduced in one month.					
4. Tom, the sales manager, sent you a memo stating that the sales forecast was incorrect. Sales are expected to increase by 20 percent starting next month. There is no inventory to meet the unexpected sales forecast.					
5. Dan, the personnel director, sent you a memo informing you that one of your employees has resigned. Your turnover rate is one of the highest in the company.					
6. Michele told you that a Bob Furry called while you were out. He asked you to return his call, but wouldn't state why he was calling. You don't know who he is or what he wants.					
7. Phil, one of your best workers, wants an appointment to tell you about a situation that happened in the shop.					
8. Tom called and asked you to meet with him and a prospective customer for your product. The customer wants to meet you.					
9. John, your boss, called and said that he wants to see you about the decrease in the quality of your product.					
10. In the mail you got a note from Randolf, the president of your company, and an article from *The Wall Street Journal*. The note says FYI (for your information).					

Behavior Model Video 7–1, Delegation, shows Steve, production manager, delegating the completion of production output forms to Dale, following the steps in Model 7–2. This video serves as a behavior model which can be used prior to conducting Skill-Building Exercise 7–2, Delegating Authority.

SKILL-BUILDING EXERCISE 7–2

Delegating Authority[59]

Preparing for Skill-Building Exercise 7–2

You should have read, and understand, the material on delegating.

Doing Skill-Building Exercise 7–2 in Class

Objective
To experience and develop skills in delegating authority.

Preparation
You should have read, and understand, the text material on delegating with the use of a model.

Experience
You will delegate, be delegated to, and observe the delegation of a task, and then evaluate the effectiveness of the delegated task. You may also see a video example of how to delegate using the delegation model.

Procedure 1 (4–8 minutes)
Break into as many groups of three as possible with the remainder in groups of two. Each person in the group picks a number 1, 2, or 3. Number 1 will be the first to delegate a task, then 2, and then 3. The level of difficulty of the delegation will increase with the number.

Each person then reads his or her delegation situation (1, 2, or 3) and plans how he or she will delegate the task. If you prefer, you can use an actual delegation from a past or present job. Just be sure to fully explain the situation to the delegatee. Be sure to follow the four delegation steps in this chapter. You may use the operational planning sheet in Figure 6–4 to help you when you delegate. An observer sheet is included at the end of this exercise for giving feedback on each delegation.

Delegation Situation 1

Delegator (No. 1). You are a college student with a paper due in three days for your 10 A.M. class. It must be typed. You don't type well, so you have decided to hire someone to do it for you. The going rate is $1.50 per page. Think of an actual paper you have done in the past or will do in the future. Plan to delegate (you may use the operational planning sheet). Be sure to include the course name, paper title, special typing instructions, and so on. Assume that you are meeting the typist for the first time. He or she doesn't know you and doesn't expect you.

Delegatee (No. 2). Assume that you do typing and are willing to do the job if the delegation is acceptable to you.

Delegation Situation 2

Delegator (No. 2). You are the manager of a fast-food restaurant. In the past, you have scheduled the workers. Your policy is to keep changing the workers' schedules. You have decided to delegate the scheduling to your assistant manager. This person has never done any scheduling but appears to be very willing and confident about taking on new responsibility. Plan your delegation (you may use the operational planning sheet).

Delegatee (No. 3). Assume that you are interested in doing the scheduling if the manager delegates the task effectively.

Delegation Situation 3

Delegator (No. 3). You own and manage your own business. You have eight employees, one of whom is the organization's secretary. The secretary presently uses an old memory typewriter, which needs to be replaced. You are not sure whether it should be replaced with a word processor or a computer (with word-processing software). You can afford to spend up to $2,500. You try to keep costs down and get the most for your money. Because the secretary will use the new machine, you believe that this employee should be involved in, or maybe even make, the decision. The secretary has never purchased equipment and you believe will be somewhat insecure about the assignment. Plan your delegation (you may use the operational planning sheet).

Delegatee (No. 1). Assume that you are able to do the job but are somewhat insecure. Accept the task if the delegator "participates" effectively.

Procedure 2 (7–10 minutes)
A. *Delegation Situation 1*. Delegator 1 delegates the task (role-play) to number 2. Number 3 is the observer. As the delegation takes place, the observer uses the form at the end of this exercise to provide feedback on the effectiveness of the delegator. Answer the questions on the form.
B. *Integration*. The observer (or number 3) leads a discussion of the effectiveness of the delegation, although all team members should participate. Do not continue until you are told to do so.

Procedure 3 (7–10 minutes)
A. *Delegation Situation 2*. Follow procedure 2A, except number 2 is now the delegator, number 3 is the delegatee, and number 1 is the observer.
B. *Integration*. Follow procedure 2B with number 3 as the observer. Do not continue until you are told to do so.

Procedure 4 (7–10 minutes)
A. *Delegation Situation 3*. Follow procedure 2A, except number 3 is now the delegator, number 1 is the delegatee, and number 2 is the observer. If you are in a group of two, be an additional observer for another group.
B. *Integration*. Follow procedure 2B with number 1 as observer.

Conclusion
The instructor may lead a class discussion and make concluding remarks.

Application (2–4 minutes)
What did I learn from this experience? How will I use this knowledge in the future?

____

____

Sharing
Volunteers give their answers to the application section.

Note: Remember that the process does not end with delegating the task; you must control (check progress at control points and help when needed) to ensure that the task is completed as scheduled.

Observer Form

During the delegation process, the observer checks off the items performed by the delegators. Items not checked were not performed. After the delegation, the delegator and delegatee also check off the items. This sheet is used for all three situations. Use the appropriate vertical column for each situation.

Delegation items for all situations	Situation 1	Situation 2	Situation 3
Did the delegator follow these steps: *Step 1.* Explain the need for delegating and the reason for selecting the employee? *Step 2.* Set an objective that defines responsibility and level of authority, and set a deadline? *Step 3.* Develop a plan? Was it effective? *Step 4.* Establish control checkpoints and hold the employee accountable?			

Did the delegatee clearly understand what was expected of him or her and how to follow the plan?

____

____

How could the delegation be improved if done again?

____

____

____

____

____

Managing Change: Culture, Innovation, Quality, and Diversity

Learning Objectives

After studying this chapter, you should be able to:

1. Identify where the forces for change initiate.
2. List the four types of changes.
3. State the difference among a fact, a belief, and a value.
4. Describe the three levels of organizational culture and their relationship.
5. Explain intrapreneurship and its three roles.
6. State the core values of TQM.
7. Describe a learning organization's culture.
8. Discuss the relationship among diversity, innovation, and quality.
9. State the difference in the use of forcefield analysis and survey feedback.
10. Explain the difference between team-building and process consultation.
11. Define the following **key terms** (in order of appearance in the chapter):

    types of change
    management information systems (MIS)
    stages of the change process
    organizational culture
    levels of culture
    core values of TQM
    learning organization
    organizational development (OD)
    OD interventions
    forcefield analysis
    survey feedback
    team-building
    process consultation
    organizational revitalization

Skill Development

1. You can develop your skill at identifying resistance to change so that you can implement change. (Skill-Building Exercise 8–1).

   Overcoming resistance to change is an organizing skill that utilizes conceptual and decision-making skills and human and communication skills. The exercise develops your interpersonal leader role and the decisional role of entrepreneur. The SCANS skill competencies of using resources, interpersonal skills, information, and systems, as well as the basic, thinking, and personal qualities foundation skills are also developed.

BM has two fundamental missions. First, the company strives to lead in the creation, development, and manufacture of the industry's most advanced information technologies, including computer systems, software, networking systems, storage devices, and microelectronics. Second, IBM translates these advanced technologies into value for its customers worldwide—through its sales and professional services units in North America, Europe/Middle East/Africa, Asia Pacific, and Latin America. The company strives to provide products and services that improve customers' competitive position, enhance their own customer service, increase their productivity, and enrich their personal lives. IBM is making technology easier to use and manage. IBM's companywide crusade is translating technology into value for customers.

IBM has six strategic imperatives: (1) Exploiting its technology. (2) Increasing its share of the client/server computing market. (3) Establishing leadership in the emerging network-centric computing world. (4) Realigning the way it delivers value to customers. (5) Rapidly expanding its position in

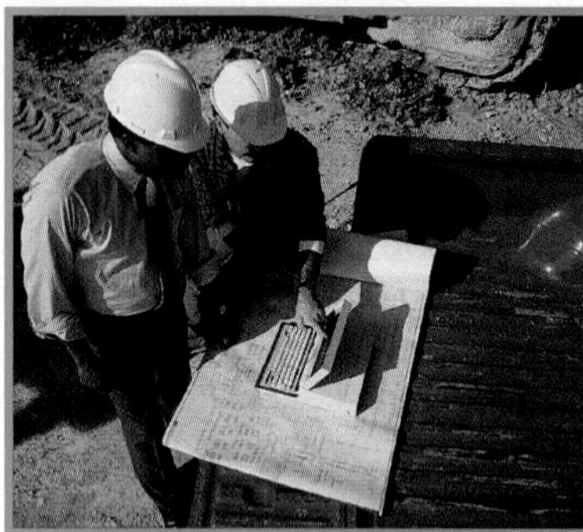
IBM's companywide crusade is translating technology into customer value.

key emerging geographic markets. (6) Leveraging its size and scale to achieve cost and market advantages.

To increase its software and networking operations, IBM acquired Lotus Development Corporation in June of 1995 for $3.52 billion, or $64 a share—the largest software deal on record. IBM's main businesses include computer hardware, software, and consulting services. Lotus's main products include 1-2-3, Freelance, Ami Pro, Notes, and cc: Mail. IBM employed around 215,000 people before acquiring Lotus's 5,550 workers.

Notes, which allows PC users at separate sites to share documents, will replace OS/2 as the strategic centerpiece in personal computer software. IBM saw Notes as the cornerstone of its strategy against Microsoft in the coming battle to control the market for "groupware" that runs on computers linked into networks. IBM planned to do a better job of marketing Notes through explaining how Notes can help big companies easily move information among employees. But IBM had to move quickly because Microsoft planned to introduce a rival to Notes, called Exchange, by year end 1995. The price of Notes was cut in half in 1995.

IBM hopes that by buying a star software company it will become a software star that can compete with Microsoft. IBM and Lotus will be making changes, and only time will tell if the acquisition will be a success.[1]

For current information on IBM, use Internet address http://www.ibm.com. For ideas on using the Internet, see the Appendix.

MANAGING CHANGE

Plato said, "Change takes place no matter what deters it." Managing change is one of the most difficult challenges that face business organizations.[2] Managers are undergoing revolutionary changes in response to the global marketplace.[3] In the diverse global business environment, change is a way of life.[4] Ability to manage change determines success.[5] American business leaders are not comfortable with managing change. Some 62 percent say they have a conservative or reluctant approach to change.[6] Your ability to flexibly change with the diversifying global environment will affect your career success.[7]

People with outdated skills are often retrained, unemployed, or underemployed. Your college education should help prepare you to continue your lifelong journey of learning and changing. In this section, you will learn about the forces for change, types of change, resistance to change, overcoming resistance to change, and change models.

Forces for Change

1. Identify where the forces for change initiate.

The Environment. The changing business environment presents many challenges.[8] An organization interacts with its external and internal environment. Following is a re-listing of environmental factors; review Chapter 2 for more details on how these factors require change in organizations and how the organization should proact and interact, rather than merely react, with the environment. The external environmental forces for change include competition, consumers, government laws and regulations, economic conditions, suppliers, labor force, shareholders, society, and technological advances.

The internal organizational forces for change include management, redefined missions and strategies, resources, the systems process, and structure. When an organization is restructured, it is changed. IBM acquired Lotus for multiple reasons, one being its mission and strategy to develop software. By acquiring Lotus it obtained Notes and other software. Major external forces included consumer demand, competition from Microsoft, and technological changes to networking computers. IBM wanted to compete in the new emerging groupware, and Lotus gave it the edge on Microsoft. However, on February 29, 1996, AT&T stated that it would pull the plug on Lotus Notes, a service enabling users to link up with one another via AT&T phone lines. The service demise dealt Lotus an external environmental blow. AT&T launched its own Internet service that, for the first year, provides long distance customers with five free hours per month of access.

The Management Functions and Change. Most plans that managers develop require changes. When managers organize and delegate tasks, they often require employees to make some changes in their regular routine. When managers hire, orient, train, and evaluate performance, change is required. Leadership calls for influencing employees, often to change in some way, and control may require new methods or techniques. Acquiring Lotus was part of IBM's plan to achieve its goal in software leadership. Adding Lotus to the company requires some reorganization of IBM. IBM will require changes at Lotus, possibly in leadership, and it will have some form of control over Lotus.

Work Application

1. Give an example of a force that resulted in a change in an organization you work or have worked for.

Types of Change

2. List the four types of changes.

The types of change refer to what the organization will actually be changing. The four **types of change** *are strategy, structure, technology, and people.* Figure 8–1 presents the four types of change. Many firms fail to implement change because they tend to look at a particular change in isolation,[9] rather than as a systems process. The proper metaphor for the systems affect for managing change is balancing a mobile because a change in one variable changes the others.[10] Because of the systems affect, you need to consider the repercussions a change in one variable (type of change) will have on the other variables and plan accordingly.

types of change
Strategy, structure, technology, and people.

Strategy. An organization may change its strategy at the corporate, business, and/or functional level. At the corporate level, IBM lost money from 1991 to 1993. During this time, IBM had a turnaround and retrenchment strategy. It sold its Federal Systems Company and cut costs by $6.3 billion over two years. In 1995, IBM stabilized and changed its strategy to growth and acquired Lotus as a related diversification growth strategy. At the business level, IBM has multiple divisions, some of which can use the prospecting, defending, and analyzing strategies. Overall, IBM tends to use a differentiation strategy and focus, rather than a low-cost leader strategy. IBM's PC unit has been having problems. It is aggressively overhauling and refocusing the whole operation. It particularly needs changes in the operations functional level. However, there are also changes in finance, marketing, and human resources. As a strategic move that required change, IBM and Toshiba planned to jointly spend $1.2 billion to build a plant in Manassas, Virginia, to manufacture next-generation memory chips.[11]

Structure. Structure commonly follows strategy (as it should). In other words, a change in strategy results in a change in structure. When IBM acquired Lotus, its organizational design changed. Over time, organizations often make changes in their structure. In the last chapter you learned about organizational structure; Figure 8–1 summarizes the areas. With the trend toward the global environment, organizations are restructuring.[12] Flat organizational structures with work centers are common,[13] and the use of self-managed work teams continues.

Work Application

2. Give one or more examples of a type of change (identify it as strategy, structure, technological, or people) you experienced in an organization you work or have worked for.

Technology. Technological changes, such as the computer, have increased the rate of speed at which change takes place. Technology has compelled businesses to undergo changes at an enormous rate.[14] Technology is a commonly used method of increasing productivity to gain competitive leverage.[15] Wal-Mart, the largest U.S. retailer, is committed to technology. Wal-Mart's operating costs are 5 percent less than its nearest competitor and, consequently, the lower cost structure equals lower prices for customers.[16]

Technology often leads to a change in strategy or structure. Lotus's new groupware was a major factor in IBM's changing its strategy and structure through the acquisition. Some of the major areas of technology change include:

- *Machines* New machinery or equipment is introduced on an ongoing basis. The computer is a sophisticated machine that is also a part of many

Figure 8–1
Types of Organizational Change

STRATEGY	STRUCTURE	TECHNOLOGY	PEOPLE
Corporate (growth, stability, and turnaround and retrenchment)	**Principles** (unity of command and direction, chain of command, span of management, division of labor, coordination, balanced responsibility and authority, delegation, and flexibility)	**Machines**	**Skills**
Business Level (prospecting, defending, and analyzing)	**Authority** (formal and informal, levels of, line and staff, and centralized and decentralized)	**Systems Process**	**Performance**
Functional (marketing, operations, finance, and human resources)	**Organizational Design** (departmentalization)	**Information Process**	**Attitudes**
	Job Design (job simplification, rotation, enlargement, enrichment, and work teams)	**Automation**	**Behavior**

other machines. The fax machine has increased the speed of doing business. Once people overcome their fear of machines through training and use, the machines lose their mystery and people views machines as another tool to use in accomplishing objectives.

- *Systems Process.* Systems process refers to how the organization transforms inputs into outputs. Changes in the systems process, such as the sequence of the work, is a technology change.
- *Information Process.* With the aid of the computer, organizations have changed the way they process information. **Management information systems (MIS)** *are formal systems for collecting, processing, and disseminating the necessary information that aids managers in decision-making.* The MIS attempts to centralize and integrate all or most of the organization's information, such as finance, production, inventory, and sales. In this way the departments can coordinate their efforts in working with the systems affect. Businesses must be proactive to change in order to successfully adapt to new technologies.[17] IBM is in the information technology business to help other organizations use information technology.
- *Automation. Automation* is the simplification or reduction of human effort to do a job. Computers and other machines have allowed robots to replace people in jobs such as inspecting, cleaning, guarding, and assembling parts. Automation does not take away jobs; it changes the types of jobs. The need for training and higher levels of skill will continue into the future, while the demand for unskilled jobs will continue to decrease. Your college education should help you to become flexible and to continue to upgrade your skills with technology changes. If you want raises and promotions, be the first to voluntarily learn new technologies.

The MIS centralizes and integrates the organization's information, including inventory and production.

management information systems (MIS)
Formal systems for collecting, processing, and disseminating the necessary information that aids managers in decision-making.

People. Tasks refer to the day-to-day things that employees do to perform their jobs, and tasks change with technology and structural changes. As tasks change, people's *skills* and *performance* must change. Organizations often attempt to change employees' *attitudes* and *behavior*. A change in organizational culture is also considered a people change. You will learn about culture in the next four major sections.

It is people that develop and implement strategy and structure. People also create, manage, and use technology; therefore, people are the most important resource.[18] What people resist is the social change brought about by technological changes. Business success is based on optimizing the integration of both people and technology (sociotechnical systems). When changing structure or

APPLYING THE CONCEPT

AC 8–1 Types of Change

Identify each type of change as:

a. strategy b. structure c. technology d. people

____ **1.** "We bought a new computer system to speed up the time it takes to bill customers."

____ **2.** "With the increasing number of competitors, we are going to have to change and spend more time and effort to keep our existing customers."

____ **3.** "Jamie, I'd like you to consider getting a college degree if you are serious about a career in management with us."

____ **4.** "We are changing suppliers so that we can get a higher quality component to put into our product."

____ **5.** "We are laying off some managers to increase the number of people reporting to one boss."

technology, you should never forget the impact of change on people. Any of these other variables will not be effective without people. So it is most important to get the input and participation of those who will be most affected by changes.

People changes can take place by hiring people, retraining people, or laying people off. IBM was not doing well, so it replaced its chairman and CEO John Akers with Louis Gerstner, who had no computer experience, to turn IBM around. IBM also laid off thousands of workers and continues to train its employees to keep up with technology changes.

Stages in the Change Process

stages of the change process Denial, resistance, exploration, and commitment.

People go through four distinct stages in the change process. *The four* **stages of the change process** *are denial, resistance, exploration, and commitment.*[19]

1. *Denial.* When people first hear the rumors though the grapevine that change is coming, they deny that it will happen at all, or to them. The "it will affect the others, but not me" reaction is common. Originally, managers at Lotus were against the sale to IBM. Lotus's chairman and CEO, Jim Manzi, told IBM that Lotus was not for sale.
2. *Resistance.* Once people get over the initial shock and realize that change is going to be a reality, they resist the change. You need to accept the fact that resistance to change is part of human nature.[20] Many organizational changes fail due to employee resistance to change.[21] In this section, you will learn the details of resistance to change and how to overcome it. Lotus began to take steps to stop the sale to IBM. There were rumors that Manzi would quit or be let go if IBM bought Lotus. Manzi did quit 99 days after the IBM takeover.
3. *Exploration.* When the change begins to be implemented, employees explore the change, often through training, and better understand how it will affect them. After discussions with CEO Gerstner, and thinking about IBM's offer for him to stay as chairman and CEO of Lotus, Manzi accepted the offer.
4. *Commitment.* Through exploration, employees determine their level of commitment to making the change a success. The level of commitment can change. For example, it can start low and stay that way or increase, or it can start high and decrease, or any combination. Manzi's resignation showed lack of commitment to Lotus being part of IBM.

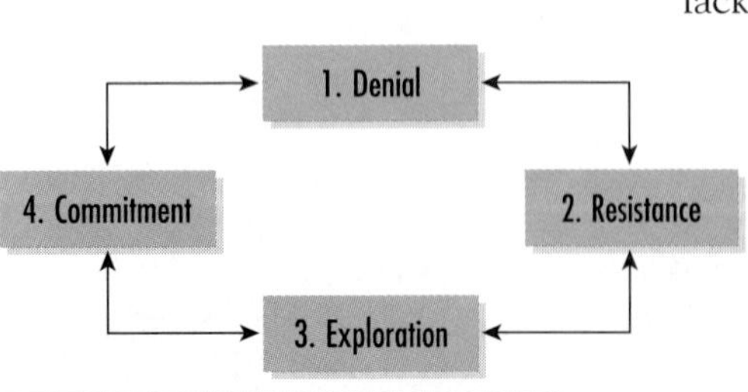

Figure 8–2
Stages in the Change Process

The better you are at overcoming resistance to change, training, and including others' input into the change, the greater your chances of successfully implementing change. Employees at both IBM and Lotus will be going through the stages of the change process. How well the change process is implemented will affect the behavior, human relations, and performance of the two businesses which are now one company. Figure 8–2 illustrates the change process. Notice that the stages are in a circular formation because change is an ongoing process not a linear one, and people can regress as the arrows show.

Resistance to Change and How to Overcome It

If you want to change strategy, structure, technology, or people, you must deal with resistance to change. Most change programs fail because of employee re-

Resistance to Change
Uncertainty
Inconvenience
Self-interest
Loss
Control
Overcoming Resistance
Trust climate for change
Plan
State why change is needed and how it will affect employees
Create a win-win situation
Involve employees
Provide support

Figure 8–3
Resistance to Change and Ways to Overcome Resistance

sistance.[22] You will now learn why people resist change, and how to overcome resistance to change. See Figure 8–3 for an overview.

Resistance to Change. Five of the major reasons employees resist change are:

- *Uncertainty*. Fear of the unknown outcome of change is common. People often get anxious and nervous and resist change in order to cope with their feelings. Employees at Lotus were uncertain about how the company would change with IBM ownership. Would their jobs change, or worse, would they be eliminated?
- *Inconvenience*. People usually do not want to disrupt the way things are because they are comfortable. At a minimum, employees have to learn new ways, and they may need training to learn new skills. Employees of Lotus will be inconvenienced by IBM.
- *Self-Interest*. People resist change that threatens their own self-interest. Employees are commonly more concerned about their best interest than the organization's. If Lotus CEO Manzi knew he would be fired if IBM bought Lotus, he may have resisted the acquisition.
- *Loss*. With change, jobs may possibly be lost. Change may require an economic loss due to a pay cut, which has happened in the airline industry. A change in work assignments or schedules may create a loss of social relationships.
- *Control*. Change can also result in an actual or perceived loss of power, status, security and especially control. People may resent the feeling that their destiny is being controlled by someone else. Lotus employees were concerned about IBM taking control. How much control, and what types of control, would IBM use?

Work Application

3. Give an example of when and how you resisted a change. Be sure to specify which of the five reasons influenced your resistance to change.

Overcoming Resistance to Change. Six of the major things you can do to overcome resistance to change follow. IBM can use all of these methods to overcome resistance to change at Lotus.

1. *Develop a Positive Trust Climate for Change*. Develop and maintain good human relations. Make employees realize you have their best interest in mind.

Because affirmative change and trust are so closely intertwined, your first concern should be to develop mutual trust. Constantly look for better ways to do things. Get employees to view change in a positive way. Encourage employees to suggest changes. Listening to and implementing their ideas is an important part of continuous improvement.

2. *Plan.* To implement changes successfully takes good planning. You need to identify the possible resistance to change and plan how to overcome it. Put yourself in the employee's position. Don't consider how you as a manager would react because managers perceive things differently. What seems very simple and logical to you may not be to an employee. Set clear objectives so employees know exactly what the change is and how it affects them. The next four methods should be part of your plan.
3. *Clearly State Why the Change Is Needed and How It Will Affect Employees.* Communication is the key to change.[23] Employees want and need to know why the change is necessary and how it will affect them both positively and negatively. Be open and honest with employees. If employees understand why the change is needed, and it makes sense to them, they will be more willing to change.[24] Remember to relate the change to the employee's values, and sell them on the benefits to them. Giving employees the facts as far in advance as possible helps them to overcome the fear of the unknown. If the grapevine starts to send incorrect facts, correct the information as quickly as possible.
4. *Create a Win-Win Situation.* Recall that the goal of human relations is to meet employee needs while achieving departmental/organizational objectives. To overcome resistance to change, be sure to answer the other parties' unasked question, "What's in it for me?" When people can see how they benefit, they are more willing to change. If the organization is going to benefit by the change, so should the employees.[25] Be willing to *negotiate*. Many companies have guaranteed that employees will not lose jobs, pay, or anything else due to specific changes.
5. *Involve Employees.* To create a win-win situation, involve employees. A commitment to change is usually critical to its successful implementation. Employees who participate in developing changes are more committed to them than employees who have changes assigned to them.[26] This is the most effective technique for overcoming resistance to change.
6. *Provide Support.* Allow employees to express their feelings in a positive way. Since training is very important to successful change, give as much advance notice and training as possible before the change takes place. Giving thorough training helps reduce frustration and helps employees realize they can be successful with the change. Remember that mistakes are both inevitable and necessary during the change process. Mistakes should be used as learning experiences toward the change.[27]

3. State the difference among a fact, a belief, and a value.

A Model for Identifying and Overcoming Resistance to Change

Before making changes, you should anticipate how employees will react to or resist them.[28] Resistance to change involves the variables of intensity, source, and focus, and explains why people are reluctant to change. Ken Hultman identifies these three variables as the major variables of resistance to change.[29]

Intensity. People have different attitudes toward change. Some thrive on it and some are upset by it; many resist it at first but gradually accept it. As a manager of change, you must anticipate employee resistance to change. Will it be strong, weak, or somewhere in between? Intensity will be lower if you use the six methods for overcoming resistance to change.

Source. There are three major sources of resistance:

1. *Facts*. The facts (statements that identify reality) of the change are often circulated inaccurately through the grapevine. People tend to use facts selectively to prove their point. Facts used correctly help to overcome fear of the unknown.
2. *Beliefs*. Facts can be proven; beliefs cannot. Beliefs are subjective opinions that can be shaped by others. Our beliefs lead us to think and feel that a change is correct or incorrect or good or bad. Differences in perception can cause resistance to change. We use our past and present experiences to predict the future change. If employees have had a bad experience with change, they may believe the new change will also be "bad."
3. *Values*. Values are what people believe are worth pursuing or doing. What we value is important to us. Values pertain to right and wrong and prioritization. Our values meet our needs and affect our behavior. Because change often requires learning new ways to do things, people view change as an *inconvenience* and place a low value on it. People analyze the facts presented from all sources and determine if they believe the change has value to them—in their *self-interest*. When the facts are clear and logical and people believe the change has value to them, they tend to have low resistance to the change.

Focus. There are three major focuses of resistance:

1. *Self*. People naturally want to know "What's in it for me? What will I gain or lose?" When the facts of change have a negative effect on employees, creating a perceived loss, employees resist the change.
2. *Others*. After considering what's in it for them, or when the change does not affect them, people tend to consider how the change will affect their friends, peers, and colleagues. If employees analyze the facts and believe the change will affect others negatively, they may be resistant to the change.
3. *Work Environment*. The work environment includes the physical setting and the climate. People like to be in control of their environment, and they resist changes that take away their control. Employees' analysis of the facts about the current versus the changed work environment will affect their resistance to the change. If employees believe the changed environment has no value to them, they will resist the change. For example, if a salesperson has a Ford Thunderbird company car and it is proposed that it be replaced with a Ford Escort, the salesperson will probably resist the change. The salesperson most likely would not resist a change from the Escort to the Thunderbird. Changes in technology are changes in the work environment.

Model 8–1
Resistance Matrix

Sources of Resistance (fact → belief → value)

Focus of Resistance (self → other → work)

1. Facts about self	4. Beliefs about self	7. Values pertaining to self
• I never did the task before. • I failed the last time I tried	• I'm too busy to learn it. • I'll do it, but don't blame me if it's wrong.	• I like the way I do my job now. Why change? • I like working in a group.
2. Facts about others	**5. Beliefs about others**	**8. Values pertaining to others**
• She has the best performance record in the department. • Other employees told me it's hard to do.	• He just pretends to be busy to avoid extra work. • She's better at it than I am; let her do it.	• Let someone else do it; I do not want to work with her. • I like working with him. Don't cut him from our department.
3. Facts about the work environment	**6. Beliefs about the work environment**	**9. Values pertaining to the work environment**
• Why don't you pay me more to do it? • It's over 100 degrees. Can't we wait?	• This is a lousy job. • The pay here is too low.	• I don't care if we meet the goal or not. • The new task will make me work inside. I'd rather be outside.

Intensity (high, medium, or low for each box)

Source: Adapted from Ken Hultman, *Resistance Matrix: The Path of Least Resistance* (Austin, Tex.: Learning Concepts, 1979).

Work Application

4. Identify your resistance to change in Work Application 3. Use the resistance matrix and identify the box number, source, and focus name.

Model 8–1 shows an adapted version of Ken Hultman's resistance matrix with examples of each area of resistance. For instance, in box 1, "Facts about Self," note that one reason given is "I never did the task before." Understanding the reasons people resist change will make you better able to anticipate and deal with those reasons. However, resistance may come from more than one focus and source (box). Use the matrix to identify the intensity, source, and focus of resistance. Once you have identified the probable resistance to change, you can work at overcoming it. Note that intensity is outside the matrix because it can be strong, moderate, or weak for each of the nine matrix boxes. In Skill-Building Exercise 8–1, you will use the resistance matrix to identify the source and focus of change.

ORGANIZATIONAL CULTURE

Organizational culture *consists of the shared values, beliefs, and assumptions of how its members should behave.* Organizational culture is an approach to understanding how organizations function, or it gives meaning to the organization's way of doing things. Think of culture as the organization's personality. Members of an organization need to understand its culture.[30] In this section, you will learn about the three levels of culture, strong and weak cultures, and changing cultures.

organizational culture
The shared values, beliefs, and assumptions of how its members should behave.

Three Levels of Culture

4. Describe the three levels of organizational culture and their relationship.

The three **levels of culture** *are behavior, values and beliefs, and assumptions.* Figure 8–4[31] illustrates the three levels of culture.

levels of culture
Behavior, values and beliefs, and assumptions.

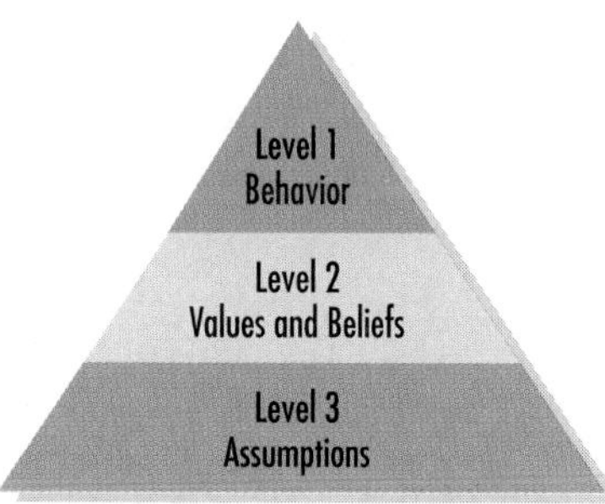

Figure 8–4
Three Levels of Culture

Level 1. Behavior. Behavior is the observable things that people do and say, or the actions employees take. *Artifacts* result from behavior and include written and spoken language, dress, material objects, and so on. Other terms used to describe Level 1 behavior include rites, celebrations, ceremonies, heroes, jargon, myths, and stories.

Managers, particularly top managers who founded the organization, have a strong influence on culture. The late Sam Walton, founder of Wal-Mart; Tom Watson, founder of IBM; and Ray Kroc, founder of McDonald's, are heroes to employees who tell stories about them. Mary Kay, founder of Mary Kay Cosmetics, has elaborate celebrations and ceremonies to reward employees with crowns, badges, jewelry, trips, and pink Cadillacs for high sales volume.

Level 2. Values and Beliefs. Values represent the way we ought to behave and beliefs represent if-then statements. If I do X, then Y will happen. Values and beliefs provide the operating principles that guide decision-making and behavior that result in Level 1 culture. We can observe behavior, but not values and beliefs. We can only infer from peoples' behavior what they value and believe. Values and beliefs often come from the mission statement; some organizations have formal statements of their values and beliefs, often called philosophy or ideology. Values identify what it takes to be successful; for example, McDonald's has "Q, S, C, V—Quality, Service, Cleanliness, and Value." Larry Robinson, head of a Cleveland-based chain of jewelry stores, says that the golden rule "Do unto others as you would have them do unto you," has been the base of the company's corporate culture which took the chain from 2 to 72 stores.

Tom Watson developed three principles stating that (1) all employees should be respected and treated with dignity, (2) the company should aim to accomplish every task in a superior way, and (3) the customer should be given the best service possible. New CEO Gerstner replaced the three principles with eight goals with heavy emphasis on serving the customer and becoming more efficient. Watson's principle 1 is Gerstner's goal 8. Organizations also use slogans to convey values, such as Ford's "Quality Is Job 1."

Level 3. Assumptions. Assumptions are values and beliefs that are deeply ingrained as unquestionably true. Employees tend to unquestionably understand how things are. Because assumptions are shared, they are rarely discussed. They serve as an automatic pilot to guide behavior. In fact, people often feel threatened when assumptions are challenged. If you question employees on why they do something, or suggest a change, they often respond with statements like, "That's the way it's always been done." Assumptions are often the most stable and enduring part of culture and are difficult to change. Notice that behavior is at the top of the diagram in Figure 8–4. However, the assumptions and values and beliefs affect the behavior, not the other way around. In fact, in the Figure 8–4 pyramid, cause and effect work from the bottom up.

Strong and Weak Cultures

Organizational cultural strength is on a continuum from strong to weak. Organizations with *strong cultures* have employees that unconsciously know the shared assumptions; consciously know the values and beliefs; agree with the shared assumptions, values, and beliefs; and behave as expected. Organizations with employees who do not agree with the shared assumptions, values, and beliefs and/or have many employees who do not behave as expected have weak cultures. When employees do not agree with the generally accepted shared values, they may become rebels and fight the culture. Companies with strong cultures include Amdahl, Boeing, Dana Corporation, Digital, Emerson Electric, Fluor, IBM, Johnson & Johnson, Marriott, Procter & Gamble, and 3M.

Work Application

5. Describe the organizational culture at all three levels for a firm you work or have worked for. Does the organization have a strong or weak culture?

The primary benefits of a strong culture include easier communication and cooperation. Unity of direction is common, and consensus is easier to reach. The primary disadvantage is the threat of becoming stagnant. To change with the environment requires questioning the assumptions, values, and beliefs and changing them when necessary. One of the major reasons Gerstner was hired as CEO of IBM was because he was an outsider not prejudiced by the culture.

Studies suggest that humor can enhance people's creativity, increase their willingness to trust others, and reduce their level of stress. Employees who work in a fun environment tend to provide better customer service.[32] Southwest Airlines CEO Kelleher works hard to maintain a strong culture based on humor. Employees value having a fun work environment.[33]

Managing and Changing Cultures

Organizational culture can be managed and changed.[34] Organizations that change and manage culture include the City of San Diego, Fiat, Ford, GM, Pacific Mutual, Pacific Telsis, Polaroid, Procter & Gamble, Tektronix, and TRW. Part of Gerstner's job when he was hired as CEO was to change IBM's culture. Successful organizations realize that managing culture is not a program with a starting and ending date. It is an ongoing organizationwide process called *organizational development* (OD).[35] You will learn about OD later in this chapter.

A change in culture is considered a *people-type* change. A survey revealed that managers are dissatisfied with many of the values and attitudes that exist in their organizational cultures.[36] When changing culture, it must be changed at all three levels. A culture of success changes over time, and businesses that fail to change their culture lose their competitive advantage.[37]

The first step in changing organizational culture is to assess the existing culture and decide what culture the organization wants to have.[38] Bull Information

Systems successfully changed its culture based on the values of partnership, respect, ownership, fun, innovation, and trust. The change involved empowering middle and senior management through coaching, delegating, and feedback systems.[39]

Culture is an important consideration when merging with or acquiring a business. A mismatch in cultures can lead to failure. It is common for larger businesses to acquire small companies and to try to change their culture to match their own without success.[40] IBM has had a history of problems with acquisitions. IBM and Lotus have different cultures. IBM is larger and more bureaucratic than freewheeling Lotus. IBM plans to maintain Lotus as a freestanding company. But, at the same time, IBM must integrate Lotus products into its own to make the entire IBM company a success.[41]

When developing or changing culture, remember that it's not what you, as a manager, say is a value; it's what you measure, reward, and control that will influence behavior. For example, if management says ethics are important, but does not punish people for unethical behavior or reward ethical behavior, employees will not be ethical.

Three popular dimensions of culture include innovation, quality, and diversity. You will learn how organizations are creating organizational cultures to manage innovation, quality, and diversity in the next three sections.

APPLYING THE CONCEPT

AC 8–2 Strong and Weak Cultures

Identify each statement as being characteristic of an organization with a

a. strong culture b. weak culture

____ **6.** "Walking around this department during my job interview, I realized I'd have to wear a jacket and tie everyday."

____ **7.** "I'm a little tired of hearing how our company founders conducted business. We all know the stories, so why do people keep telling them?"

____ **8.** "I've never attended a meeting with people who all seem to act differently. I guess I can just be me rather than trying to act in an acceptable manner to others."

____ **9.** "It's hard to say what is really important because management says quality is important. They force us to work at too fast a pace and they know we send out defective products just to meet orders."

____ **10.** "I started to tell this ethnic joke and the other employees all gave me a dirty look."

INNOVATION

Recall from Chapter 4 that *creativity* is a way of thinking that generates new ideas and an *innovation* is the implementation of a new idea. Two important types of innovations are product innovation (new things) and process innovation (new ways of doing things). *Product innovations* are changes in outputs (good and/or service) to increase consumer value, or new outputs. *Process innovations* are changes in the transformation of inputs into outputs. Innovation is commonly a technology-type change. New product innovations go through the stages of the product life cycle (Chapter 5). Large companies commonly introduce new products in a test market area and, if successful, launch the product on a national or international level. Domino's test-marketed buffalo wings, which were so successful that the company is working on other innovative products.

Organizations need to develop technological innovations to keep ahead of competition, or at least to keep up with competitors.[42] Successful companies use

Work Application

6. Give an example of an innovation from an organization you work or have worked for. Be sure to specify if it was a product or process innovation.

innovation as a competitive advantage.[43] In this section, you will learn about organizational structures and cultures that stimulate creativity and innovation.

5. Explain intrapreneurship and its three roles.

Innovative Organizational Structures

Organizational structures (Chapter 7) that stimulate innovation are commonly flat organizations with limited bureaucracy, have a generalist division of labor, coordinate with cross-functional teams, and are flexible. Use of the informal system is common and authority is decentralized. Job design includes job enrichment and work teams based on sociotechnical systems.

Large companies commonly use divisional structure to create small units that can be innovative. Innovative organizations commonly create separate systems for innovative groups,[44] such as new venture units (skunkworks). To develop the Macintosh computer, Steve Jobs took a small group of engineers and programmers and set up operations apart from the remainder of the plant. Colgate-Palmolive created Colgate Venture Company as a separate unit, and General Foods developed Culinova Group as a unit to which employees can take their ideas for possible development.

Within the human resources function, creative employees are *recruited* and *trained*, and a *reward* system that encourages creativity and innovation is developed. Rewarding innovation leads to increased creativity.[45] Many organizations provide financial and nonfinancial rewards to employees, as individuals and groups, that develop innovations. Organizations commonly use cash, prizes (such as trips), praise, and recognition to encourage people to be creative. Many companies give a percentage of the savings/earning for the first year. Monsanto gives $50,000 each year to the individual or group that develops the biggest commercial breakthrough.

Innovative Organizational Cultures

Hewlett-Packard has a strong innovative culture.

The best corporate cultures encourage creativity and innovation.[46] In other words, cultures that value innovation and develop the proper environment of believing it is possible and assume that it is part of the job have innovative employee behavior. Organizations known to have strong innovative cultures include Corning, Hewlett-Packard, Intel, Johnson & Johnson, Merck, Monsanto, Procter & Gamble, Rubbermaid, Texas Instruments, and 3M. Such organizations develop structures to match, and become a part of, their innovative culture.

Innovative organizations tend to have similar cultures that encourage experimentation. They usually have strong cultures and have innovative organizational structures as discussed. Innovative cultures commonly have the following six characteristics:

- *Encouragement of Risk-Taking.* They encourage employees to be creative without fear of punishment due to failure. Mistakes and failure are expected, but they are not punished unless due to negligence. They are viewed as a learning experience. At 3M, around 60 percent of the innovations do not succeed in the marketplace.

- *Intrapreneurship*. Intrapreneurship encourages the development of new products and services that might become separate business units. Intrapreneurship commonly has three roles in large organizations. The *inventor* is the one who comes up with the creative idea. However, inventors often lack the skill to transform the idea into an innovation. The *champion* is the one responsible for transforming the idea into an innovation. The champion, usually a middle manager, believes in the idea and promotes it by finding a sponsor to provide the resources needed for the innovation. The *sponsor*, a top-level manager, supports the innovation by providing the resources and structure for the innovation. Sponsors deal with the politics necessary to get the resources. At Texas Instruments, only creative ideas with an acknowledged inventor, champion, and sponsor are formally transformed into innovations.
- *Open Systems*. Organizational members constantly scan the environment for creative ideas. Benchmarking (Chapter 5) is commonly used.
- *Focus on Ends Rather Than Means*. They tell employees the objectives (ends) but the employees decide on the means to achieve them.
- *Acceptance of Ambiguity and Impractical Ideas*. Requiring clear, practical ideas stifles creativity. They encourage employees to work on creative ideas even when it is not clear to managers what the employees are doing, and they do not have to have an immediate practical value for the ideas. What seems ambiguous and impractical sometimes ends up as a great innovation.
- *Tolerance of Conflict*. They encourage diversity of opinions as a means of coming up with creative ideas and improving on them.

Work Application

7. Identify and explain how an organization you work or have worked for does or does not have each of the six characteristics of innovative cultures. Overall, does the organization have a creative culture?

3M is generally recognized as the leader in innovation. 3M uses six rules, listed in Figure 8–5, to stimulate innovation. These six rules, which have been copied by other companies, are deeply engraved into 3M's culture.

Figure 8–5
3M's Rules for an Innovative Culture[47]

- **Set goals for innovation.** 3M's goal is to have 25 to 30 percent of annual sales from products that are five years old or less. About one-third of 3M's revenues come from new products.
- **Commit to research and development.** 3M invests close to twice as much to R&D as the average U.S. company. 3M has a goal to cut the time it takes to introduce new products in half.
- **Inspire intrapreneurship.** Champions are allowed to manage their products as if they were running their own businesses. 3M employees can spend 15 percent of their time on personal research interests unrelated to their current job.
- **Facilitate, don't obstruct.** Divisions are small and autonomous and have access to information and technical resources throughout the entire company. Researchers with good ideas receive $50,000 Genesis grants to develop their creative ideas into innovative products.
- **Focus on the customer.** Quality is defined by the customer.
- **Tolerate failure.** Managers know that mistakes will be made and that destructive criticism kills creativity. Employees know that if an idea fails, they will be encouraged to pursue other ideas.

APPLYING THE CONCEPT

AC 8–3 Innovative and Noninnovative Cultures

Identify each statement as being characteristic of an organization with an

a. innovative culture b. noninnovative culture

____ **11.** "We have a very tall organization."

____ **12.** "I worked on trying to develop a faster rotating blade, but it didn't work. However, my boss gave me a very sincere thank you for trying."

____ **13.** "It drives me crazy when I'm delegated a task and the boss tells me the details of how to do the job. Why can't I meet the objective my way for a change?"

____ **14.** "This company makes heavy use of policies, procedures, and rules."

____ **15.** "We have jobs that are broad in scope and a lot of autonomy to do the job the way the team wants to do it."

IBM has a fairly good record of innovation. However, it has had problems with its PC unit. In 1993, IBM Personal Computer Company lost $1 billion despite $10 billion in sales. In 1994, IBM lost its leading sales position worldwide to Compaq, and fell to fourth place (behind Compaq, Apple, and Packard-Bell) in U.S. sales. IBM will need some innovations to regain its leading PC position. Lotus has a more creative structure and culture than IBM, and it is important for IBM to stimulate creativity at its traditional divisions and especially at its new Lotus division.

QUALITY

An organizational culture can value both innovation and quality. In fact, the innovation structure is essentially the same for a total quality culture. Because all organizations have different cultures, they generally don't say they have a culture of innovation, not quality, or vice versa. Both innovation and quality cultures focus on creating customer value. One slight difference is the emphasis on innovation. Organizations that focus primarily on innovation, like 3M, tend to place more emphasis on developing new products. However, organizations that focus primarily on TQM place more emphasis on continuous improvement of their products and services through their systems and processes. TQM is based on continuous innovation.

6. State the core values of TQM.

core values of TQM
(1) To focus everyone in the organization on delivering customer value and (2) to continously improve the system and its processes.

Core Values of TQM

The **core values of TQM** *are (1) to focus everyone in the organization on delivering customer value and (2) to continuously improve the system and its processes*. The values of a TQM culture emphasize the importance of trust, open communication, willingness to confront and solve problems, openness to change, cooperation (not competition), and adaptability to the environment. TQM values people as the most important resource. Employees are well trained, and they work in teams. Employees collect data and use science to improve customer value. A TQM culture is a strong culture in which values are directed toward the strategic purpose of aligning people, processes, and resources to create value for customers through continuous improvement for strategic purposes.

Work Application

8. Identify and explain TQM values that are part of the culture in an organization that you work or have worked for.

IBM has always maintained a reputation for quality products that include both goods and excellent service. Through this quality reputation, IBM has developed many loyal customers. Quality products and excellent service are a driving force for all managers' decisions.

The late W. Edwards Deming developed 14 points for creating the TQM culture. Survey and interview research results imply that Deming's points im-

1. Create constancy of purpose toward improvement of product and service, with the aim to become competitive, to stay in business, and to provide jobs.
2. Adopt a new philosophy. We are in a new economic age created by Japan. We can no longer live with commonly accepted styles of American management, nor with commonly accepted levels of delays, mistakes, or defective products.
3. Cease dependence on inspection to achieve quality. Eliminate the need for inspection on a mass basis by building quality into the product in the first place.
4. End the practice of awarding business on the basis of price tag. Instead, minimize total cost.
5. Improve constantly and forever the system of production and service to improve quality and productivity, and thus constantly decrease costs.
6. Institute training on the job.
7. Institute supervision. The aim of supervision should be to help people, machines, and gadgets to do a better job. Supervision of management is in need of overhaul, as well as supervision of production workers.
8. Drive out fear so that everyone may work effectively for the company.
9. Break down the barriers between departments. People in research, design, sales, and production must work as a team to foresee problems of production and use that may be encountered with the product or service.
10. Eliminate slogans, exhortations, and targets for the work force that ask for zero defects and new levels of productivity. Such exhortations only create adversarial relationships. The bulk of the causes of low productivity belong to the system, and thus lie beyond the power of the work force.
11. Eliminate work standards that prescribe numerical quotas for the day. Substitute aids and helpful supervision.
12. Remove the barriers that rob the hourly worker of his or her right to pride of workmanship. The responsibility of supervisors must be changed from sheer numbers to quality. Remove the barriers that rob people in management and engineering of their right to pride of workmanship. This means abolishment of the annual rating, or merit rating, and management by objectives.
13. Institute a vigorous program of education and retraining.
14. Put everybody in the company to work to accomplish the transformation.

Figure 8–6
Deming's 14 Points for Creating the Total Quality Culture

prove employee perceptions of their own job satisfaction, organization quality, productivity, overall organizational effectiveness, and organizational competitiveness.[48] Figure 8–6 presents the 14 points.

The Learning Organization

7. Describe a learning organization's culture.

Empirical research indicates a relationship between culture and quality, and between culture and employee performance.[49] Although 90 percent of major U.S. companies have instituted some form of quality improvement programs, two-thirds have not been successful.[50] TQM is not a program. Many organizations that have failed implemented TQM as a program, rather than as a culture with TQM values of continuous improvement and change.[51] A culture of resistance to change is the biggest hurdle in implementing quality initiatives.[52] Even organizations that have implemented TQM systems successfully nevertheless exhibit a reluctance to change much of their organizational culture.[53] A true quality culture is one in which the organization is willing to change its culture through continuous quality improvements.[54] A learning organization changes its culture as needed.

TQM is based on systems to develop a quality culture. The concept of the learning organization has developed out of the systems view of organizations. In a learning organization, everyone in the organization understands that the world is changing rapidly, that they must be aware of these changes, adapt to changes and, more importantly, be forces for change *The* **learning organization** *has a culture with a capacity to learn, adapt, and change with its environment to continuously increase customer value*. It values change not for the sake of change, but as a means of effectively and efficiently improving customer value. It continuously develops employees' skills and knowledge so that they can continuously contribute creativity and innovation to the organization. CEO Gerstner seems to be moving IBM toward becoming a learning organization.

learning organization
The organization has a culture with a capacity to learn, adapt, and change with its environment to continuously increase customer value.

8. Discuss the relationship among diversity, innovation, and quality.

DIVERSITY

An organizational culture can value innovation, quality, and diversity. In fact, the same organization structure supports all three values. According to the National Performance Review report, a relationship exists between quality and diversity. The report stated that before organizations can improve the quality of their services, they must first understand and address the requirements of their employees. Diversity programs must therefore be integrated into the TQM objectives.[55] In addition, a diverse work force is also more creative and innovative in dealing with the rapidly changing environment.

While all organizations have different cultures, they can develop cultures that value diversity. The approach to developing a culture that values diversity is to recognize the realities of the new work force and how this affects the efficiency and effectiveness of the organization as a system. *Valuing diversity* emphasizes training employees of different races and ethnicity, religions, genders, ages, and abilities and with other differences to function effectively together. To be creative and innovative and to continuously improve customer value, employees must work in an atmosphere of dignity and trust to work together as a team. A poor atmosphere compromises employees' ability to cooperatively execute the processes through which work gets done. Diversity affects the companies' bottom-line profits.[56] In other words, if people don't work well together, the organization does not work well.

Managing diversity emphasizes fully utilizing human resources through organizational actions that meet all employees' needs. Managing diversity can only be successful with a change in culture.[57] Managing diversity is a process that must be managed and built into the organization's culture and core value system through processes affecting everything the organization does.[58] Managing diversity requires an organizational culture that values diversity and meets the needs of all groups of workers.[59] To be part of the culture, all employees, from the top down, must place value on diversity. The way employees know what is valued is by what managers reward. Therefore, management must develop policies and practices that reward diversity, if diversity is to be a part of the organization's culture.

A diversity of employees can lead to a weak culture because people don't want to behave in a standard way. It is important to focus everyone on the really important values such as customer value and teamwork, rather than unimportant issues such as how people dress and how they do their jobs, as long as they get done.

Review Chapter 3 for the details on the benefits of diversity and how to manage diversity through top management support and commitment, diversity leadership, diversity policies and practices, and diversity training. Through valuing and managing diversity, diversity becomes a part of the organizational culture. Like any successful organization, IBM values and manages diversity.

ORGANIZATIONAL DEVELOPMENT

In the first section of this chapter, you learned about four types of change: strategy, structure, technology, and people/culture. Organizational development (OD) is the commonly used method of managing change. **Organizational development** *is the ongoing planned process of change used as a means of improving performance through interventions.* The human resources management department, discussed in the next chapter, is usually responsible for OD throughout the organization. The *change agent* is the person selected by human resources management to be responsible for the OD program. The change agent may be a member of the organization or a hired consultant. In this section, you will learn about change models, interventions, and revitalizing organizations.

organizational development (OD)
The ongoing planned process of change used as a means of improving performance through interventions.

Change Models

Lewin's Change Model. In the early 1950s, Kurt Lewin developed a technique, still used today, for changing people's behavior, skills, and attitudes. Lewin viewed change as the modification of those forces that keep a system's behavior stable (status quo). Two forces exist: (1) those striving to maintain the status quo and (2) those pushing for change. To create change, you can increase the forces that are pushing for change, decrease the forces that are maintaining the current state, or some combination of the two. Lewin contends that modifying the forces that are maintaining the status quo produces less tension and resistance than increasing forces for change; therefore, it is a more effective strategy for change. Lewin's change model consists of three steps, listed in Figure 8–7:

1. *Unfreezing*. This step usually involves reducing the forces that are maintaining the status quo. Organizations sometimes accomplish unfreezing by introducing information that shows discrepancies between desired performance and actual performance.
2. *Moving*. This step shifts the behavior to a new level. This is the change process in which employees learn the new desirable behavior, values, and attitudes. Strategy, structure, technology, and people/culture changes may take place to reach desirable performance levels.

Figure 8–7
Change Models

Lewin's Change Model	**A Comprehensive Change Model**
Step 1. Unfreezing.	*Step 1.* Recognize the need for change.
Step 2. Moving.	*Step 2.* Identify possible resistance to the change and plan how to overcome it.
Step 3. Refreezing.	*Step 3.* Plan the change interventions.
	Step 4. Implement the change interventions.
	Step 5. Control the change.

3. *Refreezing*. The desirable performance becomes the permanent way of doing things or the new status quo. Refreezing often takes place through reinforcement and support for the new behavior.

A Comprehensive Change Model. Lewin's change model requires a new formula for today's rapidly evolving business environment.[60] The model provides a general framework for understanding organizational change. Because the steps of change are broad, the author has developed a more specific model. The model consists of five steps, listed in Figure 8–7:

1. *Recognize the Need for Change*. The change agent can use a variety of techniques to diagnose problems in need of changes to solve them. Techniques include reviewing records, observing, interviewing individuals and/or groups, holding meetings, and using questionnaires. Clearly state the change needed—set objectives. Don't forget the systems effects. How will the change affect other areas of the organization?
2. *Identify Possible Resistance to the Change and Plan How to Overcome It*. Follow the guidelines in step 1.
3. *Plan the Change Interventions*. Based on the diagnosis of the problem, the appropriate intervention must be selected. You will learn some of the interventions used to facilitate change in this section. The change agent may select one or more interventions.
4. *Implement the Change Interventions*. The change agent, or someone selected, conducts the intervention to bring about the desired change.
5. *Control the Change*. Follow up to ensure that the change is implemented and maintained. Make sure the objective is met. If not, take corrective action.

Organizational Development Interventions

OD interventions
Specific actions taken to implement specific changes.

OD interventions *are specific actions taken to implement specific changes*. You will now learn about nine of the many OD interventions, listed in Figure 8–8.

Training and Development. Training and development are presented first because the other interventions often include some form of training. Training is the process of developing skills, behaviors, and attitudes to be used on the job. You will learn about training in the next chapter. Recall that training is an important part of valuing diversity. Levi Strauss & Company has a $5-million-a-year valuing diversity educational program designed to get employees to become more tolerant of personal differences.[61]

Organizations that develop TQM cultures select specific skills, such as statistical process control, that employees learn through training sessions. IBM is highly regarded as one of the top companies in commitment to and quality of its training and development programs.

9. State the difference in the use of forcefield analysis and survey feedback.

Forcefield Analysis. Forcefield analysis is particularly useful for small group (4 to 18 members) problem-solving. **Forcefield analysis** *is an OD intervention that diagrams the current level of performance, the hindering forces toward change, and the driving forces toward change.* The process begins with an appraisal of the current level of performance. The present level of performance appears in the middle of the diagram. The hindering forces holding back performance are listed on the top or left part of the diagram. The driving forces keeping performance at this level are listed on the bottom or right of the diagram. After viewing the diagram, you develop strategies for maintaining or increasing the driving forces with simultaneous steps for decreasing hindering forces. For example, Figure 8–9, on the next page, was developed for IBM's PC unit which has dropped in market share. The solution selected should focus on the production problems and sales forecasting by marketing. After group members agree on the diagram, the solution often becomes clear to them as they develop a plan to change the present situation.

forcefield analysis
An OD intervention that diagrams the current level of performance, the hindering forces toward change, and the driving forces toward change.

Survey Feedback. Survey feedback is one of the oldest and most popular OD techniques. **Survey feedback** *is an OD intervention that uses a questionnaire to gather data to use as the basis for change.* Survey feedback is commonly used in step 1 of the change model. Different change agents will use slightly different approaches; however, a commonly used survey feedback program includes six steps:

survey feedback
An OD intervention that uses a questionnaire to gather data to use as the basis for change.

1. Management and the change agent do some preliminary planning to develop an appropriate survey questionnaire.
2. The questionnaire is administered to all members of the organization/unit.
3. The survey data is analyzed to uncover problem areas for improvement.
4. The change agent feeds back the results to management.
5. Managers evaluate the feedback and discuss the results with their subordinates.
6. Corrective intervention action plans are developed and implemented.

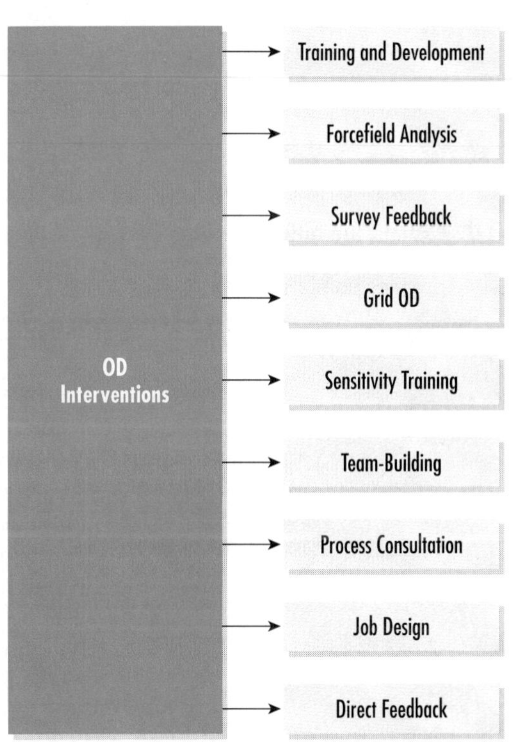

Figure 8–8
OD Interventions

Grid OD. Robert Blake and Jane Mouton developed a "packaged" approach to OD.[62] They developed a standardized format, procedures, and fixed goals. Blake and Mouton, or their associates, conduct the program for organizations. *Grid OD* is a six-phase program designed to improve management and organizational effectiveness. The six phases are:

1. *Training.* Teams of five to nine managers, ideally from different functional areas, are formed. During a week-long seminar, each team member assesses his or her leadership style by determining his or her position on the grid. (You will learn about the grid in Chapter 12.) They work at be-

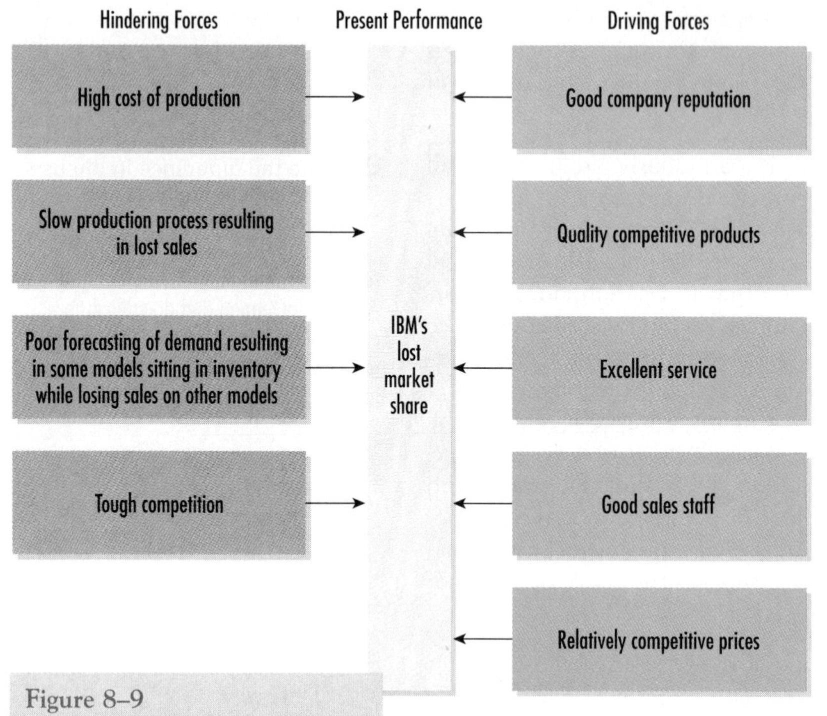

Figure 8–9
Forcefield Analysis

coming 9,9 managers by developing skills in the areas of team-building, communication, and problem-solving.

2. *Team Development.* Managers return to the job and try to use their new skills as 9,9 managers, who show high concern for production and people.
3. *Intergroup Development.* Work groups improve their ability to cooperate and coordinate their efforts. This fosters joint problem-solving activities.
4. *Organizational Goal-Setting.* Management develops an organization model it should strive to become.
5. *Goal Attainment.* The changes needed to become the model organization are determined and implemented.
6. *Stabilization.* The first five phases are evaluated to determine and stabilize positive changes and to identify areas for improvement or alteration.

Sensitivity Training. Sensitivity training includes a training group (or T-group) of 10 to 15 people. The training sessions have no agenda. People learn about how their behavior affects others and how others' behavior affects theirs. The popularity of T-groups peaked in the 1970s as organizations questioned the on-the-job value gained through the training. Although T-groups are still used, they have largely been replaced by team-building and process consultation.

10. Explain the difference between team-building and process consultation.

Team-Building. Team-building is probably the most widely used OD technique today, and its popularity will continue as more companies use work teams. Individuals work as part of a unit or department, and each small functional group of individuals that works closely and interdependently makes up a team. The effectiveness of each team and all the teams working together directly affects the results of the entire organization. Because of the importance of teams, you will be given detailed information about them.

team-building
An OD intervention designed to help work groups increase structural and team dynamics performance.

Team-building *is an OD intervention designed to help work groups increase structural and team dynamics performance.* Team-building can be used as a comprehensive OD technique in which the top executives go through the program by themselves, and then go through it with their middle managers, who then go through it with their supervisors, who then go through it with their employees. The agenda tends to change to meet the needs of each group. However, team-building is more widely used as a means of helping new or existing groups in need of improving effectiveness. For example, Dr. Miriam Hirsch was called in as a consultant by a medical center and told that there was a restructuring of administrative responsibility. The medical center changed to a three-member team management approach. Doctors were no longer sole decision-makers; they had to work with a management nurse and an administrative person. Because these managers were not used to teamwork, the consultant was asked to propose a team-building program to help them develop their skills.

The Change Agent's Responsibilities. Generally, the change agent first meets with the manager to discuss why a team-building program will be conducted. They discuss the goals of the program. The change agent assesses the manager's willingness to get feedback on how the team feels about his or her style and practices. The manager's receptiveness to the program will directly affect the potential of the team-building results.

The change agent and manager meet with the team. An atmosphere of openness and trust begins with the change agent describing the goals, agenda, and procedures of the team-building program. The change agent describes the agreement with the manager.

The change agent often observes the team at work and may interview each team member privately and confidentially to identify group problems. In addition to, or in place of, the interviews, a survey feedback questionnaire may be used. A sample questionnaire appears in Preparing for Skill-Building Exercise 12–2 in Class. The change agent conducts the team-building program in one or more days, depending on the problems and the number of members.

Team-Building Goals. The goals of team-building programs will vary considerably, depending on the group's needs and the change agent's skills. Some of the typical goals include:

- To clarify the objectives of the team and the responsibilities of each team member.
- To identify problems preventing the team from accomplishing its objectives.
- To develop team problem-solving, decision-making, objective-setting, and planning skills.
- To determine a preferred style of teamwork and to change to that style.
- To fully utilize the resources of each individual member.
- To develop open, honest working relationships based on trust and an understanding of group members.

The Team-Building Program. The team-building agendas vary with team needs and the change agent's skills. Typical programs go through six stages:

1. *Climate-building and goals.* The program begins with the change agent trying to develop a climate of trust, support, and openness. The change agent discusses the program's purpose and goals based on data gathered prior to the program. Team members learn more about each other and share what they would like to accomplish—goals—through team-building.
2. *Structure and team dynamics evaluation.* Team-building is an intervention designed to improve both how the work is done (structure) and how team members work together as they do the work (team dynamics). The team evaluates its strengths and weaknesses in both areas. Team dynamics will be explained with process consultation, the next OD intervention you will learn about.

3. *Problem identification.* The team identifies its strengths, then its weaknesses or areas where it can improve. The problems come from the change agent's interviews and/or the feedback survey. The team first lists several areas where it can improve. Then it prioritizes them in terms of how they will help the team improve performance.
4. *Problem-solving.* The team takes the top priority and develops a solution. It then moves to the second priority, followed by the third, then fourth, and so on. Forcefield analysis can be used for problem-solving.
5. *Training.* Team-building often includes some form of training that addresses the problem(s) facing the group.
6. *Closure.* The program ends with a summarization of what has been accomplished. Team members commit to specific improvements in performance. Follow-up responsibility is assigned and a future meeting is set to evaluate results.

An offshoot of team-building is *teamwork training* which is designed to give members confidence in themselves and their teammates. It uses Outward Bound types of experience where people must depend on each other to get through various obstacles such as climbing cliffs, whitewater rafting, ropes courses, and other activities.

A second offshoot of team-building is *intergroup team-building* which is designed to help different work teams work together more effectively. Members learn to better understand the other groups' situations and to deal with conflict between groups.

process consultation
An OD intervention designed to improve team dynamics.

Process Consultation. Process consultation is often part of the second stage of team-building, but it is commonly used as a separate, more narrowly focused intervention. **Process consultation** *is an OD intervention designed to improve team dynamics.* While team-building may focus on the process of getting the job itself done, process consultation focuses on how people interact as they get the job done. Team dynamics (or process) include how the team communicates, allocates work, resolves conflict, and handles leadership, and how the group solves problems and makes decisions. The change agent observes the group members as they work in order to give them feedback on team process. During team process consultation, the team discusses its process and how to improve it. Training may also be conducted to improve group process skills. The ultimate objective is to train the group so that process consultation becomes an ongoing team activity. You will learn more about team dynamics in Chapter 13.

Work Application

9. Give an example of one or more OD interventions used in an organization that you work or have worked for.

Job Design. Job design, which you already learned about in Chapter 7, is an OD intervention. Job enrichment is the commonly used intervention.

Direct Feedback. Situations occur, particularly with technology changes, in which the change agent is an outside consultant who comes in and recommends a direct solution. For example, IBM consultants work with organizations to recommend information systems. Once installed, IBM often trains the employees to operate the new system.

Organizational Revitalization

Organizational revitalization *is the planned change to realign the organization with its environment.* Many organizations have a difficult time keeping up with the rapid changes in their environment. This can be particularly true for organizations that are doing well so they become complacent and take the view that past success will continue. This happened to the American auto makers in the 1970s as they produced large, gas-guzzling, low-quality cars. The Japanese auto makers forced them to undergo organizational revitalization to realign with the environment which the oil embargo and Japanese auto makers changed. American Airlines, Disney, and many other organizations have taken the time to step back and work to revitalize their companies. Gerstner was hired to revitalize IBM, which he did. Organizational revitalization is part of the turnaround and retrenchment strategy that requires changes in culture.

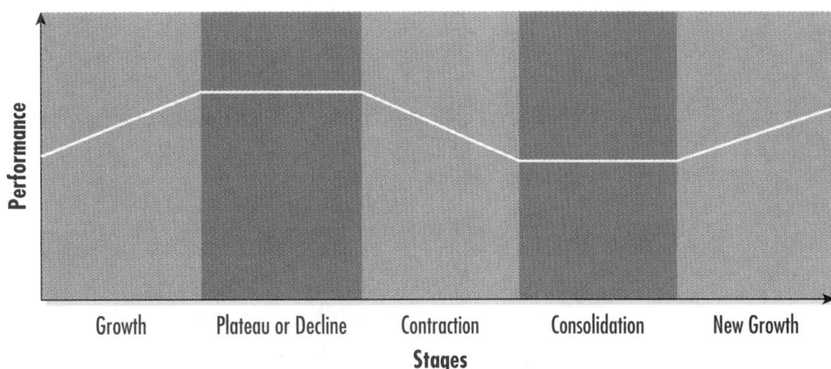

Figure 8–10
Organizational Revitalization Stages

organizational revitalization
The planned change to realign the organization with its environment.

Stages of Revitalization. Organizations do not have to go through a series of stages to revitalize. However, many organizations go through five stages of revitalization, shown in Figure 8–10. During the *growth stage*, things are going well and the firm often becomes complacent and falls out of alignment with its environment, which results in the *plateau* or *decline stage*. At this point, the firm realizes the problem and may bring in new managers, such as Gerstner at IBM. The company goes into the *contraction stage* by cutting back on its operations, eliminating unnecessary facilities, and so on. Then it learns to live with a leaner, more cost-efficient operation in the *consolidation stage*. Gerstner laid off thousands of IBM employees and cut expenses by $6.3 billion in two years. After consolidation, the firm is now ready for the *new growth stage*. Companies often infuse new capital into the orga-

APPLYING THE CONCEPT

AC 8–4 OD Interventions

Identify the appropriate OD intervention for the change in each statement as:

a. training and development
b. forcefield analysis
c. survey feedback
d. grid OD
e. sensitivity training
f. team building
g. process consultation
h. job design
i. direct feedback

____ **16.** "Things are going well, but I think we could benefit from an organizationwide intervention to improve management and organizational effectiveness."

____ **17.** "Morale and motivation have fallen throughout the division in recent months. We need an intervention that can identify the problems so we can change the situation."

____ **18.** "We have outgrown our present inventory system, which is also dated. What intervention should we use to develop a new one?"

____ **19.** "The new offset printing machine is installed. Who are we going to teach to run it and what intervention should we use?"

____ **20.** "What intervention should we use to prepare our employees to put the product together as a group rather than each person continuing to produce one part of it?"

nization and/or make new investments. IBM acquired Lotus as a growth strategy. Some companies go through drastic revitalization over an extended period of time and some even change their name. International Harvester is now Navistar International and U.S. Steel became USX.

CURRENT MANAGEMENT ISSUES

Globalization. As companies go *global*, their environments expand and the rate of change increases for strategy, structure, technology, and people/culture. Multinational companies are developing global business cultures, and they view a diverse global culture as a competitive advantage.[63] MNCs work to develop cultures that value innovation, quality, and diversity. Many large MNCs use mergers, acquisitions, joint ventures, and alliances in which blending cultures becomes important to success. General Motors and Fanuc Company of Japan formed a joint venture to create GMF Robotics Corporation which is the market leader of heavy robotics in the U.S. Both companies had very different cultures, but they worked hard and invested considerable time and effort to develop trust and to understand each other's cultures. They used OD interventions to blend cultures.

Diversity. Global companies purport to embrace multiculturalism in the workplace, but their internal cultures are much less international in nature.[64] MNCs tend to develop cultures that value *diversity*. However, they must be careful not to export their successful diversity programs to other countries with different cultural values. For example, diversity programs that promote women in the United States are successfully accepted. But, in Japan they could cause problems because women do not enjoy the level of equality with men that they do in the United States.[65]

Ethics and Social Responsibility. Although not given an entire section in this chapter, *ethics and social responsibility* are part of organizational cultures. Companies place different levels of value on ethics and social responsibility. Generally, if people in the organization have a shared expectation that employees will behave in an ethical manner, they will. Shared expectations for ethical behavior come from following the guidelines in Chapter 2. Many companies, such as Levi Strauss and Johnson & Johnson, value ethics and social responsibility. Many U.S. companies stopped doing business in South Africa due to apartheid, and many returned once it was abolished. Levi Strauss no longer outsources Dockers in China because of the country's poor record on, and slow progress toward, human rights.[66]

Productivity. Re-engineering efforts, as a means of increasing *productivity*, often fail because of a lack of total commitment to change cultures. Without a change in culture, any attempt to increase customer value will not succeed. Re-engineering should be a proactive process considered as a means rather than an end to changing culture.[67]

Quality, TQM, and Productivity. There is a debate over the compatibility of re-engineering and *TQM*. Some people believe that re-engineering will supplant TQM as the latest management tool. However, re-engineering is narrower in scope and can be part of TQM. Combining the two processes yields the best results in terms of focused and cost-effective development. TQM sets the stage for re-engineering because it paves the way for change by ingraining a culture of change in the organization.[68]

The quest for increased *productivity* can have various effects on culture. With the TQM emphasis on continuous improvements, productivity generally increases. However, when the quest for productivity focuses solely on cost-cutting, it can have negative effects. For example, Bell & Howell focused on cost-cutting, which became part of its culture. The company achieved operating profit growth of 15 percent a year, but revenue growth of only 3 percent a year. After five years, top management realized that it could not continue to keep saving its way to prosperity. Bell & Howell had to change its culture to value revenue growth. Managers worked hard to change the culture by encouraging risk-taking and spending on products and people that could speed growth. To do so, it replaced four of the five cost-cutting focused top executives with growth-oriented executives. Executives were given 30 percent of their salaries as bonuses for sales growth. The mentality of obsessive cost-cutting was a tough habit to break. Bell & Howell changed the culture, as is evident in its results of a 7 percent increase in revenue and 23 percent surge in operating income.[69]

Participative Management. In addition to strong and weak cultures, some people identify culture as participative versus nonparticipative. Participative cultures use self-managed teams. They are considered to be open and are characterized by attributes such as trust, openness in communication, information sharing, worker autonomy, and group problem-solving. The TQM culture is an open, participative culture. Rensis Likert developed a system for measuring the level of participation on a four-point scale:

No participation .... *High participation*

System I	System II	System III	System IV
Exploitative autocratic	Benevolent autocratic	Consultative	Participative team

Likert recommends that organizations determine their present level of participation, through a survey feedback questionnaire he developed, and to change the culture to a participative team. As a consultant, Likert worked with companies to transform them into a participative team.

Small Business. *Small businesses* usually change faster and are more innovative than large businesses. Researchers found that small businesses produce 2.4 times as many innovations as larger companies, despite their more limited resources.[70] According to the U.S. Office of Management and Budget, individual inventors and entrepreneurs developed more than half the major technological advances of the 20th century. Many large businesses, including Apple, McDonald's, Polaroid, Procter & Gamble, Levi Strauss, and Xerox, started as innovative small companies that grew into multibillion-dollar enterprises. Small businesses often provide higher-quality goods and services than large businesses, and many large businesses outsource to small businesses because they can provide higher quality for less cost. Large companies often use divisional departmentalization to create smaller units that can act like small entrepreneurial businesses. OD change agents in large businesses are often experts at managing change using formal interventions, whereas small business owners/mangers are the change agents who don't use formal OD interventions.

CHAPTER SUMMARY AND GLOSSARY

The chapter summary is organized to answer the 11 learning objectives for Chapter 8.

1. Identify where the forces for change initiate.
The forces for change come from the external and internal environment.

2. List the four types of change.
The four types of change are strategy, structure, technology, and people/culture.

3. State the difference among a fact, a belief, and a value.
A fact is a provable statement that identifies reality. A belief cannot be proven because it is an opinion. A value is what is important to people; values are used to prioritize.

4. Describe the three levels of organizational culture and their relationship.
Level 1 is behavior—the actions employees take. Level 2 is values and beliefs. Values represent the way we ought to behave and beliefs represent if-then statements. Level 3 is assumptions—values and beliefs that are deeply ingrained as unquestionably true. Values, beliefs, and assumptions provide the operating principles that guide decision-making and behavior.

5. Explain intrapreneurship and its three roles.
Intrapreneurship is the development of new products that might become separate business units. The *inventor* comes up with the creative idea. The *champion* is responsible for the transformation of the idea into an innovation. The champion finds a *sponsor* who provides the resources needed for the innovation.

6. State the core values of TQM.
The core values of TQM are (1) to focus everyone in the organization on delivering customer value and (2) to continuously improve the system and its processes.

7. Describe a learning organization's culture.
Learning organizations have a culture with a capacity to learn, adapt, and change with their environments to continuously increase customer value.

8. Discuss the relationship among diversity, innovation, and quality.
Diversity has a direct effect on innovation and quality. A diverse organization is generally more innovative and produces higher-quality products than nondiverse organizations.

9. State the difference in the use of forcefield analysis and survey feedback.
Forcefield analysis is used by a small group to diagnose and solve a specific problem. Survey feedback uses a questionnaire filled out by a large group to identify problems; the group does not work together to solve a problem. Forcefield analysis could be used to solve a problem identified through survey feedback.

10. Explain the difference between team-building and process consultation.
Team-building is broader in scope than process consultation. Team-building is an intervention designed to improve both how the work is done and how team members work together as they do the work (team dynamics). Process consultation is designed to improve team dynamics.

11. Define the following key terms (in order of appearance in the chapter):
Select one or more methods: (1) fill in the missing key terms from memory, (2) match the key terms from the end of the summary with their definitions below, or (3) copy the key terms in order from the list at the beginning of the chapter.

The __________ are strategy, structure, technology, and people.

__________ are formal systems for collecting, processing, and disseminating the necessary information that aids managers in decision-making.

The __________ are denial, resistance, exploration, and commitment.

__________ consists of the shared values, beliefs, and assumptions of how its members should behave.

The three __________ are behavior, values and beliefs, and assumptions.

The __________ are (1) to focus everyone in the organization on delivering customer value and (2) to continuously improve the system and its processes.

A __________ has a culture with a capacity to learn, adapt, and change with its environment to continuously increase customer value.

__________ is the ongoing planned process of change used as a means of improving performance through interventions.

__________ are specific actions taken to implement specific changes.

__________ is an OD technique that diagrams the current level of performance, the hindering forces toward change, and the driving forces toward change.

__________ is an OD technique that uses a questionnaire to gather data that are used as the basis for change.

__________ is an OD technique designed to help work groups increase structural and team dynamics performance.

__________ is an OD technique that is designed to improve team dynamics.

__________ is the planned change to realign the organization with its environment.

KEY TERMS

core values of TQM
forcefield analysis
learning organization
levels of culture
management information systems (MIS)
OD interventions
organizational culture
organizational development (OD)
organizational revitalization
process consultation
stages of the change process
survey feedback
team-building
types of change

REVIEW AND DISCUSSION QUESTIONS

1. How do the management functions relate to change?
2. How does the systems affect relate to the four types of change?
3. List the four stages in the change process.
4. Which of the five reasons for resisting change do you believe is most common?
5. Which of the six ways to overcome resistance to change do you believe is the most important?
6. What is the difference between a strong and weak organizational culture?
7. What are the two types of innovations?
8. List the six characteristics of an innovative culture.
9. Do you agree with the core values of TQM or would you recommend changing them? If yes, state your core values for TQM.
10. Which change model do you prefer? Why?
11. Have you ever worked for a firm that went through any type of organizational revitalization? If yes, explain it.

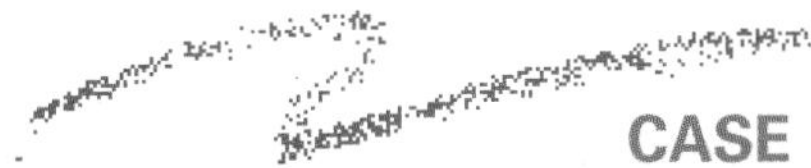

CASE

Eastman Kodak

Eastman Kodak Company was a very strong leader in the U.S. market in the 1970s. Kodak used the export global strategy of making products in several U.S. plants and shipping them to domestic and foreign customers. Kodak was losing its strong leadership position as competition increased. One of its problem areas of business, best known to the public, was its photographic products. The Japanese came out with the 35-millimeter camera, while Kodak ignored the market for too long and gave the first mover advantage to the Japanese companies. Kodak also unsuccessfully spent years and millions of dollars on developing an instant camera to compete with

Polaroid, and got sued in the process for patent infringement. In the film area it lost market share to Fuji and other companies. On top of the heavy competition, the price of silver rose dramatically. Kodak was in a crisis because silver was a critical raw material in its photographic products.

Planning for Change

Top managers identified three major factors contributing to problems at Kodak. First, costs were too high. Second, information at the bottom of the operation was not being shared throughout the company, and managers were not being held accountable for performance. Third, staff specialists developed strategic planning but it was not implemented by the line managers. In other words, the planning process was not working. Based on these factors, departmentalization was considered to be the cause of many of Kodak's problems.

Kodak's functional departments focused on manufacturing, marketing, R&D, and finance. However, the top managers believed that the company had to respond to the global environment based on businesses rather than functions. With functional departments, no one was responsible for performance. The decision was made to change from functional to divisional departmentalization. The next decision was how to plan and implement the departmental change. A common approach was to have a group of four or five managers make the new organization chart behind closed doors and then dictate the change.

Managers were concerned about making the reorganization a success, so they decided to use participative management to implement the change following these steps: The top three managers developed a new organization. Then they met with the nine line managers, who would be affected by the change, and explained the new organization and the rationale as to why it was required. Part of the rationale was to become more competitive by developing new products at a faster rate. Top managers simply told the nine line managers to go off and think about the reorganization and then come back and discuss it. Line managers were to challenge, question, understand, improve, and most importantly to feel as though it is "our" reorganization. After four months, the team of 12 had a reorganization plan.

The team of 12 was expanded to the top 50 managers who went through roughly the same process. At the end of five months, 62 managers had a reorganization plan. The 62 widened to the top 150 managers. However, their job was not to rework the departmentalization; they were to develop a specific plan for the divisional implementation.

The next step was to appoint people to the top jobs in the new organization. Appointments were made based on assessment of talent, with seniority second in importance. Most of the top 150 managers involved in the process had new jobs. But more importantly, the large majority of managers supported the reorganization regardless of their new jobs. The preparation for change took 14 months.

Implementing Change

Kodak's reorganization began with a 12 percent reduction of employees over a two-year period. Most left voluntarily for other jobs, retirement, and so on. Over time, the number of managers was reduced by about 25 percent, and Kodak stopped its habit of promoting managers from within. Over a five-year period, nearly 70 percent of the key managers were new to their jobs.

Next, nearly 30 independent business units were created and given the responsibility for developing and implementing their own strategy and worldwide profit performance. The export strategy changed, depending on the business unit, all the way to the direct investment level. The business units were grouped into traditional imaging businesses, image-intensive information technology, and plastic polymers. Kodak acquired Sterling Drug and expanded into pharmaceuticals as an additional business group.

In order to achieve better focus on the customer, markets, and technology, manufacturing and R&D were split up and distributed into the business units. The relationship between the business units and the different geographic areas where Kodak conducted its business were more clearly articulated. In simple terms, each business unit was responsible for developing the strategic thrust of the business while the geographic unit was responsible for implementation of that thrust.

Each business unit was subject to periodic evaluation of its earnings and value. Each was required to generate a return that exceeded an internally established cost of equity, reflecting its own level of risk and market conditions. Businesses unable to attain the required rate of return were put on probation, and if they did not reach the goal, they were dismantled or divested.

Kodak's reorganization was successful by most measures. It improved its financial, productivity, and market share performance. Kodak's performance improved at a rate four times the U.S. average for several years in a row.

Select the best alternative for the following questions. Be sure you are able to explain your answers.

___ 1. The forces for change at Kodak came from the ___ environment.

a. external b. internal c. both

___ 2. The type of change Kodak made was primarily a ___ change.

a. strategy c. technology
b. structure d. people

___ 3. Top management at Kodak took so long, 14 months, coming up with a plan for change because it was concerned about the ___ stage in the change process.

a. denial c. exploration
b. resistance d. commitment

___ 4. Managers at Kodak may have resisted the change for ___ reasons.

a. uncertainty d. loss
b. inconvenience e. control
c. self-interest f. all of these

___ 5. The primary way to overcome resistance to change used at Kodak was

a. develop a trust climate
b. plan
c. state why change is needed and how it will affect employees
d. create a win-win situation
e. involve employees
f. provide support

___ 6. Part of the reason for Kodak's change in departmentalization was to develop a more innovative culture.

a. true b. false

___ 7. Kodak changed to a TQM culture.

a. true b. false

___ 8. Kodak used OD in its change process.

a. true b. false

___ 9. Kodak followed the steps in the comprehensive change model.

a. true b. false

___ 10. Kodak's change can be considered an organizational revitalization.

a. true b. false

11. Discuss the systems affect of Kodak's reorganization.

12. It took 14 months to plan the change, and the organizational design was not changed dramatically from the original top three managers' plan. Would it have been faster just to have dictated the change? Using hindsight, would you have dictated the change or used participation as Kodak did?

For current information on Kodak, use Internet address http://www.kodak.com. For ideas on using the Internet, see the Appendix.

SKILL-BUILDING EXERCISE 8–1

Identifying Resistance to Change

Preparing for Skill-Building Exercise 8–1

Below are ten statements made by employees asked to make a change on the job. Identify the source and focus of their resistance using Model 8–1. Because it is difficult to identify intensity of resistance on paper, skip the intensity factor. However, when you deal with people on the job, you need to identify their intensity. Place the number of the box (1–9) that represents and best describes the major resistance.

___ 1. "But we never did the job that way before. Can't we just do it the same way as always?"

___ 2. The tennis coach asked Jill, the star player, to have Louise as her doubles partner. Jill said, "Come on, Louise is a lousy player. Betty is better; don't break us up." The coach disagreed and forced Jill to accept Louise.

___ 3. The manager, Winny, told Mike to stop letting everyone in the department take advantage of him by sticking him with extra work. Mike said, "But I like my coworkers and I want them to like me, too. If I don't help people they may not like me."

___ 4. "I can't learn how to use the new computer. I'm not smart enough to use it."

___ 5. The police sergeant asked Chris, the patrol officer, to take a rookie cop as her partner. Chris said, "Do I have to? I broke in the last rookie, Wayne. He and I are getting along well."

___ 6. The employee went to Chuck, the manager, and asked him if she could change the work-order form. Chuck said, "That would be a waste of time; the current form is fine."

___ 7. Diane, an employee, is busy at work. The manager tells her to stop what she is doing and begin a new project. Diane says, "The job I'm working on now is more important."

___ 8. "I don't want to work with that work team. It has the lowest performance record in the department."

___ 9. "Keep me in the kitchen part of the restaurant. I can't work in the bar because drinking is against my religion."

___10. "But I don't see why I have to stop showing pictures of people burning in a fire to help get customers to buy our smoke detector system. I don't think its unethical. Our competitors do it."

Doing Skill-Building Exercise 8–1 in Class

Objective
To develop your ability to identify resistance to change so that you can improve your skill at overcoming resistance and implement changes effectively.

Preparation
You should have determined the resistance to change for the ten preparation statements.

Experience
You will get feedback on how well you identified resistance to change.

Procedure (10–30 minutes)
Option 1. Break into groups of four to six and share your priorities. Try to reach a group consensus on each of the ten priorities. When the groups are finished, one member records priorities for the entire class to see. After all groups are finished, the instructor goes over the recommended answers.

Option 2. The instructor calls on students to get their priorities to each task. The instructor goes over the recommended answer for each item after a student(s) gives a priority.

Option 3. The instructor goes over the recommended answers without student involvement.

Conclusion
The instructor leads a class discussion and/or makes concluding remarks.

Application (2–4 minutes)
What did I learn from this experience? How will I use this knowledge in the future?

____

____

Sharing
Volunteers give their answers to the sharing questions.

EXERCISE 8–1
Team Building

Preparing for Exercise 8–1

Note: This exercise is designed for permanent class groups (teams that have worked together regularly). Following is a survey feedback questionnaire. There are no right or wrong answers. Answer each question as it applies to your class group. Place the number (1-5) representing your level of agreement with each statement on the line before the statement.

Strongly agree	Agree somewhat	Neutral/ between	Disagree somewhat	Strongly disagree
1	2	3	4	5

Conflict or Fight

___ 1. Our group's atmosphere is friendly.

___ 2. Our group has a relaxed (rather than tense) atmosphere.

___ 3. Our group is very cooperative (rather than competitive).

___ 4. Members feel free to say what they want.

___ 5. There is much disagreement in our group.

___ 6. Our group has problem people (people who don't talk during discussions—silent, people who dominate the discussions—talkers, people who don't participate—bored, people who change the subject—wanderers, and people who like to fight—arguers).

Apathy

___ 7. Our group is committed to its tasks (all members actively participate).

___ 8. Our group members have good attendance.

___ 9. Group members come to class prepared. (All assignments are complete.)

___ 10. All members do their share of the work.

___ 11. Our group should consider firing a member for not attending and/or doing his or her share of the work.

Decision-Making

___ 12. Our group's decision-making ability is good.

___ 13. All members participate in making decisions.

___ 14. One or two members influence most decisions.

___ 15. Our group follows the six steps of the decision-making model (Chapter 4): (1) Define the problem. (2) Set objectives and criteria. (3) Generate alternatives. (4) Analyze alternatives (rather than quickly agreeing on one) and select the most feasible. (5) Plan and implement the decision, and (6) Control.

Group Techniques

___ 16. Our group members sit in a close circle during meetings.

___ 17. We determine the approach to the task before starting.

___ 18. Only one member speaks at a time, and everyone discusses the same question.

___ 19. Each person presents answers with specific reasons for selecting the answer.

___ 20. We rotate order for presenting answers to avoid domination.

___ 21. We listen to others when they talk.

___ 22. All members defend their answers (when they believe they are correct) rather than changing to avoid discussion, conflict, or to get the task over with.

23. List other relevant questions to your group.

____

____

____

Doing Exercise 8–1 in Class

This exercise is designed for groups that have worked together for some time.

Objectives
To experience a team-building session and to improve your group's effectiveness.

Preparation
You should have answered the survey feedback questionnaire preparation.

Experience
This exercise is discussion-oriented. The procedures follow the six stages of team-building from the text.

Climate Building and Goals

Procedure 1a (5–30 minutes)
To develop a climate of trust, support, and openness, group members will learn more about each other through a discussion based on asking questions.

Rules

1. Rotate; take turns asking questions.
2. You may refuse to answer a question as long as you did not ask it (or plan to).
3. You do not have to ask the questions in the order listed.
4. You may ask your own questions. (Add them.)

As an individual and before meeting with your group, review the following questions and place the name of one or more group members to whom you want to ask the question. If you prefer to ask the entire group, put "group" next to the question. When everyone is ready, begin asking the questions.

1. How do you feel about this course?
2. How do you feel about this group?
3. How do you feel about me?
4. How do you think I feel about you?
5. Describe your first impressions of me.
6. What do you like to do?
7. How committed to the group are you?
8. What do you like most about this course?
9. What do you plan to do after you graduate?
10. What do you want out of this course?
11. How do you react to deadlines?
12. Who in the group are you the closest to?
13. Who in the group do you know the least?

Other: ______________________________

____

When the instructor tells you to do so, get together with your group members and ask each other your questions.

Procedure 1b (2–4 minutes)
Participants determine what they would like to accomplish during the team-building session—goals. Following are six major goals of team-building from the text; you may add to them. Rank them according to your preference.

To clarify the team's objectives.

To identify areas for improving group performance.

To develop team skills.

To determine and utilize a preferred team style.

To fully utilize the resources of each group member.

To develop working relationships based on trust, honesty, and understanding.

Your own goals (list them): ______________________________

____

Procedure 1c (3–6 minutes)
Participants share their answers to Procedure 1b. The group can come to a consensus on its goal(s) if it wants to.

Structure and Process

Procedure 2 (3–8 minutes)
As a team, discuss the group's strengths and weaknesses in structure and process.

Problem Identification

Procedure 3a (10–15 minutes)
As a team, answer the survey feedback questionnaire (preparation for Exercise 8–1). Place a G on the line to signify the team's answer. Don't rush; fully discuss the issues and how and why they affect the group.

Procedure 3b (3–7 minutes)
Based on the preceding information, list three to five ways in which the team could improve its performance.

____

____

____

____

____

Procedure 3c (3–6 minutes)
Prioritize the preceding list (1 = important).

Problem Solving

Procedure 4 (6–10 minutes)
Take the top-priority item. Then, list shared values (do's and don'ts) for the group to abide by in order to be more effective. List shared values for each area of improvement until time is up. Try to cover at least three areas.

____

____

____

____

____

Training

Procedure 5 (1 minute)
Team-building often includes training to address the problems facing the group. Because training takes place during most exercises, we will not do any now. Remember that the agendas for team-building vary and usually last for one or more full days, rather than one hour.

Closure

Procedure 6a (3 minutes)

1. I intend to implement the team's solutions. Why? _____
____
2. What did I learn from this experience? ____________
____
3. How can I apply this knowledge in my daily life?_______
____
4. How can I apply this knowledge as a manager? ______
____

Procedure 6b (1–3 minutes)
Group members summarize what has been accomplished and state what they will do (commit) to improve the group.

Conclusion
The instructor may lead a class discussion and/or make concluding remarks.

Sharing (4–7 minutes)
A spokesperson from each team tells the class the group's top three areas for improvement. The instructor records them on the board.

VIDEOCASE

Managing Change: Central Michigan Community Hospital

Central Michigan Community Hospital (CMCH), introduced in the Chapter 2 Videocase, has been evaluating changes in the health care environment and how it should respond to ensure the future of its regional health system.

CHCH managers and its board of directors have realized that environmental pressures from employers, consumers, and government will dictate major changes in health care delivery. To respond, CMCH is working closely with its medical staff to form an integrated health delivery system. Forming new hospital/doctor alliances is not an easy task. CMCH is also introducing many new services. An important new service is a health and wellness center. Another initiative involves recruiting new physicians. Changes related to patient care and technology are also occurring within the hospital. Many other changes have occurred or are in the planning stages.

All of these changes at CMCH must be planned and managed. Managerial skills are required to involve people and plan the implementation to achieve successful change.

Human Resources Management: Staffing

Learning Objectives

After studying this chapter, you should be able to:

1. List the four parts of the human resources management process.
2. Explain the difference between a job description and a job specification and why they are needed.
3. State the two parts of attracting employees and the difference between them.
4. Describe the difference between the group and panel interview and hypothetical and probing questions.
5. Discuss the difference between orientation and training and development of employees.
6. List the steps in job instructional training.
7. State the major components of compensation.
8. Describe the difference between the use of job analysis and job evaluation.
9. Explain why most organizations do not have labor relations.
10. Define the following **key terms** (in order of appearance in the chapter):

    human resources management process
    bona fide occupational qualification
    strategic human resources planning
    job description
    job specifications
    recruiting
    selection
    assessment centers
    orientation
    training
    development
    vestibule training
    performance appraisal
    compensation
    job evaluation
    labor relations
    collective bargaining

Skill Development

1. You can develop your skill in selection interviewing (Skill-Building Exercise 9–1).

2. You can develop your skill at training employees (Skill-Building Exercise 9–2).

Selecting and training are organizing/staffing skills that utilize human, communication, conceptual, and decision-making skills. The exercises develop your interpersonal, informational, and decisional management roles. The SCANS skill competencies of using resources-staff, interpersonal skills, informational-teaching others, and systems, as well as basic, thinking, and personal qualities foundation are developed.

citor, of Sunnyvale, California, produces goods and services in program management, systems engineering, and customized computer information systems. Founder and CEO Roger Meade has developed a unique organizational culture at Scitor based on his approach to human resources management. Meade views employees as valuable assets: "Scitor is our people; our success depends on them." He believes that the key to productivity is taking care of employee's needs, and he takes good care of them. Meade sees Scitor's human resources programs as investments, not a cost of doing business.

Human resources investments have been paying off through 15 years of profitable growth. However, Meade does not set goals for growth or profitability. His theory is that profits and growth are a byproduct of doing the job right and focusing on customer satisfaction. By satisfying the customers and making them successful, the company is successful. Meade realizes that human resources practices without goods and services that provide customer value would not be successful. Therefore, Scitor strives to create an environment where employees are not distracted from the goal of customer satisfaction. As a result, employees continually enhance customer value.

Gene Priestman (CIO), Terry Petrzelka (President), and Roger Meade (CEO) view employees of Scitor as valuable assets.

The human resources management process focuses on making life on the job as agreeable and as easy to handle as possible. Some of Scitor practices include benefits to all employees who work at least 17.5 hours per week. Scitor provides unlimited sick leave with no lost wages and no tracing of sick days taken. Scitor provides a company-paid health care plan with a $1,400 fund for each employee for dental and vision care and unreimbursed medical expenses. New mothers get 12 weeks of paid maternity leave and the option of full- or part-time work when they return. Scitor offers job sharing (two employees completing one full-time job) and flextime (employees select starting and ending times).

Scitor gives every employee tickets to one 49ers football home game. The company organizes picnics, chili cook-offs, ski trips, fishing trips, wine-tasting trips, and road rallies. Also, Scitor has an annual fiscal year kick-off meeting in a first-class resort that all employees attend. Scitor pays for transportation, food, and lodging for each employee and a guest for the three-day meeting.

Meade does not view his human resources policies as generous or liberal; it's simple economics. Everything Scitor does is driven toward increasing competitiveness and productivity. The benefits exist because they support the attract-and-retain employee objective. Turnover is 2.1 percent versus the industry average of 16.5 percent. The money saved on attracting and training new employees pays for the benefits. For example, Scitor decided to pay the cost of sick-care service for employees. It costs about $2,400 a year, and the company estimates it saves around $17,000 in lost customer billings.

1. List the four parts of the human resources management process.

human resources management process
Planning, attracting, developing, and retaining employees.

THE HUMAN RESOURCES MANAGEMENT PROCESS

The **human resources management process** *consists of planning, attracting, developing, and retaining employees*. It is also know as the *staffing* process. Figure 9–1 illustrates the process, and each of the four parts of the process is discussed as a major section of this chapter. Notice the arrows used to illustrate the systems affect. For example, planning and compensation affect attracting employees, la-

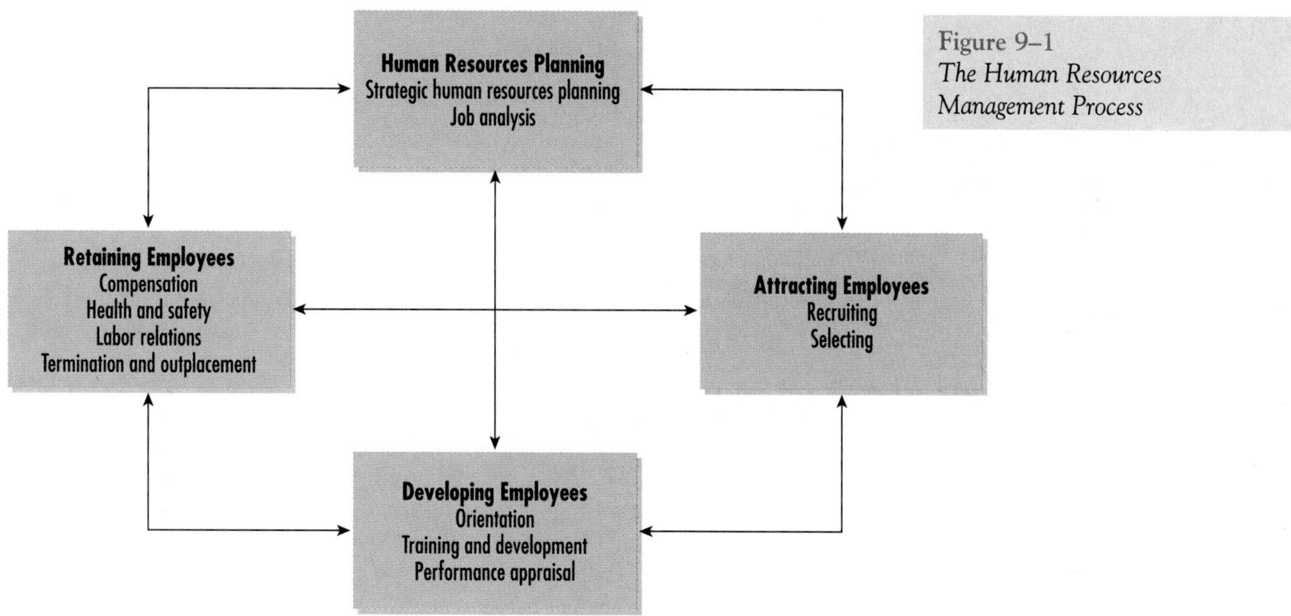

Figure 9–1
The Human Resources Management Process

bor relations affects planning, the job analysis affects training, and so on. In this section, you will learn about the legal environment and the human resources department.

The Legal Environment

The external environment, especially the competitive and legal environment, has a major impact on human resources practices. When the organization does not offer the competitive pay and benefits that competitors offer, employees may change companies. Organizations are not completely free to hire whomever they want. The human resources department usually has the responsibility of seeing that the organization complies with the law. Some of the legal considerations follow.

Major laws affecting employment are Equal Employment Opportunity (EEO) and executive orders on Affirmative Action (AA). EEO, a 1972 amendment to the Civil Rights Act of 1964, prohibits employment discrimination on the basis of sex, religion, race or color, or national origin and applies to virtually all private and public organizations that employ 15 or more employees. Who is legally considered a minority? A minority is just about anyone who is not a white male, of European heritage, or adequately educated. The EEO minority guidelines list includes Hispanics, Asians, African-Americans, Native Americans, and Alaskan natives. The EEO also protects disadvantaged young people, disabled workers, and persons over 40 years of age. Although the law protects women from discrimination in employment, they are not considered to be a legal minority because they make up half of the population, and in some situations, are a majority.

Sexual Harassment. Sexual harassment is one of the most sensitive areas of discrimination because it is often a matter of personal judgment. To help people know if they have been sexually harassed, the Equal Employment Opportunity Commission (EEOC) has defined the term as follows:

> Unwelcome sexual advances, requests for sexual favors, and other verbal or physical conduct of a sexual nature constitute sexual harassment when (1) submission to such conduct is made either explicitly or implicitly a term or condition of an individual's employment, (2) submission to or rejection of such conduct by an individual is used as the basis for employment decisions affecting such individual, or (3) such conduct has the purpose or effect of unreasonably interfering with an individual's work performance or creating an intimidating, hostile, or offensive environment.

Over 1,500 people win over $25 million annually from employers through EEO.[1]

The EEOC is responsible for legally enforcing equal opportunity for all. It has 47 field offices across the nation, and it operates a WATTS line (1-800-USA-EEOC) around the clock to provide information on employee rights. If you are not sure if what you are about to do, or are doing, is legal, call. In addition, the EEOC offers seminars for employees who feel they aren't getting a fair shake.

The Americans with Disabilities Act of 1990 prohibits discrimination against people with disabilities and requires "reasonable accommodations" so they can work.

Some of the other laws affecting staffing include the Equal Pay Act of 1963, which requires employers to provide equal pay for substantially equal work regardless of sex; the Age Discrimination in Employment Act of 1967, which prohibits discriminatory employment practices against persons ages 40 and older; the Vocational Rehabilitation Act of 1973, which requires federal contractors to take affirmative action to hire and advance employment of persons with disabilities; the Vietnam-Era Veterans' Readjustment Assistance Act of 1972 and 1974 (amended in 1980), which requires contractors to take affirmative action to hire individuals with disabilities and Vietnam-era veterans; the Pregnancy Discrimination Act of 1978, which prohibits discrimination against women because of pregnancy, childbirth, or related medical conditions, especially in the area of benefits administration; and the Americans with Disabilities Act (ADA) of 1990, which prohibits discrimination against people with disabilities and requires "reasonable accommodations" so they can work. ADA also protects recovering alcoholics or drug abusers, cancer patients in remission, and AIDS victims. The Family Medical Leave Act of 1993 allows employees to take off up to six weeks, without loss of present job, to care for family members.

Violation of any of these laws can lead to investigation by the EEOC or to becoming a defendant in class-action or specific lawsuits. Courts find discrimination when selection criteria are vague, elusive, unstructured, undefined, or poorly conceived. As a manager, you should be familiar with your organization's EEO and AA program guidelines. Besides, offering equal opportunity to a diverse work force pays. The 20 percent of companies rated highest for hiring women and minorities outperformed the stock market by 2.4 percentage points, while the worst 20 percent trailed the average by 8 points.[2]

Work Application

1. Have you or anyone you know been sexually harassed and/or asked for discriminatory information during the preemployment process? If yes, please explain the situation in language acceptable to all.

Preemployment Inquiries. On the application blank and during interviews, no member of an organization can legally ask discriminatory questions. The two major rules of thumb to follow are: (1) Every question asked should be job-related. When developing questions, you should have a purpose for using the information. Only ask legal questions you plan to use in your selection process. (2) Any general question that you ask should be asked of all candidates.

Figure 9–2 lists what you can (lawful information you can use to disqualify candidates) and cannot (prohibited information you cannot use to disqualify

Name

Can Ask: Current legal name and whether the candidate has ever worked under a different name.

Cannot Ask: Maiden name or whether the person has changed his or her name.

Address

Can Ask: Current residence and length of residence.

Cannot Ask: If the candidate owns or rents his or her home, unless it is a BFOQ.

Age

Can Ask: If the candidate is between specific age groups, 21 to 70, to meet job specifications. If hired, can you furnish proof of age? For example, an employee must be 21 to serve alcoholic beverages.

Cannot Ask: How old are you? Or to see a birth certificate. Do not ask an older person how much longer he or she plans to work before retiring.

Sex

Can Ask: Only if sex is a BFOQ.

Cannot Ask: If it is not a BFOQ. To be sure not to violate sexual harassment laws, do not ask questions or make comments remotely considered flirtatious. Do not ask about sexual preferences.

Marital and Family Status

Can Ask: If the candidate can meet the work schedule or job and whether the candidate has activities, responsibilities, or commitments that may hinder meeting attendance requirements. The same question(s) should be asked of both sexes.

Cannot Ask: To select a marital status or any questions regarding children or other family issues.

National Origin, Citizenship, Race, or Color

Can Ask: If the candidate is legally eligible to work in the United States, and if this can be proven if hired.

Cannot Ask: To identify national origin, citizenship, race or color (or that of parents and other relatives).

Language

Can Ask: To list languages the candidate speaks and/or writes fluently. The candidate may be asked if he or she speaks and/or writes a specific language if it is a BFOQ.

Cannot Ask: The language spoken off the job, or how the applicant learned the language.

Convictions

Can Ask: If the candidate has been convicted of a felony and other information if the felony is job-related.

Cannot Ask: If the candidate has ever been arrested. (An arrest does not prove guilt.) For information regarding a conviction that is not job-related.

Height and Weight

Can Ask: If the candidate meets or exceeds BFOQ height and/or weight requirements, and if it can be proven if hired.

Cannot Ask: The candidate's height or weight if it is not a BFOQ.

Religion

Can Ask: If the candidate is of a specific religion when it is a BFOQ. If the candidate can meet the work schedules or must be absent for religious reasons (holidays, etc.)

Cannot Ask: Religious preference, affiliations, or denominations.

Credit Ratings or Garnishments

Can Ask: If it is a BFOQ.

Cannot Ask: If it is not a BFOQ.

Education and Work Experience

Can Ask: For information that is job-related.

Cannot Ask: For information that is not job-related.

References

Can Ask: For the names of people willing to provide references. For the names of people who suggested the candidate apply for the job.

Cannot Ask: For a reference from a religious leader.

Military

Can Ask: For information on education and experience gained that relates to the job.

Figure 9–2
Preemployment Inquiries

Cannot Ask: Dates and conditions of discharge. Draft classification or other eligibility for military service. National Guard or reserve units of candidates. About experience in foreign armed services.

Organizations

Can Ask: To list membership in job-related organizations, such as union, professional, or trade associations.

Cannot Ask: To identify membership in any non-job-related organization that would indicate race, religion, and so on.

Disabilities

Can Ask: If the candidate has any disabilities that would prevent him or her from performing the specific job.

Cannot Ask: For information that is not job-related. Focus on abilities, not disabilities.

Figure 9–2
Continued

candidates) ask during the selection process. In all cases, the assumption is that the information asked for is not a bona fide occupational qualification (BFOQ) for the job. A **bona fide occupational qualification** *allows discrimination where it is reasonably necessary to normal operation of a particular organization.* In an example of a BFOQ upheld by its supreme court, the state of Alabama required all guards in male maximum-security correctional facilities to be male. People believing that this requirement was sexual discrimination took it to court. The supreme court upheld the male sex requirement on the grounds that 20 percent of the inmates were convicted of sex offenses, and this creates an excessive threat to the security of female guards.

bona fide occupational qualification (BFOQ)
Allows discrimination where it is reasonably necessary to normal operation of a particular organization.

APPLYING THE CONCEPT

AC 9–1 Legal or Illegal Questions

Identify the ten questions as:

a. legal (can ask) b. illegal (cannot be asked during preemployment)

____ **1.** What languages do you speak?
____ **2.** Are you married or single?
____ **3.** How many dependents do you have?
____ **4.** So you want to be a truck driver. Are you a member of the Teamsters Union?
____ **5.** How old are you?
____ **6.** Have you been arrested for stealing on the job?
____ **7.** Do you own your own car?
____ **8.** Do you have any form of handicap?
____ **9.** What type of discharge did you get from the military?
____ **10.** Can you prove you are legally eligible to work?

The Human Resources Department

As stated in prior chapters, human resources is one of the four major functional departments in an organization. It is a staff department that advises and assists all the other departments in the organization. The human resources department is responsible for the human resources management process.

In organizations large enough (usually about 100 or more employees) to have a separate human resources department, the department develops the human resources plans for the entire organization:

- It recruits employees so the line managers can select which employees to hire.
- It orients employees and trains many of them to do their jobs.
- It usually develops the performance appraisal system and forms used by managers throughout the organization.

- It determines compensation for employees.
- It is usually responsible for employee health and safety programs, works on labor relations, and is involved with the termination of employees. Employment records are kept in and by the human resource department, and it is often involved with legal matters.

Work Application

2. State your involvement with the human resources department in an organization you work or have worked for.

HUMAN RESOURCES PLANNING

In this section you will learn about strategic human resources planning and job analysis. **Strategic human resources planning** *is the process of staffing the organization to meet its objectives*. The job of the human resources department is to provide the right kinds of people, in the right quantity, with the right skills, at the right time. Human resources plans are based on the organization's strategy. If the strategy is growth, then employees will need to be hired. If the strategy is retrenchment, then there will be a layoff. If the strategy is stability, staffing levels will need to be maintained. However, even with a stability strategy, in a dynamic environment of continuous changes, the types of skills needed continually change. Strategic human resources management has become increasing important in the 1990s.[3]

strategic human resources planning
The process of staffing the organization to meet its objectives.

Based on the organization's strategy, human resources managers analyze its current human resources based on its environment and sales forecast. The next step is to forecast specific human resources needs. The final step is to develop a plan to provide the employees necessary to meet the organization's objectives. For example, at Lands' End, a mail-order business, the firm's staffing needs increase during the Christmas holiday season. Over 2,000 seasonal and temporary workers are required to fill these needs. Staffing is done according to a plan formulated as early as January of that year, when the required number of employees is estimated according to projected orders and the expected work volumes of specific jobs.[4] As Scitor continues its growth strategy, it continues to plan its human resources needs.

Job Analysis

2. Explain the difference between a job description and a job specification and why they are needed.

Strategic human resources planning determines the number of people and skills needed, but it does not specify how each job is performed. An important part of human resources planning is the review of information about the job.[5] Job design is the process of combining tasks that each employee is responsible for completing (Chapter 7). In order to design jobs, they must be analyzed. *Job analysis* is the process of determining what the position entails and the qualifications needed to staff the position. As the definition implies, job analysis is the basis for the job description and the job specifications.

The **job description** *identifies the tasks and responsibilities of a position*. In other words, it identifies what employees do to earn their compensation. The trend is to describe jobs more broadly in order to design enriched jobs.[6] Figure 9–3 lists information commonly included in a job description; Figure 9–4 shows a sample written job description.

job description
Identifies the tasks and responsibilities of a position.

Realistic Job Preview. Part of the job analysis should be to develop a realistic job preview (RJP). The RJP provides the candidate with an accurate, objective understanding of the job. Research indicates that employees who feel

Figure 9–3
Job Analysis

Job Analysis

Job Description

The job title. (Clerk, bookkeeper, technician, etc.)
Supervision. (Who you report to? Who, if anyone, reports to you?)
Location. (Where the job is performed—shop, office, etc.)
Tasks, duties, activities, etc. (What the person actually does on the job.)
Performance standards. (The level of acceptable performance, e.g., the sale of $100,000 worth of merchandise per year.)
Working conditions. (Specifies any hazards, heat, noise, etc.)
Tools, equipment, materials, etc. (Typewriters, computers, forklifts, etc.)

Job Specifications

Skills and ability. (Type 60 words per minute.)
Credentials. (College degree, teacher certification.)
Training. (Trained to operate XYZ machine.)
Experience. (Having held the same or a similar job for a certain period of time, usually stated in years of experience.)
Personal qualities. (Good judgment, initiative, personality, ambition.)
Physical effort. (Able to lift 50-pound bags.)
Sensory demands. (Specific level of sight, hearing, smell.)

they were given accurate descriptions are more satisfied with the organization, believe the employer stands behind them and is trustworthy, and express a lower desire to change jobs than do those who feel they were not given an accurate job description.[7]

job specifications
Identify the qualifications needed to staff a position.

Based on the job description, the second part of job analysis is to determine job specifications. **Job specifications** *identify the qualifications needed to staff a position*. The job specifications identify the types of people needed. Figure 9–3 provides a list of specifications that may be included as part of the job analysis.

Figure 9–4
Job Description

DEPARTMENT: Plant Engineering

JOB TITLE: Lead Sheet Metal Specialist

JOB DESCRIPTION:

Responsible for the detailed direction, instruction, and leading of sheet metal department personnel in the construction and repair of a wide variety of sheet metal equipment. Also must perform similar related or more complex phases of the work most of the time. Receives verbal or written instructions from foreman as to sequence and type of jobs or special methods to be used. Allocates work to members of the group. Directs the layout, fabrication, assembly, and removal of sheet metal units according to drawings or sketches and generally accepted trade procedures. Obtains material or supplies needed for specific jobs according to standard procedures. Trains new employees, as directed, regarding metalworking procedures and safe working practices. Checks all work performed by the group. Usually makes necessary contacts for the group with supervision or engineering personnel. May report irregularities to higher supervision but has no authority to hire, fire, or discipline other employees.

Job analysis can be performed by an expert in the field, by the manager of the job, by employees who hold the job, or by a combination of these people. The job analyst can observe an employee performing the job, interview the employee about the job, have the employee fill out a job questionnaire, or have employees keep a log of what they actually do. A combination of these methods may also be used.

The *Position Analysis Questionnaire* (PAQ) is popular for job analysis. The PAQ contains 194 questions that require specific answers. The answers serve as the basis for the job description and job specifications. The *Dictionary of Occupational Titles* (DOT), published by the federal government, may also be used. It contains information on over 20,000 jobs. Each job is coded to enable an analyst to describe its "functions." The functions determine the degree of complexity in terms of working with people, data, and things. The DOT information is often adjusted for the specific job and presented in a format appropriate for the organization.

Job analysis is an important part of human resources planning because it serves as a basis for attracting, developing, and retaining employees. For example, if you don't understand the job: How can you select employees to do the job? How can you train them to do the job? How can you evaluate their performance? How do you know how much to pay employees?

Work Application

3. Complete a job analysis for a job you hold or held; write a simple job description and job specifications.
4. Were you given a realistic job preview? Explain.

ATTRACTING EMPLOYEES

After hiring needs have been determined and jobs analyzed, the human resources department generally recruits and line managers select people to fill positions. In this section you will learn about recruiting, the selection process, and how to conduct an interview.

3. State the two parts of attracting employees and the difference between them.

Recruiting

Recruiting *is the process of attracting qualified candidates to apply for job openings.* To fill an opening, possible candidates must first be made aware that the organization is seeking employees. They must then be persuaded to apply for the jobs. Recruiting can be conducted internally and externally; Figure 9–5 lists possible recruiting sources.

recruiting
The process of attracting qualified candidates to apply for job openings.

Internal Recruiting. *Internal recruiting* involves filling job openings with current employees or people they know. Some of the advantages of internal recruiting are: it costs less in many situations; it fosters performance among those who aspire to be promoted; and it helps reduce turnover. In addition, the organization knows the strengths and weaknesses of the employee and the employee is familiar with the organization. One disadvantage of internal recruiting is the "ripple effect." The person promoted must also be replaced. Depending on the level and nature of the job, this may involve substantial shifts in personnel. One organization experienced 545 job movements to fill 195 initial openings. Another disadvantage to internal recruiting is that employees who are not promoted may be dissatisfied, particularly when their new boss is an old peer. In addition, this "inbreeding" can mean that fewer new ideas are generated. Training costs

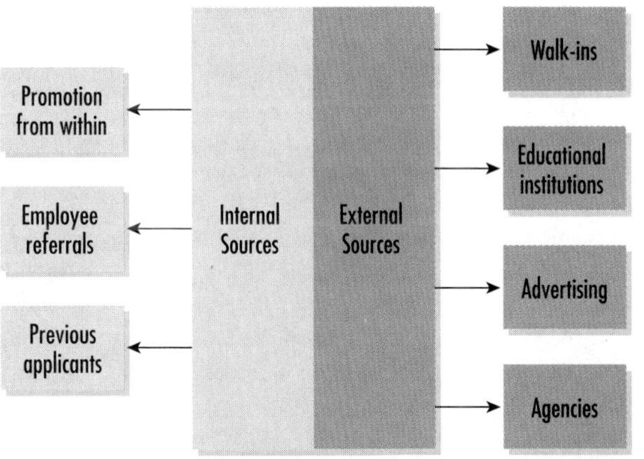

Figure 9–5
Recruiting Sources

tend to increase as well. Promotion from within and employee referral are two common types of internal recruiting. Others include previous employees, and previous applicants who can be contacted.

- *Promotions from Within*. Many organizations post job openings on bulletin boards, in company newsletters, and so on. Current employees may apply or bid for the open positions.
- *Employee Referrals*. When job openings are posted internally, employees may be encouraged to refer friends and relatives for the positions. Generally, employees will refer only good candidates. Studies have shown that referral employees tend to stay on the job for a significant length of time. However, the government has stated that the referral method is not acceptable when current employees are predominantly white or male since it tends to perpetuate the present composition of the work force, resulting in discrimination.

Work Application

5. Identify the recruiting source used to hire you for one or more jobs.

APPLYING THE CONCEPT

AC 9–2 Recruiting Sources

Select the major recruiting source that should be used for each of the five job openings described.

Internal Sources	*External Sources*	
a. promotion from within	c. walk-ins	f. agencies
b. employee referrals	d. educational institutions	g. executive recruiters
	e. advertising	

____ **11.** One of your workers was hurt on the job and will be out for one month. The person must be replaced.

____ **12.** One of the first-line supervisors is retiring in two months.

____ **13.** You need an engineer who has very specific qualifications. There are very few people who can do the job.

____ **14.** Your sales manager likes to hire young people without experience in order to train them to sell using a unique approach.

____ **15.** Your maintenance department needs a person to perform routine cleaning services.

External Recruiting. Some of the major advantages of external recruiting include more potential candidates; hiring experienced workers reduces training costs; new ideas and insights are brought in; and changes are often accomplished more easily. Some of the major disadvantages of external recruiting include: the high cost; the possibility of lowered morale of present employees; the time it takes a new person to adjust to the organization; and the risk of not knowing the candidate's true ability, including potential to fit in. The following are external recruiting sources:

- *Walk-Ins*. Without actually being recruited, good candidates may come to the organization "cold" and ask for a job. According to some estimates, one in three people gets a job by walking in and asking. However, professionals tend to send a résumé and cover letter asking for an interview.
- *Educational Institutions*. Recruiting takes place at high schools, vocational/technical schools, and colleges. Many schools offer career planning and placement services to aid the students and potential employers. Educational institutions are good places to recruit people without prior experience.
- *Advertising*. It is important to use the appropriate source to reach qualified candidates. A simple help wanted sign in the window is an advertisement. A newspaper is good for most positions, but professional and trade magazines may be more suitable for specific professional recruiting.

- *Agencies*. There are three major types of agencies: (1) *Temporary agencies*, like Kelly Services, provide part- or full-time help for limited periods. They are useful for replacing employees who will be out for a short period of time or for supplementing the regular work force during busy periods. (2) *Public agencies* are nationwide state employment services. They generally provide job candidates to employers at no, or very low, direct cost. (3) *Private employment agencies* are privately owned and charge a fee for their service. Agencies are good for recruiting people with prior experience. *Executive recruiters* are a type of private agency often referred to as "headhunters." They specialize in recruiting managers and/or those with specific high-level technical skills, like engineers and computer experts. They tend to charge the employer a large fee.

The Selection Process

Selection *is the process of choosing the most qualified applicant recruited for a job.* No set sequence is universally followed. Organizations may even use different selection methods for different jobs. Selection is important because bad hiring decisions can hang around to haunt the organization.[8] Employee turnover costs thousands of dollars per employee leaving. You will now learn about the application form, screening interviews, testing, background and reference checks, interviewing, and hiring in this section.

selection
The process of choosing the most qualified applicant recruited for a job.

Application Form. As part of the selection process, the recruited applicants will be asked to complete an application. Organizations may use different application forms for different jobs. For professional jobs, a résumé may replace the application form. The application form typically includes the following information:

Personal data: name, address, telephone number.
Education: schools attended with dates, majors, and certificates or degrees earned.
Experience: previous employers, job titles, duties, dates employed, salary, supervisor, reason for leaving, and so on.
Skills: machines operated, certifications, and so forth.
References: the names of (usually) three people who can vouch for the applicant in some way, with their addresses, telephone numbers, occupations, and relationship to the candidate.

With advances in technology, organizations including the White House, Disneyland, and Ford now use computers to read/scan application forms and résumés.[9] Before sending in a résumé, you may want to check to see if the organization uses computers. If it does, the human resources department can give you specific instructions to make sure your résumé information is scanned accurately.

The selection process can be thought of as a series of obstacles that the applicant must overcome to be offered the job. The first obstacle is typically the application. The data the applicant provides are compared to the job specifications. If they match, the applicant may progress to the next obstacle; if they do not, that candidate is out of the selection process.

Screening Interview. Specialists in the human resources department often conduct screening interviews to select the top candidates who will continue on in the selection process. This especially helps save line managers' time when there are large numbers of job applicants. Some organizations are using computers to conduct screening interviews. For example, at Great Western Bank job candidates for a teller job sit before a computer, with a microphone, which asks them to make change, respond to tough customers, and to sell products that customers don't ask for. In addition, the computer gives applicants a realistic job preview by showing tellers talking about their jobs on the screen. Applicants who do well are immediately brought into the manager's office for an interview.[10]

Testing. Tests can be used to predict job success when they meet EEO guidelines for validity (people who score high on the test do well on the job while those who score low do not do well on the job) and reliability (if people take the same test on different days, they will get approximately the same score each time). Illegal tests can result in lawsuits. Some of the major types of tests include:

1. *Achievement* tests, which measure actual performance. Examples of achievement tests include a typing test, a programming test, and a driving test. People who do well on this type of test should do well on the job. A recent survey revealed that about one-third of companies now test for basic reading and math skills.[11]
2. *Aptitude* tests, which measure potential to do the job. Intelligence quotient (IQ) tests are aptitude tests. The Dallas Cowboys and other National Football League teams use aptitude tests as predictors of a player's ability to learn the plays and to be successful in the league.
3. *Personality* tests, which measure or describe personality dimensions such as emotional maturity, self-confidence, objectivity, and subjectivity. Examples include the Rorschach inkblot tests and the Edwards Personal Preference test.
4. *Interest* tests, which measure interest in various kinds of activities. It is assumed that people perform best at what interests them. Examples include the Strong-Campbell Interest Inventory and the Kuder Preference Record. Tests available on computers score the results immediately.
5. *Physical exams*, which measure ability to perform the job. Physical exams may include drug and AIDS testing. When using physical exams, the organization must be careful not to discriminate against disabled candidates. In fact, the Americans with Disabilities Act states that physical exams can only be given after an offer for employement has been made.

assessment centers
Places where job applicants undergo a series of tests, interviews, and simulated experiences to determine their managerial potential.

Internal and external candidates for management positions are tested through assessment centers. **Assessment centers** *are places where job applicants undergo a series of tests, interviews, and simulated experiences to determine their managerial potential.* Candidates who perform well are selected for management positions.

Background and Reference Checks. Organizations should prevent poor hiring decisions and negligent hiring liability by instituting a reference-checking system to verify the information on a candidate's application form and/or résumé.[12] It has been estimated that up to one-half of all applications contain false or erroneous material. For example, people have stated that they have earned college degrees when they have never even attended college.

Organizations use references on the assumption that past performance is a good predictor of future success. Unfortunately, due to privacy legislation, many organizations will only verify employment and give the job title, dates of employment, and last salary, but will not make statements concerning the candidate's performance. People are more apt to give more accurate references orally, rather than in writing. Calling for a reference might get you the information you want.

Interviewing. The interview is the most heavily weighted selection criterion. A human resources manager for Xerox told the author that Xerox gives the résumé about 30 percent and the interview about 60 percent of the weight in the selection process. The interview is usually the final hurdle in the selection process. After the human resources department has reviewed the application, conducted a screening interview(s), tested, and checked references, the top candidates are sent to the line managers for interviewing. The interview gives both the applicant and the employer a chance to determine whether there is a match that should end in employment. The interview gives the candidate a chance to learn about the job and organization. The interview also gives a manager a chance to learn things about candidates that can't be obtained from an application, test, or references, such as the candidate's ability to communicate, personality, appearance, and motivation. Because job interviewing is so important, you will learn how to prepare for and conduct a job interview in this section.

Hiring. After obtaining information using the selection methods discussed, the manager compares the candidates without bias, and decides who is best suited for the job. Diversity should be considered when selecting a candidate. The candidate is contacted and offered the job. If the candidate does not accept the job, or accepts but leaves after a short period of time, the next best candidate is offered the job. If a qualified candidate is not available, the organization should try to determine why. Is the salary too low? Are the expectations too high? The organization may need to begin recruiting again or obtain the services of an agency or executive recruiter.

Scitor has a growth strategy; therefore, it is continually attracting employees. However, due to its reputation as an excellent company to work for, which was developed through its human resources practices, it does not have problems attracting well-qualified employees.

Work Application

6. Identify the selection methods used for a job you were offered. List each method from the selection process and state whether it was used or not. If a test was used, be sure to specify the type of test.

Selection Interviewing

Few managers are trained in the job interview process.[13] After completing this chapter, you will know how to conduct a job interview and you can develop this skill in Skill-Building Exercise 9–1.

4. Describe the difference between the group and panel interview and hypothetical and probing questions.

Types of Interviews and Questions. Figure 9–6 lists the types of interviews and questions.

Interviews. There are two classifications of interviews based on the structure and people involved. Three basic types of interviews are based on structure: (1) The *structured* interview has a list of prepared questions to ask all candidates. (2) The *unstructured* interview has no preplanned questions or sequence of topics. (3) The *semistructured* interview has a list of questions to ask, but the interviewer also asks unplanned questions. The semistructured interview is generally

Figure 9–6
Types of Interviews and Questions

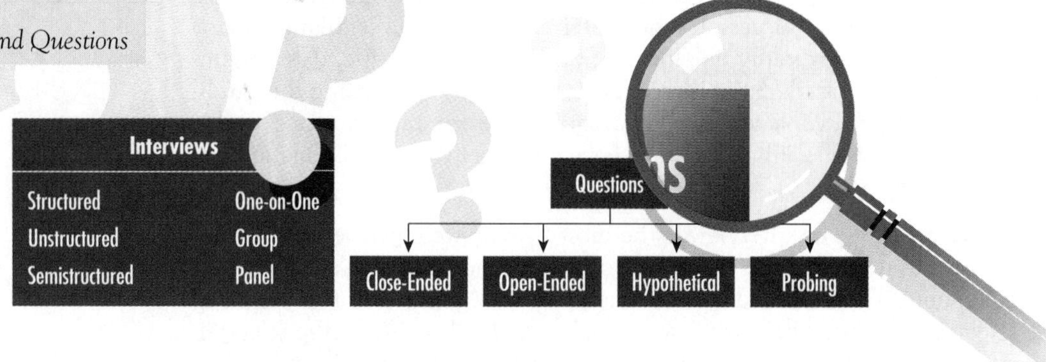

preferred because, although it helps ensure against discrimination in that the interviewer has a list of prepared questions to ask all candidates, it also allows the interviewer to ask each candidate questions relating to his or her own situation. The interviewer departs from the structure when appropriate. At the same time, using a standard set of questions makes it easier to compare candidates. Structured questions are considered more legally valid for selection purposes. The amount of structure you should use depends on your experience. The less experience you have, the more structure you need. As you develop your interviewing skills, you can be less structured. However, structured interviews generally are less susceptible to illegal discrimination.

The three classifications of interviews are based on the people involved: (1) The *one-on-one* interview is the most common. (2) The *group* interview involves several candidates being interviewed at the same time. (3) The *panel* interview involves one candidate being interviewed by more than one interviewer. The group interview allows the interviewer to compare candidates head-on, and the panel interview allows a group to work together in selecting a candidate, which helps reduce bias.

Questions. The questions you ask give you control over the interview; they allow you to get the information you need to make your decision. Questions should not just involve restating what is on the application form; use them to verify and expand on the information. All questions should have a purpose and be job-related, and ask all candidates the same set of questions. You may use four types of questions during an interview: (1) The *closed-ended* question requires a limited response, often a yes or no answer, and is appropriate for dealing with fixed aspects of the job. "Is there anything that will interfere with your working from 3:00 to 11:00?" "Do you have a class one license and can you produce it if hired?" (2) The *open-ended* question requires an unlimited response and is appropriate for determining abilities and motivation. "Why do you want to be a computer programmer for our company?" "What do you see as a major strength you can bring to our company?" (3) The *hypothetical* question requires the candidate to describe what he or she would do and say in a given situation; it is appropriate in assessing capabilities. "What would the problem be if the machine made an XYZ sound?" The Great Western Bank computer interview is based on hypothetical questions.[14] (4) The *probing* question requires a clarification response and is appropriate for improving understanding. The probing question is not planned. It is used to clarify the candidate's response to an open-

Work Application

7. What types of job interviews have you experienced?
8. Identify the types of questions you were asked during a job interview. Write down some of the questions, identifying their types.

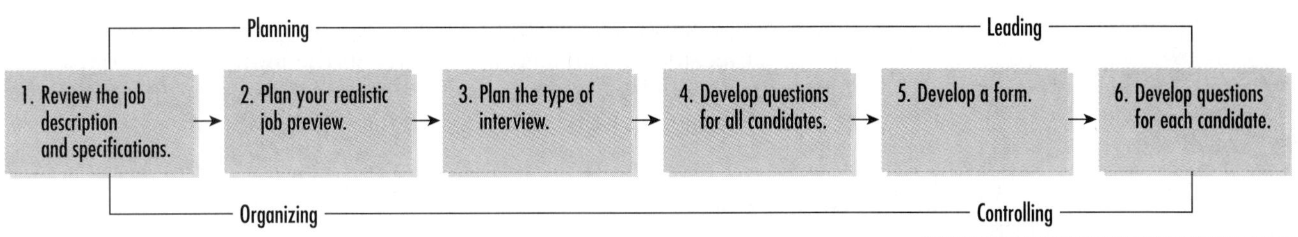

Model 9–1
Interview Preparation Steps

ended or hypothetical question. "What do you mean by 'it was tough'?" "What was the dollar increase in sales you achieved?"

Preparing for the Interview. Completing the preparation steps will help you improve your interviewing skills. Model 9–1 lists the steps.[15]

step 1. **Review the Job Description and Specifications.** You cannot effectively match the candidate to the job if you do not thoroughly understand the job. Read and become familiar with the job description and job specifications. If they are outdated, or do not exist, conduct a job analysis.

step 2. **Plan Your Realistic Job Preview.** Candidates should understand what the job is and what they are expected to do. They should know the good and bad points of the job. Plan how you will present the RJP using the job description. It often helps to give candidates a tour of the work area.

step 3. **Plan the Type of Interview.** What level of structure will you use? Will the interview be one-on-one, group, and/or panel? The interview should take place in a private, quiet place, without interruptions. It may be appropriate to begin the interview in an office and then tour the facilities while asking questions. Plan when the tour will take place and what questions will be asked. Take your form if you intend to ask several questions.

step 4. **Develop Questions for All Candidates.** Your questions should be job-related, nondiscriminatory, and asked of all candidates. Use the job description and specifications to develop questions that relate to each job task and responsibility. Use a mixture of closed-ended, open-ended, and hypothetical questions. Don't be concerned about the order of questions; just write them out at this point.

step 5. **Develop a Form.** Once you have completed your list of questions, determine the sequence. Start with the easy questions. One approach starts with closed-ended questions, moves on to open-ended questions, and then to hypothetical questions; use probing questions as needed. Another approach structures the interview around the job description and specifications; explain each and then ask questions relating to each responsibility.

Write out the questions in sequence, leaving space for checking off closed-ended responses, and room to make notes on the responses to open-ended and hypothetical questions, and for follow-up questions.[16] Add information gained from probing questions where appropriate. You are guided through the interview as you record the candidate's responses on the form. Make a copy of the form for each candidate, and a few extras for future use when filling the same job, or as a reference when developing forms for other jobs.

step 6.

Develop Questions for Each Candidate. Review each candidate's application/résumé. You will most likely want to verify or clarify some of the information given during the interview. Examples include the following: "I noticed that you did not list any employment during 1985; were you unemployed?" "On the application you stated you had computer training; what computer were you trained to operate?" Be sure the individual questions are not discriminatory; for example, do not ask only women whether they can lift 50 pounds; ask all candidates, men or women, this question.

You can either add the individual questions to the standard form, writing them in where appropriate, or you can add a list at the end of the form.

Conducting the Interview. Following the steps listed will help you do a better job of interviewing candidates. Model 9–2 lists the interviewing steps.[17]

step 1.

Open the Interview. Develop a rapport. Put the candidate at ease by talking about some topic not related to the job. You may add a little humor when appropriate. According to Adia Personnel Services, 63 percent of the personnel executives surveyed said that humor is appropriate during job interviews.[18] But be sure the humor is not sexist, racial, offensive, or discriminatory in any way. Maintain eye contact in a way that is comfortable for you and the candidate.

step 2.

Give Your Realistic Job Preview. Be sure the candidate understands the job requirements. Answer any questions the candidate has about the job and the organization. If the job is not what the candidate expected, or wants to do, allow the candidate to disqualify himself or herself and close the interview at that point.

step 3.

Ask Your Questions. Steps 2 and 3 can be combined if you like. To get the most out of a job interview, you must take notes on responses to your questions.[19] Tell the candidate that you have prepared a list of questions you will be asking, and that you plan to take notes.

During the interview, the candidate should do most of the talking. Give the

Model 9–2
Interviewing Steps

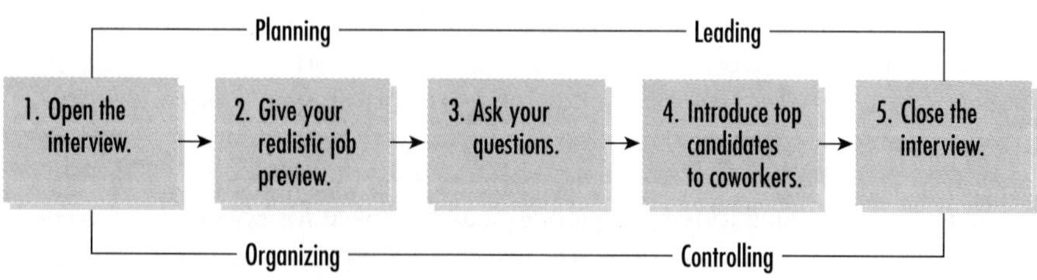
Planning
Leading
1. Open the interview.
2. Give your realistic job preview.
3. Ask your questions.
4. Introduce top candidates to coworkers.
5. Close the interview.
Organizing
Controlling

candidate a chance to think and respond. If the candidate did not give you all the information you wanted, ask an unplanned probing question. However, if it is obvious that the candidate does not want to answer the question, don't force it. Go on to the next question or close the interview. End with a closing question such as, "I'm finished with my questions. Is there anything else you want to tell me about, or ask me?"

step 4.

Introduce Top Candidates to Coworkers. Introduce top candidates to people with whom they will be working to get a sense of their interpersonal skills and overall attitude.[20] Introductions can also give you a sense if the person is a team player.[21] The more formal panel interview may also be used.

step 5.

Close the Interview. Do not lead candidates on. Be honest without making a decision during the interview. Thank candidates for their time, and tell them what the next step in the interview process is, if any. Tell candidates when you will contact them. For example, say, "Thank you for coming in for this interview. I will be interviewing over the next two days and will call you with my decision by Friday of this week." After the interview, be sure to jot down general impressions not covered by specific questions.

Work Application

9. Using Model 9–2, identify the steps used or not used when you were interviewed for a job.

Selecting the Candidate. After all interviews are completed, compare each candidate's qualifications to the job specifications to determine who would be best for the job. Be sure to get the coworkers' impressions of each candidate. If you use a panel interview, the group can make the selection decision. You may use the Kepner-Tregoe decision-making analysis (Chapter 4). Follow the guidelines presented in hiring, the last step in the selection process.

Problems to Avoid. Avoid the following problems during the selection process:

- *Rushing*. Try not to be pressured into hiring "any" candidate. Find the best person available.
- *Stereotyping*. Don't prejudge or leap to conclusions. Do a thorough review of the job description and job specifications. Match the candidate to the job based on analysis rather than instinct.
- *"Like Me" Syndrome*. Don't look for a candidate who is your clone. People who are not like you may do an excellent job. Remember the benefits of diversity.
- *Halo and Horn Effect*. Do not judge a candidate on the basis of one or two favorable or unfavorable characteristics. Make the selection on the basis of the total qualifications of all candidates.
- *Premature Selection*. Don't make your selection based on the application/résumé or after interviewing a candidate who impressed you. Do not compare candidates after each interview. The order in which you interview applicants can influence you. Be open-minded during all interviews and make a choice only after you have finished all interviews. Compare each candidate on each job specification.

DEVELOPING EMPLOYEES

After employees have been recruited and selected (attracting), they must be oriented, trained, and evaluated (developing).

5. Discuss the difference between orientation and training and development of employees.

orientation
The process of introducing new employees to the organization and their jobs.

Orientation

Orientation *is the process of introducing new employees to the organization and their jobs*. Orientation is learning the ropes or the rules of the game. Some of the benefits of effective orientation include reduced time to get the employee to perform to standard levels, reduced anxiety about doing a good job and getting along with peers, and accurate perceptions of what is expected of the employee. Employees tend to stay on the job longer (reduced turnover) and have improved attitudes and performance when they go through orientation.

Orientation Programs. The time it takes and the content of orientation vary greatly from organization to organization. At Disney World, all new employees go through an 8-hour orientation followed by 40 hours of apprenticeship training. The purpose is to familiarize them with Disney's history, tradition, policies, expectations, and ways of doing things. Starbucks Coffee encourages employees to take pride in their work and to develop a sense of purpose, commitment, and enthusiasm for their job and the company.[22]

Although orientation programs vary in formality and content, five important elements should be included; they are listed in Figure 9–7. Customize your orientation program to meet your new employee's and department's needs. Be familiar with the orientation given by the human resources department and coordinate with it. To avoid information overload, it may be best to spread the orientation over several days. Experiment and find out what works best.

Organization and department functions.
Job tasks and responsibilities.
Standing plans.
Tours.
Introduction to coworkers.

Figure 9–7
Orientation Programs

Organization and Department Functions. Talk about the organization's history, culture, and products or services. Explain what your department does and how the job relates to the department. Describe the interrelationship between your department and the other departments. State the departmental objectives and values. Develop pride in working for the organization.

Job Tasks and Responsibilities. Be sure the new employee's work station is clean and well supplied before his or her arrival. Give the employee a copy of the job description, if one exists, and review the tasks and responsibilities together. Describe any training that will be given and tell the employee when it will take place. Explain what the employee's authority is, what assistance is available, and how the employee can get help. Explain where and how to get any needed supplies, materials, tools, and so on. Clearly explain job standards; tell the employee how long it should take to reach standard levels of performance. Go over the work hours, pay rates, payment system, and benefits. Explain any overtime needs and extra duty assignments.

Standing Plans. Explain the policies, procedures, and rules of the organization and your department. Some areas to cover include break and lunch times; safety procedures and requirements; rules about eating, drinking, smoking, chewing gum, and so on; the use of time clocks or time sheets; and policies on absence and lateness.

Tours. The new employee should be given a tour of the organization and the department. Areas you should consider touring include locations of supplies, tools, equipment, files, and so forth; work stations of coworkers; restrooms and locker rooms; water fountain; lounges and cafeterias; departments the employee will work with; and location of safety equipment (such as the fire alarm, fire extinguisher, and first aid kit).

Introduction to Coworkers. Coworkers should be introduced when the new employee tours their work stations. Be enthusiastic when introducing the new employee; make him or her feel important and wanted. Say something like, "This is Surgeo Wagner; he is highly qualified and we're glad to have him as a member of our team." It is difficult to remember several people's names all at once. Reintroduce new employees on several occasions until they know everyone by name.

Work Application

10. Recall an orientation you experienced. Which parts of an orientation program did it include and exclude? Describe the entire orientation.

Training and Development

Employees will have to be taught how to perform a new job. Orientation and training may, and often do, take place simultaneously. **Training** *is the process of acquiring the skills necessary to perform a job.* Training typically develops the technical skills of nonmanagers. **Development** *is the ongoing education to improve skills for present and future jobs.* Development is less technical and aimed at developing human, communication, conceptual, and decision-making skills in managerial and professional employees.

training
The process of acquiring the skills necessary to perform a job.

development
The ongoing education to improve skills for present and future jobs.

Training and development are a good investment because they benefit individuals, their organizations, and the economy as a whole.[23] Employee training increases product quality.[24] IBM has reported spending more than $750 million a year on corporate schooling, which exceeded the entire budget of Harvard University. At General Motors' truck plant, assembly-line employees received 400 to 500 hours of training. Skilled workers received 1,000 hours of training in about six months. Motorola, Texas Instruments, and Xerox invest heavily in training and development. However, overall, American organizations underinvest in employee development. U.S. organizations spend around $30 billion annually on formal training and development, but only 11 percent of workers receive new employee training and only 10 percent receive upgrading training. Less than 1 percent of American organizations provide formal, job-related training.[25]

Off- and On-the-Job Training. Employees can learn to perform their jobs off and/or on the job.

Off-the-Job Training. As the name implies, this training is conducted away from the work site, often in some sort of classroom setting. A common method is vestibule training. **Vestibule training** *develops skills in a simulated setting.* It is used when teaching job skills at the work site is impractical. For example, many large retail stores have training rooms where new employees learn how to run the cash registers and other equipment. Once they achieve the desired level of performance, they work with the same type of equipment in the store. The training is usually conducted by a training specialist. Most organizations conduct development programs off-the-job.

vestibule training
Develops skills in a simulated setting.

On-the-Job Training (OJT). This training is done at the work site with the resources the employee uses to perform the job. The manager, or an employee

6. List the steps in job instructional training.

Model 9–3
Job Instructional Training Steps

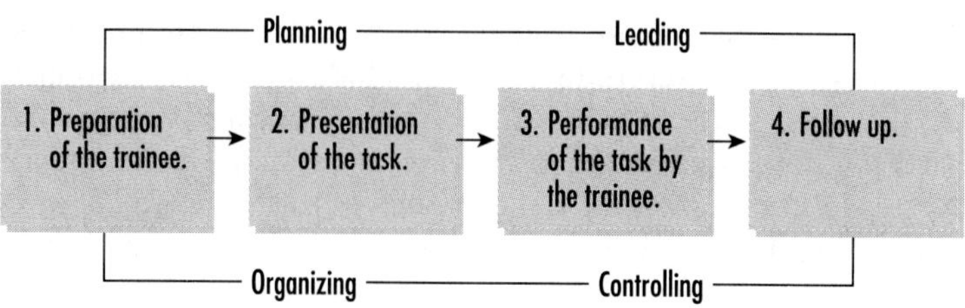

selected by the manager, usually conducts the training. Because of its proven record of success, job instructional training (JIT) is a popular method worldwide.

Job Instructional Training. JIT has four steps, presented in Model 9–3 and described here. Remember that things we know well seem very simple to use, but they are usually difficult for the new trainee.

step 1. **Preparation of the Trainee.** Put the trainee at ease as you create interest in the job and encourage questions. Explain the quantity and quality requirements and their importance.

step 2. **Presentation of the Task.** Perform the task yourself at a slow pace, explaining each step several times. Once the trainee seems to have the steps memorized, have him or her explain each step as you perform the job at a slow pace. For complex tasks with multiple steps, write them out and give a copy to the trainee.

Work Application

11. Identify which steps of JIT your trainer used to train you for a present or past job. Was the training on or off the job?

step 3. **Performance of the Task by the Trainee.** Have the trainee perform the task at a slow pace, explaining each step. Correct any errors and be willing to help the trainee perform any difficult steps. Continue until the employee can proficiently perform the task.

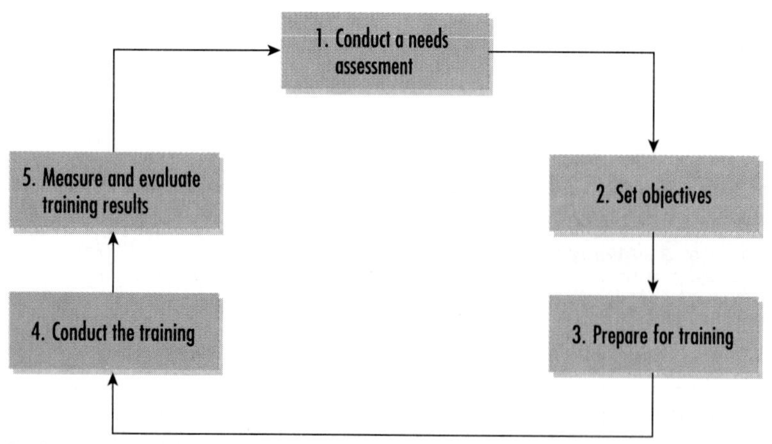

Figure 9–8
The Training Cycle

step 4. **Follow Up.** Tell the trainee who to go to for help with any questions or problems. Gradually leave the trainee alone. Begin by checking quality and quantity frequently, then decrease the amount of checking based on the trainee's skill level. Watch the trainee perform the task and be sure to correct any errors or faulty work procedures before they become a habit. As you follow up be sure to be patient and encouraging. At first, praise the employee's good effort, then praise his or her good performance as skills develop.

The Training Cycle. Following the steps in the training cycle will help ensure that training is done in a systematic way. A discussion of the five steps of the systems training cycle, presented in Figure 9–8, follows.

step 1. **Conduct a Needs Assessment.** Before you begin training, you must determine your employees' training needs. Common needs assessment methods include observation, interviews, and questionnaires. These needs will differ depending on whether you are training new or existing employees. To train inexperienced workers, you must review the job description and specifications and identify the specific skills a new employee will need. For existing employees, you need to compare actual performance to standards and, when training is the reason for poor performance, teach employees to meet the standards. Then proceed to the next step in the training cycle. An assessment center may be used to determine training needs.

step 2. **Set Objectives.** Any training program should have well-defined, performance-based objectives. As with all plans, you should begin by determining the end result you want to achieve. The criteria for your objectives should meet the criteria are discussed in Chapter 5. Three examples of training objectives that meet the criteria are: (1) Participants will type a minimum of 40 words per minute by the end of the one-week training period. (2) Assemblers will be able to assemble 10 sets per hour by the end of the one-day training period. (3) Customer service representatives will serve an average of 20 customers per hour by the end of the one-month training period.

step 3. **Prepare for Training.** Before conducting a training session you should have written plans and all the necessary materials ready. If you ever had an instructor come to class obviously unprepared, you know why preparation before training is necessary for success. As with all plans, training plans should answer the who, what, when, where, and how questions. As many as 30 hours of preparation are needed for one hour of training.

An important part of preparation is selecting the training method. You have already learned about JIT. Figure 9–9 lists other training methods. Whatever method you develop, break the task down into steps. What we do as part of our routine seems simple to us. But it may seem very complicated to the new employee. Write out each step and go through the steps to make sure they work.

step 4. **Conduct the Training.** Regardless of the training method used, follow your plan. Be sure to have your written plan with you, as well as any other materials needed. The present trend is to have line managers, rather than training specialists, train their employees, or at least take part in the training of, their own employees.[26]

step 5. **Measure and Evaluate Training Results.** One of the most important changes in the training field is the linkage between training outcomes and business results.[27] Top managers are pressuring training specialists to prove the value of their training by determining how it affects the bottom line.[28] During training and at the end of the program, you should measure and evaluate the results to determine whether or not the objectives were achieved. If they were, the training is over; if they were not, you either have to continue the training until objectives are met or take employees off the job if

Method	Definition	Skill Developed
Written material	Manuals, books, and so on.	Technical
Lecture	Spoken word; class lectures.	Technical
Video	Television; class videos.	Technical
Question and answer	After another method(s) above, the trainer and/or trainees can ask questions about what they read, heard, and/or watched.	Technical
Discussion	A topic can be presented and discussed.	Technical
Programmed learning	A computer or book is used to present material, followed by a question or problem. The trainee is asked to select a response, then is given feedback on his or her response. Based on the material presented, PL may possibly help develop human and conceptual skills.	Technical
Demonstration	The trainer shows the trainee how to perform the task. This is step 2 of job instructional training. Demonstrations can also be used as part of developing human and decision-making skills.	Technical
Job rotation	Employees learn to perform multiple jobs.	Technical and conceptual
Projects	Special assignments, such as developing a new product or doing a special report, are given. Projects that require working with people and other departments may also develop human and conceptual skills.	Technical
Role-playing	Trainees act out a possible job situation, such has handling a customer complaint, to develop skill at handling similar situations on the job.	Human and communication
Behavior modeling	It involves four steps: (1) The trainees observe how to perform the task correctly. This may be done via a live demonstration or a videotape. (2) Trainees role-play a situation using the observed skills. (3) Trainees receive feedback on how well they performed. (4) Trainees develop plans for using the new skills on the job. Behavior modeling is a feature of this book.	Human and communication
Cases	The trainee is presented with a situation and asked to diagnose and solve the problems involved. The trainee is usually asked to answer questions. There is a case at the end of each chapter in this book.	Conceptual and decision-making
In-basket exercise	The trainee is given actual or simulated letters, memos, reports, telephone messages, and so forth that would typically be found in the in-basket of a person holding the job for which training is given. Trainees are asked what, if any, action they would take for each item, and to assign priorities to the material.	Conceptual and decision-making
Management games	The trainees manage a simulated company. They make decisions in small teams and get the results back, usually on a quarterly basis, over a period of several game "years." Teams are in an "industry" with several competitors.	Conceptual and decision-making

Figure 9–9
Training Methods

Interactive video	Trainees sit at a computer and respond as directed. The job interview at Great Western Bank uses interactive video. The bank could use the same technology to train tellers how to handle complaints, as well as testing them on it during the job interview.	Any of the three skills

Figure 9–9
Continued

they cannot meet the standards. Revise and improve your written plans for future use.

Training Methods. Figure 9–9 lists some of the other training methods available, many of which can be used as part of JIT. The third column, skill development, lists the primary skill developed. However, some of the technical methods can be combined. Technical skill also includes acquiring knowledge that can be tested.

When selecting a training method, keep the following statistics in mind: People learn 10 percent of what they read, 20 percent of what they hear, and 30 percent of what they see. People learn 50 percent of what they see and hear. They learn 70 percent of what they talk over with others. People learn 80 percent of what they use and do in real life. They learn 95 percent of what they teach someone else.

Work Application

12. Explain the training methods used to teach you how to perform your present or past job.

Managerial Use of Training Methods. Managers commonly use reading, lecture, video, question-and-answer, discussion, programmed learning, demonstration, job rotation, and projects to train employees how to perform their jobs. Managers do not commonly use role-playing and behavior modeling. However, they are appropriate for managers who need to train employees how to handle human relations such as customer complaints. The manager can also teach human skills to employees by example.

Management games, in-basket exercises, and cases are commonly used to train managers, not employees. Therefore, managers may be trained with these methods, but will probably not use these training methods with their employees.

APPLYING THE CONCEPT

AC 9–3 Training Methods

Select the most appropriate training method in the following situations.

a. written material
b. lecture
c. video
d. question-and-answer
e. discussion
f. programmed learning
g. demonstration
h. job rotation
i. projects
j. role-playing
k. behavior modeling
l. management games
m. in-basket exercise
n. cases

____ **16.** You have a large department with a high turnover rate. Employees must learn several rules and regulations in order to perform their jobs.

____ **17.** You occasionally have new employees whom you must teach to handle the typical daily problems they will face on the job.

____ **18.** Your boss has requested a special report.

____ **19.** You want to be sure that employees can cover for each other if one or more of them are absent.

____ **20.** You need to teach employees how to handle customer complaints.

Performance Appraisal

performance appraisal
The ongoing process of evaluating employee performance.

After you have hired and trained employees, you must evaluate how well they perform their jobs. **Performance appraisal** *is the ongoing process of evaluating em-*

ployee performance. Managers should use performance appraisals to develop employee job performance. Most employees want their boss to give them constructive feedback about their performance. Feedback allows employees to determine their progress, helps them correct deficiencies, and helps them find ways to improve their job performance.[29]

Evaluating performance is both an organizing (staffing) and controlling technique. You will learn how to conduct a performance appraisal in Chapter 16.

Scitor has a formal orientation program. Employees are well trained to perform their present jobs, and the company is also committed to developing employees for future jobs as the industry changes quickly and the firm continues to grow. With its growth strategy, training is an ongoing necessity to achieve organizational objectives. Performance appraisal is very important at Scitor because it serves as the basis for making decisions on who gets promoted. Promotions continually become available with growth.

RETAINING EMPLOYEES

After incurring the great cost of attracting and developing employees, an organization must have human resources systems to retain employees. Employee turnover can reduce overall efficiency and profitability. According to the U.S. Department of Labor, it costs about 33 percent of a new recruit's annual salary to be replaced.[30] If compensation is not competitive, the work environment is not healthy and safe, and labor relations are not good, employees tend to leave for organizations that provide these retention methods. Recall that Scitor's human resources systems are designed to retain employees; the company has a turnover rate of 2.1 percent, versus the industry average of 16.5 percent. In this section you will learn about compensation, health and safety, labor relations, and termination and outplacement.

7. State the major components of compensation.

compensation
The total cost of pay and benefits to employees.

Compensation

Compensation *is the total cost of pay and benefits to employees*. Compensation affects both attracting and retaining employees. For example, when Salomon Brothers changed its compensation system, there was a large increase in turnover. The company was forced to make concessions to reduce the turnover.[31] An important overall compensation decision is pay level. *Pay level* refers to the choice to be a high-, medium-, or low-paying organization. Scitor is a high-paying company which results in its attracting and retaining excellent employees. Low-paying firms may save money on pay, but the savings can be lost to the high cost of turnover. We will cover pay and benefits separately.

Pay Systems. There are three general pay methods, and organizations can use all three. (1) *Wages* are paid on an hourly basis. (2) *Salary* is based on time—week, month, or year. A salary is paid regardless of the number of hours worked. (3) *Incentives* are pay for performance. Incentives include piece rate (pay based on production), commissions (pay based on sales), merit raises (the more productive workers get paid more), and bonuses. Two common types of bonus include stating a specific reward for reaching an objective and profit-sharing in which employees get a part of the profits. The use of bonuses is on the increase.[32] Organizations including Hewlett Packard, Polaroid, and West Bend are creating innovative incentive pay systems.[33] The trend is toward replacing wages with salaries and offering incentives to all employees.[34]

8. Describe the difference between the use of job analysis and job evaluation.

Pay Determination. A difficult decision is how much to pay each employee. An external approach is to find out what other organizations pay for the same or similar jobs and set the pay based on the pay level decision. An internal approach is to use job evaluation. **Job evaluation** *is the process of determining the worth of each job relative to the other jobs within the organization.* Organizations commonly group jobs into pay grades. The higher the worth/grade of the job, the higher the pay. Many managers are highly paid. Both approaches are often used together.

job evaluation
The process of determining the worth of each job relative to the other jobs within the organization.

Despite the Equal Pay Act, requiring equal pay for everyone doing the same job, women's average hourly earnings are 70 percent of men's. Over the 30 years since the law was passed, the wage gap has closed by a dime.[35] A related controversial issue important to job evaluation is comparable worth. *Comparable worth* means that jobs that are distinctly different but with similar levels of ability, responsibility, skills, working conditions, etc., that make jobs of equal value, should have the same pay scale.

Benefits. *Benefits* are the part of compensation paid for by the employer that benefit employees, and often their families. Benefits are commonly noncash and are not merit-based. Legally required benefits include *workers' compensation* to cover job-related injuries, *unemployment compensation* for when employees are laid off or terminated, and *Social Security* for retirement. Your employer matches the amount the government takes out of your pay for Social Security. Commonly offered optional benefits include health insurance; paid sick days, holidays, and vacations; and pension plans. Optional benefits can be paid in full by employers, split between employee and employer, or paid completely by the employee. Other benefits less commonly offered include dental and life insurance, counseling programs, membership to fitness centers, membership in credit unions, and tuition reimbursement.

The benefits percentage of compensation has been increasing over the years, primarily due to the high cost of health insurance. The percentage varies with the level of job from one- to two-thirds of compensation, but it has been estimated that the average employee receives slightly over 40 percent of compensation from benefits.[36] For example, if an employee's pay is $25,000 and his or her benefits cost $10,000, the compensation costs the organization $35,000. Scitor is very generous with benefits; in the beginning of this chapter, two paragraphs listed the optional benefits offered by Scitor to employees.

Work Application

13. Identify the compensation package offered by your present or past employer.

Health and Safety

The Occupational Safety and Health Act (OSHA) of 1970 requires employers to pursue workplace safety. Employers must meet OSHA safety standards, maintain records of injuries and deaths due to workplace accidents, and submit to onsite inspections. The human resources department commonly has responsibility for ensuring the health and safety of employees. It works closely with the other departments and often conducts new employee and ongoing training sessions, as well as maintaining health and safety records. As a manager, you should know the safety rules, be sure your employees know them, and enforce them to prevent accidents.

9. Explain why most organizations do not have labor relations.

labor relations
The interactions between management and unionized employees.

Labor Relations

Labor relations *are the interactions between management and unionized employees.* Labor relations are also called union–management relations and industrial relations. There are many more organizations without unions than there are with unions. Therefore, not all organizations have labor relations as part of their human resources systems. The *union* is an organization that represents employees in collective bargaining with the employer. Unions are also a source of recruitment. The National Labor Relations Act (also known as the Wagner Act, after its sponsor) established the National Labor Relations Board (NLRB) which oversees labor relations by conducting unionization elections, hears unfair labor practice complaints, and issues injunctions against offending employers.

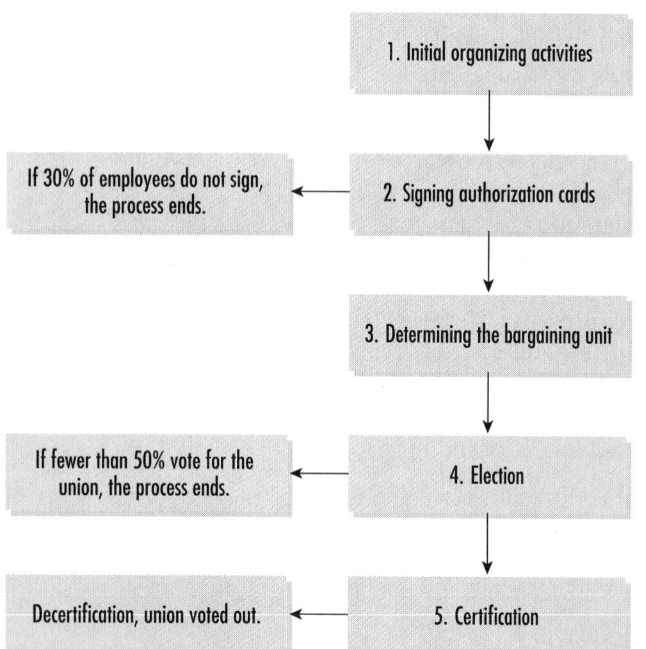

Figure 9–10
The Union-Organizing Process

The Union-Organizing Process. There are typically five stages in forming a union, which Figure 9–10 lists.

Initial Organizing Activities. The process may begin with employees contacting a union and asking its representatives to come and help them organize; or the union may come to the firm. Union organizers assist in distributing materials promoting the union, contact individual workers, and hold mass meetings.

Signing Authorization Cards. For the union to be recognized, a minimum of 30 percent of the employees must sign authorization cards stating an interest in union representation.

Determining the Bargaining Unit. The bargaining unit is the specific group the union represents in collective bargaining. The NLRB usually defines the bargaining unit using a number of criteria. If more than one union seeks recognition, the NLRB must resolve the issue. More than one union can be placed on the ballot.

The Election. The NLRB usually conducts representation elections. In recent years, the NLRB has conducted about 8,000 annual elections. Unions have won about 45 percent of the elections, down from 55 percent in 1969. A secret ballot is commonly used. The ballot is a simple vote for or against union representation. In order to win union representation, over 50 percent of the voting employees must vote for unionization. If more than one union is seeking representation, employees must make a choice. To gain certification, one union must get a majority of the votes. If no union gets a majority, a runoff is held between the two unions with the most votes. If the majority of employees votes "no union," another unionization election cannot be held for one year.

Certification. The NLRB must certify the election. This means that the union is recognized as the bargaining unit of the employees it represents. Certification requires that the employer bargain in good faith with the union over conditions of employment. Certification may end if the employees vote to change unions or to get rid of the union. This is called a *decertification* election. In recent years, there has been a steady increase in attempts to decertify labor unions.[37]

Collective Bargaining. **Collective bargaining** *is the negotiation process resulting in a contract that covers employment conditions*. Collective bargaining, a part of the democratic process, gives employees an independent voice at work.[38] The most common employment conditions covered in the contract include compensation, hours, and working conditions. But, the contract can include any issue that both sides agree to. Job security is a major bargaining issue for unions today.[39] In the late 1980s and early 1990s, unions gave in to pay concessions to help companies compete in the global environment. However, they are looking for payback time. To continue to hold pay costs down, many companies are offering lump-sum bonuses and other incentives that vary with profits and other performance measures.[40]

collective bargaining
The negotiation process resulting in a contract that covers employment conditions.

To avoid a strike or lockout (refusing to let employees work) and to handle *grievances* by either side, collective bargainers sometimes agree to use neutral third parties, called mediators, from the Federal Mediation and Conciliation Service (FMCS). A *mediator* is a neutral party who helps management and labor settle their disagreements. In cases where management and labor are not willing to compromise but do not want to call a strike or lockout, they may call in an arbitrator. An *arbitrator* is different from a mediator in that the arbitrator makes a binding decision for management and labor. The arbitrator's decision must be followed. The services of an arbitrator are more commonly used to settle grievances than to deal with impasses in collective bargaining.

Termination and Outplacement

There are three primary reasons employees leave organizations: (1) Attrition results in some employees leaving for other jobs, electing to stop working for a period of time, or retiring. In any case, employees lost to attrition often need to be replaced. Employees who leave voluntarily are often interviewed to find out the reason for leaving. The *exit interview*, usually conducted by the human resources department, can help identify problem areas that lead to turnover. (2) Firing results in employees being terminated who break the rules and do not perform to standards. In Chapter 16 you will learn how to handle problem employees. (3) Layoffs result in employees being let go. Layoffs usually occur because of economic and organizational problems and mergers and acquisitions. Apple, Boeing, General Dynamics, GM, IBM, McDonnell Douglas, and Sears laid off tens of thousands of employees during the 1990s to cut costs.

When companies have a layoff, they may offer outplacement services. *Outplacement services* help employees to find new jobs. For example, when General Electric had a layoff of 900 employees, it set up a reemployment center to help employees find new jobs or to learn new skills. GE provided counseling on how to write a résumé and conduct a job search, and it took out an ad in local newspapers saying that employees were available. Because of Scitor's human resources practices, it has little difficulty in attracting and retaining employees. It has no labor relations, low termination, and has had no need for outplacement services.

CURRENT MANAGEMENT ISSUES

The traditional name of personnel has changed to human resources management. Some organizations use more current titles. For example, Southwest Airlines, ValuJet Airlines, and Herman Miller Inc., have a vice president for people. The GM Saturn plant has a vice president for people system.[41]

Globalization. For the *global* company, the human resources management process becomes even more complex. The legal environment, methods of human resources planning—attracting, developing, and retaining employees—often vary from country to country. One problem area has been transferring managers between diverse countries. Moving U.S. managers overseas has been more of a problem than moving European and Japanese managers to other countries. The performance appraisal system has proven to be a useful way to monitor the behavior of international managers and international activities as a whole.[42]

Although U.S. companies spend billions of dollars on training, Americans spend only 1.5 percent of payroll on training, while the Europeans and Japanese spend 5 percent or more.[43] According to the Commission on Workforce Quality and Labor Market Efficiency, the U.S. government and businesses must make vast increases in investment in human resources if they want to compete successfully in the global environment.[44]

Diversity. Valuing *diversity* requires changes in the traditional human resources practices. External recruiting efforts must be broadened to include women's networks, over-50 clubs, urban job banks, training centers for the disabled, ethnic newspapers and magazines, and so on. Care must be taken to avoid discrimination. Minorities should be oriented and trained to be sure they understand the organizational culture and that their differences are appreciated. Many organizations are making special efforts to train minority employees so that they can qualify for better jobs. Mentoring programs are also being used to train minorities for advancement.[45] Diversity training continues to be used.

Many organizations are giving women the opportunity to enter jobs held traditionally by men.

In support of comparable worth, many organizations are upgrading the worth of jobs traditionally held by women to those of jobs traditionally held by men, and they are giving women the opportunity to enter the traditionally held male jobs. Many organizations are changing human resources practices to help break the *glass ceiling* (barriers to advancement) for women and minorities. Great progress has been made in middle- and low-level management jobs. However, advancement to top management is slow; 97 percent of senior managers of the 1,500 largest U.S. companies are white with about the same percentage being male.[46]

One last area of diversity is the trend of organizations to better meet the needs of their diverse workforce by creating flexible, or cafeteria, benefit programs. *Cafeteria benefits* allow employees to select from a menu of benefits the ones most relevant to them. Organizations are also trying to allow employees to better balance their work and personal life by offering work-family benefits such as dependent care and flexible work schedules.[47]

Ethics and Social Responsibility. *Ethics and social responsibility* are commonly part of the human resources department. It is often involved in developing policies, such as codes of conduct, to govern ethical behavior. Whistleblowers are commonly told where to report unethical behavior, and that place is commonly the human resources department. Social responsibility progress reports are commonly prepared by the human resources department. To be socially responsible, many organizations send employees to schools to teach, and employees often act as mentors to students.[48]

Organizations have a social responsibility to provide a healthy and safe work environment for their employees. Layoff, stress from long hours of work and increased pressure to do more with less, media glorification of violence, availability of weapons, and other factors have contributed to the increasing problem of workplace violence. Employers should screen applicants for a safer workplace.[49] Employers can ask questions that will reveal potentially violent personalities without violating the Americans with Disabilities Act.[50]

Quality and TQM. Quality people produce *quality* products and services. To ensure quality, organizations must attract, develop, and retain quality employees who are flexible and able to continue learning and adapting. In a *TQM* culture, the human resources department does not conduct job analysis without employee input. As changes are made to improve quality, people's jobs will change, making job analysis a continuing process. An important key to a TQM is training and development.[51] While traditional companies focus on training, TQM focuses on development to insure continuous improvement in customer value. Training and development are often used to stimulate change. Incentives are used to increase quality.[52]

Participative Management and Teams. Participative management empowers employees to participate in decision-making. The use of work teams requires recruiting and selecting employees who want to be team players. Team members must also be trained to work together effectively as a group.[53] Self-managed work teams are usually responsible for selecting and conducting performance appraisals of their members. To provide a culture that values team work requires a compensation system based on incentives,[54] and incentives should be based on team rather than individual performance.[55] Teams are crucial to the success of the TQM philosophy, and the NLRB has ruled that the creation and use of employee committees constituted an unfair labor practice.[56] In other words, unions have the power to say no to teams, which will have a negative effect on TQM.

Productivity. Productivity is based on human resources. The employees recruited and selected will have a direct impact on productivity. Training and development and performance appraisals are used to increase productivity.[57] Incentive compensation can motivate employees to higher levels of performance.[58] Labor relations also affect productivity, and many organizations are trying to change the old adversarial management versus union relationship to establish closer partnerships.[59] For example, at GM Saturn, plant management and the union work in collaboration.[60] See the case at the end of Chapter 7 for details.

In their effort to increase productivity, many organizations have focused on cutting back the number of employees and the resources for training and development. Unfortunately, when budgets need to be cut, training and development are often cut. There has been a great deal of uncertainity about the bottom-line effects of *downsizing*. There is evidence that downsizing does not reduce expenses as much as desired, and that sometimes expenses increase.[61] The American Management Association has shown that downsizing has not

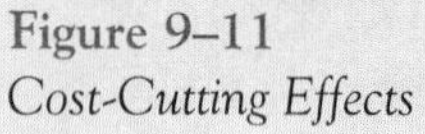

Figure 9–11
Cost-Cutting Effects

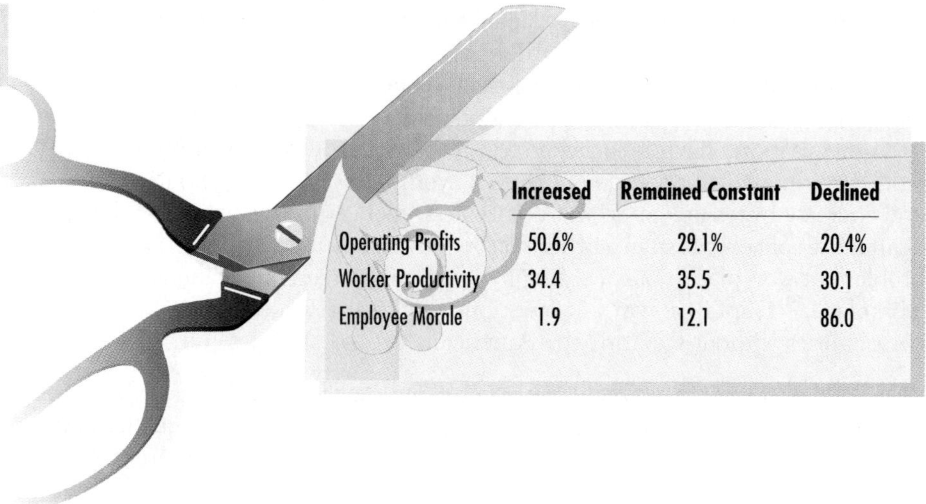

	Increased	Remained Constant	Declined
Operating Profits	50.6%	29.1%	20.4%
Worker Productivity	34.4	35.5	30.1
Employee Morale	1.9	12.1	86.0

been successful at increasing worker productivity and it has had very negative effects on employee morale.[62] See Figure 9–11 for survey results.

Re-engineering has not been successful at many organizations because management is focusing on cost-cutting and has not made the necessary investment in human resources. According to Hammer, co-author of the book that coined the term *re-engineering*, "The biggest lie told by most corporations, and they tell it proudly, is that people are our most important assets. Total fabrication. They treat people like raw materials. If you're serious about treating people as an asset, we're looking at a dramatic increase in investment in them."[63] "I tell companies they need to quintuple their investment in education. Training is about skills; education is about understanding broad knowledge. Everybody who works in a company needs to understand the business." This includes complete understanding of the mission, objectives, and strategy (Chapter 5).[64] The investment must also come through incentive compensation.

To cut costs, many organizations use contingent workers. *Contingent workers* are part-time, temporary, and freelance laborers. Organizations primarily use contingent workers because they generally do not give these workers any benefits. It is less costly to have two part-time workers than one full-time employee. Wal-Mart keeps its costs down in part by keeping its compensation level low. Contingent workers make up 25 percent of the work force and outnumber all employees of the Fortune 500 companies combined.[65] The growth in number of contingent workers is bad news for workers who want full-time jobs with benefits.[66]

Small Business. *Small businesses* commonly do not have separate human resources departments. Line mangers with other responsibilities perform the functions. Small businesses often have more trouble attracting employees because they generally have less advancement potential and compensation, particularly benefits, is lower than in large businesses. However, with downsizing, attracting and retaining employees has become easier. Without a human resources department, line managers have complete responsibility for orientation and training of their employees. On an employee basis, benefits are more expensive for small businesses. For example, insurance is less costly with larger numbers of employees. To provide better benefits, some companies are *leasing* *employees*. Through leasing companies, in essence, employees are fired by the company and hired by the leasing company who leases them back to the company. The leasing company takes over the payroll function, which provides savings in accounting. Technically, employees work for the leasing company, but still do the same jobs except they usually get better benefits. For example, employees at Ceramic Devices asked for a 401(k) pension plan. By leasing employees, the company gave them the 401(k) benefit. Over one million employees are being leased in the United States.[67]

CHAPTER SUMMARY AND GLOSSARY

The chapter summary is organized to answer the ten learning objectives for Chapter 9.

1. List the four parts of the human resources management process.

The four parts of the human resources management process are (1) human resources planning, (2) attracting employees, (3) developing employees, and (4) retaining employees.

2. Explain the difference between a job description and a job specification and why they are needed.

The job description identifies what the employee does on the job, whereas the job specification identifies the qualifications needed to get the job. Job analysis is needed because it serves as the basis for attracting, developing, and retaining employees.

3. State the two parts of attracting employees and the difference between them.

The two parts of attracting employees are recruiting and selecting. Recruiting is the process of attracting qualified candidates to apply for job openings. Selecting is the process of choosing the most qualified applicant recruited for a job.

4. Describe the difference between the group and panel interview and hypothetical and probing questions.

In the group interview, one person interviews more than one candidate. In the panel interview, one candidate is interviewed by more than one interviewer. A hypothetical question is planned; it requires the candidate to describe what he or she would do and say in a given situation. A probing question is not planned; it is used to clarify a response to an open-ended or hypothetical question.

5. Discuss the difference between orientation and training and development of employees.

Orientation is the process of introducing new employees to the organizational culture and their jobs. Training and development is the process of acquiring the skills necessary to perform present and future jobs.

6. List the steps in job instructional training.

The steps in job instructional training are (1) prepare the learner, (2) present the task, (3) performance of the task by the trainee, and (4) follow up.

7. State the major components of compensation.

The two components of compensation are pay and benefits.

8. Describe the difference between the use of job analysis and job evaluation.

A job analysis is used to determine what the job entails and the qualifications needed to staff the position. Job evaluation is used to determine how much to compensate employees for their jobs.

9. Explain why most organizations do not have labor relations.

Labor relations are the interactions between management and unionized employees. Because most organizations do not have unions, they do not have labor relations.

10. Define the following key terms (in order of appearance in the chapter):

The ______________ consist of planning, attracting, developing, and retaining employees.

A ______________ allows discrimination where it is reasonably necessary to normal operation of a particular organization.

______________ is the process of staffing the organization to meet its objectives.

The ______ identifies the tasks and responsibilities of a position.

______ identify the qualifications needed to staff a position.

______ is the process of attracting qualified candidates to apply for job openings.

______ is the process of choosing the most qualified applicant recruited for a job.

______ are places where job applicants undergo a series of tests, interviews, and simulated experiences to determine their managerial potential.

______ is the process of introducing new employees to the organization and their jobs.

______ is the process of acquiring the skills necessary to perform a job.

______ is the ongoing education to improve skills for present and future jobs.

______ develops skills in a simulated setting.

______ is the ongoing process of evaluating employee performance.

______ is the total cost of pay and benefits to employees.

______ is the process of determining the worth of each job relative to other jobs within the organization.

______ are the interactions between management and unionized employees.

______ is the negotiation process resulting in a contract that covers employment conditions.

KEY TERMS

assessment centers
bona fide occupational qualification
collective bargaining
compensation
development
human resources management process
job description
job evaluation
job specifications
labor relations
orientation
performance appraisal
recruiting
selection
strategic human resources planning
training
vestibule training

REVIEW AND DISCUSSION QUESTIONS

1. What is your opinion of allowing a bona fide occupational qualification?
2. What are the components of a job analysis?
3. What is your opinion of using promotion from within as an internal recruiting source?
4. Do you agree that the interview should be the primary criterion for selection?
5. What is the most common problem to avoid during interviewing?
6. If you work for a company with a human resources department, does this mean that, as a manager, you don't have to orient and train employees? Explain.
7. How does setting objectives affect measuring and evaluating training results in the training cycle?
8. How is compensation both an attracting and retaining part of the human resources process?
9. Why don't most employees realize how expensive benefits are and how much they contribute to compensation cost?
10. Are unions greedy because they expect more than they are worth, or is management greedy because it takes excessive salaries and gives too large a share of the profits to the owners?
11. What is the difference between a mediator and an arbitrator?

CASE

Cunningham Communication, Inc.

Andrea Cunningham started her own public relations (PR) firm in Santa Clara, California. She believed that any PR firm could package and disseminate information. Andrea developed a mission that gave the firm a competitive advantage because it keeps clients apprised of how they are perceived by the market. To live the mission, Cunningham keeps tabs on the financial community, the press, consultants, customers, and even employees within the firm. High-quality employees are critical to PR success because clients must have extreme confidence in the PR people in charge of their accounts. PR people often have to give clients bad news based on the data they gather. Client turnover is high at most PR agencies, and employee job-hopping is also common as PR representatives search for higher pay and new challenges.

Cunningham acquired some of Silicon Valley's best clients, including Borland International and Aldus Corporation software makers and Hewlett-Packard and Motorola. Andrea's Cunningham Communication revenues grew to over $3 million annually with 24 employees. However, Andrea made a common entrepreneurial error. She tried to make all the decisions herself without delegating authority. As a result, managers were constantly fighting, morale was very low, turnover of both clients and employees was very high, and Andrea faced the threat of losing money for the first time since she started the business.

Faced with problems, Andrea knew that she needed to make changes. Her first attempt was to assign clients to individual teams and give bonuses based on profitability. Unfortunately, internal competition became fierce. Turf wars developed, employees refused to share information, and there was no cooperation between teams. Andrea realized that teams were a good idea, but the team system needed to be changed.

Andrea came to the realization that she had to delegate authority if she were going have a turnaround. She decided to develop a goal-driven system with a cooperative management program called *input teams*. Andrea set annual objectives for each team to develop the necessary plans and budgets to achieve the objectives. Every employee was a member of at least one team that met for five hours per week. Andrea also realized that her human resources practices had to support the Cunningham mission and new management system. Working with her human resources manager and others, they developed the following program.

To attract and retain employees, called associates, they developed a career path system. A career path is a sequence of job assignments that leads to more responsibility with raises and promotions. The career path system was designed to develop associates to a level of competence that inspired the confidence of clients. New associates are oriented to the organizational culture, called the Cunningham Culture. They learn about the various departments, they are taught about the input teams, and they develop team skills and time-management skills. New associates attend Cunningham Communications Inc. University for a formal three-day training session.

The compensation system was also changed. All associates receive a set pay for the year and a bonus based on meeting objectives. Each associate determines his or her responsibilities, objectives, and pay. Andrea says that associates rarely request compensation that they are not worth. Frequent advisory sessions give associates feedback from their boss on how well they are meeting expectations. On occasion when associates have fallen short of their objectives, compensation has been withheld without complaint. To increase compensation, associates have to generate more revenue.

Within six months of implementing the changes, all but three members of the senior staff voluntarily terminated employment at Cunningham. Andrea was sad to see them go, but felt they were not right for the new management system. On the positive side, the company became profitable and continues to grow; the number of associates went from 24 to 59 under the new systems.

Select the best alternative for the following questions. Be sure you are able to explain your answers.

___ 1. Which of the components of the human resources management process is not discussed in the case.

a. human resources planning
b. attracting
c. developing
d. retaining employees

___ 2. Poor job analysis and poor realistic job previews were major reasons for the high turnover rate at Cunningham.

a. true b. false

___ 3. Cunningham's primary problem was in the area of

a. attracting employees
b. developing employees
c. retaining employees

___ 4. Cunningham's primary recruiting source would have to be

a. internal b. external

___ 5. Cunningham training focuses more on

a. technical skills
b. human and conceptual skills

___ 6. Advisory sessions are a ___ tool.

a. recruitingd. orientation
b. training e. selection
c. performance appraisal

___ 7. Cunningham's compensation system does not include

a. wages b. salary c. incentives

___ 8. There are good labor relations at Cunningham.

a. true b. false

___ 9. Cunningham offers outplacement services.

a. true b. false

___ 10. Cunningham's primary changes to increase performance focused on

a. globalization d. quality and TQM
b. diversity e. participative management
c. ethics

11. Are the human resources problems at Cunningham unique or are they common to other organizations?

12. Andrea went from one extreme of having total responsibility for running the business to letting the employees run the business. Would you have recommended a gradual move or extreme change?

13. Would you allow associates to set their own pay?

14. What else would you recommend Cunningham do to attract, develop, and retain associates?

Behavior Model Video 9–1, Employment Interviewing, shows Craig conducting a job interview with Betsy, following the steps in Model 9–2. This video serves as a behavior model which can be used prior to conducting Skill-Building Exercise 9–1, Selecting a Tennis Coach.

SKILL-BUILDING EXERCISE 9–1

Selecting a Tennis Coach[68]

Preparing for Skill-Building Exercise 9–1

You are in your first year as athletic director at a local high school. While planning your human resources needs, you realize the tennis coach position will be open. You must staff the position. The compensation for the job is set in the budget. It is to be paid in one lump sum at the end of the season. It is competitive with the pay of other tennis coaches in the area.

Recruiting

Because you have no recruiting budget, you do some internal recruiting and contact some athletic directors in your area to spread the word about the opening. You recruit three candidates for the coaching position. Following is a brief listing of their qualifications.

Candidate A has been a history teacher at your school for ten years. This person was the tennis coach for two years. It's been five years since the teacher coached the team. You don't know why the candidate stopped coaching or how good a job was done. Candidate A never played competitive tennis. However, someone told you the candidate plays regularly and is pretty good. You guess the teacher is about 35 years old.

Candidate B works as a supervisor on the 11 P.M. to 7 A.M. shift for a local business. This candidate has never coached before. However, the person was a star player in high school and college. Candidate B still plays in local tournaments and you see the name in the paper now and then. You guess this candidate is about 25 years old.

Candidate C has been a basketball coach and physical education teacher at a nearby high school for the past five years. The person has a master's degree in physical education. You figure it will take the person 20 minutes to get to your school. Candidate C has never coached tennis, but did play on the high school team. The candidate plays tennis about once a week. You guess the person is about 45 years old.

Preparing for the Interviews

Follow the six interview preparation steps in Model 9–1. For step 1, there are no job descriptions and specifications. Because there are only three candidates, you have decided to interview them all, even if they do not meet your job specifications.

Conducting the Interviews

During the in-class part of this exercise you will conduct a job interview. Be sure to bring your preparation—written questions on a form—material for class use.

Doing Skill-Building Exercise 9–1 in Class

Objectives
To perform a job analysis and to develop skills in employment selection interviewing.

Preparation
You should have your form with a list of questions for candidates.

Experience
You will discuss your preparation. You will also conduct a job interview, be an interviewee, and observe an interview.

Procedure 1 (5–10 minutes)
Break into groups of five or six, pass your preparation materials around to the other members, and discuss them. You may make changes to improve your preparation. For example, you may want to add some good questions you did not think of.

Procedure 2 (3–5 minutes)
Break into groups of three; do not divide into the same groups used in procedure 1. Make one or two groups of two, if necessary. Each person selects one of the three candidates (A, B, or C) he or she will role-play during the interview. Use your own name, but assume you have the person's qualifications; ad lib realistically.

Procedure 3 (25–75 minutes)
1-1. *Interview 1 takes place*. The person who chose A is the interviewer, B is the interviewee, and C is the observer. A conducts the interview using his or her interview materials, while B answers the questions. C observes quietly, and gives feedback on how well the interview went. (If there are only two in your group, B is also the observer.) You may not be able to ask all your questions in the allotted time (5 to 20 minutes). Keep the opening short and be sure to close when you are ready to or the time is up.

1-2. *Integration* (3–5 minutes). C gives his or her observation of the interview. All three group members discuss the interview and how it could be improved. Do not go on to the next interview until you are told to do so.

2-1. *Interview 2 takes place*. B is the interviewer, C is the interviewee, and A is the observer. Follow the guidelines for 1-1.

2-2. *Integration*. Follow the guidelines for 1-2.

3-1. *Interview 3 takes place*. C is the interviewer; A is the interviewee; and B is the observer. Groups of two join other triads as observers. Follow the guidelines for 1-1.

3-2. *Integration*. Follow the guidelines for 1-2.

Procedure 4 (2–4 minutes)
Individually select the candidate you would offer the job to. The instructor counts how may students would hire each candidate to determine the class selection.

Conclusion
The instructor may lead a class discussion and make concluding remarks.

Application (2–4 minutes)
What did I learn from this experience? How will I use this knowledge in the future?

____

____

Sharing
Volunteers give their answers to the application section.

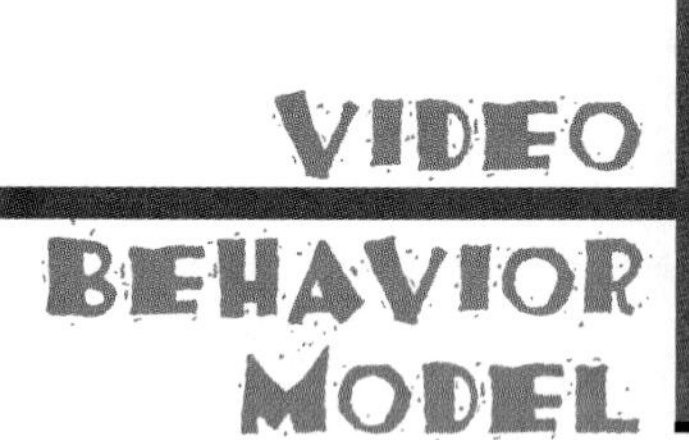

Behavior Model Video 9–2 shows Chris conducting a job instructional training session with Betsy, following the steps in Model 9–3. This video serves as a behavior model which can be used prior to conducting Skill-Building Exercise 9–2, Job Instructional Training.

SKILL-BUILDING EXERCISE 9–2

Job Instructional Training

Preparing for Skill-Building Exercise 9–2

For this exercise, you will prepare to conduct a training session using Model 9–3 by following the training cycle below:

Step 1. Conduct a Needs Assessment. Select a task you are familiar with that most people don't know how to do and can teach someone else to do in ten minutes (knitting, a job function, an athletic technique, how to play a game, conduct a magic trick, and so on).

Step 2. Set Objectives. Write down your objective(s) for the training session.

Step 3. Prepare for Training. Write out a description of your plan, following the four steps in the JIT model. Be sure to develop steps for presenting the operation. The "who" will be determined in class. The "when" and "where" will be in class. Be sure to bring the necessary material (knitting, ball, game, etc.) to class to conduct the training session.

Step 4. Conduct the Training. The training will be done in class. Be sure to bring all the materials you will need.

Step 5. Measure and Evaluate Results. This will be done in class. But make sure that your plan includes how you will measure and evaluate your training results.

Doing Skill-Building Exercise 9–2 in Class

Objective
To develop skills in designing and implementing training using the training cycle and job instructional training (JIT).

Preparation
You should have planned how to train someone to perform a task and have brought the necessary materials to conduct the training session.

Experience
You will give, receive, and observe JIT.

Procedure 1 (2–3 minutes)
Break into groups of three, preferably with people who are not familiar with the task you will be teaching. Make some groups of two, if necessary. Decide who will be the trainer (A), trainee (B), and observer (C) for the first training session. During the training session, the trainer teaches the trainee to perform the task while the observer makes notes on the integration sheet at the end of this exercise.

Procedure 2 (20–40 minutes)
1-1. *Training session 1 takes place.* Member A trains B to perform the task using JIT, as C observes and takes notes on the integration sheet.

1-2. *Integration.* When the training is over, or the time is up, observer C leads a group discussion on which JIT steps the trainer did and did not follow. Focus on how the trainer can improve his or her skills. Do not go on to the next training session until you are told to do so.

2-1. *Training session 2 takes place.* Member A is now the trainee; C becomes the trainer; and B becomes the observer.

2-2. *Integration.* Same as procedure 1-2; B leads the discussion. Do not go one to the next training until told to do so.

3-1. *Training session 3 takes place.* Each person plays the role he or she hasn't played yet; B trains C while A observes.

3-2. *Integration.* Same as procedure 1-2.

Conclusion
The instructor may lead a class discussion and/or make concluding remarks.

Application (2–4 minutes)
What did I learn from this experience? How will I use this knowledge in the future?

___

___

Sharing
Volunteers give their answers to the application section.

Integration Sheet

The observer gives feedback to the trainer on how well he or she performed each step of JIT. Focus on things done well and how to improve at each step. Refer to the text for the details of what should take place for each step.

Step 1. Preparation of the Trainee.

___

___

Step 2. Presentation of the Task.

___

___

Step 3. Performance of the task by the trainee.

___

___

Step 4. Follow up.

___

___

Communicating

Learning Objectives

After studying this chapter, you should be able to:

1. Describe the three ways communication flows through organizations.
2. List the four steps in the communication process.
3. State the major advantages of oral over written communications, and the advantages of written over oral communications.
4. State the general guide to channel selection.
5. List the five steps in the face-to-face message-sending process.
6. Describe paraphrasing and state why it is used.
7. List and explain the three parts of the message-receiving process.
8. Define reflecting response and state when it should be used.
9. Discuss what should and what should not be done to calm an emotional person.
10. Define the following **key terms** (in order of appearance in the chapter):

communication
vertical communication
horizontal communication
grapevine
communication process
encoding
communication channels
decoding
nonverbal communication
feedback
paraphrasing
message-sending process
message-receiving process
reflecting responses
empathic listening

Skill Development

1. You can develop your skill at giving instructions (Skill-Building Exercise 10–1).

   Giving instructions requires human and communication skills, and the management roles require communication skills. Communication is a part of the leadership management function. The SCANS competencies of interpersonal skills and information require communication skills. In addition, the basic and personal qualities foundation skills are based on communication skills.

2. You can develop your situational communication skills (Skill-Building Exercise 10–2).

   Skill-Building Exercise 10–2 develops your ability to know which of the four management styles is most appropriate to use with people outside your department in a given situation.

elta Airlines made the decision to cap travel agents' commissions on ticket sales. Prior to the cap, the commission was based on 10 percent of the airfare.

For example, if a flight cost $1,000, the commission was $100. However, the cap set an upper limit of $50 for domestic round-trip tickets and $25 for one-way tickets. Within a short time, other major airlines—including American, Northwest, United, and USAir—also set the same commission cap. TWA set the cap and then removed it to try to get extra business from competitors. Most travel agents were notified about the cap through a fax message from the airline.

The commission caps hurt some travel agents more than others. The travel agents that target the business travel market were hurt the most because business travel is often a last minute decision and the traveler pays top price. Travel agents that target the leisure travel market were not hurt as much because travelers plan well in advance and prices are usually lower. In addition, leisure travel agents focus on selling travel packages, including hotel and car rentals, which pay a commission of 13 to 15 percent.

National news media gave coverage of the commission cap. The American Society of Travel Agents, the major trade association, responded in

Travel agents who target the business market were hurt most by the commission cap.

protest with full-page advertisements in major newspapers. The ads failed to communicate the travel agency community's stability. The media had given travel agents their best opportunity to describe what they do and how they make money, but they failed to take advantage of the opportunity.

Many of the travel agents never communicated with their clients to explain the commission cap and how it would affect the travel agents. The failure to communicate with clients is fairly common in the travel industry. Profitable midsize accounts that switch agencies usually do not hear from the old agent for three to six months, if ever.[1]

For current information on Delta Airlines, use Internet address http://www.delta-air.com. For ideas on using the Internet, see the Appendix.

At all organizational levels, at least 75 percent of each workday is consumed in communication. Seventy-five percent of what we hear, we hear imprecisely; and 75 percent of what we hear accurately, we forget within three weeks. Communication, the skill we need the most at work, is the skill we most lack.[2] The ability to listen and convey information is one of the four top qualities employers want in their employees.[3] Good information with which to do a good job tops the list of employee motivators.[4] Organizations with effective communication systems are more likely to be successful.[5]

communication
The process of transmitting information and meaning.

Communication *is the process of transmitting information and meaning.* Two major types of communications occur: organizational and interpersonal. At the organizational level, communication takes place among organizations and among units/departments of an organization. At the interpersonal level, communication takes place among people. Communication is either effective or ineffective at transmitting information and meaning.[6] The primary barrier to effective organizational communication is its members' failure to understand the communication function.[7]

1. Describe the three ways communication flows through organizations.

ORGANIZATIONAL COMMUNICATION

Managers need to develop their communication skills.[8] Communication is one of the three major skills needed by managers (Chapter 1). The management roles (interpersonal, informational, and decisional) and management functions (planning, organizing, leading, and controlling) all require effective communi-

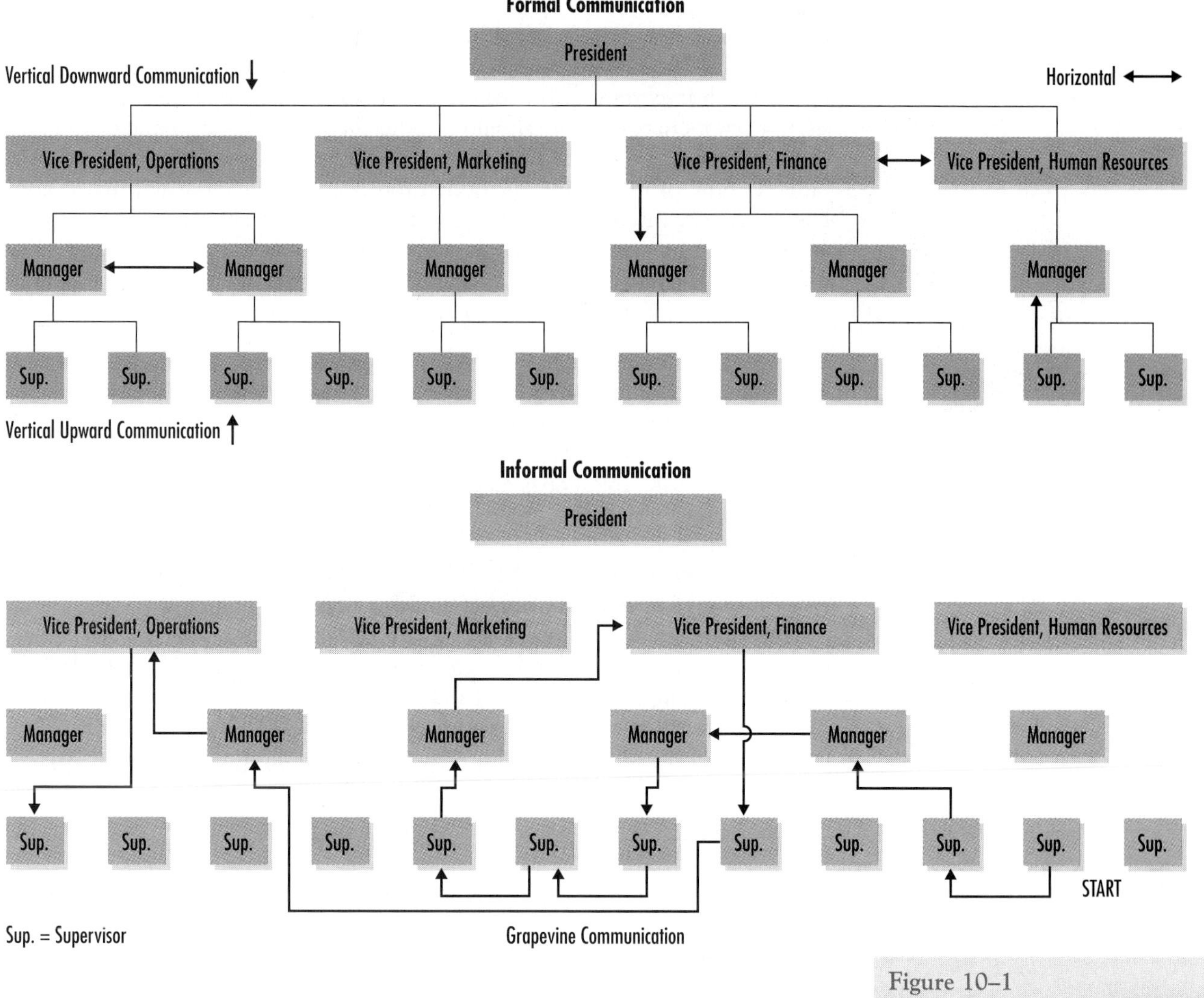

Figure 10–1
Organizational Communication

cation skills. The organizational mission, strategy, goals,[9] and culture[10] all must be communicated effectively. Lee Iacocca, former top executive credited with saving Chrysler from bankruptcy, said, "The most important thing I learned in school was how to communicate."[11]

Organizational communication flows formally in a vertical and horizontal direction and informally through the grapevine. Figure 10–1 illustrates organizational communication.

Vertical Communication

Vertical communication *is the flow of information both downward and upward through the organizational chain of command.* It is also called *formal communication* because it is recognized as officially sanctioned transmission of information and meaning.

vertical communication
The flow of information both downward and upward through the organizational chain of command.

Downward Communication. When top-level management makes decisions, policies, procedures, and so forth, they are often communicated down the chain of command to instruct employees. It is the process of higher-level managers telling those below them what to do and how to do it. The delegation process is a downward communication.

To have effective organizational communication, top management should send enough important information down to employees, especially during a crisis or a major change. There should be official communication policies and procedures to ensure accurate and effective transmission of information. To facilitate the flow of formal information throughout an organization, many firms have computer information systems with an executive who oversees all aspects of information technology such as computing, office systems, and telecommunication. The current trend gives the title of chief information officer (CIO) to the executive.[12] You will learn more about information systems in Chapter 17.

Upward Communication. When employees send a message to their bosses, they are using upward communication. Managers learn about what is going on in the organization, and often about customers, through employees. Employees gain from upward communication as they discuss issues with their managers. By listening, upper managers set a good example throughout the organization.

To help facilitate upward communication, many organizations, including Caterpillar Tractor, use an open-door policy which allows employees to feel at ease in going to managers. Connecticut Mutual Life Insurance offers free breakfasts and lunches to employees who sit with managers in a no-holds-barred question-and-answer session. Ford, Sears, and other organizations do periodic surveys to assess employees' attitudes and opinions. Ed Carlson of United Airlines coined the term *management by wandering around* (MBWA), which involves getting out of the office and talking frequently and informally with employees.

Horizontal Communication

horizontal communication
The flow of information between colleagues and peers.

Work Application

1. Give an example of vertical (upward and downward), horizontal, and grapevine communication where you work or have worked.

Horizontal communication *is the flow of information between colleagues and peers.* It is formal communication, but it does not follow the chain of command. Horizontal communication is needed to coordinate within a department and among different departments. Most employees spend more time communicating with peers than with managers. When the manager of the marketing department communicates with the manager of the production department, or other departments, horizontal communication takes place.

For effective organizational communication, many firms have computer systems that make information available to all areas of the organization. Organizations including Arco, Bell Laboratories, Reliance Insurance, and Shell use teleconferencing to link participants throughout the country and world. Managers hold meetings with people from different departments to coordinate their efforts and resolve conflicts between them.

Grapevine Communication

grapevine
The flow of information in any direction throughout the organization.

The **grapevine** *is the flow of information in any direction throughout the organization.* It is informal communication because it is not official or sanctioned by management. The grapevine, or rumor and gossip mill, can begin with anyone in the organization and can flow in any direction. Employees complain about their boss, talk about sports and news events, and whisper secrets about coworkers through the grapevine. With the trend toward downsizing, many employees hear of layoffs long before the pink slips are officially sent out.

The methods for improving formal communication also apply to informal communication. If managers hear of incorrect information being passed along the grapevine, they can use formal and/or informal means to correct the situation. When managers have new information, it can be sent through the formal channels and the grapevine to help prevent incorrect information from spreading.[13]

APPLYING THE CONCEPT

AC 10–1 Communication Flow

Identify the communication flow as:

a. vertical-downward c. horizontal
b. vertical-upward d. grapevine

____ 1. "Hey, Carl, have you heard that Paul and Helen were caught. . . ?"

____ 2. "Quanita, will you come here and hold this so I can get it straight, the way I do it for you all the time."

____ 3. "Tom, here is the letter you asked me to type. Check it and I'll make changes."

____ 4. Robbin, I have two new customers who want to set up charge accounts. Please rush the credit check so I can sell them lots of our merchandise and you can bill them for it."

____ 5. "Ted, please take this letter to the mail room for me right now."

Delta and other airlines officially communicated the commission cap to travel agents by fax notices. However, many agents first heard about the caps through the grapevine or media.

THE COMMUNICATION PROCESS AND COMMUNICATION BARRIERS

2. List the four steps in the communication process.

The **communication process** *consists of a sender who encodes a message and transmits it through a channel to a receiver who decodes it and may give feedback.* Communication models help people better visualize the relationship among the elements of the process.[14] Figure 10–2 illustrates the communication process and explains each step with common communication barriers at each stage.

communication process
Consists of a sender who encodes a message and transmits it through a channel to a receiver who decodes it and may give feedback.

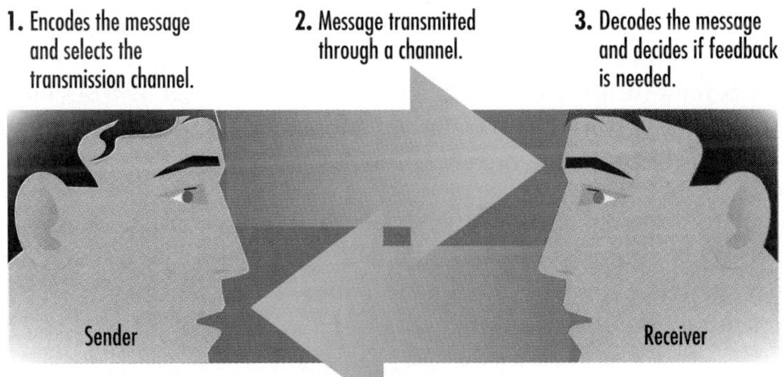
1. Encodes the message and selects the transmission channel.
2. Message transmitted through a channel.
3. Decodes the message and decides if feedback is needed.
Sender
Receiver
The sender and receiver may continually change roles as they communicate.
4. Feedback, response, or new message may be transmitted through a channel.

Figure 10–2
The Communication Process

1. The Sender Encodes the Message and Selects the Channel

encoding
The sender's process of putting the message into a form that the receiver will understand.

Encoding the Message. The *sender* of the message is the person who initiates the communication. The *message* is the information and meaning communicated. Communicators should have a clear objective for their messages.[15] **Encoding** *is the sender's process of putting the message into a form that the receiver will understand.* The sender should consider the receiver of the message, and determine the best way to encode the message to ensure transmitting information and meaning.

Perception Communication Barriers. As messages are transmitted to receivers, they use their perception to translate the message so that it makes sense to them. Watch *semantics* and *jargon* because the same word often means different things to different people. For example, the term "wicked good" can be confusing to people not familiar with the term, who do not realize it does mean good. Also, a manager gives the secretary a letter to type saying, "Please type this and then burn it." *Burn,* meaning make a copy, may be interpreted as putting a match to it.

Overcoming Perception Barriers. To overcome perception problems, you need to consider how the other person will most likely perceive the message and try to encode and transmit it appropriately. Thus, the choice of words is important. Be careful not to use jargon with people who are not familiar with the terminology.

Information Overload Communication Barriers. We all have a limit on the amount of information we can understand at any given time. Information overload commonly occurs for new employees on the first few days, because they are often presented with too much information to comprehend in that period of time. With the widespread use of computers and with so much information available, managers are often dazzled and don't know what to do with it all.[16]

Overcoming Information Overload. To minimize information overload, send messages in a quantity that the receiver can understand. When sending a message, do not talk for too long without checking to be sure the receiver understands the message as you intended. If you talk for too long, the receiver can become bored or lose the thread of the message.

communication channels
The three channels are oral, nonverbal, and written.

Selecting the Channel. The message is transmitted through a channel. *The three primary* **communication channels** *are oral, nonverbal, and written.* The sender should determine the most appropriate channel to meet the needs of the situation; you will learn how in the next section.

Channel Selection Communication Barriers. Use of an inappropriate channel can result in missed communication. For example, if a manager catches an employee in the act of breaking a rule, the manager should use one-on-one, face-to-face communication. Another channel will not be as effective.

Overcoming Channel Selection Barriers. Before sending a message, give careful thought to selecting the most effective channel. In the next major section of this chapter, you will study the appropriate use of various channels.

2. The Sender Transmits the Message

After the sender encodes the message and selects the channel, he or she transmits the message through the channel to a receiver(s). The managers at Delta Airlines selected a written fax as the channel to inform travel agents of the commission cap.

Noise Communication Barriers. Noise factors during the transmission of a message can disturb or confuse the receiver. Noise is anything that interferes with message transmission. For example, a machine or people may make noise that makes it difficult to hear, the sender may not speak loud enough for the receiver to hear well, or a radio or TV may distract the receiver, causing message interpretation errors.

Overcoming Noise Barriers. To overcome noise we need to consider the physical surroundings before transmitting the message. Try to keep noise to a minimum. If possible, stop the noise or distraction or move to a quiet location.

3. The Receiver Decodes the Message and Decides if Feedback Is Needed

The person receiving the message decodes it. **Decoding** *is the receiver's process of translating the message into a meaningful form.* The receiver combines the message with other ideas and interprets the meaning of the message. The receiver decides if feedback, a response, or a new message is needed. With oral communication, feedback is commonly given immediately. However, with written communication, it is often not necessary to reply. When Delta Airlines sent the fax stating the commission cap, the travel agents did not need to give feedback.

decoding
The receiver's process of translating the message into meaningful form.

Trust and Credibility Communication Barriers. During communication, receivers take into account the trust they have in the senders, as well as their credibility. When receivers do not trust senders,[17] and when they do not believe senders know what they are talking about, receivers are reluctant to accept the message.[18]

Overcoming Trust and Credibility Barriers. To improve your trust level, be open and honest with people. If people catch you in a lie, they may never trust you again. To gain and maintain credibility, get the facts straight before you communicate. Send clear, correct messages. Become an expert in your area.

Not Listening Barrier to Communication. People usually hear what the sender is saying, but often they do not listen to the message or understand what is being transmitted. Not listening is sometimes the result of not paying attention or noise distractions.

Overcoming Not Listening Barriers. One method to help ensure that people listen to your message involves questioning them and having them paraphrase the message back to you. When listening, you should follow the listening tips presented later in this chapter.

Emotional Barriers to Communication. Everyone has emotions, such as anger, hurt, fear, sorrow, happiness, and so on. Emotional people find it difficult to be objective and to listen.

Work Application

2. Give an example of a message that was transmitted where you work or have worked. Be sure to illustrate the four steps in the communication process, state the channel, and identify if feedback was given.
3. Give two examples of different communication barriers you encountered at work. Explain how the barrier could have been overcome.

Overcoming Emotional Barriers. When communicating, you should remain calm and be careful not to make others emotional by your behavior. Later in this chapter you will learn how to calm an emotional employee.

4. Feedback: A Response or a New Message May Be Transmitted

After the receiver decodes the message, feedback may be given to the sender. You should realize that the role of sender and receiver can change during a communication exchange. Many travel agents contacted Delta directly to complain about the commission cap, and the American Society of Travel Agents took out a full-page ad in several newspapers complaining about the cap.

Filtering Communication Barriers. *Filtering* is the process of altering or distorting information in order to project a more favorable image. For example, when people are asked to report progress toward objectives, they may stress the positive and deemphasize, or even leave out, the negative side or they may lie.

Overcoming Filtering Barriers. To help eliminate filtering, you should treat errors as a learning experience rather than as an opportunity to blame and criticize employees. You will learn about criticism later in this chapter. Using an open-door policy can create and support a two-way communication climate.

Summary. An example of the preceding stages of the communication process would be: (1) A professor (sender) prepares for a class and encodes by preparing a lecture. (2) The professor transmits the message orally through a lecture during class. (3) The students (receivers) decode the lecture (message) by listening and/or taking notes in a meaningful way. Students generally select from the lecture what to write down in notes. The notes are usually decoded rather than taken verbatim. (4) Students usually have the option of asking questions (feedback) during or after class. See Figure 10–3 for a review of the communication barriers.

APPLYING THE CONCEPT

AC 10–2 Communication Barriers

Identify the communication barriers as:

a. perception	e. trust and credibility
b. information overload	f. not listening
c. channel selection	g. emotions
d. noise	h. filtering

____ 6. "Chill out. You shouldn't be upset."

____ 7. "No questions." (Really thinking, "I was lost back on step one and don't know what to ask.")

____ 8. "We are right on schedule." (Really thinking, "We are actually behind, but we'll catch up.")

____ 9. "I said I'd do it in a little while. It's only been 15 minutes. Why do you expect it done by now?"

____ 10. You don't know what you are talking about. I'll do it my way."

3. State the major advantages of oral over written communications, and the advantages of written over oral communications.

MESSAGE TRANSMISSION CHANNELS

When encoding the message, the sender should give careful consideration to selecting the channel. Channels (the forms of the transmitted message) include oral, nonverbal, and written. Figure 10–4 lists the major channel sources.

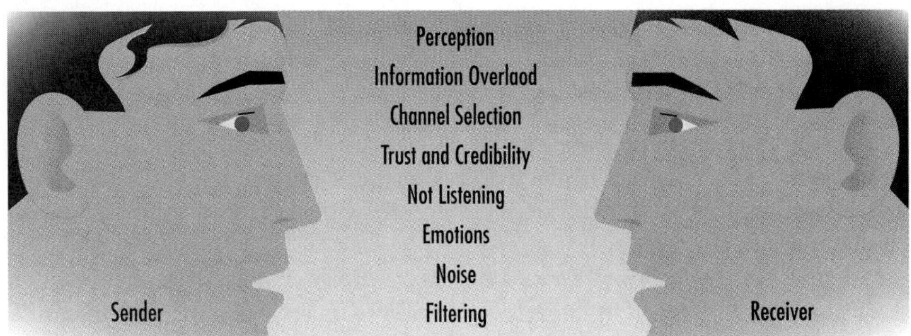

Figure 10–3
Major Communication Barriers

Applying the concepts at the end of this section gives you the opportunity to select channels for messages.

Oral Communication

Most managers prefer oral communication (channel) for sending messages.[19] The five most common media for oral communication are face-to-face, meetings, presentations, the telephone, and voice mail. The major advantage of oral over written communication is that it is usually easier and faster and encourages feedback. The disadvantages are that it is usually less accurate and provides no record.

Face-to-Face. Most managers communicate one-on-one, face-to-face with employees. Sam Walton, former founder and head of Wal-Mart, relied on face-to-face communication to keep the firm growing. Top executives visit 6 to 12 stores each week.

Face-to-face communication is the appropriate channel for delegating tasks, coaching, disciplining, sharing information, answering questions, check-

Figure 10–4
Message Transmission Channels

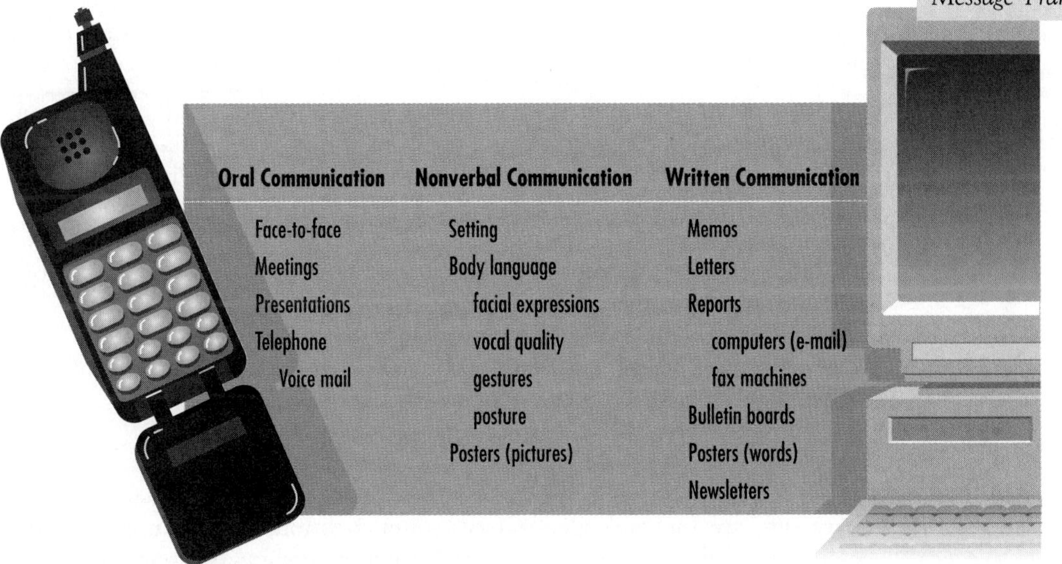

ing progress toward objectives, and developing and maintaining human relations. Managers also spend one-on-one, face-to-face time communicating with their bosses, colleagues, and peers.

Meetings. We will discuss a variety of types of meetings in Chapter 13. The manager's most common meeting is the brief, informal get-together with two or more employees. With the increased use of teams, more time is spent in meetings.[20]

Meetings are appropriate for coordinating employee activities, delegating a task to a group, and resolving employee conflicts. If your department schedule permits, brief, daily, informal department meetings should be held to exchange information, coordinate resources, and develop mutual understanding and human relations.

Presentations are common at meetings and are appropriate for explaining information.

Presentations. On occasion, you may be required to make a formal presentation. Prepare your presentations and be sure they have the following three parts: (1) Beginning—the presentation should begin with a purpose statement and an overview of the main points to be covered. (2) Middle—the presentation supports its purpose through a discussion of the main points in the detail necessary to get the message across. (3) End—the presentation should summarize the purpose, main points, and any action required of the audience.

Presentations are common at meetings and are appropriate for explaining information. The presenter can allow questions and give answers. With a small group, questions can be taken during the presentation. However, with large groups, questions should be saved until after the presentation.

Telephone. The amount of time spent on the telephone varies greatly with the job. Before making a call, set an objective[21] and write down what you plan to discuss. Use the paper to write notes during the call. When receiving a call, determine the purpose of the call and decide if you or another person should handle it. When receiving calls at inconvenient times, arrange for a callback. Conference calls (three or more people talking) are being used more frequently

The telephone is the appropriate channel for quick exchanges of information and checking up on things. It is especially useful for saving travel time. However, it is inappropriate for personal matters such as discipline.

Voice Mail. Voice mail is commonly used to replace written memos and to leave messages for people who don't answer the telephone. Voice mail memos are appropriate for sending short messages containing information not needed in written form for employees to refer to. It is also ideal for leaving a message that does or does not require the receiver to call you back. A study found that employees spend an average of 302 hours per year listening to voice mail and responding to messages.[22]

At the present time, *video conferencing* is not very commonly used. However, as the technology improves and the costs go down, video conferencing will be used more frequently.[23]

Nonverbal Communication

nonverbal communication
Messages sent without words.

Every time we use oral, face-to-face communication, we also use nonverbal communication. **Nonverbal communication** *is messages sent without words.* Nonverbal communication includes the *setting* (physical surroundings) of the communication and *body language*. Body language includes (1) facial expressions (eye contact and a wink or a smile, frown, a dirty look); (2) vocal quality (it does not refer to the "words" used but how they are said. For example, the message can be sent in a calm/excited/upset/slow/fast, soft/yelling quality to convey a message such as anger and disappointment or happiness and approval); (3) gestures (the use of body motion such as using hands, pointing and signaling, and nodding of head); and (4) posture (sitting up straight or slouching, leaning back or forward, crossing arms and/or legs). The old adage, "Actions speak louder than words," holds true. For example, if a manager gives a stern look at an employee doing something wrong, it may be more powerful than words. Also, if Amy, a manager, tells employees to do a quality job but does not do a quality job herself and does not reward quality performance, employees will most likely ignore the verbal message.

To make nonverbal communication effective, you should be aware of your nonverbal communication and make sure it is consistent with your oral and/or written communication. Be aware of, or read, other people's nonverbal communication because it tells you their feelings and attitudes toward the communication and you as a person/manager. Arrange your office so that it is conducive to open communication. Generally, you should not sit behind your desk and have the other person in front of the desk. Sitting side-by-side creates a more open atmosphere. When talking to people, use nonverbal communication to convey openness to messages. Smile, face the person, and use eye-contact comfortable for all; lean forward a bit and gesture frequently to convey that you are listening and are interested. Do not cross your arms or legs (signs of being closed to communication), and speak in a pleasant, calm tone of voice.

Written Communication

Probably nothing can reveal your weaknesses more clearly than poorly written communication. Mike Lockerd, a Texas Instruments vice president, gives this career advice: "Learn to write."[24] The major advantages of written over oral communication, is that it is usually more accurate and provides a record. The major disadvantages are that it usually takes longer and hinders feedback.

A list of commonly used written communications includes:

1. *Memos*—commonly used to send interorganizational messages.
2. *Letters*—commonly used to communicate with people outside the organization. *Computers*—electronic mail (*e-mail*) is used to send memos and letters to save time and paper.[25] *Fax machine*—also used to send memos and letters instantly. Note that e-mail and fax are not numbered because they are forms of using memos and letters.
3. *Reports*—used to convey information. Reports usually involve an evaluation, analysis, and/or recommendation to management or colleagues. Reports can also be sent by e-mail or fax.
4. *Bulletin board notices*—usually are a supplement to another form of communication.
5. *Posters (or signs)*—commonly used as reminders of important information such as the mission statement, safety instructions, quality, clean-up before you leave, etc. Posters can also be nonverbal or graphic communication. An

example is the "no" signs with a picture of what you are not supposed to do circled with a line through it.

6. *Newsletters*—used to convey general information to all employees.

Written communication is appropriate for sending general information; messages requiring future action; formal, official, or long-term messages (especially those containing facts and figures); and messages that affect several people in a related way. Ford Motor Company has over 40,000 users on its global communication system, which indicates that e-mail can be highly preferable to phoning overseas.[26]

Writing Tips. Lack of organization is the number one writing problem.[27] Before you begin writing, set an objective for your communication. Keep the audience in mind. What do you want them to do? Make an outline, using letters and/or numbers, of the major points you want to get across. Now put the outline into written form. The first paragraph states the purpose of the communication. The middle paragraphs support the purpose of the communication: fact, figures, and so forth. The last paragraph summarizes the major points and clearly states the action, if any, to be taken by you and the receivers.

Write to communicate, not to impress. Keep the message short and simple. Limit each paragraph to a single topic and an average of five sentences. Sentences should average 15 words. Vary paragraph and sentence length; however, a paragraph should not exceed one-half page. Write in the active voice (I recommend . . .) rather than the passive voice (it is recommended . . .).

Edit your work and rewrite where necessary. When you have time, wait a day or two and edit your work again. To improve sentences and paragraphs, add to them to convey full meaning, cut out unnecessary words and phrases, and/or rearrange the words. Check your work with computer spelling and grammar checkers. Have others edit your work as well.

Combining Channels

Nonverbal communication is usually combined with oral communication. You can also combine oral, nonverbal, and written communication. Repetition is often needed to ensure that the message has been conveyed with mutual understanding of the meaning. Using combined channels is appropriate when the message is important and you want to ensure that employees attend to and understand it. For example, managers sometimes send a memo and follow up with a personal visit or telephone call to see if there are any questions.

4. State the general guide to channel selection.

Selecting the Message Transmission Channel

Work Application

4. Give an example of an oral and written message you received at work. Be sure to specify the channel of the oral and written message.

Before you send a message, be sure to select the most appropriate channel of transmission. Another consideration in selecting a channel is media richness.

Media richness refers to the amount of information and meaning conveyed through the channel. The more information and meaning, the "richer" the channel. Face-to-face is the richest channel because it allows full oral and nonverbal communication to be used. The telephone is less rich than face-to-face because most of the nonverbal cues are lost when you cannot see facial expressions and gestures. All forms of oral communication are richer than written communication because oral communication allows at least some nonverbal cues which are lost with written messages.

A General Guide to Channel Selection. As a general guide, use rich oral channels for sending difficult and unusual messages, less rich written channels for transmitting simple and routine messages to several people, and combined channels for important messages that employees need to attend to and understand.

Delta selected the fax written communication channel to send the message of the commission cap. Many of the travel agents used a variety of channels to provide feedback to Delta. The American Society of Travel Agents elected written newspaper advertisements to give feedback to the airlines and to inform its members of the situation.

APPLYING THE CONCEPT

AC 10–3 Channel Selection

For each of the five communication situations, select the most appropriate channel for transmitting the message. If you would use combined media, place the letter of the second channel you would use at the end of the situation.

Oral communication	*Written communication*	
a. face-to-face	e. memo	h. bulletin board
b. meeting	f. letter	i. poster
c. presentation	g. report	j. newsletter
d. telephone		

____ **11.** You are waiting for an important letter to arrive by FedEx and you want to know if it is in the mail room yet. ____

____ **12.** Employees have been leaving the lights on in the stock room when no one is in it. You want them to shut the lights off. ____

____ **13.** Jóse, Jamal, and Sam will be working as a team on a new project. You need to explain the project to them. ____

____ **14.** John has come in late for work again; you want this practice to stop. ____

____ **15.** You have exceeded your departmental goals and want your boss to know about it because it should have a positive influence on your upcoming performance appraisal. ____

SENDING MESSAGES

Have you ever heard a manager say, "This isn't what I asked for"? When this happens, it is usually the manager's fault. Managers often make incorrect assumptions and do not take 100 percent of the responsibility for ensuring the message is transmitted with mutual understanding.

The second step in the communication process involves sending the message. Before you send a message, you should carefully select the channel and plan how you will send the message. Then, send the message using the message-sending process.

Planning the Message

Before sending a message, you should plan:

- *What.* What is the goal of the message? Is it to influence, inform, and/or to express feeling? What do you want the end result of the communication to be? Set an objective. When appropriate, consult others for information and/or to participate in defining the objective.
- *Who.* Determine who should receive the message.
- *How.* With the receiver(s) in mind, plan how you will encode the mes-

sage so that it will be understood. Select the appropriate media for the audience and situation. What will be said, done, written, etc.?

- *When*. When will the message be transmitted? Timing is important. For example, if it is going to take 15 minutes to transmit a message, don't approach an employee five minutes before quitting time. Wait until the next day. Make an appointment when appropriate.
- *Where*. Decide where the message will be transmitted (setting)—your office, his or her work place, etc. Remember to keep distractions to a minimum.

5. List the five steps in the face-to-face message-sending process.

message-sending process
(1) Develop rapport, (2) state your communication objective, (3) transmit your message, (4) check the receivers' understanding, and (5) get a commitment and follow up.

The Message-Sending Process

When sending a face-to-face message, follow the steps in *the* **message-sending process:** *(1) develop rapport, (2) state your communication objective, (3) transmit your message, (4) check the receiver's understanding, and (5) get a commitment and follow up.*

step 1. **Develop rapport.** Put the receiver at ease. It is usually appropriate to begin communication with small talk correlated to the message. It helps prepare the employee to receive the message.

step 2. **State your communication objective.** The common business communication objectives are to influence, inform, and express feelings. Objectives are also commonly combined. With the goal of influencing, it is helpful for the receiver to know the end result of the communication before covering all of the details.

step 3. **Transmit your message.** If the communication objective is to influence, tell the people what you want them to do, give instructions, and so forth. Be sure to set deadlines for completing tasks. If the objective is to inform, give the people the information. If the objective is to express feeling, do so.

step 4. **Check the receiver's understanding.** The only time you may not want to check understanding is when the objective is to express feelings. When influencing and giving information, you should ask direct questions and/or use paraphrasing. Simply asking "Do you have any questions?" does not check understanding. After step 5, you will learn how to check understanding.

step 5. **Get a commitment and follow up.** When the goal of communication is to inform or express feelings, a commitment is not needed. However, when the goal of communication is to influence, get a commitment to the action. Managers should make sure that employees can do the task and have it done by a certain time or date. In situations in which employees do not intend to get the task done, it is better to find out when sending the message, rather than waiting until the deadline. When employees are reluctant

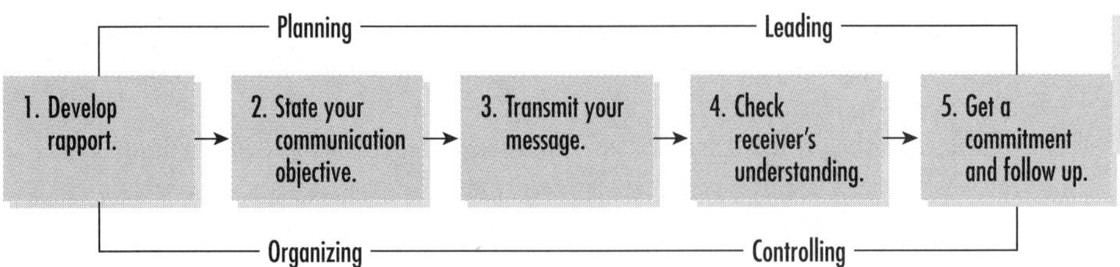

Model 10–1
The Face-to-Face Message-Sending Process

to commit to the necessary action, managers can use persuasive power within their authority. When communicating to influence, follow up to ensure that the necessary action has been taken.

Model 10–1 lists the five steps in the message-sending process.

Work Application

5. Recall a specific task that your boss assigned to you. Identify which steps the manager did and did not use in the face-to-face message-sending process.

Checking Understanding: Feedback

Feedback *is the process of verifying messages.* Questioning, paraphrasing, and allowing comments and suggestions are all forms of feedback that check understanding. Feedback when giving and receiving messages facilitates job performance.[28] Feedback motivates employees to achieve high levels of performance.[29]

6. Describe paraphrasing and state why it is used.

feedback
The process of verifying messages.

paraphrasing
The process of having the receiver restate the message in his or her own words.

Mutual understanding of the meaning of the message must exist for communication to take place. The best way to make sure communication has taken place is to get feedback from the receiver of the message through questioning and paraphrasing. **Paraphrasing** *is the process of having the receiver restate the message in his or her own words.*

The Common Approach to Getting Feedback on Messages and Why It Doesn't Work. The most common approach to getting feedback is to send the entire message, followed by asking "Do you have any questions?" Feedback usually does not follow because people tend not to ask questions. There are three good reasons why people do not ask questions:

1. *Receivers feel ignorant.* To ask a question, especially if no one else does, is often considered an admission of not paying attention or not being bright enough to understand the issue.
2. *Receivers are ignorant.* Sometimes people do not know enough about the message to know whether or not it is incomplete, incorrect, or subject to interpretation. There are no questions because what was said sounds right. The receiver does not understand the message, or does not know what to ask.
3. *Receivers are reluctant to point out the sender's ignorance.* This commonly occurs when the sender is a manager and the receiver is an employee. Employees often fear that asking a question suggests that the manager has done a poor job of preparing and sending the message. Or it suggests that the manager is wrong. Regardless of the reason, it has the same end result: Generally, employees don't ask questions when they do not understand; students don't either.

After managers send a message and ask if there are questions, they then proceed to make another common error. They assume that if no questions are asked, the communication is complete, that mutual understanding of the message exists. In reality, the message is often misunderstood. When "this isn't what I asked for" happens, the task has to be done over again. The end result is often wasted time, materials, and effort.

The most common cause of messages not resulting in communication is the lack of getting feedback that ensures mutual understanding. The proper use of questioning and paraphrasing can help you ensure that your messages are communicated.

How to Get Feedback on Messages. You should use the following four guidelines when getting feedback on messages. They are appropriate for managers and nonmanagers.

- *Be open to feedback.* There are no dumb questions. When someone asks a question, you need to be responsive and patiently answer and explain things clearly. If people sense that you get upset if they ask questions, they will not ask. Instead, praise good questions.
- *Be aware of nonverbal communication.* Make sure that your nonverbal communication encourages feedback. For example, if you say "I encourage questions," but when people ask questions you look at them as though they are stupid, or you are impatient, people will learn not to ask questions. You must also read people's nonverbal communication. For example, if you are explaining a task to Larry and he has a puzzled look on his face, he is probably confused but may not be willing to say so. In such a case, you should stop and clarify things before going on.
- *Ask questions.* When you send messages, you should know whether or not the messages are understood before taking action. That way, the action will not have to be changed or repeated. Because communicating is 100 percent the responsibility of message-senders, you should ask questions to check understanding, rather than simply asking, "Do you have any questions?" Direct questions dealing with the specific information you have given will indicate if the receiver has been listening and whether or not he or she understands enough to give a direct reply. If the response is not accurate, you need to repeat, giving more examples or elaborating more on the message. You can also ask indirect questions to attain feedback. You can ask "how do you feel?" questions about the message. You can also ask "if you were me" questions, such as "If you were me, how would you explain how to do it?" Or you can ask third-party questions, such as "How will employees feel about this?" The response to indirect questions will tell you the other's attitude.
- *Use paraphrasing.* The most accurate indicator of understanding is paraphrasing. How you ask the receiver to paraphrase will affect his or her attitude. For example, saying "Joan, tell me what I just said so that I can be sure you will not make a mistake as usual," would probably result in defensive behavior on Joan's part. Joan would probably make a mistake. Two examples of proper requests for paraphrasing follow:

"Now tell me what you are going to do so we will be sure that we are in agreement."

"Would you tell me what you are going to do so that I can be sure that I explained myself clearly?"

Notice that the second statement takes the pressure off the employee. The sender is asking for a check on his or her ability, not that of the employee. These types of requests for paraphrasing should result in a positive attitude toward the message and the sender. They show concern for the employee and for communicating effectively.

Delta Airlines' communication objective was to inform travel agents of its decision to cap their commissions. Delta selected the written fax to send the message. Delta did not check understanding because it knew the feedback would be negative. What type of feedback would you give to a person who told you that you will do the same work, but you will be paid less, possibly half as much, for doing it? The written fax was chosen because it does not often encourage a response. Many travel agents that target business travelers had their revenues cut dramatically. They needed to book passengers on airlines that did not have a cap. However, this is not always possible. Therefore, to help cut the lost revenue, they needed to pass on some of the cost to the client. Many travel agents appropriately met face-to-face with clients to go over the cap situation and discuss added fees.

Work Application

6. Recall a past or present boss. How effective was this person at getting feedback? Was the boss open to feedback and aware of nonverbal communication? Did the boss ask questions and ask you to paraphrase?

RECEIVING MESSAGES

The third step in the communication process requires the receiver to decode the message and decide if feedback is needed. With oral communication, the key to successfully understanding the message is listening.

Listening Skills

Complete Self-Assessment Exercise 10–1 to determine how good a listener you are, then read the tips for improving listening skills in the message-receiving process.

SELF-ASSESSMENT EXERCISE 10–1

Listening Skills

Select the response that best describes the frequency of your actual behavior. Place the letter A, U, F, O, or S on the line before each of the 15 statements.

A—almost always U—usually F—frequently
O—occasionally S—seldom

___ 1. I like to listen to people talk. I encourage others to talk by showing interest, smiling, nodding, and so forth.

___ 2. I pay closer attention to people who are more similar to me than people who are different from me.

___ 3. I evaluate people's words and nonverbal communication ability as they talk.

___ 4. I avoid distractions; if it's noisy, I suggest moving to a quiet spot.

___ 5. When people come to me and interrupt me when I'm doing something,

I put what I was doing out of my mind and give them my complete attention.

___ 6. When people are talking, I allow them time to finish. I do not interrupt, anticipate what they are going to say, or jump to conclusions.

___ 7. I tune people out who do not agree with my views.

___ 8. While the other person is talking, or professors are lecturing, my mind wanders to personal topics.

___ 9. While the other person is talking, I pay close attention to the nonverbal communication to help me fully understand what he or she is trying to communicate.

___ 10. I tune out and pretend I understand when the topic is difficult for me to understand.

___ 11. When the other person is talking, I think about and prepare what I am going to say in reply.

___ 12. When I think there is something missing or contradictory, I ask direct questions to get the person to explain the idea more fully.

___ 13. When I don't understand something, I let the other person know I don't understand.

___ 14. When listening to other people, I try to put myself in their position and see things from their perspective.

___ 15. During conversations I repeat back to the other person what has been said in my own words to be sure I understand what has been said.

If people you talk to regularly answer these questions about you, would they have the same responses that you selected? To find out, have friends fill out the questions using "you" (your name) rather than "I." Then compare answers.

To determine your score, give yourself 5 points for each A, 4 for each U, 3 for each F, 2 for each O, and 1 for each S for statements 1, 4, 5, 6, 9, 12, 13, 14, and 15. Place the numbers on the line next to your response letter. For items 2, 3, 7, 8, 10, and 11 the score reverses: 5 points for each S, 4 for each O, 3 for each F, 2 for each U, and 1 for each A. Place these score numbers on the lines next to the response letters. Now add your total number of points. Your score should be between 15 and 75. Place your score on the continuum below. Generally, the higher your score, the better your listening skills.

Poor listener Good listener
15—20—25—30—35—40—45—50—55—60—65—70—75

The key to effective management is sensitive listening. Listening's greatest value is that it gives the speaker a sense of worth.[30] People have a passionate desire to be heard.[31] Good human relations depend on listening.[32] Plus, you learn by listening, not talking.

7. List and explain the three parts of the message-receiving process.

The Message-Receiving Process

message-receiving process Includes listening, analyzing, and checking understanding.

The **message-receiving process** *includes listening, analyzing, and checking understanding.* To improve your listening skills, spend one week focusing your attention on listening by concentrating on what other people say and the nonverbal communications they send when they speak. Notice if their verbal and nonverbal communications are consistent. Do the nonverbals reinforce the speaker's words or detract from them? Talk only when necessary so that you can listen and see what others are saying. If you apply the following tips, you will improve your listening skills. The tips are presented in the receiving-messages process; we should listen, analyze, then check understanding, which Figure 10–5 illustrates.

Listening
Pay attention
Avoid distractions
Stay tuned in (mentally paraphrase)
Don't assume and interrupt
Watch nonverbals
Ask questions
Take notes (when appropriate)
Convey meaning

Analyzing
Think
Wait to evaluate until after listening

Checking Understanding
Paraphrase
Watch nonverbals

Figure 10–5
The Message-Receiving Process

Listening. *Listening* is the process of giving the speaker your undivided attention. As the speaker sends the message, you should listen by:

- *Paying attention.* When people interrupt you to talk, stop what you are doing and give them your complete attention immediately. Quickly relax and clear your mind so that you are receptive to the speaker. This will get you started correctly. If you miss the first few words, you may miss the message.
- *Avoiding distractions.* Keep your eyes on the speaker. Do not fiddle with pens, papers, or other distractions. For important messages, put your phone on "take a message." If you are in a noisy or distracting place, suggest moving to a quiet spot.
- *Staying tuned in.* While the other person is talking or the professor is lecturing, do not let your mind wander to personal topics. If it does wander, gently bring it back. Do not tune out the speaker because you do not like something about the person or because you disagree with what is being said. If the topic is difficult, do not tune out; ask questions. Do not think about what you are going to say in reply, just listen. As you listen, mentally paraphrase the message to stay tuned in.
- *Not assuming and interrupting.* Do not assume you know what the speaker is going to say, or listen to the beginning and jump to conclusions. Most listening mistakes are made when people hear the first few words of a sentence, finish it in their own minds, and miss the second half. Listen to the entire message without interrupting the speaker.
- *Watching nonverbals.* Understand both the feelings and the content of the message. People sometimes say one thing and mean something else. So watch as you listen to be sure that the speaker's eyes, body, and face are sending the same message as the verbal message. If something seems out of sync, get it cleared up by asking questions.
- *Asking questions.* When you feel there is something missing, contradictory, or you just do not understand, ask direct questions to get the person to explain the idea more fully.
- *Taking notes (when appropriate).* Part of listening is writing important things down so you can remember them later, and to document them when necessary, especially when listening to instructions. You should always have something to write with such as a pen and a notebook or some index cards.
- *Conveying meaning.* The way to let the speaker know you are listening to the message is to use verbal clues such as, "you feel . . . ," "uh huh," "I see," "I understand."[33] You should also use nonverbal communication such as eye contact, appropriate facial expressions, nodding of the head,

or leaning slightly forward in your chair to indicate you are interested and listening.[34]

Analyzing. *Analyzing* is the process of thinking about, decoding, and evaluating the message. Poor listening is caused in part by the fact that people speak at an average rate of 120 words per minute, while they are capable of listening at a rate of over 500 words per minute. The ability to comprehend words more than four times faster than the speaker can talk often results in wandering minds. To analyze, as the speaker sends the message, you should be:

- *Thinking.* To help overcome the discrepancy in the speed between your ability to listen and people's rate of speaking, use the speed of your brain positively. Listen actively by mentally paraphrasing, organizing, summarizing, reviewing, interpreting, and critiquing often. These activities will help you to do an effective job of decoding the message.
- *Waiting to evaluate until after listening.* When people try to listen and evaluate what is said at the same time they tend to miss part or all of the message. You should just listen to the entire message, then come to your conclusions. When you evaluate the decision, base your conclusion on the facts presented rather than on stereotypes and generalities.

Checking Understanding. *Checking understanding* is the process of giving feedback. After you have listened to the message, or during if it's a long message, check your understanding of the message by:

- *Paraphrasing.* Begin speaking by giving feedback through paraphrasing the message back to the sender.[35] When you can paraphrase the message correctly, you convey that you have listened and understood the other person. Now you are ready to offer your ideas, advice, solution, decision, or whatever the sender of the message is talking to you about.[36]
- *Watching nonverbals.* As you speak, watch the other person's nonverbals. If the person does not seem to understand what you are talking about, clarify the message before finishing the conversation.

Do you talk more than you listen? To be sure your perception is correct, ask your boss, coworkers, and friends who will give you an honest answer. If you spend more time talking than listening, you are probably failing in your communications and boring people too. Regardless of how much you listen, if you follow these guidelines, you will improve your conversation and become a person that people want to listen to instead of a person they feel they have to listen to. To become an active listener, take 100 percent of the responsibility for ensuring mutual understanding. Work to change your behavior to become a better listener. Review the 15 statements in Self-Assessment Exercise 10–1. Do items 1, 4, 5, 6, 9, 12, 13, 14, and 15. Do not do items 2, 3, 7, 8, 10, and 11. Effective listening requires responding to the message to ensure mutual understanding takes place.

When Delta Airline sent the message of the commission cap to travel agents, the agents received a message they did not want to get. Because Delta sent the message by fax, listening skills were not used. The analysis was fairly simple—a cut in revenue. To check understanding, many travel agents contacted Delta to verify the accuracy of the message; they hoped it was some type of a mistake.

Work Application

7. Refer back to Self-Assessment Exercise 10–1 and the listening tips. What is your weakest listening skill area? How will you improve your listening ability?

RESPONDING TO MESSAGES

The fourth, and last, step in the communication process involves responding to the message. However, not all messages require a response. For example, when Delta Airlines faxed the commission cap message to the travel agents it did not expect or want them all to contact Delta with a response. Managers at Delta were most likely hoping that travel agents would just accept the decreased commissions with a limited response to the bad news.

With oral communication, the sender often expects the receiver to respond to the message. When the receiver does respond, the roles are reversed as the receiver now becomes the sender of a message. Roles can continue to change throughout the conversation. In this section you will study five response styles and how to deal with emotional people.

Response Styles

As the sender transmits a message, how you as the receiver respond to the message directly affects the communication. There is no best response style. The response should be appropriate for the situation. The five response styles, which appear in Figure 10–6, are advising, diverting, probing, reassuring, and reflecting. For each response style, you will be given an example response to this employee message:

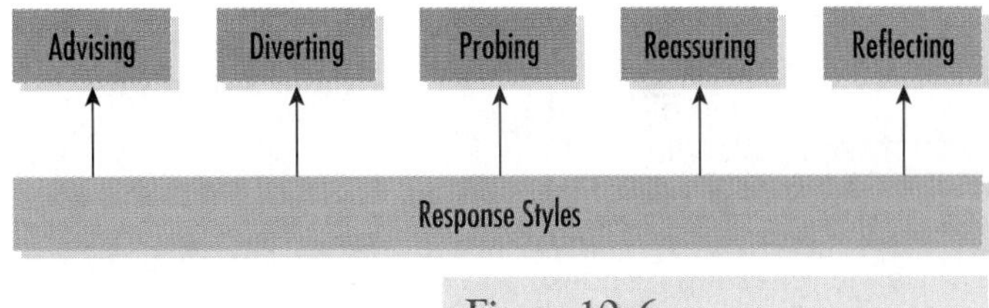

Figure 10–6
Response Styles

"You supervise me so closely that you disrupt my ability to do my job."

Advising. *Advising responses* provide evaluation, personal opinion, direction, or instructions. Employees often come to the manager for advice on how to do something or for the manager to make the decision. Advising tends to close, limit, or direct the flow of communication away from the sender to the receiver.

Appropriate Use of Advising Responses. Giving advice is appropriate when you are directly asked for it. However, quickly giving advice tends to build dependence. Managers need to develop their employee's ability to think things out and to make decisions. When asked for advice by employees who you believe don't really need it, ask questions such as, "What do you think is the best way to handle this situation?"

Example Advising Responses. An example manager's advising response to the employee's message is: "You need my directions to do a good job; you lack experience." "I disagree. You need my instructions and for me to check your work." Note that in this situation advice was not asked for, but it was given anyway.

Diverting. *Diverting responses* switch the focus of the communication to a new message; it is commonly called changing the subject. Diverting responses tend to redirect, close, or limit the flow of communication. Diverting responses used during the early stages of receiving the message may cause the sender to feel that the message is not worth discussing, or that the other party's message is more important.

Appropriate Use of Diverting Responses. The diverting response is appropriate when either party is uncomfortable with the topic. Diverting responses may be helpful when used to share personal experiences or feelings similar to those of the sender but that change the topic.

Example Diverting Response. An example manager's diverting response to the employee's message is: "You've reminded me of a manager I once had who. . . ."

Probing. A *probing response* asks the sender to give more information about some aspect of the message. It can be useful to get a better understanding of the situation. When probing, "what" questions are preferred to "why" questions.

Work Application

8. Recall two situations in which you received an oral message. State the message and your response to it. Be sure to identify your response style and use two different response styles.

Appropriate Use of Probing Responses. Probing is appropriate during the early stages of the message to ensure that you fully understand the situation. After probing, the other response styles are often needed.

Example Probing Response. An example manager's probing response to the employee's message is: "What do I do to cause you to say this?" Not: "Why do you feel this way?"

Reassuring. A *reassuring response* is given to reduce the intensity of the emotions associated with the message. Essentially you're saying, "Don't worry; everything will be OK." "You can do it." You are pacifying the sender.

8. Define reflecting response and state when it should be used.

reflecting response
Paraphrase the message and communicate understanding and acceptance to the sender.

Appropriate Use of Reassuring Responses. Reassuring is appropriate when the other person lacks confidence. Encouraging responses that give praise can help employees develop confidence.

Example Reassuring Responses. An example manager's reassuring response to the employee's message is: "Don't worry, I will not do it for much longer." "Your work is improving, so I may be able to provide less direction soon."

APPLYING THE CONCEPT

AC 10–4 Identifying Response Styles

Identify each of the six responses as:

a. advising
b. diverting
c. probing
d. reassuring
e. reflecting

Secretary: Boss, do you have a minute to talk?
Boss: Sure, what's up?
Secretary: Can you do something about all the swearing people do in the operations department? It carries through these thin walls into my work area. It's disgusting. I'm surprised you haven't done anything.
Boss:

____ **16.** "I didn't know anyone was swearing. I'll look into it."
____ **17.** "You don't have to listen to it. Just ignore the swearing."
____ **18.** "Are you feeling well today?"
____ **19.** "So you find this swearing offensive?"
____ **20.** "What specific swear words are they saying that offend you?"

Reflecting. **Reflecting responses** *paraphrase the message and communicate understanding and acceptance to the sender.* When reflecting, be sure NOT to use the senders' exact words or they may feel you are mimicking them, not understanding them, or not listening closely. Reflecting in your own words leads to the most effective communication and most effective human relations.

Appropriate Use of Reflecting Responses. Reflecting responses should be used when coaching and counseling. The sender can feel listened to, understood, and free to explore the topic in more depth. As the communication progresses, it is often appropriate to change to other response styles.

Example Reflecting Responses. An example manager's reflecting response to the employee's message is: "My checking up on you annoys you!" "You don't think I need to check up on you, is this what you mean?" Note that these responses allow the employee to express feelings and direct the communication.

Dealing with Emotional People

As a manager, an employee or customer may send you a message in an emotional state. Emotions tend to hurt communications, but they can bring about new ideas and new ways of doing things. You should understand emotions and how to deal with them.[37]

Understanding Feelings. You should realize that:

- Feelings are subjective; they tell us people's attitudes and needs.
- Feelings are usually disguised as factual statements. For example, when people are hot, they tend to say "It's hot in here" rather than "I feel hot." When they are bored, they tend to say, "This topic is boring," rather than, "I'm feeling bored by this topic." Everyone will often not be hot or bored.
- And most importantly, feelings are neither right nor wrong.

We cannot choose our feelings, or control them. However, we can control how we express feelings. For example, if Rachel, an employee, says "You *!!" (pick a swear word that would make you angry) to Louise, her manager, she will feel its impact. However, Louise can express her feelings in a calm manner, or she can yell, hit, give Rachel a dirty look, and so on. Managers should encourage people to express their feelings in a positive way. But they shouldn't allow employees to go around yelling, swearing, or hitting others. You should avoid getting caught up in others' emotions. Staying calm when dealing with an emotional person works much better than getting emotional too.

Calming the Emotional Employee. When an emotional employee comes to you, NEVER make put-down statements such as, "You shouldn't be angry," "Don't be upset," "You're acting like a baby," "Just sit down and be quiet," or "I know how you feel." (No one knows how anyone else feels. Even people who experience the same thing at the same time don't feel the same.) These types of statements only make the feelings stronger. You may get employees to shut up and you can show them who is boss, but communication will not take place. The problem will still exist and your human relations with the employee will suffer because of it, as will your relations with others who see or hear about what you said and did. When the employee complains to peers, some peers will feel you were too hard or easy on the person. You lose either way.

9. Discuss what should and what should not be done to calm an emotional person.

Reflective Empathic Responding. **Empathic listening** *is the ability to understand and relate to another's situation and feelings.* The empathic responder deals with feelings, content, and the underlying meaning being expressed in the message. Empathy is needed to develop human relationships based on trust.[38] To calm emotional people, don't argue with them. Encourage them to express

empathic listening
The ability to understand and relate to another's situation and feelings.

Work Application

9. Recall a situation in which a manager had to handle an emotional employee. Did the manager follow the guidelines for calming an emotional person? Did the manager use reflective empathic responses?

their feelings in a positive way. Empathically let them know that you understand how they feel. People want to be listened to and understood, and if you do not listen to and understand others they will avoid you.[39] Do not agree or disagree with the feelings; simply identify them verbally. Paraphrase the feeling to the person. Use statements like, "You were *hurt* when you didn't get the assignment." "You *resent* Charlie for not doing his share of the work; is that what you mean?" "You are *doubtful* that the job will be done on time; is that what you're saying?"

After you deal with emotions, you can proceed to work on content (solving problems). It may be wise to wait until a later time if emotions are very strong. You will find that just understanding others' feelings is often the solution rather than giving advice.

Criticism

Giving Criticism. Even when bosses ask, they usually don't want to hear personal criticism. In a meeting, if your boss asks you for feedback on how good a manager he or she is or how he or she can improve, it may sound like the ideal opportunity to unload your complaints, but don't criticize. In such a situation, the first rule of thumb is: never publicly criticize your boss, even if specifically asked to do so. You are better off airing criticism in private.[40] And don't criticize your boss behind his or her back; bosses often find out about it. Criticizing your boss could hurt your human relations and career.

An important part of the manager's job is to improve employee performance through criticism. Chapter 16 will show you how to do this.

Getting Criticism. If you're asking for personal feedback, remember that you are asking to hear things that may surprise, upset, insult, or hurt your feelings. If you become defensive and emotional, and it is hard not to when you feel attacked, the person will stop giving feedback. The criticizer will probably tell others what happened, and others will not give you truthful feedback either. You should realize that criticism from your boss, peers, or employees is painful. People do not really enjoy being criticized, even when it is constructive. Keep the phrase "no pain, no gain" in mind when it comes to criticism. If you want to improve your performance, and your chances of having a successful career, seek honest feedback about how you can improve your performance. When you get criticism, whether you ask for it or not, view it as an opportunity to improve, stay calm (even when the other person is emotional) and don't get defensive. Use the feedback to improve your performance.

Work Application

10. How would you rate yourself on your ability to accept criticism without getting emotional and defensive? How could you improve your ability to accept criticism?

CURRENT MANAGEMENT ISSUES

Globalization. Communicating becomes increasingly complex in a *global* environment.[41] Communication barriers intensify as people of different cultures perceive things differently. They may not trust each other, they may get emotional as they get frustrated communicating with foreigners, and they more easily reach the information overload point. Language barriers make communication difficult. Over 3,000 languages are spoken and about 100 are official national languages. To overcome this barrier, many managers at multinational corporations (MNCs) such as Citicorp, du Pont, Eastman Kodak, and General

Electric are learning other languages. Nonverbal differences further complicate communications. As a general guide, when communicating with people of different cultures, learn their culture and use simple, clear messages free of jargon and slang.

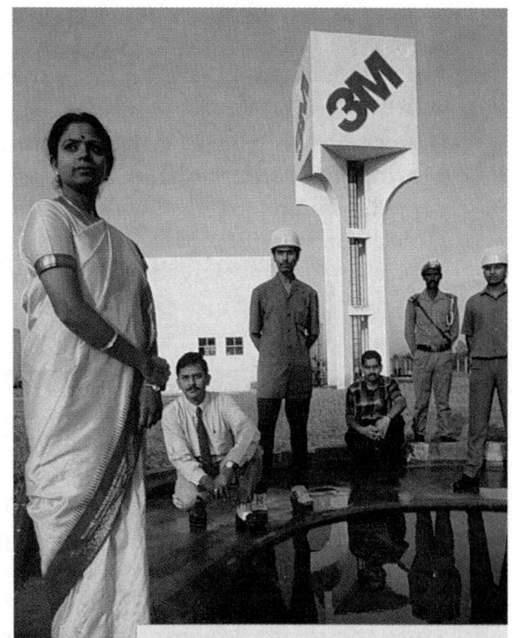

In order to communicate in a global environment, many managers at MNCs are learning other languages.

Diversity. Communicating with a *diversity* of people also complicates sending messages. Communication styles can vary widely depending on sex, race, and religion.[42] Treating all employees alike may not achieve the desired results. Therefore, communication must be tailored and adjusted to fit the persons involved.[43] At many organizations, such as Digital, memos are sent in multiple languages. Refer back to Chapter 3 for more details on managing diversity.

Ethics and Social Responsibility. Ethics is directly involved with communications. Open, honest communication is ethical. When filtering is a major distortion and includes lying, it is unethical. Open, honest communication with stakeholders in the external environment is an important part of *social responsibility*.

TQM. The *TQM* environment promotes open and complete sharing of information among all employees because the systems approach requires such openness. The TQM principles of focusing on delivering customer value and continuously improving systems and process require open and complete information. Three of Deming's 14 Points (Chapter 8) directly address issues involving communication: (1) Create constancy of purpose toward improvement of products. (8) Drive out fear, so that everyone may work effectively for the organization. (9) Break down barriers between departments. Enabling people to understand the situation breaks down communication barriers of perception, trust and credibility, and filtering. With open communication, much less gossip travels the grapevine.

Productivity. Open, honest communication contributes positively to *productivity*. When people hold back information for their own personal use and gain, the organization loses. However, in organizations that have downsized through layoffs and cutbacks without open, honest communications, the grapevine is filled with rumors. When employees view managers without trust and credibility and emotions are high, barriers result. Such communication barriers have a negative long-term effect on productivity.[44]

Participative Management and Teams. Managers in traditional top-down autocratic organizations that adopt *participative management* often find that they need to develop their interpersonal communication skills which an empowered environment greatly needs.[45] The need for good communication skills has become even more urgent with the trend toward the use of *teams*. It is only through effective communication that everyone in the team and the organization can be directed toward the same mission and objectives.[46]

Small Business. In *small businesses*, communication tends to be less formal as the chain of command usually has fewer layers of management with flatter organizational structures. However, the communication process and the need for effective communication skills does not change with the size of the organization. Communication tends to flow through the same vertical, horizontal, and grapevine channels in all organizations. The eight communication barriers are found in all sizes of organizations.

CHAPTER SUMMARY AND GLOSSARY

This chapter summary is organized to answer the ten learning objectives for Chapter 10.

1. Describe the three ways communication flows through organizations.

First, communication formally flows vertically downward and upward through the chain of command. Second, communication formally flows horizontally between colleagues and peers. Third, communication flows informally through the grapevine in any direction.

2. List the four steps in the communication process.

(1) The sender encodes the message and selects the transmission channel. (2) The sender transmits the message through a channel. (3) The receiver decodes the message and decides if feedback is needed. (4) The receiver may give feedback, make a response, or send a new message through a channel.

3. State the major advantages of oral over written communications, and the advantages of written over oral communications.

The major advantage of oral over written communication is that it is usually easier and faster and encourages feedback. The disadvantages are that it is usually less accurate and provides no record.

The major advantages of written over oral communication is that it is usually more accurate and provides a record. The major disadvantages are that it usually takes longer and hinders feedback.

4. State the general guide to channel selection.

As a general guide, use rich oral channels for sending difficult and unusual messages, less rich written channels for transmitting simple and routine messages to several people, and combined channels for important messages that employees need to attend to and understand.

5. List the five steps in the face-to-face message-sending process.

The face-to-face message-sending process involves five steps: (1) Develop rapport. (2) State your communication objective. (3) Transmit your message. (4) Check the receivers' understanding. (5) Get a commitment and follow up.

6. Describe paraphrasing and state why it is used.

Paraphrasing is the process of having the receiver restate the message in his or her own words. The receiver uses paraphrasing to check understanding of the transmitted message. If the receiver can paraphrase the message accurately, communication has taken place. If not, communication is not complete.

7. List and explain the three parts of the message-receiving process.

The three parts of the message-receiving process are: listening, analyzing, and checking understanding. Listening is the process of giving the speaker your undivided attention. Analyzing is the process of thinking about, decoding, and evaluating the message. Checking understanding is the process of giving feedback.

8. Define reflecting response and state when it should be used.

Reflecting responses paraphrase back the message and communicate the sender's understanding and acceptance. Reflecting responses are appropriate to use when coaching and counseling.

9. Discuss what should and should not be done to calm an emotional person.

To calm an emotional person, do not make statements that put the person down. Make reflective empathic responses that let the emotional person know that you understand how he or she feels. Paraphrase the feelings.

10. Define the following key terms (in order of appearance in the chapter):

Select one or more methods: (1) fill in the missing key terms from memory, (2) match the key terms from the end of the review with their definitions below, or (3) copy the key terms in order from the list at the beginning of the chapter.

______ is the process of transmitting information and meaning.

__________ is the flow of information both downward and upward through the organizational chain of command.

__________ is the flow of information between colleagues and peers.

The ______ is the flow of information in any direction throughout the organization.

The __________ consist of a sender who encodes a message and transmits the message through a channel and a receiver who decodes it and may give feedback.

______ is the sender's process of putting the message into a form that the receiver will understand.

The three primary __________ are oral, nonverbal, and written.

______ is the receiver's process of translating the message into a meaningful form.

__________ are messages sent without words.

______ is the process of verifying messages.

______ is the process of having the receiver restate the message in his or her own words.

The __________ includes: (1) develop rapport, (2) state your communication objective, (3) transmit your message, (4) check the receivers' understanding, and (5) get a commitment and follow up.

The __________ includes listening, analyzing, and checking understanding.

__________ paraphrase back the message and communicate understanding and acceptance to the sender.

__________ is the ability to understand and relate to another's situation and feelings.

KEY TERMS

communication
communication channels
communication process
decoding
empathic listening
encoding
feedback
grapevine
horizontal communication
message-receiving process
message-sending process
nonverbal communication
paraphrasing
reflecting responses
vertical communication

REVIEW AND DISCUSSION QUESTIONS

1. What is the difference among vertical, horizontal, and grapevine communication?
2. What is the difference between encoding and decoding?
3. What does perception have to do with encoding and decoding?
4. What is filtering?
5. What is the difference between nonverbal setting and body language?
6. What is the difference between voice mail and e-mail?
7. What are the three parts of a written outline?
8. As an average, how many words should a sentence have and how many sentences should there be in a paragraph?
9. What is media richness?
10. What should be included in your plan to send a message?
11. What are the four ways to get feedback on messages?
12. Why should you listen, analyze, then check understanding?
13. Which response style do you use most often?
14. When calming an emotional employee, why shouldn't you make put-down statements to him or her?

CASE

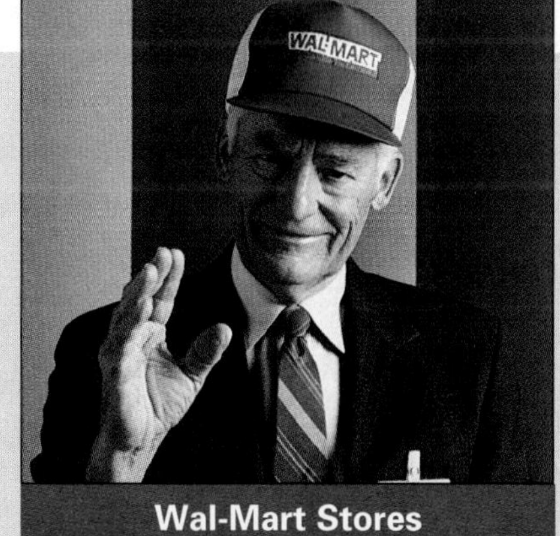

Wal-Mart Stores

Back in the 1950s, Sam Walton visited discount stores all over the United States to learn about this industry. Walton asked employees questions and wrote in his little notebook. In 1963, Sam opened his first Wal-Mart store. Before Sam retired, several hundred Wal-Mart stores had been opened, headquartered in Bentonville, Arkansas. Sam would visit all Wal-Mart stores at least once a year. He also continued to visit hundreds of competitors, looking for ideas to improve operations. Sam would simply walk through the store and talk to the employees, who are called associates, and customers. He continued to write in a notebook. Sam required all executives to visit stores. At least one hundred stores are visited every day. Sam wanted all employees involved in continuous improvements, so all managers ask every associate what he or she can do to improve store operations. All employees have access to complete financial results to keep them focused on the bottom line.

Sam Walton died in April 1992. The same year, Wal-Mart became the largest retailer in the nation based on sales of $55 billion, with stores in 43 states. Wal-Mart, which also owns Sam's Warehouse Club, SuperCenters, and Hypermarts, has grown by more than 30 percent a year for more than 20 years to over 1,900 stores. Wal-Mart continues to open about 150 stores every year and its strategic plan is to continue this growth rate and to be in all 50 states by the year 2000. Over the past ten years, average annual return to stockholders has been more than 40 percent. If you bought $1,000 worth of Wal-Mart stock in 1970, it would be worth more than $5 million today!

Sam's son Rob, chairman of the board, and David Glass, CEO, manage Wal-Mart. However, Sam's original communication system is still used today, and management is committed to continuing it. When Glass is not personally visiting stores, he maintains communication through a six-channel satellite system. The communication goal is to link every store by voice and video to facilitate store-to-store and store-to-home-office communications. The satellite also gathers store data for the master computers.

By satellite, Glass and other executives can talk via video to every store at the same time as often as they want to. They can also communicate with only a few stores. When associates come up with suggestions for improving operations, such as increasing sales or decreasing costs, the satellite system quickly transmits the information to all stores. The major advantage of the satellite is its use in merchandising, which follows the old saying: a picture is worth a thousand words. A buyer can go on video and make an announcement such as, "These are the new items for Department 12. Here is how you should display them." Associates can see how the merchandise is displayed and copy it.

In addition to store visits and the satellite system, a third major means of communication is the company magazine, *Wal-Mart World*, which is used as a combining channel to send some of the same messages. *Wal-Mart World* is also used to announce the names and show pictures of the winners of its various contests.

Select the best alternative to the following questions. Be sure you are able to explain your answers.

___ 1. When David Glass sends a message to all stores via satellite, he is using ___ communication.

a. downward c. horizontal
b. upward d. grapevine

___ 2. When store managers seek ideas from associates to improve operations, they are using ___ communication.

a. downward c. horizontal
b. upward d. grapevine

___ 3. When Wal-Mart executives and store managers walk around stores and talk to associates and customers, they are involved in ___ communication.

a. formal b. informal

___ 4. The biggest communication barrier to using the satellite to send messages is most likely

a. perception e. trust and credibility
b. information overload f. not listening
c. channel selection g. emotions
d. noise h. filtering

___ 5. The satellite system itself is a(n) ___ of communication.

a. encoding c. channel
b. decoding d. feedback

___ 6. When used for merchandising, the Wal-Mart satellite relies most heavy on ___ communication.

a. oral b. nonverbal c. written

___ 7. Wal-Mart places ___ emphasis on feedback.

a. great b. little

___ 8. At Wal-Mart, the ability to listen is considered

a. very important c. somewhat important
b. important d. not very important

___ 9. The most appropriate response for Wal-Mart executives to use when walking around and talking to associates and customers is

a. advising d. reassuring
b. diverting e. reflecting
c. probing

___ 10. Wal-Mart ___ criticism.

a. openly seeks c. does not really want
b. will listen to d. avoids

11. What message do you think Wal-Mart executives send to associates when they visit stores?

12. What effect has the satellite had on formal communication?

13. What part would you say communication has played in Wal-Mart's success?

For current information on Wal-Mart, use Internet address http://www.walmart.com. For ideas on using the Internet, see the Appendix.

SKILL-BUILDING EXERCISE 10–1

Giving Instructions

Doing Skill-Building Exercise 10–1 in Class

Objective
To develop your ability to give and receive messages (communication skills).

Experience
You will plan, give, and receive instructions for the completion of a drawing of three objects.

Preparation
No preparation is necessary except reading and understanding the chapter. The instructor will provide the original drawings.

Procedure 1 (3–7 minutes)
Read all of Procedure 1 twice. The task is for the manager to give an employee instructions for completing a drawing of three objects. The objects must be drawn to scale and look like photocopies of the originals. You will have up to 15 minutes to complete the task.

The exercise has four separate parts or steps:

1. The manager plans.
2. The manager gives the instructions.
3. The employee does the drawing.
4. The results are evaluated.

Rules. The rules are numbered to correlate with the four parts of the exercise.

1. *Planning.* While planning, the manager may write out instructions for the employee, but may not do any drawing of any kind.
2. *Instructions.* While giving instructions, the manager may not show the original drawing to the employee. (The instructor will give it to you.) The instructions may be given orally and/or in writing, but no nonverbal hand gestures are allowed. The employee may take notes while the instructions are being given, but cannot do any drawing with or without a pen. The manager must give the instructions for all three objects before drawing begins.
3. *Drawing.* Once the employee begins the drawing, the manager should watch but no longer communicate in any way.
4. *Evaluation.* When the employee is finished or the time is up, the manager shows the employee the original drawing. Discuss how you did. Turn to the integration section and answer the questions. The manager writes the answers, not the employee. The employee will write when playing the manager role.

Procedure 2 (2–5 minutes)
Half of the class members will act as the manager first and give instructions. Managers move their chairs to one of the four walls (spread out). They should be facing the center of the room with their backs close to the wall.

Employees sit in the middle of the room until called on by a manager. When called on, the employee brings a chair to the manager. The employee sits facing the manager so that he or she cannot see any managers' drawing.

Procedure 3 (Up to 15 minutes for drawing and integration)
The instructor gives each manager a copy of the drawing, being careful not to let any employees see it. The manager plans the instructions. When a manager is ready, he or she calls an employee and gives the instructions. It is helpful to use the message-sending process. Be sure to follow the rules. The employee should do the drawing on an 8½ by 11 sheet

of paper, not in this book. If you use written instructions, they may be on the reverse side of the page that the employee draws on or on a different paper. The employee has up to 15 minutes to complete the drawing and for integration (evaluation). When the drawing is finished, turn to the evaluation questions in the integration section.

Procedure 4 (up to 15 minutes)
The employees are now the managers and sit in the chairs facing the center of the room. New employees go to the center of the room until called for.

Follow Procedure 3 with a different drawing. Do not work with the same person (change partners).

Integration

Evaluating Questions. You may select more than one answer. The manager and employee discuss each question and the manager, not the employee, writes the answers.

1. The goal of communication was to:

   a. influence b. inform c. express feelings

2. The communication was:

   a. vertical-downward c. horizontal
   b. vertical-upward d. grapevine

3. The manager did an ____ job of encoding the message and the employee did an ____ job of decoding the message.

   a. effective b. ineffective

4. The manager transmitted the message through ____ communication channel(s):

   a. oral c. nonverbal
   b. written d. combined

5. The manager spent ____ time planning.

   a. too much b. too little c. the right amount of

Questions 6 to 10 relate to the steps in the message-sending process.

6. The manager developed rapport. (Step 1)

   a. true b. false

7. The manager stated the communication objective. (Step 2)

   a. true b. false

8. The manager transmitted the message (Step 3)

   a. effectively b. ineffectively

9. The manager checked understanding by using (Step 4)

   a. direct questions c. both
   b. paraphrasing d. neither

   The amount of checking was:

   a. too frequent b. too infrequent c. about right

10. The manager got a commitment and followed up. (Step 5)

    a. true b. false

11. The employee did an ____ job of listening, ____ job of analyzing, and an ____ job of checking understanding through the receiving-messages process.

    a. effective b. ineffective

12. The primary response style used by the employee was ____ and the two most appropriate response styles were ____ and ____ for this situation.

    a. advising c. probing e. reflecting
    b. diverting d. reassuring

13. The manager and/or employee got emotional.

    a. true b. false

14. When going over this integration, the manager was ____ and the employee was ____ to criticism that can help improve communication skills.

    a. open b. closed

15. Were the objects drawn to approximate scale (same size)? If not, why not?

16. Did you follow the rules? If not, why not?

17. If you could do this exercise over again, what would you do differently to improve communication?

____

____

____

Conclusion
The instructor leads a class discussion and/or makes concluding remarks.

Application (2–4 minutes)
What did I learn from this experience? How will I use this knowledge in the future?

____

____

____

Sharing
Volunteers give their answers to the application section.

VIDEO BEHAVIOR MODEL

Behavior Model Video 10–1, Situational Communications, shows two managers, Steve and Darius, meeting to discuss faulty parts. The video illustrates the four situational management styles, explained in Skill-Building Exercise 10–2.

Objectives
To better understand the four situational communication styles.

Procedure 1 (10–20 minutes)
The instructor shows Video Module 10–1, Situational Communication. As you view each of the four scenes, identify the four communication styles being used by the manager. Write the letters and number of the style on the scene line.

Scene 1. ____ Autocratic (S1A)
Scene 2.____ Consultative (S2C)
Scene 3.____ Participative (S3P)
Scene 4.____ Empowerment (S4E)

Option A. View all four scenes and identify the style used by the manager. Select the style that you would use in this situation. Are other styles also appropriate? Which style would you not use (not appropriate) for this situation. Next to each style listed, write the letter A for appropriate or N for not appropriate. After everyone is done, the instructor leads a class discussion and/or gives the correct answers.

Option B. After each scene the class discusses the style used by the manager. The instructor states the correct answer after each of the four scenes.

Conclusion
The instructor leads a class discussion and/or makes concluding remarks.

Application (2–4 minutes)
What did I learn from this exercise? How will I use this knowledge in the future?

____

____

____

Sharing
Volunteers give their answers to the application section.

SKILL-BUILDING EXERCISE 10–2

Situational Communications[47]

Preparing for Skill-Building Exercise 10–2

When you work with people outside your department, you have no authority to give them direct orders. You must use other means to achieve your goal. Situational communications is a model for conducting interpersonal communications with people outside your department or organization, or with peers and managers in higher levels of management than you. The situational communications model will teach you how to analyze a given situation and select the most appropriate style of communication.

Through this skill-building exercise you will learn the interactive process system, situational communication styles, situational variables, and how to select the most appropriate communication style in a given situation. Begin by determining your preferred communication style by completing Self-Assessment Exercise 10–2.

SELF-ASSESSMENT EXERCISE 10–2

Determining Your Preferred Communication Style

To determine your preferred communication style, select the alternative that most closely describes what you would do in each of the following 12 situations. Do not be concerned with trying to pick the correct answer; select the alternative that best describes what you would actually do. Circle the letter a, b, c, or d. Ignore all of the answer spaces for now. They will be explained later in this exercise, and will be used during the in class part of this skill-building exercise.

___ 1. Wendy, a knowledgeable person from another department, comes to you, the engineering supervisor, and requests that you design a special product to her specifications. You would:

____ time ____ information ____ acceptance
____ capability ____ communication style

a. Control the conversation and tell Wendy what you will do for her. S ___

b. Ask Wendy to describe the product. Once you understand it, you would present your ideas. Let her know that you are concerned and want to help with your ideas. S ___

c. Respond to Wendy's request by conveying understanding and support. Help clarify what is to be done by you. Offer ideas, but do it her way. S ___

d. Find out what you need to know. Let Wendy know you will do it her way. S ___

___ 2. Your department has designed a product that is to be fabricated by Saul's department. Saul has been with the company longer than you have; he knows his department. Saul comes to you to change the product design. You decide to:

____ time ____ information ____ acceptance
____ capability ____ communication style

a. Listen to the change and why it would be beneficial. If you believe Saul's way is better, change it; if not, explain why the original design is superior. If necessary, insist that it be done your way. S ___

b. Tell Saul to fabricate it any way he wants to. S ___

c. You are busy; tell Saul to do it your way. You don't have time to listen and argue with him. S ___

d. Be supportive; make changes together as a team. S ___

___ 3. Upper management has a decision to make. They call you to a meeting and tell you they need some information to solve a problem they describe to you. You:

____ time ____ information ____ acceptance
____ capability ____ communication style

a. Respond in a manner that conveys personal support and offer alternative ways to solve the problem. S ___

b. Just answer their questions. S ___

c. Explain how to solve the problem. S ___

d. Show your concern by explaining how to solve the problem and why it is an effective solution. S ___

___ 4. You have a routine work order. The work order is to be placed verbally and completed in three days. Sue, the receiver, is very experienced and willing to be of service to you. You decide to:

____ time ____ information ____ acceptance
____ capability ____ communication style

a. Explain your needs, but let Sue make the order decision. S ___

b. Tell Sue what you want and why you need it. S ___

c. Decide together what to order. S ___

d. Simply give Sue the order. S ___

___ 5. Work orders from the staff department normally take three days; however, you have an emergency and need the job today. Your colleague Jim, the department supervisor, is knowledgeable and somewhat cooperative. You decide to:

____ time ____ information ____ acceptance
____ capability ____ communication style

a. Tell Jim that you need it by three o'clock and will return at that time to pick it up. S ___

b. Explain the situation and how the organization will benefit by expediting the order. Volunteer to help in any way you can. S ___

c. Explain the situation and ask Jim when the order will be ready. S ___

d. Explain the situation and together come to a solution to your problem. S ___

___ 6. Danielle, a peer with a record of high performance, has recently had a drop in productivity. Her problem is affecting your performance. You know Danielle has a family problem. You:

____ time ____ information ____ acceptance
____ capability ____ communication style

a. Discuss the problem; help Danielle realize that the problem is affecting her work and yours. Supportively discuss ways to improve the situation. S ___

b. Tell the boss about it and let him decide what to do. S ___

c. Tell Danielle to get back on the job. S ___

d. Discuss the problem and tell Danielle how to solve the work situation; be supportive. S ___

___ 7. You are a knowledgeable supervisor. You buy supplies from Peter regularly. He is an excellent salesperson and very knowledgeable about your situation. You are placing your weekly order. You decide to:

____ time ____ information ____ acceptance
____ capability ____ communication style

a. Explain what you want and why. Develop a supportive relationship. S ___

b. Explain what you want and ask Peter to recommend products. S ___

c. Give Peter the order. S ___

d. Explain your situation and allow Peter to make the order. S ___

___ 8. Jean, a knowledgeable person from another department, has asked you to perform a routine staff function to her specifications. You decide to:

____ time ____ information ____ acceptance
____ capability ____ communication style

a. Perform the task to her specifications without questioning her. S ___

b. Tell her that you will do it the usual way. S ___

c. Explain what you will do and why. S ___

d. Show your willingness to help; offer alternative ways to do it. S ___

___ 9. Tom, a salesperson, has requested an order for your department's services with a short delivery date. As usual, Tom claims it is a take-it-or-leave-it offer. He wants your decision now, or within a few minutes, because he is in the customer's office. Your action is to:

____ time ____ information ____ acceptance
____ capability ____ communication style

a. Convince Tom to work together to come up with a later date. S ___

b. Give Tom a yes or no answer. S ___

c. Explain your situation and let Tom decide if you should take the order. S ___

d. Offer an alternative delivery date. Work on your relationship; show your support. S ___

___ 10. As a time-and-motion expert, you have been called in regard to a complaint about the standard time it takes to perform a job. As you analyze the entire job, you realize the one element of complaint should take longer, but other elements should take less time. The end result is a shorter total standard time for the job. You decide to:

____ time ____ information ____ acceptance
____ capability ____ communication style

a. Tell the operator and foreman that the total time must be decreased and why. S ___

b. Agree with the operator and increase the standard time. S ___

c. Explain your findings. Deal with the operator and/or foreman's concerns, but ensure compliance with your new standard. S ___

d. Together with the operator, develop a standard time. S ___

___ 11. You approve budget allocations for projects. Marie, who is very competent in developing budgets, has come to you with a proposed budget. You:

____ time ____ information ____ acceptance
____ capability ____ communication style

a. Review the budget, make revisions, and explain them in a supportive way. Deal with concerns, but insist on your changes. S ___

b. Review the proposal and suggest areas where changes may be needed. Make changes together, if needed. S ___

c. Review the proposed budget, make revisions, and explain them. S ___

d. Answer any questions or concerns Marie has and approve the budget as is. S ___

___ 12. You are a sales manager. A customer has offered you a contract for your product with a short delivery date. The offer is open for two days. The contract would be profitable for you and the organization. The cooperation of the production department is essential to meet the deadline. Tim, the production manager, and you do not get along very well because of your repeated request for quick delivery. Your action is to:

____ time ____ information ____ acceptance
____ capability ____ communication style

a. Contact Tim and try to work together to complete the contract. S ___

b. Accept the contract and convince Tim in a supportive way to meet the obligation. S ___

c. Contact Tim and explain the situation. Ask him if you and he should accept the contract, but let him decide. S ___

d. Accept the contract. Contact Tim and tell him to meet the obligation. If he resists, tell him you will go to his boss. S ___

To determine your preferred communication style, circle the letter you selected as the alternative in situations 1–12. The column headings indicate the style you selected.

	Autocratic (S1A)	Consultative (S2C)	Participative (S3P)	Empowerment (S4E)
1.	a	b	c	d
2.	c	a	d	b
3.	c	d	a	b
4.	d	b	c	a
5.	a	b	d	c
6.	c	d	a	b
7.	c	a	b	d
8.	b	c	d	a
9.	b	d	a	c
10.	a	c	d	b
11.	c	a	b	d
12.	d	b	a	c
Total				

Add up the number of circled items per column. The total column should equal 12. The column with the highest number represents your preferred communication style. There is no one best style in all situations. The more evenly distributed the numbers are between the four styles, the more flexible your communications. A total of 0 or 1 in any column may indicate a reluctance to use the style(s). You could have problems in situations calling for the use of this style.

The Interactive Process System

According to Anderson and Erlandson, communication has the following five dimensions, which are each on a continuum:[48]

Initiation ______________________ Response

Initiation. The sender starts, or initiates, the communication. The sender may or may not expect a response to the initiated message.

Response. The receiver replies or takes action on the sender's message. In responding, the receiver can become an initiator. As two-way communication takes place, the role of initiator (sender) and responder (receiver) may change.

Presentation ______________________ Elicitation

Presentation. The sender's message is structured, directive, or informative. A response may not be needed, although action may be called for. ("We are meeting to develop next year's budget." "Please open the door.")

Elicitation. The sender invites a response to the message. Action may or may not be needed. ("How large a budget do we need?" "Do you think we should leave the door open?")

Closed ______________________ Open

Closed. The sender expects the receiver to follow the message. ("This is a new form to fill out and return with each order.")

Open. The sender is eliciting a response as a means of considering the receiver's input. ("Should we use this new form with each order?")

Rejection ______________________________ Acceptance

Rejection. The receiver does not accept the sender's message. ("I will not fill out this new form for each order!")

Acceptance. Agreement with the sender's message. ("I will fill out the new form for each order!")

Strong ______________________________ Mild

Strong. The sender will use force or power to have the message acted on as directed. ("Fill in the form or you're fired.")

Mild. The sender will not use force or power to have the message acted on as directed. ("Please fill in the form when you can.")

Situational Communication Styles

The interactive process can be used with situational management.[49] For example, when using the autocratic style, the sender initiates a closed, strong presentation while the empowerment style uses an open, mild elicitation. The mild to strong component can be used with any of the styles, but the strong messages tend to be used more often with the autocratic and consultative styles. Acceptance or rejection can come from any of the styles because, to a large extent, it is out of the sender's control.

Following is the interactive process as it is used with each of the four situational management styles.

The **Autocratic Communication Style (S1A)** demonstrates high task/low relationship behavior (HT-LR), initiating a closed presentation. The other party has little, if any, information and is low in capability.

- *Initiation/Response.* You initiate and control the communication with minimal, if any, response.
- *Presentation/Elicitation.* You make a presentation letting the other parties know they are expected to comply with your message; there is little, if any, elicitation.
- *Closed/Open.* You use a closed presentation; you will not consider the receiver's input.

The **Consultative Communication Style (S2C)** demonstrates high task/high relationship behavior (HT-HR), using a closed presentation for the task with an open elicitation for the relationship. The other party has moderate information and capability.

- *Initiation/Response.* You initiate the communication by letting the other party know that you want him or her to buy into your influence. You desire some response.
- *Presentation/Elicitation.* Both are used. You use elicitation to determine the goal of the communication. For example, you may ask questions to determine the situation and follow up with a presentation. When the communication goal is known, little task elicitation is needed. Relationship communication is elicited in order to determine the interest of the other party and acceptance of the message. The open elicitation should show your concern for the other party's point of view and motivate him or her to follow your influence.
- *Closed/Open.* You are closed to having the message accepted (task), but open to the person's feelings (relationship). Be empathetic.

The **Participative Communication Style (S3P)** demonstrates low task/high relationship behavior (LT-HR), responding with open elicitation, some initiation, and little presentation. The other party is high in information and capability.

- *Initiation/Response.* You respond with some initiation. You want to help the other party solve a problem or get him or her to help you solve one. You are helpful and convey personal support.
- *Presentation/Elicitation.* Elicitation can occur with little presentation. Your role is to elicit the other party's ideas on how to reach objectives.
- *Closed/Open.* Open communication is used. If you participate well, the other party will come to a solution you can accept. If not, you may have to reject the other party's message.

The **Empowerment Communication Style (S4E)** demonstrates low task/low relationship behavior (LT-LR), responding with the necessary open presentation. The other party is outstanding in information and capability.

- *Initiation/Response.* You respond to the other party with little, if any, initiation.
- *Presentation/Elicitation.* You present the other party with information, structure, and so forth.
- *Closed/Open.* Open. You convey that the other party is in charge; you will accept the message.

Situational Variables

When selecting the appropriate communication style, you should consider four variables: time, information, acceptance, and capability. Answering the questions related to each of the following variables can help you select the appropriate style for the situation. These same four variables appear in Model 4–2 (Chapter 4).

Time. Do I have enough time to use two-way communication—yes or no? When there is no time, the other three variables are not considered; the autocratic style is appropriate. When time is available, any of the other styles may be appropriate, depending on the other variables. Time is a relative term; in one situation a few minutes may be considered a short time period, while in another a month may be a short period of time.

Information. Do I have the necessary information to communicate my message, make a decision, or to take action? When you have all the information you need, the autocratic style may be appropriate. When you have some of the information, the consultative style may be appropriate. When you have little information, the participative or laissez-faire style may be appropriate.

Acceptance. Will the other party accept my message without any input? If the receiver will accept the message, the autocratic style may be appropriate. If the receiver will be reluctant to accept it, the consultative style may be appropriate. If the receiver will reject the message, the participative or empowerment style may be appropriate to gain acceptance. There are situations where acceptance is critical to success, such as in the area of implementing changes.

Capability. Capability has two parts. (1) *Ability:* Does the other party have the experience or knowledge to participate in two-way communications? Will the receiver put the organization's goals ahead of personal needs or goals? (2) *Motivation:* Does the other party want to participate? When the other party is low in capability, the autocratic style may be appropriate; if he or she is moderate in capability, the consultative style may be appropriate; if he or she is high in capability, the participative style may be appropriate; if he or she is outstanding in capability, the empowerment style may be appropriate. In addition, capability levels can change from one task to another. For example, a professor may have outstanding capability in classroom teaching but be low in capability for advising students.

Selecting Communication Styles

Successful managers rely on different communication styles according to the situation. There are three steps to follow when selecting the appropriate communication style in a given situation.

Step 1. Diagnose the Situation. Answer the questions for each of the four situation variables. In Self-Assessment Exercise 10–2, you were asked to select an alternative to 12 situations. You were told to ignore the other answer spaces. Now you will complete this part in Doing Skill-Building Exercise 10–2 in class by placing the style letters (S1A, S2C, S3P, S4E) on the lines provided for each of the 12 situations.

Step 2. Select the Appropriate Style for the Situation. After analyzing the four variables, you select the appropriate style for the situation. In some situations, where variables may have conflicting styles, you should select the style of the most important variable for the situation. For example, capability may be outstanding (C-4), but you have all the information needed (S1A). If the information is more important, use the autocratic style even though the capability is outstanding. When doing the in class part of this skill-building exercise, place the letters (S1A, S2C, S3P, S4E) for the appropriate styles on the S ___ (style) lines.

Step 3. Implement the Appropriate Communication Style. During the in class part of this exercise, you will identify one of the four communication styles for each alternative action; place the S1A, S2C, S3P, or S4E on the S ___ lines. Select the alternative a, b, c, or d that represents the appropriate communication for each of the 12 situations, and place it on the line before the number of the situation.

Model 10–2 summarizes the material in this preparation for the exercise. Use it to determine the appropriate communication style in situation 1 and during the in class part of this exercise.

Determining the Appropriate Communication Style for Situation 1

Step 1. Diagnose the Situation. Answer the four variable questions from the model, and place the letters on the following four variable lines.

___ 1. Wendy, a knowledgeable person from another department, comes to you, the engineering supervisor, and requests that you design a special product to her specifications. You would:

____ time ____ information ____ acceptance
____ capability ____ communication style

a. Control the conversation and tell Wendy what you will do for her. S ___

b. Ask Wendy to describe the product. Once you understand, you would present your ideas. Let her know that you are concerned and want to help with your ideas. S ___

c. Respond to Wendy's request by conveying understanding and support. Help clarify what is to be done by you. Offer ideas, but do it her way. S ___

Model 10–2
Situational Communication

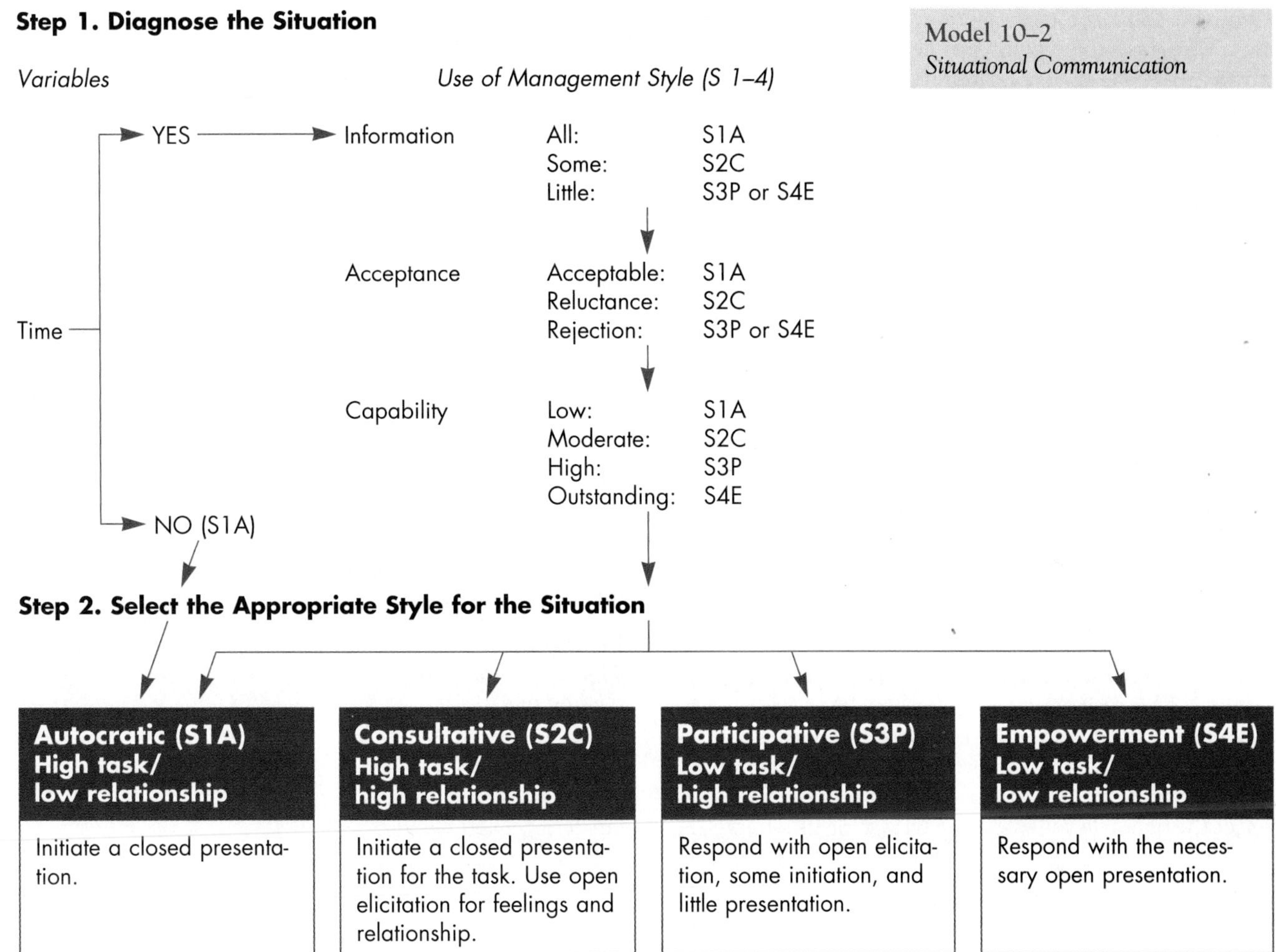

Step 3. Use the Appropriate Communication Style for the Situation.

d. Find out what you need to know. Let Wendy know you will do it her way. S ___

Step 2. Select the Appropriate Communication Style for the Situation. Review the four variables. If they are all consistent, select one style. If they are conflicting, select the most important variable as the style to use. Place its letters (S1A, S2C, S3P, or S4E) on the style line.

Step 3. Select the Appropriate Action. Review the four alternative actions. Identify the communication style for each, placing its letters on the S line, then check the appropriate match alternative.

Let's See How You Did. (1) *Time*. Time is available (or yes you have time); it can be any style. *Information*. You have little information, so you need to use a participative or empowerment style to find out what Wendy wants done: S3P or S4E. *Acceptance*. If you try to do it your way rather than Wendy's way, she will most likely reject it. You need to use a participative or empowerment style: S3P or S4E. *Capability*. Wendy is knowledgeable and has a high level of capability: S3P. (2) Reviewing the four variables, you see that there is a mixture of S3P and S4E. Since you are an engineer, it is appropriate to participate with Wendy to give her what she needs. Therefore, the choice is S3P. (3) Alternative a is S1A; this is the autocratic style, high task/low relationship. Alternative b is S2C; this is the consultative style, high task/high relationship. Alternative c is S3P; this is the participative style, low task/high relationship. Alternative d is S4E; this is empowerment style, low task/low relationship behavior. If you selected c as your action, you chose the most appropriate action for the situation. This was a three-point answer. If you selected d as your answer, this is also a good alternative; it scores two points. If you selected b, you get one point for overdirecting. If you selected a, you get zero points; this is too much directing and will most likely hurt communications.

The better you match your communication style to the situation, the more effective you will be at communicating. In the in class part of this exercise, you will apply the model to the other 11 situations in Self-Assessment Exercise 10–2 to develop your ability to communicate as a situational communicator.

Doing Skill-Building Exercise 10–2 in Class

Objectives
To develop your ability to communicate using the appropriate style for the situation.

Preparation
You should have completed the preparation for this exercise.

Experience
You will work at selecting the appropriate style for the situations 2–12 in Self-Assessment Exercise 10–2. On the time line place Y (yes), on the information, acceptance, and capability lines place the letters S1A, S2C, S3P, or S4E that are appropriate for the situation. Based on your diagnoses, select the one style you would use by placing its letters S1A, S2C, S3P, or S4E on the communication style line. On the four S lines write the letters S1A, S2C, S3P, or S4E to identify each style being used. Place the letter a, b, c, d on the line before the number that represents the most appropriate communication style for the situation.

Procedure 1 (15–20 minutes)
Behavior Model Video 10–1 is shown to illustrate the four styles. Use the form on page 349 to record answers.

Procedure 2 (5–10 minutes)
The instructor reviews the situational communications model and explains how to apply it to determine the appropriate style for situation 2.

Procedure 3 (5–10 minutes)
Students working alone complete situation 3 of Self-Assessment Exercise 10–2 using the model. Then the instructor goes over the recommended answers

Procedure 4 (20–50 minutes)
1. Break into groups of two or three. As a team, apply the model to situations 4 through 8. The instructor will go over the appropriate answers when all teams are done or the time is up.
2. Break into new groups of two or three and do situations 9 through 12. The instructor will go over the appropriate answers.

Conclusion
The instructor leads a class discussion and/or makes concluding remarks.

Application (2–4 minutes)
What did I learn from this experience? How will I use this knowledge in the future?

____

____

Sharing
Volunteers give their answers to the application section.

Motivating

Learning Objectives

After studying this chapter, you should be able to:

1. Illustrate the motivation process.
2. Describe how the Pygmalion effect influences motivation and performance.
3. Explain the performance formula and how to use it.
4. Discuss the major similarity and difference among the four content motivation theories: hierarchy of needs, ERG, two-factor, and acquired needs theories.
5. Discuss the major similarity and difference among the three process motivation theories: equity, goal-setting, and expectancy theories.
6. Explain the four types of reinforcement: positive, avoidance, extinction, and punishment.
7. State the major difference among content, process, and reinforcement theories.
8. Explain the major difference between the Japanese and U.S. approach to motivating employees.
9. Define the following **key terms** (in order of appearance in the chapter):

   motivation
   motivation process
   Pygmalion effect
   performance formula
   content motivation theories
   hierarchy of needs theory
   ERG theory
   two-factor theory
   acquired needs theory
   process motivation theories
   equity theory
   goal-setting theory
   expectancy theory
   reinforcement theory
   giving praise model

Skill Development

1. You can improve your skill in giving motivational praise (Skill-Building Exercise 11–1).

   Giving praise is a leadership management function and an interpersonal management role of a leader. Giving praise requires human and communication management skills. The SCANS competencies of interpersonal skills are developed through Skill-Building Exercise 11–1.

onna Brogle has enjoyed sewing since her childhood. Following her hobby, Donna worked as a seamstress for a major hospital. However, being married with four children, she preferred to be at home with her family. The hospital administrator decided to order new drapes and gave Donna the job. Gaining drapery experience at the hospital, Donna decided to quit working for the hospital and start her own business, "Draperies by Donna." She set goals for her business and found women in the process of retiring who gave her some help getting started. In 1989 Donna set up shop in her basement. She enjoyed the flexibility of setting her own schedule and working at home. Things went well until the recession hit in 1990–1991 and business dropped. As luck would have it, the hospital called her and asked her to come back as an employee to make drapes. Donna did not want to lose her independence, so she offered to work for the hospital as a vendor. They agreed that Donna would work at home and continue to run her business as well. After gaining more experience, and the economy turned around, the number of Donna's customers increased to the point where she no longer depended on the hospital as a customer.

Donna Brogle enjoys the flexibility of setting her own schedule and working at home.

Donna is having a problem with her employee Susan.[1] Susan is often late for work, and even though she can do a good job, She does not regularly perform to expectations. Donna had a talk with Susan to determine the cause of the problem. Susan said the money is okay and she is treated fairly, but the job is boring. Susan complained that she didn't have any say about how to do her job and that Donna continually checked up on her. If you were in Donna's position, how would you motivate Susan? In this chapter you will learn specific motivation theories and techniques that can be used to motivate Susan and a diversity of employees in all organizations.

Recall from Chapter 1 that Bonnie stated the importance of motivating employees and that having to deal with employee performance problems is the part about being a manager that she likes the least. The more you can motivate employees, the less time you will have to spend dealing with performance problems.

MOTIVATION AND PERFORMANCE

In this section you will study what motivation is and why it is important, how motivation affects performance, and how managers affect employee motivation and performance. You will also get an overview of three major theories of motivation.

1. Illustrate the motivation process.

What Is Motivation and Why Is It Important?

motivation
The willingness to achieve organizational objectives.

motivation process
Employees go from need to motive to behavior to consequence to satisfaction or dissatisfaction.

What Is Motivation? Motivation is an inner desire to satisfy an unsatisfied need. Being motivated leads to a level of willingness to achieve organizational objectives. For our purposes, **motivation** *is the willingness to achieve organizational objectives*. Have you ever wondered why people do the things they do? People primarily do what they do to meet their needs or wants.

Through the **motivation process,** *employees go from need to motive to behavior to consequence to satisfaction or dissatisfaction*. For example, you are thirsty (need) and have a drive (motive) to get a drink. You get a drink (behavior) that quenches (consequence and satisfaction) your thirst. However, if you could not get a drink, or a drink of what you really wanted, you would be dissatisfied. Satisfaction is usually short-lived. Getting that drink satisfied you, but soon you will need another drink. For this reason, the motivation process has a feedback loop:

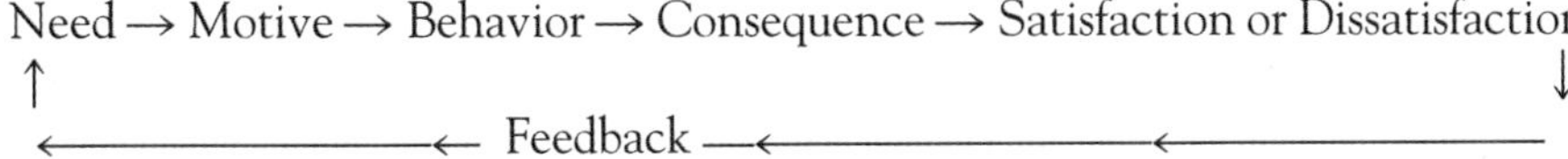

Some need or want motivates all behavior. However, needs and motives are complex; we don't always know what our needs are or why we do the things we do. Have you ever done something and not known why you did it? Understanding needs will help you understand behavior. You will gain a better understanding of why people do the things they do.

You cannot observe motives, but you can observe behavior and infer the person's motive. However, it is not easy to know why people behave the way they do because people do the same thing for different reasons. Also, people often attempt to satisfy several needs at once.

Why Is Motivation Important? Motivation is the number one problem facing business today.[2] Today's employees have less interest in extra hours, job dedication, attendance, and punctuality.[3] Knowing how to motivate will help you eliminate or reduce these performance problems. In the opening case, Donna is concerned because Susan is not motivated to work hard to achieve objectives.

Businesses lose $160 billion a year through wasted time on the job. This figure does not include the cost of absenteeism, alcoholism and drug abuse, or personal problems. Many employees just do enough to get by without being fired. They operate at about 60 percent efficiency. With proper motivation, their efficiency could be raised to 80 percent or higher.[4]

Managers have come to realize that a motivated and satisfied work force can deliver powerfully to the bottom-line profits.[5] A study determined that self-motivation is one of the three most important skills companies look for when hiring an employee. Motivation is a major part of a manager's job. Charles Shipley, a vice president of SL Industries, says that managers have to learn more about motivating and guiding workers. The ability to motivate subordinates is critical for advancement.

In the global environment, the United States is losing ground in productivity to Japan, France, Germany, and Italy. The most significant hurdle to productivity is motivation.[6] The old belief proposed that if you paid people adequately they would be motivated. However, today we realize that Americans don't work just for money. Money is not the prime motivator; job satisfaction is. Current researchers have found that motivation theories that apply in North America do not apply in other countries.[7] With cultural diversity, motivation becomes more complex.

The trend toward total quality management and self-directed teams places an emphasis on management through influence rather than control.[8] Organizations are motivating employees by giving them more power (empowerment).

2. Describe how the Pygmalion effect influences motivation and performance.

The Role of Expectations in Motivation and Performance

Pygmalion effect
Managers' attitudes toward and expectations of employees and how they treat them largely determine their motivation and performance.

The **Pygmalion effect** *states that managers' attitudes toward and expectations of employees and how they treat them largely determine their motivation and performance.* Research by J. Sterling Livingston and others has supported the Pygmalion effect theory. In a study of welding students, the foreman training the group was given the names of employees who were quite intelligent and would do well. Actually, the students were selected at random. The only difference was the foreman's expectations. The so-called intelligent students did significantly outperform the other employees. Why this happened explains the Pygmalion effect. In a sense, the Hawthorne effect (Chapter 1) is related to the Pygmalion effect because both affect motivation and performance. In the Hawthorne studies, the special attention and treatment given to the workers by the managers resulted in increased performance. We all need to have high expectations and treat people as though they are high achievers to get the best from them.

Work Application

1. Recall a person (parent, friend, teacher, coach, boss) who expected you to perform well, and treated you like you would do well, which affected your success. And/or recall a situation in which you lived up to or down to your own expectations. Describe the situation.

According to Douglas McGregor, managers motivate employees based on their assumptions about and expectations of people. A Theory X manager tends to coerce and closely control employees to motivate them, whereas Theory Y managers trust their employees and allow them to use self-control. Over the years, researchers have shown that managers with Theory Y attitudes tend to have employees with higher levels of motivation than the employees of Theory X managers. However, managers with Theory Y assumptions usually, but do not always, have higher levels of productivity in their departments. As stated in the skill-building exercises on situational management (Chapter 1), you need to use the appropriate management style for the employees being led. Use of Theory Y methods of motivation are in vogue today as managers are using higher levels of employee participation in management.

3. Explain the performance formula and how to use it.

performance formula
performance = ability × motivation × resources.

In addition to managers' expectations, employees' expectations also affect performance. Closely related to the Pygmalion effect is the *self-fulfilling prophecy*. Henry Ford said, if you believe you can, or you believe you can't; you are right. If you think you will be successful, you will be. If you think you will fail, you will, because you will fulfill your own expectations. You will live up to or down to your own expectations, so be positive, confident, and optimistic.

APPLYING THE CONCEPT

AC 11–1 The Performance Formula

Identify the factor contributing to low performance in the following five situations.

a. ability b. motivation c. resources

____ 1. Latoya went on a sales call. When she reached into her briefcase she realized that she did not have her product display book. Trying to explain the products without a visual look at the product resulted in no sale.

____ 2. Frank does not produce as much as the other department members because he does not put much effort into the job.

____ 3. "I practice longer and harder than my track teammates, Heather and Linda. I don't understand why they beat me in the running races."

____ 4. "I could get all 'As' in school if I wanted to. But I'd rather relax and have a good time."

____ 5. The government would be more efficient if it cut down on waste.

How Motivation Affects Performance

Generally, a motivated employee will try harder to do a good job than someone who is not motivated. However, performance is not simply based on motivation. Three interdependent factors determine the level of performance attained: ability, motivation, and resources. Stated as a **performance formula:** *performance = ability × motivation × resources*.

For maximum performance levels, all three factors must be high. If any factor is low or missing, the performance level will be adversely affected. As a manager, if you want to attain high levels of performance, you must be sure that you and your employees have the ability, motivation, and resources to meet objectives. When performance is not at the standard level or above, you must determine which performance factor needs to be improved, and improve it. In the opening case, Susan has the ability and resources, but lacks motivation. To increase Susan's performance, Donna needs to motivate her.

An Overview of Three Major Classifications of Motivation Theories

There is no single universally accepted theory of how to motivate people. In this chapter you will study three major classifications of motivation theories, plus subtheories, and how you can use them to motivate yourself and others. Figure 11–1 lists the major motivation theories. After studying all of the theories, you can select one theory to use, take from several to make your own theory, or ap-

Figure 11–1
Major Motivation Theories

Classification of Motivation Theories	**Specific Motivation Theory**
1. **Content motivation theories** focus on identifying and understanding employee needs.	a. **Hierarchy of needs theory** proposes that employees are motivated through five levels of needs: physiological, safety, social, esteem, and self-actualization. b. **ERG theory** proposes that employees are motivated by three needs: existence, relatedness, and growth. c. **Two-factor theory** proposes that employees are motivated by motivators (higher-level needs) rather than maintenance (lower-level needs) factors. d. **Acquired needs theory** proposes that employees are motivated by their need for achievement, power, and affiliation.
2. **Process motivation theories** focus on understanding how employees choose behaviors to fulfill their needs.	a. **Equity theory** proposes that employees will be motivated when their perceived inputs equal outputs. b. **Goal-setting theory** proposes that achievable but difficult goals motivate employees. c. **Expectancy theory** proposes that employees are motivated when they believe they can accomplish the task and the rewards for doing so are worth the effort.
3. **Reinforcement theory**	**Reinforcement theory** proposes that through the consequences for behavior employees will be motivated to behave in predetermined ways.

ply the theory that best fits the specific situation. As each motivation theory and technique is presented, you will study how Donna can apply it to motivate Susan or others.

7. State the major difference among content, process, and reinforcement theories.

4. Discuss the major similarity and difference among the four content motivation theories: hierarchy of needs, ERG, two-factor, and acquired needs theories.

content motivation theories
Focus on identifying and understanding employee needs.

CONTENT MOTIVATION THEORIES

A satisfied employee usually has a higher level of motivation and is more productive than a dissatisfied employee.[9] According to content motivation theorists, if you want to have satisfied employees you must meet their needs. When employees are asked to meet objectives they think, but usually do not ask, "What's in it for me?" The key to success for organizations is to meet the needs of employees while achieving organizational objectives.

The **content motivation theories** *focus on identifying and understanding employee needs*. In this section, you will study four content motivation theories: hierarchy of needs theory, ERG theory, two-factor theory, and acquired needs theory; and how managers use them to motivate employees.

Hierarchy of Needs

hierarchy of needs theory
Proposes that employees are motivated through five levels of needs: physiological, safety, social, esteem, and self-actualization.

The **hierarchy of needs theory** *proposes that employees are motivated through five levels of needs: physiological, safety, social, esteem, and self-actualization*. In the 1940s, Abraham Maslow developed this theory[10] based on four major assumptions: (1) Only unmet needs motivate. (2) People's needs are arranged in order of importance (hierarchy) going from basic to complex. (3) People will not be motivated to satisfy a higher-level need unless the lower-level need(s) has been at least minimally satisfied. (4) Maslow assumed that people have five classifications of needs, which are presented here in hierarchy order from low to high level of need.

Physiological needs. These include people's primary or basic needs: air, food, shelter, sex, and relief from or avoidance of pain.

Safety needs. Once they satisfy their physiological needs, people are concerned with safety and security.

Social needs. After establishing safety, people look for love, friendship, acceptance, and affection.

Esteem needs. After they meet their social needs, people focus on ego, status, self-respect, recognition for accomplishments, and a feeling of self-confidence and prestige.

Self-actualization needs. The highest level of need is to develop one's full potential. To do so, people seek growth, achievement, and advancement.

Maslow did not take into consideration that a person can be at different levels of needs based on different aspects of their lives. Nor did he mention that people can revert back to lower-level needs. Also, our needs change, and needs often exist in combination. It is difficult to set up a motivation program to satisfy needs based on Maslow's hierarchy.

Motivating Employees with Hierarchy of Needs Theory. Today people realize that needs are not on a simple five-step hierarchy. Managers should meet

Figure 11–2
How Managers Motivate with Hierarchy of Needs Theory

Self-Actualization Needs
Organizations meet these needs by developing employees' skills, the chance to be creative, achievement and promotions, and the ability to have complete control over their jobs.

Esteem Needs
Organizations meet these needs through titles, the satisfaction of completing the job itself, merit pay raises, recognition, challenging tasks, participation in decision-making, and chance for advancement.

Social Needs
Organizations meet these needs by providing employees with the opportunity to interact with others, to be accepted, and to have friends. Activities include parties, picnics, trips, and sports teams.

Safety Needs
Organizations meet these needs through safe working conditions, salary increases to meet inflation, job security, and fringe benefits (medical insurance/sick pay/pensions) that protect the physiological needs.

Physiological Needs
Organizations meet these needs through adequate salary, breaks, and safe working conditions.

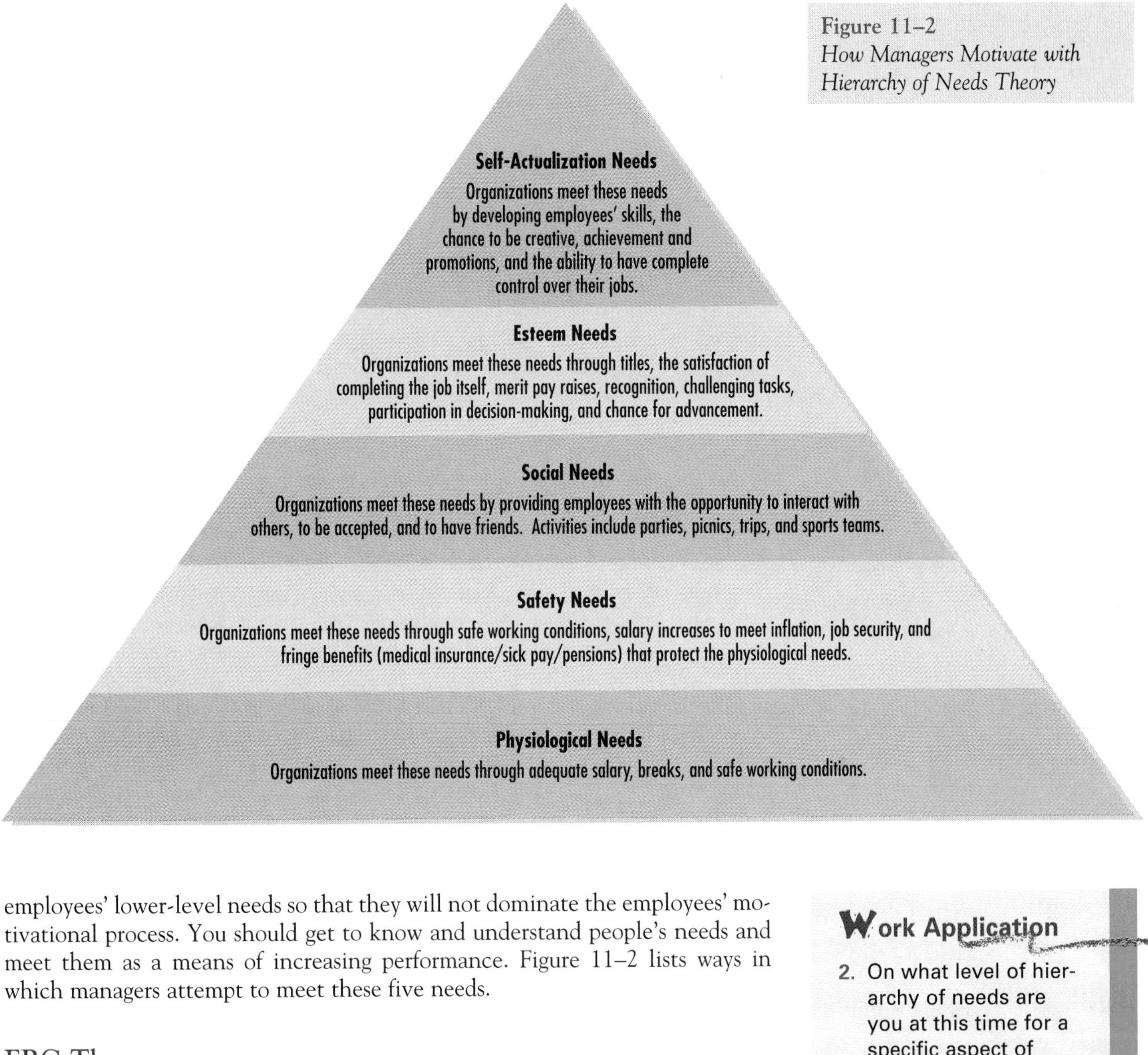

employees' lower-level needs so that they will not dominate the employees' motivational process. You should get to know and understand people's needs and meet them as a means of increasing performance. Figure 11–2 lists ways in which managers attempt to meet these five needs.

Work Application

2. On what level of hierarchy of needs are you at this time for a specific aspect of your life (profesional or personal)? Be sure to specify the level by name and explain why you are at this level.

ERG Theory

Figure 11–1 shows several motivation theories. ERG is a well-known simplification of the hierarchy of needs theory. **ERG theory** *proposes that employees are motivated by three needs: existence, relatedness, and growth.* Clayton Alderfer reorganized Maslow's needs hierarchy into three levels of needs: existence (physiological and safety needs), relatedness (social), and growth (esteem and self-actualization). Alderfer maintained the higher- and lower-order needs. He agreed with Maslow that unsatisfied needs motivate individuals, but disagreed that only one need level is active at one time.[11]

ERG theory
Proposes that employees are motivated by three needs: existence, relatedness, and growth.

Motivating Employees with ERG Theory. To use ERG theory, you must determine which needs have been met, which needs have not been met or have been frustrated, and how to meet the unsatisfied needs. You need to satisfy employee needs while achieving the organizational objectives. Donna observed Susan and took the time to talk to her to determine her needs. Susan's needs for existence and relatedness have been met. However, her need for growth has been frustrated. To motivate Susan, Donna must meet her need for growth. Donna should allow her to have more say on how she does her work and not check up on her as often, as long as Susan meets expected performance levels.

Two-Factor Theory

two-factor theory
Proposes that employees are motivated by motivators rather than maintenance factors.

In the 1950s, Frederick Herzberg classified two sets of needs that he called *factors*.[12] Herzberg combined lower-level needs into one classification he called *maintenance* or *hygiene*, and higher-level needs into one classification he called *motivators*. **Two-factor theory** *proposes that employees are motivated by motivators rather than maintenance factors*. Maintenance factors are also called *extrinsic motivators* because motivation comes from outside the job itself; they include pay, job security, and title; working conditions; fringe benefits; and relationships. Motivators are called intrinsic motivators because motivation comes from the work itself; they include achievement, recognition, challenge, and advancement.

Herzberg and associates, based on research, disagreed with the traditional view that satisfaction and dissatisfaction were at opposite ends of one continuum. Two continuums exist: not dissatisfied with the environment (maintenance) to dissatisfied, and satisfied with the job itself (motivators) to not satisfied.

Employees are on a continuum from dissatisfied to not dissatisfied with their environment. Herzberg contended that providing maintenance factors will keep employees from being dissatisfied, but it will not make them satisfied, or motivate them. In other words, maintenance factors will not satisfy or motivate employees, they will only keep them from being dissastisfied. For example, if employees are dissatisfied with their pay and they get a raise, they will no longer be dissatisfied. However, before long people get accustomed to the new standard of living and will become dissatisfied again. Employees will need another raise to not be dissatisfied again. The vicious cycle goes on. If you got a pay raise, would you be motivated and be more productive? Herzberg says that you must first ensure that maintenance factors are adequate. Once employees are no longer dissatisfied with their environment, they can be motivated through their jobs.

Employees are on a continuum from satisfied to not satisfied with the job itself. To motivate employees you need to make jobs more interesting and challenging, give employees more responsibility, provide the opportunity for growth, and give employees recognition for a job well done. Do not expect external rewards for everything you are asked to do. To be satisfied, you must seek and attain internal rewards to be self-motivated.[13] Figure 11–3 illustrates two-factor theory.

Motivating Employees with Two-Factor Theory. The best way to motivate employees is to ensure that they are not dissatisfied with maintenance factors; then focus on motivating. One successful way to motivate is to build challenge and opportunity for achievement into the job itself. Herzberg developed a method for increasing motivation, which he called *job enrichment*, which you studied in Chapter 7.

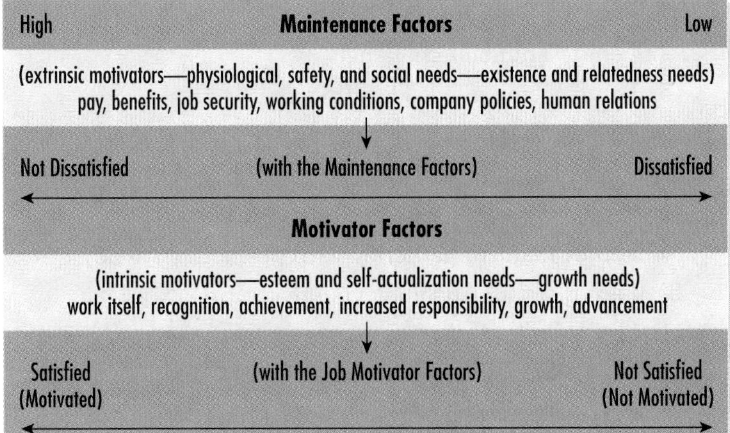

Figure 11–3
Two-Factor Theory

In the opening case, Susan said she was not dissatisfied with maintenance factors. Since Susan said the job is boring, will a pay raise or better working conditions increase her level of satisfaction? If Donna is going to motivate Susan, she will have to focus on intrinsic job motivation, not maintenance. Donna needs to give Susan more input into how she does her job.

Work Application

3. Recall a present or past job; were you dissatisfied or not dissatisfied with the maintenance factors? Were you satisfied or not satisfied with the motivators? Be sure to identify and explain your satisfaction with the specific maintenance and motivator factors.

Acquired Needs Theory

Acquired needs theory *proposes that employees are motivated by their need for achievement, power, and affiliation.* Henry Murray developed general needs theory.[14] It was adapted by John Atkinson,[15] and David McClelland developed a specific acquired needs theory.[16] McClelland does not have a classification for lower-level needs. His affiliation needs are the same as social and relatedness, and power and achievement are related to esteem and self-actualization and growth.

acquired needs theory
Proposes that employees are motivated by their need for achievement, power, and affiliation.

Unlike Maslow, McClelland believed that needs are based on personality and are developed as people interact with the environment. All people possess the need for achievement, power, and affiliation, but to varying degrees. One of the three needs tends to be dominant in each of us and motivates our behavior. Before getting into the details of each need, complete Self-Assessment Exercise 11–1 to determine your dominant or primary need.

SELF-ASSESSMENT EXERCISE 11–1

Acquired Needs

Identify each of the 15 statements according to how accurately it describes you. Place the number 1–5 on the line before each statement.

Like me		Somewhat like me		Not like me
5	4	3	2	1

___ 1. I get enjoyment out of working hard.

___ 2. I enjoy competing and winning.

___ 3. I enjoy having lots of friends.
___ 4. I enjoy a difficult challenge.
___ 5. I enjoy being in a leadership role.
___ 6. I want other people to like me.
___ 7. I want to know how I am progressing as I complete tasks.
___ 8. I confront people who do things I disagree with.
___ 9. I enjoy frequent gathering with people such as at parties.
___ 10. I enjoy setting and achieving realistic goals.
___ 11. I try to influence other people to get my way.
___ 12. I enjoy belonging to lots of groups/organizations.
___ 13. I enjoy the satisfaction of completing a difficult task.
___ 14. In a leaderless situation, I tend to step forward and take charge.
___ 15. I enjoy working with others more than working alone.

To determine your primary need, place the number 1–5 that represents your score for each statement. Each statement/column represents a specific need.

	Achievement	*Power*	*Affiliation*
	___ 1.	___ 2.	___ 3.
	___ 4.	___ 5.	___ 6.
	___ 7.	___ 8.	___ 9.
	___ 10.	___ 11.	___ 12.
	___ 13.	___ 14.	___ 15.
Totals	___	___	___

Add up the total of each column, which should be between 5 and 25 points. The column with the highest score is your dominant or primary need.

The Need for Achievement (n Ach). People with a high n Ach tend to be characterized as wanting to take personal responsibility for solving problems. They are goal oriented and they set moderate, realistic, attainable goals. They seek a challenge, excellence, and individuality; take calculated, moderate risk; desire concrete feedback on their performance, and are willing to work hard. People with a high n Ach think about ways to do a better job, how to accomplish something unusual or important, and career progression. They perform well in nonroutine, challenging, and competitive situations, while people low in n Ach do not perform well in these situations.

McClelland's research showed that only about 10 percent of the U.S. population has a dominant need for achievement. Evidence of a correlation exists between high achievement need and high performance. People with a high n Ach tend to enjoy sales and entrepreneurial-type positions. Managers tend to have a high, but not a dominant, n Ach.

Motivating Employees with a High n Ach. Give them nonroutine, challenging tasks with clear attainable objectives. Give them fast and frequent feedback on their performance. Continually give them increased responsibility for doing new things. Keep out of their way.

The Need for Power (n Pow). People with a high need for power tend to be characterized as wanting to control the situation, wanting influence or control over others, enjoying competition in which they can win (they do not like to lose), and willing to confront others. People with high n Pow think about controlling a situation, and others, while seeking positions of authority and status. People with high n Pow tend to have a low need for affiliation. Managers tend to have a dominant need for power. They understand that power is essential for successful management.

Motivating Employees with a High n Pow. Let them plan and control their jobs as much as possible. Try to include them in decision-making, especially when the decision affects them. They tend to perform best alone rather than as team members. Try to assign them to a whole task rather than just a part of it.

In the opening case, Susan's primary need seems to be power. Susan wants more say on how to do her job and wants Donna to do less checking up on her. If Donna empowers Susan by giving her more job-related responsibility, it may satisfy Susan's needs, resulting in higher performance.

People with a high need for affiliation tend to enjoy jobs where they can develop, help, and teach others.

The Need for Affiliation (n Aff). People with a high n Aff tend to be characterized as seeking close relationships with others, wanting to be liked by others, enjoying lots of social activities, and seeking to belong. They join groups and organizations. People with a high n Aff think about friends and relationships. They tend to enjoy developing, helping, and teaching others. They tend to have a low n Pow. People with high n Aff seek jobs in teaching, social work, human resources management, and in other helping professions. They tend to avoid management because they like to be one of the group rather than its leader.

Motivating Employees with High n Aff. Be sure to let them work as part of a team. They derive satisfaction from the people they work with rather than the task itself. Give them lots of praise and recognition. Delegate responsibility for orienting and training new employees to them. They make great buddies and mentors.

Donna, from the opening case, like all people, has a need for achievement, power, and affiliation. Taking the risk to start her own business indicates her need for achievement and power; her motivation to work at home so she could be with her family came from her need for affiliation.

Figure 11–4 compares the four content theories of motivation.

Work Application

4. Explain how your need for achievement, power, and/or affiliation has affected your behavior motivation, or someone you work or have worked with.

Figure 11–4
A Comparison of Four Content Motivation Theories

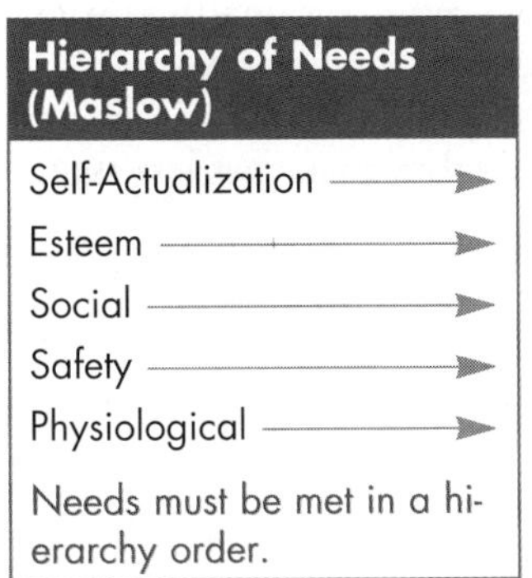

Hierarchy of Needs (Maslow)	ERG Theory (Alderfer)	Two-Factor Theory (Herzberg)	Acquired Needs Theory (McClelland)
Self-Actualization →	Growth →	Motivators →	Achievement and Power
Esteem →	Growth →	Motivators →	Achievement and Power
Social →	Relatedness →	Maintenance →	Affiliation
Safety →	Existence →	Maintenance →	Not classified
Physiological →	Existence →	Maintenance →	Not classified
Needs must be met in a hierarchy order.	Unmet needs can be at any level simultaneously.	Maintenance factors will not motivate employees.	Motivating needs are developed through experience.

5. Discuss the maor similarity and difference among the three process motivation theories: equity goal-setting, and expectancy theories.

process motivation theories
Focus on understanding how employees choose behavior to fulfill their needs.

PROCESS MOTIVATION THEORIES

Process motivation theories *focus on understanding how employees choose behavior to fulfill their needs*. Process motivation theories are more complex than content motivation theories. Content motivation theories simply focus on identifying and understanding employee needs. Process motivation theories go a step further to understand why employees have different needs, why their needs change, how and why employees choose to try to satisfy needs in different ways, the mental process employees go through as they understand situations, and how they evaluate their need satisfaction. In this section, you will study three process motivation theories: equity theory, goal-setting theory, and expectancy theory.

Equity Theory

equity theory
Proposes that employees are motivated when their perceived inputs equal outputs.

Equity theory, primarily J. Stacy Adams' motivation theory, proposes that people are motivated to seek social equity in the rewards they receive (output) for their performance (input).[17] **Equity theory** *proposes that employees are motivated when their perceived inputs equal outputs*. Based on a knowledge of equity theory, you may be able to predict behavior.

According to equity theory, people compare their inputs (effort, experience, seniority, status, intelligence, and so forth) and outputs (praise, recognition, pay, benefits, promotions, increased status, supervisor's approval, etc.) to that of relevant others. A relevant other could be a coworker or group of employees from the same or different organizations, or even from a hypothetical situation. Notice that our definition says *perceived* and not actual inputs to outputs. Equity may actually exist. However, if employees believe there is inequity, they will change their behavior to create equity. Employees must perceive that they are being treated fairly, relative to others.[18]

Unfortunately, many employees tend to inflate their own efforts or performance when comparing themselves to others. They also tend to overestimate what others earn. Employees may be very satisfied and motivated until they find out that a relevant other is earning more for the same job or earning the same for doing less work. When employees perceive inequity, they attempt to reduce it by reducing input or increasing output. A comparison with relevant others leads to three conclusions: The employee is underrewarded, overrewarded, or equitably rewarded.

Underrewarded. When employees perceive that they are underrewarded, they may reduce the inequity by trying to increase outputs (get a raise), reducing inputs (doing less work, absenteeism, long breaks, etc.), rationalizing (finding a logical explanation for inequity), changing others' inputs or outputs (get them to do more, or get less), leaving the situation (get transferred or leave for a better job), or changing the object of comparison (they make/get less than I do).

Overrewarded. Being overrewarded does not disturb most employees. However, research suggests that employees may reduce perceived inequity by increasing input (work harder or longer), reducing output (take a pay cut), rationalizing (I'm worth it), or trying to increase others' output (give them the same as me).

Equitably Rewarded. Inputs and outputs are perceived as being equal; motivation exists. Employees may believe that relevant others should have greater outputs when they have more experience, education, and so on.

Motivating with Equity Theory. Research supporting equity theory is mixed. One view of equity proposes that it is like Herzberg's maintenance factors. When employees are not dissatisfied they are not actively motivated, but maintenance factors do demotivate when employees are dissatisfied. Related to equity theory, when employees believe they are equitably rewarded they are not actively motivated. However, when employees believe they are underrewarded they are demotivated.

Using equity theory in practice can be difficult because you don't know the employees' reference group, and their view of inputs and outcomes. However, it does offer some useful general recommendations:

1. Managers should be aware that equity is based on perception, which may not be correct. Possibly, managers can create equity or inequity. Some managers have favorite subordinates who get special treatment; others don't.
2. Rewards should be equitable. When employees perceive that they are not treated fairly, morale and performance problems occur. Employees producing at the same level should be given equal rewards.
3. High performance should be rewarded, but employees must understand the inputs needed to attain certain outputs. When using incentive pay, there should be clear standards specifying the exact requirements to achieve the incentive. A manager should be able to objectively tell others why one person got a higher merit raise than another.

Work Application

5. Give an example of how equity theory has affected your motivation or someone else's you work or have worked with. Be sure to specify if you were under-, over-, or equitably rewarded.

In the opening case, Susan said that she was equitably treated. Therefore, Donna does not need to be concerned about equity theory with Susan. However, it could be an issue with another employee.

Goal-Setting Theory

The research conducted by E. A. Locke and others revealed that setting objectives has a positive effect on motivation and performance.[19] **Goal-setting theory** *proposes that achievable but difficult goals motivate employees.* Chapter 5 presented setting objectives and MBO in detail. Our behavior has a purpose, which is usually to fulfill a need. Goals give us a sense of purpose—why we are working to accomplish a given task. Setting objectives helps employees identify ways of meeting their needs, and the attainment of objectives is reinforcing in itself. According to Parkinson's Law, work expands to fill the time available for its completion. If you set difficult but achievable goals with quick deadlines, people will not take their time but will work hard to complete the task in the allotted time.

goal-setting theory
Proposes that achievable but difficult goals motivate employees.

Using Goal-Setting to Motivate Employees. When setting objectives, be sure that they are difficult, challenging, achievable, specific, measurable, have a target date for accomplishment, and are jointly set when possible (see Chapter 5 for details). Domino's Pizza used to have its well-known objective of free delivery in 30 minutes or less. However, due to delivery auto accidents resulting in lawsuits because employees placed too much emphasis on deadlines versus safety, the 30-minute time limit was dropped. However, quick delivery is still an

Work Application

6. Give an example of how a goal(s) affected your motivation and performance, or someone else's you work or have worked with.

important goal and employee performances are compared to other employees and the companywide average delivery time of 23 minutes. In the opening case, Donna could use MBO to identify objectives that could motivate Susan.

Expectancy Theory

expectancy theory
Proposes that employees are motivated when they believe they can accomplish the task and the rewards for doing so are worth the effort.

Expectancy theory is based on Victor Vroom's formula: motivation = expectancy × valence.[20] **Expectancy theory** *proposes that employees are motivated when they believe they can accomplish the task and the rewards for doing so are worth the effort.* The theory is based on the following assumptions: (1) both internal (needs) and external (environment) factors affect behavior; (2) behavior is the individual's decision; (3) people have different needs, desires, and goals; and (4) people make behavior decisions based on their perception of the outcome.

Two important variables in Vroom's formula must be met for motivation to take place.

Expectancy. Expectancy refers to the person's perception of his or her ability (probability) to accomplish an objective. Generally, the higher one's expectancy, the better the chance for motivation. When employees do not believe that they can accomplish objectives, they will not be motivated to try. Also important is the perception of the relationship between performance and the outcome or reward. Generally, the higher one's expectancy of the outcome or reward, the better the chance for motivation. If employees will certainly get the reward, they probably will be motivated. When not sure, employees may not be motivated. For example, Dan believes he would be a good manager and wants to be promoted. However, Dan has an external locus of control and believes that working hard will not result in a promotion anyway. Therefore, he will not be motivated to work for the promotion. *Locus of control* refers to the belief of who has control over one's life events. An internal locus of control means that what happens is within one's control.

Valence. Valence refers to the value a person places on the outcome or reward. Generally, the higher the value (importance) of the outcome or reward, the better the chance of motivation. For example, the supervisor, Jean, wants an employee, Sim, to work harder. Jean talks to Sim and tells him that working hard will result in a promotion. If Sim wants a promotion, he will probably be motivated. However, if Sim does not want the promotion, it will not motivate him.

Motivating with Expectancy Theory. Expectancy theory can accurately predict a person's work effort, satisfaction level, and performance,[21] but only if you plug the correct values into the formula. Therefore, this theory works in certain contexts but not in others. The following conditions should be implemented to make the theory result in motivation:

1. Clearly define objectives and the necessary doable performance needed to achieve them.
2. Tie performance to rewards. High performance should be rewarded. When one employee works harder to produce more than other employees and is not rewarded, he or she may slow down productivity.
3. Be sure rewards have value to the employee. Managers should get to know employees as individuals. Develop good human relations (Chapter 3).

4. Make sure your employees believe you will do what you say you will do. For example, employees must believe you will give them a merit raise if they do work hard. And you must do as you say you will, so employees will believe you.

Expectancy theory also works best with employees who have an internal locus of control because if they believe they control their destiny, their efforts will result in success. Expectancy theory does not work well with employees who have an external locus of control because they do not believe their efforts result in success. Believing that success is due to fate or chance, why should they be motivated to work hard?

In the opening case, if Donna can find a need with expectancy and valence, Susan will be motivated to perform to expectations, creating a win-win situation for both of them. As related to MBO, maybe Susan would agree to producing more work for more money.

Work Application

7. Give an example of how expectancy theory has affected your motivation or someone else's you work or have worked with. Be sure to specify the expectancy and valence.

REINFORCEMENT THEORY

B. F. Skinner, reinforcement motivation theorist, contended that to motivate employees managers do not need to identify and understand needs (content motivation theories) or to understand how employees choose behaviors to fulfill them (process motivation theories). Instead, managers need to understand the relationship between behaviors and their consequences and then arrange contingencies that reinforce desirable behaviors and discourage undesirable behaviors. **Reinforcement theory** *proposes that through the consequences for behavior employees will be motivated to behave in predetermined ways*. Reinforcement theory uses behavior modification (apply reinforcement theory to get employees to do what you want them to do) and operant conditioning (types and schedules of reinforcement). Skinner stated that behavior is learned through experiences of positive and negative consequences. Skinner proposes three components:[22]

reinforcement theory
Proposes that through the consequences for behavior employees will be motivated to behave in predetermined ways.

Stimulus ⟶	Responding Behavior ⟶	Consequences of Behavior—
(legal speed limit)	(speed)	Reinforcement (police officer gives speeder a negative consequence—ticket/fine—to discourage repeat performance).

Employees learn what is, and is not, desired behavior as a result of the consequences for specific behavior. The two important concepts used to modify behavior are the types of reinforcement and the schedules of reinforcement.

Types of Reinforcement

6. Explain the four types of reinforcement: positive, avoidance, extinction, and punishment.

The four types of reinforcement are: positive, avoidance, extinction, and punishment.

Positive Reinforcement. A method of encouraging continued behavior is to offer attractive consequences (rewards) for desirable performance. For example, an employee arrives on time for a meeting and is rewarded by the supervisor thanking him or her. The praise is used to reinforce punctuality. Other reinforces include pay, promotions, time off, increased status, and so forth. Positive reinforcement is the best motivator for increasing productivity.

Avoidance Reinforcement. Avoidance is also called negative reinforcement. As with positive reinforcement, you are encouraging continued desirable behavior. The employee avoids the negative consequence. For example, an employee is punctual for a meeting to avoid the negative reinforcement, such as a reprimand. Standing plans, especially rules, are designed to get employees to avoid certain behavior. However, rules in and of themselves are not a punishment. punishment is only given if the rule is broken.

Extinction. Rather than encourage desirable behavior, extinction (and punishment) attempts to reduce or eliminate it by withholding reinforcement when the behavior occurs. For example, an employee who arrives late for a meeting is not rewarded with praise. Or you withhold a reward of value, a pay raise, until the employee performs to set standards. From another perspective, managers who do not reward good performance can cause its extinction. In other words, if you ignore good employee performance, good performance may stop as employees think, "Why should I do a good job if I'm not rewarded in some way."

Punishment. Punishment can be used to provide an undesirable consequence for undesirable behavior. For example, an employee who arrives late for a meeting is reprimanded. Notice that with avoidance there is no actual punishment; it's the threat of punishment that controls behavior. Other methods of punishment include harassing, taking away privileges, probation, fining, demoting, firing and so forth. Using punishment may reduce the undesirable behavior, but it may cause other undesirable behavior, such as poor morale, lower productivity, and acts of theft or sabotage. Punishment is the most controversial method and the least effective at motivating employees. Figure 11–5 illustrates the four types of reinforcement.

Remember that employees will do what they are rewarded for doing. Within TQM, if managers say quality of production is important, but employees who do a quality job are not rewarded, and nothing happens to employees

Figure 11–5
Types of Reinforcement

As a manager, you have a secretary who makes many errors when completing correspondence. Your objective, which you discussed with the secretary, is to decrease the error rate. You have four types of reinforcement that you can use with the secretary when you next review the work:

Employee Behavior	Type of Reinforcement	Manager Action (Consequence)	Employee Behavior Modification (Future)
Improved performance →	Positive →	Praise improvements →	Repeat quality work*
Improved performance →	Avoidance →	Do not give any reprimand →	Repeat quality work
Performance not improved →	Extinction →	Withhold praise/raise →	Do not repeat poor work
Performance not improved →	Punishment →	Discipline action, i.e., written warning →	Do not repeat poor work

*Assuming the employee improved performance, positive reinforcement is the best motivator.

(extinction or punishment) who do not do a quality job, employees will not be motivated to do a quality job. If a professor tells students to read this book, but does not test students on the book (reward or punishment based on test performance)—test questions only come from lectures—what percentage of students do you think will read and study this book versus those that will simply take notes and study them for exams?

Schedule of Reinforcement

The second reinforcement consideration in controlling behavior is when to reinforce performance. The two major classifications are continuous and intermittent.

Continuous Reinforcement. With a continuous method, each and every desired behavior is reinforced. Examples of this method would be a machine with an automatic counter that lets the employee know, at any given moment, exactly how many units have been produced, piece rate of $1 for each unit produced, or a manager who comments on every customer report.

Intermittent Reinforcement. With intermittent reinforcement, the reward is given based on the passage of time or output. When the reward is based on the passage of time, it is called an *interval* schedule. When it is based on output, it is called a *ratio* schedule. When electing to use intermittent reinforcement, you have four alternatives:

1. Fixed interval schedule (giving a salary paycheck every week; breaks and meals at the same time every day).
2. Variable interval schedule (giving praise only now and then, a surprise inspection, a pop quiz).
3. Fixed ratio schedule (giving a piece rate or bonus after producing at a standard rate).
4. Variable ratio schedule (giving praise for excellent work, a lottery for employees who have not been absent for a set time).

Ratios are generally better motivators than intervals. The variable ratio tends to be the most powerful schedule for sustaining behavior.

Motivating with Reinforcement

Several organizations, including 3M, Frito-Lay, and B. F. Goodrich, have used reinforcement to increase productivity. Michigan Bell had a 50 percent improvement in attendance and above-standard productivity and efficiency level. Emery Air Freight went from 30 to 90 percent of employees meeting standard after using reinforcement. Emery estimates that its reinforcement program has resulted in a $650,000 yearly savings.

Generally, positive reinforcement is the best motivator. Continuous reinforcement is better for sustaining desired behavior; however, it is not always possible or practical. Some general guidelines include:

1. Make sure employees know exactly what is expected of them. Set clear objectives.
2. Select appropriate rewards. A reward to one person could be considered a punishment by another. Know your employees' needs.

3. Select the appropriate reinforcement schedule.
4. Do not reward mediocre or poor performance.
5. Look for the positive and give praise, rather than focusing on the negative and criticizing. Make people feel good about themselves (Pygmalion effect).
6. Never go a day without giving praise.
7. Do things for your employees, instead of to them, and you will see productivity increases.

In the opening case, Susan has been performing below expectations. If Donna talks to Susan about changing her job to better meet Susan's needs, in an MBO format, this would be positive reinforcement. Scheduling of MBO meetings could be at a fixed interval, say once every week or two, to quickly review Susan's performance. If positive reinforcement doesn't change Susan's performance, Donna can use avoidance reinforcement. Based on her authority, Donna could tell Susan that if the next time performance is below a specific level, she will receive a specific punishment, such as withholding part of her pay. If Susan does not avoid this behavior, Donna must follow up and give the punishment reinforcement. As a manager, try the positive first. Positive reinforcement is a true motivator because it creates a win-win situation by meeting both the employee's and the manager's/organization's needs. From the employees' perspective, avoidance and punishment create a lose-win situation. The organization/manager wins by forcing them to do something they really don't want to do.

Work Application

8. Give a few examples of the types of reinforcement, and the schedules used, on a present or past job.

Reinforcement for Getting Employees to Come to Work and to Be on Time

The traditional method used to get employees to come to work and to be on time is avoidance and punishment. If employees miss a specific number of days, they don't get paid. If an employee is late, the time card indicates this, and the employee receives punishment. Many managers today use positive reinforcement by offering employees rewards for coming to work and being on time. For example, ADV Marketing Group, a Stamford, Connecticut, company, uses continuous reinforcement by offering prizes simply for showing up and being on time: a $100 dinner certificate after 13 on-time weeks and an $800 vacation plus two days off after a year of on-time performance. Mediatech, a Chicago company, uses a variable ratio schedule by holding a lottery. Each week Mediatech puts up $250. On Friday they spin a wheel to determine if a drawing will be held that week. If not, the money goes into the pot for the next week. When holding a drawing, it includes only the employees who have attended on time up to the drawing.

A popular technique used by many organizations, which virtually eliminates the problem of being late for work, is *flextime*. Flextime allows employees to determine when they start and end work, provided they work their full number of hours, with certain restrictions on working hours. A typical schedule permits employees to begin work between 6:00 and 9:00 A.M. and to complete their work day between 3:00 and 6:00 P.M. Flextime helps meet the goal of good human relations because it allows employees to schedule their time to accommodate their personal needs and job requirements.

Giving Praise

In the 1940s, Lawrence Lindahl conducted a survey revealing that what employees want most from a job is full appreciation for work done. Similar studies have been performed over the years with little change in results. Another survey showed that managers want personal recognition more than salary by four to one.[23] Another survey revealed that 27 percent of workers would quit to move to a company known for giving praise and recognition; 38 percent of workers said they rarely or never get praise from the boss.[24] When was the last time your boss gave you a thank-you or some praise for a job well done? When was the last time your boss complained about your work? If you are a manager, when was the last time you praised or criticized your employees? What is the ratio of praise to criticism?

Giving praise develops a positive self-concept in employees and leads to better performance—the Pygmalion effect and self-fulfilling prophecy. Praise is a motivator (not maintenance) because it meets employees' needs for esteem/self-actualization, growth, and achievement. Giving praise creates a win-win situation. It is probably the most powerful, simplest, least costly, and yet most under used motivational technique.

Ken Blanchard and Spencer Johnson popularized giving praise through their best-selling book *The One-Minute Manager*.[25] They developed a technique that involves giving one-minute feedback of praise. Model 11–1, Giving Praise, shows an adaptation. *The steps in the* **giving praise model** *are: (1) Tell the employee exactly what was done correctly; (2) Tell the employee why the behavior is important; (3) Stop for a moment of silence; (4) Encourage repeat performance.* Blanchard calls it one-minute praise because it should not take more than one minute to give the praise. The employee need not say anything. The four steps are presented in Model 11–1 and discussed here.

giving praise model
(1) Tell the employee exactly what was done correctly; (2) Tell the employee why the behavior is important; (3) Stop for a moment of silence; (4) Encourage repeat performance.

step 1. **Tell the Employee Exactly What Was Done Correctly.** When giving praise, look the person in the eye. Eye contact shows sincerity and concern. Be very specific and descriptive. General statements such as "You're a good worker" are not as effective. On the other hand, don't talk for too long, or the praise loses its effectiveness.

Donna: "Susan, I just overheard you deal with that customer's complaint. You did an excellent job of keeping your cool; you were polite. That person came in angry and left happy."

step 2. **Tell the Employee Why the Behavior Is Important.** Briefly state how the organization, and/or person, benefits from the action. Also, tell the employee how you feel about the behavior. Be specific and descriptive.

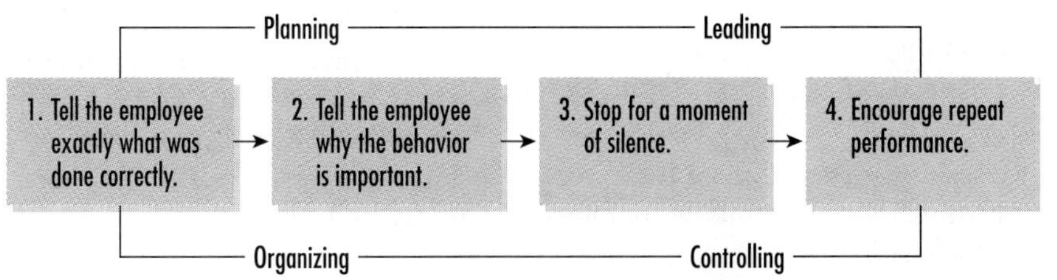

Model 11–1
Giving Praise

Donna: "Without customers, we don't have a business. One dissatisfied customer can cause hundreds of dollars in lost sales. It really made me proud to see you handle that tough situation the way you did."

step 3. **Stop for a Moment of Silence.** Being silent is tough for many managers.[26] The rationale for the silence is to give the employee the chance to "feel" the impact of the praise. It's like "the pause that refreshes." When you are thirsty and take the first sip/gulp of a refreshing drink, it's not until you stop, and say "AH," that you feel the quench.

Donna: (Silently counts to five.)

step 4. **Encourage Repeat Performance.** This reinforcement motivates the employee to continue the desired behavior. Blanchard recommends touching the employee. Touching has a powerful impact. However, he recommends it only if both parties feel comfortable. Others say don't touch employees; it could lead to a sexual harassment charge.

Donna: Thanks, Susan, keep up the good work (while touching her on the shoulder, or shaking hands).

As you can see, giving praise is easy and it doesn't cost a penny. Managers trained to give praise say it works wonders. It's a much better motivator than giving a raise or other monetary reward. One manager stated that an employee was taking his time stacking cans on a display. He gave the employee praise for stacking the cans so straight. The employee was so pleased with the praise that the display went up with about a 100 percent increase in productivity. Note that the manager looked for the positive and used positive reinforcement, rather than punishment. The manager could have given a reprimand comment such as, "Quit goofing off and get the display up faster." That statement would not have motivated the employee to increase productivity. All it would have done was hurt human rela-

APPLYING THE CONCEPT

AC 11–2 Motivation Theories

Identify the theory behind each supervisor's statement on how to motivate employees.

a. hierarchy of needs
b. ERG theory
c. two-factor
d. acquired needs
e. equity
f. goal-setting
g. expectancy
h. reinforcement

____ **6.** "I motivate employees by making their jobs interesting and challenging."

____ **7.** "I make sure I treat everyone fairly to motivate them."

____ **8.** "I know Kate likes people, so I give her jobs in which she works with other employees."

____ **9.** "Carl would yell in the halls because he knew it bothered me. So I decided to ignore his yelling, and he stopped."

____ **10.** "I got to know all of my employees' values. Now I can offer rewards that will motivate them when they achieve attainable task performance."

____ **11.** "Our company now offers good working conditions, salaries, and benefits, so we are working at developing the third need for socialization."

____ **12.** "When my employees do a good job, I thank them using a four-step model."

____ **13.** "I used to try to improve working conditions to motivate employees. But I stopped and now focus on giving employees more responsibility so they can grow and develop new skills."

____ **14.** "I tell employees exactly what I want them to do, with a tough deadline that they can achieve."

____ **15.** "I now realize that I tend to be an autocratic manager because it helps fill my needs. I will work at giving some of my employees more autonomy on how they do their jobs."

____ **16.** "I used to try to meet needs in a five-step sequence. After I heard about this new technique, I now focus on three needs and realize that needs can be unmet at more than one level at a time."

tions and it could have ended in an argument. The cans were straight. The employee was not praised for the slow work pace. However, if the praise had not worked, the manager should have used another reinforcement method.[27]

In the opening case, Donna should give Susan praise for increasing performance to encourage her to continue this behavior. Praise is an effective positive reinforcement when used with a variable interval schedule.

PUTTING THE MOTIVATION THEORIES TOGETHER WITHIN THE MOTIVATION PROCESS

Motivation is important because it helps to explain why employees behave the way they do. At this point, you may be wandering: How do these theories fit together? Is one the best? Should I try to pick the correct theory for a given situation? The groups of theories are complementary; each group of theories refers to a different stage in the motivation process. Each group of theories answers a different question. Content motivation theories answer the question; What needs do employees have that should be met on the job? Process motivation theories answer the question; How do employees choose behavior to fulfill their needs? Reinforcement theory answers the question; What can managers do to get employees to behave in ways that meet the organizational objectives?

In the first section of this chapter you found that the motivation process went from need to motive to behavior to consequence to satisfaction or dissatisfaction. Now let's make the motivation process a little more complex by incorporating the motivation theories, or answers to the preceding questions, into the process. See Figure 11–6 for an illustration. Note that Step 4 loops back to Step 3 because, according to reinforcement theory, behavior is learned through consequences. Step 4 does not loop back to Steps 1 or 2 because reinforcement theory is not concerned with needs, motives, or satisfaction; it focuses on getting employees to behave in predetermined ways, through conseuqences provided by managers. Also note that Step 5 loops back to Step 1 because meeting needs is ongoing; meeting our needs is a never-ending process. Finally, be aware that, according to two-factor theory, Step 5, satisfaction or dissatisfaction, is not on one continuum but on two separate continuums (satisfied to not satisfied or dissatisfied to not dissatisfied), based on the level of need being met (motivator or maintenance).

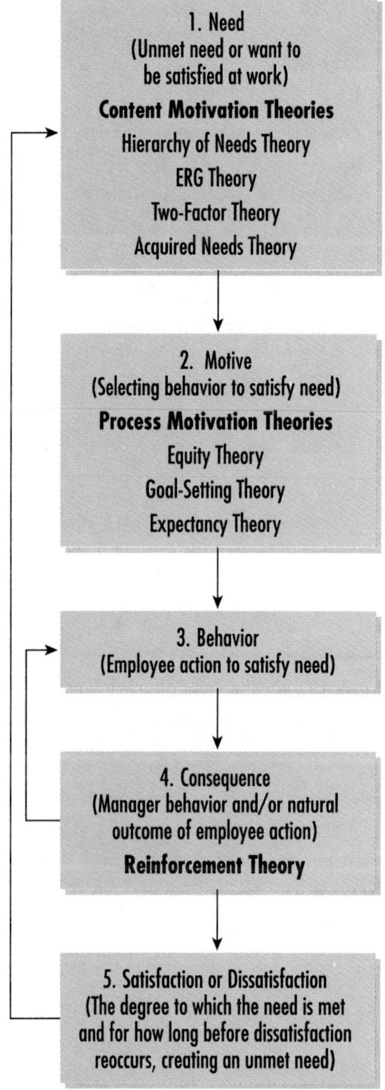

Figure 11–6
The Motivation Process with the Motivation Theories

CURRENT MANAGEMENT ISSUES

Organizational *reward systems* (pay, benefits, and so on, Chapter 9) must be designed to motivate employees. A reward system is effective if it attracts new people to apply to work for the organization, motivates employees to achieve organizational objectives, and motivates them to stay with the organization. According to equity theory, people will compare the reward system of the organization they work for to others. If they feel they can get a better deal elsewhere, they may go there. Organizations, including Du Pont, have developed new reward systems to increase motivation and productivity. Some of the current trends in rewards include pay for performance to reward productive workers with higher pay; an all-salaried work force (no more time clocks); skills-based systems in which employees are paid based on how many different skills they

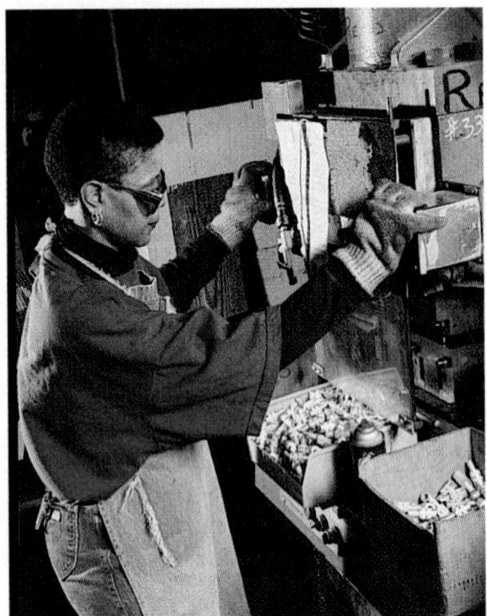

Women tend to place more importance on convenient work hours, good interpersonal relations, and the opportunity to learn.

8. Explain the major difference between the Japanese and U.S. approach to motivating employees.

have (organizations, including General Foods and Texas Instruments, offer the opportunity to increase skills to attain raises); a variety of bonuses (cash, gifts, trips, etc.) for suggestions for improvements; profit-sharing programs (at Lincoln Electric, employees in recent years have received approximately their annual wages and double in profit-sharing payouts alone).

Diversity. Within the United States, we have a *diversified work force;* what motivates one person may not motivate another. For example, men tend to place more importance on having a lot of autonomy in their jobs, whereas women place more importance on convenient work hours, good interpersonal relations, and the opportunity to learn.[28] However, there are always exceptions; don't over generalize. The needs of a student working part time, a single parent working full time, a person who is not married working full time, and a retired person working part time will tend to be different.

Globalization. When you expand the business to other countries, the diversity continues to increase in complexity. The motivation theories you have studied were developed largely in America. As organizations become *global,* managers must be aware of the cultural limitation to theory generalizations. In 1980 it was recognized that motivational concerns vary globally.[29] A survey revealed distinct differences among U.S. salespeople and Japanese and Korean salespeople, but not between salespeople in the two Asian countries.[30] An example from NAFTA countries includes a U.S. firm in Mexico that gave workers a raise to motivate them to work more hours. The raise actually motivated the employees to work less hours because they could now make enough money to live and enjoy life (one of their primary values) in less time, so why should they work more hours? In Sweden there is a very high tax rate on overtime pay that makes it very difficult to motivate employees to work more hours based on money.

Intrinsic motivation of higher-level needs tends to be more relevant to developed countries than to Third World countries in which most people are on a lower level of hierarchy of need than those in developed countries. The term *self-actualization* is not translatable in the Chinese language. Even in developed countries, the level of needs focus varies. In the United States, people tend to be motivated by higher-level needs of self-actualization (do your own thing) and esteem; in Greece and Japan security is more important, while in Sweden, Norway, and Denmark, people are more concerned with social needs. McClelland's acquired need for achievement is more predominant in the United States. *Achievement* is difficult to translate into most other languages. Therefore, acquired achievement need has limited use outside of the United States and Canada unless managers are willing to train employees to acquire the need for achievement.

One major cultural difference is in the focus on individualistic versus group approaches to business. Individualistic societies (the United States, Canada, Great Britain, Australia) tend to value self-accomplishment. Collective societies (Japan, Mexico, Singapore, Venezuela, Pakistan) tend to value group accomplishment and loyalty.[31] Cultural differences suggest that self-actualization, achievement, and esteem needs tend to be met from group membership in Japan and from individualism in the United States.

Expectancy theory holds up fairly well, cross-culturally, because it is flexible. It allows for the possibility that there may be differences in expectations and valences across cultures. For example, societal acceptance may be of higher value than individual recognition in collective societies.[32]

Participative Management and Teams. The late Dr. W. Edwards Deming, often credited with making Japan a world business leader, said in an interview with *The Wall Street Journal:*[33]

> We are all born with intrinsic motivation, self-esteem, dignity, an eagerness to learn. Our present system of management crushes that all out. Instead of working for the company, people compete with each other. The Japanese are more successful than the U.S. because they live by cooperation, not competition. American firms will have to learn to support each other, rather than continue with the everybody for him or herself approach. That's how business should be.

Deming was saying that America must change from an individualistic society to a collective society if it is to survive in the global economy. He was pessimistic that U.S. businesses would make the changes he thought are necessary to compete. However, U.S. businesses have been moving toward the use of more *teams and participative management*.[34] The trend toward TQM is a case in point.[35]

Productivity. Equity theory advocates pay for performance. Pay for individual performance tends to be more of a motivator in individualistic countries than it is in collective countries where people tend to prefer equality where all are paid the same regardless of output. Even within the United States, unions tend to favor equal pay. In collective countries, pay for performance should be group- rather than individual-based. When employees are paid less and perceive their performance to be as high as employees being paid more for performance, you can have motivation problems. Therefore, with pay for performance, you must have objective measures to avoid perception problems of who is a better worker.

TQM. The trend is toward improving *quality* through TQM. Through the principles of TQM, managers create a culture (Chapter 8) in which employees direct their motivation and behaviors toward customer satisfaction through working in teams to design and execute work processes, using data to improve work processes, and acting to maximize the value of individual input and minimize rework and waste. Employees need information, training, tools, and the authority to act so that quality products and services are the result. The practices of TQM create a culture and set of management actions that give direction to employee motivation and accomplishing organizational objectives. TQM supports goal-setting theory because it gives employees a sense of their purpose and what their role is in accomplishing organizational objectives. Employees should always realize that the ultimate goal is customer satisfaction. As stated in an Eastman Kodak

APPLYING THE CONCEPT

AC 11–3 Japanese versus American Motivation Techniques

For each statement, identify which country it is more closely associated with:

a. America b. Japan.

____ **17.** Tends to focus on motivating groups versus individuals.

____ **18.** Would be the country where you would tend to get the best results with acquired needs theory.

____ **19.** Is the country in which managers provide the greater job security.

____ **20.** Is the country were managers develop a system of giving pins/stars/etc. as a symbol of achievement of high performance.

poster, "Total quality is more than a goal. It's an obsession." However, recall that TQM does not support MBO (Chapter 5).

Ethics. *Ethics* and equity theory are related in the sense that managers should treat all employees fairly. However, when working with a *diverse work force* it is recommended that managers treat people as individuals. This can be in contradiction with equity theory because when managers treat employees as individuals they run the risk of being called prejudiced by giving preferential treatment to someone. As a manager you may find it difficult to treat all employees fairly (as perceived by all employees) when you treat people as individuals. If employees do complain, you should use the complaint-handling model (Chapter 3).

Small business entrepreneurs have a high need for achievement; it tends to be the force that drives them to succeed. The motivation process and theories apply to both small and large business. This chapter includes examples of how managers in both large and small businesses motivate employees.

CHAPTER SUMMARY AND GLOSSARY

The chapter summary is organized to answer the eight learning objectives for Chapter 11.

1. Illustrate the motivation process.
Employees go through the five-step process to met their needs. Note that this is a circular process because needs reoccur.

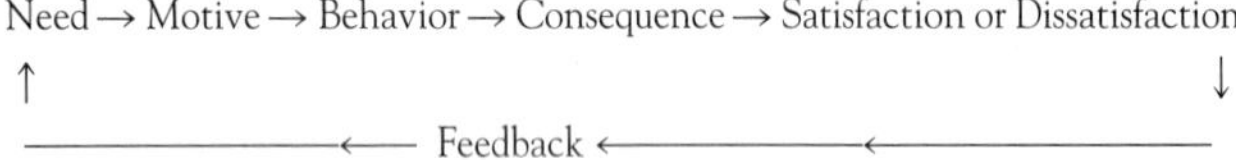

2. Describe how the Pygmalion effect influences motivation and performance.
The Pygmalion effect proposes that managers can have a positive or negative effect on employee motivation and performance because employees will live up to or down to managers' expectations, which are expressed through managers' attitudes.

3. Explain the performance formula and how to use it.
The performance formula proposes that performance is based on ability, motivation, and resources. If any of these three components are low, performance will be negatively affected. When a performance problem occurs, managers need to determine which component of the performance formula is the reason for the performance level and take appropriate action to correct the problem.

4. Discuss the major similarity and difference among the four content motivation theories: hierarchy of needs, ERG, two-factor, and acquired needs theories.
The similarity between the four content motivation theories is their focus on identifying and understanding employee needs. The theories identify similar needs, but are different in the way they classify the needs. Hierarchy of needs theory includes physiological, safety, social, esteem, and self-actualization needs. ERG theory includes existence, relatedness, and growth needs. Two-factor theory includes motivators and maintenance factors. Acquired needs theory includes achievement, power, and affiliation needs. (See Figures 11–1 and 11–4 for a comparison of the four content theories of motivation.)

5. Discuss the major similarity and difference among the three process motivation theories: equity, goal-setting, and expectancy theories.
The similarity among the four process motivation theories is their focus on understanding how employees choose behaviors to fulfill their needs. However, they are very different in how they perceive employees are motivated. Equity theory proposes that employees are motivated when their perceived inputs equal outputs. Goal-setting theory proposes that achievable but difficult goals motivate employees. Expectancy theory proposes that employees are motivated when they believe they can accomplish the task and the rewards for doing so are worth the effort.

6. Explain the four types of reinforcement: positive, avoidance, extinction, and punishment.
With positive reinforcement you provide the employee with a reward consequence for performing the desired behavior. With avoidance reinforcement you encourage employees to perform the desired behavior in order to avoid a negative consequence. With extinction rein-

forcement you withhold a positive consequence to get the employee to stop performing undesirable behavior. With punishment reinforcement you give the employee a negative consequence to get him or her to stop performing undesirable behavior.

7. State the major difference among content, process, and reinforcement theories.
Content motivation theories focus on identifying and understanding employee needs. Process motivation goes a step further to understand how employees choose behavior to fulfill their needs. Reinforcement theory is not concerned about employee needs; it focuses on getting employees to do what managers want them to do through the consequences provided by managers for their behavior. The use of rewards is the means of motivating employees.

8. Explain the major difference between the Japanese and U.S. approach to motivating employees.
The Japanese tend to focus their motivational systems on a group basis whereas the Americans tend to focus their motivational systems on an individual basis.

9. Define the following key terms (in order of appearance in the chapter).
Select one or more methods: (1) fill in the missing key terms from memory, (2) match the key terms from the end of the review with their definitions below, or (3) copy the key terms in order from the list at the beginning of the chapter.

______ is the willingness to achieve organizational objectives.

Through the __________, employees go from need to motive to behavior to consequence to satisfaction or dissatisfaction.

The __________ states that managers' attitudes and expectations of employees and how they treat them largely determine their motivation and performance.

In the __________ performance = ability × motivation × resources.

__________ focus on identifying and understanding employee needs.

The __________ proposes that employees are motivated through five levels of needs: physiological, safety, social, esteem, and self-actualization.

______ proposes that employees are motivated by three needs: existence, relatedness, and growth.

__________ proposes that employees are motivated by motivators rather than maintenance factors.

__________ proposes that employees are motivated by their need for achievement, power, and affiliation.

__________ focus on understanding how employees choose behavior to fulfill their needs.

__________ proposes that employees are motivated when their perceived inputs equal outputs.

__________ proposes that achievable but difficult goals motivate employees.

__________ proposes that employees are motivated when they believe they can accomplish the task and the rewards for doing so are worth the effort.

__________ proposes that through the consequences for behavior employees will be motivated to behave in predetermined ways.

The steps in __________ are as follows: (1) Tell the employee exactly what was done correctly. (2) Tell the employee why the behavior is important. (3) Stop for a moment of silence. (4) Encourage repeat performance.

KEY TERMS

acquired needs theory
content motivation theories
equity theory
ERG theory
expectancy theory
giving praise model
goal-setting theory
hierarchy of needs theory
motivation
motivation process
performance formula
process motivation theories
Pygmalion effect
reinforcement theory
two-factor theory

REVIEW AND DISCUSSION QUESTIONS

1. What is motivation and why is it important to know how to motivate employees?
2. Do you agree that managers' attitudes and expectations affect employee motivation and performance? Explain your answer.
3. Do you agree with the performance formula? Will you use it on the job?
4. Do people really have a diversity of needs?
5. Which of the four content motivation theories do you prefer? Why?

6. Which of the three process motivation theories do you prefer? Why?

7. What reinforcement methods have been used to get you to go to work and to be on time?

8. Reinforcement theory is unethical because it is used to manipulate employees. Do you agree with this statement? Explain your answer.

9. Which motivation theory do you feel is the best? Explain why.

10. What is your motivation theory? What are the major methods, techniques, etc., you plan to use on the job as a manager to increase motivation and performance.

11. Do you agree with Deming's statement that Americans need to change to a group approach to compete in a global economy?

CASE

Friedman Microwave Motivation Techniques

The following conversation takes place between Art Friedman and Bob Lussier. In 1970, Art Friedman implemented a new business technique. At that time the business was called Friedman's Appliances. It employed 15 workers in Oakland, California. Friedman's is an actual business that uses the technique you will read about.

Bob: What is the reason for your success in business?

Art: My business technique.

Bob: What is it? How did you implement it?

Art: I called my 15 employees together and told them, "From now on I want you to feel as though the company is ours, not mine. We are all bosses. From now on you decide what you're worth and tell the accountant to put it in your pay envelope. You decide which days and hours you work and when to take time off. We will have an open petty cash system that will allow anyone to go into the box and borrow money when they need it."

Bob: You're kidding, right?

Art: No, it's true. I really do these things.

Bob: Did anyone ask for a raise?

Art: Yes, several people did. Charlie asked for and received a $100-a-week raise.

Bob: Did he and the others increase their productivity to earn their raises?

Art: Yes, they all did.

Bob: How could you run an appliance store with employees coming and going as they pleased?

Art: The employees made up schedules that were satisfactory to everyone. We had no problems of under- or overstaffing.

Bob: Did anyone steal from the petty cash box?

Art: No.

Bob: Would this technique work in any business?

Art: It did work, it still works, and it will always work!!

In 1976, Art Friedman changed his strategy. Art's present business is Friedman's Microwave Ovens. It is a franchise operation, which still utilizes his technique of making everyone a boss. In its first three years, Art's business grew from one store in Oakland to 20 stores, which sold over 15,000 microwaves. In 1988 Art had over 100 stores nationwide. Friedman's now sells around 125,000 microwaves per year.

Select the best alternative for the following questions. Be sure to be able to give an explanation to support your answers.

___ 1. Art's new techniques focus on motivation and performance.

a. true b. false

___ 2. Art focused on which factor in the performance formula?

a. ability b. motivation c. resources

___ 3. Art's employees appear to be on which needs level for their job?

a. physiological d. esteem
b. safety e. self-actualization
c. social

___ 4. Art is focusing on which level of ERG needs?

a. existence b. relatedness c. growth

___ 5. Art's technique has less emphasis on meeting which need?

a. achievement b. power c. affiliation

___ 6. Herzberg would say Art is using

a. maintenance b. motivators

___ 7. Vroom would agree that Art uses expectancy motivation theory.

a. true b. false

___ 8. Adams would say Art has

a. equitable rewards
b. underrewards
c. overrewards

___ 9. Art uses goal-setting theory.

a. true b. false

___ 10. Art uses which types of reinforcement?

a. positive c. extinction
b. avoidance d. punishment

11. Do you know of any organizations that use Art's or any other unusual techniques? If yes, what is the organization's name? What does it do?

12. Could Art's technique work in all organizations? Explain your answer.

13. In a position of authority, would you use Art's technique? Explain your answer.

Behavior Model Video 11–1, Giving Praise, shows a bank branch manager, Laura, giving praise to Kelly, a teller, for successfully handling an angry customer. Laura follows the steps in Model 11–1 on pages 377–378. This video serves as a behavior model which can be used prior to conducting Skill-Building Exercise 11–1.

SKILL-BUILDING EXERCISE 11–1

Giving Praise

Preparing for Skill-Building Exercise 11–1

Think of a job situation in which you did something well, deserving of praise and recognition. For example, you may have saved the company some money, you may have turned a dissatisfied customer into a happy one, and so on. If you have never worked or done something well, interview someone who has. Put yourself in a management position and write out the praise you would give to an employee for doing what you did.

Briefly describe the situation:

____

____

____

Step 1. Tell the employee exactly what was done correctly.

____

____

____

Step 2. Tell the employee why the behavior is important.

____

____

____

Step 3. Stop for a moment of silence. (Count to five silently.)

Step 4. Encourage repeat performance.

____

____

____

Doing Skill-Building Exercise 11–1 in Class

Objective
To develop your skill at giving praise.

Preparation
You will need your prepared praise.

Experience
You will give and receive praise.

Video (5–10 minutes)
Behavior Model Video 11–1, Giving Praise, may be shown to illustrate how to give praise.

Procedure (12–17 minutes)
Break into groups of four to six. One at a time, give the praise.

1. Explain the situation.
2. Select a group member to receive the praise.
3. Give the praise. (Talk; don't read it off the paper.) Try to select the position you would use if you were actually giving the praise on the job. (Both standing, both sitting, etc.)
4. Integration. The group gives the giver of praise feedback on how he or she did:

   Step 1. Was the praise very specific and descriptive? Did the giver look the employee in the eye?

   Step 2. Was the importance of the behavior clearly stated?

   Step 3. Did the giver stop for a moment of silence?

   Step 4. Did the giver encourage repeat performance? Did the giver of praise touch the receiver (optional)?

Did the praise take less than one minute? Was the praise sincere?

Conclusion
The instructor leads a class discussion and/or makes concluding remarks.

Application (2–4 minutes)
What did I learn from this experience? How will I use this knowledge in the future?

____

____

Sharing
Volunteers give their answers to the application section.

EXERCISE 11–1

Job Motivators and Maintenance Factors

Preparing for Exercise 11–1 (Self-Assessment)

SELF-ASSESSMENT EXERCISE 11–1

What Movivates You?

Following are 12 job factors that contribute to job satisfaction. Rate each according to how important it is to you by placing the number 1–5 on the line before each factor.

Very important ——— Somewhat important ——— Not important
5 ——— 4 ——— 3 ——— 2 ——— 1

___ 1. An interesting job I enjoy doing.
___ 2. A good boss that treats people fairly.
___ 3. Getting praise and other recognition and appreciation for the work that I do.
___ 4. A satisfying personal life at the job.
___ 5. The opportunity for advancement.
___ 6. A prestigious or status job.
___ 7. Job responsibility that gives me freedom to do things my way.
___ 8. Good working conditions (safe environment, nice office, cafeteria, etc.).
___ 9. The opportunity to learn new things.
___ 10. Sensible company rules, regulations, procedures, and policies.
___ 11. A job I can do well and succeed at.
___ 12. Job security.

Place the numbers 1–5 that represent your answers below.

Motivating Factors Score		*Maintenance Factors Score*
1. ___		2. ___
3. ___		4. ___
5. ___		6. ___
7. ___		8. ___
9. ___		10. ___
11. ___		12. ___
___	Total points	___

Add each column vertically. Did you select motivators or maintenance factors as being more important to you?

Doing Exercise 11–1 in Class

Objectives
To help you better understand how job factors affect motivation. To help you realize that people are motivated by different factors. What motivates you may turn someone else off.

Preparation
You should have completed the preparation for this exercise.

Experience
You will discuss the importance of job factors.

Procedure 1 (8–20 minutes)
Break into groups of four to six and discuss job factors selected by group members in the preparation for this exercise. Come to a consensus on the three factors that are most important to the group. They can be either motivators or maintenance factors. If the group mentions other job factors not listed, such as pay, you may add them.

Procedure 2 (3–6 minutes)
A representative from each group goes to the board and writes its group's three most important job factors.

Conclusion
The instructor leads a class discussion and/or makes concluding remarks.

Application (2–4 minutes)
What did I learn from this experience? How will I use this knowledge in the future?

____

____

Sharing
Volunteers give their answers to the application section.

Leading

Learning Objectives

After studying this chapter, you should be able to:

1. State the difference among trait, behavioral, and situational leadership theorists.
2. Explain why the terms *management* and *leadership* are not interchangeable.
3. Describe leadership trait theory and, according to Ghiselli, the most important leadership trait.
4. Discuss the major similarity and difference between two-dimensional leadership styles and the leadership grid.
5. Identify the management levels that are the focus of charismatic, transformational, transactional, and symbolic leadership.
6. State the primary difference between the contingency leadership model and the other situational leadership models.
7. Discuss the major criticism shared by the continuum leadership model and the path-goal leadership model.
8. Describe the major characteristic shared by the normative leadership model and the situational leadership model.
9. Define the following **key terms** (in order of appearance in the chapter):

   leadership
   leadership trait theorist
   behavioral leadership theorist
   leadership style
   two-dimensional leadership styles
   leadership grid model
   charismatic leadership
   transformational leadership
   transactional leadership
   symbolic leadership
   situational leadership theorist
   contingency leadership model
   leadership continuum model
   path-goal model
   normative leadership model
   situational leadership model
   substitutes for leadership

Skill-Development

1. You can develop your ability to select the appropriate leadership style for a given situation using the leadership continuum model (Skill-Building Exercise 12–1).

2. You can develop your ability to select the appropriate leadership style for a given situation using the situational leadership model (Skill-Building Exercise 12–2).

   Leadership skill is one of the four functions of management and requires human and communication and often decision-making skills. Leadership requires interpersonal management roles of leader and liaison; informational roles of monitor, disseminator, and spokesperson; and decisional roles of disturbance handler and negotiator. The SCANS competencies of interpersonal skills and information are developed, as well as basic and thinking skills and personal qualities foundation skills, through the exercises.

iz Claiborne worked in the clothing industry and developed a reputation as a top-notch women's fashion designer. In the 1970s, as the number of career women increased, Liz saw a gap between the casual slacks and jeans look and the boardroom-career suit with bow tie look. She believed that women wanted clothing that would give them style, quality, fit, and value. A huge market existed for relaxed yet functional and coordinated separates that career women could mix and match.

In January 1976, Liz and her husband Arthur Ortenberg started Liz Claiborne Inc. with $50,000 of savings and $200,000 from family and friends. After only one year, sales reached $200 million. People in the fashion industry referred to Liz as "visionary" and "the great pathfinder." After only 11 years, Liz Claiborne was included in the Fortune 500 largest company list. Liz Claiborne was one of the youngest companies, and only one of two companies started by a woman to make the Fortune 500. Liz Claiborne grew to become the largest women's apparel company in the world, and it does not own any manufacturing facilities, nor does it have a sales force on the road. Claiborne outsources manufacturing to independent suppli-

Through her coaching leadership style, Liz Claiborne has a positive relationship with her employees.

ers overseas. Liz built the business into a $2 billion-plus fashion empire before turning over the leadership position to Jerome Chazen, an original partner in the firm.

Liz Claiborne grew to become the top-selling women's clothing label for two important reasons. First, Liz and her employees really listen to their customers and design the clothing to fit their lifestyles and build a whole wardrobe around what they want. Liz Claiborne offers customer value. There are 150 specialists who visit stores, talk to customers, and give seminars to salespeople. Retailers say that Liz Claiborne responds to the customer better than any other apparel company. This is especially important in the global marketplace where women in different countries have very different preferences. Liz Claiborne entered the continental European market in the 1980s.

Second, the company's success resulted from Liz's leadership. Liz wanted employees to feel as though they are a part of the company. She wanted employees with team sprit. Therefore, Liz spent part of each work day with the teams of designers. Liz did not do the designs herself; she worked with the teams to develop their design skills. Liz delegated responsibility to the teams and rewarded their success. Through her coaching leadership style, Liz built positive relationships with employees.

1. State the difference among trait, behavioral, and situational leadership theorists.

LEADERSHIP AND TRAIT THEORY

In this section, you will study leadership and its importance in organizations, the difference between leadership and management, and trait theory.

Leadership

leadership
The process of influencing employees to work toward the achievement of organizational objectives.

Leadership *is the process of influencing employees to work toward the achievement of organizational objectives*. Leadership is one of the most talked-about, researched, and written-about management topics. Ralph Stogdill's well-known *Handbook of Leadership* contains over 3,000 references on the topic, and Bass's revision of it contains well over 5,000 publications on leadership.[1] Survey results have revealed that academicians and practitioners alike agree that leadership is the most important topic of all within the realm of organizational behavior/human relations.[2] According to a leadership study of more than 25,000 employees, 69 percent of employee job satisfaction stems from the leadership skills of the employee's manager.[3] The major reason for employee failure is poor leadership.[4] Leadership is probably the most important characteristic people need to have to be effective on the job.[5] Management experts believe that leadership could be the number one strategic concern of businesses in the 21st century.[6]

Leadership and Management Are Not the Same

2. Explain why the terms *management* and *leadership* are not interchangeable.

People tend to use the terms *manager* and *leader* interchangeably. However, managers and leaders differ.[7] Leadership is one of the four management functions (planning, organizing, leading, and controlling). Management is broader in scope than leadership; leading is only one of the management functions. A manager can have this position without being a true leader. There are managers—you may know of some—who are not leaders because they do not have the ability to influence others. There are also good leaders who are not managers. The informal leader, an employee group member, is a case in point. You may have worked in a situation where one of your peers had more influence in the department than the manager. It has been said that organizations are overmanaged and underled.[8] Liz Claiborne is both an effective manager and leader.

Leadership Trait Theory

3. Describe leadership trait theory and, according to Ghiselli, the most important leadership trait.

An organized approach to studying leadership began in the early 1900s. The early studies were based on the assumption that leaders are born, not made. Researchers wanted to identify a set of characteristics or traits that distinguished leaders from followers or effective from ineffective leaders. **Leadership trait theorists** *attempt to determine a list of distinctive characteristics accounting for leadership effectiveness*. Researchers analyzed physical and psychological traits, or qualities, such as appearance, aggressiveness, self-reliance, persuasiveness, and dominance in an effort to identify a set of traits that all successful leaders possessed. The list of traits would be a prerequisite for promotion of candidates to leadership positions. Only candidates possessing all the identified traits were to be given leadership positions.

leadership trait theorists
Attempt to determine a list of distinctive characteristics accounting for leadership effectiveness.

Inconclusive Findings. In 70 years, over 300 trait studies were conducted.[9] However, no one compiled a universal list of traits that all successful leaders possess. In all cases, there were exceptions. For example, several lists identified successful leaders as being tall. However, Napoleon was short. On the other hand, some organizations came up with a list of traits and found people who possessed them all, only to find that these people were not successful leaders. In addition, some people were successful in one leadership position but not in another. People also questioned whether traits like assertiveness and self-confidence were developed before or after one became a leader. Peter Drucker says there is no such thing as "leadership qualities or a leadership personality."[10] Indeed, if leaders were simply born and not made (in other words, if leadership skills could not be developed), there would be no need for courses in management.

The Ghiselli Study. Edwin Ghiselli conducted probably the most widely publicized trait theory study. He studied over 300 managers from 90 different businesses in the United States and published his results in 1971.[11] He concluded that there are traits important to effective leadership, though not all are necessary for success. Ghiselli identified the following six traits, in order of importance, as being significant traits for effective leadership: (1) Supervisory abil-

Work Application

1. Of Ghiselli's six traits, explain which ones your present/past boss does and does not posses?

ity. Getting the job done through others. Basically, the ability to perform the four functions of management you are studying in this course. (2) Need for occupational achievement. Seeking responsibility. The motivation to work hard to succeed. (3) Intelligence. The ability to use good judgment, reasoning, and thinking capacity. (4) Decisiveness. The ability to solve problems and make decisions competently. (5) Self-assurance. Viewing oneself as capable of coping with problems. Behaving in a manner that shows others that you have self-confidence. (6) Initiative. Self-starting in getting the job done with a minimum of supervision from one's boss. Liz Claiborne has demonstrated supervisory ability, and probably all of the other traits as well.

Even though it is generally agreed that there is no universal set of leadership traits or qualities, people continue to study and write about leadership traits. For example, in Chapter 1 you completed Self-Assessment Exercise 1–1 which answered the question, What are the most important traits for success as a manager? They included integrity, industriousness, and ability to get along with people.

BEHAVIORAL LEADERSHIP THEORIES

By the late 1940s, most of the leadership research had changed from trait theory to focus on what the leader did. In the continuing quest to find the one best leadership style in all situations, researchers attempted to identify the differences in the behavior of the effective leaders versus the ineffective leaders. **Behavioral leadership theorists** *attempt to determine distinctive styles used by effective leaders*. Recall that Douglas McGregor, a behavioral theorist, developed Theory X and Theory Y (Chapters 1 and 11). Complete Self-Assessment Exercise 12–1 to determine your leadership behavior according to Theory X and Theory Y.

behavioral leadership theorists Attempt to determine distinctive styles used by effective leaders.

SELF-ASSESSMENT EXERCISE 12–1

McGregor Theory X and Theory Y Behavior

For each of the following ten statements, place the letter (U, F, O, S) that best describes what you would do as a manager on the line preceding the statement. There are no right or wrong answers.

Usually (U) Frequently (F) Occasionally (O) Seldom (S)

___ 1. I would set the objectives for my department alone, rather than include employee input.

___ 2. I would allow employees to develop their own plans, rather than develop them myself.

___ 3. I would delegate several tasks I enjoy doing to employees, rather than do them myself.

___ 4. I would allow employees to make decisions to solve problems, rather than make them myself.

___ 5. I would recruit and select new employees alone, rather than include employees' input.

___ 6. I would orient and train new employees myself, rather than have employees do it.

___ 7. I would tell employees only what they need to know, rather than give them access to anything they want to know.

___ 8. I would spend time praising and recognizing my employees' work efforts, rather than just give criticism.

___ 9. I would set several controls for employees to ensure that objectives are met, rather than allow employees to set their own controls.

___ 10. I would frequently observe my employees to ensure that they are working and meeting deadlines, rather than leave them alone.

To better understand your own behavior toward employees, score your answers. For items 1, 5, 6, 7, 9, and 10, give yourself one point for each usually (U) answer; two points for each frequently (F) answer; three points for each occasionally (O) answer; and four points for each seldom (S) answer. For items 2, 3, 4, and 8, give yourself one point for each seldom (S) answer; two points for each occasionally (O) answer; three points for each frequently (F) answer; and four points for each usually (U) answer. Total all points. Your score should be between 10 and 40. Place your score here ______. Theory X and Theory Y are on opposite ends of a continuum. Some people's behavior falls somewhere between the two extremes. Place a checkmark on the continuum that represents your score.

Theory X Behavior (Autocratic)	10———20———30———40	Theory Y Behavior (Participative)

The lower your score (10), the stronger the Theory X behavior, and the higher your score (40), the stronger the Theory Y behavior. A score of 20–30 could be considered balanced between the two theories. Your score may not be an accurate measure of how you would behave in an actual job. However, it should help you to understand your own behavior toward your employees.

In this section you will study the basic leadership styles, two-dimensional leadership styles, the leadership grid, and contemporary perspectives on behavior leadership.

Basic Leadership Styles

Leadership style *is the combination of traits, skills, and behaviors managers use to interact with employees.* Note that behavioral theorists focus on the leaders' behavior. However, leader behaviors are based on their traits and skills.

leadership style
The combination of traits, skills, and behaviors managers use to interact with employees.

In the 1930s, before behavioral theory became popular, Kurt Lewin, Ronald Lippitt, and Ralph White conducted studies at the University of Iowa that concentrated on the leadership style of the manager. Their studies identified three basic leadership styles: (1) *Autocratic:* The leader makes the decisions, tells employees what to do, and closely supervises employees—similar to Theory X behavior. (2) *Democratic:* The leader encourages employee participation in decisions, works with employees to determine what to do, and does not closely supervise employees—similar to Theory Y behavior. (3) *Laissez-Faire:* The leader takes a leave-the-employees-alone approach, allowing them to make the decisions, decide what to do, and does not follow up. The Iowa studies contributed to the behavioral movement (Chapter 1) and led to an era of behavioral rather than trait research.

Liz Claiborne used the democratic style as she worked with the design teams rather than making the designs for them or just leaving them alone. However, Liz Claiborne also left design teams alone to make decisions as she used the laissez-faire leadership style.

4. Discuss the major similarity and difference between two-dimensional leadership styles and the leadership grid.

Two-Dimensional Leadership Styles

two-dimensional leadership styles Based on job structure and employee consideration, which result in four possible leadership styles.

Two-dimensional leadership styles *are based on job structure and employee consideration, which result in four possible leadership styles.* The two dimensions are structuring (job-centered) and consideration (employee-centered).

Structuring and Consideration Styles. In 1945, the Personnel Research Board of Ohio State University, under the principal direction of Ralph Stogdill, began a study to determine effective leadership styles. In the attempt to measure leadership styles, they developed an instrument known as the Leader Behavior Description Questionnaire (LBDQ). Respondents to the questionnaire perceived their leader's behavior toward them on two distinct dimensions:

1. *Initiating structure.* The extent to which the leader takes charge to plan, organize, lead, and control as the employee performs the task. It focuses on getting the job done.
2. *Consideration.* The extent to which the leader communicates to develop trust, friendship, support, and respect. It focuses on developing relationships with employees.

Job-Centered and Employee-Centered Styles. At approximately the same time the Ohio State studies began, the University of Michigan's Survey Research Center began leadership studies under the principal direction of Rensis Likert. Their research identified the same two dimensions or styles of leadership behavior. However, they called the two styles *job-centered* (the same as initiating structure) and *employee-centered* (the same as consideration).

Work Application

2. Recall a present or past boss. Which of the four leadership styles, based on the two-dimensional leadership style, did your boss use most often? Describe the behavior of your boss.

Using Two-Dimensional Leadership Styles. When interacting with employees, the manager can focus on getting the job done through directing (initiating structure, job-centered behavior) and/or developing supportive relationships (consideration, employee-centered behavior). Combinations of the two dimensions of leadership result in four leadership styles, which Figure 12–1 illustrates. The Ohio State and University of Michigan Leadership Models differ because UM placed the two dimensions at opposite ends of the same continuum. OSU considered the two dimensions independent of one another.

With the design teams, Liz Claiborne tended to use a high structure (job-centered) and high consideration (employee-centered) leadership style. However, sometimes she left the design teams alone, using low structure (job-centered) and low consideration (employee-centered).

Ohio State University

Consideration

High

Low Structure and High Consideration [quadrant C]*

High Structure and High Consideration [quadrant B]

Low Structure and Low Consideration [quadrant D]

High Structure and Low Consideration [quadrant A]

Low

Initiating Structure

Low → High

*Quadrant letters A, B, C, D added by the text author.

University of Michigan

Job Centered —— Employee Centered

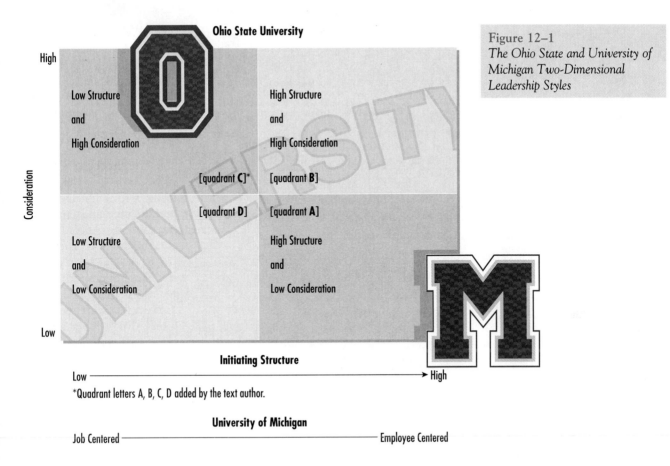

Figure 12–1
The Ohio State and University of Michigan Two-Dimensional Leadership Styles

The Leadership Grid®

Robert Blake and Jane Mouton developed the Managerial Grid[12] which later became the Leadership Grid,[13] with Anne Adams McCanse replacing Mouton. The Leadership Grid is based on the same two leadership dimensions, which they called "concern for production" and "concern for people." *The* **leadership grid model** *identifies the ideal leadership style as having a high concern for both production and people*. They used a questionnaire to measure the concern for both people and production on a scale from 1 to 9. Therefore, the grid has 81 possible combinations of concern for production and people. Figure 12–2 is an adaptation of the Leadership Grid. However, they identify five major styles:

leadership grid model
Identifies the ideal leadership style as having a high concern for both production and people.

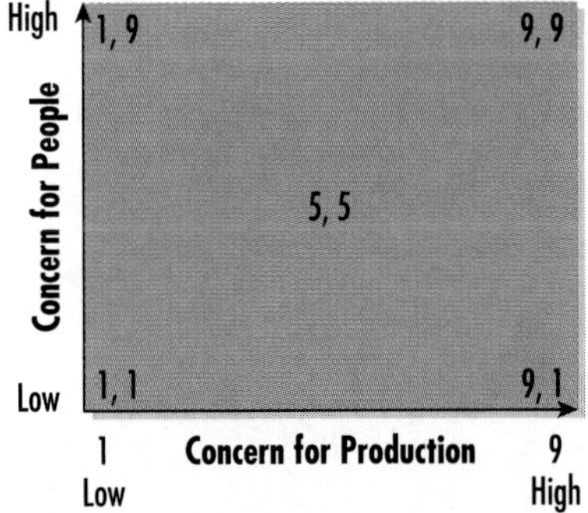

Figure 12–2
Blake, Mouton, and McCanse Leadership Grid

(1,1) *The impoverished leader* has low concern for both production and people. The leader does the minimum required to remain employed in the position.

(9,1) *The authority-compliance leader* has a high concern for production and a low concern for people. The leader focuses on getting the job done as people are treated like machines.

(1,9) *The country club leader* has a high concern for people and a low concern for production. The leader strives to maintain a friendly atmosphere without regard for production.

APPLYING THE CONCEPT

AC 12–1 The Leadership Grid

Identify the five statements by their leader's style.

a. 1,1 (impoverished)
b. 1,9 (country club)
c. 9,1 (authority-compliance)
d. 5,5 (middle of the road)
e. 9,9 (team manager)

____ 1. The group has very high morale; its members enjoy their work. Productivity in the department is one of the lowest in the company. The leader is highly concerned for people but not for production.

____ 2. The group has adequate morale. They have an average productivity level. The leader is somewhat concerned for both people and production.

____ 3. The group has one of the lowest levels of morale. It is one of the top performers. The leader is highly concerned for production but not for people.

____ 4. The group is one of the lowest producers. It has a low level of morale. The leader is not concerned for people or production.

____ 5. The group is one of the top performers. They have high morale. The leader is highly concerned for both people and production.

(5,5) *The middle of the road leader* has balanced, medium concern for both production and people. The leader strives to maintain minimal satisfactory performance and morale.

(9,9) *The team leader* has a high concern for both production and people. This leader strives for maximum performance and employee satisfaction. According to the behavioral theorists, the team leadership style is the most appropriate style to use in all situations. However, researchers have found this to be a myth.[14] Liz Claiborne most likely changed management styles, but commonly used the team leader style.

Work Application

3. Recall a present or past boss. Which of the five leadership grid styles did your boss use most often? Describe the behavior of your boss.

5. Identify the management levels that are the focus of charismatic, transformational, transactional, and symbolic leadership.

charismatic leadership
Based on a leadership style that inspires loyalty, enthusiasm, and high levels of performance.

transformational leadership
Based on change, innovation, and entrepreneurship as the top manager continually takes the organization through three acts.

Contemporary Perspectives

Current researchers focus on top-notch managers who exhibit certain behaviors that make them outstanding despite the possibility of wide variations in individual leadership styles.[15] Some of the current behavioral researchers focus on charismatic, transformational, transactional, and symbolic leadership.

Charismatic Leadership. **Charismatic leadership** *is based on a leadership style that inspires loyalty, enthusiasm, and high levels of performance.* The term *charismatic* has been applied to many leaders[16] including Pope John Paul II and Mother Theresa (Catholic Church leaders), Martin Luther King, Jr. (Civil Rights leader), Michael Jordan (basketball), Mary Kay Ashe (Mary Kay Cosmetics), Liz Claiborne (Liz Claiborne), Lee Iacocca (Chrysler), and Bill Gates (Microsoft). Charismatic leaders have an idealized goal or vision, have a strong personal commitment to that goal, communicate the goal to others, display self-confidence, and are viewed as being able to make the radical changes to reach the goal.[17] The followers in turn trust the leaders' beliefs, adopt those beliefs themselves, feel affection for the leaders, obey the leaders, and develop an emotional involvement with the goal, which leads to higher levels of performance. Researchers have recommended that top-level managers should attempt to develop the charismatic roles of leadership as part of organizational culture.[18]

Transformational Leadership. **Transformational leadership** *is based on change, innovation, and entrepreneurship as the top manager continually takes the organization through three acts.* Transformational leadership focuses on top-level managers, primarily CEOs of large organizations who are considered to be charismatic leaders. Transformational leaders perform, or take the organization through, three acts, on an ongoing basis:[19]

Act 1. Recognizing the need for revitalization. The transformational leader recognizes the need to change the organization in order to keep up with the rapid changes in the environment and to keep ahead of the global competition, which is becoming more competitive all the time.

Act 2. Creating a new vision. The transformational leader visualizes the changed organization and motivates people to make it become a reality.

Act 3. Institutionalizing change. The transformational leader guides people as they make the vision become a reality. A recent study found that transformational leadership had a positive effect on organizational commitment, employee satisfaction, and social behavior and some effect on performance.[20] Liz Claiborne was a successful transformational leader because she continually scanned the environment and made the necessary changes to stay ahead of the competition.

A charismatic leader, such as Martin Luther King, Jr., inspires loyalty, enthusiasm, and high levels of performance.

Transactional Leadership. Transformational leadership has been contrasted with transactional leadership.[21] **Transactional leadership** *is based on leadership style and exchange*. The exchange is based on the principle of you do this work for me and I'll give this reward to you. The manager may engage in both task and consideration leadership behavior with employees during the exchange. Transactional leadership focuses more on middle and first-line management. However, top level managers usually approve of monitary rewards used by the lower-level managers in exchanges.

transactional leadership
Based on leadership style and exchange.

symbolic leadership
Based on establishing and maintaining a strong organizational culture.

Symbolic Leadership. **Symbolic leadership** *is based on establishing and maintaining a strong organizational culture* (Chapter 8). Employees learn the culture (shared values, beliefs, and assumptions of how they should behave in the organization) through leadership. Liz Claiborne took a team approach to leadership in designing women's clothing. She emphasized sharing ideas and open communication when working with design teams. Employees throughout the organization recognized and adopted these values. Symbolic leadership starts with top management and should flow down to middle and first-line managers.

Work Application

4. Recall the top manager from an organization you work or have worked for. Would you call this CEO a charismatic transformational leader? Why or why not?

SITUATIONAL LEADERSHIP THEORIES

Both the trait and behavioral leadership theories were attempts to find the best leadership style in all situations. In the late 1960s, it became apparent that there is no best leadership style in all situations. Managers need to adapt different leadership styles to different situations.[22]

Situational leadership theorists *attempt to determine the appropriate leadership style for various situations*. In this section you will study some of the most popular situational or contingency leadership theories, including contingency leadership theory, leadership continuum, normative leadership theory, situational leadership, and path-goal theory. You will also learn about leadership substitutes and neutralizers.

situational leadership theorists
Attempt to determine the appropriate leadership style for various situations.

6. State the primary difference between the contingency leadership model and the other situational leadership models.

Contingency Leadership Model

In 1951, Fred E. Fiedler began to develop the first situational leadership theory. He called the theory "Contingency Theory of Leader Effectiveness."[23] Fiedler believed that one's leadership style reflects one's personality (trait theory oriented) and remains basically constant. Leaders do not change styles. *The* **contingency leadership model** *is used to determine if one's leadership style is task- or relationship-oriented and if the situation matches the leader's style.*

contingency leadership model
Used to determine if one's leadership style is task- or relationship-oriented and if the situation matches the leader's style.

Leadership Style. The first major factor is to determine one's leadership style as being task or relationship oriented. To do so, the leader fills in the Least Preferred Coworker (LPC) scales. The LPC essentially answers the question, Are you more task oriented or people relationship oriented in working with others? The two leadership styles are *task* and *relationship*. Note that unlike two-dimensional leadership, there are only two, not four leadership styles.

Situational Favorableness. After determining your leadership style, you determine the situational favorableness. Situation favorableness refers to the degree a situation enables the leader to exert influence over the followers. The three variables, in order of importance, are:

1. *Leader-member relations.* Is the relationship good or poor? Do the followers trust, respect, accept, and have confidence in the leader? Is it a friendly, tension-free situation? Leaders with good relations have more influence. The better the relations, the more favorable the situation.
2. *Task structure.* Is the task structured or unstructured? Do employees perform repetitive, routine, unambiguous, standard tasks that are easily understood? Leaders in a structured situation have more influence. The more repetitive the jobs, the more favorable the situation.
3. *Position power.* Is position power strong or weak? Does the leader have the power to assign work, reward and punish, hire and fire, and give raises and promotions? The leader with position power has more influence. The more power, the more favorable the situation.

Determining the Appropriate Leadership Style. To determine whether task or relationship leadership is appropriate, the user answers the three questions per-

APPLYING THE CONCEPT

AC 12–2 Contingency Leadership Theory

Using Figure 12–3, match the situation number with its corresponding appropriate leadership style. Select two answers.

a. 1 b. 2 c. 3 d. 4 e. 5 f. 6 g. 7 h. 8
a. task oriented b. Relationship oriented

____ ____ **6.** Saul, the manager, oversees the assembly of mass-produced containers. He has the power to reward and punish. Saul is viewed as a hard-nosed boss.

____ ____ **7.** Karen, the manager, is from the corporate planning staff. She helps the other departments plan. Karen is viewed as being a dreamer; she doesn't understand the various departments. Employees tend to be rude in their dealings with Karen.

____ ____ **8.** Juan, the manager, oversees the processing of canceled checks for the bank. He is well liked by the employees. Juan's boss enjoys hiring and evaluating his employees' performance.

____ ____ **9.** Sonia, the principal of a school, assigns teachers to classes and other various duties. She hires and decides on tenure appointments. The school atmosphere is tense.

____ ____ **10.** Louis, the chairperson of the committee, is highly regarded by its volunteer members from a variety of departments. The committee members are charged with recommending ways to increase organizational performance.

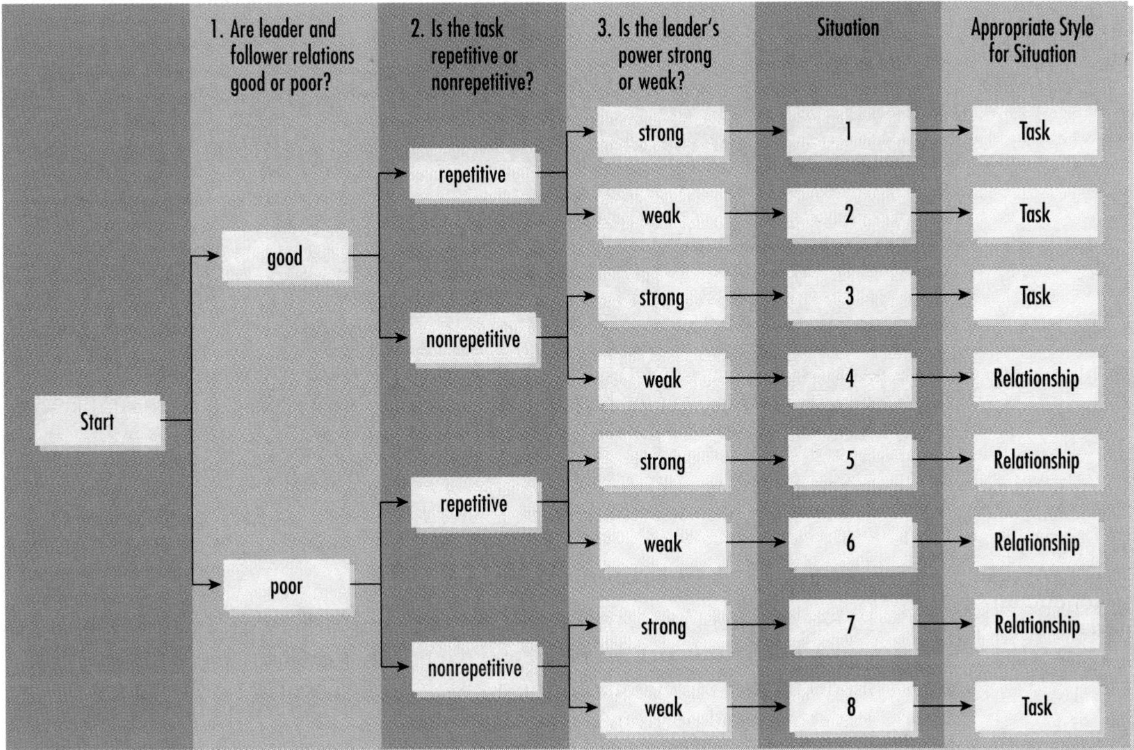

Figure 12–3
Fiedler Contingency Leadership Model

taining to situational favorableness, using the Fiedler contingency theory model. Figure 12–3 shows an adapted model. The user starts with question 1 and follows the decision tree to *good* or *poor* depending on the relations. The user then answers question 2 and follows the decision tree to *structured* or *unstructured*. When answering question 3, the user ends up in one of eight possible situations. Situations range from favorable for leader (1) to unfavorable (8). If the LPC preferred leadership style does not match the situation, Fiedler recommends (and trains people to) change the situation, rather than their leadership styles.

Even though Fiedler's theory is based on 80 studies conducted over more than a decade and in a variety of situations, it has many critics. One of the major criticisms concerns the view that the leader should change his or her style rather than the situation. The other situational writers in this chapter suggest changing leadership styles, not the situation. Fiedler has helped contribute to the other contingency theories. More recently, Fiedler has written about the leader knowing when to lead and when to stand back.[24]

Liz Claiborne had good relations with design teams, the task is unstructured or nonrepetitive, and Liz had strong position power as CEO. This is Situation 3, in which the appropriate leadership style is task. If Liz's preferred style were task, Fiedler would say do nothing. However, if Liz's preferred style was relationship, Fiedler would suggest that Liz change the situation to meet her preferred leadership style.

Work Application

5. Classify your present or past boss's preferred style as being task or relationship oriented. Using the Contingency Model, identify your boss's situation by number and the appropriate style to use for this situation. Does the boss's preferred style match the situation? Or, in other words, does or did the boss use the appropriate style?

Figure 12–4
Tannenbaum and Schmidt's Leadership Continuum Model

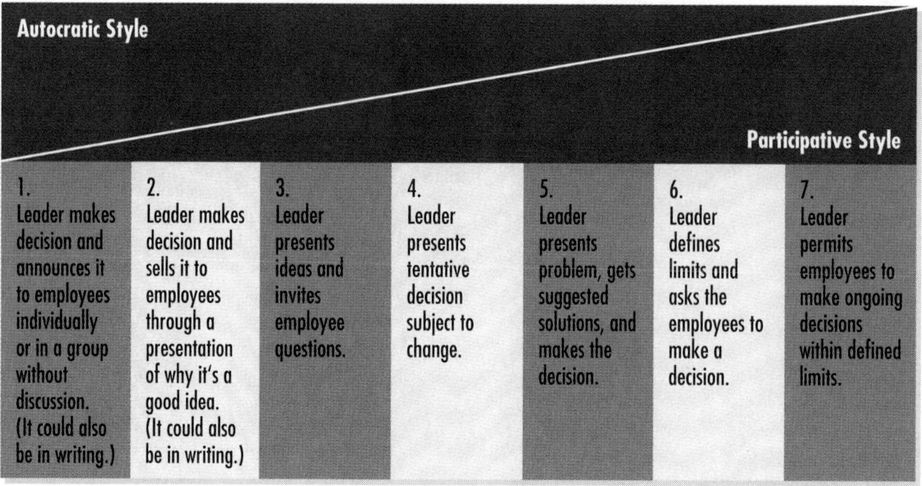

Autocratic Style
Participative Style
1. Leader makes decision and announces it to employees individually or in a group without discussion. (It could also be in writing.)
2. Leader makes decision and sells it to employees through a presentation of why it's a good idea. (It could also be in writing.)
3. Leader presents ideas and invites employee questions.
4. Leader presents tentative decision subject to change.
5. Leader presents problem, gets suggested solutions, and makes the decision.
6. Leader defines limits and asks the employees to make a decision.
7. Leader permits employees to make ongoing decisions within defined limits.

7. Discuss the major criticism shared by the continuum leadership model and the path-goal leadership model.

Leadership Continuum Model

Robert Tannenbaum and Warren Schmidt stated that leadership behavior occurs on a continuum from boss-centered to employee-centered leadership. Their model focuses on who makes the decisions. They identify seven major styles the leader can choose from. Figure 12–4, an adaptation of their model, lists the seven styles.[25] *The* **leadership continuum model** *is used to determine which of seven styles to select based on one's use of boss-centered versus employee-centered leadership.*

leadership continuum model
Used to determine which of seven styles to select based on one's use of boss-centered versus employee-centered leadership.

Before selecting one of the seven leadership styles, the leader must consider the following three factors or variables:

The Manager. The leader's preferred style, based on experience, expectation, values, background, knowledge, feeling of security, and confidence in the subordinates is considered in selecting a leadership style.

The Subordinates. The subordinates' preferred style for the leader, based on experience, expectation, and so on is considered in selecting a leadership style. Generally, the more willing and able the subordinates are to participate, the more freedom of participation should be used, and vice versa.

The Situation. The environmental considerations, such as the organization's size, structure, climate, goals, and technology, are considered in selecting a leadership style. Upper-level managers also influence leadership styles. For example, if a middle manager uses an auto-

APPLYING THE CONCEPT

AC 12–3 Leadership Continuum

Using Figure 12–4, match the five statements with their style.

a. 1 b. 2 c. 3 d. 4 e. 5 f. 6 g. 7

____ **11.** "Chuck, I selected you to be transferred to the new department, but you don't have to go if you don't want to."

____ **12.** "Sam, go clean off the tables right away."

____ **13.** "From now on, this is the way it will be done. Does anyone have any question about the procedure?"

____ **14.** "These are the two weeks we can go on vacation. You select one."

____ **15.** "I'd like your ideas on how to stop the bottleneck on the production line. But I have the final say on the solution we implement."

cratic leadership style, the supervisor may tend to use it too. The time available is also another consideration.

In a follow-up to their original 1973 article, Tannenbaum and Schmidt recommended that the leader become a group member when allowing the group to make decisions; that the leader clearly state the style (subordinate's authority) being used; that the leader should not try to trick the followers into thinking they made a decision that was actually made by the leader; and that it's not the number of decisions the followers make, but, rather, their significance that counts.[26]

Even though the continuum leadership model was very popular, one of the major criticisms concerns the fact that the three factors to consider when selecting a leadership style are very subjective. In other words, determining which style to use when is difficult. Although Liz Claiborne changed leadership styles to meet the needs of the situation, she tended to make greater use of the participative styles.

Work Application

6. Using the leadership continuum model, identify your boss's most commonly used leadership style by number. Would you say this is the most appropriate leadership style based on the manager, subordinates, and situation? Explain.

Path-Goal Model

Robert House developed the path-goal leadership model.[27] *The* **path-goal model** *is used to determine employee objectives and to clarify how to achieve them using one of four styles*. It focuses on how leaders influence employees' perceptions of their goals and the paths they follow toward goal attainment. As shown in Figure 12–5 (an adaptation of the model), the model uses the situational factors to determine the leadership style which affects goal achievement through performance and satisfaction.

path-goal model
Used to determine employee objectives and to clarify how to achieve them using one of four styles.

Situational Factors. *Subordinate* situational characteristics include: (1) authoritarianism—the degree to which employees defer to and want to be told what to do and how to do the job; (2) locus of control—the extent to which employees believe they control goal achievement (internal) or if goal achievement is controlled by others (external); and (3) ability—the extent of employee ability to perform tasks to achieve goals. *Environment* situational factors include: (1) task structure—the extent of repetitiveness of the job; (2) formal authority—the extent of the leader's power; and (3) work group—the extent to which coworkers contribute to job satisfaction.

Leadership Styles. Based on the situational factors, the leader can select the most appropriate leadership style by following these general guidelines:

1. *Directive*. The leader provides high structure. Directive leadership is appropriate when the subordinates want authority leadership, have external locus

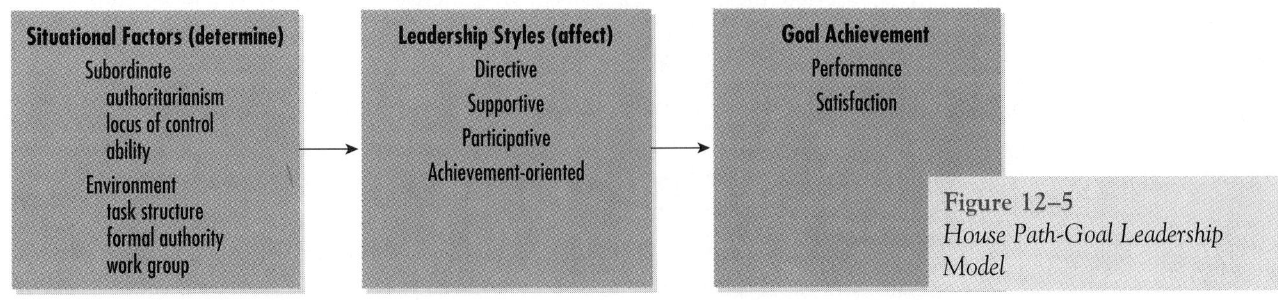

Figure 12–5
House Path-Goal Leadership Model

of control, and their ability is low. Directive leadership is also appropriate when the environmental task is complex or ambiguous, formal authority is strong, and the work group provides job satisfaction.

2. *Supportive*. The leader provides high consideration. Supportive leadership is appropriate when the subordinates do not want autocratic leadership, have internal locus of control, and their ability is high. Supportive leadership is also appropriate when the environmental tasks are simple, formal authority is weak, and the work group does not provide job satisfaction.
3. *Participative*. The leader includes employee input into decision-making. Participative leadership is appropriate when subordinates want to be involved, have internal locus of control, and their ability is high. Participative leadership is also appropriate when the environmental task is complex, authority is either strong or weak, and job satisfaction from coworkers is either high or low.
4. *Achievement-Oriented*. The leader sets difficult but achievable goals, expects subordinates to perform at their highest level, and rewards them for doing so. In essence, the leader provides both high structure and high consideration. Achievement-oriented leadership is appropriate when subordinates are open to autocratic leadership, have external locus of control, and their ability is high. Achievement-oriented leadership is also appropriate when the environmental task is simple, authority is strong, and job satisfaction from coworkers is either high or low.

Work Application

7. Identify your boss's most commonly used path-goal leadership style (directive, supportive, participative, achievement-oriented). Would you say this is the most appropriate leadership style based on the situational factors? Explain.

Although path-goal theory is more complex and specific than the leadership continuum, it also has been criticized because it is difficult to know which style to use when. As you can see, many situations occur in which the six situational factors are exactly as presented in the guidelines. Judgment calls are needed to select the appropriate style. Liz Claiborne tended to use the participative leadership style most often with her design teams.

8. Describe the major characteristic shared by the normative leadership model and the situational leadership model.

Normative Leadership Model

normative leadership model A decision tree that enables the user to select one of five leadership styles appropriate for the situation.

Based on empirical research into managerial decision-making, Victor Vroom and Philip Yetton attempted to bridge the gap between leadership theory and managerial practice by developing a model.[28] *The* **normative leadership model** *is a decision tree that enables the user to select one of five leadership styles appropriate for the situation*. Vroom and Arthur Jago worked to refine the model and expanded it to four models.[29] The four models are based on two factors: individual versus group decisions and time-driven versus development-driven decisions.

Leadership Styles. Vroom and Yetton identified five leadership styles. Two are autocratic (AI and AII), two are consultative (CI and CII), and one is group-oriented (GII).

AI. The leader makes the decision alone using available information.

AII. The leader gets information from subordinates but makes the decision alone. Subordinates may or may not be told what the problem is. They are not asked for input into the decision.

CI. The leader meets individually with subordinates, explains the situation, and gets information and ideas on how to solve the problem. The leader makes the final decision alone. The leader may or may not use the subordinates' input.

CII. The leader meets with subordinates as a group, explains the situation, and gets information and ideas on how to solve the problem. The leader makes the decision alone after the meeting. Leaders may or may not use the subordinates' input.

GII. The leader meets with the subordinates as a group, explains the situation, and the decision is made by the group with the help, but not with the over-influence, of the leader.

Determining the Appropriate Leadership Style. To determine the appropriate style for a specific situation, you answer eight questions, some of which may be skipped based on prior answers. The questions are sequential and are presented in a decision-tree format similar to the Fiedler model in which you end up with the one best style to use. The eight questions are:

1. Is there a quality requirement such that one solution is likely to be more rational than another?
2. Do I have sufficient information to make a high-quality decision?
3. Is the problem structured?
4. Is the subordinates' acceptance of the decision critical to effective implementation?
5. If I were to make the decision by myself, is it reasonably certain that it would be accepted by my subordinates?
6. Do subordinates share the organizational goals to be attained in solving the problem?
7. Is conflict among subordinates likely in the preferred solution (not relevant to individual problems)?
8. Do subordinates have sufficient information to make a high-quality decision?

Work Application

8. Identify your boss's most commonly used normative leadership decision-making style (AI, AII, CI, CII, GII). Would you say this is the most appropriate leadership style based on the eight questions to determine the appropriate style? Explain.

Vroom and Yetton's model is popular in the academic community because it is based on research. Vroom conducted research concluding that managers using the style recommended in the model have a 65 percent probability of a successful outcome, while not using the recommended style allows only a 29 percent probability of a successful outcome.[30] However, the model is not as popular with managers because they find it cumbersome to select from four models and to pull out the model and follow an eight-question decision tree every time they have to make a decision.

Liz Claiborne changed leadership styles, but tended to use the GII group approach to leadership and decision-making.

Situational Leadership Model

Paul Hersey and Ken Blanchard developed the situational leadership model.[31] *The* **situational leadership model** *is used to select one of four leadership styles that match the employees' maturity level in a given situation.* For the most part, situational leadership takes the two-dimensional leadership styles of the Ohio State model (four quadrants, see Figure 12–1), and gives names to the four leadership styles:

situational leadership model
Used to select one of four leadership styles that match the employees' maturity level in a given situation.

APPLYING THE CONCEPT

AC 12–4 Situational Leadership

For each of the following situations, identify the maturity level of the employees and the appropriate leadership style, by quadrant in Figure 12–6, for you to use as the manager to get the job done.

a. Low Maturity (M1) of employee. The manager should use the *telling* style (high structure/low consideration).
b. Low to Moderate Maturity (M2) of employee. The manager should use the *selling* style (high structure/high consideration).
c. Moderate to High Maturity (M3) of employee. The manager should use the *participating* style (low structure/low consideration).
d. High Maturity (M4) of employee. The manager should use the *delegating* style (low structure/low consideration).

____ **16.** Mary Ann has never done a report before, but you know she can do it with a minimum of help from you.

____ **17.** You told John to fill the customer order to your specifications. However, he deliberately ignored your directions. The customer returned the order to you with a complaint.

____ **18.** Tina is an enthusiastic employee. You have decided to expand her job responsibilities to include a difficult task which she has never done before.

____ **19.** Part of Pete's job, which he has done properly many times, is to take out the trash in your office when it's full. It is full now.

____ **20.** Carl usually does an excellent job and gets along well with coworkers. For the past two days you have noticed a drop in the quality of his work and saw him arguing with coworkers. You want Carl to return to his usual level of performance.

Telling (lower right quadrant A—high structure, low consideration)

Selling (upper right quadrant B—high structure, high consideration)

Participating (upper left quadrant C—high consideration, low structure)

Delegating (lower left quadrant D—low consideration, low structure).

Hersey and Blanchard went beyond the behavioral theory by developing a model that tells the leader which style to use in a given situation. To determine the leadership style, the leader determines the followers' maturity level. Maturity level does not mean how grown up the employees act. Maturity means the level of employee development (based on competence and commitment) or readiness to do the job (based on ability and willingness). If the leadership style is:

Low (M1), the leader uses a telling style.

Moderate to low (M2), the leader uses a selling style.

Moderate to high (M3), the leader uses the participating style.

High (M4), the leader uses a delegating style.

Work Application

9. Identify your boss's most commonly used situational leadership style (telling, selling, participating, delegating). Would you say this is the most appropriate leadership style based on the maturity level of the employees? Explain.

Hersey and Blanchard's model also differs from the Ohio State approach in another way. They place a bell-shaped curve within the four quadrants, and below the four quadrants they list the four maturity levels going from left (mature), to right (immature). Figure 12–6 shows an adaptation.

Situational management, in Skill-Building Exercise 1–1, is an adaptation of Hersey and Blanchard's situational leadership. Skill-Building Exercises 4–2, Situational Decision-Making, 10–2, Situational Communications, and 13–2, Situational Group Leadership are adapted from Hersey and Blanchard and Vroom and Yetton. Situational leadership has also been modified by others.[32]

Managers tend to like situational leadership because it is simple to use on the job. However, academic types prefer normative leadership theory because situational leadership lacks research and consistency in its instruments and model.[33] However, one common characteristic of situational leadership and normative leadership theory is that they both provide one clear leadership style to use in the given situation. Liz Claiborne changed styles, but tended to use the participative leadership style.

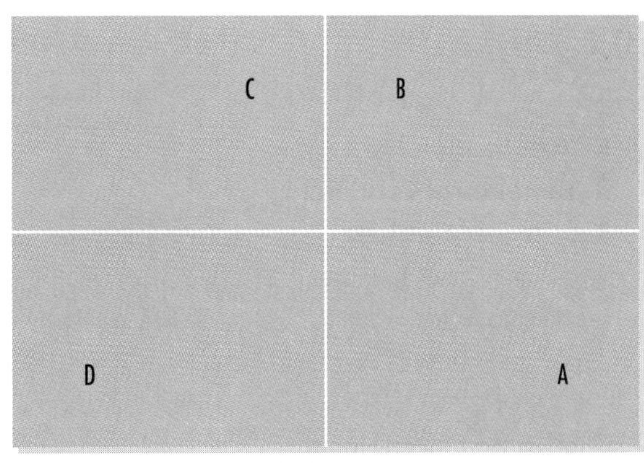

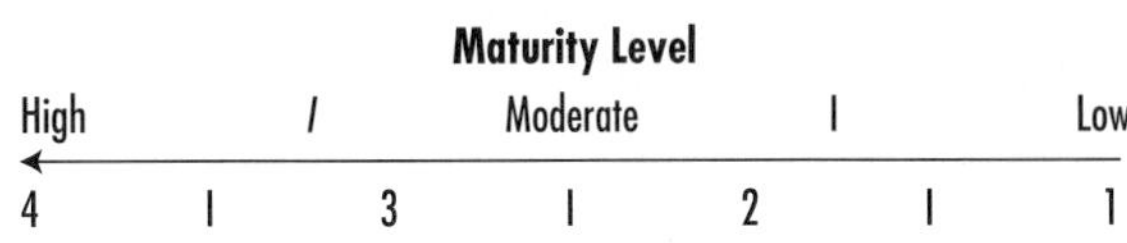

Figure 12–6
Hersey and Blanchard Situational Leadership Model

Leadership Substitutes Theory

The leadership theories presented assume that some leadership style will be effective in each situation. Steven Kerr and John Jermier argued that certain situational variables prevent leaders from affecting subordinates' attitudes and behaviors.[34] **Substitutes for leadership** *are three characteristics that replace the need for a leader*. The three characteristics of the task, subordinates, or organization can also have the effect of counteracting or neutralizing the effect of leadership behavior.[35]

substitutes for leadership
Three characteristics that replace the need for a leader.

The following may substitute for or neutralize leadership by providing direction and/or support rather than a leader:

1. *Characteristics of subordinates*. Ability, knowledge, experience, training. Need for independence. Professional orientation. Indifference toward organizational rewards.
2. *Characteristics of task*. Clarity and routine. Invariant methodology. Provision of own feedback concerning accomplishment. Intrinsic satisfaction.
3. *Characteristics of the organization*. Formalization (explicit plans, goals, and areas of responsibility). Inflexibility (rigid, unbending rules and procedures). Highly specified and active advisory and staff functions. Closely knit, cohesive work groups. Organizational rewards not within the leader's control. Spatial distance between superior and subordinates.

A study of nursing work indicated that the staff nurses' education, the cohesion of the nurses, and work technology substituted for the head nurse's leadership behavior in determining the staff nurses' performance.[36] In other words, a leader providing direction and support was not necessary.

Although Liz Claiborne provided strong leadership when she was with the design groups, there were multiple design groups and Liz did not try to manage them. Primarily the groups provided the leadership substitutes.

Work Application

10. Identify your present or past boss. Could the characteristics of subordinates, task, or organization substitute for this leader? In other words, is your boss necessary? Explain.

PUTTING THE LEADERSHIP THEORIES TOGETHER

So far in this chapter you have studied three approaches to classifying leadership theories (trait, behavioral, situational) with seven behavioral leadership theories (basic, two-dimensional, leadership grid, charismatic, transformational, transactional, and symbolic leadership) and six situational leadership theories (contingency, leadership continuum, path-goal, normative, situational, and leadership substitutes); plus, you studied situational management in Chapter 1. Figure 12–7 puts all of these leadership theories together. This figure should help you to better understand the similarities and differences between these theories. The models use the two dimensions of leadership; therefore, the boxed theories indicate the four possible leadership styles. Because different authors use different names to indicate the same two dimensions, we will use directive and supportive behavior to represent the other terms.

Work Application

11. Identify the one leadership theory/model you prefer. State why?
12. Describe the type of leader that you want to be.

	Two-Dimensional Leadership Styles			
	$H^{+}D^{*}/L^{++}S^{**}$	HD/HS	LD/HS	LD/LS
I. Trait Leadership	X	X	X	X
II. Behavioral Leadership				
Basic Leadership Styles	Autocratic	Democratic		Laissez-faire
Two-Dimensional [quadrant]	A	B	C	D
Leadership Grid	9,1 Authority	9,9 Team; moderate D&S 5,5 Middle road	1,9 Country	1,1 Impoverished
Charismatic Leadership	X	X	X	X
Transformational Leadership	X	X	X	X
Transactional Leadership	X	X	X	X
Symbolic Leadership	X	X	X	X
III. Situational Leadership				
Contingency Leadership	Task		Relationship	
Leadership Continuum	1	2 & 3	4 & 5	6 & 7
Path-Goal	Directive	Achievement	Supportive	
			Participative	
Normative Leadership	AI & AII	CI & CII		GII
Situational Leadership	Telling	Selling	Participating	Delegating
Situational Management	Autocratic	Consultative	Participative	Empowerment
Leadership Substitutes	X	X	X	X

$^{+}$ High $^{++}$ Low * Directive ** Supportive
X no two-dimensional leadership style used with this theory.

Figure 12–7
Putting the Leadership Theories Together

CURRENT MANAGEMENT ISSUES

Globalization. Global companies, like McDonald's with restaurants in 73 countries, realize that successful leadership styles can vary greatly from place to place.[37] In Europe managers have more cultural than technical aspects as they deal with diverse value systems and religious backgrounds. Management is organized more as a language than as a set of techniques. Companies look for graduates with an international openness who can master the complexity of the global economy.[38]

Back in the 1970s, Japan increased its rate of productivity at a faster pace than the United States. William Ouchi found that Japanese firms were managed and led differently than U.S. organizations. Ouchi identified seven major differences between the two countries. The Japanese (1) have a longer length of employment, (2) use more collective decision-making, (3) use more collective responsibility, (4) evaluate and promote employees more slowly, (5) use more implicit mechanisms of control, (6) have more unspecialized career paths, and (7) have a more holistic concern for employees.[39] Ouchi combined practices of U.S. and Japanese companies in what he called Theory Z. Over the years, many American companies have begun to use more collective decision-making and responsibilities.

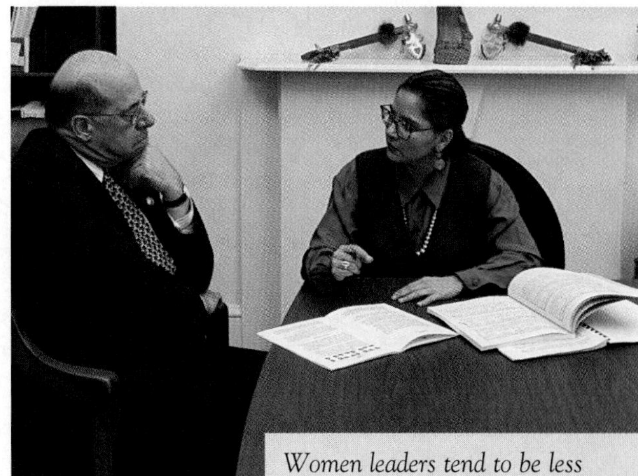

Women leaders tend to be less competitive, more cooperative and consensus-seeking, and more participative than men.

Diversity. Managers of the future will have to be effective in dealing with a *diversity* of people.[40] A variety of studies have tried to determine *gender* and *race* differences of leaders. Some studies have found no differences,[41] while others have found differences. A major study that found a difference stated that women tend to be transformational leaders while men tend to be transactional leaders.[42] It has also been reported that women are less competitive, more cooperative and consensus-seeking, and more participative leaders than men.[43] However, no clear agreement shows that gender and race differ among managers. And even if there are clear differences, based on situational leadership theory, one cannot conclude that people of one gender or race are better managers.

One of the reasons for the "glass ceiling" stems from the fact that women have often been stereotyped as followers rather than leaders. Stereotyping occurs more frequently in organizations with few senior women managers.[44] Bosses require women to prove themselves and exhibit personal strength, while they are more lenient to men of an equal position.[45] However, gender roles have a stronger effect on emergent leadership than sex. Masculine, rather than feminine, subjects are most likely to emerge as leaders regardless of sex.[46] The key to effective leadership in organizations is to take a situational approach to leadership. There are some excellent and poor male and female leaders among whites and people of color. In selecting leaders, managers must value and manage diversity (Chapter 3). Women recommend that other women who want to be managers plan their way to success.[47] This also applies to men.

Ethics and Social Responsibility. People, not organizations, are *ethical* and *socially responsible*. Managers' leadership style example behaviors tend to be copied by employees. Charismatic leadership has been applied to many business leaders, yet it does not distinguish between ethical and unethical leadership.[48] For example, Adolph Hitler and Charles Manson were considered very charismatic leaders and very unethical. In a recent study of desirable traits of leaders, honesty ranked as the top priority.[49] Researchers, in a study conducted to determine if women are more ethical than men, reported that males and females are ethically equivalent.[50]

TQM. TQM focuses on creating customer value and continuous improvement of systems and processes. A total quality culture (Chapter 8), conveyed through leadership, is important to TQM success.[51] Therefore, symbolic leadership is part of TQM. Managers get the quality job done through employees, and the various leadership models provide a context and methods for leading employees to achieve organizational missions and objectives.

Productivity. For several years now, it has been recognized that the key to increased *productivity* is not simply technology but people. People come up with the creative ideas that lead to innovation. To foster creativity and innovation, managers have been empowering employees by leaving them alone to do the job their way.[52] Leaders of the future need the ability to express an organizational vision and values and to serve as change agents.[53] These are characteristics and behaviors of charismatic, transformational, and symbolic leaders.

Participative Management and Teams. Managers are changing from autocratic to *participative leadership* and *teamwork*, or they often lose their jobs. The effectiveness of the team leader largely determines the success of teams.[54] Unfortunately, it is often difficult to change behaviors, and team leaders rate their performance higher than their team members do.[55] The role of the team leader differs from traditional management. The role of the leader is to help the team solve problems, to develop members' skills, and to bring out the creative ideas of all member.[56] With re-engineering, which is based on participative teamwork, the manager's job changes radically to include three major areas: (1) The leader is concerned about how to fill work orders and design products. (2) The leader acts as a coach who teaches and develops people. (3) The leader motivates by creating an environment where people get the job done.[57]

Small Business. Some entrepreneurs who run *small businesses* use different leadership styles than managers of large organizations. Some entrepreneurs tend to have a clear vision of what they want and how they want it done. They are often more autocratic to ensure that employees complete the job the entrepreneur's way. Entrepreneurs often have trouble expanding their business because they want to maintain autocratic control and make the important decisions, rather than delegating authority, which is necessary in large businesses. Entrepreneurs can be charismatic, but they can be very job centered and insensitive to others' needs.

CHAPTER SUMMARY AND GLOSSARY

The chapter summary is organized to answer the nine learning objectives for Chapter 12.

1. State the difference among trait, behavioral, and situational leadership theorists.

Trait theorists try to find a list of distinctive characteristics accounting for leadership effectiveness. Behavioral theorists try to determine distinctive styles used by effective leaders and they tend to seek the one best leadership style in all situations. Situational theorists try to find the appropriate style for various situations and they believe the best leadership style varies from situation to situation.

2. Explain why the terms *management* and *leadership* are not interchangeable.

Management is broader in scope and includes planning, organizing, leading, and controlling. Leadership is the process of influencing employees to work toward the achievement of organizational objectives. A person can be a manager who is a poor leader, and a person can be a good leader without being a manager.

3. Describe leadership trait theory and, according to Ghiselli, the most important leadership trait.

Leadership trait theory assumes that distinctive characteristics account for leadership effectiveness. According to Ghiselli, supervisory ability is the most important leadership trait. Supervisory ability is the ability to perform the four management functions of planning, organizing, leading, and controlling.

4. Discuss the major similarity and difference between two-dimensional leadership styles and the leadership grid.

Both theories use the same two dimensions of leadership, but use different names for the dimensions. The major difference is that two-dimensional leadership theory has four major leadership styles (high structure/low consideration, high structure/high consideration, low structure/high consideration, low structure/low consideration), whereas, the leadership grid has five leadership styles (1,1 impoverished, 9,1 authority-compliance, 1,9 country club, 5,5 middle of the road, and 9,9 team leadership styles).

5. Identify the management levels that are the focus of charismatic, transformational. transactional, and symbolic leadership.

Charismatic and transformational leadership focus on top-level management. Transactional leadership focuses on middle and first-line management. Symbolic leadership starts with top management and should flow down to middle and first-line management.

6. State the primary difference between the contingency leadership model and the other situational leadership models.

The contingency leadership model recommends changing the situation, not the leadership style. The other situational leadership models recommend changing the leadership style, not the situation.

7. Discuss the major criticism shared by the continuum leadership model and the path-goal leadership model.

The continuum leadership model and path-goal model are subjective making which leadership style to use when difficult or unclear.

8. Describe the major characteristic shared by the normative leadership model and the situational leadership model.

The major characteristic shared by situational leadership and normative leadership theory is that they both provide one clear leadership style to use in a given situation.

9. Define the following key terms (in order of appearance in the chapter).

Select one or more methods: (1) fill in the missing key terms from memory, (2) match the key terms from the end of the review with their definitions below, or (3) copy the key terms in order from the list at the beginning of the chapter.

______ is the process of influencing employees to work toward the achievement of organizational objectives.

__________ attempt to determine a list of distinctive characteristics that account for leadership effectiveness.

__________ attempt to determine distinctive styles used by effective leaders.

__________ is the combination of traits, skills, and behaviors managers use to interact with employees.

__________ is based on job structure and employee consideration, which result in four possible leadership styles.

The __________ identifies the ideal leadership style as having a high concern for both production and people.

__________ is based on a leadership style that inspires loyalty, enthusiasm, and high levels of performance.

__________ is based on change, innovation, and entrepreneurship as the top manager continually takes the organization through three acts.

__________ is based on leadership style and exchange.

__________ is based on establishing and maintaining a strong organizational culture.

__________ attempt to determine the appropriate leadership style for various situations.

The __________ is used to determine if one's leadership style is task- or relationship-oriented and if the situation matches the leader's style.

The __________ is used to determine which one of seven styles to select based on one's use of boss-centered versus employee-centered leadership.

The __________ is used to determine employee objectives and then to clarify how to achieve them using one of four styles.

The __________ is a decision tree that enables the user to select one of five leadership styles appropriate for the situation.

The __________ is used to select one of four leadership styles that matches the employees' maturity level in a given situation.

__________ are aspects of the task, subordinates, or organization that replace the need for a leader.

KEY TERMS

behavioral leadership theorist
charismatic leadership
contingency leadership model
leadership
leadership continuum model
leadership grid model
leadership style
leadership trait theorist
normative leadership model
path-goal model
situational leadership model
situational leadership theorist
substitutes for leadership
symbolic leadership
transactional leadership
transformational leadership
two-dimensional leadership styles

Review and Discussion Questions

1. What is leadership and why is it important?
2. What traits do you think are important to leaders?
3. Based on Self-Assessment Exercise 12–1, is your behavior more Theory X or Y?
4. What are the three parts of leadership style?
5. What are the two dimensions of leadership and the four possible leadership styles?
6. What are the five leadership grid leadership styles?
7. What is the difference between transformational and transactional leadership?
8. What are the two leadership styles of the contingency leadership model?
9. What are the two dimensions at the ends of the leadership continuum model?
10. What are the four leadership styles of the path-goal leadership model?
11. What are the five leadership styles of the normative leadership model?
12. What are the four leadership styles of the situational leadership model?
13. What are the three substitutes for leadership?
14. Do you believe men and women lead differently?

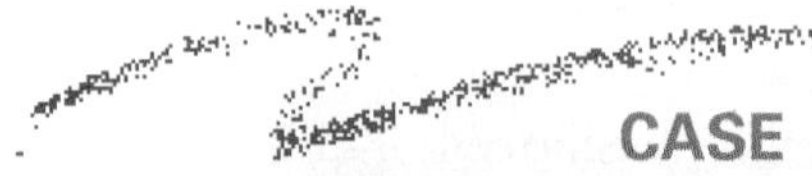

CASE

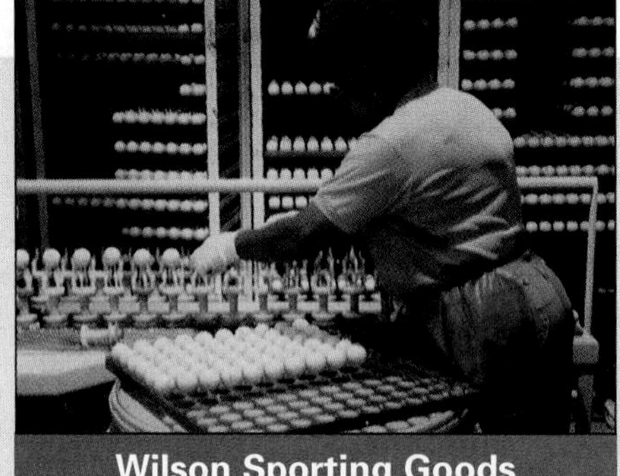

Wilson Sporting Goods

The Humboldt, Tennessee, facility was considered to be one of the least efficient plants within the Wilson Sporting Goods corporation. The facility produces golf balls and consistently lost money year after year. Major problems in the following areas caused Humboldt's lack of profitability: productivity, quality, cost, safety, morale, and housekeeping. The management and employee attitude toward each other was it's us against them. The plant manager Al Scott wanted to change the situation by solving these problems. He wanted Humboldt to make the best golf balls and have the most efficient production facilities in the world. With this vision in mind, Al developed the following mission statement: "Our mission is to be recognized . . . as the premier manufacturer of golf balls." To achieve the mission, Al developed the following five guiding philosophies, or what he wanted to become shared values: employee involvement, total quality management, continuous improvement, lowest total manufacturing cost, and just-in-time manufacturing.

Al held meetings with groups of employees to tell them about the vision, mission, and values he wanted them to share. He asked everyone to radically change their way of doing business. Al stressed the need to change from the old dictator management style to the new employee involvement style. Employees were referred to as associates and empowered to find new solutions to old problems. Managers were trained in employee involvement and developed skills to include employees in decision-making. They were also trained to develop teams, to develop better human relations, to coach employees, to better manage time, and to manage total quality (statistical process control, cause and effect analysis, etc.). The old attitude of "we cannot do it or cannot afford to do it" was changed to "we can do it and we cannot afford NOT to do it." The leadership style did change at Humboldt, and in turn employee loyalty, morale, enthusiasm, and level of performance increased.

To solve Humboldt's problems, Al instituted a voluntary employee participation program called Team Wilson. Humboldt developed teams of associates to participate in problem-solving in the areas of productivity, quality, cost, safety, morale, and housekeeping. Teams focused on reducing operating expenses, increasing cash flow, reducing inventory, and improving safety and housekeeping. To ensure team success, Humboldt gave all associates on teams similar training given to managers at the beginning of the change in process.

Many of the team leaders were associates, even though coaches (managers) were members of the team. However, leaders do not make the decisions; the teams do. Each team had the authority to spend up to $500 for each project they selected without management approval. More expensive projects were presented by the team to a management team that would accept the proposal and authorize the funds or explain why it denied the project.

With a new vision and mission and a changed management style, within a few years 66 percent of associates had formed voluntary teams, which dramatically changed the Humbold facility. Each team represented a specific area of the plant. The teams created their own unique logo, T-shirt, and posters which hang in the plant. Wilson holds several cookouts, picnics, and parties each year to show its appreciation to all associates. To recognize team accomplishments, Humboldt chooses three Team Wilson teams each quarter for awards.

Some team accomplishments include an increase in market share from 2 to 17 percent, an increase in inventory turns from 6.5 to 85, two-thirds reduction in inventory, reduction of manufacturing losses caused by scrap and rework by 67 percent, and an increase in productivity by 121 percent. The Humboldt plant produces over 1 billion golf balls each year, and the volume is growing. *Industry Week* magazine named it one of the "Best Plants in America."

Select the best alternative to the following questions. Be sure you are able to explain your answers.

___ 1. Al Smith called for a change in basic management style from ___ to ___.

a. democratic to laissez-faire
b. autocratic to laissez-faire
c. laissez-faire to democratic
d. autocratic to democratic

___ 2. Based on two-dimensional leadership (Figure 12–1) and situational leadership (Figure 12–6), within the Team Wilson teams, the team leader primarily uses the ___ leadership style.

a. telling—high structure/low consideration
b. selling—high structure/high consideration
c. participating—low structure/high consideration
d. delegating—low structure/low consideration

___ 3. Al Smith ___ be considered a charismatic leader.

a. should b. should not

___ 4. Al Smith should be considered a ___ leader.

a. transformational b. transactional

___ 5. Al Smith ___ focus on symbolic leadership at the Humboldt plant.

a. did b. did not

___ 6. Based on the original situation at Humboldt before Al made changes, determine Al's situation and the appropriate style using Figure 12–3.

a. 1, task
b. 2, task
c. 3, task
d. 4, relationship
e. 5, relationship
f. 6, relationship
g. 7, relationship
h. 8, task

___ 7. Based on the continuum model, Figure 12–4, the leadership style used was ___.

a. 1 b. 2 c. 3 d. 4 e. 5 f. 6 g. 7

___ 8. The management style at Humboldt was changed to the ___ path-goal leadership style.

a. directive
b. supportive
c. participative
d. achievement-oriented

___ 9. The normative leadership style used by the teams is ___.

a. AI b. AII c. CI d. CII e. GII

___ 10. Al ___ create substitutes for leadership at the Humboldt plant.

a. did b. did not

11. What role did leadership play in the improvements at Wilson's Humboldt plant?

12. Would the methods used by Al Scott work at an organization you work or have worked for? Explain your answer.

SKILL-BUILDING EXERCISE 12–1

A Leadership Continuum Role-Play[58]

Preparing for Skill-Building Exercise 12–1

You are an office manager with four subordinates who all do typing on regular typewriters. You will be receiving a word processor to replace one of the present typewriters. Everyone knows about it because several salespeople have been in the office. You must decide who gets the new word processor. Some information about each subordinate follows.

Pat has been with the organization for 20 years, is 50 years old, and presently has a two-year-old typewriter.

Chris has been with the organization for 10 years, is 31 years old, and presently has a one-year-old typewriter.

Fran has been with the organization for 5 years, is 40 years old, and presently has a three-year-old typewriter.

Sandy has been with the organization for 2 years, is 23 years old, and presently has a five-year-old typewriter.

Using the leadership continuum model, Figure 12–4, select the leadership style by number 1–7. You are not asked to select the employee who gets the word processor, only to select the style to be used in making the selection. Place your selection here ___ .

Doing Skill-Building Exercise 12–1 in Class

Objectives
To experience leadership in action. To identify the leadership style, and how using the appropriate versus inappropriate leadership style affects the organization.

Experience
You may role-play one of the employees or the manager in making the word-processing decision. You will observe the role-playing and try to determine the style used by the managers.

Preparation
You should have selected a leadership style in the preceding preparation section.

Procedure 1 (5–10 minutes)
Break into groups of three to six, but try to have a total of six groups. As a group, select the leadership continuum style (1–7) your group would use to make the word-processing decision.

Procedure 2 (5–10 minutes)

1. Four volunteers from different groups go to the front of the class. Take out a sheet of 8 × 11 paper and write the name of the person you are role-playing (in big, dark letters), fold it in half, and place it in view of the class. While the managers are planning, turn to the end of this exercise and read your role and the roles of your colleagues. Try to put yourself in the person's position and do and say what he or she actually would during the role-play. No one but the typist should read this additional subordinate role information.
2. The instructor will tell each group which leadership style their manager will role-play; it may or may not be the one your group selected. Be sure to review the continuum model in Figure 12–4 to fully understand the style.
3. The group selects a manager to do the actual role-play of making the decision; and the group plans how the manager will use the style given by the instructor.

Procedure 3 (1–10 minutes)
One manager volunteers, or is selected by the instructor, to go to the front of the class and conduct the leadership role-play.

Procedure 4 (1–5 minutes)
The class members (other than the group being represented) vote for the style (1–7) they think the manager portrayed. Then the manager reveals the style. If several class members didn't vote for the style portrayed, a discussion of why can take place.

Procedure 5 (25–40 minutes)
Continue to repeat Procedures 3 and 4 until all managers have their turn or the time runs out.

Procedure 6 (2–3 minutes)
The entire class individually determines the style they would use when making the decision. The class votes for the style to use in this situation. The instructor gives his or her recommendation and/or the author's.

Conclusion
The instructor may lead a class discussion and/or make concluding remarks.

Application (2–4 minutes)
What did I learn from this experience? How will I apply this knowledge in the future?

___

___

___

Sharing
Volunteers give their answers to the integration and/or application section.

Subordinate Roles

Additional information for subordinate role-players only.

Pat—You are happy with the way things are now. You do not want to learn how to use a word processor. Be firm and assertive in your stance.

Chris—You are bored with your present job. You really want to learn how to run a word processor. Being second in seniority, you plan to be aggressive in trying to get the word processor. You are afraid that the others will complain because you got the last new typewriter, so you have a good idea. You will take the word processor and Sandy can have your typewriter.

Fran—You are interested in having the word processor. You spend more time each day typing than any of the other employees. Therefore, you believe you should get the word processor.

Sandy—You want the word processor. You believe you should get it because you are by far the fastest typist and you have the oldest typewriter. You do not want a hand-me-down typewriter.

SKILL-BUILDING EXERCISE 12–2

The Situational Leadership Model

Preparing for Skill-Building Exercise 12–2

Think of a leadership situation, preferably from a present or past job. Describe the situation in enough detail so that others can understand it and determine the maturity level of the employees. Write the situation information below. If you have trouble thinking of a situation, refer back to Chapter 1, Skill-Building Exercise 1–1, Situational Management, for 12 examples.

____

____

____

____

For your situation, determine the maturity level of the follower(s) and select the situational leadership style appropriate for the situation (M1, low telling; M2, moderate to low selling; M3, moderate to high participating; M4, high delegating).

Doing Skill-Building Exercise 12–2 in Class

Objectives
To develop your skill at determining the appropriate leadership style to use in a given situation.

Experience
You may present your leadership situation to others for them to determine the appropriate leadership style, and you will hear others' leadership situations for you to determine the appropriate leadership style

Preparation
You should have a written leadership situation for others to analyze.

Procedure (10–50 minutes)
Option A. One at a time, volunteers or those selected by the instructor, come to the front of the class and present their situation. After the statement, the class may ask questions to clarify the situation. The class members take a minute to determine the appropriate leadership style (telling, selling, participating, or delegating) for the situation. The student or instructor asks the class how many selected each of the four styles. The student may or may not tell the class the style he or she selected. The instructor may lead a class discussion of the most appropriate leadership style for the situation.

Option B. Break into groups of five or six. One at a time, present your situation to the group. Each group member determines the style he or she would use. Then the group members share styles and discuss the most appropriate. It is not necessary to come to a consensus.

Option C. Same as option B, but the group selects one example to be presented to the entire class using option A format. The members of the group do not vote for the most appropriate style.

Conclusion
The instructor may lead a class discussion and/or make concluding remarks.

Application (2–4 minutes)
What did I learn from this experience? How will I apply this knowledge in the future?

____

____

____

Sharing
Volunteers give their answers to the integration and/or application section.

VIDEOCASE

Leadership: Sunshine Cleaning Systems

Sunshine Cleaning Systems (SCS) is a privately held company, founded in 1976, headquartered in Fort Lauderdale, Florida. Larry Calufetti, a former professional baseball player, started the business by cleaning windows himself after his baseball career had ended. Today, Sunshine is one of the largest contract cleaning companies in Florida. Sunshine specializes in cleaning windows, carpets, ceilings, and construction sites as well as pressure cleaning. Sunshine also cleans entire facilities inside and out. Clients include sports facilities, office buildings, stores and malls, and the Fort Lauderdale Airport. Their slogan is "We Guarantee a Brighter Day."

In addition to having been a professional baseball player, Larry Calufetti had been a minor league and college baseball coach. He applied his "coaching" style of leadership in founding and building Sunshine Cleaning Systems. Larry considers his company, and its hundreds of employees as a team. Larry's team includes everyone from the janitorial workers to executives who work at headquarters. Larry believes that employees should be properly trained and then be prepared to "play their positions" in cleaning some of the most important facilities in South Florida. Employees who perform at a high level are eligible for special recognition as members of "Larry's Dream Team." Managers throughout Sunshine emulate this "coaching" style. Larry attributes a large measure of his company's success to employees' responsiveness to his "coaching" style of leadership.

Group and Team Development

Learning Objectives

After studying this chapter, you should be able to:

1. Describe the major differences between groups and teams.
2. State the group performance model.
3. List and explain the three dimensions of group types.
4. Define the three major roles played in groups
5. Explain the differences between rules and norms.
6. Describe cohesiveness and why it is important to teams.
7. List the four major stages of group development and state the level of commitment and competence and the appropriate leadership style.
8. Explain the difference between a group manager and a team leader.
9. Discuss the three parts of meetings.
10. Define the following **key terms** (in order of appearance in the chapter):

group	group process
team	group process dimensions
group performance model	group roles
group structure dimensions	norms
group types	group cohesiveness
command groups	status
task groups	stages of group development
group composition	team leaders

Skill-Development

1. You can develop your skill at analyzing a group's development stage and selecting the appropriate leadership (Skill-Building Exercise 13–1).

   Group skills are an important part of the leadership function of management. Group skills require interpersonal roles, particularly the leader and liaison roles; informational roles of monitor, disseminator, and spokesperson; and decisional roles of disturbance handler, resource allocator, and negotiator. The SCANS competencies of interpersonal skills, information, and systems are developed, and basic, thinking, and personal qualities are developed through the exercise.

Methodist Medical Center (MMC) of Oak Ridge, Tennessee, is a fully accredited, nonprofit organization that has grown into a 300-bed facility with 24 specialty departments, 140 physicians, 1,280 employees, and 200 volunteers. MMC's primary goal is to deliver quality health care.

In the mid-1980s, the health care market became increasingly competitive. President and CEO Marshall Whisnant took action to improve performance. After a few failed attempts, he decided to take a systems approach to MMC. New initiatives included employee involvement, long-term thinking, pride in work quality, and an emphasis on teamwork to get the job done. With the help of consultants from QualPro, MMC launched "Quality Together."

Quality Together has four principles: (1) Quality assessment is to be performed by the employees doing the procedures by forming teams who use statistics to monitor work processes and make improvements on a continuous basis. (2) The number one rule is to satisfy customers, whether they are patients, physicians, corporate clients, or third-party payers. Measures of performance are customer-focused. (3) The focus of improving performance should be on making the overall customer satisfaction system and its processes function better, not on the management of employees or discrete events. (4) Top management focuses on the interrelationship of the entire system, and the other levels are responsible for reducing variation caused by special events and problems that deviate from the normal system.

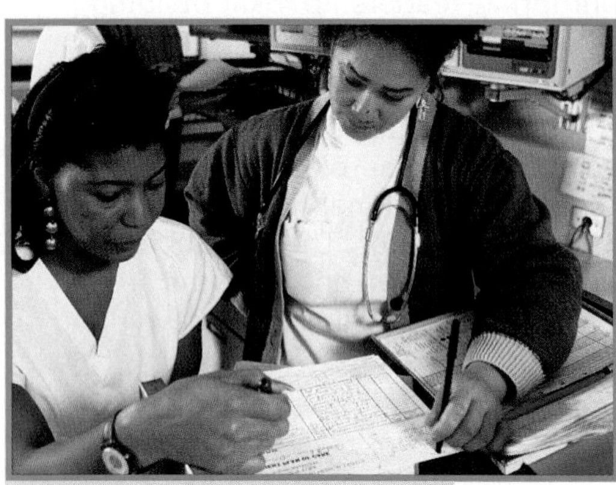

MMC's "Total Quality" program emphasizes employee involvement and teamwork to get the job done.

To implement Quality Together value principles, QualPro consultants led MMC through four phases: (1) *Commitment.* A needs assessment was conducted to determine areas for improvement. The top management team went though team training. The team selected several process improvement projects. (2) *Initial Success.* Teams of managers and employees were formed to work on the projects selected in Phase 1. Team members were trained in teamwork, and QualPro consultants led the groups through applying an improvement process to their projects. The teams had great success at improving the processes of their projects. (3) *Implementation.* Many new teams were formed to focus on improving interdepartmental processes throughout the system. Members were trained in teamwork and building interdepartmental teams. (4) *Self-Sufficiency.* During the final phase, QualPro consultants trained MMC employees, called facilitators, to conduct the teamwork training, to train team leaders to run the team meeting, and to serve on teams as resource persons.

Managers developed teams within their own departments and kept informed on team progress by visiting team meetings. The managers provided support and resources to implement team recommendations. Managers were also encouraged to request interdepartmental project teams to improve specific process areas. Through this process, MMC implemented teams throughout the system, emphasizing the involvement of all employees.

THE LESSON OF THE GEESE

When you see geese heading south for the winter flying in a "V" formation, you might be interested in knowing what scientists have discovered about why they fly that way. It has been learned that as each bird flaps its wings, it creates an uplift for the bird immediately following. By flying in a "V" formation, the flock adds at least 71 percent more flying range than if each bird flew on its own.

Basic truth #1. People who share a common direction and sense of community can get where they are going quicker and easier because they are traveling on the thrust of one another. . . . Whenever a goose falls out of formation, it suddenly feels the drag and resistance of trying to go it alone and quickly gets back into formation to take advantage of the lifting power of the bird immediately in front.

Basic truth #2. There is strength and power and safety in numbers when traveling in the same direction as others with whom we share a common goal. . . . When the lead goose gets tired, he or she rotates back in the wing and another goose flies point.

Basic truth #3. It pays to take turns doing hard jobs. . . . The geese honk from behind to encourage those up front to keep up their speed.

Basic truth #4. We all need to be remembered with active support and praise. . . . Finally, when a goose gets sick or is wounded and falls out, two geese fall out of formation and follow him or her down to help and protect. They stay with the downed goose until the crisis resolves, and then they launch out on their own or with another formation to catch up with their group.

Basic truth #5. We must stand by each other in times of need.

GROUPS AND TEAMS AND PERFORMANCE

Groups are the backbone of organizations because of the systems effect in which each group/department is affected by at least one other group and each department affects the performance of the total organization. Researchers have shown that performance can be improved when organizations use a systems approach.[1]

Managers are evaluated on the results of their departments as a whole, rather than on the results of each employee. Managers report spending 50 to 90 percent of their time in some form of group activity. Management performance depends on team performance, and leadership behavior affects team performance.[2] The better you understand groups and their performance, the more effective you will be as both a group member and leader. It is recommended that you have team experience on your résumé to help you get a job.[3]

In this section you will study the differences between groups and teams, about factors that affect group performance, and how organizational context affects performance.

Groups and Teams

1. Describe the major differences between groups and teams.

group
Two or more members with a clear leader who perform independent jobs with individual accountability, evaluation, and rewards.

team
A small number of members with shared leadership who perform interdependent jobs with both individual and group accountability, evaluation, and rewards.

Although the terms *group* and *team* are used interchangeably, in recent years a distinction has been made.[4] Distinctions between groups and teams and their levels of autonomy are presented in Figure 13–1. All teams are groups, but not all groups are teams. Therefore, *when the term* groups *is used throughout this chapter, it can also refer to a team.*

To summarize the differences between groups and teams, they are defined as follows. A **group** *is two or more members with a clear leader who perform independent jobs with individual accountability, evaluation, and rewards.* A **team** *is a small number of members with shared leadership who perform interdependent jobs with both individual and group accountability, evaluation, and rewards.*

Differences Between Groups and Teams

Characteristics	Group	Team
Size	Two or more; can be large.	Small number, often 5 to 12.
Leadership	One clear leader making decisions.	Shared leadership.
Jobs	Members perform one clear job; individual members do one independent part of a process (make one part of the product and pass it on to next person to do the next part).	Members share job responsibility by performing many interdependent tasks with complementary skills; the team completes an entire process (makes the entire product).
Accountability and Evaluation	Leader evaluates employees' individual performance.	Members evaluate each other's individual performance and group performance.
Rewards	Members are rewarded based on individual performance only.	Members are rewarded for both individual and group performance.
Objectives	Organizational.	Organizational and those set by the team.

Level of Autonomy

Group Management-Directed	Semi-Autonomous	Team Self-Directed

Figure 13–1
Groups versus Teams

As shown in the bottom of Figure 13–1, groups and teams are on a continuum; it's not always easy to make a clear distinction. The terms *management-directed, semi-autonomous*, and *self-managed* (or directed) are commonly used to differentiate along the continuum. Management-directed is clearly a group, self-directed is clearly a team, and semi-autonomous is between. The U.S. Congress, workers on a traditional assembly line, and traditional sales forces are groups, not teams. Congress will probably never be a team. However, some companies are getting away from the assembly line, such as Volvo, and having teams build the entire product. Saturn is using more of a team approach to producing cars. Salespeople are also becoming teams in some organizations with a focus on customer satisfaction rather than just the number of products sold.[5] Geese are more of a team than a group, although large numbers of them sometimes fly together. The teams at Methodist Medical Center (MMC) are closer to being a group than a team because they are problem-solving groups for an area rather than teams of workers actually getting the job done on a day-to-day basis.

Although it is not always easy to make a clear distinction between a group and a team, do so. Also, be aware that the trend is toward developing teams.[6] David

APPLYING THE CONCEPT

AC 13–1 Group or Team

Based on each statement, identify it as characteristic of:

a. group b. team

____ **1.** "My boss conducts my performance appraisals, and I get good ratings."

____ **2.** "We don't have any departmental goal; we just do the best we can to accomplish the mission."

____ **3.** "My compensation is based primarily on my department's performance."

____ **4.** "I get the assembled product from Jean, I paint it and send it to Tony for packaging."

____ **5.** "There are about 30 people in my department."

Packard and William Hewlett used teams to make Hewlett-Packard a leading global computer company. With teams, Pitney Bowes reduced inventories by 60 percent, reduced needed space by 25 percent, and improved cycle time in one area by 94 percent.[7] AES, a producer of power, has increased revenue an average of 23 percent with profits increasing sixfold since starting to use teams in 1990.[8]

Work Application

1. Recall a present or past job. Did you work in a group or team? Explain using each of the six characteristics in Figure 13–1. *Note:* You may want to select one job and use it to answer the work applications throughout this chapter.

The Group Performance Model

The performance of groups is based on four major factors and can be listed as a formula. *In the* **group performance model,** *group performance is a function of organizational context, group structure, group process, and group development stage.* The group performance model is illustrated in Figure 13–2. Organizational context has been covered in other chapters, so in this section it will be explained briefly. However, the other three factors affecting group performance will be covered in detail in separate sections.

2. State the group performance model.

group performance model
Group performance is a function of organizational context, group structure, group process, and group development stage.

Organizational Context

A number of overall organizational and environmental factors affect how groups function and their level of performance. These organizational context factors have been discussed in prior chapters. However, a few of these factors will be explained as they relate directly to the use of groups or teams and their performance.

In response to the global *environment,* many organizations are changing their *missions* and *strategies* to be more competitive. To meet this productivity challenge, many organizations are changing from groups to teams to increase performance. The type of *culture* that values teamwork will tend to use teams rather than groups.

Within the organizational *structure* (Chapter 7), centralized versus decentralized authority affects the use of groups or teams. As shown in Figure 13–1, centralized management-directed autonomy calls for the use of groups, and self-directed decentralized authority calls for the use of teams. The way jobs are designed also affects the use of groups or teams. Independent, simplified jobs call for groups and interdependent, enriched jobs for teams. Figure 13–1 suggests the difference in job designs of groups and teams. The physical layout of where people work affects the use of groups and teams. Team members need to be relatively close to each other in an open area to work together. However, technol-

Figure 13–2
Group Performance Model

Group Performance	(f)	Organizational Context	Group Structure	Group Process	Group Development Stage
High to Low		Environment	Type	Roles	Orientation
		Mission	Size	Norms	Dissatisfaction
		Strategy	Composition	Cohesiveness	Resolution
		Culture	Leadership	Status	Production
		Structure	Objectives	Decision-making	Termination
		Systems and Processes		Conflict resolution	

(f) = a function of

ogy such as teleconferencing and computers helps groups function more like teams; this will be discussed in Chapter 17.

The *systems and processes* for converting inputs into outputs also affect the use of groups or teams and their performance. With an individual evaluation and reward system, there is little incentive to create teams. Groups, and especially teams, need good feedback systems so that they can evaluate group performance and continuously improve processes.

GROUP STRUCTURE

group structure dimensions
Include group type, size, composition, leadership, and objectives.

Group structure dimensions *include group type, size, composition, leadership, and objectives*. Each of these five components of group structure is described in this section.

3. List and explain the three dimensions of group types.

Group Types

group types
Include formal or informal, functional or cross-functional, and command or task.

Dimensions of **group types** *include formal or informal, functional or cross-functional, and command or task.*

Formal or Informal Groups. *Formal groups*, such as departments and smaller subparts, are created by the organization as part of the formal structure; the groups generally have their own formal structure for conducting business. *Informal groups* are not created by the organization as part of the formal structure. They are spontaneously created when members join together voluntarily because of similar interests. People from any part of the organization who get together for breaks, lunch, and after work make up an informal group, which may be referred to as a *clique*. Membership in informal groups tends to be more open and changes at a faster rate than membership in formal groups. Throughout this text, the focus is on formal groups and teams.

Functional or Cross-Functional Groups. *Functional*, or vertical, *groups* have members who perform jobs within one limited area. Work units/departments make up a functional group. For example, the marketing, finance, operations, and human resources departments are functional groups. *Cross-functional*, or horizontal, *groups* have members from different areas and possibly different levels. Generally, the higher the management level, the more cross-functional the responsibility.

Each manager in the organization serves as the link between each group. Ideally, all functional groups coordinate their activities through the aid of the managers who are responsible for linking the activities together. Rensis Likert calls this the *linking-pin role*. Figure 13–3 illustrates functional and cross-functional groups with managers acting as linking pins. The current trend is toward using more cross-functional groups to better coordinate the functional areas of the organization.

command groups
Comprised of managers and their employees.

Command or Task Groups. **Command groups** *are comprised of managers and their employees*. People are hired to be a part of a command group. Command groups are distinguished by department membership as being functional or cross-functional. In Figure 13–3, the president and the vice presidents are a cross-functional command group, while the vice presidents and their managers are functional command groups.

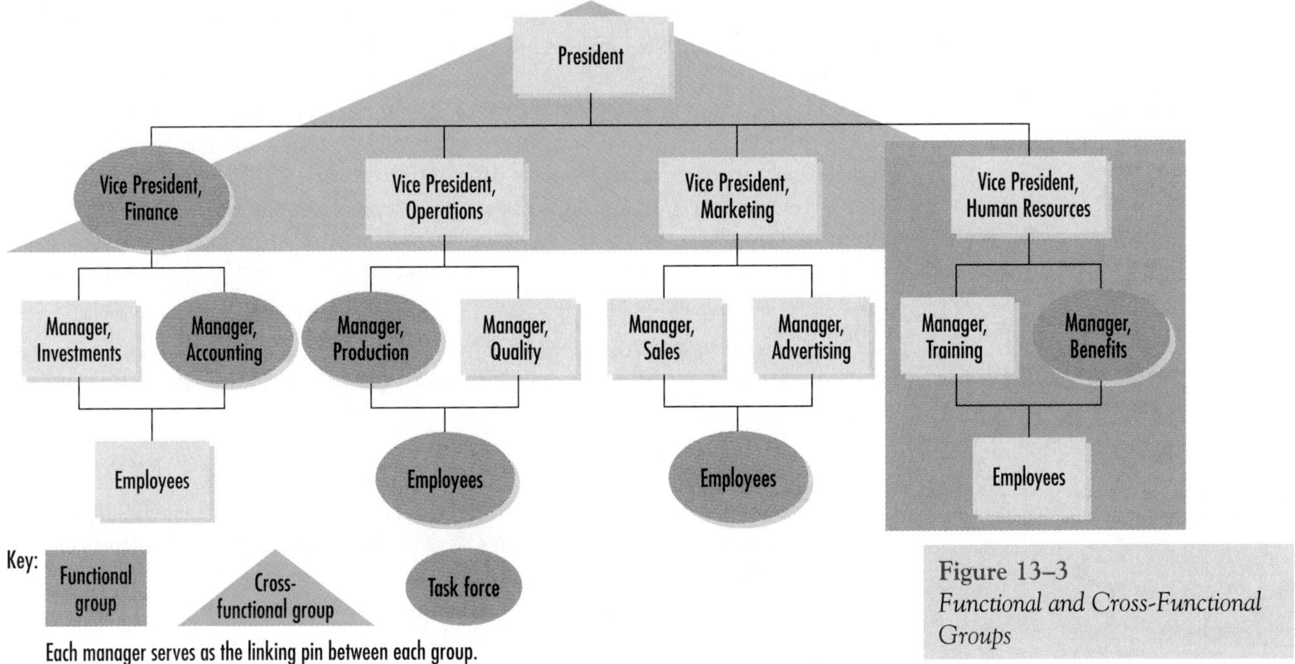

Figure 13–3
Functional and Cross-Functional Groups

task groups
Comprised of employees selected to work on a specific objective.

Task groups *are comprised of employees selected to work on a specific objective.* Task groups are usually called *committees*. There are two primary types of task groups: task forces and standing committees.

A *task force*, or ad hoc committee, is a temporary group formed for a specific purpose. For example, part of Phase 1 at MMC was to form a group to identify several process improvement projects. Once the list was completed, the committee was disbanded. Managers can also form cross-functional task teams to work on interdepartmental problems. Project teams, using a matrix structure (Chapter 7), are a form of task group in which employees have a functional boss and work with cross-functional departments as needed. In Figure 13–3, the purpose of the task force is to select three top candidates to present to the board of directors as potential replacements for the current president who will retire in six months. One employee from each of the functional areas, selected by their peers, serves on the task force.

A *standing committee* is a permanent group that works on continuing organizational issues. For example, the functional teams at MMC continue to meet in order to provide continuous improvement, and it always has a budget committee because it creates a new budget every year. Membership on standing committees is often rotated every year so that new ideas are brought to the group. For example, membership may be for three years, with one-third of the committee replaced every year.

Many organizations have a variety of standing committees. For example, environmental scanning standing committees to conduct an ongoing SWOT analysis (Chapter 5) and budget committees to allocate resources are common. Some organizations, including Dow, GE, Monsanto, Westinghouse, and Union Carbide have venture groups that develop new products and lines of business to enter. 3M has at least 24 venture groups developing new lines of business at one

Work Application

2. Identify task groups used in an organization you work or have worked for. Be sure to specify each group as a task force or standing committee.

time, and six of its current divisions grew out of these venture groups. At MMC a cross-functional steering committee makes the decisions on projects over $500.

There are a couple of major differences between a command and task group. One difference is the membership. Command groups tend to be functional, while task groups are often cross-functional. Another difference is in who belongs to which type of group. Everyone in an organization belongs to a command group, but employees may work for an organization for many years without ever being a member of a cross-functional task group. Generally, the higher the level of management, the more variety and time spent in task groups and their meetings.

Group Size

Is There an Ideal Group Size? There is no consensus on the ideal size for groups; some say three to nine, others say five or six to eight, while still others say up to twenty. The number varies depending on the purpose. Groups tend to be larger than teams. At Titeflex teams of six to ten manufacture fluid and gas-holding systems. EDS has project teams of 8 to 12 members. Johnsonville Foods uses self-managed teams of around 12. Digital Equipment Corporation believes the ideal size team is 14 or 15. In flat organization structures, it is common to have one boss with 30 or more employees forming a group.

Task groups/teams are often smaller than command groups. Fact-finding groups can be larger than problem-solving groups. These larger groups generate more alternatives and higher-quality ideas as they benefit from diverse participation.[9]

If the group is too small, it limits ideas and creativity. It tends to be too cautious and the workload is not distributed over enough members. On the other hand, if a group is too large, it tends to be too slow and not everyone gets to participate. With 20 or more members, you have a group rather than a team because there are too many members to get consensus on decisions, and members tend to form subgroups. In large groups, free-riding is a problem. *Free-riding* occurs when members rely on others to carry their share of the workload.

How Size Affects Leadership. Group size affects leadership, members, and the group's process of completing the job.[10] The appropriate leadership style may vary with group size. The larger the size, the more formal or autocratic the leadership needs to be to provide direction. Managers tend to be more informal and participative when they have smaller teams. Group members are more tolerant and appreciative, at times, of autocratic leadership in large groups. Larger groups tend to inhibit equal participation. Generally, participation is more equal in groups of around five. This is why teams are small in size. The larger the group, the greater need there is for formal structured plans, policies, procedures, and rules.[11]

Leadership Implications. Usually, managers have no say in the size of their command groups. However, if you have a large department, you can take a larger group and break it into teams. As the chair of a committee, you may be able to select the group size. In doing so, keep the group size appropriate for the task and be sure to get the right group composition.

Group Composition

What Is Group Composition? **Group composition** *is the mix of members' skills and abilities*. Group and team performance, regardless of type and size, is affected by its composition. Without the right mix of skills and abilities, groups will not perform at high levels.

group composition
The mix of members' skills and abilities.

People with a high need for affiliation tend to make better team players than people with a high need for power, who work better in groups. Managers tend to have a high need for power and a low need for affiliation, which contributes to their use of groups and their resistance to changing to teams.

Leadership Implications. One of the most important group leadership functions it to attract, select, and retain the best people for the job. When selecting group or team members, be sure to include a diversity of members. Recall (Chapter 3) that diverse groups tend to outperform homogeneous groups. With teams you want members with complementary skills, rather than selecting people with the same skills. Cross-functional teams provide diversity and complementary skills.

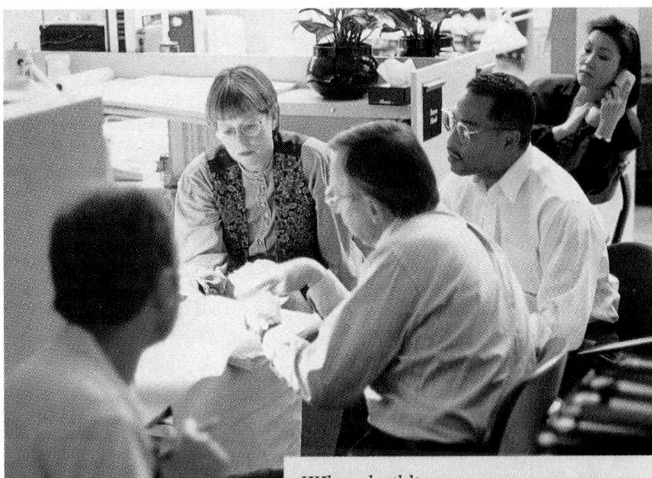

When building a group or team, be sure to include members with a diversity of skills and abilities.

Group Leadership and Objectives

Leadership. To a large extent, the leader provides and determines group structure. In Figure 13–1, you learned that the leadership style is different in groups and teams. In Chapter 12, you learned that group performance is affected by the team leader,[12] and how the role is changing from group to team leadership through higher levels of participation.[13] In this section, you learned that group size affects the type of leadership style needed. Throughout the rest of this chapter you will learn more about group and team leadership.

Objectives. In Chapter 5 you learned the benefits of setting objectives; they apply to both individuals and groups. Researchers have shown that acceptance of and commitment to difficult but specific objectives improves performance.[14] In groups, the objective is commonly very broad—usually to fulfill the mission. However, teams develop their own objectives. One of the reasons why teams tend to outperform groups is because they have their own objectives; groups do not. Objectives help to provide the structure required to identify organizational need to achieve the objective.

Leadership Implications. Companies in the Forbes top 25 are focusing on developing team leadership and goal-setting skills.[15] As a manager, you need to provide the appropriate leadership style for the situation. Part of leadership responsibility is to be sure the size and composition are appropriate for the situation. As a group or team leader, or as a member with leadership skills, be sure that the group or team has clear objectives. When setting objectives, follow the guideline in Chapter 5.

Work Application

3. Recall a present or past job. State the type of group/team you belonged to and describe its size, composition, leadership, and objectives.

MMC has groups in all three dimensions of group type. It has moved from groups to teams. The Quality Together program includes command and task

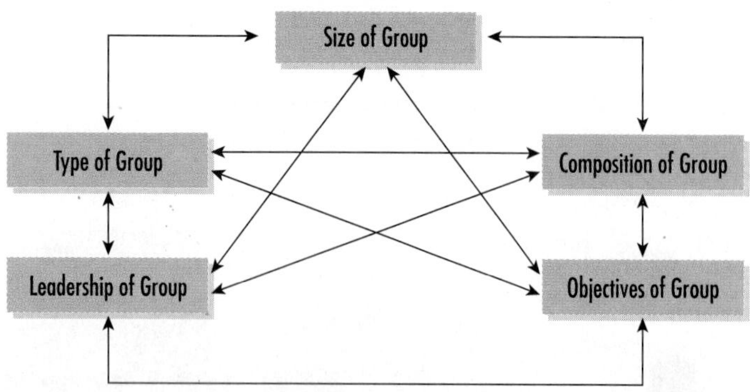

The arrows indicate the effect (or systems interrelationship) each dimension has on the others.

Figure 13–4
Group Structure Dimensions

groups of various sizes. MMC teams have leaders, but they share leadership responsibilities with members. When managers develop teams, they do consider composition and the teams develop their own objectives.

In summary, group structure dimensions include group type, size, composition, leadership, and objectives. See Figure 13–4 for a review of group structure dimensions.

GROUP PROCESS

group process
Refers to the patterns of interactions that emerge as members perform their jobs.

When team members work together to get the job done, how they interact affects their performance as individuals and as a group.[16] **Group process** *refers to the patterns of interactions that emerge as members perform their jobs*. Group process is also called *group dynamics* and the process can change over time. Employees find themselves in a group but few are actually trained to develop group process skills.[17] However, team members need training in group process to be successful.[18] Attention to group process improves the performance of groups, particularly in the areas of communication and decision-making.[19] Regardless of the type of groups you work in, your ability to understand group process and to develop these skills will affect your performance, the group's performance, and all members' job satisfaction.

group process dimensions
Include roles, cohesiveness, status, decision-making, and conflict resolution.

Group process dimensions *include roles, norms, cohesiveness, status, decision-making, and conflict resolution*. These components are presented in this section.

4. Define the three major roles played in groups.

Group Roles

As a group works toward achieving its objectives, it has to perform certain functions. As functions are performed, people develop roles. *Job roles* are shared expectations of how group members will fulfill the requirements of their position. It is important that employees have clear roles so they know their responsibilities. Job descriptions help to clarify functional roles. People often have multiple roles within the same position. For example, a professor may have the roles of teacher, researcher, writer, consultant, advisor, and committee member. Job roles vary greatly but group roles have just three classifications.

group roles
Task, maintenance, and self-interest.

Classifying Group Roles. The three primary **group roles** *are task, maintenance, and self-interest*. In Chapter 12, you learned that when managers interact with employees, they can use task behavior or maintenance behavior;[20] in addition, both behaviors or neither can be used to develop the four leadership styles. These same two dimensions are performed by group members as they interact.

Group task roles are played when members do and say things that directly aid in the accomplishment of the group's objectives. Terms used to describe task roles include structuring, job-centered, production, task-oriented, and directive.

Group maintenance roles are played when members do and say things to develop and sustain the group process. Terms used to describe maintenance roles include consideration, employee-centered, relationship-oriented, and supportive.

Self-interest roles are played when members do and say things that help the individual while hurting the group. When group members put their own needs before those of the group, its performance suffers. For example, if a member supports an alternative solution rather than the best solution because he or she is only concerned about getting his or her own way, a self-interest is being met.

As a team member, watch for self-interest roles and hidden agendas as you learn to distinguish between a self-interest that benefits both the individual and the organization (a win-win situation) and one that benefits the individual and hurts the organization (a win-lose situation) as you strive to achieve objectives. It has been said that group performance can increase dramatically if its members are not concerned about who gets credit for the idea.

Work Application

4. Recall a present or past job. Identify group/team members, including yourself, and state the primary role they played in the group.

How Roles Affect Group Performance. To be effective, a group must have members who play task roles and maintenance roles, while minimizing self-interest roles. Groups that only have task performers may suffer performance problems because they do not deal with conflict effectively, and because the job will be boring if there is no maintenance. Its group process will hurt performance. On the other hand, groups who have a great time but do not have members playing task roles will not get the job done. Any group whose members are playing self-interest roles will not produce to its fullest potential.

Leadership Implications. When in a group, the leader should be aware of the roles its members play. If the members are not playing the task and/or maintenance roles required at a given time, the leader should play the role. If the group has a leader who does not provide the proper roles when the members do not, any group member can provide the necessary leadership. The leader should also make the group aware of the need to play these roles and the need to minimize self-interest roles. In the next major section, you will learn about group development and how the leader should use task and maintenance roles to help the group develop. Team members at MMC and many other organizations get training to help them to understand group roles.

APPLYING THE CONCEPT

AC 13–2 Roles

Identify each statement by the role it fulfills:

a. task b. maintenance c. self-Interest

____ 6. "Wait. We can't make the decision because we haven't heard Rodney's idea yet."

____ 7. "I don't understand. Could you explain why we are doing this again?"

____ 8. "We tried that before you came to work here; it did not work. My idea is much better."

____ 9. "What does this have to do with the problem we are working on? We are getting sidetracked."

____ 10. "I like Ted's idea better than mine. Let's go with his idea instead of mine."

Group Norms

5. Explain the differences between rules and norms.

Command groups generally have policies, procedures, and rules to help provide the necessary guidelines for behavior, while task groups do not. However, standing plans cannot be complete enough to cover all situations. All groups tend to form their own unwritten norms about how things are done. **Norms** *are the*

norms
The group's shared expectations of its members' behavior.

group's shared expectations of its members' behavior. Norms determine what should, ought, or must be done in order for the group to maintain consistent and desirable behavior.

How Norms Develop. Norms are developed spontaneously as the members interact through the group's routine. Each group member has cultural values and past experience. The group's beliefs, attitudes, and knowledge influence the type of norms developed. For example, the group decides, without ever actually talking about it and agreeing this would be a rule, what is an acceptable level of work. If the group members develop a shared expectation that this level is desirable, members will produce it. The use of certain words or jokes, like swearing and ethnic jokes, are considered acceptable or not. If a member swears or tells an ethnic joke, and members look at the person like he or she is strange or make comments against it, members will tend not to use these words or jokes. On the other hand, if everyone else jumps in with swearing or jokes, members will use these behaviors. Norms can change over time to meet the needs of the group. Diversity training tends to discourage ethnic jokes.

How Groups Enforce Norms. If a group member does not follow the norm, the other members try to enforce compliance. The common ways groups enforce norms include ridicule, ostracism, sabotage, and physical abuse. For example, if a member, Sal, produces more than the accepted level of performance, other members may kid or ridicule him. If Sal continues to break the norm, members could use physical abuse or ostracize him to enforce compliance with the norm. Members could also damage his work or take his tools or supplies to slow down his production.

Work Application

5. Recall a present or past job. Identify at least two group/team norms. Explain how you know they are norms and how the group enforces these norms.

Leadership Implications. Group norms can be positive, helping the group meet its objectives, or they can be negative, hindering the group from meeting its objectives. For example, if the company's production standard is 110 units per day, a group norm of 100 is a negative norm. However, if the standard were 90, it would be a positive norm. Leaders should be aware of their group's norms. They should work toward maintaining and developing positive norms, while trying to eliminate negative norms. Leaders should confront groups with negative norms and try to work out agreeable solutions to make them positive.

6. Describe cohesiveness and why it is important to teams.

Group Cohesiveness

group cohesiveness
The extent to which members stick together.

The extent to which a group will abide by and enforce its norms depends on its degree of cohesiveness. **Group cohesiveness** *is the extent to which members stick together*. The more cohesive the group, the more it sticks together as a team. The more desirable group membership is, the more willing the members are to behave according to the group's norms. For example, in a highly cohesive group all members would produce about the same amount of work. However, in a moderate or low cohesive group, members could produce at different levels without the norm being enforced. Also, if some group members take drugs, and the group develops a norm of taking drugs together, cohesive members will sometimes behave in ways they really don't agree with to be accepted by the group.

Factors Influencing Cohesiveness. Six factors influence cohesiveness:

1. *Objectives*. The stronger the agreement and commitment made to the achievement of the group's objectives, the higher the cohesiveness of the group.
2. *Size*. Generally, the smaller the group, the higher the cohesiveness. The larger the group, the more difficulty there is in gaining consensus on objectives and norms. Three to nine members seems to be a good group size for cohesiveness.
3. *Homogeneity*. Generally, the more similar the group members are, the higher the cohesiveness; but diverse groups usually make better decisions. People tend to be attracted to people who are similar to themselves.
4. *Participation*. Generally, the more equal the level of participation among group members, the higher the group's cohesiveness. Groups dominated by one or a few members tend to be less cohesive.
5. *Competition*. The focus of the competition affects cohesiveness. If the group focuses on internal competition, its members will try to outdo each other, and low cohesiveness results. If the group focuses on external competition, its members tend to pull together as a team to beat its rivals.
6. *Success*. The more successful a group is at achieving its objectives, the more cohesive it tends to become. Success tends to breed cohesiveness, which in turn breeds more success. People want to be on a winning team. Have you ever noticed that losing teams tend to argue more than winning teams? Members complain and blame each other for failing.

How Cohesiveness Affects Group Performance. Many research studies have compared cohesive and noncohesive groups and concluded that cohesive groups tend to have a higher level of success at achieving their objectives with greater satisfaction. Cohesive group members tend to miss work less often, are more trusting and cooperative, and have less tension and hostility. S. E. Seashore conducted one of the most highly recognized studies on this subject several years ago. The results of the study, which are basically substantiated by a recent study by Robert Keller,[21] reveal that cohesiveness is associated with performance in the following ways:

- Groups with the highest level of productivity were highly cohesive and accepted management's level of productivity.
- Groups with the lowest levels of productivity were also highly cohesive, but rejected management's level of productivity; they set and enforced their own level below that of management. This can happen in organizations with unions that have the "us against them" attitude.
- Groups with intermediate levels of productivity were low cohesive groups, irrespective of their acceptance of management's level of productivity. The widest variance of individual group members' performance was among the groups with the lower cohesiveness. They tended to be more tolerant of nonconformity with group norms.

Leadership Implications. As a leader, you should strive to develop cohesive groups that accept a high level of productivity. The use of participation helps the group develop cohesiveness while it builds agreement and commitment toward its objectives.[22] The use of coaching helps to encourage and develop cohesiveness.[23] While some intragroup competition may be helpful, leaders should focus primarily on intergroup competition.[24] It helps to develop a cohesive winning team, which in turn motivates the group to higher levels of success. However, recall the many advantages of managing a diverse group, and meet the challenge of developing a cohesive diversified group.

Work Application

6. Recall a present or past job. Identify the group/team's level of cohesiveness as high, medium, or low. Be sure to explain the level.

Status within the Group

As group members interact, they develop respect for one another on numerous dimensions. The more respect, prestige, influence, and power a group member has, the higher his or her status within the group. **Status** *is the perceived ranking of one member relative to other members in the group.*

status
The perceived ranking of one member relative to other members in the group.

The Development of Status. Status is based on several factors, including member's performance, job title, wage or salary, seniority, knowledge or expertise, interpersonal skills, appearance, education, race, age, sex, and so on. Group status depends on the group's objectives, norms, and cohesiveness. Members who conform to the group's norms tend to have higher status than members who do not. A group is more willing to listen to and overlook a high-status member who breaks the norms. High-status members also have more influence on the development of the group's norms and the decisions made by the group. Lower-level members' ideas are often ignored, and they tend to copy high-status members' behavior and agree with their suggestions to be accepted.

Work Application

7. Recall a present or past job. List each member, including yourself, and identify each person's level of status within the group as high, medium, or low. Explain why each member has the level of status you assigned.

How Status Affects Group Performance. The high-status members have a major impact on the group's performance. In a command group, the boss is usually the member with the highest status. The leader's ability to manage affects the group performance. In addition to the leader, high-status members of command groups also affect performance. If high-status members support positive norms and high productivity, chances are the group will too.

Another important factor influencing group performance is status congruence. *Status congruence* is the acceptance and satisfaction members receive from their group status. Members who are not satisfied with their status may not be active participants of the group. They may physically or mentally escape from the group and not perform to their full potential. Or they may cause group conflict as they fight for a higher status level. Leadership struggles can go on for a long period and/or may never be resolved. The group member(s) who is dissatisfied with status may lower performance level for the group.

APPLYING THE CONCEPT

AC 13–3 Group Process

Identify each statement by a dimension of the group process:

a. roles c. cohesiveness e. decision-making
b. norms d. status f. conflict resolution

____ 11. "Although we do have occasional differences of opinion, we really get along well and enjoy working together."

____ 12. "When you need advice on how to do things, go see Shirley; she knows the ropes around here better than anyone."

____ 13. "I'd have to say that Carlos is the peacemaker around here. Every time there is a disagreement, he tries to get the members to work out the problem."

____ 14. "Kenady, you're late for the meeting. Everyone else was on time, so we started without you."

____ 15. "What does this have to do with solving the problem? We are getting sidetracked."

Leadership Implications. To be effective, the leader needs to have high status within the command group. The leader should maintain good human relations with the group, particularly with the high-status informal leader(s), to be sure they endorse positive norms and objectives. In addition, the leader should be aware of conflicts that may be the result of lack of status congruence. Ideally, status should be about equal within the group.

Decision-Making and Conflict Resolution

The decisions made by groups and teams have a direct effect on performance. With groups, decision-making authority is held by the manager. However, with teams, decision-making authority is held by the members. Creative problem-solving and decision-making have already been covered in Chapter 4. You may want to review the parts that relate to groups.

A conflict exists when group members are in disagreement. Conflict is common in groups and teams, and unresoloved conflicts can have a negative effect on performance. In the next chapter you will develop your skills at resolving conflict.

The managers, team leaders, and team members at MMC were trained to develop their group process skills. MMC leaders try to provide clear roles for all members, develop positive norms, build highly cohesive teams, have relatively equal status within the group, make participative decisions with everyone's input, and resolve conflicts. If you understand and develop group process skills, you will be a more effective group/team member and leader. Figure 13–5 summarizes the six dimensions of group process/dynamics.

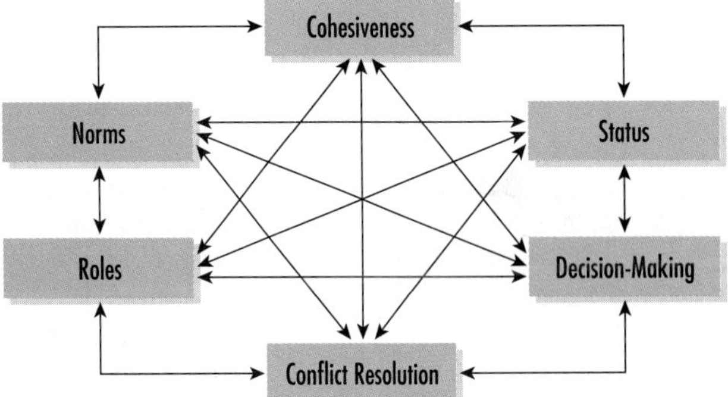

The arrows indicate the effect (or systems interrelationship) each dimension has on the others.

Figure 13–5
Group Process Dimensions

GROUP DEVELOPMENT STAGES AND LEADERSHIP STYLES

7. List the four major stages of group development and state the level of commitment and competence and the appropriate leadership style.

All groups have unique organizational context, group structure, and group processes that change over a period of time. However, it is generally agreed that all groups go through the same stages as they grow from a collection of individuals to a smoothly operating and effective group or team.[25] *The* **stages of group development** *are orientation, dissatisfaction, resolution, production, and termination.*[26]

stages of group development
Orientation, dissatisfaction, resolution, production, and termination.

Situational leadership can be applied to the stages of group development.[27] In other words, the appropriate leadership style changes with the level of group development. In this section, you will study the five stages of group development and the appropriate leadership style for each stage.

Stage 1. Orientation

The orientation stage, also known as the *forming* stage, is characterized by low development level (D1)—high commitment and low competence. When people first form a group, they tend to come to the group with a moderate to high commitment to the group. However, because they have not worked together, they do not have the team competence to do the job.

During orientation, members have *group structure issues* over the leadership and objectives of the group. The size of the group and its composition are checked out. With regard to type of group, command groups are rarely started with all new members. This stage is more characteristic of task groups that have clear new beginnings. *Group process issues* include anxiety over how members will fit in (status), what will be required of them (roles and norms), what the group will be like (cohesiveness), how decisions will be made, and how members will get along (conflict). These group structure and group process issues must be resolved to progress to the next stage of group development.

Leadership Style. During the orientation stage, the appropriate leadership style is autocratic (high task/low maintenance). When a group first comes together, the leader needs to spend time helping the group clarify its objectives, providing clear expectations of members. The leader should also allow some time for group members to start to get to know one another.

Stage 2. Dissatisfaction

The dissatisfaction stage, also known as the *storming* stage, is characterized by moderate development level (D2)—lower commitment and some competence. As members work together for some time, they tend to become dissatisfied with the group. Members start to question: Why am I a member? Is the group going to accomplish anything? Why don't other group members do what is expected? and so forth. Often the task is more complex and difficult than anticipated; members become frustrated and have feelings of incompetence. However, the group does develop some competence to perform the task.

During the dissatisfaction stage, the group needs to work on resolving its group structure and process issues. What is expected should become clearer; norms, status, and cohesiveness develop, decisions need to be made, and conflicts arise. These group structure and process issues must be resolved before the group can progress to the next stage of development. Groups can get stuck in this stage of development and never progress to being satisfied with the group and learning to perform as a team.

Leadership Style. During the dissatisfaction stage, the appropriate leadership style is consultative (high task/high maintenance). When satisfaction drops, the leader needs to focus on playing the maintenance role to encourage members to continue to work toward the objectives. The leader should help the members meet their needs as they develop the appropriate group structure and process. At the same time, the leader needs to continue to provide the task behavior necessary to help the group develop its level of competence.

Stage 3. Resolution

The resolution stage, also called the *norming* stage, is characterized by high development level (D3)—variable commitment and high competence. With time, members often resolve the differences between initial expectations and realities in relation to the objectives, tasks, skills, and so forth. As members develop competence, they often become more satisfied with the group.

Relationships develop that satisfy group members' affiliation needs. Members learn to work together as they develop a group structure and process with acceptable leadership, norms, status, cohesiveness, and decision-making. During periods of conflict or change, the group needs to resolve these issues.

Commitment can vary from time to time as the group interacts. If the group does not deal effectively with group process issues, the group may regress to stage 2 or plateau, fluctuating in commitment and competence. If the group is successful at developing a positive group structure and process, it will develop to the next stage.

Leadership Style. During the resolution stage, the appropriate leadership style is participative (low task/high maintenance). Once group members know what to do and how to do it, there is little need to provide task behavior. The group needs the leader to play a maintenance role.

When commitment varies, it is usually due to some problem in the group's process, such as a conflict. The leader needs to focus on maintenance behavior to get the group through the issue(s) it faces. If the leader continues to provide task directives that are not needed, the group can become dissatisfied and regress or plateau at this level.

Stage 4. Production

The production stage, also called the *performing* stage, is characterized by outstanding development level (D4)—high commitment and high competence. At this stage commitment and competence do not fluctuate much. The group works as a team with high levels of satisfaction. The group maintains a positive group structure and process. The fact that members are very productive helps lead to positive feelings. The group structure and process may change with time, but the issues are resolved quickly and easily; members are open with each other.

Leadership Style. During the production stage, the appropriate style is empowerment (low task/low maintenance). Groups that develop to this stage have members who play the appropriate task and maintenance roles; the leader does not need to play either role, unless there is a problem, because the group has effective shared leadership.

Stage 5. Termination

The termination stage, also called the *adjuring* stage, is not reached in command groups unless there is some drastic reorganization. However, task groups do terminate. During this stage, members experience feelings about leaving the group. In groups that have progressed through all four stages of group development, the members usually feel sad that the group is ending. However, for groups that did not progress through the stages of development, a feeling of relief is often experienced. The group may talk about its termination over a period of time or only at the last meeting. It tends to vary with the meaningfulness of the relationship, and whether the members will be seeing each other at all after the group terminates.

MMC has a variety of types of groups. Different groups make it to different levels of development. However, to help ensure that groups develop, MMC em-

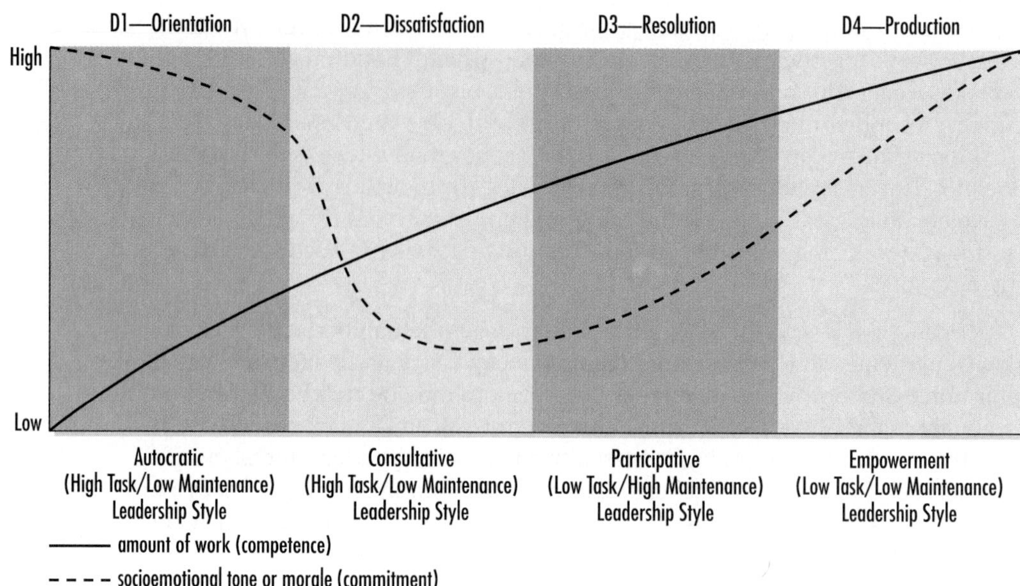

Figure 13–6
Group Development Stages and Leadership

Work Application

8. Recall a present or past job. Identify the group's stage of development and the leader's situational management style. Does the leader use the appropriate style? Explain what can be done to improve the group's structure and/or process.

ployees are trained to develop group process skills. Teams tend to develop to higher levels than groups. As a leader or member of a group/team be aware of the group's development stage and use the appropriate leadership style to help it develop to the productivity level.

Changes in Group Development and Leadership Style. The two key variables identified through each stage of group development are work on the task (competence) and the socioemotional tone or morale (commitment). The two variables do not progress in the same manner. Competence tends to continue to increase through each of the first four stages, while commitment tends to start high in stage 1, drops in stage 2, then rises through stages 3 and 4. This is illustrated in Figure 13–6, along with the appropriate leadership style for each stage of development at the bottom. In Skill-Building Exercise 13–1, Situational Management of Teams, you will develop your ability to identify group development stages and the appropriate leadership style for the group/team.

8. Explain the difference between a group manager and a team leader.

DEVELOPING GROUPS INTO TEAMS

As shown in Figure 13–1, groups and teams are different. The trend is toward the empowerment of teams because teams are more produtive than groups.[28] To turn groups into teams, first consider the size of the department/group. If you have 20 or more members, break the group into two or three teams. In this section you will learn about training, planning, organizing and staffing, leading, and controlling teams and the difference between a group manager and a team leader.

Training

If you expect a group to function as a team, members need training in group process skills so they can make decisions and handle conflict. A team-building program, as discussed in Chapter 8, is also very helpful in turning groups into teams.[29] At MMC, management did not just place people into teams and expect them to be successful; they trained them to be successful.

The management functions are handled differently in groups and teams. In this section, you will learn how the job of the manager is changing.

Planning

Important parts of planning are setting objectives and decision-making. Both groups and teams need clear objectives, well-developed plans to achieve the objectives, and effective decision-making to perform at high levels. A major difference between groups and teams is who develops the objectives and plans and who makes the decisions. To go from a group to a team, the manager must allow the members, along with the manager, to set objectives, develop plans, and make the decisions. The manager's role changes to focusing on involving members and making sure they know the objectives and that they accept them and are committed to achieving them.

Organizing and Staffing

The important parts of organizing and staffing are assigning members to jobs and authority and selecting, evaluating, and rewarding members. In groups, members have clearer, distinct jobs assigned by the manager and perform one independent part of the process; in teams, jobs are more interchangeable and are assigned by the members as they perform dependent parts of the entire process.

In both groups and teams, it is important that members have a clear understanding of their level of authority (inform, recommend, report, full) for the situation. In groups, authority is held by the manager; in teams, the members have higher levels of authority. At MMC the teams have full authority to spend up to $500. To spend more money, the team must get the approval of the steering committee.

In groups, the manager makes the selection decision on who is hired; in teams, the members make the selection. In groups, the manager evaluates individual performance; in teams, the members evaluate each others' individual and group performance. Through the human resources department, reward systems are commonly determined throughout the organization. Where teams are valued, group rewards are given.

Leading

In groups, there is one clear leader; in teams, leadership is shared. However, most teams do identify a specific person as the leader. But, the leader shares this responsibility. The leader does not focus on telling employees what to do and assigning individuals to do it. Effective team leaders are highly skilled in group process and team-building. The leader focuses on developing group structure and process. Much of the leader's time is spent in communications to ensure that roles are clear, norms are positive, the group is cohesive, status is not a problem, decisions are made with the input and consensus of the members, and conflicts are resolved satisfactorily. Effective leaders work to bring the team to

Work Application

9. Recall a present or past boss. Identify the boss as a group manager or a team leader. Explain why you classified the boss as you did.

the development production level; they change leadership styles with the level of group development.

Controlling

In groups, the manager is responsible for monitoring progress toward achievement of objectives and overseeing corrective action, when needed. Specific employees are responsible for making the good and/or performing the service, and others are responsible for checking the quality. In teams, the members are responsible for monitoring progress, taking corrective action, and performing quality control.

Group Manager versus Team Leader

team leaders
Team leaders empower members to take responsibility for performing the management functions while focusing on developing effective group structure, group process, and group development.

In summary, the roles of the group manager and team leader are different. The group manager takes responsibility for performing the four functions of management. **Team leaders** *empower members to take responsibility for performing the management functions while focusing on developing effective group structure, group process, and group development.* At MMC, in general, the role of managers has changed to team leader. In fact, in some teams managers are not even the official leader. Because the trend is toward team leadership, it is critically important that you understand group structure, process, and development, and are able to develop team skills.

MEETING LEADERSHIP SKILLS

With a group structure, managers spend a great deal of time in management meetings. There are generally few meetings involving employees. However, most teams include employees, and it is common for teams to have daily meetings. With the trend toward teams, meetings are taking up an increasing amount of time. Therefore, the need for meeting management skills is stronger than ever.[30] The success of meetings depends on the leader's skill at managing group process.[31] Common complaints about meetings are that there are too many of them, they are too long, and they are unproductive. Meeting leadership skills can lead to more productive meetings. Ford spent $500,000 to send 280 employees to a three-day meeting with three one-day meetings to follow as an investment to improve performance.[32] In this section, you will learn how to plan and conduct a meeting and how to handle problem group members.

Planning Meetings

The leaders' and members' preparation for the meeting have a direct effect on the meeting. Unprepared leaders tend to conduct unproductive meetings. There are at least five areas where planning is needed: objectives, selecting participants and making assignments, the agenda, the time and place for the meeting, and leadership. A written copy of the plan should be sent to members prior to the meeting (see Figure 13–7).

Objectives. Probably the single greatest mistake made by those who call meetings is that they often have no clear idea and purpose for the meeting.

Figure 13–7
Meeting Plans

Content

- **Time.** List date, place (if it changes), and time (both beginning and ending).
- **Objective.** State the objectives and/or purpose of the meeting. The objectives can be listed with agenda items, as shown below, rather than as a separate section. But be sure objectives are specific.
- **Participation and Assignments.** If all members have the same assignment, if any, list it. If different members have different assignments, list their names and assignments. Assignments may be listed as agenda items as shown below for Ted and Karen.
- **Agenda.** List each item to be covered in priority order with its approximate time limit. Accepting the minutes of the last meeting may be an agenda item.

Example

GOLD TEAM MEETING

November 22, 199X, Gold Room, 9:00 to 10:00 A.M.

Participation and Assignments

All members will attend and should have read the six computer brochures enclosed before the meeting. Be ready to discuss your preferences.

Agenda

1. Discussion and selection of two PCs to be presented to the team at a later date by PC representatives—45 minutes. (Note that this is the major objective; the actual selection takes place later.)
2. Ted will give the Venus project report—5 minutes.
3. Karen will present an idea for changing the product process slightly without discussion—5 minutes. Discussion will take place at the next meeting after you have given the idea some thought.

Before calling a meeting, you should clearly define its purpose and set objectives to be accomplished during the meeting. The only exception may be at regularly scheduled information-dissemination or brainstorming meetings.

Participants and Assignments. Before calling the meeting, you should decide who should attend the meeting. When too many members attend a meeting, the speed of completing the work will often slow down. Does the full group/team need to attend? Should some nongroup specialist be invited to provide input? On controversial issues, the leader may find it wiser to talk with the key members before the meeting to discuss the issue. Participants should know in advance what is expected of them at the meeting. If any preparation is expected (read material, do some research, make a report, and so forth), they should have adequate advance notice.

Agenda. Before calling the meeting, you should identify the activities that will take place in order to achieve the objective. The agenda tells the members what is expected and how the meeting will progress. Having a set time limit for each agenda item helps keep the group on target; needless discussion and getting off the subject is common at meetings. When this happens, someone needs to speak up to get back on the topic. However, you need to be flexible and allow more time when really needed. Members may also submit agenda items to include. If you get agenda items that require action, they should have objectives.

Place agenda items in order of priority. Then, if the group does not have time to cover every item, the least important items will carry forward. The author has attended too many meetings where the leader puts all the so-called quick items first. The group gets bogged down and either rushes through the important items or puts them off until later.

Date, Place, and Time. To determine which day(s) and time(s) of the week are best for meetings, get members' input. Members tend to be more alert early in the day. When members are close, it is better to have more frequent shorter meetings focusing on one or just a few items. However, when members have to travel, fewer longer meetings are needed. Be sure to select an adequate place for the meeting and plan for the physical comfort of the group. Be sure seating provides eye contact for small discussion groups, and plan enough time so that the members do not have to rush. If reservations are needed for the meeting place, make them far enough in advance to get a proper meeting room.

With advances in technology, telephone conferences/meetings are becoming quite common. Videoconferences are also gaining popularity. These techniques save travel costs and time, and they may result in better and quicker decisions. Some of the companies using videoconferencing include Aetna, Arco, Boeing, Ford, IBM, TRW, and Xerox. The personal computer is said to be the most useful tool for running meetings since Robert's Rules of Order. The personal computer can be turned into a large-screen "intelligent chalkboard" that can dramatically change meeting results. Minutes (notes on what took place during a meeting) can be taken on the personal computer and a hard copy can be distributed at the end of the meeting.

Leadership. The leader should determine the appropriate leadership style for the meeting. Each agenda item may need to be handled differently. For example, some items may simply call for disseminating information, while others require a discussion, vote, or a consensus; still other items require a simple quick report from a member, and so forth. An effective way to develop group members' ability is to rotate the role of the group moderator/leader for each meeting.

9. Discuss the three parts of meetings.

Conducting Meetings

The First Meeting. At the first meeting, the group is in the orientation stage. The leader should use the high-task role. However, the members should be given the opportunity to spend some time getting to know one another. Introductions set the stage for subsequent interactions. A simple technique is to start with introductions, then move on to the group's purpose, objectives, and members' job roles. Some time during or following this procedure, have a break that enables members to interact informally. If members find that their social needs will not be met, dissatisfaction may occur quickly.

The Three Parts of Meetings. Meetings should have the following three parts:

1. *Identify objectives*. Begin the meeting on time; waiting for late members penalizes the members who are on time and develops a norm for coming late. Begin by reviewing progress to date, the group's objectives, and the purpose/objective for the specific meeting. If minutes are recorded, they are usually approved at the beginning of the next meeting. For most meetings, it is recommended that a secretary be appointed to take minutes.
2. *Cover agenda items*. Be sure to cover agenda items in priority order. Try to keep to the approximate times, but be flexible. If the discussion is constructive and members need more time, give it to them; however, if the discussion is more of a destructive argument, move ahead.
3. *Summarize and review assignments*. End the meeting on time. The leader should summarize what took place during the meeting. Were the meeting's objectives achieved? Review all of the assignments given during the meeting. Get a commitment to the task that each member should perform for the next or a specific future meeting. The secretary and/or leader should record all assignments. If there is no accountability and follow-up on assignments, members may not complete them.

Leadership. The team leader needs to focus on group structure, process, and development. As stated, the leadership style needed changes with the group's level of development. The leader must be sure to provide the appropriate task and/or maintenance behavior when it is needed.

Handling Problem Members

As members work together, personality types tend to emerge. Certain personality types can cause the group to be less efficient than possible. Some of the problem members you may have in your group are the following: silent, talker, wanderer, bored, and the arguer.

Silent. To be fully effective, all group members should participate. If members are silent, the group does not get the benefits of their input.

It is the leader's responsibility to encourage silent members to participate without being obvious or overdoing it. One technique the leader can use is the rotation method, in which all members take turns giving their input. This method is generally less threatening than directly calling on them. However, the rotation method is not appropriate all the time. To build up the silent members' confidence, call on them with questions they can easily answer. When you believe they have convictions, ask them to express them. Watch their nonverbal communication as indicators of when to call on them. If you are a silent type, try to participate more often. Know when to stand up for your views and be assertive.

Talker. Talkers have something to say about everything. They like to dominate the discussion. However, if they do dominate, the other members do not get to participate. The talker can cause intragroup problems such as low cohesiveness and conflicts.

It is the leader's responsibility to slow talkers down, not to shut them up. Do not let them dominate the group. The rotation technique is also effective with talkers because they have to wait their turn. When not using a rotation method, gently interrupt the talker and present your own ideas or call on other specific members to present their ideas. Prefacing questions with statements such as, "Let's give those who have not answered yet a chance" can also slow the talker down. With a problem talker, the leader may need to talk to the person outside of the meeting to make the talker understand the behavior, and why it needs to change.

If you tend to be a talker, try to slow down. Give others a chance to talk and do things for themselves. Good leaders develop others' ability in these areas.

Wanderer. Wanderers distract the group from the agenda items, they tend to change the subject, and often like to complain.

The leader is responsible for keeping the group on track. If the wanderer wants to socialize, cut it off. Be kind, thank the member for the contribution, then throw a question out to the group to get it back on track. However, if the wanderer has a legitimate and solvable complaint, allow the group to discuss it. Group structure issues should be addressed and resolved. However, if it is not resolvable, get the group back on track. Griping without resolving anything tends to reduce morale and commitment to task accomplishment. If the wanderer complains about unresolvable issues, make statements such as, "We may be underpaid, but we have no control over our pay. Complaining will not get us a raise; let's get back to the issue at hand."

If you tend to be a wanderer, try to be aware of your behavior and stay on the subject at hand.

Bored. Your group may have one or more members who are not interested in the job. The bored person may be preoccupied with other issues and not pay attention or participate in the group meeting. The bored member may also feel superior and wonder why the group is spending so much time on the obvious.

The leader is responsible for keeping members motivated. Assign the bored member a task such as recording ideas on the board and recording the minutes. Call on bored members; bring them into the group. If you allow them to sit back, things may get worse and others may decide not to participate either.

If you tend to be bored, try to find ways to help motivate yourself. Work at becoming more patient and in control of behavior that can have negative effects on other members.[33]

Arguer. Like the talker, the arguer likes to be the center of attention. This behavior can occur when you use the devil's advocate approach, which is helpful in developing and selecting alternative courses of action. However, arguers enjoy arguing for the sake of arguing, rather than helping the group. They turn things into a win-lose situation, and they cannot stand losing.

The leader should resolve conflict, but not in an argumenta-

APPLYING THE CONCEPT

AC 13–4 Group Problem People

Identify the problem type as:

a. silent b. talker c. wanderer d. bored e. arguer

____ **16.** Charlie is always first or second to give his ideas. He is always elaborating on ideas. Because Charlie is so quick to respond, others sometimes make comments to him about it.

____ **17.** One of the usual active group members is sitting back quietly today for the first time. The other members are doing all the discussing and volunteering for assignments.

____ **18.** As the group is discussing a problem, Billy asks the group if they heard about the company owner and the mail room clerk.

____ **19.** Eunice is usually reluctant to give her ideas. When asked to explain her position, She often changes her answers to agree with others in the group.

____ **20.** Dwayne enjoys challenging members' ideas. He likes getting his own way. When a group member does not agree with Dwayne, he makes wise comments about the member's prior mistakes.

tive way. Do not get into an argument with arguers; that is exactly what they want to happen. If an argument starts, bring others into the discussion. If it is personal, cut it off. Personal attacks only hurt the group. Keep the discussion moving on target. As with the problem talker, the leader may need to speak to the argurer outside of the meeting to change the behavior.

If you tend to be an arguer, strive to convey your views in an assertive debate format, not as an aggressive argument. Listen to others' views and be willing to change if they have better ideas.

Working with Group Members. Whenever you work in a group, do not embarrass, intimidate, or argue with any members, no matter how much they provoke you. If you do, the result will make martyrs of them and a bully of you to the group. If you have serious problem members who do not respond to the preceding techniques, confront them individually outside of the group. Get them to agree to work in a cooperative way.

Work Application

10. Recall a meeting you attended. Did you receive an agenda prior to the meeting? How well did the leader conduct the meeting? Give ideas on how the meeting could have been improved. Did the group have any problem members? How well did the leader handle them?

CURRENT MANAGEMENT ISSUES

Global. To a large extent, the global trend toward teamwork has come from Japan. Japanese companies have been very productive largely because of their culture of group-oriented teamwork. Although culture has an effect on group work versus individualism, the Japanese have been successful at implementing teams in other countries. Japan's Mazda built a plant in Flat Rock, Michigan, based on work teams. However, managers were very careful at selecting and developing the company's American employees. Managers realize that not everyone is suited for teamwork. Job applicants were assessed in interpersonal skills, motivation, aptitude for learning and relearning, and to determine their interest in teamwork and participation. Employees hired were given a three-week training program that focused on helping them understand how to function better as individuals, and more importantly, as team members. After team training came ten weeks of technical training before they were put to work as members of a Mazda team. Mazda invested $40 million, or $13,000 per employee.

Japanese companies have been very productive using teamwork. They have also been successful at implementing teams in other countries.

Diversity. As covered in detail in Chapter 3, *diversity* is critical for success in teams. In general, diverse work teams outperform homogeneous teams.[34] Being a member of a team helps to get individual commitment to achieving organizational objectives.[35]

Ethics. Being open and honest is *ethical* behavior. The level of trust, which leads to ethical behavior, is higher in teams than in groups. When teams are ethical, the organization tends to be more *socially responsible*.

TQM, Participative Management, and Teams. The fourth principle of TQM is the use of *teams* to focus on system and process and to make continuous improvements to ensure customer value. In TQM, teams are empowered to use *participative management* to perform the management functions.[36] Quality circles were a starting point in participation. *Quality circles* are small groups that meet to make improvements in functional areas. Quality circles have lost popularity because they were task forces or committees. Today, continuous improvement is the teams' ongoing responsibility. Ford began TQM in the early 1980s with quality problem-solving teams (quality circles). In 1995 the Ford Milan, Michigan, plant switched to team manufacturing.[37]

Productivity. *Re-engineering* is a major reorganization that takes the entire firm from groups to teams to increase *productivity*. Re-engineering, with proper training in team skills, has been very successful in many organizations. However, downsizing to increase productivity does not focus on converting groups into teams. The usual approach is to reduce the number of group members and to require the rest of the members to maintain the prior level of group production. Downsizing does not work. Massive layoffs tend to be short-term fixes followed by lackluster results, low morale, overwork, and even sabotage by disgruntled survivors.[38]

Small Business. *Small businesses* are at somewhat of an advantage because they have smaller numbers of employees. It is easier to have teamwork with smaller numbers. However, many small businesses do not have the resources to train their employees and develop their team skills. In addition, many entrepreneurs are more autocratic than participative. In other words, many entrepreneurs are group managers rather than good team leaders.

CHAPTER SUMMARY AND GLOSSARY

This chapter summary is organized to answer the ten learning objectives for Chapter 13.

1. Describe the major differences between groups and teams.

The major differences are based on size, leadership, jobs, accountability and evaluation, rewards, and objectives. A group is two or more members with a clear leader who perform independent jobs with individual accountability, evaluation, and rewards. A team has a small number of members with shared leadership who perform interdependent jobs with both individual and group accountability, evaluation, and rewards.

2. State the group performance model.

Group performance is a function of organizational context, group structure, group process, and group development stage.

3. List and explain the three dimensions of group types.

The three group type dimensions are formal or informal, functional or cross-functional, and command or task. Formal groups are created as part of the organizational structure; informal groups are not. Functional group members come from one area, while cross-functional members come from different areas. Command groups include managers and their employees, while task groups include selected employees who work on a specific objective. A task force is temporary, while a standing committee is ongoing.

4. Define the three major roles played in groups.

Group task roles are played when members do and say things that directly aid in the accomplishment of the group's objectives. Group maintenance roles are played when members do and say things that develop and sustain the group process. Self-interest roles are played when members do and say things that help the individual while hurting the group.

5. Explain the differences between rules and norms.

Rules are formally established by management or by the group itself. Norms are the group's shared expectations of its members' behavior. Norms are not developed by management or agreed to by the groups; they develop as members interact.

6. Describe cohesiveness and why it is important to teams.

Group cohesiveness is the extent to which members stick together. Group cohesiveness is important because highly cohesive groups that accept management's level of productivity have a higher level of productivity than groups with low levels of cohesiveness.

7. List the four major stages of group development and state the level of commitment and competence and the appropriate leadership style.
Group development stages: (1) Orientation is characterized by low development level (D1)-high commitment and low competence and the appropriate leadership style is autocratic. (2) Dissatisfaction is characterized by moderate development level (D2)-lower commitment and some competence and the appropriate leadership style is consultative. (3) Resolution is characterized by high development level (D3)-variable commitment and high competence and the appropriate leadership style is participative. (4) Production is characterized by outstanding development level (D4)-high commitment and high competence and the appropriate leadership style is empowerment.

8. Explain the difference between a group manager and a team leader.
The group manager takes responsibility for performing the four functions of management. The team leader empowers the members to take responsibility for performing the management functions, while focusing on developing effective group structure, group process, and group development.

9. Discuss the three parts of meetings.
Meetings should begin with covering the objectives for the meeting. During the meeting, agenda items should be covered in priority order. The meeting should end with a summary of what took place and assignments to be completed for future meetings.

10. Define the following key terms (in order of appearance in the chapter):
Select one or more methods: (1) fill in the missing key terms from memory, (2) match the key terms from the end of the review with their definitions below, or (3) copy the key terms in order from the list at the beginning of the chapter.

A ______ is two or more members with a clear leader who perform independent jobs with individual accountability, evaluation, and rewards.

A ______ is a small number of members with shared leadership who perform interdependent jobs with both individual and group accountability, evaluation, and rewards.

In the __________, group performance is a function of organizational context, group structure, group process, and group development stage.

__________ include group type, size, composition, leadership, and objectives.

__________ include formal or informal, functional or cross-functional, and command or task.

______ are comprised of managers and their employees.

______ are comprised of employees selected to work on a specific objective.

______ is the mix of member skills and abilities.

______ refers to the patterns of interactions that emerge as members perform their jobs.

__________ include roles, norms, cohesiveness, status, decision-making, and conflict resolution.

______ include task, maintenance, and self-interest.

______ are the group's shared expectations of its members' behavior.

______ is the extent to which members stick together.

______ is the perceived ranking of one member relative to other members in the group.

__________ are orientation, dissatisfaction, resolution, production, and termination.

______ empower members to take responsibility for performing the management functions while focusing on developing effective group structure, group process, and group development.

KEY TERMS

command groups
group
group cohesiveness
group composition
group performance model
group process
group process dimensions
group roles
group structure dimensions
group types
norms
stages of group development
status
task groups
team
team leaders

REVIEW AND DISCUSSION QUESTIONS

1. Which are usually larger, groups or teams?
2. Which level of management has the most influence over organizational context?
3. Is there an ideal group size?
4. Why is diversity important to group composition?
5. Why are objectives important to groups?
6. How do groups enforce norms?
7. Which type of groups tends to terminate and which do not?
8. Does the level of commitment to the group continue to increase through all four stages of group development?
9. Are the four functions of management important to both groups and teams?
10. Why is it important to keep records of meeting assignments?
11. Describe the five types of problem members in meetings. How does each cause a problem to the group?

CASE

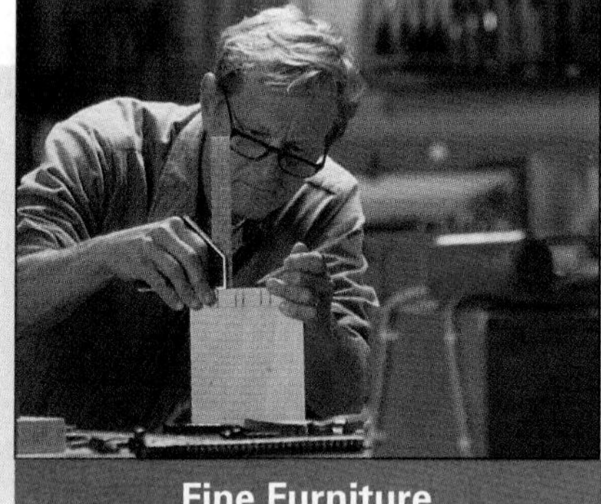

Saul Fine worked for the State of Vermont highway department. But, in his spare time he made wood furniture, mostly tables and chairs, which he sold to a local furniture store. Saul got to the point of having many more orders than he could fill working only nights and weekends. Plus, he was tired of working so many hours. With 20 years of service to the state, he retired at age 42 with a small pension and opened Fine Furniture. Even working full time, he could not keep up with the demand for his furniture. Over a few years, as his business grew, he moved out of his basement into a shop and hired more employees. Saul has three separate areas or departments making furniture. Each department has seven or eight employees and the crew leader. All three departments make one standard size set and each department makes a few other different products as well. The crew leaders are Joel, Samantha, and Carl.

Saul was happy with the size of his operation, so he did not want to grow any more. However, he was not satisfied with the rate of productivity. Saul had very few meetings with his crew leaders, and they were not informed of each other's productivity rates. Crew leaders worked alongside the employees. The only real management responsibilities they had were staffing and leadership. Saul did the planning, organizing, and controlling for all three crews. Saul set up independent jobs and evaluated and rewarded employees on an individual basis. However, everyone was paid about the same wages. Crew leaders trained the other employees and helped them if they had problems. The three crew leaders were very good furniture makers and, as Fine Furniture expanded, Saul appointed them crew leaders without giving them any management training. Saul made the following observations about each crew.

Samantha's crew has the highest rate of productivity. Members help each other and get along well; they usually go on breaks and to lunch together. Samantha and all crew members seem to do about the same amount of work.

Joel's crew has the middle rate of productivity. Members seem to be split. Joel and three employees get along well and produce at about the same high rate. The other four members seem to be individual-oriented. One is very fast, one produces at about the same rate as the group of three, and the other two are slow. They just seem to take it slow and easy and Joel and the others do not say anything to them about their productivity level.

Carl's crew has the lowest productivity rate. All but one of the members seems to work at a slow, easy pace. Carl and the one fast worker get along well, but the two of them do not get along well with the rest of the crew members who seem to want the other members to slow down the production rate to their level.

Saul called a meeting with Joel, Samantha, and Carl to discuss his observations and to discuss ways of increasing productivity throughout the company.

Select the best alternative to the following questions. Be sure you are able to explain your answers.

1. At Fine Furniture, the three crews are primarily

a. groups b. teams

2. Saul, Joel, Samatha, and Carl make up a ___ group/team.

a. command
b. task force
c. standing committee

3. Leadership has a ___ impact on crew productivity.

a. major b. minor

4. ___'s crew has the most negative norms.

a. Samantha b. Joel c. Carl

5. Which leader's crew is not highly cohesive?

a. Samantha b. Joel c. Carl

6. Cohesiveness has a ___ effect on productivity.

a. major b. moderate c. minor

7. Which crew member has the lowest status within his or her crew?

a. Samantha b. Joel c. Carl

8. Samantha's crew appears to be at the ___ stage of development and the appropriate leadership style is ___ (select two answers).

a. orientation c. resolution
b. dissatisfaction d. production

a. autocratic c. participative
b. consultative d. empowerment

9. Joel's crew appears to be at the ___ stage of development and the appropriate leadership style is ___ (select two answers).

a. orientation c. resolution
b. dissatisfaction d. production

a. autocratic c. participative
b. consultative d. empowerment

10. Carl's crew appears to be at the ___ stage of development and the appropriate leadership style is ___ (select two answers).

a. orientation c. resolution
b. dissatisfaction d. production

a. autocratic c. participative
b. consultative d. empowerment

11. Do you think that promoting employees to supervisory positions without management training has had any effect on the present situation? Explain.

12. What would you recommend doing to increase productivity in each of the three crews?

SKILL-BUILDING EXERCISE 13–1

Group Situational Management[39]

Preparing for Skill-Building Exercise 13–1

To determine your preferred group leadership style, complete Self-Assessment Exercise 13–1.

SELF-ASSESSMENT EXERCISE 13–1

Determining Your Preferred Group Leadership Style

In the following situations, select the response that represents what you would actually do as the group's leader. Ignore the D and S lines; they will be used in class as part of Skill-Building Exercise 13–1.

1. Your group works well together; members are cohesive with positive norms. They maintain a fairly consistent level of production that is above the organizational average, as long as you continue to provide maintenance behavior. You have a new assignment for them. To accomplish it you would: D___
   a. Explain what needs to be done and tell them how to do it. Oversee them while they perform the task. S___
   b. Tell the group how pleased you are with its past performance. Explain the new assignment, but let them decide how to accomplish it. Be available if they need help. S___
   c. Tell the group what needs to be done. Encourage them to give input on how to do the job. Oversee task performance. S___
   d. Explain to the group what needs to be done. S___
2. You have been promoted to a new supervisory position. The group appears to have little talent to do the job, but they do seem to care about the quality of the work they do. The last supervisor was terminated because of the department's low productivity level. To increase productivity you would: D___
   a. Let the group know you are aware of its low production level, but let them decide how to improve it. S___
   b. Spend most of your time overseeing group members as they perform their jobs. Train them as needed. S___
   c. Explain to the group that you would like to work together to improve productivity. Work together as a team. S___
   d. Tell the group how productivity can be improved. With their ideas, develop methods and make sure they are implemented. S___
3. Your department continues to be one of the top performers in the organization. The members work well as a team. In the past, you generally let them take care of the work on their own. You decide to: D___
   a. Go around encouraging group members on a regular basis. S___
   b. Define members' roles and spend more time overseeing performance. S___
   c. Continue things the way they are; leave them alone. S___
   d. Hold a meeting. Recommend ways to improve and get members' ideas as well. After agreeing on changes, oversee the group to make sure it implements the new ideas and does improve. S___
4. You have spent much of the past year training your employees. However, they do not need you to oversee production as much as you used to. Several group members no longer get along as well as they did in the past. You've played referee lately. You: D___
   a. Have a group meeting to discuss ways to increase performance. Let the group decide what changes to make. Be supportive. S___
   b. Continue things the way they are now. Supervise them closely and be the referee when needed. S___
   c. Let the group alone to work things out for themselves. S___
   d. Continue to supervise closely as needed, but spend more time playing maintenance roles; develop a team spirit. S___
5. Your department has been doing such a great job that it has increased in size. You are surprised at how fast the new members were integrated. The team continues to come up with ways to improve performance on its own. Due to the growth, your department will be moving to a new, larger location. You decide to: D___
   a. Design the new layout and present it to the group to see if the members can improve upon it. S___
   b. In essence become a group member and allow the group to design the new layout. S___
   c. Design the new layout and put a copy on the bulletin board so employees know where to report for work after the move. S___
   d. Hold a meeting to get employee ideas on the layout of the new location. After the meeting, think about their ideas and finalize the layout. S___
6. You are appointed to head a task group. Because of the death of a relative, you had to miss the first meeting. At the second meeting, the group seems to have developed

objectives and some ground rules. Members have volunteered for assignments that have to be accomplished. You: D___

a. Take over as a strong leader. Change some ground rules and assignments. S___

b. Review what has been done so far, and keep things as they are. However, you take charge and provide clear direction from now on. S___

c. Take over the leadership but allow the group to make the decisions. Be supportive and encourage them. S___

d. Seeing that the group is doing so well, leave and do not attend any more meetings. S___

7. Your group was working at, or just below, standard. However, there has been a conflict within the group. As a result, production is behind schedule. You: D___

a. Tell the group how to resolve the conflict. Then closely supervise to make sure it does what you say and production increases. S___

b. Let the group work it out. S___

c. Hold a meeting to work as a team to come up with a solution. Encourage the group members to work together. S___

d. Hold a meeting to present a way to resolve the conflict. Sell the members on its merits, include their input, and follow up. S___

8. The organization has allowed flextime. Two of your employees have asked if they could change work hours. You are concerned because all busy work hours need adequate coverage. The department is very cohesive with positive norms. You decide to: D___

a. Tell them things are going well; we'll keep things as they are now. S___

b. Hold a department meeting to get everyone's input, then reschedule their hours. S___

c. Hold a department meeting to get everyone's input; then reschedule their hours on a trial basis. Tell the group that if there is any drop in productivity, you will go back to the old schedule. S___

d. Tell them to hold a department meeting. If the department agrees to have at least three people on the job during the busy hours, they can make changes, giving you a copy of the new schedule. S___

9. You have arrived 10 minutes late for a department meeting. Your employees are discussing the latest assignment. This surprises you because, in the past, you had to provide clear direction and employees rarely would say anything. You: D___

a. Take control immediately and provide your usual direction. S___

b. Say nothing and just sit back. S___

c. Encourage the group to continue, but also provide direction. S___

d. Thank the group for starting without you, and encourage them to continue. Support their efforts. S___

10. Your department is consistently very productive. However, occasionally the members fool around and someone has an accident. There has never been a serious injury. You hear a noise and go to see what it was. From a distance you can see Sue sitting on the floor, laughing, with a ball made from company material in her hand. You: D___

a. Say and do nothing. After all, she's OK, and the department is very productive; you don't want to make waves. S___

b. Call the group together and ask for suggestions on how to keep accidents from recurring. Tell them you will be checking up on them to make sure the behavior does not continue. S___

c. Call the group together and discuss the situation. Encourage them to be more careful in the future. S___

d. Tell the group that's it; from now on you will be checking up on them regularly. Bring Sue to your office and discipline her. S___

11. You are at the first meeting of an ad hoc committee you are leading. Most of the members are second- and third-level managers from the marketing and financial areas; you are a supervisor from production. You decide to start by: D___

a. Working on developing relationships. Get everyone to feel as though they know each other before you talk about business. S___

b. Going over the group's purpose and the authority it has. Provide clear directives. S___

c. Asking the group to define its purpose. Because most of the members are higher-level managers, let them provide the leadership. S___

d. Start by providing both direction and encouragement. Give directives and thank people for their cooperation. S___

12. Your department has done a great job in the past. It is now getting a new computer, somewhat different from the old one. You have been trained to operate the computer, and you are expected to train your employees to operate it. To train them you: D___

a. Give the group instructions and work with them individually, providing direction and encouragement. S___

b. Get the group together to decide how they want to be instructed. Be very supportive of their efforts to learn. S___

c. Tell them it's a simple system. Give them a copy of the manual and have them study it on their own. S___

d. Give the group instructions. Then go around and supervise their work closely, giving additional instructions as needed. S___

Scoring. To determine your preferred group leadership style, circle the letter you selected as the alternative you chose in situations 1–12. The column headings indicate the style you selected.

	Autocratic (S1A)	Consultative (S2C)	Participative (S3P)	Empowerment (S4E)
1.	a	c	b	d
2.	b	d	c	a
3.	b	d	a	c
4.	b	d	a	c
5.	c	a	d	b
6.	a	b	c	d
7.	a	d	c	b
8.	a	c	b	d
9.	a	c	d	b
10.	d	b	c	a
11.	b	d	a	c
12.	d	a	b	c
Total	___	___	___	___

Add up the number of circled items per column. The total column should equal 12. The column with the highest number represents your preferred group leadership style. There is no one best style in all situations.

The more evenly distributed the numbers are between the four styles, the more flexible you are at leading groups. A total of 0 or 1 in any column may indicate a reluctance to use the style(s). You could have problems in situations calling for this style.

Is your preferred group leadership style the same as your preferred situational management style (Chapter 1) and situational communication style (Chapter 10)?

As discussed in the group development stages and leadership styles section of this chapter, first determine the level of development then use the appropriate leadership style. For a review and for use in the in-class part of this exercise, see Model 13–1.

Doing Skill-Building Exercise 13–1 in Class

Objectives
To help you understand the stages of group development and to use the appropriate group situational management style.

Preparation
You should understand the group development stages and have completed Self-Assesment Exercise 13–1.

Experience
You will discuss your selected management styles for the 12 preparation situations, and you will be given feedback on your accuracy in selecting the appropriate style to meet the situation.

Procedure 1 (3–10 minutes)
The instructor reviews Model 13–1 and explains how to apply it to situation 1. The instructor states the group's developmental stage, the leadership style of each of the four alternative actions, and the scoring for each alternative. Follow the three steps below, as you try to select the most appropriate alternative action for each of the 12 situations.

Step 1. For each situation, determine the group's level of development. Place the number 1, 2, 3, or 4 on the D line.

Step 2. Identify each management style of all four alternatives A–D. Place the letters A, C, P, or E on the S lines.

Step 3. Select the appropriate management style for the group's level of development. Circle its letter, either a, b, c, or d.

Procedure 2
Option A (3–5 minutes). The instructor gives the class the recommended answers to situations 2–12, as in procedure 1, without any explanation.

Option B (15–45 minutes). Break into teams of two or three and go over the number of situations stated by the instructor. The instructor will go over the recommended answers as in Option A.

Model 13–1
Group Situational Management

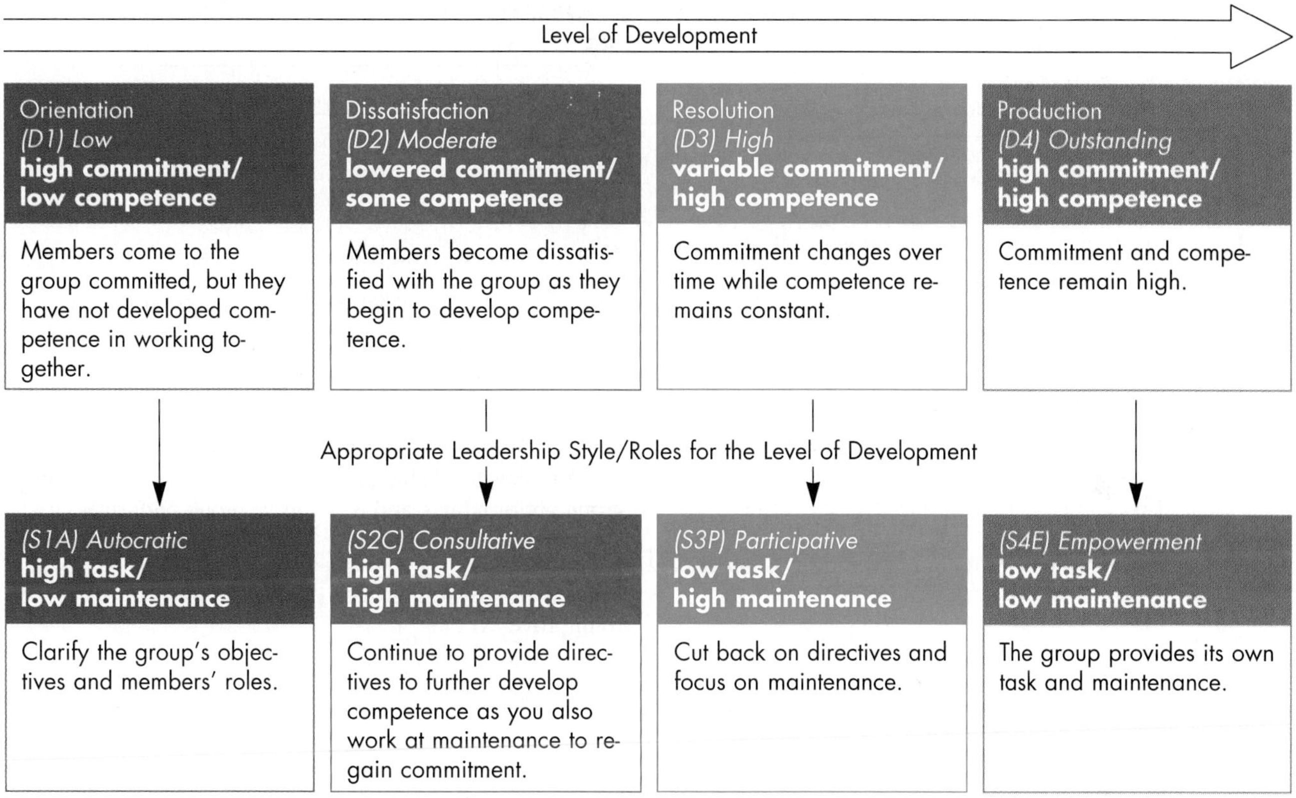

Level of Development →

Orientation *(D1) Low* **high commitment/ low competence**	Dissatisfaction *(D2) Moderate* **lowered commitment/ some competence**	Resolution *(D3) High* **variable commitment/ high competence**	Production *(D4) Outstanding* **high commitment/ high competence**
Members come to the group committed, but they have not developed competence in working together.	Members become dissatisfied with the group as they begin to develop competence.	Commitment changes over time while competence remains constant.	Commitment and competence remain high.

Appropriate Leadership Style/Roles for the Level of Development

(S1A) Autocratic **high task/ low maintenance**	*(S2C) Consultative* **high task/ high maintenance**	*(S3P) Participative* **low task/ high maintenance**	*(S4E) Empowerment* **low task/ low maintenance**
Clarify the group's objectives and members' roles.	Continue to provide directives to further develop competence as you also work at maintenance to regain commitment.	Cut back on directives and focus on maintenance.	The group provides its own task and maintenance.

Conclusion
The instructor leads a class discussion and/or makes concluding remarks.

Application (2–4 minutes)
What did I learn from this experience? How will I use this knowledge in the future?

Sharing
Volunteers give their answers to the application section.

Exercise 13–1
Group Performance

Preparing for Exercise 13–1

Note: This exercise is designed for class groups that have worked together for some time. (Five or more hours of prior classwork are recommended.)
Answer the following questions as they apply to your class group/team.

1. Using Figure 13–1, would you classify your members as a group or a team? Why?

Group Structure

2. What type of group/team are you? [formal/informal, functional/cross-functional (by majors), command/task]
3. What is the size of your group/team? The size is (too large, too small, good).
4. What is the group/team composition?

5. Is there a clear leader? (Who is/are the leader[s])
6. Does your group/team have clear objectives?
7. List some ways in which group structure could be improved to increase group performance.

___

___

Group Process

8. List each group member, including yourself, and the major role(s) each plays.

   1. ______ 4. ______
   2. ______ 5. ______
   3. ______ 6. ______

9. Identify at least three group norms. Are they positive or negative? How does the group enforce them?
10. How cohesive is your group (high, moderate, low)?
11. List each group member, including yourself, in order of status.

   1. ______ 4. ______
   2. ______ 5. ______
   3. ______ 6. ______

12. How are decisions made in your group/team?
13. How is conflict resolved in your group/team?
14. List some ways in which group process could be improved to increase group performance.

___

___

Group Development Stage

15. At what stage of group development is your group/team? Explain.
16. List some ways in which your group/team can develop to a higher level of development to increase group performance.

___

___

Meetings

17. List some ways in which your meetings could be improved to increase group performance.

___

___

18. Does your group have any problem members? What can be done to make them more effective?

Doing Exercise 13–1 in Class

Note: This exercise is designed for groups that have worked together for some time. (Five or more hours are recommended.)

Objectives
To gain a better understanding of the group structure, process, development, and meetings and how they affect group performance, and to improve group performance.

Experience
You will discuss your group's performance and develop plans to improve it.

Preparation
You should have answered the 18 preparation questions.

Procedure 1 (10–20 minutes)
Groups/teams get together to discuss their answers to the 18 preparation questions. Be sure to fully explain and discuss your answers. Try to come up with some specific ideas on how to improve your group's structure, process, development, and meetings.

Conclusion
The instructor leads a class discussion and/or makes concluding remarks.

Application (2–4 minutes)
What did I learn from this experience? How will I use this knowledge in the future?

___

___

Sharing
Volunteers give their answers to the application section.

VIDEOCASE

A Study in Teamwork: Valassis Communications

Valassis Communications, which prints coupon inserts for various publications, developed a corporate culture of teamwork to help it achieve its goals of satisfying customer demands. Top management believed strongly that teamwork was needed so that workers could benefit from each other's knowledge in meeting tough challenges. For example, teams figure out how to reduce waste in paper consumption.

The teamwork culture is supported by cross-training, visiting other departments, and working in open cubicles. Closely related to teamwork is companywide goal-setting in which teams of workers gear their activities to reaching corporate goals.

Power, Politics, Conflict, and Stress

Learning Objectives

After studying this chapter, you should be able to:

1. Define *power* and the difference between position and personal power.
2. Explain the difference among reward, legitimate, and referent power.
3. Discuss how power and politics are related.
4. Describe how money and power have a similar use.
5. Explain what networking, reciprocity, and coalition have in common.
6. List and define the five conflict management styles.
7. List the steps in the initiating conflict resolution model.
8. Explain the stress tug-of-war analogy.
9. Define the following **key terms** (in order of appearance in the chapter):

   power
   politics
   networking
   reciprocity
   coalition
   conflict
   functional conflict
   initiating conflict resolution model
   BCF model
   mediator
   arbitrator
   stress
   stressors

Skill-Development

1. You can develop your skill at using power and negotiation (Skill-Building Exercise 14–1). Power is a leadership management function. Power requires the use of interpersonal, informational, and decision-making management roles. The SCANS competencies of interpersonal skills and information, as well as basic, thinking, and personal qualities are developed through the exercise.

2. You can develop your collaborative conflict management skills (Skill-Building Exercise 14–2). Conflict management is a leadership management function. Conflict management requires the use of interpersonal, informational, and decision-making management roles. The SCANS competencies of interpersonal skills and information, as well as basic, thinking, and personal qualities are developed through the exercise.

egend has it that Ross Perot started his business career as a boy delivering newspapers in a Texarkana, Texas, ghetto and became a successful young salesperson for IBM by meeting his annual sales quota in the first month. According to Doron Levin, author of *Irreconcilable Differences: Ross Perot versus General Motors,* Perot's motives are money, attention, and power. His need for attention and power influenced his decision to spend millions of dollars running for the presidency of the United States, although he officially withdrew, and to later work to develop a third political party to compete with the Republican and Democratic parties.

Perot's power-based personality is illustrated in his motto, which he quotes from Winston Churchill, "Never give in. Never." When Perot decides to do something, he is convinced that he is right, and those who disagree with him become his enemies. He exerts power and politics and creates conflict and stress in others to get what he wants. He has been known to discredit competitors and use political arm-twisting to win business deals. When one of his business facilities in California voted to organize a union, Perot shut the facility down rather than tolerate a union. However, Perot is supportive of employees who are loyal to him. People who have worked for him have stated that they are a bit afraid of him, in awe of him, sometimes angry with him, but they like working for him!

Ross Perot's motto is, "Never give in. Never."

Perot started Electronic Data Systems, Inc. (EDS) and became a powerful self-made billionaire. EDS assists client organizations in the development of computer information systems designed to address and solve business problems. He went on to sell EDS to General Motors (GM) and became a member of GM's board of directors and a GM stockholder. Perot was very outspoken against GM management practices and was pressing for drastic changes. He was so powerfully intimidating and successful at building a political network that GM management decided to buy his GM stock at a premium price to get rid of him. He went on to recruit EDS employees away from GM when he created a competing company, Perot Systems. Although Ross Perot is basically an autocratic leader, he has always been against bureaucracy and hierarchy and for informal communication.

Today, EDS employs over 72,000 people in 38 strategic business units based on industry served and has annual revenues of over $8 billion. EDS has the largest project organizational structure in the world. EDS is a loosely connected collection of project teams. Self-managed teams of 8 to 12 programmers and systems experts last for 9 to 18 months. The team structure consists of individual performers, subproject team leaders, and formally designated team leaders, all of whom tend to report to one another. Employees move on and off teams informally according to project needs. Project managers recruit members from other teams. The teams live the "close to the customer" concept by physically working within the client organizations.

For current information on EDS, use Internet address http://www.eds.com. For ideas on using the Internet, see the Appendix.

Besides excellent work, what does it take to get ahead in an organization? To climb the corporate ladder, you will have to gain power, engage in politics, and manage your conflicts and stress.

POWER

To be effective in an organization, you must understand how power is gained and used. You will study the importance of power in organizations, the bases of power, and how to increase your own power.

Organizational Power

1. Define *power* and the difference between position and personal power.

Some people view power as the ability to make people do what they want them to do, or the ability to do something to people or for people. These definitions may be true, but they tend to give power a manipulative, negative connotation, as does Plato's saying, "Power corrupts and absolute power corrupts absolutely." For our purposes, having **power** *is the ability to influence others' behavior*. Ross Perot is considered a powerful person because of his ability to influence others' behavior.

power
The ability to influence others' behavior.

Within an organization, power should be viewed in a positive sense. Without power, managers could not achieve organizational objectives. Leadership and power go hand in hand. Employees are not influenced without a reason, and the reason is often the power a manager has over them. You do not actually have to use power to influence others. Often it is the perception of power, rather than the actual power, that influences others.

Power starts at the top of the organization, and today top managers are giving more power to employees (*empowerment*). Organizations, including AT&T, Corning, GE, and Motorola, have an office of the CEO with a team, rather than one autocratic leader. CEOs are not asking what should *I* do, but what should *we* do. Teams work out decisions. CEOs are pushing teamwork downward.[1]

There are two types of power: position and personal. *Position power* is derived from top management and is delegated down the chain of command. *Personal power* is derived from the follower based on the individual's behavior. *Charismatic leaders have personal power*. Therefore, personal power can be gained or lost. It is best to have both position power and personal power. There is no universal acceptance of which source of power is more important. However, with the trend toward empowered teams, personal power is becoming more important than position power.

Bases of Power and How to Increase Your Power

2. Explain the difference among reward, legitimate, and referent power.

The seven bases of power, along with their sources, are presented in Figure 14–1 and each base of power is discussed along with how to increase it. You can build your power base,[2] without taking power away from others. Generally, power is given to those who get results and have good human relations skills.

Coercive Power. The use of *coercive power* involves threats and/or punishment to influence compliance. Out of fear of reprimands, probation, suspension, or dismissal, employees often do as their boss requests. Other examples of coercive power include verbal abuse, humiliation, and ostracism. Group members may use coercive power to enforce norms. Ross Perot has been known to use coercive power to get what he wants.

Appropriate Use of Coercive Power. Coercive power is appropriate to use in maintaining discipline when enforcing rules. When employees are not willing to do as requested, coercive power may be the only way to gain compliance.

Position Power			►◄			Personal Power
Coercive	Connection	Reward	Legitimate	Referent	Information	Expert

Figure 14–1
Sources and Bases of Power

However, employees resent managers' use of coercive power.[3] Keep the use of coercive power to a minimum because it hurts human relations and often productivity as well.

Increasing Coercive Power. Generally, to have coercive position power you need to have a management job that enables you to gain and maintain the ability to hire, discipline, and fire your employees. However, some people can pressure others to do what they want without position authority.

Connection Power. *Connection power* is based on the user's relationship with influential people. You rely on the use of contacts or friends who can influence the person you are dealing with. The right connections can give power or at least the perception of having power. If people know you are friendly with people in power, they are more apt to do as you request. For example, if the boss's son has no position power but wants something done, he can gain compliance by making a comment about speaking to his father or mother.

In spite of Plato's warning, power should be viewed in a positive sense in organizations when used correctly.

Appropriate Use of Connection Power. When you are looking for a job or a promotion, connections can help. There is a lot of truth in the statement, "It's not what you know, it's who you know." Connection power can also help you get the resources you need and increased business.

Increasing Connection Power. To increase your connection power, expand your network of contacts with important managers who have power. Join the "in crowd" and the "right" clubs. Sports such as golf may help you meet influential people. When you want something, identify the people who can help you attain it, make alliances, and win them over to your side. Get people to know your name. Get all the publicity you can. Make your accomplishments known to the people in power; send them notices. Connections are developed through political networking, the topic of the next section. When Ross Perot entered politics, he realized how important connection power can be.

Reward Power. *Reward power* is based on the user's ability to influence others with something of value to them. It is based on transactional leadership. In a management position, use positive reinforcement with incentives such as praise, recognition, pay raises, and promotions to influence others' behavior. With peers, you can exchange favors as a reward, or give something of value to them. Reward power affects performance expectations and achievement.[4] Employees at EDS get a variety of rewards for doing a good job.

Appropriate Use of Reward Power. Let people know what's in it for them. If you have something attractive to others, use it. For example, when Professor

Jones is recruiting a student aide, he tells candidates that if they are selected and do a good job, he will recommend them for an MBA fellowship at Suffolk University, where he has connection power. As a result, he gets good, qualified help for minimum wages, while helping both his student aide and his alma mater.

Increasing Reward Power. Get a management position and gain and maintain control over evaluating your employees' performance and determining their raises and promotions. Find out what others value and try to reward them in that way. Using praise can help increase your power. Employees who feel they are appreciated rather than being used will give the manager more power.

Legitimate Power. *Legitimate power* is based on the user's position power given by the organization. Employees tend to feel that they ought to do what the boss says within the scope of the job. For example, the manager asks an employee to take out the trash. The employee does not really want to do it, but thinks, "The boss made a legitimate request and I ought to do it," and takes it out.

Appropriate Use of Legitimate Power. The use of legitimate power is appropriate when asking people to do something that is within the scope of their job. Day-to-day manager-employee interactions at EDS and other organization are based on legitimate power.

Increasing Legitimate Power. Get a management job and let people know the power you possess, and work at gaining people's perception that you do have power. Remember that people's perception that you have power gives you power.

Referent Power. *Referent power* is based on the user's personal power relationship with others. It is based primarily on personality. For example, say "Will you please do it for me?" not "This is an order." Identification stems primarily from the employee's attractiveness to the person using power, and the personal feelings of "liking" or the desire to be liked by the power holder.

Appropriate Use of Referent Power. The use of referent power is particularly appropriate for people with weak, or no, position power. Referent power is needed in self-managed teams because leadership should be shared.

Increasing Referent Power. To gain referent power, develop your human relations skills (Chapter 3). Remember that your boss's success depends on you. Gain his or her confidence in order to get more power; work at your relationship with your boss.

Information Power. *Information power* is based on data desired by others. Managers rely on information from others. Organizational recruiters are looking for people who can convey information successfully.[5] The information is usually related to the job, but not always. Some secretaries have more information and are more helpful answering questions than the managers they work for.

Appropriate Use of Information Power. An important part of the manager's job is to convey information. Employees often come to managers for information on what to do and how to do it. As a consulting firm, EDS gets its clients because of the information it has about how to set up computer information systems to help client organizations solve business problems. EDS gives organizational members information power. At EDS, information flows freely through informal channels.

Increasing Information Power. Have information flow through you. Know what is going on in the organization. Provide service and information to other departments. Serve on committees because it gives you both information and a chance to increase connection power. To keep lines of communication open, treat people with good, neutral, and bad news in essentially the same way.[6]

Work Application

1. Identify a present or past boss. Which power base does/did the boss use most often? Explain. Also, give a least one example of another power base you saw the boss use.
2. Which one or two suggestions for increasing your power base are the most relevant to you? Explain.

Expert Power. *Expert power* is based on the user's skill and knowledge. Being an expert makes other people depend on you. Employees with expert power are often promoted to management positions. Expert power requires technical and conceptual management skills. People often respect an expert, and the fewer people who possess an expertise, the more power the individual has. For example, because there are few jobs and not many people possessing the ability to become top athletes, like basketball star Michael Jordan, they command multimillion dollar contracts. It's a supply and demand issue.

Appropriate Use of Expert Power. Managers are often, but not always, experts within their departments. Expert power is essential to people who have to work with employees from other departments and organizations. They have no direct position power to use, so being seen as an expert gives credibility and power. EDS also gets its clients based on its expertise in setting up computer systems needed by clients.

Increasing Expert Power. To become an expert, take all the training and educational programs your organization provides. Keep up with the latest technology. Volunteer to be the first to learn something new. Stay away from routine tasks in favor of more complex, hard-to-evaluate tasks. Project a positive image.

In conclusion, power is commonly viewed with contingency theory. The type of power to use to be the most effective at maximizing performance is based on the situation. You have studied the appropriate use of the seven bases of power.

Why do some people want and seek power while others will not take it even if its offered to them? McClelland's acquired needs theory of motivation (Chapter 11) states that the answer is based on one's need for power. Effective managers have a high need for power, but not simply for personal power. They have a concern for influencing others on behalf of the organization so

APPLYING THE CONCEPT

AC 14–1 Using Power

Identify the appropriate power to use in each situation.

a. coercive c. reward or legitimate e. information or expert
b. connection d. referent

____ 1. Bridget, one of your best workers, needs little direction from you. However, recently her performance level has dropped. You are quite sure Bridget has a personal problem affecting her work.

____ 2. You want a new personal computer to help you do a better job. PCs are allocated by a committee, which is very political in nature.

____ 3. One of your best workers, Jean, wants a promotion. Jean has talked to you about getting ahead and has asked you to help prepare her for when the opportunity comes.

____ 4. John, one of your worst employees, has ignored one of your directives again.

____ 5. Whitney, who needs some direction and encouragement from you to maintain production, is not working to standard today. As she does occasionally, she claims that she does not feel well but cannot afford to take time off. You have to get an important customer order shipped today.

that all stakeholders benefit. Was your score for the need for power high or low in Self-Assessment Exercise 11–1? Do you want to influence others? Do you plan to follow the suggestions in the text to increase your power base?

ORGANIZATIONAL POLITICS

In this section, you will study the nature of politics, political behavior, and guidelines for developing political skills. Begin by determining your use of political behavior by completing Self-Assessment Exercise 14–1.

SELF-ASSESSMENT EXERCISE 14–1

Use of Political Behavior

Select the response that best describes your actual or planned use of the following behavior on the job. Place the number 1–5 on the line before each statement.

(1) rarely (2) seldom (3) occasionally (4) frequently (5) usually

___ 1. I get along with everyone, even those considered to be difficult to get along with.
___ 2. I avoid giving my personal opinion on controversial issues, especially when I know others don't agree with them.
___ 3. I try to make people feel important by complimenting them.
___ 4. I compromise when working with others and avoid telling people they are wrong.
___ 5. I try to get to know the key managers and find out what is going on in all the organizational departments.
___ 6. I dress the same way as the people in power and take on the same interests (watch or play sports, join the same clubs, etc.).
___ 7. I purposely seek contacts and network with higher level managers so they will know who I am by name and face.
___ 8. I seek recognition and visibility for my accomplishments.
___ 9. I get others to help me to get what I want.
___ 10. I do favors for others and use their favors in return.

To determine your political behavior, add the ten numbers you selected as your answers. The number will range from 10 to 50. The higher your score, the more political behavior you use. Place your score here ___ and on the continuum below.

Nonpolitical 10———20———30———40———50 Political

3. Discuss how power and politics are related.
4. Describe how money and power have a similar use.

politics
The process of gaining and using power.

The Nature of Organizational Politics

Political skills are a part of power.[7] **Politics** *is the process of gaining and using power*. Politics is a reality of organizational life.[8] None of the current trends—such as globalization, diversity, total quality management, teams, and so on—have eliminated politics.[9]

Like power, politics often has a negative connotation due to people who abuse political power. A positive way to view politics is to realize that it is simply a medium of exchange. Like money, politics in and of itself is neither good nor bad. It is simply a means of getting what we want. In our economy, money is the medium of exchange; in an organization, politics is the medium of exchange.

Managers cannot meet their objectives without the help of other people and departments over which they have no authority or position power. For example, Chris, a production department manager, needs materials and supplies to make the product, but must rely on the purchasing department to acquire them. If Chris does not have a good working relationship with purchasing, materials may not be there when needed. This is especially true for rush jobs.

The amount and importance of politics varies from organization to organization. However, larger organizations tend to be more political; and the higher the level of management, the more important politics becomes. A survey of executives revealed that 20 percent of their time is spent on politics.[10]

Politics requires communication, and like communication, your politics should flow in a vertical, horizontal, and grapevine direction. You need to have a good working relationship with your boss and employees, with your colleagues and peers, and with people throughout your organization and in other organizations.

5. Explain what networking, reciprocity, and coalition have in common.

Political Behavior

Networking, reciprocity, and coalitions are important political behaviors.

networking
The process of developing relationships for the purpose of socializing and politicking.

Networking. **Networking** *is the process of developing relationships for the purpose of socializing and politicking*. Management activities and the time spent on each area have been studied and classified into four areas: traditional management, communication, human resources management, and networking. Of these four activities, networking has the most relative contribution to management success because it helps get the job done. Successful managers spend around twice as much time networking as average managers.[11]

reciprocity
Involves creating obligations and developing alliances and using them to accomplish objectives.

Reciprocity. Using **reciprocity** *involves creating obligations and developing alliances and using them to accomplish objectives*. When people do something for you, you incur an obligation that they may expect to be repaid. When you do something for people, you create a debt that you may be able to collect at a later date when you need a favor. You should work at developing a network of alliances that you can call on for help in meeting your objectives.

coalition
A network of alliances that will help a manager achieve an objective.

Coalitions. A **coalition** *is a network of alliances that will help a manager achieve an objective*. Reciprocity is used to achieve ongoing objectives, whereas coalitions are developed for achieving a specific objective. For example, Pete, a team member, has an idea for a new service to be offered by EDS. By himself, Pete has no authority to offer a new service. A suggested procedure for building a coalition would be for Pete to first go to his boss or bosses. Pete would present the idea to his boss and get approval to get wider support. Pete would then get peers and people at other levels as allies. It is important to align yourself with powerful people who can help.[12] Pete may offer payoffs from the new service in return for support, time, money, and other resources that peers and others contribute. The focus is on telling others how they will benefit if the service is provided. With a coalition in place, Pete would then go to the person with the power to approve the new service. A formal presentation is often required. When higher-level managers know that the lower levels are in favor of the idea, and it is a good one, approval is often given. If the service is approved, Pete may be the team leader to offer it, and his coalition members may be on the team.

Guidelines for Developing Political Skills

If you want to climb the corporate ladder, you should develop your political skills. More specifically, review the ten statements in Self-Assessment Exercise 14–1 and the three political behaviors and consciously increase your use of these behaviors. Successfully implementing these behaviors results in increased political skills. However, if you don't agree with one of the political behaviors, don't use it; you don't have to use all of them to be successful. Learn what it takes in the organization where you work as you follow the guidelines in Figure 14–2.

Learn the Organizational Culture. Learn the cultural shared values and beliefs (Chapter 8) and how business and politics operate where you work. Learn to read between the lines. For example, a boss asked a new employee to select one of two project teams to work on. The employee selected one and told the boss his selection. The boss told him to rethink the decision. In talking to others, the new employee found out that the manager of the team was disliked by the new CEO. No matter how good the idea or how well the team did, the team was doomed to fail, and so would the employee.

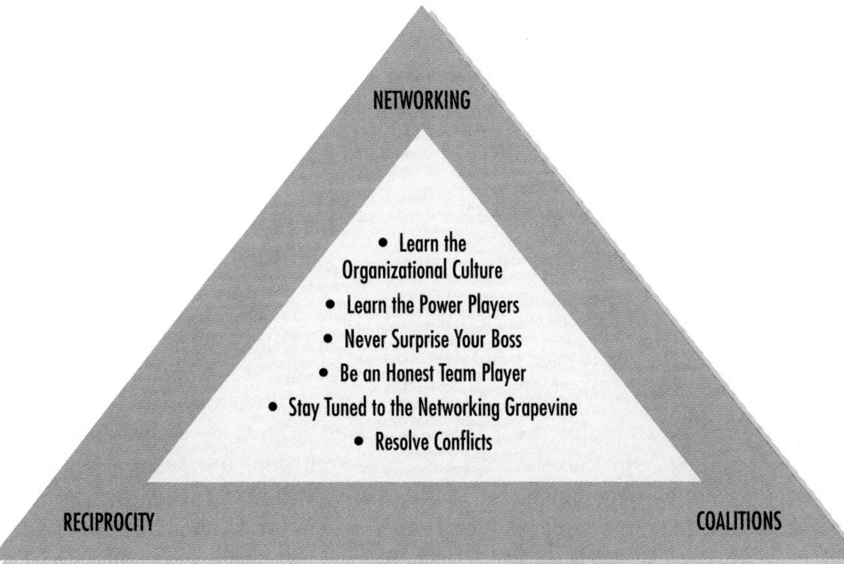

Figure 14–2
Political Behaviors and Guidelines for Developing Political Skills

Learn the Power Players. It is natural, especially for young people, to take a purely rational approach to a job without considering politics. But don't do this because many business decisions are very nonrational and are simply based on power and politics.[13] For example, a specific location of a new business facility is often chosen simply based on where the person in power wants to live.

In all organizations, there are some powerful key players. Don't just find out who they are, gain an understanding of what makes each of them tick. By understanding them, you can tailor the presentation of your ideas and style to fit the needs of each individual. Your boss is a key player to you. For example, some managers want to see detailed financial numbers and statistics, while others don't. Some managers expect you to continually follow up with them, while others will think you are annoying them. When developing coalitions, get key players.

Never Surprise Your Boss. If you want to get ahead, you should have a good working relationship with your boss. Get to know what your boss expects from you and do it. It's common to put off telling the boss bad news. But, if you are having a job problem, let your boss know early. If you are behind schedule to meet an important deadline and your boss finds out about it from others, it is embarrassing, especially if your boss finds out from his or her boss. And don't show your boss up in public, such as during a meeting. If you do, don't be surprised if the next time you open your mouth at a meeting your boss embarrasses you. When developing a coalition, include your boss.

Work Application

3. Give a job example of how networking, reciprocity, or a coalition was used to achieve an organizational objective.
4. Which one or two suggestions for developing political skills are the most relevant to you? Explain.

Be an Honest Team Player. Some backstabbing gossips may get short-term benefits from their behavior, but in the long run they are generally unsuccessful because others gossip about them in return. In any organization, you must earn others' respect, confidence, and trust. Once caught in a lie, it's difficult to regain trust. There are very few, if any, jobs in which organizational objectives can be achieved without the support of a group/team of individuals. Even lone wolf salespeople are subject to the systems effect and need the help of production to make the product, transportation to deliver it, and service to maintain it. The trend is toward teamwork, so if you are not a team player, work at it.

Stay Tuned to the Networking Grapevine. Find out what is going on through the grapevine. The grapevine can help you to learn the organizational culture and key players to include in your coalitions. Your grapevine should include a network of people within and outside your organization. Join trade or professional associations and attend meetings. You will be surprised at how much others know about your organization. It's not unusual for people to hear about what is going on in

APPLYING THE CONCEPT

AC 14–2 Political Behavior

Identify the behavior in each situation as effective or ineffective political behavior.

a. effective b. ineffective

____ 6. Jill is taking golf lessons so she can join the Saturday golf group that includes some higher-level managers.

____ 7. Paul tells his boss's boss about mistakes his boss makes.

____ 8. Sally avoids socializing so that she can be more productive on the job.

____ 9. John sent a very positive performance report to three higher-level managers to whom he does not report. They did not request copies.

____ 10. Carlos has to drop off daily reports by noon. He brings them around 10:00 on Tuesday and Thursday so that he can run into some higher-level managers who meet at that time near the office where the report goes. On the other days, Carlos drops the report off around noon on his way to lunch.

their organization from people who don't work there. But, use the grapevine to check rumors, not to spread them.

Resolve Conflicts. When climbing the corporate ladder, you may have to be careful not to get thrown off it. Following the preceding guidelines can help you avoid a political fight. However, if you are suddenly left out of the information loop and everything you say gets rejected or ignored, or if your coworkers or boss start treating you differently, find out why. Use your networking grapevine to find out if someone is trying to undermine you and why. You need to understand where your enemies are coming from, how they operate, who's behind them, and what weapons they might use. Confront individuals or groups suspected of instigating conflict.[14] If you did something to offend your adversary, an apology may clear the air. In any case, confront your adversary to resolve the conflict using the ideas in the next section.

MANAGING CONFLICT

A **conflict** *exists whenever people are in disagreement and opposition*. In the workplace, conflict is inevitable;[15] you cannot avoid it. Managers need strong conflict resolution and negotiation skills if they want to be successful.[16] Constructive conflict management is one of the most important skills you can acquire.[17] How well you handle conflict affects your job satisfaction and success. To this end, many organizations offer conflict resolution programs.[18]

conflict
Exists whenever people are in disagreement and opposition.

In this section you will learn that conflict can be functional or dysfunctional, about types and sources of conflict, and five conflict management styles.

Conflict Can Be Dysfunctional or Functional

People often think of conflict as fighting and view it as disruptive. When conflict prevents the achievement of organizational objectives, it is negative or *dysfunctional conflict*. However, it can be postive. **Functional conflict** *exists when disagreement and opposition support the achievement of organizational objectives*. Functional conflict increases the quality of group decisions.[19] The question today is not whether conflict is negative or positive, but how to manage conflict to benefit the organization.

functional conflict
Exists when disagreement and opposition support the achievement of organizational objectives.

Too little or too much conflict is usually dysfunctional. If people are not willing to disagree and optimize, or if they fight too much without resolution, objectives may not be met and performance will be lower than optimal. Too much conflict, and not knowing how to resolve it, results in violence.[20] A balance of conflict is functional to organizations because it optimizes performance outcomes. Challenging present methods and presenting innovative change causes conflict, but leads to improved performance. Figure 14–3 illustrates the effects conflict has on performance. One of the

Figure 14–3
Conflict and Performance

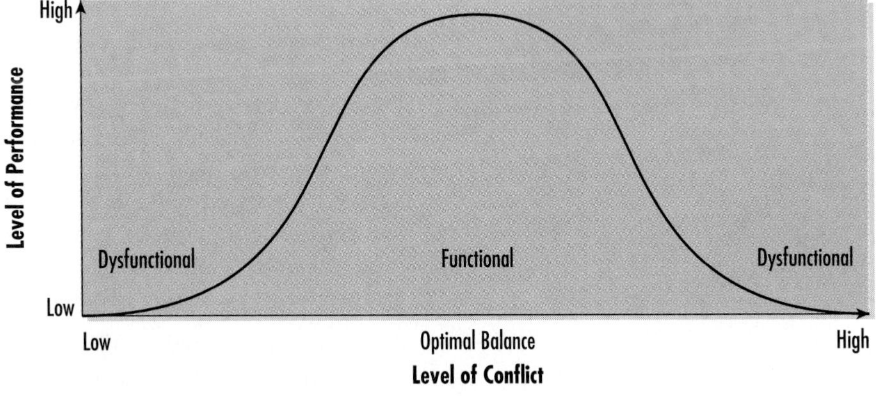

reasons that EDS is so successful is because employees are able to optimally balance conflict so that it is functional.

Types and Sources of Conflict

Types of Conflict. Conflict can be classified by the people involved. There are at least five types of conflict: (1) *Conflict within the individual* is common when a person is faced with conflicting priorities. If you are asked to work overtime and have another commitment, what would you do? (2) *Interpersonal conflict* occurs between two or more people who disagree. (3) *Conflict between an individual and a group* occurs when a group member breaks the group's norms. (4) *Intergroup conflict* occurs between two different groups/departments within the same organization. (5) *Conflict between organizations* occurs when competing in a free enterprise system leads to conflict through opposition.

Sources of Conflict. There are at least five major sources of, or reasons for, conflict:

1. With a *diversity* of people comes conflict.
2. People tend to use different sources of *information*. At times the sources do not agree, or the same information is interpreted differently. The better your communication skills, the fewer conflicts you will have.[21]
3. Individuals and groups sometimes have *different objectives* with incompatible roles. For example, the salesperson's objective is to sell as much as possible, while the credit person's objective is to give credit only to good credit risks. These two groups are known to have their conflicts.
4. *Changes* in the environment call for changes in the organization; conflict occurs over what to change and how.
5. Employees and departments often have to compete for *scarce organizational resources*. Conflict is common during the budget process. People are also territorial; conflict can occur if one person or group of people try to infringe on another's turf.

People at EDS, and all organizations, have to deal with these types and sources of conflict.

6. List and define the five conflict management styles.

Conflict Management Styles

When you are in conflict, you have five conflict management styles to choose from. The five styles are based on two dimensions of concerns—concern for others' needs and concern for your own needs—which result in three types of behavior. A low concern for your own needs and a high concern for others' needs results in passive behavior. A high concern for your own needs and a low concern for others' needs results in aggressive behavior. A moderate or high concern for your own needs and others' needs results in assertive behavior. Each conflict behavior style results in a different combination of win-lose situations. The five styles, along with concern for needs and win-lose combinations, are presented in Figure 14–4 and discussed in the following section in order of passive, aggressive, and assertive behavior.

Avoiding Conflict Style. The *avoiding conflict style* user attempts to passively ignore the conflict rather than resolve it. When you avoid a conflict, you

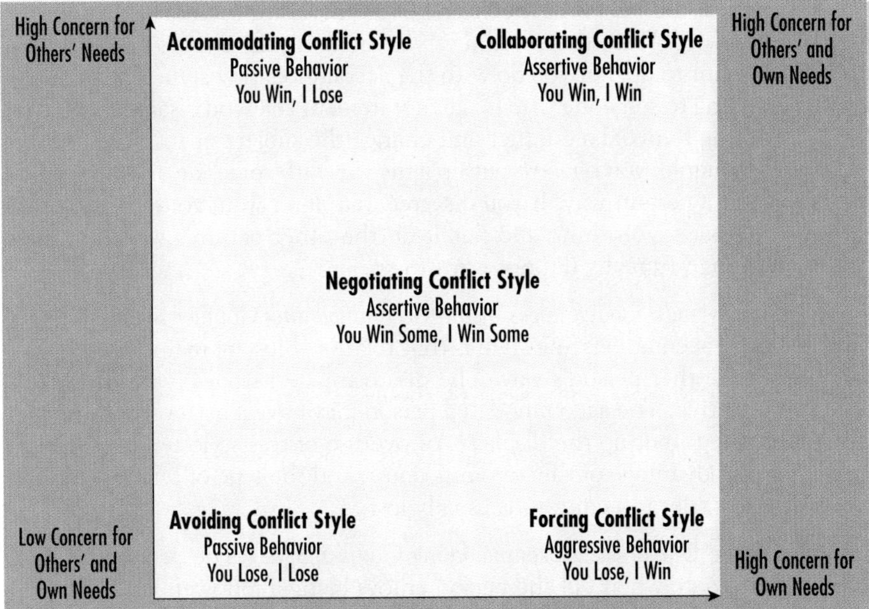

Figure 14–4
Conflict Management Styles

are being unassertive and uncooperative. People avoid the conflict by refusing to take a stance, escaping the conflict by mentally withdrawing, and by physically leaving. A lose-lose situation is created because the conflict is not resolved.

Advantages and Disadvantages of the Avoiding Conflict Style. The advantage of the avoiding style is that it may maintain relationships that would be hurt through conflict resolution. The disadvantage of this style is the fact that conflicts do not get resolved. An overuse of this style leads to conflict within the individual. People tend to walk all over the avoider. Some managers allow employees to break rules without confronting them. Avoiding problems usually does not make them go away; the problems usually get worse. And the longer you wait to confront others, the more difficult the confrontation usually is.

Appropriate Use of the Avoiding Conflict Style. The avoiding style is appropriate to use when: (1) the conflict is trivial, (2) your stake in the issue is not high, (3) confrontation will damage an important relationship, (4) you don't have time to resolve the conflict, or (5) emotions are high. When you don't have time to resolve the conflict or people are emotional, you should confront the person(s) later. However, it is inappropriate to repeatedly avoid confrontation until you get so upset that you end up yelling at the other person(s). This passive-aggressive behavior tends to make the situation worse by hurting human relations. Often people do not realize they are doing something that bothers you (that you are in conflict) and, when approached properly, are willing to change. The proper approach is explained with the collaborating conflict style.

Accommodating Conflict Style. The *accommodating conflict style* user attempts to resolve the conflict by passively giving in to the other party. When you use the accommodating style you are being unassertive but cooperative. You attempt to satisfy the other party while neglecting your own needs by letting others get their own way. A win-lose situation is created.

A common difference between the avoiding and accomodating styles is based on behavior. With the avoiding style you don't have to do anything you really don't want to do, but you do with the accommodating style. For example, if you are talking to someone who makes a statement that you disagree with, you can say nothing to avoid a conflict and change the subject or stop the conversation. For example, you have to put up a display with someone and the person wants to do it a certain way. If you disagree and don't want to do it the other person's way but say nothing and put it up the other person's way, you have done something you really did not want to do.

Advantages and Disadvantages of the Accommodating Conflict Style. The advantage of the accommodating style is that relationships are maintained by doing things the other person's way. The disadvantage is that giving in may be counterproductive. The accommodated person may have a better solution, such as a better way to put up the display. An overuse of this style tends to lead to people taking advantage of the accommodator, and the type of relationship the accommodator tries to maintain is usually lost.

Appropriate Use of the Accommodating Conflict Style. The accommodating style is appropriate when (1) the person enjoys being a follower, (2) maintaining the relationship outweighs all other considerations, (3) the changes agreed to are not important to the accommodator, but are to the other party, (4) the time to resolve the conflict is limited, and (5) you have an autocratic boss who uses the forcing style.

Forcing Conflict Style. The *forcing conflict style* user attempts to resolve the conflict by using aggressive behavior to get his or her own way. When you use the forcing style you are uncooperative and aggressive; you do whatever it takes to satisfy your own needs at the expense of others. Forcers use authority, threaten, intimidate, and call for majority rule when they know they will win. Forcers commonly enjoy dealing with avoiders and accommodators. If you try to get others to change without being willing to change yourself, regardless of the means, then you use the forcing style.[22] A win-lose situation is created.

Advantages and Disadvantages of the Forcing Style. The advantage of the forcing style is that better organizational decisions, rather than less effective, compromised decisions will be made when the forcer is correct. The disadvantage is that overuse of this style leads to hostility and resentment toward its user. Forcers tend to have poor human relations. However, some of them do not care about people.

Appropriate Use of the Forcing Style. Some managers commonly use their position power to force others to do things their way. The forcing style is appropriate to use when (1) unpopular action must be taken on important issues, (2) commitment by others to proposed action is not crucial to its implementation (in other words, people will not resist doing what you want them to do), (3) maintaining relationships is not critical, and (4) the conflict resolution is urgent.

Negotiating Conflict Style. The *negotiating conflict style* user attempts to resolve the conflict through assertive give-and-take concessions. It is also called the *compromising style*. When you use the compromising approach you are moderate in assertiveness and cooperation. An I-win-part-I-lose-part situation is created through compromise.

Advantages and Disadvantages of the Negotiating Conflict Style. The advantage of the negotiating conflict style is that the conflict is resolved relatively quickly, and working relationships are maintained. The disadvantage is that the compromise often leads to counterproductive results such as suboptimum decisions. An overuse of this style leads to people playing games such as asking for twice as much as they need in order to get what they want. It is commonly used during collective bargaining.

Appropriate Use of the Negotiating Conflict Style. The negotiating conflict style is appropriate to use when (1) the issues are complex and critical and there is no simple and clear solution, (2) parties have about equal power and are interested in different solutions, (3) a solution will only be temporary, and (4) time is short.

Work Application

5. Select a present or past boss. Which conflict management style did the boss use most often? Explain through a typical example.
6. Which one of the five conflict management styles do you tend to use most often? Explain.

Collaborating Conflict Style. The *collaborating conflict style* user assertively attempts to jointly resolve the conflict with the best solution agreeable to all parties. It is also called the *problem-solving style*. When you use the collaborating approach you are being assertive and cooperative. Although avoiders and accommodators are concerned about others' needs and forcers are concerned about their own needs, the collaborator is concerned about finding the best solution to the problem that is satisfactory to all parties. Unlike the forcer, the collaborator is willing to change if a better solution is presented. While negotiating is often based on secret information, collaboration is based on open and honest communication. This is the only style that creates a true win-win situation.

A common difference between negotiating and collaborating is the solution. Continuing the putting up a display example: With negotiation, the two people may trade off by putting up one display one person's way and the next display the other person's way. This way they win and lose. With collaboration, the two people work together to develop one display method that they both like. It may be some form of both or simply one person's, if after an explanation, the other person really agrees that the method is better. The key to collaboration is agreeing that the solution is the best possible one.

APPLYING THE CONCEPT

AC 14–3 Selecting Conflict Management Styles

Identify the most appropriate conflict management style as:

a. avoiding
b. accommodating
c. forcing
d. negotiating
e. collaborating

____ **11.** You have joined a committee in order to meet people. Your interest in what the committee does is low. While serving on the committee, you make a recommendation that is opposed by another member. You realize that you have the better idea. The other party is using a forcing style.

____ **12.** You are on a task force that has to select a new computer. The four alternatives will all do the job. It's the brand, price, and service that people disagree on.

____ **13.** You are a sales manager. Beth, one of your competent salespeople, is trying to close a big sale. The two of you are discussing the next sales call she will make. You disagree on the strategy to use to close the sale.

____ **14.** You're late and on your way to an important meeting. As you leave your office, at the other end of the work area you see Chris, one of your employees, goofing off instead of working.

____ **15.** You're over budget for labor this month. It's slow so you asked Kent, a part-time employee, to leave work early. Kent tells you he doesn't want to go because he needs the money.

Advantages and Disadvantages of the Collaborating Style. The advantage of the collaborating style is that it tends to lead to the best solution to the conflict using assertive behavior. The disadvantage is that the skill, effort, and time it takes to resolve the conflict are usually greater and longer than with the other styles. There are situations, mentioned under negotiation, where collaboration is difficult and when a forcer prevents its use. The collaborative style offers the most benefit to the individual, group, and organization.

Appropriate Use of the Collaborating Conflict Style. The collaborating style is appropriate when (1) you are dealing with an important issue that requires an optimal solution; compromise would result in suboptimizing; (2) people are willing to place the group goal before self-interest; members will truly collaborate; (3) maintaining relationships is important; (4) time is available; and (5) it is a peer conflict.

The situational perspective states that there is no one best style for resolving all conflicts. A person's preferred style tends to meet his or her needs. Some people enjoy forcing, while others prefer to avoid conflict, and so forth. As with all management functions, success lies in one's ability to use the appropriate style to meet the situation. At EDS employees do use all five styles. However, the emphasis at EDS is on teamwork and collaboration.

During a job interview you may be asked how you resolved conflicts in the past.[23] Of the five styles, the most difficult to implement successfully, due to the complexity and level of skill needed, is the collaborative style. It is most likely the most underutilized when appropriate. Organizations around the globe, including EDS, are training employees to resolve conflicts using collaboration.[24] Therefore, the collaborative style is the only one that will be given detailed coverage, in the next section, in order to develop your conflict skills.

THE COLLABORATING CONFLICT MANAGEMENT STYLE

Although you can help prevent conflict, you will not eliminate it completely nor should you try to because it is functional. You will develop your skill to assertively confront (or be confronted by) people you are in conflict with, in a manner that resolves the conflict without damaging interpersonal relationships. Model 14–1 provides the steps you can follow when initiating, responding to, and mediating a conflict resolution. Before discussing the model steps, which

Model 14–1
The Collaborating Conflict Style

Planning — Leading

Initiating Conflict Resolution
- Step 1. Plan a BCF statement that maintains ownership of the problem.
- Step 2. Present your BCF statement and agree on the conflict.
- Step 3. Ask for, and/or give, alternative conflict resolutions.
- Step 4. Make an agreement for change.

Responding to Conflict Resolution
- Step 1. Listen to and paraphrase the conflict using the BCF model.
- Step 2. Agree with some aspect of the complaint.
- Step 3. Ask for, and/or give, alternative conflict resolutions.
- Step 4. Make an agreement for change.

Mediating Conflict Resolution
- Step 1. Have each party state his or her complaint using the BCF model.
- Step 2. Agree on the conflict problem(s).
- Step 3. Develop alternative conflict resolutions.
- Step 4. Make an agreement for change.
- Step 5. Follow up to make sure the conflict is resolved.

Organizing — Controlling

are explained in detail, let's be sure you understand the difference between forcing and collaborating.

Forcing versus Collaborating Styles

When people do things that really bother you (i.e., smoke in your space, tell sexual or racial jokes, use words that are offensive to you) don't use the avoiding conflict style. Confront them early in a calm manner using the collaborating style. If you tell someone that they are doing something that bothers you, they may tell you that you do something that bothers them. When this happens, you need to be collaborative by your willingness to change your behavior.

When others do things that bother you, do things differently than you would, and don't want to do things your way, examine your own needs. If all you want to do is change others to be the way you want them to be, get people to do what you want them to do, or get people to do things your way, and you are not willing to change your behavior, then you are using the forcing not the collaborating style.

Initiating Conflict Resolution

7. List the steps in the initiating conflict resolution model.

An initiator is the person who confronts the other person(s) to resolve the conflict. When initiating a conflict resolution using the collaborating style, use the following model: *The* **initiating conflict resolution model** *steps are to (1) plan a BCF statement that maintains ownership of the problem, (2) present your BCF statement and agree on the conflict, (3) ask for and/or give alternative conflict resolutions, and (4) make an agreement for change.* This is Model 14–1.

initiating conflict resolution model
The steps are to: (1) plan a BCF statement that maintains ownership of the problem, (2) present your BCF statement and agree on the conflict, (3) ask for and/or give alternative resolutions, and (4) make an agreement for change.

step 1. **Plan a BCF Statement That Maintains Ownership of the Problem.** Planning is the beginning management function and starting point of initiating a conflict resolution. Let's begin by stating what "maintains ownership of the problem" means. Assume you don't smoke and someone who is smoking visits you. Is it you or the smoker who has a problem? The smoke bothers you, not the smoker. It's your problem. Open the confrontation with a request for the respondent to help you solve your problem. This approach reduces defensiveness and establishes an atmosphere of problem-solving that will maintain the relationship.

The **BCF model** *describes a conflict in terms of behavior, consequences, and feelings.* When you do B (behavior), C (consequences) happens, and I feel F (feelings). An example of a BCF statement is: "When you smoke in my room (behavior), I have trouble breathing and become nauseous (consequence), and I feel uncomfortable and irritated (feeling)." You can vary the sequence and start with a feeling or consequence to fit the situation and to provide variety. For example, "I fear (feeling) that the advertisment is not going to work (behavior), and that we will lose money (consequences)."

BCF model
Describes a conflict in terms of behavior, consequences, and feelings.

When developing your opening BCF statement, as shown in the preceding examples, be descriptive, not evaluative. Keep the opening statement short. The longer the statement, the longer it will take to resolve the conflict. People get defensive when kept waiting for their turn to talk. Avoid trying to determine who is to blame for something or who is right and wrong. Both parties are usually partly to blame or partly correct. Fixing blame or correctness only gets people defensive, which is counterproductive to conflict resolution. Timing is also important. If others are busy, see them later to discuss the conflict. In addition, don't confront a person on several unrelated issues at once.

After planning your BCF statement, you should practice saying it before confronting the other party.[25] In addition to planning and practice, think of some possible alternatives you can offer to resolve the conflict. However, be sure your ideas show high concern for others rather than just for yourself. Try to put yourself in the other person's position. If you were the other person, would you like the ideas presented by the confronter?

step 2.

Present Your BCF Statement and Agree on the Conflict. After making your short planned BCF statement, let the other party respond. If the other party does not understand or avoids acknowledgment of the problem, persist. You cannot resolve a conflict if the other party will not even acknowledge its existence. Repeat your planned statement several times by explaining it in different terms until you get an acknowledgment or realize that it's hopeless. But don't give up too easily.

step 3.

Ask For, and/or Give, Alternative Conflict Resolutions. Begin by asking the other party what can be done to resolve the conflict. If you agree, great; if not offer your resolution. However, remember that you are collaborating not simply trying to change others. When the other party acknowledges the problem, but is not responsive to resolving it, appeal to common goals. Make the other party realize the benefits to him or her and the organization as well.

Work Application

7. Use the BCF model to describe a conflict you face or have faced.

step 4.

Make an Agreement for Change. Try to come to an agreement on specific action you will both take to resolve the conflict. Clearly state, or better yet for complex change, write down the specific behavior changes necessary by all parties to resolve the conflict. Again, remember that you are collaborating, not forcing.

Skill-Building Exercise 14–2 gives you the opportunity to develop your skill at initiating a conflict resolution.

Responding to Conflict Resolution

As the responder, an initiator has confronted you. Here's how to handle the role of responder to a conflict. Most initiators do not follow the model. Therefore, the responder must take responsibility for successful conflict resolution by following the conflict resolution model steps: (1) Listen to and paraphrase the conflict using the BCF model. (2) Agree with some aspect of the complaint. (3) Ask for, and/or give, alternative conflict resolutions. (4) Make an agreement for change. This is Model 14–2.

step 1.

Listen to and Paraphrase the Conflict Using the BCF Model. If someone confronts you when you don't have time to talk, explain your situation and set an appointment to discuss it. When discussing a conflict, listen. Do not get defensive and justify your actions as your first response. Even when you disagree, listen to the other party's position. Avoid discussing and agreeing on who is to blame or who is correct.

Let people blow off some steam as long as they don't verbally attack you. If they do, calmly tell them you are willing to discuss a genuine problem, but you will not tolerate personal attacks or scapegoating. When a person is too emotional, it may be better to postpone the discussion until everyone is calm. Deal with emotions following the communication guidelines in Chapter 10.

Using the BCF Model. The untrained initiator often makes general statements and simply blames the responder. To resolve the conflict, you must transform the general and personal accusations into specific descriptions of behavior. To do this, use the BCF model:

1. Ask for a specific behavioral example (when I do B). "Can you give me a specific example of what I do that causes the conflict/problem?" Keep at it until you clearly understand the specific behavior.
2. Have the initiator describe the consequences of the behavior (C happens). "When I do X, what are the results?" Keep at it until you understand the consequences of your behavior.
3. Ask the person how he or she feels, if feelings were not expressed (you feel F). Paraphrase the model back to the initiator. "When I get back from break late (B), you have to wait on my customer (C), and you get upset (F). Is that your complaint?" If the complainer agrees to the problem, go to step 2. If not, keep paraphrasing until you get it. Paraphrasing does not mean you agree with the initiator's complaint. It simply shows your true understanding of the complaint.

step 2.

Agree with Some Aspect of the Complaint. This is important but difficult, especially when you do not agree with the complaint. It is tempting to change from the collaborative style to the avoiding, forcing, accommodating, or compromising style. But don't. State your position in an assertive and cooperative way. Find a point you can agree on. Even in the most exaggerated complaints, there is generally a grain of truth. If there is nothing you agree with, at least agree on the person's perception. For example, "I agree that my behavior is upsetting to you."

Again, you are not agreeing with the total complaint, nor are you conceding your position. Being agreeable will lead to problem-solving. Generally, people who complain have a long list of arguments to support their positions. They will keep them coming until you agree with something. The longer it takes to agree on something, the broader the base of the argument will be and the longer it will take to resolve it.

step 3.

Ask For, and/or Give, Alternative Conflict Resolutions. In asking for solutions, you show your regard for the initiator and shift the focus away from the negative past to the positive future. Together you try to find a a win-win solution that is satisfactory to all parties. Unless absolutely necessary, don't change conflict management styles to compromise or accommodate, and you should not force or avoid.

step 4.

Make an Agreement for Change. Come to an agreement on a resolution and develop a plan stating each party's responsibility for change. If possible, have each person paraphrase what he or she agrees to do in the future; for complex conflicts, write down the changes.

Mediating Conflict Resolution

mediator
A neutral third party who helps resolve a conflict.

Frequently, conflicting parties cannot resolve their dispute alone. In these cases, a mediator should be used. A **mediator** *is a neutral third party who helps resolve a conflict.* In nonunionized organizations, managers are commonly the mediators. But some organizations have trained and designated employees as mediators. In unionized organizations, the mediator is usually a professonal from outside the organization. However, a conflict resolution should be sought internally first.

Before bringing the conflicting parties together, the mediator should decide whether to start with a joint meeting or conduct individual meetings. If one employee comes to complain, but has not confronted the other party, or if there is a serious discrepancy in employee perceptions, meet one-on-one with each party before bringing them together. On the other hand, when both parties have a similar awareness of the problem and motivation to solve it, you can begin with a joint meeting when all parties are calm. The manager should be a mediator, not a judge. Get the employees to resolve the conflict, if possible. Remain impartial, unless one party is violating company policies. Don't belittle the parties in conflict. Don't make comments such as, "I'm disappointed in you two" or "you're acting like babies."

When bringing conflicting parties together, follow the mediating conflict model steps: (1) Have each party state his or her complaint using the BCF model. (2) Agree on the conflict problem(s). (3) Develop alternative conflict resolutions. (4) Make an agreement for change. (5) Follow up to make sure the conflict is resolved. This is Model 14–3.

step 1.

Have Each Party State His or Her Complaint Using the BCF Model. Teach the employees the BCF model and have them state their complaints using it. It is helpful to have them write out their complaints first.

step 2.

Agree on the Problem(s). Do not try to place the blame on any one party. If either party blames the other, make a statement such as, "We are here to resolve the conflict; placing blame is not productive." Focus on how the conflict is affecting their work. Discuss the issues by addressing specific behavior, not personalities. If a person says, "We cannot work together because of a personality conflict," ask him or her to state the specific behavior in question. The discussion should make the parties aware of their behavior and its consequences. The mediator may ask questions or make statements to clarify what is being said. The mediator should develop one problem statement that is agreeable to all parties, if possible. If not, take each party's statement separately. But clarify the conflict before working to develop a resolution.

Develop Alternative Conflict Resolutions. Have all parties suggest possible solutions to the problem(s). Focus on the changes in behavior needed to eliminate the negative consequences and feelings. Combining ideas is often helpful. The mediator may suggest alternatives, but as a neutral party should collaborate rather than try to force the parties to accept them. Be sure the resolution creates a win-win situation for all parties including the organization.

step 4.

Make an Agreement for Change. Come to a solution satisfactory to all parties. Have each party state what he or she will or will not do in the future. The mediator should paraphrase the statements of all parties to ensure all are in agreement and to get a commitment to the changed behavior. "To summarize, Saul, you agree to do X, and Whitney, you are going to do X. Do you both agree to this action?"

step 5.

Follow Up to Make Sure the Conflict Is Resolved. Two follow-up methods include (1) watching parties interact over a period of time to make sure the conflict is resolved, and (2) setting a follow-up meeting to sit down and discuss if the conflict has been resolved.

If the conflict has not been resolved, an arbitrator may be used. *An* **arbitrator** *is a neutral third party who makes a binding decision to resolve a conflict*. The arbitrator is like a judge and his or her decision must be followed. However, the use of arbitration should be kept to a minimum because it is not a collaborative style. Arbitrators commonly use a negotiating style in which each party wins some and loses some. Mediation and then arbitration tend to be used in management labor negotiations when collective bargaining breaks down and the contract deadline is near.

arbitrator
A neutral third party who makes a binding decision to resolve a conflict.

Dealing with power, politics, and conflict can be very stressful. Therefore, in the next section you will study the causes and consequences of stress and how to manage it.

STRESS

People react to external environmental stimuli internally. **Stress** *is the body's reaction to environmental demands made on it*. Body reactions can be emotional and/or physical reactions to environmental activities and events. Dealing with power, politics, and conflict can be stressful. Organizations, including EDS, offer stress management programs to better enable employees to handle stress.

stress
The body's reaction to environmental demands made on it.

Stress Can Be Functional or Dysfunctional

Stress is functional when it helps improve performance by challenging and motivating people to meet objectives. People perform best under some pressure. When deadlines are approaching, adrenaline flows and people rise to the occasion with top-level performance. In order to meet deadlines, managers often have to apply some pressure to themselves and their employees. However, too much stress is dysfunctional because it is harmful to the individual and to the organization. Situations in which too much stress exists are known as stressors. **Stressors** *are situations in which people feel overwhelmed by anxiety, tension, and pressure*. On the other hand, if the situation is stress-free, people usually perform at lower levels.

stressors
Situations in which people feel overwhelmed by anxiety, tension, and pressure.

Stress is an individual matter. In the same situation one person may be very comfortable and stress-free while another feels it is a stressor situation. In other words, abilities to handle pressure vary.

Causes of Stress

There are five common job stressors: personality type, organizational culture, management behavior, work performed, and human relations. The combination of these factors play an important role in determining *job satisfaction*. Generally, the lower the job satisfaction, the higher the stress. Complete Self-Assessment Exercise 14–2 to determine your personality type as it relates to stress.

SELF-ASSESSMENT EXERCISE 14–2

Stress Personality Type

Identify how frequently each item applies to you at work or school. Place the number 1–5 on the line before each statement.

(5) usually (4) often (3) occasionally (2) seldom (1) rarely

___ 1. I enjoy competition and I work/play to win.
___ 2. I skip meals or eat fast when there is a lot of work to do.
___ 3. I'm in a hurry.
___ 4. I do more than one thing at a time.
___ 5. I'm aggravated and upset.
___ 6. I get irritated or anxious when I have to wait.
___ 7. I measure progress in terms of time and performance.
___ 8. I push myself to work to the point of getting tired.
___ 9. I work on days off.
___ 10. I set short deadlines for myself.
___ 11. I'm not satisfied with my accomplishments for very long.
___ 12. I try to outperform others.
___ 13. I get upset when my schedule has to be changed.
___ 14. I consistently try to get more done in less time.
___ 15. I take on more work when I already have plenty to do.
___ 16. I enjoy work/school more than other activities.
___ 17. I talk and walk fast.
___ 18. I set high standards for myself and work hard to meet them.
___ 19. I'm considered a hard worker by others.
___ 20. I work at a fast pace.
___ Total. Add up the numbers (1–5) you have for all 20 items. Your score will range from 20 to 100. Place an X on the continuum that represents your score.

Type A 100—90—80—70—**60**—50—40—30—20 Type B

The higher your score the more characteristic you are of the Type A stress personality. The lower your score, the more characteristic you are of the Type B stress personality. An explanation of these two stress personality types appears in this section.

Personality Types. The degree to which stressors affect us is due, in part, to our personality type. Since our body reacts to external stimuli internally, the things we do can cause us stress. The *Type A personality* is characterized as fast-moving, hard-driving, time-conscious, competitive, impatient, and preoccupied with work. The Type B personality is the opposite of Type A. The 20 statements of Self-Assessment Exercise 14–2 relate to the personality styles. The number 5 (usually) represents Type A behavior, and the number 1 (rarely) represents Type B behavior. People with Type A personalities have more cardiovascular disorders than people with Type B personalities.[26] If you have a high score, Type A personality, you could end up with some of the problems associated with stress.

Organizational Culture. The amount of cooperation, motivation, and morale affects stress levels. The more positive the organizational culture, the less stress there is. Organizations that push employees to high levels of performance create a stressful situation. A change from a group to a team culture without team training can be stressful.

Management Behavior. The better managers supervise their employees, the less stress there is. Calm, participative management styles are less stressful. Workers with bad bosses are five time as likely to report stress-related lost sleep, headaches, and upset stomachs.[27]

Work Performed. Some types of work are more stressful than others. But part of the stress comes from the perception of the enjoyment of the work itself. People who have jobs in which they enjoy the work itself derive satisfaction and handle stress better than those who do not. In some cases, changing to a job with enjoyable work is a wise move that can lower or rid one of stressors.

Human Relations. When people do not get along, conflict exists which can be very stressful. Human relations is a very important factor in job satisfaction. People who don't really like the work performed but enjoy the people they work with can have job satisfaction. However, people who don't like the work or the people face a stressful situation, and they usually have high absenteeism.

EDS has a positive culture and the team structure creates less management behavior through more employee involvement. Employees perform interesting work and get to select which teams to work on, which in turn creates better human relations and overall job satisfaction.

Consequences of Stress

Two out of three workers consider stress to be their primary health concern and deem work-related stress to be a direct cause of their health-related problems.

Current estimates indicate that job stress costs employers more than $200 billion per year in absenteeism, tardiness, lower productivity, high turnover, workers' compensation, and rising health care premiums.[28] Employees under stress do not work up to potential, have decreasing performance, and display poor attitudes.[29] Increased stress results in missed deadlines and decreased customer service.[30]

Signs of Stress. A few of the mild signs of stress include an increased breathing rate and amount of perspiration. When stress continues for a period of time, it tends to lead to disillusionment, irritableness, headaches and other body tension, the feeling of exhaustion, and stomach problems. Headaches cost employers an estimated $50 billion a year in medical expenses and absenteeism.[31] When you continually feel pressured and fear that you will not meet deadlines, you are experiencing stress. People watch TV/movies, drink, take drugs, eat, or sleep more than usual to escape stress.

Burnout. Stress that is constant, chronic, and severe can lead to burnout over a period of time. *Burnout* is the constant lack of interest and motivation to perform one's job due to stress. People sometimes experience temporary burnout during busy periods, as is the case with students studying for exams and retailers trying to cope with Christmas. However, when things slow down again, the interest and motivation come back. When the interest and motivation do not return, permanent burnout occurs.

Stress Management

Stress management is the process of eliminating or reducing stress. Managers need to understand their job stressors, avoid stressful events when possible, plan how to handle stressful situations (such as initiating conflict resolution using the model), and use stress management techniques.[32] You can better control stress by following a three-stage stress management plan: (1) identify stressors, (2) determine their causes and consequences, and (3) plan to eliminate or decrease the stress. There are six stress management techniques you can use: time management, relaxation, nutrition, exercise, positive thinking, and support network.

Spending time doing enjoyable activities with family and friends is an excellent stress-management technique.

Time Management. Generally, people with good time management skills experience less job stress. Refer back to Chapter 6 for details on time management.

Relaxation. Relaxation is an excellent stress management technique.[33] Get enough rest and sleep; have some fun and laugh. If you are a Type A personality, slow down and enjoy yourself. Participate in activities that are pleasurable and relaxing.[34] Have some enjoyable off-the-job interests. People without a balanced career and personal life commonly suffer burnout.[35] Some of the things you can do to relax include socializing with friends, prayer, meditation, music, reading, TV, movies, hobbies, and so forth.

Relaxation Exercises. When you feel stress, you can perform some simple relaxation exercises. One of the most popular and simplest is deep breathing because it relaxes the entire body. If you feel tension in one muscle, you may do a specific relaxation exercise; or you may relax your entire body going from head to toe, or vice versa. Figure 14–5 lists relaxation exercises that you can do al-

Muscles Relaxed	**Exercise** (Tighten muscles as much as you can without straining, and perform as many tightening-relaxing repetitions as needed to feel relaxed without straining.)
All	Take a deep breath, hold it for around 5 seconds, then let it out slowly. See the deep breathing discussion in the text for more specific details. Deep breathing may be performed during and/or between other relaxation exercises.
Forehead	Wrinkle your forehead by trying to make your eyebrows touch your hairline for 5 seconds. Relax.
Eyes, nose	Close your eyes tightly for 5 seconds. Relax.
Lips, cheeks, jaw	Draw the corners of your mouth back tightly (grimace) for 5 seconds. Relax.
Neck	Drop your chin to your chest, then slowly rotate your head without tilting it back. Relax.
Shoulders	Lift your shoulders up to your ears and tighten for 5 seconds. Relax.
Upper arms	Bend your elbows and tighten your upper arm muscles for 5 seconds. Relax.
Forearms	Extend your arms out against an invisible wall and push forward with your hands for 5 seconds. Relax.
Hands	Extend your arms in front of you; clench your fists tightly for 5 seconds. Relax.
Back	Lie on your back on the floor or bed and arch your back up off the floor, while keeping your shoulders and buttocks on the floor, and tighten for 5 seconds. Relax.
Stomach	Suck in and tighten your stomach muscles for 5 seconds. Relax. Repeating this exercise several times throughout the day can help reduce the size of your waistline.
Hips, buttocks	Tighten buttocks for 5 seconds. Relax.
Thighs	Press your thighs together and tighten them for 5 seconds. Relax.
Feet, ankles	Flex your feet with toes pointing up as far up as you can and tighten for 5 seconds; then point your toes down and tighten for 5 seconds. Relax.
Toes	Curl your toes under and tighten for 5 seconds then wiggle them. Relax.

Figure 14–5
Relaxation Exercises

most anywhere. Deep breathing can be done during and/or between the other exercises; how to breathe deeply is explained in more detail next.

Deep Breathing. You simply take a slow deep breath, preferably through your nose, hold it for a few seconds (you may count to five), then let it out slowly, preferably through lightly closed lips. To breathe deeply you must inhale by expanding the stomach, not the chest. Breathe in without lifting your shoulders and/or expanding your chest. Think of your stomach as a balloon and slowly fill it then empty it. As you inhale, think and visualize breathing in healing energy that makes you feel better, more energetic, less pain, and so on that results from stress. As you exhale think and visualize breathing out the tension, pain, illness, and so on that stress you. This same positive thinking technique can also be used during the other relaxation exercises.

Energy. Stress depletes your energy. Even feeling pressured and worrying about a stressor to come depletes your energy without physically doing anything. Mental stress can be more exhausting than physical stress. Remember that air (breathing), relaxation (especially sleep), and nutrition (food—our next topic) are major sources of the energy you need to resist stress. Contrary to the belief of many, proper exercise (our topic after nutrition) also increases your energy level rather than depleting it.

Nutrition. Good health is essential to everyone's performance, and nutrition is a major factor in health. Underlying stress can lead to overeating and compulsive dieting,[36] and being overweight is stressful. When you eat, take your time and relax because rushing is stressful and can cause stomach upset. Also, when people eat slower they tend to eat less.

Breakfast is considered the most important meal of the day. Getting up and going to work without eating until lunch is stressful. A good breakfast increases your ability to resist stress, and a good breakfast may include eggs. Current empirical medical researchers report that eggs do not negatively increase cholesterol.[37]

Watch your intake of junk foods because they are stressful to your body. Consume fat (fried meat and vegetables including french fries and chips), sugar (pastry, candy, fruit drinks, soda—many cans of soda contain 10 teaspoons), caffeine (coffee, tea, soda), and salt (combined with the others and put on food from a shaker) in moderation. Eat more natural foods such as fruits and vegetables and drink their juice. Realize that poor nutrition and the use of overeating, smoking, alcohol, and drugs to reduce stress often create other stressful problems over a period of time.

Exercise. Physical exercise is an excellent way to improve health while releasing stress. Aerobic exercise, in which you increase the heart rate and maintain it for 20 to 30 minutes three or more days per week, is generally considered the best type of exercise. Exercises such as fast walking or jogging, biking, swimming, and aerobic dance/exercise fall into this category. Other exercises that require you to increase your heart rate, but not maintain a constant rate for 20 or more minutes, include sports like racketball, tennis, and basketball. These are not aerobic, because of the stop and go action, but they are also very beneficial.

Before starting an exercise program, check with a doctor to make sure you are able to do so safely. Always remember that the objective is to relax and reduce stress. The no pain–no gain mentality applies to competitive athletes, not to stress management. Besides, if you don't enjoy exercising it may be because you are pushing yourself too hard, and if you do, you will most likely quit anyway.

Work Application

8. Follow the stress management plan steps: (1) identify your major stressors, (2) determine their causes and consequences, and (3) plan to eliminate or decrease the stress. Be sure to identify each step and the stress management techniques you will use.
9. At which of the six time management techniques are you best and worst? What can you do to improve your stress management skills?

Positive Thinking. People with an optimistic attitude generally have less stress than pessimists. Remember the self-fulfilling prophecy (Chapter 10). Once you start having doubts about your ability to do what you have to do, you become stressed. Make statements to yourself in the affirmative, such as "This is easy," or "I will do it." The statements to repeat while doing deep breathing are positive. But be realistic. Positive thinking will not guarantee that you will not get a stress headache, but many people have talked themselves into having headaches or other illnesses.

Don't Procrastinate or Be a Perfectionist. Procrastinating gives you more time to think about what you have to do and to get stressed before you start. You do a good quality job, but perfectionism stresses you as you perform rework.

Support Network. Talking to others in a support network can help reduce stress.[38] Develop a network of family and friends you can go to for help with your problems. But don't continually lean on others to help you or use stress to get attention. Political reciprocity and coalitions can be used to help you and your network to reduce each others' stress.

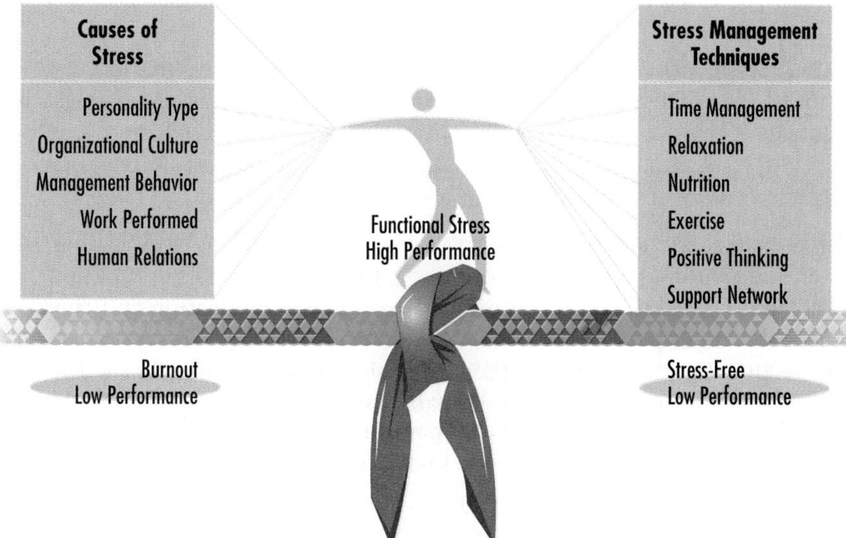

Figure 14–6
The Stress Tug-of-War

The Stress Tug-of-War

8. Explain the stress tug-of-war analogy.

Think of stress as a tug-of-war with you in the center, as illustrated in Figure 14–6. On your left are causes of stress (ropes) trying to pull you to the left to burnout. On your right are stress management techniques (ropes) you pull to keep you in the center. Recall that when stress is too high or too low, performance is lowered; performance is maximized with moderate stress. If the stress becomes too powerful it will pull you off center, to the left, and you lose as you suffer burnout. The stress tug-of-war is an ongoing game. On easy days you move to the right, and on overly tough days you move to the left. Your main objective is to stay in the center and avoid burnout. Generally, as a manager, if you don't keep working on stress management, you will experience stressors that will lower your performance levels.

Stress management does not require the use of all six techniques. Use the ones that work best for you. If you use stress management and experience permanent burnout, you should seriously consider getting out of the situation. Ask yourself two questions: "Is my long-term health important?" and "Is this situation worth hurting my health for?" If you answer yes and no, a change of situations/jobs is advisable. Drop the ropes and walk away to a new tug-of-war.

APPLYING THE CONCEPT

AC 14–4 Stress Management Techniques

Identify each statement by the technique being used:

a. time management c. nutrition e. positive thinking
b. relaxation d. exercise f. support network

____ **16.** "I've been repeating statements to myself to be more optimistic."

____ **17.** "I've set up a schedule for myself."

____ **18.** "I've been getting up earlier and eating breakfast."

____ **19.** "I've been talking to my partner about my problems."

____ **20.** "I've been praying."

Current Management Issues

Global. As the business environment continues to become more *global*, the need for conflict resolution, including negotiation skills, increases in importance.[39] The use of power and politics does vary from country to country. However, power and politics are a reality of all organizations. And interacting with others all over the world can be stressful.

Diversity. People have a *diversity* of styles in acquiring and dealing with power and politics. Conflict is more likely in a diverse group than a homogeneous one. However, when dealing with conflict, stop reacting and trying to change the other person. Sort out the situation, identify personal needs, and shift to a new way of treating others to solve problems.[40] In other words, you should not simply use the forcing style and try to make people become like you, but rather use a collaborating style. When focusing on diversity by gender, it has been reported that few women know how to play the "corporate game" (power and politics).[41] Women tend to be more collaborative and less forcing when resolving conflicts than men. However, job stress seems to be similar for men and women.[42] When women work full time and have families they usually do more of the household tasks and may have more total stress than men.

Ethics. *Ethics* becomes an important issue with power and politics. Power and politics can be used ethically.[43] Power and political behavior are ethical when they create a win-win situation so that all stakeholders and the organization benefit. However, they are unethical when they create a win-lose situation so that an individual(s) benefits at the expense of others and/or the organization. Ethics, diversity, and conflict resolution skills can be developed.[44]

TQM, Participative Management, and Teams. In the quest to increase quality (*TQM*) based on *participative management, teams* have become commonplace in U.S. companies.[45] In teams, power is left to the group and becomes an important issue. Ideally, power should change based on what needs to be done and team members' skills. However, if members struggle for power, conflict can result as members are not satisfied with their status in the team. Conflict power struggles can be very stressful to the team, and recall that dysfunctional stress decreases performance. Managing conflict is necessary for successful TQM[46] and teams.[47] Organizations using teams, including Corning and EDS, are training team members to resolve conflict.[48] Therefore, the topics of this chapter, especially conflict resolution, become more important as organizations increase their use of teams.

Productivity. In the quest to increase *productivity*, many organizations have downsized and re-engineered. With both approaches, employees are expected to do more with less, which results in increased stress for workers.[49] Through the planning and implementation process of downsizing and re-engineering, political power struggles are common. Conflict is heightened and stress levels increase dramatically.

Small Business. In general, power and politics is more of an issue in large businesses. In *small businesses*, it is more common for the owner to maintain control of the power. However, as the owner appoints other managers and eventually steps down, the process of replacement often results in political power struggles. Conflict and stress are common to all businesses.

CHAPTER SUMMARY AND GLOSSARY

The chapter summary is organized to answer the nine learning objectives for Chapter 14.

1. Define *power* and the difference between position and personal power.

Power is the ability to influence others' behavior. Position power is derived from top management and delegated down the chain of command, while personal power is derived from the followers based on the individual's behavior.

2. Explain the difference among reward, legitimate, and referent power.

The difference is based on how the person with power influences others. Reward power is based on the user's ability to influence others with something of value to them. Legitimate power is based on the user's position power given by the organization. Employees feel that they should be influenced. Referent power is based on the user's personal power relationship with others.

3. Discuss how power and politics are related.

Power is the ability to influence the behavior of others. Politics is the process of gaining and using power. Therefore, political skills are a part of power.

4. Describe how money and power have a similar use.

Money and power have a similar use because they are mediums of exchange. In our economy, money is the medium of exchange. In an organization, politics is the medium of exchange.

5. Explain what networking, reciprocity, and coalition have in common.

Networking, reciprocity, and coalitions are all political behaviors. Networking is the process of developing relationships for the purpose of socializing and politicking. Reciprocity involves creating obligations and developing alliances and using them to accomplish objectives. Coalitions are a network of alliances that will help the person achieve an objective.

6. List and define the five conflict management styles.

(1) The *avoiding conflict style* user attempts to passively ignore the conflict rather than resolve it. (2) The *accommodating conflict style* user attempts to resolve the conflict by passively giving in to the other party. (3) The *forcing conflict style* user attempts to resolve the conflict by using aggressive behavior to get his or her own way. (4) The *negotiating conflict style* user attempts to resolve the conflict through assertive give-and-take concessions. (5) The *collaborating conflict style* user assertively attempts to resolve the conflict with the best solution agreeable to all parties.

7. List the steps in the initiating conflict resolution model.

The steps in the initiating conflict resolution model are: (1) plan a BCF statement that maintains ownership of the problem, (2) present your BCF statement and agree on the conflict, (3) ask for, and/or give, alternative conflict resolutions, and (4) make an agreement for change.

8. Explain the stress tug-of-war analogy.

Under the stress tug-of-war, you are in the center where stress is functional and performance is high. On your left are the causes of stress trying to pull you off center. On your right are the stress management techniques you use to keep you in the center. If the causes of stress pull you off center, you burn out and performance decreases. If there is an absence of stress, performance is also decreased.

9. Define the following key terms (in order of appearance in the chapter):

Select one or more methods: (1) fill in the missing key terms from memory, (2) match the key terms from the end of the review with their definitions below, or (3) copy the key terms in order from the list at the beginning of the chapter.

______ is the ability to influence others' behavior.

______ is the process of gaining and using power.

______ is the process of developing relationships for the purpose of socializing and politicking.

______ involves creating obligations and developing alliances and using them to accomplish objectives.

A ______ is a network of alliances that will help the person achieve an objective.

A ______ exists whenever people are in disagreement and opposition.

__________ exists when disagreement and opposition support the achievement of organizational objectives.

The __________ steps are: (1) plan a BCF statement that maintains ownership of the problem, (2) present your BCF statement and agree on the conflict, (3) ask for, and/or give, alternative conflict resolutions, and (4) make an agreement for change.

The ______ describes a conflict in terms of behavior, consequences, and feelings.

A ______ is a neutral third party who helps resolve a conflict.

An ______ is a neutral third party who makes a binding decision to resolve a conflict.

______ is the body's reaction to environmental demands placed on it.

______ are situations in which people feel overwhelmed by anxiety, tension, and pressure.

KEY TERMS

arbitrator
BCF model
coalition
conflict
functional conflict
initiating conflict resolution model
mediator
networking
politics
power
reciprocity
stress
stressors

REVIEW AND DISCUSSION QUESTIONS

1. What are the seven bases of power?
2. Can management order the end of power and politics in the organization? If yes, should they?
3. Why should you learn the organizational culture and identify power players where you work?
4. How do you know when you are in conflict?
5. What is the difference between functional and dysfunctional conflict and how does each affect performance?
6. What is the primary reason for your conflicts?
7. What is meant by "maintain ownership of the problem"?
8. How is the BCF model used?
9. What is the difference between a mediator and an arbitrator?
10. What are the characteristics of a Type A personality?
11. What are the six stress management techniques?

CASE

Ohio Mutual Insurance Company

Ohio Mutual is a national insurance company. One of its locations is in Akron, Ohio.[50] At this facility, Debbie Townson is manager of the claims department. She is going to be promoted in one month. Debbie has been asked to select her replacement as manager of the claims department. She has narrowed down her selection to two finalists: Ted Shea and Libby Lee. Ted and Libby know they are competing for the promotion because Debbie told them that she will select one of them as the new manager on the day before she leaves for her new job. Their years of experience and quality and quantity of work are about the same. Following is some of the political behavior each has been using to help get the promotion.

Ted is good at sports and has been playing golf and tennis with some of the upper-level managers for over a year now. In the department, especially with

Debbie, Ted drops names as he refers to conversations with managers all the time. When Ted does something for someone, he or she can expect to do a favor in return. Ted really wants this promotion, but he fears that with more women and minorities being promoted to management positions, Libby will get the job just because she is a woman and minority. To increase his chances of getting the job, Ted occasionally reminds Debbie of past errors that Libby has made, and he makes negative remarks to everyone about her behind her back.

Libby has been going to night classes and company training programs in management to prepare herself for the promotion. Knowing that Debbie was an officer in a local chapter of a national insurance businesswomen's organization, Libby joined the club six months ago and now serves on a committee. At work, Libby talks regularly to Debbie about the women's organization. Libby makes an effort to know what is going on throughout the organization. She gets along well with everyone. Libby is very upbeat and goes out of her way to be nice to people and to compliment them.

Ted and Libby used to cooperate until they heard that they were competing for Debbie's management job. A few of Libby's friends have told her that Ted is talking negatively about her behind her back. One of Libby's friends has suggested that she talk about Ted to get even; another suggested talking to Ted and telling him to stop it; and a third suggested that Libby tell Debbie what he is doing. Libby is not sure what to do. Libby is too polite to talk negatively about Ted, and she really does not want to be a tattletale. In Libby's opinion, her only real option is to confront Ted about his behavior. However, her Asian cultural background and family upbringing have taught her to be cooperative. Just the thought of confronting anyone, especially Ted, makes her feel anxiety. Libby is stressed but has decided to wait and see if things get better.

Debbie is aware of the situation because one of her employees told her about Ted, and she has observed both of them being uncooperative. At this point, Debbie is wondering if she should do anything. And if she does do something what she should do or how to handle the situation. After all, there are only two more weeks before she is promoted and leaves the department.

Select the best alternative to the following questions. Be sure you are able to explain your answers.

___ 1. Debbie has ___ power.

a. position b. personal

___ 2. To be promoted, Ted has worked to develop a ___ power base. Refer to the opening statement about Ted.

a. coercive
b. connection
c. reward
d. legitimate
e. referent
f. information
g. expert

___ 3. To be promoted, Libby has worked to develop a ___ power base. Refer to the opening statement about Libby.

a. coercive
b. connection
c. reward
d. legitimate
e. referent
f. information
g. expert

___ 4. The case states that Ted uses ___ political behavior, but it does not say Libby does.

a. networking b. reciprocity c. coalitions

___ 5. Debbie and Libby belong to the insurance professional association, which is ___ political behavior.

a. networking b. reciprocity c. coalitions

___ 6. ___ has conducted the most effective political behavior to identify "the power players" to get this promotion.

a. Ted b. Libby

___ 7. In Libby's conflict with Ted, she is using the ___ conflict management style.

a. avoiding
b. accommodating
c. forcing
d. negotiating
e. collaborating

___ 8. In the conflict between Ted and Libby, ___ should maintain ownership of the problem.

a. Ted b. Libby

___ 9. Debbie is in the position to be the ___ of the conflict between Ted and Libby.

a. initiator b. responder c. mediator

___ 10. Libby's primary cause of stress is

a. personality type
b. organizational culture

c. management behavior
d. work performed
e. human relations

11. What action, if any, should Libby take? What would you do if you were in her situation?

12. What do you think of Ted's talking about Libby to discredit her? Is this ethical behavior?

13. What action, if any, should Debbie take to resolve the conflict?

14. Should Libby's being an Asian woman affect the promotion decision? Should Ted's recent behavior affect the decision? In Debbie's situation, who would you select for your job?

15. Could Debbie have handled this promotion situation more effectively? In Debbie's situation, how would you have handled selecting your replacement?

SKILL-BUILDING EXERCISE 14–1

Car Dealer Negotiation[51]

Preparing for Skill-Building Exercise 14–1

You should have read and understand the seven power bases.

____

____

____

Doing Skill-Building Exercise 14–1 in Class

Objective
To develop your understanding of power and to build negotiation skills.

Experience
You will be the buyer or seller of a used car.

Procedure 1 (1–2 minutes)
Break up into groups of two and sit facing each other so that you cannot read each other's confidential sheet. Each group should be as far away from other groups as possible so that they cannot overhear each others' conversations. If there is an odd number of students in the class, one student will be an observer or work with the instructor. Decide who will be the buyer and who will be the seller of the used car.

Procedure 2 (1–2 minutes)
The instructor goes to each group and gives the buyer and seller their confidential sheets, which do not appear in this textbook.

Procedure 3 (5–6 minutes)
Buyers and sellers read their confidential sheets and jot down some plans (what will be your basic approach, what will you say) for the lunch meeting.

Procedure 4 (3–7 minutes)
Negotiate the sale of the car. Try not to overhear your classmates' conversations. You do not have to buy or sell the car. After you make the sale, or agree not to sell, read your partner's confidential sheet and discuss the exerience.

Integration (5–7 minutes)
Answer the following questions:

1. Did you set a specific objective price to pay or accept? Should you have one? ___
   a. yes b. no
2. Did you get ___ what you wanted to pay/accept for the car?
   a. more than b. less than c. exactly
3. The appropriate type of plan for this situation was a ___?
   a. general single-use project plan.
   b. detailed standing-policy plan
4. The most relevant power base to help you successfully negotiate this car deal was ___?
   a. coercive e. referent
   b. connection f. information
   c. reward g. expert
   d. legitimate

5. Was this a conflict situation?

   a. yes b. no

6. Did this exercise create some stress (faster heart rate, perspiration; did you feel anxiety, tension, or pressure)?

   a. yes b. no

7. When negotiating, it is better to appear to be dealing with ___ power. In other words, should you try to portray that you have other options and don't really need to make a deal with this person. Or, should you appear to be in need of a deal.

   a. strong b. weak

8. Can having the power to intimidate others be helpful in negotiations?

   a. yes b. no

9. When negotiating, it is a good practice to ask for more than you expect to pay/receive.

   a. yes b. no

10. When negotiating, is it better to be the one to ___ the initial offer?

   a. give b. receive

Conclusion
The instructor leads a class discussion or simply gives the answers to the integration questions and makes concluding remarks.

Application (2–4 minutes)
What did I learn from this experience? How will I use this knowledge in the future?

____

____

____

Sharing
Volunteers give their answers to the application section.

Behavior Model Video 14–1, Initiating Conflict Resolution, shows Alex initiating a conflict resolution over an advertising account with coworker Catherine. Alex follows the steps in Model 14–1 on pages 469–470. This video serves as a behavior model which can be used prior to conducting Skill-Building Exercise 14–2.

SKILL-BUILDING EXERCISE 14–2

Initiating Conflict Resolution[52]

Preparing for Skill-Building Exercise 14–2

During class you will be given the opportunity to role-play a conflict you are facing, or have faced, in order to develop your conflict skills. Students and workers have reported that this exercise helped prepare them for a successful initiation of a conflict resolution with roommates and coworkers. Fill in the following information:

Other party(s) (You may use fictitious names) ____________

Describe the conflict situation:

____

____

____

List pertinent information about the other party (i.e., relationship to you, knowledge of the situation, age, background, etc.):

____

____

____

Identify the other party's possible reaction to your confrontation. (How receptive will he or she be to collaborating? What might he or she say or do during the discussion to resist change?)

____

____

____

How will you overcome this resistance to change?

____

____

____

Following the initiating conflict resolution model steps, write out your planned opening BCF statement that maintains ownership of the problem.

____

____

____

Doing Skill-Building Exercise 14–2 in Class

Objective
To experience and develop skills in resolving a conflict.

Preparation
You should have completed the conflict information questions in the preparation for this exercise.

Experience
You will initiate, respond to, and observe a conflict role-play, and then evaluate the effectiveness of its resolution.

Video (4½ minutes)
Behavior Model Video 14–1, Initiating Conflict Resolution, may be shown

Procedure 1 (2–3 minutes)
Break into as many groups of three as possible. If there are any people not in a triad, make one or two groups of two. Each member selects the number 1, 2, or 3. Number 1 will be the first to initiate a conflict role-play, then 2, followed by 3.

Procedure 2 (8–15 minutes)

A. Initiator number 1 tells or gives his or her information from the preparation to number 2 (the responder) to read. Once number 2 understands, role-play (see B). Number 3 is the observer.

B. Role-play the conflict resolution. Number 3, the observer, writes his or her observations on the feedback sheet at the end of this exercise.

C. Integration. When the role-play is over, the observer leads a discussion on the effectiveness of the conflict resolution. All three group members should discuss the effectiveness. Number 3 is not a lecturer. Do not go on to the next procedure until told to do so.

Procedure 3 (8–15 minutes)
Same as procedure 2, only number 2 is now the initiator, number 3 is the responder, and number 1 is the observer.

Procedure 4 (8–15 minutes)
Same as procedure 2, only number 3 is the initiator, number 1 is the responder, and number 2 is the observer.

Conclusion
The instructor leads a class discussion and/or makes concluding remarks.

Application (2–4 minutes)
What did I learn from this experience? How will I use this knowledge in the future?

____

____

Sharing
Volunteers give their answers to the application section.

Feedback Form

Try to have positive improvement comments for each step in initiating conflict resolution. Remember to be DESCRIPTIVE and SPECIFIC, and for all improvements have an alternative positive behavior (APB) (i.e., if you would have said/done . . . , it would have improved the conflict resolution by . . .).

Initiating Conflict Resolution Model Steps
Step 1. Plan a BCF statement that maintains ownership of the problem. (Did the initiator have a well-planned, effective BCF statement?)

____

____

Step 2. Present your BCF statement and agree on the conflict. (Did the initiator present the BCF statement effectively? Did the two agree on the conflict?)

____

____

Step 3. Ask for, and/or give, alternative conflict resolutions. (Who suggested alternative solutions? Was it done effectively?)

____

____

Step 4. Make an agreement for change. (Was there an agreement for change?)

____

____

In Behavior Model Video 14–2, Mediating Conflict Resolution, Peter brings Alex and Catherine together to resolve their advertising account conflict. They follow the steps in Model 14–3 on pages 472–473. There is no Skill-Building Exercise to follow up this mediating conflict video.

Control Systems: Financial Control and Productivity

Learning Objectives

After studying this chapter, you should be able to:

1. List the four stages of the systems process and describe the type of control used at each stage.
2. Describe the appropriate feedback process among the functional areas/departments.
3. List the four steps in the control systems process.
4. Describe the difference among the three control frequencies.
5. Explain the difference between line-item versus program budgets, static versus flexible, and incremental versus zero-based budgeting.
6. Define *capital expenditures budget* and explain how it is different from the expense budget.
7. List the three primary financial statements and what is presented in each of them.
8. State how to measure productivity and list the three ways to increase it.
9. Define the following **key terms** (in order of appearance in the chapter):

controlling
preliminary control
concurrent control
rework control
damage control
control systems process
standards
critical success factors
control frequency
management audit
budget
operating budgets
capital expenditures budget
financial statements
productivity

Skill-Development

1. You should improve your skill at developing a control system for an organization/department (Skill-Building Exercise 15–1).

2. You should improve your skill at calculating cost-volume profit analysis, which includes break-even (Skill-Building Exercise 15–2).

These exercises focus on the control management function which requires technical, conceptual, and decision-making skills. Controlling requires the use of interpersonal roles, especially the monitor informational role, and decisional management roles. The SCAN competencies of resources, information, and systems, as well as basic skills, especially math, are developed through this exercise.

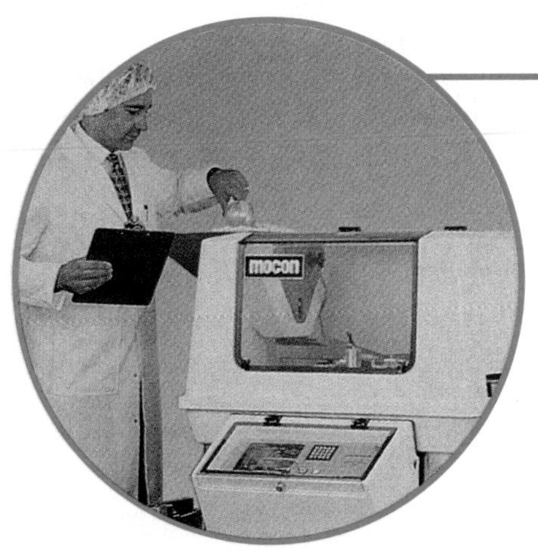

odern Control, Inc. (MOCON®) is an international company with headquarters in Minneapolis, Minnesota. Its shares are traded on the NASDAQ Stock Market under the symbol MOCON. The following information and the financial data presented later in this chapter are taken from the *MOCON 1994 Annual Report.*

MOCON is a leading developer, manufacturer, and marketer of high technology instrumentation designed to test packages and packaging materials, films, and pharmaceutical products. The company employs several patented technologies to measure permeation of various gases, to gauge thickness and weight variation during production of materials, and to test for leakage in quality control applications. MOCON testing instrumentation is used in research laboratories, production environments, and quality control applications in the food, plastics, medical, and pharmaceutical industries.

MOCON has three major lines of business: (1) Permeation products address the needs of film converters and food packagers working on new or better packaging material. (2) Packaging products are used to test for leaks in finished food and snack

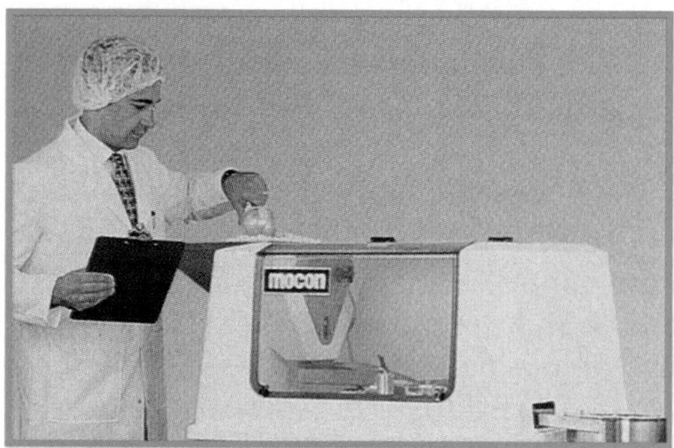

MOCON *is in the business of helping other companies control their operations.*

packages. (3) Weighing and sorting systems serve pharmaceutical capsule and tablet manufacturers.

In other words, MOCON is in the business of helping other companies control their operations. However, like all organizations, the management function of controlling is critical to MOCON's success.

Unfortunately, some students don't place a high priority on understanding accounting and finance. Those who are not accounting and finance majors tend to believe that accounting and finance are not too important. This is a grave mistake if they want to climb the corporate management ladder because they will have to develop budgets and make important decisions based on financial information. Accounting is referred to as the language of business and it is the primary measure of business success.

1. List the four stages of the systems process and describe the type of control used at each stage.

ORGANIZATIONAL AND FUNCTIONAL AREA CONTROL SYSTEMS

controlling
The process of establishing and implementing mechanisms to ensure that objectives are achieved.

As defined in Chapter 1, **controlling** *is the process of establishing and implementing mechanisms to ensure that objectives are achieved.* In this section you will learn about controlling the organizational system and its functional areas.

Organizational Systems Control

Organizational performance is important not only to managers but to all stakeholders who evaluate performance when making decisions. For example, customers evaluate product performance and service after the sale when making purchasing decisions. Suppliers (on credit) and lenders evaluate the organization's ability to pay them. Investors evaluate profitability potential before buying stock. Competitors benchmark against each other and copy good ideas. Present and potential employees evaluate the organization when keeping a job or taking a job offer.

An important part of determining performance is measuring and controlling it. With multiple types of organizations and stakeholders, there is no universally accepted performance measure or control system. Based on the contingency approach to management, the controls must fit the situation. However,

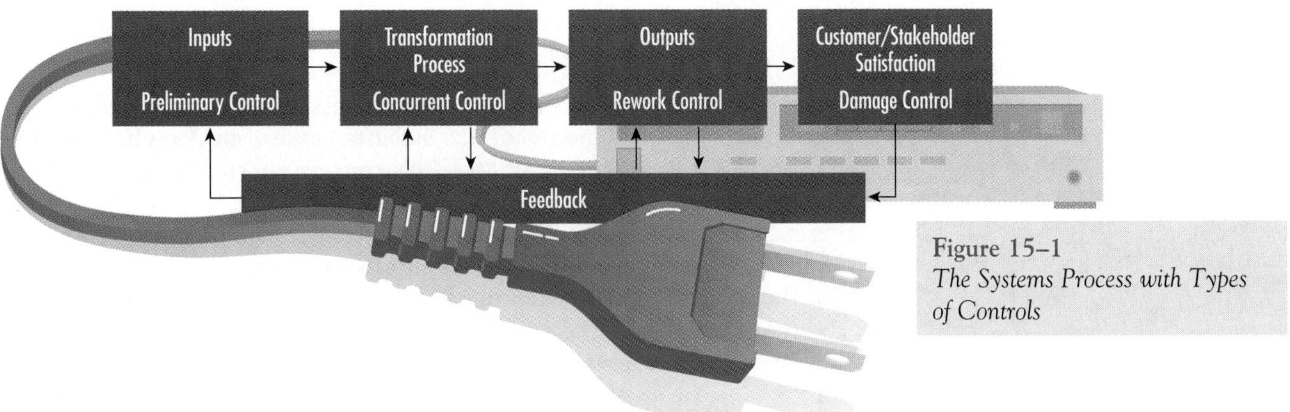

Figure 15–1
The Systems Process with Types of Controls

within the controlling section of this chapter, the focus will be on integrating various controls through the systems approach.

In Chapter 2, you learned about the systems process of inputs, transformation, and outputs, which are now expanded to include types of controls at each stage. Figure 15–1 illustrates the systems process with types of controls. Also, recall the means-ends process. Customer/stakeholder satisfaction is the desired end result, and preliminary, concurrent, rework, and damage controls are all means to achieve customer satisfaction. The downward arrows in Figure 15–1 represent sending feedback to earlier stages of the systems process through the appropriate upward arrow.

Top managers use control systems to guide and effect changes in the organizations they lead.[1] Controlling starts at the top of the organization with long-range strategic planning and flows down the organization to the day-to-day operations. At the different stages of the systems process, the four different types of controls are needed as explained next.

Work Application

1. Using Figure 15–1, identify the primary organizational inputs, transformational process, outputs, and customers of a firm you work or have worked for. Also, identify the level of customer satisfaction.

Preliminary Control (Inputs). **Preliminary control** *is designed to anticipate and prevent possible problems.* A major difference between successful and unsuccessful managers is their ability to anticipate and prevent problems, rather than solving problems after they occur.

preliminary control
Designed to anticipate and prevent possible problems.

Planning and organizing are the keys to preliminary control, which is also called *feedforward control.* The organization's mission and objectives serve to guide the use of all organizational resources so that the mission and objectives are achieved. Standing plans (Chapter 6) are designed to control employee behavior in recurring situations to prevent problems, and contingency plans tell employees what to do if problems occur. However, flexibility is needed in fast-changing environments. Strict adherence to organizational hierarchy of authority, standing plans, well-defined job descriptions, and budgets is called *bureaucratic control.*

A common preliminary control is preventive maintenance. Many production departments and transportation companies/departments routinely tune up their machines and engines to prevent breakdowns that would cause problems later. Another important preliminary control is purchasing only quality inputs from other organizations to prevent product problems. For example, if Johnson & Johnson buys a MOCON weighing and sorting system for its Tylenol products and it does not work properly, it will have an adverse effect on J&J's transformation process and outputs.

concurrent control
Action taken as inputs are transformed into outputs to ensure that standards are met.

Concurrent Control (Transformation Process). **Concurrent control** *is action taken as inputs are transformed into outputs to ensure standards are met.* The key to success is quality control. MOCON test instruments to be sold to customers are checked to make sure they meet quality standards as the products are being made. It is usually more economical to reject faulty input parts than to wait and find out that the finished output does not work properly. Employees spend time checking quality during the transformation process, and managers spend time overseeing employees as they work. Using effective process controls will help ensure that your departmental objectives are met.

rework control
Action taken to fix an output.

Rework Control (Outputs). **Rework control** *is action taken to fix an output.* Rework is necessary when preliminary and concurrent controls have failed. Most organizations inspect the final output before it is sold to the customer or sent as an input to other departments within the organization. When the outputs don't meet standards, they need to be reworked. Sometimes rework is not cost effective or possible, and outputs have to be accepted as is, discarded, or sold for salvage, which can be costly. For example, if MOCON has a bad year and loses money (outputs), it is too late; it cannot change the past. However, past performance can be used to improve preliminary controls for the next year.

damage control
Action taken to minimize negative impacts on customers/stakeholders due to faulty outputs.

Damage Control (Customer/Stakeholder Satisfaction). **Damage control** *is action taken to minimize negative impacts on customers/stakeholders due to faulty outputs.* When a faulty output gets to the customer, damage control is needed. Warranties, a form of damage control, require refunding the purchase price, fixing the product or reperforming the service (a form of rework), or replacing the product with a new one. Apologizing and promising to do better in the future are also important damage controls that can help keep customers.

Feedback. An important part of the systems process is the feedback loop, particularly from the customer and other stakeholders. The only way to continually increase customer satisfaction is to use feedback from the customer to continually improve the products offered at the input, transformation process, and output stages. Too many organizations today focus on the outputs as the ends, rather than the means, and do not actively seek external feedback. In some organizations, external and internal feedback is even ignored and denied, rather than used to make changes to improve the system.

Within the organization, the outputs should give feedback to the transformation process and inputs. And the transformation process should give feedback to the inputs for continuous improvement throughout the systems process.

Work Application

2. Continuing your answer from work application 1, give an example of preliminary, concurrent, rework, and damage control for the organization you work or have worked for.

Focus on Preliminary and Concurrent Types of Controls. Why is it that so many managers cannot find the time to use preliminary and concurrent controls, but they always find time to use rework and damage controls? Remember that focusing on the first two cuts down on the use of the latter two.

Relying on rework control is not effective because it is more costly to do things twice that to do it right the first time by using effective preliminary and concurrent controls. Using rework to control performance means wasted resources, unpredictable delivery schedules, and extra inventory as safety stock. In addition, with a focus on rework, faulty products slip through inspection and get to customers, which requires damage control and warranty cost. This is particularly problematic with services, such as manicures and haircuts and auto repairs, which are delivered as they are produced. The best solution is to prevent poor quality from ever happening in the first place. Doing so creates a win-win situation by minimizing warranty cost and maximizing customer satisfaction.

Functional Area/Department Control Systems

Although in most organizations the only functional area that actually transforms the inputs into the outputs of goods and services (which are called *products*) that are sold to customers is the operations department, all functional departments use the systems process. Figure 15–2 illustrates how this is done; it

Figure 15–2
Systems Processes for Functional Areas/Departments

Systems Process

Inputs Preliminary Control	→	Transformation Process Concurrent Control	→	Outputs Rework Control	→	Customer for Output Damage Control

Feedback

Operations Department Systems Process

Raw Materials	→	Make the Product	→	Finished Product	→	Marketing Department

Marketing Department Systems Process

Finished Product	→	Sales Presentation	→	Completed Sale	→	Customer

Human Resources Department Systems Process

Recruited and Present Employees	→	Attracting, Developing, and Retaining Systems	→	New and More Productive Employees	→	Employees are a Major Input to All Departments

Finance Department Systems Process

Revenues, Borrowed Funds, and Owners' Funds	→	Recording Transactions and Overseeing the Budgeting Process	→	Budgeted Funds, Financial Statements, and Other Reports	→	Inputs to All Departments and Payments to Stakeholders

Information (MIS) Department Systems Process

Data Collection from All Departments and External Sources	→	Transforming Data Into Information	→	Information	→	Inputs to All Appropriate Employees in All Departments

New Product Development Systems Process

Data Collection from Potential Customers, Actual Customers, and All Departments	→	Transforming Ideas into New Products (Major Changes to a Product Can Be Considered New)	→	Plan for a New Product	→	Inputs to the Operations Department that Creates the Product, and to All Appropriate Employees in All Departments Involved with the New Product

will be explained with each functional area in the following section. Note that damage control with the customer is primarily the function of the marketing department. The other department outputs stay within the organization and go to stakeholders, not the customer, and internal damage control is necessary when outputs are faulty.

Recall from Chapters 1 and 7 that firms are commonly organized into four major functional departments: operations, marketing, human resources, and finance. Information is a fifth major functional area that may be a standalone department or may fall under the finance functional area. Organizations have other departments as well, but you will only study the five key functional areas.

Operations Function. The operations, also called production and manufacturing, department is the functional area that is responsible for actually making the goods or performing the service. Figure 15–1 illustrates the operations process. In Chapter 17, you will learn more about the operations process and controls. MOCON describes itself as a leading developer and manufacturer of technology instrumentation.

Marketing Function. The marketing, also called sales, department is the functional area that is responsible for selling the products. The four key areas (called the four Ps) of marketing are pricing, promoting (personal selling, advertising), placing (sales locations), and products that are sold (features, packaging, brands, installation, instructions). Marketing also determines the target market for the products. MOCON refers to itself as a leading marketer of testing instrumentation used in research laboratories, production environments, and quality control applications in the food, plastics, medical, and pharmaceutical industries.

The systems process for the marketing department generally includes the finished product as the major input, the sales presentation as the transformation process, and the completed sale as the output. It is primarily the marketing department that deals with the customer and uses damage control outside the organization, while other departments use damage control within the organization.

Marketing is the department that works directly with the customer. Therefore, an important part of the job is to provide feedback from customers to the other departments as the basis for continually increasing customer value. In addition, because marketing people directly compete for sales with competitors, they should also provide information regarding competitor actions such as lowering prices and offering product innovations and entirely new products to other departments for use in strategic planning.

Market control is commonly used by organizations that conduct business in highly competitive environments. *Test marketing* is used to determine the sales potential of a new product in limited areas. If the product sells well in a limited area, it is sold on a national and/or international level. For example, McDonald's test marketed pizza before offering it nationally. However, companies, including Sara Lee, Ralston Purina, and Frito-Lay, are doing very limited quick market testing and going right to full-scale national and international marketing. The reason for the change is to get a good first mover advantage (Chapter 5) on the competition. As stated previously, competitive marketers will report the test market activity, and the competitors may also develop the new product and have it ready at the same time, or shortly after, for mass marketing. Although no, or quick, test marketing is risky and may result in major losses, it also has a major profit potential. In addition, test marketing does not guarantee success. Many McDonald's franchises stopped selling pizza. Commonly used market measurement and control ratios include market share, profit margin on sales, and sales to sales presentation, which will be presented later in this chapter.

Human Resources Function. The human resources, formerly called personnel, department is responsible for attracting (recruiting and selecting), developing (orientation, training and development, and performance appraisal), and retaining (compensation, health and safety, and labor relations) employees. For details on human resources processes, other than performance appraisal, see Chapter 9. Because performance appraisal, which includes coaching and discipline, is so important to all managers, it will be covered in detail in the next chapter. Human resources ratios of turnover, absenteeism, and work force composition will be presented later in this chapter. Most large organizations, including MOCON, have a professional human resources staff to control employees.

The systems process for the human resources department generally includes recruited and present employees as inputs; attracting, developing, and retaining systems as the transformation process. Its outputs are new and more productive employees, and employees are a major input to all departments.

Finance Function. The finance, or accounting, department is the functional area that is responsible for recording all financial transactions (primarily paying for inputs and the sale of outputs), for obtaining funds needed to pay for inputs (loans, the sale of bonds and stocks), and for investing any surplus funds (various forms of savings accounts and purchasing assets such as other company stocks). Part of this responsibility includes preparing the budgets and financial statements. The majority of this chapter is devoted to financial controls. You will study budgeting, cost-volume-profit analysis, financial statements, and ratios (from MOCON).

The systems process for the finance/accounting department generally includes collected revenues, borrowed funds, and owners' funds as inputs. The transformation process includes recording transactions and overseeing the budgeting process. Outputs include budgets, financial statements, and other reports (such as tax returns, employee tax withholding, and annual reports). Its primary customers are the other departments through their budgets and payments to stakeholders such as employee paychecks, and payments to suppliers and lenders for their inputs.

Because of the importance of finance, particularly budgeting, many organizations have a high-level manager with the title controller, sometimes called *comptroller*. The *controller* is responsible for assisting the other managers with the controlling function by gathering information and generating reports. Because of the information part of the controller's job, the head of the information department often reports to the controller. In the past, the controller strictly focused on the finance function. However, in organizations including Coors, EDS, Hyundai, and United Parcel Services controllers have been given broader control responsibilities.

Information Function. The management information systems (MIS) department is responsible for controlling information in a central location. MIS departments generally run the computers for the entire organization. You will learn more about controlling information in Chapter 17.

The MIS department collects data from all departments and external sources as its inputs. *Data* includes unorganized facts and figures. The data is transformed into information. *Information* is data organized in a meaningful way to assist employees in making decisions. For example, the accounting transactions (debits and credits) are data. But, when you put them all together over a period of time and create an income statement, you have information. Information becomes the input to all appropriate employees in all departments. With the trend toward empowering employees, information that was once deemed appropriate for managers only is being given to all employees. MOCON has a sophisticated MIS department and most information is available to all employees. Its products provide data and information to other companies.

Work Application

3. Continuing work application questions 1 and 2, using Figure 15–2, illustrate the systems process for a department you work or have worked for within the organization. Be sure to give examples of preliminary, concurrent, rework, and damage controls for your department.

New Product Development Function. All organizations do not have new product development departments or teams. Therefore, it is not listed as one of the four major functional departments. However, it is an important function in many firms. For example, auto makers introduce new models of their cars every few years. As illustrated in Figure 15–2, ideas for major improvements or totally new products should come from external sources, especially potential customers, and from all areas of the firm that will be involved with the new product. For example, the Ford Motor Company Sigma Project for the Taurus changed the new model to appeal to new and existing customers by having the marketing function collect data. The operations team members give input into the practical aspects of producing the new Taurus. The finance team members give input into the cost and the effects on pricing of the car. The final plan for the production of the Taurus goes to the operations department. The marketing department plans how to promote and sell the new Taurus. The finance department works on the cost and budget for the Taurus and keeps records (information) on performance. The human resources department may need to make personnel changes or attract creative engineers to the company.

2. Describe the appropriate feedback process among the functional areas/departments.

The Feedback Process within and among Functional Areas/Departments. Within each deparment, each employee also uses the systems process to transform inputs into outputs. Other department members may receive their outputs rather than other departments. For example, on a production line making the Taurus, each person works on one part of the car. When the work is done that person's output moves down the line as the next person's input, and so on until the Taurus is completed. Each employee should also be using preliminary, concurrent, rework, and damage control.

Figure 15–3
The Feedback Process among Functional Areas/Departments

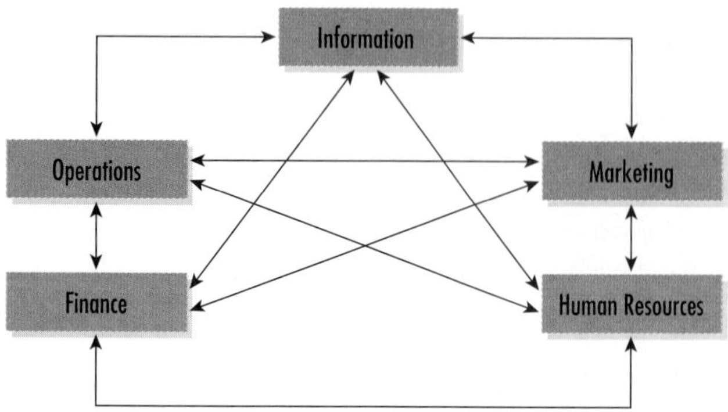

The arrows represent the flow of feedback throughout the systems process

As illustrated in Figure 15–2, within each functional department, feedback and preliminary, concurrent, and rework are collectively used to continually improve the internal systems process. In additon, damage control is used with the other departments receiving the outputs as their inputs.

Throughout the systems process, feedback should be circulated among all the functional areas/departments in order to improve organizational performance in the input, transformation, and output processes while continually increasing customer satisfaction. Figure 15–3 illustrates the effective feedback process among the functional departments. Note that operations, marketing, finance, and human resources provide feedback to each other and to the information department. To be effective, feedback should be given to all departments, not just to the information department for dissemination to the other departments.

Work Application

4. Continuing work application questions 1 through 3, illustrate the systems process you personally use within your department. Be sure to give an example preliminary, concurrent, rework, and damage control you personally use.

ESTABLISHING CONTROL SYSTEMS

In this section you will study the four steps in the control systems process and about ten control methods that can be used during the process.

The Control Systems Process

The **control systems process** *steps are (1) set objectives and standards, (2) measure performance, (3) compare performance to standards, and (4) correct or reinforce.* See Model 15–1 for an illustration of the control process. The same control systems process steps should be followed on an organizational level and within each functional area.

3. List the four steps in the control systems process.

control systems process
(1) Set objectives and standards. (2) Measure performance. (3) Compare performance standards. (4) Correct or reinforce.

step 1. **Set Objectives and Standards.** Planning and controlling are inseparable. Part of planning should be to develop controls. Setting objectives (Chapter 5) is the starting point to both planning and controlling.[2] Setting objectives and standards is part of the input process and they are preliminary controls.

Objectives, in a sense, are standards. However, additional standards are also used to measure whether you are meeting the objectives. For example, if one of MOCON's operations departments has an objective of assembling 200 instrumentation machines per day, it must set additional standards for each team of employees to achieve this goal. With five teams, the team standard could be the assembly of 40 (200 machines divided by 5 teams) machines per day. Assembly of 39 or less is below standard; assembly of 41 or more machines is above standard. On a per-hour basis, each team should assemble five machines (40 machines divided by 8 hours) per hour to be at the standard production level.

Model 15–1
The Control Systems Process

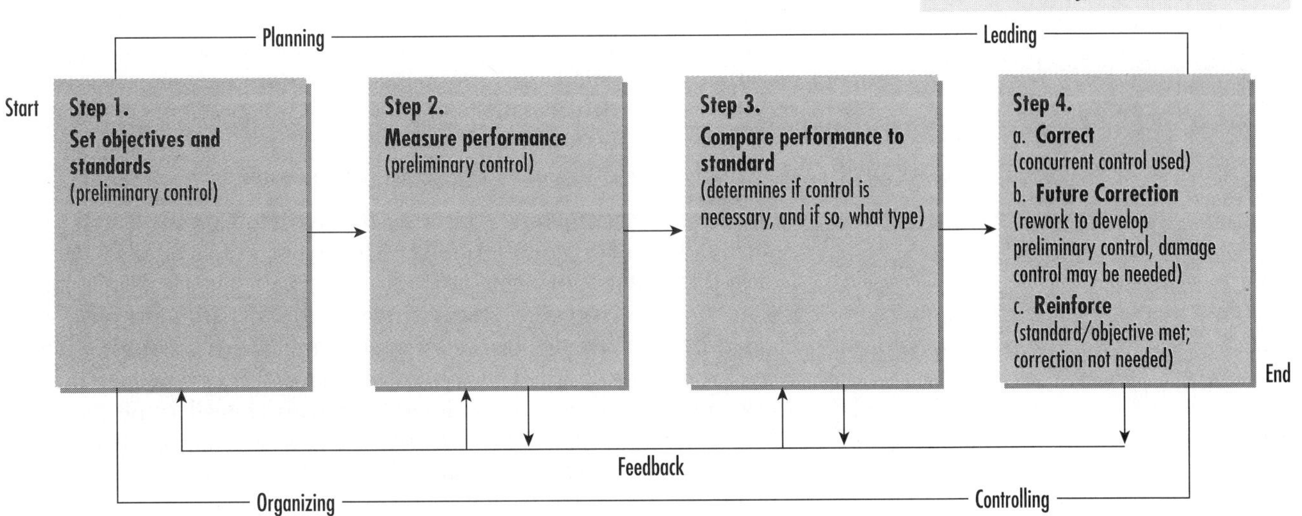

As a manager, some standards will have been established before you got the job. Others may be set by people outside your department. For example, industrial engineers may conduct time and motion studies to determine production standards. Cost accountants may determine how much it should cost to produce your department's output. Your boss will also establish standards for you. But there will be situations in which you establish the standards.

standards
Measure performance levels in the areas of quantity, quality, time, cost, and behavior.

For standards to be complete, they should cover five major areas. **Standards** *measure performance levels in the areas of quantity, quality, time, cost, and behavior.* Incomplete standards usually lead to negative results. For example, if employees are only given high quantity standards with a fast time limit, they will tend to focus only on how many products are produced and may ignore quality. Employees respond to what is measured so the development of balanced standards is a key management function that drives business results.

- *Quantity*. How many units should employees produce to earn their pay? Some examples of quantity standards include the number of words a secretary should type, the number of loans a loan officer must make, and the number of classes a professor must teach. It is relatively easy to measure performance with quantitative standards.
- *Quality*. How well must a job be done? How many errors are acceptable? Quality is a relative term. There is a trade-off between cost and benefits. For some products, such as parachutes, defects are unacceptable because the cost of a life is too high, traded off against the cost of doing a quality job. For other products, the standard of zero defects is too costly. In any situation, you should set quality standards and follow through to make sure employees meet them. If you don't, employees may not produce quality work. Some examples of quality standards include the number of typing errors a secretary may make; the number or percentage of delinquent loans a loan officer may make; and the acceptable number or percentage of poor student evaluations an instructor may get. Quality standards are often difficult to establish and measure. For example, how does an educational supervisor determine how "good" the teachers are? It's not easy, but quality must be measured and evaluated.
- *Time*. When should the task be completed? Or how fast? When assigning a task, it is important to specify a time period. Deadlines are one form of a time-based standard. Performance may also be measured against a specific time period. Examples include how many words per minute a secretary types; how many loans a loan officer makes per month; and how many courses a professor teaches per semester or year.
- *Cost*. How much should it cost to do the job? How sophisticated a cost system should an organization have? The answers to these questions depend on the situation. Some production departments use cost-accounting methods to ensure accuracy, whereas other departments have a set budget. Some examples of cost standards include: a secretary's typing cost may be reflected in a salary limit; a loan officer's cost may include an expense account to wine and dine customers, as well as the cost of an office, secretarial help, and so on. Or cost could be determined on the basis of delinquent loan losses only. The professor's cost may include a salary limit and an overhead cost.

- *Behavior*. What should employees do and not do? Standing plans, especially rules, help control or limit behavior.[3] In addition, there may be specific things to do and say to customers. For example, a secretary may be expected to answer the telephone with a specific greeting. A loan officer may be expected to process a loan in a certain manner. A professor may be expected not to date current students. You will learn more about controlling behavior in the next chapter.

In the previous paragraphs we discussed standards in terms of each of the five areas separately. Now we will set standards for the secretary, loan officer, and instructor that combine all five areas, as effective standards should. The secretary's standard may be to type 50 words (quantity) per minute (time) with two errors or less (quality) at a maximum salary of $12.00 per hour (cost) and to answer the telephone with a specific greeting (behavior). The loan officer's standard may be to make $100,000 (quantity) in loans per quarter (time) with delinquency not to exceed $5,000 (quality and cost) while following procedures (behavior). The instructor's standard is to teach 24 semester hours (quantity) per year (time), with an acceptable department chair performance evaluation (quality) without dating current students (behavior) at a salary of less than $50,000 (cost). Each of these jobs would have additional standards as well.

Work Application

5. Give an example of a standard from an organization you work or have worked for that has the five characteristics of a complete standard.

step 2.

Measure Performance. By measuring its performance, an organization knows if it is successful, and to what level, and how to improve success. If you don't measure performance how do you know if the organization's mission and objectives are being met? An important consideration in the control process is what to measure and how frequently to measure it.[4] What to measure and its frequency are inputs and require preliminary controls.

critical success factors
The limited number of areas in which satisfactory results will ensure successful performance to achieve the objective/standard.

After setting objectives, but possibly while setting standards, the next step is to identify the critical success factors (CSF). **Critical success factors** *are the limited number of areas in which satisfactory results will ensure successful performance to achieve the objective/standard.* In other words, you cannot control everything, so the organization, department/team, and individual should identify the few most important things to control. For example, at the organizational level in supermarkets (including Edwards, Food Mart, Kroger, Safeway, and Stop & Shop), maintaining the right product mix in each local store, having the products on the shelves, having them advertised effectively to pull shoppers into the store, and having them priced correctly (since profit margins are low in this industry) are the critical success factors. At the departmental and employee level, these CSFs must be implemented and monitored.

The critical success factors at a supermarket are having the right product mix, having products on the shelves, advertising effectively, and pricing correctly.

For a performance to be measured as a CSF, it must meet the following criteria:

- *Critical*. If a problem occurs in the CSF performance area, it affects the performance of the entire organization/department and each individual.
- *Timeliness*. It must be possible to identify deviations from the standard in the CSF performance area before serious consequences occur.

Work Application

6. Give an example of the critical success factors for a job you have/had. Be sure to place them in priority order (first most important) and to explain why they are critical.

Concurrent control action is taken to ensure that the standard is met. Rework control is not desirable and damage control is too late.

- *Economical.* The specific control method used to measure and monitor the CSF performance areas must have a greater benefit than the cost. Zero defects and security personnel are not always economical.

Notice that in Model 15–1 there is a feedback loop. It is important to realize that when you determine CSF and measures, you may need to rework the objectives and standards.

CSFs can change greatly from job to job. If you want to climb the corporate ladder, you must determine the CSFs for your job and control them with preliminary and concurrent controls. Remember that your boss is the primary person that will measure your performance. Learn the CSFs your boss uses to evaluate you.

How often should you measure performance and what methods of control should you use? According to contingency theory, it depends on the situation. For example, large expensive products are each monitored several times during the transformation process. Inexpensive products may only be measured at the output stage. But when sample inspection is used, only some of the products are tested to accept or reject the entire batch of products. MOCON has sophisticated measurements, and it makes products that other companies use to measure their performance.

There are three primary measures of performance based on frequency of use: constant, periodic, and occasional. You will learn how to measure performance through specific control methods you can use to control CSFs, once we finish the control process.

step 3. **Compare Performance to Standards.** After determining what, when, and how frequently performance is to be measured, you must follow up by comparing the actual results to the objective or standard in order to know if you are on schedule to achieve (or have achieved) the objective/standard. This step is relatively easy if you have performed the first two steps correctly. This comparison determines the type of control, if any, needed in step 4. The productivity section of this chapter focuses on measuring and comparing productivity rates to standards.

A performance or variance report, such as the one shown in Figure 15–4, is commonly used to measure and evaluate performance. Performance reports usually show standards, actual performance, and deviations from standards. In Figure 15–4, the results, although under production and over cost, are excellent because they are both under one percent deviation from standard (standard divided by deviation). When variances are significant, they should be explained. This will be covered in more detail under the exception principle of occasional control methods later in this section.

step 4. **Correct or Reinforce.** During the transformation process, concurrent controls are used to correct performance in order to meet standards. MOCON focuses on preliminary and concurrent controls internally, as do the products it sells to customers.

Outputs and Inputs	Standard/Budget	Actual	Variance
Units produced (outputs)	10,000	9,992	−8
Production cost (inputs)			
Labor, including overtime	$ 70,000	$ 69,895	$+105
Materials	95,500	95,763	−263
Supplies	4,750	4,700	+50
Totals	$170,250	$170,358	−108

Figure 15–4
Operations Performance Report, January 1997

When performance is complete and it is too late to take corrective action to meet the standard, the corrective action is to: (1) analyze why the standard was not met. (2) use the information to develop preliminary control. (3) feed back the preliminary control to take the corrective action necessary to meet the objective/standard next time. When performance affects others, also use damage control, such as the action taken in the following example.

Bob called Anthony's Pizza to have two pizzas delivered. He specified that he wanted them by 4:30. Anthony guaranteed on-time delivery. At 4:40, Bob called to find out why the pizzas were not at his house yet. Anthony said they were on the way. Shortly before 5:00, Bob called Anthony back to cancel the pizzas because he had to leave. Anthony apologized and stated that the delivery person got lost and could not find the house. Apologizing again, Tony told Bob his next order was on him. The next night Bob called back, got free pizza, and continued to do business with Anthony's. If Anthony did not use effective damage control, not only would he have been stuck with two cold pizzas and lost delivery time, he would have lost a customer. Anthony analyzed the cost of giving away free pizza to the benefit of possible future business.

When the objective/standard has been met, there is no need for corrective action. However, do not be like most managers and end the control process here. Reinforce the behavior through rewarding employees for a job well done with techniques such as praise. By letting employees know that they are meeting, or have met, objectives/standards and that you appreciate their efforts motivates them to higher levels of performance through continuous improvements. Refer back to Chapter 11 for details on how to motivate employees to meet standards.

Work Application

7. Identify a situation in which corrective action was needed to meet an objective/standard. Describe the corrective action taken to meet the objective/standard.

Resistance to Control. When establishing control systems, especially the standards, it is important to consider employee reactions to them and their possible resistance to the changes. Managing change methods (Chapter 8) should be used when establishing control systems. Allowing employees to be involved in establishing the control system is very helpful at overcoming resistance to control.

Control Frequency and Methods

4. Describe the difference among the three control frequencies.

There are ten specific methods you can use to measure and control performance. These ten methods fall into three categories of control frequency. **Control frequency** *is: constant, periodic, and occasional.*

control frequency
Constant, periodic, and occasional.

Constant Controls. *Constant controls* are in continuous use and include self-control, clan control, and standing plans.

- *Self-Control.* If managers are not watching or somehow monitoring performance, will employees do the job? In any job, there is an element of self-control. The real issue is the degree of self-control employees are given versus imposed control by managers (such as standing plans). Too much or too little imposed control can cause problems. You will learn more about self- versus imposed control in the next chapter.
- *Clan Control. Clan, or group, control* is a form of human resources control in which the organization relies heavily on its culture and norms to ensure specific behavior. Organizations that use teams tend to rely on clan control. Refer back to Chapter 13 for details on group control. Self- and clan control are used in all phases of the systems process with the four types of controls.
- *Standing Plans.* Policies, procedures, and rules are developed to influence employees' behavior in recurring predictable situations. When standards are developed, they are similar to standing plans that are in constant use. When standing plans and standards are developed, they are preliminary controls. When standing plans and standards are implemented, they become concurrent, rework, or damage controls.

Periodic Controls. *Periodic controls* are used on a regular fixed basis, such as once per hour or day, every week, or at the end of the month, quarter, or year. Period controls include regular reports, budgets, and audits.

- *Regular Reports.* Regular reports can be oral or written. Regularly scheduled daily, weekly, and monthly meetings with one or more employees to discuss progress and any problems are common in all organizations. Regular written reports are commonly used. For example, at MOCON the production manager may get a daily report on the number of products produced. The sales manager may get a weekly sales report. A vice president may get a monthly income statement. The information (MIS) department is commonly responsible for period reports. Regular reports are designed as preliminary control. But, the report itself is used as a concurrent, rework, or damage control depending on the situation.
- *Budgets.* Budgets are one of the most widely used control tools. You will learn budgeting details in the next two sections of this chapter. When preparing a new budget, it is a preliminary control. As the year progresses, it becomes a concurrent control. At year end, it is reworked for the next year. A budget may also require damage control if significant changes such as overspending take place for some reason.
- *Audits.* There are two major types of audits: internal and external accounting and management. Part of the accounting finance function is to maintain records of the organization's transactions and assets. Most large organizations, including MOCON, have an *internal auditing* person or entire department that checks periodically to make sure the assets are reported accurately and to keep theft levels at a minimum. In addition to performing internal audits, many organizations hire outside accountants to verify the organization's financial statements through an *external accounting audit* firm, usually a certified public accounting (CPA) firm. The

auditor states whether the statements reflect the true financial position and if they were prepared in accordance with generally accepted accounting principles. Companies that sell securities to the public, including MOCON, must be audited annually. The auditors come in once a year, but very few people know exactly when they will arrive. Lastly, the **management audit** *analyzes the organization's planning, organizing, leading, and controlling functions for improvements*. The analysis focuses on the past, present, and future. The management audit can be conducted both internally and externally.

management audit
Analyzes the organization's planning, organizing, leading, and controlling functions for improvements.

Audits may also be occasional controls when used sporadically; for example, auditors may make unannounced visits at irregular intervals. The audit is designed as a preliminary control, but it is used to ensure accurate records and to control theft.

Occasional Controls. *Occasional controls* are used on a sporadic basis when needed. They include observation, exception principle, special reports, and project controls. Unlike periodic controls, they do not involve set time intervals.

- *Observation*. Managers personally watch and talk to employees as they perform their jobs. Recall that Sam Walton personally visited all of his Wal-Mart stores and that personal store visits remain an important part of managers' jobs. Observation is also done by video camera. Observation can be used with any of the four types of control. Management by walking around (MBWA) is a specific method of personal observation that increases performance.[5] MBWA is a coaching technique and will be explained in the next chapter.
- *Exception Principle*. In this instance, control is left up to the employees unless problems occur, in which case employees go to the manager for help. Corrective action is taken to get the performance back on schedule. For example, Carolyn, a production worker, has to produce 100 units per day as her standard. If she produces less than 90 units for any reason, such as the machine breaks down or the necessary materials run out, she informs her manager, Julio, immediately so he can help by taking corrective action. The exception principle can be very effective if used correctly. However, people are often reluctant to ask for help or to report that they are not performing up to standard until it is too late to take corrective action. Therefore, it is important for the manager and employees to agree on what constitutes an exception. The exception principle is designed as a preliminary control, but can be used with any of the other three types of controls.
- *Special Reports*. When problems are identified, management often requests a special report to be compiled by one employee, a committee within the department/organization, or outside consultants who specialize in that area. These reports vary in content and nature but are often designed to identify the cause of a problem as well as a solution, or an opportunity and a way to take advantage of it. When developing new products at MOCON, special reports are given before the product is manufactured and sold to customers. Special reports are designed as a preliminary control, but can be used with any of the other three types of controls.

Figure 15–5
Types and Frequency and Methods of Control

Types of Control	*Frequency* and Methods of Control		
	Constant Controls	*Periodic Controls*	*Occasional Controls*
Preliminary (input)	Self	Regular Reports	Observation
Concurrent (transformation process)	Clan	Budgets	Exception Principle
Rework (output)	Standing Plans	Audits	Special Reports
Damage (customer satisfaction)			Project

Work Application

8. Give an example of a constant, a periodic, and an occasional control method used by an organization you work or have worked for. Identify each by name and explain why it is classified as such.

- *Project Controls*. With nonrecurring or unique projects, the project manager needs to develop a control system to ensure the project is completed on time. Because planning and controlling are so closely linked, planning tools, such as Gantt charts and PERT networks (Chapter 6) are also project control methods. Project controls are designed as a preliminary control, but can be used with any of the other three types of controls.

For a review of the systems process with its four types of controls and the methods of control categorized by frequency, see Figure 15–5. The types and frequency and methods of control are listed separately because all four types of control may be used with any method. Recall how a budget changes its type of control over time, and that more than one control method can be used at once. You need to be aware of the stage of the systems process you are working in and the type of control used in that stage (Figure 15–1) and then select the appropriate method(s) for the type of control.

In Skill-Building Exercise 15–1, you will be asked to develop a control system for Bolton Employment Agency using the four steps of the control systems process.

BUDGETING

budget
Planned quantitative allocation of resources for specific activities.

Preparing and following a well thought out budget for a business will ensure smoother financial management.[6] A **budget** *is a planned quantitative allocation of resources for specific activities*. Notice that the term *budget* does not include money. This is because all types of resources can be allocated. For example, in Figure 15–4 units of output were budgeted. Human resources, machines, time, space, and so on can also be budgeted. However, for our purposes, when we use the term *budgeting* in this chapter, we are referring to the narrower, more commonly used financial budget.

The Master Budgeting Process

The *master budgeting process steps* are to develop the (1) revenue and expenditure operating budgets, (2) capital expenditures budget, and (3) financial budgeted cash flow, income statement, and balance sheet. The three steps are illustrated with their substeps in Figure 15–6. Notice the feedback loop which takes into account possible revisions in a prior budget due to other budget developments. Each of the operating budgets and the capital expenditures budget will be explain in this section; the financial budgets will be covered in the next section.

The budget usually covers a one-year period, broken down by month, and the finance *controller* is responsible for the budgeting process that results in a *master budget* for the entire organization. In other words, it is the end result of the budgeting process. Although it is common for organizations to follow the three steps in the master budget process, the use of power and politics (Chapter 14) and the details of how each separate budget is actually developed do vary from organization to organization.

During the budgeting process, many controllers use a *budget committee* to aid in developing the master budget. A top-down and/or or bottom-up approach can be used. However, the focus of budgeting should be to enable the organization to meet its mission and objectives.[7] In other words, the budget is a means to the ends; the objectives are the end. It is effective to use both approaches by having the controller/committee request that the functional department managers each submit a proposed budget for the next year. It is common for the controller/committee to let the departments know if increases or even decreases in the budget are needed based on current and projected future performance.

Each department submits its proposed budget to the controller/committee for approval. However, during the budgeting process, the use of power and politics is common, and the negotiating conflict management style (Chapter 14) is typically used to resolve expected conflicts that exist when allocating scarce resources. The controller/committee may negotiate recommended revisions with department managers and/or use its position power to require revisions.

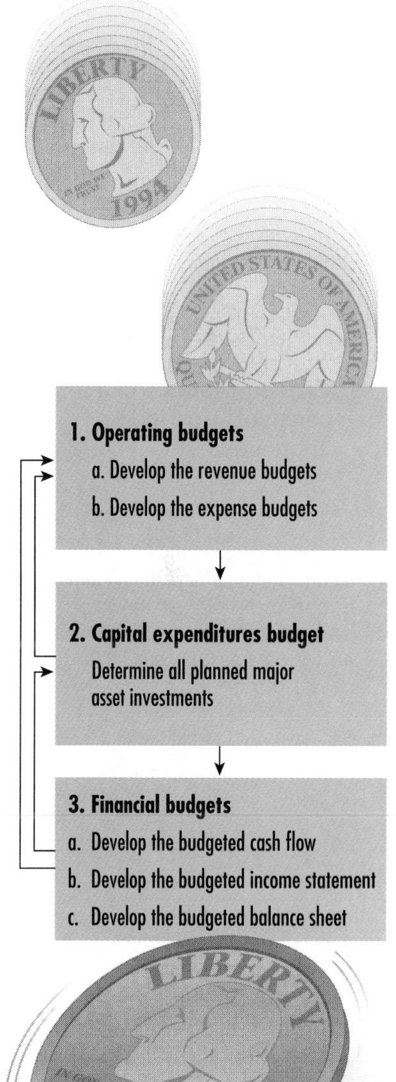

1. Operating budgets
a. Develop the revenue budgets
b. Develop the expense budgets
2. Capital expenditures budget
Determine all planned major asset investments
3. Financial budgets
a. Develop the budgeted cash flow
b. Develop the budgeted income statement
c. Develop the budgeted balance sheet

Figure 15–6
The Master Budgeting Process Steps

Operating Budgets

The **operating budgets** *include the revenue and expense budgets.* As you have learned from experience, you must first determine how much money you have, or will have, before you can plan how you are going to spend it. Therefore, the first step in the master budgeting process is to determine the revenue then the expenditure (operating) budgets.

operating budgets
Include the revenue and expense budgets.

Revenue Budgets. A *revenue budget* is the forecast of total income for the year. Although sales is the most common form of revenue, many organizations, including MOCON, have revenue from investments. And nonprofit organizations often get income from fees, donations, grants, and fund raisers. The revenue budget projects and adds all sources of income, such as sales for each product and/or location, together. The marketing/sales department commonly provides the revenue figures for the entire firm.

The revenue budget is primarily based on the sales forecast. Refer back to Chapter 6 for the details on sales forecasting. In a sense, the sales forecast revenue budget is the most important budget because the other budgets are based on it.

Expense Budgets. An *expense budget* is the forecast of total operating spending for the year. It is common for each functional area/department manager to have an expenditure budget. Many managers fear budgets because they have weak math or accounting skills. In reality, budgeting requires planning skills rather than math and accounting skills. And using a computer makes the job even easier. Through the systems effect, all department budgets affect the others and managers need to share information. For example, the operations department needs the sales forecast to determine how much it will produce, and the human resources department needs to determine organizationwide employee needs to develop its budget.

As stated, the budget process varies. First-line managers may submit their budgets to their middle-manager boss, who submits a combined budget for the combined functional area/departments, who in turn submit their budget to the top manager/controller. Next, you will learn more about expenditure budgets. However, let's first talk about profit centers.

Profit Centers. Organizations that identify the revenue and expenses of their units have *profit centers*. Profit centers are commonly used with the divisional structure (Chapter 7) in which the company has lines of business (companies within a company) that are given their own separate budgets. For example, Philip Morris Corporation has Philip Morris Cigarettes, Miller Beer, Kraft, and General Foods divisions which are each profit centers that calculate their own revenue minus expenses to determine profits. At the corporate level, managers evaluate profit center performance, and combine the business units' revenue and expenses to determine corporate performance.

5. Explain the difference between line-item versus program budgets, static versus flexible, and incremental versus zero-based budgeting.

Expense Budget Alternatives

Major expenditure budget alternatives include line-item versus program budgets, static versus flexible, and incremental versus zero-based budgets. Before we discuss these alternatives, let's define two important types of cost that are important to expenditure budgets. *Fixed costs* remain unchanged in total amount over a wide range of activities. For example, the cost of rent is the same regardless of how often the facility is actually used. *Variable costs* change in total amount as activity increases. For example, the cost of sales catalogs and mailing will increase with the number printed and mailed. You will learn more about cost in Exercise 15–1.

Line-Item vs. Program Budgets. When projecting expenses, the format generally takes one of two forms, or it can combine them. A *line-item budget* identifies the major expenses of the department/organization, and is the most commonly used form. With the functional organizational structure (Chapter 7), each department is a cost center with its own line-item budget; these are combined to form the expense budget for the master budget.

A *program budget* identifies the expenses of specific organizational activities or units. See Figure 15–7 for separate line-item and programmed budgets for the current year (adopted) and the next year (proposed). The ten line items are the major school system expenses, and the school system has six major programs. Notice that the total budget expenses are the same for both forms of budgets. It is only the presentation of the expenses that changes. Also, notice that expenses do not include payments for major assets such as buildings and equipment that will last for several years. For example, Milford has a two-year-old school which will be paid off over a 20-year loan, and it is still paying off two others. However, it does not show up on the expense budget because it is not part of operating the school system. Payments for major assets are part of the capital budget and will be explained in more detail later in this section.

A program budget is similar to a profit center in that the expenses can be identified for a unit of the business; however, the revenues from the units cannot be. For example, the school system has no revenue from any of its programs; revenues come from the city taxes.

See Figure 15–7, bottom, for a combined budget showing both line items and programs together for the current year only. Notice that line items and total columns remain the same. All you do is identify the amount for each program. With separate programs/units, the combined budget gives a more detailed account of where the money is being spent. In Skill-Building Exercise 15–2, you will take a line-item budget and make it a combined line-item and program budget.

Figure 15–7
City of Milford School System Line-Item, Program Budget, and Combined Budget for the Fiscal Year Ending June 30

Line Budget

	Adopted Budget 1995–96	Proposed Budget 1996–97
Teachers' Salaries	$ 980,000	$1,050,000
Administrative salaries	120,000	132,000
Clerical salaries	70,000	75,000
Maintenance salaries	80,000	85,000
School supplies	90,000	105,000
Maintenance supplies	20,000	26,000
Utilities	38,000	46,000
Other facilities expenses	28,000	30,000
Miscellaneous expenses	24,000	25,000
Transportation	150,000	176,000
Total	$1,600,000	$1,750,000

Program Budget

	Adopted Budget 1995–96	Proposed Budget 1996–97
Primary education	$ 655,000	$ 712,000
Secondary education	729,000	786,000
Student enrichment programs	90,000	98,000
Adult education	58,000	67,000
Athletic programs	53,000	62,000
Community service programs	15,000	25,000
Total	$1,600,000	$1,750,000

Combined Line Item and Program Budget

Adopted Budget 1995–96

	Primary Educa.	Second. Educa.	Student Enrich.	Adult Educa.	Athletic	Comm. Service	**Total**
Teacher's salaries	$392,000	$490,000	$58,000	$32,000	$ 6,000	$ 2,000	**$ 980,000**
Administrative salaries	65,000	40,000	6,000	3,000	4,000	2,000	**120,000**
Clerical salaries	34,000	28,000	4,000	2,500	1,000	500	**70,000**
Maintenance salaries	40,000	30,000	1,500	500	6,500	1,500	**80,000**
School supplies	38,000	43,000	3,000	4,000	1,000	1,000	**90,000**
Utilities	18,000	12,000	3,000	1,000	3,500	500	**38,000**
Maintenance supplies	8,000	6,000	700	500	4,500	300	**20,000**
Other facilities expenses	8,000	6,300	500	500	12,000	700	**28,000**
Miscellaneous expenses	1,000	1,700	300	12,000	6,000	3,000	**24,000**
Transportation	51,000	72,000	13,000	2,000	8,500	3,500	**150,000**
Total	**$655,000**	**$729,000**	**$90,000**	**$58,000**	**$53,000**	**$15,000**	**$1,600,000**

Figure 15–8
Springfield College Training and Development Services Flexible Budget (and Conversion to Line-Item Budget)

Income				
Revenue	100%	$15,000	$20,000	$25,000
Expenses				
Trainer's salary	50%	7,500	10,000	12,000
Overhead	20%	3,000	4,000	5,000
Expenses	10%	1,500	2,000	2,500
College Surplus	20%	3,000	4,000	5,000
S.C. Line-Item Budget (Account Number and Title)				
1. Salaries (50% of revenue)			10,000	
2. Labor (part of expenses)			500	
3. Supplies (part of expenses)			1,100	
4. Travel (part of expenses)			400	
5. Equipment			0	

Static versus Flexible Budgets. A *static budget* has only one set of expenses, while a *flexible budget* has a series of expenses for a range of activities. The static budget is appropriate in a stable environment in which there is little change in demand for the product. The Milford School System budget is a static budget. A flexible budget is appropriate in a turbulent environment in which demand for the product changes over a range of activities with variable cost.

At Springfield College, a professor started a training and development (SCT&DS) consulting business for the college. SCT&DS was started as a profit center. The professor's role as director was a part-time addition to his job as he continued to teach his full course load of four classes per semester, so he did not have a lot of time to devote to the profit center. In the first year, the director had no previous sales to use as the basis for forecasting revenue or expenses. Having developed the profit center based primarily on variable cost and with an uncertain demand for the services, he developed the flexible budget shown in Figure 15–8. The flexible budget had to be placed within the college line-item budget. This is shown at the bottom of the budget for the one set of figures that was actually put into the computerized master budget.

Work Application

9. Identify the major source of revenue(s) and expenses where you work or have worked. State which budget alternatives (line-item vs. program, static vs. flexible, and incremental vs. zero-based) are used at this organization. If you are not sure, call or talk to your present or past boss and find out.

Incremental versus Zero-Based Budgets. Incremental and zero-based budgets do not change the presentation of the funds like the line-item versus program and static versus flexible budgets do. Their focus is on how the budgeted figures are derived based on their justification.

With *incremental budgeting,* past funds are allocated with only new expenses being justified and approved. With *zero-based budgeting* (ZBB) all funds must be justified each year. ZBB assumes that the previous year's budget should not be the base on which to rework the budget for the next year. The zero-base focus is on the mission and objectives and the determination of what it will cost to achieve them. ZBB is especially appropriate in turbulent environments in which some departmental activities/products are increasing dramatically while others are decreasing. Departments with decreasing activity should not simply be given their prior-year budget; it should be cut. At Springfield College, the first four line items, Figure 15–8, are incremental while item 5 equipment is a ZBB.

Capital Expenditures Budget

6. Define *capital expenditure budget* and explain how it is different from the expense budget.

capital expenditures budget Includes all planned major asset investments.

The second step in developing the master budget is to develop the capital expenditures budget. *The* **capital expenditures budget** *includes all planned major asset investments*. Major assets are owned by the organization and last for, and are paid for, over several years. The major assets budgeted for may include land, new buildings, whole new product lines or projects, or acquiring an existing company. On a lower level, other decisions include whether to replace existing assets such as machinery with new ones, to buy or lease assets, to make components yourself or to buy them through outsourcing, or to rework defective outputs or to sell or scrap them. But, in every case, the objective is to earn a satisfactory return on the invested funds. Raising the money to buy the capital asset is an important finance function.[8]

Capital expenditures are difficult decisions because they are often based on long-range forecast under the condition of uncertainty (Chapter 4). These decisions are critical because (1) large sums of money are often involved, (2) funds are committed for long periods of time, and (3) once the decision is made and a project is begun, it may be difficult or impossible to reverse the effects of a poor decision.

When making capital expenditures, various financial calculations can be made to aid in decision-making. Three commonly used technique are return on investment, discounted cash flow, and cost-volume-profit analysis. A simple definition of *discounted cash flow* is that it is what you have left over after paying for the investment, or it is the time value of money. Cost-volume-profit analysis, which includes break-even analysis, is used to predict profits based on various selling prices and cost. In Skill-Building Exercise 15–2, you will use cost-volume-profit analysis to determine if you should run an aerobics dance class. The decision is based on your objectives and the profitability of the program. With either of the three methods, or a combination, you rank each investment opportunity and select the one(s) with the greatest benefit to the organization.[9]

It is true that controlling expenses is important. However, focusing on controlling costs of products that are decreasing in customer value and sales will only postpone business failure. There seems to be a strong link between capital budgets and long-term success of new product development.[10] Capital expenditure budgeting is the most important budget because it is based on developing ways to bring in additional revenues through new and improved products and projects that will create customer value. MOCON and other companies continually work to develop new products and plan to take advantage of opportunities. MOCON's recent capital expenditures budget included offering new products (which included discounted cash flow and cost-volume profit analysis) and opening additional sales offices in Pennsylvania, New Jersey, and New York (which included a buy or lease decision). Each new product and sales office requires an operating expense budget. Hence, the need for the feedback loop from capital budgeting back to operating budgets in the master budgeting process (Figure 15–6).

Work Application

10. Identify the major capital asset expenditures your present or past organization invested in.

FINANCIAL STATEMENTS AND BUDGETS

The primary financial controls revolve around the three primary financial statements in their completed and budgeted formats, which are the topics of this section. Financial statement ratio analysis, covered in the first part of this section, is an easily understood measure of performance.[11] Financial statements and their analysis are also used by others, such as suppliers, creditors, and investors, to evaluate the financial integrity of the organization when making decisions to conduct business with the firm.[12]

Managers are expected to understand financial statements and how business transactions affect each statement.[13] Therefore, in this section you will learn about the three financial statements and financial budgets, and in Applying the Concept 15–2 you will determine which financial statement areas are affected by given business transactions.

7. List the three primary financial statements and what is presented in each of them.

financial statements
Include the income statement, balance sheet, and cash flow statement.

Financial Statements

The three primary **financial statements** *are the income statement, balance sheet, and cash flow statement.* They are presented in the order in which they appear in annual reports.

The Income Statement. The *income statement* presents revenues and expenses and the profit or loss for the stated time period. The income statement primarily covers one year. However, monthly and quarterly income statements are also developed to measure interim performance and to use concurrent control when necessary. When revenue exceeds expenses, there is a net income. When expenses exceed revenues, there is a net loss. Figure 15–9 is MOCON's income statement as reported in its 1994 annual report. Losses are indicated by parentheses. Note that MOCON has a loss on investment income.

The two primary ways to increase net income are to (1) increase revenues and (2) decrease expenses. A combination of the two expedites income increases. The capital expenditure budget focuses on increasing revenues, while the expense budget can be used to focus on decreasing costs.

The Balance Sheet. The *balance sheet* presents the assets and liabilities and owners' equity. Assets are owed by the organization. Liabilities are its debts owed to others. Owners'/stockholders' equity is the assets minus the liabilities, or the share of assets owed. It is called a balance sheet because the total of the assets always equals the total of the liabilities plus owners' equity for a particular point in time. Figure 15–10 is MOCON's balance statement as reported in its 1994 annual report.

Figure 15–9
Consolidated Statements of Income, Modern Controls, Inc. Year Ended December 31

Revenue	**1994**	**1993**
Sales	$10,612,752	$10,404,555
Cost of sales	3,941,933	3,911,938
Gross profit	6,670,819	6,492,617
Expenses		
Selling, general administrative expenses	3,353,291	3,252,597
Research and development expenses	897,729	814,402
Investment income	(366,178)	(394,625)
	3,884,842	3,672,374
Income before income taxes	2,785,977	2,820,243
Income taxes	933,000	931,000
Net income	**$ 1,852,977**	**$ 1,889,243**
Net income per common share (primary and fully diluted)	$ .39	$ .39

The operating budgets project the current assets and liabilities. The capital expenditure budget affects the major assets, commonly called property/plant and equipment, and the long-term liabilities. The long-term liabilities are the payments for the major assets made over several years, such as mortgages payable and bonds payable. Notice in Figure 15–10 that MOCON has property

Figure 15–10
Consolidated Balance Sheet, Modern Controls, Inc.

	December 31	
	1994	1993
Assets		
Current assets		
Cash and temporary cash investments	$ 246,265	$ 846,079
Marketable securities, current	5,664,849	3,228,464
Accounts receivable		
Trade, less allowance for doubtful accounts of $147,000 in 1994 and $150,000 in 1993	1,511,700	935,920
Other receivables	151,480	171,315
Inventories	1,733,760	1,812,736
Prepaid expenses	177,061	119,251
Deferred income taxes	358,000	456,000
Total current assets	9,843,115	7,569,765
Marketable securities, noncurrent	2,367,003	5,464,182
Property and equipment	1,827,421	1,730,246
Less accumulated depreciation & amortization	1,310,824	1,055,960
	516,597	674,286
Other assets	401,656	368,787
	$13,128,371	**$14,077,020**
Liabilities and Stockholders' Equity		
Current liabilities		
Accounts payable	$ 347,121	$ 185,111
Accrued compensation	365,598	210,788
Other accrued expenses	246,457	242,970
Estimated product warranties	140,000	161,000
Accrued income taxes	252,243	201,379
Dividends payable	233,905	241,929
Total current liabilities	1,585,324	1,243,177
Deferred income taxes	29,000	18,000
Stockholders' equity		
Common stock—$.10 par value; authorized 10,000,000 shares; issued and outstanding 4,526,231 shares in 1994 and 4,819,925 shares in 1993	452,623	481,992
Capital in excess of par value	—	1,398,629
Retained earnings	11,171,424	10,935,222
Net unrealized loss on noncurrent marketable equity securities	(110,000)	—
Total stockholders' equity	11,514,047	12,815,843
	$13,128,371	**$14,077,020**

and equipment assets, and its only long-term liability is deferred income taxes. Therefore, its major assets are paid for and owned by MOCON. This limited liability provides ability to invest in capital expenditures.

Cash Flow Statement. The *cash flow statement* presents the cash receipts and payments for the stated time period. It commonly has two sections: operating and financial activities. Checks are considered cash. Cash flow statements typically cover one year. However, monthly and quarterly statements are also developed to measure interim performance and to use concurrent control when necessary. The operating budgets and capital expenditures budget affect the cash flow statement as cash revenue is received and cash expenses and expenditures are paid.

The cash flow indicates when the firm will have surplus cash it can invest and when it will have a cash deficit and will need to borrow money. Accurate cash flow statements are especially important to seasonal businesses. For example, most of Head snow ski sales take place in the winter months. Therefore, during the winter months it will have a surplus of cash and during the summer months it will have negative cash flow. Head may take the cash surplus in the winter and put it into short-term investments to earn interest and have it available during the summer months to pay its bills. If Head budgets for a bad year in which cash payments will exceed receipts, it can plan to borrow short-term money to pay its bills in the summer. The cash flow statement also indicates the firm's ability to finance capital expenditures and aids in the selection process.[14]

APPLYING THE CONCEPT

AC 15–1 Financial Statements

Identify the accounts affected by each business transaction for a retail store. (*Hint:* Transactions require two- or three-letter answers based on cash versus credit activities.)

Income Statement	*Balance Sheet*	*Cash Flow Statement*
a. Revenue (sales)	c. Current assets (cash, accounts receivable, inventory to sell)	h. Cash receipts i. Cash payments
b. Expenses (operating bills)	*d. Property and equipment* e. Current liabilities (accounts payable) f. Long-term liabilities (mortgage payable) g. Owners' equity *(stock, retained earnings)*	

____ **1.** You sent a check to pay for the building you own; there are ten years of payments left.

____ **2.** You took the money and charge slips out of the cash register to record today's sales, and they totaled $5,000.

____ **3.** You sent a check to Wrangler to pay for the jeans you bought on credit 30 days ago to sell to your customers.

____ **4.** You need cash to open another store, so you sold $25,000 worth of stock to a friend.

____ **5.** You gave your employees their weekly paychecks today.

____ **6.** Chris, a personal friend, came to your store, after you were closed, and bought $500 worth of clothes. Chris will pay for them at the end of the month. Because you were closed, you decided to make a separate transaction rather than add it to today's or tomorrow's sales.

____ **7.** You ordered and received $2,000 worth of Nike sneakers on credit.

____ **8.** You received a check for $30,000 for your customer credit card sales from the bank/VISA.

____ **9.** You bought a new computer cash register system that will keep accurate records of merchandise sold and in inventory, on a monthly, three-year installment credit payment plan.

____ **10.** You were given a check for $35 for the sale of your old cash register.

Comparisons. Note that the income statement and cash flow statement cover up to one year. However, the balance sheet shows the cumulative effect of business transactions since starting the organization, up to the date of the statement. Two or more years of figures are commonly presented with all three financial statements for comparison purposes as a measure of performance progress, or lack thereof.

The income statement is often considered the most important financial statement to managers and investors. The cash flow statement is often considered more important to suppliers of credit and lenders, such as banks, because it indicates the organization's ability to pay them back. An income statement can conceal cash outflow and report a profit while the cash flow budget indicates negative cash flow.[15] However, the three statements together allow better assessment of overall financial performance.

Work Application

11. Does the company you work or have worked for make its financial statements available to the public? If it does, get a copy and review it. Also, does the organization develop operating, capital expenditures, and financial budgets? If it does, try to get copies for review. If you are not sure, call or talk to your present or past boss and find out.

Financial Budgets

The third step in the master budgeting process is to prepare financial budgets. In other words, before the year begins, the controller forecasts what each statement will be at year end. The financial budgets are prepared last because the operating and capital expenditure budget figures are needed to prepare them. The cash flow budget is the first financial statement prepared because it is needed to prepare the other two. The income statement budget is prepared second because it is needed to prepare the balance sheet. If the budgeted financial statements do not meet expectations, the capital expenditures budget and/or operating budgets may need to be revised. Hence the need for the feedback loop in the master budget process in Figure 15–6. Revisions are common when a net loss is projected.

Each statement is commonly budgeted for the year with each month and quarter presented. The difference between the budget, also called pro forma, statement and actual statements is that the term *budget* or *pro forma* is placed before each statement's name. One reports past results and the other projects future results. Budgets are preliminary control and actual statements are rework control.

Following the control systems process: (1) The budgeted statements are standards which serve as preliminary controls. (2 and 3) Performance is measured monthly and compared to the budget. Corrective, concurrent control is taken, when necessary, to reach the yearly budget. (4) At year end, the budgeted and actual financial statements serve as the basis for next year's budget or, in other words, the budget goes through rework controls. Damage control may be needed during the control systems process.

Corporations that are owned by shareholders with stock sold through the New York, American, or NASDAQ stock markets must make their annual reports, which include financial statements, available not only to the shareholders, but to the general public. However, there is no such requirement for budgets. Most corporations keep their budgets private for competitive reasons. And not all organizations have a master budget with operating, capital expenditures, and financial budgets.

PRODUCTIVITY

8. State how to measure productivity and list the three ways to increase it.

Since the United States went from being an industrial power to a struggling player in the international economy, productivity has been a premiere issue.[16] Compared to the 1970s and 1980s, there has been very little growth in productivity in the 1990s.[17] Employees would like to get paid more. However, if they are paid more without producing any more, the common approach is to raise product prices to offset the wage cost to maintain profits. In simple terms, this combined effect causes inflation. The only real way we can increase our standard of living is to increase productivity. As a manager, you should understand how to measure and increase productivity, and to do so in the functional areas.

Measuring Productivity

The U.S. government measures productivity rate on a macro level for various industries and has been criticized for the methods it uses.[18] As a result, the U.S. Bureau of Economic Analysis created new and more accurate rules for measuring productivity.[19] Measuring productivity can be complex when determining cost, but it doesn't have to be and we'll keep it simple, yet realistic, enough for you to use on the job. We will focus on measuring productivity on the micro company level.

productivity
A performance measure relating outputs to inputs.

Productivity *is a performance measure relating outputs to inputs*. In other words, productivity is measured by dividing the outputs by the inputs. For example, a trucking company wants to measure productivity on a delivery. The truck traveled 1,000 miles and used 100 gallons of gas. Its productivity was 10 miles to the gallon:

$$\frac{\text{output: 1,000 miles traveled}}{\text{inputs: 100 gallons of gas}} = \text{productivity: 10 mpg}$$

The inputs selected can be in a variety of forms. In the preceding example, the inputs were gallons of gas. Inputs could also be labor hours, machine hours, number of workers, the cost of labor, and so on.

Another fairly simple example, following a four-step process, involves measuring the productivity of an accounts payable department. (1) Select a base period of time, such as an hour, day, week, month, quarter, or year. We'll use a week. (2) Determine how many bills were sent out during that period of time (outputs): 800—We checked the records. (3) Determine the cost of sending out the bills (inputs). Determining cost can become complicated if you use overhead, depreciation, and so forth. We'll calculate cost based on direct labor charges. We have three employees. Each is paid $7 per hour. They all worked 40 hours during the week, or a total of 120 hours. The total cost is $7 per hour times 120 hours, or $840. (4) Divide the number of output bills by the input costs to determine the productivity rate of .95 (800 ÷ $840 = .95).

The performance of .95 can be stated differently. It is usually stated as a ratio (in this case, .95:1), or as a percentage (95 percent). It can also be stated as a labor cost per unit. To determine the *labor cost per unit*, you reverse the process and divide the input by the output. In this case, it cost $1.05 to send out each bill ($840 ÷ 800).

Calculating Productivity Percentage Changes. The .95 productivity rate is set as the base standard. In the next week, the accounting department sent out 800 bills, but due to machine problems, concurrent corrective action of having employees work overtime was needed to meet the standard output at an additional cost of $100. The productivity rate went down to .85 (800 ÷ $940). And the labor cost per unit went up to $1.175 ($940 ÷ 800). To determine the percentage change, use this formula:

Current productivity rate	85
− Base standard productivity rate	95
= Change	10

Change ÷ base productivity rate (10 ÷ 95) = .1053 or
there was a 10.53 percent decrease in productivity

Note that it is not necessary to use the decimal for .95 and .85, and when the base current productivity rate is less than the standard you have a decrease in productivity, but it is not necessary to use a negative number.

Production versus Productivity. It is important to calculate productivity rather than just production output because you can increase production while decreasing your productivity. For example, if the accounts payable department sends out 850 bills (production) but it takes 10 hours of overtime (which cost time-and-a-half at $10.50 per hour × 10 hours = $105), productivity has decreased to .90 (850 ÷ 945) from .95. The same thing could happen if they hired a full- or part-time employee rather than pay overtime. In other words, if you only measure output production and it increases, you can be fooled into thinking you are doing a better job, when in reality you are doing a worse job. So, measure productivity not simply production, and work to continuously increase productivity to provide greater customer value.

Increasing Productivity

There are three ways to increase productivity:

- Increase the value of the outputs while maintaining the value of the inputs (↑ O ↔ I)
- Maintain the value of the outputs while decreasing the value of the inputs (↔ O ↓ I)
- Increase the value of the outputs while decreasing the value of the inputs (↑ O ↓ I)

The preceding accounts payable department example will be used as the standard to illustrate the three methods with unrelated situations.

(↑ O ↔ I) The manager conducted a training program for the employees. As a result of the training, they sent out 850 bills the following week (outputs increased), without getting a raise in pay (inputs maintained). The current productivity increase is figured as follows: 850 ÷ $840 = 1.01. As a ratio it is 1.01:1. As a percentage it is 101%. The percentage increase was 6.32% (101 − 95 = 6 ÷ 95 = .0632). The labor cost per unit decreased to .9882 cents ($840 ÷ 850) or by 6.18 cents each (1.05 − .9882).

(↔ O ↓ I) Bill, one of the employees, was out sick on Thursday. Bill is a salaried employee but he used up his paid sick days, so he was docked $56 from his pay. Cost decreases to $784 ($840 − $56). The manager helped out a little on Friday and convinced the other two employees to push hard to maintain the 800 billing level. The current productivity level is 1.02 (800 ÷ $784). As a ratio it is 1.02:1. As a percentage it is 102%. The percentage increase was 7.37% (102 − 95 = 7 ÷ 95 = .0737). The labor cost per unit decreased to .98 cents ($784 ÷ 800) or by 7 cents each (1.05 − .99).

(↑ O ↓ I) Through the capital expenditures budget, the manager bought a new computer with a new accounts payable software program. The three employees were given jobs in another department. An experienced computer operator was hired at $12 per hour for a 40-hour workweek ($480 per week). During the week, 900 bills were sent out. The current productivity level is 1.88 (900 ÷ $480). As a ratio it is 1.88:1. As a percentage it is 188%. The percentage increase was 97.89% (188 − 95 = 93 ÷ 95). The labor cost per unit decreased to .5333 cents ($480 ÷ 900) or by .5167 cents each (1.05 − .5333), which is about half the previous cost.

APPLYING THE CONCEPT

AC 15–2 Measuring Productivity

The standard monthly productivity rate in your department is:

$$\frac{\text{outputs: 6,000 units}}{\text{inputs: \$9,000 cost}} = .67$$

For the first five months of the year, calculate the current productivity rate and show it as a ratio and percentage. Also, calculate the percentage productivity change, compared to the standard, stating if it was an increase or decrease.

11. January: outputs 5,900, inputs $9,000 ____ ratio, ____ %, ____ % change ↑ ↓

12. February: outputs 6,200, inputs $9,000 ____ ratio, ____ %, ____ % change ↑ ↓

13. March: outputs 6,000, inputs $9,300 ____ ratio, ____ %, ____ % change ↑ ↓

14. April: outputs 6,300, inputs $9,000 ____ ratio, ____ %, ____ % change ↑ ↓

15. May: outputs 6,300, inputs $8,800 ____ ratio, ____ %, ____ % change ↑ ↓

Input Cost. Note that in the three examples the capital expenditure cost of the old investment in the prior system and the new computer is not included in the inputs cost. Nor have any other costs been added to the labor cost such as paper and envelopes. The only input cost is direct labor cost. The cost of labor is a good source in most industries because wages account for two-thirds of business expenses.[20]

The important thing to realize is that the capital expenditure for the computer has increased productivity significantly. Due to the new computer, a new standard must be set for future comparisons, which means that it is not necessary to add the cost of the new computer to your inputs in measuring productivity in this situation. It will, however, affect the total cost per unit. Direct labor is commonly two-thirds of total cost. In large organizations, the accounting department can help you determine the total cost of your department inputs. You will learn more about costs, such as overhead, in Skill-Building Exercise 15–2.

Productivity Comparisons. Productivity measures are more meaningful when they are compared to other productivity rates.[21] For example, you can compare your department's productivity to that of other organizations and/or departments. This is done is Skill-Building Exercise 15–1. Most importantly, you should compare your productivity during one period to your productivity in other periods. This comparison will enable you to identify increases or decreases in productivity over time. A productivity rate can also be set as the standard, and you can compare your productivity to the standard on an ongoing basis. This is done in Applying the Concept 15–2.

Productivity has been referred to as a state of mind because everyone should be constantly thinking of ways to increase it. As a manager, you should be working with your employees to measure productivity and continually work to increase it in order to provide customer value. Productivity comparisons should be made in the functional areas, which is our next topic.

APPLYING THE CONCEPT

AC 15–3 MOCON Financial Ratios

Using MOCON's income statement and balance sheet, Figures 15–9 and 15–10, calculate the following ratios for 1994 using the calculations in Figure 15–11.

____ % **16.** Net profit margin. (Profitability ratios are commonly reported as percentages.)

____

____ % **17.** Return on investment.

____

____ :1 **18.** Current ratio. (Liquidity ratios are commonly reported as a ratio compared to one.)

____

____ :1 **19.** Debt to equity. (Leverage ratios are commonly reported as ratios. But you should realize that MOCON owns about 86% of its assets.) You need to add total current assets and deferred income taxes to get total liabilities.

____

_____ times **20.** Inventory turnover. (Operations ratios are reported as the number of times per year.) MOCON does not provide data to determine average inventory, so use the inventories number.

____

How would you say MOCON is doing financially based on these ratios?

____

Productivity Measures in the Functional Areas

The basic concepts of productivity measurement can be applied to all functional areas in the organization. Productivity is a *ratio* measure; in other words, it shows the relationship between two numbers. Ratios are used in the functional areas as productivity measures and to indicate strengths and areas for improvement through comparisons.[22] All productivity measures are indications of how well the organization is managed. See Figure 15–11 for a list of ratios in the functional areas. Although the ratios are separated by function, due to the systems effect they are interrelated.

Information and Financial Productivity Measures. The role of the information (MIS) department is to take input data and transform it into output information that can be used by organization members. Therefore, the individual numbers are data which are transformed through math to provide information, which is listed in the last column in Figure 15–11. You will learn about controlling information (MIS) in Chapter 17.

The numbers used to calculate the financial ratios are taken from the income statement and balance sheet; the cash flow statement is not used. As indicated in Figure 15–11, ratios are easy to calculate and to understand and they are commonly used in the control system as the means of measurement.[23] Some generally accepted liquidity financial ratio standards are: current ratio 2:1 and quick ratio 1:1.[24] Other ratio standards tend to vary by industry. In Applying the Concept 15–3, you calculate the 1994 financial ratios for MOCON. In addition, you can calculate the ratios for 1993 to compare them to 1994.

Although the financial ratios indicate performance, they do not measure the performance of the finance department itself. For example, the profitability ratios are based heavily on sales, which is a marketing function. We'll discuss others with their functions. However, the performance of the other departments is affected by how well the finance department does its job. For example, the finance department controls the budget which helps the other departments.

Work Application

12. Does a company you work or have worked for calculate financial ratios? If you are not sure, call or talk to your present or past boss and find out. If it does, identify which ones it calculates and give the ratios. If it does not calculate ratios, or you cannot get them, but it does provide financial statements, calculate them yourself.

Area	Ratio	Calculation	Information
Finance			
Profitability	Gross profit margin	$\frac{\text{Sales} - \text{COGS}}{\text{Sales}}$	Shows efficiency of operations and product pricing
	Net profit margin	$\frac{\text{Net profit/income}}{\text{Sales}}$	Shows product profitability
	Return on investment	$\frac{\text{Net profit/income}}{\text{Total assets}}$	Shows return on total capital expenditures, or assets' ability to generate profit
Liquidity	Current ratio	$\frac{\text{Current assets}}{\text{Current liabilities}}$	Shows ability to pay short-term debt
	Quick ratio	$\frac{\text{Current assets} - \text{inventory}}{\text{Current liabilities}}$	Shows stronger measure of bill-paying ability because inventory may be slow to sell for cash
Leverage	Debt to equity	$\frac{\text{Total liabilities}}{\text{Owners' equity}}$	Shows proportion of the assets owned by the organization. The higher the ratio, the more solvent the firm and the easier to get credit/funds.
Operations	Inventory turnover	$\frac{\text{Cost of goods sold}}{\text{Average inventory}}$	Shows efficiency in controlling investment in inventory. The larger the number the better because products are sold faster.
Marketing	Market share	$\frac{\text{Company sales}}{\text{Total industry sales}}$	Shows the organization's competitive position. The larger the better because it is outselling competitors.
	Sales to presentation	$\frac{\text{Sales completed}}{\text{Sales presentations made}}$	Shows how many presentations it takes to make one sale. The lower the better because less time is spent making nonproductive presentations.
Human Resources	Absenteeism	$\frac{\text{No. of absent employees}}{\text{Total no. of employees}}$	Shows the ratio/percentage of employees not at work for a given time period
	Turnover	$\frac{\text{No. of employees leaving}}{\text{Total no. of employees}}$	Shows ratio/percentage of employees that must be replaced for a given time period, usually one year
	Work force composition	$\frac{\text{No. of a specific group}}{\text{Total no. of employees}}$	Shows ratio/percentage of women, Hispanics, African-Americans, and so on

Figure 15–11
Functional Area Ratios

Also, the marketing department sells the products on credit, but it is the finance department that collects the payments and pays for the purchases made throughout the organization.

Marketing and Operations Productivity Measures. The marketing and operations areas of an organization are like the heart and lungs of the body. The key to business success is for these two areas, with the aid of the others, to continually increase customer value. If the marketing and operations areas/heart and lungs do not work well and together, the entire organization/body will not function properly/will be sick and may go bankrupt/die. The financial profitability ratios of gross profit margin and net profit margin are also considered marketing ratios because they are based on sales.

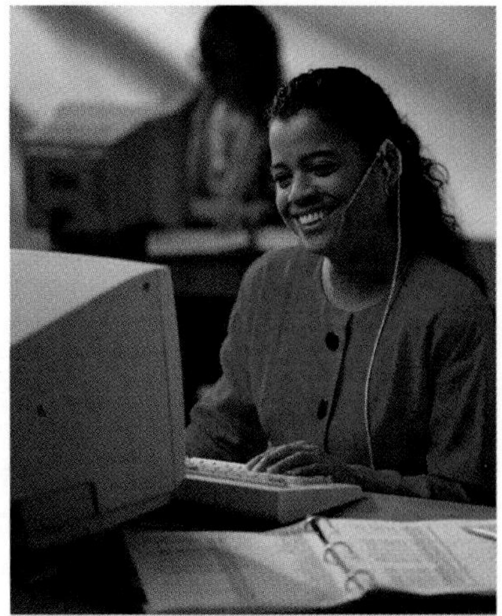
The key to business success is for marketing and operations to continually increase customer value.

Market share and sales to presentation are shown in Figure 15–11. However, these figures do not come from the financial statements. Market share is calculated in many industries by the government and professional/trade organizations for large businesses. When it is not, total industry sales are often given, and the organization can do the calculations as shown in the figure. Increasing market share is a common marketing objective. General Motors has lost market share as Ford has increased market share. Ford has the objective to pass GM to be the market leader in the auto industry.

Sales to presentations made is also important in developing and comparing employees. In industries like telemarketing, sales employees commonly use this ratio. It is helpful to the employees' egos to realize that they are only expected get one sale out of every 20 or so calls. Employees who make only one sale per 30 calls are not doing well comparatively. The sales to presentations can be calculated in, and it is an issue of, Skill-Building Exercise 15–1.

The operations function does not have a separate section in Figure 15–11 because it tends to use the basic productivity measure, which is more focused on input-output relations than other departments. However, the operations inventory turnover financial ratio in Figure 15–11 is primarily the operations department's responsibility. However, it is dependent on the marketing department for its sales forecast which it uses as the basis for its production budget. If sales are too optimistic, operations will produce too much and it will sit in inventory, which decreases the turnover rate. You will learn more about controlling operations and quality in Chapter 17.

The U.S. government provides business operations ratio information to the general public. For example, *The U.S. Department of Transportation Air Travel Consumer Report* lists the ten largest airlines ranked by on-time performance for the present and past period. Southwest ranked number one in October 1995 with 87 percent, as compared to its 1994 number one rank with 82.5 percent.[25]

Human Resources Productivity Measures. The numbers for calculating the human resource ratios shown in Figure 15–11 do not come from the financial statements. The numbers for these calculations, which are commonly reported as percentages, are computed by the human resources or information (MIS) departments.

Work Application

13. Describe how performance is measured in a functional department you work or have worked for. Is it measured as production or productivity? Explain. As the manager, how would you measure and increase productivity?

While there are no specific financial human resources ratios, all organizational performance is based on the employees it is responsible for attracting, developing, and retaining. In other words, the human resources department has a systems effect on the performance of all departments.

In the next chapter you will learn about the performance appraisal system and tools that are used to measure employee performance. In addition, you will develop skills in taking corrective action when employees are not performing to standards.

CURRENT MANAGEMENT ISSUES

Global. In response to *global* competition, some organizations have increased productivity by working better and faster with fewer employees. For example, Xerox halved both the number of employees and the amount of time needed to design a product. Harley-Davidson reduced total plant employment by 25 percent while cutting the time it takes to make a motorcycle by more than half.

Diversity. The four-step control systems process model and general productivity measures can be used globally with little, if any, changes for the *diversity* of people. However, accounting standards are diversified around the globe. Therefore, changes in financial statements and budgets must be made to account for local accounting practices, and for various tax considerations.

Ethics and Social Responsibility. In an ideal world, profits and *ethical principles* co-exist. In the real world, it's not so easy.[26] While unethical behavior cannot be completely eliminated, controls can help to minimize it. When controlling all organizational resources, especially human resources, managers need to be ethical when using power and politics. While some managers have not been *socially responsible* by intentionally reporting wrong numbers on budgets and financial statements to make their performance look better, this is not common practice. Constant, periodic, and occasional control methods, especially audits, should be used to help prevent such unethical behavior.

Quality and TQM. Controlling quality is a key component of *TQM*. Companies are emphasizing continuous quality improvement.[27] With the TQM focus on systems and processes, many organizations now develop budgets based on processes and their related costs instead of traditional itemized costs, as presented in this chapter. Analysis of the processes involved allows better evaluation of what is effective and what can be eliminated, and contributes to better long-term planning. This process approach is more popularly known as *activity-based budgeting* (ABC).[28] However, ABC should be re-engineered into the traditional cost accounting system rather than completely replacing it. This synthesis can result in a more focused, less expensive system that generates more precise product costs and enables managers to control their costs.[29]

Productivity. Downsizing and re-engineering have been used to increase *productivity*. Downsizing has emphasized cutting cost. Wages are a major cost that account for two-thirds of business expenses.[30] Two other areas of high cost are health insurance and workers' compensation insurance.[31] To cut cost in these areas, over the years large companies have been laying off employees. The economy tends to lose more than it gains through downsizing in the long run because workers who lose their jobs tend to fail to find equal jobs.[32] At the same time, the number of people without health insurance, or who have less extensive coverage, has gone up. On the bright side, layoffs have declined in the mid 1990s.[33] But, some companies cut costs too far and many manager now suffer from a cost-cutting focus.[34] Top managers who focus more on the external environment can better forecast business and manage their companies than managers who focus more on the internal environment, such as expenditure budgets.[35] In other words, to be successful in the long run, managers need to focus on capital expenditures to continually increase customer value and income.

Participative Management and Teams. Through the use of *participative management and teams*, employees are becoming more involved in the budgeting process. Recall the use of budget committees. Employee teams are also being empowered to revise existing control systems, to develop their own new control systems, to measure their own productivity, and to implement methods to increase productivity without requesting permission to do so. If this empowerment is encouraged through rewards that will motivate employees (Chapters 9 and 11), productivity will continue to increase.

Small Business. Both large and *small businesses* can use the control systems process. However, many very small business don't even use budgets, don't measure productivity, and don't calculate ratios, and tend to have simple accounting systems. Large businesses tend to follow the master budget process, have sophisticated accounting systems, calculate ratios and measure productivity several ways and compare their performance to competitors. However, preparing and following a well-planned budget will ensure smoother financial management for any size firm.[36] In fact, most banks require budgeted/pro forma financial statements before they will lend money to a small business.

Another area of diversity between large and small businesses is their ability to obtain external sources of funding. It is much more difficult, and more costly, for small businesses to obtain funding. Many banks that make business loans will not give them to small businesses, and, when funds are tight, those that do give them to the larger businesses first. This is one of the major reasons the Small Business Administration (SBA) was started and continues today. The SBA has a variety of small business loan programs.[37] If you start your own small business, be sure to pursue the SBA for funds and use the knowledge and skills from this chapter, along with that from all the other chapters.

CHAPTER SUMMARY AND GLOSSARY

The chapter summary is organized to answer the nine learning objectives for Chapter 15.

1. List the four stages of the systems process and describe the type of control used at each stage.
The first stage of the systems process is inputs. Preliminary control is designed to anticipate and prevent possible input problems. The second stages is the transformation process. Concurrent control is action taken as inputs are transformed into outputs to ensure standards are met. The third stage is outputs. Rework control is action taken to fix an output. The forth stage is customer/stakeholder satisfaction. Damage control is action taken to minimize negative impacts on customers/stakeholders due to faulty outputs. During the four stages feedback is used to improve upon the process to continually increase customer satisfaction.

2. Describe the appropriate feedback process among the functional areas/departments.
Throughout the systems process, feedback is circulated among all the functional areas in order to improve organizational performance in the input, transformation, and output processes while continually increasing customer satisfaction.

3. List the four steps in the control systems process.
The control systems process steps are: (1) set objectives and standards, (2) measure performance, (3) compare performance to standards, and (4) correct or reinforce, with a feedback loop for continuous improvement.

4. Describe the difference among the three control frequencies.
Constant controls are in continuous use. Periodic controls are used on a regular, fixed basis such as once a day or week. Occasional controls are used on a sporadic basis when needed.

5. Explain the difference between line-item versus program budgets, static versus flexible, and incremental versus zero-based budgeting.

The line-item budget identifies the major expenses of the organization/department, while the program budget identifies the expenses of specific organizational activities or units. A static budget has only one set of expenses, while a flexible budget has a series of expenses for a range of activities. With incremental budgeting, past funds are allocated with only new expenses being justified and approved. With zero-based budgeting, all funds must be justified each year.

6. Define *capital expenditures budget* and explain how it is different from the expense budget.
The capital expenditures budget includes all planned major asset investments. It consists of funds allocated for investments in major assets that will last, and be paid for, over several years. The expense budget contains funds allocated to pay for operating cost during the budgeting year. With expense budgets, the focus is on cost control. With capital expenditures, the focus is on the more important role of developing ways to bring in additional revenues through new and improved products and projects that will create customer value.

7. List the three primary financial statements and what is presented in each of them.
The income statement presents revenue and expenses and the profit or loss for the stated time period. The balance sheet presents assets, liabilities, and owners' equity. The cash flow statement presents the cash receipts and payments for the stated time period.

8. State how to measure productivity and list the three ways to increase it.
Productivity is measured by dividing the outputs by the inputs. Productivity is increased by (1) increasing the value of the outputs while maintaining the value of the inputs, (2) maintaining the value of the outputs while decreasing the value of the inputs, and (3) increasing the value of the outputs while decreasing the value of the inputs.

9. Define the following key terms (in order of appearance in the chapter):

Select one or more methods: (1) fill in the missing key terms from memory, (2) match the key terms from the end of the review with their definitions below, or (3) copy the key terms in order from the list at the beginning of the chapter.

______ is the process of establishing and implementing mechanisms to ensure that objectives are achieved.

______ is designed to anticipate and prevent possible problems.

__________ is action taken as inputs are transformed into outputs to ensure standards are met.

__________ is action taken to fix an output.

__________ is action taken to minimize negative impacts on customers/stakeholders due to faulty outputs.

The ______________ steps include: (1) set objectives and standards, (2) measure performance, (3) compare performance to standards, and (4) correct or reinforce.

______ measure performance levels in the areas of quantity, quality, time, cost, and behavior.

______________ are the limited number of areas in which satisfactory results will ensure successful performance to achieve the objective/standard.

__________ includes constant, periodic, and occasional.

The __________ analyzes the organization's planning, organizing, leading, and controlling functions for improvements.

A ______ is a planned quantitative allocation of resources for specific activities.

The __________ include the revenue and expense budgets.

The ______________ includes all planned major asset investments.

The three primary __________ are the income statement, balance sheet, and cash flow statement.

______ is a performance measure relating outputs to inputs.

KEY TERMS

budget
capital expenditures budget
concurrent control
control frequency
controlling
control systems process
critical success factors
damage control
financial statements
management audit
operating budgets
preliminary control
productivity
rework control
standards

REVIEW AND DISCUSSION QUESTIONS

1. Why is damage control important?
2. Why should you focus on preliminary and concurrent types of control rather than rework and damage control?
3. Who are the primary customers/stakeholders for the outputs of the operations, marketing, human resources, finance, and information functional areas/departments?
4. What are the five areas of performance that standards measure?
5. Why is measuring performance important to an organization?
6. What is shown in a performance report?
7. What is the role of reinforcement in the control systems process?
8. What are the three constant control methods, the three periodic control methods, and the four occasional control methods?
9. What are the three steps in the master budgeting process?
10. Why is the capital expenditures budget the most important budget?
11. What is the difference between financial statements and financial budgets?
12. Why should you measure productivity rather than just production?
13. What are some of the major ratio measures in the functional areas of finance, marketing, and human resources?

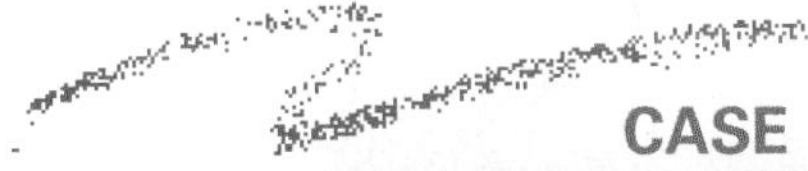

CASE

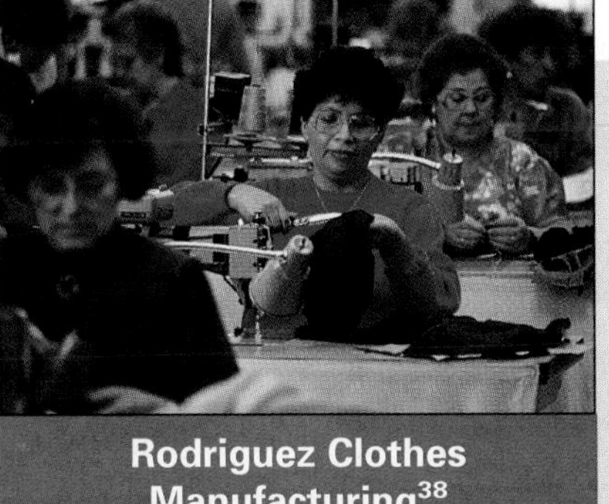

Rodriguez Clothes Manufacturing[38]

Carmen Rodriguez started his small business about 15 years ago in the Garment District in New York City. Carmen employs around 50 people who work in five different manufacturing teams. One of Rodriguez's teams presently makes quality shirts for men's clothing stores on basic manufacturing sewing machines. The cutting team provides them with the material which they sew together into a shirt. The shipping deparment team commonly adds a label and package with the store name for an additional fee prior to shipment. The five teams at Rodriguez work in one big room in which all clothes are made.

Carmen works in his separate office and spends his time on marketing, finance, and human resources management. He does not spend much time with the manufacturing employees. Each team has a leader who works individually like everyone else. Team leader responsibility is to keep team production records and the hours worked, to train the members, and to help them when there is a problem. Team leaders do not get involved with discipline or other problems; they report them to Carmen and he takes care of them.

Before Carmen came up with a new way to increase the workers' speed, employees made around 48 shirts per eight-hour day. Unlike some competitors, Carmen does not want to run a sweat shop, so he pays employees a salary rather than a low piece rate for actual work performed. However, if employees don't produce an average of 48 shirts, they lose their jobs. Carmen's employees have a higher rate of job satisfaction than the competitors', and Rodriguez has a quality reputation.

With all the competition, Carmen is not making much money. Carmen wanted to get employees to produce more shirts. Carmen thought about buying new machines as a capital expenditure, but he really does not have the money or the desire because his present machines are working fine. Carmen has also considered changing to piece-rate pay. However, he figured that if he pays employees more to produce more it will have an offsetting effect which will not benefit him much unless he takes a sweat shop approach, which he does not want to do. He also feared that if he went to piece rate pay he would have quality problems, which he did not want to risk. Carmen prides himself on being ethical and socially responsible to all stakeholders.

Carmen came up with the idea of setting a new quota in addition to the 48-shirt standard. Employees could leave work early once they met the new 53-shirt quota. Carmen figured he was not pushing his employees too hard and that they could get out of work around a half-hour early each day. Most of the employees were women with children, so he decided to try the new control system. He figured he would try the new quota system with the shirt team and if it worked, he could expand the idea to other teams as well.

Carmen met with the employees in the shirt team and told them, "I want to try a new idea for the next two weeks which I think is fair to everyone. If you produce 53 shirts you can go home for the day and get your full pay. I figure you can get out around 4:30 instead of 5 o'clock without having to rush your work. The same level of quality is required and will be checked as usual. You can continue to produce 48 shirts and work the full eight hours. What do you think of the idea?" They discussed the new system and they all liked the idea of working less hours for the same pay. The employees agreed to work a little faster to get out early. So Carmen said they'd try it for two weeks and evaluate the results and possibly make changes that were fair to everyone. If it did not work, they would go back to the old system.

After the first week, on the following Monday, Carmen got his weekly production reports from each team which state the number of units made by each worker and the hours each employee worked. Carmen got around to reading them after closing time, as usual. He went right to the shirt team report to see how the new system was working. Carmen was happy to see that everyone was producing 53 shirts and getting out around 4:30. However, on Friday, Maria made 53 shirts but left at 2:30. Carmen did not understand how this was possible. He decided to talk to Maria to see what was going on.

On Tuesday morning Carmen visited Maria at work and asked her how it was possible to get out at 2:30. Maria said, "All I did was adjust my machine and place this new gadget on it to speed it up. Plus I developed a new procedural sequence in which I make the shirt. Watch how much faster I can sew now; especially placing buttons on is so much faster." Carmen watched her make a shirt in amazement. He did not know what to say. Carmen told her to keep up the good work and went back to his office.

As Carmen walked back to his office he wondered to himself: "Should I continue to let her leave that early? Do the other workers think it's fair for Maria to get out so much earlier than they do? This is only a two-week trial that is subject to changes that are fair to everyone. What is the fair thing to do?"

Select the best alternative to the following questions. Be sure you are able to explain your answers.

___ 1. Carmen's allowing employees to go home early when they finished their work was a ___ control.

a. preliminary c. rework
b. concurrent d. damage

___ 2. The primary customer for the operations products is the ___.

a. customer b. marketing c. finance

___ 3. Carmen did not make the new standard clear in the area of ___.

a. quantity d. cost
b. quality e. behavior
c. time

4. In establishing the new policy that employees can leave when they complete their work, Carmen primarily used the ___ control method.

Constant	*Periodic*	*Occasional*
a. self-	d. regular reports	g. observation
b. clan	e. budgets	h. exception principle
c. standing plans	f. audits	i. special reports
		j. project controls

___ 5. The primary control method Carmen used in letting employees leave when they met the quota/standard was ___.

Constant	*Periodic*	*Occasional*
a. self-	d. regular reports	g. observation
b. clan	e. budgets	h. exception principle
c. standing plans	f. audits	i. special reports
		j. project controls

___ 6. In this case, Carmen is focusing on ___.

a. operating budgets c. financial budgets
b. capital expenditures d. productivity

___ 7. Carmen's new leave-early control system has a meaningful direct effect on ___ financial statement(s).

a. the income statement c. the cash flow
b. the balance sheet d. none of the

___ 8. Carmen's new control focuses on increasing

a. production b. productivity

___ 9. Carmen's new control technique focuses on

a. Increasing the value of the outputs while maintaining the value of the inputs.

b. Maintaining the value of the outputs while decreasing the value of the inputs.

c. Increasing the value of the outputs while decreasing the value of the inputs.

___ 10. Carmen's new control technique has the greatest potential to affect the ___ ratio because it measures the manufacturing department's performance.

a. profitability d. operations
b. liquidity e. marketing
c. leverage f. human resource

11. Did Carmen Rodriguez follow the four steps in the control systems process in this case? Explain your answer listing the steps he did and/or did not follow.

12. Calculate the production/productivity increase percentage change from before and after the new control method was introduced.

13. Is there any potential problem with Maria adjusting her machine?

14. Should Carmen keep the control system the way it is now and continue to let Maria leave two hours earlier than the other employees? If not, what should he do?

15. Is there any potential threat to employees with the increased production/productivity? Explain.

SKILL-BUILDING EXERCISE 15–1

Bolton Control System

Preparing for Skill-Building Exercise 15–1

Marie Bolton owns and operates the Bolton Clerical Employment Agency. As the name indicates, her agency focuses on providing clerical employees to its small business clients. Its service is recruiting clerical workers through newspaper advertising and word of mouth for walk-ins. They have a file of clerical employees looking for jobs, or better jobs. When employers place job orders with the agency, the agency recruiter tries to find a person who fits the job specifications. The agency sends possible candidates to the employer. The employment agencies charge the employer a fee only when one of their referred candidates is hired by the company. The fee is based on the employee's first-year salary. The average fee paid by employers is $1,000. The recruited clerical workers pay nothing for the service.

The small business clients could recruit their own employees, but without their own human resources staff, they feel that paying the average fee of $1,000 per employee hired is worth it. Each agency recruiter gets 35 percent of the fee charged as a salary. Pay is 100 percent commission. Refunds are made if the person placed does not stay on the job for a set period of time, usually three months for Bolton.

Marie has two employees called recruiters. With only two employees, Marie is also a full-time recruiter. She does the management functions in addition to recruiting. Marie takes care of the weekly advertising which brings in a steady flow of workers. Workers with immediate potential for job placement are interviewed by a recruiter. At the end of the interview, the recruiter asks if the candidate knows anyone who is looking for a clerical job. Marie follows up on these referrals if it's not busy, but this does not happen too often.

Bolton has a good relationship with several client employers who call the recruiters to fill jobs as they open. However, clients do tend to work with more than one employment agency, so speed is a factor in getting placements. Marie, not the recruiters, is also responsible for bringing in new client employers. If business is slow, Marie will call to develop new client employers seeking job openings. But, this does not happen very often.

Marie has no formal control methods because her two recruiters are very competent professionals who are paid only by commission; she places minimal restriction on them. Marie is somewhat satisfied with the way her business is operating. However, through a professional association she found out that her business is not doing as well as the average employment agency. Being competitive by nature, Marie does not want to be below average.

Marie has asked you to set up a control system to help her improve her agency's performance. She has provided you with the following performance report comparing her agency figures to those of the average agency. The professional association forecasts that revenues for next year will not increase for the industry.

Performance Information Report for Last Year

	Bolton	Average
Placement Revenue (refunds deducted, not taxes)	$230,000	$250,000
Recruiter commissions paid	$80,500	$87,500
Refunds	$8,000	$10,000
Number of placements	230	250
Number of company interviews	*	1,000
Number of full-time recruiters (including owners who recruit)	3	3

*Bolton does not keep records of the number of candidates it sends to companies for interviews.

Identify the systems process for Bolton by identifying its primary:

Inputs	*Transformation Process*	*Outputs*	*Customers/ Stakeholders*

Identify major types of control for each stage of the systems process:

Preliminary	*Concurrent*	*Rework*	*Damage*

To set up a control system for Bolton, follow the steps in the control systems process.

Step 1. Set Objectives and Standards

Marie's objective is to earn $250, 000 in revenue for the next year, which is the industry average. Establish standards for the year that will enable Marie to reach her objective.

Quantity of interviews and placements per recruiter: _____ _____

Calculate the number of additional interviews needed to meet the standard per recruiter _____ and the percentage increase _____ %.

Quality. Dollar value and number of acceptable refunds per recruiter: $ _____ _____

Time. State the time period in which the quantity and quality standards should be met: _____

Cost. State the cost based on commisions per recruiter: $ _____

Behavior. Identify any new behavior employees should change in order to help them meet the standards

____

____

Step 2. Measure Performance

What are the critical success factors for employment agencies? Have you identified the critical success factors within your standards? If not, rework them.

How often should Marie measure performance and what methods of control should she use?

Time frequency to measure performance: _______________

Quantity of interviews and placements per recruiter for time period: _____ _____

Specific control methods to use: ____________________

____

____

____

____

Step 3. Compare Performance to Standards

How should Marie compare her agency performance to her new standards? ____________________

____

____

____

Step 4. Correct or Reinforce

What type of corrective action should Marie take if standards are not being met, or reinforcement if they are? _____

____

____

____

Assume that Bolton does exactly meet the standard.

1. Calculate the rate of productivity for Bolton's past performance and for the new performance standard (average agency). ___ ___ Is there a change in productivity? ___ yes ___ no If yes, did it increase or decrease by what percentage? ______ Base the inputs on recruiter commissions only.
2. Calculate the past commission per employee and the new commission per employee (average agency). ___ ___ What percentage of a pay increase do recruiters get ___?
3. Do profits increase with the new standards being met? __

____

____

____

How do you think the employees will react to your proposed control system? Do you think they will resist the control? Why or why not?

____

____

____

Doing Skill-Building Exercise 15–1 in Class

Objective
To improve your skill at developing a control system for an organization/department.

Preparation and Experience
You should have developed a control system for Bolton Clerical Employment Agency in the preparation section of this exercise. In class you may work in a group to develop the control system.

Procedure (15–50 minutes)
Option A. The instructor goes over a possible control system for Bolton.

Option B. The instructor calls on one or more students to present their control system to the class.

Option C. Break into groups of four to six and develop the best control system for Bolton. Have one member be the spokesperson and write down the group's answers and report them to the class. The instructor will give you a set time, such as 10 to 15 minutes, for developing the control system.

Conclusion
The instructor may lead a class discussion and/or make concluding remarks about the exercise.

Application (2–4 minutes)
What did I learn from this exercise? How will I use this knowledge in the future?

____

____

Sharing
Volunteers give their answers to the application sections.

SKILL-BUILDING EXERCISE 15–2

Budgeting and Cost-Volume-Profit Analysis

Preparation for Skill-Building Exercise 15–2

In this chapter, you learned about budgeting, but not cost-volume-profit analysis (CVPA). Therefore, we'll cover CVPA then do a budgeting problem followed by a CVPA problem.

Cost-volume-profit analysis is a method of predicting what will happen to profits when there is a change in selling price, product mix, cost, and so on. CVPA uses break-even analysis but goes behind it to answer questions such as: What sales volume is needed to earn a specific profit?

What will happen to sales volume and profits if the selling price is increased or decreased? What will profits be if we buy new equipment? What price should we charge for a new product? What will happen to profits if we change the sales mix?

To answer these kinds of questions, CVPA is more appropriate than break-even analysis. The decisions made using CVPA are only as good as the sales forecast (Chapter 6) and cost allocations, which we cover next. CVPA is more reliable as an approximation rather than as a specific expectation.

Fixed versus Variable and Total Cost

Fixed costs remain unchanged in total amount over a wide range of activities. For example, the cost of rent is the same regardless of how often the facility is actually used. Note, however, that fixed cost per unit will decrease as the level of activity increases. If you pay $1,000 per month rent and are open for business 200 hours, rent costs you $5.00 per hour. If you are open 300 hours, rent costs you $3.00 per hour. Other examples are insurance and salaries.

Variable costs change in total amount as activity increases. For example, the more (or less) a retail store sells, the more (or less) its merchandise will cost. Variable costs change in direct proportion to changes in the level of activity. For example, each unit of merchandise costs the same ($20.00); therefore, if you sell one unit, it costs $20.00; if you sell ten units they cost $200. Other variable costs include materials and supplies.

Not all costs can be easily identified as fixed or variable since some have an element of both. They are called *semi-variable* or *mixed costs*. An example is a car you rent for $25.00 per day, plus $0.10 per mile.

Total cost (TC) is simply the addition of the total fixed costs plus variable costs.

Direct versus Indirect Cost

Direct cost (DC) can be identified with a specific activity (product, department, program, and so forth). Examples include a product's direct labor and material costs.

Indirect, overhead, cost cannot be identified with a specific activity. Examples include indirect labor, which includes people who help the line departments do their job while working for several of them. Indirect costs can be top management salaries or human resources and other staff departments such as maintenance staff who service other departments.

Break-Even Point

Break-even is the point at which there is no profit or loss. In addition to fixed and variable costs, other components of the formula must be identified. They include:

Selling price (SP) is the price charged for the sale of each product.
The number of units (NU) of products sold. Simply the total of all items sold.
Revenue (R) is the selling price times the number of units.

Contribution margin (CM) is the amount of revenue that the sale of each unit contributes toward payment of the fixed cost (FC). It is calculated by subtracting the variable cost per unit (VC) from the selling price per unit (SP)

$$\text{The break-even formula: BE} = \frac{\text{TFC}}{\text{CM}} \quad (\text{SP} - \text{VC})$$

If total fixed costs are $1,000, the selling price is $2.50, and variable costs are $0.50, what is the break-even point in units and dollars?

$$\text{BE} = \frac{\$1{,}000}{\$2.50 \quad -.50} \qquad \frac{\$1{,}000}{\$2.00}$$

$$\text{BE} = 500 \text{ units}$$
$$500 \text{ units} \times \$2.50 = \$1{,}250$$

Allocating Cost

In order to determine actual cost, both direct and indirect costs must be allocated to each activity. Direct costs are fairly easy to allocate because they are identifiable with the specific product. However, indirect costs (overhead) are not as easy to allocate. In order to determine actual costs, they must be allocated. When allocating indirect (overhead) costs you are allocating the cost of the support or service expenses to the revenue departments.

For example, at your college, the major revenue departments are the faculty-taught courses. However, courses cannot be offered without the aid of support (indirect cost) departments which include the nonteaching administrators, student activities staff, admissions, registrar, business office, physical plant department, police security, and so forth. The cost of all these services must be allocated to the teaching departments in order to determine the real cost of offering courses. What Springfield College actually does is to calculate the total indirect cost (overhead) and divide it by the total direct labor costs (faculty salaries). The actual percentage used is 50 percent. What is the direct labor cost plus overhead of one course if the average professor costs

$7,312.50 per course ($45,000 per year salary, plus 30 percent benefits divided by eight courses taught per year)?

$7,312.50 + 50% = $10,968.75

How many students are needed to break even at a tuition rate of $900 per course?

$10,968.75 ÷ $900 = 12.1875 or 13 students

As you know, some professors cost more or less than this amount, and some classes have more or less than the number of students enrolled. The college gets funds from sources other than tuition in order to help keep the cost of tuition lower than the actual cost. Springfield College tries to keep total revenue equal to, or greater than, its total cost.

When allocating costs, the two most popular methods are specific cost and percentage of use. The *specific cost method* is primarily for costs that can be identified with a specific program. For example, if two programs are using the same copy machine or mailings, a record of copies would be kept and each department would be charged for its actual use. This method is accurate, but it is time-consuming to keep records.

Percentage of use method does not keep records of use of such things as copying or mailing for each department. The total cost of copies and mailing is determined and allocated on a predetermined basis, such as 60 percent and 40 percent. Another example is rent. It can be allocated based on square footage (percent of use) with the commonly used areas' cost allocated in some predetermined way such as 50 percent for both programs.

Calculating Overhead Cost Based on Direct Labor

In labor-intensive organizations, it is possible to allocate the indirect overhead cost based on the cost of direct labor. The formula is as follows:

$$\frac{\text{Indirect cost (overhead)}}{\text{direct labor cost}} = \text{the percentage of overhead applied to direct labor}$$

To illustrate the calculation, turn to Figure 15–7, Combined Line Item and Program Budget, the Primary Education column. The first step is to calculate the overhead cost. Begin by identifying each line item as a direct or indirect cost. The only direct costs are teachers' salaries ($392,000) and school supplies ($38,000). All other costs are indirect overhead costs. Either take the total cost $65,000 minus direct cost $392,000 minus $38,000, which is $225,000; or add the overhead costs $65,000, $34,000, $40,000, $18,000, $8,000, $1,000, and $51,000, which equal $225,000. The overhead percentage rate is:

$$\frac{\text{Overhead}}{\text{direct labor}} = \frac{\$225{,}000}{\$392{,}000} = 57\%$$

PROBLEM 1 Converting a Line-Item Budget into a Combined Budget and Determining Overhead Cost

East Coast YMCA Budget 1997

		Youth	Adult
___ Executive Director's Compensation	$ 30,000		
___ Youth Programs' Compensation (2 employees)	40,000		
___ Adult Programs' Compensation (2 employees)	50,000		
___ Office Staff Compensation (2 employees)	18,000		
___ Maintenance Compensation	10,000		
___ Rent	10,000		
___ Utilities	2,000		
___ Program Materials and Expenses—Youth	2,000		
___ Program Materials and Expenses—Adult	1,000		
___ Supplies, Mail, Miscellaneous	2,000		
Total Expenses	$165,000	$75,800	$89,200

1. Place a F or V to the left of each line item to identify it as Fixed or Variable. Calculate the total F ___ and V ___ costs.
2. Place an I or D to the left of each line item, with its fixed or variable cost, to identify it as an indirect or direct cost. Calculate the total I ___ and D ___ costs.
3. To the right of the line-item budget, develop a program budget for the youth and adult programs. If the cost is direct you place it in one column and 0 in the other. If the cost is indirect, you allocate it between the two programs. Assume that the executive director and office staff (supplies) spend equal time with each program. The adult programs occupy 40 percent of the building, the

youth group 20 percent; the remaining 40 percent is used by both groups equally. After you finish allocating the line-item cost to each program, add up the totals. If they don't equal the total figures, you made an error.

4. If the direct revenue from the adult programs is $60,000 and the direct revenue from the youth programs is $50,000, which program is performing best? How did you make your decision?

5. Calculate the overhead rate based on direct labor for each program and both programs combined.

   Youth ______________________________

   Adult ______________________________

   Combined ______________________________

6. A youth program worker's compensation is $20,000; what is the direct labor overhead? Use the youth overhead percentage figure from question 5.

   ____

PROBLEM 2 Cost-Volume-Profit Analysis

East Coast YMCA Continued

The East Coast YMCA is considering offering an aerobic dance class for non-full-time YMCA members.

Cost-Volume-Profit Analysis. To make your decision to offer or not to offer an aerobic dance class, you decide to use CVPA. The options are much wider than the information presented here. For simplicity, while still being realistic, the options are limited for you as presented below.

Computer software spreadsheet programs, such as Lotus or Excel, make budgeting and CVPA easier and faster to do. If you have access to one, do this problem on a computer. It will do most of the calculations for you; all you need to do is plug in the numbers.

1. Calculate the total amount of adult staff time in hours and direct labor cost to implement the aerobic dance class assuming:
   - The class will run for a half-hour three times per week for 4 weeks. (Note: The number of weeks could be any number you select.) You also estimate it will take 24 hours to do the CVPA, advertise the class, and make other preparations for the classes.
   - The compensation of your full-time adult instructor is $400 per week. She works a 40-hour week. This will be an added responsibility with no additional pay. (Note: You could have used a part-time instructor at additional labor cost.)

   Total number of hours ___ × $ ___ cost per hour = $ ___ direct labor cost (DLC)

2. Calculate the total fixed cost assuming:
   - Advertising will cost $150 per ad and you plan to run only one ad. The instructor will also make up posters to be placed around the Y to get full-time members to tell their friends about the class. Poster cost is within overhead. (Note: You could use a variety of sizes of ads for different prices, and you could have used other promotions like radio, TV, and direct mail.)
   - Overhead cost was calculated in Problem 1 to be 76 percent for adult programs.

   Ad. cost ___ + DLC ___ + overhead ___ = $ ___ FC

3. Calculate the break-even (BE) number of participants needed assuming:
   - *Selling price (SP)*. You want to keep the price of the class low; use $20 per class member.
   - *Variable cost (VC)*. You estimate the additional expense to be only $0.25 for a membership card.
   - Round up to the next member regardless of the decimal because you at least want to know the point at which you will not lose money by running the class.

   FC $ ___ FC ___
   SP ___ − VC = CM ___ CM ___ = BE ___

4. Calculate the break-even (BE) number of participants needed assuming that you change the fixed cost by running two ads instead of one, and that you change the selling price to $30.

   FC $ ___ FC ___
   SP ___ − VC = CM ___ CM ___ = BE ___

5. Calculate the break-even (BE) number of participants needed assuming that you change the fixed cost by running three ads instead of one, and that you change the selling price to $35.

   FC $ ___ FC ___
   SP ___ − VC = CM ___ CM ___ = BE ___

   (Note: You could use any number of other assumptions to run "what if" scenarios. This job is easy with a computer software program.)

6. Calculate "what if" scenarios by filling in the figures for revenue, fixed cost, profit or loss, out-of-pocket cost (In other words, how much "cash" would it cost. Remember overhead is not a cash cost.), and out-of-pocket recovery (In other words, how much "cash" would you have if you run the class—revenue − O/P/C) based on 15 to 45

(maximum the room will hold) class members assuming that selling price is $25 and you run two ads.

Part	*Revenue*	−*FC*	−*VC*	=*O/P/Cost*	*O/P/Recovery*
15	___	___	___	___	___
25	___	___	___	___	___
35	___	___	___	___	___
45	___	___	___	___	___

(Note: You could use any number of participants, such as in increments of five, and other assumptions to run "what if" scenarios. This job is easy with a computer software program.)

As you can see, forecasting the sales demand (Chapter 6) for the program at various prices is very important when determining cost-volume-analysis. For example, if you make the decision to run the class based on a forecast of 30 participants and you only get 15, you will not realize the profit or out-of-pocket recovery you planned for.

7. What price $ ___ and how many ads ___ would you run? Remember the law of supply and demand with elastic supply. The lower the price, the more people will sign up; the higher the price, the less people will sign up. Feel free to run the numbers for your decision.
8. Make the decision to offer or not to offer the aerobic dance class assuming that the sales forecast is for 25 people and your selling price is $25 and you run two ads. Using your figures from step 6, would you run the program? Yes ___ No ___. Recall that throughout the text we have been stating the importance of objectives. Make the decision to offer or not to offer the class based on the following two objectives:

   Objective
   To make a profit.
   Would you run the class? Yes ___ No ___.

   Objective
   To increase adult membership by 5 percent in 1997. You are considering offering an aerobic dance class as a way to increase membership. Your target market is housewives and working women. You think that if you can get these women to sign up for the class, you can get several to sign up as regular members.
   Would you run the class? Yes ___ No ___.
9. Based on the two objectives, would your answer change for question 6? State why and how.

   ____
   ____
   ____
   ____

Doing Skill-Building Exercise 15–2 in Class

Objective
To improve your skill at cost-volume-profit analysis.

Preparation and Experience
You should have completed the preparation for this exercise. In class you may work in a group to go over the problems.

Procedure (15–50 minutes)
Option A. The instructor goes over the answers to the problems.

Option B. Break into groups of four to six and go over the answers to problems 1 and/or 2. The instructor will give you a set time, such as 10 to 15 minutes.

Conclusion
The instructor may lead a class discussion and/or make concluding remarks about the exercise.

Application (2–4 minutes)
What did I learn from this exercise? How will I use this knowledge in the future?

____
____
____
____

Sharing
Volunteers give their answers to the application questions.

VIDEOCASE

Control Systems: Sunshine Cleaning Systems

Sunshine Cleaning Systems (SCS) is a privately held company, founded in 1976, headquartered in Fort Lauderdale, Florida. Today, Sunshine has offices in Tampa, Orlando, and West Palm Beach, in addition to Fort Lauderdale. Sunshine is one of the largest contract cleaning companies in Florida. They clean entire facilities, inside and out. Sunshine also specializes in cleaning windows, carpets, ceilings, and construction sites and pressure cleaning. Clients include sports facilities, office buildings, stores and malls, the Orlando Convention Center, and the Fort Lauderdale Airport.

Given that Sunshine has four regional offices, hundreds of employees, and hundreds of customers with differing needs, control systems and procedures must be implemented to ensure quality and consistency. Sunshine has developed a multilevel inspection program which serves as the major element in its quality assurance program. The inspection program incorporates training, scheduling, workload assignments, supervision, and inspection. If an area does not pass inspection, an "Action Alert" will result and special effort will be focused to improve results. In addition to the inspection program, a number of other control mechanisms have been developed to ensure quality and consistency throughout the corporation.

Human Resources Control Systems

Learning Objectives

After completing this chapter, you should be able to:

1. Explain the two types of performance appraisal.
2. Describe the difference between the informal and formal steps in the performance appraisal process.
3. Explain the concept, "You get what you reward."
4. State the primary criterion for determining the degree of imposed control versus self-control.
5. Explain the importance of positive motivational feedback in coaching.
6. List the four steps in the coaching model.
7. Explain the manager's role in counseling and the role of the employee assistance program staff.
8. List the five steps in the discipline model.
9. List the steps in conducting the evaluative and developmental performance appraisal interviews.
10. Define the following **key terms** (in order of appearance in the chapter):

    - performance appraisal
    - developmental performance appraisal
    - evaluative performance appraisal
    - critical incident file
    - rating scale
    - behaviorally anchored rating scale
    - coaching
    - management by walking around
    - discipline
    - management counseling
    - employee assistance program

Skill-Development

1. You can develop your skill at coaching employees to improve performance (Skill-Building Exercise 16–1).

2. You can develop your skill at disciplining an employee (Skill-Building Exercise 16–2).

Ensuring human resources performance is a controlling management function. It requires human relations and communications skills. The management roles of interpersonal leader, informational monitor, and decisional are needed for effective performance control. The SCANS competencies of resources, interpersonal skills, information, and systems, as well as basic and thinking skills and personal qualities are developed through each of these exercises.

W. K. Kellogg was a successful entrepreneur in the breakfast cereal industry who later became a visionary philanthropist. He strongly believed that the greatest return on dollars spent could be found in human potential. He held an unwavering confidence in the ability of people to define their own problems and to implement appropriate solutions—given the opportunity and encouragement to do so.

It was this belief, along with the desire to be a good steward of his rapidly growing cereal wealth, that motivated him to establish the nonprofit W. K. Kellogg Foundation in 1930. "I'll invest my money in people," he said, determined to create an innovative philanthropic organization that would provide help and encouragement to individuals and organizations throughout the world. By 1995, the Foundation's endowment, to which Mr. Kellogg donated more than $66 million, has grown to more than $6 billion. Revenue generated by these resources has enabled the Foundation to award more than $2.7 billion in grants over the course of its history.

The Kellogg Foundation of Battle Creek, Michigan, provides grant money to educational and service projects of potential national or international importance that emphasize the application of knowledge in addressing significant human problems.

The major interest areas and geographical areas for grants are listed here along with the money granted in 1995.[1]

W. K. Kellogg believed that the greatest return on dollars spent could be found in human potential.

As a nonprofit organization in the business of giving away money to help people help themselves, the W. K. Kellogg Foundation has approximately 300 employees, 100 of whom have formal supervisory roles. Managers use human resources performance control systems that include the informal coaching and discipline, and formal performance appraisal.

Areas of Interest

Health Care	$ 63,218,175	27%
Food Systems and Rural Development[a]	23,468,153	10%
Youth Development and Higher Education[b]	53,497,270	23%
Philanthropy and Volunteerism	19,872,180	8%
Leadership	23,999,600	10%
Special Opportunities		
Special Programming Opportunities	22,611,699	10%
Emerging Programs	9,984,893	4%
Battle Creek Programming	4,798,833	2%
Other[c]	1,240,978	1%
Programs Operated	11,351,309	5%
	$234,243,090	100%

Includes:

[a]Agriculture and Rural Development in southern Africa.

[b]Basic Education and Youth/Higher Education in southern Africa, Basic Education and Youth in Latin America and the Caribbean.

[c]Program Development (Latin America and the Caribbean), Study Grants and Bursaries (southern Africa), Study Grant Fellowships (Latin America and the Caribbean) under goals and strategies adopted in 1995.

Geographical Areas

United States	$173,008,682	74%
Africa (southern)	11,429,744	5%
Latin America and the Caribbean	29,156,241	12%
Other International Programs	20,648,423	9%
	$234,243,090	100%

In Chapter 1, you learned about the systems effect among the management functions. The interrelationship between the leading (Chapters 10–14) and controlling human resources performance functions is strong. In other words, it takes leading skills to control employee performance. In Chapter 9 you learned about the human resources process of attracting, developing, and retaining employees. Performance appraisal (PA) is an important part of developing employees. It is both an organizing and controlling function, which requires leadership skills. In Chapter 15 we discussed human resources control from the human resources department function because within that department it is primarily an organizing function. However, for the managers in all departments, controlling human resources performance is a leadership and controlling function. The human resources department has the organizing function of developing a performance appraisal system for the entire organization, while all departments implement the system using leadership skills. The human resources department can assist managers in conducting performance appraisals.[2]

The focus of human resources control is on controlling performance, not on manipulating people. In other words, you are ensuring that people perform their jobs to standard levels of performance and rewarding them for doing so. Recall that in Chapter 11 you learned about how reinforcement theory uses consequences for behavior to motivate behavior in predetermined ways. We now narrow reinforcement motivation theory to focus on the predetermined behavior it takes to meet performance standards. As a manager, you should reward employees who meet the performance standards (positive reinforcement) and take corrective action (avoidance, extinction, and/or punishment) when they do not. You are going to learn how to do so in this chapter.

THE PERFORMANCE APPRAISAL PROCESS

As stated in Chapter 9, **performance appraisal** *is the ongoing process of evaluating employee performance*. Performance appraisal (PA) is also called performance evaluation, performance review, merit rating, and performance audit. Regardless of the name, bosses hate to give them and workers hate to get them.[3] Performance appraisal is one of the manager's most important, yet most difficult, functions and is becoming even more demanding.[4] Handled properly, it can increase productivity, motivation, and morale and decrease absenteeism and turnover.[5] But handled poorly, it can decrease performance.

performance appraisal
The ongoing process of evaluating employee performance.

In this section you will learn the two types of performance appraisal, the PA process, and that the control systems process is included within the PA process.

Types of Performance Appraisal

1. Explain the two types of performance appraisal.

The two types of performance appraisal are developmental and evaluative. PA has two separate but related uses based on whether a developmental or administrative decision is being made. They are related because the developmental plans are always based on an evaluative performance appraisal. However, the primary purpose of PA should be to help employees improve their performance.[6]

Developmental performance appraisal *is used to make decisions and plans for performance improvements*. To improve future performance, appraisers must give employees feedback on how well they are doing their jobs. Areas of strength and improvement must be clear, and a plan for improvement must be developed so

developmental performance appraisal
Used to make decisions and plans for performance improvements.

that the employee knows what it takes to get a higher evaluation rating on the next performance review.

evaluative performance appraisal Used to make administrative decisions including pay raises, transfers and promotions, and demotions and terminations.

Evaluative performance appraisal *is used to make administrative decisions including pay raises, transfers and promotions, and demotions and terminations.* Managers are held legally accountable for administrative decisions because they must meet the EEOC Uniform Guidelines on Employee Selection Procedures (Chapter 9). Managers are not completely free to promote or discharge anyone they please; administrative decisions should not be discriminatory. Effective performance appraisal can prevent company litigation.[7] Decisions should be based on objective job performance criteria; employees must know exactly where they stand, what their responsibilities are, and the standards of performance they are expected to achieve.[8]

Work Application

1. Give a developmental and administrative decision your present or past boss made based on your performance.

When both the developmental and evaluative performance appraisals are conducted together, which they commonly are, the development is often less effective, especially when the employee disagrees with the evaluation. Most managers are not good at performance appraisals because they don't know how to be both a judge and a coach.[9] The evaluative PA focuses on the past, whereas the developmental PA focuses on the future. Therefore, separate meetings make the two uses clear and can help the manager be both a judge and a coach. You will learn how to conduct both types of formal performance reviews later in this chapter.

2. Describe the difference between the informal and formal steps in the performance appraisal process.

The Performance Appraisal Process

The performance appraisal process steps are: (1) job analysis, (2) develop standards and measurement methods, (3) informal PA—coaching and discipline, and (4) prepare for and conduct the formal PA interview. See Figure 16–1 for an illustration of the performance appraisal process. The four steps are briefly described below, and steps 2 to 4 are explained in more detail throughout the chapter. The Kellogg Foundation has a formal performance appraisal system, and it trains its managers to be effective in conducting performance appraisals.

Figure 16–1
The Performance Appraisal Process

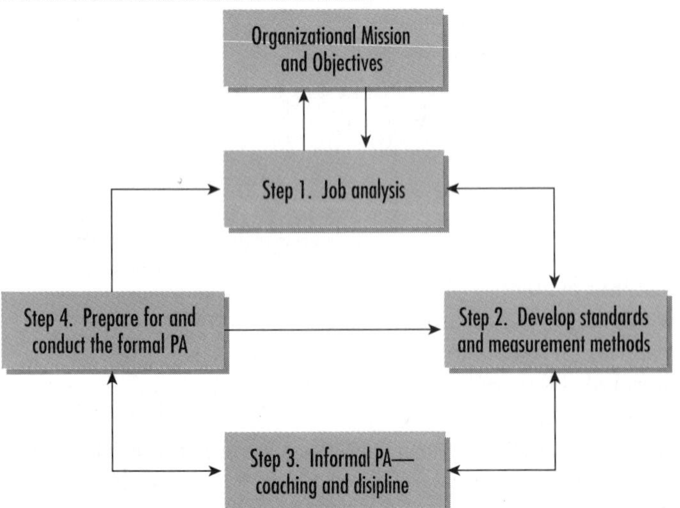

In Figure 16–1, note the connection between the organization's mission and objectives and the performance appraisal process. The feedback loop indicates the need for the PA to control human resources performance in order to meet the mission and objectives. Based on the organization's mission and objectives (Chapter 5), employees' performance should be measured against the achievement of these goals.[10]

step 1. **Job Analysis.** The job analysis (Chapter 9) includes determining the job description and job specification. The job description responsibilities should be ranked in order of importance and the critical success factors identified and distinguished (Chapter 15). Refer back to Chapter 9 for details on conducting a job analysis.

step 2.

Develop Standards and Measurement Methods. After determining what it takes to do the job, standards and methods for measuring performance can be developed. In the next section of this chapter, we will discuss setting standards and describe several common performance appraisal methods.

step 3.

Informal Performance Appraisals—Coaching and Discipline. A performance appraisal should not just consist of the once-a-year formal interview.[11] As stated in its definition, PA is an ongoing process. Employees need regular informal feedback on their performance. Coaching involves giving praise for a job well done to maintain performance, or taking corrective action when standards are not met. The employee performing below standard may need daily or weekly coaching or discipline to meet standards. In the third and fourth sections of this chapter, we will discuss coaching and discipline.

step 4.

Prepare for and Conduct the Formal Performance Appraisal. In Figure 15–1, note that the feedback loop has a return arrow from step 3 to 2, and from 2 to 1, but it does not have a return arrow from 4 to 3. The reason for this is that, at step 4, it is too late to change the past; the formal performance appraisal is used to influence the future. At step 4 you have three options on which step to proceed to. You may skip going back to step 1 if the job has not changed. If the job has not changed, the standards do not need to be changed; if you have a developmental plan, you may skip step 2 and go directly forward to step 3.

Failure to plan for the performance appraisal is planning to fail. In the fifth section of this chapter, we will discuss how to prepare for the interview and problems to avoid when conducting the interview. In the fifth section, we also discuss the steps to follow when conducting the formal performance appraisal interview.

The Kellogg Foundation has a performance management system. At the Foundation, performance management is a system that helps employees to manage their efforts in support of the organization's mission, vision, and guiding principles. Managers believe that it is important for employees and supervisors to meet on a regular basis to discuss performance. It is through regular coaching and feedback that team members know whether their efforts are meeting performance standards and expectations. In this regard, the performance management system provides opportunities for discussing problems, achieving so-

APPLYING THE CONCEPT

AC 16–1 The Performance Appraisal Process

Identify which step in the performance appraisal process is represented by the following statements.

a. step 1 c. step 3
b. step 2 d. step 4

____ **1.** "You really did a great job of fixing that copier; it works great."

____ **2.** "Review this job description, and then we will go over it together to make sure you understand your job."

____ **3.** "Have a seat. As you know, we are going to evaluate your performance over the past year."

____ **4.** "Pete, you are late for work again. I'm giving you a verbal warning that action will be taken the next time you are late."

____ **5.** "We use this form during our performance appraisals."

lutions, and developing new opportunities that are consistent with employees' interests and talents and the goals of the Foundation.

How the Control Systems Process Is Included within the PA Process

You should realize the performance appraisal process does include the steps in the control systems process. The steps in the control systems process (Chapter 15) are listed here with their corresponding steps in the performance appraisal system.

step 1. **Set Objectives and Standards.** The performance appraisal control process begins at step 2 with developing standards and measurement methods. Their development is a preliminary control.

step 2. **Measure Performance.** Performance is measured in the performance appraisal process in steps 3, informal PA, and 4, formal PA. The measurement process is a preliminary control.

step 3. **Compare Performance to Standards.** Comparing performance to standards also takes place in PA steps 3 and 4.

step 4. **Correct or Reinforce.** When employee performance is below standard, corrective action is taken. Corrective action takes place as a concurrent control through informal PA step 3, coaching and discipline. At step 4, the formal PA, it is too late to take corrective action. Therefore, rework control is needed to make development plans as a preliminary control for the next formal performance appraisal. Damage control may also be needed. When employees are meeting or exceeding standards, you should reinforce the behavior by giving them good performance appraisals and motivating rewards (Chapter 11) such as praise, increased responsibility, more challenging work, pay increases, promotions, and so on.

STANDARDS AND MEASUREMENT METHODS

Step 2 in a performance appraisal process is developing standards and measurement methods. This is the topic of this section.

Developing Performance Standards

Standards are the backbone of a performance appraisal. Employees need to be aware that their work is measured according to a standard.[12] The author is amazed at how many students tell him that they had no standards for their jobs. He asks them, "How do you and your boss know if you are doing a good job, and how good of a job?" They don't have an answer, because they don't know.

As a manager, make sure that your employees know what the standards are. If you give an employee an average rather than a good rating, you should be able to clearly explain why. The employee should understand what needs to be done during the next performance period to get the higher rating. With clear standards, there shouldn't be any surprise disagreements over performance during the formal performance appraisal. Courts do not look favorably on surprises and subjective disagreements over performance.

See Chapter 15 for details on how to set standards in the areas of quantity, quality, time, cost, and behavior. Be sure that your standards cover the critical success factors (CSF). In addition, standards for performance appraisals should encompass a range to motivate employees to excel. For example, the standard range for typing could be as follows: 70 words per minute (WPM)—excellent; 60 WPM—good; 50 WPM—average; 40 WPM—satisfactory; 30 WPM—unsatisfactory. Remember that standing plans are standards.

Work Application

2. Describe the performance standards for a job you have or have had. Describe how you would improve them.

Standards and Rewards

3. Explain the concept, "You get what you reward."

You Get What You Reward. One of the most important things you should learn in this course is that people will do what they are rewarded for doing. People seek information concerning what activities are rewarded, and then seek to do (or at least pretend to do) those things, often to the exclusion of activities not rewarded. The extent to which this occurs depends on the attractiveness of the rewards offered.[13]

For example, if a professor gives a class a reading list of several sources, but tells students (or they realize without being told) they will not discuss them in class or be tested on them, how many students will acquire and read them? Or, "A, B, and C from this chapter are important and I'll test you on them, but X, Y, and Z are not." Will students spend equal time studying both?

In the business setting, if the manager repeatedly says quality is important, but the standard of evaluation includes only quantity and meeting scheduled shipments, how many employees will ship poor quality products to meet the scheduled shipment, and how many will miss the scheduled shipment and take a reprimand for missing it and get a poor performance review in order to do a quality job? Incomplete standards measuring only quantitative output that is highly visible and easy to measure are a common problem.[14]

The Folly of Rewarding A, While Hoping for B. Reward systems are mixed up in that the types of behavior rewarded are those the rewarder is trying to discourage, while the behavior desired is not being rewarded at all. Steven Kerr calls this problem "the folly of rewarding A, while hoping for B." Figure 16–2 illustrates such folly.[15] How common are these follies? In a survey, 90 percent of respondents said they are prevalent in corporate America today. Over half concluded that the folly is "widespread" in their companies. Figure 16-2 includes their examples.

When asked, "What is the most formidable obstacle in dealing with the folly?" common responses included: (1) The inability to break out of the old ways of thinking about reward and recognition practices, particularly including nonquantifiable standards and those that are system focused rather than job or functionally dependent. (2) Lack of a holistic or overall systems view of performance factors and results. (3) Continuing focus on short-term results by managers and shareholders.[16] The answer to the overall question, "What is wrong?" is "It's the reward system, stupid!"[17]

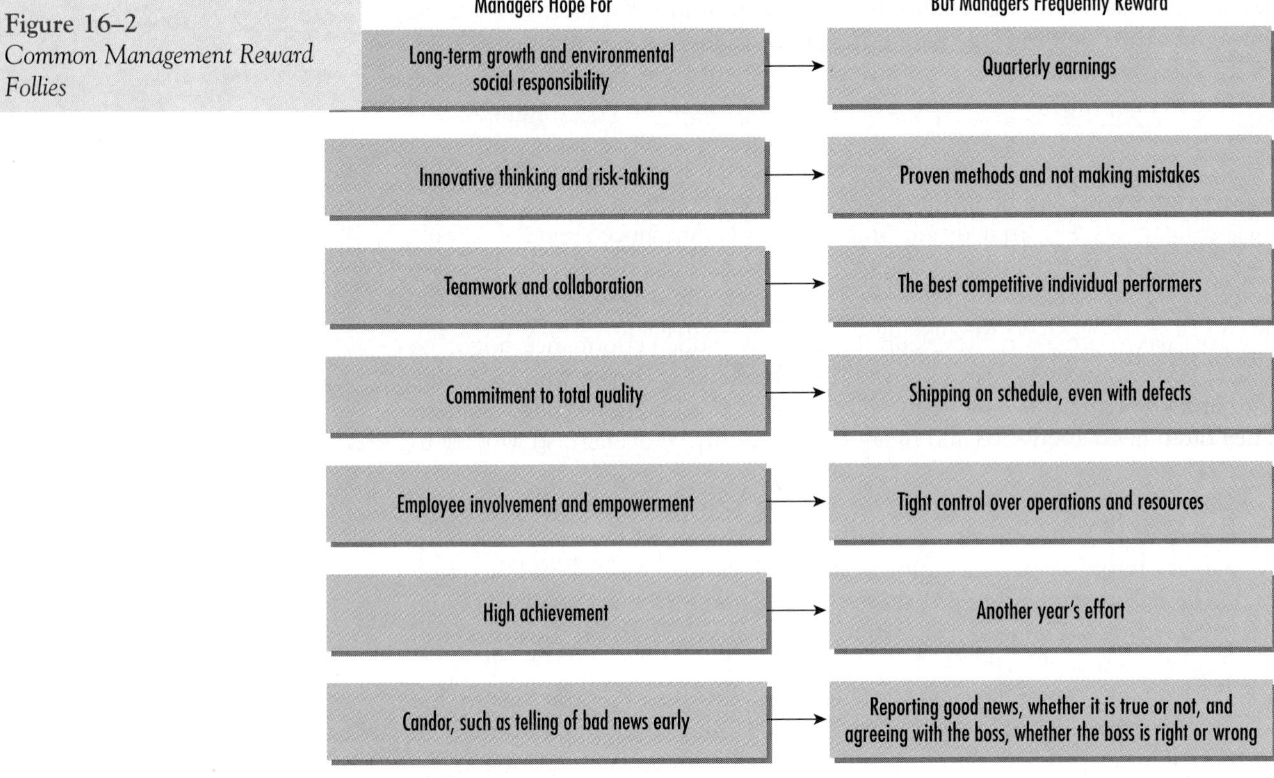

Managers Hope For
But Managers Frequently Reward
Long-term growth and environmental social responsibility
Quarterly earnings
Innovative thinking and risk-taking
Proven methods and not making mistakes
Teamwork and collaboration
The best competitive individual performers
Commitment to total quality
Shipping on schedule, even with defects
Employee involvement and empowerment
Tight control over operations and resources
High achievement
Another year's effort
Candor, such as telling of bad news early
Reporting good news, whether it is true or not, and agreeing with the boss, whether the boss is right or wrong

Figure 16–2
Common Management Reward Follies

Deming's Criticism of Current Performance Appraisal Systems

The late W. E. Deming, quality guru (Chapter 8), stated that performance appraisal practices of American industry are the root cause of its quality problems. He has identified four recurring problems.[18]

1. *Performance appraisal practices are unfair.* They are unfair because they hold the worker responsible for errors that may be the result of faults within the system rather than within the employee. Deming believed that over 90 percent of quality problems of American industry are the result of faults built into the system due to prior decisions, defects in material inputs, flaws in the design of the system, or some managerial shortcoming, rather than an error on the employees' part. Therefore, judging workers according to their output can result in gross injustice.

In support of Deming's view, a Texas hotel had problems with its banquet staff. Managers wanted to know why employees were habitually late and inefficient. The results revealed that poor performance was due to weak job qualifications, insufficient training, inefficient procedures, and weak performance appraisal. Performance was significantly increased with the same staff by improving the system. The system was changed by providing better training, using task checklists, giving employees regular performance feedback, setting objectives, and using bonuses.[19]

2. *Performance appraisal practices promote behavior that compromises quality.* When managers focus on quantity standards, workers focus on the tar-

gets and quotas and ignore quality to meet them. Employees will ship out defective products to meet managers' schedules/standards.

3. Performance appraisal practices discourage workers who cease trying to excel. When PA methods that are based on subjective relative ranking with the use of measures such as average and satisfactory, there is a tendency to equate "average" with "unsatisfactory." There is nothing wrong with this when there are clear objective standards specifying average, such as sales and piecework counts of output. (But, recall that below-average performance can be due to the system, not the employee.) When standards are subjective, which they often are, good performance might be designated simply because it is low relative to that of others in the group. Conversely, poor performance might be judged acceptable simply because it falls in the middle. People who are trying hard and know that they are doing a good job do not like to be called average. They often get demoralized and figure they will only be average, so why try to excel.

4. Performance appraisal practices rob employees of pride in their work. You may have heard the expression, "Americans don't take pride in their work like the Japanese." While it may be true for some, it is not true in general. The answer to the question "Why don't employees take pride in their work?" is It's the PA system, as items 1–3 point out, and "It's the reward system, stupid!" If managers set quality standards and reward employees for doing a quality job, they will do a quality job and they will have pride in their work.

A decade of surveys support Kerr and Deming's criticisms of current performance appraisal practices because unhappiness with PA systems runs deep. Many workers see evaluations as superficial, inconsistent, and unreliable with scant relevance to actual duties or pay levels.[20]

Measurement Methods

The formal performance appraisal is often conducted based on a standard form, usually rating scales or BARS, developed by the human resources department to measure employee performance. See Figure 16–3 for a list of the commonly used performance appraisal measurement methods on a continuum based on their use in administrative and developmental decisions.

Figure 16–3
Performance Appraisal Measurement Methods with Their Decision Use

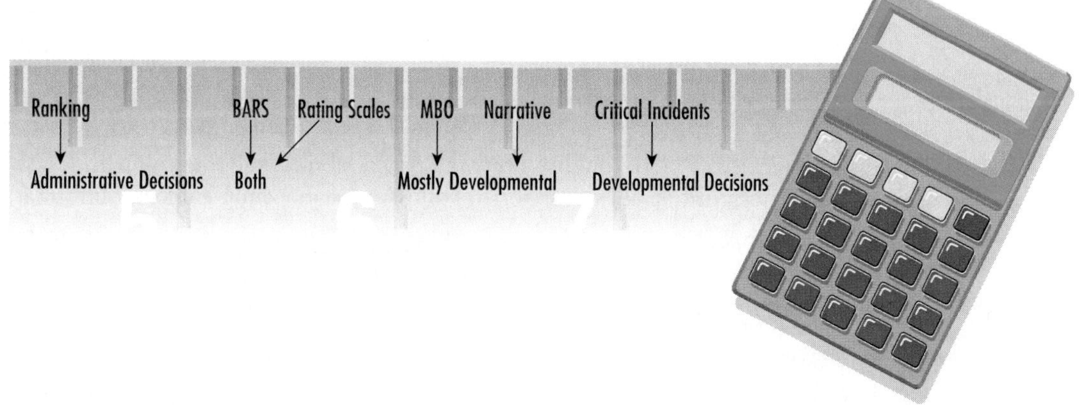

critical incident file
A record of an employee's positive and negative performance.

Critical Incident File. The **critical incident file** *is a record of an employee's positive and negative performance*. Because the formal review period is usually six months to one year, it is very difficult to remember an employee's performance from appraisal to appraisal. The critical incident file provides a record of performance by date. It also provides documentation, which is needed in this litigious environment.

There are no hard and fast rules as to what a critical incident file should contain. Basic guidelines include: (1) Keep a record of uncommonly good or poor performance. Most managers only focus on the negative; don't. (2) As the name is critical incidents, focus on critical success factors. (3) Record the facts, including the date, soon after the incident. (4) A simple system includes having a file folder for each employee. Make critical incident notes on the inside of the folder itself, or notes on a sheet of paper, and store performance forms inside the folder. (5) Some managers make weekly summaries of performance. (6) Deming would recommend keeping records of incidents that are within employees' control, or their fault, not the system's—including the manager. (7) Be specific and descriptive so that others, such as a jury, can understand what you wrote. For example, see the following list:

1/10/9X: 10 minutes late for work. Stated the reason was car trouble.

1/14/9X: Absent. Stated the reason was to attend mother's funeral.

1/18/9X: Voluntarily stayed a half hour late to finish a job.

1/23/9X: Took an extra 15 minutes for lunch.

2/03/9X: Pushed to meet a contract deadline; produced 10 extra units.

2/14/9X: Produced five units below standard.

2/19/9X: Merchandise returned defective. Reworked and sent back to customer.

Decisions. Critical incident files are appropriate for developmental decisions. They are not very appropriate when used alone for administrative decisions such as pay raises and promotions. Referring to critical incidents can help change an employee's performance. For example, if you want to improve an employee's lateness record, don't say, "You're always late." (This is too general.) The employee will probably say, "No, I'm not." Say, "On January 5, 11, and 17 you were late." (This is specific.) It is difficult to argue with accurate facts.

The critical incident file was presented first because it is recommended and can be used with any performance appraisal form. It is rarely, if ever, used as the sole measure of performance. The critical incidents are used when filling out another form.

rating scale
A form on which the manager simply checks off the employee's level of performance.

Rating Scale. The **rating scale** *is a form on which the manager simply checks off the employee's level of performance*. Some of the possible areas evaluated include quantity of work, quality of work, dependability, judgment, attitude, cooperativeness, initiative, and so forth. Following is an example check-off format:

Quantity of work: ____superior ____above average ____average
____ below average ____ unacceptable

Four common problems exist with rating scales: (1) They are often subjective ratings. In the preceding example, how do you know what superior quantity of work is? What is the difference between above, average, and below average? What is unacceptable? (2) Because rating scales are generally generic to all departments, they often do not focus on the employee's critical success factors. (3) Rating scale forms tend to have multiple performance measures. However, these factors are seldom ranked or weighted for importance. You can have ten items all given equal weight, when in reality one of them may be a true critical success factor, while the other nine are not. In such a case, the one critical success factor should be considered more important than the other nine combined. (4) Employee performance should be compared to the scales, not to the performance of other employees. However, managers tend to make their rating based on peer comparisons to get some employees in the average rating. This is Deming's point 3.

Decisions. Objective rating scales geared to the specific job are appropriate for both developmental and administrative decisions. The scales indicate strengths and areas where improvement is needed. They can be used to develop objectives and plans for improved performance. They can also be used as the basis for pay raises, promotions, and other administrative decisions. Rating scales for all employees can be compared to identify superior performers.

Behaviorally Anchored Rating Scales (BARS). The **behaviorally anchored rating scales** *consist of a form with descriptive statements which managers select from to measure employee performance*. Rather than just a rating of excellent, good, average, and so on, the form includes a statement that describes the employee's performance. Standards are clearer when objective BARS are developed as shown below for an employee handling customer returns:

behaviorally anchored rating scales (BARS)
Consist of a form with descriptive statements which managers select from to measure employee performance.

1. Always deals with customers in a polite and calm manner.
2. Almost always deals with customers politely, but occasionally is upset.
3. Is almost always calm, but is occasionally rude.
4. Is occasionally rude, but is frequently upset.
5. Is occasionally upset, but is frequently rude.
6. Is very frequently upset and rude.

This appraisal method is growing in popularity because it is more objective and accurate than the other methods. In courts, BARS tend to be viewed more favorably than rating scales. BARS are very job-specific and cannot be used for a variety of different jobs as the rating scales can. Therefore, BARS can focus on critical success factors, while rating scales often do not. However, like rating scales, BARS also tend not to rank or weight the performance measures. The major drawback to BARS is the time it takes to develop the instrument. And, there is an element of subjectivity in the terms used—such as almost always, occasionally, frequently, and so on.

Decisions. Like the rating scales, BARS can be used to make both developmental and administrative decisions.

Management by Objectives (MBO). Management by objectives, or *goal setting*, specifies that managers and their employees jointly set objectives for employees, periodically evaluate their performance, and reward the employees based on the results. (See Chapter 5 for details.) Management by objectives is more popularly used with professional employees who do not have routine jobs. With routine jobs, such as assembly workers, standards work fine.

Decisions. Management by objectives is appropriate for developmental decisions for both professional and routine jobs. It is often difficult to make administrative decisions based on MBO alone.

Narrative. With the *narrative* method, the manager writes a description of the employee's performance. How this is done can vary. Managers may be allowed to write whatever they like, or they may be required to write answers to specific questions about the employee's performance. The free-form narrative often becomes subjective. Answering a series of questions makes the method more objective and uniform.

Some prefer the written statement to other measurement methods, especially for managers and professionals with complex jobs with responsibility that changes frequently. However, the written statement is not popular, possibly because it is more subjective and difficult to use. The narrative is often combined with another method. In addition, many managers lack the writing skills for this method to be effective.

Decisions. The narrative is appropriate for developmental decisions because the objectives and plans can be written down. Like management by objectives, it can be difficult to use the narrative method for administrative decisions involving employees who have different managers because there is no uniform measurement.

Ranking. *Ranking* is used to compare employee performance. It is used to compare employees to each other rather than comparing them to a standard measurement. Employees are often rated too high during appraisals. To offset this, some organizations require a ranking in addition to the rating scales and BARS because all employees may perform the job well, but only one can be the best. An offshoot of ranking is the *forced distribution method*. A predetermined percentage of employees are placed in each performance category, for example, excellent, 5 percent; above average, 15 percent; average, 60 percent; below average, 15 percent; and poor, 5 percent.

Decisions. Ranking methods are appropriate for administrative decisions such as merit pay raises that reward for performance and promotions. They are more accurate when the ranking is based on a standard measure such as rating scales or BARS.

Ranking is not appropriate for development decisions. Ranking causes employees to compete

APPLYING THE CONCEPT

AC 16–2 Selecting Performance Appraisal Methods

Select the performance appraisal method that is most appropriate for the given situation.

a. critical incidents
b. rating scales
c. BARS
d. ranking
e. MBO
f. narrative

____ 6. You started a small company with ten employees. You are overworked, but you want to develop one performance appraisal form you can use with all employees.

____ 7. You have been promoted from a supervisory position to a middle management position. You have been asked to select your replacement.

____ 8. Winnie is not performing up to standard. You have decided to talk to her in order to improve her performance.

____ 9. You want to create a system for developing each employee.

____ 10. Your small business has grown to 50 employees. Employees have complained that the one form does not work well for different types of employee jobs. You have decided to hire a professional to develop a performance appraisal system that is more objective and job specific with PA forms for your various employee groups.

against each other which impairs effective cooperation and teamwork.[21] Deming's point 3 is a problem because most of the employees know they cannot be the best, so they don't try. Let all employees have a chance to be winners. Don't rank them for development; compare them to the standard.

Which Performance Appraisal Method Is Best? The answer to the question of choosing an appraisal method depends on the objectives of the system and the decision being made (Contingency Management Theory, Chapter 1). A combination of methods is usually superior to using any single method. For developmental objectives, the critical incident file, MBO, and narrative work well. For administrative decisions, a ranking method based on rating scales or BARS works well. Remember that critical incidents and narrative are commonly used together with another method.

At the Kellogg Foundation, the performance review form combines a rating scale and narrative formats with aspects of MBO in reference to goal-setting requirements and assessments. However, the form is not the sole component of the Foundation's performance review system. The Foundation's performance management cycle consists of three phases: performance planning, feedback and coaching, and performance review. Thus, completion of the review form as part of the formal year-end review is only one component of the performance management cycle.

Work Application

3. Identify the measurement method used to evaluate performance for a job you have or have had. If you were never formally evaluated, ask your boss/coworkers which method is used for your job or a similar one in the department.

The real success of performance appraisal does not lie in the method or form used. It depends on the manager. The effective manager will have success with any format because he or she will communicate standards clearly. The ineffective supervisor can have the best format in the world and do a poor job.

The performance appraisal system and measurement method are often selected by the human resources department. If you do not like the procedures or forms, offer suggestions on how to improve them, rather than complaining and criticizing. To be more specific, request permission to develop the performance appraisal systems for your department, following the four steps to avoid the folly, with the input of your employees. If you cannot get permission to develop your own departmental PA system, you can at least use management by objectives to do it indirectly.

Imposed Control versus Self-Control

4. State the primary criterion for determining the degree of imposed control versus self-control.

The formal performance appraisal interview is commonly done once or twice a year; some organizations, including Hoffmann-La Roche, require a quarterly coaching session. Therefore, the frequency of measurement and control method is more relevant to the ongoing process of informal evaluation. Recall from Chapter 15 that control methods include constant, periodic, and occasional. A major issue in human resources performance control is imposed control versus self-control.

Imposed control is the extent to which the manager relies on the control system to control employee performance. The control system includes devices, such as counters to measure performance output quantity and especially the manager personally checking up on the employee through direct observation. *Self-control* is the extent to which the manager relies on employees to control their own performance. With imposed control, the manager takes the active role for controlling: measuring performance (which may be through systems) and comparing it to standard and getting employees to take corrective action when necessary. With self-control, the employees take the active role in controlling.

The degree of imposed versus self-control is the determining factor in the success of the human resources control system. The primary factor in determining the degree of imposed versus self-control is based on employee capability level, which has two parts: ability to be self-controlled and the motivation to be self-controlled. Capability is on a continuum from low to outstanding. Based on the capability level, the manager selects the appropriate degree of imposed versus self-control, which is reflected in one of four management styles. For more

Model 16–1
Determining the Degree of Imposed Control versus Self-Control

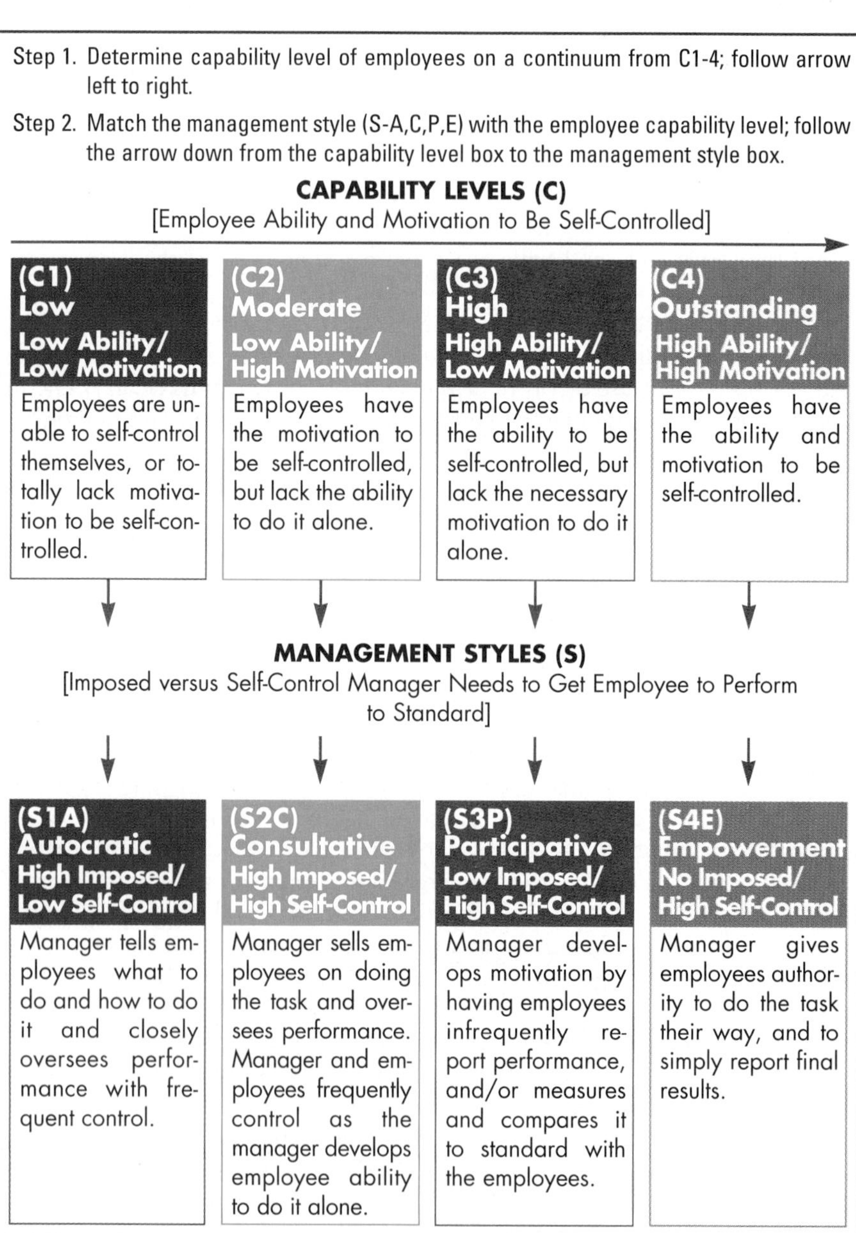
Step 1. Determine capability level of employees on a continuum from C1-4; follow arrow left to right.
Step 2. Match the management style (S-A,C,P,E) with the employee capability level; follow the arrow down from the capability level box to the management style box.
CAPABILITY LEVELS (C)
[Employee Ability and Motivation to Be Self-Controlled]
(C1) Low
Low Ability/ Low Motivation
Employees are unable to self-control themselves, or totally lack motivation to be self-controlled.
(C2) Moderate
Low Ability/ High Motivation
Employees have the motivation to be self-controlled, but lack the ability to do it alone.
(C3) High
High Ability/ Low Motivation
Employees have the ability to be self-controlled, but lack the necessary motivation to do it alone.
(C4) Outstanding
High Ability/ High Motivation
Employees have the ability and motivation to be self-controlled.
MANAGEMENT STYLES (S)
[Imposed versus Self-Control Manager Needs to Get Employee to Perform to Standard]
(S1A) Autocratic
High Imposed/ Low Self-Control
Manager tells employees what to do and how to do it and closely oversees performance with frequent control.
(S2C) Consultative
High Imposed/ High Self-Control
Manager sells employees on doing the task and oversees performance. Manager and employees frequently control as the manager develops employee ability to do it alone.
(S3P) Participative
Low Imposed/ High Self-Control
Manager develops motivation by having employees infrequently report performance, and/or measures and compares it to standard with the employees.
(S4E) Empowerment
No Imposed/ High Self-Control
Manager gives employees authority to do the task their way, and to simply report final results.

details, refer to Skill-Building Exercise 1–1 in Chapter 1. Model 16–1 illustrates selecting the degree of imposed versus self-control. Managers at the Kellogg Foundation try to use self-control rather than imposed control.

Managers who over- or undercontrol will have human resources problems. For example, if a manager has an outstanding employee, and the manager is constantly checking up on the employee, the employee will be frustrated and demotivated to do a good job. Many employees who know that their work is going to be checked and corrected by someone else, are not motivated to do a good job. On the other hand, if an employee is not capable of performing to standard alone, but the manager does not provide the necessary control, the employee will fail to meet standards. Conscientious employees who don't meet standards because they do not get the support they need, such as proper training, become very frustrated because they want to do a good job. Ideally, the manager works with employees to develop their ability to become self-controlled. When the employees are self-controlled, the manager can spend more time on the other management functions.

Work Application

4. Identify your capability level for being self-controlled on your present or past job. Did the manager use the appropriate level of imposed control versus self-control? If not, explain how you were over- or under-controlled.

Developing Effective Standards and Measures of Performance

To develop effective standards and measures that help to avoid the problems identified in this section, follow these guidelines:

- Include employee input throughout the process.
- Determine the critical success factors.
- Set complete standards in all five areas of quantity, quality, time, cost, and behavior for each critical success factor.
- a. Rank critical success factors in order of importance and weight them. For example, CSF 1 may be 50 percent of the overall PA, CSF 2 may be 30 percent, CSF 3 may be 10 percent, while CSF 4 and 5 may be 5 percent.
  b. If you have been working with employees to develop the standards through steps 1–3, then they should clearly understand them and be committed to achieving them. If employees have not been involved or don't agree, make it clear what you want them to do; communicate standards in steps 1–3.
- Use the appropriate degree of imposed versus self-control with each employee.
- Reward employees for doing what you want them to do (meeting standards). Do not reward employees who do not meet standards, at least to the same degree as the ones that do. This is known as *pay for performance*. Otherwise, some employees who work hard and excel, but get the same rewards as employees who take it easy, will tend to say, "Why bother working hard?" and become average. An average employee will have no incentive to excel. However, do not use ranking, and limit the numbers who excel. There is usually no good reason why most employees cannot excel to challenging high standard levels of performance.

These five steps are summarized in Figure 16–4.

Figure 16–4
Developing Effective Performance Standards and Measures

- Include employee input throughout the process.
- Determine the critical success factors.
- Set complete standards.
- Rank critical success factors in order of importance and weight them.
- Use the appropriate degree of imposed versus self-control with each employee.
- Reward employees for doing what you want them to do (meeting standards).

COACHING

As our definition states, performance appraisal is an ongoing process. The third step in the performance appraisal process is informal PA, which includes coaching and discipline. In this section you will learn about coaching and in the next section about counseling, which is a form of coaching, and discipline. Managers at the Kellogg Foundation are encouraged to coach employees as feedback and coaching is the second phase in its three-phase performance management cycle. Managers meet with employees on a regular basis to discuss performance. Through feedback, employees determine if they are meeting performance standards and expectations. Coaching sessions provide opportunities for discussing problems and solutions. Foundation managers are trained to be effective in all three phases of performance appraisal.

coaching
The process of giving motivational feedback to maintain and improve performance.

Coaching *is the process of giving motivational feedback to maintain and improve performance. Discipline* is the process of taking corrective action to get employees to meet standards. In other words, with coaching you are fine-tuning performance, but with discipline you are dealing with a problem employee. While the formal performance appraisal commonly takes place only once or twice a year, coaching should be a daily activity and discipline should be used when needed.

When some people hear the word *coaching,* they think of athletes. The word is taken from athletics because like the athletic coach, managers should be looking for steady performance and constant improvement. If you have ever had a good coach, think about the behavior used that helped to maintain and improve your performance and that of other team members. The next time you watch a sporting event, keep an eye on the coaches and learn some ways to coach employees.

The next time you watch a Chicago Bulls game, keep an eye on Phil Jackson and learn some ways to coach employees.

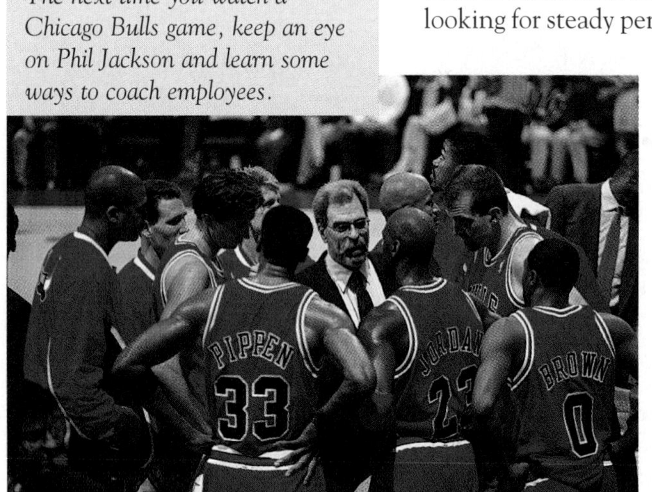

Coaching boosts performance.[22] Nine out of ten workers who have received job coaching think it is an effective developmental tool. However, only 38 percent of workers are being coached.[23] Developing your coaching skills is an important part of increasing employee performance. In this section, we'll cover the role of feedback in coaching to maintain and improve performance, determining corrective coaching action, management by walking around, and increasing performance with the coaching model.

5. Explain the importance of positive motivational feedback in coaching.

The Importance of Positive Feedback in Coaching to Maintain and Improve Performance

Before reading on, recall the best and worst boss you ever had. Which of the two bosses were you more motivated to work for? To maintain or improve performance, employees need feedback on how they are doing.[24] As implied in our definition of coaching, feedback is the central part of coaching, and it should be motivational. In other words, focus on the positive and keep criticism to a minimum.

Give More Positive Than Negative Feedback. As a manager, one simple technique to determine the ratio of positive to negative feedback is to keep a 3 by 5 card in your pocket. Every time you give positive feedback put a plus (+)

on one side of the card. Every time you give negative feedback put a minus (−) on the other side of the card. After a typical week, add up the number of plus and minus signs. The typical manager has more minus signs. If this is true in your case, you should work at giving more positive feedback.

Jack Falvey takes the positive versus negative feedback ratio to the point of recommending only positive feedback:

> Criticism is to be avoided at all costs (there is no such thing as constructive criticism; all criticism is destructive). If you must correct someone, never do it after the fact. Bite your tongue and hold off until the person is about to do the same thing again and then challenge the person to make a more positive contribution.[25]

This may seem at bit extreme, but later in this section you will learn how to give feedback, which can be considered criticism, in a positive way in the coaching model. Did your best boss give you more positive feedback than your worst boss? Did the feedback affect your motivation selection between the two bosses?

Reward to Maintain and Improve Performance. Monetary rewards such as pay increases are usually only given during the formal performance appraisal. However, rewards can be given all year long. Recall (Chapter 11) that giving praise and recognition for a job well done is a powerful reward that costs nothing but a minute of time.

Demotivating. Unfortunately, many managers spend much more time giving negative criticism than praise. Negative managers take the attitude, "Why should I thank employees for doing their job?" Managers who only communicate the bad news when employees slip up tend to demotivate them. Many employees take the attitude, "My boss doesn't appreciate my work. All the manager does is criticize me, so why should I work hard to do a good job?" Such employees take the play-it-safe road by doing the minimum, taking no risk, and focusing on not making errors and covering up any errors so they aren't criticized. Employees also tend to avoid overly critical bosses. They feel stress just seeing the boss coming over to them. They think, "What did I do this time?"

These negative managers treat employees like machines—as a means to get the job done. If you have never heard of managers like this, here is a true example. A manager and his wife were having a baby, so he told his boss that he would be attending the delivery and taking a few days off to help out at home. After returning, his boss came in and yelled at him, asking where he had been for the past few days. After he reminded the boss about his baby, the boss did not remember and went right into dealing with the reason he was looking for the manager. A few days later, the manager and his boss were together and the manager made a comment about his son. His boss said, "Why didn't you tell me you had a baby?" Do you want your boss to take a personal interest in you? Is this the type of environment you want to work in and create? Was the worst boss you ever had negative and somewhat like this?

Motivating. Why should you be positive and thank employees for doing their jobs? The reason is simple: it motivates employees to maintain and increase performance. We all want our efforts to be appreciated. We tend to find what we are looking for, so we find the best in people. Focusing on the positive builds employees up. They feel like winners and are more willing to try to main-

Work Application

5. Does your present or past boss give you more positive or negative feedback? Estimate the ratio of positive to negative feedback.

tain and improve performance. If you want to increase productivity, try saying thank you.[26] An effective way of saying thank you is by using the giving praise model (Chapter 11) to motivate employees. Was the best boss you ever had positive and somewhat like this?

Determining Corrective Coaching Action

According to contingency theory, there is no single corrective coaching action for all situations. When an employee is not performing to potential, even when acceptable standards are being met, the first step is to determine the reason why using the performance formula (Chapter 11):

$$\text{Performance} = \text{Ability} \times \text{Motivation} \times \text{Resources}$$

Ability. If the employee's ability is what is keeping his or her performance from being optimal, the corrective coaching action is training. Like the athletic coach, when an employee is not performing a task as effectively as possible, work with the employee to improve it. Following the job instructional training model in Chapter 9, point out inefficiency, then demonstrate appropriate behavior, watch the employee perform the task, and continually give feedback for ongoing improvements.

Motivation. If the employee has the ability, but lacks the motivation to do a good job, training is not the answer. Examine the reward system. Are you caught in the folly of really rewarding employees for doing A, while hoping employees will do B? Is the performance appraisal system fair? Does it discourage workers to excel and/or rob workers of pride in their work? If the system is OK, then use the motivational theories from Chapter 11. An important part of motivation is encouraging with positive feedback. Also, talk to the employee to try to determine why he or she is not motivated, and develop a plan together to motivate the person.

Resources. The performance appraisal system, including rewards, is actually a resource. However, because resources are such an important contributor to motivation, they were discussed with motivation. Other relevant resources not directly related to motivation include all areas of the systems process of inputs, transformation, and outputs. Deming believed that over 90 percent of quality problems of American industry are the result of faults built into the system due to prior decisions, defects in material inputs, flaws in the design of the system, or some managerial shortcoming, rather than an error on the employees' part. Remember to focus on the system, not on blaming the employees for their lack of motivation. Use employee input to improve the system to ensure continuing customer value.

Management by walking around is an effective way to increase performance in the resource area, especially facilitating, and the coaching model is effective in dealing with ability and motivation problems.

management by walking around (MBWA)
The three major activities are listening, teaching, and facilitating.

Management by Walking Around

Management by walking around (MBWA) *has three major activities: listening, teaching, and facilitating.*[27]

Listening. To find out what is going on, managers must do a lot more listening than talking, and be open to feedback. Penalizing employees for speaking their minds will stop communication. Learn to talk last, not first. Open with a simple question like, "How is it going?" Then use the communication skills from Chapter 10.

Teaching. Teaching does not mean telling employees what to do. It means helping them to do a better job by solving their own problems. Teach employees how to be more innovative. Use coaching statements such as, "What do you think should be done?" Do not encourage employees to blame others. When interacting with employees, values should be transmitted directly and indirectly. If quality is important, managers should talk and act as though it is and reward it.

Facilitating. *Facilitating* means taking action to help employees get their jobs done. The focus is primarily on improving the system to increase performance. When listening, find out what's getting in the way or slowing employees down. This will seldom be big things. Problems are usually caused by petty annoyances that employees believe are too trivial to bother the manager with. The manager's job is to run interference, to remove the stumbling blocks for the employees to improve the system. (Recall the upside-down organization chart, Chapter 7.) Employees who tell the manager what's going on should be told what will be done about a given problem, if anything, and when. Managers who listen but don't facilitate through corrective action will find that employees will stop talking. The result is that the manager will lose the most valuable source of input for improving the system.

Improving Performance with the Coaching Model

6. List the four steps in the coaching model.

The four steps in the coaching model are presented here and summarized in Model 16–2. They are illustrated in Behavior Module Video 11, Coaching.

step 1. **Describe Current Performance.** In detail using specific examples, describe the current behavior that needs to be changed. Tell the employees exactly what they are not doing as well as they can. Notice the positive; don't tell them only what they are doing wrong.

For example, don't say, "You are picking up the box wrong." Say, "Billie, there is a more effective way of picking the box up off the floor than bending at the waist."

step 2. **Describe Desired Performance.** Tell the employees exactly what the desired performance is in detail. If performance is *ability* related, demonstrate the appropriate way. If the employees know the proper way, it is *motivational*, and demonstration is not needed. Just describe desired performance as you ask the employees to state why the performance is important.

Model 16–2
Coaching Model

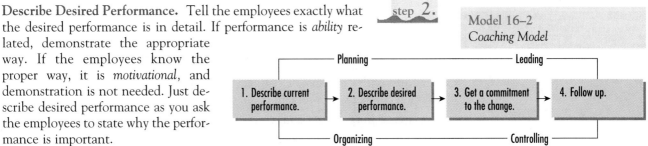

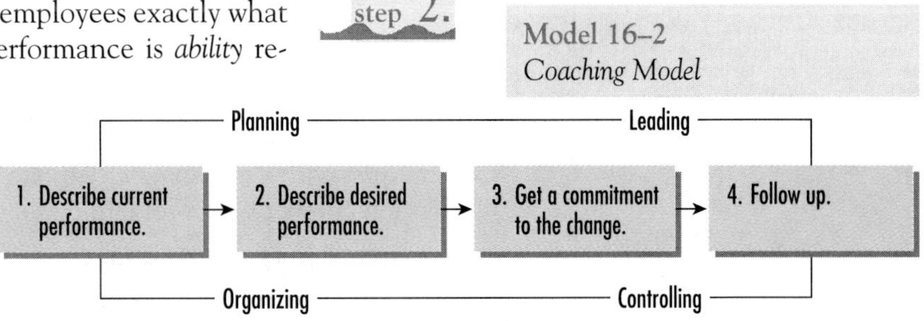
Planning
Leading
1. Describe current performance.
2. Describe desired performance.
3. Get a commitment to the change.
4. Follow up.
Organizing
Controlling

For example: *Ability*—"If you squat down and pick up the box using your legs instead of your back, it is easier and there is less chance of injuring yourself. Let me demonstrate for you." "Motivation—"Why should you squat and use your legs rather than your back to pick up boxes?"

step 3. **Get a Commitment to the Change.** When dealing with an *ability* performance issue, it is not necessary to get employees to verbally commit to the change if they seem willing to make it. However, if employees defend their way, and you're sure it's not as effective, explain why your proposed way is better. If you cannot get the employees to understand and agree, get a verbal commitment. This is also important for *motivation* performance issues because, if the employees are not willing to commit to the change, they will most likely not make the change.

For example: *Ability*—In the box example, the employee will most likely be willing to do it correctly, so skip the step. *Motivation*—"Will you squat rather than use your back from now on?"

step 4. **Follow Up.** Remember, some employees (those with low and moderate capability for self-control) do what managers inspect (imposed control), not what they expect. You should follow up to ensure that the employees are behaving as desired.

When dealing with an *ability* performance issue, and the person was receptive and you skipped step 3, say nothing. But, watch to be sure it is done correctly in the future. Coach again, if necessary. For a *motivation* problem, make a statement that you will follow up and that there are possible consequences for repeat performance.

For example: *Ability*—say nothing, but observe. *Motivation*—"Billie, picking up boxes with your back is dangerous; if I catch you doing it again, I will take disciplinary action." We deal with disciplinary action next.

Work Application

6. How would you rate your present or past boss's coaching ability? Explain your answer using critical incidents.

COUNSELING AND DISCIPLINING

When coaching, you are fine-tuning performance; with counseling and disciplining, you are dealing with a problem employee who is not performing to standards, or is violating standing plans (policies, procedures, and rules). **Discipline** *is corrective action to get employees to meet standards and standing plans*. The two most common discipline offenses are absenteeism and poor performance.[28] In this section, you will learn about problem employees, counseling, guidelines for effective discipline, and how to use the discipline model.

discipline
Corrective action to get employees to meet standards and standing plans.

Problem Employees

You will learn about the four types of problem employees, how to recognize an employee with a problem, why solving employee problems is important, and the relationship between problem employees and the management functions.

Types of Problem Employees. There are four types of problem employees: (1) Employees who do not have the *ability* to meet the job performance standards. This is an unfortunate situation, but after training such employees and realizing they cannot do a good job, they should be dismissed. Many employees are hired on a trial basis; this is the time to say, "Sorry, but you have to go." During the trial period, disciplinary action is not needed, but afterwards it is. (2) Employees who do not have the *motivation* to meet job performance standards often need discipline. Hopefully, discipline action will motivate this type of employee to meet standards. (3) Employees who intentionally *violate standing plans*. As a manager, it is your job to enforce the rules through disciplinary action. (4) Employees with *problems*. These employees may have the ability and motivation, but have a problem that affects job performance. The problem may not be related to the job. It is common for personal problems, such as child care and relationship/marital problems, to affect job performance. The employee with problems should be counseled before he or she is disciplined.

The late employee	The employee with a family problem
The absent employee	The insubordinate employee
The dishonest employee	The employee who steals
The violent or destructive employee	The sexual or racial harasser
The alcoholic or drug user	The safety violator
The nonconformist	The sick employee
The employee who's often socializing or doing personal work	

Figure 16–5
Problem Employees

We'll discuss counseling in the next part of this section, and how to deal with motivation and intentional violation of standing plans later in this section. But first, Figure 16–5 lists some problem employees you may encounter. In reviewing the figure, you can see that it is not always easy to distinguish between the types of problem employees. Therefore, it is often advisable to start with coaching/counseling and change to discipline if the problem persists.

Recognizing an Employee with a Problem. As a manager, be aware of changes in employee behavior and try to catch the problem before it becomes serious. Realize that behavior is a symptom that a problem exists, but may not be the problem itself. Following are some of the changes that indicate a problem.

Changed Personality. The employee is not the same person. He or she may be moody or irritable. An employee who used to get along well with coworkers is now getting into fights.

Changed Quality and Quantity of Work. The employee who made few mistakes begins to make frequent errors. The productive worker of the past no longer meets the standard level of output.

Increased Time Off. The employee with a good attendance record misses work more frequently. The employee who used to be on time begins to be late. The employee takes longer breaks and lunches and is not at the work station when he or she should be.

Signs of Alcohol or Drug Use. The employee is not as coordinated as he or she was in the past. The employee smells of alcohol or is using something to mask its smell. The employee's appearance has changed. The employee's eyes look different. He or she has less regard for personal appearance.

Why Solving Employee Problems Is Important. Too often managers choose to ignore problems, hoping that the problem will be solved without their input; or they take the attitude, "It's not my problem." When employee problems affect job performance, it *is* the manager's problem. Over the years, a training consultant asked managers if ignoring problem employees makes things better or worse. Almost everyone agrees that ignoring the problem usually makes it worse and the longer you wait the harder it is to solve. Action should be taken when employees fail to conform to performance expectations.[29]

Problem employees left unchecked don't just negatively affect their own productivity, they cause more work for managers and other employees. They lower employee morale as employees resent them because they are not pulling their weight and others have to do their work for them. When employees observe others not meeting standards or violating standing plans, and no disciplinary action is taken, they often perform the same undesirable behavior. Problem employees should be dealt with for the good of all.

Intentional disobedience, especially when the employee challenges a manager's authority in the presence of other workers, is an important area of discipline. Failure to do acceptable job-related behavior as requested is inexcusable and merits stern punishment. Its not unusual for an older, more experienced worker to challenge a new, young manager. If disciplinary action is not taken, the manager's authority will be undermined as others generally will also challenge the manager. This can result in a chaotic and unproductive work environment in which the manager is not respected and is without position power.[30]

Work Application

7. Identify a problem employee you observed on the job. Describe how the person affected the department's performance.

Problem Employees and the Management Functions. How you perform the four management functions, and the management skills you have, will directly affect the number and intensity of problems you will have with employees. Generally, the better the manager and the system, including performance appraisal, the fewer the problems. The best preliminary control the manager can use to prevent problem employees is effective staffing. The manager should be careful not to hire candidates who will become problem employees.

7. Explain the manager's role in counseling and the role of the employee assistance program staff.

Management Counseling

As mentioned, the first thing a manager should do with a person experiencing a personal problem is to attempt to help the employee solve the problem. This is usually done through counseling, which is a form of coaching.

When most people hear the term *counseling*, they think of psychological counseling or psychotherapy. That type of sophisticated help should not be attempted by nonprofessionals such as a manager. Instead, **management counseling** *is the process of giving employees feedback so they realize that a problem is affecting their job performance, and referring employees with problems to the employee assistance program.*

management counseling
The process of giving employees feedback so they realize that a problem is affecting their job performance, and referring employees with problems to the employee assistance program.

Most managers do not like to hear the details of personal problems. This is not a requirement. Instead, the manager's role is to help employees realize that they have problems and that those problems affect their work. The manager is getting the employee back on track. Management counseling involves a one-on-one exchange of thoughts, ideas, and feelings. The employee is given the opportunity to get things off his or her chest. For example, the manager could say, "I've noticed that you are not yourself. You made three errors on this report. Is something wrong I should know about?"

The manager should not give advice on how to solve personal problems such as marital difficulty. When professional help is needed, the manager should refer the employee to the human resources department for professional help through the employee assistance program. *The* **employee assistance program (EAP)** *consists of a staff of people who help employees get professional assistance in solving their problems.* The employee assistance staff should have a list of counselors and other resources available in the community. Some large companies even have some

employee assistance program (EAP)
Consists of a staff of people who help employees get professional assistance in solving their problems.

full- and part-time professional employee counselors. Many large organizations pay the counseling cost, such as alcohol and drug abuse programs.

To make the referral, a manager could say something like, "Are you aware of our employee assistance program? Would you like me to set up an appointment with Jean in the human resources department to help you get professional assistance with your problem?"

However, if job performance does not return to standard, discipline is appropriate because it often makes the employee realize the seriousness of his or her problem and the importance of maintaining job performance. Some time off from work, with or without pay depending on the situation, often helps the employee deal with the problem.

The Kellogg Foundation has a comprehensive employee assistance program. The purpose of the program is to provide access to professional counseling that will assist employees and their immediate families in resolving personal problems that may affect their well-being and, in some cases, job performance. The EAP's team of professional counselors provides assistance and services in the following areas: communication and interpersonal skills, family/marital stress, alcohol and drug abuse, legal and financial problems, difficulties with children, depression and anxiety, aging parents, career counseling, stress, and information regarding community resources for educational, recreational, and medical needs. To access services, the employee and/or his or her immediate family make direct contact with the EAP provider. This service is kept strictly confidential between the EAP provider and the employee and/or his or her family. The initial assessment and short-term counseling are free to any Foundation employee or immediate family member.

Disciplining

Coaching, which includes counseling, should generally be the first step in dealing with a problem employee. However, an employee may be unwilling or unable to change or a rule may be broken. In such cases, discipline is necessary. The major objective of discipline is to change behavior. Secondary objectives may be to (1) let employees know that action will be taken when standing plans or performance requirements are not met and (2) when challenged, to maintain authority.

The human resources department handles many of the disciplinary details and provides written discipline guidelines. Written policy procedures usually outline grounds for specific sanctions and dismissal based on the violation. Common offenses include theft, sexual or racial harassment, verbal or substance abuse, and safety violations.[31] You will learn some discipline guidelines and about progressive discipline and discipline without punishment in the following sections.

The Kellogg Foundation does not have formal written discipline guidelines. At the Foundation, they believe a philosophy of supervision is more appropriate and more effective than rigid policies. This philosophy includes statements that describe the ways and means by which they wish to have all interactions occur and, therefore, convey important ideas to everyone who is a part of their staff. Statements of philosophy give supervisors the flexibility to respond to individual needs and yet ensure that the work is accomplished in a timely, efficient, and consistent manner throughout the Foundation.

Work Application

8. Identify some of the rules and penalties for violating them in an organization you work or have worked for.

Figure 16–6
Guidelines for Effective Discipline

- Clearly communicate the standards and standing plans to all employees.
- The punishment should fit the crime.
- Follow the standing plans yourself.
- Take consistent, impartial action when the rules are broken.
- Discipline immediately, but stay calm and get all the necessary facts before you discipline.
- Discipline in private.
- Document discipline.
- When the discipline is over, resume normal relations with the employee.

Discipline Guidelines. Figure 16–6 lists eight guidelines for effective discipline, which are explained here.

Clearly Communicate the Standards and Standing Plans to All Employees. It may sound obvious, but you would be surprised how many employees are disciplined for behavior they did not know they were not supposed to do. This is why it is safe to start with coaching as a reminder for minor rules that employees may not know, or could have forgotten.

The Punishment Should Fit the Crime. Offenders of major violations should be given severe discipline, but minor offenders should not. Major offenses, such as stealing, are often grounds for dismissal on the first violation, while being late subjects the employee to progressive discipline, which will be explained in this section.

Follow the Standing Plans Yourself. Lead by example. Don't expect employees to follow the rules if you don't.

Take Consistent, Impartial Action When the Rules Are Broken. There is a difference between consistency and impartiality. The manager who enforces rules sporadically causes frustration and resentment. Employees will make comments such as, "Tom did it yesterday and nothing happened to him. Betty can break the rules because she's the boss's pet." To be impartial, the manager should focus on the act, not the person. The employee should realize that discipline is not personal; it's just a specific behavior that needs to be changed.

Discipline Immediately, but Stay Calm and Get All the Necessary Facts before You Discipline. Discipline should take place soon after the violation occurs to reinforce the desired behavior. However, stay calm. Unmanaged anger can interfere with your ability to function in a rational manner, inhibit effective communication, and create external and internal distress by negatively affecting your relationship with your employee, not to mention your physical health and well-being.[32] If you and/or the employee is upset, make an appointment to discuss the violation at a set time, say one hour later. This will give you time to rationally plan your discipline. Also, do not jump to conclusions. Do not discipline on hearsay evidence. If someone tells you that an employee is breaking a rule, try to catch that employee in the act. When you do catch a person in the act, give him or her a chance to explain before you discipline. Things are not always as they seem.

Discipline in Private. Normally, no one should observe you disciplining an employee. Even if someone challenges you in front of others, don't get into a shouting match. If you do, some employees may think you won, while others may think the employee won. Some employees will feel you were too hard on the employee, while others will think you were too soft. In any case, you lose. So discipline in private. For example, if an employee challenges you in front of other employees, say something like, "Meet me in my office at 10:00 so that we can calm down and discuss this in a rational manner." All employees will realize that discipline will take place.

Document Discipline. It is extremely important to document violations and the action taken. The critical incident file is appropriate for recording what happened. However, it is also advisable to have the employee sign and receive a copy of a written document stating that a warning has been given and why. The document can be handwritten, but preferably should be on company letterhead. It should state the date and time and the specifics of the violation; briefly report what took place during the discipline session; include a statement of the employee's commitment to change, if given, or reasons for the refusal to change; and describe the penalty for future violations. If the employee disagrees with the written statement, try to get an agreement, making a minor change if necessary. If the employee refuses to sign an accurate document, have a company official, such as your boss, witness the refusal and sign it as proof that the employee was given the warning and refused to sign the statement. Proof that the employee did receive a written warning and was informed of the consequences for future violations will make it difficult for the organization or a court of law to overturn your action.

APPLYING THE CONCEPT

AC 16–3 Guidelines for Effective Discipline

Identify which guideline is being followed, or not being followed, in the following statements.

Use the guidelines in Figure 16–6 as the answers. Place the letters A–H in sequence before each guideline and place the letter of the guideline on the line before its statement.

____ **11.** "The boss must have been upset to yell that loud."

____ **12.** "It's not fair. The manager comes back from break late all the time; why can't I?"

____ **13.** "When I leave the place a mess, the manager reprimands me. When Chris does it, nothing is ever said."

____ **14.** "The boss gave me a verbal warning for smoking in a restricted area and placed a note in my file."

____ **15.** "I want you to come into my office so that we can discuss this matter."

When the Discipline Is Over, Resume Normal Relations with the Employee. Do not hold a grudge or treat the violator as a criminal. The self-fulfilling prophecy applies: if you treat the employee like a criminal, he or she will probably live up to your expectations and be a repeat offender. If you treat the employee as though it was a one-time mistake which you don't expect to happen again, that will probably be the end of it.

Work Application

9. Review the discipline guidelines. Identify any guidelines your present or past boss did not follow.

Progressive Discipline. Many organizations have a series of more severe disciplinary actions. The progressive disciplinary steps are (1) oral warning, (2) written warning, (3) suspension, and (4) dismissal. For minor violations, such as being late for work, all four steps are commonly followed. However, for more important violations, such as stealing, steps may be skipped. Be sure to document each step. Discipline without punishment is a form of progressive discipline.

Discipline without Punishment. Over 30 years ago, John Huberman developed discipline without punishment[33] and it is still being written about and used successfully by organizations including Bay Area Rapid Transit, General Electric, GTE, Pennzoil, Procter & Gamble, Tampa Electric, and the Texas Department of Mental Health.[34] Discipline is viewed as positive and punishment as negative. Punishment should be avoided because it produces fear, anxiety, and more punishment. There are three major differences between discipline and punishment: (1) *Responsibility*. With discipline, the employee is responsible for changing behavior. With punishment, the manager is responsible for making the employee obey the rules. (2) *Focus*. Discipline focuses on changing future behavior. Punishment focuses on penalizing past violations. (3) *The manager's role*. The manager is a coach when disciplining and a judge when punishing.

Discipline without punishment involves four steps:

1. *The employee is given an oral warning.* It focuses on making the employee responsible for changing future behavior.
2. *The employee is given a written reminder*. If the employee fails to change and repeats the violation after the oral warning, he or she gets a written reminder not to do it again.
3. *The employee is given decision-making leave*. If a third warning is needed, the employee is given a day off, with pay, to determine whether he or she wishes to remain with the organization. If the employee chooses to stay on the job, he or she realizes the need for change, because a fourth violation will result in termination.
4. *The employee is terminated*. A fourth violation results in the employee's being fired.

The Kellogg Foundation does not have progressive disciplinary steps. However, the results of progressive discipline are achieved through application of its philosophy of supervision and effective coaching. The Foundation has trained its managers to be effective at disciplining employees. However, the emphasis is placed on effective communication for maintaining productive working relationships and performance coaching.

8. List the five steps in the discipline model.

The Discipline Model

The steps in the discipline model should be followed each time an employee must be disciplined. What will change is the discussion based on the level of progression in discipline and the discipline given.

The five steps in the discipline model are presented here and summarized in Model 16–3. They are also illustrated in Behavior Model Video 16–1, Discipline.

step 1. **Refer to Past Feedback.** Begin the interview by refreshing the employee's memory. If the employee has been coached/counseled about the behavior, or if he or she has clearly broken a known rule, state that.

For example: *Prior coaching*—"Billie, remember my telling you about the proper way to lift boxes with your legs?" *Rule violation*—"Billie, you know the safety rule about lifting boxes with your legs."

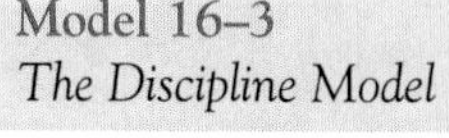

Model 16–3
The Discipline Model

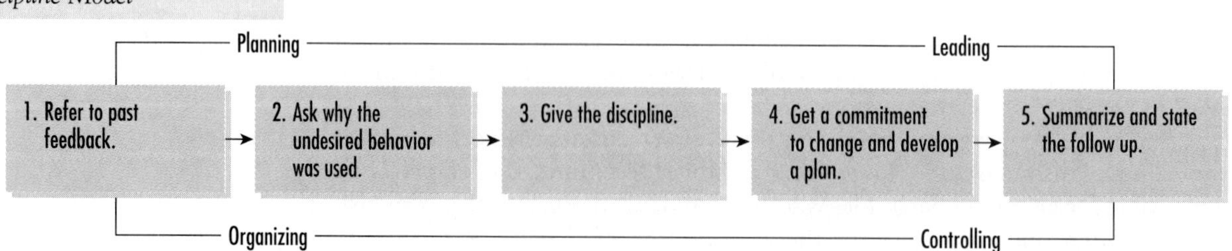
Planning
Leading
1. Refer to past feedback.
2. Ask why the undesired behavior was used.
3. Give the discipline.
4. Get a commitment to change and develop a plan.
5. Summarize and state the follow up.
Organizing
Controlling

step 2. **Ask Why the Undesired Behavior Was Used.** As in the guideline, you are giving the employee a chance to explain the behavior as part of getting all the necessary facts before you discipline. If you used prior coaching and the employee committed to changing the behavior, ask why the behavior did not change. If the behavior had changed, discipline would not be needed. Again, be sure to describe specific critical incidents to support your contention that behavior has not changed at all or has not changed enough to be at standard.

For example: *Prior coaching*—"Two days ago you told me that you would use your legs, rather than your back, to lift boxes. Why are you still using your back?" *Rule violation*—"Why are you breaking the safety rule and using your back, rather than your legs, to lift the box?"

step 3. **Give the Discipline.** If there is no good reason for the undesirable behavior, give the discipline. The discipline will vary with the stage in the discipline progression.

For example: *Prior coaching*—"Because you have not changed your behavior, I'm giving you an oral warning." *Rule violation*—"Because you have violated a safety rule, I'm giving you an oral warning.

step 4. **Get a Commitment to Change and Develop a Plan.** Try to get a commitment to change. If the employee will not commit, make note of the fact in the critical incidents file or use the procedures for a written warning. A plan for change may have been developed in the past. If it has, the manager may try to get the employee to commit to it again. Develop a new plan, if necessary. A statement such as, "Your previous attempt has not worked; there must be a better way," is often helpful. With a personal problem, offer professional help again.

For example: *Prior coaching or rule violation*—"Will you lift with your legs from now on?" "Is there a way to get you to remember to use your legs instead of your back when you lift?"

step 5. **Summarize and State the Follow Up.** Summarize the discipline and state the follow-up disciplinary action to be taken. Part of follow up is to document the discipline. At the written warning and suspension stage, get the employee's signature. If necessary, take the next step in the discipline model until dismissal.

For example: *Prior coaching or rule violation*—"So you agree to use your legs instead of your back when you lift. If I catch you again, you will be given a written warning, which is followed by a suspension and dismissal if necessary."

FORMAL PERFORMANCE APPRAISAL INTERVIEWS

The Kellogg Foundation has a formal performance appraisal in which employees are evaluated once a year with an optional midyear review. Managers are trained to conduct performance appraisal interviews. Recall that it is recommended to have separate evaluative and developmental PA interviews. In this section you will learn how to prepare for and conduct separate evaluative and developmental PA interviews. But first, you will learn some common problems to avoid when conducting performance appraisal interviews.

Problems to Avoid When Conducting Performance Appraisals

Memory and recency	Central tendency
Activity trap	Leniency
Bias	Strictness
Halo effect	Interruptions
Horn effect	Rushing

Figure 16–7
Problems to Avoid When Conducting Performance Appraisals

Truthful and realistic performance appraisals are not only ethical, they can prevent company litigation.[35] Complaints of unfairness found in the literature have focused on the inaccuracies and errors resulting from appraisal methods.[36] Figure 16–7 lists ten of these inaccuracies and errors to avoid when conducting a performance appraisal, which are explained here.

Memory and Recency. It is difficult to remember what happened six months to a year ago. Managers who don't keep a critical incidents files tend to give more weight to recent performance during the evaluation. Keeping a good critical incidents file will help you remember past performance.

Activity Trap. Do not evaluate employees based on how active or busy they appear to be. Evaluate results. The employee who appears to be the busiest may actually be the least productive.

Bias. Evaluate actual performance, not friendship, personality, race, religion, and so forth. Managers develop feelings for employees based on work-related interactions. Be aware of your feelings toward each employee. Separate objective judgment from subjective feelings when evaluating performance.

Halo Effect. The halo effect means that you rate the employee favorably on all criteria based on performance in a few. When evaluating performance, you should deal with each criterion separately. An employee may be outstanding in some areas and poor in others.

Horn Effect. The horn effect is the opposite of the halo effect. You rate the employee low on all criteria based on unfavorable performance in a few.

Central Tendency. The central tendency means that you rate most employees as average or that all ratings in a single evaluation are within a narrow range. There should be some distribution of ratings because employees do not perform at the same level all the time or on every task.

Leniency. Leniency means that you rate employees higher than actual performance warrants. Supervisors generally give

APPLYING THE CONCEPT

AC 16–4 Performance Appraisal Problems

Identify the performance appraisal problem or mistake made by the manager. Use the items in Figure 16–7 as the answers. Place the letters A–J in sequence before each item and place the letter of the item on the line before its statement.

____ **16.** "I went five months without making a mistake. This month I made one and got a good rating instead of very good."

____ **17.** "I'm not concerned about how I perform because I always get the same rating. Almost everyone gets an average rating."

____ **18.** "I don't type well. I only type about 20 percent of the time anyway. But because of typing, the manager rates me low on other items."

____ **19.** "I take my time and pace myself. I do more work than many of the people in the department. But because I don't pretend to be really pushing it when the boss walks around, like some others do, I don't get high evaluations."

____ **20.** "Although Chris, the manager, did not say it, she gave me a low rating because of the way I dress. Chris is always making comments about my clothes."

their subordinates higher performance ratings than they actually deserve. Inflated appraisals do not encourage employees to improve and can be used by discharged employees as litigation weapons.[37]

Strictness. The opposite of leniency is strictness. You rate employees lower than actual performance warrants. This may reflect a manager's negative bias about employees.

Interruptions. It is important to avoid interruptions during a performance appraisal. It is very distracting to both the manager and employee. Before beginning the interview, tell others not to disturb you unless an extreme emergency arises.

Rushing. Managers often underestimate the time the appraisal will take. When pressed for time, they rush through the end of the appraisal. Be sure to leave plenty of time. Do not plan anything for some time after you think the appraisal will end so that you can carry on until a natural ending. Do not schedule the appraisal too late in the work day.

Work Application

10. Recall an appraisal of your performance. Did the manager avoid all ten problems? If not, which problems did the manager have.

The Evaluative Performance Appraisal Interview

9. List the steps in conducting the evaluative and developmental performance appraisal interviews.

It is recommended that you plan before you act for performance appraisal interviews. Therefore, this section is separated into preparing for and conducting the PA interview. Because the evaluative interview is the basis for the development interview, it is completed first. However, recall that the primary purpose of the PA should be to help employees improve their performance.[38]

Preparing for an Evaluative Interview. When preparing for this interview, follow the steps in the evaluative performance appraisal process, Model 16–4, which are explained here.

step 1. **Make an Appointment.** About one week before you plan to conduct the performance appraisal interview, make an appointment with the employee. Agree on a date, time, and place. Let the employee select the place—your office, the employee's work area, or a neutral area such as a conference room (reserve it). Don't break the appointment; this sends a signal that the employee is not important.

Model 16–4
The Evaluative Performance Appraisal

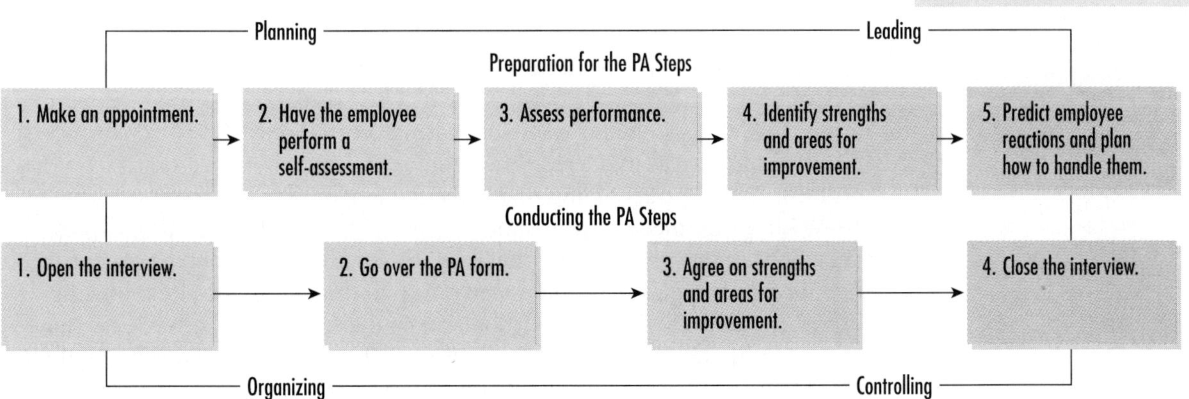
Planning
Leading
Preparation for the PA Steps
1. Make an appointment.
2. Have the employee perform a self-assessment.
3. Assess performance.
4. Identify strengths and areas for improvement.
5. Predict employee reactions and plan how to handle them.
Conducting the PA Steps
1. Open the interview.
2. Go over the PA form.
3. Agree on strengths and areas for improvement.
4. Close the interview.
Organizing
Controlling

step 2.

Have the Employee Perform a Self-Appraisal. When you make the appointment, give the employee a copy of the evaluation form. Ask him or her to fill it out (explain how, if necessary) and bring it to the interview. Also ask the employee to identify strengths and areas for improvement.

step 3.

Assess Performance. Gather the data you need to make the assessment: employee records, critical incidents file, and so on. Fill out the evaluation form, but not in final form. You may change your evaluation during the interview. Review the ten problem areas, and be sure you avoid them all.

step 4.

Identify Strengths and Areas for Improvement. Notice that I did not say weaknesses. That term has a negative connotation. An employee may say, "I have no weaknesses," but there are always areas where improvement is possible.

step 5.

Predict Employee Reactions and Plan How to Handle Them. Managers who know their employees should have a good idea of how the employee will react to the evaluation. Be aware that it is natural for employees to rate themselves higher than managers and their peers.[39] Having a list of specific critical incidents to back up your evaluation will help you overcome disagreement. Be prepared to clearly explain why the employee did not get a higher rating on all items and what it takes to get it.

Conducting an Evaluation Interview. Encourage the employee to talk. The appraisal should be a give-and-take interview with both parties contributing on a 50–50 basis. The steps to follow when conducting the evaluative performance appraisal interview are listed in Model 16–4, and discussed here.

step 1.

Open the Interview. Put the employee at ease. Develop a rapport by discussing some topic of interest to the employee, such as sports, hobbies, and so forth. Nonoffensive humor is appropriate for performance reviews. Once a rapport is established, state the purpose of the interview.

step 2.

Go Over the Form. You can start with the first item and go over the items on the form in order. You can begin with the employee's self-evaluation and his or her reason for the rating. Follow with the rating you gave on the item and your reasons for it. Use critical incidents to support the rating. You can also begin with your rating on the item and reasons it was selected, using critical incidents. You then ask for the employee's rating and reason for it. Taking turns going first is recommended.

With either method, you should praise good performance and express appreciation. In most interviews, there will be at least one area of disagreement on the rating the employee should receive. When this occurs, do the following: (1) Listen to the employee's side without becoming hostile, defensive, or argumentative. (2) Be willing to change the rating if the employee is correct. (3) Stand firm if you are correct. Do not let the employee bluff you into changing ratings if you disagree. If the employee continues to disagree, tell him or her to submit a written statement. The statement can be written directly on the form—several include space for this purpose—or it can be attached to the form.

step 3. **Agree on Strengths and Areas for Improvement.** After going over each item on the form, ask the employee to describe his or her strengths. You should also describe what you believe are the employee's strengths and then come to an agreement. Follow the same procedure to identify areas for improvement. Keep the latter to two or three items, at most. Unless the employee has low capability, this is a good time to tell him or her to develop objectives and plans for improvements in these areas. If you have the authority to give pay raises, the amount of the raise can be discussed at this point. You can also set up the appointment for the developmental interview.

step 4. **Close the Interview.** Summarize the meeting with an overall rating of the employee's performance. End on a positive note such as, "I'm glad we had a chance to discuss your performance," "You're doing a great job," "I'm sure that if we work together, you can improve the evaluation next time," and so on.

The Developmental Performance Appraisal Interview

As with the evaluative interview, you should prepare for and conduct the developmental performance appraisal.

Preparing for a Developmental Interview. After the evaluation is completed, you should prepare for the developmental interview. To do this, follow the steps in Model 16–5, which are explained here.

step 1. **Make an Appointment.** Set a date, time, and place for the developmental interview. This date can be set at the end of the evaluation interview or later. Schedule the developmental interview about a week after the evaluation.

Model 16–5
The Developmental Performance Appraisal

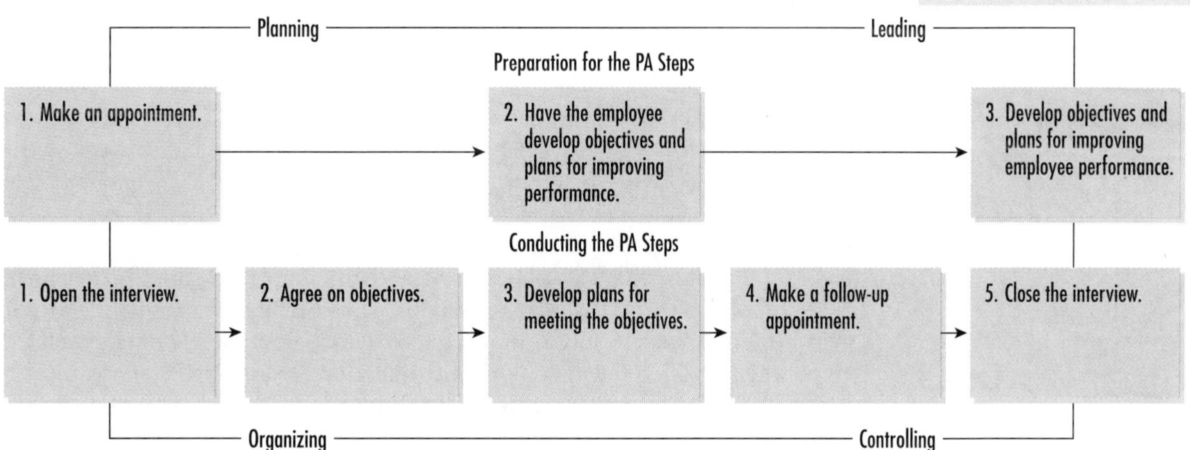
Planning
Leading
Preparation for the PA Steps
1. Make an appointment.
2. Have the employee develop objectives and plans for improving performance.
3. Develop objectives and plans for improving employee performance.
Conducting the PA Steps
1. Open the interview.
2. Agree on objectives.
3. Develop plans for meeting the objectives.
4. Make a follow-up appointment.
5. Close the interview.
Organizing
Controlling

step 2.

Have the Employee Develop Objectives and Plans for Improving Performance. During the evaluation interview, you and the employee should have agreed on strengths and areas for improvement. The areas for improvement serve as the basis for developmental objectives and plans.

step 3.

Develop Objectives and Plans for Improving Employee Performance. The degree of detail in the objectives and plans you develop should depend on the employee's capability level. Use the management style (discussed in Chapter 1) appropriate to the situation. With a low-capability employee, you should have more details worked out than with a high-capability employee. As with management by objectives, you should both have a copy, review progress, and evaluate the next item based on performance. If the employee implements the plan successfully, he or she should get a higher rating for the item on the next performance appraisal.

Conducting the Developmental Interview. To do this, follow the steps in Model 16–5, which are explained here.

step 1.

Open the Interview. Open the interview by developing rapport, as you did with the evaluation interview.

step 2.

Agree on Objectives. Keep the number of objectives to two or three, at most. This discussion depends on the employee's capability level. Use the management style (discussed in Chapter 1) appropriate to the situation. In any case, you should both write each objective down, preferably on an operational planning sheet (Chapter 6), following the criteria for effective objectives (Chapter 5).

step 3.

Develop Plans for Meeting Objectives. To meet each objective, a plan must be developed. How much guidance you give depends on the employee's capability level. The lower the level, the more guidance is needed; the higher the level, the less guidance is needed. But, be sure to use as much employee participation as possible so that the employee feels as though it is his or her plan, rather than yours. In any case, each objective and the plans should be written down, preferably on an operational planning sheet. Be sure to set control checkpoints to review progress in meeting the objectives.

step 4.

Make a Follow-Up Appointment. Be sure to schedule a meeting to review progress at the first control checkpoint.

step 5.

Close the Interview. You and the employee should each have copies of the operational plans, or make arrangements to get copies. You may review action items. Close with a positive statement such as, "I'm confident that you will achieve the objectives."

After reviewing the coaching, disciplining, and formal performance appraisal system steps, some people, especially those who have worked full time and have been through a formal review interview, state that their managers did not follow these steps. This is true in most cases. However, the objective of this book is not to teach you poor practices that are commonly used. It is to present tried and proven methods that can work, if you work to develop the skill through using the models. It is not difficult to pull out your book and follow these steps when the performance appraisal interview is coming.

CURRENT MANAGEMENT ISSUES

Global. Managers of *global* companies must be concerned with ensuring that human resources control methods can be used on an international level. Deming believed that his four criticisms of performance appraisal systems are global problems, but are less of a problem in Japan where his methods have been widely adopted.

Diversity. During all stages of the performance appraisal, managers should realize that they lead a *diversity* of employees. Employees do differ concerning how well and how conscientiously they do their work.[40] Therefore, it is important to use the appropriate level of imposed versus self-control based on the capability of each employee. To reward positive behavior, more organizations are implementing pay-for-performance programs.[41] Another current issue is whether an organization should control the way its employees dress. Many organizations are instituting dress-down policies that allow more diversity. Many managers believe that employees will be more productive if they are comfortable. Besides, with today's technology, in many industries employees never come face-to-face with people outside the organization. However, many organizations set boundaries to define casual wear.[42]

Ethics and Social Responsibility. The entire performance appraisal system should be *socially responsible*. *Ethics* is always an issue in PA. Truthful and realistic PA can be difficult but worthwhile.[43] Employees generally will not or cannot improve performance without effective measures and feedback. Important ethical questions are the right to privacy and the degree of imposed control. Today's technology makes spying on employees very easy. Tiny video surveillance cameras can be mounted throughout a workplace. Telephones can be bugged. Computer drives can be read in their entirety. Software can even monitor every keystroke so there's no guessing about when employees are working and when they're not. As a manager, you have the ability to spy.[44] The question is, "Is it ethical?" In addition, corporate America has been criticized for its drive for success and profits to the point of denigrating employees and that its drive helps foster workplace violence. The needs of people must have as much importance as success and profits.[45]

Total Quality Management. *TQM's* quality focus makes setting quality standards and measuring quality an important issue. Being a quality expert, Deming's four criticisms of current performance appraisal systems focus on quality issues. Deming also criticized the current PA focus for being on outputs only. In keeping with the systems process, Deming called for performance appraisal in the areas of input, transformation processes, and output. In addition, he recommended the focus of control be on the process, not controlling employee behavior.[46] With the TQM emphasis on teams, team members are taking on greater responsibility for performance appraisal.

Participative Management and Teams. If you really want to develop a performance appraisal system that avoids the problems identified in this chapter, you need to use *participative management* and actively involve all those who are affected by the PA.[47] One of the current trends in participative management and *teams* is to increase the number of people involved in conducting PA. The use of self-evaluations, peer evaluations, and peers evaluating their bosses is on the increase. While these evaluations can increase information used in the PA process, there are some problems with them. Self-ratings tends to be biased and lenient when the rater has a direct interest in receiving high ratings. Honest team reviews from peers can instruct—and sting. Organizations including AT&T, Baxter International, Dow Chemical, and Eastman Chemical are a few of the many using team evaluations.[48] Peer ratings among friends can also lead to bias and leniency. Peer reviews are more useful when they are anonymous and used for developmental rather than administrative decisions. Subordinates who are dissatisfied with their boss tend to be subject to bias, the horn effect, and strictness. To help overcome these problems, these evaluations should be used, but the direct supervisor should have ultimate authority for the performance appraisal.[49] For example, Abbott Laboratories' Diagnostic Division has salespeople evaluate the sales managers to help make the sales units work together and more efficiently. The evaluations give regional managers who do not see the sales managers on a daily basis a better idea as to their management style and effectiveness. However, the boss evaluations are only part of the regional managers' evaluation of the sales managers.[50]

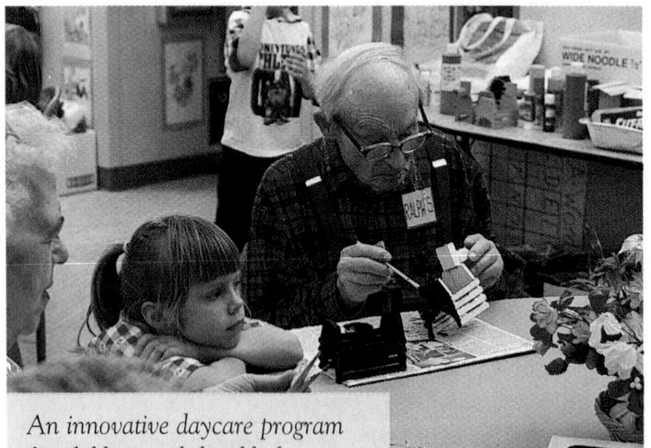

An innovative daycare program for children and the elderly at Lancaster Laboratories greatly reduces employee absenteeism.

Productivity. In the quest for productivity, three million jobs were cut in seven years.[51] However, re-engineering efforts are more successful if the implementation emphasizes a shift in performance that is geared toward increasing *productivity*.[52] An area of concern to productivity is absenteeism, which is on the increase. Only 45 percent of absenteeism is due to personal illness, while dealing with family issues accounts for 27 percent of unscheduled time off. An uncertain percentage are not so much sick as they are sick and tired and take the day off to escape stress.[53] In a survey, 72 percent of 300 companies stated that on-site or back-up daycare services would "greatly" reduce worker absenteeism. However, only 6 percent of companies offer the service.

Small Business. Many *small businesses*, especially those with fewer than 100 employees, do not have human resources departments with professionals who develop performance appraisal systems with clear standards and measurement methods, employee assistance programs, and discipline policies. Many don't even hold formal performance appraisals once a year. However, this does not mean that PA is any less important in small businesses than it is in large businesses. Some small businesses, including the Kellogg Foundation because it only has 300 employees, do have a formal PA process as discussed throughout this chapter.

CHAPTER SUMMARY AND GLOSSARY

This chapter summary is organized to answer the ten learning objectives for Chapter 16.

1. Explain the two types of performance appraisal.

The two types of performance appraisal are developmental and evaluative. Developmental PA is used to make decisions and plan for performance improvements. Evaluative PA is used to make administrative decisions including pay raises, transfers and promotions, and demotions and termination.

2. Describe the difference between the informal and formal steps in the performance appraisal process.

Performance appraisal is the ongoing process of evaluating employee performance. The informal PA is the ongoing process of concurrent control. The formal PA interview takes place once or twice a year and serves primarily as a rework control.

3. Explain the concept, "You get what you reward."

People seek information concerning what activities are rewarded, and then seek to do (or at least pretend to do) those things, often to the exclusion of activities not rewarded.

4. State the primary criterion for determining the degree of imposed control versus self-control.

The primary criterion for determining the degree of imposed control versus self-control is the capability of the employees to meet standards using self-control. The lower the capability level, the more imposed control should be used. The higher the capability level, the more self-control should be used.

5. Explain the importance of positive motivational feedback in coaching.

The objective of coaching is to improve performance. Positive feedback, such as giving praise, is used to motivate employees to maintain and improve their performance.

6. List the four steps in the coaching model.

The four steps in the coaching model are (1) describe current performance, (2) describe desired performance, (3) get a commitment to the change, and (4) follow up.

7. Explain the manager's role in counseling and the role of the employee assistance program staff.

The manager's role in counseling is to give employees feedback so they realize that a problem is affecting their job performance, and to refer employees with problems to the employee assistance program. The role of the employee assistance program staff is to help employees get professional help to solve their problems.

8. List the five steps in the discipline model.

The five steps in the discipline model are (1) refer to past feedback, (2) ask why the undesired behavior was used, (3) give the discipline, (4) get a commitment to change and develop a plan, and (5) summarize and state the follow up.

9. List the steps in conducting the evaluative and developmental performance appraisal interviews.

The four steps in conducting the evaluative interview are (1) open the interview, (2) go over the PA form, (3) agree on strengths and areas for improvement, and (4) close the interview. The five steps in conducting the developmental interview are (1) open the interview, (2) agree on objectives, (3) develop plans for meeting the objectives, (4) make a follow-up appointment, and (5) close the interview.

10. Define the following key terms in order of appearance in the chapter.

Select one or more methods: (1) fill in the missing key terms from memory, (2) match the key terms from the end of the review with their definitions below, or (3) copy the key terms in order from the list at the beginning of the chapter.

______ is the ongoing process of evaluating employee performance.

______________ is used to make decisions and plans for performance improvements.

______________ is used to make administrative decisions including pay raises, transfers and promotions, and demotions and terminations.

The __________ is a record of an employee's positive and negative performance.

The __________ is a form on which the manager simply checks off the employee's level of performance.

The ______________ is a form with descriptive statements which managers select from to measure employee performance.

__________ is the process of giving motivational feedback to maintain and improve performance.

______________ has three major activities: listening, teaching, and facilitating.

__________ is corrective action to get employees to meet standards and standing plans.

______________ is the process of giving employees feedback so they realize that a problem is affecting their job performance, and to refer employees with problems to the employee assistance program.

The ______________ consists of a staff of people who help employees get professional assistance in solving their problems.

KEY TERMS

behaviorally anchored rating scale
coaching
critical incident file
developmental performance appraisal
discipline
employee assistance program
evaluative performance appraisal
management by walking around
management counseling
performance appraisal
rating scale

REVIEW AND DISCUSSION QUESTIONS

1. What are the steps in the performance appraisal process?
2. Why should performance appraisal be an ongoing process?
3. How is the control systems process included within the performance appraisal process?
4. Should standards be absolute or cover a range? Why?
5. What is the folly of rewarding A, while hoping for B?
6. What are Deming's four criticisms of current performance appraisal systems?
7. What is the difference between rating scales and behaviorally anchored rating scales?
8. What are appropriate and inappropriate decisions based on ranking?
9. What is the role of critical success factors in developing effective standards and measures of performance?
10. What is the objective of coaching?
11. How do managers commonly demotivate employees?
12. What is the performance formula and how is it used with coaching?
13. What are the three activities of management by walking around and what is the role of facilitating?
14. What is the difference among coaching, counseling, and disciplining?
15. What is the relationship between problem employees and the management functions?
16. Which of the eight discipline guidelines is most relevant to you personally? Explain.
17. What are the three differences between discipline and punishment?
18. Which of the ten problems to avoid when conducting a performance appraisal is most relevant to you personally? Explain.

CASE

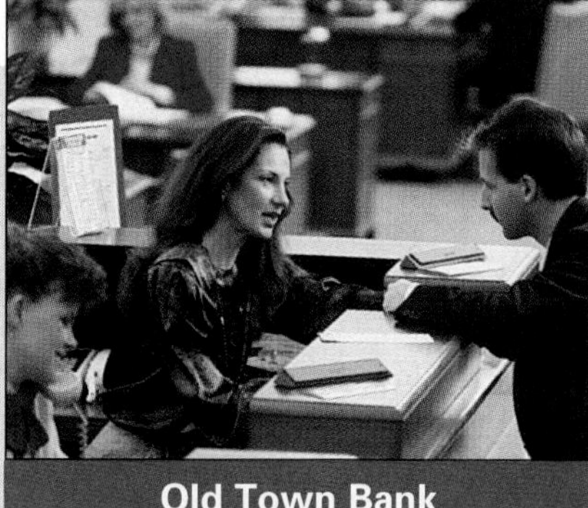
Old Town Bank

Old Town Bank has ten branches in the Fremont, Nebraska, area. It has a formal performance appraisal system in which all employees are evaluated once a year by the branch manager. Steve Tomson is the manager of the 10th Street branch. Following is his performance appraisal interview with his bank teller, Jean Jones (nicknamed JJ), who is getting her first yearly performance appraisal.[54]

Steve: JJ, I called you into my office because it's time for your first yearly performance appraisal.

JJ: It's gone by fast.

Steve: The checkmarks on this two-page form show how I evaluated you. I want you to look at the form and sign it.

JJ: (several minutes later) You only gave me an average mark of 4 down the form and overall! Why? I'm a better teller than most of the people in this branch.

Steve: You are a good teller. You see, the human resources manager says that even though there is a range from 1 to 7, managers cannot give anyone a 1 for superior, because no one is that good. Plus, only two employees can get a 2, and I have to give one worker a 7. New workers like you usually get a 5. So, you are doing a good job with a 4.

JJ: This doesn't make sense to me. I'm doing a good job, and I should get a good evaluation, not average.

Steve: I can understand your feelings, but it's out of our control. Besides, everyone gets the same raise as long as you don't get the poor evaluation. The person with the poor PA does not get a raise.

JJ: I understand your explanation, but it still seems strange to me.

Steve: Well, you can write a note and attach it to the form. The form is sent to the human resources director, who will read it.

JJ: I'll sign it, but I'm not going to write a note.

Steve: Overall, you're doing a good job, and you're getting the standard raise. Thank you for coming in for this meeting. I'm glad to have you in my branch.

JJ: I'll see you later.

Select the best alternative to the following questions. Be sure you are able to explain your answers.

1. This interview was a(n) ___ performance appraisal.

   a. developmental b. evaluative

2. Steve is in the ___ step of the performance appraisal process.

   a. 1st. b. 2nd c. 3rd c. 4th

3. Performance standards are clear.

   a. true b. false

4. The bank performance appraisal system is guilty of the folly of rewarding A, while hoping for B.

   a. true b. false

5. Deming would say that the bank performance appraisal practices ______.

   a. are unfair
   b. compromise quality
   c. discourage workers from excelling
   d. rob employees of pride in their work
   e. all of these

6. The form Steve filled out and JJ signed is a ___ performance appraisal measurement method.

   a. critical incident file
   b. rating scales
   c. BARS
   d. ranking
   e. MBO
   f. narrative

7. The PA practice that Steve described to JJ required Steve to use the ___ performance appraisal method

a. critical incident file d. ranking
b. rating scales e. MBO
c. BARS f. narrative

8. Coaching seems to be an important part of the performance appraisal system at the bank.

a. true b. false

9. Requiring one employee to get a poor performance appraisal is ______.

a. coaching b. counseling c. disciplining

10. The major problem with the bank's performance appraisal system is ______.

a. interruptions f. halo effect
b. rushing g. horn effect
c. memory/recency h. central tendency
d. activity trap i. leniency
e. bias j. strictness

11. Explain your answer to question 5.

12. If you were in JJ's position, would you attach a note to express your feeling about the PA system?

13. What, if any, changes would you recommend in the PA system?

Behavior Model Video 16–1, Coaching, shows Sarah coaching Dan. Dan is an Internet Web page designer who is not meeting deadlines. Sarah follows the Steps in Model 16–2 on pages 553–554. This video serves as a behavior model which can be used prior to conducting Skill-Building Exercise 16–1, Coaching, below.

SKILL-BUILDING EXERCISE 16–1

Coaching[55]

Preparing for Skill-Building Exercise 16–1

You should have read and understand the text material on coaching. You may also view Video Behavior Module 16–1, which illustrates how to conduct a coaching session using the coaching model.

Doing Skill-Building Exercise 16–1 in Class

Objective
To develop your skill at improving performance through coaching.

Experience
You will coach, be coached, and be observed coaching using Model 16–2.

Procedure 1 (2–4 minutes)
Break into groups of three. Make some groups of two, if necessary. Each member selects one of the following three situations in which to be the manager, and a different one in which to be the employee. In each situation, the employee knows the standing plans; he or she is not motivated to follow them. You will take turns coaching and being coached.

Three Problem Employee Situations

1. Employee 1 is a clerical worker. The person uses files, as do the other ten employees in the department. The employees all know that they are supposed to return the files when they are finished so that others can find them when they need them. Employees should have only one

file out at a time. The supervisor notices that Employee 1 has five files on the desk, and another employee is looking for one of them. The supervisor thinks that Employee 1 will complain about the heavy workload as an excuse for having more than one file out at a time.

2. Employee 2 is a server in an ice cream shop. The employee knows that the tables should be cleaned up quickly after customers leave so that new customers do not have to sit at dirty tables. It's a busy night. The supervisor finds dirty dishes on two of this employee's occupied tables. Employee 2 is socializing with some friends at one of the tables. Employees are supposed to be friendly; Employee 2 will probably use this as an excuse for the dirty tables.
3. Employee 3 is an auto technician. All employees at the garage where this person works know that they are supposed to put a paper mat on the floor of each car so that the carpets don't get dirty. When the service supervisor got into a car Employee 3 repaired, the car did not have a mat and there was grease on the carpet. Employee 3 does excellent work and will probably make reference to this fact when coached.

Procedure 2 (3–7 minutes)
Prepare for coaching to improve performance. Below, each group member writes an outline of what he or she will say when coaching Employee 1, 2, or 3, following the steps below:

1. Describe current performance. ____________________

    ____

2. Describe the desired behavior. (Don't forget to have the employee state why it is important.)

    ____

    ____

3. Get a commitment to the change. ____________________

    ____

4. Follow up. ____________________________________

    ____

Procedure 3 (5–8 minutes)

a. Role-playing. The manager of Employee 1, the clerical worker, coaches him or her as planned. (Use the actual name of the group member playing Employee 1.) Talk—do not read your written plan. Employee 1, put yourself in the worker's position. You work hard; there is a lot of pressure to work fast. It's easier when you have more than one file. Refer to the workload while being coached. Both the manager and the employee will have to ad lib.

The person not playing a role is the observer. He or she makes notes on the observer form below. Try to make positive comments and point out areas for improvement. Give the manager alternative suggestions for what he or she could have said to improve the coaching session.

OBSERVER FORM

1. How well did the manager describe current behavior?

    ____

    ____

2. How well did the manager describe desired behavior? Did the employee state why the behavior is important?

    ____

    ____

3. How successful was the manager at getting a commitment to the change? Do you think the employee would change?____________________________________

    ____

4. How well did the manager describe how he or she was going to follow up to ensure that the employee performed the desired behavior? ____________________

    ____

b. Feedback. The observer leads a discussion of how well the manager coached the employee. (This should be a discussion, not a lecture.) Focus on what the manager did well and how the manager could improve. The employee should also give feedback on how he or she felt and what might have been more effective in getting him or her to change. Do not go on to the next interview until you are told to do so. If you finish early, wait for the others to finish.

Procedure 4 (5–8 minutes)
Same as procedure 3, but change roles so that Employee 2, the server, is coached. Employee 2 should make a comment about the importance of talking to customers to make them feel welcome. The job is not much fun if you can't talk to your friends.

Procedure 5 (5–8 minutes)
Same as procedure 3, but change roles so that Employee 3, the auto technician, is coached. Employee 3 should comment on the excellent work he or she does.

Conclusion
The instructor leads a class discussion and/or makes concluding remarks.

Application (2–4 minutes)
What did I learn from this experience? How will I use this knowledge in the future?

____

____

Sharing
Volunteers give their answers to the application section.

In Behavior Model Video 16–2, Discipline, Dan continues to miss deadlines so Sarah disciplines him following the steps in Model 16–3 on pages 560–561. This video serves as a behavior model which can be used prior to conducting Skill-Building Exercise 16–2, Disciplining, below.

SKILL-BUILDING EXERCISE 16–2

Disciplining[56]

Preparing for Skill-Building Exercise 16–2

You should have read and understand the text material on disciplining. You may also view Video Behavior Module 16–2 which illustrates how to conduct a discipline session using the discipline model.

Doing Skill-Building Exercise 16–2 in Class

Objective
To develop your ability to discipline an employee.

Experience
You will discipline, be disciplined, and observe a discipline session using Model 16–3. This is a follow-up exercise to Skill Building Exercise 16–1.

Procedure 1 (2–4 minutes)
Break into groups of three. Make some groups of two, if necessary. Each member selects one of the three situations from Skill-Building Exercise 16–1. Decide who will discipline Employee 1, the clerical worker; Employee 2, the ice cream shop server; and Employee 3, the auto technician. Also select a different group member to play the employee being disciplined.

Procedure 2 (3–7 minutes)
Prepare for the discipline session. Write a basic outline of what you will say to Employee 1, 2, or 3; follow the steps in the discipline model below.

1. Refer to past feedback. (Assume that you have discussed the situation before, using the coaching model.)

   ____

   ____

2. Ask why the undesired behavior was used. (The employee should make up an excuse for not changing.)

   ____

   ____

3. Give the discipline. (Assume that an oral warning is appropriate.) ____________________

   ____

4. Get a commitment to change and develop a plan.

5. Summarize and state the follow up.

Procedure 3 (5–8 minutes)

a. Role-play. The manager of Employee 1, the clerical worker, disciplines him or her as planned. (Use the actual name of the person playing the employee.) Talk—do not read your written plan. Employee 1, put yourself in the worker's position. You work hard; there is a lot of pressure to work fast. It's easier when you have more than one file. Both the manager and employee will need to ad lib.

The person not playing a role is the observer. He or she makes notes on the observer form below. For each of the following steps, try to make a statement about the positive aspects of the discipline and a statement about how the manager could have improved. Give alternative things the manager could have said to improve the discipline session. Remember, the objective is to change behavior.

OBSERVER FORM

1. How well did the manager refer to past feedback?

2. How well did the manager ask why the undesired behavior was used?

3. How well did the manager give the discipline?

4. Did the manager get a commitment to change? Do you think the employee will change his or her behavior?

5. How well did the manager summarize and state the follow up? How effective will the follow up be?

b. Feedback. The observer leads a discussion of how well the manager disciplined the employee. The employee should also give feedback on how he or she felt and what might have been more effective in getting him or her to change. Do not go on to the next interview until you are told to do so. If you finish early, wait until the others finish or the time is up.

Procedure 4 (5–8 minutes)
Same as procedure 3, but change roles so that Employee 2, the ice cream server, is disciplined. Employee 2, put yourself in the worker's position. You enjoy talking to your friends, and you're supposed to be friendly to the customers.

Procedure 5 (5–8 minutes)
Same as procedure 3, but change roles so that Employee 3, the auto technician, is disciplined. Employee 3, put yourself in the worker's position. You are an excellent technician. Sometimes you forget to put the mat on the floor.

Conclusion
The instructor leads a class discussion and makes concluding remarks.

Application (2–4 minutes)
What did I learn from this experience? How will I use this knowledge in the future?

Sharing
Volunteers give their answers to the application section.

VIDEOCASE

Human Resources: Next Door Food Stores

Next Door Food Stores is a family-run business of thirty convenience stores in two states. The stores sell gasoline and over 3,000 individual grocery and merchandise items. The customer base is quite diverse and each store must adapt to meet the needs of its customers. Next Door's strategy is to meet the needs of its target market of the consumer in a hurry. It has recently added a Subway sandwich shop to each store so its customers can pick up a sandwich when they stop at one of the stores.

Next Door uses independent wholesalers to supply its stores. This reduces its need for expensive warehouse facilities and trucking systems and reduces its overall number of employees. A significant majority of employees are located in stores, resulting in a small headquarters staff.

Next Door has a central headquarters and a human resources department consisting of three employees and a separate training facility consisting of one employee. Much of the human resources function is maintained at corporate headquarters, but some responsibility has been decentralized to the convenience stores.

This video will explain the human resources department's responsibilities, identify typical problems in human rsources, and explain the centralized/decentralized aspect of human resources.

Operations, Quality, and Information Control Systems

Learning Objectives

After completing this chapter, you should be able to:

1. Describe time-based competition and state why it is important.
2. Explain the difference among the three tangibilities of products, the three levels of customer involvement, the four flexibilities of operations processes, and the three intensities of resources.
3. Discuss what is meant by "quality is a virtue of design."
4. Explain product, process, cellular, and fixed-position types of facility layouts in terms of their customer involvement and flexibility.
5. Describe priority scheduling and list its three priorities.
6. Explain the difference among inventory control, just-in-time (JIT) inventory, and materials requirement planning (MPR).
7. Explain how statistical process control (SPC) charts and the exception principle are used in quality control.
8. Describe the three primary types of information systems and their relationship.
9. List the components of an information network.
10. Define the following **key terms** (in order of appearance in the chapter):

time-based competition
operations
product
customer involvement
operations flexibility
technology
facility layout
capacity
routing
priority scheduling
inventory
inventory control
just-in-time (JIT) inventory
materials requirement planning (MRP)
quality control
statistical process control (SPC)
information
types of information systems
computer networks
information networks
International Standards Organization (ISO)

Skill-Development

1. You can develop your skill at determining the economic order quantity (Skill-Building Exercise 17–1).

   Ordering the economic quantity of materials and supplies is a controlling management function that is based on mathematical technical skill. Doing so requires the decisional management role which is based on the informational role. The SCAN competencies of resources, information, and systems, as well as basic and thinking foundation skills are developed through this exercise.

PepsiCo Inc. has business units in beverages Pepsi), restaurants (KFC, Pizza Hut, Taco Bell), and snack foods (Frito-Lay). Frito-Lay is the undisputed market leader in the $17 billion global snack-food market. Potato chips are far and away the world's most popular snack with a $4 billion market, or 24 percent of the snack-food market. Frito-Lay's primary product lines, in order by sales dollar volume, are Doritos, Lays and Ruffles, Chee-tos, Fritos, Tostitos, Rold Gold, Sun Chips, and Santitas which have a combined U.S. market share greater than 50 percent.

While Bud may be the king of beers, Frito-Lay is the king of snack foods and is chewing up the competition. In late 1995, Anheuser-Bush put its Eagle Snacks business up for sale, highlighting the danger of trying to compete against Frito-Lay. England's United Biscuits Holdings also put its snack business up for sale in 1995; Borden sold off many of its regional snack companies in 1994; and dozens of regional companies collapsed during these years. The dropout rate is not due to a shrinking market. Americans continue to eat more than 20 pounds of salty snacks a year, and the international market has great potential growth with less competition. Yet Frito-Lay seems to be the only player to reap the benefits.

Potato chips are the world's most popular snack food—with a $4 billion market.

Frito-Lay also kills the competition with its distribution. Over its 35-year history, the company has built a network of 42 plants with more than 900 tractor trailers, 13,000 salespeople, and nearly 400,000 retail customers. The company was one of the first to give its drivers hand-held computers to transmit sales back to headquarters.

Frito-Lay also kills the competition with its advertising budget of more than $60 million versus Eagle's, which is less than $2 million, while regional companies often have no budget. But competitors say that it is Frito-Lay's tactics with retailers that make it an invincible foe. Because many retailers are charging more and more for shelf space, $40,000 a foot annually in some instances, many regional companies say Frito-Lay is paying retailers to squeeze out competing brands who cannot afford to pay. However, both analysis and industry experts say that the key to Frito-Lay's success has been a balance of wild innovation in creating new products and operating discipline in bringing the products to store shelves.[1]

For current information on Frito-Lay, use Internet address http://www.pepsi.com. For ideas on using the Internet, see the Appendix.

1. Describe time-based competition and state why it is important.

TIME-BASED COMPETITION AND OPERATIONS

Before we get into the details of the chapter, you should understand time-based competition and operations.

Time-Based Competition

time-based competition
Strategies to increase the speed of going from creativity to delivery.

Time-based competition *refers to strategies to increase the speed of going from creativity to delivery*. The organization that can take a creative idea, turn it into an innovation (introduction of something new, either a product—new thing or service—or process—new way of doing things; Chapter 4), sell it, and deliver it to continually increase customer value has a first-mover competitive advantage (Chapter 5). In 1996, Puma, which had been in business for many years before Nike and Reebok entered the business, took pride in being the first to ship a next-generation athletic shoe, beating the other companies to market.[2]

All types of organizations, including Frito-Lay, are setting objectives for time-saving tactics.[3] Beer companies are benefitting from switching from lager to faster-brewed ale.[4] Because the mission of all organizations revolves around providing products, the operations department is the primary focus of speed as it is critical to the success of all organizations. To be time-based competitive, the operations department must work with the marketing and other departments to create continuing customer value.

operations
The function in which resource inputs are transformed into product outputs.

product
A good, a service, or a combination of the two.

Operations

Operations *is the function in which resource inputs are transformed into product outputs*. A **product** *is a good, a service, or a combination of the two*. IBM manufactures computer goods, but its service is of equal importance to many customers. In the past, the making of goods was called *manufacturing and production*, and the offering of services was called *operations*. Today, the term *operations* is used to refer to both because the basic concepts apply to both goods and services, as you will learn in the next section. Although operations take place in all departments and are performed by all employees, as was illustrated in Chapter 15, in this chapter we focus on the operations department. Figure 17–1 lists the three major functions of managing operations, which are discussed in this chapter.

Work Application

1. Is your present or past organization concerned about time-based competition? If yes, what functional areas are primarily responsible for speed?

CLASSIFYING OPERATIONS SYSTEMS

2. Explain the difference among the three tangibilities of products, the three levels of customer involvement, the four flexibilities of operations processes, and the three intensities of resources.

Operations can be classified by the tangibility of products, customer involvement, flexibility, and resources and technology used.

Tangibility of Products

Tangibility of products refers to whether they are tangible, intangible, or mixed.

Tangible Products. *Tangible products* include goods such as Frito-Lay snack foods, Gateway 2000 computers, and this textbook.

Intangible Products. *Intangible products* include services, such as a hair cut, dry cleaning, or legal advice.

I. Classifying Operations Systems	II. Designing Operations Systems	III. Managing Operations Systems
• Tangibility of products • Customer involvement • Flexibility • Resources and technology	• Product mix and design • Facility layout • Facility location • Capacity planning	• Organizing and leading • Forecasting and scheduling • Inventory control • Materials requirement planning • Quality control

Figure 17–1
Operations

Mixed Products. *Mixed products* include both tangible and intangible qualities, for example, TWA airplanes are tangible, but the airline flight is an intangible service. Today, many organizations focus on products, not just goods. For example, major appliance retail stores, like Sears Brand Central, not only sell major appliances, but they offer extended warranties and they service what they sell. Even though Frito-Lay sells products, its service is very important to many of its customers because the snack-food delivery person comes frequently and places the products on the shelf for the store. The store has no, or little, inventory to store and shelve.

Customer Involvement

customer involvement Operations are made-to-stock, made-to-order, or assemble-to-order.

Customer involvement *refers to whether operations make to stock, make to order, or assemble to order.*

Made to Stock (MTS). *Made-to-stock* operations produce products in anticipation of demand with a common design and price. Therefore, there is a low level of customer involvement. Most products that you see in retail stores, including Frito-Lay's, are from made-to-stock operations. Retail store operations are primarily made to stock as well. Products are designed for all potential customers, rather than customized for a specific customer. Most services cannot be made to stock, such as a hair cut. However, some can, such as scheduled transportation such as airline flights and train and and bus trips.

Made to Order (MTO). *Made-to-order* operations are only produced after receipt of an order from a specific customer. Therefore, there is a high level of customer involvement. Many services, such as auto repair, tailoring, development of an accounting system, a legal criminal defense, and medical services have to be made to order. Retailers who simply resell merchandise, such as the Gap, use made-to-order operations. Some goods are also made to order, such as custom clothes and drapes and a family portrait.

Assemble to Order (ATO). *Assemble-to-order* operations produce a standard product with some customized features. Some goods can only be produced after the receipt of an order, or to stock with different features. However, services can only be assembled to order after receipt of an order. Therefore, there is a moderate level of customer involvement. Relatively expensive goods, such as automobiles, mainframe computer systems, and furniture are commonly assembled to order. McDonald's primarily makes its hamburgers and other products made to stock, while Burger King emphasizes "have it your way" with assemble to order by offering a standard burger, with customized toppings.

Relatively expensive goods, such as automobiles, are commonly assembled to order.

Service can also be assembled to order. For example, standard training consulting packages and accounting and legal services can be customized to fit the needs of an organization. The models in this book are standardized, but could be customized by developing scenarios that are organization-specific to apply them to. Accountants and lawyers have template forms, such as a tax return and a will, that are filled in with the customers' information.

Flexibility

Operations flexibility *refers to whether the products are produced continuously, repetitively, in batches, or individually.* Flexibility of operations is based on product volume and variety. *Volume* refers to how many units of one product are produced, and *variety* refers to how many different products the operation produces. The four operations are presented in order by least to most flexibility.

APPLYING THE CONCEPT

AC 17–1 Customer Level of Involvement

Identify each product by its level of customer involvement.

a. made to stock b. assembled to order c. made to order

____ **1.** A hair cut by Pier.

____ **2.** A soft drink in a can by 7-UP.

____ **3.** Coffee ice cream in a sugar cone by Friendly's Ice Cream.

operations flexibility
Products are produced continuously, repetitively, in batches, or individually.

Continuous Process Operations (CPO). *Continuous process operations* produce outputs that are not in discrete units, such as gas and oil, electricity, chemicals, and pulp. They produce goods rather than services. Continuous process operations have no, or very little, variety and high volume, making them the least flexible operations systems. Therefore, they are used with *made to stock goods* operations.

Repetitive Process Operations (RPO). *Repetitive process operations* produce outputs in an assembly-line-type structure. Operations employees and equipment are quite specialized in function and location. Each unit of output follows the same path through labor and equipment. All kinds of consumer and industrial goods, such as automobiles and tableware, are repetitive process operations outputs. Some services can also be assembly-line oriented, such as an automatic car wash or dog grooming service. The first person on the line washes the dog, then sends it down the line to the next person who dries it, who passes it along to the third person who cuts its hair. Repetitive process operations have some variety and a high volume of similar units. Therefore, they are primarily used with *made-to-stock or assemble-to-order goods* operations. Frito-Lay snacks can be produced on a repetitive process operations system.

Batch Process Operations (BPO). *Batch process operations* produce different outputs with the same resources. When both the volume and variety of products are moderate, flexibility is needed. Organizations often cannot justify the investment required to dedicate labor or equipment to a single product, so they have multiple uses. For example, a wood furniture maker could use the same people and machines and spend one week making dining room tables and chairs, the next week making desks, and the next making bedroom dressers, and so on. Batches are commonly made by number of units rather than time. Most of Frito-Lay's snacks are fried, so the same fryer can be used at different times to fry a variety of snacks. A few services, such as cleaning services who have business accounts, can also use *batch process operations*. For example, a cleaning crew goes to a set number of businesses each day. The assigned batch of businesses for each crew for the day can vary, and the cleaning requirements can also vary by business specifications. Batch process operations have moderate variety and volume of similar units. Therefore, they are primarily used with *made-to-stock or assemble-to-order goods* operations.

Batch process operations require more controls than continuous process and repetitive process operations in coordinating the inputs, the transformation process, and the inventory of finished outputs. The starting point is how many of each batch to make. Then each batch is different; therefore, each may require a different flow sequence in the transformation process. Also, all batches are produced with the same resources; therefore, it takes coordination to schedule the resources to avoid having one or more resources with a bottleneck of units waiting to be worked on, while other resources wait idly for something to do. You have to be sure not to sell all of one product or have too much of it in stock.

Individual Process Operations (IPO). *Individual process operations* produce outputs to customer specifications. They have high variety and low volume. Therefore, they are *made-to-order goods and service* operations. Refer back to made-to-order examples of goods and services that are individual process operations. Individual process operations are the most flexible operations system. In manufacturing operations, the term for individual process operations is *job shop*. Because the large majority of retailers and service organizations use individual process operations, they do not usually classify their type of flexibility like manufacturers do.

As with batch process operations, individual process operations require more controls than continuous process and repetitive process operations in coordinating the inputs and the transformation process. It has similar control challenges as batch process operations in that: (1) Each order is different; therefore, each may require a different flow sequence in the transformation process. (2) All orders are produced with the same resources; therefore, it takes coordination to schedule the resources to avoid having one or more resources with a bottleneck of units waiting to be worked on, while other resources wait idly for something to do. It does not have the batch process operation challenges of: (1) Size of batches to make—you make the number the customer requested. (2) Output inventory—you sell all you make to the customer.

Project Process Operations (PPO). Project process operations are another area of process that does not fit the more popular flexibility by volume and variety. Project process operations produce low-volume outputs that require a relatively long period of time to complete. Project process operations are commonly completed by sending the resources to the customer's site, rather than completing the project at the seller's facilities. Project process operations are used in the construction industry to build office buildings and business locations and homes. Other examples include building an oil tanker or supercomputer, which are usually managed as projects. Consulting services often blend individual process with project process operations, as the client gives the consultant a project to complete. The work may be divided between the two sites.

APPLYING THE CONCEPT

AC 17–2 Flexibility of Operations

Identify each product by the operations system that would produce it.

a. CPO b. RPO c. BPO d. IPO

____ **4.** A Whirlpool refrigerator.

____ **5.** A swimming pool sold and installed by Teddy Bear Pools.

____ **6.** The asphalt for a driveway delivered by Juan's Asphalt Company.

____ **7.** Packages of Trident gum.

Resources and Technology

While operations is the function in which inputs are transformed into product outputs, **technology** *is the process used to transform inputs into outputs*. Important decisions include the use of labor and capital intensity to make the product, how the customer will be served, and how the manufacturing or service technology will be managed.

technology
The process used in transforming inputs into outputs.

Capital-Intensive Operations. In *capital-intensive operations*, machines do most of the work. Manufacturing companies that use the continuous and repetitive operations processes (such as oil, automobile, and steel companies) are capital-intensive because they invest large sums in the machines that make the goods. These companies tend to use high levels of technology that is often developed by other companies, such as Modern Controls products discussed in Chapter 15. Advanced design tools help Hewlett-Packard succeed in a highly competitive market.[5] Manufacturing firms are generally more capital-intensive than service organizations. Frito-Lay snacks are produced by capital-intensive repetitive operations process machines.

Labor-Intensive Operations. In *labor-intensive operations*, human resources does most of the work. Organizations that use the individual operations process tend to be labor-intensive. Retail and service organizations are generally less capital-intense than manufacturing firms, and they tend to use lower levels of technology. But, not always. Education and consulting, as well as personal services such as hair cutting, auto repair, accounting, and legal services, tend to be very labor-intensive.

Balanced-Intensity. Manufacturing firms use a balance of labor and capital in batch and individual operations processes because it takes skilled workers to use the flexible machines. Many large retailers have a balance of capital (because of the high cost of rent at malls or buying a store in a good location) and labor (they have a lot of employees). Frito-Lay snack distribution is labor-intensive with 12,800 delivery people, but it is also capital-intensive with 900 tractor trailers and a smaller truck for each delivery person.

Serving Customers. Customers can be served by people, machines, or both. Most of Frito-Lay snacks are sold to retailers who hire people to sell the product. However, the company also sells snacks in vending machines. Candy, cigarettes, and food are also sold in machines. Some small banks service their customers only by personal tellers, while large banks tend to use both tellers and automatic teller machines. If you call to get information about movies and a variety of other things, you will probably get a recorded message. Also, where is the customer served—his or her home or office or the business's. Today, some banks send a loan officer to your home or office to take a mortgage loan application; others will do it over the phone. Some banks will let you make transactions, such as transferring funds between accounts and paying bills, over the phone or by computer.

Managing Manufacturing Technology. Two important areas of manufacturing technology used in organizations are (1) *automation*, the process of designing work to be performed by machine and (2) *computer-assisted manufacturing*, the process of using computers to design or manufacture goods. Computer-assisted manufacturing includes *computer-aided design (CAD)*, *computer-aided manufacturing (CAM)*, and *computer-integrated manufacturing (CIM)*. CAD uses computers to design parts and complete goods and to simulate performance so that a prototype does not need to be constructed. Automakers use it to speed up car designs, GE used it to change the design of circuit breakers, and Benneton uses CAD to design new styles and products. CAD is usually combined with CAM to ensure that the design is coordinated with its production. CAM is especially useful with individual operations processes when reorders come in because it can quickly produce the desired product, prepare labels and copies of orders, and deliver it. CIM links CAD and CAM together, and all manufacturing activities are controlled by computer. With CIM, the computer can access the company's information systems and adjust machine placements and settings automatically to enhance both the complexity and flexibility of scheduling. Robots perform functions ordinarily thought to be appropriate for human beings and are commonly used in CIM.

Computer-integrated manufacturing is a powerful and complex management control system which is relatively expensive, and therefore is more commonly used with high-volume continuous and repetitive operations processes, rather than batch and individual processes. It is recommended that flexibility be based on sales volume and technical change. With high volume and low technical change, continuous process or repetitive process operations work well; with lower sales volume and high technical change, batch process operations work well; with high volume and change, combined repetitive process and batch process operations work well.[6]

Managing Service Technology. It is the manufacturers who create the innovative products, such as computer hardware and software, that are commonly used by service firms to make them competitive. For example, VISA customers' credit card transactions are recorded and billed electronically. Hotels use technology to accept and record room reservations. Health care providers use technology to manage patient records, dispatch ambulances, and monitor patient vital signs.

Combining Classification Methods. Figure 17–2 combines the four classification methods. Notice that the focus on the left is on manufacturing goods; the focus on the right is on providing services; and in the middle the focus is on integrating the two. However, it is not always easy to make a clear classification between closely related operations as processes should be seen as being part of a continuum,[7] as they are in Figure 17–2. For example, with tangibility of products it's difficult to say exactly where the mix cut off is or the exact balance of capital and labor intensity resources. There is some overlap in flexibility between continuous process and repetitive process operations, repetitive process and batch process operations, and batch process and individual process operations. The trend today, with the fast-changing environment, is toward more flexible operations systems. Some organizations are designing repetitive process operations that try to gain the benefits of batch process operations.[8]

Some organizations have more than one type of operation within the same system. For example, Frito-Lay could use repetitive process operations for its best-selling items, and batch process operations for its lower-selling items. It could have one assembly line making potato chips all day long and another being changed over to make more than one product. It could also use individual

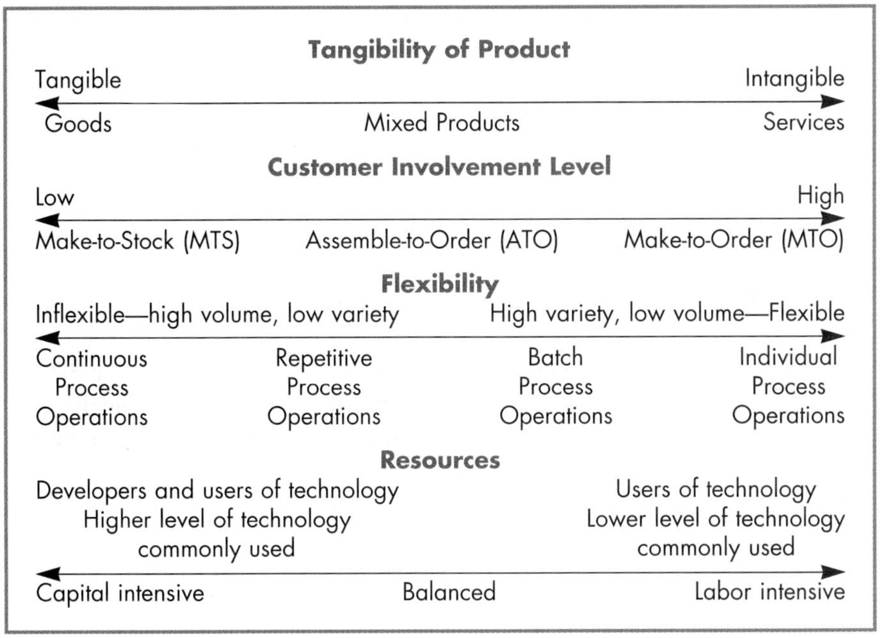

Tangibility of Product		
Tangible		Intangible
Goods	Mixed Products	Services
Customer Involvement Level		
Low		High
Make-to-Stock (MTS)	Assemble-to-Order (ATO)	Make-to-Order (MTO)

Flexibility			
Inflexible—high volume, low variety			High variety, low volume—Flexible
Continuous Process Operations	Repetitive Process Operations	Batch Process Operations	Individual Process Operations

Resources		
Developers and users of technology Higher level of technology commonly used		Users of technology Lower level of technology commonly used
Capital intensive	Balanced	Labor intensive

Figure 17–2
Classifying Operations Systems

process operations to make snacks for customers by placing them in bags with the customer's name on it, such as Safeway or Edwards food stores.

Work Application

2. Using Figure 17–2, identify the operation system where you work or have worked based on tangibility, customer involvement, flexibility, and resources. Be sure to classify the operations by using the names below the continuum lines.

DESIGNING OPERATIONS SYSTEMS

With the classification of the operation system, the operations that will take inputs (materials, workers, machines, technology, information, etc.) and transform them into product outputs that customers will value must be designed. In a changing environment, the operation systems must be continually redesigned in the interrelated areas of product mix and design, facility layout, facility location, and capacity planning. Hewlett-Packard is continually refining its production process.[9]

Product Mix and Design

Product Mix. Based on the organization's mission and objectives, top-level managers select the product mix. The *product mix* includes the number of product lines, the number of products within each line offered, and the mixture of goods and services within each line. With existing products, the product mix is set, but can be changed. For example, computer clone manufacturers (such as Dell and Gateway) used to focus on goods, but over the years they have increased their service.

Frito-Lay's product lines are listed at the beginning of the chapter. Each line includes a variety of flavors in various sizes and packaging. Frito-Lay has had double-digit growth, half of which comes from its traditional lines, and half from new healthier products such as Baked Lays, Baked Tostitos, and Rold Gold Fat-Free Pretzels. Its cheesier Doritos have turned a sleepy chip into a billion-

Work Application

3. List the product mix for an organization you work or have worked for. Be sure to identify the number of major product lines, the number of products within the one major line offered, and the mixture of goods and services within the one major line.

dollar brand, and spicier flavors, including sour cream and onion and cool ranch, have made Lays the number one potato chip.

Product Design. *Product design* refers to new or improved product development. Large manufacturing companies generally have engineers who design products and a separate operations department that produces the products. In the past, engineers were told what to design, and they designed the product without coordination among the various departments. Today, successful companies, including Hewlett-Packard, integrate design and manufacturing rather than treat them as separate steps in product development.[10]

3. Discuss what is meant by "quality is a virtue of design."

Quality Is a Virtue of Design. *Quality is a virtue of design* means that if products are designed with cross-functional team input to provide customer value, there will be fewer operations problems, the product will be easier to sell, and it will be less costly to service the product. Conversely, if the product is not designed properly, there will be operations, sales, and service problems. Therefore, it is important for all functional areas to work together on the design of new products.

Design and the Systems Effect. Cross-functional teams are now designing products. The marketing function is to find out what the customers value, to forecast the sales of a new product, and to sell the products. The finance function provides the input to determine if the new product will be profitable enough to make the investment, and it provides the capital budgeting necessary to pay for the product investment. The designers make the product specifications with marketing input to ensure customer value, with operations input to make the manufacturing process run smoothly, and with service input to ensure the product is easy to service after the sale. It is also helpful to get the actual customers to talk to the design, operations, and service people rather than using marketing people as intermediaries. The operations department function is to produce the products that offer customer value. The human resources function provides the employees to make and sell the new product, as well as other support services such as delivery. The information department provides information to all the other departments to help make the design decisions. The cross-functional team members must work together effectively because quality is a virtue of design.

The Need to Balance Time-Based Competition and Design. The Japanese auto makers have the time-based competitive advantage over U.S. auto makers in designing the product from concept to assembly line. The current average time is 32 months, and all the auto makers have goals to cut the time.[11]

However, the answer to speeding up the process is not to rush through the design. For example, GM's Pontiac Fiero sports car lacked virtue of design. One design error was that the trunk had a small spare tire. When a driver got a flat tire and put on the spare, the regular tire would not fit into the trunk, with a small two-seat sports car interior, there was really no room for the tire. There were all kinds of small problems that ran up the service costs, and because of the problems, the cars were hard to sell. The Fiero had one of the worst records for repeat buyers. Pontiac eventually discontinued the Fiero. The Ford Edsel and the Chrysler K cars were not successful because they lacked customer value. Ford, GM, and Chrysler are using cross-functional teams to design cars. Ford spent heavily on product design to make the Taurus the number one selling car in America.[12]

Facility Layout

4. Explain product, process, cellular, and fixed-position types of facility layouts in terms of their customer involvement and flexibility.

facility layout
Whether operations use product, process, cellular, or fixed-position layouts.

Facilities are the physical resources used in the operations process. The building, machines, furniture, and so on are part of the facility. *Layout* refers to the spatial arrangement of operations units relative to each other. **Facility layout** *refers to whether operations use product, process, cellular, or fixed-position layouts*. The facility layout selected is based on the classification of operations system and the product design. An important consideration in layout is the flow of the product through its transformation.[13]

Product Layout. *Product layout* uses make-to-stock and/or assemble-to-order customer involvement, repetitive process or continuous process ooperations flexibility, and tends to be more capital-intensive.

Organizations with high volume and low variety have to decide what the sequence of assembly line flow will be. Frito-Lay makes snacks and IBM produces PCs on a product layout. American, Southwest, TWA, and the other airlines provide a service using product layout. Air travelers go to the check-in area, to the boarding area, and on the plane; when they arrive, passengers get off the plane, go to the luggage pickup, and to ground transportation.

Process Layout. *Process, or functional, layout* uses made-to-order customer involvement, individual operations process flexibility, and tends to be labor-intensive or balanced.

Organizations with high variability and lower volume with products/customers that will have different needs and use only some processes/functions have to decide how they should be arranged. Most offices are set up functionally with assigned areas/departments, such as human resources and finance. Retail stores use process layouts so customers can go to departments to find what they need. Elegant restaurants make each meal to order and arrange the kitchen away from the dining area, and the operations are arranged so cooks can move about in adequate work space to process numerous meals at the same time. In a health care facility, the patient is sent to the functions(s) necessary to treat the patient, such as x-ray, laboratories, internal medicine, pharmacy, and so on.

Cellular Layout. *Cellular layout* uses made-to-stock and/or assemble-to-order batch operations process, and tends to have balanced capital and labor intensity.

Organizations with moderate variability and volume products must decide how to *group technology* so that all the activities involved in creation of the product are located near one another. Grouping technology into cells provides some of the efficiencies of both product and process layouts. Multiple cells make it easy for employees with different skills to work together to deliver the final product. Self-managed teams (Chapter 13) are commonly used with each cell. Edy's Ice Cream uses cells with self-managed teams to make its various flavors in batches.

Flexible manufacturing systems group technology to take advantage of a product layout without creating a batch environment by using automated technology to produce both high volume and high variety products.[14] However, they still produce in batches. For example, Mazda's Japan Ujina plant can build up to eight different car models on a single assembly line. Most U.S. assembly lines, which can be an entire facility, make one model. If demand for the car goes down the entire line/plant is closed or retooled. Flexible manufacturing also gives Mazda a time-based competitive advantage by building an assembled-to-

Boeing uses a fixed-position layout and assemble-to-order project process operations because planes are a low-volume product that take a relatively long time to complete.

order car in one week compared to the average three weeks, dramatically increased efficiency, and higher profits per car. The use of flexible manufacturing will continue to increase with the rapidly changing global environment. However, recall the control issues of batch process operations.

Fixed-Position Layout. Fixed-position layout uses made-to-order and/or assemble-to-order project process operations and tends to have balanced capital and labor intensity.

Organizations with low-volume products that take a relatively long period of time to complete each unit, must determine the sequence of steps of workers who come to the product during its construction. Most contractors construct buildings, Boeing makes planes, and Newport News makes ships using fixed-position layout.

Figure 17–3 summarizes and compares the four types of layouts with their level of customer involvement and types of flexibility of operations process and provides an illustration of each systems process.

APPLYING THE CONCEPT

AC 17–3 Facilities Layout

Identify each product by the facility layout that would produce it.

a. product b. process c. cellular d. fixed-position

____ **8.** A container of blueberry ice cream at Bonnie's Gourmet Ice Cream Shop.

____ **9.** A VCR by RCA.

____ **10.** A bridge being built by Smith Contractors, Inc.

____ **11.** A set of fingernails by Jean's Manicures.

Facility Location

Location is the physical geographic site of facilities. The facility location must be based on the classification of operating systems, its product mix, layout requirements, and capacity planning. Some of the major factors that are considered when making the location decision include the following.

Cost. Cost includes the cost of the land and facility (or rent); the expenses of human resources to staff it; and operating expenses such as utilities, taxes, and insurance.

Work Application

4. Identify the facility layout used where you work or have worked. Draw a layout of the facilities.

Near Inputs, Customers, and/or Competitors. Some locations need to be near inputs. For example, General Mills and Pillsbury are both located in Minneapolis to get easy access to grains from Midwest farmers for processing into flour and other products to be sold to retail stores. On the other hand, some locations need to be easy to get to for customers. For example, retail stores are common in malls in major suburbs. Fast food restaurants are commonly located on major thoroughfares. Some businesses want to locate away from competitors to be convenient to customers, while others want to be close to competitors. For example, Joe's Burger is at a distance while McDonald's and Burger King are often located across from each other.

Figure 17–3
Facilities Layout

Product layout uses made-to-stock (MTS) and/or assemble-to-order (ATO) customer involvement with repetitive process operations (RPO) or continuous process operations (CPO) flexibility.

Inputs → *Transformation* → *Transformation* → *Transformation* → *Output*

Process, or functional, layout uses made-to-order (MTO) customer involvement with individual operations process (IPO) flexibility.

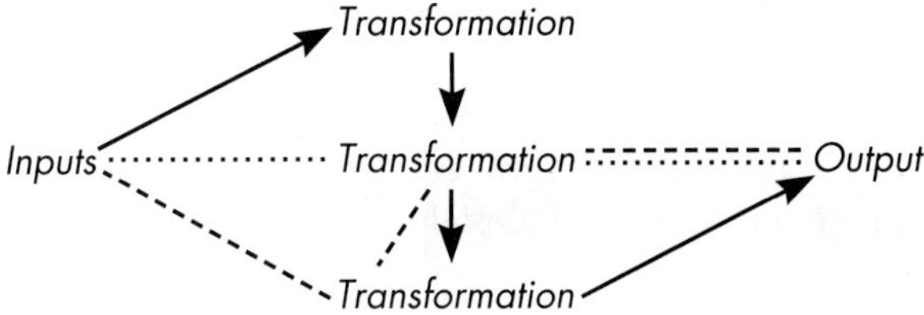

Cellular layout uses made-to-stock (MTS) and/or assemble-to-order (ATO) with batch operations process (BPO) flexibility.

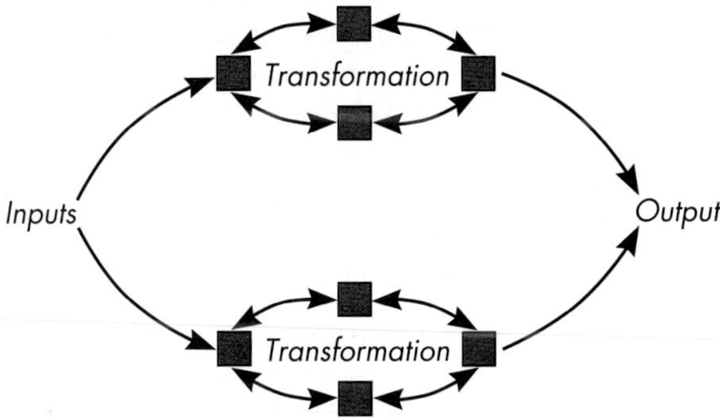

Fixed-position layout uses made-to-order (MTO) and/or assemble-to-order (ATO) with project process operations (PPO) flexibility.

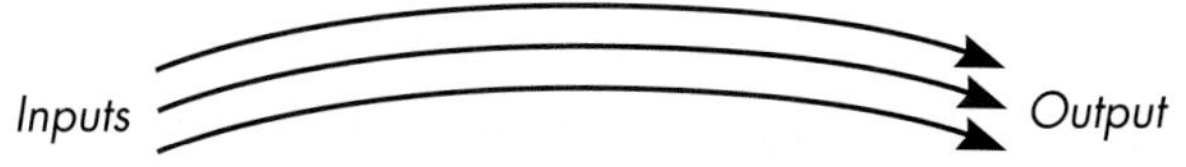

Transporation. For manufacturers, this includes access to air, rail, truck, and sea transportation to get inputs and to deliver product outputs. For retailers, this includes getting merchandise delivered for sale, and whether employees and customers can easily get to the location. Parking has been one of the problems that has caused the failure of many downtown businesses. Many of these businesses have relocated to malls.

Access to Human Resources. Certain types of skilled labor can be more easily found in certain locations. For example, high-tech firms tend to go to the technology highway, Route 128 in the Boston area and Silicon Valley in California.

Community Interest. To gain jobs, many communities have offered incentives, such as cheap land and low taxes, to attract businesses to their area. Incentives were considered in the foreign automobile companies' decision to locate plants in the Southern states.

Quality of Life Issues. The quality of local schools, the availability of recreational and cultural facilities, crime rates, and an overall community environment that will contribute to the firm's ability to attract and retain high-caliber employees, especially managers, are given some consideration in the location decision. Based on these factors, and possibly others, a cost-benefit analysis is made to select a location. Frito-Lay is headquartered in Dallas, Texas, while its parent PepsiCo is based in Purchase, New York.

Another important consideration is the number of facilities. Frito-Lay has increased its facilities to 42 over the years to make and deliver its products to customers all over the United States. In the other direction, many companies have downsized and closed facilities. For example, GE decided that it did not need six facilities to make circuit breakers. So, it invested heavily in capital intensity to automate one plant and closed the other five.

Capacity Planning

capacity
The amount of products an organization can produce.

Another part of the facility decision is capacity and planning. **Capacity** *is the amount of products an organization can produce*. Should a facility be built to produce 2,000 or 5,000 units per day? How many checkouts/teller stations should a supermarket/bank have? Should a restaurant have 50 or 100 tables? How many rooms should a hotel build?

In most cases, capacity planning is made under uncertainty or at least a high risk (Chapter 4) because it usually requires a large capital investment, and the decision is made based on a long-term sales forecast (Chapter 6).

Under Capacity. If the organization selects to build a facility to produce 2,000 units per day, and the demand is 5,000 per day, it will lose sales, revenues, and profits. Modulate Corporation incorrectly forecasted capacity needs and at a high cost moved its head office six times in seven years. Some organizations select a facility location taking into consideration the ability to expand capacity if necessary. Buying a larger building than needed and renting out part of it, then taking it back if necessary, is a capacity strategy.

Excess Capacity. Excess capacity is common in businesses with fluctuation demand such as restaurants. It is not unusual to have twice as many people going out on a Friday or Saturday night than on the other nights of the week, or for a hotel to be overbooked during peak season and underbooked during off season. Excess capacity can be expensive as assets must be paid for even though they are not being used.

Optimizing Capacity. It is necessary for many organizations to optimize capacity.[15] Ideally, organizations with fluctuating demand should maximize revenue by turning away some business during peak periods while not having too much excess capacity during the slow periods. For example, a restaurant that could fill 80 to 100 tables on a good weekend night but only 30 during the week should probably have 50 to 60 tables to maximize capacity. Hotels do the same and their occupancy rate was 63.5 percent in 1991 and the forecast for 1996 was 71 percent.[16]

Another way to optimize capacity is by offering products that are used at different times. For example, McDonald's started out selling only lunch and dinner so its restaurants were idle during the morning, so they began to offer breakfast. Dunkin' Donuts was busiest during the morning, so it offered soup and sandwiches on a croissant to increase afternoon business.

After capacity is set, there are some scheduling techniques that can be used to adjust capacity to help optimize it. But, this falls under managing operations systems, which is our next topic.

Work Application

5. Does the organization you work or have worked for have under, excess, or optimal capacity utilization? Explain your answer.

MANAGING OPERATIONS

After the operations systems have been designed, they must be managed. In this section you will study organizing and leading, forecasting and scheduling, inventory control, and materials requirement planning in operations.

Organizing and Leading

The principles of organization—authority, delegation, and especially organizational design and job design (Chapter 7)—are used with operations systems and control. The leadership theories (Chapter 12) as well as all the functional areas, can be used in operations.

Operations and Departmentalization. A one-location firm that uses functional departmentalization will have one operations department. A firm that uses product departmentalization will have at least one operations department per business line. Frito-Lay is one of PepsiCo's business lines with its own operations departments at each of its 42 facilities. PepsiCo's soft-drink companies and restaurants have their own operations departments. With decentralized product departmentalization, it is common for leadership to be shared.

Facility Layouts and Job Designs With a product layout organizational structure, which is based on repetitive process operations, the job design used is commonly job simplification. With a process layout organizational structure, which is based on individual process operations, the job design used is commonly job expansion. With a cellular layout organizational structure, which is based on batch process operations, the job design is commonly work teams. With a fixed-position layout, which is based on project process operations, job simplification, job expansion, and/or work teams can be used as the various inputs come to the site to perform the transformation part of the output. With a cellular layout using teams, leadership is often shared at lower levels more than with the other layouts.

Planning: Forecasting and Scheduling

As with all plans, operations managers must plan to answer who, what, when, where, and how questions. The first step in planning operations is to determine the planning horizon. The *planning horizon* is based on how long it takes to get the inputs and to transform them into outputs. A contractor of major buildings may have a planning horizon of a year. A retail store manager may have a monthly time frame. A restaurant manager may only need to plan operations a few days ahead. Three important parts of planning are forecasting sales demand, scheduling operations to meet demand, and adjusting capacity to meet operations demand.

Forecasting. Forecasting operations to transform inputs into outputs is based on the sales forecast, which is a marketing function. For details on *qualitative* and *quantitative sales forecasting techniques* refer back to Chapter 6.

If the sales forecast is lower than actual demand, operations will not produce enough products and the organization will lose sales. If the sales forecast is greater than actual demand, operations will produce too many goods and the organization will have excess inventory. If the sales forecast is accurate, sales and inventory will be maximized. Based on the sales forecast, operations can schedule to produce the products needed to meet the predicted demand.

Scheduling. *Scheduling* is the process of listing activities that must be performed to accomplish an objective; activities are listed in sequence with the time needed to complete each one (Chapter 6). Scheduling answers the planning questions: Who (which employees) will make which products? What specific products will be produced? When will they be produced? Where will they be produced? And how will products be produced and how many of each? An important part of scheduling is routing. **Routing** *is the path and sequence of transformations a product takes to become an output.* Routing is illustrated for each of the four facility layouts in Figure 17–3. Notice that with process and cellular layouts, routing is more complex. Routing is interrelated with priority scheduling, so it is discussed further there.

routing
The path and sequence of transformations a product takes to become an output.

Three popular scheduling tools are the *Gantt chart*, *PERT*, and the *planning sheet*; for details on these techniques refer back to Chapter 6. Gantt charts and PERT are commonly used with process and cellular layouts. PERT is commonly used with a fixed-position layout because of the importance of sequencing resources as the product is built. With a product layout using made-to-stock, Gantt and PERT are commonly not needed because the sequence of operations is already inflexibly predetermined. However, Gantt and PERT are used with assemble-to-order to keep track of customized orders. The planning sheet is more commonly used by employees in the other departments, rather than in the operations department.

5. Describe priority scheduling and list its three priorities.

priority scheduling
The continuing evaluation and reordering of the sequence in which products will be produced.

Priority Scheduling. **Priority scheduling** *is the continuing evaluation and reordering of the sequence in which products will be produced.* Priority scheduling depends on the layout used. With product layout made-to-stock, continuous process and repetitive process operations, prioritization and routing are relatively easy. With a fixed layout, the issue is scheduling resources to go to the job in sequence. When there are multiple jobs, employees with other resources cannot be at more than one site at a time. With process, individual process operations and cellular, batch process operations layouts, priority scheduling and routing are complex and critical to successful operations. Three simple prioritization methods are used to schedule operations:

- *First Come-First Served*. Jobs are scheduled in the order they are received. This is common in service organizations.
- *Earliest Due Date*. The job with the earliest promised delivery date is scheduled first.
- *Shortest Operating Time*. Jobs that take the least time are scheduled first.
- *Combination*. Many organizations use a combination of the three methods.

Work Application

6. Identify which priority scheduling method(s) the organization you work or have worked for uses.

Scheduling to Adjust Capacity. When comparing the forecast and schedule to the capacity, adjustments in capacity can be made to coordinate operations and demand in the following ways:

- *Fluctuating Demand.* When there are times when operations vary, a few things can be done to smooth capacity and demand. You should stagger work shifts so that there are more resources during busy times. For example, a restaurant will have more employees on a weekend night and order more food. Businesses with fluctuating demand commonly use part-time, on-call, and temporary employees. You can offer incentives to get people to use the product during low-demand periods. Examples are lower-priced luncheon and early bird specials, lower long-distance telephone rates on nights and weekends, or off-season rates at resorts. You can use appointments for haircuts and reservations for dinner to smooth operations and demand to help prevent long waiting lines that can result in lost sales.
- *Limited Resources and Economies of Scale.* To get the most out of your resources, you can limit the number of products and outsource part of the operations process. If demand increases temporarily, you can have employees work overtime. If the demand increase will be permanent, add a shift. Hospitals and many manufacturers are open 24 hours a day with three shifts. In some cases, you can open more hours. With batch process operations, you can maximize the sizes of batches. In some businesses, you can have a fixed schedule, such as with airline flights or a dance class.
- *Demand Exceeds Capacity.* If the business is at the point where demand exceeds capacity and the other methods are not effective, managers can decide to stay with the present facility or expand. If they stay with the present facility, they can turn down business; create a waiting line, as at a restaurant; or set up appointments, as done by a dentist. Expansion can often take place within the existing facility or a new facility can be occupied. The new facility can be in addition to or in place of the old one. Opening multiple locations is a common strategy for organizations, such as McDonald's and Frito-Lay.

Classifying the operations system, designing it, and scheduling are all preliminary control methods. Inventory control, our next topic, however, uses preliminary, concurrent, rework, and damage control.

Inventory Control

Inventory *is the stock of materials held for future use.* Inventory is an idle resource. Controlling inventory, also called *materials control,* is an important responsibility of the operations manager because in many organizations materials (which includes purchasing, moving, storing, insuring, and controlling) are the single major cost item. The U.S. Department of Commerce reported that the value of inventory held in the manufacturing sector averaged 13.4 percent of sales.[17] Clearly, the decisions that determine the flow of materials (routing) through operations are among the most important.[18]

6. Explain the difference among inventory control, just-in-time (JIT) inventory, and materials requirement planning (MRP).

inventory
The stock of materials held for future use.

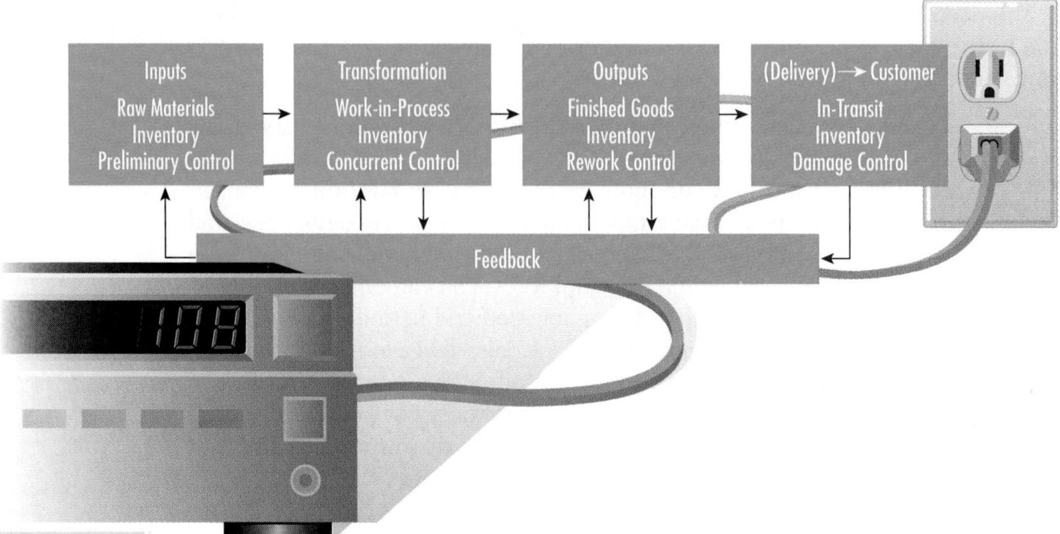

Figure 17–4
Inventory Control within the Systems Process

inventory control
The process of managing raw materials, work-in-process, finished goods, and in-transit goods.

Inventory Control. **Inventory control** *is the process of managing raw materials, work-in-process, finished goods, and in-transit goods.* Figure 17–4 illustrates inventory control within the systems process, and each type of inventory is explained here.

- *Raw Materials.* Raw materials are input material that has been received but has not been transformed in any way by the operations department, such as eggs at a restaurant or steel at an auto maker. Important preliminary controls in manufacturing, including food preparation, are the *purchasing* of raw materials and *scheduling* to have them delivered to your facility when needed. Routing is also an important part of raw materials and work-in-process.
- *Work-in-Process.* Work-in-process is material that has had some transformation, but is not yet an output, such as an egg that has been scrambled or is being cooked or a car on the assembly line. Concurrent controls are used to ensure that products meet standards before they become finished goods.
- *Finished Goods.* Finished goods are transformed outputs that have not yet been delivered to customers, such as the cooked scrambled eggs sitting on the plate waiting to be served to the customer or a car sitting at the factory waiting to be shipped to a dealer. Rework control may be needed, such as if the eggs get cold while waiting for the server, they may be reheated, or if the car cannot be driven off the assembly line, it will be fixed.
- *In-Transit (Pipeline) Goods.* In-transit goods are finished goods being delivered to the customer, such as the server walking to the table with the eggs or the truck delivering the cars to the dealer. Damage control may be needed; for example, if the server drops the eggs on the way to the table, the order will be redone; or if the car is damaged in delivery, it may need to be returned or fixed at the dealer at the manufacturer's expense.

Deliverers of products commonly have insurance to cover the cost of damages and lost goods.

Retailing and Services Inventory. The classifications of raw materials and work-in-process are used in manufacturing of goods, including food preparation, but they are not used by retailers and services.

Retail inventory control, including *purchasing,* consists almost exclusively of finished goods for resale as is. However, many, but not all, retailers do have in-transit inventory, such as the Home Shopping Network and catalog seller L.L. Bean, and major furniture and appliance stores. Inventory control has become an essential measure of productivity to retailers who track every movement of their merchandise through computer systems that connect purchasing, receiving, cash register sales, and delivery.[19]

Most service organizations do not have inventory control purchasing of finished goods. Services deal only with the finished goods inventory they create by providing the service. However, some services have in-transit inventory; accounting statements and legal documents are commonly delivered to the client.

Just-In-Time (JIT) Inventory. The objective of inventory control is to have the correct amount of all four types of inventory available at the time they are needed and where they are needed, while minimizing the total cost. To accomplish this objective, many organizations now use JIT. **Just-in-time (JIT) inventory** *is a method that has necessary parts and raw materials delivered shortly before they are needed.* The time frame varies among industries. For example, many auto repair shops including Midas Muffler keep a small inventory of low-cost, commonly used parts in stock. However, for more costly, less commonly used parts, they call the auto parts stores who typically will deliver the part in 20 to 30 minutes. For manufacturers *shortly* commonly means having parts and raw materials delivered 24 to 48 hours before they are needed. Depending on the size of the store, Frito-Lay commonly makes frequent deliveries to keep the shelves stocked so that little or no back-room storage is needed. For FedEx and UPS, same-day and overnight delivery make JIT easier to control.

just-in-time (JIT) inventory
A method that has necessary parts and raw materials delivered shortly before they are needed.

JIT provides organizations with a better way to control inventory by ensuring timely arrival of the product as well as better forecasting of demand for the product.[20] Generally, the shorter the sales forecast, the more accurate it is. JIT helps meet the objectives of making raw materials available at the time they are needed and where they are needed. JIT also minimizes the total cost objective by reducing the investment in raw materials and parts, reducing the storage space for nonidle activities, and insuring inventory cost.

JIT does, however, require a close working relationship between the organization and its suppliers to coordinate schedules. If the parts and raw materials arrive too early, there is no room to store them. If they come too late, facilities may be idle as they wait. It is important to schedule enough, but not too much, lead time.[21] Johnson Control and Chrysler successfully use JIT. Johnson makes seats and delivers them 75 miles to Chrysler so they arrive two hours before they are needed.

Work Application

7. Identify the type of inventory and how it is controlled where you work or have worked.

Materials Requirement Planning (MRP)

Materials requirement planning (MRP) *is a system that integrates operations and inventory control with complex ordering and scheduling.* MRP develops a system to

materials requirement planning (MRP)
A system that integrates operations and inventory control with complex ordering and scheduling.

order raw materials and components in the right quantity and to have them arrive shortly before scheduled transformation into outputs, while having appropriate work-in-process ready as needed. JIT is part of inventory control, which is part of MRP.

MRP is commonly used by companies that have different delivery systems and lead times. Errors in lead time can be costly.[22] Companies including Boise-Cascade, Lockheed, Texas Instruments, and Westinghouse use MRP because they need hundreds of parts in vastly different quantities with arrival times that vary from hours to months. Coordinating and controlling such a complex system is virtually impossible for any manager. However, MRP uses computer software to manage the system fairly easily.

Materials requirement planning has four steps:

1. The manager specifies the inventory needed for a project and figures out when it should arrive.
2. The manager determines existing inventories.
3. The MRP system then specifies an ordering and arrival time for inventory that is not currently in stock.
4. The software generates reports that tell the manager when to place orders and what quantities of each inventory to specify in each order.

Economic Order Quantity (EOQ). EOQ is a mathematical model that determines the optimal quantity to order when placing each reorder. The more often you reorder, the higher the ordering cost; but if you order less often, your holding cost goes up. So you use EOQ to optimize ordering and holding cost, without running out of stock.

EOQ is a part of MRP. However, many organizations, especially small businesses, don't need MRP. Therefore, EOQ can be easily determined using a calculator as follows:

$$\text{EOQ} = \sqrt{\frac{2RS}{H} \;\; \frac{2(5{,}000)(25)}{2}} = 5{,}000 \times 25 = 125{,}000 \times 2 = \frac{250{,}000}{2}$$

$$= 125{,}000 \sqrt{} = 353.55$$

EOQ	= optimal quantity to reorder	354
R	= total required over planning horizon (usually one year)	5,000
S	= cost of preparing one order (or setup)	$25.00
H	= cost to holding one unit for the planning horizon	$ 2.00

The actual optimization of EOQ is based on the accuracy of R, S, and H values. One of the problems with EOQ is managers' ability to forecast sales and the operations quantity to match demand correctly. It is also difficult to estimate the cost of S and H; managers commonly understate the cost of S and H. People within the accounting department often do the calculations for line managers. Managers should be concerned with continuously lowering the costs that are plugged into the formula.

QUALITY CONTROL

Quality control is one of the functions of managing operations systems. However, because quality is such an important issue it is has been covered extensively throughout the text and is covered in a separate section now as we compare quality control to TQM, present statistical quality control, and state contributions made by quality gurus.

TQM and Quality Control Are Different

TQM was discussed extensively in Chapters 2 and 8 as well as in the current management issues sections of every chapter. To quickly review, the four major TQM principles are: (1) Focus on delivering customer value. (2) Continually improve systems and processes. (3) Focus on managing processes rather than people. (4) Use teams to continually improve. A few of the differences between TQM and quality control are as follows:

- TQM is much broader in scope because part of its core value is to make it everyone in the organization's job to improve quality. Under quality control, the operations department is responsible for quality control. So, quality control is only one part of TQM.
- With TQM, quality is determined by customers through the comparison of actual use to requirements to determine value, or purchasing benefits. With quality control, quality is determined by the standards set for quality acceptability.
- With TQM, the focus is not on acceptance or rejection of the product. With quality control, if products don't meet quality requirements, corrective action is needed to make them acceptable or they are rejected.

Quality Control. **Quality control** *is the process of ensuring that all four types of inventory meet standards*. As you can tell by the definition, quality control and inventory control overlap. In Figure 17–4, the top row shows the systems process steps, the middle row shows the four inventory stages, and the bottom row shows the four types of quality control. The eggs at a restaurant and the steel at an auto maker are quality control examples placed with each of the four types of inventory. Quality control is just as important for goods as it is for services. The scrambled eggs can be considered a service and the car as a good.

quality control
The process of ensuring that all four types of inventory meet standards.

Quality assurance means that you must "build in" quality; you cannot "inspect it in." Recall, from Chapter 15, that the quality focus should be on preliminary and concurrent control, not rework and damage control. Also, recall that quality is a virtue of design. This is the quality assurance approach. Companies that have established quality assurance programs have increased performance.[23]

Striving for TQM does not guarantee success. JIT can have a negative effect on quality control because, when there is not enough lead time, performance quality is bound to suffer.[24] Following are some examples of recent quality problems by organizations that strive for TQM: Honda and Nissan recalled cars with seat belt problems.[25] Philip Morris sold eight billion cigarettes with filter contaminants at an estimated recall cost of about $200 million.[26] Intel has had quality problems with its Pentium computer microchips' ability to calculate complex math problems, and the speed of the chip was exaggerated by an estimated 10 percent.[27] Compaq delayed shipping computers with Intel's Pentium Pro because the chip encountered problems in network servers with some combination of internal cards.[28]

1. Put people before things.
2. Always be nice—no matter how busy you are.
3. Take your time with people.
4. Be polite: say please, thank you, and you're welcome.
5. Don't discriminate with your service.
6. Avoid jargon.

Figure 17–5
Six Rules of Customer Human Relations

Customer Quality Control. We have been focusing on creating customer value throughout this entire book. Figure 17–5 lists six rules that help ensure quality customer service,[29] which are explained here. If you follow these rules, you will increase your chances of developing effective human relations skills. When reading the rules, remember that they don't only apply to people in marketing who deal with external customers. The outputs of everyone in the other departments go to an internal customer. (Go back to Chapter 15 and review Figure 15–2, The Systems Process in the Functional Areas.) In other words, everyone you deal with is a customer.

The six rules that help ensure quality customer service are as follows:

1. *Put people before things.* How many times, and for how long, have you been kept waiting before being acknowledged; did you like it? Acknowledge people immediately and quickly; put things aside so you can give the person your *full attention.* Things will not walk away, but the person might.
2. *Always be nice—no matter how busy you are.* We are all busy; it's not an excuse for being rude. The customer wants your *full attention.* If you appear too busy, the customer may go elsewhere. The next time someone at work asks you, "How's it going," say "Great! How can I help you?" Imagine if everyone did?
3. *Take your time with people.* Let's face it; unless you are waiting on customers, most people who stop by or call are interrupting you when you are in the middle of something. Rushing threatens customers who need your *full attention.* Don't do other things like type or talk to anyone else unless it pertains to the person. It is better to let the person know it is not a good time for you, rather than rushing them. Rushing makes you seem uninterested, and it makes people feel like they are not important. When appropriate, make an appointment to meet or talk over the phone. Change your mindset. Customers are not an interruption; they are your business. Remember, the people you don't need now, you may need later.
4. *Be polite: say please, thank you, and you're welcome.* Being polite means giving others your *full attention.* Part of being polite is saying "please" when you make requests of people, even if you are their boss. When someone does something for you, which includes buying something, cheerfully smile and say "thank you," rather than grunting something like "there ya go." When someone thanks you for doing something, say "you're welcome," rather than grunting something like "un-huh."
5. *Don't discriminate with your service.* All customers should be given your *full attention* and the royal treatment, not just a select few. You don't have to apologize for not realizing that the customer is special, such as treating a big boss, or friend of one, as unimportant until you find out who they are. Remember, people you don't think are important to you now, you may need later.
6. *Avoid jargon.* When dealing with customers, remember that they usually don't have the technical vocabulary (jargon) that you have. To give customers your *full attention,* you must speak at a level they understand. When jargon is important, take your time and explain technical terms as you use them. Remember to send messages to communicate, not to impress. Besides, you're not impressing anyone with your knowledge of what they don't know.

Statistical Quality Control

7. Explain how statistical process control (SPC) charts and the exception principle are used in quality control.

In Chapter 1 you read about management science theory which is the use of math to aid in decision-making. *Statistical quality control* is a management science technique that uses a variety of statistical tests based on probability to improve quality through decision-making. Statistics improve the probability of identifying and eliminating quality problems.[30] The most common test is statistical process control, which is a standard TQM technique.

Statistical process control (SPC) *aids in determining if quality is within the acceptable standard range*. It is called a process control because quality is measured and corrected during the transformation process as a *concurrent control*. SPC is used to monitor operations and to minimize variances in the quality of products.[31] McDonald's goes to great lengths to ensure that the quality of its Big Mac is the same all over the country; a burger in Texas should test the same as one in Maine.

statistical process control (SPC) Aids in determining if quality is within the acceptable standard range.

Following are the four steps to implementing SPC, followed by an example that is illustrated in Figure 17–6.

step 1. **Set the Desired Quality Standard and a Range.** The range includes the highest (upper control limit, UCL) and the lowest (lower control limit, LCL) level of acceptable quality, with the desired standard in the middle called the *mean*, which is an average. The narrower the range, the higher the quality consistency between products.

step 2. **Determine the Frequency of Measuring Performance and the Sampling Technique.** *Sampling technique* refers to how many products will be inspected; the range is from 0 to 100 percent. There are statistical models to help determine the percentage.[32] As a general rule, the more critical it is to stay within quality range, the more frequent the measures and the larger the sample inspected.

step 3. **Measure Performance and Plot it on the Chart.** You statistically analyze the variance in performance from each sample mean to the desired mean.[33]

step 4. **Use the Exception Principle and Do Nothing if Performance Is Within Range, but Do Take Corrective Action if It Is Out of Control Limits.**

Example. Frito-Lay is very concerned about quality and uses SPC. However, for illustrative purposes, here is a made up example. Lay's potato chips come in a one-pound bag in Figure 17–6.

Figure 17–6
Statistical Process Control Chart by Ounces and Time of Day

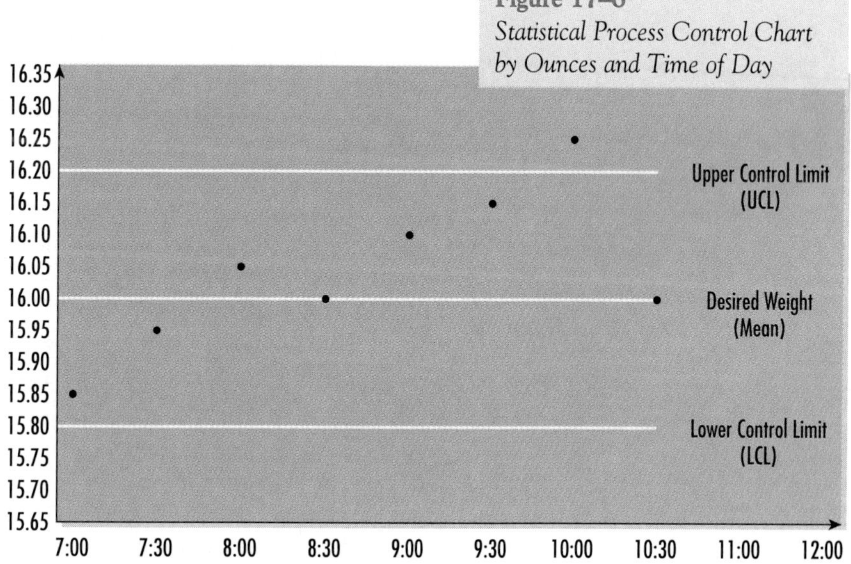

(1) The desired quality, as measured by weight, is 16 ounces. However, weighing every bag on a very accurate scale is too costly. It is cheaper to give away a few extra chips or give a few people legally less chips than it is to make every bag exactly one pound. So, you have an acceptable range of say .40 ounces; this give you a high of 16.20 and a low of 15.80 ounces. If measured on a cheaper scale, both bags would legally weigh 16 ounces.

(2 & 3) Let's say you take five bags every one-half hour, and get the average (mean) weight, and plot it on Figure 17–6 with an asterisk.

(4) If the machine produces bags with more or less weight, it is *out of control* and production is stopped to correct the problem. Notice that this happened at 10:00, but at 10:30 weight was back within standard range.

Companies, including Modern Control (Chapter 15), make machines that automatically produce statistical process control charts as frequently as per unit. With computerized statistical process control charts, all employees have to do is look at the chart to know when corrective action is needed.

Work Application

8. Explain quality control in an organization where you work or have worked.

Service Organizations. Service organizations also use statistical process control. A SPC system was created to help a credit company achieve timeliness goals for its car loans and to monitor setting up accounts for customer groups. The SPC method helped the loan-processing department in dispatching labor assignments and speeding up other operating procedures that caused delay. SPC also led to increased labor productivity and better response times and it minimized the duration of poor service.[34]

Quality Guru Contributions

Walter A. Shewhart. The beginning of the quality revolution goes back to May 16, 1924, when Walter Shewhart wrote a memo to his boss at Bell Labs stating that he wanted to use statistics to improve the quality of Bell telephones. At that time, and still today in some organizations, the focus was on having inspectors weed out badly finished products. Shewhart started the focus on concurrent control by delegating the role of inspector to the employees.

W. Edwards Deming. W. Edwards Deming met Shewhart in 1938 and applied his statistical methods. He went to Japan to teach quality in the 1950s and is credited with being instrumental in turning Japanese industry into an economic world power. The highest Japanese award for quality is the Deming Prize. Deming said that improving quality will automatically improve productivity. You capture the market with lower prices and better quality. Deming called for a focus on customer value and continuous improvement. He called managers' attention to the fact that most quality problems, up to 90 percent, are not the fault of employees; the system is to blame. Refer back to Chapter 8, Figure 8–6, for a list of Deming's world famous 14 points to improve quality.

Joseph M. Juran. Joseph M. Juran also knew Shewhart. Juran also went to Japan, shortly after Deming. He was less of an advocate for statistical quality control. However, he developed the *Pareto chart* that plots the reasons for being in the out of control range. He stated that 20 percent of the reasons for being out of control caused 80 percent of the quality problems. He called this the *Pareto principle*, which is commonly known as the "80–20" *rule*. When performance is out of control, you first look at the usual "vital few" reasons (20 percent) and most of the time (80 percent) you have a standing-plan solution. Or, only 20 percent of the time will the variance be caused by some other unexpected reason. Did you ever notice how manufacturers commonly have a place in the product manual that says, "If you have a problem try 1,2,3,4"?

Juran emphasized that "managers" should pursue quality improvement on two levels: (1) the mission of the firm as a whole, and (2) the mission of individual departments. Managers need to focus on setting quality goals, developing plans to achieve them, and implementing them. Hence, the emphasis on quality in strategic planning. In a recent interview, Juran explained that senior managers must be involved in attaining better quality, and that there should be a staff or office dedicated to quality.[35]

Armand V. Feigenbaum. Armand V. Feigenbaum became General Electric's top quality expert at age 24. He made his world mark in the 1950s by publishing "total quality control" material, which is now more commonly called TQM. He focused on improving quality as an important way to lower costs. Feigenbaum worked to fight the myth that maintaining quality is expensive. In fact, he said that investing in quality improvement pays better dividends than any other investment a company can make. Hence, the emphasis on quality in capital budgeting. In a recent article, a model was presented that can be used to include quality in capital budgeting decisions concerning new equipment.[36]

Philip B. Crosby. Philip B. Crosby popularized the concepts "quality is free," "do it right the first time," and "zero defects" in the late 1970s. Crosby believed that it is possible to measure the cost of poor quality, and it is necessary to measure it in order to combat the notion that quality is expensive. He advocates that quality is not only free, it's easy. In a recent interview, Crosby claimed that quality is still free, and that a well-run quality program can save a company 20 to 25 percent of revenues.[37]

Genichi Taguchi. Genichi Taguchi focused primarily on the design stage of the process through "quality engineering." He was concerned about the losses a product imparts to society from the time it is shipped to the customer. To limit such losses, he advocated that quality must be designed into each product. Hence, the emphasis on quality as a virtue of design.

Steven Kerr. Steven Kerr, although not a TQM guru, contributed indirectly to TQM by popularizing the ideas that "you get what you reward" and "the folly of rewarding A, while hoping for B" (Chapter 16). In other words, if you want people to do a quality job, you have to develop a system that really rewards employees for doing a quality job.

Work Application

9. Are any of the gurus' quality contributions used where you work or have worked? Explain how.

INFORMATION SYSTEMS

As discussed so far, information plays an important part in operations and quality control. In this section, you will learn about information and technology, the information systems (IS) process, computer hardware and software, functional area IS, types of IS, and integrating IS.

Important Terms. *Data* includes unorganized facts and figures. **Information** *is data organized in a meaningful way to assist employees in doing their jobs and making decisions.*

information
Data organized in a meaningful way to assist employees in doing their jobs and making decisions.

Information and Technology

Who can dispute that our lives, and society in general, have become more complex? The fast rate of change brought about by technology, and especially "information" technology, will not slow down. Technological advances occur virtually every day. Manufacturers who make the best use of information technology to meet their customers' needs stand the best chance of beating their competition,[38] Frito-Lay being an excellent example. Because of rapid changes, even leading companies outsource some of their information technology functions.[39]

Failure to keep up with innovative change can threaten a firm's competitive position and possibly even its survival. Wal-Mart passed Sears and Kmart to become the leading retailer, as well as the low-cost leader, primarily based on information technology. Frito-Lay was one of the first to give its drivers handheld computers to transmit sales back to headquarters.

Technology has led to the rapid changes we go through as time seems to go by more quickly, and time is becoming more important with *time-based competition*, which depends on information.[40] Organizations seek applicants that can convey information.[41] Clearly, your understanding of information systems is important to your career success.

The Information Age. In the 1980s the emphasis began to shift from the technology to its applications, and the information age was born. In the information age, the computer is used as a tool that helps managers use information as an important organizational resource. Information is a critical component of time-based competition. Information systems have changed the way we do business and the way we manage organizations.

Information and the Management Skills and Functions. The use of information has always been an important part of the manager's job. However, with the information age, using and managing information is growing in importance.

Management Skills. Your use of information affects your management skills. In Chapter 1 you learned that technical, communications and human relations, and conceptual and decision-making skills are important to managers. The use of information and computers is a technical skill. In Chapter 10, *communication* was related to the leadership function. Because information is a vital part of communication, how you use information affects your management and leadership skills. The use of information also affects your *decision-making* skills. Managers use computer information to improve decision-making (Chapter 4); you will learn how in this section.

Management Functions. Your use of information affects your skill at performing the four management functions. Computers are used to aid in the *planning* process (Chapters 5 and 6). A focus on information has become a competitive advantage for organizations, including Wal-Mart. IS have helped managers change organizational structures (Chapter 6) and increase their span of management/control, which has led to flatter structures and fewer staff positions. With IS, organizations can be decentralized, while managers maintain control. IS affect the way we communicate, motivate, and lead individuals and teams (Chapters 11–14). They enable managers to lead by using higher levels of participative management. Managing information is a vital part of *controlling*. IS makes it possible to obtain more complete and accurate information in the measuring phase of controlling. Control monitoring can be much faster with information systems, and corrective action can be taken before major problems occur (Chapters 15–17).

Characteristics of Effective Information. To be effective, information should be:

- *Accurate*. It needs to be correct and of quality. Sales forecasts are often inaccurate. The speed of the Pentium chip was overestimated by 10 percent.
- *Timely*. It needs to be current. Have you ever gotten a message or seen a media ad about an event that already happened?
- *Complete*. It needs to contain all the facts. Kroger Supermarkets used to give a lot of shelf space to store brands because they had a higher markup per item than the national brands. After a while, they realized that they were selling more of the national brands. Therefore, focusing on profits, rather than markups, Kroger reallocated more shelf space to national brands.
- *Relevant*.It needs to be appropriate for the situation. Managers in the United States have gone global using what works in America, only to find out that the information was irrelevant in the other country. (Motivation techniques don't work in different countries, Chapter 11.) Also, have you ever had so much information that you could not figure out what was really important or what to do with it all (information overload)? This is our next topic.

Frito-Lay would not be the leading snack food company if it was not effective at using data and information.

Work Application

10. Give an example, from an organization you work or have worked for, of when information did not meet one of the four characteristics of effective information. Explain the consequences.

Controlling Information Overload. The information age has brought us to the point of information overload. Organizations are developing IS based on critical success factors (CSF).[42] Controlling the IS helps to eliminate the problem of information overload. However, here is a simple personal guide to controlling information overload. As you come upon data and information, ask yourself these two question about its relevance: "Will this information help me to meet my objectives? Does the information affect my critical success factors?" If you answer yes, use the information; if not, use *information dump* and be aware of it for future reference, file it, or discard it. A good filing system is a time management technique (Chapter 6) that is critical to controlling information.

The Information Systems Process

Figure 17–7 illustrates the information systems process. Notice that the information department is placed in the center to show its staff role in getting data from the external and internal environments (Chapter 2) and converting it into information (Chapter 15) that can be used by all the organizational departments. Information is also sent to external stakeholders. Improving the internal and external linkage is an important current management issue for IS.[43]

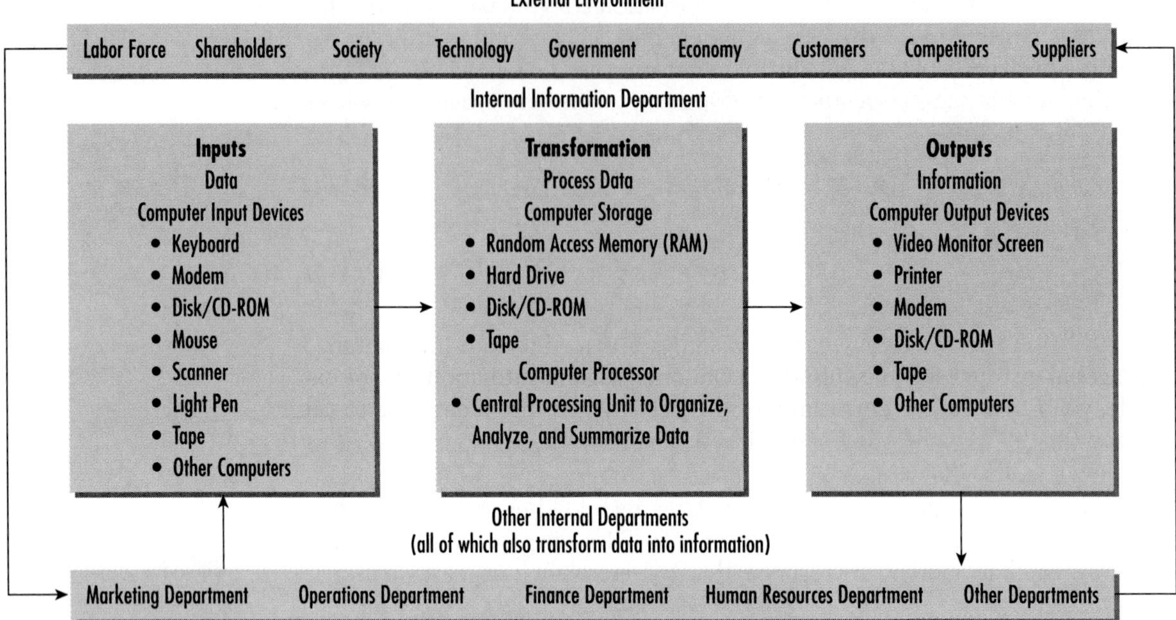

Figure 17–7
The Information Systems Process

Because most information departments are computerized, the computer devices are listed for each subsystem to illustrate how the computer transforms data into information. All people in an organization also continually transform data into information without the use of computers, although many do use computers as well. The information systems process is commonly used in organizations, such as Frito-Lay.

Hardware and Software

Hardware. Hardware is the basic physical components of a computer. The computer input, storage, processor, and output devices, listed in Figure 17–7 are all hardware. All three types of computers—mainframes, minicomputers, and microcomputers, better known as personal computers or PCs—require hardware.

Software. *Software* is a computer program, or set of commands, that instructs hardware to perform various operations, such as reading, analyzing, processing, and storing data. No matter what type of computer hardware is used, you need software to make it run. A variety of software has been developed for various functional areas in business, such as CAD/CAM for operations. Many

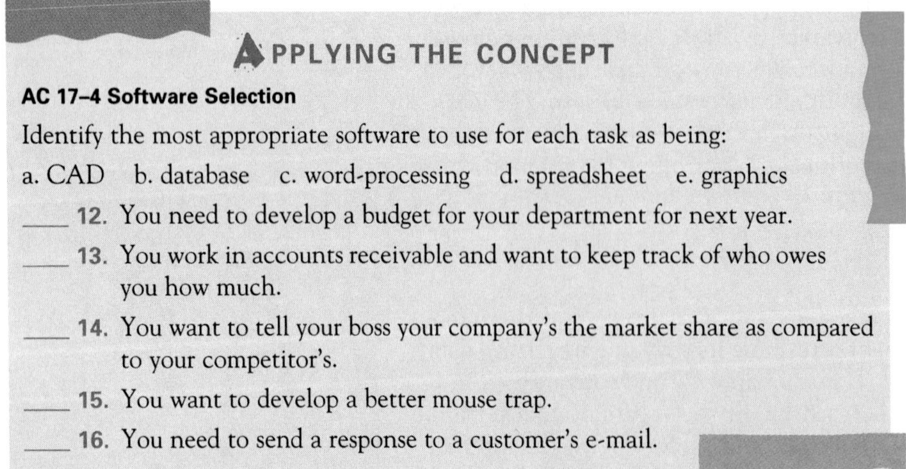

APPLYING THE CONCEPT

AC 17–4 Software Selection

Identify the most appropriate software to use for each task as being:

a. CAD b. database c. word-processing d. spreadsheet e. graphics

____ **12.** You need to develop a budget for your department for next year.

____ **13.** You work in accounts receivable and want to keep track of who owes you how much.

____ **14.** You want to tell your boss your company's the market share as compared to your competitor's.

____ **15.** You want to develop a better mouse trap.

____ **16.** You need to send a response to a customer's e-mail.

organizations have computer programmers who develop software to meet specific needs.

Four popular software programs commonly used in IS include: *databases*, which permit the user to organize and manipulate primarily numerical data in interconnected ways, such as customer accounts; *word-processing*, which allows creating and editing written material; *spreadsheets*, which permit arranging numbers or words in a matrix of rows and columns and performs mathematical calculations; *graphics*, which allows drawing of graphs, charts, and other illustrations. Software makers now offer these products independently and in combined packages.

Integrated Software. The trend in software is to integrate it. Combined packages allow the user to bring work from one program into another. For example, you can write a report using word-processing, go into a database to get data, and include graphics and spreadsheets in your work.

Groupware. *Groupware* is software that can be shared by multiple users. Internal networks use groupware to store and process data. Frito-Lay uses data and information using these software and groupware programs.

Functional Area Information Systems

All departments also get data and convert it into information and send data and information to other departments and external stakeholders, as the arrows directly to and from the external environment to the other departments illustrate in Figure 17–7. In the box listing the functional departments, there are no lines to illustrate that there is a free flow of data and information among all departments. All departments in organizations, including Frito-Lay, also have information systems they use for internal use.

As you read about each functional area, remember that it is common for each to have its own computer hardware, and many have their own special software programs. Also, the use of groupware will increase. Remember that each area gives and receives data and information from the information department on an ongoing basis.

Finance. The processing of accounting data is commonly the first area to be computerized. Determining profit performance is computerized for speed and accuracy. Subsystems of accounting include accounts payable and receivable, payroll, sales and invoices, inventory control, and financial reports.

Accounting gets data from all departments, and IS provide managers in other departments with control information such as cost accounting and budgets. Accounting also sends information in the form of annual reports to external shareholders, it pays taxes to the government, it collects money from customers, pays suppliers, and so on.

Operations. In this chapter you have learned how organizations use computerized CAD, CAM, and CIM for designing, scheduling, and operations control; MRP for inventory control; and SPC for quality control to improve performance. Operations needs to get data in the form of a sales forecast from marketing in order to schedule production. Operations develops and uses technology with input and output to and from external sources.

Manufacturing operations often use a value-added network (VAN) to link operations with their external customers and suppliers. The VAN system is explained in the next section with computer networks.

Marketing. Marketing is responsible for the four Ps of selecting the *products*, the *price* to charge, the *place* where they will be sold, and the *promotion* used to sell the product. As you have read in this chapter, Frito-Lay has very strong marketing. Marketing needs to be in constant contact with its potential customers to gather data and to forecast sales that affect all departments.

The most important part of marketing is selling the products. Marketing information such as ads, brochures, and reports is produced on computer desktop publishing work stations. Many sales presentations today are created by a sales rep with the aid of high-quality computerized multimedia sources, and some video presentations replace a salesperson altogether.

Human Resources. The human resources department needs to communicate with the external labor force to recruit new employees. It also gets data from all departments to retain employees and to calculate absenteeism and turnover rates. The selection, development, and rewarding processes are based on information from both internal and external sources. The human resources department keeps benefits records and works with external insurance companies to control cost. It may also need to complete EEO, OSHA, and workers' compensation reports and may need to work with labor relations with both internal employees and external labor unions. The human resources department commonly keeps a file of data and information on each employee, which can be in paper and/or computerized form.

Work Application

11. Explain the information system used within the functional department you work or have worked for.

Office Management Systems. The use of computer word-processors has made the job of written communications much easier, and so has e-mail. With the use of computers, many organizations have cut back the number of secretaries needed as managers are expected to use computer word-processors to complete their own communications. With voice mail, and answering machines, less secretarial time is spent writing down messages. Computerized copiers feed the sheets into the machine and collate them, and computer printers are often used to make copies. Computers and other office equipment make communicating data and information among all departments easy.

8. Describe the three primary types of information systems and their relationship.

types of information systems
Transaction processing, management information, and decision support.

Types of Information Systems

The three primary **types of information systems** *are transaction processing, management information, and decision support.*

Transaction Processing Systems (TPS). Transaction processing systems are used to handle routine and recurring business matters. Computers were first used for data processing to replace manual clerical functions in the finance area. Most organizations, including Frito-Lay, use transaction processing systems to record accounting transactions, such as accounts receivable and payable and payroll. Most large retail organizations use scanners to record marketing sales transactions at the checkout counter. Banks process checks and deposits and record credit card transactions. Stockbrokers buy and sell stock for clients. Airlines and travel agents make flight reservations. College registrars register students for classes and record grades.

Transaction processing systems are usually designed for a narrow range of activities. The user must follow specific procedures, which he or she cannot change, to accomplish the transaction. The computer often cannot perform any other function.

Transaction processing systems are especially useful for totaling individual transactions. For example, a finance manager may not be too concerned about specific account transactions. However, the total of accounts receivable and payable is a very important part of a financial statement. A regional Frito-Lay manager may not be too concerned about how much each store sells, but total regional sales are a critical measure of success.

Management Information Systems (MIS). MIS transform data into the information managers need from the database to do their work. Managers' work usually consists of running their units/departments, and the information is commonly used for making routine (programmed, Chapter 4) decisions. For example, Frito-Lay's operations managers need to know the sales forecast to schedule routine production. Figure 17–7, the Information Systems Process, is an example of a MIS.

Executive Information Systems (EIS). Executive information systems are a form of MIS used by top-level managers. They provide information on the organization's critical success factors (Chapter 15). Executive information systems place greater emphasis on integrating external data and information with internal information in the critical success factors,[44] which are often industry-specific. The external sources are often more important at higher levels in the organization, especially when they are related to, and can affect, the organization's mission and strategic objectives (Chapter 5). In other words, executive information systems focus more on strategy development and revision, while MIS focus more on strategy implementation.

Decision Support Systems (DSS). Decision support systems use a manager's insights in an interactive computer-based process to assist in making nonroutine (nonprogrammed, Chapter 4) decisions. They use decision rules, decision models, and comprehensive databases. Decision support systems have been used for more than 20 years, and their role and benefits are widely recognized around the world.[45]

Decision support systems are more flexible than MIS. However, the DSS interact with the MIS by applying specific mathematical operations to the information available in the MIS. These math tools allow managers to evaluate the possible effects of alternative decisions. For example, capital budgeting decisions (Chapter 15) and cost-volume-profits analysis (Skill-Building Exercise 15–2, Chapter 15, problem 2) can be done with DSS. Also, linear programming, queuing theory, and probability theory (Chapter 4) can be done with decision support systems.

Frito-Lay was the first in its business to use decision support systems to help it make marketing decisions. Managers can estimate the effects a specific price discount promotional offer (such as a $1.49 bag of Lay's chips being sold for $1.25, .99 cents, and so on) will have on sales, and make the decision to discount or not, and how much to discount by. The salespeople are armed with hand-held computers, that transmit sales back to the office daily. Today, with the decision support systems, Frito-Lay managers know in days, rather than months, how a discounting promotion is affecting sales. They can also spot a competitor's challenge before it does too much damage.

APPLYING THE CONCEPT

AC 17–5 Types of Information Systems

Identify the type of IS as:

a. TP b. MIS c. EIS d. DSS e. expert systems

____ **17.** A manager wants to know if an important order has been shipped yet.

____ **18.** A manager wants to determine how many checkout counters to have in a new store.

____ **19.** A small business owner/manager wants to use an accounting software program.

____ **20.** A manager intuitively knows how to schedule customers. A top manager wants to help others do a good job of scheduling too.

Artificial Intelligence (AI). Artificial intelligence is the attempt to create computers that simulate human decision processes. Artificial intelligence is a form of decision support system that incorporates qualitative as well as quantitative information. It allows the user to inject intuition (fuzzy logic) into the simulation model provided by the computer. Artificial intelligence is being used in robotics and in designing expert systems.

Expert Systems. Expert systems imitate the thought processes of a human being. They build on series of rules ("if-then" scenarios) to move from a set of data to a decision. Boeing uses an expert system called CASE (connector assembly specification expert). CASE produces assembly procedures for each of the five thousand electrical connectors on its airplanes. It now takes the computer a few minutes to get a computer printout for a specific connector, rather than about 45 minutes of searching through 20,000 pages of printed material.

Summary. Transaction processing systems are used to record routine repetitive transactions. MIS, which also include transaction processing system totals, are used by managers to make routine decisions. Executive information systems are a form of MIS, but are used for strategic decisions while MIS is used for strategy implementation. Decision support systems, using MIS, are used by managers to make nonroutine decisions. Artificial intelligence and expert systems are extended forms of DSS used when making specific routine decisions.

Integrating Information Systems

Database Management. With computers, each department can tie its data and information together, and the information department can tie all departments' data together and provide them with information through database management. *Databases* integrate department IS data and information in one central database. A database is created in order to reduce the duplication of information, effort, and cost and to provide controlled access to this information by employees in all departments. Figure 17–7 illustrates database management which focuses primarily on MIS, including transaction processing system totals.

Integrating IS, however, is not only difficult but it is not always possible with existing equipment, especially after departments have independently set up their own systems. For example, marketing may be using Apple equipment, operations a Wang system, and human resources an IBM system. To set up a new system, or convert an old incompatible system all at once is very expensive.

Even designing a system that will be implemented over a period of years is no guarantee of success. It is difficult to anticipate future needs, and with the rapid change in technology, the new design could be obsolete before it is implemented. Frito-Lay uses database management.

The trend today is to integrate the functional area IS. For example, at PepsiCo's Taco Bell, orders are placed (marketing—sales) and sent to be filled (operations) by computer. The system is also used to collect the money (finance) to keep track of inventory (operations), and to reorder food and supplies. The IS also records which employee is using the system (human resources). If an employee has more sales than money received (finance), action can be taken. Hospitals are also integrating IS to facilitate their financial, patient, and administrative support functions to better service patients.[46]

Professional Help with Integrating Information Systems. Big computer companies including IBM, Unisys, Digital Equipment, and Hewlett-Packard sell fully developed and integrated information systems. EDS (Chapter 14) will take basic equipment and write custom software for an organization's IS needs. Some firms hire experienced managers to set up and run their IS; they are commonly given the title of chief information officer (CIO). Organizations are now getting professional help in setting up integrated IS using networks, which is covered in the next section.

INFORMATION NETWORKS

The Age of the Information Network Is Here

9. List the components of an information network.

computer networks
Connect independent computers so that they can function in interrelated ways.

Computer networks *connect independent computers so that they can function in interrelated ways*. Networks are commonly described as computers communicating or talking with each other. Networks are a way of integrating information systems. As shown in Figure 17–7, one computer's data can become another computer's input, and a third computer can be an output source of the information. For example, you could get an e-mail (input), use the e-mail data (process), and send your e-mail to someone else (output).

Lou Gerstner of IBM and Bill Gates of Microsoft agree that network-centric computing is the wave of the future. Failure to use networks in business will generate wider failure, as workers will lack the tools to be competitive. New information system skills will need to be assimilated, with network management, systems integration, and remote systems management representing future needs.[47]

information networks
Connect all employees from headquarters and remote facilities to each other, to suppliers and customers, and into databases.

Information networks *connect all employees from headquarters and remote facilities to each other, to suppliers and customers, and into databases*. Figure 17–8 illustrates the information network, and its components are discussed next.

Connecting All Employees

Internal computer networks are changing the way companies—and their employees—do business.[48] With internal computer networks, employees in an organization have direct access to each other and to the information they need to do their work. All employees can do their jobs in a more informed and efficient manner by using the shared database and by having direct contact with others.

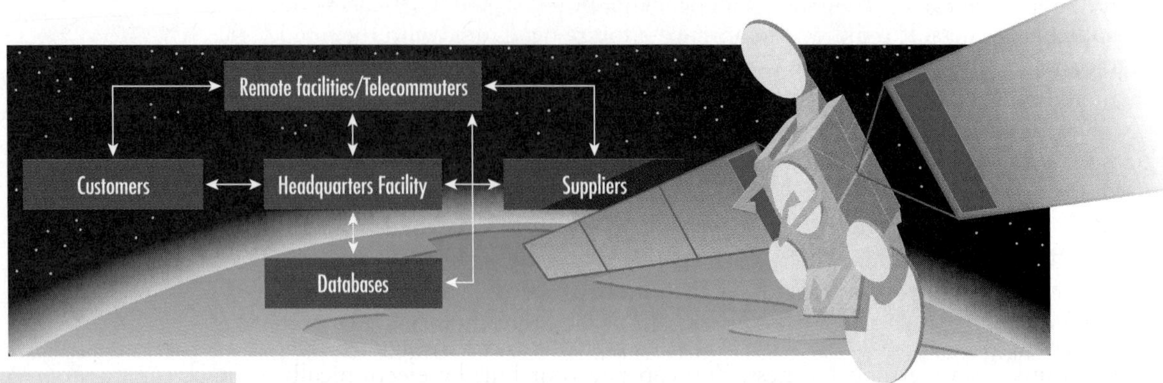

Figure 17–8
Information Network

Lotus uses its own Notes groupware to link up its programmers around the world so they have instantaneous access to each other's work.

Local-Area Networks (LAN). Local-area networks directly link everyone via computers within one facility. In Figure 17–8, headquarters and each remote facility would use a local-area network.

Wide-Area Networks (WAN). Wide-area networks link employees in different facilities via computers using telephone lines or long-range communications devices. In Figure 17–8, headquarters and each remote facility would be connected by wide-area network, as well as each remote facility to the others.

The Virtual Office and Telecommunications

With information networks it is no longer necessary to have all employees in one facility. Within the *virtual office*, people who are spread out in remote locations work as though they were in one place using wide-area networks.

The virtual office is made possible by telecommunications (machines linked by telephone) technology networks of telephones, centralized voice mail, e-mail, fax machines, and teleconferencing (also called videoconferencing, people can see and talk to each other from different locations). Sam Walton used teleconferencing for Saturday meetings with employees.

Telecommuters. With a virtual office, *telecommuters* transmit and receive required data and information to and from other employees and locations. Salespeople who have to travel and stay overnight, including those from Frito-Lay, have portable virtual offices they use on the road.[49]

Telecommuters' remote location is commonly their home. Telecommuters only go to the central office at set intervals, such as once a week, and/or for special purposes. Telecommuting saves on expenses for office space, commuting, clothing, and going out to lunch when all employees work in one place. The virtual office and telecommuting allow employees in all departments in all locations to easily communicate data and information. With the dropping cost of a virtual office (equipment costs less than $3,000), telecommuting will continue to increase in the future.[50] However, to be successful, telecommuters need to have clear standing plans with lots of communication to guide their performance.[51]

Note that in Figure 17–8 telecommuters are in a sense a remote facility; that is why they are in the same box. The figure represents any organization. It could be a bank with a headquarters, often called the main branch, and any number of remote facility branches. It may also have telecommuters who are connected to everyone else in the information system.

Customers and Suppliers

Customers. Information networks facilitate faster response to customers' problems and needs. When a customer calls, or a salesperson reports a customer problem, networks allow a single employee to get the information, or person, who can help solve the problem.

Some situations, such as banking at home by computer, use a computer network to link customer and business. You can pay your bills by electronically transferring money from your account into the company's account. However, note that customers are often not connected by computer in the information network, as in the following example.

At Hewlett-Packard, when a customer calls with a technical problem, the call is routed to one of four engineering hubs around the world, depending on the time of day. This way customers have 24-hour access to technical support. The employee places data about the problem and customer into the system. All four hubs have access to information on how the problem was solved. When other customers with the same or similar problems call, employees have the information to solve that customer's problem. In a sense, they use the Pareto principle so they all know the common problems that will occur and they all know how to solve them quickly (80 percent of the time). Or, employees will be working on new problems only 20 percent of the time. Another major advantage of the network system is that problem areas are identified and can be eliminated in the new computer models.

Suppliers. Through networks, companies can place orders for materials and supplies instantly via e-mail. Computerized material requirements planning also help companies to know when and how much to order.

Customers and Suppliers. Manufacturing operations often use a *value-added network* (VAN) to link operations with their external customers and suppliers. The value added network system allows for instant transfer of information about current inventories and will automatically place an order for new goods for shipment from operations to retailers when products are low. It helps keep retail inventories at a minimum level and results in cost saving through just-in-time inventories. Value-added networks are controlled through *electronic data interchange (EDI)*, or the scanners cashiers use to ring up your sale at retail stores.

Databases

On-Line Services and the Internet. Networks are commonly used to tap into databases such as on-line services which may provide access to the Internet and its World Wide Web. However, America Online, CompuServe, Genie, Prodigy and other on-line services are being threatened by direct-access companies that allow users to bypass on-line services and access the Internet directly.[52] Due to this threat, Prodigy owners Sears and IBM sold Prodigy to investors including Grupo Caso.[53] America Online and others realize that the Net and Web are bewildering and difficult to use for the new or casual computer users. They see a booming business guiding these users through the Net's often chaotic and unmapped regions. The Internet is creating software challenges.[54]

As network systems become more prevalent and as modems are increasingly used to share documents, integrated hardware and software will become even more important. They will enable IS to evolve into the highly effective control and communication tools they are capable of being. Recall from Chapter 8 that IBM acquired Lotus primarily to get its Notes "groupware" to run network software on its hardware. In 1996, IBM chairman Lou Gerstner promised heavy investment in its Lotus Notes line and unveiled a new version of the software that integrates Internet features.[55]

Other Databases. Although the Internet is used by business and for doing business, many businesses make greater use of other databases. For example, many businesses contact a database to check on the credit rating of a customer or supplier, or to find out whether a customer has adequate credit to cover the cost of the current purchase.

Work Application

12. Explain how an organization you work or have worked for uses network telecommunications.

Integrated Services Digital Networks (ISDN)

Integrated services digital networks are the new technology that links computers and other machines through the use of digital cabling, which acts much like telephone wires. ISDNs enable exact copies of a company's forms to be transmitted from one unit to another. ISDN is in the development stage as this book is being written. However, with the rapid technological advances, it may be common before the next edition of this book is printed.

CURRENT MANAGEMENT ISSUES

Global. Time-based competition is important in the *global* environment. Information networks have helped to improve operations by connecting facilities all over the world. Global markets create growth opportunities. Frito-Lay is rapidly expanding overseas, where snacking isn't a national sport. The overseas snack business brings in more than $3.25 billion in sales from more than 30 countries, and there is enormous opportunity for growth. Frito-Lay is already the world's largest producer of snack chips outside the United States; it has more snack manufacturing experience and technological expertise than any other company. However, there can be quality problems with operating facilities outside of the United States. Frito-Lay's overseas market has mainly grown by buying foreign competitors or entering into joint ventures. Products acquired and sold only in international markets include Walkers and Hostess. This strategy led to unpredictable quality. Overseas chips were sometimes too thick, too thin, or overcooked and were occasionally made with low-grade oil or damaged potatoes. To correct these problems, higher-quality control standards have been set, and new and better packaging, ad campaigns, and overhaul in manufacturing techniques are being implemented.

Diversity. In this chapter you have learned about a *diversity* of operation systems. The trend is toward more flexibility,[56] and there is great diversity in the use of information systems. There is a diversity of quality globally. The

International Standards Organization (ISO) certifies organizations that meet set quality standards. Manufacturing and services companies seeking ISO 9000 certification are required to document practices that affect the quality of products. They need to comply with the applicable guidelines embodied in standards ISO 9000 through 9003.[57] Many companies are seeking ISO 9000 certification because of the benefits associated with meeting the international quality standards that have become the hallmark of excellence. So far, over 7,500 U.S. companies have gained certification. This number will grow dramatically as major companies, including GM and Ford, require their suppliers to be certified.[58]

International Standards Organizaiton (ISO)
Certifies organizations that meet set quality standards.

Ethics and Social Responsibility. With computers comes the issue of *ethics* and *social responsibility*. With easy access to information through networks, companies have had problems keeping their secrets. Proprietary documents are showing up in the hands of competitors or in the media.[59] Competitors are unethically stealing the information or buying the information from unethical employees. E-mail and on-line network information is considered socially responsible because it cuts down on the use of paper, which saves trees.[60]

TQM, Participative Management, and Teams. TQM includes quality control and is broadly accepted in the United States. It has been estimated that 60 to 80 percent of Fortune 500 companies have implemented or are experimenting with TQM and employee empowerment.[61] TQM empowers *teams* as a *participative management* technique. Clearly, information networks facilitate teamwork as members can keep in constant contact through e-mail as they have instant access to each other's work.

Productivity. Information systems, including networks, have clearly increased *productivity* at Frito-Lay and many other organizations. They have helped in the downsizing and re-engineering of organizations because it takes fewer people to process work when employees have instant access to the information they need. There has been a debate about whether information systems should be centralized or decentralized. With only a mainframe computer, central control was not an issue. However, when PCs became common, there was a fear of decentralized information systems. There is an argument that decentralized information systems at the department level allow better customer service.[62] On the other hand, there is an argument that centralized information systems are less expensive and reduce duplication of efforts.[63] Today, with information networks you have the best of both worlds. Hewlett-Packard attributes its success in rapid product turnover to its information network.[64]

Small Business. Small businesses are often successful with time-based competition. Small companies have been known to act quickly and to be more flexible than big businesses. However, with the aid of information networks, many large business are acting more quickly and becoming more flexible. While small businesses can use any form of operation system, due to size limitations continuous and repetitive operation processes are not as commonly used as they are in big business. Quality is equally important for all organizations. Many smaller businesses that have a major big businesses customer are being forced to get ISO certification to retain it. One form of small business customer value advantage is often the personal contact in customer service. Information systems and networks are more common with large businesses, but with the cost dropping, as with the use of PCs, networks will increase in use.

Chapter Summary and Glossary

The chapter summary is organized to answer the ten learning objectives for Chapter 17.

1. Describe time-based competition and state why it is important.

Time-based competition refers to strategies to increase the speed of going from creativity to delivery. It is important because speed gives the organization a first-mover competitive advantage.

2. Explain the difference among the three tangibilities of products, the three levels of customer involvement, the four flexibilities of operations processes, and the three intensities of resources.

A product can be a tangible good, intangible service, or a combination of both. The three levels of customer involvement refer to whether the operation makes-to-stock with a standard product, makes-to-order with customer-specific products, or assembles-to-order with a standard product with some customized features. Flexibility refers to whether the products are produced continually in nondiscrete units, repetitively on an assembly line for one product, in batches with the same resources used for multiple products, or individually to customer specifications. Intensity of resources refers to capital in which machines do most of the work, labor in which human resources do most of the work, or a balance of the two.

3. Discuss what is meant by "quality is a virtue of design."

"Quality is a virtue of design" means that if products are designed with cross-functional team input to provide customer value, there will be fewer operations problems, the product will be easier to sell, and it will be less costly to service the product. Therefore, it is important for cross-functional teams to work together on the design of new products.

4. Explain product, process, cellular, and fixed-position types of facility layouts in terms of their customer involvement and flexibility.

Product layout uses make-to-stock and/or assemble-to-order customer involvement with repetitive or continuous process operations flexibility. Process layout uses make-to-order customer involvement with individual operations process flexibility. Cellular layout uses make-to-stock and/or assemble-to-order with batch operations process flexibility. Fixed-position layout uses made-to-order and/or assemble-to-order with project process operations flexibility.

5. Describe priority scheduling and list its three priorities.

Priority scheduling is the continuous evaluation of and reordering of the sequence in which products will be produced. Its three priorities are first come-first served, earliest due date, and shortest operating time; a combination of these may be used.

6. Explain the relationship among inventory control, just-in-time (JIT) inventory, and materials requirement planning (MRP).

Inventory control is the process of managing raw materials, work-in-process, finished goods, and in-transit goods. JIT is an inventory control method that has necessary parts and raw materials delivered shortly before they are needed. MRP is a system that integrates operations and inventory control. JIT is part of inventory control and both are part of MRP.

7. Explain how statistical process control (SPC) charts and the exception principle are used in quality control.

The statistical process control chart is used to graph actual performance to see if it is within the standard range. According to the exception principle, if performance is within standard range, do nothing; if performance is out of control range, take corrective action.

8. Describe the three primary types of information systems and their relationship.

Transaction process systems (TPS) are used to record routine repetitive transactions. Management information systems (MIS) are used by managers to perform their work and to make routine decisions. Decision support systems (DDS) are used by managers to make nonroutine decisions. TPS is related to MIS because its totals are included in the MIS. DSS is related to MIS, which includes TPS totals, because it uses MIS databases.

9. List the components of an information network.

The components of an information network include connecting all employees from headquarters and remote locations to each other, to suppliers and customers, and into databases.

10. Define the following key terms (in order of appearance in the chapter):

Select one or more methods: (1) fill in the missing key terms from memory, (2) match the key terms from the end of the review with their definitions below, or (3) copy the key terms in order from the list at the beginning of the chapter.

_______________ refers to strategies to increase the speed of going from creativity to delivery.

______ is the function in which resource inputs are transformed into product outputs.

A ______ is a good, service, or a combination of the two.

__________ refers to whether operations make-to-stock, make-to-order, or assemble-to-order.

__________ refers to whether the products are produced continuously, repetitively, in batches, or individually.

______ is the process used in transforming inputs into outputs

__________ refers to whether operations use product, process, cellular, or fixed-position layout.

______ is the amount of products an organization can produce.

______ is the path and sequence of transformations a product takes to become an output.

__________ is the continuing evaluation and reordering of the sequence in which products will be produced.

______ is the stock of materials held for future use.

__________ is the process of managing raw materials, work-in-process, finished goods, and in-transit goods.

_______________ is a method that has necessary parts and raw materials delivered shortly before they are needed.

_______________ is a system that integrates operations and inventory control with complex ordering and scheduling.

__________ is the process of ensuring that the four types of inventory meet standards.

_______________ aids in determining if quality is within the acceptable standard range.

______ is data organized in a meaningful way to assist employees in doing their jobs and making decisions.

_______________ include transaction processing, management information, and decision support.

__________ connect independent computers so that they can function in interrelated ways.

__________ connect all employees from headquarters and remote locations to each other, to suppliers and customers, and into databases.

The _______________ certifies organizations that meet set quality standards.

KEY TERMS

capacity
computer networks
customer involvement
facility layout
information
information networks
inventory
inventory control
International Standards Organization (ISO)
just-in-time (JIT) inventory
materials requirement planning (MRP)
operations
operations flexibility
priority scheduling
product
quality control
routing
statistical process control (SPC)
technology
time-based competition
types of information systems

REVIEW AND DISCUSSION QUESTIONS

1. What does the operations department do?
2. Which level of customer involvement is the highest? Why?
3. Which type of process operations is the most and least flexible?
4. Which type of process operations is most commonly used by retailers and service organizations?
5. Are most services more capital- or labor-intensive than manufacturers?
6. Why is it important to balance time-based competition and design?
7. Which two facility layouts are the most flexible and which two are the least flexible?
8. Why is capacity planning so important?
9. Why is sales forecasting important to operations?
10. What are the four types of inventories?
11. What does materials requirement planning integrate?

12. What is the relationship between inventory and quality control?
13. What are the six rules of customer relations?
14. What is the relationship between information and the management function?
15. What are the two questions you should ask yourself when dealing with information overload?
16. What takes place during the information systems process?
17. What is the difference among hardware, software, and groupware?
18. What is the function of database management?
19. What is the difference between a computer network and an information network?

CASE

Gitano

Haim and Isaac Dabah once successfully owned and managed Gitano Group, Inc. Haim headed the marketing area and created the high-fashion ads that established Gitano's young, slick, and sassy image. Haim's strategy was to sell Gitano, Gloria Vanderbilt, and Regatta Sport brands through department stores. Gitano focused on customers who shunned high-priced designers like Calvin Klein but who wanted the glitz of a label on their clothes at a moderate price. Gitano clothes sold at a high profit margin in department stores. However, when Haim changed strategies and also began to sell clothes to discount retail stores including Wal-Mart, profit margins dropped. Wal-Mart bargains hard with suppliers.

Isaac managed the operations area. He acquired operations facilities in Mississippi, Guatemala, and Jamaica. Isaac had no experience or much skill at designing operations and controlling them. For example, the Jamaica plant wasted five times the industry average, or a full 20 percent of its materials. Rather than rework jeans that had been dyed the wrong colors, employees simply threw them away. There were no controls in any of the plants to determine where clothes were in the production process. Several thousand dollars' worth of inventory disappeared somehow. Isaac did not do any sales forecasting; he simply had manufacturing facilities run at full capacity so they had large inventories ready to ship when orders came in. Despite large inventories, it often took weeks or even months to ship orders, and they sometimes shipped the wrong merchandise, which wasted more time. Although Gitano's operations were managed poorly, surprisingly, quality of products was not a real problem.

Despite operations problems, Gitano did well through the 1980s. In fact, in 1989, it sold around $600 million worth of clothes with a net profit of $31 million. However, when the recession of the early 1990s hit, Gitano was caught without any strategic plans. During the recession, many prior customers stopped buying Gitano clothes. Isaac was years too late at cutting back production and he continued to produce at full capacity. Gitano got to the point of having at least three years' worth of most products on hand in finished inventory.

Because Isaac was running at full capacity without forecasting demand, Gitano had far too many outdated clothes and not enough of some newer styles. Gitano regularly substituted products to fill orders. Many of the stores did not realize that they were not getting the actual clothes they ordered. However, Wal-Mart ordered its vendors to begin tagging merchandise with bar codes. Wal-Mart could easily compare every pair of jeans against what it had actually ordered. Haim convinced Wal-Mart that it was developing a bar-coding system while it continued to substitute orders.

With at least three years of back inventory, Haim decided that the best way to get rid of it was to open Gitano's own retail stores. In four years it opened around 100 stores. But, the stores did not help much. As new inventory came in, it was placed on top of the old merchandise. Eventually, stores were so backlogged that everything was marked down below cost in an attempt to get rid of it. At the urging of their bankers, the Dabah brothers hired Robert Gregory to run the business. Gregory was formerly the president and chief operating officer of VF Corporation, the maker of Lee jeans. His first priority was to establish a badly needed control system and to downsize operations. But the attempt was too little too late.

While Wal-Mart was unhappily waiting for Gitano to bar code its products, the Dabah brothers pleaded guilty to a scheme to avoid import quotas and agreed to pay $2 million in fines in December 1993. Wal-Mart pulled its Gitano account, saying it would not do business with a company that engaged in unethical and socially irresponsible behavior. A few months later, Gitano announced it was filing for Chapter 11 bankruptcy protection and selling its assets to Fruit of the Loom, Inc., for $100 million.

How was Gitano able to make millions of dollars with no strategic plan, no forecasting, no budgets, and no control systems? Robert Gregory gave an assessment of the rise and fall of Gitano. He stated that back in the 1980s you could be successful with good marketing of high-profit margin products that covered the cost of poor management planning and control systems, but not in the highly competitive global market of the 1990s and beyond.

Select the best alternative for the following questions. Be sure you are able to explain your answers.

1. Gitano's level of customer involvement was.

a. made-to-stock c. assembled-to-order
b. made-to-order

2. Gitano's flexibility of operations was.

a. continuous process c. batch process
b. repetitive process d. individual process

3. Gitano's operations resources were.

a. capital-intensive
b. labor-intensive c. balanced

4. Product mix was important to Gitano's success.

a. true b. false

5. Gitano's facility layout was.

a. product b. process c. cellular c. fixed

6. Gitano's facility location selections were most likely based on.

a. cost e. community interest
b. proximity f. quality of life
c. transportation
d. access to human resources

7. Gitano was ______ at priority scheduling and scheduling to adjust operations capacity.

a. effective b. ineffective

8. Using statistical quality control would have led to major improvement in solving Gitano's problems.

a. true b. false

9. Gitano seemed to have ______ coordination and sharing of information among different departments.

a. little b. some c. great

10. The best way that Gitano could have controlled its operations problems would have been to have developed a type of ______ network.

a. local-area d. value-added
b. wide-area e. database
c. virtual office

11. Describe Gitano's primary operations transformation process.

12. What was Gitano's approach to capacity planning and how could it be improved?

13. What was Gitano's approach to scheduling to adjust capacity and how could it be improved?

14. What was Gitano's approach to inventory control, and how could it be improved?

15. What type(s) of information systems and networks would you recommend Gitano use?

SKILL-BUILDING EXERCISE 17–1

Economic Order Quantity

Preparing for Skill-Building Exercise 17–1

Calculate the EOQ for each of the four following situations:

___ 1. R = 2,000, S = $15.00, H = $5.00

___ 2. H = $10.00, R = 7,500, S = $40.00

___ 3. R = 500, H = $15.00, S = $35.00

___ 4. S = $50.00, H = $25.00, R = 19,000

Doing Skill-Building Exercise 17–1 in Class

Objective
To develop your skill at calculating EOQ.

Preparation
You should have calculated EOQ for the four situations in the preparation section.

Procedure 1 (10–20 minutes)
Option A. The instructor goes over the correct EOQ answers in class.
Option B. The instructor has students come to the front of the class and go over the EOQ answers.

Conclusion
The instructor leads a class discussion and/or makes concluding remarks.

Application (2–4 minutes)
What did I learn for this experience? How will I use this knowledge in the future?

____

____

Sharing
Volunteers give their answers to the application section.

EXERCISE 17–1

Implementing the Management Functions

Preparation for Exercise 17–1

You should have studied planning, organizing and staffing, leading, and controlling.

Doing Exercise 17–1 in Class

Objective
To develop skill at implementing the management functions.

Preparation
The preparation is to have studied the prior chapters covering the management functions.

Experience
During the in-class exercise, you will be either a member of Production Company that produces a product to make a profit or a customer and supplier who buys the product and sells materials. Your organization will compete against other class groups to earn the most profit. Your group will have to bid on how many products it will make and how much inventory to buy. Turn to the Production Company Contracts with Customers and Suppliers and Profit or Loss Statement to get an idea of bidding and purchasing supplies agreements you will make during the exercise.

Procedure 1 (3–4 minutes)
Break into as many groups of five as possible while still having at least half as many students as the number of teams. The students in the groups are members of Production Company and will produce the product described below. This is not an ongoing product that is sold; it is a one-time order from one customer. All other students will be customers and suppliers. At least one student must be assigned to each group as its customer and/or supplier; if necessary, customer/suppliers may have more than one group. Teams should spread out as much as possible. Suppliers are given stacks of paper to sell to the groups. Customers/suppliers should sit close to their Production Company team and listen and observe. However, they may not communicate in any way with the team.

Procedure 2 (10 minutes)
Suppliers give each Production Company team ten free papers for planning purposes. Using the contract with customer and supplier (and profit or loss statement) sheet accompanying this exercise, each production team must plan its bid on how many products it will make during the ten-minute time period of the contract, and how much raw materials paper it will buy. In doing so, the team must plan how it will produce the products, as well as organize and staff, lead, and control its operations.

Production Company Contracts with Customer and Supplier and Profit or Loss Statement (To be filled out by customer/supplier with Production Company)

Customer Contract

Bid: number of products Production Company contracts to build during the period. ________*
The customer will not buy any products above the bid amount.
Agreed price per product that meets inspection: $25,000.
Number of products accepted ______ × $25,000 = $ ________
Agreed penalty charge of $30,000 for each product not delivered on time.
Number not produced ______ × $30,000 = – $ ________
Check paid by customer to Production Company. $ ________
Fine for unethically making products before or after time period; if caught deduct $100,000 from amount of check to be paid to customer.

Supplier Contract

Number of raw material paper purchased ________ × $10,000 = $ ________*
Raw material of unused paper cannot be used for other jobs. However, the supplier agrees to buy it back at a penalty.
Number of returned unfolded papers ________ × $8,000 = – $ ________
All work-in-process cannot be sold after the contract period, nor returned to the supplier at a penalty fee. However, the supplier will buy it as scrap.
Number of folded papers ________ × $5,000 = – $ ________
Cost of Goods Sold (CGS) Check given to supplier from Production Company. $ ________

Profit or Loss Job Statement

Revenue (amount of check received from customer)		$ ________
Cost of Goods Sold (variable cost, check given to supplier)	–	________
Gross Profit		$ ________
Expenses (fixed cost for the period including labor, overhead, etc.)	–	$ 250,000 .
Profit or Loss Before Taxes		$ ________
Taxes (If you have a profit, multiply 25% tax rate times profit)	–	$ ________
Net Income or Loss		$ ________

*Filled out prior to production. All others lines filled-out after production period.

Steps for Making the Product

1. Fold the paper in half; unfold. Then fold it in half in the other direction; unfold.

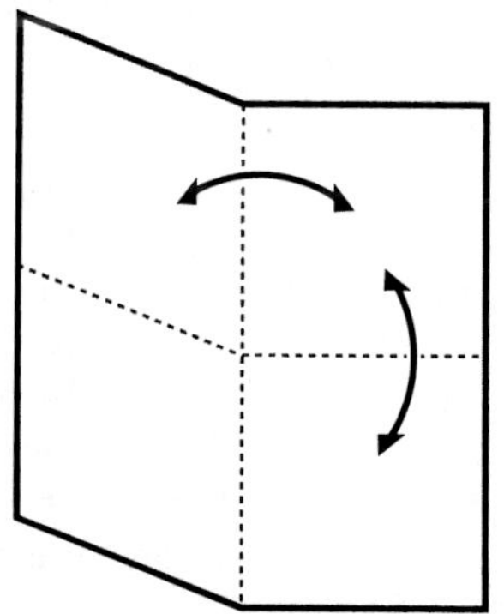

2. Turn the paper over. Fold the paper in half diagonally; unfold. Then fold it in half diagonally in the other direction.

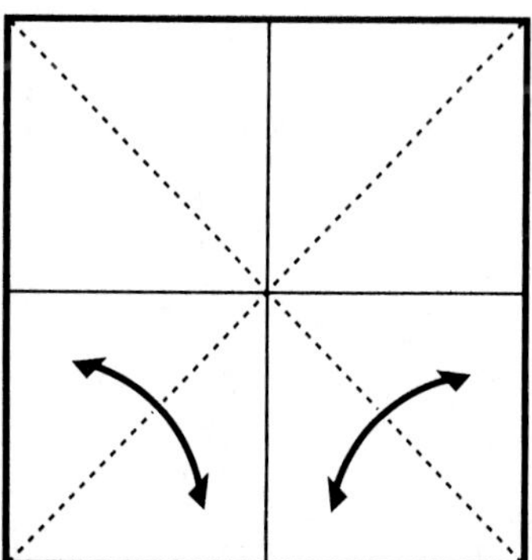

3. Fold each corner toward the middle.

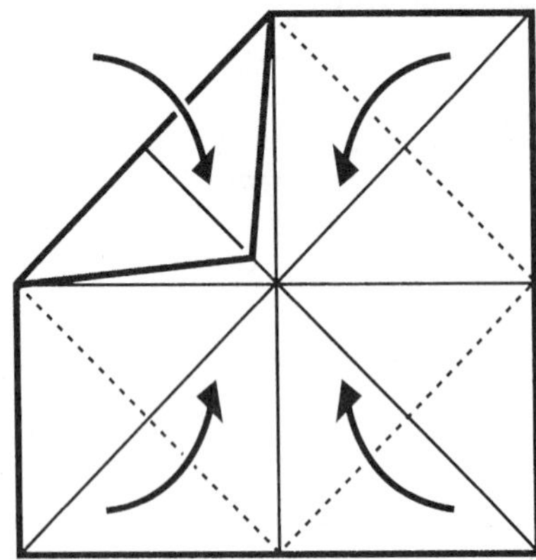

4. Turn the paper over. Fold each corner toward the middle.

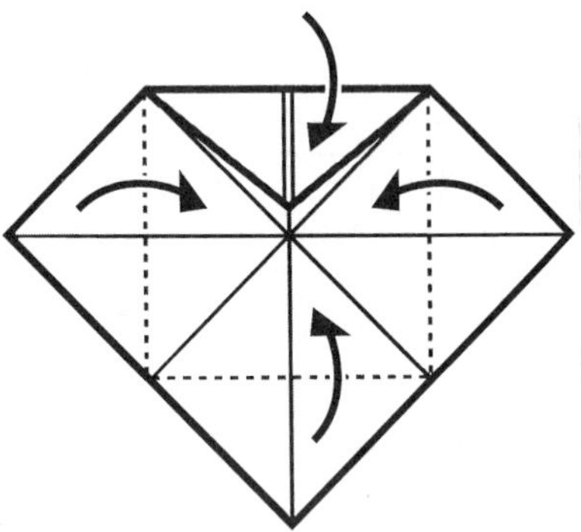

5. Fold it in half; unfold. Then fold it in half in the other direction; unfold.

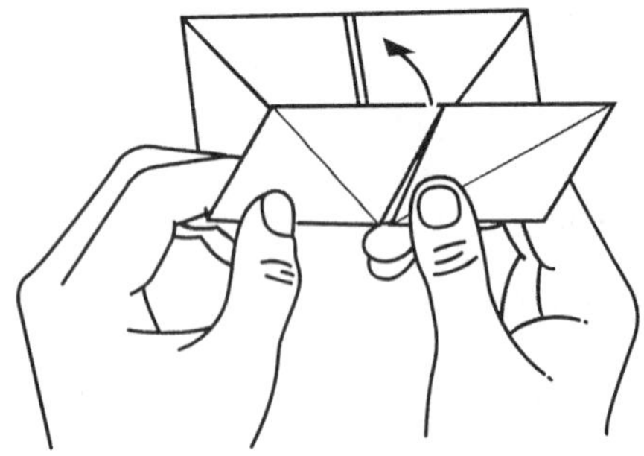

6. Stick your thumbs and index fingers under flaps on undersides.

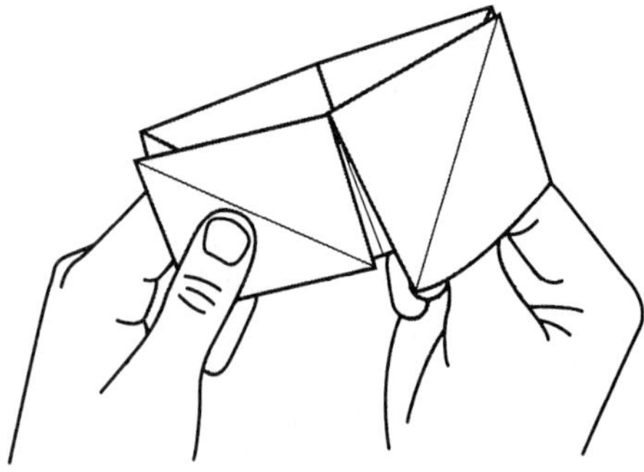

7. Be sure the paper looks like it is supposed to and that it folds easily in both directions. If it does, it should pass inspection by your team and the customer. If not, fix it so that it does or scrap it at a cost of $7,000 each. Remember that you have exactly ten minutes of production time for the period.

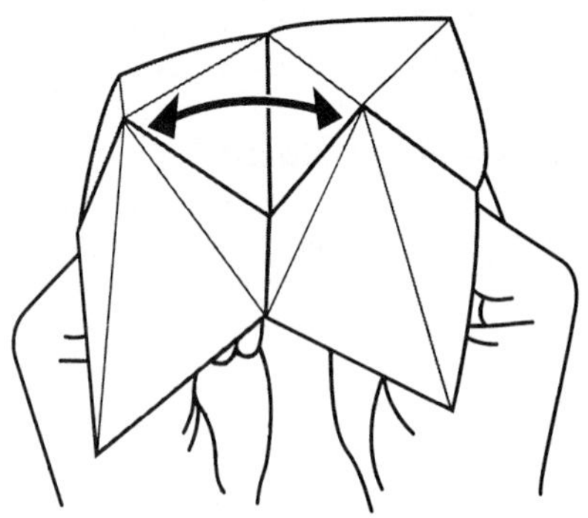

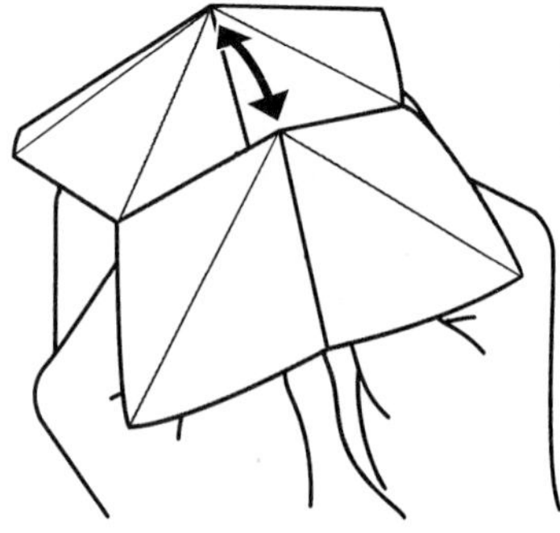

Procedure 3 (3–6 minutes)
The customer/supplier goes to the Production Company and takes back the ten papers. If they are not used, they are placed with good sheets; if they are folded, they are discarded. On the contract sheet the customer writes in the bid and the supplier sells (gives) the paper and writes in the

dollar amount of raw material purchased. Teams may not start manufacturing products until told to do so. Beginning work is unethical behavior, and if caught, a $100,000 fine will be imposed by the customer. Customers, watch your Production Company team members. If you catch them in unethical behavior, you save money.

Procedure 4 (10 minutes)
Production teams have ten minutes to make the product. The instructor will announce when there are two minutes left, one minute left, 30 seconds left, 15 seconds left, and time to stop. When told to stop, all team members must stop. To finish the product is unethical behavior. All team members caught working after they are told to stop will be fined $100,000 by the customer.

Procedure 5 (8–10 minutes)
The customer/supplier goes to the Production Company and inspects the goods and buys the ones that pass inspection (look like they are supposed to and open and close in both directions). The supplier buys back any raw and work-in-process goods. Fill in the lines to determine the revenue, cost of goods sold, and profit or loss statement. The customer/supplier records the team's bid, actual number produced, number of papers bought, and profit or loss statement for all teams to see. With all comparative information recorded, the team with the greatest net income is the winner. However, every team that makes a profit also wins.

Integration (12–20 minutes)
Option A. Individually, everyone answers the following questions to identify how your team implemented the management functions, followed by the instructor going over the answers.
Option B. As a team, answer the following questions, followed by the instructor going over the answers.
Option C. The instructor goes over the answers to the following questions as individuals answer them.

Planning Skills (Chapters 4–6)

1. What were the important decisions that needed to be made to be successful in this exercise?______________

____

2. The decisions in this exercise were ____ programmed ____ unprogrammed and the condition was ____ certainty ____ risk ____ uncertainty.
3. Our major decisions were made by ____ one individual ____ the group.
4. Our bid ____ was ____ was not the team objective, and our team ____ exactly made the bid or ____ did not produce enough ____ could have done more.
5. What was Production Company's basic mission or goal?______________________________

____

6. As an environmental analysis, what were your team's strengths and weaknesses? How did your team stack up against the competition?
7. Our Production Company developed ____ strategic ____ operational plans.
8. The appropriate plans were ____ standing ____ single-use.
9. Forecasting in the area of ____ sales ____ operations was important in this exercise.
10. Time management ____ was ____ was not important in this exercise.

Organizing Skills (Chapters 7–9)

11. Our team members ____ developed a chain of command ____ were all basically equal.
12. Our team had ____ line ____ line and staff positions.
13. Jobs were ____ simplified (each person did one part of making each product) ____ job expansion (each person made an entire product). ______________ was our fastest production worker.
14. Our group ____ was ____ was not a work team.
15. Managing change and innovation ____ were ____ were not very important in this exercise.
16. There ____ was ____ was not diversity within our team.
17. During this exercise the most relevant human resources process was ____ human resources planning ____ attracting employees ____ developing employees ____ retaining employees.

Leading Skills (Chapters 10–14)

18. Communications flowed ____ vertically ____ horizontally ____ grapevine.
19. Our team primarily used ____ oral ____ nonverbal ____ written communication.
20. Our team was ____ effective ____ ineffective at sending, receiving (listening to each other), and responding to messages.
21. Overall, our team members ____ were ____ were not motivated to win.
22. Being in competition ____ did ____ did not meet any member's need for power. In other words, were the peo-

ple with a high need for power pushing more to win, and were they upset if they lost?

23. The most relevant process motivation theory in this exercise was _____ equity _____ goal-setting _____ expectancy theory.
24. The type of reinforcement used was _____ positive _____ avoidance _____ extinction _____ punishment.
25. Our team focused more on _____ task _____ relationship behavior.
26. Our team's primary leadership style was _____ autocratic _____ consultative _____ participative _____ empowerment.
27. Members were primarily influenced by _____ one member _____ a few members _____ shared leadership. However, I'd say our primary leader was __________.
28. We were a _____ group _____ team.
29. We had the following group types: _____ formal _____ informal; _____ functional _____ cross-functional; _____ command _____ task.
30. We made _____ effective _____ ineffective decisions, and we were _____ effective _____ ineffective at resolving conflict.
31. Our team progressed to the following stage of group development: _____ orientation _____ dissatisfaction _____ resolution _____ production _____termination.
32. I'd say the most powerful group member was __________.
33. I'd say the person displaying the most effective political behavior was __________.
34. I'd say the person most effective at handling conflict in our team was __________.
35. Overall, our team found this exercise to be _____ stressful _____ nonstressful.

Controlling Skills (Chapters 15–17)

36. Our team's systems process was __________.
37. The preliminary, concurrent, rework, and damage controls our team used were: ______________________________

____
38. This exercise focused primarily on the _____ finance _____ marketing _____ operations _____ human resources functional area.
39. During this exercise, our team followed the steps in the control systems process (check all that apply): _____ set objectives and standards _____ measure performance _____ compare performance to the standard _____ correct, future correct, reinforce.
40. We had standards in the area of (check all that apply): _____ quantity _____ quality _____ time _____ cost _____ behavior.
41. Our team used the following control methods (check all that apply): _____ constant _____ periodic _____ occasional.
42. The type of budget we developed was (check all that apply): _____ revenue _____ expense _____ capital expenditure.
43. Our expense budget was primarily _____ line-item _____ program; _____ static _____ flexible; _____ incremental _____ zero-based.
44. Our team developed the following financial statements (check all that apply): _____ income _____ balance sheet _____ cash flow.
45. Our team's level of productivity or cost per unit was __________ (outputs [number of products sold] divided by inputs [cost of goods sold plus expenses of $250,000]).
46. Our team focused more on _____ imposed control _____ self-control.
47. Our team _____ did _____ did not use coaching.
48. Our team _____ did _____ did not use discipline.
49. This exercise _____ was _____ was not a time-based competition.
50. Our team product is classified as _____ tangible _____ intangible; _____ made-to-stock _____ made-to-order _____ assembled-to-order; _____ continuous _____ repetitive _____ batch _____ individual process operations; operations were _____ capital-intensive _____ labor-intensive.
51. Our team facility layout for this exercise was _____ product _____ process _____ cellular _____ fixed-position.
52. Our inventory control resulted in _____ no _____ few _____ many raw material returns; _____ no _____ few _____ many work-in-process sold for scrap; _____ no _____ few _____ many finished goods rejected for sale. Overall, our materials requirement planning was _____ effective _____ ineffective and our quality control was _____ effective _____ ineffective.
53. Information _____ was _____ was not very important in this exercise.
54. The type of computer information system that would be most helpful in this exercise is _____ transaction processing _____ management information systems _____ decision support systems.
55. The information network in this exercise included (check all that apply): _____ connecting all employees _____ customers _____ suppliers _____ databases.

Procedure 6 (15–18 minutes)
Procedures 3–5 may be repeated one or more times. However, the customers/suppliers should change roles with team members.

Conclusion
The instructor may lead a class discussion and/or make concluding remarks.

Application (2–4 minutes)
What did I learn from this exericse? How will I use this knowledge in the future?

____

____

____

VIDEOCASE

A Study in Quality: Wainwright

Wainwright Industries, a family-owned supplier to the automotive and aerospace industries, decided to upgrade its quality to remain competitive. To move the company forward, top management used the Baldrige Award criteria as guides to quality improvement. Wainwright emphasized training and empowering employees, customer satisfaction, and continuous improvement based on employee input and involvement. Team rewards replaced individual rewards. The company first focused on employee satisfaction. Satisfied employees would then be better able to respond to customer needs. Key results from quality improvement included lower costs, better safety, and higher profits. Through its efforts, Wainwright won the Baldrige Quality Award in the Small Business classification.

Appendix: How to Research Case Material Using the Internet

There was a time when it was hard to find a nugget of information regarding a company that was being discussed in a case at the end of a chapter or in a textbook. This statement was true up until the mid-1990s. Today there is a whole new science to conducting research to find company material. It is virtually impossible to go anywhere without hearing about the Internet.

The advantage of this in-house, on-line data search is the fact that you reduce the need to visit a physical library. Although is will be necessary to frequently visit a library, home access to the Net allows you to find much more information on business topics without leaving your home or dormitory room.

Assuming you have found an access to the Net, the next question is, "What do you do there?" The following are possibilities: you may go directly to the Web site of the case company or you may use the reference desk, access the Hoover Database, and use the company name as the key topic/word.

Going Directly to the Company's Web Site

You can go directly to the Web site of the company you wish to research. A Web site is a location on the Net that a company has set up to disperse information about its products. Information can be gathered by accessing the World Wide Web on your service provider. For instance, Digital has set up an elaborate Web site which can be found by typing in http://www.digital.com. Pages of company information, from financial information to corporate strategies, are provided.

National services such as America Online (AOL), CompuServe, and Prodigy also provide windows to the Internet where you can once again go directly to a company's Web site (for example, by typing http://www.kodak.com) and acquire company information. *At the ends of the opening and closing cases of each chapter are the Web site addresses of companies that had Web addresses* when the book was published. Other sites may now be available.

Limitation of Web Sites and the Need for at Least Two Sources of Information

The only limitation to a company's Web site is that the information is provided by the company and may not be indicative of what magazines and journals are writing about the company. You should realize that researching the Web site or one journal/magazine (no matter which one) is not enough to validate findings. You need to use at least two sources of information to support your findings. In other words, simply using a Web site is not enough. You need to use jour-

Source: Dr. David C. Kimball, Assistant Professor of Management, Elms College, Chicopee, Massachusetts.

nals/magazines, too. The Internet can also be used, as well as library databases, to find updated information on companies, as discussed next.

Finding Journal/Magazine Company Information on the Internet

The simplest way to gain access to the Internet is to sign up with America Online, CompuServe, Prodigy, or any other national service. These service providers charge about $10.00 a month for five hours of access time. Once online, you enter the reference desk area and, after accessing the Hoover Database, you can start doing word searches for key topics such as "Wal-Mart," "The Metropolitan Museum of Art," or any other business topic related to the case. You can continue your search (this is called surfing) by entering the Marketplace database which is a collection of magazines and journals that each service has contracted to provide. For example, AOL provides the ability to search current and previous issues of *BusinessWeek* for any keyword you desire. This type of database gives you access to complete articles about the company you are researching. Additionally, the information can be as current as last month, last week, yesterday, or today's issue of whichever journal/magazine you are searching on the Net. If a Web site is not listed for an opening case or closing case, you can try to do a journal/magazine search; if it is a large organization, there may be information on it. However, small companies usually do not make the press.

Referencing Internet Material

Finding information on the Net does not allow you to bypass proper bibliography procedures. Referencing material found on the Internet is not quite as straightforward as citing books, journals, and magazines. Databases on the Internet can be found anywhere in cyberspace. Material is only acceptable if you can specifically document its origins as if you were writing a traditional reference. Students must write down:

- The author's name
- Title of the article
- Name of publication
- Date and page numbers

Your instructor will provide you with more details on his or her expectations of how to use Internet material.

Endnotes

Chapter 1

1. Bill Walsh, "Information Please!" *Forbes* (February 1995), Vol. 155, No. 5, p. S19.
2. Timothy Schellhardt, "Managing Your Career." *The Wall Street Journal*, April 20, 1994, p. B1
3. John Byrne, "Belt-Tightening the Smart Way," *Business Week*, Annual 1993, p. 34.
4. Hal Lancaster, "Managing Your Career," *The Wall Street Journal*, October 8, 1994, p. B1.
5. "Diverse Work Teams," *The Wall Street Journal*, June 15, 1993, p. 1,
6. *The Wall Street Journal*, November 14, 1980, p. 33.
7. Ted Pollock, "A Personal File Stimulating Ideas, Little Known Facts and Daily Problem Solvers." *Supervision*. (January 1994), Vol. 55, No. 1, pp. 24–26.
8. Gary Esterling, "How to Refine Management Skills." *Industrial Distribution*, (June 1994), Vol. 8, No. 6, p. 8.
9. Robert Katz, "Skills of an Effective Administrator." *Harvard Business Review*, September/October 1974, pp. 90–102.
10. John Schlegel, "Tips on Leading the Association Effectively." *Association Management*, (January 1995), Vol. 47, No. 1, p. L42.
11. Gene Epstein, "The Participation Equation: Which Plan Makes Workers Work Best?" *Barron's* (December 5, 1994), Vol. 74, No. 49, pp. 48–49.
12. Tom Brown, "Ten Commandments for Business." *Industry Week* (January 9, 1995), Vol. 244, No. 1, p. 27.
13. Andrew Kinder and Ivan Robertson, "Do You have the Personality to be a Leader?" *Leadership & Organizational Development Journal* (January 1994), Vol. 15, No. 1, pp. 3–12.
14. Leonard Marcus, "More Conflict Means More Need for Resolution Skills." *American Medical News* (December 13, 1993), Vol. 36, No. 46, pp. 42–43.
15. Edwin Ghiselli, *Explorations in Management Talent* (Santa Monica, CA: Goodyear Publishing, 1971).
16. Laura Leach, "A Planning Primer for Small Associations." *Association Management* (April 1994), Vol. 46, No. 4, pp. 83–87.
17. W. James Ludlow, "The Road to Wealth." *Business Credit* (March 1994), Vol. 96, No: 3, pp. 10–11.
18. Laura Leach, "A Planning Primer for Small Associations." *Association Management* (April 1994), Vol. 46, No. 4, pp. 83–87.
19. Micheal Verespes, "To Lead or not to Lead?" *Industry Week* (January 9, 1995), Vol. 244, No. 1, pp. 17–18.
20. Pete Bissonette, *News Letter* (Wayzata, MN: Learning Strategies Corporation, February 1995), p. 1.
21. W. James Ludlow, "The Road to Wealth." *Business Credit* (March 1994), Vol. 96, No. 3, pp. 10–11.
22. Lance Kurke and Howard Aldrich, "Mintzberg Was Right!: A Replication and Extension of *The Nature of Managerial Work*." *Management Science*, 1983, Vol. 29, pp. 975–984.
23. Cynthia Pavett and Alan Lau, "Managerial Work: The Influence of Hierarchical Level and Functional Specialty." *Academy of Management Journal*, 1983, Vol. 26, pp. 170–177.
24. Colin Hales, "What Do Managers Do? A Critical Review of the Evidence." *Journal of Management Studies*, 1986 Vol. 23, pp. 88–115.
25. Henry Mintzberg, *The Nature of Managerial Work* (New York: Harper & Row, 1973).
26. Barrie Gibbs, "The Effect of Environment and Technology on Management Roles." *Journal of Management* (Fall 1994), Vol. 20, No. 3, p. 581.
27. "Automaker Plans More Cuts in Its Management Levels." *The Wall Street Journal*, April 6, 1994, p. B4.
28. Gerald d'Amboise and Marie Muldowney, "Management Theory for Small Business: Attempts and Requirements." *Academy of Management Review*, April 1988, pp. 226–240.
29. Joseph Paolillo, "The Manager's Self-Assessment of Managerial Roles: Small vs. Large Firms." *American Journal of Small Business*, January/March 1984, pp. 61–62.
30. Martha Mangelsdorf, "Big vs. Small," *INC.*, May 1989, p. 22.
31. Hal G. Rainey, "Public Management: Recent Research on the Political Context and Managerial Roles, Structures, and Behaviors." *Journal of Management*, June 1989, pp. 229–250.
32. Frederick Winslow Taylor, *Principles of Scientific Management* (New York: Harper and Brothers, 1911).
33. Henri Fayol, *General and Industrial Management*, translated by J.A. Conbrough (Geneva: International Management Institute, 1929).
34. Fritz Roethlisberger and William Dickson, *Management and the Worker* (Boston: Harvard University Press, 1939).
35. Abraham Maslow, *Motivation and Personality*, 2nd ed. (New York: Harper & Row, 1970).
36. Douglas McGregor, *The Human Side of Enterprise* (New York: McGraw-Hill, 1960).
37. Russell Ackoff, *Creating the Corporate Future* (New York: Wiley, 1981).
38. Harold Koontz, "The Management Theory Jungle Revisited." *Academy of Management Review* (April 1980), Vol. 5, p. 175.
39. Daniel Katz and Robert Khan, *The Social Psychology of Organizations*, 2nd ed. (New York: Wiley, 1978)
40. E. L. Trist and K. W. Bamforth, "Some Social and Psychological Consequences of the Long Wall Method of Coal Getting." *Human Relations*, 1951, Vol. 4, pp. 3–38. F. E. Emery and E. I. Trist, *Socio-Technical Systems, Vol. 2 of Management Science: Methods and Techniques* (London: Pergamon, 1960).
41. Tom Burns and George Stalker, *The Management of Innovation* (London: Tavistock, 1961).
42. Laurie Epting, Sandra Glover, and Suzan Boyd, "Managing Diversity." *Health Care Supervisor* (June 1994), Vol. 12, No. 4, pp. 73–83.
43. Anonymous, "Competitive Advantage Through Managing Diversity." *Franchising World* (January/February 1994), Vol. 26, Iss.: 1, p. 35.
44. Raymond Pomerleau, "A Desideratum for Managing the Diverse Workplace." *Review of Public Personnel Administration* (Winter 1994), Vol. 14, No. 1, pp. 85–100
45. Dean Elmuti, "Managing Diversity in the Workplace: An Immense Challenge." *Industrial Management* (July/August 1993), Vol. 35, No. 4, pp. 19–22.
46. Christopher Washington, "Diversity Without Performance Is a Ticket to Mediocrity: A Rejoinder." *Human Resource Development Quarterly* (Fall 1993), Vol. 4, No. 3, pp. 291–293.
47. Anonymous, "Mixed Blessings." *Management Today*, December 1993, pp. 89–90.
48. Shari Caudron, "Successful Companies Realize That Diversity Is a Long-Term Process,

Not a Program." *Personnel Journal* (April 1993), Vol. 72, No. 4, pp. 54–55.
49. Geoffrey Soutar, Margaret McNeil, and Caron Molster, "The Impact of the Work Environment on Ethical Decision Making: Some Australian Evidence." *Journal of Business Ethics* (May 1994), Vol. 13, No. 5, pp. 327–339.
50. Patrick Flanagan, "The Rules of Purchasing Are Changing." *Management Review* (March 1994), Vol. 83, No. 3, pp. 28–32.
51. Joe Batten, "A Total Quality Culture." *Management Review* (May 1994), Vol. 83, No. 5, p. 61.
52. Gary Vasilash, "Don't Solve Problems—Work on Solutions." *Production* (May 1994), Vol. 106, No. 5, pp. 64–65.
53. Edward Lawler, *High Involvement Management* (San Francisco: Jossey-Bass, 1991).
54. Thomas Tang, Peggy Tollison, and Harold Whiteside, "Differences Between Active and Inactive Quality Circles in Attendance and Performance." *Public Personnel Management* (Winter 1993), Vol. 22, No. 4, pp. 579–590.
55. Janet Snieze, "Group Decision Making." *Organizational Behavior & Human Decision Process* (June 1992), Vol. 52, No. 1, pp. 124–155.
56. James Davis, "Some Compelling Intuitions about Group Consensus." *Organizational Behavior & Human Decision Process* (June 1992), Vol. 52, No. 1, pp. 3–38.
57. Kathryn Hegar and Robert N. Lussier, *Study Guide with Experiential Exercises* to accompany *Management: Concepts and Practices* (3rd ed.). (Boston: Allyn and Bacon, 1986), pp. 257–260 and 264–266. Adapted with permission of the publisher.
58. Ken Blanchard, "The Blanchard Management Report." *Manage* (October 1993), Vol. 45, No. 2, p. 25.
59. Kathryn Hegar and Robert N. Lussier, *Study Guide with Experiential Exercises* to accompany *Management: Concepts and Practices* (3rd ed.). (Boston: Allyn and Bacon, 1986), pp. 15–16. Adapted with permission of the publisher.

Chapter 2

1. Material throughout Chapter 2 is taken from the Federal Express Information Packet available to anyone upon request by calling 901-395-3460.
2. "Managers View." *The Wall Street Journal*, December 13, 1994, p. 1.
3. "Give Me a Voice." *The Wall Street Journal*, December 6, 1994, p. 1.
4. "Dr. W. Edwards Deming 1988/1989 Winner of Dow Jones Award." *ESB*, Spring 1989, p. 3.
5. "What We Have Here Is a Failure by Employer to Communicate." *The Wall Street Journal*, January 30, 1990, p. 1.
6. Russell Ackoff, *Creating the Corporate Future* (New York: Wiley, 1981).
7. Greg Bounds, Greg Dobbins, and Oscar Fowler, *Management: A Total Quality Perspective* (Cincinnati, OH: South-Western, 1995)
8. Taken from Juran's work in Brian Joiner, *Fourth Generation Management* (New York: McGraw-Hill, 1994), pp. 33–34.
9. "What Goes Around Comes Around." *News from . . . Cally Curtis*, Vol. 8, No. 1, p. 3. [no year listed on pub.]
10. "Federal Express." *The Wall Street Journal*, April 12, 1995, p. 1.
11. "RJR Nabisco." *The Wall Street Journal*, May 8, 1995, p. 1.
12. Peter Drucker, "Planning for Uncertainty." *The Wall Street Journal*, July 22, 1992, p. A14.
13. Jim Calton, "Sega Leaps Ahead by Shipping New Player Early." *The Wall Street Journal*, May 11, 1995, p. B1.
14. "Sony Sets Unexpectedly Low Price." *The Wall Street Journal*, May 12, 1995, p. 1.
15. "Microsoft Will Announce." *The Wall Street Journal*, April 24, 1995, p. 1.
16. Joann Lublin, "Disabilities Act Will Compel Businesses to Change Many Employment Practices." *The Wall Street Journal*, July 7, 1992, p. B1.
17. "The Accent's on Competition." *Inc.* (May 1994), Vol. 16, Iss. 5, p. 3.
18. Russell Ackoff, *Redesigning the Future* (New York: Wiley, 1974), pp. 22–31.
19. Eileen Davis, "Global Trotting in the Information Age." *Management Review* (April 1995), Vol. 84, Iss. 4, p. 17.
20. Peter Cherry, "Making Globalization Work." *Design News* (December 19, 1994), Vol. 49, Iss. 24, p. 140.
21. "The Discreet Charm of the Multicultural Multinational." *The Economist* (July 30, 1994), Vol. 332, Iss. 7874, p. 57.
22. "Fortune's Global 500." *Fortune* (July 26, 1993), Vol. 128, Iss. 2, p. 226.
23. Mark Hordes, J. Anthony Clancy, and Julie Baddaley, "A Primer for Global Start-ups." *The Academy of Management Executives* (May 1995), Vol. IX, Iss. 2, pp. 7–11.
24. Robert Lussier, Robert Baeder, and Joel Corman, "Measuring Global Practices: Global Strategic Planning Through Company Situational Analysis." *Business Horizons* (September-October 1994), Vol. 37, Iss. 5, p. 56.
25. "Global Companies Reexamine Corporate Culture." *Personnel Journal* (August 1994), Vol. 73, Iss. 8, p. S12.
26. Stefan Wills and Kevin Barham, "Being an International Manager." *European Management Journal* (March 1994), Vol. 12, Iss. 1, pp. 49–58.
27. "Multinationals Can Aid Some Foreign Workers." *The Wall Street Journal*, April 24, 1995.
28. Chetan Sankar, William Boulton, Nancy Davidson, and Charles Snyder, with Richard Ussert, "Building a World-Class Alliance: The Universal Card-TSYS Case." *The Academy of Management Executives* (May 1995), Vol. IX, Iss. 2, pp. 20–29.
29. J. D. Power, "Car Companies Going Global." *Knight-Ridder/Tribune Business News*, August 19, 1993, p. 9.
30. Robert Lussier, Robert Baeder, and Joel Corman, "Measuring Global Practices: Global Strategic Planning Through Company Situational Analysis." *Business Horizons* (September/October 1994), Vol. 37, Iss. 5, pp. 56–63.
31. Kerry Hannon, "Career Guide 1995." *U.S. News & World Report* (October 31, 1994), Vol. 117, Iss. 17, p. 94.
32. Tim Stevens, "Managing Across Boundaries." *Industry Week* (March 6, 1995), Vol. 244, Iss. 5, p. 24.
33. Joann Lublin, "Firms Ship Unit Headquarters Abroad." *The Wall Street Journal*, December 1992, p. B1.
34. "Global Dinner." *The Wall Street Journal*, April 27, 1995, p. 1.
35. Stephenie Overman, "Going Global." *HRMagazine* (September 1993), Vol. 38, Iss. 9, p. 47.
36. Peter Druker, "The New World According to Drucker." *Business Month* (May 1989), Vol. 133, Iss. 5, pp. 50–56.
37. Joel Corman, Robert N. Lussier, and Robert Baeder, "Global Strategies for the Future: Large vs. Small Business," *Journal of Business Strategies* (Fall 1991), Vol. 8, Iss. 2, pp. 86–93.
38. Kate Brown, "Using Role Play to Integrate Ethics into the Business Curriculum," *Journal of Business Ethics* (February 1994), Vol. 13, Iss. 2, p. 105.
39. Catherine Vannace-Small, "Battling International Bribery." *OECD Observer* (February-March 1995), Iss. 192, p. 16.
40. Robert Armstrong and Jill Sweeney, "Industry Type, Culture, Mode of Entry and Perceptions of International Marketing Ethics." *Journal of Business Ethics* (October 1994), Vol. 13, Iss. 10, p. 775.
41. John Hallaq and Kirk Steinhorst, "Business Intelligence Methods—How Ethical." *Journal of Business Ethics* (October 1994), Vol. 13, Iss. 10, p. 787.
42. Donna Holmquist, "Ethics—How Important Is It in Today's Office?" *Personnel Management* (Winter 1993), Vol. 22, Iss. 4, pp. 537–544.
43. "The '90s May Tame the Savage M.B.A." *The Wall Street Journal*, June 14, 1991, p. B1.
44. "Hi-Tech Interviews." *The Wall Street Journal*, March 22, 1994, p. 1
45. Patrick Primeaux and John Stieber, "Profit Maximation: The Ethical Mandate of Business." *Journal of Business Ethics* (April 1994), Vol. 13, Iss. 4, pp. 287–294.

46. Barry Castro, "Business Ethics: Know Ourselves." *Business Ethics Quarterly* (April 1994), Vol. 4, Iss. 2, p. 181.
47. "More Big Businesses Set Up Ethics Offices," *The Wall Street Journal*, May 10, 1993, p. B1
48. Roy Simerly, "Corporate Social Performance and Firms' Financial Performance: An Alternative Perspective." *Psychological Reports* (December 1994), Vol. 75, Iss. 3, pp. 1091–1114.
49. Wallace Davidson, Dan Worrell, and Chun Lee, "Stock Market Reactions to Announced Corporate Illegalities." *Journal of Business Ethics* (December 1994), Vol. 13, Iss. 12, pp. 979–988.
50. Robert Gildea, "Consumer Survey Confirms Corporate Social Action Affects Buying Decisions." *Public Relations Quarterly* (Winter 1994), Vol. 39, Iss. 4, pp. 20–21.
51. Dwight Lee and Richard McKenzie, "Corporate Failure as a Means to Corporate Responsibility." *Journal of Business Ethics* (December 1994), Vol. 13, Iss. 12, pp. 969–979.
52. S. Prakesh Sethi, "Conversion of a Corporate CEO into a Public Persona." *Business and Society Review* (Fall 1994), Iss. 91, pp. 42–45.
53. Max Clarkson, "A Stakeholder Framework for Analyzing and Evaluating Corporate Social Performance." *Academy of Management Review* (January 1995), Vol. 20, Iss. 1, pp. 92–117.
54. "Productivity Perils." *The Wall Street Journal*, March 9, 1993, p. 1.
55. "Profits Tied to Revamps Can Prove to Be Costly Down the Road." *The Wall Street Journal*, April 6, 1995, p. 1.
56. James Martin, "Remember the Merging '80s?" *America* (December 31, 1994), Vol. 171, Iss. 20, pp. 6–8.
57. Michael Hammer and James Champy, "Re-Engineering Authors Reconsider Re-Engineering." *The Wall Street Journal*, January 17, 1995, p. B1.
58. Michael Hammer and James Champy, "Managers Beware: You're Not Ready for Tomorrow's Job." *The Wall Street Journal*, January 24, 1995 p. B1.
59. Berry William, "HRIS Can Improve Performance, Empower and Motivate Knowledge Workers." *Employment Relations Today* (Autumn 1993), Vol. 20, Iss. 3, pp. 297–303.
60. Information taken from Thomas Bateman and Carl Zeithaml, *Management: Functions & Strategy* (Burr Ridge, IL: Irwin, 1993), p. 172.

Chapter 3

1. Digital Equipment Corporation data throughout the chapter was supplied by Digital, and Thomas Bateman and Carl Zeithaml, *Management*, 2nd ed. (Burr Ridge, IL: Irwin, 1993), p. 376.
2. Christopher Washington, "Diversity Without Performance Is a Ticket to Mediocrity: A Rejoinder." *Human Resource Development Quarterly* (Fall 1993), Vol. 4, Iss. 3, pp. 291–293.
3. "Mixed Blessings," *Management Today*, December 1993, pp. 89–90.
4. Shari Caudron, "Successful Companies Realize That Diversity Is a Long-Term Process, Not a Program." *Personnel Journal* (April 1993), Vol. 72, Iss. 4, pp. 54–55.
5. Farrell Bloch, "Affirmative Action Hasn't Helped Blacks." *The Wall Street Journal*, March 1, 1995, p. A14.
6. Leon Wynter, "Diversity Is Often All Talk, No Affirmative Action." *The Wall Street Journal*, December 21, 1994, p. B1.
7. Leon Wynter, "Education Is the Best Defense of Affirmative Action." *The Wall Street Journal*, April 26, 1995, p. B1.
8. Ibid.
9. Leon Wynter, "Diversity Is Often All Talk, No Affirmative Action." *The Wall Street Journal*, December 21, 1994, p. B1.
10. "Global Companies Reexamine Corporate Culture." *Personnel Journal* (August 1994), Vol. 73, Iss. 8, p. S12.
11. "Competitive Advantage Through Managing Diversity." *Franchising World* (January/February 1994), Vol. 26, Iss. 1, p. 35.
12. Eileen Davis, "Global Trotting in the Information Age." *Management Review* (April 1995), Vol. 84, Iss. 4, p. 17.
13. Raymond Pomerleau, "A Desideratum for Managing the Diverse Workplace." *Review of Public Personnel Administration* (Winter 1994), Vol. 14, Iss. 1, pp. 85–100.
14. William Johnson and Arnold Packer, "Executive Summary." *Workforce 2000: Work and Workers for the Twenty-First Century* (Indianapolis: Hudson Institute, June 1987), pp. xii–xiv.
15. Mailyn Loder and Judy Rosner, *Workforce America!* (Burr Ridge, IL: Business One-Irwin, 1991).
16. "Two-Income Marriages Are Now the Norm." *The Wall Street Journal*, June 13, 1994, p. B1.
17. "Sex Still Shapes Sharing of Chores." *The Wall Street Journal*, December 11, 1991, p. B1.
18. "Three Decades After the Equal Pay Act, Women's Wages Remain Far from Parity." *The Wall Street Journal*, June 9, 1993, p. B1.
19. Nancy Adler, "Women Managers in a Global Economy." *Training & Development* (April 1994), Vol. 48, Iss. 4, pp. 22–25.
20. "Women Hold." *The Wall Street Journal*, July 10, 1990, p. B1.
21. Nancy Adler, "Women Managers in a Global Economy." *Training & Development* (April 1994), Vol. 48, Iss. 4, pp. 22–25.
22. Mailyn Loder and Judy Rosner, *Workforce America!* (Burr Ridge, IL: Business One-Irwin, 1991).
23. "Middle-Aged Growth Sweeps the States." *The Wall Street Journal*, March 10, 1995, p. B1.
24. "Fired Up." *The Wall Street Journal*, April 25, 1995, p. 1.
25. Mailyn Loder and Judy Rosner, *Workforce America!* (Burr Ridge, IL: Business One-Irwin, 1991).
26. "Disabilities Act Will Compel Businesses to Change Many Employment Practices." *The Wall Street Journal*, July 7, 1992, p. B1.
27. "U.S. Agency Issues Set of Definitions on the Disabled." *The Wall Street Journal*, March 16, 1995, p. B10.
28. "Most Disabled People Aren't Working." *The Wall Street Journal*, June 7, 1994, p. 1.
29. "The Handicapped Worker." *The Wall Street Journal*, May 19, 1987, p. 1.
30. "Boss May Be Personally Liable If Firing Violates Disability Law." *The Wall Street Journal*, May 2, 1995, p. B1.
31. Mailyn Loder and Judy Rosner, *Workforce America!* (Burr Ridge, IL: Business One-Irwin, 1991).
32. Thomas Bateman and Carl Zeithaml, *Management*, 2nd ed. (Burr Ridge, IL: Irwin, 1993), pp. 385–387; Ann Morrison, *The New Leaders: Guidelines on Leadership Diversity in America* (San Francisco: Jossey-Bass, 1992), pp. 18–27.
33. "English-Only Rules." *The Wall Street Journal*, April 4, 1995, p. 1.
34. Lisa Harrington, "Why Managing Diversity Is So Important." *Distribution* (November 1993), Vol. 92, Iss. 11, pp. 88–92.
35. Lisa Jenner, "Diversity Management: What Does It Mean?" *HR Focus* (January 1994), Vol. 7, Iss. 1, p. 11.
36. Ibid.
37. "Nonprofits May Be Model." *The Wall Street Journal*, April 20, 1995, p. 1
38. "In Re-Engineering, What Really Matters Are Workers' Lives." *The Wall Street Journal*, March 1, 1995, p. B1
39. "Diversity Is Up." *The Wall Street Journal*, March 21, 1995, p. 1.
40. Delvin Benjamin, "Stereotypes: Where Do They Come From?" *LIMRA's MarketFacts* (May/June 1994), Vol. 13, Iss. 3, pp. 30–31.
41. Shari Caudron, "Successful Companies Realize That Diversity Is a Long-Term Process, Not a Program." *Personnel Journal* (April 1993), Vol. 72, Iss. 4, pp. 54–55.
42. Ibid.
43. Catherine Ellis and Jeffrey Sonnenfeld, "Diverse Approaches to Managing Diversity." *Human Resource Management* (Spring 1994), Vol. 33, Iss. 1, pp. 79–109.
44. "Re-Engineering Authors Reconsider Re-Engineering." *The Wall Street Journal*, January 17, 1995, p. B1.

45. Robin Tierney, "Diversity." *World Trade* (December 1993), Vol. 6, Iss. 11, pp. 22–25.
46. "Putting on a Japanese Face." *International Business* (February 1994), Vol. 7, Iss. 2, p. 90.
47. Bruno Dufour, "Dealing with Diversity: Management Education in Europe." *Selections* (Winter 1994), Vol. 10, Iss. 2, pp. 7–15.
48. Michael Johnson, "Doing Le Business." *Management Training*, February 1992, pp. 62–65.
49. Robin Tierney, "Diversity." *World Trade* (December 1993), Vol. 6, Iss. 11, pp. 22–25.
50. Michael Johnson, "Doing Le Business," *Management Training*, February 1992, pp. 62–65.
51. "Global Companies Reexamine Corporate Culture." *Personnel Journal* (August 1994), Vol. 73, Iss. 8, p. S12.
52. Robert N. Lussier, *Supervision: A Skill-Building Approach* (2nd ed.). (Chicago: Richard D. Irwin, Inc., 1994), pp. 551–552. Adapted with permission of the publisher.

Chapter 4

1. Information provided by Coca-Cola Company, *Financial Topics, Facts, Figures and Features*, and *1994 Annual Report*
2. Hal Lancaster, "Managing Your Career." *The Wall Street Journal*, January 3, 1995, p. B1.
3. Peggy Wallace, "LAN Training: Finding the Right Fit." *InfoWorld (April 18, 1994), Vol. 16, Iss. 16, pp. 67–70.*
4. Charles Johnson, "A Free Market View of Business Ethics." *Supervision* (May 1994), Vol. 55, Iss. 5, pp. 14–17.
5. Hillel Einhorn and Robin Hogarth, "Decision Making: Going Forward in Reverse." *Harvard Business Review*, January-February 1987, p. 66.
6. Michael Pacanowsky, "Team Tools for Wicked Problems." *Organizational Dynamics* (Winter 1995), Vol. 23, Iss. 3, pp. 36–152.
7. David Budescu, Ramzl Suleiman, and Amnon Rapoport, "Positional Order and Group Size Effects in Resource Dilemmas with Uncertainty." *Organizational Behavior & Human Decision Process* (March 1995), Vol. 61, Iss. 3, pp. 225–239.
8. Raymond McLeod, Jack Jones, and Carol Saunders, "The Difficulty in Solving Strategic Problems: The Experiences of Three CIOs." *Business Horizons* (January-February 1995), Vol. 38, Iss. 28, pp. 2839.
9. William Bulkeley and Don Clark, "Lotus Has Everything to Lose—or Gain," and Bart Ziegler, "Will Buying a Software Star Make IBM One?" *The Wall Street Journal*, June 7, 1995, p. B1.
10. "Lotus Agreed." *The Wall Street Journal*, June 12, 1995, p. 1.
11. Peter Meyer, "A Surprisingly Simple Way to Make Better Decisions." *Executive Female* (March-April 1995), Vol. 18, Iss. 2, pp. 13–15.
12. Anne O'Leary-Kelly, Joseph Martocchio, and Dwight Frink." *Academy of Management Journal* (October 1994), Vol. 37, Iss. 5, pp. 1285–1292.
13. Christer Carlsson and Robert Fuller, "Multiple Criteria Decision Making: The Case for Interdependence." *Computers & Operations Research* (March 1995), Vol. 22, Iss. 3, pp 251–261.
14. Allen Ward, Jeffrey Liker, John Cristiano, and Durward Sobeck, "The Second Toyota Paradox: How Delaying Decisions Can Make Better Cars Faster." *Sloan Management Review* (Spring 1995), Vol. 36, Iss. 3, pp. 43-62.
15. Lawrence Ladin, "Selling Innovation: Tips for Commercial Success." *The Wall Street Journal*, March 20, 1995, A14.
16. James Higgins, "Creating Creativity." *Training & Development* (November 1994), Vol. 48, Iss. 11, pp. 11–16.
17. Betty Morris and Peter Waldman, "The Death of Premier." *The Wall Street Journal*, March 10, 1989, p, B14
18. "How Pitney Bowes Establishes Self-Directed Work Teams." *Modern Materials Handling*, February 1993, pp. 58–59.
19. Roberta Bhasin, "What to Do When They Don't Trust You." *Pulp & Paper* (April 1995), Vol. 69, Iss. 4, pp. 30–40.
20. Ernst Diehl and John Sterman, "Effects of Feedback Complexity on Dyamic Decision Making." *Organizational Behavior & Human Decision Processes* (May 1995), Vol. 62, Iss. 2, pp. 198–216.
21. Scott Highhouse and Karen Bottrill, "The Influence of Social (mis) Information on Memory for Behavior in an Employment Interview." *Organizational Behavior & Human Decision Process* (May 1995), Vol. 62, Iss. 2, pp. 220–230.
22. Anton Kuhberger, "The Framing of Decision: A New Look at Old Problems." *Organizational Behavior & Human Decision Processes* (May 1995), Vol. 62, Iss. 2, pp. 230–241.
23. Venessa Houlder, "Back to the Future." *The Financial Times*, February 7, 1995, pp. 15–16.
24. Kenneth MacCrimmon and Christian Wagner, "Stimulating Ideas Through Creativity Software." *Management Science* (November 1994), Vol. 10, Iss. 11, pp. 1514–1533.
25. Christopher Neck and Charles Manz, "From Groupthink to Teamthink: Toward the Creation of Constructive Thought Patterns in Self-Managing Teams." *Human Relations* (August 1994), Vol. 47, Iss. 8, pp. 929–954.
26. Floyd Hurt, "Better Brainstorming." *Training & Development* (November 1994), Vol. 48, Iss. 11, pp. 57–60.
27. Elizabeth Mannix, "Orgainizations as Resources Dilemmas: The Effect of Power Balance on Coalition Formation in Small Groups." *Organizational Behavior & Decision Processes* (June 1993), Vol. 55, Iss. 1, pp. 1–22.
28. "How Pitney Bowes Establishes Self-Directed Work Teams." *Modern Materials Handling*, February 1993, pp. 58–59.
29. Gail Kay, "Effective Meetings Through Electronic Brainstorming." *Management Quarterly* (Winter 1994), Vol. 35, Iss. 4, pp. 15–27.
30. Michael Wolfe, "A Theoretical Justification for Japanese Nemawashi/Rngi Group Decision Making and an Implementation." *Decision Support Systems* (April 1992), Vol. 8, Iss. 2, pp. 125–140.
31. Jeffrey Hornsby, Brian Smith, and Jatinder Gupta, "The Impact of Decision-Making Methodology on Job Evaluation Outcomes: A Look at Three Consensus Approaches." *Group & Organizational Management* (March 1994), Vol. 19, Iss. 1, pp. 112–128.
32. Peter Meyer, "A Surprisingly Simple Way to Make Better Decisions." *Executive Female* (March-April 1995), Vol. 18, Iss. 2, pp. 13–15.
33. Birger Wernerfelt, "A Rational Reconstruction of the Compromise Effect: Using Market Data to Infer Utilities." *Journal of Consumer Research* (March 1995), Vol. 21, Iss. 4, pp. 627–634.
34. Christopher Neck and Charles Manz, "From Groupthink to Teamthink: Toward the Creation of Constructive Thought Patterns in Self-Managing Teams." *Human Relations* (August 1994), Vol. 47, Iss. 8, pp. 929–954.
35. Anton Kuhberger, "The Framing of Decision: A New Look at Old Problems." *Organizational Behavior & Human Decision Processes* (May 1995), Vol. 62, Iss. 2, pp. 230–241.
36. Chip Heath and Rich Gonzalez, "Interaction with Others Increases Decision Confidence But Not Decision Quality: Evidence Against Information Collection Views of Interactive Decision Making." *Organizational Behavior & Human Decision Processes* (March 1995), Vol. 61, Iss. 3, pp. 305–327.
37. Kathryn Hegar and Robert Lussier, *Study Guide with Experiential Exercises* to accompany *Management: Concepts and Practices* (3rd ed.) (Boston: Allyn and Bacon, 1986), pp. 104–106 and 110. Adapted with permission of the publisher.

Chapter 5

1. The information on Peter Clark came from a personal interview with the author. Information on Pennzoil and Jiffy Lube International was taken from the 1994 annual report.
2. Alecia Swasy, "Diaper's Failure Shows How Poor Plans, Unexpected Woes Can Kill New

Products." *The Wall Street Journal,* October 9, 1990, p. B1.
3. Ibid.
4. Louise Lee, "A Company Failing from Too Much Success." *The Wall Street Journal,* March 17, 1995, p. B1.
5. Dave Martin, "It's Time to Bridge the Gap Between Levels." *Mediaweek,* November 26, 1992, pp. 12–13.
6. Sharon Dorn and Debora Perrone, "Charting a Course for Success." *Fund Raising Management* (January 1995), Vol. 25, Iss. 1, pp. 30–34.
7. Jo Wright, "Vision and Positive Image." *The Public Manager: The New Bureaucrat* (Winter 1994), Vol. 23, Iss. 4, pp. 55–57.
8. Gavin Chalcraft, "Like All Good Things, Strategic Planning Takes a Little Time." *Brandweek,* February 20, 1995, pp. 17–18.
9. "Taking Charge of Your Destiny: The New Age of Enterprise Computing." *Chief Executive,* November-December 1994, pp. S2–6.
10. Abble Griffin, Greg Gleason, Rich Pries, and Dave Shevenaugh, "Best Practice for Customer Satisfaction in Manufacturing Firms." *Sloan Management Review* (Winter 1995), Vol. 36, Iss. 2, pp. 87–99.
11. Alistair Davidson and Sharon Weller-Cody, "Software Tools for the Strategic Manager." *Planning Review* (March-April 1995), Vol. 23, Iss. 2, pp. 32–36.
12. Gavin Chalcraft, "Like All Good Things, Strategic Planning Takes a Little Time." *Brandweek,* February 20, 1995, pp. 17–18.
13. David Baron, "Integrated Strategy: Market and Nonmarket Components." *California Management Review* (Winter 1995), Vol. 37, Iss. 2, pp. 47–66.
14. Sharon Dorn and Debora Perrone, "Charting a Course for Success." *Fund Raising Management* (January 1995), Vol. 25, Iss. 1, pp. 30–34.
15. Michael Porter, "How Competitive Forces Shape Strategy." *Harvard Business Review* (March-April 1979), Vol. 57, Iss. 2, pp. 137–145.
16. "SWOT or go under." *The Economist,* Vol. 327, Iss. 7810, pp. 35–37.
17. Jon Berry, "Getting Naked with Wal-Mart: Inside the SWOT Papers." *Brandweek,* March 8, 1993, pp. 12–13.
18. Michael Hitt, Beverly Tyler, Camilla Hardee, and Daewoo Park, "Understanding Strategic Intent in the Global Marketplace." *The Academy of Management Executives* (May 1995), Vol. IX, Iss. 4, pp. 12–19.
19. Gavin Chalcraft, "Like All Good Things, Strategic Planning Takes a Little Time." *Brandweek,* February 20, 1995, pp. 17–18.
20. Stephen Smith, "Innovation and Market Strategy in Italian Industrial Cooperatives." *Journal of Economic Behavior & Organization* (May 1994), Vol. 23, Iss. 3, pp. 303–321.
21. Jeffrey Pfeffer, "Producing Sustainable Competitive Advantage Through the Effective Management of People." *The Academy of Management Executives* (February 1995), Vol. IX, Iss. 1, pp. 55–68.
22. Shelby Hunt and Robert Morgan, "The Comparative Advantage Theory of Competition." *Journal of Marketing* (April 1995), Vol. 59, Iss. 2, pp. 1–16.
23. "Doughty Sets Up CAB Show with Woodward." *Marketing,* May 19, 1994, p. 1.
24. Beverly Geber, "An Interview with C. K. Prahalad." *Training* (November 1994), Vol. 31, Iss. 11, pp. 33–39.
25. "Meals on Wheels." *The Wall Street Journal,* May 25, 1995, p. 1.
26. Ann Wiley, "A Target That Beckons." *Technical Communication* (August 1994), Vol. 41, Iss. 3, pp. 532–537.
27. Michael Ames, "Rethinking the Business Plan Paradigm: Building the Gap Between Plans and Plan Execution." *Journal of Small Business Strategy* (Spring 1994), Vol. 5, Iss. 1, pp. 69–76.
28. Ibid.
29. Jon Berry, "Getting Naked with Wal-Mart: Inside the SWOT Papers." *Brandweek,* March 8, 1993, pp. 12–13.
30. Ibid.
31. "Paper Chased." *The Wall Street Journal,* April 9, 1992, p. 1
32. Jane Bird, "Born to Float." *Management Today,* October 1994, pp. 90–93.
33. "GTE Is Negotiating." *The Wall Street Journal,* January 13, 1995, p. 1.
34. "Re-Engineering's Buzz May Fuzz Results." *The Wall Street Journal,* June 30, 1994, p. 1.
35. Robert Rodgers and John Hunter, "The Discard of Study Evidence by Literature Reviewers." *Journal of Applied Behavioral Science* (September 1994), Vol. 30, Iss. 3, pp. 329–346.
36. Brenda Mullins and Bill Mullins, "Coaching Winners." *Canadian Insurance* (January 1994), Vol. 99, Iss. 1, p. 34.
37. "ITT's Board." *The Wall Street Journal,* May 10, 1995, p. 1.
38. "James River Said." *The Wall Street Journal,* March 30, 1995, p. 1.
39. "Sears Plans." *The Wall Street Journal,* March 23, 1995, p. 1
40. "Strategic Alliances." *The Wall Street Journal,* April 20, 1995, p. 1.
41. "Two Makers." *The Wall Street Journal,* May 23, 1995, p. 1.
42. "First Data." *The Wall Street Journal,* June 14, 1995, p. 1.
43. "Crown Cork & Seal." *The Wall Street Journal,* May 23, 1995, p. 1.
44. "Maytag Agreed to Sell." *The Wall Street Journal,* May 31, 1995, p. 1.
45. Marcus Alexander, Andrew Campbell, and Michael Goold, "A New Model for Reforming the Planning Review Process." *Planning Review* (January/February 1995), Vol. 23, Iss. 1.
46. Michael Porter, *Competitive Strategy: Techniques for Analyzing Industries and Competitors* (New York: The Free Press, 1980).
47. Jim Carlton, "Apple's Choice: Preserve Profits or Cut Prices." The *Wall Street Journal,* February 22, 1994, p. B1.
48. Alan Meekings, John Dransfield, and Jules Goddard. "Implementing Strategic Intent: The Power of an Effective Business Management Process." *Business Strategy Review* (Winter 1994), Vol. 5, Iss. 4, pp. 17–32.
49. Johny Johansson and George Yip, "Exploiting Globalization Potential: U.S. and Japanese Strategies." *Strategic Management Journal* (October 1994), Vol. 15, Iss. 8, pp. 579–603.
50. Suresh Kotha, Roger Dunbar, and Allen Bird, "Strategic Action Generation: A Comparison of Emphasis Placed on Generic Competitive Methods by U.S. and Japanese Managers." *Strategic Management Journal* (March 1995), Vol. 16, Iss. 3, pp. 195–221.
51. Alan Singer, "Strategy as Moral Philosophy." *Strategic Management Journal* (March 1994), Vol. 15, Iss. 3, pp. 191–204.
52. Larue Tone Hosmer, "Strategic Planning as If Ethics Mattered." *Strategic Management Journal* (Summer 1994), Vol. 15, Iss. Special, pp. 17–35.
53. Roy Simerly and Anisya Thomas, "Strategic Orientation and Corporate Social Performance." *Journal of Business Strategies* (Fall 1994), Vol. 11, Iss. 2, pp. 113–123.
54. Thomas Powell, "Total Quality Management as a Competitive Advantage." *Strategic Management Journal* (January 1995), Vol. 16, Iss. 1, pp. 15–38.
55. Daniel Leemon, "Marketing's Core Role in Strategic Reengineering." *Planning Review* (March/April 1995), Vol. 23, Iss. 2, pp. 8–15.
56. Barbara Ettorre, "A Strategy Session with C. K. Prahalad." *Management Review* (April 1995), Vol. 84, Iss. 4, pp. 50–53.
57. "Taking Charge of Your Destiny: The New Age of Enterprise Computing." *Chief Executive* (November-December 1994), Iss. 99, pp. S2–6.
58. Robert N. Lussier, "A Nonfinancial Business Success Versus Failure Prediction Model for Young Firms." *Journal of Small Business Management* (January 1995), Vol. 33, Iss. 1, pp. 8–20.
59. Joel Corman, Robert Lussier, and Robert Baeder, "Global Strategies for the Future: Large vs. Small Business." *Journal of Business Strategies* (Fall 1991), Vol. 8, Iss. 2, pp. 86–93.
60. Philip Olson and Donald Bokor, "Strategy Process-Content Interaction: Effects on Growth Performance in Small Start-up Firms." *Journal of Small Business Management* (January 1995), Vol. 33, Iss. 1, pp. 34–45.

61. Mark Stevens, "Seven Steps to a Well-Prepared Business Plan." *Executive Female* (March-April 1995), Vol. 18, Iss. 2, pp. 30–32.

Chapter 6

1. This case is based on an actual consultant, but the name and other information have been changed to provide confidentiality for the consultant.
2. Darrell Rigby, "Managing the Management Tools." *Planning Review* (September/October 1994), Vol. 22, Iss. 5, pp. 20–25.
3. Gregory Johnson, "Shippers Exhaust Contingency Plans as Strike Shows No Sign of Ending." *Journal of Commerce and Commercial*, April 28, 1994, p. 12A.
4. "Microsoft," *The Wall Street Journal*, July 3, 1995, p. 1
5. Joseph Arkin, "Contracting Insights: Proper Use of a Sales Budget and Forecast." *Air Conditioning, Heating & Refrigeration News*, September 12, 1994, p. 8.
6. Dick Outcalt and Pat Johnson, "Sales Forecasting: Part Art, Part Science." *Gift & Decorative Accessories* (June 1994), Vol. 95, Iss. 6, pp. 30–32.
7. "Forecasts Are Fallible: Broadway Stores Prizes Error Detection." *Chain Store Age Executive with Shopping Center Age* (September 1994), Vol. 70, Iss. 9, pp. 50–52.
8. Anthony Rutigliano, "Cloudy with a Change of Leads." *Sales & Marketing Management* (August 1994), Vol. 146, Iss. 8, p. 6.
9. Joe Burt, "Managing Inventory: Headache or Home Run?" *Chain Store Age Executive with Shopping Center Age* (January 1994), Vol. 70, Iss. 1, p. 13MH.
10. Theodore Modis, "Life's Ups and Downs." *The Guardian*, January 12, 1995, p. S7.
11. "Jet Manufacturers." *The Wall Street Journal*, June 22, 1995, p. 1.
12. See case on Bill Gates, CEO Microsoft, at the end of Chapter 1 for more details.
13. "Interactive Retail." *The Wall Street Journal*, July 6, 1995, p. 1
14. William Keenan, "Numbers Racket: Are Your Salespeople Contributing to the Effort to Predict Tomorrow's Business Results?" *Sales & Marketing Management* (May 1995), Vol. 147, Iss. 5, pp. 64–71.
15. Bobb Peck, "Tools for Teams Addressing Total Customer Satisfaction." *Industrial Engineering* (January 1995), Vol. 27, Iss. 1, pp. 30–33.
16. Richard Ligus, "Enterprise Agility: Jazz in the Factory." *Industrial Engineering* (November 1994), Vol. 26, Iss. 11, pp. 18–20.
17. W.H. Weiss, "Guidelines for Planning and Scheduling Work for Employees." *Supervision* (January 1995), Vol. 56, Iss. 1, pp. 14–17.
18. Gail Roberts, "Logging in the Hours: Using Computers for Staff Scheduling Is Enhancing Customer Service and Increasing Productivity." *Supermarket News*, February 7, 1994, pp. 11–13.
19. Ching-Jong Liao, Chien-Lin Sun, and Wen-Ching You, "Flow-Shop Scheduling with Flexible Processors." *Computers & Operations Research* (March 1995), Vol. 22 , Iss. 3, pp. 297–307.
20. Ahiwei Zhu and Ronald Heady, "A Simplified Method of Evaluating PERT/CPM Network Parameters." *IEEE Transaction on Engineering Management* (November 1994), Vol. 41, Iss. 4, pp. 426–431.
21. C. Li and Y. Wu, "Minimal Cost Project Networks: The Cut Set Parallel Difference Method." *Omega* (July 1994), Vol. 22, Iss. 4, pp. 401–408.
22. Grover Norwood, "Just a Matter of Time: Review of How You Do Business." *Managers Magazine* (July 1994), Vol. 69, Iss. 7, pp. 32–34.
23. Grover Norwood, "Time Has Come: Consumers Want It Now." *Managers Magazine* (May 1994), Vol. 69, Iss. 5, pp. 32–33.
24. "Cycle-Time Reduction: A Minute Saved Is a Minute Earned." *Industrial Engineering* (March 1994), Vol. 26, Iss. 3, pp. 19–21.
25. Phil Van Ahken, "A New Strategy for Time Management." *Supervision* (January 1995), Vol. 56, Iss. 1, pp. 3–7.
26. Gene Levine, "Finding Time." *Bobbin* (June 1994), Vol. 35, Iss. 10, pp. 113–114.
27. Michael Adams, "Time Warp." *Successful Meetings* (February 1994), Vol. 42, Iss. 2, pp. 44–48.
28. Amy Feldman, "We'll Make You Scary." *Forbes*, February 14, 1994, p. 96.
29. Rick Wartzman, "Billable Hours." *The Wall Street Journal*, March 14, 1995 p. 1.
30. Lucy Kellaway, "Waring: This Weapon can Backfire." *The Financial Times*, Iss. 32288, p. 11.
31. Hyrum Smith, "10 Natural Laws." *Executive Excellence* (January 1994), Vol. 11, Iss. 1, pp. 5–6.
32. Jeffrey Underwood, "Where Hath the Time Gone?" *Real Estate Today* (March 1995), Vol. 28, Iss. 3, pp. 20–24.
33. "Go Home." *The Wall Street Journal*, August 23, 1994, p. 1
34. Jennifer Laabs, "Executives on Hold." *Personnel Journal* (January 1994), Vol. 11, Iss. 1, pp. 18–20.
35. Jeffrey Underwood, "Where Hath the Time Gone?" *Real Estate Today* (March 1995), Vol. 28, Iss. 3, pp. 20–24.
36. Rick Wartzman, "Billable Hours." *The Wall Street Journal*, March 14, 1995, p. 1.
37. Ann Reeves, "Six Strategies for Entrepreneurs: How to Get Time on Your Side." *Communication World* (May 1995), Vol. 12, Iss. 5, pp. 15–18.
38. Ibid.
39. Ibid.
40. Ted Pollock, "Fifteen Commonsense Ways to Manage Your Time Better." *Production* (February 1994), Vol. 106, Iss. 2, p. 10.
41. Bryon Thompson and Janis Huston, "How to Break Down Tasks So They Don't Break You: Coping with Overwhelming Demands on Your Time." *Health Care Supervisor* (March 1994), Vol. 12, Iss. 3, pp. 39–43.
42. Mark Landouceur, "Four Dimensions." *Executive Excellence* (January 1994), Vol. 11, Iss. 1, p. 11.
43. Lucy Kellaway, "Warning: This Weapon Can Backfire." *The Financial Times*, Iss. 32288, p. 11.
44. Stephen Covey, "First Things First." *Success* (April 1994), Vol. 41, Iss. 3, pp. 8A–8D.
45. Ibid.
46. Amy Feldman, "We'll Make You Scary." *Forbes*, February 14, 1994, p. 96.
47. Bryon Thompson and Janis Huston, "How to Break Down Tasks So They Don't Break You: Coping with Overwhelming Demands on Your Time." *Health Care Supervisor* (March 1994), Vol. 12, Iss. 3, pp. 39–43.
48. Gene Levine, "Finding Time." *Bobbin* (June 1994), Vol. 35, Iss. 10, pp. 113–114.
49. Nick Costa, "Taming Your Desk." *Fund Raising Management* (May 1994), Vol. 25, Iss. 3, pp. 20–23.
50. "Customer Demand Forecasting." *Journal of Business Forecasting* (Fall 1994), Vol. 13, Iss. 3, pp. 2–5.
51. Grover Norwood, "Time Has Come: Consumers Want It Now." *Managers Magazine* (May 1994), Vol. 69, Iss. 5, pp. 32–33.
52. Ibid.
53. Farzad Mahmoodi and G. E. Martin, "Optimal Supplier Delivery Scheduling to JIT Buyers." *The Logistics and Transportation Review* (December 1994), Vol. 30, Iss. 4, pp. 353–362.
54. C. Richard Weylman, "Making Sure Your Marketing Plan Becomes Reality." *National Underwriter Life & Health-Financial Services Edition*, January 2, 1995, p. 18.
55. Kathryn Hegar and Robert N. Lussier, *Study Guide with Experiential Exercises* to accompany *Management: Concepts and Practices* (3rd ed.). (Boston: Allyn and Bacon, 1986), pp. 361–365. Adapted with permission of the publisher.
56. Robert N. Lussier, *Supervision: A Skill-Building Approach* (2nd ed.). (Chicago: Richard D. Irwin, Inc., 1994), p. 587. Adapted with permission of the publisher.

Chapter 7

1. S. A. Ravid and E. F. Sudit, "Power Seeking Managers, Profitable Dividends and Financing Decisions." *Journal of Economic Behavior* (October 1994), Vol. 25, Iss. 2, pp. 241–256.

2. Frank Haflich, "Reliance Linking Up New Chain of Command." *American Metal Market*, July 15, 1994, p. 4.
3. George Hattrup and Brian Kleiner, "How to Establish the Proper Span of Control for Managers." *Industrial Management* (November-December 1993), Vol. 35, Iss. 6, pp. 28–30.
4. Paul Lawrence and Jay Lorsch, *Organization and Environment* (Homewood, IL: Irwin, 1967).
5. Linda Hill, "Maximizing Your Influence." *Working Woman* (April 1995), Vol. 20, Iss. 4, pp. 21–24.
6. Gary Krieger, "Accountability Must Be Restored to Health Care Systems." *American Medical News*, May 22, 1995, pp. 24–26.
7. Ted Pollock, "Secrets of Successful Delegation." *Production* (December 1994), Vol. 106, Iss. 12, pp. 10–12.
8. Charles Handy, "Trust and the Virtual Organization." *Harvard Business Review* (May-June 1995), Vol. 73, Iss. 3, pp. 40–49.
9. Rekha Karambayya, Jeanne Brett, and Anne Lytle, "Effects of Formal Authority and Experience on Third-party Roles, Outcomes, and Perception of Fairness." *Academy of Management Journal* (June 1992), Vol. 35, Iss. 2, pp. 426–439.
10. Richard Brouillet, Barbara Calfre, Jill Follows, Vincent Maher, and Lois McBirde, "Out of Line?" *Nursing*, Vol. 24, Iss. 11, pp. 18–19.
11. Peter Block, "The Next Revolution in the Workplace." *Executive Female* (September-October 1994), Vol. 17, Iss. 5, pp. 42–46.
12. Jac Fitz-enz, "HR's New Score Card." *Personnel Journal* (February 1994), Vol. 73, Iss. 2, pp. 84–88.
13. Ron Zemke and Susan Zemke, "Partnering: A New Slant on Serving the Internal Customer." *Training* (September 1994), Vol. 31, Iss. 9, pp. 37–54.
14. John Purcell, "Be a Uniting Force in a Divided Firm." *People Management*, April 6, 1995, pp. 26–29.
15. Shawn Tully, "What Team Leaders Need to Know." *Fortune*, February 20, 1995, pp. 93–94.
16. Elaine Underwood, "Jean-etic Licenses: Sears Rides Canyon River into $8 Billion Jeans Market." *Brandweek*, May 29, 1995, pp. 1–2.
17. "Deloitte & Touche." *The Wall Street Journal*, February 2, 1995, p. 1.
18. "IBM." *The Wall Street Journal*, May 6, 1994, p. 1
19. "McDonnel Douglas." *The Wall Street Journal*, August 10, 1992, p. 1
20. Esther Gal-Or, "Departmentalization and Stochastic Dissimilarity." *European Economic Review* (February 1995), Vol. 39, Iss. 2, pp. 293–318.
21. "Philip Morris." *The Wall Street Journal*, January 4, 1995, p. 1
22. Berry William, "HRIS Can Improve Performance, Empower and Motivate Knowledge Workers." *Employment Relations Today* (Autumn 1993), Vol. 20, Iss. 3, pp. 297–303.
23. Kimberly Baytos and Brian Kleiner, "New Developments in Job Designs." *Business Credit* (February 1995), Vol. 97, Iss. 2, pp. 22–26.
24. William Fox, "Sociotechnical Systems Principles and Guidelines: Past and Present." *Journal of Applied Behavioral Science* (March 1995), Vol. 31, Iss. 1, pp. 91–114.
25. Berry William, "HRIS Can Improve Performance, Empower and Motivate Knowledge Workers." *Employment Relations Today* (Autumn 1993), Vol. 20, Iss. 3, pp. 297–303.
26. Keith Denton, "`!*# I Hate the Job." *Business Horizons* (January/February 1994), Vol. 37, Iss. 1, pp. 46–52.
27. Ibid.
28. Berry William, "HRIS Can Improve Performance, Empower and Motivate Knowledge Workers." *Employment Relations Today* (Autumn 1993), Vol. 20, Iss. 3, pp. 297–303.
29. Douglas May and Catherine Schwoerer, "Employee Health by Design: Using Employee Involvement Teams in Ergonomic Job Redesign." *Personnel Psychology* (Winter 1994), Vol. 47, Iss. 4, pp. 861–877.
30. Michael Morley and Noreen Heraty, "The High-Performance Organization: Developing Teamwork Where It Counts." *Management Decisions* (March 1995), Vol. 33, Iss. 2, pp. 56–64.
31. Thomas Hemmer, "On the Interrelation Between Production Technology, Job Design, and Incentives." *The Journal of Accounting and Economics* (March-May 1995), Vol. 19, Iss. 2-3, pp. 209–247.
32. Joel Greshenfeld, et al. "Japanese Team-Based Work Systems in North America: Explaining the Diversity." *California Management Review* (Fall 1994), Vol. 37, Iss. 1, pp. 42–65.
33. Richard Hackman and Greg Oldham, *Work Redesign* (Reading, MA: Addison-Wesley, 1980).
34. Jim Temme, "Learn to Manage Competing Priorities by Focusing on What Is Important—Urgent." *Plant Engineering* (February 1994), Vol. 48, Iss. 2, pp. 78–80.
35. Marg Connolly, "Are You Drowning in Detail?" *Supervisory Management* (January 1994), Vol. 39, Iss. 1, pp. 1–2.
36. Steve Stecklow, "Management 101." *The Wall Street Journal*, December 9, 1994, p. 1.
37. This section and Skill-Building Exercise 7–1 are adapted from Harbridge House Training Materials (Boston).
38. Michael Adams, "Time Warp." *Successful Meetings* (February 1994), Vol. 42, Iss. 2, p. 11.
39. Ted Pollock, "Fifteen Commonsense Ways to Manage Your Time Better." *Production* (February 1994), Vol. 106, Iss. 2, p. 10.
40. Nick Costa, "Taming Your Desk." *Fund Raising Management* (May 1994), Vol. 25, Iss. 3, pp. 20–23.
41. Jim Temme, "Learn to Manage Competing Priorities by Focusing on What Is Important—Urgent." *Plant Engineering* (February 1994), Vol. 48, Iss. 2, pp. 78–80.
42. Gene Levine, "Finding Time." *Bobbin* (June 1994), Vol. 35, Iss. 10, pp. 113–114.
43. "Delegation: It's Often a Problem for Agency Owners." *Agency Sales Magazine* (May 1995), Vol. 25, Iss. 5, pp. 35–38.
44. Ted Pollock, "Secrets of Successful Delegation." *Production* (December 1994), Vol. 106, Iss. 12, pp. 10–12.
45. Jack Ninemeier, "10 Tips for Delegating Tasks." *Hotels* (June 1995), Vol. 29, Iss. 6, pp. 20–21.
46. "Delegation: It's Often a Problem for Agency Owners." *Agency Sales Magazine* (May 1995), Vol. 25, Iss. 5, pp. 35–38.
47. Ted Pollock, "Secrets of Successful Delegation." *Production* (December 1994), Vol. 106, Iss. 12, pp. 10–12.
48. Rebecca Morgan, "Guidelines for Delegating Effectively." *Supervision* (April 1995), Vol. 56, Iss. 4, pp. 20–22.
49. "Delegation: It's Often a Problem for Agency Owners." *Agency Sales Magazine* (May 1995), Vol. 25, Iss. 5, pp. 35–38.
50. Ted Pollock, "Secrets of Successful Delegation." *Production* (December 1994), Vol. 106, Iss. 12, pp. 10–12.
51. Jack Ninemeier, "10 Tips for Delegating Tasks." *Hotels* (June 1995), Vol. 29, Iss. 6, pp. 20–21.
52. Rebecca Morgan, "Guidelines for Delegating Effectively." *Supervision* (April 1995), Vol. 56, Iss. 4, pp. 20–22.
53. Paula Dwyer, et al. "Tearing Up Today's Organization Chart." *Business Week*, November 18, 1994, pp. 80–87.
54. John Purcell, "Be a Uniting Force in a Divided Firm." *People Management*, April 6, 1995, pp. 26–29.
55. "Eastman Kodak." *The Wall Street Journal*, January 17, 1995, p. 1.
56. Berry William, "HRIS Can Improve Performance, Empower and Motivate Knowledge Workers." *Employment Relations Today* (Autumn 1993), Vol. 20, Iss. 3, pp. 297–303.
57. Alan Brumagim and Richard Klavans, "Conglomerate Restructuring in the 1980's: A Study of Performance/Strategy Linkage." *Journal of Business Strategies* (Fall 1994), Vol. 11, Iss. 2, pp. 141–155.
58. Robert Simmson and Oscar Suris, "Racing Cars." *The Wall Street Journal*, July 18, 1995, p. 1.
59. Kathryn Hegar and Robert N. Lussier, *Study Guide with Experiential Exercises* to accompany

Management: Concepts and Practices (3rd ed.). (Boston: Allyn and Bacon, 1986), pp. 31–36. Adapted with permission of the publisher.

60. Kathryn Hegar and Robert N. Lussier, *Study Guide with Experiential Exercises* to accompany *Management: Concepts ad Practices* (3rd ed.). (Boston: Allyn and Bacon, 1986), pp. 151–156. Adapted with permission of the publisher.

Chapter 8

1. Information for the opening case was taken from *IBM Annual Report* (1994) and *The Wall Street Journal,* June 7, 1995 pp. B1 and B6, and June 12, 1995, pp. A3 and A4. Because the IBM acquisition of Lotus took place as the text chapter was being written, throughout the chapter possible issues and options for the companies are presented rather than actual events, as given in most chapters.

2. Neil Fitzgerald, "Change Directions." *CA Magazine* (May 1995), Vol. 99, Iss. 1066, pp. 6–9.

3. David Bottoms, "Facing Change or Changing Faces." *Industry Week,* May 1, 1995, pp. 17–19.

4. Brenda Mullins and Bill Mullins, "Coaching Winners." *Canadian Insurance* (January 1994), Vol. 99, Iss. 1, p. 34.

5. Barry Spiker, "Making Change Stick." *Industry Week,* March 7, 1994, p. 45.

6. Albert Vicere, Maria Taylor, and Virginia Freeman, "Executive Development in Major Corporations: A Ten-Year Study." *Journal of Management Development* (1994), Vol. 13, Iss. 1, pp. 4–22.

7. Brenda Mullins and Bill Mullins, "Coaching Winners." *Canadian Insurance* (January 1994), Vol. 99, Iss. 1, p. 34.

8. Robert Nozar, "Managing Change." *Hotel & Motel Management,* March 20, 1995, pp. 22–24.

9. Neil Fitzgerald, "Change Directions." *CA Magazine* (May 1995), Vol. 99, Iss. 1066, pp. 6–9.

10. Jeanie Duck, "Managing Change: The Art of Balancing." *Harvard Business Review* (November/December 1993), Vol. 7, Iss. 6, pp. 109–118.

11. "IBM and Toshiba." *The Wall Street Journal,* August 8, 1995, p. 1.

12. Michael Hammer and James Champy, "Avoid the Hottest New Management Cure." *Inc.* (April 1994), Vol. 16, Iss. 4, pp. 25–26.

13. William Cotton, "Relevance Regained Downunder." *Management Accounting* (May 1994), Vol. 75, Iss. 11, pp. 38–42.

14. John Zimmerman, "The Principles of Managing Change." *HR Focus* (February 1995), Vol. 72, Iss. 2, pp. 15–17.

15. Jeffrey Pfeffer, "Competitive Advantage Through People." *California Management Review* (Winter 1994), Vol. 36, Iss. 2, pp. 9–28.

16. Loretta Roach, "Wal-Mart's Top Ten." *Discount Merchandiser* (August 1993), Vol. 33 , Iss. 8, pp. 76–77.

17. Peter Flatow, "Unappreciated Task: Managing Change; Yet It Should Be a Core Competency." *Advertising Age,* March 27, 1995, pp. 14–15.

18. Jeffrey Pfeffer, "Competitive Advantage Through People." *California Management Review* (Winter 1994), Vol. 36, Iss. 2, pp. 9–28.

19. Larry Reynolds, "Understand Employees' Resistance to Change." *HR Focus* (June 1994), Vol. 71, Iss. 6, p. 17.

20. Ken Matejka and Ramona Julian, "Resistance to Change Is Natural." *Supervisory Management* (October 1993), Vol. 38, Iss. 10, pp. 10–11.

21. Barry Spiker and Eric Lesser, "We Have Met the Enemy." *Journal of Business Strategy* (March-April 1995), Vol. 16, Iss. 2, pp. 17–22.

22. Larry Reynolds, "Understand Employees' Resistance to Change." *HR Focus* (June 1994), Vol. 71, Iss. 6, pp. 17–18.

23. Brenda Sunoo, "HR Positions U.S. Long Distance for Further Growth." *Personnel Journal* (January 1994), Vol. 73, Iss. 1, pp. 78–91.

24. Janice Tomlinson, "Human Resources—Partners in Change." *Human Resource Management* (Winter 1993), Vol. 32, Iss. 4, pp. 545–554.

25. Paul Strebel, "New Contracts: The Day to Change." *European Management Journal* (December 1993), Vol. 11, Iss. 4, pp. 387–402.

26. John Burbidge, "It's a Time of Participation." *Journal of Quality & Participation* (December 1993), Vol. 16, Iss. 7, pp. 30–37. Janice Tomlinson, "Human Resources—Partners in Change." *Human Resource Management* (Winter 1993), Vol. 32, Iss. 4, pp. 545–554.

27. Edgar Schein, "How Can Organizations Learn Faster? The Challenge of Entering the Green Room." *Sloan Management Review* (Winter 1992), Vol. 34, Iss. 2, pp. 85–92.

28. John Ward and Craig Aronoff, "Preparing Successors to Be Leaders." *Nation's Business* (April 1994), Vol. 82, Iss. 4, pp. 54–55.

29. Ken Hultman, *The Path of Least Resistance* (Austin, TX: Learning Concepts, 1979).

30. Ronald Recard, "Overcoming Resistance to Change." *National Productivity Review* (Spring 1995), Vol. 14, Iss. 2, pp. 5–13.

31. Edgar Schein, *Organizational Culture and Leadership* (San Francisco: Jossey-Bass, 1985).

32. Bob Filipczal, "Are We Having Fun Yet?" *Training* (April 1995), Vol. 32, Iss. 4, pp. 48–56.

33. Brenda Sunoo, "How Fun Flies at Southwest Airlines." *Personnel Journal* (June 1995), Vol. 74, Iss. 6, pp. 62–72.

34. Jacqueline Hood and Christine Koberg, "Patterns of Differential Assimilation and Acculturation for Women in Business Organizations." *Human Relations* (February 1994), Vol. 47, Iss. 2, pp. 159–181.

35. Matti Dobbs, "San Diego's Diversity Commitment." *Public Manager* (Spring 1994), Vol. 23, Iss. 1, pp. 59–62.

36. Brian Moskal, "A Shadow between Values & Reality." *Industry Week,* May 16, 1994, pp. 23–26.

37. Ronald Clement, "Culture, Leadership, and Power: The Keys to Organizational Change." *Business Horizons* (January/February 1994), Vol. 37, Iss. 1, pp. 33–39.

38. Robert Greene, "Culturally Compatible HR Strategies." *HRMagazine* (June 1995), Vol. 40, Iss. 6, pp. 115–122.

39. Richard Allen and John Thatcher, "Achieving Cultural Change: A Practical Case Study." *Leadership & Organization Development Journal* (February 1995), Vol. 16, Iss. 2, pp. 16–24.

40. Suresh Gopalan, John Dittrich, and Reed Nelson, "Analysis of Organizational Culture: A Critical Step in Mergers and Acquisitions." *Journal of Business Strategies* (Fall 1994), Vol. 11, Iss. 2, pp. 124–140.

41. William Bulkeley and Don Clark, "Lotus Has Everything to Lose-or Gain." *The Wall Street Journal,* June 7, 1995, p. B1.

42. Stuart Kauffman, "Escaping the Red Queen Effect." *The McKinsey Quarterly* (Winter 1995), Iss. 1, pp. 118–130.

43. Adigun Abiodun, "21st Century Technologies: Opportunities or Threats for Africa?" *Futures* (November 1994), Vol. 26, Iss. 9, pp. 944–964.

44. Joseph Bower and Clayton Christensen, "Disruptive Technologies: Catching the Wave." *Harvard Business Review* (January-February 1995), Vol. 73, Iss. 1, pp. 43–54.

45. "Producer Power." *The Economist,* March 4, 1995, pp. 98–99.

46. Michael Barrier, "Beyond the Suggestion Box." *Nation's Business* (July 1995), Vol. 83, Iss. 7, pp. 34–37.

47. R. Mitchell, "Masters of Innovation." *Business Week,* April 10, 1989, pp. 58–63.

48. Dean Elmuti and Taisier AlDiab, "Improving Quality and Organizational Effectiveness Go Hand in Hand Through Deming's Management System." *Journal of Business Strategies* (Spring 1995), Vol. 12, Iss. 1, pp. 86–98.

49. Andrew Klein, Ralph Masi, and Ken Weidner, "Organization Culture, Distribution and Amount of Control and Perceptions of Quality: An Empirical Study of Linkages." *Group & Organization Management* (June 1995), Vol. 20, Iss. 2, pp. 122–149.

50. Timothy Keiningham, Anthony Zahorik, and Roland Rust, "Getting Return on Quality." *Journal of Retail Banking* (Winter 1994), Vol. 16, Iss. 4, pp. 7–13.

51. "Quality Street May Lead to a Dead End." *Management Decision* (September 1994), Vol. 32, Iss. 5, pp. 12–14.

52. "Quality Initiatives Lack Employee Focus." *IRS Employment Trends*, January 15, 1995, pp. 4–5.
53. Judith Neal and Cheryl Tromley, "From Incremental Change to Retrofit: Creating High-Performance Work Systems." *The Academy of Management Executive* (February 1995), Vol. 9, Iss. 1, pp. 42–54.
54. Judith Messey, "Cultural Resolution." *Computing*, February 23, 1995, pp. 30–32.
55. Matti Dobbs, "Managing Diversity: A Unique Quality Opportunity." *The Public Manager: The New Bureaucrat* (Fall 1994), Vol. 23, Iss. 3, pp. 39–43.
56. Christine Taylor, "Building a Business Case for Diversity." *Canadian Business Review* (Spring 1995), Vol. 22, Iss. 1, pp. 12–16.
57. James Rodgers, "Implementing a Diversity Strategy." *LIMRA's MarketFacts* (May/June 1993), Vol. 12, Iss. 3, pp. 26–29.
58. Tia Freeman-Evans, "The Enriched Association: Benefiting from Ulticulturalsim." *Association Management* (February 1994), Vol. 46, Iss. 2, pp. 52–56.
59. Laurie Epting, Sandra Glover, and Suzan Boyd, "Managing Diversity." *Health Care Supervisor* (June 1994), Vol. 12, Iss. 4, pp. 73–83.
60. Beverly Goldberg and John Sifonis, "Keep On Keepin' On." *Journal of Business Strategy* (July-August 1994), Vol. 15, Iss. 4, pp. 23–25.
61. Lisa Jenner, "Diversity Management: What Does It Mean?" *HR Focus* (January 1994), Vol. 7, Iss. 1, p. 11.
62. Robert Blake and Jane Mouton, *The Managerial Grid III: Key to Leadership Excellence* (Houston, TX: Gulf Publishing, 1985).
63. Jennifer Chatman and Karen Jehn. "Assessing the Relationship Between Industry Characteristics and Organizational Culture: How Different Can You Be?" *Academy of Management Journal* (June 1994), Vol. 37, Iss. 3, pp. 522–553.
64. "From Multilocal to Multicultural: This Way for the Rainbow Corporation." *The Economist*, June 24, 1995, pp. S14–S16.
65. Cornelius Grove and Willa Hallowell, "Can Diversity Initiatives Be Exported?" *HRMagazine* (March 1995), Vol. 40, Iss. 3, pp. 78–80.
66. John McClenahen, "Good Enough?" *Industry Week*, February 20, 1995, pp. 58–62.
67. Paul Allen and Sandra Cespedes, "Reengineering Is Just a Catalyst in Bank Culture Change." *The Bankers Magazine* (May-June 1995), Vol. 178, Iss. 3, pp. 46–53.
68. Hans Allender, "Is Reegineering Compatible with Total Quality Management?" *Industrial Engineering* (September 1994), Vol. 26, Iss. 9, pp. 41–43.
69. Bernard Wysocki, "Lean—and Frail." *The Wall Street Journal*, July 5, 1995, p. 1.
70. John Byrne, "Entreprise: How Entrepreneurs Are Reshaping the Economy—And What Big Companies Can Learn." *Business Week/Enterprise*, Special Issue 1993, pp. 11–18.

Chapter 9

1. "Sexual Harassment." *The Wall Street Journal*, May 24, 1994, p. 1
2. "Equal Opportunity Pays." *The Wall Street Journal*, May 4, 1993, p. 1.
3. Elmer Burack, Marvin Burack, Diane Miller, and Kathleen Morgan, "New Paradigm Approaches in Strategic Human Resource Management." *Group & Organizational Management* (June 1994), Vol. 19, Iss. 2, pp. 141–160.
4. Jennifer Jaabs, "Strategic Holiday Staffing at Lands' End." *Personnel Journal* (December 1994), Vol. 73, Iss. 12, pp. 28–31.
5. James Clifford, "Job Analysis: Why Do It, and How Should It Be Done?" *Public Personnel Management* (Summer 1994), Vol. 23, Iss. 2, pp. 321–341.
6. Peter LeBlance and Michael McInerney, "Need a Change? Jump on the Banding Wagon." *Personnel Journal* (January 1994), Vol. 73, Iss. 1, pp. 72–77.
7. G. Stephen Taylor, "Realistic Job Previews in the Trucking Industry." *Journal of Managerial Issues* (Winter 1994), Vol. 6, Iss. 4, pp. 457–474.
8. Don James, "Bad Hiring Decisions Can Hang Around to Haunt Companies." *Houston Business Journal*, September 16, 1994, pp. 53–54.
9. "Revolution in Résumés: Companies Let Computers Do the Reading." *The Wall Street Journal*, May 16, 1995, p. 1.
10. William Bulkeley, "Replaced by Technology: Job Interviews." *The Wall Street Journal*, July 22, 1994, p. B1.
11. Catherine Romano, "Training ABCs." *Management Review* (September 1994), Vol. 83, Iss. 9, pp. 7–8.
12. Mark Disney, "Reference Checking to Improve Hiring Decisions." *Industrial Management* (March-April 1994), Vol. 36, Iss. 2, pp. 31–33.
13. "Less Instinct, More Analysis." *Industry Week*, July 17, 1995, pp. 11–12.
14. "Revolution in Résumés: Companies Let Computers Do the Reading." *The Wall Street Journal*, May 16, 1995, p. 1.
15. Adapted from Robert Lussier, "Selecting Qualified Candidates Through Effective Job Interviewing." *Clinical Laboratory Management Review* (July/August 1995), Vol. 9, Iss. 4, pp. 267–275.
16. "How to Hire the Right Person." *Supervision* (May 1995), Vol. 56, Iss. 5, pp. 10–12.
17. Adapted from Robert Lussier, "Selecting Qualified Candidates Through Effective Job Interviewing." *Clinical Laboratory Management Review* (July/August 1995), Vol. 9, Iss. 4, pp. 267–275.
18. "Going for Laughs." *The Wall Street Journal*, July 16, 1987, p. 31
19. "Less Instinct, More Analysis." *Industry Week*, July 17, 1995, pp. 11–12.
20. Ibid.
21. George Henderson, "Quality Is the Key to Success." *Estates Gazette*, May 27, 1995, pp. S41–S43.
22. Bob Filipczak, "Trained by Starbucks." *Training* (June 1995), Vol. 32, Iss. 6, pp. 73–78.
23. Terri Bergman, "Training: The Case for Increased Investment." *Employment Relations Today* (Winter 1994), Vol. 21, Iss. 4, pp. 381–392.
24. Richard Bakka, "Comprehensive Training Is Key: To Simply Tell Someone How to Do Things Without Providing Them a Measure of Their Effectiveness Is Useless." *Beverage World* (January 1995), Vol. 114, Iss. 1583, pp. 104–105.
25. Terri Bergman, "Training: The Case for Increased Investment." *Employment Relations Today* (Winter 1994), Vol. 21, Iss. 4, pp. 381–392.
26. "Training Salespeople." *The Wall Street Journal*, April 18, 1995, p. 1.
27. Beverly Geber, "A Rabble-Rousing Roundtable." *Training* (June 1995), Vol. 32, Iss. 6, pp. 61–67.
28. Beverly Geber, "Does Your Training Make a Difference? Prove It!" *Training* (March 1995), Vol. 32, Iss. 3, pp. 27–35.
29. Paul Clolery, "Employee Evaluations That Really Work." *The Practical Accountant* (November 1994), Vol. 27, Iss. 11, pp. 9–10.
30. Gerald White, "Employee Turnover: The Hidden Drain on Profits." *HR Focus* (January 1995), Vol. 72, Iss. 1, pp. 15–18.
31. "Salomon Brothers." *The Wall Street Journal*, April 18, 1995, p. 1.
32. "Look Movie Tickets." *The Wall Street Journal*, September 27, 1994, p. 1.
33. Donna Hogarty, "New Ways to Pay." *Management Review* (January 1994), Vol. 83, Iss. 1, pp. 34–37.
34. "The Role of Rewards on a Journey to Excellence." *Management Decision* (September 1994), Vol. 32, Iss. 5, pp. 46–48.
35. U.S. Census Bureau reported in Joan Rigdon, "Three Decades After the Equal Pay Act Women's Wages Remain Far from Parity." *The Wall Street Journal*, June 9, 1993, p. B1.
36. U.S. Chamber of Commerce, *Employee Benefits 1991* (Washington, D.C.: U.S. Government Printing Office, 1992).
37. "Union No?" *The Wall Street Journal*, August 15, 1995, p. 1.
38. Lynn Williams, "The Challenges Ahead." *Labor Law Journal* (August 1994), Vol. 45, Iss. 8, pp. 525–529.
39. David Hage, "Unions Feel the Heat." *U.S.*

New & World Report, January 24, 1994, pp. 57–61.
40. Fred Bleakley, "The Outlook—Unions Are Preparing for Tough Bargaining." *The Wall Street Journal*, April 10, 1995, p. 1.
41. "You Can't Ask for Personnel." *The Wall Street Journal*, June 13, 1995, p. 1.
42. Maddy Janssens, "Evaluating International Managers' Performance: Parent Company Standards as Control Mechanism." *International Journal of Human Resource Management* (December 1994), Vol. 5, Iss. 4, pp. 853–874.
43. "The Checkoff." *The Wall Street Journal*, December 14, 1993, p. 1.
44. Stephen Wildstrom, "A Failing Grade for the American Workforce." *Business Week*, September 11, 1989, p. 22.
45. "Take Our Mentors to Work." *The Wall Street Journal*, April 27, 1995, p. 1.
46. "Glass Ceiling." *The Wall Street Journal*, March 14, 1995, p. 1.
47. Sue Shellenbarger, "Work & Family—Home Life Matters More to Employees." *The Wall Street Journal*, August 31, 1994, p. B1.
48. "Mentoring in Schools." *The Wall Street Journal*, May 9, 1995, p. 1.
49. Louis DiLorenzo and Darren Carroll, "Screening Applicants for a Safer Workplace." *HR Magazine* (March 1995), Vol. 40, Iss. 3, pp. 55–59.
50. Michael Barrier, "When Laws Collide." *Nation's Business* (February 1995), Vol. 83, Iss. 2, pp. 23–24.
51. Brian Niehoff and Donita Bammerlin, "Don't Let Your Training Process Derail Your Journey to Total Quality Management." *SAM Advanced Management Journal* (Winter 1995), Vol. 60, Iss. 1, pp. 39–46.
52. L. Kate Beatty, "Pay and Benefits Break Away from Tradition." *HR Magazine* (November 1994), Vol. 39, Iss. 11, pp. 63–68.
53. Anat Arkin, "From Supervision to Team Leader." *Personnel Management* (February 1994), Vol. 26, Iss. 2, pp. 48–50.
54. Shari Caudron, "Tie Individual Pay to Team Success." *Personnel Journal* (October 1994), Vol. 73, Iss. 10, pp. 40–46.
55. Scott Snell and James Dean, "Strategic Compensation for Integrated Manufacturing: The Moderating Effects of Jobs and Organizational Inertia." *Academy of Management Journal* (October 1994), Vol. 37, Iss. 5, pp. 1109–1141.
56. Randall Hanson, Rebecca Porterfield, and Kathleen Ames, "Employee Empowerment at Risk: Effects of Recent RLRB Ruling." *The Academy of Management Executive* (May 1995), Vol. IX, Iss. 2, pp. 45–54.
57. Joan Rigon, "Workplace—Using New Kinds of Corporate Alchemy, Some Firms Turn Lesser Lights into Starts." *The Wall Street Journal*, May 3, 1993, p. B1.
58. Jaclyn Fierman, "Beating the Mid-life Career Crisis." *Fortune*, September 6, 1993, pp. 52–62.
59. Ted Kuster, "The Challenge of Partnerships Between Union and Management." *New Steel* (November 1994), Vol. 10, Iss. 11, pp. 16–21.
60. Stephen Anderson, "Unions/Management Create Collaborative Culture." *Communication World* (April 1994), Vol. 11, Iss. 4, pp. 16–19.
61. William McKinley, Carol Sanchez, and Allen Schick, "Organizational Downsizing: Constraining, Cloning, Learning." *The Academy of Management Executives* (August 1995), Vol. IX, Iss. 3, pp. 32–42.
62. Bernard Wysocki, "Lean—and Frail, Some Companies Cut Costs Too Far, Suffer Corporate Anorexia." *The Wall Street Journal*, July 5, 1995, p. 1.
63. Hal Lancaster, "Managing Your Career—Re-Engineering Authors Reconsider Re-Engineering." *The Wall Street Journal*, January 17, 1995, p. B1.
64. Hal Lancaster, "Managing Your Career—Managers Beware: You're Not Ready for Tomorrow's Jobs." *The Wall Street Journal*, January 24, 1995, p. B1.
65. Sue Shellenbarger, "Work & Family." *The Wall Street Journal*, February 1, 1995, p. B1.
66. "The Boom in the Temporary-Help Business." *The Wall Street Journal*, April 11, 1995, p. 1.
67. "Lease Don't Hire." *The Wall Street Journal*, March 16, 1993, p. 1
68. Kathryn Hegar and Robert N. Lussier, *Study Guide with Experiential Exercises* to accompany *Management: Concepts and Practices* (3rd ed.). (Boston: Allyn and Bacon, 1986), pp. 193–194 and 207–209. Adapted with permission of the publisher.

Chapter 10

1. Wade Nichols, "What We Have Here . . . (Poor Communications Following Airlines' Decision to Cap Travel Agents' Commissions)." *Travel Weekly*, July 3, 1995, pp. 22–23.
2. Robert Maidment, "Listening—The Overlooked and Underdeveloped Other Half of Talking." *Supervisory Management*, August 1985, p. 10.
3. Hal Lancaster, "Managing Your Career." *The Wall Street Journal*, January 3, 1995, p. B1.
4. Shari Caudron, "The Top 20 Ways to Motivate Employees." *Industry Week*, April 3, 1995, pp. 12–16.
5. "Only Communicate." *The Economist*, June 24, 1995, pp. S18–S19.
6. Martha Peak, "Can We Talk: One-Size-Fits-All Doesn't Work When It Comes to Communications and Learning Styles." *Management Review* (February 1995), Vol. 84, Iss. 2, p. 1.
7. Tom Geddle, "Leap Over the Barriers of Internal Communication." *Communication World* (Winter 1994), Vol. 11, Iss. 2, pp. 12–15.
8. Michael Dennis, "Effective Communication Will Make Your Job Easier." *Business Credit* (June 1995), Vol. 97, Iss. 6, p. 45.
9. Donald McNerney, "Improve Your Communication Skills." *HR Focus* (October 1994), Vol. 71, Iss. 10, p. 22.
10. David Fagiano, "Altering the Corporate DNA." *Management Review* (December 1994), Vol. 83, Iss. 12, p. 4.
11. Lee Iacocca, *Iacocca* (New York: Bantam Books, 1985), p. 15.
12. "The CIO's Seat Grows But Remains Difficult to Define." *The Wall Street Journal*, September 21, 1995, p. 1.
13. Timothy Galpin, "Pruning the Grapevine." *Training & Development* (April 1995), Vol. 49, Iss. 4, pp. 28–33.
14. Charles Beck, "Theory and Profession." *Technical Communication* (February 1995), Vol. 42, Iss. 1, pp. 133–142.
15. Richard Barger, "Aim Projects with Objectives." *Communication World* (May 1995), Vol. 12, Iss. 5, pp. 33–34.
16. Herbert Corbin, "Tracking the New Thinkers." *Public Relations Quarterly* (Winter 1994), Vol. 39, Iss. 4, pp. 38–41.
17. Quarterly Burger, "Why Should They Believe Us?" *Communication World* (January/February 1995), Vol. 12, Iss. 1, pp. 16–17.
18. Harriet Lawrence and Albert Wiswell, "Feedback Is a Two-Way Street." *Training & Development* (July 1995), Vol. 49, Iss. 7, pp. 49–52.
19. Deborah Tannen, "The Power of Talk: Who Gets Heard and Why." *Harvard Business Review* (September/October 1995), Vol. 73, Iss. 5, pp. 138–148.
20. Hal Lancaster, "Managing Your Career." *The Wall Street Journal*, May 2, 1995, p. B1.
21. Richard Barger, "Aim Projects with Objectives." *Communication World* (May 1995), Vol. 12, Iss. 5, pp. 33–34.
22. "Playing Phone Tag." *The Wall Street Journal*, June 22, 1995, p. 1.
23. "Behind E-Mail." *Inc.* (Summer Special Bonus Issue), Vol. 47, Iss. 4, pp. 27–29.
24. Hal Lancaster, "Managing Your Career." *The Wall Street Journal*, May 2, 1995, p. B1.
25. Greg Davis and Robert Barker, "The Legal Implications of Electronic Documents." *Business Horizons* (May/June 1995), Vol. 38, Iss. 3, pp. 51–55.
26. "E-Mail Etiquette." *The Wall Street Journal*, October 12, 1995, p. 1.
27. Gary Blake, "It Is Recommended That You Write Clearly." *The Wall Street Journal*, April 2, 1995, p. A14.
28. Harriet Lawrence and Albert Wiswell,

"Feedback Is a Two-Way Street." *Training & Development* (July 1995), Vol. 49, Iss. 7, pp. 49–52.

29. Shari Caudron, "The Top 20 Ways to Motivate Employees." *Industry Week*, April 3, 1995, pp. 12–16.

30. Edgar Wycoff, "The Language of Listening." *Internal Auditor* (April 1994), Vol. 5, Iss. 2, pp. 26–28.

31. Anonymous, "Communicating: Face-to-Face." *Agency Sales Magazine* (January 1994), Vol. 24, Iss. 1, pp. 22–23.

32. Edgar Wycoff, "The Language of Listening." *Internal Auditor* (April 1994), Vol. 5, Iss. 2, pp. 26–28.

33. Jacob Weisberg, "Listen to Me." *Telemarketing Magazine* (March 1994), Vol. 12, Iss. 9, pp. 69–70; Edgar Wycoff, "The Language of Listening." *Internal Auditor* (April 1994), Vol. 5, Iss. 2, pp. 26–28.

34. Ibid.

35. Jacob Weisberg, "Listen to Me." *Telemarketing Magazine* (March 1994), Vol. 12, Iss. 9, pp. 69–70.

36. Stephen Boyd, "Put Yourself in Someone Else's Shoes." *Chemical Engineering* (March 1994), Vol. 101, Iss. 3, pp. 139–140.

37. Tom Brown, "The Emotional Side of Management." *Industry Week*, May 1, 1995, pp. 30–33.

38. Harriet Lawrence and Albert Wiswell, "Feedback Is a Two-Way Street." *Training & Development* (July 1995), Vol. 49, Iss. 7, pp. 49–52.

39. Jacob Weisberg, "Listen to Me." *Telemarketing Magazine* (March 1994), Vol. 12, Iss. 9, pp. 69–70.

40. Joan Rigdon, "Managing Your Career." *The Wall Street Journal*, October 10, 1994 p. B1.

41. "Only Communicate: Thoroughly Modern Corporations Know No Borders." *The Economist*, June 24, 1995, p. S18.

42. Deborah Tannen, "The Power of Talk: Who Gets Heard and Why." *Harvard Business Review* (September/October 1995), Vol. 73, Iss. 5, pp. 138–148.

43. Martha Peak, "Can We Talk: One-Size-Fits-All Doesn't Work When It Comes to Communications and Learning Styles." *Management Review* (February 1995), Vol. 84, Iss. 2, p. 1.

44. Chester Burger, "Why Should They Believe Us?" *Communication World* (January-February 1995), Vol. 12, Iss. 1, pp. 16–17.

45. Penny Swinburne, "Management with a Personal Touch." *People Management*, April 6, 1995, pp. 38–39.

46. Donald McNerney, "Improve Your Communication Skills." *HR Focus* (October 1994), Vol. 71, Iss. 10, p. 22.

47. Kathryn Hegar and Robert N. Lussier, *Study Guide with Experiential Exercises* to accompany *Management: Concepts and Practices* (3rd ed.). (Boston: Allyn and Bacon, 1986), pp. 285–290, 295–297. Adapted with permission of the publisher.

48. Bruce Anderson and David Erlandson, from *Early Behavioral Classification Systems*, in "Communication Patterns: A Tool for Memorable Leadership Training." *Training*, January 1984, pp. 55–57.

49. Eugene Anderson, "Communication Patterns: A Tool for Memorable Leadership Training." *Training*, January 1984, pp. 55–57.

Chapter 11

1. Donna Brogle is the owner of Drapery Designs by Donna, but she does not have an employee named Susan. However, this motivation problem is common and throughout the chapter you will learn how to motive using Susan as an example.

2. Tom Watson, "Linking Employee Motivation and Satisfaction to the Bottom Line." *CMA Magazine* (April 1994), Vol. 68, Iss. 3, p. 4.

3. Karen Down and Leanne Liedtka, "What Corporations Seek in MBA Hires: A Survey." *Selections* (Winter 1994), Vol. 10, Iss. 2, pp. 34–39.

4. Peggy Wallance, "LAN Training: Finding the Right Fit." *InfoWorld*, April 18, 1994, pp. 67–70.

5. Thomas Van Tassel, "Productivity Dilemmas." *Executive Excellence* (April 1994), Vol. 11, Iss. 4, pp. 16–17.

6. Selwyn Feinstein, "Pointing Workers to a Common Goal." *The Wall Street Journal*, February 16, 1988, p. 1.

7. Alan Dubinsky, Masaaki Kotabe, Chae Un Lim, and Ronald Michaels, "Differences in Motivational Perceptions Among U.S., Japanese, and Korean Sales Personnel." *Journal of Business Research* (June 1994), Vol. 30, Iss. 2, pp. 175–185.

8. Karen Down and Leanne Liedtka, "What Corporations Seek in MBA Hires: A Survey." *Selections* (Winter 1994), Vol. 10, Iss. 2, pp. 34–39.

9. Ibid.

10. Abraham Maslow, "A Theory of Human Motivation." *Psychological Review* (1943), Vol. 50, pp. 370–96, and *Motivation and Personality* (New York: Harper & Row, 1954).

11. Clayton Alderfer, "An Empirical Test of a New Theory of Human Needs." *Organizational Behavior and Human Performance*, April 1969, pp. 142–175. Clayton Alderfer, *Existence, Relatedness, and Growth* (New York: Free Press, 1972).

12. Frederick Herzberg, "One More Time: How Do You Motivate Employees?" *Harvard Business Review*, January-February 1968, pp. 53–62.

13. Karen Down and Leanne Liedtka, "What Corporations Seek in MBA Hires: A Survey." *Selections* (Winter 1994), Vol. 10, Iss. 2, pp. 34–39.

14. Henry Murray, *Explorations in Personality* (New York: Oxford Press, 1938).

15. John Atkinson, *An Introduction to Motivation* (New York: Van Nostrand Reinhold, 1964).

16. David McClelland, *The Achieving Society* (New York: Van Nostrand Reinhold, 1961). David McClelland and D. H. Burnham, "Power Is the Great Motivator." *Harvard Business Review*, March-April 1978, p. 103.

17. J. Stacy Adams, "Toward an Understanding of Inequity." *Journal of Abnormal and Social Psychology* (1963), Vol. 67, pp. 422–436.

18. Erica Gordon Sorochan, "Healthy Companies." *Training & Development* (March 1994), Vol. 48, Iss. 3, pp. 9–10.

19. E. A. Locke, K. N. Shaw, L. M. Saari, and G. P. Latham, "Goal Setting and Task Performance." *Psychological Bulletin* (August 1981), Vol. 90, pp. 125–152. Gary Lapham and Edwin Loack, "Goal Setting—A motivational Technique That Works." *Organizational Dynamics*, Autumn 1979, pp. 68–80. Edwin Locke and Douglas Henne, "Work Motivation Theories." In Cary I. Cooper and I. Robertson, eds., *Review of Industrial and Organizational Psychology* (Chichester, England: John Wiley & Sons, 1986). Edwin Locke and Gary Latham, *Goal Setting: A Motivational Technique That Works* (Englewood Cliffs, NJ: Prentice Hall, 1984). "Re-Engineering's Buzz May Fuzz Results; High Goals and Focus Work Best." *The Wall Street Journal*, June 30, 1994, p. A1.

20. Victor Vroom, *Work and Motivation* (New York: John Wiley & Sons, 1964).

21. Daniel Ilgen, Delbert Nebeker, and Robert Pritchard, "Expectancy Theory Measures: An Empirical Comparison in an Experimental Simulation." *Organizational Behavior and Human Performance* (1981), Vol. 28, pp. 189–223.

22. B. F. Skinner, *Beyond Freedom and Dignity* (New York: Alfred A. Knopf, 1971).

23. "A Pat on the Back." *The Wall Street Journal*, January 3, 1989, p. 1. "Odds and Ends." *The Wall Street Journal*, April 18, 1989, p. B1.

24. "Odds and Ends." *The Wall Street Journal*, April 18, 1989, p. B1.

25. Kenneth Blanchard and Spencer Johnson, *The One-Minute Manager* (New York: Morrow, 1982).

26. This statement is based on Robert N. Lussier's consulting experience.

27. This paragraph is based on Robert N. Lussier's consulting experience.

28. Itzhak Harpaz, "The Importance of Work Goals: An International Perspective." *Journal of International Business Studies*, First Quarter 1990, pp. 75–93.

29. Greet Hofestede, "Motivation, Leadership, and Organizations: Do American Theories Apply Abroad?" *Organizational Dynamics*, Summer 1980, p. 55.

30. Alan Dubinsky, Masaaki Kotabe, Chae Un Lim, and Ronald Michaels, "Differences in Motivational Perceptions Among U.S., Japanese, and Korean Sales Personnel." *Journal of Business Research* (June 1994), Vol. 30, Iss. 2, pp. 175–185.
31. C. Kagitcibasi and J. W. Berry, "Cross-Culture Psychology: Current Research and Trends." *Annual Review of Psychology* (89), Vol. 40, pp. 493–531.
32. N. J. Alder, *International Dimensions of Organizational Behavior* (Boston: Kent, 1986).
33. "Deming's Demons." *The Wall Street Journal*, June 4, 1990, pp. R39, R41.
34. Erica Gordon Sorochan, "Healthy Companies." *Training & Development* (March 1994), Vol. 48, Iss. 3, pp. 9–10.
35. Brenda Mullins and Bill Mullins, "Coaching Winners." *Canadian Insurance* (January 1994), Vol. 99, Iss. 1, p. 34.

Chapter 12

1. Bernard Bass, *Stogdill's Handbook of Leadership*, rev. ed. (New York: Free Press, 1981). F. R. Manfred and Kets des Vries, "The Leadership Mystique." *The Academy of Management Executive* (August 1994), Vol. 8, Iss. 3, pp. 73–92.
2. James Meindle and Sanford Ehrlich, "The Romance of Leadership and the Evaluation of Performance." *Academy of Management Journal*, March 1987, p. 92.
3. Ceel Pasternak, "Work Satisfaction Linked to Manager." *HRMagazine* (May 1994), Vol. 39, Iss. 5, p. 27.
4. Frank Pacetta and Roger Gittines, "Fire Them UP!" *Success* (May 1994), Vol. 41, Iss. 4, pp. 16A–16D.
5. Richard Fulwiler, "Leadership Skills: Key to Increasing Individual Effectiveness." *Occupational Hazards* (May 1995), Vol. 57, Iss. 5, pp. 63–72.
6. Meryl Davids, "Where Style Meets Substance." *Journal of Business Strategy* (January-February 1995), Vol. 16, Iss. 1, pp. 48–59.
7. Larry Van Meter, "Lead Before Managing: The Team Concept Approach." *Business Credit* (June 1995), Vol. 97, Iss. 6, pp. 9–10.
8. John Malcom, "10 Steps to the Right Candidate." *Folio*, May 1, 1994, pp. 37–38.
9. Bernard Bass, *Stogdill's Handbook of Leadership*, rev. ed. (New York: Free Press, 1981).
10. Peter Drucker, "Leadership: More Doing Than Dash." *The Wall Street Journal*, January 6, 1988, p. 24.
11. Edwin Ghiselli, *Explorations in Management Talent* (Santa Monica, CA: Goodyear, 1971).
12. Robert Blake and Jane Mouton, *The Managerial Grid III: Key to Leadership Excellence* (Houston, TX: Gulf Publishing, 1985).
13. Robert Blake and Anne Adams McCanse, *Leadership Dilemmas—Grid Solutions* (Houston, TX: Gulf Publishing, 1991).
14. Paul Nystrom, "Managers and the Hi-HI Leader Myth." *Academy of Management Journal* (June 1978), Vol. 21, Iss. 3, pp. 325–331.
15. Judith Komaki, "Emergence of the Operant Model of Effective Supervision or How an Operant Conditioner Got Hooked on Leadership." *Leadership & Organizational Development Journal* (August 1994), Vol. 15, Iss. 5, pp. 27–32.
16. Jane Howell and Bruce Avolio, "Charismatic Leadership: Submission or Liberation?" *Business Quarterly* (Autumn 1995), Vol. 60, Iss. 1, pp. 62–70.
17. Jay Kconger and Rabindra Kanugo, "Toward a Behavioral Theory of Charismatic Leadership in Organizational Settings." *Academy of Management Review* (1987), Vol. 12, Iss. 3, pp. 637–647.
18. F. R. Manfred and Kets des Vries, "The Leadership Mystique." *The Academy of Management Executive* (August 1994), Vol. 8, Iss. 3, pp. 73–93.
19. Noel Tichy and Mary Anne Devanna, *The Transformational Leader* (New York: John Wiley & Sons, 1986).
20. William Koh, Richard Steers, and James Terborg, "The Effects of Transformational Leadership on Teacher Attitudes and Student Performance in Singapore." *Journal of Organizational Behavior* (July 1995), Vol. 16, Iss. 4, pp. 319–323.
21. Peter Bycio, Rick Hackett, and Joyce Allen, "Further Assessments of Bass's (1985) Conceptualization of Transactional and Transformational Leadership." *Journal of Applied Psychology* (August 1995), Vol. 80, Iss. 4, pp. 468–478.
22. Richard Gordon, "Substitues for Leadership." *Supervision* (July 1994), Vol. 55, Iss. 7, pp. 17–20.
23. Fred Fiedler, *A Theory of Leadership Effectiveness* (New York: McGraw-Hill, 1967).
24. Fred Fiedler, "When to Lead, When to Stand Back." *Psychology Today*, February 1988, pp. 26–27.
25. Robert Tannenbaum and Warren Schmidt, "How to Choose a Leadership Pattern." *Harvard Business Review*, May-June 1973, p. 166.
26. Robert Tannenbaum and Warren Schmidt, "How to Choose a Leadership Pattern." *Harvard Business Review*, July-August 1986, p. 129.
27. Robert House, "A Path-Goal Theory of Leader Effectiveness." *Administrative Science Quarterly* (1971), Vol. 16, Iss. 2, pp. 321–329.
28. Victor Vroom and Philip Yetton, *Leadership and Decision Making* (Pittsburgh: University of Pittsburgh Press, 1973).
29. Victor Vroom and Arthur Jago, *The New Leadership: Managing Partipation in Organizations* (Englewood Cliffs, NJ: Prentice Hall, 1987).
30. Victor Vroom, "Can Leaders Learn to Lead?" *Organizational Dynamics*, Winter 1976, pp. 17–28.
31. Paul Hersey and Kenneth Blanchard, *Management of Organizational Behavior: Utilizing Human Resources*, 4th ed. (Englewood Cliffs, NJ: Prentice Hall, 1982).
32. O. M. Irgens, "Situational Leadership: A Modification of Hersey and Blanchard's Model." *Leadership & Organizational Development Journal*, Vol. 16, Iss. 2, pp. 36–40.
33. Claude Graeff, "The Situational Leadership Theory: A Critical Review." *Academy of Management Review*, August 8, 1983, pp. 285, 290.
34. Steven Kerr and Jermier Jermier, "Substitutes for Leadership: The Meaning and Measurement." *Organizational Behavior and Human Performance* (1978), Vol. 22, pp. 375–403.
35. Ibid., and Richard Gordon, "Substitutes for Leadership." *Supervision* (July 1994), Vol. 55, Iss. 7, pp. 17–20.
36. J. E. Sheridan, D. J. Vredenburgh, and M. A. Abelson, "Contextual Model of Leadership Influence in Hospital Units." *Academy of Management Journal* (1984), Vol. 27, Iss. 1, pp. 57–78.
37. "Global Companies Reexamine Corporate Culture." *Personnel Journal* (August 1994), Vol. 73, Iss. 8, pp. S12–13.
38. Bruno Dufour, "Dealing with Diversity: Management Education in Europe." *Selections* (Winter 1994), Vol. 10, Iss. 2, pp. 7–15.
39. William Ouchi, *Theory Z—How American Business Can Meet the Japanese Challenge* (Reading, MA: Addison-Wesley, 1981).
40. Jay Klagge, "Unity and Diversity: A Two-Headed Opportunity for Today's Organizational Leaders." *Leadership & Organizational Development Journal* (April 1995), Vol. 16, Iss. 4, pp. 45–48.
41. Cynthia Epstein, "Ways Men and Women Lead." *Harvard Business Review*, January/February 1991, pp. 150–160. David Van Fleet and Julie Saurage, "Recent Research on Women in Leadership and Management." *Akron Business and Economic Review* (1984), Vol. 15, pp. 15–24.
42. Ibid.
43. Sally Helgesen, *The Female Advantage: Women's Ways of Leadership* (New York: Doubleday, 1990).
44. Robin Ely, "The Power in Demography: Women's Social Construction of Gender Identity at Work." *Academy of Management Journal* (June 1995), Vol. 38, Iss. 3, pp. 589–634.
45. Marian Ruderman, Patricia Ohlott, and Kathy Kram, "Promotion Decisions as a Diversity Practice." *Journal of Management Development* (February 1995), Vol. 14, Iss. 2, pp. 6–24.
46. Russell Kent and Sherry Moss, "Effects of Sex and Gender Role on Leader Emergence." *Academy of Management Journal* (October 1994), Vol. 37, Iss. 5, pp. 1335–1337.
47. Ruth Herrmann Siress, "How You Can

Carry the Leadership Torch." *Women in Business* (July-August 1995), Vol. 47, Iss. 4, pp. 46–48.
48. Jane Howell and Bruce Avolio, "Charismatic Leadership: Submission or Liberation?" *Business Quarterly* (Autumn 1995), Vol. 60, Iss. 1, pp. 62–71.
49. Christopher Selvarajah, Patrick Dunignan, Chandraseagran Suppiah, Terry Lane, and Chris Nuttman, "In Search of the ASEAN Leader: An Exploratory Study of the Dimensions That Relate to Excellence in Leadership." *Management International Review* (January 1995), Vol. 35, Iss. 1, pp. 29–45.
50. Andrew Sikula and Adelmiro Costa, "Are Women More Ethical Than Men?" *Journal of Business Ethics* (November 1994), Vol. 13, Iss. 11, pp. 859–872.
51. John Nicholls, "The Strategic Leadership Starr: A Guiding Light in Delivering Value to the Customer." *Management Decision* (December 1994), Vol. 32, Iss. 8, pp. 21–28.
52. Tom Peters, "When Muddling Through Can Be the Best Strategy." *Washington Business Journal,* January 27, 1995, pp. 19–20.
53. "Leadership Competencies." *Journal of Business Strategy* (January-February 1995), Vol. 16, Iss. 1, pp. 58–60.
54. Mark Frohman, "Nothing Kills Teams Like Ill-prepared Leaders: These Survival Rules and Techniques Will Help to Provide Effective Leadership." *Industry Week,* October 2, 1995, pp. 72–75.
55. Judith Kolb, "Leader Behavior Affecting Team Performance: Similarities and Differences Between Leader/Member Assessments." *The Journal of Business Communication* (July 1995), Vol. 32, Iss. 3, pp. 32–35.
56. Lawrence Holpp, "New Roles for Leaders: An HRD Reporters' Inquiry." *Training & Development* (March 1995), Vol. 49, Iss. 3, pp. 46–51.
57. Hal Lancaster, "Managing Your Career (A Re-engineering Interview with Champy and Hammer)." *The Wall Street Journal,* January 29, 1995, p. B1.
58. Kathryn Hegar and Robert N. Lussier, *Study Guide with Experiential Exercises* to accompany *Management: Concepts and Practices* (3rd ed.) (Boston: Allyn and Bacon, 1986), pp. 261–263. Adapted with permission of the publisher.

Chapter 13

1. "West Point Pointers." *The Wall Street Journal,* June 22, 1995, p. 1
2. Judith Kolb, "Leader Behaviors Affecting Team Performance: Similarities and Differences Between Leader/Member Assessments." *The Journal of Business Communication* (July 1995), Vol. 32, Iss. 3, pp. 233–249.
3. "Team Spirit." *The Wall Street Journal,* March 23, 1995, p. 1.
4. Jon Katzenback and Douglas Smith, "The Discipline of Teams." *Harvard Business Review* (March/April 1993), Vol. 70, Iss. 2, pp. 111–120.
5. "More Companies Link Sales Pay to Customer Satisfaction." *The Wall Street Journal,* March 29, 1994, p. 1.
6. Hal Lancaster, "Managing Your Career." *The Wall Street Journal,* January 29, 1995, p. 1.
7. "How Pitney Bowes Establishes Self-Directed Work Teams." *Modern Materials Handling* (February 1993), Vol. 48, Iss. 2, pp. 58–59.
8. Alex Markels, "Team Approach." *The Wall Street Journal,* July 3, 1995, p. 1
9. Brent Gallupe, Alan Dennis, William Cooper, Joseph Valcich, Lana Bastianutti, and Jay Nunamaker, "Electronic Brainstorming and Group Size." *Academy of Management Journal* (June 1992), Vol. 35, Iss. 2, pp. 350–369.
10. Hsin-Ginn Hwang and Jan Guynes, "The Effect of Group Size on Group Performance in Computer-Supported Decision Making." *Information & Management* (April 1994), Vol. 26, Iss. 4, pp. 189–198.
11. Jeffrey Waddle, "Management Styles That Make Meetings Work." *Association Management* (November 1993), Vol. 45, Iss. 11, pp. 40–44.
12. Mark Frohman, "Nothing Kills Teams Like Ill-Prepared Leaders: These Survival Rules and Techniques Will Help Provide Effective Leadership." *Industry Week,* October 2, 1995, pp. 72–25.
13. Lawrence Holpp, "New Roles for Leaders: An HRD Reporters' Inquiry." *Training & Development* (March 1995), Vol. 49, Iss. 3, pp. 46–50. Hal Lancaster, "Managing Your Career." *The Wall Street Journal,* January 29, 1995, p. B1.
14. Paul Buller and Cecil Bell, "Effects of Team Building on Goal Setting and Productivity: A Field Experiment." *Academy of Management Journal,* June 1986, p. 307.
15. "West Point Pointers." *The Wall Street Journal,* June 22, 1995, p. 1.
16. Aaron Nurick, "Facilitating Effective Work Teams." *SAM Advanced Management Journal* (Winter 1993), Vol. 58, Iss. 1, pp. 22–27.
17. Patricia Buhler, "Managing in the 90s." *Supervision* (May 1994), Vol. 55, Iss. 5, pp. 8–10.
18. "Winning Team Play." *Supervisory Management* (June 1994), Vol. 39, Iss. 6, pp. 8–9.
19. Marilyn Lewis Lanza, and Judith Keefe, "Group Process and Success in Meeting the Joint Commission on Accreditation." *Journal of Mental Health Administration* (Spring 1994), Vol. 21, Iss. 2, pp. 210–216.
20. Patricia Buhler, "Managing in the 90s." *Supervision* (May 1994), Vol. 55, Iss. 5, pp. 8–10.
21. Robert Keller, "Predictors of the Performance of Project Groups in R&D Organizations." *Academy of Management Journal,* December 1986, pp. 715–726.
22. Darlene Russ-Eft, "Predicting Organizational Orientation Toward Teams." *Human Resource Development Quarterly* (Summer 1993), Vol. 4, Iss. 2, pp. 125–134.
23. Robert Keller, "Predictors of the Performance of Project Groups in R&D Organizations." *Academy of Management Journal,* December 1986, pp. 715–726.
24. Pamela Hayes, "Using Group Dynamics to Manage Nursing Aides." *Health Care Supervisor* (September 1992), Vol. 11, Iss. 1, pp. 16–20.
25. B. W. Tuckman, "Developmental Sequence in Small Groups." *Psychological Bulletin,* Vol. 63 1965. Connie Gersick, "Marking Time Predictable Transitions in Task Groups." *Academy of Management Journal* (June 1989), Vol. 32, pp. 274–309.
26. R. B. Lacoursiere, *The Life Cycle of Groups: Group Development Stage Theory* (New York: Human Service Press, 1980).
27. Donald Carew, Eunice Carew, and Kenneth Blanchard, "Group Development and Situational Leadership." *Training and Development Journal,* June 1986, p. 48.
28. Tom Peters, "When Muddling Through Can Be the Best Strategy." *Washington Business Journal,* January 27, 1995, pp. 19–20.
29. "West Point Pointers." *The Wall Street Journal,* June 22, 1995, p. 1.
30. Blanchard Smith, "A Survivor's Guide to Facilitating." *Journal for Quality & Participation* (December 1991), Vol. 14, Iss. 6, pp. 56–62.
31. Robert Levasseur, "People Skills: What Every Professional Should Know About Designing and Managing Meetings." *Interfaces* (March/April 1992), Vol. 22, Iss. 2, pp. 11–14.
32. "More Meetings?" *The Wall Street Journal,* May 30, 1995, p. 1.
33. Patricia Buhler, "Managing in the 90s." *Supervision* (May 1994), Vol. 55, Iss. 5, pp. 8–10.
34. "Diverse Work Teams." *The Wall Street Journal,* June 15, 1993.
35. Jeongkoo Baker Yoon and Ko Jong-Wook Mouraine, "Interpersonal Attachment and Organizational Commitment." *Human Relations* (March 1994), Vol. 47, Iss. 3, pp. 329–351.
36. "West Pointers." *The Wall Street Journal,* June 22, 1995, p. 1.
37. "More Meetings?" *The Wall Street Journal,* May 30, 1995, p. 1.
38. "A New Book Challenges the Wisdom of Mass Layoffs." *The Wall Street Journal,* October, 3, 1995, p. 1.
39. Robert N. Lussier, *Supervision: A Skill-Building Approach* (2nd ed.). (Homewood, IL: Richard D. Irwin, 1994), pp. 521–524. Adapted with permission.

Chapter 14

1. Gilbert Fuchsberg, "Chief Executives See Their Power Shrink." *The Wall Street Journal,* March 15, 1993, p. B1.

2. Richard Weylman, "Building Your Power Base with Insider Information." *National Underwriter*, July 3, 1995, p. 16.
3. Dallas Brozik, "The Importance of Money and the Reporting of Salaries." *Journal of Compensation and Benefits* (January/February 1994), Vol. 9, pp. 61–64.
4. Jeffrey Vancouver and Elizabeth Morrison, "Feedback Inquiry: The Effect of Source Attributes and Individual Difference." *Organizational Behavior and Human Decision Processes* (June 1995), Vol. 62, pp. 276–285.
5. Hal Lancaster, "Manageing Your Career." *The Wall Street Journal*, January 3, 1995, p. 1.
6. Jacob Weisberg, "Building Your Information Power Base." *Folio*, April 15, 1995, pp. 34–35.
7. Patricia Wilson, "The Effects of Politics and Power on the Organizational Commitment of Federal Executives." *Journal of Management* (Spring 1995), Vol. 21, pp. 101–118.
8. Hal Lancaster, "Ignore the Psychics and Stick with What You Find Meaningful." *The Wall Street Journal*, April 25, 1995.
9. John Byrne, "How to Succeed: Same Game Different Decade." *Business Week*, April 17, 1995, p. 48.
10. "Executives Point the Finger at Major Time Waster." *Personnel Journal* (August 1994), Vol. 73, p. 16.
11. Stephen Robbins and David De Cenzo, *Fundmentals of Management* (Englewood Cliffs, NJ: Prentice Hall, 1995), pp. 10–11.
12. Nancie Fimbel, "Communicating Realistically: Taking Account of Politics in Internal Business Communications." *Journal of Business Communications* (January 1994), Vol. 31, pp. 7–26.
13. Richard Mason, "Securing: One Man's Quest for the Meaning of Therefore." *Interfaces* (July/August 1994), Vol. 24, pp. 67–72.
14. "Executives Point the Finger at Major Time Waster." *Personnel Journal* (August 1994), Vol. 73, p. 16.
15. Joseph Goldstein, "Alternatives to High-Cost Litigation." *The Cornell Hotel and Restaurant Administration Quarterly* (February 1995), Vol. 36, pp. 28–33.
16. Jill Sherer, "Resolving Conflict (the Right Way)." *Hospital & Health Network*, April 20, 1994, pp. 52–55.
17. "Nordstrom: Respond to Unreasonable Customer Requests!" *Planning Review* (May/June 1994), Vol. 22, Iss. 3, pp. 17–18.
18. Joseph Goldstein, "Alternatives to High-Cost Litigation." *The Cornell Hotel and Restaurant Administration Quarterly* (February 1995), Vol. 36, pp. 28–33.
19. Ichiro Innami, "The Duality of Group Decision, Group Verbal Behavior, and Intervention." *Organizational Behavior and Human Decision Process* (December 1994), Vol. 60, pp. 409–430.
20. Sonny Weide and Gayle Abbott, "Management on the Hot Seat: In an Increasingly Violent Workplace, How to Deliver Bad News." *Employment Relations Today* (Spring 1994), Vol. 21, pp. 23–34.
21. Kenneth Kaye, "The Art of Listening." *HR Focus* (October 1994), Vol. 71, p. 24.
22. "Keeping Hot Buttons from Taking Control." *Supervisory Management* (April 1995), Vol. 40, p. 1.
23. Stephenie Overman, "Bizarre Questions Aren't the Answer." *HR Magazine* (April 1995), Vol. 40, p. 56.
24. Elizabeth Niemyer, "The Case for Case Studies." *Training and Development* (January 1995), Vol. 49, pp. 50–52.
25. Sonny Weide and Gayle Abbott, "Management on the Hot Seat: In an Increasingly Violent Workplace, How to Deliver Bad News." *Employment Relations Today* (Spring 1994), Vol. 21, pp. 23–34.
26. John Schaubroeck, Daniel Ganster, and Barbara Kemmeret, "Job Complexity, Type A Behavior and Cardiovascular Disorder." *Academy of Management Journal* (April 1994), Vol. 37, Iss. 2, pp. 426–439.
27. "Lousiet Bosses." *The Wall Street Journal*, April 4, 1995, p. 1.
28. Brian Seaward, "Job Stress Takes a Global Toll." *Safety and Health* (January 1995), Vol. 151, pp. 64–66.
29. Katherine Andrews, "Impression Management: Trying to Look Bad at Work." *Harvard Business Review* (July/August 1995), Vol. 73, pp. 13–14.
30. "Hiring Freezes Thaw." *The Wall Street Journal*, April 18, 1995, p. 1.
31. "Checkoffs." *The Wall Street Journal*, April 4, 1995, p. 1.
32. W. H. Weiss, "Coping with Work Stress." *Supervision* (April 1994), Vol. 55, pp. 3–5.
33. Brian Seaward, "Job Stress Takes a Global Toll." *Safety and Health* (January 1995), Vol. 151, pp. 64–66.
34. W. H. Weiss, "Coping with Work Stress." *Supervision* (April 1994), Vol. 55, pp. 3–5.
35. Richard Federico, "Are You Doing More with Less, or Doing More with More." *Employee Benefits Journal* (December 1994), Vol. 19, p. 32–34.
36. "Food for Thought." *The Wall Street Journal*, May 4, 1993, p. 1.
37. It was reported in *The Wall Street Journal* that participants in a study ate two hard boiled eggs every day for a month. At the end of the month, overall cholesterol was up a bit, but the good cholesterol level versus the bad cholesterol level increased by six percent.
38. Sonny Weide and Gayle Abbott, "Management on the Hot Seat: In an Increasingly Violent Workplace, How to Deliver Bad News." *Employment Relations Today* (Spring 1994), Vol. 21, pp. 23–34.
39. Richard Pascale, "Intentional Breakdowns and Conflicts by Design." *Planning Review* (May/June 1994), Vol. 22, Iss. 3, pp. 52–55.
40. "Keeping Hot Buttons from Taking Control." *Supervisory Management* (April 1995), Vol. 40, p. 14.
41. "The Corporate Game." *The Wall Street Journal*, June 13, 1988, p. 1.
42. Barbara Noble, "Now He's Stressed, She's Stressed." *New York Times*, October 9, 1994, p. 21, Section 3. William Hendrix, Barbara Spencer, and Gail Gibson, "Organizational and Extraorganizational Factors Affecting Stress, Employee Well Being, and Absenteeism for Males and Females." *Journal of Business and Psychology* (Winter 1994), Vol. 9, pp. 103–128.
43. Mancie Fimbel, "Communicating Realistically: Taking Account of Politics in International Business Communications." *Journal of Business Communications* (January 1994), Vol. 31, pp. 7–26.
44. Elizabeth Niemyer, "The Case for Case Studies." *Training and Development* (January 1995), Vol. 49, pp. 50–52.
45. "Teams Become Commonplace." *The Wall Street Journal*, November 28, 1995, p. 1.
46. Gail Combs, "Take Steps to Solve Dilemma of Team Misfits." *HR Magazine* (May 1994), Vol. 39, Iss. 5, pp. 127–128.
47. Jerry Wisinski, "What to Do About Conflict." *Supervisory Management* (March 1995), Vol. 40, p. 11.
48. Glenn Ray, Jeff Hines, and Dave Wilcox, "Training Internal Facilitators." *Training and Development* (November 1994), Vol. 48, p. 45–48.
49. John Guaspari, "A Cure for 'Intiative Burnout'." *Management Review* (April 1995), Vol. 84, pp. 45–49. Richard Federico, "Are You Doing More with Less, or Doing More with More." *Employee Benefits Journal* (December 1994), Vol. 19, pp. 32–33.
50. The company name and location are made up. However, the case situation could happen in many organizations.
51. The car dealer negotiation confidential information is from Arch G. Woodside, Tulane University. The Car Dealer Game is part of a paper, "Bargaining Behavior in Personal Selling and Buying Exchanges," that was presented at the 1980 Eighth Annual Conference of the Association for Business Simulation and Experiential Learning (ABSEL). It is used with Dr. Woodside's permission.
52. Kathryn Hegar and Robert N. Lussier, *Study*

Guide with Experiential Exercises to accompany *Management: Concepts and Practices* (3rd ed.). (Boston: Allyn and Bacon, 1986), pp. 317–318. Adapted with permission of the publisher.

Chapter 15

1. Robert Simons, "How New Top Managers Use Control Systems as Levers of Strategic Renewal." *Strategic Management Journal* (March 1994), Vol. 15, Iss. 3, pp. 169–189.
2. Ibid.
3. Ibid.
4. Ibid.
5. Tom Peters and Nancy Austin, *A Passion for Excellence* (New York: Random House, 1985), pp. 378–392.
6. Carolyn Brown, "The Bottom Line on Budgets." *Black Enterprise* (November 1995), Vol. 26, Iss. 4, pp. 40–41.
7. Stephen Rehnberg, "Keep Your Head Out of the Cockpit." *Management Accounting* (July 1995), Vol. 77, Iss. 13, pp. 34–38.
8. Ginna Jacobson, "Raise Money Now: Successful Entrepreneurs and Veteran Financiers Reveal the Best Strategies for Finding Capital." *Success* (November 1995), Vol. 42, Iss. 9, pp. 39–47.
9. Deryck Williams, "Foolproof Projects," *CA Magazine* (September 1995), Vol. 128, Iss. 7, pp. 35–37.
10. C.W. Neale, "Successful New Product Development: A Capital Budgeting Perspective." *Journal of Marketing Management* (May 1994), Vol. 10, Iss. 4, pp. 283–297.
11. Larry Aeilts, "The Ratio Report." *Mass Transit* (March-April 1995), Vol. 21, Iss. 2, pp. 32–35.
12. John McCann, "Financial Statement Analysis—Mexican Companies." *Business Credit*, Vol. 97, Iss. 2, pp. 26–29.
13. Mark Coggins, "Accounting for Tangible Fixed Assests." *Accountancy* (April 1995), Vol. 115, Iss. 1220, pp. 86–88.
14. Carolyn Brown, "The Bottom Line on Budgets." *Black Enterprise* (November 1995), Vol. 26, Iss. 4, pp. 40–41.
15. James Bandler, "Statement of Choice." *Journal of Business Strategy* (March-April 1995), Vol. 16, Iss. 2, pp. 55–58.
16. Judy Rice, "U.S. Business—Guilty as Charged." *National Productivity Review* (Winter 1994), Vol. 14, Iss. 1, pp. 1–8.
17. Stephen Oliner and William Wascher, "Is a Productivity Revolution Under Way in the United States?" *Challenge*, November-December 1995, pp. 18–30.
18. Joseph Spiers, "Why Can't the U.S. Measure Productivity Right?" *Fortune*, October 16, 1995, pp. 55–57.
19. "Productivity and the Hubble Constant." *The Economist*, October 14, 1995, p. 19.
20. "The Economy Is Likely to Lose Luster in 1995." *The Wall Street Journal*, December 19, 1995, p. 1.
21. Kevin MacLatchie, "Know the Numbers: Reviewing the Income Statement for Accuracy." *Journal of Property Management* (March-April 1995), Vol. 60, Iss. 2, pp. 26–29.
22. Ibid.
23. Larry Aeilts, "The Ratio Report." *Mass Transit* (March-April 1995), Vol. 21, Iss. 2, pp. 32–35. Mark Coggins, "Accounting for Tangible Fixed Assets." *Accountancy* (April 1995), Vol. 115, Iss. 1220, pp. 86–88.
24. James Kristy, "Conquering Financial Ratios: The Good, the Bad, and the Who Cares?" *Business Credit* (February 1994), Vol. 96, Iss. 2, pp. 14–18.
25. Scott McCartney, "How to Make an Airline Run on Schedule." *The Wall Street Journal*, December 22, 1995, p. B1.
26. F.C. "What Price Principles?" *Entrepreneur*, January 1996, p. 20.
27. Judy Rice, "U.S. Business—Guilty as Charged," *National Productivity Review* (Winter 1994), Vol. 14, Iss. 1, pp. 1–8.
28. John McClenahem, "Generally Accepted: Practice: The Plusses—and Minuses—of Activity-Based Budgeting." *Industry Week*, November 6, 1995, pp. 13–14.
29. Daniel Keegan and Robert Eiler, "Let's Reengineer Cost Accounting." *Management Accounting* (August 1994), Vol. 76, Iss. 2, pp. 26–32.
30. "The Economy Is Likely to Lose Luster in 1995." *The Wall Street Journal*, December 19, 1995, p. 1.
31. Carmeneric Church and Elyse Cherry, "Workers' Compensation and Health Insurance." *Supervision* (September 1995), Vol. 56, Iss. 9, pp. 14–17.
32. Stephen Oliner and William Wascher, "Is a Productivity Revolution Under Way in the United States?" *Challenge*, November-December 1995, pp. 18–30
33. Bernard Wysocki, "Big Corporate Layoffs are Slowing Down," *The Wall Street Journal*, June 12, 1995, p. 1.
34. Bernard Wysocki, "Lean—and Frail," *The Wall Street Journal*, July 5, 1995, p. 1.
35. "An Exterior View May Be What Some Companies Need," *The Wall Street Journal*, December 14, 1995.
36. Carolyn Brown, "The Bottom Line on Budgets." *Black Enterprise* (November 1995), Vol. 26, Iss. 4, pp. 40–41
37. Janean Chun, "Capital Crunch." *Entrepreneur*, January 1996, p. 102.
38. There is no Rodriguez Clothes Manufacture; this is a fictional case based on a possible situation.

Chapter 16

1. Information taken from the *1994 Annual Report of the W.K. Kellogg Foundation*.
2. John Adams, "Playing Hardball and Getting Through on Performance." *HRMagazine*, Vol. 40, Iss. 10, pp. 8–9.
3. Joann Lublin, "It's Shape-Up Time for Performance Reviews." *The Wall Street Journal*, October 3, 1994, p. B1.
4. Jai Ghorpade and Milton Chen, "Creating Quality-Driven Performance Appraisal Systems." *The Academy of Management Executive* (February 1995), Vol. 9, Iss. 1, pp. 32–40.
5. Joseph Rosenberger, "How'm I Doing?" *Across the Board* (September 1995), Vol. 32, Iss. 8, pp. 27–31.
6. Jai Ghorpade and Milton Chen, "Creating Quality-Driven Performance Appraisal Systems." *The Academy of Management Executive* (February 1995), Vol. 9, Iss. 1, pp. 32–40.
7. John Adams, "Playing Hardball and Getting Through on Performance. *HRMagazine*, Vol. 40, Iss. 10, pp. 8–9.
8. Joann Lublin, "It's Shape-Up Time for Performance Reviews." *The Wall Street Journal*, October 3, 1994, p. B1
9. Ibid.
10. Jai Ghorpade and Milton Chen, "Creating Quality-Driven Performance Appraisal Systems." *The Academy of Management Executive* (February 1995), Vol. 9, Iss. 1, pp. 32–40.
11. Joann Lublin, "It's Shape-Up Time for Performance Reviews." *The Wall Street Journal*, October 3, 1994, p. B1.
12. Joseph Rosenberger, "How'm I Doing?" *Across the Board* (September 1995), Vol. 32, Iss. 8, pp. 27–31.
13. Steven Kerr, "On the Folly of Rewarding A, While Hoping for B." *The Academy of Management Executive* (February 1995), Vol. 9, Iss. 1, pp. 32–40.
14. Ibid.
15. Based on examples from Steven Kerr, "On the Folly of Rewarding A, While Hoping for B." *The Academy of Management Executive* (February 1995), Vol. 9, Iss. 1, pp. 32–40; The Editors, "More on Folly," the same issue, pp. 15–16.
16. Ibid, Editors.
17. Ibid, Editors.
18. Jai Ghorpade and Milton Chen, "Creating Quality-Driven Performance Appraisal Systems." *The Academy of Management Executive* (February 1995), Vol. 9, Iss. 1, pp. 32–40.
19. Tobias LaFleur and Cloyd Hyten, "Improving the Quality of Hotel Banquet Staff Performance." *Journal of Organizational Behavior*

Management (Spring-Fall 1995), Vol. 15, Iss. 1–2, pp. 29–94.

20. Joann Lublin, "It's Shape-Up Time for Performance Reviews." *The Wall Street Journal*, October 3, 1994, p. B1

21. Jai Ghorpade and Milton Chen, "Creating Quality-Driven Performance Appraisal Systems." *The Academy of Management Executive* (February 1995), Vol. 9, Iss. 1, pp. 32–40.

22. Karen Rancourt, "Real-Time Coaching Boosts Performance." *Training & Development* (April 1995), Vol. 49, Iss. 4, pp. 53–57

23. "Buddy System." *The Wall Street Journal*, December 12, 1995.

24. Karen Rancourt, "Real-Time Coaching Boosts Performance." *Training & Development* (April 1995), Vol. 49, Iss. 4, pp. 53–57.

25. Jack Falvey, "To Raise Productivity, Try Saying Thank You." *The Wall Street Journal*, December 6, 1982.

26. Ibid.

27. Tom Peters and Nancy Austin, *A Passion for Excellence* (New York: Random House, 1985), pp. 378–392.

28. "Discipline at Work." *IRS Employment Trends* (September 1995), Iss. 591, pp. 4–11.

29. William Bransford and Jerry Shaw, "Poor Performance: How Much Due Process?" *The Public Manager: The New Bureaucrat* (Summer 1995), Vol. 24, Iss. 2, pp. 17–20.

30. William Lissey, "Employee's Intentional Disobedience." *Supervision* (September 1995), Vol. 56, Iss. 9, pp. 17–19.

31. "Discipline at Work." *IRS Employment Trends* (September 1995), Iss. 591, pp. 4–11.

32. "All the Rage." *Entrepreneur*, January 1996, p. 98.

33. John Huberman, "Discpline Without Punishment." *Harvard Business Review*, July-August 1964, p. 62.

34. Jo McHale, "How to Deal with People Who Are Distrupting Performance." *People Management*, May 31, 1995, pp. 50–51. Dick Grote, "Discipline Without Punishment." *The Wall Street Journal*, Manager's Journal, May 25, 1994, p. A7.

35. John Adams, "Playing Hardball and Getting Through on Performance." *HRMagazine*, Vol. 40, Iss. 10, pp. 8–9.

36. Jai Ghorpade and Milton Chen, "Creating Quality-Driven Performance Appraisal Systems." *The Academy of Management Executive* (February 1995), Vol. 9, Iss. 1, pp. 32–40.

37. Jonathan Segal, "Evaluating the Evaluators." *HRMagazine* (October 1995), Vol. 40, Iss. 10, pp. 46–51.

38. Jai Ghorpade and Milton Chen, "Creating Quality-Driven Performance Appraisal Systems." *The Academy of Management Executive* (February 1995), Vol. 9, Iss. 1, pp. 32–40.

39. Judith Kolb, "Leader Behavior Affecting Team Performance: Similarities and Differences between Leader/Member Assessments." *The Journal of Business Communication* (July 1995), Vol. 32, Iss. 3, pp. 233–249.

40. Jai Ghorpade and Milton Chen, "Creating Quality-Driven Performance Appraisal Systems." *The Academy of Management Executive* (February 1995), Vol. 9, Iss. 1, pp. 32–40.

41. "What Benefits?" *The Wall Street Journal*, November 14, 1995, p. 1.

42. Mark Henricks, "Informal Wear." *Entrepreneur*, January 1996, pp. 79–80.

43. John Adams, "Playing Hardball and Getting Through on Performance." *HRMagazine*, Vol. 40, Iss. 10, pp. 8–9.

44. Robert McGarvey, "I Spy." *Entrepreneur*, December 1995, pp. 73–75.

45. Arun Gandhi, "Nonviolence and Us." *Business Horizons* (March-April 1995), Vol. 38, Iss. 2, pp. 1–3.

46. Jai Ghorpade and Milton Chen, "Creating Quality-Driven Performance Appraisal Systems." *The Academy of Management Executive* (February 1995), Vol. 9, Iss. 1, pp. 32–40.

47. Ibid.

48. Sue Shellenbarger, "Reviews from Peers Instruct—and Sting." *The Wall Street Journal*, October 4, 1994, p. B1.

49. Jai Ghorpade and Milton Chen, "Creating Quality-Driven Performance Appraisal Systems." *The Academy of Management Executive* (February 1995), Vol. 9, Iss. 1, pp. 32–40.

50. "Your Next Review May Come from Salespeople." *Sales & Marketing Management* (July 1995), Vol. 147, Iss. 7, pp. 41–43.

51. "Grim Countdown; Three Million Jobs Are Cut in Seven Years." *The Wall Street Journal*, December 12, 1995, p. 1.

52. Joseph Rosenberger, "How'm I Doing?" *Across the Board* (September 1995), Vol. 32, Iss. 8, pp. 27–31.

53. "Missing Persons." *Entrepreneur*, January 1996, p. 10.

54. This case is based on an actual bank and its performance appraisal system. However, for confidentiality, it has been given a fictional name and location in Nebraska. This is the common discussion during a performance appraisal interview.

55. Robert N. Lussier, *Supervision: A Skill-Building Approach* (2nd ed.). (Homewood IL: Richard D. Irwin, Inc., 1994), pp. 419–420. Adapted with permission of the publisher.

56. Ibid., pp. 487–488.

Chapter 17

1. Robert Frank, "Frito-Lay Devours Snack-Food Business." *The Wall Street Journal*, October 27, 1995, p. B1. Robert Frank, "Potato Chips to Go Global—Or so Pepsi Bets." *The Wall Street Journal*, November 30, 1995, pp. B1, B6. PepsiCo Inc. 1994 Annual Report.

2. "Puma AG." *The Wall Street Journal*, January 11, 1996, p. 1.

3. "What Does the Future Hold?" *The Wall Street Journal*, December 28, 1995, p. 1 Valerie Reitman and Robert Semison, "Japanese Car Makers Speed Up Car Making." *The Wall Street Journal*, December 29, 1995, p. B1. John Birge and Marilyn Maddox, "Bounds on Expected Project Tardiness." *Operations Research* (September-October 1995), Vol. 42, Iss. 5, pp. 838–851.

4. "Brew Pubs." *The Wall Street Journal*, January 11, 1996, p. 1

5. Jonah McLeod, "Thriving with a Rapid Product Turnover." *Electronics*, March 13, 1995, pp. 15–16.

6. Glenn Wilson, "Changing the Process of Production." *Industrial Management* (January-February 1995), Vol. 37, Iss. 1, pp. 1–3.

7. Ibid.

8. Scott Shafer, Bennett Tepper, Jack Meredith, and Robert Marsh, "Comparing the Effects of Cellular and Functional Manufacturing on Employee's Perceptions and Attitudes." *Journal of Operations Management*, Vol. 12, Iss. 2, pp. 63–75.

9. Jonah McLeod, "Thriving with a Rapid Product Turnover." *Electronics*, March 13, 1995, pp. 15–16.

10. Ibid.

11. "What Does the Future Hold?" *The Wall Street Journal*, December 28, 1995, p. 1 Valerie Reitman and Robert Semison, "Japanese Car Makers Speed Up Car Making." *The Wall Street Journal*, December 29, 1995, p. B1.

12. "Ford Faces." *The Wall Street Journal*, January 10, 1996, p. 1.

13. Paul Adler, Avi Mandelbaum, Vien Nguyen, and Elizabeth Schwerer, "From Project to Process Management: An Empirically-Based Framework for Analyzing Product Development Time." *Management Science* (March 1995), Vol. 41, Iss. 3, pp. 458–485.

14. Scott Shafer, Bennett Tepper, Jack Meredith, and Robert Marsh, "Comparing the Effects of Cellular and Functional Manufacturing on Employee's Perceptions and Attitudes." *Journal of Operations Management*, Vol. 12, Iss. 2, pp. 63–75.

15. Joseph Mazzola and Robert Schantz, "Single-Facility Resource Allocation Under Capacity-Based Economies and Diseconomies of Scope." *Management Science* (April 1995), Vol. 41, Iss. 4, pp. 669–680.

16. "U.S. Hotel Occupancy." *The Wall Street Journal*, January 11, 1996, p. 1.

17. James Dilworth, *Operations Management* (New York: McGraw-Hill, 1992), p. 8.

18. Paul Adler, Avi Mandelbaum, Vien Nguyen, and Elizabeth Schwerer, "From Project to Process Management: An Empirically-Based Framework for Analyzing Product Development Time." *Management Science* (March 1995), Vol. 41, Iss. 3, pp. 458–485.
19. "Introduction and Overview." *Chain Store Age Executive with Shopping Center Age* (December 1995), Vol. 71, Iss. 12, p. IM2.
20. Allison Lucas, "Through Thick and Thin, But Just-In-Time." *Sales & Marketing Management* (December 1995), Vol. 147, Iss. 12, pp. 70–71.
21. John Birge and Marilyn Maddox, "Bounds on Expected Project Tardiness." *Operations Research* (September-October 1995), Vol. 43, Iss. 5, pp. 838–851.
22. Ibid.
23. Fredrik Williams, Derrick D'Souza, Martin Rosenfeldt, and Massoud Kassaee, "Manufacturing Strategy, Business Strategy and Firm Performance in a Mature Industry." *Journal of Operations Management* (July 1995), Vol. 13, Iss. 1, pp. 19–34.
24. Randall Cyr, "What Ever Happened to the Idea of Lead Time?" *Industrial Management* (January-February 1995), Vol. 37, Iss. 1, p. 32.
25. "Federal Regulators." *The Wall Street Journal*, May 22, 1995, p. 1.
26. "Philip Morris." *The Wall Street Journal*, May 30, 1995, p. 1.
27. "Intel Said." *The Wall Street Journal*, January 8, 1995, p. 1.
28. "Compaq Plans." *The Wall Street Journal*, November 2, 1995, p. 1.
29. Adapted from Nancy Friedman, "Six Cardinal Rules of Customer Service." *National Business Association Newsletter*, February 1993, p. 14.
30. Rohit Verma and John Goodale, "Statistical Power in Operations Management Research." *Journal of Operations Management* (August 1995), Vol. 13, Iss. 2, pp. 19–34.
31. Chris Rauwendaal, "Statistical Process Control in Extrusion." *Plastics World* (March 1995), Vol. 53, Iss. 3, pp. 59–64.
32. Ross Fink and Thomas Margavio, "Economic Models for Single Sample Acceptance Sampling Plans, No Inspection, and 100 Percent Inspection." *Decision Sciences* (July-August 1994), Vol. 25, Iss. 4, pp. 625–654.
33. Chris Rauwendaal, "Statistical Process Control in Extrusion." *Plastics World* (March 1995), Vol. 53, Iss. 3, pp. 59–64
34. Joyce Mehring, "Achieving Multiple Timeliness Goals for Auto Loans: A Case for Process Control." *Interfaces* (July-August 1995), Vol. 25, Iss. 4, pp. 81–92.
35. Tracy Kirker, "Dr. Juran." *Industry Week*, April 4, 1994, pp. 12–16.
36. Ross Fink and Thomas Margavio, "Economic Models for Single Sample Acceptance Sampling Plans, No Inspection, and 100 Percent Inspection." *Decision Sciences* (July-August 1994), Vol. 25, Iss. 4, pp. 625–654.
37. Tim Stevens, "Quality Is Still Free." *Industry Week*, June 19, 1995, pp. 13–15.
38. Sue Reese, "Sharpen Your Competitive Edge: Information Systems Help Manufacturing Companies Stay a Step Ahead." *Industry Week*, December 5, 1994, pp. 26–27.
39. Stev Alexander, "Make or Buy?" *Computerworld*, October 9, 1995, pp. S35–38.
40. Kathleen Gow, "No Pain, No Gain." *Computerworld*, October 9, 1995, pp. S27–30.
41. Hal Lancaster, "Managing Your Career." *The Wall Street Journal*, January 3, 1995, p. 1.
42. P.C. Chu, "Conceiving Strategic Systems." *Journal of Systems Management* (July-August 1995), Vol. 46, Iss. 4, pp. 36–42.
43. Ibid.
44. P.C. Chu, "Conceiving Strategic Systems." *Journal of Systems Management* (July-August 1995), Vol. 46, Iss. 4, pp. 36–42.
45. C.M. "Decision Support Systems: An Extended Research Agenda." *Omega* (April 1995), Vol. 23, Iss. 2, pp. 221–230.
46. Charles Austin, Jerry Trimm, and Patrick Sobczak, "Information Systems and Strategic Management." *Health Care Management Review* (Summer 1995), Vol. 20, Iss. 3, pp. 26–34.
47. Charles Babcock, "New World Demands New Skills." *Computerworld*, November 27, 1995, pp. 126–127.
48. Christian Hill, "All Together Now." *The Wall Street Journal*, January 23, 1996, p. R1.
49. Sandra Sullivan and Robert Lussier, "Flexible Work Arrangements as a Management Tool." *Supervision* (August 1995), Vol. 56, Iss. 8, pp. 14–17.
50. Ibid.
51. Sandra Sullivan and Robert Lussier, "Flexible Work Arrangements from Policy to Implementation." *Supervision* (September 1995), Vol. 57, Iss. 9, pp. 10–113.
52. Jared Sandberg and Bart Ziegler, "Web Trap." *The Wall Street Journal*, January 18, 1996, p. 1.
53. "IBM and Sears." *The Wall Street Journal*, May 7, 1996, p. 1.
54. Jared Sandberg and Bart Ziegler, "Web Trap." *The Wall Street Journal*, January 18, 1996, p. 1
55. "IBM's Chairman Promised." *The Wall Street Journal*, January 23, 1996, p. 1.
56. Glenn Wilson, "Changing the Process of Production." *Industrial Management* (January-February 1995), Vol. 37, Iss. 1, pp. 1–3.
57. Jay Velury, "Integrating ISO 9000 into the Bigh Picture." *IIE Solutions* (October 1995), Vol. 27, Iss. 10, pp. 26–30.
58. "ISO 9000: To Be or Not to Be?" *Modern Material Handling* (November 1995), Vol. 50, Iss. 13, pp. 10–12.
59. Milo Gevelin, "Why Many Businesses Can't Keep Their Secrets." The *Wall Street Journal*, November 20, 1995, p. B1.
60. "Personal Technology." *The Wall Street Journal*, March 23, 1995, p. 1.
61. Randall Hanson, Rebecca Porterfield, and Kathleen Ames, "Employee Emplowerment at Risk: Effects of Recent NLRB Rulings." *Academy of Management Executive* (May 1995), Vol. 9, Iss. 2, pp. 45–54.
62. Stuart Lieberman, "Should IS be Centralized: Or Decentralized?" *Computerworld*, November 27, 1995, pp. 97–99.
63. Claude Marais, "Should IS be Centralized: Or Decentralized?" *Computerworld*, November 27, 1995, pp. 96–98.
64. Johan McLeod, "Thriving with a Rapid Product Turnover." *Electronics*, March 13, 1995, pp. 15–16

Company Index

G

H

I

J

L

Subject Index

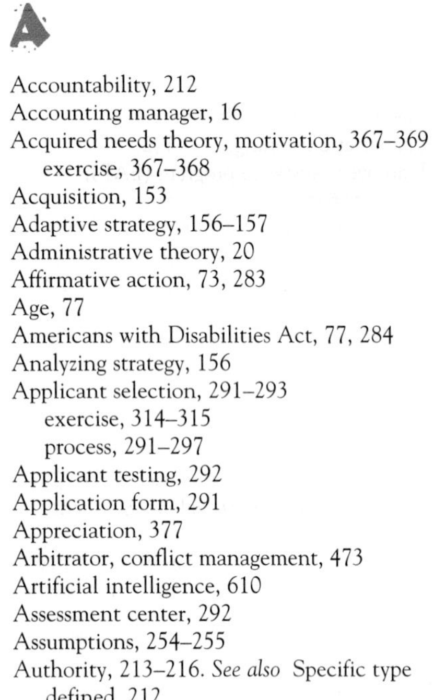

O

P

Q

R